*For a summary of general treatment categories, see the Chapter 16 Summary. For a summary of research techniques, see Tables 7-2 and 7-3.*

## ABOUT THE COVER

*Cortical Columns*, 2013
21K, 18K, and 12K gold, ink, dye, and metal powder on aluminized panel
36" × 48"

The front cover depicts Dr. Greg Dunn's work *Cortical Columns*, which he describes as "an ode to one of the brain's most iconic and beautiful regions, the cerebral cortex. Neurons are separated by vertical layer, and are grouped into loose columns that act as local processing units. The cortex is responsible for a huge variety of brain-related functions, everything from eye tracking, logical comprehension, from movement, sensation, planning, vision, hearing, decision making, and more. Evolution has adapted the cortex's unique structure to take on a staggering number of tasks, and there is no part of the human brain which greater differentiates us as a species."

You can find more information about this piece, as well as other brain- and mind-themed artwork, at gregadunn.com.

SEVENTH EDITION

# AN INTRODUCTION TO
# BRAIN AND BEHAVIOR

**BRYAN KOLB** ▪ **IAN Q. WHISHAW** ▪ **G. CAMPBELL TESKEY**

University of Lethbridge · University of Lethbridge · University of Calgary

**worth publishers**
Macmillan Learning
New York

This book is dedicated to the patients described within its pages—in particular, Fred Linge, who is the first patient mentioned in Chapter 1 and the last patient mentioned in Chapter 16. Fred was a clinical psychologist who coined the term "posttraumatic growth," to characterize his own nonconventional therapy of "faith, hope, and love." He recently passed away after 40 years of growth with his injury. The many other patients described in the book have allowed us to introduce a wide range of neurological disorders to students, and we hope their stories have added some reality to the many complex topics that are discussed.

Executive Vice President & General Manager:
  Charles Linsmeier
Vice President, Social Sciences & High School: Shani Fisher
Executive Program Manager for Psychology: Daniel DeBonis
Development Editor: Andrew Sylvester
Assistant Editor: Talia Green
Executive Marketing Manager: Katherine Nurre
Marketing Assistant: Claudia Cruz
Senior Media Editor, Social Sciences: Stefani Wallace
Senior Director, Content Management Enhancement:
  Tracey Kuehn
Senior Managing Editor: Lisa Kinne
Senior Content Project Manager: Vivien Weiss
Senior Project Manager: Aravinda Doss, Lumina Datamatics, Inc.
Senior Media Project Manager: Eve Conte
Senior Workflow Project Manager: Paul Rohloff
Production Supervisor: Robert Cherry
Executive Permissions Editor: Cecilia Varas
Photo Researcher: Richard Fox, Lumina Datamatics, Inc.
Director of Design, Content Management: Diana Blume
Senior Design Services Manager: Natasha Wolfe
Senior Cover Design Manager: John Callahan
Art Manager: Matthew McAdams
New Illustrations: Eli Ensor and Lumina Datamatics, Inc.

Composition: Lumina Datamatics, Inc.
Printing and Binding: Lakeside Book Company

Library of Congress Control Number: 2021952854

ISBN-13: 978-1-319-25438-4
ISBN-10: 1-319-25438-1

International Edition:
ISBN-13: 978-1-319-49856-6
ISBN-10: 1-319-49856-6

1  2  3  4  5  6          27  26  25  24  23  22

Macmillan Learning
120 Broadway
New York, NY 10271
www.macmillanlearning.com

Deborah Muirhead

**Bryan Kolb** received his Ph.D. from Pennsylvania State University in 1973. He conducted postdoctoral work at the University of Western Ontario and the Montreal Neurological Institute. He then moved to the University of Lethbridge in 1976, where he is Professor of Neuroscience and holds a Board of Governors Chair in Neuroscience. His current research examines how neurons of the cerebral cortex change in response to various factors—including hormones, experience, psychoactive drugs, neurotrophins, and injury—and how these changes are related to behavior in the normal and diseased brain. Kolb has received the distinguished teaching medal from the University of Lethbridge. He is a Fellow of the Royal Society of Canada and of the Canadian Psychological Association (CPA), the American Psychological Association, and the Association of Psychological Science. A recipient of the Hebb Prize from the CPA and from the Canadian Society for Brain, Behaviour, and Cognitive Science, Kolb has also received four honorary doctorates. He is a Senior Fellow of the Child Brain Development program of the Canadian Institute for Advanced Research. In 2017, he was appointed as an Officer of the Order of Canada. He and his wife train and show horses in Western riding events.

David Benard

**Ian Q. Whishaw** received his Ph.D. from Western University and is a Professor of Neuroscience at the University of Lethbridge. He has held visiting appointments at The University of Texas at Austin, the University of Michigan, Cambridge University, and the University of Strasbourg. He is a fellow of Clair Hall, Cambridge, and of the Canadian Psychological Association, the American Psychological Association, and the Royal Society of Canada. Whishaw has received the Canadian Humane Society Bronze Medal for Bravery and the Ingrid Speaker Gold Medal for Research, as well as the Distinguished Teaching Award from the University of Lethbridge and the ASTech Award for Distinguished Science. He has received the Key to the City of Lethbridge and has honorary doctorates from the University of British Columbia, Thompson Rivers University, and the University of Lethbridge. His research addresses the evolution and neural basis of skilled hand movement and the neural basis of brain disease, and the Institute for Scientific Information includes him in its list of most cited neuroscientists. His hobby is training horses for Western performance events.

Tannis Teskey

**G. Campbell Teskey** received his Ph.D. from Western University in 1990 and then conducted postdoctoral work at McMaster University. In 1992, he relocated to the University of Calgary, where he is a professor in the Department of Cell Biology and Anatomy and at the Hotchkiss Brain Institute. His current research programs examine the development, organization, and plasticity of the motor cortex, as well as how seizures alter blood flow, brain function, and behavior. Teskey has won numerous teaching awards, has developed new courses, is a founder of the bachelor of science in neuroscience program, served as Education Director for the Hotchkiss Brain Institute, and chaired the Education Committee of Campus Alberta Neuroscience. His hobbies include hiking, biking, kayaking, and skiing.

# CONTENTS

**CHAPTER 4**
BSIP SA/Alamy Stock Photo

# How Do Neurons Use Electrical Signals to Transmit Information? . . . . . . . . . . 111

## CHAPTER 5 — How Do Neurons Communicate and Adapt?

ANDRZEJ WOJCICKI/
SCIENCE PHOTO LIBRARY/
Getty Images

## CHAPTER 6 — How Do Drugs Influence Brain and Behavior?

Meletios Verras/Getty
Images

NEIL M. BORDEN/Science Source

**CHAPTER 7**

# How Do We Study the Brain's Structures and Functions? . . . . . . 211

Aynur_sib/Getty Images

**CHAPTER 8**

# How Does the Nervous System Develop and Adapt? . . . . . . . . . . . . . . . . . . . . . 248

## CHAPTER 9 How Do We Sense, Perceive, and See the World? . . . . . . . . . 287

*Science Photo Library/Alamy*

## CHAPTER 10 How Do We Hear, Speak, and Make Music? . . . . . . . . . . . . . . . . . 325

*SCIENCE PHOTO LIBRARY/Science Source*

How Does the Nervous
System Respond
to Stimulation
and Produce
Movement?

CHAPTER 11

Tim Gainey/Alamy Stock Photo

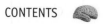

## CHAPTER 14

Russell Kightley/Science Source

# How Do We Learn and Remember? ..... 483

## CHAPTER 15

Movus/Getty Images

# How Does the Brain Think?........... 525

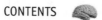

**CHAPTER 16**

# What Happens When the Brain Misbehaves?

William Taufic/Getty Images

# PREFACE

**Like the prior editions, this seventh edition** of *An Introduction to Brain and Behavior* incorporates the latest research and technological advancements to give students a foundation in behavioral neuroscience as it is understood and practiced today. New material on genetics and epigenetics, genetic mutations, connectomics, brain imaging, genetic engineering and transgenic techniques, and our understanding and categorization of diseases and disorders of the brain are included throughout the text.

In addition to these updates, we have made some significant changes within some sections to reflect the current understanding of the concepts and better communicate that knowledge to the student. For example, the list of 10 principles of nervous system function, a hallmark of the text that is referenced throughout the chapters, has been revised to highlight the central role of neuronal circuits in the processes of sensation, integration, and movement. Chapter 4 has been reorganized to give students a complete understanding of excitation and inhibition in graded potentials before detailing the propagation and phases of an action potential. The discussion of hormones has been moved from Chapter 6 to Chapter 5, where it facilitates a comparison of the functions of hormones and neurotransmitters. The discussion of habituation and sensitization has been moved from Chapter 5 to Chapter 14, where it is presented in the context of brain plasticity. Chapter 7 includes a new section on computational neuroscience and deep learning, and includes a discussion of the emerging field of neuroethics. The discussion of sleep disorders in Chapter 13 has been revamped to adhere more closely to the broad categories outlined in the *International Classification of Sleep Disorders*. These examples are just a few of the updates and revisions found throughout the seventh edition.

The range of updates and new coverage in the seventh edition exposition and Focus features is listed, chapter by chapter, in the margins of these Preface pages. You can easily see the breadth and scope of the revision. Yet these changes have not added to the length of the text. To keep the student focused on the material, judicious cuts have been made throughout to compensate for the new additions.

Changes in each new edition are always made with the goal of maintaining the voice and style that have helped make *An Introduction to Brain and Behavior* successful, and this seventh edition preserves the tools and features developed in the prior editions. Reflecting the encouraging feedback received from readers, the book's learning apparatus continues to feature sets of self-test questions at the end of the major sections in each chapter. These Section Reviews help students track their understanding as they progress through the text and the course. Answers appear at the back of the book.

We continue to expand the popular margin notes. Beyond offering useful asides to the text narrative, these marginalia increase the reader's ease in finding information, especially when related concepts are introduced early in the text and then elaborated on in later chapters. Readers can return quickly to an earlier discussion to refresh their knowledge or jump ahead to learn more. The margin notes also help instructors move through the book to preview later discussions. Margin callouts are also deployed to highlight places where the 10 principles of nervous system functioning, introduced in Chapter 2, correspond directly to the material in each chapter. Although this feature is by no means comprehensive, by reiterating these principles in key places where the connection is sharpest, we help students gain a deeper understanding of these core concepts and the nervous system functioning they reflect.

The illustrated Experiments, another of the book's most popular features, show readers how researchers design experiments—that is, how they approach the study of brain–behavior relationships. The Basics features let students brush up or get up to speed on their science foundation—knowledge that helps them comprehend behavioral neuroscience.

## SEVENTH EDITION KEY REVISIONS

### CHAPTER 1

**REVISED** Section 1-1 touches on the topic of neurodiversity and artificial intelligence in the discussion of why we study brain and behavior.

**REVISED** Section 1-2 concludes with a discussion of contemporary theories of consciousness.

**NEW** subsection in Section 1-4 explores the significance of human intelligence, and issues related to our ability to define and measure it.

### CHAPTER 2

**UPDATED** Clinical Focus 2-3 discusses new neuroimaging and other treatments for stroke, and explains the FAST method for detecting stroke.

**REVAMPED** discussion of the 10 principles of the nervous system, with revised order, updated descriptions throughout, and a new Principle 1 highlighting the role of neuronal circuits.

### CHAPTER 3

**UPDATED** discussion in Section 3-1 on Barbara Webb's work and approaches to robot intelligence and AI.

**UPDATED** discussion of glial cells and functions in Section 3-1, including discussion of tripartite synaptosomics in the study of astrocytes.

**UPDATED** discussion of genetic engineering techniques in Section 3-3, including an expanded presentation of CRISPR (with figure).

### CHAPTER 4

**REORGANIZED** discussion of electrical activity at the synapse across Sections 4-2 and 4-3, which now presents integration and summation of inputs before explaining action potentials.

**UPDATED** Clinical Focus 4-4 discusses recent clinical trials focusing on the brain–machine interface in the treatment of ALS.

We have made some big changes, but much of the book remains familiar. Shaping the content throughout is our ongoing emphasis on examining the nervous system with a focus on function, on how our behavior and our brain interact. Along the way, we ask the key questions that both students and neuroscientists ask:

- Why do we have a brain?
- How is the nervous system organized—functionally as well as anatomically?
- How do drugs affect our brain and our behavior?
- How does the brain learn?
- How does the brain think?
- Why do we sleep and dream?

Every chapter's central question highlights the brain–behavior relationship. When we first describe how neurons communicate in Chapter 5, for example, we also describe how synapses can change based on experience. Later, in Section 14-4, we expand on synaptic plasticity as we explore learning and memory.

Just as it was when we wrote the first edition, our goal in this new edition is to bring coherence to a vast subject by helping students understand the big picture. Asking fundamental questions about the brain has another benefit: it piques students' interest and challenges them to join us on the journey of discovery that is brain science.

Scientific understanding of the human brain and human behavior continues to grow at an exponential pace. We want to communicate the excitement of recent breakthroughs in brain science as well as relate some of our own experiences of studying brain and behavior, both to make the field's developing core concepts and latest revelations understandable and to transport uninitiated students to the frontiers of physiological psychology.

# Areas of Emphasis

To convey the excitement of neuroscience as researchers understand it, we interweave evolution, genetics, and epigenetics; psychopharmacology; and neural plasticity and connectivity, including central nervous system (CNS) and enteric nervous system (ENS) interactions, throughout the book.

**EVOLUTION** Our perspective—neuroscience in an evolutionary context—recurs in almost every chapter. Focusing on comparative behavior and anatomy, we address nervous system evolution in depth in Chapters 1 and 2, evolution of the synapse in Section 5-1, and evolution of visual pathways in Section 9-2. We discuss how evolution might have influenced behaviors related to aggression and mate selection in Section 12-1, the evolutionary theories of sleeping and dreaming in Section 13-4, and the evolutionary origins of memory in Section 14-3. We describe the evolution of sex differences in spatial cognition and language in Section 15-5 and links between our evolved reactions to stress and anxiety disorders in Section 16-2.

**GENETICS AND EPIGENETICS** We introduce the foundations of genetic and epigenetic research in Sections 1-3 and 2-1, and then begin to elaborate on them in Section 3-3. Chapter 5 discusses metabotropic receptors and DNA. The interplay of genes and drug action is integral to Chapter 6, as are the developmental roles of genes and gene methylation to Chapter 8. Section 9-4 explains the genetics of color vision, and the genetics of sleep disorders anchors Section 13-6. Section 14-4 highlights the role of epigenetics in memory. Section 16-3 considers the roles of genetics and of prions in understanding the causes of behavioral disorders.

**PSYCHOPHARMACOLOGY** Chapter 5 explores the roles of hormones in regulating behavior, and Chapter 6 continues this investigation by examining the effects of drugs on behavior, topics we revisit often throughout the book. You will find coverage of drugs and cellular communication in Section 5-3, and synthetic biology and drug manipulations in Section 7-1. Section 12-7 covers drugs and emotional behavior;

Section 13-6, drugs and sleep disorders; and Section 14-4, neuronal changes with drug use. Sections 16-2 and 16-3 explore drugs used as treatments for a range of behavioral disorders.

**CONNECTIVITY** Neural plasticity is a hallmark of this book. We introduce this concept in Section 1-1, detail it in Section 2-1, develop it further in Section 2-6, and expand on it throughout. At the conclusion of Section 14-4, we elaborate seven guiding principles of brain plasticity. In Section 1-4, we introduce the emerging field of connectomics, which we explore further throughout Chapter 15. The new field of psychobiotics, which identifies the connection between the gut microbiome and its effects on the ENS, as well as on the CNS, appears in Sections 2-5. The emerging study of computational neuroscience, which explores the organization of neural networks and applies that knowledge to research in deep learning and artificial intelligence, is covered in Section 7-7.

# Scientific Background Provided

We describe the journey of discovery in neuroscience in a way that students beginning to study the brain and behavior can understand; and we provide clinical examples to tie its relevance problems we face. Our approach provides the background that students need to understand introductory brain science. Multiple illustrated Experiments (found in 13 chapters) help students in visualizing the scientific method with how scientists think. The Basics features (found in 6 chapters) address the fact that understanding brain function requires understanding information from all the basic sciences.

Some encounters with neuroscience can be surprising to students who come to the course without a science background. The Basics features in Chapters 1 and 2 address relevant evolutionary and anatomical background. In Chapter 3, The Basics provides a short introduction to chemistry before the text describes the brain's chemical activities. In Chapter 4, The Basics addresses electricity before exploring the brain's electrical activity.

Readers already comfortable with this material can easily skip it; less experienced readers can learn it and use it as a context for neuroscience. Students with this background can tackle brain science with greater confidence. For students with limited knowledge of basic psychology, we review the stages of behavioral development in Chapter 8 and forms of learning and memory in Chapter 14.

Students in social science disciplines often remark on the amount of biology and chemistry in the book, and an equal number of students in biological sciences remark on the amount of psychology. More than half the students enrolled in the bachelor of science in neuroscience program at the University of Lethbridge switched from an initial biochemistry or psychology major after taking this course. Neuroscience is exciting!

Chapter 7 showcases the range of methods that behavioral neuroscientists use to measure and manipulate brain and behavior—both traditional methods and cutting-edge techniques such as optogenetics, optical tomography, resting-state fMRI, chemogenetics, GRAB, DREADD, and CRISPR. Expanded discussions of these techniques appear where appropriate, especially in the Research Focus features, including Focus 4-3, Optogenetics and Light-Sensitive Ion Channels; Focus 7-2, Brainbow: Rainbow Neurons; Focus 7-3, Brain Organoids and Personalized Medicine; Focus 11-1, Neuroprosthetics; and Focus 16-1, Posttraumatic Stress Disorder, which includes treatments based on virtual reality (VR) exposure therapies.

Because critical thinking is vital to progress in science, selected discussions throughout the book center on the philosophical problems addressed by brain research. Section 1-2 concludes with "The Separate Realms of Science and Belief." Section 7-8 presents a variety of ethical considerations in neuroscience research and practice now being explored under the umbrella of neuroethics, as well as issues related to animal welfare in scientific research. Section 15-2 discusses the rise and fall of mirror neurons, demonstrating how the media—and even scientists—can fail to question the validity of

---

## SEVENTH EDITION KEY REVISIONS

### CHAPTER 8

**UPDATED** Clinical Focus 8-2 discusses the connection between gray-matter volume and ASD.

**NEW** subsection in Section 8-2 discusses research into neurogenesis in adulthood.

**NEW** subsection in Section 8-4 focuses on environmental influences on brain development, including a discussion of SES and cognitive enrichment, and expanded coverage (and new figure) on the relationships between gut bacteria and brain development.

### CHAPTER 9

**NEW** Figure 9-2 depicts a flowchart for simplified sensory pathways.

**UPDATED** Clinical Focus 9-3 discusses treatments for glaucoma involving the mTOR signaling pathway and other treatments.

**NEW** Section 9-6 on plasticity in the visual pathways.

### CHAPTER 10

**REVISED** Research Focus 10-1 focuses on the connection between music and language in the cognitive mechanisms that allow rhythmic vocalizations in hominins.

**NEW** Clinical Focus 10-5 describes the experience of cochlear implants for a child who was born deaf.

### CHAPTER 11

**UPDATED** Clinical Focus 11-1 on the brain–computer interface and the computer–brain interface.

**UPDATED** discussion of the use of nanotechnology in the treatment for spinal cord injury in Section 11-1.

**EXPANDED** discussion of pain gates in Section 11-4.

**REVISED** presentation of body and action maps in Section 11-5.

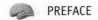

research results. Section 12-5—and particularly Research Focus 12-3, The Brain Gender Continuum—explores the idea that gender identity comprises a broad spectrum rather than a simple female–male dichotomy.

# Clinical Focus Maintained

Neuroscience is a human science. Everything in this book is relevant to our lives and the lives of those we know, and everything in our lives is relevant to neuroscience. Understanding neuroscience helps us understand how we learn, how we develop, and how we can help people with brain and behavioral disorders. Knowledge of how we learn, how we develop, and what the symptoms of brain and behavioral disorders provide insights into neuroscience.

Clinical material also helps make neurobiology relevant to students who plan to seek a career in psychology, social work, or another profession related to mental health, as well as to students of the biological sciences. We integrate clinical information throughout the text with Clinical Focus features, and we expand on it in Chapter 16, the book's capstone, as well.

In *An Introduction to Brain and Behavior*, the placement of some topics is novel relative to traditional treatments. We include brief descriptions of brain diseases close to discussions of basic associated processes. For example, coverage of Parkinson disease is integrated throughout Chapter 5, How Do Neurons Communicate and Adapt? This strategy helps first-time students repeatedly forge close links between what they are learning and real-life issues.

To provide a consistent disease nomenclature, the seventh edition follows the system advocated by the World Health Organization for diseases named after their putative discoverers. "Down syndrome," for example, has largely replaced "Down's syndrome" in the popular and scientific literature. We extend that convention to Parkinson disease and Alzheimer disease, among other eponymous diseases and disorders.

The nearly 150 disorders we cover are cross-referenced in the Index of Disorders inside the book's front cover. Chapter 16 expands on the nature of neuroscience research and the multidisciplinary treatment methods for neurological and psychiatric disorders described in preceding chapters.

We emphasize questions that relate to the biological bases of behavior. For us, the excitement of neuroscience lies in understanding how the brain explains what we do, whether it is talking, sleeping, seeing, or learning. Readers will therefore find nearly as many illustrations focusing on behavior as illustrations depicting the brain. This emphasis on explaining the biological foundations of behavior is another reason we include a mix of Clinical, Research, and Comparative Focus features throughout the text.

# Abundant Chapter Pedagogy

Building on the innovative teaching devices described so far, numerous in-text pedagogical aids adorn every chapter, beginning with an outline and an opening Focus feature that draws students into the chapter's topic. Focus features dot each chapter to connect brain and behavior to relevant clinical or research experience. Within chapters, definitions of boldface key terms introduced in the text appear in the margins as reinforcement, margin notes link topics together, and end-of-section Review self-tests help students check their grasp of major points.

Each chapter ends with a Summary (several of which include summarizing tables or illustrations to help students visualize or review big-picture concepts); a list of Key Terms, each referencing the page number on which the term is defined; and a list of dynamic digital resources available through Macmillan's Achieve platform. Following this Preface, the Media and Supplements section describes the wide array of supplemental materials designed exclusively for students and teachers using the seventh edition.

# Superb Visual Reinforcement

Our most important learning aid appears on nearly every page in the book: an expansive and, we believe, exceptional set of illustrations. Overwhelmingly, readers agree that, hand in hand with our words, these diagrams vividly describe and illuminate the nervous system. Important anatomical illustrations are presented in a large format to ease their perusal. We have selected relevant and engaging photos that enliven and enrich the discussion, ranging from a dance class for individuals with Parkinson disease in Section 5-3, to VR clinic rooms that allow patients and neurosurgeons to interact directly with VR models in Section 7-3, to a seniors' bridge game to illustrate the discussion of cognitively stimulating activities in Section 16-3.

Illustrations are presented in a consistent manner from chapter to chapter so that they reinforce one another. We consistently color-code diagrams that illustrate each aspect of the neuron, depict each structural region in the brain, and demarcate nervous system divisions. We include many varieties of micrographic images to show what a particular neural structure actually looks like. These illustrations and images are included in our PowerPoint presentations and integrated as labeling exercises in our Study Guide and Testing materials.

# Teaching Through Metaphors, Examples, and Principles

If a textbook is not enjoyable, it has little chance of teaching well. We heighten students' interest through abundant use of metaphors and examples. Students read about patients whose brain injuries offer insights into brain function, and we examine car engines, robots, and prehistoric flutes for the same purpose. A wealth of illustrated Experiments, comparative biology examples, and representative Comparative Focus features help students understand how much we humans have in common with creatures as distant from us as sea slugs and as close to us as chimpanzees.

We also facilitate learning by reemphasizing the main points and by distilling sets of principles about brain function that offer a framework to guide students' thinking. Thus, Section 2-6 introduces 10 key principles that explain how the parts of the nervous system work together. Section 14-4 summarizes seven guiding principles of neuroplasticity. Collectively, these sets of principles form the basis of many discussions throughout the book. Margin notes also remind readers when they encounter these principles again—and indicate where they can review them in depth.

# Big-Picture Emphasis

One challenge in writing an introductory book on any topic is deciding what to include and what to exclude. We have organized the discussions in this text to focus on the bigger picture—a focus exemplified by the 10 principles of nervous system function introduced in Section 2-6, revised for this edition, and echoed throughout the book. Any set of principles may be arbitrary yet nevertheless afford students a useful framework for understanding the brain's activities.

In Chapters 8 through 16, we tackle behavioral topics in a more general way than most contemporary books do. In Section 16-4, Research Challenges, we outline the challenges in the treatment of brain diseases. In Chapter 12, for instance, we revisit experiments and ideas from the 1960s to understand why animals behave as they do, then consider emotional and motivated behaviors as diverse as eating and anxiety attacks in humans. In Chapter 14, the larger picture of learning and memory is presented alongside a discussion of recovery from traumatic brain injury.

This broad focus helps students grasp the big picture that behavioral neuroscience paints. While broadening our focus requires us to leave out some details, our

## SEVENTH EDITION KEY REVISIONS

### CHAPTER 15

**REVISED** discussion of executive function in the presentation of planning in Section 15-2.

**UPDATED** discussion of mirror neurons in Section 15-2.

**UPDATED** discussion of brain connectomes, mapping, and parcellation in Section 15-3.

**REVISED** Clinical Focus 15-3 on neuropsychological assessment.

**NEW** presentation of network neuroscience theory in Section 15-6.

**REVAMPED** discussion of the neural basis of consciousness in Section 15-7, with a new presentation of global neuronal workspace theory.

### CHAPTER 16

**EXPANDED** discussion of clinical neuroscience in Section 16-1.

**UPDATES** throughout the discussions of psychiatric disorders and neurological disorders and their treatments in Sections 16-2 and 16-3.

**REVISED** presentation of multiple sclerosis under the new subheading "Disorders of Myelin."

**NEW** presentation of amyloid beta and tau protein in the discussion of prion disorders in Section 16-3.

**REVAMPED** Section 16-5, which now addresses recovery in terms of post-traumatic growth.

experience with students and teachers through six earlier editions confirms that discussing the larger problems and issues in brain and behavior is of greater interest to students—especially those new to this field—and is more often remembered than are myriad details without context.

As in preceding editions, we have been selective in our citations of the truly massive literature on the brain and behavior in this seventh edition, because we believe that too many citations can disrupt the text's flow, distracting students from the task of mastering concepts. We provide citations to classic works by including the names of the researchers and by mentioning where the research was performed. In areas where controversy or new breakthroughs predominate, we include detailed citations to papers (especially reviews) from the years 2018 to 2021. An end-of-book References section lists, by chapter, all the literature used in developing the book, reflecting the addition of many new citations in this edition and the elimination of other, now superseded, research.

# Acknowledgments

We sincerely thank the many people who contributed to the development of this edition. The staff at Macmillan Learning is remarkable and makes doing revisions a joy. We thank our executive program manager, Daniel DeBonis, who was more than ably assisted by Talia Green; our senior content project manager, Vivien Weiss; and senior workflow project manager Paul Rohloff; as well as senior project manager Aravinda Doss, and the composition team at Lumina. Andrew Sylvester took over from Barbara Brooks as development editor for the sixth edition and has continued with this edition. He has done a wonderful job in coordinating the contributions of three authors to ensure that the book continues to have a single voice and encouraging us to write simply and clearly for students encountering neuroscience for the first time.

We thank senior cover design manager John Callahan for a striking cover and senior design services manager Natasha Wolfe for a fresh, inviting, accessible new interior design. Thanks also to Cecilia Varas for coordinating the photo research and to Richard Fox, who found photographs and other illustrative materials that we would not have found on our own. We are indebted to Macmillan art manager Matt McAdams and Eli Ensor for their excellent work in creating new illustrations.

Our colleagues, too, have helped in the development of every edition. We would like to thank the following colleagues and students for making important contributions: Javad Karimi Abadchi, Mike Antle, Jaideep Bains, Nicole Burma, Tim Bussey, Richard Dyck, Jonathan Epp, Paolo Federico, Richard Frayne, Robbin Gibb, Matthew Hill, Lisa Siksida, Simon Spanswick, Peter Stys, Catherine Thomas, Masami Tatsuno, Roger Thompson, Tuan Trang, and Alicia Zumbusch.

And for their help in shaping the seventh edition, we are especially indebted to the reviewers who provided extensive comments on selected chapters and illustrations: Francis R. Bambico, *Memorial University*; Mark E. Basham, *Regis University*; Kristine A. Camacho, *Worcester State University*; Rochelle Caroon-Santiago, *University of the Incarnate Word*; Laurence S. David, *Alexander College*; Amanda ElBassiouny, *California Lutheran University*; Michael Emond, *Laurentian University*; Kelly M. Fischer, *Ball State University*; Tom Fischer, *Wayne State University*; Veronica V. Galvan, *University of San Diego*; Jeffrey W. Grimm, *Western Washington University*; Joseph Hall, *Binghamton University—State University of New York*; Adam Howorko, *Concordia University College*; Brittany M. Jeye, *Worcester State University*; Artur Luczak, *University of Lethbridge*; Eliza L. Nelson, *Florida International University*; Kimberly A. Paul, *Southeast Community College Area*; Ruth E. Propper, *Montclair State University*; Jeffrey Rudski, *Muhlenberg College*; Dr. Lesley A. Schimanski, *Simon Fraser University*; James O. Taylor, *Utah Valley University*; Sarah Thackray, *University of Calgary*; Jennifer Thomson, *Messiah College*; Melanie M. Trowbridge, *William Jessup University*; Alicia A. Walf, *Rensselaer Polytechnic Institute*; Andrew Weeks, *Nipissing University*; Keith L. Williams, *Oakland University*; and Carly A. Yadon, *Missouri State University Springfield*. We would also like to thank the Writing Diversely team, particularly Gulnaz Saiyed and Juno Baker, for their review of selected chapters to help ensure greater equity and inclusivity in the presentation.

Likewise, we continue to be indebted to the colleagues who provided extensive comments during the development of previous editions of this book: Chana Akins, *University of Kentucky*; Michael Anch, *Saint Louis University*; Barry Anton, *University of Puget Sound*; Karen Atkinson-Leadbeater, *Mount Royal University*; Mark Basham, *Regis University*; Nancy Blum, *California State University, Northridge*; R. Bruce Bolster, *University of Winnipeg*; Kelly Bordner, *Southern Connecticut State University*; Richard Brown, *LaGuardia Community College, CUNY*; James Canfield, *University of Washington*; Edward Castañeda, *University of New Mexico*; Benjamin Clark, *University of New Mexico*; Richard Conti, *Kean University*; Pam Costa, *Tacoma Community College*; Russ Costa, *Westminster College*; Renee Countryman, *Austin College*; Kristen D'Anci, *Salem State University*; Darragh P. Devine, *University of Florida*; Carol DeVolder, *St. Ambrose University*; Benjamin DeVore, *Virginia Tech*; Francine Dolins, *University of Michigan–Dearborn*; Evelyn Field, *Mount Royal University*; Roslyn Fitch, *University of Connecticut*; Merage Ghane, *Virginia Polytechnic Institute and State University*; Trevor Gilbert, *University of Calgary*; Nicholas Grahame, *Indiana University–Purdue University Indianapolis*; Kenneth Green, *California State University, Long Beach*; Bradley Gruner, *College of Southern Nevada*; Trevor James Hamilton, *Grant MacGewn University*; Kenneth Troy Harker, *University of New Brunswick*; Christian Hart, *Texas Woman's University*; Matthew Holahan, *Carleton University*; Sandra Holloway, *Saint Joseph University*; Adam Hutcheson, *Georgia Gwinnett College*; Jason Ivanoff, *St. Mary's University*; Eric Jackson, *University of New Mexico*; Chris Jones, *College of the Desert*; Joy Kannarkat, *Norfolk State University*; Daniel Kay, *Brigham Young University*; Jennifer Koontz, *Orange Coast College*; Dwight Kravitz, *The George Washington University*; Ralph Lydic, *University of Tennessee, Knoxville*; Lisa Lyons, *Florida State University*; Kate Makerec, *William Paterson University of New Jersey*; Vincent Markowski, *SUNY Geneseo*; Paul Meyer, *The State University of New York at Buffalo*; Maura Mitrushina, *California State University, Northridge*; Daniel Montoya, *Fayetteville State University*; Michael Nadorff, *Mississippi State University*; Michael Nelson, *University of Missouri, Rolla*; Michael Neelon, *University of North Carolina–Asheville*; Jaime Olavarria, *University of Washington*; Barbara Oswald, *Miami University of Ohio*; Gabriel Radvansky, *University of Notre Dame*; Christopher Robison, *Florida State University*; Joshua S. Rodefer, *University of Iowa*; Carlos Rodriguez, *The University of New Mexico*; Jackie Rose, *Western Washington University*; Neil Sass, *Heidelberg University*; Claire Scavuzzo, *University of Alberta*; Steven Schandler, *Chapman University*; Sarah Schock, *University of Ottawa*; Maharaj Singh, *Marquette University*; Andra Smith, *University of Ottawa*; Robert Stackman, *Florida Atlantic University*; Richard Straub, *University of Michigan–Dearborn*; Sandra Trafalis, *San Jose State University*; Charlene Wages, *Francis Marion University*; Douglas Wallace, *Northern Illinois University*; Patricia Wallace, *Northern Illinois University*; Paul Wellman, *Texas A&M University*; Ilsun White, *Morehead State University*; Matthew Will, *University of Missouri, Columbia*; Manda Williamson, *University of Nebraska–Lincoln*; Edie Woods, *Madonna University*; and Harris Philip Zeigler, *Hunter College*. The methods chapter was new to the third edition and posed the additional challenge of taking what easily could read like a seed catalog and making it engaging to readers. We therefore are indebted to Margaret G. Ruddy, *The College of New Jersey*, and Ann Voorhies, *University of Washington*, for providing extensive advice on the initial version of Chapter 7. Sheri Mizumori, *University of Washington*, deserves special thanks for reading the entire second edition manuscript for accuracy and providing fresh ideas that proved invaluable.

Finally, we must thank our tolerant wives for putting up with sudden changes in plans as chapters returned, in manuscript or in proof, with hopes for quick turnarounds. We also thank our colleagues Robbin Gibb and Masami Tatsuno at the University of Lethbridge, who use the book and have provided much feedback, as well as our colleagues at the University of Calgary who also use the book and/or provided advice, including Michael Antle, Jadeep Bains, Richard Dyck, Jonathan Epp, Matthew Hill, Ken Lukowiak, Alex McGirr, Vilten Nicola, and Quentin Pittman. In addition, we are grateful to our undergraduate and graduate students, technicians, and postdoctoral fellows, who kept our research programs moving forward when we were engaged in revising the book.

*Bryan Kolb, Ian Q. Whishaw, G. Campbell Teskey*

*An Introduction to Brain and Behavior*, Seventh Edition, features a wide array of supplemental materials designed exclusively for students and teachers of the text. For more information about any of the items, please visit the Macmillan Learning catalog at www.macmillanlearning.com.

# For Students

## NEW! Achieve

Achieve is the new learning platform that sets a whole new standard for teaching. It brings together all of the features that instructors and students loved about our previous platform, LaunchPad—an interactive e-book, LearningCurve adaptive quizzing, immersive learning activities, and extensive instructor resources—in a powerful new platform with a cleaner, more intuitive, mobile-friendly interface.

Achieve was co-designed with instructors and students, on a foundation of years of learning research, and rigorous testing over multiple semesters. The result is superior content, organization, and functionality. Achieve is effective for students at all levels of motivation and preparedness, whether they are high achievers or need extra support. Macmillan Learning offers deep platform integration with all LMS providers, including Blackboard, Brightspace, Canvas, and Moodle. With integration, students can access course content and their grades through one sign-in. And you can pair Achieve with course tools from your LMS, such as discussion boards, chat, and gradebook functionality. LMS integration is also available with Inclusive Access. For more information, visit MacmillanLearning.com or talk to your local sales representative.

Achieve was built with accessibility in mind. Macmillan Learning strives to create products that are usable by all learners and meet universally applied accessibility standards. In addition to addressing product compatibility with assistive technologies such as screen reader software, alternative keyboard devices, and voice recognition products, we are working to ensure that the content and platforms we provide are fully accessible. For more information, visit MacmillanLearning.com/College/US/Our-Story/Accessibility.

Achieve for *An Introduction to Brain and Behavior*, Seventh Edition, includes the following resources:

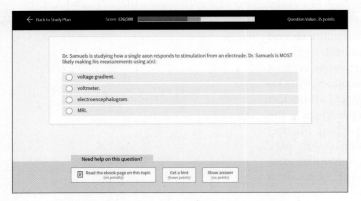

- **NEW! NEUROSCIENCE IN ACTION ACTIVITIES, VOLUMES I AND II,** are a collection of online activities that enable students to deepen their understanding of neuronal processes. The seventh edition features the debut of Volume II of the collection, adding more than 10 new activities and bringing the total collection to over 25. These activities show, through vivid animations, the foundational processes that the reader can only imagine when reading the text. Students come away with a fuller understanding of topics such as the conduction of the action potential, the integration of neural inputs, synaptic transmission, and the action of neurotransmitters. A perfect accompaniment to an online or hybrid course, each activity is fully assessable with multiple-choice questions. This collection is indispensable for bringing fundamental neuroscience concepts to life.

- **THE LEARNINGCURVE** adaptive quizzing system is designed based on the latest findings from learning and memory research. It combines adaptive question selection, immediate and valuable feedback, and a gamelike interface to engage students in a learning experience that is unique to them. Students experience learning that is customized to their level of knowledge, and instructors receive state-of-the-art reporting on the progress of each student, as well as the class as a whole.

- **PRACTICE QUIZZES** provide another way for students and instructors to rehearse their knowledge. Each quiz is written on the topics discussed throughout each chapter and features a variety of multiple-choice questions presented to students randomly from question pools. Valuable to both student and instructor, these practice quizzes are fully editable and make robust assessment quick and easy to set up.

- **AN INTERACTIVE E-BOOK** allows students to highlight, bookmark, and make notes, just as they would with a printed textbook. The search function and in-text glossary definitions make the text ready for the digital age.

- **STUDENT VIDEO ACTIVITIES** include engaging modules that instructors can easily assign for student assessment. Videos cover a variety of topics and are sure to spark discussion and encourage critical thinking.

# For Instructors

### Instructor's Resources

This invaluable tool, for new and experienced instructors alike, was revised by Catherine Smith of Carleton University. It includes chapter-by-chapter learning objectives and chapter overviews, detailed lecture outlines, thorough chapter summaries, chapter key terms, in-class demonstrations and activities, springboard topics for discussion and debate, ideas for research and term paper projects, homework assignments and exercises, and suggested readings from journals and periodicals. Course-planning suggestions and a guide to videos and Internet resources are also included.

# Assessment Tools

### Test Bank

The entire Test Bank for the seventh edition has been revised by text author G. Campbell Teskey and Simon Spanswick (both of the University of Calgary). The collection comprises more than 1300 multiple-choice and short-answer test questions. Each item is keyed to the page in the textbook on which the answer can be found. All the questions have been thoroughly reviewed and edited for accuracy and clarity.

# Presentation

### Illustration Slides and Lecture Slides

Available for download from Achieve, these slides can either be used as they are or customized to fit the needs of your course. They feature the main points of the chapter with selected figures and illustrations.

# What Are the Origins of Brain and Behavior?

# 1

Callista Images/Cultura/Getty Images

## ◎ CLINICAL FOCUS 1-1

# Living with Traumatic Brain Injury

Fred Linge, a clinical psychologist with a degree in brain research, wrote this description 12 years after the car crash that resulted in his head injury:

> In the second it took for my car to crash head-on, my life was permanently changed, and I became another statistic in what has been called "the silent epidemic."
>
> During the next months, my family and I began to understand something of the reality of the experience of head injury. I had begun the painful task of recognizing and accepting my physical, mental, and emotional deficits. I couldn't taste or smell. I couldn't read even the simplest sentence without forgetting the beginning before I got to the end. I had a hair-trigger temper that could ignite instantly into rage over the most trivial incident. . . .
>
> Two years after my injury, I wrote a short article: "What Does It Feel Like to Be Brain Damaged?" At this point in my life, I began to involve myself with other brain-damaged people. It brought me an enormous outpouring of letters, phone calls, and personal visits that continue to this day. Many were struggling as I had struggled, with no diagnosis, no planning, no rehabilitation, and most of all, no hope. . . . The catastrophic effect of my injury was such that I was shattered and then remolded by the experience, and I emerged from it a profoundly different person with a different set of convictions, values, and priorities. (Linge, 1990)

Adapting to an injured brain can come to dominate the lives of those who experience brain injury and disease as well as the lives of their friends and family members. In the absence of proper diagnosis and treatment, the challenges of brain injury often exceed the support that health systems and the community can provide.

Globally, brain disease and injury is the leading cause of disability and the second leading cause of death (GBD 2016 Neurology Collaborators, 2019). The National Institute of Neurological Disorders and Stroke estimates that 1.7 million U.S. residents receive medical attention each year after experiencing a **traumatic brain injury (TBI)** — a wound to the brain that results from a blow to the head or a **concussion**.

TBI frequently occurs from playing sports, from falls, and from vehicle accidents, and is the most common cause of discharge from military service. Throughout this book, you will encounter many of the 2000 or more disorders of the brain (see the index of major disorders on the inside front cover of this book). Disorders of the brain are among the challenges faced by individuals working in the field of *neuroscience*, the multidisciplinary study of the brain. Most people who suffer from TBI have to cope, at least to some degree, with Linge's forecast of "no diagnosis, no planning, no rehabilitation, and most of all, no hope."

Neuroscience looks at not only brain disease, but also the anatomy of the brain, its chemistry, physics, computational processes, influences on psychological functioning, and influences on sociological and economic factors. Neuroscience research can provide insights into individual differences, including differences in sexual orientation, cognitive function, and social behavior, and consciousness. It can address the challenges outlined by Linge by, for example, supporting improved diagnoses through imaging the anatomy, chemistry, and electrical activity of the brain and rehabilitation using computer-assisted training and prosthetics.

Fred Linge died in 2021 at the age of 84, but during his life he displayed *posttraumatic growth*—he came to terms with his TBI and found meaning in life with the nontraditional therapy of "faith, hope and love." We take up posttaumatic growth in Section 16-5.

---

**traumatic brain injury (TBI)** Wound to the brain that results from a blow to the head.

**concussion** Alteration in brain function that results from sudden shaking or blows to the head and can lead to severe brain damage especially after repeated injury; symptoms may be temporary and affect memory, consciousness, vision, coordination, and mood, and other effects.

The purpose of this book is to take you on a journey toward understanding the link between brain and behavior—to explore how the brain is organized to produce behavior. This book also invites you to become a participant in the study of your own brain and behavior. Understanding the brain will change how you think about yourself and others, change how you view education and social interactions, and perhaps spur your interest in a career in neuroscience.

As you work through this book, it will become clear that neuroscience is not merely the study of brain function and brain disease—such as those described in Clinical Focus 1-1: Living with Traumatic Brain Injury—but is also intertwined with many other areas of study, including philosophy, psychology, and economics, to name a few.

## 1-1

# The Brain in the Twenty-First Century

The purpose of this chapter is to describe the relationship between brain and behavior. In this opening section, we first present the ideas that led to our current understanding of the role of the brain in behavior. Next, we describe the brains or brain-like structures of some of the 1.5 million animal species that have one. We end by discussing what makes the brain of each animal species, including humans, special.

**Learning Objectives**
- Describe the research and societal benefits of the study of brain and behavior.
- Describe the human brain by identifying some of the defining components and by explaining its relationship to behavior.

The developing field of *neuroethics* addresses issues related to diversity, equity, and inclusion both with respect to training in neuroscience and with respect to research. A growing number of programs in research-funding agencies and in universities are directed toward making the field of neuroscience more diverse in terms of the research that is funded and through efforts to expand networks and career opportunities for historically underrepresented groups (Jones-London, 2020). In 2021, the National Institutes of Health (NIH) launched its UNITE initiative to help combat historical racial inequalities across a wide variety of biomedical and health sciences. Recent diversity and inclusion efforts by the Society for Neuroscience and other institutions have sought to address inequities in representation and enhance career and research opportunities among historically under-represented groups. We will address neuroethical issues throughout this introduction to brain and behavior.

## Why Study Brain and Behavior?

The *brain* is a physical object, a living tissue, a body organ. *Behavior* is action, momentarily observable but fleeting. Brain and behavior differ greatly, yet are also linked. They have evolved together: one is responsible for the other, which is responsible for the other, and so on. There are five reasons for linking the study of the brain to the study of behavior:

Illustrated Experiments throughout the book reveal how neuroscientists conduct research, beginning with Experiment 1-1 in Section 1-2.

1. *How the brain produces behavior is a major scientific question.* Scientists and students study the brain to understand humanity. A better understanding of brain function will allow us to better understand many aspects of our world, including educational systems, economic systems, and social systems. Understanding our brain will also help us to understand our many cultural, religious, and sexual differences. In short, understanding our brain will help us understand why we—that is, humans—are the most behaviorally diverse species.

2. *The brain is the most complex organ on Earth and is found in many groups of animals.* We study the brain to understand its place in the biological order of our planet. The importance we place on the brain extends deep into our cultures, as reflected in the many science fiction depictions of alien life, which assume that this life will include animals with brains. This chapter describes the basic function and evolution of the brain on our planet, especially the human brain.

3. *A growing list of behavioral disorders can be explained and treated as we increase our understanding of the brain.* As we have noted, more than 2000 disorders may be in some way related to brain abnormalities. As indicated in the Index of Disorders on the inside front cover of this book, we detail relationships between brain disorders and behavioral disorders in every chapter, especially in the Focus features. Understanding our brain helps us to understand the physical, mental, and emotional changes that occur as we develop and age, including disorders that emerge in childhood and continue to impact us throughout our lives. The better educated we are about the nature of brain and brain disorders, the better equipped we will be to develop effective treatments for these disorders.

4. *Study of the brain leads to an understanding of diversity.* The study of neuroscience gives us a more expansive understanding of the developmental complexity and individual differences, which can reduce stigma and break down social barriers that often pose challenges for individuals with disorders. Although the field of neuroscience has not been immune to the influence of bias and prejudice, research geared toward obtaining a better understanding of brain disorders and differences has often operated ahead of social progress and is an important tool in combating stereotypes and misconceptions.

The concept of *neurodiversity*, originally developed by sociologist Judy Singer in the late 1990s, seeks to contextualize cognitive and behavioral disorders within a wider spectrum of normal variation across individuals.

5. *Study of the brain brings insights to other fields of knowledge and is a source of employment.* The field of neuroscience is becoming more diverse, as witnessed by the emergence of new areas of study, including neuropsychology, neurophilosophy, neuroeconomics, neurobiology, and neuroethics. Neuroscience is also having an

**neuron** Specialized nerve cell engaged in information processing.

**glial cells** Brain cells that support the function of neurons.

**central nervous system (CNS)** The brain and spinal cord, which together mediate behavior.

**peripheral nervous system (PNS)** All the neurons in the body outside the brain and spinal cord.

**cerebrum (forebrain)** Major structure of the forebrain, which consists of two mirror-image hemispheres (left and right) and is responsible for most conscious behavior.

**neocortex (cortex)** The outermost part of the brain that is visibly folded in humans and other large-brained mammals.

**hemisphere** Literally, half a sphere, referring to one side of the cerebrum.

**brainstem** Central structure of the brain; responsible for most unconscious behavior.

**cerebellum** Major brainstem structure specialized for learning and coordinating movements; assists the cerebrum in generating many behaviors.

Chapter 2 describes the brain's functional anatomy.

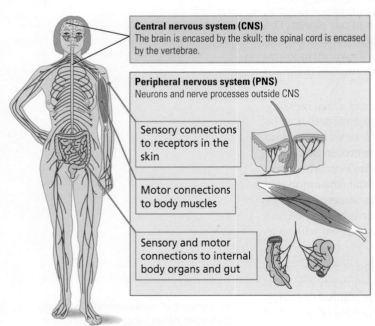

Central nervous system (CNS)
The brain is encased by the skull; the spinal cord is encased by the vertebrae.

Peripheral nervous system (PNS)
Neurons and nerve processes outside CNS

Sensory connections to receptors in the skin

Motor connections to body muscles

Sensory and motor connections to internal body organs and gut

**FIGURE 1-1 Major Divisions of the Human Nervous System** The brain and spinal cord together make up the central nervous system. All of the nerve processes radiating out beyond the brain and spinal cord and all of the neurons outside the CNS connect to sensory receptors, muscles, and internal body organs to form the peripheral nervous system.

impact on business, as shown by the application of neuroscience discoveries to a wide variety of industries, including medicine, drug development, data storage and analysis, and robotics. For example, deep learning, a kind of *artificial intelligence* (AI) developed from the study of brain networks, is becoming so sophisticated that scientists can create machines with truly brain-like properties.

None of us can predict how the knowledge we gain about the brain and behavior may prove useful. A former psychology major wrote to tell us that she took our course because she was unable to register in a preferred course. She felt that, although our course was interesting, it was "biology, not psychology." After graduating and getting a job in a social service agency, she has found—to her great delight—that understanding the links between brain and behavior is actually a source of insight into many of her clients' disorders and the treatment options available for them.

# What Is the Brain?

*Brain* is the Anglo-Saxon word for the tissue found within the skull. The brain, along with its vast connections with the organs of the body, is a part of the human nervous system (**Figure 1-1**). In subsequent sections, we will describe the relationships between the many animal species that have nervous systems and the subset of those species that have nervous systems that include some type of brain.

The human nervous system is composed of cells, as is the rest of the body. Just over half of these nervous system cells (86 billion of them) are called **neurons**. Neurons are specialized in that they interconnect with each other and with the muscles and organs of the body and are involved with information processing. The other half of the nervous system cells (85 billion) are called **glial cells**, and they support the function of the neurons. These two cell types are described in detail in Chapter 2.

Through interconnections, neurons send electrical and chemical signals to communicate with one another, with sensory receptors in the skin, with muscles, and with internal body organs. Most of the interconnections between the brain and body are made through the spinal cord, a tube of nervous tissue encased in our vertebrae. The spinal cord, in turn, sends nerve fibers out to our muscles and internal body organs and receives fibers from sensory receptors on many parts of our body.

Together, the brain and spinal cord make up the **central nervous system (CNS)**, the part of our nervous system encased in bone. The CNS is called *central* because it is both the nervous system's physical core and the core structure that mediates behavior. All the processes that radiate out beyond the brain and spinal cord constitute the **peripheral nervous system (PNS)**.

The human brain comprises many structures, but we will focus on two major divisions here. The **cerebrum (forebrain)**, shown in **Figure 1-2**A, has two nearly symmetrical halves, called **hemispheres**, one on the left and one on the right. The forebrain features a large number of structures, but the most prominent in the human brain is the neocortex. The **neocortex** ("new cortex"), often *cortex* for short (*cortex* means "bark" in Latin), is the crinkly tissue covering most of the rest of the brain. The cortex is proposed to be responsible for our conscious behavior.

The cortex enfolds the **brainstem** (Figure 1-2B), the set of structures responsible for most of our unconscious behavior. The dominant part of the human brainstem, the **cerebellum**, is specialized for learning and coordinating our movements. Although the forebrain and brainstem are associated with different general functions, they cannot manage these functions without each other. Thus, as will be discussed in later chapters, our conscious and unconscious behaviors are inextricably intertwined.

**(A) Cerebrum (forebrain)**

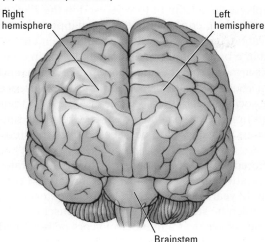

Right hemisphere

Left hemisphere

Brainstem

**(B) Right hemisphere of cerebrum**

Brainstem

Cerebellum

**FIGURE 1-2 The Human Brain (A)** Shown head-on, as oriented within the human skull, are the nearly symmetrical left and right hemispheres of the cerebrum. **(B)** A cut through the middle of the brain from back to front reveals the right hemispheres of the cerebrum and cerebellum and the right side of the brainstem. The spinal cord (not shown) emerges from the base of the brainstem.

So far, we have focused on the major components of the brain and nervous system, but there is more to the story. For his graduate research, our colleague Harvey chose to study the electrical activity of the brain in paralyzed animals. He speculated that it might be possible for a brain to live on in a bottle after the body died, and to continue functioning without receiving sensory information from the body or controlling bodily movements. He expected that his research would eventually allow a bottled brain to communicate with others who could read its electrical signals.

Harvey clearly proposed to preserve not just the brain but the *self*—consciousness, those processes such as language and memory that give us self-awareness and allowed us to interact with others. This meaning of *brain* refers to something other than the organ found inside the skull. It is what we intend when we describe a person who is clever as being "a brain" or when we speak of the computer that guides a spacecraft as being the vessel's brain. The term *brain*, then, signifies both the organ itself and the fact that this organ produces behavior.

To return to Harvey's experiment, the effect of placing even the entire CNS in a bottle would be to separate it from the PNS and, therefore, from the sensations and movements the PNS mediates. Could the brain remain awake and conscious without sensory information and without the ability to move? This question is relevant to theories of behavior as well as to many fascinating experiments and observations that have presented us with information relevant to this question.

One theory, called **embodied behavior**, proposes that our thoughts and our movements are inseparable (Conca et al., 2021). For example, we understand one another not only by listening to words but also by observing gestures and other body language. We think not only with silent language but also with overt gestures and body language. According to this view, the brain, as an intelligent entity, cannot be divorced from the body's activities.

In the 1920s, Edmond Jacobson proposed that even when motionless, we still make subliminal movements related to our thoughts. The muscles of the larynx subliminally (imperceptibly) move when we think in words, for instance, and we make subliminal eye movements when we imagine or visualize some action or a person, place, or thing. Jacobson had participants practice "total" relaxation and later asked them what the experience was like. They reported a condition of mental emptiness, as if the brain had gone blank (Jacobson, 1932).

**embodied behavior** Theory that the movements we make and the movements we perceive in others are central to communication with others.

**locked-in syndrome** Condition in which a patient is aware and awake but cannot move or communicate verbally because of complete paralysis of nearly all voluntary muscles except the eyes.

**minimally conscious state (MCS)** Condition in which a person can display some rudimentary behaviors, such as smiling or uttering a few words, but is otherwise not conscious.

**clinical trial** Consensual experiment directed toward developing a treatment.

**deep brain stimulation (DBS)** Neurosurgery in which electrodes implanted in the brain stimulate a targeted area with a low-voltage electrical current to facilitate behavior.

**persistent vegetative state (PVS)** Condition in which a person is alive but unaware, unable to communicate or to function independently at even the most basic level.

Martin Pistorius

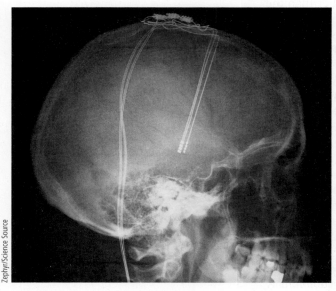

**FIGURE 1-3 Deep Brain Stimulation** X-ray image showing electrodes implanted in the thalamus, a structure deep in the brain near the tip of the brainstem, for DBS. DBS can treat disorders such as Parkinson disease and depression (see Section 16-3) and aid recovery from TBI (see Section 14-5).

Woodburn Heron took Jacobson's investigations a step further when, in 1957, he conducted experiments on sensory deprivation, a form of torture used in the Korean War (1950–1953). He asked, How does the brain cope without sensory input? Heron examined the effects of *sensory deprivation,* including feedback from movement, by having student volunteers lie on a bed in a bare, soundproof room and remain completely still. Padded tubes covered their arms so that they had no sense of touch, and translucent goggles cut off their vision. The participants reported that the experience was unpleasant, not just because of the social isolation but also because they lost their focus. Some even hallucinated, as if their brain were somehow trying to create the sensory experiences that they suddenly lacked. Most asked to be released from the study before it ended.

Evidence from people who have suffered nervous system injuries further illustrates the importance of understanding the relationship between overt behavior and consciousness. When Martin Pistorius was 12 years old, his health began to deteriorate. He lapsed into a coma, a condition in which he seemed completely unconscious. His parents placed Martin in a nursing home, where over a number of years he remained completely paralyzed.

Martin's condition persisted until, when he was 25, a nurse noticed him making some small facial movements. He seemed to be trying to communicate. Martin was not unconscious, but rather was suffering from **locked-in syndrome**—a condition in which a person is conscious but unable to move. With rehabilitation, he made excellent progress toward recovering movement in his head and arms. Using a voice synthesizer, he was eventually able to communicate verbally, and even gave a TED talk in 2015. He is married, has a child, and works as a Web developer. His 2011 book *Ghost Boy* describes his frustration and helplessness during years of enduring unrecognized locked-in syndrome. Pistorius's story shows that consciousness can persist in the absence of most overt movement.

Another case study offers further insight into the importance of arousal, or being awake, for consciousness. The patient, a 38-year-old man with brainstem damage, had lingered in a **minimally conscious state (MCS)** for more than 6 years after an assault. He was occasionally able to follow simple commands and to communicate with single words. He could make a few movements but could not feed himself despite 2 years of inpatient rehabilitation and 4 years in a nursing home.

Nicholas Schiff and his colleagues (Edlow et al., 2021) reasoned that if they could stimulate the remaining brainstem in this patient by administering a small electrical current, they could improve his level of wakefulness and so enhance his behavioral abilities. As part of a **clinical trial** (a consensual experiment directed toward developing a treatment), they implanted thin wire electrodes in the patient's brainstem so they could administer a small electrical current.

Through these electrodes, which are visible in the X-ray image shown in **Figure 1-3**, the investigators applied electrical stimulation for 12 hours each day—a procedure called **deep brain stimulation (DBS)**. The researchers observed dramatic improvements in the patient's arousal. For the first time since his assault, he was able to feed himself and swallow food. During brain stimulation, he could interact with his caregivers and watch television, and showed further improvement in response to rehabilitation. Clearly, wakefulness and consciousness are connected.

Another remarkable line of investigation illustrates that consciousness can be present in the absence of all voluntary movement. Patients who have experienced a brain injury so severe that it places them in **persistent vegetative state (PVS)** are alive, but are unable to communicate and show no signs of any cognitive function. Adrian Owen and his colleagues asked whether by imaging the brains of some of these patients, they could assess the extent to which the patients were conscious. Using a magnetic resonance imaging (MRI) procedure that measures brain function in terms of oxygen use, Owen's group discovered that some comatose patients are conscious and can communicate when given the opportunity. (For a discussion of Owen's experiments and their relevance to contemporary medical recommendations, see Scolding et al., 2021.)

Owen's group devised ways to communicate with these patients by using the signals in their brains' activity patterns (just as our colleague Harvey imagined could be done). When imaging the brains of control participants, Owen's group asked them to imagine hitting a tennis ball with a racket. When they did so, the researchers observed that their brain activity changed in association with the imaginary act. Next, the researchers asked the patients to imagine hitting a tennis ball. In response, some patients did exhibit activity similar to that of the control participants, showing that they understood the instructions. Owen's study demonstrated that some patients were conscious, which then allowed him to proceed with further efforts geared toward communication and rehabilitation.

Taken together, these studies reveal that the brain can be conscious to a great extent even in the absence of much overt behavior. They also show that in the absence of overt behavior, the brain can communicate through the signals generated by its activity, as Harvey proposed. Whether the brain can maintain consciousness with the absence of *all* sensory experience and movement—one of the challenges of Harvey's brain in a bottle experiment—remains an open question, though one that may be answered from an unexpected source.

Work with artificial intelligence (AI) shows that computers can do amazing things, including beating master players at the complex games of chess and GO. Many lines of investigation are ongoing to determine whether a computer can be conscious without directly experiencing the world in the way humans do, such as going to school, checking social media, or playing sports—in short, sensing and responding in the way we do each day. The answer to the question of whether a computer, such as your laptop or tablet, can be conscious in the absence of embodied behavior will provide insight into human consciousness (Blum & Blum, 2021).

# What Is Behavior?

Irenäus Eibl-Eibesfeldt began his classic textbook *Ethology: The Biology of Behavior* (1970) with the following definition: "Behavior consists of patterns in time." These patterns can be made up of movements, vocalizations, or changes in appearance, such as the facial movements associated with smiling. The expression *patterns in time* includes thinking. We cannot directly observe someone's thoughts. As we described earlier, though, the changes in the brain's electrical and biochemical activity that are associated with thought show that thinking, too, is a behavior that forms patterns in time.

The behavioral patterns of animals vary enormously, and these variations indicate the diverse functions of the brain. Animals produce behavior that is largely dependent on *heredity*, meaning they can perform a behavior with little or no previous experience. For these behaviors to occur, their brains must come equipped with the requisite organization to produce these behaviors. Animals can also *learn*, meaning that they can acquire new behaviors with experience and practice. These behaviors depend on the brain's **plasticity**, its ability to change in response to a learning experience.

**Figure 1-4** illustrates the contributions of inheritance and learning to the eating behaviors of two animal species, crossbills and roof rats. A crossbill's beak seems awkwardly crossed at the tip, yet it is exquisitely evolved for eating pinecones. If its shape is changed even slightly, the bird is unable to eat the pinecones it prefers until its beak grows back. For crossbills, eating does not require much modification through learning. Roof rats, in contrast, are rodents with sharp incisor teeth that appear to have evolved to cut into anything. Pinecones are an unusual food for the rats, although they have been found to eat them. But roof rats can eat pinecones efficiently only if an experienced mother teaches them to do so. This eating strategy is not only learned but also *cultural*, in that parents teach it to offspring. We expand on the concept of culture in Section 1-5.

We refer to people who voluntarily take part in research studies as *participants* and to those who are in treatment for brain or behavioral impairments as *patients*; nonhuman animals are referred to as *subjects*.

More research on TBI and other neurological disorders as well as treatments for these conditions are discussed in Sections 7-1, 14-5, and 16-3. Concussion is the topic of Clinical Focus 16-3.

A crossbill's beak is specifically designed to open pine cones. This behavior is innate.

A baby roof rat must learn from its mother how to eat pine cones. This behavior is learned.

**FIGURE 1-4 Innate and Learned Behaviors** Some animal behaviors are largely innate and fixed (*top*). Others are largely learned (*bottom*). Learning is a form of cultural transmission. Top: Information from Weiner (1995). Bottom: Information from Terkel (1995).

**plasticity** Body's potential for physical or chemical change; enhances its adaptability to environmental change and its ability to compensate for injury. (In the brain and nervous system, this potential is called *neuroplasticity*.)

The lesson from the variations exhibited by different animal species with respect to inbuilt and acquired behaviors is that much of its organization prepares the brain not only to produce behavior but also to change. For example, through selective breeding we can produce herding dogs that are prepared to learn how to herd sheep or cattle, but training is also needed for these animals to actually become successful herding dogs. Like other animals, humans retain many inherited ways of responding, such as the sucking response of a newborn infant. Most of our body functions—including heartbeat, digestion, and respiration—are controlled by unconscious nervous system activity. Throughout our lives, our preparedness to learn influences our ability to learn. Our school systems are based on the idea that our maturation is related to our capacity for learning. Nevertheless, because the majority of humans' most complex behaviors, including reading, writing, mathematics, and using smartphones, were learned long after our brain evolved its present form, we have obviously inherited a versatile brain.

The composite influence of innate abilities and learning presents researchers with many experimental questions. How does the brain inherit the organization needed to produce organized behavior? How does the brain learn? Are the brain processes that produce inherited behaviors and learned behaviors the same? These questions are also relevant in robotics, as we build machines that have inbuilt (innate) learning, and in AI, as we build machines designed to be self-educated. In subsequent chapters, we will take up these questions in our discussions of genetics, nervous system changes that mediate learning, and networks that produce both human intelligence and AI.

## 1-1 Review

**Before you continue, check your understanding. Answers to Self-Test appear at the back of the book.**

1. _____ is a wound to the brain that results from a blow to the head.

2. The brain and spinal cord together make up the _____. All of the nerve fibers radiating out beyond the brain and spinal cord as well as all of the neurons outside the brain and spinal cord form the _____.

3. The brain has two major divisions: the _____ supports conscious behavior and enfolds the _____, which supports unconscious behavior.

4. A simple definition of *behavior* is any kind of movement in a living organism. Every behavior has both a cause and a function, but behaviors vary in complexity and in the degree to which they are _____, or innate, and the degree to which they depend on _____.

5. What is meant by the concept of *embodied behavior*?

6. Explain how inventions relying on robotics and AI mimic the behaviors of the brain.

**Learning Objectives**

- Chart the historical understanding of the mind from ancient concepts of psyche through mentalism, dualism, and materialism.
- Explain the impact of genetics and inheritance on our contemporary understanding of brain and behavior.
- Summarize our contemporary understanding of consciousness.

## 1-2

# Theories of Brain and Behavior

Let's return to our central topic: how the study of brain and the study of behavior are related. Many people have reasoned about the causes of behavior. Their speculations can be classified into three theories: mentalism, dualism, and materialism. After describing each theory, we explain why contemporary brain investigators subscribe to the materialist theory. In reviewing these theories, you will recognize that we are still influenced by each. Melanie Challenger (2021) in her book, *How to Be an Animal*, outlines many of the conflicts these theories pose for us, as she asks questions such as "Why do we accept cloning a monkey but not cloning a human?"

# Aristotle and Mentalism

The hypothesis that the mind (or soul) controls behavior is found in the thinking of many cultures. This idea is embodied in the character of Psyche from ancient Greco-Roman mythology. Psyche, a mortal, became the wife of the young god Cupid. Venus, Cupid's mother, opposed his marriage, so she harassed Psyche with almost impossible tasks. Psyche performed the tasks with such dedication and compassion that she was made immortal, thus removing Venus's objection to her.

The Greek philosopher Aristotle (384–322 B.C.E.) was alluding to this story when he suggested that all human intellectual functions are produced by a person's *psyche*. The **psyche** is a nonmaterial entity that is independent of the body, but responsible for consciousness, perceptions, and emotions and for such processes as imagination, opinion, desire, pleasure, pain, memory, and reason. The psyche, Aristotle argued, is essential for life, and its departure from the body results in death.

Aristotle's account of behavior marks the beginning of contemporary psychology—and the brain played no role in it. Aristotle thought the brain existed to cool the blood. Even if he had thought that the brain produced behavior, as did some other philosophers and physicians of his time, it would have made little difference in the absence of any idea of how a body organ could produce behavior (Gross, 1995). In formulating the concept of a soul, various religions have adopted Aristotle's view that a nonmaterial entity governs our behavior and that our essential consciousness survives our death.

The word *psyche* is translated into English as *mind*, the Anglo-Saxon word for *memory*. The philosophical position that a person's mind (psyche) is responsible for behavior is called **mentalism**. Mentalism continues to influence modern behavioral science because many psychological terms crafted to describe functions of the mind—*consciousness, sensation, perception, attention, imagination, emotion, motivation, memory,* and *volition* among them—are still used today as descriptions of behavior. Indeed, we use these terms in this book, and they frequently appear as chapter titles in contemporary psychology and neuroscience textbooks.

# Descartes and Dualism

In the first book on brain and behavior, *Treatise on Man*, French philosopher René Descartes (1972/1664) proposed a theory of behavior in which he retained the mind's prominence but gave the brain a role. Descartes placed the seat of the mind in the brain and linked the mind to the body. He stated in the first sentence of the book that mind and body "must be joined and united to constitute people."

Descartes was influenced by a variety of machines that were popular in Paris at the time, including gears, clocks, and waterwheels, and he realized that mechanical and physical principles could explain most activities of the body and brain—such as motion, digestion, and breathing. For example, in the water gardens in Paris, one device caused a hidden statue to extend outward and spray water when an unsuspecting stroller walked past it. The statue's actions were triggered when the person stepped on a pedal hidden in the sidewalk. Descartes proposed that the mechanical principles that produced this reflex action could also explain bodily functions.

But Descartes could not imagine how consciousness could be reduced to a mechanistic explanation. Therefore, he proposed that the mind interacts with the body to produce movement, working through a small structure at the brain's center, the pineal body (*pineal gland*). The mind instructs the pineal body, which lies beside fluid-filled brain cavities called *ventricles*, to direct fluid from them through nerves and into muscles (**Figure 1-5**). When the fluid expanded the muscles, Descartes imagined, the body would move.

The idea that behavior is controlled by two entities—a material body and a nonmaterial mind—is known as **dualism** (from Latin, meaning "two"). The argument against dualism is that there is no way for a nonmaterial entity to influence the body: doing so requires the spontaneous generation of energy, which violates the physical law of conservation of matter and energy. The difficulty in explaining how a nonmaterial mind and a physical brain might interact is called the **mind–body problem**.

**psyche** Synonym for *mind*; a nonmaterial entity once proposed to be the source of human behavior (specifically, consciousness, imagination, opinion, desire, pleasure, pain, memory, and reason).

**mentalism** Explanation of behavior as a function of the nonmaterial mind.

**dualism** Philosophical position that both a nonmaterial mind and a material body contribute to behavior.

**mind–body problem** Difficulty of explaining how a nonmaterial mind and a material body interact.

Aristotle's conceptualization of the psyche as separate from, but linked to, the body influenced many later cultures, including Islamic scholarship's study and treatment of mental disorders.

François Gérard, *Psyche and Cupid* (1798)

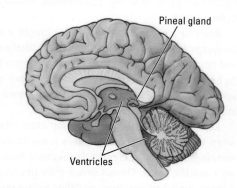

**FIGURE 1-5 Dualist Hypothesis** To explain how the mind controls the body, Descartes suggested that the mind resides in the pineal gland, where it directs the flow of fluid through the ventricles and into the muscles to move the body. The pineal gland actually influences daily and seasonal biorhythms; see Section 13-2.

The 2014 film *The Imitation Game* dramatizes Turing's efforts during World War II to crack the Nazis' Enigma code. The "imitation game" references the hypothetical interaction between a questioner and a computer, with a judge deciding whether the computer is conscious.

Nevertheless, Descartes proposed two tests for the presence of mind, based on the ability to use language and the ability to remember. He proposed that nonhuman animals and machines would be unable to pass the tests because they lacked a mind.

A contemporary version of Descartes's tests, the Turing test, is named for Alan Turing, an English mathematician. In 1950, Turing proposed his *imitation game* (now called the Turing test), in which a machine could be judged conscious if an interrogator or judge could not distinguish its answers from those of a human. Although contemporary computers can seemingly pass the Turing test, the critical component in the imitation game is the subjective assessment of the human judge—our willingness to interpret the appearance of intelligence as evidence of consciousness. Simone Natale (2021), in discussing the history of human–machine interactions, makes the point that the imitation game is not static; that is, AI is changing humans, and as it does so, it changes how we judge the imitation game.

Experimental research has also cast doubt on Descartes's view that nonhuman animals cannot pass "consciousness" tests. Studies of communication in apes and other animals partly seek to discover whether other species can speak and reason about things that are not present. Comparative Focus 1-2: The Speaking Brain summarizes a contemporary approach to studying communication in animals.

## ◎ COMPARATIVE FOCUS 1-2

# The Speaking Brain

No area of research has generated a literature as diverse and imaginative as the study of human language origins. In their book *Why Only Us*, Robert Berwick and Noam Chomsky (2016) argue that among animals, only humans have evolved language because of their unique ability to "merge" words and concepts to create an infinite number of concepts. In making this argument, they confront evolutionary theory, which suggests that language is unlikely to have appeared initially in the full-blown form seen in modern humans. While accepting the uniqueness of human language, the study of brain and behavior can contribute to our understanding of language origins by asking how the brain plays a role in communication in diverse species of animals. Many animal species with a small cerebrum, including fish and frogs, are capable of elaborate vocalizations, and vocalization is still more elaborate in species having a large cerebrum, such as birds, rodents, whales, and primates. In language studies with chimpanzees, humans' closest living relatives, scientists have investigated language learning, spontaneous vocalizations and gestures, and brain anatomy.

Beatrice and Alan Gardner (1969) taught a version of American Sign Language (ASL) to a chimpanzee named Washoe. Sue Savage-Rumbaugh and her coworkers (1999) then taught a bonobo (a chimp species thought to be an even closer relative of humans than others) named Kanzi the symbolic language Yerkish. Kanzi also displayed clear evidence of understanding complex human speech.

Kanzi's spontaneous vocalizations when interacting with people and when eating reveal that he makes many sounds associated with their meanings, or semantic context. For example, Kanzi associates various peeps with specific foods. Chimps smack their lips using the same rhythm that humans use when speaking, and they emit a raspberry or extended grunt sound in a specific context to attract the attention of others, including humans. They gesture with facial and arm movements when they vocalize to signal intent. They also use one distinct call to attract others to feeding locations and another call to initiate a trip. Stewart Watson and colleagues (2015) report that in two chimpanzee colonies, the animals used different

referential calls (names) for apples. When the groups were combined, both modified their calls and adopted a common call, an example of gestural drift analogous to people adopting the speech patterns of those around them.

Anatomical studies show that the brain regions in the cortex that are important for human language are also present in chimpanzees. Imaging of blood flow in these brain structures indicates that the same brain regions become activated in humans and chimpanzees when they communicate. Imaging studies of the pathways in the brain also show that chimpanzees that voluntarily learn to use sounds to attract human investigators show structural changes in these same brain regions compared to chimps that do not use such signals.

In summarizing the wealth of information collected in chimpanzee studies, Sam Roberts and Anna Roberts (2020) point to chimpanzees' communication ability as a behavioral trait that allows a large number of animals to live together in groups. Michael Wilson (2021) argues that the language-like behavior displayed by chimps is antecedent to the same behaviors displayed by modern humans.

Barcroft/Getty Images

Kanzi

Descartes's theory of mind led to some bad results. Based on dualism, some people have argued that young children as well as persons who are diagnosed as mentally ill must lack minds because they often fail to reason appropriately. (Colloquially, you may hear someone described as having "lost their mind.") Some proponents of dualism also reasoned that if someone lacked a mind, the person was simply a machine, who was not due either respect or kindness. Cruel treatment of animals, children, and the mentally ill were seemingly justified by Descartes's theory. It is unlikely that Descartes himself intended these interpretations. Reportedly he was kind to his own dog, Monsieur Grat.

> Note that the term "mentally ill," historically used to describe individuals with a variety of disorders, is inaccurate and often stigmatizing, and is therefore avoided in current practice.

# Darwin and Materialism

By the mid-nineteenth century, the theory known as *materialism* came to prominence when it was supported by the evolutionary theory proposed by Alfred Russel Wallace and Charles Darwin. **Materialism** advanced the idea that the workings of the brain and the rest of the nervous system alone fully explain behavior.

## Evolution by Natural Selection

The observations that many animal species display similarities in their appearance and that animal species have behavioral specialties that adapt them to their environment have been noted throughout history, from Aristotle to Taoist thinkers in the third century B.C.E. China to the ninth-century C.E. Islamic scholar Al-Jahiz. However, it was not until the mid-nineteenth century that Wallace and Darwin independently proposed the explanation: all living things are related. Darwin elaborated this idea of descent with modification in his book *On the Origin of Species by Means of Natural Selection*, published in 1859, which cemented his reputation as the founder of modern evolutionary theory (Darwin, 1963/1859). Darwin proposed that small changes in the physical and behavioral traits of animals, which were then passed from parents to their offspring, resulted in all species of living things.

**Natural selection** is the theory explaining how new species evolve and how existing species change over time. A **species** is usually defined as a group of organisms that can breed among themselves. Individual organisms of any species vary in their **phenotype**, the characteristics we can see or measure. No two individuals of any species are exactly alike. Some are big, some are small, some are fat, some are fast, some are light-colored, and some have large teeth.

> Figure 2-1 illustrates this principle of *phenotypic plasticity*.

Individual organisms whose characteristics best help them to survive in their environment are likely to leave more offspring than are less-fit members. This unequal ability of individual members to survive and reproduce leads to a gradual change in a species' population over time. Natural selection is nature's blueprint for the methods of artificial selection practiced for centuries by plant and animal breeders to produce animals and crops with desirable traits.

## Natural Selection and Heritable Factors

Neither Darwin nor Wallace understood the basis of the variation in plant and animal species they observed. A monk, Gregor Mendel, discovered one principle underlying phenotypic variation and how traits pass from parents to their offspring. Through experiments conducted on pea plants in his monastery garden beginning about 1857, Mendel deduced that heritable factors, which we now call *genes*, govern various physical traits displayed by the species.

The principles of inheritance that Mendel demonstrated through his experiments have led to countless discoveries related to what is now called **Mendelian genetics**. (If you are not familiar with Mendelian genetics, consult **Experiment 1-1**.) Members of a species that have a particular genetic makeup, or **genotype**, are likely to *express* (turn on) similar traits, or phenotypes. If parents pass the gene or combination of genes for a specific trait on to their offspring, the offspring will express the same trait. The unequal ability of individual organisms to survive and reproduce is related to the

---

**materialism** Philosophical theory that behavior can be explained as a function of the nervous system without recourse to the mind.

**natural selection** Darwin's theory explaining how new species evolve and how existing species change over time. Differential success in the reproduction of different characteristics (phenotypes) results from the interaction of organisms with their environment.

**species** Group of organisms that can interbreed.

**phenotype** Set of individual characteristics (physical or behavioral traits) that can be seen or measured.

**Mendelian genetics** Principles of inheritance, demonstrated in experiments by Gregor Mendel, based on the observation that heritable factors (genes) pass from parent to offspring.

**genotype** Particular genetic makeup of an individual.

····> **EXPERIMENT 1-1**

Question: How do parents transmit heritable factors to offspring?

**Procedure**

Members of a species that have a particular genotype are likely to express a similar phenotype, or individual characteristics. If the gene or combination of genes for a specific trait (say, flower color) is passed on to offspring, the offspring will express the trait. Two white-flowered pea plants produce white-flowered offspring in the first generation, or $F_1$ in the accompanying figure, and purple-flowered parents produce purple-flowered offspring. Observing this result, Mendel reasoned that two alternative heritable elements govern the trait flower color.

Mendel experimented with crossbreeding $F_1$ purple and white pea plant flowers. The second-generation ($F_2$) offspring all expressed the purple phenotype. Had the factor that expresses white flowers disappeared? To find out, Mendel crossbred the $F_2$ purple flowers. The third generation, $F_3$, produced flowers in the ratio of roughly one white to three purple blooms.

**Results**

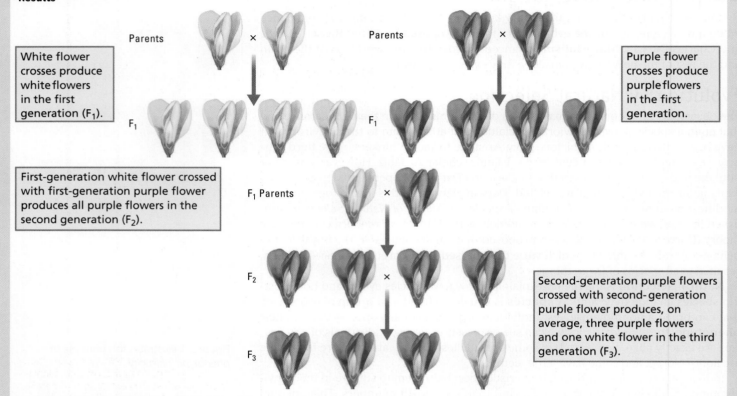

White flower crosses produce white flowers in the first generation ($F_1$).

First-generation white flower crossed with first-generation purple flower produces all purple flowers in the second generation ($F_2$).

Parents

$F_1$

$F_1$ Parents

$F_2$

$F_3$

Parents

Purple flower crosses produce purple flowers in the first generation.

Second-generation purple flowers crossed with second-generation purple flower produces, on average, three purple flowers and one white flower in the third generation ($F_3$).

*Conclusion:* This result suggested to Mendel that the trait for white flowers had not disappeared but rather was hidden by the trait for purple flowers. He concluded that individuals inherit two factors, or genes, for each trait, but one may dominate and hide (suppress) the other in the individual's phenotype.

different genes they inherit from their parents. By the same token, similar characteristics within or between species are usually due to similar genes. For example, the genes that produce similar features in the nervous systems in different animal species are similar.

## Interplay of Genes, Environment, and Experience

Gene inheritance alone cannot explain all traits or all features of all traits—an organism's phenotype. Even Mendel realized that the environment participates in the expression of traits; for example, planting tall peas in poor soil reduces their height. Experience likewise plays a part. The experience of children who attend a substandard school, for instance, is different from that of children who attend a model school.

We now know that genes and their effects are not static; that is, genes can be active at different times and under different conditions during our life. The field of **epigenetics**

Section 3-3 explains some basic genetic and epigenetic principles, including what constitutes a gene, how genes function, and how genes can change, or *mutate*.

**epigenetics** Differences in gene expression related to environment and experience.

(meaning "beyond genes") studies how gene expression is turned on or off at different times and how environment and experience influence our behavior through their effects on our genes.

## Summarizing Materialism

The theories of natural selection, genetic inheritance, and epigenetics are the foundations of materialistic approaches to neuroscience. These theories have four important implications for studying the brain and behavior:

1. *Because all animal species are related, their brains must be related.* A large body of research confirms, first, that all animals' brain cells are so similar that these cells must be related and, second, that all animals' brains are so similar that they must be related as well. Brain researchers study the nervous systems of animals as different as slugs, fruit flies, rats, and monkeys, knowing that they can extend their findings to the human nervous system.

2. *Because all animal species are related, their behaviors must be related.* In his book *The Expression of the Emotions in Man and Animals*, Darwin (1965/1872) argued that emotional expressions are similar in humans and other animals because all animals inherited them from a common ancestor. **Figure 1-6** offers evidence for this assertion. That people the world over display the same behavior suggests that the trait is inherited.

3. *Brains and behaviors in complex animals such as humans evolved from simpler animals' brains and behaviors.* Coming up in Section 1-3, we trace the evolution of nervous systems and their increasingly complex repertoires of actions, from a simple netlike arrangement to a multipart nervous system with a brain that is conscious.

4. *Consciousness and other processes attributed to the mind must be the product of the nervous system.* In the following sections, we describe experiments that reveal aspects of consciousness, a topic that we will take up in subsequent chapters as well.

Section 3-1 describes the varieties of neurons and other brain cells.

More on emotions and their expression in Sections 12-6 and 14-3.

# Toward Contemporary Perspectives on Consciousness

Can contemporary brain and behavior research explain consciousness? In his 1949 book *The Organization of Behavior*, psychologist Donald O. Hebb provided the first explanation of consciousness that relied only on brain function. He proposed that as a result of learning, small groups of neurons forge new connections with one another to

**FIGURE 1-6  An Inherited Behavior** People the world over display the same emotional expressions that they recognize in others—these smiles, for example. This evidence supports Darwin's suggestion that emotional expression is an inherited behavior.

form a *cell assembly,* which is the substrate for a memory. Cell assemblies interact: one cell assembly becomes connected to another. This linking of cell assemblies is therefore the linking of memories, which Hebb suggested is what produces our consciousness of our own and others' actions.

Hebb summarized this view in a folksy way:

> Modern psychology takes completely for granted that behavior and neural function are perfectly correlated, that one is completely caused by the other. There is no separate soul or life force to stick a finger into the brain now and then and make neural cells do what they would not otherwise. (Hebb, 1949, p. iii)

In her book *Neurophilosophy* (1986), Patricia Churchland summarizes this position by arguing that if attributes such as consciousness, pain, and attention can be explained by physical mechanisms, it is unnecessary to appeal to mental explanations.

More recent approaches to brain structure and function have provided further insights into consciousness, including the idea that our consciousness is supported by a dedicated network of brain structures and their connections. Giulio Tononi (2012), in his *integrated information theory of consciousness* (IIT; also known as Phi theory), proposes that the Phi network turns off when we sleep and turns back on again when we awake. According to Tononi, the Phi network's waking activity produces what we experience as consciousness.

Tonini's theory is derived from new approaches to using MRI to image brain structure and function. MRI is a technique that senses electromagnetic signals from the brain to describe its structure and connections. A method called *functional magnetic resonance imaging* (fMRI) monitors the flow of oxygenated blood and provides information about which brain structures work together. fMRI has revealed that functions such as consciousness are supported by *networks,* interactions of many regions and their connections.

The neural basis of consciousness and Phi theory (IIT) is taken up in detail in Section 15-7.

## The Separate Realms of Science and Belief

Some people may question materialism's tenet that only the brain is responsible for behavior because they think it denies religion. In reality, materialism is neutral with respect to religion. Many of the world's major religions accept both evolution and the brain's centrality in behavior as scientific theories. Fred Linge, introduced in Clinical Focus 1-1, has religious beliefs, as do the other members of his family. They used their religious strength to aid in his recovery. Yet, despite their religious beliefs, they realize that Linge's brain injury caused his changed behavior and that learning to compensate for his impairments caused his brain function to improve.

We will take up the topic of consciousness in our discussions of sleep (Chapter 13) and thinking (Chapter 14).

Many behavioral scientists hold religious beliefs and see no contradiction between them and their engagement with science. Science is not a belief system, but rather a set of procedures designed to allow investigators to confirm answers to a question independently. As outlined in Experiment 1-1, this four-step procedure allows anyone to *replicate,* or repeat, their original conclusions—or to find that they cannot.

The four-step experimental procedure is (1) formulate a theory, (2) make a prediction (hypothesis), (3) test it, and (4) confirm or modify the theory.

## **1-2** Review

Before you continue, check your understanding. Answers to Self-Test appear at the back of the book.

1. The theory that behavior is the product of an intangible entity called the mind (psyche) is _____. The theory that the immaterial mind acts through the material brain to produce language and rational behavior is _____. The theory that brain function fully accounts for all behavior, a view that guides contemporary research on the brain and behavior, is _____.

2. The implication that the brains and behaviors of complex animals such as humans evolved from the brains and behaviors of simpler animals draws on the theory of _____.

3. A person who has sustained a brain injury and is occasionally able to communicate or to follow simple commands, but is otherwise not conscious, is considered to be in a _____.

4. The two fields of investigation to explain phenotype are _____ and _____.

5. Describe why language and memory take central stage in the study of consciousness.

6. Briefly describe how Hebb's theory of consciousness is different from the dualist account of consciousness.

---

**1-3**

# Evolution of Brains and of Behavior

We can reconstruct the evolution of the human brain and behavior by describing (1) animals that first developed a nervous system and muscles with which to move, (2) how the nervous system grew more complex as the brain evolved to mediate complex behavior, and (3) how the human brain evolved its present complexity, which we cover in Section 1-4.

One approach to reconstructing brain evolution uses the principle of *common ancestry*. A **common ancestor** is a forebear from which two or more lineages or family groups arise. To illustrate the difference between a common ancestor and a relative, consider the following story told to us by a colleague.

Two people named Joan Campbell are introduced at a scientific convention, and their names provide a rich conversation starter. Although both belong to the Campbell lineage (family line), one Joan is not descended from the other. The two women live in different parts of North America, one in Texas and the other in Ontario, and both their families have been there for many generations.

Nevertheless, after comparing family histories, the two Joans discover that they have ancestors in common. The Texas Campbells are descended from Jeeves Campbell, brother of Matthew Campbell, from whom the Ontario Campbells are descended. Jeeves and Matthew both boarded the same fur-trading ship when it stopped for water in the Orkney Islands north of Scotland before sailing to North America in the seventeenth century.

The Joan Campbells' common ancestors, then, were the mother and father of Jeeves and Matthew. Both the Texas and the Ontario Campbell family lines are descended from this man and woman. If the two Joan Campbells were to compare their genes, they would find similarities that correspond to their common ancestors, the parents of Jeeves and Matthew.

In much the same way, humans and other apes are descended from common ancestors. But unlike the Joan Campbells, we do not know exactly who those distant ancestors were. By comparing the brain and behavioral characteristics of humans and related animals and by comparing their genes, however, scientists can reconstruct lineages based on common ancestors.

Some living animal species display characteristics more similar to those of a common ancestor than do others. For example, in some ways chimpanzees are proposed to be more similar to the common ancestor of humans and chimpanzees than are modern humans. Therefore, chimpanzees can be used as a stand-in for that ancestor, even though we recognize that chimpanzee evolutionary history is as long as our own. In the following sections, we use the principle of common ancestry to trace some major evolutionary events that led to human brains and human behavior.

## Origin of Brain Cells and Brains

Earth formed about 4.5 billion years ago, and the first life-forms arose about a billion years later. About 700 million years ago, animals evolved the first brain cells, and by 250 million years ago, the first brain had evolved. A humanlike brain first developed only about 6 million years ago, and our modern human brain has been around for only the past 200,000 years or so.

This history tells us that though life arose early in our planet's history, brain cells and brains evolved only recently. In evolutionary terms, large, complex brains, such

**Learning Objectives**
• Explain the importance of common ancestry in our understanding of nervous system development across species.
• Chart the evolutionary steps that led from the earliest forms of simple nervous system plans to the complex brains and nervous systems of the chordate phylum.

**common ancestor** Forebear of two or more lineages or family groups; ancestral to both groups.

## ◎ THE BASICS

## Classification of Life

*Taxonomy* is the branch of biology concerned with naming and classifying species by grouping representative organisms according to their common characteristics and their relationships to one another.

As shown in the left column of the Taxonomy of Modern Humans figure, which illustrates the human lineage, the broadest unit of classification is a kingdom, with more subordinate groups being phylum, class, order, family, genus, and species. This taxonomic hierarchy is useful in helping us trace the evolution of brain cells and the brain.

We humans belong to the animal kingdom, the chordate phylum, the mammalian class, the primate order, the great ape family, the genus *Homo*, and the species *sapiens*. Animals are usually identified by their genus and species names. So we humans are called *Homo sapiens sapiens*, meaning "wise, wise human."

The branches in the Cladogram figure, which shows the taxonomy of the animal kingdom, represent the evolutionary sequence (phylogeny) that connects all living organisms. Cladograms are read from left to right: the most recently evolved organism (animal) or trait (muscles and neurons) is farthest to the right.

Of the five kingdoms of living organisms represented in the cladogram, only the one most recently evolved, Animalia, contains species with muscles and nervous systems. It is noteworthy that muscles and nervous systems evolved together to underlie the forms of movement (behavior) that distinguish members of the animal kingdom.

The Evolution of the Nervous System figure shows the taxonomy of the 15 groups, or *phyla*, of Animalia, classified according to increasing complexity of nervous systems and movement. In proceeding to the right from a *nerve net*, we find that nervous systems in somewhat more recently

Taxonomy classifies groups of representative living organisms into increasingly specific, subordinate groups.

**Taxonomy of Modern Humans**

**Living organisms**

Classified in five main kingdoms: Monera (bacteria), Protista (single cells), Plantae (plants), Fungi (fungi), Animalia (animals)

**Kingdom:** Animals

Characteristics: Neurons and muscles used for locomotion

**Phylum:** Chordates

Characteristics: Brain and spinal cord

**Class:** Mammals

Characteristics: Large brains and social behavior

**Order:** Primates

Characteristics: Visual control of hands

**Family:** Great apes

Characteristics: Tool use

**Genus:** Human

Characteristics: Language

**Species:** Modern human

Characteristics: Complex culture

Modern humans are the only surviving species of the genus that includes numerous extinct species of humanlike animals.

as ours, appeared an eyeblink ago. If you are familiar with the principles of taxonomic classification, which names and orders living organisms according to their evolutionary relationships, read on. If you prefer a brief review before you continue, turn first to The Basics: Classification of Life.

## Evolution of Nervous Systems in Animals

A nervous system is not essential for life. In fact, most organisms, including plants and bacteria, both past and present, have done without one. In animals that do have a nervous system, evidence suggests that this nervous system evolved along the following general steps:

**Cladogram**

Brain cells, nervous systems, and muscles first evolved in animals.

Monera (bacteria)

Protista (single cells)

Plantae (plants)

Fungi (fungi)

Animalia (animals)

**Muscles and neurons**

**Multicells**

Common ancestor of animals

**True cells (nuclei and organelles)**

evolved phyla, such as flatworms, have more complex structure. These organisms have heads and tails, and their bodies show both *bilateral symmetry* (one half of the body is the mirror image of the other half) and *segmentation* (the body is composed of similarly organized parts). The structure of the human spinal cord resembles this segmented nervous system.

**Nerve net:** Simple nervous system, organized as a net, with no brain

**Segmented nerve trunk:** Bilaterally symmetrical organization

**Ganglia:** Structures that resemble and function somewhat like a brain

**Brain:** True brain and spinal cord

Sea anemone

Flatworm

Squid

Ganglia

Frog

Common ancestor of animals

Complexity of movement

**Evolution of the Nervous System**

1. *Neurons and muscles.* Brain cells and muscles evolved together, enabling animals to move. Neurons and muscles likely have their origins in single-cell animals (such as amoebas), which developed numerous ways of moving about. These traits later became more specialized in multicellular animals.

2. *Nerve net.* The nervous system found in evolutionarily older phyla, such as jelly-fishes and sea anemones, is quite simple. It consists of a diffuse **nerve net**, which has no structure that resembles a brain or spinal cord, but rather consists entirely of neurons that receive sensory information and connect directly to other neurons that move muscles. Look again at Figure 1-1 and imagine that the brain and spinal cord have been removed. The human PNS is reminiscent of the nerve net observed in phylogenetically simpler animals.

**nerve net** Simple nervous system that has no center, but rather consists of neurons that receive sensory information and connect directly to other neurons that move muscles.

**bilateral symmetry**  Body plan in which those organs or parts present on both sides of the body are mirror images in appearance. For example, the hands are bilaterally symmetrical, whereas the heart is not.

**segmentation**  Division into a number of parts that are similar; refers to the idea that many animals, including vertebrates, are composed of similarly organized body segments.

**ganglia**  Collection of nerve cells that function somewhat like a brain.

**chordate**  Animal that has both a brain and a spinal cord.

**cladogram**  Phylogenetic tree that branches repeatedly, suggesting a taxonomy of organisms based on the time sequence in which evolutionary branches arise.

Figure 2-30 maps the human spinal cord's segments.

3. *Bilateral symmetry*. In more complex animals such as flatworms, the nervous system is more organized, and it features **bilateral symmetry**: the nervous system on one side of the animal mirrors that on the other side. The human nervous system is also bilaterally symmetrical (see Figure 1-1).

4. *Segmentation*. The body of an animal such as an earthworm consists of a series of similar muscular segments. Its nervous system features similar repeating segments. The human spinal cord and brain display such **segmentation**: the vertebrae contain the similar repeating nervous system segments of the spinal cord.

5. *Ganglia*. Still more recently evolved invertebrate phyla, including clams, snails, and octopuses, possess clusters of neurons called **ganglia**, which resemble primitive brains and function somewhat like them in that they are command centers. In some phyla, *encephalization* (having the ganglia in the head) is a distinctive characteristic. For example, insects' ganglia are sufficiently large to merit the term *brain*.

6. *Spinal cord*. In relatively highly evolved **chordates**—animals that have both a brain and a spinal cord—a single nervous system pathway connects the brain with sensory receptors and muscles. Chordates get their name from the *notochord*, a flexible rod that runs the length of the back. In humans, the notochord is present only in the embryo; by birth, bony vertebrae encase the spinal cord.

7. *Brain*. The chordate phylum, of which amphibians, reptiles, birds, and mammals are class members, displays the greatest degree of encephalization: a true brain. Of all chordates, humans have the largest brain relative to body size, but many other chordates have large brains as well. Although built to a common plan, the brain of each chordate species displays specializations related to the distinctive behaviors of that species.

## Chordate Brain

A chart called a **cladogram** (from the Greek word *clados*, meaning "branch") is used to display the hypothetical phylogenetic relationships among animal species. In a cladogram, the branch points (nodes) indicate the points at which each of the two branches had a common ancestor—the living species on a preceding branch can stand in for the common ancestor. The distance between branch points represents the distance of relationships.

The cladogram in **Figure 1-7** depicts seven of the nine classes to which the approximately 38,500 extant chordate species belong. Wide variation exists among the nervous systems of chordates, but common to all is the basic structural pattern of bilateral symmetry, segmentation, and a spinal cord and brain encased in cartilage or bone.

The increase in brain size in chordates is related to new forms of locomotion and movement. For example, all chordates have a brainstem, but birds and mammals have a large

**FIGURE 1-7 Representative Classes of Chordates**  This cladogram illustrates evolutionary relationships among animals that have a brain and spinal cord. The distance between branches represents distance in relationships, and branch points represent divergence from a common ancestor. Brain size increased with the evolution of limbs in Amphibia. Birds and mammals are the most recently evolved chordates, and both classes have large brains relative to body size.

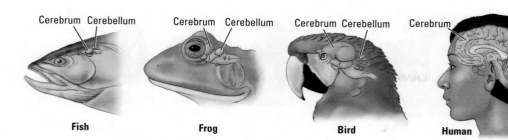

**FIGURE 1-8 Brain Evolution** The brains of representative chordate species have many structures in common, illustrating a single basic brain plan.

forebrain and cerebellum, as illustrated in **Figure 1-8**. In many large-brained mammals, both structures are extensively folded, which greatly increases their surface area while allowing them to fit into a small skull, just as folding a large piece of paper enables us to put it inside a small envelope. Increased size and folding are pronounced in primates, animals with large brains relative to their body size. The increase in the sizes of these structures accommodates complex movements including manipulation of the mouth and hands for eating, improved learning ability, and highly organized social behavior.

Research Focus 2-1 elaborates cerebellar function by describing a man born without a cerebellum.

## 1-3 Review

Before you continue, check your understanding. Answers to Self-Test appear at the back of the book.

1. Brain cells evolved at about the same time as _____, showing that the two have a close relationship.

2. Evolutionary relationships among the nervous systems of animal lineages are classified by increasing complexity, progressing from a simple _____ to a complex _____.

3. A branching diagram that represents groups of related animals is called a _____.

4. Why is the study of movement central to understanding the evolution of the brain?

5. Comment on this statement: "If you want to understand humans, you should study only humans."

1-4

# Evolution of the Human Brain and Behavior

Anyone can see similarities among humans, apes, and monkeys. Those similarities extend to the brain as well. In this section, we first consider how our brain and behavior link to those of other primates. We then explore the relationship between brain complexity and behavior across the various human species that gave rise to modern humans. We conclude by surveying theories about how brains become large and discuss how large brains are capable of producing complex behavior.

## Humans: Members of the Primate Order

We humans are members of the primate order, a subcategory of mammals that includes tarsiers and lemurs, Old World monkeys, New World monkeys, and apes (**Figure 1-9**). We are but one of an estimated 376 primate species. Primate brains are, on average, larger than those of animals in other mammalian orders, such as rodents (mice, rats, beavers, squirrels) and carnivores (wolves, bears, cats, and dogs).

   Primates' brain size is related to their unique behavioral traits. Primates have excellent vision, with the eyes positioned at the front of the face to enhance depth perception.

**Learning Objectives**
- Correlate the increase in brain size with behavioral capacity across human species.
- Describe methods of measuring brain size and explain the benefit of mapping methods in describing brain complexity.
- Describe the behavioral changes that attended the evolutionary development of the hominin brain.

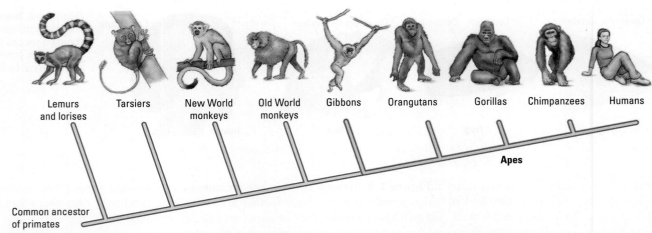

Lemurs and lorises | Tarsiers | New World monkeys | Old World monkeys | Gibbons | Orangutans | Gorillas | Chimpanzees | Humans

Apes

Common ancestor of primates

**FIGURE 1-9 Representatives of the Primate Order** This cladogram illustrates hypothetical relationships among members of the primate order. Humans are members of the great ape family (which also includes orangutans, gorillas, and chimpanzees). In general, brain size increases across the groupings, with humans having the largest brain of all primates.

**hominin** General term referring to primates that walk upright, including all forms of humans, living and extinct.

Australian Raymond Dart coined *Australopithecus* in naming the skull of a child he found among fossilized remains from a limestone quarry near Taung, South Africa, in 1924. His choice of a name that represented his native land probably was no accident.

**(A)**

*Australopithecus*

**(B)**

H. sapiens        "Lucy"

**FIGURE 1-10 *Australopithecus africanus***
**(A)** The hominin *Australopithecus* walked upright with free hands, as do modern humans, but its brain was about one-third the size of ours and comparable to that of nonhuman apes. **(B)** Human and *Australopithecus* figures compared on the basis of the most complete *Australopithecus* skeleton yet found, a young female about 1 meter tall, popularly known as Lucy, who lived 3 million years ago.

They use their highly developed visual sense to deftly guide their arm and hand movements. Female primates usually have only one infant per pregnancy. Primates also spend a great deal more time caring for their young than most other animals do. Most primates are social animals.

Humans are members of the great ape family, which includes orangutans, gorillas, and chimpanzees. Apes have the largest brains among all primates. These animals are diurnal, meaning they are active in daylight, and they have trichromatic vision, which allows them to distinguish a great variety of colors. Apes have limber shoulders and can make skilled finger movements. They can brachiate in trees (swing from one handhold to another)—a trait retained by humans, even though we generally do not live in trees these days. Nevertheless, freeing the arms at the shoulder and skilled finger movements are handy for all sorts of human activities, from traversing monkey bars on the playground to competing in the Olympic hammer toss to raising a hand to ask a question in class to typing on a computer.

Among the apes, we are most closely related to members of the genus *Pan*, which includes chimpanzees and bonobos. *Pan* members had a common ancestor between 5 million and 10 million years ago. Between that common ancestor and present-day humans, many **hominins**—primates that walk upright—in our lineage evolved. We are the only surviving hominin species, but tracing our family history reveals that many hominin species coexisted until about the last 20,000 years, when modern humans became the only hominin species.

## *Australopithecus*: Our Distant Ancestor

One of our hominin ancestors is probably an *Australopithecus* species (from the Latin *austral*, meaning "southern," and the Greek *pithekos*, meaning "ape"). **Figure 1-10** shows reconstructions of the face and body of one such animal, *Australopithecus africanus*. Many species of *Australopithecus* are believed to have existed, with some living at the same time, but evidence suggests that *Australopithecus africanus* is our common ancestor.

These early hominins were among the first primates to show such human traits as walking upright and using tools. Scientists have deduced their upright posture from the shape of their back, pelvic, knee, and foot bones and from fossilized footprints left by australopiths as they walked through freshly fallen volcanic ash some 3.8 million years ago. These footprints feature impressions of a well-developed arch and an unrotated big toe—more like humans than other apes. Although analysis of their hand bones shows that australopiths retained the ability to skillfully climb trees, their bone structure also suggests that they used tools. Nevertheless, their brain morphology (form) was similar to that of nonhuman apes (Gunz et al., 2020).

## The First Humans

The skull of the first animal to be designated as genus *Homo* (human) was found by Mary and Louis Leakey in the Oldupai Gorge in Tanzania in 1964. The Leakeys named this species *Homo habilis* ("handy human") to signify that its members were toolmakers. To date, the earliest member of the many species of *H. habilis*, found in Ethiopia, dates to about 2.8 million years ago. The fossils reveal a jaw and teeth much smaller than those in any *Australopithecus* species but characteristic to humans, and a brain larger than that of *Australopithecus* and possessing humanlike features, such as a larger forebrain (Villmoare et al., 2015).

The first humans who spread beyond Africa migrated into Europe and Asia. This species was named *Homo erectus* ("upright human") because of the mistaken notion that its predecessor, *H. habilis*, had a stooped posture. The first of the many subspecies of *H. erectus* first appear in the fossil record about 1.6 million years ago. As shown in **Figure 1-11**, these early humans had a large brain, overlapping in size with the measurements of present-day human brains. This subspecies also featured reduced sexual dimorphism and elongated lower limbs, traits that allowed it to travel and become widely dispersed across Europe and Asia. Because various subspecies of *H. erectus* survived for nearly 2 million years, they may have made many migrations out of and back to Africa during that time and interbred along the way.

The tools made by *H. erectus* were more sophisticated than those made by *H. habilis*, and this improved tool use was no doubt enabled by their larger brain. An especially small subspecies of *H. erectus*, about 3 feet tall, was found on the Indonesian island of Flores. Named *Homo floresiensis,* these hominins lived up to about 13,000 years ago (Gordon et al., 2008). This point again emphasizes the fact that it is only comparatively recently that only one hominin species has existed on our planet.

A number of *H. sapiens* species appeared within the past million years; these are collectively referred to as archaic humans. *H. neanderthalis*, named for the Neander Thal (Valley), Germany, where the first Neanderthal skulls were found, were widespread in Europe and East Asia. Because they were the first fossilized human ancestor

Early humans may have followed such proposed routes in and out of Africa, Asia, and Europe, and eventually to Australia, and finally to the Americas.

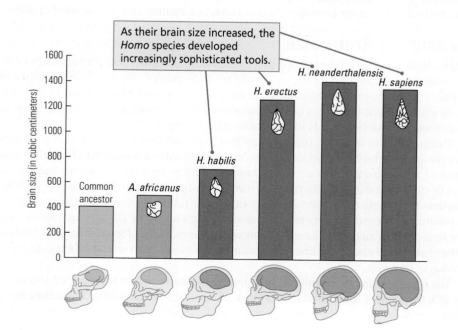

**FIGURE 1-11 Increases in Hominin Brain Size** The brain of *Australopithecus* was about the same size as that of living nonhuman apes, but succeeding members of the human lineage display increased brain size. Data from Johanson & Edey, 1981.

**FIGURE 1-12 Neanderthal Woman** A facial reconstruction by Elisabeth Daynes made from a casting of the skull. The female, whom the discoverers called Pierrette, died a violent death between the ages of 17 and 20. Her 36,000-year-old remains were discovered in western France in 1979, lying near tools from the Neanderthal period.

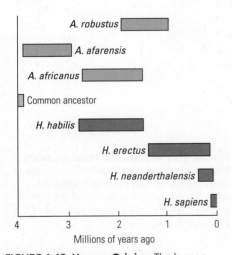

**FIGURE 1-13 Human Origins** The human lineage and a lineage of extinct *Australopithecus* probably arose from a common ancestor about 4 million years ago. The ancestor of the human lineage *Homo* was probably a hominin similar to *A. africanus*.

**encephalization quotient (EQ)** Jerison's quantitative measure of brain size obtained from the ratio of actual brain size to expected brain size, according to the principle of proper mass, for an animal of a particular body size.

to be discovered, and because so many fossils have been found, Neanderthals have been featured in more than 1500 scientific papers. Modern humans, *H. sapiens sapiens*, appeared about 200,000 years ago. In Europe, they coexisted and interbred with archaic Neanderthals, until they finally replaced Neanderthals between 20,000 and 40,000 years ago.

Neanderthals had brains as large as, and perhaps a little larger than, those of modern humans, used similar tools, and wore jewelry and makeup. They lived in family groups similar to modern humans, made music, cared for their elders, and buried their dead. From these archeological findings, we can infer that Neanderthals probably communicated using language and held religious beliefs. Zwir and colleagues (2021) have suggested that Neanderthals and modern humans might share common genes for emotionality, self-control, and self-awareness—traits necessary for creativity.

We do not know how modern humans came to completely replace archaic human species worldwide, but proposed advantages related to their toolmaking, language use, or social organization likely played a role. Contemporary genetic evidence shows that modern European humans who have inherited Neanderthals' genes often have a genetic makeup that enables them to adapt well to the cold, better ward off some diseases, and perhaps have light-colored skin that better absorbs vitamin D. People susceptible to severe COVID-19 disease may also owe this tendency to a gene inherited from Neanderthals as well (Zeberg & Pääbo, 2020). Reconstructions like the one in **Figure 1-12** suggest how closely Neanderthals resembled present-day humans.

One possible human lineage is shown in **Figure 1-13**. A common ancestor gave rise to the *Australopithecus* lineage, and one member of this group gave rise to the *Homo* lineage. The bars in Figure 1-13 are not connected because many more hominin species have been discovered than are shown, and exact direct ancestors are uncertain. The bars overlap because many hominin species coexisted until quite recently.

# Relating Brain Complexity and Behavior

In the study of brain evolution, there are three main ways to describe brain complexity: size, numbers of cells, and organization. Unfortunately, the fossil record provides skulls from which only a measure of brain size can be calculated, so size tends to dominate these discussions. Where brain tissue can be harvested, cells can be considered, and as a result counts of brain cells have become useful. When accurate measures of brain size and cell number are available, other features, such as cell size and packing density, can be estimated. As brain size and cell count increase, so, too, does the brain's complexity, as illustrated in maps that summarize the brain's organization. Here we discuss insights into brain and behavior provided by brain size, cell counts, and organizational maps.

## Measuring Brain Size

Harry Jerison (1973) has proposed that even if little is known about an animal's behavior, that animal's relative brain size could provide clues to its behavioral complexity. Jerison devised an index of relative brain size that provides a ratio of brain size to body size across species. His calculation shows that as body size increases, brain size increases at about two-thirds the increase in body weight.

Using the ratio of actual brain size to this expected brain size provided a quantitative measure, which Jerison called the **encephalization quotient (EQ)**, that could be used to compare brains across all animal species. Jerison defined an average animal (a domestic cat was his pick) as having an EQ of 1. The diagonal trend line in **Figure 1-14** plots the expected brain–body size ratio of a number of animal species in relation to a trend line representing animals with an EQ of 1. Some species lie below the line: their brain size is smaller than would be expected for an animal of that size. Other species lie above the line: their brain size is larger than would be expected for an animal of that size.

The lower an animal's brain falls relative to the trend line in Figure 1-14, the smaller its EQ; the higher an animal's brain lies relative to the trend line, the larger its EQ.

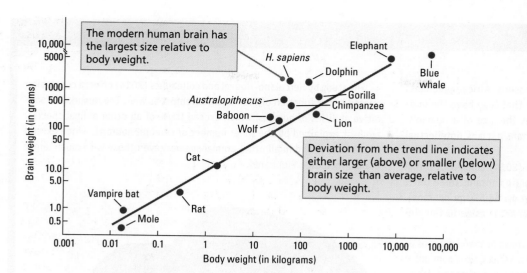

The modern human brain has the largest size relative to body weight.

Deviation from the trend line indicates either larger (above) or smaller (below) brain size than average, relative to body weight.

**FIGURE 1-14 Ratios of Brain to Body Size in Common Mammals** As represented logarithmically on this graph, average brain size relative to body weight falls along a diagonal trend line, where you find the cat. Data from Jerison, 1973.

Notice that the rat's brain is a little smaller (lower EQ) and the elephant's brain a little larger (higher EQ) than the ratio predicts. Modern humans, who are farther above the line than any other animal, have the highest EQ.

Jerison's EQ provides a rough estimate of comparative brain size, but because body size and brain size can vary independently, and behavioral complexity can deviate from that predicted by brain size, researchers were faced with several puzzles (**Figure 1-15**, top). Some apes, such as the gorillas, are specialized in having large bodies, while others, such as humans, are specialized in having large brains. Additionally, dolphins' EQ is almost as large as that of modern humans, but the behavior of dolphins seems not as complex. Some of the weakness of the EQ as a metric can be overcome by using additional methods, such as counting brain cells and measuring brain cell size.

## Counting and Measuring Brain Cells

Counting brain cells is another way to estimate the behavioral capacity of a brain. Consider the 1-mm-long roundworm *Caenorhabditis elegans,* the first animal to have its genome sequenced and the first animal to have all its brain cells and their connections described. The roundworm has 959 cells, 302 of which are neurons. In contrast, the blue whale—the largest animal that has ever lived, weighing as much as 200 tons—has a brain weighing 15,000 grams (33 lb).

Based on EQs, we would predict that *C. elegans*, with one-third of its body made up of neurons, would have a more complex behavioral repertoire than a blue whale, with 0.01% of its body made up of brain cells. But it makes no sense to suggest that a worm's behavior is more complex than that of a whale. Counting brain cells provides a better measure.

Suzana Herculano-Houzel (2019) devised method of dissolving and dissociating brain cells and then counting them using a counting machine, which is quicker than counting them one by one on stained brain slices. This technique can be used to estimate the number of neurons in a brain or a part of the brain and, therefore, the neurons' *packing density*. For example, two similar-sized brains could consist of either diffusely distributed large neurons or closely packed small neurons. Brain cell counts reveal that a blue whale has 30 billion neurons, which is a lot more than the 302 neurons of *C. elegans,* and the differences in these numbers provide a better explanation of their behaviors than a relative size measure.

Measures of cell counts and packing density show that the number of neurons per unit area is relatively constant in the primate lineage, so EQ and brain cell counts both provide a good comparison of their brain sizes (Figure 1-15, bottom). Based on these measures, *Australopithecus* likely had about 30 billion neurons (a count similar to the chimpanzee), *H. habilis* about 60 billion, and *H. erectus* about 75 billion, whereas

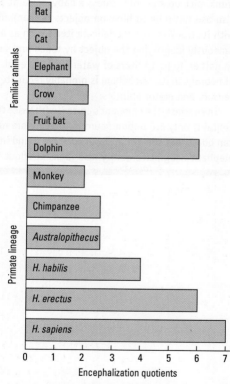

**FIGURE 1-15 Comparing EQs** The EQs of some familiar mammals are ranked at the top of the chart, and members of the primate lineage are ranked at the bottom. Clearly, intelligence is widespread among animals.

## ◉ COMPARATIVE FOCUS 1-3

# The Elephant's Brain

The elephant's brain can teach us a number of lessons. African elephants are enormous animals. It is not surprising, then, that they have the largest brain of all terrestrial animals—three times the size of a human's. With such a large brain, why don't elephants share humans' intellectual abilities?

Suzana Herculano-Houzel and her colleagues (2014) made a neuronal count of an African elephant and found that its brain contains three times as many neurons as the human brain (257 billion vs. 86 billion neurons). But remarkably, 251 billion of those neurons (97.5%) reside in the elephant's cerebellum.

The elephant's cerebellum contains nearly 45 times as many neurons as its cortex, whereas this ratio is 4-to-1 in primates. What does this number tell us about the elephant's behavior? An elephant has almost infinite degrees of freedom in the use of its trunk: it can use it to bathe, lift a tree trunk, pick up a peanut, caress a baby, or paint a picture. An elephant can also use its trunk to blow on objects to manipulate them, create suction with its trunk to pick up delicate items such as a tortilla chip while simultaneously identifying the object by touch and smell, and expand its trunk to gather up to 10 liters of water (Schultz et al., 2021). The vast number of neurons in its cerebellum is probably requisite to controlling the trunk's sensory and motor abilities.

In contrast, the elephant's cortex, with twice the mass of that of humans, contains only 5.6 billion neurons. That's more neurons than most animals can boast, but somewhat fewer than are found in chimpanzees' cortex. The elephant's cognitive ability also ranks at about that of a chimp.

The study by Herculano-Houzel and colleagues (2014) offers a conclusion related to the function of the human cerebrum as well. The remarkable cognitive abilities of humans, which exceed those of all other animal species, are best explained by the sheer number of cerebral neurons, which exceed the number found in all other animal species, even those with much larger brains, including elephants.

**An African Elephant's Brain** In the African elephant, which has the largest brain of all terrestrial animals, both the cerebrum (*left*) and the cerebellum (*right*) are gigantic compared to those of the human brain. But the cerebellum contains 97.5% of the neurons. Reproduced or adapted from our websites at http://www.brains.rad.msu.edu and http://brainmuseum.org, supported by the U.S. National Science Foundation.

modern humans have about 86 billion neurons. Brain cell counts suggest that modern humans have more brain cells than other apes because the modern human brain is larger.

Comparisons of brain cell numbers are more difficult to make between lineages because cell size—and thus packing density—can vary, as can cell counts in different brain regions. As detailed in Comparative Focus 1-3: The Elephant's Brain, pachyderms have an enormous number of neurons, but most are found in the cerebellum, an area associated with motor behavior; in contrast, the number of neurons in its cortex, an area associated with cognitive processes, is equivalent to that in chimpanzees. These neuron counts suggest that apes and elephants should have equivalent cognitive abilities, which they do. Furthermore, the dolphin, another animal with a very large brain, has a total of 30 billion neurons, a number similar to the number in chimpanzees—and many fewer than in the smaller human brain—because dolphin neurons are not densely packed. Suzana Herculano-Houzel (2018) concludes that when it comes to cognitive function, it is the number of neurons in the cortex that matters: "what distinguishes humans from other species is not how small or large, dense or scarce our cortical neurons are, but simply how many of them we have to do the job of navigating through life." As a nod to the idea that all of those neurons are related to social behavior, man's best friend the dog has the most cortical neurons of all of the carnivores. Future research on brain size and brain cell numbers will undoubtedly include the comparative counts of the types of neurons and their locations within the brain.

The utility of relating neuron number to behavioral complexity is not limited to mammals. Researchers have found that the clever behavior of birds, such as parrots and crows, is related to the larger number of densely packed neurons they have in their cerebrum relative to other birds.

## Brain Cell Connections and Brain Maps

The addition of neurons changes the structure of the brain and disproportionately increases the overall number of connections between neurons. A helpful analogy can be made to human living arrangements: as villages grow into towns and then into cities, more highways and roads are needed to connect them. Eventually, finding one's way around requires a map.

**Figure 1-16** illustrates one view of how the complexity of the brain evolves as more neurons are added. The first column in the figure uses different colors to illustrate the functions of neurons. Most of the cerebrum of a smaller brain (bottom), such as that of a fish, is devoted to the primary senses and movement. It has neurons for vision, hearing, touch, olfaction, and movement. The neurons with different functions do not occupy specific regions but have a "salt and pepper" organization.

For animals with successively larger brains, the neurons representing the primary functions aggregate to keep their connections short (as shown in the top two figures). As their numbers increase, they also begin to form new regions (gray shading). For example, visual pathways to motor regions in a fish direct whole-body movements to guide the fish from one place to another. Visual pathways in a primate not only guide locomotion, but also guide control of the arm and hand for reaching. This new function requires both a new region and new connections.

The maps in the first column of Figure 1-16 are **topographic**, representing the brain's different functional areas—for instance, areas that control vision, hearing, touch, olfaction, and movement. The second column shows a second kind of map, **connectome** maps, representing the connections through which each of these regions influences the others. These two different ways of describing the brain are similar to the maps that a computer provides of a city—that is, a scene map of buildings versus a street map of routes. Topographic and connectome descriptions of the brain are featured throughout this book.

# Why the Hominin Brain Became More Complex

The evolution of modern humans—from when humanlike creatures first appeared until modern humans emerged—spans more than 4 million years. This may seem like a long time, but the brain and behavior evolution that occurred in hominins was extremely rapid, given that other animal species did not undergo as many changes over the same time period. What caused these changes? Why did hominins evolve a large brain with so many cells, and why did their behavior become more complex? Why didn't hominins just remain apes with ape-sized brains?

In the sections that follow, we explore four leading hypotheses about how humans acquired their unique brains: lifestyle influences, rate of maturation, climate change, and genetic mutation. We will conclude by noting that combinations of influences were likely instrumental in the development of a human brain.

## The Primate Lifestyle

British anthropologist Robin Dunbar (1998) argues that a primate's social group size, a cornerstone of its lifestyle, is correlated with brain complexity. His conclusion: the average group size of about 150 favored by modern humans explains their brain. As evidence for his hypothesis, Dunbar notes that 150 is the estimated group size of hunter-gatherer groups and the average group size of many contemporary institutions—a company in the military, for instance—and coincidentally, the number of people whom each of us can gossip about (keep in mind, Dunbar was writing before the advent of social media).

Consider how group size might affect the way primates forage for food. Foraging is important for all animals, but while some foraging activities are simple, others are complex. Eating grass or vegetation is an individual pursuit: an animal need only munch and

**FIGURE 1-16 Evolution of Complexity in the Cortex** The first column provides a topographic view of how a brain might change with the addition of neurons. Each color represents a function, such as vision, touch, or hearing. Gray shading represents new areas associated with new functions of the different regions. The second column provides a connectome view of how connections might change when neurons are added as topographic regions separate and become larger.

**topographic** Representing the different functional areas of the CNS.

**connectome** All the pathways connecting regions of the CNS.

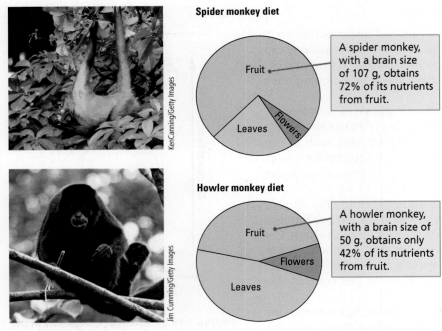

**Spider monkey diet**

Fruit

Leaves

Flowers

A spider monkey, with a brain size of 107 g, obtains 72% of its nutrients from fruit.

**Howler monkey diet**

Fruit

Flowers

Leaves

A howler monkey, with a brain size of 50 g, obtains only 42% of its nutrients from fruit.

**FIGURE 1-17 Picky Eaters** Katharine Milton examined the feeding behavior and brain size of two New World monkeys that have the same body size but different brain sizes and diets.

A small jaw distinguishes the earliest *Homo* fossils yet discovered.

move on. Vegetation eaters such as gorillas do not have especially large brains relative to their body size. In contrast, apes that eat fruit, such as chimpanzees and humans, have relatively large brains.

Katharine Milton (2003) documented the relationship between fruit foraging and larger brains by examining the feeding behavior and brain size of two South American (New World) monkeys of the same body size. As illustrated in **Figure 1-17**, spider monkeys obtain nearly three-fourths of their nutrients from fruit and have a brain twice as large as that of the howler monkey, which obtains less than half its nutrients from fruit.

What is so special about eating fruit? Fruit harvesting requires good sensory skills such as color vision to see it, good motor skills to reach and manipulate it, good spatial skills to find it, good memory to return to it, and having friends to help find it and ward off competitors. Having a parent who can teach fruit-finding skills and being a good learner are also useful. The payoff in eating fruit is its nutritional value for nourishing a large, energy-dependent brain that uses more than 20% of the body's resources. These same skills are useful for obtaining other temporary and perishable types of food, such as those obtained through scavenging, hunting, and gathering—human food acquisition strategies.

A neuron's metabolic (energy) cost is believed to be relatively constant across different species but also high relative to that of other types of body cells. As a consequence, any adaptive advantage from having more neurons must support that energy cost. Fonseca-Azevedo and Herculano-Houzel (2012) suggests that both cold and hot cooking contribute to hominin brain evolution. Cold cooking involves the use of tools to prepare food for ingestion and hot cooking involves the use of heat to prepare food for digestion (thereby maximizing caloric gain). A high degree of male–male, female–female, and female–male cooperation in food gathering and cooking, which is characteristic of the hominin lifestyle, further supports the evolution of a human brain. Were humans unable to cook, they would be confined to a lifestyle similar to that of other apes that spend most of their waking hours foraging for food.

Cooking food makes it easier to eat. This, in turn, might foster genetic mutations associated with many other physical features, including those associated with the exchange of movement strength for movement skill and the more delicate musculature of the hands and face—for example, the masticatory muscles (Marcé-Nogué et al., 2020).

## Altered Maturation

All animal species' life history can be divided into stages. *Heterochrony* (from the Greek, meaning "different times") is the study of processes that regulate life stages (gestation, infancy, childhood, adulthood) and their developmental speed and duration. Several proposals suggest that altered heterochronicity accounts for the large human brain and other distinctive human features.

In **neoteny**, juvenile stages of predecessors become adult features of descendants, rendering those features more baby-like. Neoteny is common in the animal world. Flightless birds are neotenic adult birds, domesticated dogs are neotenic wolves, and sheep are neotenic goats. Many anatomical features link us with the juvenile stages of other primates, including a small face, vaulted cranium, unrotated big toe, upright posture, and primary distribution of hair on the head, armpits, and pubic areas.

Because a human infant's head is large relative to body size, neoteny has also led to adults with proportionally larger bodies and larger skulls to house larger brains. The shape of a baby chimpanzee's head is more similar to the shape of an adult human's

**neoteny** Process in which juvenile stages of predecessors become adult features of descendants; idea derived from the observation that more recently evolved species resemble the young of their common ancestors.

head than to an adult chimpanzee's head (**Figure 1-18**). Along with this physical morphology, human adults retain some behaviors of primate infants, including play, exploration, and intense interest in novelty and learning. The brain processes that support learning thus are retained in adulthood.

Evidence for neoteny includes the fact that each stage of human development—gestation, infancy, childhood, adulthood—is prolonged relative to such ancestral species as chimpanzees. Prolonged infancy allows for the production and development of more neurons, resulting in a bigger brain. Prolonged childhood enhances learning time; and prolonged adolescence allows for the growth of a bigger body (Li et al., 2020) and, as described earlier, more brain cells.

**FIGURE 1-18 Neoteny** The shape of an adult human's head more closely resembles that of a juvenile chimpanzee's head (*left*) than that of an adult chimp's head (*right*). This observation leads to the hypothesis that we humans may be neotenic descendants of our more apelike common ancestors.

## Climate and the Evolving Hominin Brain

Climate changes have driven many physical changes in hominins, ranging from brain changes to the emergence of human culture. Evidence suggests that each new hominin species appeared after climate changes devastated the old environments and led to new ones (Challa et al., 2021).

About 8 million years ago, a massive tectonic event (deformation of Earth's crust) produced the Great Rift Valley, which runs through the eastern part of Africa from south to north. The reshaped landmass left a wet jungle climate to the west and a much drier savannah climate to the east. To the west, the apes continued unchanged in their former habitat. But the fossil record shows that in the drier eastern region, apes evolved rapidly into upright hominins in response to the selective environmental pressures that formed their new home.

Thereafter, the climate in East Africa did not remain static, but rather underwent a number of alterations. Some of these alterations isolated populations of hominins, whereas others threw different populations together. The appearance of *H. habilis* 3 million years ago and the appearance of *H. erectus* 1 million years ago were associated with these climatic alterations. Climatic changes also track the *disappearance* of other members of the human family. For instance, the warming in Europe that ended the ice age as recently as 30,000 years ago contributed to modern humans prospering and to the Neanderthal and other archaic European and Asiatic human groups disappearing.

One specific physiological adaptation to a warmer climate that may have given a special boost to larger brain size in our human ancestors is a change in the morphology of the skull. Dean Falk (Kunz & Iliadis, 2007) developed the radiator hypothesis from a remark by her automobile mechanic: to increase the size of a car's engine, you also have to increase the size of the radiator that cools it. Falk reasoned that if the brain's radiator—the circulating blood—evolved to form a more effective cooling system, brain size could increase in tandem. Brain cooling is important because the brain's metabolic activity generates a great deal of heat and the brain is at risk for overheating under conditions of exercise or heat stress. Falk argued that, unlike australopith skulls, *Homo* skulls contain holes through which cranial blood vessels pass. These holes suggest that, compared to earlier hominins, *Homo* species had a much more widely dispersed blood flow from the brain, which would have greatly enhanced brain cooling.

Ape species living in a wetter climate to the west of Africa's Great Rift Valley were cut off from species that evolved into hominins and thus adapted to a drier climate to the east.

## The Human Genome

The influences on hominin evolution described previously must have been mediated by genetic changes. But what were these changes? Scientists have an incomplete data sample for investigating the origins of the hominin *genome* (a catalogue of all of a species' genes) because only the genomes of the apes, archaic humans, and modern humans have been sequenced (i.e., the entire set of genes has been described). Although apes and modern humans have about 96% of their genes in common, their genes have many small differences, making it difficult to determine what each difference contributes.

A different approach to understanding the origins of the hominin genome is to ask whether gene changes occurred with the appearance of each new hominin (Changeux et al., 2021). Some genes are active when the cerebrum is developing and play a role in determining the number of neurons that compose the cerebrum. Genetic mutations may have occurred in these genes at key points—say, 3.4, 2.4, and 1 million years ago. Such mutation events may be associated with the jumps in brain size that occurred in *H. habilis, erectus,* and *sapiens,* respectively. Although the real story is unlikely to be quite this simple, the results from genome research encourage us to search for other connections between gene changes and human evolution.

## 1-4 Review

Before you continue, check your understanding. Answers to Self-Test appear at the back of the book.

1. Modern humans share a _____ with our closest living ape relatives, the _____.

2. Modern humans evolved from a lineage in which multiple _____ species existed concurrently.

3. A comparison between species that relies solely on brain size and neuron counts would be incomplete because it does not factor in neuron _____, defined as the number of neurons per area.

4. All neurons require about the same _____ to function.

5. Describe the hypothesized role of cooking in human brain evolution.

6. Describe how brain cell analyses can contribute to our understanding of the behavior of various animal species.

---

**1-5**

# Modern Human Brain Size, Intelligence, and Culture

In *The Descent of Man,* Charles Darwin detailed the following paradox:

> No one, I presume, doubts the large proportion which the size of man's brain bears to his body, compared to the same proportion in the gorilla or orang, is closely connected with his higher mental powers. . . . On the other hand, no one supposes that the intellect of any two animals or of any two men can be accurately gauged by the cubic contents of their skulls. (Darwin, 1871, p. 37)

Ignoring Darwin, many have tried to tie individual intelligence to gross brain size, and the ensuing debate about brain size and intelligence has lessons to teach us. In the following sections, we discuss issues related to brain size, intelligence, and culture and elaborate on Darwin's words of caution.

The evolutionary approach we have been using to explain how the large human brain evolved is based on comparisons between species. Special care is warranted when extending evolutionary principles and physical comparisons within species, especially biological comparisons within or among groups of modern humans. In this section, we first illustrate the difficulty of within-species comparisons by considering the complexity of correlating human brain size with intelligence (Deary, 2000). Then we turn to another aspect of studying the brain and behavior in modern humans: the fact that so much modern human behavior—unlike the behavior of other animals—is culturally learned.

# The Significance of Human Brain Size Comparisons

Stephen Jay Gould, in his 1981 book *The Mismeasure of Man*, criticizes the many studies that suggested that brain size and intelligence are related. He points out that though measuring a person's brain is difficult, measuring intelligence is considerably more difficult, and the primary motivation for much of the research in this area has been to support preconceived notions about sex, group, or racial superiority. We will elaborate further on why the study of individual differences can be meaningful, whereas mismeasure is not.

When attempting to measure brain size, a tape measure placed around a person's head will not allow us to factor in skull thickness. However, researchers also disagree about whether volume or weight is a better measure. And even when a more sophisticated measurement is used, we must still consider body size. The human brain varies in weight from about 1000 grams to more than 2000 grams, but people also vary in body mass. To what extent should we factor in body mass in deciding whether a particular brain is large or small? And how should we measure body mass, given that a person's total weight can fluctuate widely over time?

Large differences between the brains of individual people do exist, but the reasons for these differences are numerous and complex. Consider some examples. People may have larger or smaller brain cells. Larger people are likely to have a larger brain than smaller people because they have a larger muscle mass to control. Men have a somewhat larger brain than women, but again men are also proportionately physically larger. Nevertheless, girls mature more quickly than boys do, so in adolescence the brain and body size differences that characterize adults may not exist. As people age, they generally lose brain cells, so their brain shrinks.

Neurological diseases associated with aging accelerate the age-related decrease in brain size. Brain injury near the time of birth often results in a dramatic reduction in brain size, even in regions distant from the damage. Stress associated with physical or behavioral deprivation in infancy also reduces brain size (Herringa et al., 2013). Neurological disorders associated with a parent's chronic use of alcohol or other drugs are associated with conditions such as *fetal alcohol spectrum disorder* (*FASD*), in which the brain can be greatly reduced in size. *Autism spectrum disorder* (*ASD*), a largely genetic condition affecting development, produces a wide variety of brain changes, including either increases or decreases in brain size in different individuals.

Brain size may also change over an individual's life span. For example, just as good nutrition in the early years of life can be associated with larger body size, so this factor can be associated with an increase in brain size. The brain's plasticity—its ability to change—can be affected by an enriched environment, which promotes growth of existing brain cells and thus an increase in brain size and behavioral function (Tooley et al., 2021). Furthermore, one way in which the brain stores new skills and memories is to form new connections among brain cells, and these connections in turn contribute to increased brain size.

To find information on specific conditions, consult the index of disorders on the inside front cover of this book.

Sections 2-1 and 2-6 elaborate on plasticity, Research Focus 8-1 and Section 8-4 on environment and brain development, Section 11-3 on skilled movement, and Section 14-1 on memory.

# The Significance of Human Intelligence

Defining and measuring intelligence is also problematic. When we compare behavior across species, we are comparing **species-typical behavior**—behavior displayed by all members of a species. For example, lamprey eels do not have limbs and cannot walk, whereas salamanders do have limbs and can walk: the difference in brain size *between* the two species can be correlated with this trait. When we compare behavior (such as intelligence) *within* a species, however, we are usually comparing how well one individual performs a certain task in relation to others of the same species—how well one salamander walks relative to how well another salamander walks, for instance. The differences we are examining are likely comparatively small, vary according to the conditions under which the measurements are made, and are difficult to define objectively.

Sea lamprey        Salamander

**species-typical behavior** Behavior that is characteristic of all members of a species, such as walking in salamanders.

Measures of intelligence have often been misused to support discriminatory social policies, including arguments for eugenic policies. Issues in conceptualizing and measuring intelligence are discussed further in Section 15-6.

Section 15-3 discusses various approaches to mapping brain networks; Section 15-6 relates network efficiency to intelligence.

Saint Ambrose, who lived in the fourth century, was reportedly the first person who could read silently.

---

**culture** Learned behaviors that are passed on from one generation to the next through teaching and imitation.

**meme** An idea, a behavior, or a style that spreads from person to person within a culture.

Early in the twentieth century, Charles Spearman carried out the first formal performance analysis of the various tests used to rate intelligence in humans. He found a positive correlation among tests and suggested that a single common factor explained them. Spearman named it *g* for *general intelligence factor*, but it turns out that *g* also varies. Many factors unrelated to inherent ability—among them opportunity, interest level, training, motivation, and health—influence individual performance on a task.

For example, when IQ (intelligence quotient) tests that were given to young adults of one generation are given to the next generation, scores increase by as much as 25 points (a massive increase of one standard deviation), a phenomenon called the *Flynn effect* (Flynn, 2012). Taken at face value—though it shouldn't be—the increase suggests that human *g* has risen to such a degree in two generations that most young adults fall in the superior category relative to their grandparents. Obviously, the score change has not been accompanied by a similar increase in brain size. Education and other life experiences explain the Flynn effect.

Howard Gardner (2006) proposed a different view of intelligence when he argued that humans have a number of intelligences—verbal, musical, mathematical, social, and so on. Each type of intelligence is proposed to be dependent on the function of a particular brain region or regions. C. Branton Shearer (2020) has analyzed resting neural networks and behavior associated with a variety of behavioral tests given in brain imaging studies and found that a number of networks map onto the kinds of intelligence described by Gardner's multiple intelligences theory. Shearer further argues that personalized instruction in schools can potentiate the various latent intelligences of individuals—in other words, instruction in areas such as art, math, or creative writing can foster latent abilities in those endeavors. Nevertheless, Gardner's proposal has also received criticism, the most obvious of which is that it seems easy to add or subtract one or another kind of intelligence from the total count.

Missed in debates about intelligence is the adaptive value that variation in abilities provides to a group. A group composed of individuals with a variety of traits may be more adaptive than a hypothetical homogeneous group. A recognized principle in evolutionary biology is the importance of genetic and phenotypic variation (Conroy et al., 2021). Populations that lack variation, perhaps due to inbreeding or bottleneck events that leave only a few survivors, are at increased risk from environmental change and disease. Similarly, a group whose individual members possess behavioral variability can innovate in novel and beneficial ways. Just as nonhuman animal populations with low genetic variability are at risk, a human population with low individual variability may also be at risk.

## The Significance of Human Culture

The most remarkable thing that our brains have made possible is ever more complex and diverse **culture**—learned behaviors passed from generation to generation through teaching and experience. Humans speak thousands of different languages, have numerous social and religious practices, and adapt to the world in which they live in a remarkable number of ways. Most of this culture originated long after our brains evolved.

Cultural growth and adaptation render many contemporary human behaviors distinctly different from those of *H. sapiens* living 200,000 years ago. Only 30,000 years ago, modern humans made the first artistic relics: elaborate paintings on cave walls and carved ivory and stone figurines. Agriculture appeared still more recently, about 15,000 years ago, and reading and writing were invented only about 7000 years ago.

Most forms of mathematics and many of our skills in using mechanical and digital devices have still more recent origins. Computer programming languages, for example, date to the 1950s. We are currently experiencing an age of smartphones and social media unique in human history. Apparently, the things that the human brain did evolve to do contained the elements necessary for adapting to more sophisticated skills.

Maxime Derex and Alex Mesoudi (2020) suggest that cultural elements, ideas, behaviors, or styles that spread from person to person—called **memes** (after genes, the elements of physical evolution)—can also be studied within an evolutionary framework. They propose that individual differences in brain structure may favor the development of certain memes. Once developed, memes would in turn exert selective pressure on further brain development. For example, chance variations in individuals' brain structure may have favored tool use in some individuals. Tool use proved so beneficial that toolmaking itself exerted selective pressure on a population to favor individuals well skilled in tool fabrication.

Similar arguments can be made with respect to other memes—from language to soccer strategies, from mathematics to art. This reasoning supports brain science's ongoing expansion into seemingly disparate disciplines, including linguistics, the arts, business, and economics. Studying the human brain, instead of simply examining a body organ's structure, means investigating how it acquires culture and fosters adaptation as the world changes and as the brain changes the world.

Section 15-3 explores some of neuropsychology's expanding frontiers.

# 1-5 Review

**Before you continue, check your understanding. Answers to Self-Test appear at the back of the book.**

1. Behavior that is displayed by all members of a species is called _____.

2. Spearman called his general intelligence factor _____ .

3. The finding that the scores on IQ tests can increase from one generation to the next is called _____.

4. Gardner proposed the theory of _____.

5. Cultural _____ are analogous to physical genes.

6. Explain the reasoning behind this statement: what is true for evolutionary comparisons across different species may not be true for comparisons within a single species.

7. How could variation in intelligence contribute to group success?

# Summary

## 1-1 The Brain in the Twenty-First Century

Studying the brain and behavior can help us better understand our origins, our human nature, our cultures and individual differences, the causes of many behavioral disorders, and the rationale behind treatment for disorders.

The human nervous system is composed of the CNS, which includes the brain and the spinal cord, and the PNS, through which the brain and spinal cord communicate with sensory receptors, with muscles and other tissues, and with the internal organs. The cerebrum and the cerebellum have undergone the most growth in large-brained animal species.

We define behavior as any kind of movement, including mental processes such as thinking and imagining. In animals, behavior is caused by nervous system activity. Behavioral flexibility and complexity vary greatly across species, as does the nervous system.

For some species, including humans, the brain is the organ that exerts control over behavior. The brain seems to need ongoing sensory and motor stimulation to maintain its intelligent activity.

## 1-2 Theories of Brain and Behavior

Mentalism views behavior as a product of an intangible entity called the mind (psyche); the brain has little importance. Dualism is the notion that the immaterial mind acts through the material brain to produce language, memory, and rational behavior, whereas the brain

alone is responsible for the "lower" actions that we have in common with other animal species.

Materialism is the view that brain function fully accounts for all behavior—language and reasoning included; it guides contemporary research on the brain and behavior. Support for the materialistic view comes from the study of natural selection—the evolutionary theory proposing that behaviors such as human language evolved from the simpler language abilities of human ancestors—and from discoveries about how genes function. Experiments follow the process of science: (1) formulate a theory, (2) generate a question (hypothesis), (3) design a procedure to test it, and (4) evaluate the results to confirm or modify the theory.

After severe TBI, the brain demonstrates a remarkable ability to recover, but after either mild or severe injury, a person can be left with a permanent disability that prevents full recovery to former levels of function. Brain imaging techniques can confirm severe disabilities such as MCS, locked-in syndrome, and PVS.

## 1-3 Evolution of Brains and of Behavior

Behavioral neuroscientists subscribe to the evolutionary principle that all living organisms are descended from a common ancestor. Brain cells and muscles are quite recent developments in the evolution of life on Earth. Because they evolved only once, a similar basic pattern exists in the nervous systems of all animals.

The nervous systems of some animal lineages have become more complex, with evolution featuring first a nerve net, followed by a bilaterally symmetrical and segmented nervous system, a nervous system controlled by ganglia, and eventually, in chordates, a nervous system featuring a brain and spinal cord.

Mammals are a class of chordates characterized by a large brain relative to body size. Modern humans belong to the primate order, which is distinguished by especially large brains, and to the family of great apes, whose members' limber shoulders allow them to brachiate (hang and swing by the arms), and in the case of humans, to throw things with great force and accuracy.

## 1-4 Evolution of the Human Brain and Behavior

One of our early hominin ancestors was probably an *Australopithecus*, who lived in Africa several million years ago. It is from an australopith species that *Homo* evolved through species such as *H. habilis* and *H. erectus*. Modern humans, *H. sapiens sapiens*, appeared about 200,000 years ago.

Since *Australopithecus*, the hominin brain has increased in size almost threefold, as has its number of brain cells. These increases were associated with changes in both the brain's area (topography) and its connections (connectome). The EQ describes brain size relative to body size, but a complete comparison of different species' brains requires brain cell counts. Among the factors hypothesized to have stimulated

brain evolution in human species are environmental challenges and opportunities, such as climate changes that favored the natural selection of adaptability and more complex behavior patterns. Brain and behavior changes in hominins were mediated by perhaps only a few genes that appeared *de novo* in hominins. Also proposed as factors underlying brain evolution in human species are lifestyle changes such as social cooperation and cooking food, changes in physiology, and changed maturation rate.

## 1-5 Modern Human Brain Size, Intelligence, and Culture

Evolutionary principles learned from studying the brain and behavior *across* species do not easily apply to the brain and behavior *within* a single species, such as *H. sapiens*. People vary widely in body size, brain size, and, likely, the number of brain cells and the connections between brain cells. They also vary in culture, which is both a product of the brain and an important influence on the brain. Any of these factors can contribute to the development of different kinds of intelligence, making a simple comparison of brain size and general intelligence unwise.

Recognizing the great extent to which modern human behavior results from cultural learning and transmission, rather than being inherent in our nervous systems, is paramount to understanding how our brains function. Memes may spread from person to person and from culture to culture.

# Key Terms

bilateral symmetry, p. 18

brainstem, p. 4

central nervous system (CNS), p. 4

cerebellum, p. 4

cerebrum (forebrain), p. 4

chordate, p. 18

cladogram, p. 18

clinical trial, p. 6

common ancestor, p. 15

concussion, p. 2

connectome, p. 25

culture, p. 30

deep brain stimulation (DBS), p. 6

dualism, p. 9

embodied behavior, p. 5

encephalization quotient (EQ), p. 22

epigenetics, p. 12

ganglia, p. 18

genotype, p. 11

glial cells, p. 4

hemisphere, p. 4

hominin, p. 20

locked-in syndrome, p. 6

materialism, p. 11

meme, p. 30

Mendelian genetics, p. 11

mentalism, p. 9

mind–body problem, p. 9

minimally conscious state (MCS), p. 6

natural selection, p. 11

neocortex (cortex), p. 4

neoteny, p. 26

nerve net, p. 17

neuron, p. 4

peripheral nervous system (PNS), p. 4

persistent vegetative state (PVS), p. 6

phenotype, p. 11

plasticity, p. 7

psyche, p. 9

segmentation, p. 18

species, p. 11

species-typical behavior, p. 29

topographic, p. 25

traumatic brain injury (TBI), p. 2

# Selected Resources from  Achieve

**Neuroscience in Action:** Evolution of Brains and Behavior

**Videos**

Research Methods

**LearningCurve**

**Practice Quiz**

Science Photo Library - ROGER HARRIS/Getty Images

# What Is the Nervous System's Functional Anatomy?

2

**Throughout this book,** we examine the nervous system with a focus on function—how our brains generate behavior and how, in turn, our behavior influences our brains. In this chapter, we consider the human nervous system's anatomical and functional organization and how its basic components work together to produce behavior. Moreover, we consider how our brains change in the context of plasticity, as illustrated in Research Focus 2-1, Agenesis of the Cerebellum.

First, we emphasize the brain's anatomy, and then we elaborate on how the brain works in concert with the rest of the nervous system to produce behavior. Throughout the chapter, we describe how elements of nervous system anatomy, function, and plasticity suggest foundational principles underlying nervous system organization. These principles, described in detail in Section 2-6, apply equally to the micro and macro views of the nervous system presented in this chapter and to the broader picture of behavior that emerges in later chapters.

Note that we are using the word *function* two different ways. *Function* can refer to the purpose of the brain—its function is to produce behavior (recall *functionalism* from Chapter 1)—or it can refer to how the brain works, how it functions.

---

## RESEARCH FOCUS 2-1

# Agenesis of the Cerebellum

When an adult's brain is damaged, as in *traumatic brain injury*, for example, we see a pattern of behavioral changes that offer insight into brain functions, as described by Fred Linge in Clinical Focus 1-1, Living with Traumatic Brain Injury. Naturally occurring brain injuries rarely remove a single structure completely, leaving the rest of the brain intact. However, *agenesis*, defined as the failure of brain regions to develop, offers researchers a unique window into the brain's organization and function. In these rare cases, a complete structure is absent, yet the rest of the brain appears normal.

Historically, the cerebellum was viewed as a motor structure, with the most obvious sign of damage being *ataxia*, a failure of muscular coordination and balance. We now know that the cerebellum's functions are much more extensive than movement control (e.g., Sokolov et al., 2017). Adult patients with damage to the cerebellum do have motor disturbances, but they also have cognitive deficits in, for example, abstract thinking and language as well as emotional control.

The cerebellum contains the most neurons of any brain region, accounting for 80% of humans' neurons and a whopping 97.5% of elephants' neurons—believed to be related to the dexterity of the elephant's trunk. What would happen if the cerebellum failed to develop but the rest of the brain developed apparently normally? We humans would be missing 80% of our neurons!

Studies of people with cerebellar agenesis reveal a heterogeneous set of symptoms, but neuropsychological assessments show behavioral deficits reminiscent of people with damage to the frontal and parietal cortical regions of the brain (e.g., Baumann et al., 2015), even though these cerebral regions are intact. While people with cerebellar agenesis typically have more slowly developing language and motor functions, they show remarkable improvement over time and seem able to compensate for many of their symptoms.

The accompanying images contrast the brain of a person whose brain developed normally (A and B) to the brain of a young man born with agenesis of the cerebellum (C and D). This young man had severe visuomotor spatial disabilities as a child and adolescent, but by age 30 he showed significant improvement (Jeremy D. Schmahmann and Janet C. Sherman, personal communication). Even though he lacks 80 percent of his neurons, his behavioral capacities are remarkable—he holds an office job and

Courtesy of Jeremy Schmahmann

MRI brain scans of a person with a typical cerebellum (A, B) compared to a person with cerebellar agenesis (C, D) of the same age. A and C are viewed in the coronal plane, B and D in the midsagittal plane. For more about this condition, see www.npr.org/blogs/health/2015/03/16/393351760.

lives alone. Nevertheless, his behavior is not typical. He has a distinctive speaking pattern, an awkward gait, and difficulties with balance, as well as deficits in planning and abstract thinking. His social skills and long-term memory are good, though, as is his proficiency with routine activities.

In people with cerebellar agenesis, it is thought that brain plasticity in response to early perturbations allows for compensation as regions of the cerebral cortex begin to function more efficiently. Interestingly, it has been reported that people with cerebellar agenesis appear to have some of the symptoms of *autism* early in life. This observation comports with evidence that dysfunction (rather than absence) of the cerebellum is related to autism (detailed in Clinical Focus 8-2, Autism Spectrum Disorder).

# Overview of Brain Function and Structure

The brain's primary function is to produce *movement,* and collectively these movements are termed **behavior**. To produce effective behavior, we take in sensory information—such as vision, audition, olfaction, gustation, and somatosensation—as we search, explore, and manipulate our environment. Without stimuli, the brain cannot properly orient the body and direct it to produce appropriate behaviors. The nervous system's sensory organs gather information about the world and convert this information into biological activity that constructs perceptions—what we see, hear, smell, taste, and feel. This subjective reality is essential to carrying out any complex behavior.

When a ringtone sounds on your phone, for example, your brain directs your body to reach for it as your nervous system responds to vibrating air molecules by producing the subjective experience of a phone's ringtone. We perceive this stimulus as sound and react to it as if it actually exists, when in fact the ringtone is merely a fabrication of the brain. That fabrication is produced by a chain reaction that takes place when vibrating air molecules hit the eardrum. Without the nervous system, especially the brain, perception of sound does not exist—only the movement of air molecules.

But there is more to hearing a phone's ringtone than simply vibrating air molecules. Our mental construct of reality is based on not only the sensory information we receive, but also the cognitive processes we might use to interact with that incoming information. Hearing a ringtone when we are expecting a call has a meaning vastly different from hearing the same sound at 3 A.M., when we are not expecting a call.

The subjective reality the brain constructs can be better understood by comparing the sensory realities of two different kinds of animals. You are probably aware that dogs perceive higher-pitched sounds that humans do not perceive. This difference in perception does not mean that a dog's nervous system is better than ours or that our hearing is poorer. Rather, the perceptual world constructed by a dog brain simply differs from the world constructed by human perception. Neither experience is "correct." The difference in subjective experience is merely due to two divergently evolved systems for processing sensory stimuli.

When it comes to visual perception, humans' world is rich with color, whereas dogs see very little color. Human brains and dog brains construct different realities. Subjective differences in brains exist for good reason: they allow different animals to exploit different features in their environments. Dogs use their hearing to detect the movements of prey, such as mice in the grass; early hominids probably used color vision for identifying ripe fruit in trees. Evolution, then, created *adaptations,* solutions to long-standing historical challenges, which equipped each species with a view of the world that helped it survive.

## Plastic Patterns of Neural Organization

The brain is *plastic*: neural tissue has the capacity to change in response to the world by altering how it is organized. Just as the brain of the young man profiled in Research Focus 2-1 adapted to cerebellar agenesis, a person who is blind from birth has enhanced auditory capacities because some of the brain's visual regions have been co-opted for hearing. The brain is also plastic in the sense that connections among neurons in a given functional system are constantly changing in response to experience.

For us to learn and remember anything new, neural circuits must change to represent and store this knowledge. As we learn to play a musical instrument or speak a new language, the particular cortical regions taking part can actually increase in size as they accommodate the new skill. An important aspect of human learning and brain plasticity is related to the development of language and to the expansion of the brain regions associated with language. Humans have learned to read, to calculate, to compose and

**Learning Objectives**
- Describe neuroplasticity and the role that it plays in adapting.
- Identify the major geographic structures and internal features of the brain.
- List the major divisions of the nervous system and describe how they interact.

Chapter 10 describes the steps through which sound waves are translated into nervous system signals, and explores the neural anatomy associated with our processing of this auditory stimulation.

**Principle 9:** The nervous system produces movement in a perceptual world the brain constructs.

Section 9-1 elaborates on the nature of sensation and perception.

**behavior** a collection of coordinated movements that are internally generated, often in response to external stimuli.

**neuroplasticity** The nervous system's potential to modify itself physically or chemically in response to environmental change and to compensate for age-related changes and injury.

**phenotypic plasticity** An individual's capacity to develop into a range of phenotypes.

**Principle 10:** Neuroplasticity is the hallmark of nervous system functioning.

Section 1-2 introduces the genotype, phenotype, and epigenetics in an evolutionary context.

**FIGURE 2-1 Phenotypic Plasticity** These two mice are genetically identical but express very different phenotypes because their mothers were fed different supplements when pregnant.

Figure 1-1 provides an anatomical illustration of the human CNS and PNS.

**FIGURE 2-2 Parsing the Nervous System** The nervous system can be conceptualized **(A)** anatomically and **(B)** functionally. The functional approach employed in this book focuses on how the four parts of the nervous system interact.

play music, and to develop the sciences. While the human nervous system evolved long before we mastered these achievements, it is still able to learn and remember these new abilities because of brain plasticity.

In turn, culture plays a dominant role in shaping our behavior. Because we drive cars and communicate electronically, we—and our nervous system—are modified in some new ways compared to those of our ancestors who did not engage in these activities. The basis for change in the nervous system is **neuroplasticity**, the nervous system's fundamental potential to physically or chemically modify itself in response to a changing environment and to compensate for age-related changes and injury.

Although it is tempting to see neuroplasticity as a trait unique to animals' nervous systems, it is really part of a larger biological capacity called **phenotypic plasticity**, the individual's capacity to develop a range of *phenotypes*—the characteristics we can see or measure. (See Gilbert and Epel [2009] for a wonderful discussion of biological plasticity.) For instance, our skin responds to ultraviolet rays by incorporating more melanin, causing it to darken as a protective measure. Stated simply, an individual's *genotype* (genetic makeup) interacts with the environment to elicit a specific phenotype. This phenotype emerges from a large genetic repertoire of possibilities, a phenomenon that in turn results from *epigenetic* influences.

Epigenetic factors do not change genes, but rather influence how the genes inherited from parents express specific traits. The two mice pictured in **Figure 2-1** appear very different: one is large, one is small; one has light fur, the other has dark fur. Yet these mice are clones, genetically identical. They have different appearances because their mothers were fed different diets while pregnant. The dietary supplements added chemical markers, or epigenetic tags, on specific genes. These tags determine whether the gene is available to influence cells, including neurons, leading to differences in body structure and eating behavior.

# Functional Organization of the Nervous System

From an anatomical standpoint, the brain and spinal cord together make up the central nervous system. The nerve fibers radiating out beyond the brain and spinal cord, as well as all the neurons outside the brain and spinal cord, form the peripheral nervous system. **Figure 2-2**A charts this *anatomical* organization. Nerves in the peripheral nervous system (PNS) transmit sensory information to the central nervous system (CNS), and they carry motor instructions from the CNS to the body's muscles and tissues, including those that perform such functions as blood circulation and digestion.

Now look at Figure 2-2B. In a *functional* organization, the focus is on how the parts of the system work together. Neurons in the somatic division of the PNS connect through the cranial and spinal nerves to receptors on the body's surface and on its muscles. Somatic neurons gather sensory information for the CNS and convey information from the CNS to move muscles of the head, neck, face, trunk, and limbs. Similarly, the autonomic division of the PNS enables the CNS to govern the workings of your body's internal organs—your heartbeat, urination, pupillary response, and the

**(A) Anatomical organization**

**(B) Functional organization**

diaphragm movements that inflate and deflate your lungs. The enteric nervous system, which is often considered part of the autonomic nervous system, controls digestion and stomach contractions.

From a functional standpoint, the major PNS divisions, along with the CNS, form an interacting four-part system:

- The CNS includes the brain and the spinal cord—the nervous system core, which mediates behavior.

- The **somatic nervous system (SNS)** includes all the spinal and cranial nerves carrying sensory information to the CNS from the muscles, joints, and skin. It also transmits outgoing motor instructions that produce movement.

- The **autonomic nervous system (ANS)** produces the rest-and-digest response through the *parasympathetic* (calming) *nerves* and its opposite, the fight-or-flight response, and vigorous activity through the *sympathetic* (arousing) *nerves*.

- The **enteric nervous system (ENS)**, formed by a mesh of neurons embedded in the lining of the gut, controls the gut. The ENS can communicate with the CNS via the ANS but mostly operates autonomously.

The directional flow of neural information is important. **Afferent** (incoming) information is sensory, coming into the CNS or one of its parts. In contrast, **efferent** (outgoing) information leaves the CNS or one of its parts. When you step on a tack, the afferent sensory signals are transmitted from the body into the brain and then perceived as pain. Efferent signals from the brain cause a motor response: you lift your foot (**Figure 2-3**).

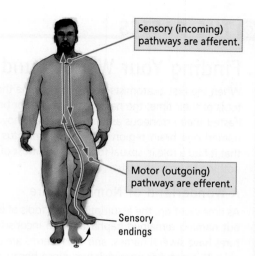

Sensory (incoming) pathways are afferent.

Motor (outgoing) pathways are efferent.

Sensory endings

**FIGURE 2-3 Neural Information Flow**

# The Brain's Surface Features

When buying a car, people like to look under the hood and examine the engine, the part of the car responsible for its behavior. All that most of us can do is gaze at the maze of tubes, wires, boxes, and fluid reservoirs in wonder—what we see makes no sense except in the most general way. We know that the engine somehow generates power to make the car move and to run the sound system, lights, and wipers. But knowing this tells us nothing about what all the many engine parts do.

When it comes to our behavior, the brain is the engine. In many ways, examining a brain for the first time is similar to looking under the hood of a car. We have a vague sense of what the brain does, but most of us have no sense of how its parts accomplish these tasks. We may not even be able to identify those parts. If you are familiar with the anatomical terms and orientations used in drawings and images of brains, read on. If you prefer to review this terminology before you continue, consult The Basics: Finding Your Way Around the Brain.

## Protecting the Nervous System

We start our functional overview by opening the hood and observing the brain snug in its home in the skull. The first thing you actually encounter is not the brain itself, but rather a tough triple-layered protective covering, the **meninges (Figure 2-4)**. The

Spinal reflexes are discussed in detail in Section 11-4 and illustrated in Figure 11-21.

---

**somatic nervous system (SNS)** Part of the PNS that includes the cranial and spinal nerves to and from the muscles, joints, and skin, which produce movement, transmit incoming sensory input, and inform the CNS about the position and movement of body parts.

**autonomic nervous system (ANS)** Part of the PNS that regulates the functioning of internal organs and glands.

**enteric nervous system (ENS)** Mesh of neurons embedded in the lining of the gut, running from the esophagus through the colon; controls the gut.

**afferent** Conducting toward a CNS structure.

**efferent** Conducting away from a CNS structure.

**meninges** Three layers of protective tissue—dura mater, arachnoid, and pia mater—that encase the brain and spinal cord.

Skull
Dura mater
Arachnoid membrane } Meninges
Pia mater
Subarachnoid space (filled with CSF)
Brain

**FIGURE 2-4 Cerebral Protection**

# ◎ THE BASICS

# Finding Your Way Around the Brain

When the first anatomists began to examine the brain with the archaic tools of their time, the names they chose for brain regions often manifested their erroneous assumptions about how the brain works. They named one brain region the *gyrus fornicatus* because they thought that it had a role in sexual function, but most of this region actually has nothing to do with sexual activity.

## A Wonderland of Nomenclature

As time went on, the assumptions and tools of brain research improved, but naming remained haphazard and inconsistent. Many brain structures have several names, and those terms are often used interchangeably. This peculiar nomenclature arose because research on the brain and behavior spans several centuries and includes scientists of many nationalities and languages.

Early investigators named structures after objects (the *pulvinar*, e.g., was thought to look like a pillow) or ideas (the *limbic system* was thought to be responsible for sexuality and emotions). They used various languages, especially Latin and Ancient Greek. They did so because the meanings of words derived from these dead languages are static—they do not change with time, whereas words in living languages do. More recently, investigators have often used numbers or letters to identify structures, but even this system lacks coherence because the numbers may be Arabic or Roman and are often used in combination with Greek or Latin letters.

The naming of structures in the brain and body was largely completed by the end of nineteenth century by scientists in Western Europe who worked primarily in English, which had become the standard language of scientific discourse by that point. The nomenclatures were

**Brain–Body Orientation**

Structures toward the brain's midline are *medial*; those located toward the sides are *lateral*.

Structures atop the brain or a structure within the brain are *dorsal*.

Medial

Posterior

Anterior

Lateral

*Anterior* is in front; *posterior* is at the back.

Structures toward the bottom of the brain or one of its parts are *ventral*.

disseminated through scientific journals and the proceedings of various societies, and then widely adopted by researchers from other cultures and languages. As a result of this legacy and despite the global nature of research, scientific journals and societies continue to use English as the standard language, and modern contributions, regardless of their origin, are typically written in English.

## Describing Locations in the Brain

Many names for nervous system structures reflect their anatomical locations with respect to other anatomical structures (e.g., the hypothalamus lies below the thalamus), with respect to their relative spatial

**Spatial Orientation**

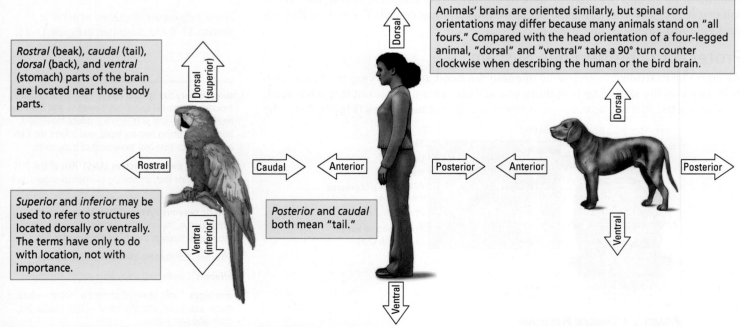

*Rostral* (beak), *caudal* (tail), *dorsal* (back), and *ventral* (stomach) parts of the brain are located near those body parts.

Animals' brains are oriented similarly, but spinal cord orientations may differ because many animals stand on "all fours." Compared with the head orientation of a four-legged animal, "dorsal" and "ventral" take a 90° turn counter clockwise when describing the human or the bird brain.

Dorsal (superior)

Dorsal

Dorsal

Rostral

Caudal

Anterior

Posterior

Anterior

Posterior

*Superior* and *inferior* may be used to refer to structures located dorsally or ventrally. The terms have only to do with location, not with importance.

Ventral (inferior)

*Posterior* and *caudal* both mean "tail."

Ventral

Ventral

locations (the lateral ventricles lie lateral to the other ventricles), and with respect to a viewer's perspective (the anterodorsal nucleus of the thalamus is in the front and above the other thalamic nuclei):

- Brain–body orientation illustrates brain structure location from the frame of reference of the human face.

- Spatial orientation illustrates brain structure location in relation to other body parts and body orientation.

- Anatomical orientation illustrates the direction of a cut, or section, through the human brain (part A) from the perspective of a viewer (part B).

These orienting terms are derived from Latin. Consult the accompanying table "Glossary of Anatomical Location and Orientation" for easy reference. It is common practice to combine orienting terms. A structure described as dorsolateral, for example, lies up and to the side, as in the case of the dorsolateral prefrontal cortex.

Finally, the nervous system, like the body, is bilaterally symmetrical: it has a left side and a right side. Structures that lie on the same side are *ipsilateral*; if they lie on opposite sides, they are *contralateral* to each other. Structures that occur in each hemisphere are *bilateral*. Structures that are close to one another are *proximal*; those far from one another are *distal*.

**Anatomic Orientation**

**(A) Plane of section**

**(B) View of brain**

Coronal section

Frontal view

A *coronal section* is cut in a vertical plane, from the crown of the head down, yielding a frontal view of the brain's internal structures.

Horizontal section

Dorsal view

A *horizontal section*, so-called because the view or the cut falls along the horizon, is usually viewed looking down on the brain from above—a dorsal view.

Sagittal section

Medial view

A *sagittal section* is cut lengthways from front to back and viewed from the side. (Imagine the brain split by an arrow—in Latin, *sagitta*.) Here, a cut in the *midsagittal plane* divides the brain into symmetrical halves, a medial view.

## Glossary of Anatomical Location and Orientation

| Term | Meaning with respect to the nervous system | Term | Meaning with respect to the nervous system |
|------|--------------------------------------------|------|--------------------------------------------|
| Anterior | Near or toward the front of the animal or the front of the head (see also *frontal* and *rostral*) | Lateral | Toward the side of the body or brain |
| Caudal | Near or toward the tail of the animal (see also *posterior*) | Medial | Toward the middle, specifically the body's midline; in reference to brain sections, a side view of the central structures |
| Coronal | Cut vertically from the crown of the head down; used to reference the plane of a brain section that reveals a frontal view | Posterior | Near or toward the animal's tail (see also *caudal*); for the human spinal cord, at the back |
| Dorsal | On or toward the back of a four-legged animal (equivalent to posterior for the human spinal cord); in reference to human brain nuclei, above, and to brain sections, viewed from above | Rostral | Toward the beak (front) of the animal (see also *anterior* and *frontal*) |
| Frontal | Of the front (see also *anterior* and *rostral*); in reference to brain sections, a viewing orientation from the front | Sagittal | Cut lengthways from front to back of the skull to reveal a medial view into the brain from the side; a cut in the midsagittal plane divides the brain into symmetrical halves |
| Horizontal | Cut along the horizon; used to reference the plane of a brain section that reveals a dorsal view | Superior | Above (see also *dorsal*) |
| Inferior | Below (see also *ventral*) | Ventral | On or toward the belly of four-legged animals (see also *inferior*); in reference to human brain nuclei, below |

Living Art Enterprises/Science Source

The brain is made up of two hemispheres, left and right.

**Frontal view**
Cerebral cortex is the brain's thin, outer "bark" layer.

Your right hand, if made into a fist, represents the positions of the lobes of the left hemisphere of your brain.

Parietal lobe

Frontal lobe

Occipital lobe

Temporal lobe

Arthur Glauberman/Science Source

Bumps in the brain's folded surface are called gyri, and cracks are called sulci.

Lobes define broad divisions of the cerebral cortex.

Parietal lobe (knuckles)

Occipital lobe (wrist)

Frontal lobe (fingers)

Temporal lobe (thumb)

**FIGURE 2-5 The Cerebral Cortex** Each cerebral hemisphere is divided into four lobes: frontal, parietal, temporal, and occipital, shown at left as oriented in the head. The brain's outer layer, or cerebral cortex, shown in the frontal view, is the layered tissue, which is heavily folded to fit inside the skull. Your right fist can map the orientation of the left hemisphere and its lobes.

outer *dura mater* (from Latin, meaning "hard mother") is a tough durable layer of fibrous tissue that is attached to the skull and encloses the brain and spinal cord in a kind of loose sac. In the middle is the *arachnoid layer* (from Greek, meaning "like a spider's web"), an ultrathin sheet of delicate connective tissue that follows the brain's contours. The inner layer, or *pia mater* (from Latin, meaning "soft mother"), is a moderately tough membrane of connective tissue that clings to the brain's surface.

Between the arachnoid layer and the pia mater flows **cerebrospinal fluid (CSF)**, a colorless solution containing sodium, chloride, and other ions. CSF cushions the brain so that it can move or expand slightly without pressing on the skull. The symptoms of meningitis—that is, infection of the meninges and CSF—are described in Clinical Focus 2-2, Meningitis and Encephalitis.

## Cerebral Geography

After removing the meninges, we can examine the brain's surface features, most prominently its two nearly symmetrical left and right hemispheres. **Figure 2-5** diagrams the left hemisphere of a typical human forebrain oriented in the upright human skull. The outer forebrain consists of folded and layered tissue, the **cerebral cortex**, detailed in the frontal view in Figure 2-5. The word *cortex*, Latin for "bark," is an apt choice for this structure, considering the cortex's heavily folded surface and its location, covering most of the rest of the brain. Unlike the bark on a tree, however, the brain's folds are not random but rather demarcate its functional cortical zones.

Make a fist with your right hand and hold it up, as shown on the right in Figure 2-5, to represent the positions of the forebrain's broad divisions, or *lobes*, in the skull. Each lobe is simply named for the skull bone it lies beneath:

- Immediately above your thumbnail, your fingers correspond to the location of the **frontal lobe**, which performs the brain's executive functions, such as decision making and generating voluntary movement.

- The **parietal lobe** is at the top of the skull, as represented by your knuckles, behind the frontal lobe. Parietal functions include directing our movements toward a goal or to perform a task, such as grasping an object.

**cerebrospinal fluid (CSF)** Clear solution of sodium, chloride, and other ions that is produced in the ventricles inside the brain and circulates around the brain and spinal cord until it is absorbed beneath the arachnoid layer in the subarachnoid space.

**cerebral cortex** Heavily folded and layered tissue that forms the outer structure of the forebrain; composed of neocortex and allocortex.

**frontal lobe** Part of the cerebral cortex, which performs the brain's executive functions, such as decision making, and voluntary movement; lies anterior to the central sulcus and beneath the frontal bone of the skull.

**parietal lobe** Part of the cerebral cortex that directs movements toward a goal or to perform a task, such as grasping an object; lies posterior to the central sulcus and beneath the parietal bone at the top of the skull.

## CLINICAL FOCUS 2-2

# Meningitis and Encephalitis

Harmful viruses or microorganisms, such as bacteria, fungi, and protozoa, sometimes invade and multiply in the layers of the meninges, particularly the pia mater and the arachnoid layer, as well as the CSF flowing between them. Their presence in the brain leads to an infection known as *meningitis* (literally "inflammation of the meninges"). In response to the infection, the body produces white blood cells designed to attack and consume these invaders. This inflammatory response increases the pressure within the cranium, which in turn impairs the functioning of the brain. Unrelieved cranial pressure can lead to delirium and, if the infection progresses, to drowsiness, stupor, coma, and even death.

Usually the earliest symptom of meningitis is severe headache and a stiff neck (cervical rigidity). Head retraction (tilting the head backward) is an extreme form of cervical rigidity. Convulsions, a symptom commonly seen in children, indicate that the inflammation is affecting the brain. Meningitis is treated with antibiotics when the cause is microorganisms and sometimes with antiviral drugs for viral infections. Survivors of meningitis can have long-term consequences, such as deafness, epilepsy, hydrocephalus, and cognitive deficits.

Infection of the brain itself is called *encephalitis* (inflammation of the brain). Like meningitis, encephalitis can be caused by a number of different invading viruses or microorganisms. For example, the COVID-19 virus (SARS-CoV2) can gain access to the brain via the olfactory pathway, cranial nerves, and white blood cells when the blood–brain barrier is compromised (Keyhanian et al., 2020). The virus then enters neurons and glial cells, particularly those in the cardiac and respiratory brainstem centers. Virus-induced damage to these centers is a likely contributor to cardiac or respiratory arrest, which are often the proximate causes of death in COVID-19 cases. As of October 2021, more than 4.9 million people worldwide are confirmed to have died from this virus.

Vaccinations are a highly effective protection against certain types of encephalitis, although many vulnerable populations have not yet been

Pus, consisting of dead white blood cells, bacteria with tissue debris, and serum, is visible over the surface of this brain infected with meningitis.

CDC/Dr. Edwin P. Ewing, Jr.

vaccinated. Experts estimate that encephalitis affected 4.3 million people and resulted in 150,000 deaths worldwide in 2015, the most recent year for which figures are available.

---

- The forward-pointing **temporal lobe** lies at the side of the brain below the parietal lobe, in approximately the same place as the thumb on your upraised fist. The temporal lobe constructs higher order hearing, language, and musical abilities, as well as facial recognition and emotional processing.

- The area at the back of each hemisphere, near your wrist, constitutes the **occipital lobe**, where visual scene processing begins.

## Examining the Brain's Surface from All Angles

As we look at the dorsal view in **Figure 2-6**A, the brain's wrinkled left and right hemispheres constitute the cerebrum, which is the major forebrain structure and the most recently expanded feature of the mammalian CNS. Visible from the opposite ventral view in Figure 2-6B is the brainstem, including the wrinkly hemispheres of the smaller *cerebellum* (Latin for "little brain"). Both the cerebrum and the brainstem are visible in the lateral and medial views in Figure 2-6C and D.

Much of the crinkled-up cerebral cortex is invisible from the brain's surface. All we can see are hills, or **gyri (sing. *gyrus*)**, and valleys, or **sulci (sing. *sulcus*)**. The really deep sulci are called *fissures*. The longitudinal fissure runs between the cerebral hemispheres and the lateral fissure travels along the sides of the brain. Both are shown in

The brain has several visual-based systems that perform different functions, such as regulating pupil size and providing input to the circadian (day/night cycle) system. *Visual scene* is the visual system that gives rise to our perception of the visual world.

---

**temporal lobe** Part of the cerebral cortex that includes hearing, language, musical abilities, facial recognition, memory, and emotional processing; lies below the lateral fissure, beneath the temporal bone at the side of the skull.

**occipital lobe** Part of the cerebral cortex where visual scene processing begins; the most posterior part of the neocortex, it lies beneath the occipital bone.

**gyri (sing. *gyrus*)** Small protrusions or bumps formed by the folding of the cerebral cortex.

**sulci (sing. *sulcus*)** Grooves in brain matter; most are in the neocortex or cerebellum.

**FIGURE 2-6 Examining the Human Brain** Locations of the lobes of the cerebral hemispheres, shown in dorsal, ventral, lateral, and medial (*top*, *bottom*, *side*, and *midline*) views, as are the cerebellum, longitudinal and lateral fissures, and central sulcus.

various views in Figure 2-6, along with the central sulcus that runs from the lateral fissures across the top of the cerebrum.

Looking at the bottom of the brain, the ventral view in Figure 2-6B, we see a smooth, whitish structure with little tubelike protrusions attached, which is located in the midst of the wrinkled cerebrum and ventral to the cerebellum. This is the brainstem, the area responsible for critical functions of life, including heart rate, breathing, sleeping, and eating. The tubelike protrusions are the cranial nerves that run to and from the brain as part of the SNS.

## Cerebral Circulation

The brain's surface is covered with blood vessels. As in the rest of the body, the arteries feed oxygenated blood to the brain, and the veins carry the oxygen-depleted blood back to the kidneys and lungs for waste removal and oxygenation. The cerebral arteries emerge from the neck to wrap around the outside of the brainstem, cerebrum, and cerebellum, finally penetrating the brain's surface to nourish its inner regions.

Three major arteries send blood to the cerebrum—the anterior, middle, and posterior cerebral arteries, shown in **Figure 2-7**. Because the brain is highly sensitive to blood loss, a blockage or break in a cerebral artery is likely to lead to the death of the affected region. This condition, known as **stroke**, is marked by the sudden appearance of neurological symptoms as a result of severely reduced blood flow. Because the three cerebral arteries supply different parts of the brain, strokes can disrupt different brain functions, depending on the artery affected.

Because the many of the brain's connections are crossed, stroke in the left hemisphere affects sensation and movement on the right side of the body. The opposite is true for people who develop strokes in the right hemisphere. Clinical Focus 2-3, Stroke, describes some disruptions that stroke can cause, both to the person who has it and to those who care for stroke survivors.

## The Brain's Internal Features

The simplest way to examine the inside of something is to cut it in half. Of course, the orientation of the cut affects what we see. Consider slicing through a pear. If we cut from side to side, we cut across the core, providing a dorsal view; if we cut from

---

The effects and treatments for stroke are covered in detail in Section 16-3.

**Principle 4:** Many brain circuits are crossed.

**stroke** Sudden appearance of neurological symptoms as a result of severely reduced blood flow in the brain.

**Anterior cerebral artery**  **Middle cerebral artery**  **Posterior cerebral artery**

Dorsal view    Lateral view    Ventral view

Lateral view    Medial view    Medial view

**FIGURE 2-7 Major Cerebral Arteries** Each of the three major arteries that feed blood to the cerebral hemispheres branches extensively to supply the regions shaded in pink. Section 16-3 elaborates on the effects of stroke and its treatment.

top to bottom, we cut parallel to the core, providing a medial view. Our impression of the inside of a pear is clearly influenced by how we slice it. The same is true of the brain.

## Macroscopic Inspection: Regions and Hemispheres

We can reveal the brain's inner features by slicing it parallel to the front of the body, downward through the middle in a coronal section (**Figure 2-8**A). The resulting frontal view, shown in Figure 2-8B, immediately reveals that the brain's interior is not homogeneous. Both dark grayish and lighter regions of tissue are visible. Although these regions may not be as distinctive as car engine parts, they nevertheless represent different brain components.

The darker regions, called **gray matter**, are largely composed of cell bodies and capillary blood vessels. Within the gray matter, neurons collect and modify information before sending it along. The lighter regions, called **white matter**, are mostly nerve fibers covered by myelin sheaths that have a high fat content. These fibers produce the white appearance, much as fat droplets in milk make it appear white. White matter fibers form longer-distance connections between and among some of the brain's neurons.

**gray matter** Areas of the nervous system composed predominantly of neuronal cell bodies that collect and modify information and capillary blood vessels that support this activity.

**white matter** Areas of the nervous system containing fat-rich, myelin-sheathed neuronal axons that form the connections between neurons.

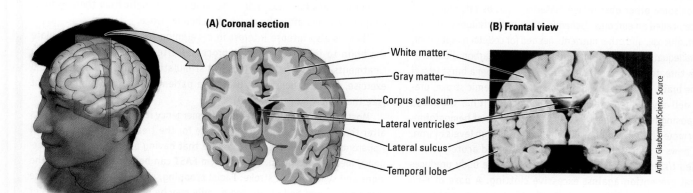

**(A) Coronal section**    **(B) Frontal view**

White matter
Gray matter
Corpus callosum
Lateral ventricles
Lateral sulcus
Temporal lobe

Arthur Glauberman/Science Source

**FIGURE 2-8 Coronal Brain Section (A)** The brain is cut down the middle parallel to the front of the body; then a coronal section is viewed at a slight angle. **(B)** This frontal view displays white matter, gray matter, and the lateral ventricles. Visible above the ventricles, a large bundle of whitish fibers, the corpus callosum, joins the hemispheres.

# Stroke

According to the World Health Organization, stroke is the second leading cause of death worldwide (behind ischemic heart disease). Approximately every minute in the United States, someone has a stroke that produces obvious visible symptoms — a rate that translates into more than half a million people having stroke every year. Acute symptoms may include facial droop, motor weakness in limbs, speech difficulties, visual disturbance, and sudden onset of severe headache.

Even with the best, fastest medical attention, most stroke survivors have some residual motor, sensory, or cognitive deficit. For every 10 people who have a stroke, 2 die, 6 are disabled to varying degrees, and 2 recover but still have a diminished quality of life (Goyal et al., 2015). Of those who survive, 1 in 10 is at increased risk for another stroke.

The consequences of strokes are significant for the people who have them, as well as for their family and lifestyle. Consider Mr. Anderson, a 45-year-old electrical engineer who took his three children to the movies one Saturday afternoon and collapsed. He had a massive stroke of the middle cerebral artery in his left hemisphere. The stroke has impaired Mr. Anderson's language ever since, and because the brain's connections are crossed, his right-side motor control is affected as well.

Ten years after his stroke, Mr. Anderson remains unable to speak, although he understands simple conversations. Severe difficulties in moving his right leg require him to use a walker. He cannot move the fingers of his right hand, so he has difficulty feeding himself, among other tasks. Mr. Anderson will probably never return to his engineering career or drive or get around on his own.

Like Mr. Anderson, most other stroke survivors require help to perform everyday tasks. In the United States and many other countries, caregivers are disproportionately female and are often relatives who give up their own careers and other pursuits (see Sharma et al., 2016, for more on gender disparities among caregivers and gender differences in the impact of caregiving; as the study indicates, more research is needed). Half of these caregivers develop emotional illness, primarily depression or anxiety, or both, after a year or so. Lost income and stroke-related medical bills significantly affect the family's living standard.

We tend to speak of stroke as a single disorder, but there are actually two major categories of strokes — ischemic and hemorrhagic. In the more common *ischemic stroke*, a blood vessel is blocked by either a blood clot, also known as a thrombus, or some other obstructive material, such as fat, clumps of bacteria, or cancer, called an embolus. *Ischemia* refers to the failure to deliver sufficient oxygen, glucose, and other nutrients needed for cellular metabolism, as well as the inadequate removal of metabolic waste like carbon dioxide.

The more life-threatening *hemorrhagic stroke* results from a burst vessel bleeding into the brain. While the hemorrhage, like an ischemic stroke, prevents sufficient delivery and removal of critical molecules, it has the added detriment of exposing neurons directly to the toxic effects of hemoglobin, the gas-carrying molecule in red blood cells that contains high levels of iron.

The hopeful news is that ischemic stroke can be treated acutely with a medication called *tissue plasminogen activator* (t-PA). The body produces t-PA as a natural prevention against excessive clotting. A dose of t-PA administered within 3 hours of the onset of ischemic symptoms will boost a patient's t-PA levels to about 1000 times the normal level, which helps break up clots and allows normal blood flow to return to an affected region. Unfortunately, there is no treatment for hemorrhagic stroke, for which the use of clot-busting t-PA would be disastrous.

Simon Fraser/Science Source

Dorsal view of a brain with a stroke, imaged by computed tomography (CT). The dark area in the right hemisphere has been damaged by the loss of blood flow.

When patients receive t-PA, the number who make a nearly complete recovery increases by about 25 percent compared with those who receive a placebo (Hatcher & Starr, 2011). In addition, impairments are reduced in the remaining patients who survive the stroke, when the t-PA medication has at least some effectiveness. Unfortunately, in a small percentage of patients who do not receive any benefit from t-PA, their outcomes are worsened by this treatment. The risk of hemorrhage is about 6% in t-PA–treated patients relative to no risk in placebo-treated patients.

By taking advantage of developments in neuroimaging, it has become possible to remove some clots from cerebral vessels mechanically (Goyal et al., 2015). This is achieved by using advanced radiographic imaging techniques to guide a long, thin catheter tube with a springlike mechanism on the end, which is inserted into the femoral artery near the groin. The tube is threaded through the body into the brain and to the clot. Then, the springlike mechanism can either grab the clot or break it up. These new procedures have expanded the window of benefit from therapy to as long as 12 hours after the onset of ischemic stroke.

There is also intense interest in developing treatments that stimulate the brain to initiate reparative processes after suffering a stroke. Such treatments, which include electrical stimulation, drugs, stem cells, and exercise, are designed to facilitate the patient's functional improvement (see the review by Zeiler, 2019).

Most stroke victims do not visit an emergency room until about 24 hours after their symptoms appear — too late for the treatment to be effective. Apparently, most people fail to realize that having a stroke requires emergency medical attention. The acronym **FAST** can be used to remember the signs and symptoms of stroke: **F**acial drooping, where one side of the face may be drooping and numb, and a smile may be uneven; **A**rm weakness or numbness on one side, with one arm pointing downward; **S**peech difficulty, including slurred or incomprehensible speech, or trouble speaking at all; and **T**ime to call 911 or get the individual to the hospital if they show any of the preceding symptoms, even if those symptoms are no longer apparent.

**(A) Lateral view of brain**

Right lateral ventricle

Left lateral ventricle

Third ventricle

Fourth ventricle

**(B) Frontal view of brain**

Lateral ventricle

Cerebral aqueduct

Third ventricle

Fourth ventricle

**FIGURE 2-9 Interconnected Cerebral Ventricles** The lateral ventricles are symmetrical, one in each hemisphere. The third and fourth ventricles lie in the brain's midline and connect to the cerebral aqueduct, which runs the length of the spinal cord.

A second feature, apparent at the center of our frontal view in Figure 2-8B, are the lateral **ventricles**—two wing-shaped cavities that contain CSF. The brain's four ventricles, shown in **Figure 2-9**, are filled with CSF made by a network of blood vessels, called the *choroid plexus,* which lines the ventricles. All four ventricles are connected, so CSF flows from the two lateral ventricles to the third and fourth ventricles, which lie on the brain's midline, and into the *cerebral aqueduct,* a canal that runs down the length of the spinal cord. CSF bathes the brain and circulates in the space between the lower layers of the meninges, where it is absorbed and deposited into the venous bloodstream (see Figure 2-4).

The CSF performs several vital brain functions. This fluid suspends the brain, making it neutrally buoyant so that it acts as if it is 1/30 of its actual mass. The CSF also acts as a shock absorber, providing the brain with important protection from mild blows to the head. The chemical content of the CSF is precisely regulated to provide a stable environment for optimal brain function. Slight changes to its chemical composition can cause dizziness and fainting. The brain also produces and distributes approximately 25 mL of CFS an hour, which accounts for about one-fifth of its total volume. In this way, substances are efficiently delivered to brain cells and waste products cleared away.

Cutting through the brain vertically from front to back produces a sagittal section (**Figure 2-10**A). If we make our cut down the brain's midline—that is, in the midsagittal plane—we divide the cerebrum into its two hemispheres, revealing several distinctive structures in the resulting medial view (Figure 2-10B). One feature is a long band of white matter that runs for much of the length of the cerebral hemispheres. This band, called the **corpus callosum**, contains about 200 million nerve fibers that join the two hemispheres and allow them to communicate.

Figure 2-10B clearly shows that the neocortex covers the cerebral hemispheres above the corpus callosum; below it are various internal *subcortical regions.*

**ventricles** Cavities in the brain that make and contain CSF.

**corpus callosum** Band of white matter containing about 200 million nerve fibers, which connects the two cerebral hemispheres to provide a route for direct communication between them.

**FIGURE 2-10 Sagittal Brain Section (A)** A section in the midsagittal plane separates the hemispheres, allowing **(B)** a medial view of the brain's midline structures, including the subcortical structures that lie ventral to the corpus callosum.

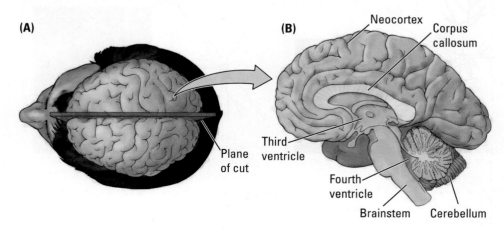

**(A)**

Plane of cut

**(B)**

Neocortex

Corpus callosum

Third ventricle

Fourth ventricle

Brainstem    Cerebellum

**Principle 3:** The CNS functions on multiple levels and is organized hierarchically and in parallel.

**Principle 6:** The brain is symmetrical and asymmetrical.

Section 10-3 details the functional anatomy of the auditory system, including an illustration of the neocortical auditory areas in Figure 10-13, and includes a discussion of lateralization of function.

Human brains contain approximately 86 billion neurons and 85 billion glia. Section 3-1 examines their structures and functions in detail.

---

**nuclei (sing. *nucleus*)** A group of neurons forming a cluster that can be identified using special stains.

---

Subcortical regions make intimate reciprocal connections with cortical areas that process sensory, perceptual, cognitive, and motor functions. When the cortical areas perceive a threat, such as an angry dog, they communicate with subcortical regions that have already begun to increase breathing and heart rate via the sympathetic nervous system. This relation between the cortical and subcortical areas illuminates another principle of CNS organization: redundant and overlapping functions exist at many levels of the nervous system.

If you were to compare medial views of the left and right hemispheres, you would be struck by their symmetry. The brain has two of most of its structures, one on each side, and they are nearly identical. In contrast, structural asymmetry in our species can be found in the neocortical auditory areas; in right-handed people, the *planum temporale*, which is responsible for understanding speech, is larger in the left hemisphere, whereas *Heschl's gyrus*, which is responsible for analyzing music, is larger on the right.

A few one-of-a-kind structures, such as the third and fourth ventricles, lie along the brain's midline (see Figure 2-9B). Another one-of-a-kind structure is the pineal gland, which straddles the two hemispheres.

## Microscopic Inspection: Cells and Fibers

The brain's fundamental units—its cells—are so small that they can be viewed only with the aid of a microscope. A microscope quickly reveals that the brain has two main types of cells, illustrated in **Figure 2-11**. *Neurons* carry out the brain's communicative and information processing functions, whereas *glial cells* have a variety of critical functions including aiding and modulating the neurons' activities—for example, by insulating their axons. Both neurons and glia come in many forms, each marked by the work that they do.

We can see the brain's internal structures in even greater detail by dyeing their cells with special stains (**Figure 2-12**). For example, if we use a dye that selectively stains cell bodies, we can see that the neurons in the cortical gray matter lie in layers, revealed by the bands of tissue in Figure 2-12A and C. Each layer contains cells that stain in characteristic ways. Figure 2-12A and B shows that stained subcortical regions are composed of clusters, or **nuclei (sing. *nucleus*)**, of similar cells.

Although layers and nuclei appear very different, both form functional units in the brain. Whether a particular brain region has layers or nuclei is largely a product of evolution. By using a stain that selectively dyes neuronal fibers, as shown in Figure 2-12B and D, we can see the borders of the subcortical nuclei more clearly.

**FIGURE 2-11 Brain Cells** Branches emanate from the cell bodies of a prototypical neuron (*left*) and a glial cell (*right*). This branching organization increases the cell's surface area. Such a neuron is called a *pyramidal cell* because the cell body is shaped somewhat like a pyramid; the glial cell is called an *astrocyte* because of its star-shaped appearance.

Neuron (pyramidal cell)

Glial cell (astrocyte)

Cell body

Cell body

Kasthuri and Lichtman, Harvard University

Nancy Kedersha/Science Photo Library/Science Source

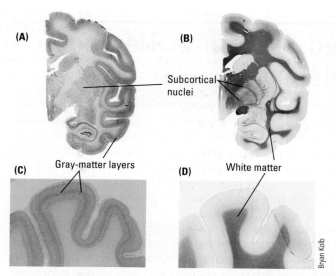

**(A)**

**(B)**
Subcortical
nuclei

**(C)** Gray-matter layers

**(D)** White matter

Bryan Kolb

**FIGURE 2-12 Cortical Layers and Glia** Brain sections from the left hemisphere of a monkey (midline is to the left in each image), viewed through a microscope. Cells are stained with **(A** and **C)** a selective cell body stain for neurons (gray matter) and **(B** and **D)** a selective fiber stain for insulating glial cells, or *myelin* (white matter). The images reveal very different views of the brain at the macro **(A** and **B)** and microscopic **(C** and **D)** levels.

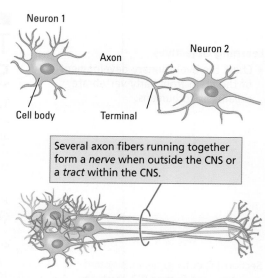

Neuron 1

Axon

Neuron 2

Cell body          Terminal

Several axon fibers running together form a *nerve* when outside the CNS or a *tract* within the CNS.

**FIGURE 2-13 Neuronal Connections**

In addition, we can see that the stained cell bodies lie in regions adjacent to those with most of the fibers.

A key feature of neurons is that they are connected to one another by fibers known as *axons*. When axons run along together, much like the wires that run from a car engine to the dashboard, they form a **nerve** or **tract** (**Figure 2-13**). By convention, a *tract* is a collection of nerve fibers in the brain and spinal cord, whereas bundles of fibers outside the CNS are typically called nerves. Thus, the pathway from the eye to the brain is the optic nerve, whereas the pathway from the cerebral cortex to the spinal cord is the corticospinal tract.

**nerve** Large collection of axons coursing together *outside* the CNS.

**tract** Large collection of axons coursing together *inside* the CNS.

## 2-1 Review

Before you continue, check your understanding. Answers appear at the back of the book.

1. The nervous system's function is to produce movement, or _____, in a perceptual world constructed by the _____.

2. The left and right cerebral hemispheres are each divided into four lobes: _____, _____, _____, and _____.

3. The human nervous system has evolved the potential to change—for example, to adapt to changes in the world or to compensate for injury. This attribute is called _____.

4. The two main types of neural tissue are (1) _____, which forms the connections among cells, and (2) _____, which collects and processes incoming (afferent) sensory or outgoing (efferent) information.

5. Bundles of nerve fibers (axons) in the brain and spinal cord are called _____. Outside the brain and spinal cord these bundles are called _____.

6. Chart the human nervous system's functional organization.

**Learning Objectives**
• Chart the evolutionary development of the brain from early vertebrate organisms to humans.

Section 1-3 outlines nervous system evolution, and Section 8-2 charts the development of the nervous system in humans from fertilization through childhood.

## 2-2

# The Conserved Pattern of Nervous System Development

The nervous system's basic structural plan is present in developing, embryonic brains, and the striking similarity of the main divisions in embryos as diverse as amphibians and mammals is evident in the earliest stages of development. Because evolution works by tinkering with the developmental programs that give rise to brain structures, simpler and evolutionarily more archaic forms have not been discarded and replaced, but rather modified and added to. As a result, all anatomical and functional features of simpler nervous systems are present in and form the basis for the most complex nervous systems, including our own.

The bilaterally symmetrical nature of the nervous system of simple worms, for example, is also found in complex nervous systems. Indeed, we can recognize in humans the spinal cord that constitutes most of the simplest fishes' nervous system. The same is true of the brainstem of more complex fishes, amphibians, and reptiles. The neocortex, although particularly large and complex in humans, is clearly the same organ found in other mammals.

## Comparative Brain Evolution

In a vertebrate embryo, the nervous system begins as a sheet of cells. This sheet folds into a hollow tube and develops into three regions—forebrain, midbrain, and hindbrain—which are recognizable as a series of three enlargements at the end of the embryonic spinal cord (**Figure 2-14**A). The adult brain of a fish, an amphibian, or a reptile is roughly equivalent to this three-part brain. The *prosencephalon* (front brain) is responsible for olfaction, the sense of smell; the *mesencephalon* (middle brain) is the seat of vision and hearing; and the *rhombencephalon* (hindbrain) controls movement and balance. The spinal cord is part of the hindbrain.

In mammalian embryos (Figure 2-14B), the prosencephalon develops further to form the subcortical structures known collectively as the *diencephalon* (between brain) and the cerebral hemispheres and cortical areas, or *telencephalon* (endbrain). The

**FIGURE 2-14 Comparative Brain Evolution and Development** As the mammalian brain has evolved, the forebrain has expanded dramatically.

**(A) Vertebrate embryo**

Prosencephalon (forebrain)
Mesencephalon (midbrain)
Rhombencephalon (hindbrain)
Spinal cord

**(B) Mammalian embryo**

Telencephalon
Diencephalon
Mesencephalon
Myelencephalon
Spinal cord
Metencephalon

**(C) Fully developed human brain**

Telencephalon
Diencephalon
Mesencephalon
Metencephalon
Myelencephalon
Spinal cord

| (A) Vertebrate embryo | (B) Mammalian embryo | (C) Fully developed human brain | |
|---|---|---|---|
| Prosencephalon (forebrain) | Telencephalon (endbrain) | Neocortex, basal ganglia, allocortex, olfactory bulb, lateral ventricles | Forebrain |
| | Diencephalon (between brain) | Thalamus, hypothalamus, pituitary gland, pineal body, third ventricle | |
| Mesencephalon (midbrain) | Mesencephalon | Tectum, tegmentum, cerebral aqueduct | Brainstem |
| Rhombencephalon (hindbrain) | Metencephalon (across brain) | Cerebellum, pons, fourth ventricle | |
| | Myelencephalon (spinal brain) | Medulla oblongata, fourth ventricle | |
| Spinal cord | Spinal cord | Spinal cord | Spinal cord |

mammalian hindbrain develops further into the *metencephalon* (across brain), which includes the cerebellum, and the *myelencephalon* (spinal brain), including the spinal cord.

The human brain is particularly complex, possessing especially large cerebral hemispheres but retaining most other mammalian brain features (Figure 2-14C). Various human cerebral areas necessary to produce language—regions in the frontal, temporal, and parietal lobes—are proportionally larger compared to the corresponding regions in the brains of other primates. Language is thought to have fostered a novel worldview—in the way we think, reflect on our own thoughts, and imagine.

# The Nervous System and Intelligent Behavior

A given behavior is the product not of a single locus in the brain, but rather of many interacting brain areas and levels. These several nervous system regions do not simply replicate function; instead, each region adds a different dimension to the behavior. This hierarchical organization affects virtually every behavior. Abnormalities associated with brain injury and brain disease that might seem bizarre in isolation are actually the normal manifestation of parts of a hierarchically organized brain. Our evolutionary history, our developmental history, and our own personal history are integrated at the various anatomical and functional levels of the nervous system.

**Principle 3:** The CNS functions on multiple levels and is organized hierarchically and in parallel.

Is the vertebrate nervous system the only path to evolving intelligent behavior? No, it is not. Invertebrate animals, such as the octopus, have traveled on an evolutionary pathway separate from that of vertebrates for more than 700 million years. The octopus's nervous system, while strikingly different from ours, is complex. Might the octopus learn much as vertebrate animals do?

Italian biologists Graziano Fiorito and Pietro Scotto (1992) placed individuals of *Octopus vulgaris* (the common octopus) in separate tanks, each with an independent water supply, and allowed them to interact visually for 2 hours. As illustrated in the Procedure section of **Experiment 2-1**, the observer octopus watched the demonstrator octopus from an adjacent tank through a transparent wall. The demonstrator was being conditioned to learn that a red ball was associated with a reward, whereas a white ball was associated with a weak electric shock.

As noted in the Results section, the demonstrator animals quickly learned to distinguish between the colored balls. The observers were then placed in isolation. When tested later, they selected the same object the demonstrators had, responded faster than the demonstrators did during their conditioning, and performed the task correctly for 5 days without significant error or further conditioning.

## `2-2` Review

Before you continue, check your understanding. Answers appear at the back of the book.

1. In vertebrate embryos, a sheet of cells folds to form a hollow tube, which will become the spinal cord, and three basic brain regions: _____, _____, and _____.

2. What do Fiorito and Scotto's experiments with octopi demonstrate about the emergence of intelligence?

3. In a brief paragraph, explain how the evolution of the forebrain in mammals reinforces the principle that the CNS functions on multiple levels.

····> **EXPERIMENT 2-1**

Question: Does intelligent behavior require a vertebrate nervous system organization?

**Procedure**

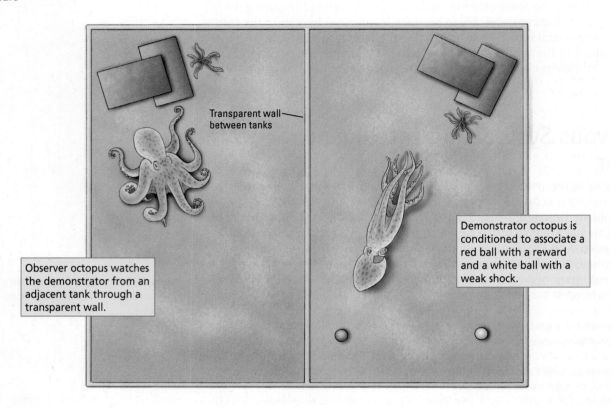

Transparent wall between tanks

Observer octopus watches the demonstrator from an adjacent tank through a transparent wall.

Demonstrator octopus is conditioned to associate a red ball with a reward and a white ball with a weak shock.

**Results**

1. The demonstrator animal quickly learned to distinguish between the colored balls.

2. When placed in isolation and tested later, the observer animals selected the same object as the demonstrators, responded more quickly, and performed the task correctly for 5 days without significant error.

*Conclusion:* Invertebrates display intelligent behavior, such as learning by observation.

Research from G. Fiorito and P. Scotto. (1992). Observational learning in *Octopus vulgaris. Science, 256,* 545–547.

**2-3**

# Central Nervous System: Mediating Behavior

When we look under the hood of a car, we can make some pretty good guesses about what certain parts of a car engine do. For example, the battery must provide electrical power to run the car's computer and lights. Because a battery has to be charged, the engine must also contain some mechanism for charging it. We can use a similar approach to deduce how the parts of the brain function. The part connected to the optic nerve coming from each eye must have something to do with vision. Structures connected to the auditory nerve coming from each ear must have something to do with hearing.

From such simple observations, we can begin to understand how the brain is organized. The real test comes when we analyze actual brain function—how this seeming jumble of parts produces experiences as complex as human thought. The best place to start is the brain's functional anatomy; learning the name of a particular CNS structure is pointless without also learning something about what it does. We focus now on the names and functions of the three major CNS components: spinal cord, brainstem, and forebrain.

## Spinal Cord

Although the brain's principal function is to produce movement, ultimately the spinal cord, with its connections to muscles, *executes* most of those body movements, usually following instructions from the brain but at times acting independently via the somatic nervous system. To understand how important the spinal cord is, think of the old saying "running around like a chicken with its head cut off." When a chicken's head is lopped off with an axe, the chicken is still capable of running around the barnyard until it collapses from loss of blood. The chicken accomplishes this feat because its spinal cord is acting independently of its brain.

Grasping the spinal cord's complexity is easier once you realize that it is not a single structure but rather a set of segmented switching stations. As detailed in Section 2-4, each spinal segment receives information from a discrete part of the body and sends out commands to that area. Spinal nerves, which are part of the SNS, carry sensory information to the cord from the skin, muscles, and related structures and, in turn, send motor instructions to control each muscle.

You can demonstrate movement controlled by the spinal cord in your own body by tapping your patellar tendon, just below your kneecap (the patella), as shown in **Figure 2-15**. The sensory input causes your lower leg to kick out. Try as you might, it is very hard to prevent the movement. Your brain, in other words, has trouble inhibiting this *spinal reflex*: it is automatic.

**FIGURE 2-15 Spinal Reflex** Reflexes are explained in Section 11-4.

## Brainstem

The **brainstem** begins where the spinal cord enters the skull and extends upward into the lower areas of the forebrain. This structure receives afferent signals coming in from the body's senses, and it sends efferent signals out to the spinal cord to control virtually all of the body's movements except the most complex movements of the fingers and toes. The brainstem, then, both creates a sensory world and directs movements.

In some vertebrates, such as frogs, the entire brain is largely equivalent to the mammalian or avian brainstem. Frogs get along quite well in life, demonstrating that the brainstem is a sophisticated piece of machinery. If we had only a brainstem, we would still be able to construct a world, but it would be a far simpler sensorimotor world, more like the world a frog experiences.

The brainstem, which is responsible for most life-sustaining behavior, can be divided into three regions: hindbrain, midbrain, and diencephalon (which means "between brain," referring to the fact that it borders the brain's upper and lower parts). **Figure 2-16**A illustrates the locations of these three brainstem regions under the cerebral hemispheres. Figure 2-16B compares the shape of the brainstem regions to the lower part of your arm when held upright. The hindbrain is long and thick like your forearm, the midbrain is short and compact like your wrist, and the diencephalon at the end is bulbous like a fist.

The hindbrain and midbrain are essentially extensions of the spinal cord; they developed first as vertebrate animals evolved a brain at the anterior end of the body. It makes sense, therefore, that these lower brainstem regions should retain a division between structures having sensory functions and those having motor functions. Thus, the sensory structures lie in a dorsal position and the motor structures are in a ventral position; in upright humans, the corresponding orientations are posterior and anterior, respectively.

Each brainstem region performs more than a single task, and each contains various groupings of nuclei that serve various purposes. In fact, all three regions have both

Here's a trick to help you remember the difference: alphabetically, *afferent* comes before *efferent*; sensory signals enter the brain before an outgoing signal results in a motor response.

**Principle 2:** Sensory and motor divisions pervade the nervous system.

**brainstem** Central structure of the brain (including the hindbrain, midbrain, thalamus, and hypothalamus) that is responsible for most life-sustaining behavior.

**FIGURE 2-16 Brainstem Structures (A)** The medial view shows the relationship between the brainstem and the cerebral hemispheres. **(B)** The shapes and relative sizes of the brainstem's three parts are analogous to your fist, wrist, and forearm.

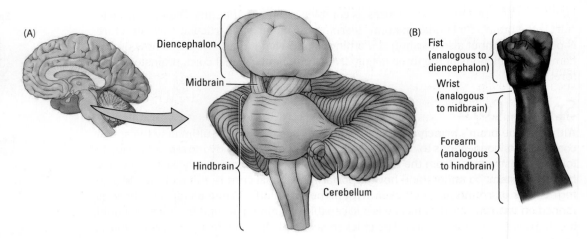

**hindbrain** Evolutionarily the oldest part of the brain; contains the pons, medulla, reticular formation, and cerebellum, the structures that coordinate and control most voluntary and involuntary movements.

**reticular formation** Midbrain area in which nuclei and fiber pathways are mixed, producing a netlike appearance; associated with sleep–wake behavior and behavioral arousal.

sensory and motor functions. However, the hindbrain is especially important in motor functions, the midbrain in sensory functions, and the diencephalon in integrative sensorimotor tasks. Here, we consider the central functions of these three regions; later chapters contain more detailed information about them.

## Hindbrain

The **hindbrain** controls motor functions ranging from breathing to balance to fine movements, such as those used in dancing. Its most distinctive structure, and one of the largest in the human brain, is the cerebellum. Its relative size increases with the physical speed and dexterity of a species.

Animals that move relatively slowly (such as a sloth) have a relatively small cerebellum for their body size. Animals that can perform rapid acrobatic movements (such as a hawk or a cat) have a very large cerebellum relative to overall brain size. The human cerebellum, which resembles a cauliflower in the medial view shown in **Figure 2-17**, likewise is important in controlling complex movements. But cerebellar size in humans is also related to cognitive capacity. Relative to other mammals, apes show an expansion of the cerebellum that correlates with increased capacity for planning and executing complex behavioral sequences, including tool use and language (Barton, 2012).

As we look beyond the cerebellum at the rest of the hindbrain, shown in Figure 2-17, we find three subparts: the reticular formation, the pons, and the medulla. Extending the length of the entire brainstem at its core, the **reticular formation** is a netlike

**FIGURE 2-17 Hindbrain** The principal hindbrain structures integrate voluntary and involuntary body movements. The reticular formation is sometimes called the *reticular activating system*. Like the cerebrum, the human cerebellum has left and right hemispheres, an extensively folded cortex with gray and white matter, and subcortical nuclei.

mixture of neurons (gray matter) and nerve fibers (white matter). This nerve net gives the structure the mottled appearance from which its name derives (from Latin *rete*, meaning "net"). The reticular formation's nuclei are localized into small patches along its length. Each has a special function in stimulating the forebrain, such as in waking from sleep.

The *pons* and *medulla* contain substructures that control many vital body movements. Nuclei in the pons receive inputs from the cerebellum and actually form a bridge from it to the rest of the brain (in Latin, *pons* means "bridge"). At the rostral tip of the spinal cord, the medulla's nuclei regulate such vital functions as breathing and the cardiovascular system. For this reason, a blow to the back of the head can kill you: your breathing stops if the hindbrain control centers are injured.

## Midbrain

In the **midbrain**, a sensory component called the **tectum** (roof) is located dorsally (posteriorly in upright humans), whereas a motor structure called the **tegmentum** (floor) is found ventrally (anteriorly in humans; **Figure 2-18**A). The tectum receives a massive amount of sensory information from the eyes and ears. The optic nerve sends a large bundle of fibers to the *superior colliculus*, whereas the *inferior colliculus* receives much of its input from auditory pathways. The colliculi not only process sensory information, but also produce **orienting movements** related to sensory inputs, such as turning your head to see a sound's source.

This orienting behavior is not as simple as it might seem. To produce it, the auditory and visual systems must share a map of the external world so that the ears can tell the eyes where to look. If the auditory and visual maps differed, it would be impossible to use the two together. In fact, the colliculi also have a tactile map. After all, if you want to look at what's making your leg itch, your visual and tactile systems need a common representation of where that place is so you can scratch the itch by moving your arm and hand.

Lying ventral to the tectum, the tegmentum (shown in Figure 2-18B in cross section) is composed of many nuclei, largely with movement-related functions. Several tegmental nuclei control eye movements. The *red nucleus* controls limb movements (and is absent in snakes). The *substantia nigra* connects to the forebrain, a connection especially important in initiating movements and in placing value on things that are rewarding to us. (Clinical Focus 5-2 explains that the symptoms of Parkinson disease are related to the destruction of the substantia nigra.) The *periaqueductal gray matter* (*PAG*), made up of cell bodies that surround the aqueduct joining the third and fourth ventricles, contains circuits that control species-typical behaviors (e.g., female sexual behavior). These nuclei also play an important role in how opioid drugs can modulate pain, a topic explored further in Chapter 6.

## Diencephalon

The **diencephalon**, shown in sagittal section in the center of **Figure 2-19**, integrates sensory and motor information on its way to the cerebral cortex. Its two principal structures are the hypothalamus and the thalamus. The thalamus—one in each hemisphere—lies just to the left of the brainstem's tip, and the hypothalamus (in Latin, *hypo* means "below") lies below the thalamus in each hemisphere.

The **hypothalamus** in each hemisphere lies along the brain's midline; it is composed of about 22 small nuclei and the nerve fiber systems that pass through it. Its critical function is to control the body's production of hormones, which it accomplishes via its interactions with the pituitary gland, shown at left in Figure 2-19. Although it constitutes only about 0.3 percent of the brain's weight, the hypothalamus plays a

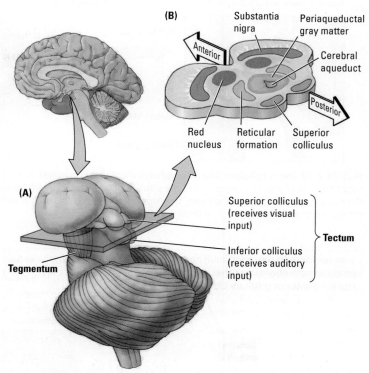

**(B)** Substantia nigra · Periaqueductal gray matter · Cerebral aqueduct · Posterior · Anterior · Red nucleus · Reticular formation · Superior colliculus

**(A)** Tegmentum · Superior colliculus (receives visual input) · Inferior colliculus (receives auditory input) · Tectum

**FIGURE 2-18 Midbrain (A)** Structures in the midbrain are critical for producing orienting movements, simple pattern recognition of visual and auditory stimuli, species-specific behaviors, and pain perception. **(B)** The tegmentum in cross section, revealing various nuclei. *Colliculus* comes from *collis*, Latin for "hill." The colliculi resemble four little hills on the midbrain's posterior surface.

**Principle 8:** The brain divides sensory input for object recognition and movement.

**midbrain** Central part of the brain; contains neural circuits for hearing and seeing as well as for orienting movements.

**tectum** Roof (area above the ventricle) of the midbrain; its functions are sensory processing, particularly visual and auditory, and the production of orienting movements.

**tegmentum** Floor (area below the ventricle) of the midbrain; a collection of nuclei with movement-related, species-specific, and pain perception functions.

**orienting movement** Movement related to sensory inputs, such as turning the head to see the source of a sound.

**diencephalon** The "between brain," which integrates sensory and motor information on its way to the cerebral cortex.

**hypothalamus** Diencephalon structure that contains many nuclei associated with temperature regulation, eating, drinking, and sexual behavior.

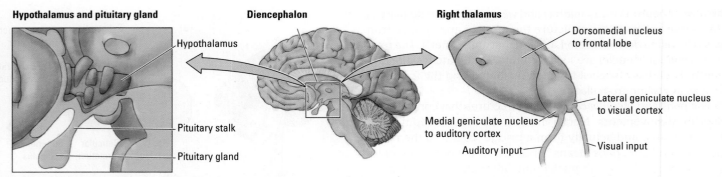

**FIGURE 2-19 Diencephalon** The diencephalon (*center*) is composed of the epithalamus, which includes the pineal gland, the thalamus (shown at *right*), the hypothalamus (the posterior portion of the pituitary gland, shown at *left*), and the subthalamus. Thalamic regions connect to discrete cortical regions. Below the thalamus, at the base of the brain, the hypothalamus (in Latin, *hypo* means "below") and pituitary lie above the roof of the mouth. The hypothalamus is composed of many nuclei, each with distinct functions.

**1** In response to sensory stimuli and cognitive activity, the hypothalamus produces neurohormones that enter the anterior pituitary through veins and the posterior pituitary through axons.

**2** On instructions from these releasing hormones, the pituitary sends hormones into the bloodstream to target endocrine glands.

**3** Endocrine glands release their own hormones that stimulate target organs, including the brain.

**FIGURE 2-20 Hormonal Hierarchy**

**thalamus** Diencephalon structure through which information from all sensory systems is organized, integrated, and projected into the appropriate region of the neocortex.

We examine how thalamic sensory nuclei process incoming information in Sections 9-2, 10-2, 11-4, and 12-2 and look at memory pathways in Section 14-3.

**forebrain** Evolutionarily the most recent addition to the brain; coordinates advanced cognitive functions such as thinking, planning, and language; contains the allocortex, neocortex, and basal ganglia.

role in nearly all aspects of behavior, including feeding, sleeping, temperature regulation, sexual and emotional behavior, and movement.

As just noted, the hypothalamus, acting in concert with the pituitary gland, has a central role in the orchestration of hormone production. **Figure 2-20** shows how the hypothalamus produces neurohormones that stimulate the pituitary gland to secrete releasing hormones into the circulatory system. The pituitary hormones, in turn, influence the endocrine glands to release appropriate hormones into the bloodstream to act on various targets in the body and send feedback to the brain about the need for more or less hormone release.

The other principal structure of the diencephalon, the **thalamus**, is much larger than the hypothalamus, as are its 20 or so nuclei. Perhaps the most distinctive thalamic function is its role as an organizer and integrator of sensory information traveling to the cerebral cortex from all sensory systems. The optic tract, for example, sends information through a large fiber bundle to a thalamic region called the *lateral geniculate nucleus* (*LGN*), shown at the right tip of the thalamus in Figure 2-19. In turn, the LGN processes some of this information and then sends it to the visual region in the occipital lobe in each hemisphere.

The routes to the thalamus may be indirect. For example, the route for olfaction traverses several synapses before entering the *dorsomedial thalamic nucleus* on its way to the forebrain. This nucleus, which projects to the frontal lobe, performs integrative tasks; thus, it plays a vital role in attention, planning, abstract thinking, and memory. Analogous sensory regions of the thalamus receive auditory and tactile information, which is subsequently relayed to the respective auditory and tactile cortical regions in each hemisphere. Other thalamic regions have motor functions, as they receive input from those regions where decisions about possible movements are made and, in turn, relay information to movement planning areas in the neocortex.

## Forebrain

The largest and most recently evolved region of the mammalian brain is the **forebrain**. Its major internal and external structures are shown in **Figure 2-21**. Each of its two principal structures has multiple functions. To summarize briefly, the *cerebral cortex* regulates a host of mental activities ranging from perception to planning to emotions and memory; the *basal ganglia* control voluntary movement and also have a role in cognitive functioning.

Extending our analogy between the brainstem and your forearm, imagine that the fist (the diencephalon) is thrust inside a watermelon—the forebrain, with the neocortex as the rind and the allocortex and basal ganglia as the fruit inside. Just as watermelons come in various sizes, so do brains, which in a sense is what evolution has done: the forebrain varies considerably in size across species.

## Cerebral Cortex

The forebrain contains the cerebral cortex (derived from Latin for "bark"), which can be viewed as a series of concentric rings of three-layered cortex, four-layered cortex, and six-layered cortex. For simplicity, we use the name **allocortex** (literally, "other bark") to refer to both the three- and four-layered cortex. A structure found in the brains of other chordates (including birds, reptiles, and mammals), the allocortex plays a role in controlling motivational and emotional states as well as in certain forms of memory. The six-layered **neocortex** (literally, "new bark") is the tissue visible when we view the brain from the outside, as in Figure 2-5. The more recently expanded neocortex is unique to mammals; its primary function is to construct a perceptual world and respond to that world. Although the neocortex and allocortex have anatomical and functional differences, most neuroscientists usually refer to both types of tissue simply as *cortex*.

Measured by volume, the cortex makes up most of the forebrain, constituting 80% of the human brain overall (but recall that 80% of our neurons are contained in the cerebellum). This brain region has expanded the most over the course of mammalian evolution. The human neocortex has a surface area as large as 2500 square centimeters but a thickness of only 2.3 to 2.8 millimeters—an area equivalent to about four pages of this book. By contrast, the chimpanzee, humans' closest relative, has a cortical area equivalent to about one page (**Figure 2-22**).

The pattern of sulci and gyri formed by the folding of the neocortex varies across species. Smaller-brained mammals, such as rats and mice, have no sulci or gyri and thus have a smooth, or *lissencephalic*, brain. Larger-brained mammals, including carnivores such as cats, have gyri that form a longitudinal pattern. In primates, the sulci and gyri form a more complex pattern. These *gyrencephalic* brains are the result of a relatively large neocortical sheet repeatedly folding in upon itself so that it fits into the restricted space of the skull. One line of research suggests that the gyrus/sulcus pattern is not random (van Essen & Glasser, 2018). Evidence from this research indicates that most connections of cells of the cortex are to neighboring cells, and tend to pull those neighboring cells toward each other. Therefore, cells in a functional area that have many connections fold toward each other, producing a gyrus bordered by sulci. Consequently, many cortical gyri appear to be closely related to particular cortical functions.

## Allocortex

The allocortex is composed of several distinct three- and four-layer structures, including the hippocampus, part of the amygdala, the cingulate cortex, several structures that make up the olfactory system, and other related areas.

The hippocampus together with its dentate gyrus look astoundingly like a seahorse, which is how it got its name (see the comparison in **Figure 2-23**). This brain structure is involved in *consolidation*, the process whereby short-term memories are solidified into long-term memories. Destruction of the hippocampus leads to problems with navigation, finding our way around, as well as difficulties with word finding.

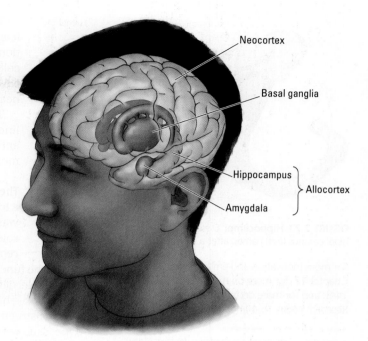

**FIGURE 2-21 Forebrain Structures** The major internal and external forebrain structures integrate sensation, motivation, emotion, and memory to enable such advanced cognitive functions as thinking, planning, and using language.

Why is the cerebellum, which contains 80 percent of our neurons, so much smaller than the forebrain? Because the cerebellum's neurons are smaller and more densely packed.

*Lissencephalic* refers to smooth brains, those without gyri or sulci. *Gyrencephalic* refers to wrinkled brains consisting of gyri and sulci.

**allocortex** Part of the cerebral cortex ("outer bark"), composed of three or four layers; plays a role in controlling motivational and emotional states as well as in certain forms of memory.

**FIGURE 2-22 Three Primate Brains** The brains of a Rhesus monkey, chimpanzee, and human, shown here to scale, differ dramatically in size and in surface appearance. With an encephalization quotient (EQ) of 2.0, the Rhesus monkey's brain is a little more than one-fourth the size of a human's (EQ 7.0). The chimp's brain (EQ 2.5) is a bit more than one-third as large (see Figure 1-15).

Buena Vista Images/Getty Images

**FIGURE 2-23 Hippocampi** Dissected human hippocampus (*left*) named after a seahorse (*right*).

For more motivation and emotion, see Chapter 12; for more on memory, see Section 14-3; and for more on brain disorders, see Research Focus 16-1 and Section 16-4.

**neocortex** Most recently expanded outer layer ("new bark") of the forebrain, composed of about six layers of gray matter. Its name is a misnomer, as it actually arose at the same time during evolution as other forms of cortex. It is also called *isocortex* because it almost always contains six layers, with a few exceptions.

**limbic system** A conceptual system controlling affective and motivated behaviors and certain forms of memory, with key anatomy lying between the neocortex and brainstem; includes the cingulate cortex, amygdala, and hippocampus, among other structures.

**vomeronasal organ (VNO)** Collection of neurons that detect pheromones; this organ plays a role in reproduction and social behavior in many mammals, although its specific function in humans is disputed.

Section 12-3 considers the chemical senses smell and taste in the context of emotional and motivated behavior.

**FIGURE 2-24 Sense of Smell** Our small olfactory bulbs lie at the base of the forebrain, connect to receptor cells that lie in the nasal cavity, and send most of this input to the pyriform cortex en route to the amygdala and thalamus.

Olfactory bulb

To pyriform cortex

Pyriform cortex

Sensory input from nose

The amygdala (meaning "almond") plays a critical role in anxiety and fear. Removal of the amygdala produces truly startling changes in emotional behavior. A cat with its amygdala removed will wander through a colony of monkeys, completely undisturbed by their hooting and threats. No self-respecting, normally functioning cat would be caught anywhere near such bedlam.

The cingulate cortex lies above the corpus callosum, close to the midline. It is involved with emotion formation and processing, learning, and memory, and is highly influential in linking behavioral outcomes to motivation.

**The Concept of the Limbic System** The concept of a **limbic system** has a long and controversial history in neuroscience. In the 1930s, psychiatry was dominated by the theories of Sigmund Freud, who emphasized the roles of sexuality and emotion in human behavior. At the time, the brain regions controlling these behaviors had not yet been identified. Coincidentally, the function of the border, or *limbus*, of the brain—that area between the subcortical nuclei of the brainstem and the neocortex, which the astute reader will recognize as allocortex—had not been determined. It was a simple step to thinking that perhaps the limbic structures played a central role in sexuality and emotion.

One issue with the limbic system concept is that neuroscientists have never agreed on which anatomical structures should be considered part of it. Another issue is that the original view that the limbic system was the emotional center and the neocortex was the home of cognition doesn't work because cognition depends on acquisition and retention of memories—and the hippocampus, an allocortical structure, plays a primary role in those functions. Thus, several neuroscientists have argued that the term *limbic system* should be abandoned because it is obsolete. A more recent view is that specific circuits for specific functions can be traced through several allocortical, neocortical, and brainstem structures.

**Olfactory System** At the very front of the brain lie the olfactory bulbs, the organs responsible for detecting odors and providing input to other brain areas responsible for our perception of smell. The olfactory system is unique among human senses, as **Figure 2-24** shows, because it is almost entirely a forebrain structure. The other sensory systems project most of their inputs from the sensory receptors to the midbrain and thalamus. Olfactory inputs take a less direct route: the olfactory bulb sends most of its inputs to a specialized region, the *pyriform cortex*, which is also part of the allocortex, on the brain's ventral surface. From there, sensory input progresses to the amygdala and the dorsomedial thalamus (see the right side of Figure 2-20), which routes it to the frontal cortex.

Smell is one of the first senses to have evolved in animals, yet curiously, the olfactory system lies at the front of the human brain and is considered part of the forebrain (see the ventral view in Figure 2-6B). The olfactory bulbs lie near the olfactory receptors in the nasal cavity. Although evolution has led to these organs sending their inputs to the pyriform cortex in mammals, their input to the brainstem is more direct in simpler brains.

Compared with the olfactory bulbs of rats, cats, and dogs, which rely more heavily on smell than we do, the human olfactory bulb is relatively small. Nonetheless, it is very sensitive, allowing us to distinguish a surprisingly large number of odors. Smell plays an important role in various aspects of our feeding and sexual behavior.

The **vomeronasal organ (VNO)** contains sensory neurons that detect pheromones, molecules that carry information between individuals of the same species. The axons from these neurons project to the accessory olfactory bulb, which connects to the amygdala and in turn to the hypothalamus. The VNO has an important role in reproduction and social behavior in many mammals, but its presence and functionality in humans remain controversial.

# Neocortical Layers

In the neocortex, six layers of gray matter sit atop the corpus callosum, the white matter structure that is composed of neocortical axons that join the two cerebral hemispheres. The six layers of the neocortex have distinct characteristics:

- Different layers have different types of cells.
- The cell density varies from layer to layer, ranging from virtually no cells in layer I (the top layer) to very dense cell packing in layer IV (**Figure 2-25**).
- Other differences in appearance are both regional and functional.

These visible differences led neuroanatomists to map the neocortex over a century ago. In 1909, Korbinian Brodmann published the map shown in **Figure 2-26**. Based on cytology (the study of cell characteristics), this kind of depiction is called a **cytoarchitectonic map**. For example, viewed through a microscope, the sensory neocortex in the parietal lobe (shown in red in Figure 2-25) has a large layer IV, and the motor cortex in the frontal lobe (shown in blue in Figure 2-25) has a large layer V. Layer IV is afferent; layer V is efferent. It makes sense that a sensory region has a large input layer, whereas a motor region has a large output layer.

In contrast to Brodmann's anatomically based map, contemporary multimodal brain maps integrate information obtained from magnetic resonance imaging (MRI). Brodmann's regions still form the basis for the newer, more complex maps, and they also correspond quite closely to regions discovered using other methods. These relationships give rise to the *FACT* definition of a functional area: each area is defined by its **F**unction, **A**natomy, **C**onnections, and **T**opography. Using the FACT definition, many of Brodmann's areas can be further subdivided, giving rise to a map that has 180 cortical areas, compared to Brodmann's 52 areas (Glasser et al., 2016)—we will return to this mapping convention in Section 15-3.

Staining neocortical tissue can reveal chemical differences between cells and layers. Some regions are rich in one chemical; others are rich in another. These differences presumably relate to functional specialization of the different neocortical areas.

One significant difference between the organization of the neocortex and the organization of other brain parts is the neocortex's range of connections. Unlike most structures, which connect only to certain brain regions, the neocortex is connected to almost all other parts of the brain. The neocortex, in other words, is the ultimate meddler. It takes part in everything—a fact that not only makes it difficult to identify specific neocortical functions, but also complicates our study of the rest of the brain because we must always consider the neocortex's role in other brain regions.

Consider your perception of clouds. You have no doubt gazed up at clouds on a summer day and imagined sailing ships, elephants, faces, and countless other objects. Although a cloud does not really look like an elephant, you can concoct an image of one if you impose your frontal cortex—that is, your imagination—on the sensory inputs. This kind of cortical activity is considered *top-down processing* because the top level of the nervous system, the neocortex, influences how information is processed in lower regions of the hierarchy—in this case, the midbrain and hindbrain.

The neocortex influences many other behaviors besides object perception. It influences our cravings for foods, our desire for things (or people), and how we interpret the meaning of abstract concepts, words, and images. The neocortex ultimately creates our reality, and one reason it serves this function is that it is so well connected.

# Cortical Lobes

To review, the human cortex consists of the nearly symmetrical left and right hemispheres, which are separated by the longitudinal fissure, shown at left in **Figure 2-27**. As shown on the right side of this figure, each hemisphere is subdivided into four lobes corresponding to the skull bones overlying them: frontal, parietal, temporal,

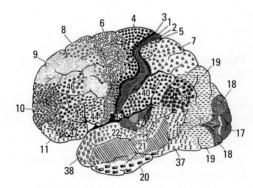

**FIGURE 2-25 Neocortical Layering** Layer IV is relatively thick in the sensory cortex and relatively thin in the motor cortex. This is because abundant afferent sensory information from the thalamus connects to layer IV. Conversely, layers V and VI are relatively thick in the motor neocortex and thin in the sensory neocortex. Efferent motor information in layer V makes up the corticospinal tract, connecting the motor neocortex to the spinal cord to generate movement, and layer VI connects to other cortical areas.

**FIGURE 2-26 Early Brain Map** In his cytoarchitectonic map of the neocortex, Brodmann (1909) defined areas based on the organization and characteristics of the cells he examined. The regions shown in color are associated with the simplest sensory perceptions: touch (red), vision (purple), and hearing (orange). As we shall see, the neocortical areas that process sensory information are far more extensive than Brodmann's basic areas.

**cytoarchitectonic map** Map of the neocortex based on the organization, structure, and distribution of the cells.

**FIGURE 2-27 Cortical Boundaries**

**Principle 1:** Neuronal circuits are the functional units of the nervous system.

*Cortex* is often used as shorthand for the neocortex or neocortical layers. However, this term may refer to any and all layered structures in the forebrain. In this book, we use the terms *neocortex* and *allocortex* only when making a distinction *between* those structures.

**Principle 5:** Brain functions are localized and distributed.

The anatomical features presented in Section 9-2 define occipital lobe boundaries.

and occipital. Unfortunately, bone location and brain function are unrelated. As a result, the cortical lobes are rather arbitrarily defined anatomical regions that include many functional zones.

Nevertheless, we can attach some gross functions to each lobe. The frontal lobe is sometimes called the brain's *executive* because it integrates sensory and motor functions, formulates plans of action, and contains the primary motor cortex. The three posterior lobes have sensory functions: the parietal lobe is tactile; the temporal lobe is visual, auditory, and gustatory; and the occipital lobe is visual. We can also predict some effects of injuries to each lobe:

- Individuals with *frontal lobe* injuries may have difficulty organizing and evaluating their ongoing behavior, as well as planning for the future.

- Injuries to the *parietal lobe* make it difficult to identify or locate stimulation on the skin and may contribute to deficits in moving the arms and hands to points in space.

- *Temporal lobe* injuries result in difficulty recognizing sounds, although, unlike people with occipital injuries, individuals with temporal injury can still recognize that they are hearing something. Temporal lobe injuries can also cause difficulties in processing complex visual information, such as faces.

- People with an injured *occipital lobe* have deficits in processing visual information. Although they may perceive light versus dark, for example, they may be unable to identify either the shape or the color of objects.

Fissures and sulci often establish the boundaries of cortical lobes (Figure 2-27, right). For instance, in humans, the central sulcus and lateral fissure form the boundaries of each frontal lobe, as well as the boundaries of each parietal lobe lying posterior to the central sulcus. The lateral fissure demarcates each temporal lobe, forming its dorsal boundary. The occipital lobes are separated from the parietal lobes by the parieto-occipital sulcus.

## Basal Ganglia

The **basal ganglia**, a collection of nuclei that lie in the forebrain just below the white matter of the cortex, consist of three principal structures: the *caudate nucleus*, the *putamen*, and the *globus pallidus* (**Figure 2-28**). Together with the thalamus and two closely associated nuclei (the substantia nigra and subthalamic nucleus), the basal ganglia perform three main functions: (1) they connect sensory regions of the cortex to motor regions of the cortex, (2) they regulate movement so that it is fluid, and (3) they are involved in associative learning—that is, learning by which one stimulus or event is associated with another, something necessary to coordinate sensory and motor skills.

**basal ganglia** Subcortical forebrain nuclei that coordinate voluntary movements of the limbs and body; connected to the thalamus and to the midbrain.

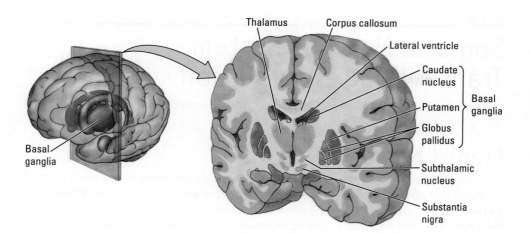

**FIGURE 2-28 Basal Ganglia** A coronal section through the cerebral hemispheres reveals a frontal view of the basal ganglia relative to the surrounding forebrain structures. Two associated structures that are likewise instrumental in controlling and coordinating movement, the substantia nigra and subthalamic nucleus, are also shown.

We can observe the functions of the basal ganglia by analyzing the behavior resulting from the many diseases that interfere with their healthy functioning. **Parkinson disease**, a motor system disorder characterized by severe tremors, muscular rigidity, and a reduction in voluntary movement, is among the most common movement disorders among the elderly population. People with Parkinsonism take short, shuffling steps; display bent posture; and may need a walker to get around. Many have almost continuous hand tremors and sometimes head tremors as well. Another disorder of the basal ganglia is **Tourette syndrome**, which is characterized by various motor tics, involuntary vocalizations (sometimes including curse words and grunting sounds), and odd, involuntary body movements, especially of the face and head.

Neither Parkinsonism nor Tourette syndrome is a disorder of *producing* movements, as in paralysis. Rather, they are disorders of *controlling* movements. The basal ganglia, therefore, must play a critical role in controlling and coordinating movement patterns rather than in activating the muscles to move.

**Parkinson disease** Disorder of the motor system correlated with a loss of dopamine from the substantia nigra and characterized by tremors, muscular rigidity, and a reduction in voluntary movement.

**Tourette syndrome** Disorder of the motor system characterized by involuntary vocalizations (sometimes including curse words and grunting sounds) and odd, involuntary movements of the body, especially of the face and head.

Details on Parkinson disease appear in Clinical Focus features 5-2, 5-4, and 5-5, as well as in Sections 11-3 and 16-3. Clinical Focus 11-3 details Tourette syndrome.

## 2-3 Review

Before you continue, check your understanding. Answers appear at the back of the book.

1. The _____ receives sensations from the skin and muscles and produces movements independent of the brain.

2. The brainstem includes three functional regions: the _____ is an extension of the spinal cord; the _____ is the first brain region to receive sensory inputs; and the _____ integrates sensory and motor information on its way to the cerebral cortex.

3. The _____ coordinates fine motor movements and is related to an animal's capacity for various cognitive functions, such as planning and executing complex behavioral sequences.

4. The two types of cerebral cortex are the three- and four-layered _____ and the _____, which features six layers that vary in density and that perform _____, _____, and _____ functions.

5. In the analysis of brain function, the acronym FACT stands for _____.

6. What is unique about the connectivity of the neocortex, in comparison to other parts of the brain?

**2-4**

# Somatic Nervous System: Transmitting Information

The SNS is monitored and controlled by the CNS—the cranial nerves by the brain and the spinal nerves by the spinal cord segments.

## Cranial Nerves

The linkages provided by the **cranial nerves** between the brain and various parts of the head and neck as well as various internal organs are illustrated and tabulated in **Figure 2-29**. Cranial nerves can have afferent functions, carrying sensory signals to the brain from the eyes, ears, mouth, and nose, or they can have efferent functions, such as carrying motor commands to the facial muscles, tongue, and eyes. Some cranial nerves have both sensory and motor functions, such as modulation of both sensation and movement in the face.

The 12 pairs of cranial nerves are known both by their numbers and by their names, as listed in Figure 2-29. One set of 12 controls the left side of the head, whereas the other set controls the right side. This arrangement makes sense for innervating duplicated parts of the head (such as the eyes), but why separate nerves should control the right and left sides of a singular structure (such as the tongue) is not so clear. Yet that is how the cranial nerves work. If you have ever received lidocaine (often called Novocaine) for dental work, you know that when the dentist injects the drug into the gums on one side of your mouth, the same side of your tongue also becomes numb. The rest of the skin and muscles on each side of the head are similarly controlled by cranial nerves located on the same side.

In later chapters, we consider many cranial nerves in detail when we discuss vision, hearing, olfaction, taste, and stress responses. For now, you simply need to know that the cranial nerves form part of the SNS, providing inputs to the brain from the head's

**cranial nerves** The 12 nerve pairs that control sensory and motor functions of the head, neck, and internal organs.

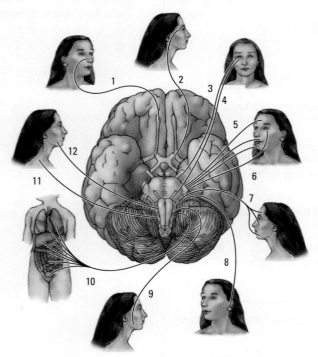

| Cranial nerve | Name | Function |
|---|---|---|
| 1 | Olfactory | Smell |
| 2 | Optic | Vision |
| 3 | Oculomotor | Eye movement |
| 4 | Trochlear | Eye movement |
| 5 | Trigeminal | Masticatory movements and facial sensation |
| 6 | Abducens | Eye movement |
| 7 | Facial | Facial movement and some taste sensation |
| 8 | Auditory vestibular | Hearing and balance |
| 9 | Glossopharyngeal | Tongue and pharynx movement and sensation |
| 10 | Vagus | Heart, blood vessels, viscera, movement of larynx and pharynx |
| 11 | Spinal accessory | Neck movement |
| 12 | Hypoglossal | Tongue movement |

**FIGURE 2-29 Cranial Nerves** Each of the 12 pairs of cranial nerves has a different function. A common mnemonic device for learning the order of the cranial nerves is "**O**n **O**ld **O**lympus's **T**owering **T**op, **A** **F**inn and **G**erman **V**iew **S**ome **H**ops." The first letter of each word is, in order, the first letter of the name of each nerve.

sensory organs and muscles and controlling head and facial movements. Some cranial nerves also contribute to maintaining autonomic functions by connecting the brain and internal organs (the vagus, cranial nerve 10) and by influencing other autonomic responses, such as salivation.

For the optic nerve, see Section 9-2; for the auditory nerve, see Section 10-2; and for the olfactory nerve, see Section 12-3.

## Spinal Nerves

The spinal cord lies inside the bony spinal column, which is made up of a series of small bones called **vertebrae (sing. *vertebra*)**. The vertebrae are categorized into five anatomical regions from top to bottom: cervical, thoracic, lumbar, sacral, and coccygeal (**Figure 2-30**A). You can think of each vertebra in these five groups as a short segment of the spinal column. The corresponding spinal cord segment in each vertebral region functions as that segment's minibrain.

This arrangement may seem a bit odd, but it has a long evolutionary history. Think of an animal with a relatively simple body plan, such as a snake. A snake's body is a segmented tube. In that tube is another tube, the spinal cord, which is also segmented. Each of the snake's nervous system segments receives nerve fibers from sensory receptors in the part of the body adjacent to it, and that nervous system segment sends back fibers to the muscles in that body part. Each segment, therefore, works independently.

A complication arises in animals such as humans, whose limbs may originate at one spinal segment level but, because we stand upright, extend past other segments of the spinal column. Your shoulders, for example, may begin at C5 (cervical segment 5), but your arms hang down well past the sacral segments. So unlike the snake, which has spinal cord segments that connect to body segments fairly directly adjacent to them, the human body's segments fall schematically into more of a patchwork pattern, as shown in Figure 2-30B. This arrangement makes sense if the arms are extended as they are when we walk on all fours.

Our body segments correspond to spinal cord segments. Each of these body segments is called a **dermatome** (meaning "skin cut"). A dermatome has a sensory nerve that sends information from the skin, joints, and muscles to the spinal cord, as well as a motor nerve that controls the muscle movements in that particular body segment.

These sensory and motor nerves, which are collectively known as *spinal* (or *peripheral*) *nerves*, are functionally equivalent to the cranial nerves of the head. Whereas the cranial nerves receive information from sensory receptors in the eyes, ears, facial skin, and so forth, the spinal nerves receive information from sensory receptors in the rest of the body—that is, in the PNS. Similarly, whereas the cranial nerves move the muscles of the eyes, tongue, and face, the peripheral nerves move the muscles of the limbs and trunk.

## Somatic Nervous System Connections

Like the CNS, the SNS is bilateral (two-sided). Just as the cranial nerves control functions on the side of the head where they are found, the spinal nerves on the left side of the spinal cord control the left side of the body, and those on the right side of the spinal cord control the body's right side.

**Figure 2-31**A shows the spinal column in cross section. Look first at the nerve fibers entering its posterior side (in red). These posterior fibers (dorsal in four-legged animals) are afferent: they carry in information from the body's sensory receptors. The fibers gather as they enter a spinal cord segment, and this collection of fibers is called a *posterior root* in humans (*dorsal root* in four-legged animals).

**vertebrae (sing. *vertebra*)** The bones that form the spinal column.

**dermatome** Body segment corresponding to a segment of the spinal cord.

Sections 11-2 and 11-4 review the spinal cord's contributions to movement and to somatosensation.

**FIGURE 2-30 Spinal Segments and Dermatomes (A)** Medial view showing the five spinal cord segments: cervical (C), thoracic (T), lumbar (L), sacral (S), and coccygeal. **(B)** Each segment corresponds to a region of body surface (a dermatome) identified by the segment number (e.g., C5 at the base of the neck and L2 in the lower back).

**(A)**

**1** Fibers entering the posterior root bring sensory information from sensory receptors.

**2** Fibers leaving the anterior root carry motor information to the muscles.

**3** Collateral branches of sensory neurons may cross to the other side and influence motor neurons there.

**4** White-matter fiber tracts carry information to and from the brain.

Posterior root (sensory)

Sensory neuron

Motor neuron

Anterior root (motor)

Gray matter

White matter

**(B)**

VideoSurgery/Science Source

**FIGURE 2-31 Spinal Nerve Connections (A)** A cross section of the human spinal cord, viewed from the front. The butterfly-shaped inner regions consist of neural cell bodies (gray matter), and the outer regions consist of nerve tracts (white matter) traveling to and from the brain. **(B)** A posterior view shows the intact human spinal cord exposed.

Sections 11-1 and 11-4 explore spinal cord injuries and treatments.

The law of Bell and Magendie and the condition Bell palsy are both namesakes of Sir Charles Bell—a renowned surgeon, neurologist, anatomist, physiologist, artist, and philosophical theologian.

Fibers leaving the spinal cord's anterior side (in blue) are efferent, carrying information out from the spinal cord to the muscles. They, too, are bundled together as they exit the spinal cord, forming an *anterior root* (*ventral root* in four-legged animals). The outer part of the spinal cord, pictured in Figure 2-31B, consists of white matter, or CNS nerve tracts. These tracts are arranged so that, with some exceptions, posterior tracts are sensory and anterior tracts are motor. The inner part of the cord, which has a butterfly shape, is gray matter composed largely of cell bodies.

The observation that the posterior/dorsal spinal cord is sensory and the anterior/ventral side is motor in all vertebrates is one of the nervous system's very few established laws, the **law of Bell and Magendie**. Combined with an understanding of the spinal cord's segmental organization, this law enables neurologists to make accurate inferences about the location of spinal cord damage or disease on the basis of changes in sensation or movement. For instance, if a person has numbness in the fingers of the left hand but can still move the hand fairly normally, one or more of the posterior (dorsal) nerves in spinal cord segments C7 and C8 must be damaged. In contrast, if sensation in the hand is normal but the person cannot move the fingers, the anterior (ventral) roots of the same segments must be damaged. Clinical Focus 2-4, Bell Palsy, further explores the loss of motor function.

# Integrating Spinal Functions

So far we have emphasized the spinal cord's segmental organization, but the spinal cord must also somehow coordinate inputs and outputs across different segments. For example, many body movements require coordinating muscles controlled by different segments, just as many sensory experiences require coordinating sensory inputs to different parts of the spinal cord. How is this coordination accomplished? The answer is that the spinal cord segments are interconnected in such a way that adjacent segments can operate together to direct rather complex coordinated movements.

Integrating spinal cord activities does not require the brain's participation, which is why the headless chicken can run around. Nevertheless, a close working relationship must exist between the brain and the spinal cord. Otherwise, how could we consciously plan and execute our voluntary actions?

Somehow, information must be relayed back and forth, and numerous examples of this information sharing are readily evident. For instance, tactile information from sensory nerves in the skin travels not just to the spinal cord but also to the cerebral cortex through the thalamus. Similarly, the cerebral cortex and other brain structures can control movements through their connections to the spinal cord's anterior roots. So even though the brain and spinal cord can function independently, the two are intimately connected in their CNS functions.

**law of Bell and Magendie** Sensory fibers are dorsal/posterior and motor fibers are ventral/anterior, with an exception.

## ⊙ CLINICAL FOCUS 2-4

# Bell Palsy

C.T. woke up one morning and proceeded with his usual routine. He sat at the kitchen table in front of the daily newspaper and began to eat his breakfast cereal. The cereal and milk fell out of his mouth. He cleaned it up and tried again with the same result. He then looked in a mirror and discovered that the left side of his face was completely paralyzed. He couldn't move his left eyebrow or left smile muscles or any other expressive muscles on the left side of his face. He couldn't wink with the left eye but could close both eyes. Sensation from the left side felt normal, and sensation and movement of the right side of his face was completely normal. He immediately sought medical attention. C.T., a neuroscientist, figured he had Bell palsy, which his family doctor confirmed.

Bell palsy is diagnosed by exclusion. Many factors can cause facial paralysis, and they need to be ruled out one by one. C.T. underwent blood tests to rule out diabetes and Lyme disease, a neurological exam to rule out stroke, and a computed tomography (CT) scan to rule out tumor.

Bell palsy is caused by inflammation of the facial (seventh) nerve, probably brought on by infection with a virus or some other inflammatory agent. The seventh nerve travels through the longest bony canal in the body, known as the fallopian canal. Nerves swell when inflamed, but when the swelling is constricted by the confines of a bony canal, pressure on the nerve stops them from functioning—hence the paralysis. If the pressure continues unabated for more than 3 weeks, the axons all die. The primary treatment is to reduce inflammation.

For the first 2 weeks after the abrupt onset of his Bell palsy, C.T. had complete paralysis on the left side of his face. He taped his left eye shut at night to prevent it from drying out and damaging his cornea. His speech was slurred, and he didn't really sound like himself. The muscles of the right side of his face were pulled the left side, giving him an asymmetric look (see the accompanying photographs). Eating was a challenge. Drinking was made easy with a straw. At about the 2-week mark, to his great relief, C.T. started to regain some minimal movement in his left eyebrow. As the weeks went by, he became able to move more and more of the left side of his face. By the sixth week, his friends and colleagues said he looked and sounded like himself again, yet he still had about 40 percent paralysis of the left side.

Bell palsy afflicts about 1 in 65 people at some time in their life. While most people, including C.T., fully recover, a small percentage will have some permanent paralysis, which can profoundly affect their lives. Smiling is an important social signal; when it is impaired, people interpret this as disapproval. This can lead to social isolation, which itself can lead to psychological problems.

Courtesy of Tannis Teskey

**(A)** Relaxed face. Strong muscles on the right side of the face pull the nose to the right, while paralyzed muscles on the left side do not pull back.
**(B)** An attempt to smile and raise both eyebrows is achieved on the right side of the face but fails on the paralyzed left side. **(C)** An attempt to frown and lower both eyebrows is achieved on the right side of the face but fails on the paralyzed left side.

# 2-4 Review

**Before you continue, check your understanding. Answers appear at the back of the book.**

1. Two sets of SNS nerves, the _____ and the _____, receive sensory information or send motor signals to muscles, or both.

2. SNS nerves on the left side of the spinal cord control function on the _____ side of the body.

3. The cranial nerves have both sensory and motor functions, receiving and sending information to the _____ and to the _____.

4. Define the law of Bell and Magendie and explain why it is important.

Section 5-3 explains CNS–ANS communication, Figure 5-22 diagrams the stress response, and Section 16-2 discusses how mood affects reactivity to stress.

**Principle 7:** The nervous system works by juxtaposing excitation and inhibition.

**sympathetic division** Part of the autonomic nervous system that arouses the body for action, such as mediating the involuntary fight-or-flight response to alarm by increasing heart rate and blood pressure.

**parasympathetic division** Part of the autonomic nervous system that acts in opposition to the sympathetic division—for example, preparing the body to rest and digest by reversing the alarm response or stimulating digestion.

## 2-5

# Autonomic and Enteric Nervous Systems: Visceral Relations

Control of the viscera (internal organs), including the heart, gut, liver, and lungs, requires complex neural systems. Yet the ANS and ENS are hidden partners, functioning in the background as the CNS controls our perceptions and behaviors. If we had to focus consciously on visceral activities, we might do little else. The ANS and ENS interact with the CNS, but each has distinctive anatomy and functions.

## ANS: Regulating Internal Functions

Even without our conscious awareness, the ANS stays on the job: it keeps the heart beating, the liver releasing glucose, the pupils of the eyes adjusting to light, and so forth. Without the ANS, which regulates the internal organs and glands via connections through the SNS to the CNS, our lives would end rather quickly. Although we can learn to exert some level of conscious control over some of these vegetative activities, such conscious interference is normally unnecessary. An important reason is that the ANS must keep working during sleep, when conscious awareness is off duty. Even so, psychological stressors can often affect ANS functions, as in the case of a racing or pounding heartbeat. Psychological therapies are often effective in reducing stress if such ANS symptoms persist.

It is tempting to think that because the ANS functions outside our conscious awareness, its organization must be pretty simple. In reality, like the SNS, the ANS has a surprisingly complex organization. The two ANS divisions work in opposition. The **sympathetic division** arouses the body for action, for example, by stimulating the heart to beat faster and inhibiting digestion when we exert ourselves during exercise or times of stress—the familiar fight-or-flight response. The **parasympathetic division** calms the body down, for example, by slowing the heartbeat and stimulating digestion to allow us to rest and digest after exertion and during quiet times.

Like the SNS, the ANS interacts with the rest of the nervous system and forms ipsilateral connections. Activation of the sympathetic division starts in the thoracic and lumbar spinal cord regions, although the spinal nerves do not directly control the target organs. Instead, the spinal cord is connected to autonomic control centers—collections of neural cells called *ganglia*. The ganglia control the internal organs, and each acts as a minibrain for specific organs.

The sympathetic ganglia are located near the spinal cord, on each side, forming chains that run parallel to the cord, as illustrated at left in **Figure 2-32** for one set of ganglia. The parasympathetic division also is connected to the spinal cord—specifically, to the sacral region—but the greater part of it derives from three cranial nerves: the vagus nerve, which calms most of the internal organs, and the facial and oculomotor nerves, which control salivation and pupil dilation, respectively (review Figure 2-29). In contrast with the sympathetic division, the parasympathetic division connects with ganglia that are found near the target organs, as shown at right in Figure 2-32.

## ENS: Controlling the Gut

The ENS functions largely independently of the ANS. Digestion is complicated, and evolution has provided this dedicated nervous system to control it. Some evolutionary biologists have proposed that the CNS evolved from the gut of very early multicellular organisms.

In fact, the ENS is sometimes called the *second brain* because, like the CNS, it contains a wide range of neuron types, the same chemical transmitters, a profusion of glial cells, and complex integrated neural circuits. Its estimated 200 million to 500 million neurons roughly equal the number of neurons found in the spinal cord. The gut

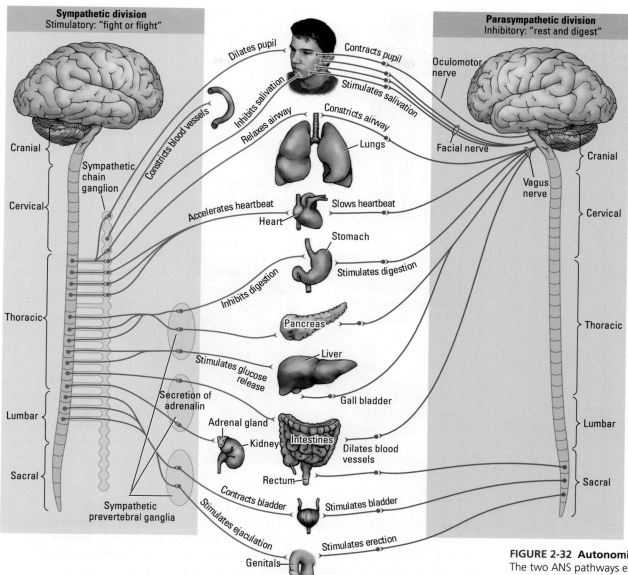

**FIGURE 2-32 Autonomic Nervous System**
The two ANS pathways exert opposing effects. All fibers connect at "stops" formed by ganglia en route from the CNS to target ANS organs. *Left:* Arousing sympathetic fibers connect to a chain of ganglia near the spinal cord. *Right:* Calming parasympathetic fibers connect to individual ganglia near target organs.

Section 12-4 explores the link between the ENS and eating. Section 12-6 expands on how emotions and the ENS interact.

reacts to a range of hormones and other chemicals with exquisitely nuanced neural responses. The ENS functions to control bowel motility, secretion, and blood flow to permit fluid and nutrient absorption and to support waste elimination (Avetisyan et al., 2015). This is no simple task, given the number and balance of nutrients needed to support the body.

ENS neurons are located in a sheet of tissue (*plexus*) lining the esophagus, stomach, small intestine, and colon. As shown in **Figure 2-33**, ENS neurons and glia form ganglia connected by nerve fibers found in two layers of gut tissue. The brain and ENS connect extensively through the ANS, especially via the vagus nerve. Although we are not aware of our gut "thinking," the ENS sends information directly to the brain—information that affects our mental state—and the brain can modify gut function in response. Indeed, a growing body of evidence implicates the ENS in many behavioral disorders, and stress and anxiety commonly modify gut function, leading to such symptoms as nausea and diarrhea.

The ENS interacts with gut bacteria, known collectively as the *microbiome*. Approximately $3.9 \times 10^{13}$ microbiota populate the adult gut, outnumbering the host

**FIGURE 2-33 Enteric Nervous System** The ENS is formed by a network of neurons embedded in the lining of the gastrointestinal tract. Congregations of neurons form ganglia that send projections to the ANS and CNS, in part through the vagus nerve (cranial nerve 10), to control gut function.

Gastrointestinal tract

Nerve

Artery

Vein

Mesentery attaches the gut to the internal body wall.

Submucosal plexus (ganglia)

Lumen, where digestion occurs. No nerves enter this area.

Myenteric plexus (ganglia)

cells by a factor of 1.3 (Sender et al., 2016). The microbiota influence nutrient absorption and are a source of neurochemicals that regulate an array of physiological and psychological processes. This relationship has inspired the development of a class of compounds known as *psychobiotics*, live microorganisms used to treat behavioral disorders. Thus, the microbiota can influence both the CNS and ENS, leading to changes in behavior.

## 2-5 Review

**Before you continue, check your understanding. Answers appear at the back of the book.**

1. The ANS interacts with the CNS and SNS via sets of autonomic control centers called _____, which act as minibrains to control the internal organs.

2. The _____ division of the ANS arouses the body for action (fight or flight), and the _____ division calms the organs (rest and digest).

3. Describe the essential role of the ANS in regulating our bodies.

4. Why is the ENS called a second brain?

5. What are psychobiotics?

# Ten Principles of Nervous System Function

Knowing the parts of the nervous system and some general notions about what they do is only the beginning. Learning how the parts work together allows us to proceed to a closer look, in the chapters that follow, at how the brain produces behavior. A deeper appreciation of how the nervous system works also comes with an understanding of the principles of CNS organization and function.

We have identified 10 principles related to the nervous system's functioning. Here we elaborate on each one. As you progress through this book, review these ideas regularly with an eye toward understanding the concept rather than simply memorizing the principle. Soon you will find yourself applying the principles of function as you encounter new information about the brain and behavior.

## Principle 1: Neuronal Circuits Are the Functional Units of the Nervous System

Edgar Adrian described how neurons work and Charles Scott Sherrington described how neurons form connections within the nervous system, breakthroughs that earned each a share of the 1932 Nobel Prize. Individual neurons cannot carry out functions in isolation of each other. In animals, sensation, integration, and movement are performed by neuronal circuits. A **neuronal circuit** is composed of a series of neurons interconnected by synapses that subserve a function when activated.

The simplest neuronal circuits consist of only two interconnected neurons—a sensory neuron that makes a single synaptic connection with a motor neuron. These circuits, termed *monosynaptic* (one synapse), are the fastest because there is no delay of routing signals through the brain. Found in the spinal cord, they mediate simple reflexes like the patellar reflex (illustrated in Figure 2-15).

*Polysynaptic* circuits, in which at least one *interneuron* comes between a sensory neuron and a motor neuron, thereby increasing the total number of synapses, are slower than monosynaptic circuits. The action of withdrawing your finger after touching something hot is mediated by a polysynaptic circuit, as illustrated in **Figure 2-34**.

Each synapse in a neuronal circuit adds about a 1- to 4-millisecond delay. Thus, the larger the number of synaptically connected neurons linked in a given circuit, the slower that circuit will be. Furthermore, single neurons can make synaptic connections with more than one downstream neuron, giving rise to larger and more complex circuits. When neural circuits interconnect with one another, they form large-scale brain networks, such as those underlying visual scene processing (Chapter 9) and music and language processing (Chapter 10).

Biological neural circuits have served as a template for the design of artificial neural circuits that have given rise to deep learning systems and some forms of artificial intelligence—a topic covered in Chapter 7.

## Principle 2: Sensory and Motor Divisions Pervade the Nervous System

The segregation of sensory and motor functions described by the Bell and Magendie law exists throughout the nervous system. Spinal nerves are either sensory or motor. Some cranial nerves are exclusively sensory; some are exclusively motor; and some have two parts, one sensory and one motor, much like spinal nerves serving the skin and muscles.

The lower brainstem regions—hindbrain and midbrain—are essentially extensions of the spinal cord. They retain the spinal cord's division, with sensory structures located posteriorly and motor structures anteriorly in humans. An important midbrain function

**Learning Objectives**
- List the ten principles of nervous system function.
- Define neuronal circuits and explain their importance in facilitating behavior.
- Explain why neural plasticity is described as the hallmark of nervous system functioning.

Sherrington and Adrian's groundbreaking conceptualization of the neuron as an excitable cell that communicates with other neurons paved the way for our modern understanding of brain and behavior.

**FIGURE 2-34 A Polysynaptic Circuit** As can be seen in this simplification, in a polysynaptic circuit, at least one interneuron bridges the connection between the sensory neuron and the motor neuron.

Review cranial nerve and spinal nerve connections in Figures 2-29 and 2-30.

**neuronal circuit** A series of neurons interconnected by synapses that subserve a function when activated.

Figures 2-16 through 2-20 illustrate brainstem structures.

is orienting the body to stimuli, which requires sensory input from the midbrain's colliculi (posterior in the human tectum) and motor output, which the tegmentum (anterior) controls. Distinctions between motor and sensory functions become more subtle in the forebrain.

Distinct sensory nuclei are present in the thalamus, too, although their positions are not segregated, as they are in lower structures. Because all sensory information reaches the forebrain through the thalamus, it is not surprising to find separate nuclei associated with vision, hearing, and touch in this structure. Separate thalamic nuclei also control movements. Other nuclei have neither sensory nor motor functions but rather connect to cortical areas, such as the frontal lobe, that perform more integrative tasks.

Finally, sensory and motor functions are divided in the cortex in two ways:

1. Separate sensory and motor cortical regions process a particular set of sensory inputs, such as vision, hearing, or touch. Other regions control fine movements of discrete body parts, such as the fingers.

2. The entire cortex is organized around the sensory and motor distinction. As diagrammed in Figure 2-25, layer IV of the cortex always receives sensory inputs, layers V and VI always send motor outputs, and layers I, II, and III integrate sensory and motor operations.

Keep in mind that the sensory and motor systems work together at all levels. For example, the pupil—a motor structure composed of muscles—controls the amount of light that falls on the sensory retina. Also, within muscles, a sensory system called the *intrafusal muscle system* detects the amount and rate of change of the *extrafusal muscles*, which actually do the work.

# Principle 3: The CNS Functions on Multiple Levels and Is Organized Hierarchically and in Parallel

In relatively simple animals, such as worms, the nerve cord essentially constitutes the nervous system. More complex animals, such as fishes, have a brainstem as well, and even more complex animals, like mammals, have also evolved a forebrain. Each of these additions to the CNS added a new level of behavioral capacity without discarding previous levels of control. As animals evolved legs, for example, brain structures simultaneously evolved to move the legs. New brain areas add new levels of nervous system control. These new levels are not autonomous, but rather are integrated into existing neural systems as refinements and elaborations of the control that earlier levels provided.

Multiple levels of function can be seen not only in the addition of forebrain areas to refine brainstem control but also in the forebrain itself. As mammals evolved, they developed an increased capacity to represent the world in the cortex, an ability related to the addition of more maps. The new maps are related to the older ones, however, and again are simply an elaboration of the perceived sensory world that existed before. Levels of CNS function are extensively interconnected to integrate their processing and produce unified perceptions or movements.

The nature of neural connectivity leads to the principle that the brain has both serial (or hierarchical) and parallel circuitry. A hierarchical circuit hooks up a linear series of regions that are all concerned with a particular function. Consider vision. In a serial system, the information from the eyes goes to regions that detect the simplest properties, such as color or brightness. This information is passed along to another region that determines shape, then to another region that measures movement, and so on until at the most complex level the information is understood to be, say, your grandmother. Information therefore flows sequentially from regions that make simpler discriminations to regions that make more complex discriminations in the hierarchy, as illustrated in **Figure 2-35**A.

**FIGURE 2-35 Models of Neural Information Processing (A)** Simple hierarchical model of serial cortical processing. **(B)** In a distributed hierarchical processing model, each of several processing streams has multiple levels. Areas at each level interconnect.

However, functionally related brain structures are not always linked linearly. Although the brain has many serial connections, many expected connections are missing. In the visual system, not all cortical regions are connected to one another. The simplest explanation is that the unconnected regions must have widely differing functions.

Parallel circuits operate on a different principle, which can also be illustrated by referring to the visual system. Imagine looking at a cup. One set of visual pathways processes information about its nature, such as color and shape, whereas another set of pathways processes information about movements, such as those necessary to lift the cup to your mouth. These two visual systems are independent of each other, but must interact somehow. When you lift the cup, you do not perceive two different representations—the cup's size, shape, and color on the one hand and the lifting movements on the other hand. When you lift the cup, you have the impression of unity in your conscious experience.

Figure 2-35B illustrates the information flow in such a distributed hierarchy. By tracing the flow from the primary area to levels 2, 3, and 4, you follow the parallel pathways. While these multiple parallel pathways are also connected to one another, those connections are more selective than the connections in a purely serial circuit.

The brain's subsystems are organized into multiple parallel pathways, yet our conscious experiences are unified. As we explore this conundrum throughout the book, keep in mind that your common-sense impressions of how the brain works might not always be correct.

## Principle 4: Many Brain Circuits Are Crossed

Most brain inputs and outputs are crossed—that is, they serve the opposite side of the body. Each hemisphere receives sensory stimulation from the opposite (contralateral) side of the body and controls muscles on the contralateral side. Crossed organization explains why people who have a stroke or other damage to the left cerebral hemisphere may have difficulty sensing stimulation to the right side of the body or in moving body parts on the right side. The opposite is true of people whose stroke occurs in the right cerebral hemisphere.

A crossed nervous system must somehow join both sides of the perceptual world together. To do so, innumerable neural connections link the brain's left and right sides. The most prominent connecting cable is the corpus callosum, whose roughly 200 million nerve fibers join the left and right cerebral hemispheres, allowing them to interact.

Four important exceptions to the crossed-circuit principle are olfactory sensation and the somatic, autonomic, and enteric PNS connections. Olfactory information does not cross, but rather projects directly into the same (ipsilateral) side of the brain. The cranial and spinal nerves that constitute the SNS are connected ipsilaterally, as are the sympathetic and parasympathetic ANS division connections. Likewise, ipsilateral ENS connections link to the ANS on both sides.

As described in Sections 11-2 and 11-4, many motor and somatosensory pathways between the brain and the body cross in the spinal cord.

## Principle 5: Brain Functions Are Localized and Distributed

A great debate in the early days of brain research focused on whether different functions are localized to specific brain regions. Some argued that specific functions are distributed, and no particular region is of prime importance. Others argued for localization, including Paul Broca and Karl Wernicke, who demonstrated decisively that two specific language functions are localized. Broca found that when damage occurs to the ventroposterior region of the frontal lobes, people are unable to produce spoken language. Wernicke found that when damage occurs to a different region, the left posterior superior temporal gyrus, pronounced deficits in language comprehension result. In essence, Broca, Wernicke, and others showed us that particular functions are localized and that some regions in the brain are of prime importance, at least in adults.

Broca's and Wernicke's areas are described in more detail throughout Chapter 10. A discussion of Penfield's work on functional mapping of these areas appears in Section 10-4.

But does this mean that function is not distributed? Not at all. Consider how particular brain regions operate. Neurons in a specific region receive inputs, make a multitude of internal connections within that region, and then send outputs. Small lesions within a specific region do not necessarily produce any noticeable disruptions. That is because within a brain region, the function is distributed among the neurons that do the information processing: if some neurons are destroyed, the remaining neurons can continue carrying out the function. Only when the majority of neurons within a specific functional region are destroyed do we see catastrophic failure for the associated function.

Because functions are both localized to specific areas and distributed within those areas, we can see paradoxical effects when certain types of brain damage occur. For instance, complete or nearly complete damage to a fairly localized region can cause irreversible loss of function, whereas widespread but diffuse damage may leave an individual's functional abilities intact. In fact, one characteristic of dementia-type diseases is that people can endure widespread deterioration of the cortex yet maintain remarkably normal language functions until late stages of the disease. **Alzheimer disease** is a degenerative brain disorder related to aging that first appears as progressive memory loss and only much later develops into generalized dementia.

## Principle 6: The Brain Is Symmetrical and Asymmetrical

The brain's left and right hemispheres look like mirror images, but they have some dissimilar features. Notably, cortical asymmetry is essential for integrative tasks, including language and body control.

Consider speaking. If a language zone existed in both hemispheres, each connected to one side of the mouth, we would actually be able to talk out of both sides of our mouth at once. That would make talking awkward, to say the least. One solution is to locate language control of the mouth on one side of the brain. Organizing the brain in this way allows us to speak with a single voice.

A similar problem arises in controlling body movements in space. We would not want the left and right hemispheres each trying to take us to a different place. Again, if a single brain area controls this sort of spatial processing, then the problem is solved.

Language control is typically situated on the left side, and spatial functions are typically found on the right. The brains of many species have such symmetrical and asymmetrical features. In the bird brain, the control of singing is in one hemisphere (usually the left side), as is the case for human language. It is likely that birds and humans evolved the same solution independently—namely, to assign the control to only one side of the brain.

## Principle 7: The Nervous System Works by Juxtaposing Excitation and Inhibition

We have emphasized the brain's role in *making* movements, but we must also recognize that the brain *prevents* movements. To make a directed movement, such as picking up a glass of water, we must refrain from other movements, such as waving the hand back and forth. In producing movement, then, the brain uses both **excitation** (increased neural activity) to produce some action and **inhibition** (decreased neural activity) to prevent other actions.

Brain injury or disease can produce either a *loss* or a *release* of behavior by changing the balance between excitation and inhibition. A brain injury in a region that normally initiates speech may render a person unable to talk—a loss of behavior. A person with an abnormality in a region that inhibits inappropriate language (such as swearing) may be unable to inhibit this form of speech. Such a release of behavior can be seen in some individuals with Tourette syndrome.

For Alzheimer neurochemistry, see Section 5-3; for incidence and possible causes, see Clinical Focus 14-3; and for a discussion of anatomical correlates and treatments, see Section 16-3.

**Alzheimer disease** Degenerative brain disorder related to aging that first appears as progressive memory loss and later develops into generalized dementia.

**excitation** Increase in the activity of a neuron or brain area.

**inhibition** Decrease in the activity of a neuron or brain area.

People with Parkinson disease may develop uncontrollable shaking of the hands because the neural system that inhibits such movements has failed. Paradoxically, they often have difficulty initiating movements and appear frozen because they cannot generate the excitation needed to produce deliberate movements.

The juxtaposition of excitation and inhibition, which is central to the way the brain produces behavior, can also be seen at the level of individual neurons. All neurons evince a spontaneous activity rate that can be either increased (excitation) or decreased (inhibition). Some neurons excite others; some inhibit them. Both effects are produced by neuronal communication via neurochemicals that cause specific ion channels to open.

Tourette syndrome and Parkinsonism are dysfunctions of the basal ganglia, which coordinates voluntary movement.

Chapter 3 details nervous system cell structure; Chapter 4 describes how neurons transmit and integrate information; and Chapter 5 discusses neuronal communication and adaptation.

## Principle 8: The Brain Divides Sensory Input for Object Recognition and Movement

Sensory systems evolved first for influencing movement, not for recognizing things. Simple organisms can detect stimulation such as light and move to or from it. It is not necessary to perceive an object to direct movements toward or away from it. Animals began to represent their environment only as their brains became more complex. Animals with complex brains evolved separate systems for recognizing objects and for moving. The human visual systems for visual scene perception and for visually guided movements exemplify this separation well (recall the cup from Principle 3).

Visual information in the cortical circuit travels from the eyes to the thalamus to visual regions of the occipital lobe. From the occipital cortex, this information then diverges along two separate pathways: the *ventral stream*, which leads to the temporal lobe for object identification, and the *dorsal stream*, which goes to the parietal lobe to guide movements relative to objects (**Figure 2-36**). People with ventral stream injuries are blind for object recognition: they cannot distinguish a cup from a spoon. Nevertheless, they shape their hands appropriately when asked to reach for objects that they cannot identify. In contrast, people with dorsal stream injuries can recognize objects, but they make clumsy reaching movements because they do not form appropriate hand postures until they contact objects. Only then do they shape the hand, on the basis of tactile information.

Recognizing that perception for movement and perception for object recognition are independent processes has three important implications for understanding brain organization:

1. The dorsal and ventral visual systems also exemplify parallel information processing in the brain (Principle 3).

2. Although we may think we are aware of our entire sensory world, the sensory analysis required for some movements clearly is not conscious.

3. Unconscious and conscious brain processing underlies an important difference in our cognitive functions. The unconscious movement system is always acting in the present and in response to ongoing sensory input. In contrast, the conscious object recognition system allows us to escape the present and bring to bear information from the past, thus forming the neural basis of enduring memory.

**FIGURE 2-36 Neural Streams** The dorsal and ventral streams mediate vision for action and recognition, respectively.

Sections 9-2 and 9-3 review the evidence that led to our understanding of the visual streams' functions and visual information processing.

## Principle 9: The Nervous System Produces Movement in a Perceptual World the Brain Constructs

The nervous system's fundamental function is to produce movements that make up behaviors. Movements are not performed in a vacuum, but rather are related to sensations, memories, and myriad other forces and factors. Your mental representation of the world depends on the information sent to your brain, your previous experiences, and the neural architecture of your nervous system. People who are color-blind perceive the world very differently from people who perceive color. The perceptual world of people who have perfect pitch differs from that of people without perfect pitch.

Although we tend to think that the world we perceive is what is actually there, individual realities, both between and within species, clearly are mere approximations of what is actually present. The brain of each individual develops in a particular set of environmental circumstances on a plan common to that species. The behavior that the brain produces, in other words, is directly related to the world that the brain has constructed.

# Principle 10: Neuroplasticity Is the Hallmark of Nervous System Functioning

Experience alters the brain's organization, and this neuroplasticity is requisite to learning and memory. In fact, the nervous system stores information *only* if neural connections change. Forgetting is presumably due to a loss of the connections that represented the memory.

As Experiment 2-1 on page 50 demonstrates, neuroplasticity is a characteristic not just of the mammalian brain; it is found in the nervous systems of all animals, even the simplest worms. Nonetheless, larger brains have more capacity for change, so their neural organization is likely to show more plasticity.

Plasticity can be beneficial in recovering from disorders such as brain injuries and diseases, as well as in normal aging. This characteristic also allows the brain to compensate for developmental abnormalities, an extreme example being agenesis of brain structures, as discussed in Research Focus 2-1. Although beneficial in such circumstances, neuroplasticity can have drawbacks in case of extreme stimulation or disease states. Brain analyses of animals given addicting doses of drugs such as cocaine or morphine reveal broad changes in neural connectivity suspected of underlying some maladaptive behaviors related to addiction. Among many other examples of pathological neuroplasticity are those associated with pain, epilepsy, and dementia.

Find details on plasticity and drug addiction in Section 14-4, on feeling and treating pain in Section 11-4, and on epilepsy in Clinical Focus 4-1. Section 16-3 covers the diagnosis and treatment of epilepsy and dementias.

## 2-6 Review

Before you continue, check your understanding. Answers appear at the back of the book.

1. What is a neuronal circuit, and why is it described as the functional unit of the nervous system?

2. Many of the brain's input and output circuits are crossed. In the nervous system, four exceptions to this principle are the_____, the_____, the_____, and the_____.

3. One aspect of neural activity that resembles the on–off language of digital devices is the juxtaposition of_____ and_____.

4. Explain this statement: Perception is not reality.

# Summary

## 2-1 Overview of Brain Function and Structure

The brain's primary function is to produce movements that make up behavior in a perceptual world the brain constructs. This perceptual world is ever-changing. To adapt to the dynamic environment, the brain must also change, a property referred to as neuroplasticity.

To study how the nervous system works, we abandon the anatomical divisions between the central nervous system and the peripheral nervous system to focus instead on function—that is, on how the CNS interacts with the divisions of the PNS: the somatic, autonomic, and enteric nervous systems.

## 2-2 The Conserved Pattern of Nervous System Development

Over generations, the vertebrate nervous system evolved from a relatively simple structure mediating reflex-like behaviors to the complex human brain mediating advanced cognitive processes. To allow for more complex behavior in an increasingly sophisticated perceptual world, archaic forms have not been replaced but rather have been adapted and modified as new structures have evolved.

The principles of nervous system organization and function generalize across the three vertebrate brain regions—hindbrain, midbrain, and forebrain—leading to multiple levels of functioning. The evolution of neural levels of control thus adds flexibility to behavioral control.

## 2-3 Central Nervous System: Mediating Behavior

The CNS includes the brain and the spinal cord. The spinal cord receives sensations from the skin and muscles and produces movements independent of the brain. The brain can be divided into the brainstem and the forebrain, each of which is made up of hundreds of parts. The brainstem both directs movements and constructs a sensory world through its connections with the sensory systems, spinal cord, and forebrain. The forebrain modifies and elaborates basic sensory and motor functions; regulates cognitive activity, including thought and memory; and ultimately controls movement. The most elaborate parts of the brain, the cerebral cortex and cerebellum, are relatively large in humans.

## 2-4 Somatic Nervous System: Transmitting Information

The SNS consists of two sets of spinal nerves that enter and leave the spinal column, connecting with muscles, skin, and joints in the body, and the cranial nerves that link the facial muscles and some internal organs to the brain. Both sets of SNS nerves are symmetrical: one set controls each side of the body. Some cranial nerves are sensory, some are motor, and some combine both functions. The spinal cord acts as a minibrain for the peripheral (spinal) nerves that enter and leave its five segments. Each spinal segment works independently, although CNS fibers interconnect them and coordinate their activities.

## 2-5 Autonomic and Enteric Nervous Systems: Visceral Relations

The ANS controls the body's glands and internal organs and operates largely outside conscious awareness. Its sympathetic (arousing) and parasympathetic (calming) divisions work in opposition to each other. The parasympathetic division directs the organs to rest and digest, whereas the sympathetic division prepares for fight or flight.

The ENS controls the gut over its entire length, from the esophagus to the colon, interacting with the brain via the ANS. ENS activity can affect our behavior and mental state. In turn, the ENS is affected by the microbiome, the roughly 39 trillion bacteria that inhabit our gut.

## 2-6 Ten Principles of Nervous System Function

Ten principles listed in the right column below form the basis for discussions throughout this book. Understanding them fully will enhance your study of brain and behavior.

## Ten Principles of Nervous System Function

| | |
|---|---|
| 1 | Neuronal circuits are the functional units of the nervous system |
| 2 | Sensory and motor divisions pervade the nervous system. |
| 3 | The CNS functions on multiple levels and is organized hierarchically and in parallel. |
| 4 | Many brain circuits are crossed. |
| 5 | Brain functions are localized and distributed. |
| 6 | The brain is symmetrical and asymmetrical. |
| 7 | The nervous system works by juxtaposing excitation and inhibition. |
| 8 | The brain divides sensory input for object recognition and movement. |
| 9 | The nervous system produces movement in a perceptual world the brain constructs. |
| 10 | Neuroplasticity is the hallmark of nervous system functioning. |

# Key Terms

afferent, p. 37
allocortex, p. 55
Alzheimer disease, p. 70
autonomic nervous system (ANS), p. 37
basal ganglia, p. 58
behavior, p. 35
brainstem, p. 51
cerebral cortex, p. 40
cerebrospinal fluid (CSF), p. 40
corpus callosum, p. 45
cranial nerves, p. 60
cytoarchitectonic map, p. 57
dermatome, p. 61
diencephalon, p. 53

efferent, p. 37
enteric nervous system (ENS), p. 37
excitation, p. 70
forebrain, p. 54
frontal lobe, p. 40
gray matter, p. 43
gyri (sing. *gyrus*), p. 41
hindbrain, p. 52
hypothalamus, p. 53
inhibition, p. 70
law of Bell and Magendie, p. 62
limbic system, p. 56
meninges, p. 37

midbrain, p. 53
neocortex, p. 56
nerve, p. 47
neuronal circuit, p. 67
neuroplasticity, p. 36
nuclei (sing. *nucleus*), p. 46
occipital lobe, p. 41
orienting movement, p. 53
parasympathetic division, p. 64
parietal lobe, p. 40
Parkinson disease, p. 59
phenotypic plasticity, p. 36
reticular formation, p. 52
somatic nervous system (SNS), p. 37

stroke, p. 42
sulci (sing. *sulcus*), p. 41
sympathetic division, p. 64
tectum, p. 53
tegmentum, p. 53
temporal lobe, p. 41
thalamus, p. 54
Tourette syndrome, p. 59
tract, p. 47
ventricles, p. 45
vertebrae (sing. *vertebra*), p. 61
vomeronasal organ (VNO), p. 56
white matter, p. 43

---

# Selected Resources from  Achieve

**Neuroscience in Action:** Finding Your Way Around the Brain

**Neuroscience in Action:** Anatomy of the Brain

**Concept Practice:** Lower Brain Structures

**Concept Practice:** The Cerebral Cortex

**Concept Practice:** Divisions of the Nervous System

**Videos**

The Central Nervous System: Spotlight on the Brain

**LearningCurve**

**Practice Quiz**

Lichtman Lab/Harvard University

# What Are the Nervous System's Functional Units?

**3**

**dystonia** Disorder in which muscles contract involuntarily, causing repetitive or twisting movements.

The Beery twins' remarkable story, described in Research Focus 3-1, highlights how neuroscientists apply advances in genetics to treat brain disorders. Understanding genes, proteins, and cellular function allows us to understand healthy brain functioning as well.

We begin this chapter by describing nervous system cell structure and function. Brain cells give the nervous system its structure and mediate its moment-to-moment activity, the activity that underlies our behavior. We conclude the chapter by describing Mendelian genetics and the new genetic science of epigenetics that complements Mendel's theory.

**Learning Objectives**
- Name the major structures of the neuron and their basic functions in information processing.
- List the five major types of neurons and describe their primary functions.
- Describe the five main types of glial cells and explain their functions.

### 3-1

# Cells of the Nervous System

The theory that the specialized cell of the nervous system, the *neuron*, is the building block of the nervous system and of our behavior emerged from a controversy between the Italian Camillo Golgi and the Spaniard Santiago Ramón y Cajal. Both men were awarded the Nobel Prize for medicine in 1906, in recognition of their work describing the cells of the nervous system.

Imagine that you are Camillo Golgi, at work in your laboratory, staining and examining nervous system tissue. You immerse a thin slice of brain tissue in a solution containing silver nitrate and other chemicals, a technique used at the time to produce

## ◉ RESEARCH FOCUS 3-1

### A Genetic Diagnosis

Fraternal twins Alexis and Noah Beery seemingly acquired brainstem damage perinatally (at or near birth). Typically, such children, who are diagnosed with cerebral palsy, do not get worse with age, but the twins' condition continued to deteriorate. They had poor muscle tone and could barely walk or sit. Noah drooled and vomited; Alexis suffered from tremors.

Their mother, Retta Beery, found a 1991 news report that described a child first diagnosed with cerebral palsy who was then discovered to have a rare condition, dopa-responsive **dystonia** (abnormal muscle tone). This condition stems from a deficiency in dopamine, a neurochemical produced by a relatively small cluster of cells in the midbrain (we discuss dopamine and its role in the process of neurotransmission in more depth in Chapters 5 and 6). When the twins received a daily dose of L-dopa, a chemical that brain cells convert into dopamine, they showed remarkable improvements. "We knew that we were witnessing a miracle," Retta recalled.

A few years later, in 2005, Alexis began to experience new symptoms marked by difficulty breathing. At the time, the twins' father, Joe, worked for Life Technologies, a biotechnology company that makes equipment used for sequencing DNA, the molecule that codes our genetic makeup. Joe arranged for the twins' blood samples to be sent to the Baylor College of Medicine's sequencing center.

The twins' genome was sequenced and compared to that of their parents and close relatives. The analysis revealed that the twins had an abnormality in a gene for an enzyme that enhances the production of not only dopamine but also serotonin, another chemical made by brainstem cells (Bainbridge, 2011).

When the twins' doctors added the chemical 5-hydroxytryptophan, which is converted to serotonin, to their L-dopa regimen, both twins improved. Their motor abilities improved so significantly that Alexis was able to compete in junior high school track, and Noah in volleyball at the Junior Olympics.

Reeta, Noah, Zach (the twins' brother), Alexis, and Joe at an event promoting the research done by the National Institutes of Health.

Courtesy Retta Beery

Theirs is the first diagnosis established through genome sequencing that has led to a treatment success — a scientific miracle indeed.

The Human Genome Project, a 13-year, international effort directed toward identifying all human genes, has launched new fields of scientific research and exciting new applications, including genome sequencing for the Beery twins. The discovery and successful treatment of dopa-responsive dystonia in the Beery twins has led to the field of *precision medicine*, in which a genetic diagnosis is used to identify individualized therapies (Sisodiya, 2021).

**(A)**

Biophoto Associates/Science Source

**(B)**

**FIGURE 3-1 Two Views of a Cell (A)** Tissue preparation revealing human *pyramidal cells* stained using the Golgi technique. **(B)** Cajal's drawing of a single *Purkinje neuron* made from Golgi-stained tissue.

---

**cell body (soma)** Core region of the cell containing the nucleus and other organelles for making proteins.

**dendrite** Branching extension of a neuron's cell membrane; greatly increases the cell's surface area; collects information from other cells.

**axon** Root, or single fiber, of a neuron that carries messages to other neurons.

---

black-and-white photographs. A contemporary method, shown in **Figure 3-1**A, produces a color-enhanced microscopic image that resembles the images Golgi saw. The image is certainly beautiful and intriguing, but what do you make of it? To Golgi, this structure suggested that the nervous system is an interconnected network of fibers. He thought that information flowed around this "nerve net," like water running through pipes, and so produced behavior.

Santiago Ramón y Cajal used Golgi's stain to study chick embryos' brain tissue and came to a different conclusion. He assumed that the chick's developing nervous system would be simpler and easier to understand than that of an adult chicken. Figure 3-1B shows an image he rendered from the neural cells using the Golgi stain. Cajal concluded that the nervous system is made up of discrete cells, which begin life as rather simple structures and become more complex with age. When mature, each cell consists of a main body with many extensions projecting from it (Ramón y Cajal, 1909–1911).

This structure looks something like a plant, with branches coming out the top and roots coming out the bottom. Cajal showed that these neurons come in many shapes and sizes and can be distinguished from the glial cells that make up the other half of brain tissue. Cajal's *neuron theory*—that neurons are the nervous system's functional units—is now the accepted theory of brain organization. The neuron theory also includes the ideas that the interactions between neurons enables behavior and that the more neurons an animal has, the more complex its behavior will be.

In the century since Golgi's and Cajal's pioneering work, scientists have developed many additional staining methods for visualizing neurons, including methods to view living cells that are cultured in a dish with nurturing fluids. Tiny microscopes, called *endoscopes* or *microendoscopes* (so named because they are small microscopes that look into tissue), can even be implanted in the brain to view the structure and activity of its neurons. Thus, a wide variety of visualization techniques are used to investigate different problems related to how neurons produce behavior. Subsequent research has also seemingly confirmed that a structure similar in appearance to Golgi's nerve net, called a *perineuronal net*, forms around neurons as they mature (Carulli & Verhaagen, 2021), though this covering does not function in the way that Golgi proposed. Today, investigators are examining the role of the perineuronal net in stabilizing the structure of neurons once they mature, in preserving well-learned behavior, and in influencing addictions to drugs and diseases of memory loss that occur as some people age—topics that we will take up in later chapters.

**Figure 3-2** shows the three basic subdivisions of a neuron. The core region is called the **cell body**, or **soma** (from the Greek for "body"; the root of words such as *somatic*). A neuron's branching extensions, or **dendrites** (from the Greek for "tree"), collect information from other cells, and its main root is the single **axon** (from the Greek for "axle"), which carries messages to other neurons. A neuron has only one axon, but most neurons have many dendrites. In fact, some neurons have so many dendrites that they look like a garden hedge, as Cajal's drawing in Figure 3-1B illustrates.

The human nervous system contains 86 billion neurons and 85 billion glial cells that support their function, a ratio of about 1:1 that characterizes the brains of all

Golgi never revealed just how he came to develop his staining technique.

Recall that in Chapter 1 we provided evidence that the number of neurons is a better measure of brain function than brain size, a conclusion consistent with Cajal's neuron theory.

Perineuronal net are discussed in the context of brain development in Section 8-4.

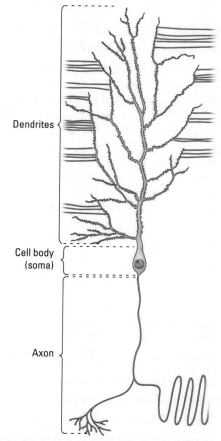

Dendrites

Cell body
(soma)

Axon

**FIGURE 3-2 Basic Structure of a Neuron** Dendrites gather information from other neurons, the cell body (soma) integrates the information, and the axon sends the information to other cells. Although a neuron may have many dendrites, it has only one axon.

animals (Herculano-Houzel et al., 2014). All neurons share a common plan, so examining how one neuron works offers insights that can be generalized to other neuron types. As you learn to recognize different types of neurons and glial cells, you will begin to understand how their specialized structures contribute to their functions in your body.

# Neurons: The Basis of Information Processing

As the information-processing units of the nervous system, neurons acquire information, store it as memory, interpret it, and pass the information along to other neurons to produce behavior. In doing so, they regulate body processes such as breathing, heartbeat, and body temperature, to which we seldom give a thought. They also regulate cognitive processes including learning, decision making, and thought. Scientists think that neurons work together in groups of many hundreds to many thousands to produce most behavior. It is important, then, to understand not only how individual neurons and glial cells function, but also how they interconnect and influence one another.

Functional groups of neurons, or **neural networks**, connect wide areas of the brain and spinal cord. The loss of a neuron or two from a network is no more noticeable than the loss of one or two voices from a cheering crowd. It is the crowd that produces the overall sound, not each person. An ongoing research effort aims to map the structural connectivity—the physical wiring, or *connectome*—of the entire human brain.

Each neuron's appearance is distinctive, but neurons are also the essence of plasticity. When living brain tissue is viewed through a microscope, the neurons appear surprisingly active, producing new branches, losing old ones, and making and losing connections with one another as you watch. This dynamic activity underlies both the constancies and the changes in our moment-to-moment behavior.

## Structure and Function of the Neuron

**Figure 3-3** details the external and internal features common to neurons. The cell's surface area is increased immensely by its extensions into dendrites and an axon (Figure 3-3A and B). The dendritic area is further increased by many small protrusions called **dendritic spines** (Figure 3-3C). A neuron may have up to 20 dendrites, each dendrite may have one to many branches, and the spines on the branches may number in the thousands. Dendrites vary in structure and function in different animal species. In mammals, dendrites collect information from other cells, and the spines are important points of contact with those neurons. The extent of a cell's branches and its spine number correspond to its information-processing capacity.

Each neuron has but a single axon to carry messages to other neurons. The axon begins at one end of the cell body, at an expansion known as the **axon hillock** (little hill), shown in Figure 3-3D. From there, the axon may branch out into one or many hundreds of **axon collaterals**, which usually emerge from it at right angles, as shown at the bottom of Figure 3-3B. These projections enable the neuron to send messages to many other neurons.

The axon collaterals may divide into multiple smaller branches (*telodendria*, or end branches). At the end of each telodendrion is a knob called a **terminal button**, or an **end foot**. The terminal button sits very close to, but usually does not touch, a dendritic spine or some other part of another cell (Figure 3-3C). This near-connection between two neurons, called a **synapse**, includes the surfaces of the end foot and the neighboring dendritic spine as well as the space between them.

Chapter 4 describes in detail how neurons transmit information via the synapse; here, we simply generalize about neuronal function by examining shape. Imagine looking down on a river system from an airplane. You see many small streams merging to

---

**Principle 1:** Neuronal circuits are the functional units of the nervous system.

The connectome is introduced in Section 1-4.

**Principle 10:** Neuroplasticity is the hallmark of nervous system functioning.

---

**neural network** Functional group of neurons that connects wide areas of the brain and spinal cord.

**dendritic spine** Protrusion that greatly increases the dendrite's surface area; typical point of dendritic contact with the axons of other cells.

**axon hillock** Juncture of soma and axon.

**axon collateral** Branch of an axon.

**terminal button (end foot)** Knob at the tip of an axon that conveys information to other neurons.

**synapse** Spatial junction between one neuron and another; forms the information transfer site between neurons.

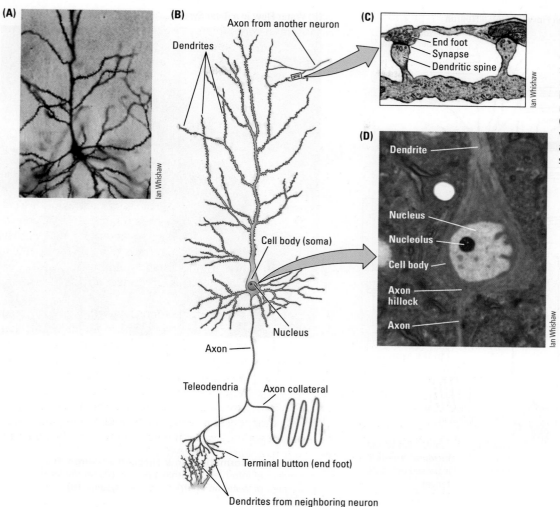

**FIGURE 3-3 Major Parts of a Neuron (A)** A Golgi-stained neuron reveals its dendrites and cell body. **(B)** The neuron's basic structures identified. **(C)** An electron micrograph captures the synapse between an axon from another neuron and a dendritic spine. **(D)** High-power light microscopic view inside the cell body. Note the axon hillock at the junction of the soma and the axon.

make creeks, which join to form tributaries, which join to form the main river channel. As the river reaches its delta, it breaks up into many smaller channels again before discharging its contents into the sea.

The general shape of a neuron suggests that it works in a broadly similar way to a river. As illustrated in **Figure 3-4**, the neuron collects information from thousands of other neurons on its dendrites. It channels this information to its axon, which can send out only a single message over all of its collaterals and teledendria. The synapse is the main information transfer site between neurons. Because it integrates information from thousands of inputs into a meaningful signal that is then passed on to other neurons, the human neuron serves as the model for the large-scale computer construction principle of *neuromorphic computing,* which seeks to emulate structural and operational elements of the human brain necessary for abstraction (Wang et al., 2021).

## Three Functions of Neurons

Neurons of varying shapes and sizes are structured to perform three specialized functions. **Sensory neurons** (**Figure 3-5**A) conduct information from the sensory receptors in or on the body into the spinal cord and brain. **Interneurons** (Figure 3-5B) associate sensory and motor activity in the central nervous system (CNS). **Motor neurons** (Figure 3-5C) carry information from the brain and spinal cord out to the body's muscles.

**sensory neuron** Cell that detects or carries sensory information into the spinal cord and brain.

**interneuron** Association cell interposed between a sensory neuron and a motor neuron; in mammals, interneurons constitute most of the brain's neurons.

**motor neuron** Cell that carries efferent information from the brain and spinal cord to make muscles contract.

**(A) Information Flow through a Neuron**

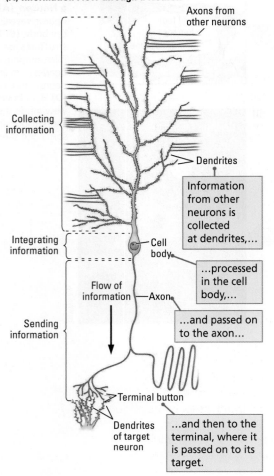

Axons from other neurons

Collecting information

Dendrites

Information from other neurons is collected at dendrites,...

Integrating information

Cell body

...processed in the cell body,...

Flow of information

Axon

...and passed on to the axon...

Sending information

Terminal button

Dendrites of target neuron

...and then to the terminal, where it is passed on to its target.

**(B) Water Flow in a River System**

Scott Camazine/Science Source

**FIGURE 3-4 Information Flow Through a Neuron** The movement of information within a neuron **(A)** resembles the movement of water and nutrients in river systems **(B)**.

**Sensory Neurons** Sensory neurons are structurally the simplest of the three types of neurons. A **bipolar neuron** found in the retina of the eye, for example, has a single short dendrite on one side of its cell body and a single short axon on the other side. Bipolar neurons transmit afferent (incoming) sensory information from the retina's light receptors to the neurons that carry information into the brain's visual centers.

A bit more structurally complicated is the **somatosensory neuron**, which brings sensory information from the body into the spinal cord, a long distance. Structurally,

**(A) Sensory neurons**

Bring information to the central nervous system

Dendrite

Axon

Bipolar neuron (retina)

Somatosensory neuron (skin, muscle)

**(B) Interneurons**

Associate sensory and motor activity in the central nervous system

Dendrites

Dendrites

Axon

Axon

Stellate cell (thalamus)

Pyramidal cell (cortex)

Purkinje cell (cerebellum)

**(C) Motor neurons**

Send signals from the brain and spinal cord to muscles

Dendrites

Axon

Motor neuron (spinal cord)

**FIGURE 3-5 Neuron Shape and Function (A)** Sensory neurons of many types detect stimulation or collect information and pass it on to **(B)** an interneuron. The multibranched interneuron dendrites collect information from varied sources and link to **(C)** motor neurons, which are distinctively large and which pass on commands to muscles to move. Cells are not drawn to scale.

the somatosensory dendrite connects directly to its axon, so the cell body sits to one side of this long pathway.

**Interneurons** Also called *association cells* because they link up sensory and motor neurons, interneurons branch extensively to collect information from many sources. A specific type of interneuron, the *stellate* (star-shaped) *cell*, is characteristically small, with many dendrites extending around the cell body. Its axon is difficult to see within the maze of dendrites. One of the main reasons brain sizes vary between species is that larger brains contain many more interneurons than smaller brains do, with the interneuron number being correlated with behavioral complexity.

A **pyramidal cell** has a long axon, a pyramid-shaped cell body, and two sets of dendrites. The apical set of dendrites projects from the cell body apex, and the basal set from the base of its cell body. Pyramidal interneurons carry information from the cortex to the rest of the brain and spinal cord. A **Purkinje cell** (named for its discoverer) is a distinctive interneuron with extremely branched dendrites that form a fan shape. It carries information from the cerebellum to the rest of the brain and spinal cord.

**Motor Neurons** To collect information from many sources, motor neurons have extensive dendritic networks, large cell bodies, and long axons that connect to muscles. Motor neurons are found in the lower brainstem and spinal cord. All efferent (outgoing) neural information must pass through them to reach the muscles.

## Neuronal Networks

Sensory neurons collect afferent (incoming) information from the body and connect to interneurons that process the information and pass it on to motor neurons. The motor neurons' efferent connections move muscles and so produce behavior. Throughout this text, we discuss many approaches to brain function that feature networks, but all networks feature these same three organizational aspects of function: input, association, and output.

Neurons that project for long distances, such as somatosensory neurons, pyramidal neurons, and motor neurons, are relatively large. In general, neurons with a large cell body have long extensions, whereas neurons with a small cell body, such as stellate interneurons, have short extensions.

Long extensions carry information to distant parts of the nervous system; short extensions are engaged in local processing. For example, the dendrite tips of some somatosensory neurons are in your big toe, whereas some targets of their axons are at the base of your brain. These sensory neurons send information over a distance as much as 2 meters—and even farther in very large animals. The axons of some pyramidal neurons must reach from the cortex as far as the lower spinal cord, a distance that can be as long as a meter. The imposing size of this pyramidal cell body accords with the work it must do in providing nutrients and other cellular supplies for its axons and dendrites.

## The Language of Neurons: Excitation and Inhibition

Neurons are avid networkers with elaborate interconnections, but how do they communicate? Simply put, neurons either excite (turn on) or inhibit (turn off) other neurons. Like digital computers, neurons send yes or no signals to one another; the yes signals are excitatory, and the no signals are inhibitory. Because a neuron can receive thousands of excitatory and inhibitory signals every second and vary its message in relation to those signals, it functions as does a radio or speaker; that is, it can produce a variable signal.

The neuron's response to all those inputs is reasonably democratic: it sums them. A neuron is spurred into action and sends messages to other neurons if its excitatory inputs exceed its inhibitory inputs. If the reverse occurs and inhibitory inputs exceed excitatory inputs, the neuron does not communicate.

**pyramidal cell** Distinctively shaped interneuron found in the cerebral cortex.

**Purkinje cell** Distinctively shaped interneuron found in the cerebellum.

**Principle 2:** Sensory and motor divisions permeate the nervous system.

**Principle 7:** The nervous system works by juxtaposing excitation and inhibition.

Section 4-2 explains how neurons summate excitatory and inhibitory signals.

Courtesy of Barbara Webb, University of Edinburgh, photo by Le Zhu

**FIGURE 3-6 Nervous System Mimics** Barbara Webb (pictured on the right) programmed rules she developed from studying cricket behavior into her Lego cricket robot (shown in all three images). Over time, Webb's robots have become increasingly more sophisticated, with miniaturized parts and more connections.

**glial cell** Nervous system cell that provides insulation, nutrients, and support and that aids in repairing neurons and eliminating waste products.

**TABLE 3-1** Types and Functions of Glial Cells

| Type | Appearance | Features and function |
|------|-----------|----------------------|
| Ependymal cell | | Small ovoid; secretes cerebrospinal fluid (CSF) |
| Astrocyte | | Star shaped; contributes to neuronal nutrition, support, and repair; contributes to forming the blood–brain barrier and to healing scarring after injury; contributes to information transfer between neurons |
| Microglial cell | | Small, derived from blood; defensive function is to remove dead tissue |
| Oligodendroglial cell | | Forms myelin around CNS axons in the brain and spinal cord |
| Schwann cell | | Wraps around peripheral nerves to form myelin |

By exciting or inhibiting one another, members of a neuronal network can detect sensory information and "decide" what kind of motor response to make to that information. Earlier we considered how neuronal function can be modeled in computer engineering. To confirm whether they understand how an entire neural network produces behavior, scientists might also create a model, such as a robot, intended to function in the same way. Robots, after all, engage in goal-oriented actions, just as animals do. A robot's computer must somehow sense the world, coordinate its actions in response, and perform much as an animal's nervous system performs. Researchers construct robotic models based on computer-based learning methods to help confirm hypotheses about how the nervous system functions and then use the information derived from this exercise to further refine subsequent robot models to more closely function like an animal's nervous system.

This two-way modeling process lies at the heart of neuromorphic computing, machine learning, and other approaches to robotic intelligence, or *artificial intelligence* (*AI*), based on principles of nervous system function. For example, Barbara Webb's cricket robot (**Figure 3-6**) is designed to mimic a female cricket, which listens for the source of a male's chirping song and then travels to it (Webb, 2020). Efforts by Webb and other AI researchers are driving the construction of more intelligent robots designed to process and respond to uncertainty and ambiguity in the natural world, much as we humans do. **Experiment 3-1** presents another example of the ways that inhibition and excitation might produce a cricket robot's behavior.

## Classes of Glial Cells

**Glial cells** (from the Greek for "glue") are the nervous system's support cells. Although many types of glial cells exist, we will describe only five types in this section. Although they do not usually transmit information themselves, glial cells help neurons carry out this task, binding them together (some *do* act as glue) and providing support, nutrients, and protection, among other functions. **Table 3-1** lists five classes of glia, along with their characteristic structures and functions.

## ····> EXPERIMENT 3-1

Question: Can the principles of neural excitation and inhibition control the activity of a simple robot that behaves like a cricket?

### Procedure A

In approaching a male, a female cricket must avoid open, well-lit places where a predator could detect her. The female must often choose between competing males, and may prefer, for example, the male that makes the longest chirps. If we insert sensory neurons between the microphone for sound detection on each side of a hypothetical robot cricket and on the motor on the opposite side, we need only two rules to instruct the female robot to seek out a chirping male cricket:

**Rule 1** When a microphone detects a male cricket's song, an excitatory message is sent to the wheel's motors, activating them so the robot moves toward the cricket.

**Rule 2** If the chirp is coming from the robot's left or right side, it will be detected as being louder by the microphone on that side, which will make one wheel turn a little faster, ensuring that the robot turns directly toward the sound.

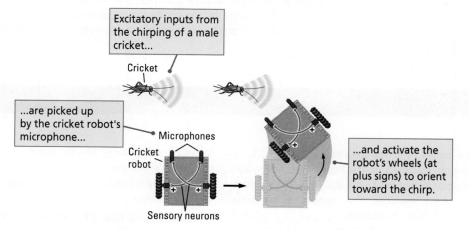

### Procedure B

Now we add two more sensory neurons, coming from photoreceptors on the robot. When activated, these light-detecting sensory neurons inhibit the motor neurons leading to the wheels and prevent the robot from moving toward a male cricket. Now the female cricket robot will move only when it is dark and "safe."

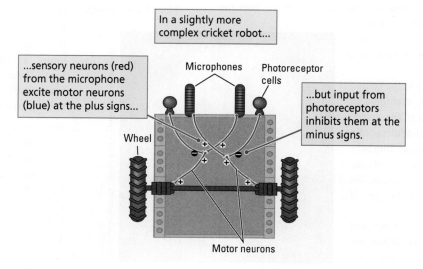

### Result

This hypothetical arrangement mimics the functions of sensory and motor neurons and the principle of summating excitatory and inhibitory signals—but with only six neurons and each neuron connected to only one other neuron!

### Conclusion

Today, *anthropomimetic robots*, so called because their parts are constructed to mimic the parts of a human body, including its billions of neurons, are being designed to model complex behavior and act as replacements for lost or impaired limbs (Webb, 2020). Entire robots are also being constructed to mimic many aspects of human behavior.

**tumor**  Mass of new tissue that grows in an uncontrolled manner and is independent of the surrounding structures.

**ependymal cell**  Glial cell that makes and secretes CSF; found on the walls of the brain's ventricles.

Figure 2-9 shows the location of the cerebral aqueduct and the four ventricles.

Glial cells differ from neurons in that most types of glial cells are produced throughout an organism's life, and errors in their replication are a main source of abnormal growths—namely, brain tumors. Clinical Focus 3-2: Brain Tumors describes the results of such uncontrolled glial cell growth.

## Ependymal Cells

On the walls of the ventricles, the fluid-filled cavities inside your brain are **ependymal cells**, which produce and secrete the cerebrospinal fluid (CSF) that fills the ventricles. CSF is constantly being secreted, and it flows through the ventricles toward the base of the brain, where it is absorbed into the blood vessels. CSF serves several purposes: it acts as a shock absorber when the brain is jarred, carries away waste products, assists the brain in maintaining a constant temperature, and is a source of nutrients for parts of the brain adjacent to the ventricles.

As CSF flows through the ventricles, it passes through some narrow passages, especially from the cerebral aqueduct into the fourth ventricle, which runs through the brainstem.

---

### ◎ CLINICAL FOCUS 3-2

## Brain Tumors

One day while watching a movie in a neuropsychology class, R. J., a 19-year-old college sophomore, collapsed on the floor, displaying symptoms of a seizure. The instructor helped her to the university clinic, where she recovered except for a severe headache. R. J. reported to the clinic providers that she had repeated severe headaches.

A few days later, a computed tomography (CT) scan showed a tumor over her left frontal lobe. The tumor was removed surgically, and R. J. returned to classes after an uneventful recovery. Her symptoms have not recurred.

A **tumor** is an uncontrolled growth of new tissue that is independent of the surrounding structures. No region of the body is immune from the development of these masses, but the brain is a site for more than 120 kinds of tumors. Such growths are a common cause of brain cancer in children.

The incidence of brain tumors in the United States is about 20 per 100,000, according to the Central Brain Tumor Registry of the United States (Ostrom et al., 2020). In adults, brain tumors grow from glia or other supporting cells rather than from neurons. In contrast, in infants, tumors may grow from developing neurons. The rate of tumor growth depends on the type of cell affected.

Some tumors are benign, as R. J.'s was, and not likely to recur after removal. Others are malignant, likely to progress and invade other tissue, and apt to recur after removal. Both benign and malignant tumors can pose a risk to life if they develop in sites from which removal is difficult.

The earliest symptoms of brain tumor usually result from the increased pressure on surrounding brain structures exerted by the growing mass of cells. They can include headaches, vomiting, mental dullness, changes in sensory and motor

The red area in this false-color CT scan is a meningioma, a noncancerous tumor arising from the meninges, which cover the brain. Large meningiomas may compress the brain but usually do not invade brain tissue.

*Dept. of Clinical Radiology, Salisbury District Hospital/Science Photo Library/Science Source*

abilities, and seizures, like the one R. J. had. Many symptoms depend on the tumor's location.

The three major types of brain tumors are classified according to how they originate:

1. *Gliomas* arise from glial cells and are the most common brain tumor. They are slow growing, rarely malignant, and relatively easy to treat if they arise from astrocytes. Gliomas that arise from the precursor *blast* or *germinal* cells that grow into glia are more often malignant, grow more quickly, and often recur after treatment. Beau Biden, U. S. President Joe Biden's son, passed away from a glioma in 2015 at the age of 42.

2. *Meningiomas*, such as R. J.'s tumor, attach to the meninges and grow entirely outside the brain, as shown in the accompanying CT scan. These tumors are usually encapsulated (contained), and if the tumor is accessible to surgery, chances of recovery are good.

3. *Metastatic tumors* become established when cells from one region of the body move into another area (which is what *metastasis* means). Typically, metastatic tumors are present in multiple locations, making treatment difficult. Symptoms of the underlying condition often first appear when the tumor cells reach the brain.

Treatment for brain tumors is usually surgical, and surgery also remains a main diagnostic tool. Chemotherapy is less successful in treating brain tumors than tumors elsewhere in the body because the blood–brain barrier blocks the chemicals' entry into the brain. Radiation therapy (X-ray treatment) is more useful for destroying brain tumor cells but can have negative effects, especially on the developing brain. Alternative treatments currently under investigation include genomic identification of a tumor and its subsequent destruction by targeting its unique genetic composition (Anirudh et al., 2021).

If these passages become fully or partly blocked, fluid flow will be restricted. Because CSF is continuously being produced, this blockage causes a buildup of pressure that begins to expand the ventricles, which in turn push on the surrounding brain.

If such a blockage develops in a newborn infant, before the skull bones are fused, the pressure on the brain is conveyed to the skull, and the baby's head swells. This condition, called **hydrocephalus** (literally, "water brain"), can cause severe intellectual impairment and even death. To treat it, doctors insert one end of a tube, called a *shunt*, into the blocked ventricle and the other end into a vein to allow excess CSF to drain into the bloodstream.

## Astroglia

**Astrocytes** (star-shaped glia, shown in Table 3-1), also called *astroglia*, provide structural support to the CNS. Their extensions attach to blood vessels and to the brain's lining, forming a scaffolding that holds neurons in place. These same extensions provide pathways for certain nutrients to move between blood vessels and neurons. Astrocytes also secrete chemicals that keep neurons healthy and help them heal if injured. *Satellite cells* (muscle stem cells) have a somewhat similar function in the peripheral nervous system (PNS).

At the same time, astrocytes contribute to the structure of a protective partition between blood vessels and the brain, the **blood–brain barrier**. As shown in **Figure 3-7**, the ends of astrocytes attach to blood vessel cells, causing the vessels to bind tightly together. These tight junctions prevent an array of substances, including many toxins, from entering the brain through the blood vessel walls. The molecules (smallest units) of these substances are too large to pass between the blood vessel cells unless the blood–brain barrier is somehow compromised. The downside of this protective barrier is that many useful drugs, including antibiotics used to treat infections, cannot pass through the blood–brain barrier to enter the brain. As a result, brain infections are difficult to treat. Scientists can bypass the blood–brain barrier by inserting small tubes into the brain that allow the delivery of a drug directly to a targeted brain region.

Yet another important function of astrocytes is to enhance brain activity. When you engage in any behavior, whether that activity is reading or running, the neuronal network responsible for that behavior requires more fuel in the form of oxygen and glucose. In response to neuronal activity, the blood vessels that supply them expand, allowing greater oxygen- and glucose-carrying blood flow. What triggers the blood vessels to dilate? This is where astrocytes come in. They pass along signals from the neurons to the blood vessels, thereby contributing to increased blood flow and fuel supply (Kenny et al., 2018).

Astrocytes also promote the healing of damaged brain tissue. If the brain is injured by a blow to the head or penetrated by some object, astrocytes form a scar to seal off the damaged area. Although the scar tissue is beneficial in healing the injury, it can also act as a barrier to the regrowth of damaged neurons. One of the many experimental approaches to repairing brain tissue seeks to get the axons and dendrites of CNS neurons to grow around or through a glial scar.

The newest area of research into astrocyte function is *tripartite synaptsomics* ("tripartite" indicates two connecting neurons and the astrocyte), which studies the role astrocytes play in neuron-to-neuron communication (Takano & Soderling, 2021). In a number of locations in the nervous system, astrocytes function in close proximity to synapses and many neurochemical interactions occur between the two connecting neurons and the astrocyte. This evidence suggests that astrocytes have a role in the many functions of synaptic connections, including information flow and learning and memory.

## Microglia

Unlike other glial cells, which originate in the brain, **microglia** originate in the blood as an offshoot of the immune system and migrate throughout the nervous system, where they make up about 20% of all glial cells. The blood–brain barrier prevents most

**hydrocephalus** Buildup of fluid pressure in the brain and, in infants, swelling of the head, if the flow of CSF is blocked; can result in intellectual impairment and death.

**astrocyte** Star-shaped glial cell that provides structural support to CNS neurons and transports substances between neurons and blood vessels.

**blood–brain barrier** Protective partition between blood vessels and the brain formed by tight junctions between the cells that compose the blood vessels in the brain; prohibits entry of an array of substances, including toxins, into the brain.

**microglia** Glial cells that originate in the blood, aid in cell repair, and scavenge debris in the nervous system.

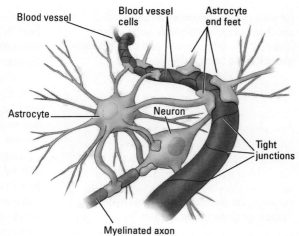

**FIGURE 3-7 Blood–Brain Barrier** Astrocyte processes attach to neurons and to blood vessel cells, stimulating them to form tight junctions and so form the blood–brain barrier. Astrocytes also move nutrients and other chemicals between blood vessels and neurons, support brain structures, and stimulate repair of damaged brain tissue.

**FIGURE 3-8 Detecting Brain Damage (A)** Arrows indicate the red nucleus in a rat brain. **(B)** Close-up of cresyl violet-stained neurons (the large dark bodies) in the healthy red nucleus. **(C)** After exposure to a neurotoxin, only microglia, the small dark objects in the micrograph, survive.

Growth factors, described in Section 8-2, are chemicals that stimulate and support brain cell growth, survival, and perhaps even plasticity (see Section 14-4).

immune system cells from entering the brain. Microglia, however, play an important part in monitoring and maintaining the health of brain tissue. They identify and attack foreign tissue, as illustrated in **Figure 3-8**. When brain cells are damaged, microglia invade the area to provide *growth factors* that aid in repair.

Several kinds of microglia exist, which take different shapes depending on the role they are performing. Microglia engulf any foreign tissue and dead brain cells, an immune process called *phagocytosis*. The fully stuffed and no-longer-functioning microglia have a distinctive appearance; they can be detected as small dark bodies, shown in Figure 3-8C, in and near damaged brain regions.

For more on understanding and treating Alzheimer disease, see Section 16-3.

Because microglia are frontline players in protecting the nervous system and removing its wastes, considerable research has focused on the extent to which microglia are involved in protecting the nervous system from disease. One characteristic of Alzheimer disease, a degenerative brain disorder commonly associated with aging, is the deposit of distinctive bodies called *plaques* in regions of damage—in a healthy system, microglia would remove this plaque. Microglia also interact with astrocytes to promote brain healing. Unfortunately, microglia may sometimes play a harmful role, consuming inflamed tissue rather than protecting it. Although small, as their name suggests, microglia play a mighty role in maintaining the brain's health and may even play a role in the production on new brain neurons (Pérez-Rodríguez et al., 2021).

## Oligodendroglia and Schwann Cells

Acting much like the plastic insulation on electrical wires, **myelin** prevents adjacent neurons from "short-circuiting." Myelinated neurons send information much faster than do neurons without myelin, so they also speed communication. Neurons that send messages over long distances quickly, including sensory and motor neurons, are heavily myelinated to increase their messaging speed.

Section 4-2 describes how myelin speeds up the neuron's information flow.

Two kinds of glial cells insulate neuronal axons: oligodendroglia and Schwann cells. **Oligodendroglia** myelinate axons in the brain and spinal cord by sending out large, flat branches that enclose and separate adjacent axons. (The prefix *oligo-* means "few" and here refers to the fact that these glia have few branches in comparison with astrocytes; see Table 3-1.) **Schwann cells** myelinate axons in the PNS. Each Schwann cell wraps itself repeatedly around a part of an axon, forming a structure somewhat like beads on a string. In addition to myelination, Schwann cells and oligodendroglia contribute to a neuron's nutrition and functioning by absorbing chemicals that the neuron releases and releasing chemicals that the neuron absorbs.

## Glial Cells, Disease, and Neuron Repair

The multifaceted relationships among neurons and glia provide insights into nervous system diseases and into brain injury and recovery. The consequences of damage to

**myelin** Glial coating that surrounds axons in the central and peripheral nervous systems; prevents adjacent neurons from short-circuiting.

**oligodendroglia** Glial cells in the CNS that myelinate axons.

**Schwann cell** Glial cell in the PNS that myelinates sensory and motor axons.

the oligodendroglia and Schwann cells can be as debilitating as damage to the neurons themselves. For example, multiple sclerosis (MS), a degenerative nervous system disorder and the most common autoimmune disease, is associated with damage to oligodendroglia that leaves a scar (*sclerosis* means "scar"), rather than myelin, on neurons in nervous system pathways. As a result, information flow along affected nerves is hindered, producing impaired movement and cognitive function.

Glia can also aid in nervous system repair. A deep cut on your body—on your arm or leg, for instance—may cut the axons connecting your spinal cord to muscles and to sensory receptors. Severing of motor neuron axons will render you unable to move the affected part of your body, whereas severing of sensory fibers will result in loss of sensation from that body part. Cessation of both movement and sensation is called **paralysis**. Weeks to months after motor and sensory axons are severed, however, movement and sensation may return. What mediates this recovery?

Both microglia and Schwann cells participate in repairing damage to the PNS. When a PNS axon is cut, it degenerates back to the cell body, as shown at the top of **Figure 3-9**. Microglia remove all of the debris left behind by the dying axon. Meanwhile, the Schwann cells that provided the axon's myelin shrink and divide to form numerous smaller glial cells along the path the axon formerly took. The cell body then sends out axon sprouts that search for and follow the path formed by the Schwann cells.

Eventually, one sprout reaches the intended target and becomes the new axon; all other sprouts retract. The Schwann cells envelop the new axon, forming new myelin and restoring function. In the PNS, then, Schwann cells serve as signposts to guide axons to their appropriate end points. Axons can get lost, however, as sometimes happens after surgeons reattach a severed limb. If axons destined to innervate one finger end up innervating another finger instead, the wrong finger will move when a message is sent along that axon.

When the CNS is damaged—as happens, for example, when the spinal cord is cut—regrowth and repair do not occur, even though the distance that the damaged fibers must bridge may be short. The fact that recovery takes place in the PNS but not in the CNS is puzzling. Regrowth in the CNS may not occur in part because as neuronal circuits mature, they become exquisitely tuned to mediate individualized behavior and, in doing so, develop chemical strategies that prevent the proliferation of new cells or the regrowth of existing cells. The oligodendrocytes that myelinate CNS cells do not behave like PNS Schwann cells to encourage brain repair. In fact, they may

**paralysis** Loss of sensation and movement due to nervous system injury.

Multiple sclerosis, which is caused by a loss of myelin, is discussed in depth in Clinical Focus 4-2.

Sections 11-1 and 11-4 detail causes of and treatments for spinal cord injury.

1 When a peripheral axon is cut, the axon dies.

Axon    Cut    Schwann cell

Cell body

2 Schwann cells first shrink and then divide, forming glial cells along the axon's former path.

Axon sprouts    Degenerating axon

Dividing Schwann cells

3 The neuron sends out axon sprouts, one of which finds the Schwann-cell path and becomes a new axon.

Schwann cells form myelin

4 Schwann cells envelop the new axon, forming new myelin.

Axon

Myelin

**FIGURE 3-9 Neuron Repair** Schwann cells aid the regrowth of axons in the somatic nervous system.

actually play a role in protecting the existing structure of the CNS by inhibiting neuron regrowth (Hernaiz-Llorens et al., 2021). Understanding how regrowth is inhibited is one approach to finding ways for the damaged CNS to repair itself.

## 3-1 Review

Before you continue, check your understanding. Answers to Self-Test appear at the back of the book.

1. The two classes of nervous system cell are _____ and _____.

2. Neurons, the information-conducting units of the nervous system, act either by _____ or _____ one another through their connecting synapses.

3. Five types of neurons are _____, _____, _____, _____, and _____.

4. Five types of glial cells are _____, _____, _____, _____, and _____.

5. Tripartite synaptsomics refers to the field of study in which _____ play a role in the communication between neurons.

6. Explain the two-way relationship between the fields of robotics and neuroscience.

7. Describe how the brain serves as a model for research in artificial intelligence.

## 3-2

# Internal Structure of a Cell

What is it about the structure of neurons that generates the remarkable ability to receive, process, store, and send a seemingly limitless amount of information? The first step in answering this question requires that we look inside a neuron to see what its components are and understand what they do. Although neurons are minuscule, when we view them with an electron microscope, we find packed inside hundreds of interrelated parts that do the cell's work.

To a large extent, a cell's proteins determine its characteristics and functions. Each cell can manufacture thousands of proteins, which variously take part in building the cell and in aiding in its communication with other cells. When memories are formed, proteins are involved; when a neuron malfunctions or contains errors, proteins are involved; and to restore function after brain injury, proteins are involved. In this section, we explain how the different parts of a cell contribute to protein manufacture, describe what a protein is, and detail some functions of proteins in the nervous system.

Water, salts, and ions play prominent parts in the cell's functions, as you will learn in this and the next few chapters. If you already understand the structure of water and know what salt and ions are, read on. If you prefer a brief chemistry review first, turn to The Basics: Chemistry Review.

## The Cell as a Factory

A cell can be compared to a miniature factory, containing work centers that cooperate to make and ship the cell's products—which include proteins. To investigate the cell's internal parts—the organelles—and how they function, we begin with a quick overview of the cell's internal structure.

**Figure 3-10** displays many external and internal cellular components. A factory's outer wall separates it from the rest of the world and affords some security. Likewise, a cell's double-layered outer wall, the *cell membrane* (or *plasmalemma*; *lemma* is Latin for "lining"), separates the cell from its surroundings and allows it to regulate what enters and leaves its domain. The cell membrane envelops the neuron's contents and contributes to forming its cell body, its dendrites and their spines, and its axon and terminals. In this way, it creates a boundary around a continuous intracellular compartment.

### Learning Objectives

- Use a factory analogy to describe the cell's internal structure.
- Explain how the cell membrane regulates the flow of substances into and out of the cell.
- Describe how proteins are manufactured in the cell and the role these proteins play at the cell membrane.

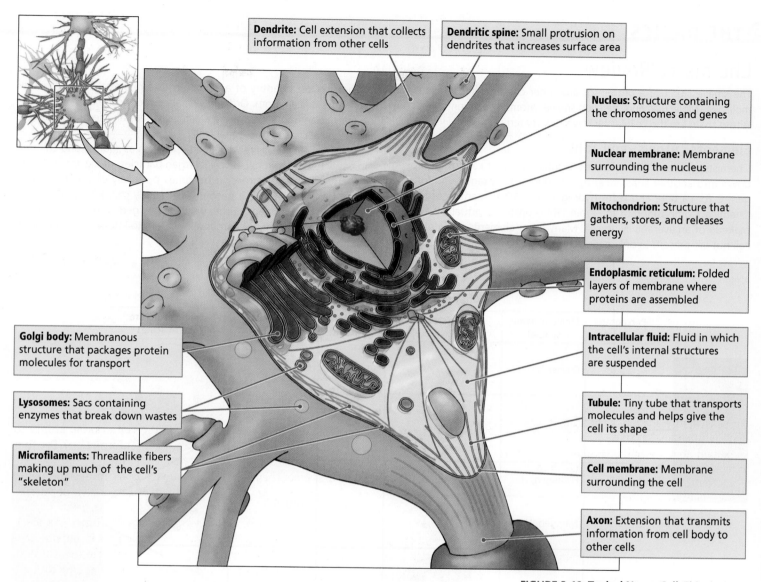

**Dendrite:** Cell extension that collects information from other cells

**Dendritic spine:** Small protrusion on dendrites that increases surface area

**Nucleus:** Structure containing the chromosomes and genes

**Nuclear membrane:** Membrane surrounding the nucleus

**Mitochondrion:** Structure that gathers, stores, and releases energy

**Endoplasmic reticulum:** Folded layers of membrane where proteins are assembled

**Intracellular fluid:** Fluid in which the cell's internal structures are suspended

**Tubule:** Tiny tube that transports molecules and helps give the cell its shape

**Cell membrane:** Membrane surrounding the cell

**Axon:** Extension that transmits information from cell body to other cells

**Golgi body:** Membranous structure that packages protein molecules for transport

**Lysosomes:** Sacs containing enzymes that break down wastes

**Microfilaments:** Threadlike fibers making up much of the cell's "skeleton"

**FIGURE 3-10  Typical Nerve Cell** This view of the outside and inside of a neuron reveals its overall structure and internal organelles and other components.

Only a few substances can enter or leave a cell spontaneously, but the cell membrane can regulate the passage of many substances. Proteins made by the cell are embedded in the cell membrane, where they facilitate the transport of substances into and out of the cell. These proteins thus serve as the cellular factory's gates. The selectivity of the cell membrane with respect to substances that can cross it is why it is called a *semipermeable membrane*.

Although neurons and glia appear to be packed tightly together, like all other cells, they are separated by *extracellular fluid* composed mainly of water, along with dissolved salts and many other chemicals. A similar *intracellular fluid* is found inside a cell. The most important factor governing the flow of substances into and out the cell is the cell membrane's semipermeability, which ensures that concentrations of substances inside and outside the cell are different.

Within the cell shown in Figure 3-10 are membranes that surround its *organelles*, similar to the work areas demarcated by a factory's interior walls. Each organelle membrane is also relatively impermeable, so it concentrates needed chemicals within its borders while keeping out unneeded ones.

The prominent *nuclear membrane* surrounds the cell's *nucleus*. Within the nucleus, the genetic blueprints for the cell's proteins are stored, copied, and sent to the "factory floor," the *endoplasmic reticulum* (*ER*). The ER is an extension of the nuclear membrane;

## ◎ THE BASICS

# Chemistry Review

The smallest unit of a protein or any other chemical substance is the molecule. Molecules and the even smaller atoms of elements that constitute them are the cellular factory's raw materials.

## Elements, Atoms, and Ions

Chemists represent each element (a substance that cannot be broken down into another substance) by a symbol—for example, O for oxygen, C for carbon, and H for hydrogen. The 10 elements listed in the Chemical Composition of the Brain table constitute virtually the entire makeup of an average living cell. Many other elements are vital to the cell but are present in only minute quantities.

The smallest quantity of an element that retains the properties of that element is an atom. Ordinarily, as shown opposite in part A of the Ion Formation figure, atoms are electrically neutral: their total positive and negative charges are equal.

Atoms of chemically reactive elements such as sodium and chlorine can easily lose or gain negatively charged particles, or electrons. When an atom gives up electrons, it becomes positively charged; when it takes on extra electrons, it becomes negatively charged, as illustrated in part B of Ion Formation. Either way, the charged atom is now an ion. Ions' positive or negative charges allow them to interact. This property is central to cell function.

## Chemical Composition of the Brain

| Percentage of weight | Element name, symbol | Atomic structure (not to scale) | Percentage of weight | Element name, symbol | Atomic structure (not to scale) |
|---|---|---|---|---|---|
| 65.0 | Oxygen, O | | 0.4 | Potassium, K | |
| 18.5 | Carbon, C | | | | |
| 9.5 | Hydrogen, H | | 0.2 | Sulfur, S | |
| 3.5 | Nitrogen, N | | | | |
| 1.5 | Calcium, Ca | | 0.2 | Sodium, Na | |
| 1.0 | Phosphorus, P | | 0.2 | Chlorine, Cl | |

Together, oxygen, carbon, and hydrogen account for more than 90% of a cell's makeup.

Some symbols derive from an element's Latin name—K for *kalium* (Latin for *potassium*) and Na for *natrium* (Latin for *sodium*), for example.

## Ions Critical to Neuronal Communication

| | |
|---|---|
| $Na^+$ | Sodium |
| $K^+$ | Potassium |
| $Ca^{2+}$ | Calcium |
| $Cl^-$ | Chloride |

Ions formed by loss of electrons are represented by an element's symbol followed by one or more plus signs.

Ions formed by gain of electrons are represented by an element's symbol followed by one or more minus signs.

## Ion Formation

### (A) Atoms

Total positive (+) and negative (−) charges in atoms are equal. The nucleus contains *neutrons* (no charge) and *protons* (positive charge). Orbiting the nucleus are *electrons* (negative charge).

Outer orbit contains 7 electrons

Outer orbit contains 1 electron

Cl atoms have 17 protons and 17 electrons.

Na atoms have 11 protons and 11 electrons.

### (B) Ions

The outer orbit gains an electron.

The outer orbit disappears because it lost its only electron.

Charged chloride ion (Cl⁻)    Charged sodium ion (Na⁺)

## Chemistry of Water

### (A) Water molecule

Two hydrogen atoms share electrons unequally with one oxygen atom, creating a polar water molecule positively charged on the hydrogen end and negatively charged on the oxygen end.

H    H

$O$

H    H

$O$

$H_2O$

### (B) Hydrogen bonds

Hydrogen bonds join water molecules to a maximum of four partners.

$H^+$ and $O^{2-}$ ions in each water molecule are attracted to nearby water molecules.

Because water molecules are polar, they are attracted both to other electrically charged substances and to one another. Part B of Chemistry of Water illustrates this attracting force, called a hydrogen bond. Hydrogen bonding enables water to dissolve electrically neutral salt crystals into their component ions. For this reason, salts cannot retain their shape in water; they dissolve. As illustrated in the Salty Water figure, the polar water molecules muscle their way into the $Na^+$ and $Cl^-$ lattice, surrounding and separating the ions.

Essentially, it is salty water that bathes our brain cells, provides the medium for their activities, supports their communications, and constitutes the brain's CSF. Sodium chloride and many other dissolved salts, including KCl (potassium chloride) and $CaCl_2$ (calcium chloride), are among the constituents of the brain's salty water.

## Molecules: Salts and Water

Salt crystals form bonds via the electrical attraction between ions. The formula for table salt, NaCl (sodium chloride), means that this molecule consists of one sodium ion and one chloride ion. KCl, the formula for the salt potassium chloride, indicates that this molecule is composed of one potassium ion ($K^+$) and one chloride ion ($Cl^-$).

Atoms bind together to form molecules, the smallest units of a substance that retain all of its properties. For example, a water molecule ($H_2O$) is the smallest unit of water that retains the properties of water. Breaking down water any further would release its component elements, the gases hydrogen and oxygen. The symbol $H_2O$ indicates that a water molecule is the union of two hydrogen atoms and one oxygen atom.

Ionic bonds hold salt molecules together, but the atoms of water molecules share electrons, and electron sharing is not equal: H electrons spend more time orbiting the O atom than orbiting each H atom. As shown in part A of the Chemistry of Water figure, this structure gives the oxygen region of the water molecule a slight negative charge and leaves the hydrogen regions with a slight positive charge. Like atoms, most molecules are electrically neutral, but water is polar: it carries opposite charges on opposite ends.

## Salty Water

Negative $Cl^-$ ions attract the positive poles of water molecules. Positive $Na^+$ ions attract the negative poles of water molecules.

Salt (NaCl)

Water ($H_2O$)

Polar water molecules surround $Na^+$ and $Cl^-$ ions in a salt crystal, dissolving it.

here, the cell's protein products are assembled in accordance with instructions from the nucleus. Once those proteins are assembled, many are packaged and sent throughout the cell. The *Golgi bodies* are "mailrooms," where proteins are wrapped, addressed, and shipped.

Other cell components include three kinds of *tubules*: microtubules, neurofilaments, and microfilaments. *Microfilaments* and *neurofilaments* reinforce the cell's structure, giving a cell its distinctive shape but also allowing the cell to change its shape and function throughout its lifetime. *Microtubules* form the transportation network that carries proteins to their destinations, much as roads allow a factory's trucks and forklifts to deliver goods to their destinations.

The various tubules are themselves constructed of proteins that have a globular or fibrous structure and are positively charged on one end and negatively charged on the other. These opposing charges enable components to link together to form scaffolds (think of a building that is under construction) or tracks (much like the rails of a railroad) that provide the structure of a cell and its communication lines. Disease that disrupts the scaffold results in the cell losing its shape (imagine if you pulled the support beams from a building); disease that disrupts the transport tracks renders the cell nonfunctional. Degenerative diseases such as some forms of Alzheimer disease are characterized by cell shrinkage. Disease due to brain trauma, such as concussion, may be associated with the malfunction of the transport systems of neurons.

Two other important parts of the cellular factory shown in Figure 3-10 are the *mitochondria* (sing. *mitochondrion*)—the cell's power plants, which supply its energy needs—and the *lysosomes*, vesicles that transport incoming nutrients and remove and store waste. Interestingly, more lysosomes are found in old cells than in young ones. Cells apparently have trouble disposing of all their garbage, just as human societies do.

Many different mitochondrial diseases, which are mainly genetic in origin, result in symptoms that include chronic fatigue. *Primary mitochondrial diseases* are genetic conditions in which mitochondria in one or more body organs fail to produce enough energy to carry out normal function. *Secondary mitochondrial disease* occurs in association with other diseases (including Alzheimer, diabetes, and cancer).

## Cell Membrane: Barrier and Gatekeeper

In the CNS, the extracellular fluid is CSF.

The cell membrane separates the intracellular fluid from the extracellular fluid, allowing the cell to function as an independent unit. The membrane's double-layered structure, shown in **Figure 3-11**A, regulates the movement of substances, including water, into and out of the cell. If too much water enters a cell, it will burst; if too much water leaves a cell, it will shrivel. The cell membrane's structure helps ensure that neither of these events happens.

The cell membrane also regulates the differing concentrations of salts and other chemicals on its inner and outer sides. This regulation is important because, if its concentrations of chemicals are unbalanced, the cell will not function normally. Which properties of a cell membrane allow it to regulate water and salt concentrations? One property is its special molecular construction. These molecules, called *phospholipids*, are named for their structure, shown close up in Figure 3-11B.

Figure 3-11C shows a space-filling chemical model of the phospholipid molecule's structure. The molecule has a head containing the element phosphorus (P) bound to some other atoms, and it has two tails, which are lipids, or fat molecules. The head has a polar electrical charge, with a positive charge in one location and a negative charge in another, as do water molecules. The tails consist of hydrogen and carbon atoms that tightly bind to one another by their shared electrons; hence, the fatty tail has no polar regions.

The polar head and the nonpolar tails are the underlying reasons a phospholipid molecule can form cell membranes. The heads are *hydrophilic* (from the Greek *hydro*, meaning "water," and *philia*, meaning "love") and so are attracted to one another and to polar water molecules. The nonpolar lipid tails have no such attraction for water. They are *hydrophobic*, or water hating (from the Greek word *phobia*, meaning "fear").

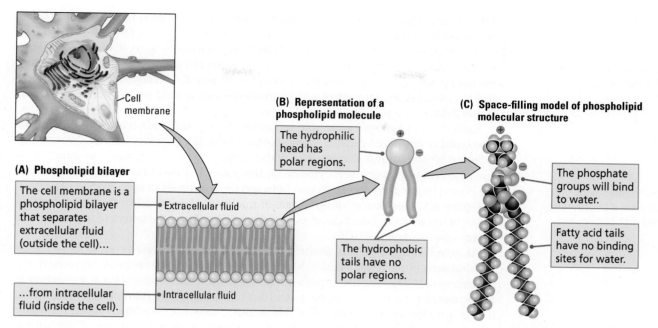

**(A) Phospholipid bilayer**

The cell membrane is a phospholipid bilayer that separates extracellular fluid (outside the cell)...

Extracellular fluid

Intracellular fluid

...from intracellular fluid (inside the cell).

**(B) Representation of a phospholipid molecule**

The hydrophilic head has polar regions.

The hydrophobic tails have no polar regions.

**(C) Space-filling model of phospholipid molecular structure**

The phosphate groups will bind to water.

Fatty acid tails have no binding sites for water.

**FIGURE 3-11 Bilayer Cell Membrane Structure (A)** Double-layered cell membrane close up. **(B)** Detail of a phospholipid molecule's polar head and electrically neutral tails. **(C)** Space-filling model shows why the phosphate head's polar regions (positive and negative poles) are hydrophilic, whereas its nonpolar fatty acid tail is hydrophobic.

Quite literally, then, the head of a phospholipid loves water and the tails hate it. To avoid water, the tails of phospholipid molecules point toward each other, and the hydrophilic heads align with one another and point outward to the watery intracellular and extracellular fluid. As a result, the cell membrane consists of a bilayer (two layers) of phospholipid molecules (see Figure 3-11A).

The bilayer cell membrane is flexible, yet forms a formidable barrier to a wide variety of substances. It is impenetrable to intracellular and extracellular water because polar water molecules cannot pass through the hydrophobic tails on the membrane's interior. Ions in the extracellular and intracellular fluid also cannot penetrate this membrane because they carry charges and so cannot pass by the polar phospholipid heads. This is why only few small molecules, such as oxygen ($O_2$), carbon dioxide ($CO_2$), and the sugar glucose, can traverse the phospholipid bilayer.

**gene** DNA segment that encodes the synthesis of a particular protein.

**FIGURE 3-12 Chromosome** The nerve cell's nucleus contains paired chromosomes of double-stranded DNA molecules bound together by a sequence of nucleotide bases.

## The Nucleus and Protein Synthesis

In our factory analogy, the nucleus is the cell's executive office, where the blueprints for making proteins and RNA are stored, copied, and sent to the factory floor. These blueprints, called **genes**, consist of segments of DNA that encode the synthesis of particular proteins. Genes are contained within the *chromosomes*, the double-helix structures that hold an organism's entire DNA library.

The chromosomes have been likened to books of blueprints. Each chromosome contains thousands of genes. Each gene is the blueprint, or code, for making one protein. The location of the chromosomes in the cell nucleus, the appearance of a chromosome, and the structure of the DNA within a chromosome are shown in **Figure 3-12**.

This static picture of chromosomes does not represent the way they actually look in living cells. Videos of cell nuclei show that chromosomes are constantly changing shape and moving in relation to one another, jockeying to occupy the best locations within the nucleus. By changing shape, chromosomes expose

Chromosome

Each chromosome is a double-stranded molecule of DNA.

DNA

A C G T

Adenine (A) binds with thymine (T). Guanine (G) binds with cytosine (C).

In humans, the reproductive cells are the sperm (male) and the egg (female).

*Chromosome* means "colored body"; chromosomes are so named because they can be readily stained with certain dyes.

different genes to the surrounding fluid, thus allowing these genes to begin the process of making proteins.

A human somatic (body) cell has 23 pairs of chromosomes, or 46 chromosomes in all. (In contrast, there are only 23 chromosomes within a reproductive cell, and they are not paired.) Each chromosome is a double-stranded molecule of *deoxyribonucleic acid* (*DNA*). The two strands of a DNA molecule coil around each other, as shown in Figure 3-12.

Each strand possesses a variable sequence of four *nucleotide bases*, the constituent molecules of the genetic code: *adenine* (A), *thymine* (T), *guanine* (G), and *cytosine* (C). Adenine on one strand always pairs with thymine on the other, whereas guanine on one strand always pairs with cytosine on the other. The two strands of the DNA helix are bound together by the attraction between the two bases in each pair, as illustrated in Figure 3-12. Sequences of hundreds of nucleotide bases within the chromosomes spell out the genetic code. Scientists represent this code by the letters of the nucleotide bases—for example, ATGCCG.

As noted earlier, a gene is a segment of a DNA strand. A gene's code is its sequence of thousands of nucleotide bases. Much as a sequence of letters spells out a word, the sequence of ACTG base pairs spells out the order in which *amino acids*, the constituent molecules of proteins, should be assembled to construct a certain protein. Each gene has, on average, approximately 30,000 base pairs, but some have many more; the entire human genome contains about 3 billion base pairs. A printed version of the human genome would fill 175 large books, each containing nearly 1500 pages on which the letters of the code are printed in the appropriate order (Brooks, 2016).

To begin to make a protein, the appropriate gene segment of the DNA strand unwinds to expose its bases. The exposed sequence of nucleotide bases on the DNA strand then serves as a template that attracts free-floating molecules called *nucleotides*. The nucleotides attach to the DNA to form a complementary strand of *ribonucleic acid* (*RNA*). The single-stranded nucleic acid molecule then detaches from the DNA and leaves the cell, carrying within its structure the code for protein synthesis. This process, called *transcription*, is shown in steps 1 and 2 of **Figure 3-13**. (To transcribe means "to copy," as in copying part of a message you receive in a text.)

**FIGURE 3-13 Protein Synthesis**
Information in a cell flows from DNA to mRNA to protein (peptide chain).

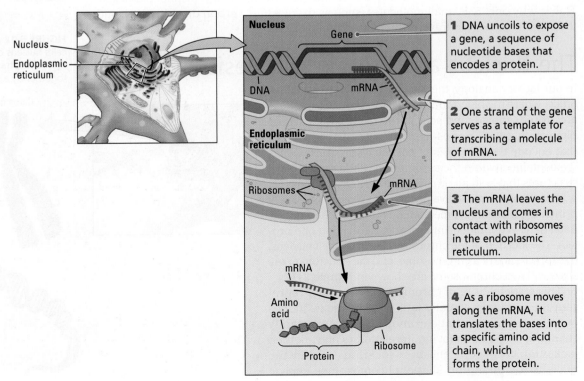

**Nucleus**

**Endoplasmic reticulum**

Nucleus

Endoplasmic reticulum

Gene

DNA

mRNA

Ribosomes

mRNA

mRNA

Amino acid

Protein

Ribosome

**1** DNA uncoils to expose a gene, a sequence of nucleotide bases that encodes a protein.

**2** One strand of the gene serves as a template for transcribing a molecule of mRNA.

**3** The mRNA leaves the nucleus and comes in contact with ribosomes in the endoplasmic reticulum.

**4** As a ribosome moves along the mRNA, it translates the bases into a specific amino acid chain, which forms the protein.

## The Endoplasmic Reticulum and Protein Manufacture

When RNA is produced through transcription, it forms a chain of bases much like a single strand of DNA, except that the base *uracil* (U) takes the place of thymine. Uracil is attracted to adenine, as is thymine in DNA; otherwise, the base codes of RNA and DNA are similar. The transcribed strand of RNA is called *messenger RNA* (mRNA) because it carries the protein code (the message) out of the nucleus to the ER, where proteins are manufactured.

Steps 3 and 4 in Figure 3-13 show that the ER consists of membranous sheets folded to form numerous channels. A distinguishing feature of the ER is that it may be studded with *ribosomes*, protein structures that act as catalysts to facilitate the building of proteins. When a mRNA molecule reaches the ER, it passes through a ribosome, where its genetic code is read. During this process of *translation*, a particular sequence of nucleotide bases in the mRNA is transformed into a particular sequence of amino acids. *Transfer RNA* (tRNA) assists in translating nucleotide bases into amino acids.

As shown in **Figure 3-14**, each group of three consecutive nucleotide bases along an mRNA molecule encodes one particular amino acid. These three-base sequences are called *codons*. For example, the codon uracil, guanine, guanine (UGG) encodes the amino acid tryptophan (Trp), whereas the codon uracil, uracil, uracil (UUU) encodes the amino acid phenylalanine (Phe). The sequence of codons on the mRNA strand determines the sequence of the resulting amino acid chain.

The human body utilizes 20 different amino acids, all structurally similar, as illustrated in **Figure 3-15**A. Each amino acid consists of a central carbon atom (C) bound to a hydrogen atom (H), an *amino group* ($NH^{3+}$), a *carboxyl group* ($COO^-$), and a *side chain* (represented by the letter R). The side chain varies in chemical composition from one amino acid to another. Each amino group is bound to the carboxyl group of the adjacent amino acid by a *peptide bond*, which gives the amino acid chain its alternative name, *polypeptide chain* (Figure 3-15B).

Just as a remarkable number of words can be made from the 26 letters of the English alphabet, a remarkable number of polypeptide (meaning "many peptides") chains can be made from the 20 amino acids. These amino acids can form 400 (20 × 20) dipeptides (two-peptide combinations), 8000 (20 × 20 × 20) tripeptides (three-peptide combinations), and almost countless polypeptides.

In summary, protein production by the genetic code is conceptually quite simple: a gene (a portion of a DNA strand) is transcribed into a strand of mRNA, and ribosomes translate the mRNA into a molecular chain of amino acids, a polypeptide chain, which forms a protein. We will discuss some other mechanisms of protein formation in the next section, but this sequence of events in building a protein is given the following designation:

$$DNA \rightarrow mRNA \rightarrow protein$$

## Proteins and RNA: The Cell's Products

A polypeptide chain and a protein are related, but they are not always the same. The relationship is analogous to the relationship between a length of ribbon and a bow that can be made from the ribbon. Long polypeptide chains have a strong tendency to twist into helices (spirals) or to form pleated sheets, which in turn have a strong tendency to fold together to form more complex shapes, as shown in **Figure 3-16**. A **protein** is a folded-up polypeptide chain; its shape is important to the function that it serves.

Proteins can vary somewhat in structure and still remain functional. Cells have mechanisms for ensuring that proteins are correctly pleated and folded and mechanisms for removing incorrectly folded proteins. However, these mechanisms are not always successful: misfolded proteins wreak havoc in more than 100 nervous system diseases. Prions (derived from the term for infectious proteins) are misfolded proteins that cause other proteins to misfold. They are implicated in many degenerative brain diseases, including Creutzfeldt-Jakob disease (colloquially known as "mad cow disease"), wasting diseases in sheep, and some forms of Alzheimer and Parkinson diseases.

A neuron, similar to all body cells, contains as many as 20,000 genes that produce RNAs that are translated into proteins, and 25,000 genes that produce RNAs that have other

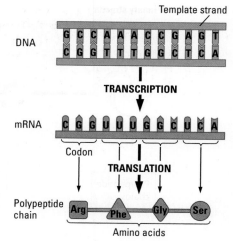

**FIGURE 3-14 Transcription and Translation** In protein synthesis (see Figure 3-13), a particular sequence of nucleotide bases in a strand of DNA (*top*) is transcribed into mRNA (*center*). Each sequence of three nucleotide bases in the mRNA strand (a codon) encodes one amino acid. In translation, the amino acids, directed by the codons, link together to form a chain (*bottom*). The amino acids are tryptophan (Trp), phenylalanine (Phe), glycine (Gly), and serine (Ser).

**(A) Amino acid structure**

The chemical composition of the R group distinguishes one amino acid from another.

Amino group          Carboxyl group

**(B) Polypeptide chain**

Peptide bond

A chain of amino acids forms a protein.

**FIGURE 3-15 Properties of Amino Acids** **(A)** Each amino acid consists of a central carbon atom (C) attached to an amine group ($NH^{3+}$), a carboxyl group ($COO^-$), and a distinguishing side chain (R). **(B)** The amino acids are linked by peptide bonds to form a polypeptide chain.

Prion diseases are discussed in more detail in Section 16-3.

**protein** Folded-up polypeptide chain that serves a particular function in the body.

**Primary structure**

Polypeptide chains...

**Secondary structures**

Pleated sheet    Helix

...form pleated sheets or helices.

**Tertiary structure**

Sheets and helices fold to form a protein.

**Quaternary structure**

A number of proteins combine to form a more complex protein.

**FIGURE 3-16 Four Levels of Protein Structure** Whether a polypeptide chain forms a pleated sheet or a helix and what its three-dimensional shape ultimately will be are determined by the amino acid sequence in the primary structure.

functions. Just under 20,000 RNAs are involved in gene translation; because these RNAs are not translated into proteins, they are called noncoding RNAs (ncRNA) (Salzberg, 2018). The number of proteins that can ultimately be produced by a neuron is far larger than the number of its genes, however. Although each gene codes for one protein, a protein can be cleaved into pieces—by enzymes, for example—to form two or more proteins, or it can be combined with other proteins in a variety of cellular processes to form still other proteins.

A protein's shape and its ability to change shape and to combine with other proteins are central to its function. Proteins can modify the length, shape, and behavior of other proteins and so act as enzymes, proteins that enhance chemical reactions. Proteins embedded in a cell membrane can regulate the flow of substances across the membrane. In addition, proteins can be exported from one cell to another and so act as messenger molecules.

# Golgi Bodies and Microtubules: Protein Packaging and Shipment

Getting proteins to the right destination is the task of cellular components that package, label, and ship them. These components operate much like a postal or shipping service.

To reach their appropriate destinations, protein molecules that have been synthesized in the cell are wrapped in membranes and marked with addresses to indicate where they are to go. This wrapping and labeling take place in the organelles called *Golgi bodies*. The packaged proteins are then loaded onto motor molecules that move along the many microtubules radiating through the cell, carrying each protein to its destination. Protein export is illustrated in **Figure 3-17**.

If a protein is destined to remain within the cell, it is unloaded into the intracellular fluid. If it is to be incorporated into the cell membrane, it is carried to the membrane,

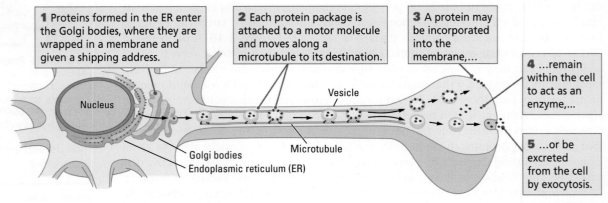

**1** Proteins formed in the ER enter the Golgi bodies, where they are wrapped in a membrane and given a shipping address.

**2** Each protein package is attached to a motor molecule and moves along a microtubule to its destination.

**3** A protein may be incorporated into the membrane,...

**4** ...remain within the cell to act as an enzyme,...

**5** ...or be excreted from the cell by exocytosis.

Nucleus

Vesicle

Microtubule

Golgi bodies

Endoplasmic reticulum (ER)

**FIGURE 3-17 Protein Export** Exporting a protein entails packaging, transporting, and assigning its fate at the destination.

where it inserts itself. If it is to be exported from the cell, it is usually transferred out in a process called *exocytosis* (meaning "out of the cell"). The membrane, or *vesicle*, in which the protein is wrapped fuses with the cell membrane, and the protein is excreted into the extracellular fluid.

# Crossing the Cell Membrane: Channels, Gates, and Pumps

Some proteins are embedded in the cell membrane. These proteins serve many functions, including transporting small molecules, such as salts, sugar, and other chemicals, across the membrane. We now consider how three types of membrane proteins—channels, gates, and pumps—perform the transport function. In each case, the particular protein's function is an emergent property of its shape.

A protein's shape and its ability to change shape derive from the precise amino acid sequence that composes the protein molecule. Some proteins change shape when other chemicals bind to them; others change shape as a function of temperature; and still others change shape in response to changes in electrical charge. The protein molecule's ability to change shape is analogous to a lock in a door. When a key of the appropriate size and shape is inserted into the lock and turned, the locking device activates and changes shape, allowing the door to be locked or unlocked.

Such a shape-changing protein is illustrated in **Figure 3-18**. The surface of this protein molecule has a groove, called a *receptor*, analogous to a keyhole. Small molecules, such as glucose, or other proteins can bind to a protein's receptors and cause the protein to change shape. Changes in shape allow the proteins to serve some new function.

Some membrane proteins form **channels** through which substances can pass. Different-sized channels regulate the passage of different-sized substances. **Figure 3-19**A illustrates a protein with a particular shape forming a channel large enough for potassium ($K^+$) to pass through, but not other ions. Other protein channels allow sodium ions or chloride ions to pass into or out of the cell. Still others allow the passage of various other substances.

Figure 3-19B shows a protein molecule that acts as a **gate** to regulate the passage of substances. Like the protein in Figure 3-18, gates change their shape in response to some trigger. The protein allows substances to pass through when its shape forms a channel and prevents substances' passage when its shape leaves the channel closed.

Changes in a protein's shape can also allow it to act as a **pump**. Figure 3-19C shows a protein that changes its shape to pump $Na^+$ and $K^+$ across the membrane, exchanging the $Na^+$ on one side for the $K^+$ on the other.

Channels, gates, and pumps play important roles in allowing substances to enter and leave a cell. Again, this passage of substances is critical in explaining how neurons send messages. Chapter 4 explores how neurons use electrical activity to communicate.

**FIGURE 3-18 Receptor Binding** When substances bind to a protein's receptors, the protein changes shape, which may change its function.

The role and function of membrane proteins in the process of neurotransmission are detailed in Chapters 4 and 5.

**channel** Opening in a protein embedded in the cell membrane that allows the passage of ions.

**gate** Protein embedded in a cell membrane that allows substances to pass through the membrane on some occasions but not on others.

**pump** Protein in the cell membrane that actively transports a substance across the membrane.

**(A) Channel**

Ions can cross a cell membrane through the appropriately shaped channel.

**(B) Gated channel**

Gates open / Gate closed

A gated channel changes shape to allow the passage of substances when gates are open...

...and to prevent passage when one or both gates are closed.

**(C) Pump**

Extracellular fluid

Intracellular fluid

A pump transporter changes shape...

...to carry substances across a cell membrane.

**FIGURE 3-19 Transmembrane Proteins** Channels, gates, and pumps are proteins embedded in the cell membrane.

## 3-2 Review

Before you continue, check your understanding. Answers to Self-Test appear at the back of the book.

1. Some constituent parts of the cell include _____, _____, _____, _____, _____, and _____.

2. Proteins in the cell membrane serve many functions, including acting at the cell membrane as _____, _____, and _____ to regulate movement of substances across the membrane.

3. The basic sequence of events in building a protein is that _____ makes _____, which in turn makes _____.

4. Once proteins are formed in the _____, they are wrapped in membranes by _____ and transported by _____ to their designated sites in the neuron or its membrane or exported from the cell by _____.

5. Briefly explain how the production of proteins in a cell contributes to behavior.

6. Describe how disease can result from abnormalities in protein production.

## 3-3

# Genes, Cells, and Behavior

Your *genotype* (genetic makeup) influences your physical and behavioral traits, which combine to form your *phenotype* (individual characteristics, including behavioral characteristics). Genetic analysis conducted by the Human Genome Project cataloged the human genome—all 30,000 or so genes in our species—and today individual genomes are routinely sequenced. (Recall the Beery twins in Research Focus 3-1.) Craig Venter, the co-describer of the human genome, was the first person to have his genome sequenced (Check, 2007).

Researchers have also sequenced the genomes of some of our extinct ancestors, including the Neanderthal genome. You can have your genome sequenced to reveal many aspects of its coding functions, including your possible relationship to Neanderthals, which you likely have if you are of European ancestry. The cost is about $100. (Before you decide to pursue such sequencing, you may want to check on any required information sharing with employers and insurers.)

Studying how genes influence our traits is the objective of Mendelian genetics, named for Gregor Mendel, whose research led to the concept of the gene. Studying how the environment influences gene expression is the objective of epigenetics. In this section, we describe how both factors influence our phenotypes.

## Mendelian Genetics and the Genetic Code

The nucleus of each human somatic cell contains 23 pairs of chromosomes, or 46 in all. One member of each pair comes from the mother, and the other member comes from the father. The chromosome pairs are numbered from 1 to 23, roughly according to size, with chromosome 1 being the largest (**Figure 3-20**).

Chromosome pairs 1 through 22 are called *autosomes*, and they contain the genes that contribute most to our physical appearance and behavior. The twenty-third pair consists of the *sex chromosomes*, which contribute to our physical and behavioral sexual characteristics. The two mammalian sex chromosomes are referred to as X and Y, shown at the right in Figure 3-20. Ordinarily, female mammals have two X chromosomes, whereas males have an X and a Y. The Y chromosome contains

### Learning Objectives

- Explain how allele combinations can influence physical and behavioral traits, and how genetic mutations can be acquired across an individual's lifetime.
- Describe the role of dominant and recessive alleles in diseases like Tay-Sachs and Huntington disease and in chromosomal abnormalities.
- Describe several techniques for genetic modification.
- Explain how epigenetic mechanisms influence the expression our genetic code.

**FIGURE 3-20 Human Chromosomes** The nucleus of a human cell contains 23 chromosomes derived from the father and 23 from the mother. Sexual characteristics are determined by the twenty-third pair, the X and Y (sex) chromosomes.

Nucleus

the SRY (sex-determining region) gene that makes the sex-determining region Y (SRY) protein, which triggers testes development and hence the male phenotype.

Because all but your sex chromosomes are matched pairs, each cell contains two copies of every gene—one inherited from your mother, the other from your father. These two copies of a gene are called **alleles**. The term *matched* here does not necessarily mean identical, as the nucleotide sequences in a pair of alleles may be either identical or different. If they are identical, the two alleles are **homozygous** (*homo-* means "the same"). If they are different, the two alleles are **heterozygous** (*hetero-* means "different").

The nucleotide sequence most common in a population is called the **wild-type** allele, whereas a less frequently occurring sequence is called a **mutation**. Any wild-type allele may have a number of mutations—some beneficial, some neutral, and some harmful.

## Dominant and Recessive Alleles

If both alleles in a gene pair are homozygous, the two encode exactly the same protein. In contrast, if the two alleles in a pair are heterozygous, they encode proteins that can vary. Three possible outcomes attend the heterozygous condition when these proteins express a physical or behavioral trait: (1) only the allele from the mother may be expressed, (2) only the allele from the father may be expressed, or (3) both alleles may be expressed simultaneously.

A member of a gene pair that is routinely expressed as a trait is called a *dominant* allele; an unexpressed allele is *recessive*. Alleles can vary considerably in their dominance. In complete dominance, only the allele's own trait is expressed in the phenotype. In incomplete dominance, the allele's own trait is expressed only partially. In *codominance*, both the allele's own trait and that of the other allele in the gene pair are expressed completely.

Each gene makes an independent contribution to the offspring's inheritance, even though that contribution may not always be visible in the offspring's phenotype. When paired with a dominant allele, a recessive allele is often not expressed. Even so, it can be passed on to future generations and influence their phenotypes when not masked by the influence of some dominant trait. Patterns of hair color in humans and the remarkable coat colors of horses illustrate how combinations of many alleles expressed in various homozygous and heterozygous combinations result in color pattern variation.

## Genetic Mutations

The mechanism described in Section 3-2 for reproducing genes and passing them on to offspring is fallible. Errors can arise in the nucleotide sequence when reproductive cells make gene copies. The altered alleles that arise in this way are called *mutations*.

A mutation may be as small as a change in a single nucleotide base, called a *single nucleotide polymorphism* (SNP, pronounced "snip"). This one-base change results in a change in a codon and a resulting change in one amino acid in a protein. A single amino acid change is also a mutation, which is often sufficient to alter the protein's function.

Because the average gene has thousands of nucleotide bases, an enormous number of SNPs as well as more complex losses and changes in bases can occur on a single gene. For example, the *BRCA1* (BReast CAncer) gene, found on chromosome 17, is a caretaker gene that contributes to preventing breast cancer and other cancers in both men and women. More than 1000 mutations of this gene have been found. Thus, in principle, there are more than 1000 ways in which to have a predisposition to, or increased resistance to, a cancer just from this gene.

A mutation in a nucleotide or the addition of a nucleotide to a gene sequence can be beneficial or disruptive, or both. For example, a SNP in which a T base is substituted for an A base in the *HBB* (hemoglobin) gene on chromosome 11 causes *sickle-cell anemia*, a condition in which blood cells take on an abnormal sickle shape. The sickle shape offers some protection against malaria, but sickle cells also have poor oxygen-carrying capacity, which weakens the person who possesses them. Sickle-cell anemia is the most common genetic blood disease, affecting millions of people worldwide, including 80,000

**allele** Alternative form of a gene; a gene pair contains two alleles.

**homozygous** Having two identical alleles for a trait.

**heterozygous** Having two different alleles for the same trait.

**wild type** Typical allele (most common in a population).

**mutation** Alteration of an allele that yields a different version of its protein.

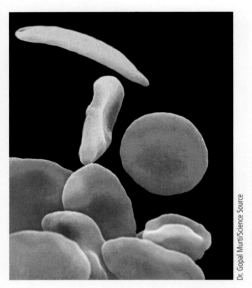

In this micrograph, a sickle cell (*top left*) is surrounded by healthy (rounded) blood cells.

Dr. Gopal Murti/Science Source

people in the United States. Later in this section, we describe various processes for editing gene sequences, potentially allowing for correction for genetic diseases, such as sickle-cell anemia.

Neuroscientists cannot yet explain human behavior in relation to genes, but we know the severe behavioral consequences of about 2000 genetic abnormalities that affect the nervous system. For example, an error in a gene could produce a protein that should be an ion channel but does not allow the appropriate substance to pass. It may produce a pump that will not pump or a protein that the cell's transportation system refuses to transport.

**Acquired Genetic Mutations**   The genetic mutations just described may be inherited by offspring from their parents. However, each of us also acquires a surprisingly large number of genetic mutations during our lifetime. These acquired mutations are not inheritable, but they have the potential to affect the behavior of the individual carrier. Some mutations are due to *mitotic* (cell division) errors that occur during our development, some occur as a cell's DNA engages in its routine activity of producing proteins, and some seem to be related to aging.

Different mutations may be localized in different parts of the body or brain, or even in individual brain cells. Given that the human brain consists of 86 billion neurons and 85 billion glial cells, all of which arose by cell division from a single cell, it is not surprising that mutations occur. And because most neurons are with us for life and remain metabolically active for life, it is not surprising that they can accumulate mutations. One estimate of single human neuron mutations found that errors in each neuron accumulate at a remarkable rate. At 1 year of age, a neuron may have up to 300 to 900 mutations; by 80 years of age, it may have as many as 2000 mutations. Do the math: 173 billion brain cells multiplied by up to 2000 mutations per cell is a lot of mutations in a lifetime (Miller et al., 2021).

The analysis of the DNA changes in the aging brain is called *genosenium* (for "aging genome"). One theory about such genomic changes proposes that aging is the result of all these genetic mutations. In short, we are accustomed to hearing that our genome is inherited from our parents, but it actually gets modified a lot as we develop and age.

# Applying Mendel's Principles

Gregor Mendel introduced the concept of dominant and recessive alleles in the nineteenth century, when he studied pea plants. Today, scientists describe this form of inheritance as *Mendelian genetics*. Many kinds of brain disorders are associated with this form of inheritance.

Experiment 1-1 describes one of Mendel's experiments.

## Allele Disorders That Affect the Brain

We will describe two rare brain diseases to illustrate Mendel's principles of dominant and recessive alleles: Tay-Sachs and Huntington disease. **Tay-Sachs disease** is caused by a dysfunction in a gene that produces HexA (hexosaminidase A). HexA breaks down a class of lipids (fats) in brain cells. If HexA is nonfunctional, the lipids accumulate in brain cells, resulting in cell damage.

Scientists Warren Tay and Bernard Sachs first described the disorder.

Symptoms usually appear a few months after birth. The baby begins to have seizures, deteriorating eyesight, and degenerating motor and mental abilities. Inevitably, the child dies within a few years. Tay-Sachs mutations appear with high frequency among certain ethnic groups, including Ashkenazi Jews and French Canadians, but the mutation in different populations can be different.

The dysfunctional Tay-Sachs HexA enzyme is caused by a recessive (nonfunctioning) allele of the *HEXA* gene on chromosome 15. Two copies of the nonfunctional allele (one from the mother and one from the father) are needed for the disorder to manifest. Thus, a baby will develop Tay-Sachs disease only when both parents pass on the recessive allele.

**Tay-Sachs disease**   Inherited birth defect caused by the loss of genes that encode the enzyme necessary for breaking down certain fatty substances; appears 4 to 6 months after birth and results in intellectual disability, physical changes, and death by about age 5.

Because both parents have survived to adulthood, both must also possess a corresponding dominant wild-type *HEXA* allele for that particular gene pair. The egg and sperm cells produced by this man and woman will therefore contain a copy of the

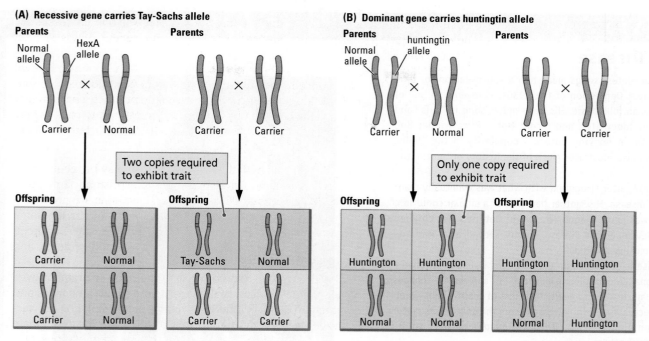

**(A) Recessive gene carries Tay-Sachs allele**

Parents
Normal allele    HexA allele
×
Carrier    Normal

Parents
×
Carrier    Carrier

Two copies required to exhibit trait

Offspring
| Carrier | Normal |
| Carrier | Normal |

Offspring
| Tay-Sachs | Normal |
| Carrier | Carrier |

**(B) Dominant gene carries huntingtin allele**

Parents
Normal allele    huntingtin allele
×
Carrier    Normal

Parents
×
Carrier    Carrier

Only one copy required to exhibit trait

Offspring
| Huntington | Huntington |
| Normal | Normal |

Offspring
| Huntington | Huntington |
| Normal | Huntington |

**FIGURE 3-21 Inheritance Patterns (A)** *Recessive condition:* If a parent has one mutant allele, the parent will not show symptoms of the disease but will be a carrier. If both parents carry a mutant allele, each of their offspring stands a 25% chance of developing the disease. **(B)** *Dominant condition:* A person with a single allele will develop the disease. If this person mates with a noncarrier, offspring have a 50–50 chance of developing the disease. If both parents are carriers, both will develop the disease, and offspring have a 75% chance of developing it.

wild type, or the mutation of these two alleles. Which allele is passed on is determined completely by chance.

In any child born of two Tay-Sachs carriers, then, this situation gives rise to three possible gene combinations, as shown in **Figure 3-21**A. The child may have two wild-type alleles, in which case he or she will be spared the disorder and cannot pass it on. The child may have one normal allele and one Tay-Sachs allele, in which case he or she, like the parents, will be a carrier. Or the child may have two Tay-Sachs alleles, in which case he or she will develop the disease.

The chance of a child of two carriers having two normal alleles is 25%, the chance of being a carrier is 50%, and the chance of having Tay-Sachs disease is 25%. If one parent is a Tay-Sachs carrier and the other is normal, any child has a 50–50 chance of being normal or a carrier. Such a couple has no chance of conceiving a baby who develops Tay-Sachs disease.

The Tay-Sachs allele operates independently of the dominant allele. As a result, it still produces the defective HexA enzyme, so the person who carries it has a higher-than-normal lipid accumulation in the brain. Because this person also has a normal allele that produces a functional enzyme, however, the abnormal lipid accumulation is not enough to cause Tay-Sachs disease.

A blood test can detect whether a person carries the Tay-Sachs allele. People who find that they are carriers can then make informed decisions about conceiving children. If they avoid having children with another Tay-Sachs carrier, none of their children will have the disorder, although some will probably be carriers. Where genetic counseling has been effective, the disease has been eliminated.

**Huntington disease** is a condition in which the abnormal *HTT* (huntingtin) allele is dominant and the recessive allele is normal, and the one defective allele causes the disease. In this disorder, the buildup of an abnormal version of the huntingtin protein kills brain cells of the basal ganglia and cortex. Huntington disease is a landmark disease for neuroscience because it has revealed much about the relationship between a single gene and the nervous system and, perhaps more importantly, because this knowledge can in principle lead to a cure for the disease.

Symptoms of Huntington disease can begin at any time from infancy to old age, but they most often start in midlife and include abnormal involuntary movements—which is why the disorder was once called a *chorea* (from the Greek word for "dance"). Other symptoms include memory loss and eventually a complete deterioration of behavior, followed by death.

**Huntington disease** Hereditary disease characterized by chorea (ceaseless involuntary jerky movements) and progressive dementia, ending in death.

## ⊙ CLINICAL FOCUS 3-3

# Huntington Disease

Woody Guthrie, whose protest songs made him a spokesperson for farm workers during the Great Depression of the 1930s, is revered as one of the founders of American folk music. His best-known song is "This Land Is Your Land." Singer, songwriter, and recent Nobel Prize winner Bob Dylan was instrumental in reviving Guthrie's popularity in the 1960s. Guthrie's life, however, also illustrates much of the history of Huntington disease.

Guthrie died in 1967, after struggling with what was eventually diagnosed as Huntington disease. His mother had died of a similar condition, although her illness was never diagnosed. Two of Guthrie's five children from two marriages developed the disease, and his second wife, Marjorie, became active in promoting its study.

Huntington disease is devastating, characterized by memory impairment; *choreas* (abnormal, uncontrollable movements); and marked changes in personality, eventually leading to nearly total loss of healthy behavioral, emotional, and intellectual functioning. Even before the onset of its motor symptoms, Huntington disease impairs *theory of mind,* a person's ability to assess the behavior of others.

The symptoms of Huntington disease result from neuronal degeneration in the basal ganglia and cortex. Symptoms can appear at any age but typically start in midlife. In 1983, the geneticist Nancy Wexler collected blood samples from patients with Huntington disease; by examining these samples, she was able to find on chromosome 4 the *HTT* (huntingtin) gene responsible for forming the abnormal huntingtin protein.

The *HTT* gene has been a source of insights into the transmission of genetic disorders. Part of the gene contains repeats of the base sequence CAG. The CAG codon encodes the amino acid glutamine. If the number of CAG repeats exceeds about 40, then the carrier, with 40 or more glutamine amino acids in the huntingtin protein, has an increased likelihood of experiencing Huntington symptoms.

As the number of CAG repeats increases, the onset of symptoms occurs earlier in life, and the disease progresses more rapidly. Typically, non-Europeans have fewer repeats than do Europeans, among whom the disease is more common. The number of repeats can also increase with transmission from the father but not from the mother.

John Springer Collection/Getty Images

Because of his celebrity and the advocacy of his wife Marjorie, who helped found the Huntington's Disease Society of America, Woody Guthrie's death helped to raise awareness for Huntington disease. His unpublished lyrics and artwork are archived at woodyguthrie.org.

Investigations into why brain cells change in Huntington disease and into potential treatments use transgenic animal models. Mice, rats, and monkeys that have received the *HTT* gene produce the abnormal huntingtin protein and display symptoms of Huntington disease (Stricker-Shaver et al., 2018). Modification of the *HTT* gene using modern genetic engineering, including the CRISPR method, described in this chapter, is in principle a cure for the disease (Bonnerjee & Bagh, 2021).

Figure 3-21B illustrates the inheritance patterns associated with a dominant allele on chromosome 4 that produces Huntington disease. If one parent carries the defective allele, offspring have a 50% chance of inheriting the disorder. If both parents have the defective allele, the chance of inheritance increases to 75%. As discussed further in Clinical Focus 3-3: Huntington Disease, because the abnormal *huntingtin* allele usually is not expressed until midlife—that is, after the people who possess it may have already had children—it may unwittingly be passed down to offspring even though it is lethal.

As with the allele that causes Tay-Sachs disease, a genetic test can determine whether a person carries the allele that causes Huntington disease. If so, the person can elect not to procreate. A decision not to have children in this case will reduce the incidence of the abnormal *huntingtin* allele in the human gene pool.

## Chromosome Abnormalities

Genetic disorders are not caused solely by single defective alleles. Some nervous system disorders are caused by copy number variations—that is, aberrations in a part of a chromosome or even an entire chromosome. Copy number variations have been linked to a variety of disorders, including autism, schizophrenia, and learning disabilities. Often, though, copy number variation has little obvious consequence or is even beneficial. For example, humans average about 6 copies of the *AMY1* (amylase) gene but may have as many as 15 copies. This gene is an adaptation that improves the ability to digest starchy foods (Yang & Ye, 2021).

One condition that results from a change in chromosome number in humans is **Down syndrome**, which affects approximately 1 in 700 children. Down syndrome is usually the result of an extra copy of chromosome 21. One parent (usually the mother) passes on to the child two copies of chromosome 21 rather than the normal single chromosome. Combining these two with one chromosome from the other parent yields three copies of chromosome 21, an abnormal number called a *trisomy* (**Figure 3-22**).

Although chromosome 21 is the smallest human chromosome, its trisomy can dramatically alter a person's phenotype. People with Down syndrome have characteristic facial features and short stature. They are susceptible to heart defects, respiratory infections, and intellectual impairment. They are prone to developing leukemia and Alzheimer disease. Although people with Down syndrome usually have a shorter-than-normal life span, some live to middle age or beyond. Improved educational opportunities can also enrich the lives of children with Down syndrome.

**Down syndrome** Chromosomal abnormality resulting in intellectual impairment and other abnormalities, usually caused by an extra chromosome 21.

# Genetic Engineering

As our understanding of gene structure and function has advanced, scientists have invented methods to influence the traits that genes express. This approach collectively defines the science of *genetic engineering*. In its simplest forms, genetic engineering entails manipulating a genome, removing a gene from a genome, or modifying or adding a gene to the genome. Its techniques include selective breeding, cloning, and transgenics.

## Selective Breeding

The oldest means of influencing genetic traits is the selective breeding of animals and plants. Beginning with the domestication of wolves into dogs more than 30,000 years ago, humans have domesticated many animal species by selectively breeding males and females that display particular traits. The selective breeding of dogs, for example, has produced the species with the most diverse traits of all animal species: breeds that can run fast, haul heavy loads, retrieve prey, dig for burrowing animals, climb rocky cliffs in search of sea birds, herd sheep and cattle, or sit on an owner's lap and cuddle. Selective breeding has influenced the dog's brain by making it smaller than a wolf's

**FIGURE 3-22 Chromosome Aberration** *Left*: Down syndrome, also known as trisomy 21, is caused by an extra chromosome 21 (colored red, bottom row at left). *Right*: Chris Burke, the first person with Down syndrome to play a leading role on a television series—*Life Goes On*, in the 1990s—is now in his fifties and remains an advocate for individuals with Down syndrome.

BSIP/Getty Images

Djamilla Rosa Cochran/Getty Images

brain but also by giving it the largest number of cortical neurons for a carnivore of its size, which may account for its sociability with humans (Jardim-Messeder et al., 2017).

Maintaining spontaneous mutations is one objective of selective breeding. Using this method, researchers can produce whole populations of animals possessing some unusual trait that originally arose as an unexpected mutation in only one individual or in a few animals. In laboratory colonies of mice, for example, multiple spontaneous mutations have been discovered and nurtured to produce more than 450 different mouse strains.

Some of the strains of mice make abnormal movements, such as reeling, staggering, and jumping. Other strains have diseases of the immune system; still others are blind or cannot hear. Some mice are smart, some mice are not; some have big brains, some small; and many display distinctive behavioral traits. Some mice are also designed to have neurons that incorporate proteins that produce specialized channels and fluorescent proteins. Some of these fluorescent proteins are so bright that they can be visualized through the skull. If the fluorescence is activated by a metabolic change in a single cell, this cell's activity can be observed through the skull (Rynes et al., 2021). As a result, the neural and genetic bases of the altered behavior in the mice can be studied systematically to understand and treat human disorders.

Unlike other animals, humans can consent to experimental procedures. Section 7-8 frames debates on the benefits and ethics of conducting research using nonhuman animals.

Sections 7-1 and 7-5 review genetic methods used in neuroscience research.

## Cloning

More direct approaches to manipulating the expression of genetic traits include altering early embryonic development. One such method is *cloning*—producing an offspring that is genetically identical to another animal.

To clone an animal, scientists begin with a cell nucleus that contains DNA (usually from a living animal donor), place it in an egg cell from which the nucleus has been removed, and, after stimulating the egg to start dividing, implant the new embryo in the uterus of a female—a cloning method called *nuclear transfer*. Because each individual animal that develops from these cells is genetically identical to the donor, clones can be used to preserve valuable traits, to study the relative influences of heredity and environment, or to produce new tissue or organs for transplant to the donor. Dolly, a female sheep born in 1996, was the first cloned mammal.

A team of researchers in Scotland cloned Dolly in 1996. As an adult, she mated and bore a lamb.

Cloning has matured from an experimental manipulation to a commercial enterprise to produce better strains of domestic animals, preserve rare animal species, and even bring back extinct species. You can have your pet cloned for less than $50,000. The first horse to be cloned was Charmayne James's horse Scamper, the mount she rode to 11 world championships in barrel racing. The clone, named Clayton, was born in 1999. The first cloned cat, shown in **Figure 3-23** and named Copycat, was born in 2001. Over the past two decades, many other species have been cloned, including cattle, pigs, goats, camel, and several species of fish. The first primate species cloned using the nuclear transfer method was a Macaque monkey in 2017.

Investigators interested in *de-extinction* propose to use preserved cells from species such as the extinct passenger pigeon or from frozen carcasses of the extinct mastodon to clone those animals. The first rare species cloned, in 2000, was an Asian gaur, an animal related to the cow, though he lived less than 2 days. In 2009, the first extinct animal, a Pyrenean ibex, was cloned, though the clone lived only a few minutes. Cloning also has the benefit of bringing genetic diversity to endangered populations. In 2020, a Przewalski's horse named Kurt was cloned, and in 2021 a black-footed ferret named Elizabeth Ann was cloned; both species are critically endangered.

With respect to cloning animals for economic reasons, it is debatable whether cloning has advantages over selective breeding. Any attempt to clone humans would confront the uncertainty of success and many ethical issues.

**FIGURE 3-23 A Clone and Her Mom**
Copycat (*left*) and Rainbow (*right*), the cat that donated the cell nucleus for cloning. Although the cats' genomes are identical, their phenotypes, including fur color, differ. One copy of the X chromosome is randomly inactivated in each cell, which explains the color differences. Even clones are subject to epigenetic plasticity: they retain the capacity to develop into more than one phenotype.

Photos used with permission from Texas A&M College of Veterinary Medicine & Biomedical Sciences

## Transgenic Techniques

Transgenic technology enables scientists to introduce genes into an embryo or to remove genes from it. In *knock-in technology*, a number of genes or a single gene from one species is added to the genome of another species, passed along, and expressed in subsequent generations of **transgenic animals**. For instance, researchers have introduced into lines of mice, rats, and Rhesus monkeys the human *HTT* gene that causes Huntington disease (Stricker-Shaver et al., 2018). The animals express the abnormal allele and display humanlike Huntington symptoms, allowing investigators to test potential treatments for the disease (see Clinical Focus 3-3).

*Knockout technology* can be used to inactivate a gene—for example, so that a line of laboratory animals fails to express it. The line can then be examined to determine whether the targeted gene is responsible for a specific function or a human disorder and to examine possible therapies. In the past, knockout technology has been used to produce a line of mice that display the emotional and cognitive symptoms of human childhood attention-deficit/hyperactivity disorder in an effort to explore methods of treatment (Meng et al., 2021).

## Gene Modification

A new method for modifying genes involves altering its code—that is, its base pairs. Jennifer Doudna of the United States and Emmanuelle Charpentier of France were awarded the 2020 Nobel Prize for their discovery of the *CRISPR*/Cas9 genetic scissors (*Cas* refers to a "CRISPR-associated gene"). The CRISPR (pronounced "crisper") machinery was discovered as part of the immune system of bacteria. Recall the role of RNA in the transcription process, illustrated in Figure 3-14. A CRISPR RNA base sequence in the bacteria seeks out a matching DNA sequence in an invading virus and cuts the virus DNA, thereby inactivating the virus.

**Figure 3-24** describes the main features of the CRISPR machinery. CRISPR stands for "clustered regularly interspaced short palindromic repeat." The "repeats" are sequences of DNA that contain a series (cluster) of base pairs—usually 20 to 40 base pairs long—which are separated by short sequences of DNA that act as spacers. The repeats are palindromic because the sequence of base pairs in one strand of a repeat is the same as the sequence in the adjacent strand when read in reverse. Each spacer between two repeats is different and corresponds to a DNA sequence in a virus that has previously attacked the bacteria.

Cas9 is a CRISPR-associated protein that is coded for by DNA adjacent to the CRISPR DNA sequence. The Cas9 protein can identify the target DNA, unzip it, and cut out a portion with a scissors-like action. Essentially, the CRISPR DNA tells the Cas9 protein which portion to cut. In bacteria, the Cas9 protein seeks out DNA that contains a segment matching the spacer DNA corresponding to that virus. It then cuts the bacterial DNA at that location, thereby inactivating it.

Spacer DNA in bacteria produces RNA that Cas9 can use to identify an invading virus. In the laboratory, an RNA sequence can be produced to identify a specific part of the DNA in any gene. The identified gene can then be cut, deleting a portion of its DNA sequence. In the normal process of transcription and translation, damaged DNA is repaired by a cell; however, if a new piece of DNA is introduced into the cell via CRISPR, it can be incorporated into the cut segment of the DNA. If this insertion is successful, the gene is modified. This type of gene editing is similar to the way that you edit a sentence with your word processor to delete words, add words, or correct spelling mistakes.

Applications of the CRISPR technology include making plants or animals resistant to viral or bacterial infections, identifying cancer cells (including brain cancer) to kill them, and creating animal models to study almost any aspect of behavior, including emotion, memory, and motor behavior. For example, CRISPR technology has been used to study the olfactory behavior of mosquitoes and ants in the hopes that the genes of these insects can be modified so that they do not identify humans as targets to bite. CRISPR technology is also being used to facilitate *gene drives*, the introduction of genes into a population that affect the incidence of expressed genes. For example, a gene alteration that produces only daughterless offspring can, over the course of one generation, eliminate a population of disease-carrying mosquitoes, fruit flies that destroy a fruit crop, or an invasive species of animal, such as the rabbits in Australia, that is disrupting an ecosystem.

**transgenic animal** Product of technology in which one or more genes from one species is introduced into the genome of another species to be passed along and expressed in subsequent generations.

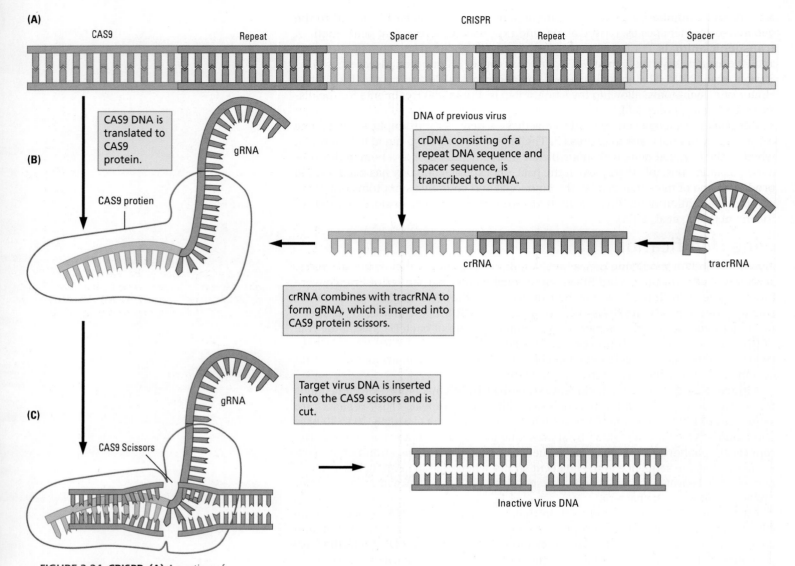

**(A)**

CAS9    Repeat    CRISPR    Spacer    Repeat    Spacer

**(B)**

CAS9 DNA is translated to CAS9 protein.

gRNA

CAS9 protien

DNA of previous virus

crDNA consisting of a repeat DNA sequence and spacer sequence, is transcribed to crRNA.

crRNA    tracrRNA

crRNA combines with tracrRNA to form gRNA, which is inserted into CAS9 protein scissors.

**(C)**

gRNA

CAS9 Scissors

Target virus DNA is inserted into the CAS9 scissors and is cut.

Inactive Virus DNA

**FIGURE 3-24  CRISPR  (A)** A portion of bacteria DNA that has genes for producing CAS9 and CRISPR RNA (crRNA). **(B)** Tracer RNA (tracrRNA) attaches to crRNA to form guide RNA (gRNA) to be inserted into the CAS9 protein. **(C)** When virus DNA is fed into the CAS9 scissors, the spacer portion of gRNA identifies the virus by a complimentary portion of its DNA, and inactivates it by cutting.

For more information on the CRISPR method, see Section 7-1.

**epigenetic** Difference in gene expression related to environment or experience.

   CRISPR technology can, in principle, also be used to identify and fix genes that are implicated in various diseases. The first successful application of CRISPR to human disease was aimed at editing the gene of a small number of people with sickle-cell anemia (recall our earlier discussion), a blood disorder caused by a mutation of one base pair of a gene responsible for making red blood cells (Urnov, 2021).

## The Epigenetic Code

Our genotype is not sufficient to explain our phenotype. Indeed, every individual displays the capacity to develop into more than one phenotype. Each of the 248 cell types in your body is derived from a single cell type. In the first half of the twentieth century, British developmental biologist Conrad Waddington coined the term **epigenetic** (meaning "in addition to genetic") to describe the variations that occur in the developmental process and eventually produce all of these cell types from a single genome. Waddington recognized that environmental influences—from neighboring cells and from the external environment—could shape this development. For example, variations in temperature during their development can modify the phenotype of fruit flies (Waddington, 1956).

   One example of such an alteration in the phenotypes of brain anatomy is illustrated in strains of genetically identical mice, some of which develop a brain with no corpus callosum (**Figure 3-25**). The absence of this hemispheric connector results from an epigenetic influence that determines whether the trait is expressed in a particular mouse. It occurs in the embryo at about the time the corpus callosum should form.

A lack of *concordance* (incidence of similar behavioral traits) is also observed in patterns of disease incidence in human identical twins, who share the same genome. The concordance rate between identical twins for a vast array of diseases—including schizophrenia, Alzheimer disease, multiple sclerosis, Crohn disease (a form of inflammatory bowel disease), asthma, diabetes, and prostate cancer—is between 30% and 60%. For cleft palate and breast cancer, identical twins' concordance rate is about 10%. The expectation from Mendelian genetics is 100% concordance. These less-than-perfect concordance rates point to the ability of epigenetic factors to alter the way traits are expressed in individuals.

Epigenetic mechanisms create phenotypic variations without altering the base pair nucleotide sequence of the genes. Through these mechanisms, experience and the environment can allow a gene to be expressed or can prevent its expression. Epigenetics is viewed as a second code, with the first code being the genome. In essence, epigenetics describes how a single genetic code produces each of the various somatic cell types, explains how a single genome can code for many phenotypes, and describes how cell functions go astray to produce diseases ranging from cancer to brain dysfunction. It also describes how experience throughout a lifetime produces changes in behavior.

## Applying the Epigenetic Code

The genes expressed in a cell are influenced by factors both within the cell and in the cell's environment. Once a fertilized egg begins to divide, each new cell finds itself in a somewhat different environment from that of its parent cell. The cell's environment will determine which genes are expressed and, in turn, which kind of tissue it becomes, including which kind of nervous system cell it becomes. Environmental influences do not end at birth, of course. Our environment changes daily throughout our lives, as does its influence on our genes.

Epigenetic mechanisms can influence gene function either by blocking a gene to prevent transcription or by unlocking a gene so that it can be transcribed. This is where experiential and environmental influences come into play. To review, each of your chromosomes consists of a long, double-stranded chain of nucleotide bases that forms your DNA. Each gene on a chromosome is a segment of DNA that encodes the synthesis of a particular protein (see Figure 3-13).

Chromosomes are wrapped around supporting molecules of a protein called *histone*. Histone wrapping allows the many yards of a chromosome to be packaged in a small space, much as yards of thread are wrapped around a spool. For any gene to be transcribed into messenger RNA, its DNA must be unspooled from the histone. Once unspooled, each gene must be instructed to transcribe mRNA. Then the mRNA must be translated into an amino acid chain that forms the protein. **Figure 3-26** illustrates some ways that each step can be either enabled or blocked:

1. *Histone modification*. DNA may unwrap or be stopped from unwrapping from the histone. At the top of Figure 3-26, a methyl group ($CH_3$) or other molecule binds to the tails of histones to block DNA from unspooling. The DNA's genes cannot be exposed for transcription with the block in place (left), but the DNA's genes can be opened for transcription (right) if the block is absent or removed.

2. **Gene (DNA) methylation**. Transcription of DNA into mRNA may be enabled or blocked. In the center of Figure 3-26, one or more methyl groups bind to CG base pairs to block transcription.

3. *mRNA modification*. mRNA translation may be enabled or blocked. At the bottom of Figure 3-26, noncoding RNA (ncRNA) binds to mRNA, blocking translation.

An environmental influence can either induce or remove one or more blocks, thus allowing the environment to regulate gene expression and influence behavior. In other words, exposure to stress or environmental pollution can produce epigenetic changes that can result in disease. Likewise, stress reduction and improvements in the environment can reverse these epigenetic changes. It is through these epigenetic mechanisms

**(A)**  Corpus callosum

Anterior commissure

**(B)**

Republished with permission of Springer Science+Business Media, Plenum Press, New York, from Douglas Wahlsten, Hiroki S. Ozaki, "Defects of the Fetal Forebrain in Acallosal Mice," Advances in Behavioral Biology Volume 42, pp. 125–133; ©1994, Figure 1. Permission conveyed through Copyright Clearance Center, Inc.

**FIGURE 3-25  Gene Expression** Identical coronal sections through the brains of mice with identical genotypes reveal frontal views of distinctly different phenotypes. **(A)** This mouse had a corpus callosum. **(B)** This mouse did not.

The cloned mice shown in Figure 2-1 exemplify phenotypic plasticity.

Just as the Human Genome Project has described the genetic code, the International Human Epigenome Consortium (IHEC) mandate is to describe the epigenetic code.

Methylation dramatically alters gene expression during brain development (see Sections 8-2 and 12-5) and can affect memory and brain plasticity (see Section 14-4).

**gene (DNA) methylation** Epigenetic process in which a methyl group attaches to the DNA sequence, suppressing or enabling gene expression.

**FIGURE 3-26 Epigenetic Mechanisms**

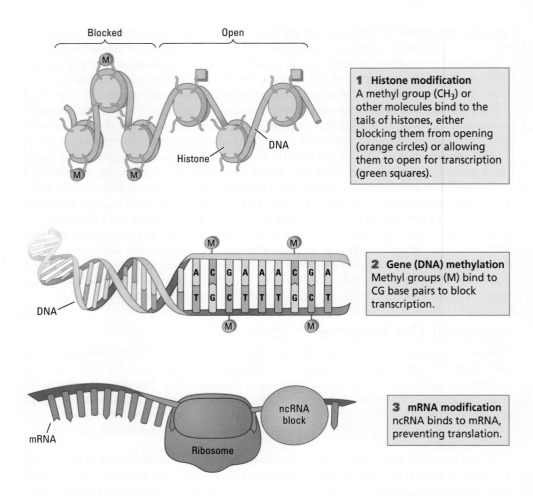

**1 Histone modification**
A methyl group (CH₃) or other molecules bind to the tails of histones, either blocking them from opening (orange circles) or allowing them to open for transcription (green squares).

**2 Gene (DNA) methylation**
Methyl groups (M) bind to CG base pairs to block transcription.

**3 mRNA modification**
ncRNA binds to mRNA, preventing translation.

that cells are instructed to differentiate into various body tissues and that our unique environment and experience induce the changes in our brain that make us unique individuals.

## A Case of Inheriting Experience

Most epigenetic changes that a genome acquires are erased in sexual reproduction when a sperm and an egg combine to form a fertilized egg. This process, called *reprogramming*, allows the cells of the fetus to essentially start afresh and make their own genetic and epigenetic future. Nevertheless, some epigenetic changes can be passed from one generation to the next. This *transgenerational epigenetic inheritance* shows that some life experience of ancestors can be inherited in their offspring, at least for a few generations.

Lars Olov Bygren and colleagues (Kaati et al., 2007) have described transgenerational epigenetic inheritance in a human population. These investigators focused on Norrbotten, a sparsely populated northern Swedish region. In the nineteenth century, Norrbotten was virtually isolated from the outside world. If the harvest there was bad, people starved. According to historical records, the years 1800, 1812, 1821, 1836, and 1856 saw total crop failures. The years 1801, 1822, 1828, 1844, and 1863 brought good harvests and abundance.

Using historical records, Bygren and his colleagues identified a sample of individuals who had been subjected to famine or to plenty in the years just before they entered puberty. Then the researchers examined the health records and longevity of these people's children and grandchildren.

The findings seem to defy logic. The descendants of the "plenty" group had higher rates of cardiovascular disease and diabetes and had a life expectancy more than 7 years shorter than that of the "famine" group! Notably, these effects were found only in male offspring of males and female offspring of females.

Bygren and colleagues propose that diet during a critical period can modify the genetic expression of sex chromosomes—the Y chromosome in males and the X chromosome in females. Furthermore, this change can be passed on to subsequent generations. Dietary experience in the prepubertal period, just before the onset of sexual maturity, is important: this is the time at which gene expression on the sex chromosomes begins.

Growing support for transgenerational inheritance is also found in studies of other human populations that have been subject to the stress of famine and war, as well as in numerous experimental studies with animals. Yet several central questions remain unanswered: How are such influences passed from one generation to the next? Which influences are most likely to be inherited? Which chromosomes and genes are most likely to be influenced? How might these epigenetic influences affect genetic inheritance? Experiments with the small roundworm *Caenorhabditis elegans* have led Natalya Frolows and Alyson Ashe (2021) to suggest that the mechanism underlying transgenerational inheritance may involve cytoplasmic ncRNA. Not only can this RNA be passed from the egg or sperm to a fertilized egg, but ncRNA can also influence subsequent physical development and may permit learned behavior to be transmitted from one generation to the next.

Section 8-4 examines critical periods, limited time spans during which events have long-lasting influences on development.

Section 7-5 describes additional experiments that demonstrate how experience can change gene expression.

## 3-3 Review

**Before you continue, check your understanding. Answers to Self-Test appear at the back of the book.**

1. Each of our _____ chromosome pairs contains thousands of genes, and each gene contains the code for one _____.

2. The genes we receive from our parents may include slightly different _____ of particular genes.

3. Abnormalities in a gene, caused by a(n) _____ can result in an abnormally formed protein, hence in abnormal cell function.

4. Chromosome abnormality can result in abnormal functioning of many genes. _____, for example, is caused by an extra copy of chromosome 21, a(n) _____.

5. Tay-Sachs disease results from a(n) _____ allele being expressed; Huntington disease results from the expression of a(n) _____ allele.

6. _____ is a new technology that allows for faster and easier gene modification. In this method, a(n) _____ identifies the DNA to be cut and _____ does the cutting.

7. _____ is an epigenetic mechanism that either enables or blocks transcription.

8. What distinguishes Mendelian genetics from epigenetics?

9. Describe how the genome of your brain cells changes throughout a lifetime.

# Summary

### 3-1 Cells of the Nervous System

The nervous system is composed of two kinds of cells: neurons, which transmit information, and glia, which support neuronal function. Sensory neurons may act as receptors to convey information from the body to the brain, motor neurons command muscles to move, and interneurons link up sensory and motor neuron activities.

Like neurons, glial cells can be grouped by structure and function. Ependymal cells produce CSF. Astrocytes structurally support neurons, help to form the blood–brain barrier, and seal off damaged brain tissue. Microglia aid in brain cell repair and waste removal. Oligodendroglia and Schwann cells myelinate axons in the CNS and in the somatic division of the PNS, respectively.

A neuron is composed of three parts: a cell body, or soma; multiple branching extensions called dendrites, designed to receive information; and a single axon that passes information along to other neurons. Numerous dendritic spines greatly increase a dendrite's surface area. An axon may have branches (axon collaterals), which further divide into telodendria, each ending at a terminal button (end foot). A synapse is the almost-connection between a terminal button and another cell's membrane.

### 3-2 Internal Structure of a Cell

A surrounding cell membrane protects the cell and regulates what enters and leaves it. Within the cell are a number of organelles, also enclosed in membranes. These compartments include the nucleus (containing the cell's chromosomes and genes), the endoplasmic reticulum (where proteins are manufactured), the mitochondria (where energy is gathered and stored), the Golgi bodies (where protein molecules are packaged for transport), and lysosomes (which break down wastes). A cell also contains a system of tubules (microfilaments) that aid its movements, provide structural support, and act as highways for transporting substances.

To a large extent, the work of cells is carried out by proteins. The nucleus contains chromosomes—long chains of genes, each encoding a specific protein the cell needs. Proteins perform diverse tasks by virtue of their diverse shapes. Some act as enzymes to facilitate chemical reactions; others serve as membrane channels, gates, and pumps; still others are exported for use in other parts of the body.

A gene is a segment of a DNA molecule made up of a sequence of nucleotide bases. Through transcription, a copy of a gene is produced in a strand of messenger RNA. The mRNA travels to the endoplasmic reticulum, where a ribosome moves along the mRNA molecule, translating it into a sequence of amino acids. The resulting amino acid chain is called a *polypeptide*. Polypeptides fold and combine to form protein molecules with distinctive shapes that serve specific purposes in the body.

## 3-3 Genes, Cells, and Behavior

From each parent, we inherit one of each chromosome in the 23 chromosome pairs that constitute the human genotype. Because all but the sex chromosomes are matched pairs, a cell contains two alleles of every gene. Sometimes the paired alleles are homozygous (the same), and sometimes they are heterozygous (different).

An allele may be dominant and expressed as a trait, recessive and not expressed, or codominant and expressed along with the other allele in the organism's phenotype. One allele of each gene is designated as the wild type—the most common in a population—whereas the other alleles are called mutations. A person might inherit any of these alleles from a parent, depending on the parent's genotype.

Genes have the potential to undergo many mutations—of a single base pair, of part of the chromosome, or of the entire chromosome. Mutations can be inherited by offspring from parents, or they can be acquired as we develop and age. Acquired mutations can be localized to different parts of the body, organs (including the brain), or even individual cells. Mutations can be beneficial, harmful, or neutral in their effects on nervous system structure and behavioral function. Genetic research is seeking ways to prevent the expression of genetic and chromosomal abnormalities and to find cures for disorders caused by such expression.

Selective breeding is the oldest form of genetic manipulation. In genetic engineering, an animal's genome is artificially altered. The genetic composition of a cloned animal is identical to that of a parent or sibling. In transgenic animals, a new or altered gene may be added or a gene removed. CRISPR, a technology for editing a gene, is faster and easier to perform and allows researchers to identify, cut, and replace specific DNA sequences in the genome.

The genome can express a range of phenotypes. The phenotype that is ultimately produced is determined by epigenetics, which is influenced by experience and the environment. Epigenetic mechanisms can influence whether genes are transcribed or their transcription is blocked, albeit without changing the genetic code itself. Some epigenetic instructions can be transgenerational.

# Key Terms

allele, p. 99

astrocyte, p. 85

axon, p. 77

axon collateral, p. 78

axon hillock, p. 78

bipolar neuron, p. 80

blood–brain barrier, p. 85

cell body (soma), p. 77

channel, p. 97

dendrite, p. 77

dendritic spine, p. 78

Down syndrome, p. 103

dystonia, p. 76

ependymal cell, p. 84

epigenetic, p. 106

gate, p. 97

gene, p. 93

gene (DNA) methylation, p. 107

glial cell, p. 82

heterozygous, p. 99

homozygous, p. 99

Huntington disease, p. 101

hydrocephalus, p. 85

interneuron, p. 79

microglia, p. 85

motor neuron, p. 79

mutation, p. 99

myelin, p. 86

neural network, p. 78

oligodendroglia, p. 86

paralysis, p. 87

protein, p. 95

pump, p. 97

Purkinje cell, p. 81

pyramidal cell, p. 81

Schwann cell, p. 86

sensory neuron, p. 79

somatosensory neuron, p. 80

synapse, p. 78

Tay-Sachs disease, p. 100

terminal button (end foot), p. 78

transgenic animal, p. 105

tumor, p. 84

wild type, p. 99

# Selected Resources from  Achieve

**Neuroscience in Action:** Build a Neuron

**Concept Practice:** Neural Communication

**Videos**

Genes and Personality

Behavioral Genetics

**LearningCurve**

**Practice Quiz**

# How Do Neurons Use Electrical Signals to Transmit Information?

**4**

## ◎ CLINICAL FOCUS 4-1

# Epilepsy

J. D. worked as a disc jockey for a radio station and at parties in his off-hours. One evening, he set up on the back of a truck at a rugby field to emcee a jovial and raucous rugby party. Between musical sets, he made introductions, told jokes, and exchanged toasts.

At about 1 A.M., J. D. suddenly collapsed, making unusual jerky motions, then passed out. He was rushed to a hospital emergency room, where he gradually recovered. The attending physician noted that he was not intoxicated, released him to his friends, and recommended that a series of neurological tests be run the next day. Neuroimaging with state-of-the-art brain scans can usually reveal brain abnormalities (Cendes et al., 2016), but it did not do so in J. D.'s case.

The EEG detects electrical signals given off by the brain in various states of consciousness, as explained in Sections 7-2 and 13-3. Section 16-3 details the diagnosis and treatment of epilepsy.

When the electrical activity in J. D.'s brain was recorded while a strobe light was flashed before his eyes, the resulting *electroencephalogram* (EEG) displayed a series of abnormal electrical patterns characteristic of epilepsy. The doctor prescribed Dilantin (diphenylhydantoin), an antiseizure drug, and advised J. D. to refrain from drinking alcohol. He was required to give up his driver's license because he was considered to be at high risk of having a seizure while driving. And he lost his job at the radio station.

After 3 uneventful months, the medication was stopped, and J. D.'s driver's license was restored. J. D. convinced the radio station that he could resume work, and subsequently he has remained seizure free.

Epilepsy is a common neurological disease marked by periods of excessive neural synchrony called **electrographic seizures**. The disease is electrical in nature. The brain is normally electrically active; if this activity becomes abnormal, even infrequently, the consequences, including loss of conscious awareness, can be severe.

Electrographic seizures often follow innocuous stimuli — events that would not typically cause seizures in people who do not have epilepsy. The core concept is that the brain of a person with epilepsy has a chronically low seizure threshold and so is subject to self-generated and recurrent seizures. Approximately half of all cases of epilepsy have been linked to specific neural causes, among them infections, trauma, tumors, structural abnormalities, or genetic mutations in the proteins that make up ion channels (Beghi, 2020). But that leaves the remaining 50% without a clear cause.

If seizures occur repeatedly and cannot be controlled by drug treatment, as occurs in about 30% to 40% of people with epilepsy, other options may include a high-fat/low-carbohydrate ketogenic diet, deep brain stimulation, and surgical resection of the seizure focus (Rho et al., 2010). Removing this small area of brain tissue may also prevent seizures or keep them from spreading to other brain regions.

**electrographic seizures** Abnormal rhythmic neuronal discharges; may be recorded by an electroencephalogram.

Descartes was the first to propose a mechanistic theory of behavior; see Section 1-2.

**FIGURE 4-1 Descartes's Theory of Information Flow**

The most reproduced drawing in behavioral neuroscience is nearly 350 years old, pre-dating our understanding of the electrical basis of epilepsy by centuries. Taken from René Descartes's book *Treatise on Man* (1664) and reproduced in **Figure 4-1**, it represents the first serious attempt to explain how information travels through the nervous system. Descartes proposed that the carrier of information is cerebrospinal fluid flowing through nerve tubes.

Descartes reasoned that when the fire burns the man's toe, it stretches the skin, which tugs on a nerve tube leading to the brain. In response to the tug, a valve in a brain ventricle opens, and cerebral spinal fluid (CSF) flows down the tube, filling the leg muscles and causing them to contract and pull the toe back from the fire. The flow of fluid through other tubes to other muscles of the body (not shown in Figure 4-1) causes the head to turn toward the painful stimulus and the hand to rub the injured toe.

Descartes's theory was incorrect, yet it is remarkable because he isolated the three basic questions that underlie a behavioral response to stimulation:

1. How do our nerves detect a sensory stimulus and inform the brain about it?
2. How does the brain decide what response to make?
3. How does the brain command muscles to move?

Descartes was trying to explain the very same things that scientists have sought to explain in the intervening centuries. Even if it is not triggered by stretched skin tugging on a nerve tube, the message must still be initiated somehow. Even if opening valves does not initiate the flow of CSF to convey information, the information must still be sent. Even if filling the muscles with fluid does not produce movements, the muscles must still contract by some other mechanism.

These mechanisms are the subject of this chapter. We begin by describing the clues and tools that were first used to explain the nervous system's electrical activity. We then explore how electrical activity on the dendrite and cell body increases or decreases the chance of activating the information impulse—the *action potential*. Next, we consider how the action potential is generated at the initial segment (where the axon meets the cell body) and propagated down the axon, as shown in **Figure 4-2**. We wrap up our discussion by examining how neurons convey information from the environment throughout the nervous system and ultimately activate muscles to produce movement.

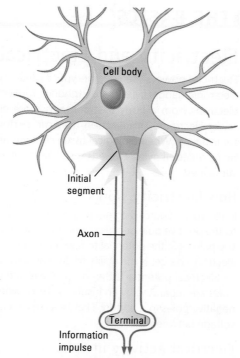

**FIGURE 4-2 The Action Potential** In Section 4-2, we describe how graded potentials (EPSPs and IPSPs) over the dendrite and cell body are spatially and temporally summed together. If their summed voltage at the initial segment surpasses the threshold, an action potential is generated; it then propagates down the length of the axon, as explained in Section 4-3.

## 4-1

# Searching for Electrical Activity in the Nervous System

The first hints about how the nervous system conveys its messages came in the eighteenth century, following the discovery of electricity. Early discoveries about the nature of electricity quickly led to proposals that it plays a role in conducting information in the nervous system. We describe a few milestones that led from this idea to an understanding of how the nervous system really conveys information. If you have a basic understanding of how electricity works and how it is used to stimulate neural tissue, read on. If you prefer to brush up on electricity and electrical stimulation first, turn to The Basics: Electricity and Electrical Stimulation.

## Early Clues That Linked Electricity and Neuronal Activity

In a dramatic demonstration in 1731, Stephen Gray, an amateur scientist, rubbed a rod with a piece of cloth to accumulate electrons on the rod. Then he touched the charged rod to the feet of a boy suspended on a rope and raised a piece of metal foil to the boy's nose. The foil was attracted to the boy's nose, causing it to bend on its approach; as foil and nose touched, electricity passed from the rod through the boy to the foil.

Gray speculated that electricity might be the messenger that spreads information through the nervous system. Two other lines of evidence, drawn from electrical stimulation and electrical recording studies, implicated electrical activity in the nervous system's flow of information.

## Electrical Stimulation Studies

When the Italian scientist Luigi Galvani, a contemporary of Gray, observed that frogs' legs hanging on a wire in a market twitched during a lightning storm, he surmised that sparks of electricity from the storm were activating the leg muscles. Investigating this possibility, he found that if an electrical current is applied to an exposed nerve, the muscle connected to that nerve contracts. While it was unclear how the process worked, Galvani had discovered **electrical stimulation**: passing an electrical current from the uninsulated tip of an electrode onto a nerve to produce behavior—a muscular contraction.

Among the many researchers who used Galvani's technique to produce muscle contraction, two mid-nineteenth-century scientists, Gustav Theodor Fritsch and Eduard Hitzig, demonstrated that electrical stimulation of the neocortex causes movement. They studied several animal species, including rabbits and dogs, and may even have

### Learning Objectives

- Explain how the squid axon, oscilloscope, and microelectrodes led to a breakthrough in our understanding of neuron activity.
- Describe the process by which ions move along concentration and voltage gradients.

Gray's experiment resembles accumulating electrons by combing your hair. Hold a piece of paper near the comb, and the paper bends toward it. Negative charges on the comb push negative charges on the paper to its backside, leaving the front side positively charged. Because opposite charges attract, the paper bends toward the comb.

**electrical stimulation** Passage of an electrical current from the uninsulated tip of an electrode through tissue, resulting in changes in the electrical activity of the tissue.

## ⊙ THE BASICS

# Electricity and Electrical Stimulation

Electricity powers the lights in your home and the batteries that run so many electronic gadgets, from smartphones to electric cars. *Electricity* is the flow of electrons from a body that contains more electrons to a body that contains fewer electrons. This electron flow can perform work—lighting an unlit bulb, for instance. When biological tissue contains an electrical charge, the charge can be recorded; if living tissue is sensitive to an electrical charge, the tissue can be stimulated.

## How Electricity Works

In the Power Source diagram to the right, negatively charged electrons are attracted to the positive pole because opposite charges attract. The electrons on the negative pole have the potential to flow to the positive pole. This *electrical potential*, or electrical charge, is the ability to do work using stored electrical energy.

Electrical potential difference is measured in *volts*. The negative and positive poles are separated by an insulator. Thus, when not connected, the positive and negative poles in a battery, like the poles in each wall socket in your home, hold voltage between the poles.

## Electrical Activity in Cells

If the bare tip of an insulated wire, or *electrode*, from each pole of a battery comes into contact with biological tissue, current will flow from the electrode connected to the negative pole into the tissue and from the tissue into the electrode connected to the positive pole. The stimulation comes from the electrode's uninsulated tip. Microelectrodes can record from or stimulate tissues as small as parts of a single living cell.

Electrical stimulation, illustrated in part A of the Studying Electrical Activity in Animal Tissue diagram, is most effective when administered in brief pulses. A timer in the stimulator turns the current on and off to produce the pulses. During electrical recording, the voltage can be seen on the dial of a voltmeter, a recording device that measures the voltage of a battery or of biological tissue (part B).

**Power Source**

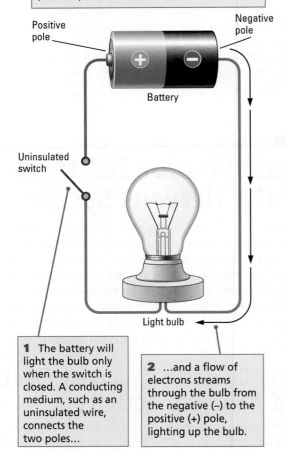

Because electrons carry a negative charge, the negative pole has more electrons than the positive pole.

Positive pole

Negative pole

Battery

Uninsulated switch

Light bulb

**1** The battery will light the bulb only when the switch is closed. A conducting medium, such as an uninsulated wire, connects the two poles…

**2** …and a flow of electrons streams through the bulb from the negative (–) to the positive (+) pole, lighting up the bulb.

---

## Studying Electrical Activity in Animal Tissue

**(A) Electrical stimulation**

Current leaves the stimulator through a wire lead (red) that attaches to an electrode. From the uninsulated tip of the electrode, the current enters the tissue and stimulates it. The current flows back to the stimulator through a second lead (green) connected to a reference electrode.

**1** A stimulating electrode delivers current (electrons) ranging from 2 to 10 milliamps, intensities sufficient to produce a response without damaging cells.

**2** The reference electrode contacts a large surface area that spreads out the current and thus does not excite the tissue here.

Stimulator

Reference electrode

Stimulating electrode

Uninsulated tip

Nerve

Current flow

**(B) Electrical recording**

The difference in voltage between the tip of a recording electrode and a reference electrode deflects a needle that indicates the electric potential difference.

Voltmeter

Reference electrode

Recording electrode

Current flow

stimulated the neocortex of a person whom they were treating for head injuries sustained on a Prussian battlefield. These scientists observed their subjects' arm and leg movements in response to the stimulation of specific parts of the neocortex.

Roberts Bartholow is credited with being the first researcher to describe, in 1874, the effects of human brain stimulation. One of his patients, Mary Rafferty, had a skull defect that exposed part of her neocortex. Bartholow stimulated her exposed brain tissue to examine the effects. In one of his observations, he wrote:

> Passed an insulated needle into the left posterior lobe so that the non-insulated portion rested entirely in the substance of the brain. The reference was placed in contact with the dura mater. When the circuit was closed, muscular contraction in the right upper and lower extremities ensued. Faint but visible contraction of the left eyelid, and dilation of the pupils, also ensued. Mary complained of a very strong and unpleasant feeling of tingling in both right extremities, especially in the right arm, which she seized with the opposite hand and rubbed vigorously. Notwithstanding the very evident pain from which she suffered, she smiled as if much amused. (Bartholow, 1874)

As you might imagine, Bartholow's report was not well received! His publication met with heated criticism on ethical as well as technical grounds. Despite his audacious and unethical experiment, Bartholow demonstrated the basic principles of human cortical mapping (Patra et al., 2019). Importantly, we acknowledge and pay sincere tribute to Mary Rafferty, whose sacrifice should be remembered in medical history.

## Electrical Recording Studies

A less invasive line of evidence indicating that information flow in the brain is partly electrical came from the results of electrical recording experiments. Richard Caton, a physician who lived a century ago, was the first to measure the brain's electrical currents with a sensitive device that measured electric current between two bodies. When he placed electrodes on a human subject's skull, Caton reported fluctuations in his recordings. Today, one type of brain recording of the electric potential differences, called an **electroencephalogram (EEG)**, is a standard tool used for, among other things, monitoring sleep stages and detecting the excessive neural synchrony that characterizes electrographic seizures, as described in Clinical Focus 4-1: Epilepsy.

These pioneering studies provided evidence that neurons send electrical messages, but it would be incorrect to conclude that nerves and tracts carry the same kind of electrical current that powers your car battery or the lights in your home. Hermann von Helmholtz, a nineteenth-century scientist, stimulated a nerve leading to a muscle and measured the time the muscle took to contract. The nerve conducted information at only 30 to 40 meters per second, whereas electricity flows along a wire about a million times faster.

Information flow in the nervous system, then, is much too slow to be a flow of electricity (based on electrons). To explain the electrical signals of a neuron, Julius Bernstein suggested in 1886 that neuronal chemistry (based on ions) produces an electrical potential. He also proposed that the electric potential could change, so it could act as a signal. Bernstein's idea was that the movement of ions constitutes the message conveyed by the neuron.

Moreover, it is not the ions themselves that travel along the axon but rather a *wave* of ionic potential. To understand the difference, consider other kinds of waves. If you drop a stone into a pool of still water, the contact produces a wave that travels away from the site of impact, as shown in **Figure 4-3**. The water itself moves up and down and does not travel away from the impact site. Only the *change in pressure* moves, shifting the height of the water surface and producing the wave effect.

Similarly, when you speak, you induce pressure waves in air, and these waves carry your voice to a listener. If you flick a towel, a wave travels to the other end of the towel. Just as waves through the air send a spoken message, Bernstein's idea was that waves of chemical change travel along an axon to deliver a neuron's message.

**electroencephalogram (EEG)** Graph of electrical activity from the brain, which is mainly composed of graded potentials from many neurons.

By the 1960s, the scientific community had established ethical standards for research on human and nonhuman subjects (see Section 7-8). Today, low-intensity and nondamaging brain stimulation is standard in many neurosurgical procedures (see Section 16-3).

Details on these EEG applications appear in Sections 7-2, 13-3, and 16-3.

**FIGURE 4-3 Wave Effect** Waves formed by dropping stones into still water do not entail the water's forward movement but rather pressure differences that change the height of the water surface.

Franklin Kappa/Getty Images

**FIGURE 4-4 Wave of Information** Neurons can convey information as a wave, induced by stimulation of the cell body, that travels down the axon to its terminal. A voltmeter detects the wave's passage.

**voltmeter** Device that measures the strength of electrical voltage by recording the difference in electrical potential between two points.

1 micrometer (also called a micron) (μm) = one-millionth of a meter, or one-thousandth of a millimeter (mm).

# Tools for Measuring a Neuron's Electrical Activity

Waves that carry messages in the nervous system are minute and are restricted to the surfaces of neurons. Despite these constraints, we can produce these waves using conventional electrical stimulation and measure them using electrical recording techniques to determine how they are produced. When a single axon is stimulated, it produces a wave of excitation. If an electrode connected to a **voltmeter** is placed on a single axon, as illustrated in **Figure 4-4**, the electrode can detect a change in electrical potential on that axon's membrane as the wave passes.

As simple as this process may seem, recording a wave and determining how it is produced requires a neuron large enough to record, a recording device sensitive enough to detect a tiny electrical impulse, and an electrode small enough to be placed on the surface of a single neuron. The fortuitous discovery of the giant axon of the squid, the invention of the oscilloscope, and the development of microelectrodes met all these requirements.

## Giant Axon of the Squid

The neurons of most animals, including humans, are tiny, on the order of 1 to 20 micrometers (μm) in diameter—too small to be seen by the naked eye. The zoologist J. Z. Young, when dissecting the North Atlantic squid *Loligo vulgaris*, noticed that it has giant axons, as large as a millimeter (mm; 1000 μm, or about 1/25 inch) in diameter. **Figure 4-5** illustrates *Loligo* and the giant axons leading to its body wall, or mantle, which contracts to propel the squid through the water.

Measuring only about 1 foot long, *Loligo* is not a giant squid. But its axons are giant, as axons go. Each is formed by the fusion of many smaller axons. Because larger axons send messages faster than smaller axons do, these giant axons allow the squid to quickly jet-propel away from predators.

**(A)**

**(B)**

**FIGURE 4-5 Laboratory Specimen (A)** The North Atlantic squid propels itself both with fins and by contracting its mantle to force water out for propulsion. **(B)** The stellate ganglion projects giant axons to contract the squid's mantle.

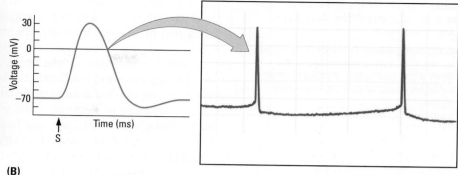

**(A)**

**(B)**

**FIGURE 4-6 Oscilloscope Recording**
**(A)** Basic wave shapes are displayed on a digital oscilloscope, a versatile electronic instrument used to visualize and measure electrical signals as they change. **(B)** On the graph of a trace produced by an oscilloscope, S stands for stimulation. The horizontal axis measures time, and the vertical axis measures voltage. By convention, the axon voltage is represented as negative, in millivolts (mV). On the right, one trace of two action potentials from an individual neuron as displayed on a digital oscilloscope screen.

In 1936, Young suggested to Alan Hodgkin and Andrew Huxley, neuroscientists at Cambridge University in England, that *Loligo*'s axons were large enough to be used for electrical recording studies. They dissected a giant axon out of the squid and kept it alive and functioning in a bath of salty liquid that approximated the squid's body fluids. In this way, Hodgkin and Huxley (1939) determined the neuron's ionically based electrical activity. In 1963, they received the Nobel Prize for their accomplishment.

## Oscilloscope

Hodgkin and Huxley's experiments were made possible by the invention of the **oscilloscope**, a voltmeter with a screen sensitive enough to display the minuscule electrical signals emanating from a nerve or neuron over time (**Figure 4-6**A). As shown in the graph in Figure 4-6B, the units used when recording the electrical charge from a nerve or neuron are millivolts (mV; 1 mV is one-thousandth of a volt) and milliseconds (ms; 1 ms is one-thousandth of a second). Computers interfaced with recording equipment have largely replaced oscilloscopes.

## Microelectrodes

The final device needed to measure a neuron's electrical activity is an electrode small enough to be placed on or in an axon—that is, a **microelectrode**. A microelectrode can deliver electrical current to a single neuron as well as record from it. One way to create a microelectrode is to etch the tip of a piece of thin wire to a fine point, about 1 mm in size, and insulate the rest of the wire with a synthetic polymer, like plastic. The tip is placed on or in the neuron, as shown in the left-hand image in **Figure 4-7**A.

A microelectrode can also be made from a thin glass tube tapered to a very fine tip (Figure 4-7A, right image). The tip of a hollow glass microelectrode can be as small as 1 μm. When the glass tube is filled with salty water, a conducting medium through which electrical current can readily travel, it acts as an electrode. A wire in the salt solution connects the electrode to either a stimulating device or a recording device.

Microelectrodes can record from axons in many ways. The tip of a microelectrode placed on an axon provides an extracellular measure of the electrical current from a tiny part of the axon. The tip of one electrode can be placed on the surface of the axon, and the tip of a second electrode can be inserted into the axon. This technique can be used to measure voltage across the cell membrane.

An even more refined use of a glass microelectrode is to place its tip on the neuron's membrane and apply a little suction until the tip is sealed to a

**oscilloscope** A specialized device that serves as a sensitive voltmeter, registering changes in voltage over time.

**microelectrode** A microscopic insulated wire or a saltwater-filled glass tube whose uninsulated tip is used to stimulate or record from neurons.

**(A)**

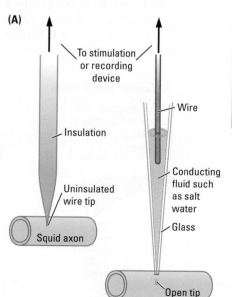

To stimulation or recording device

Wire

Insulation

Uninsulated wire tip

Squid axon

Conducting fluid such as salt water

Glass

Open tip

**(B)**

Microelectrode

Ion channel

Membrane

**FIGURE 4-7 Uses of Microelectrodes**
**(A)** A squid axon is larger than the tip of either a wire (*left*) or a glass (*right*) microelectrode. Both can be placed on an axon or in it. (Drawings are not to scale.) **(B)** A glass microelectrode can record from only a small area of an axon by suctioning the membrane up onto its tip.

**diffusion** Movement of ions from an area of higher concentration to an area of lower concentration through random motion.

**concentration gradient** Difference in the relative abundance of a substance among regions of a container; allows the substance to diffuse from an area of higher concentration to an area of lower concentration.

The Basics, on pages 90–91, covers ions. The Salty Water illustration shows how water molecules dissolve salt crystals.

patch of the membrane, as shown in Figure 4-7B. This technique, which is analogous to placing the end of a soda straw against a piece of plastic wrap and sucking, allows a recording to be made from only the small patch of membrane sealed to the microelectrode tip.

Using the giant axon of the squid, an oscilloscope, and microelectrodes, Hodgkin and Huxley recorded the electrical voltage on an axon's membrane and learned that the *nerve impulse* is a change in the concentration of specific ions across the cell membrane. The basis of electrical activity in nerves is the movement of intracellular and extracellular ions, which carry positive and negative charges across the cell membrane. We discuss the role of electrical activity in cell functioning in the next section. To understand Hodgkin and Huxley's results, though, you first need to understand the principles underlying the movement of ions.

## How Ion Movement Produces Electrical Charges

The intracellular fluid within a neuron and the extracellular fluid surrounding it contain various ions, including $Na^+$ (sodium) and $K^+$ (potassium)—both positively charged, as the plus signs indicate—and negatively charged $Cl^-$ (chloride). These fluids also contain numerous protein molecules, most of which hold an overall negative charge ($A^-$). Positively charged ions are called *cations*, and negatively charged ions, including protein molecules, are called *anions*. Three factors influence the movement of anions and cations into and out of cells: *diffusion*, the *concentration gradient*, and the *voltage gradient*.

Because molecules move constantly, they tend to spread out from a point of high concentration. This spreading out is called **diffusion**. Diffusion requires no additional energy, but rather results from the random motion of molecules as they move and bounce off one another to gradually disperse in a solution. Diffusion results in a dynamic equilibrium, with a relatively equal number of molecules found everywhere in the solution.

Smoke, for example, gradually diffuses through the air in a room until every bit of air contains roughly the same number of smoke molecules. Dye poured into water diffuses in the same way—from its point of contact to every part of the water in the container. Salt placed in water dissolves; the individual ions dissociate and become surrounded by water molecules. The ions and their associated water molecules then diffuse throughout the solution until they reach equilibrium, at which point every part of the container has the same ion concentration.

The **concentration gradient** describes the relative abundance of a substance in a space. Ions are initially highly concentrated where they enter at the top of a beaker of water, as illustrated in **Figure 4-8**, compared to the bottom of the beaker. As time passes, concentration gradients flow down due to diffusion.

**FIGURE 4-8 Moving to Equilibrium**

**(A) Concentration gradient**

**1** Ink dropped into water diffuses from the initial point of contact...

**2** ...until it is equally distributed throughout the water.

Ink

Time

**(B) Voltage gradient**

**3** If a salty solution is poured into water,...

**4** ...the positive and negative ions will flow down their electrostatic gradients until positive and negative charges are everywhere equal.

Salt water

Time

Because ions carry an electrical charge, and because like charges repel one another, ion movement can be described by both a concentration gradient, the difference in the number of ions between two regions, and a **voltage gradient**, the difference in charge between two regions. Ions move down a voltage gradient from an area of higher electric potential to an area of lower electric potential, just as they move down a concentration gradient from an area of higher concentration to an area of lower concentration.

Figure 4-8B illustrates this process. When salt is dissolved in water, the diffusion of its ions can be described either as movement down a concentration gradient (for sodium and chloride ions) or movement down a voltage gradient (for the positive and negative charges). In a container that allows unimpeded movement of ions, the positive and negative charges eventually balance.

A thought experiment will illustrate how a cell membrane influences ion movement. **Figure 4-9**A shows a container of water divided in half by a solid membrane that is impermeable to water and ions. If we place a few grains of table salt (NaCl) in the left half of the container, the salt dissolves. The ions diffuse down their concentration and voltage gradients until the water in the left compartment is in equilibrium.

In the left side of the container, there is no longer a gradient for either sodium or chloride ions because they occur everywhere with the same relative abundance. There are no gradients for these ions on the other side of the container either, because the solid membrane prevents the ions from entering that side. But there are concentration gradients for both sodium and chloride ions *across* the membrane—that is, from the salty side to the freshwater side.

Transmembrane protein molecules embedded in a cell membrane form channels, some with gates, and pumps that allow specific kinds of ions to pass through the membrane. Returning to our thought experiment, we can insert a few chloride channels into the membrane that divides the container of water, making the membrane semipermeable—that is, permeable to chloride but not to sodium, as illustrated at the left in Figure 4-9B. Chloride ions will now diffuse through the channels and cross the membrane by moving down their concentration gradient to the side of the container that previously had no chloride ions, shown in the middle of Figure 4-9B. The sodium ions, in contrast, cannot pass through the chloride channels and remain on one side of the cell membrane.

If the only factor affecting the movement of chloride ions were the chloride concentration gradient, the efflux (outflow) of chloride from the salty side to the freshwater side of the container would continue until chloride ions were in equilibrium on both sides. But this is not what happens. Remember that opposite charges attract—so the chloride ions, which carry a negative charge, are attracted to the positively charged sodium ions they left behind. Because they are pulled back toward the sodium ions, the chloride ions cannot diffuse completely. Consequently, the concentration of chloride ions remains somewhat higher in the left side of the container than in the right, as illustrated at the right in Figure 4-9B.

**voltage gradient** Difference in electric potential between two regions that allows a flow of current if the two regions are connected.

The cell membrane is an insulator that is impermeable to salty solutions: dissolved ions, surrounded by water molecules, do not pass through the membrane's hydrophobic tails (review Figure 3-11).

Even though dissolved sodium ions are smaller than chloride ions, they hold water molecules more strongly. As a result, they act as if they are bulkier and cannot pass through a narrow chloride channel.

**(A) Impermeable membrane**  **(B) Semipermeable membrane**  **FIGURE 4-9 Modeling the Cell Membrane**

**1** Salt placed in one side of a beaker of water that is divided by a barrier dissolves.

**2** Positive and negative ions distribute themselves evenly throughout half of the container but cannot cross the barrier.

**3** If the barrier has a channel through which Cl⁻ can pass but Na⁺ cannot, Cl⁻ will diffuse from the side of high concentration through the hole in the barrier.

**4** Cl⁻ will not be equally distributed on the two sides, because of the voltage gradient pulling them back toward the positive sodium ions.

**5** At equilibrium, one half of the container will be positively charged,...

**6** ...the other half will be negatively charged, and the voltage difference will be greatest close to the membrane.

Salt (NaCl)

Cell membrane

Time   Time   Time

In other words, the efflux of chloride ions down the chloride concentration gradient is counteracted by the influx (inflow) of chloride ions up the chloride voltage gradient. In this situation, the chemical driving force and the electrical driving force are in opposition. At some point, an equilibrium is reached: the force pushing chloride ions to the right of the beaker by diffusion is balanced by the electric force (the attraction between negative and positive) pulling chloride ions to the left. In brief:

$$\text{concentration gradient} = \text{voltage gradient}$$

The balance of the movement of ions across a membrane is referred to as *equilibrium potential*, a concept to which we will return in the next section.

In this equilibrium, the different concentrations of the chloride ions on the two sides of the membrane produce a difference in electric potential—that is, a voltage difference. The left side of the container is more positively charged because some chloride ions have migrated out of this side, leaving a preponderance of positively charged ($Na^+$) ions. The right side of the container is more negatively charged because some chloride ions have entered that chamber, where none were before. The voltage difference is highest on the surface of the semipermeable membrane, the area at which positive and negative ions accumulate. Much the same process happens at the semipermeable membranes of cells.

## 4-1 Review

Before you continue, check your understanding. Answers to Self-Tests appear at the back of the book.

1. Based on his experiments with charged rods, Stephen Gray speculated that _____ might be the messenger that sends information through the nervous system.

2. Experimental results obtained over hundreds of years from electrical _____ and more recently from electrical _____ implicated electrical activity in the nervous system's flow of information.

3. The electrical activity of neuronal axons entails the diffusion of ions. Ions may move down a(n) _____ and down a(n) _____.

4. What three technical problems did scientists in the mid-twentieth century resolve that allowed them to measure the changes in electrical potential that travel like a wave along an axon's membrane?

5. In what three ways does the semipermeable cell membrane affect the movement of ions in the nervous system?

## 4-2

# Electrical Activity at the Dendritic and Cell Body Membrane

**Learning Objectives**

- Explain the mechanisms in the semipermeable cell membrane that allow the neuron to maintain its resting potential.
- Describe how the ion flow produces fluctuations in polarity across the cell membrane.
- Explain temporal and spatial summation of inhibitory and excitatory inputs.

A neuron typically receives input on its dendrite and cell body. In this section, we will consider changes in ionic flow across these membranes, but will refer to them simply as the membrane. Most biological membranes are semipermeable because they have ion channels embedded within them. Electrical activity in neurons is the movement of specific ions through channels *across* neuronal membranes. It is this process that allows the waves of electrical activity moving *along* membranes to convey information throughout the nervous system. So how are changes in the movement of ions across neuronal membranes achieved?

## Resting Potential

**Figure 4-10** shows how the voltage difference is recorded when one microelectrode is placed on the outer surface of an axon's membrane and another is placed on its inner surface. In the absence of stimulation, this difference is about 70 mV. Although the

...while another records the inner surface.

Axon

One electrode records the outer surface of an axon...

By convention, the extracellular side of the membrane is given a charge of 0 mV;...

...therefore the intracellular side of the membrane is –70 mV relative to the extracellular side. This measurement is the membrane's resting potential.

**FIGURE 4-10 Resting Potential** The electrical potential across a resting cell membrane stores potential energy.

charge on the outside of the membrane is actually positive, by convention it is given a charge of zero. Therefore, the inside of the membrane at rest is –70 mV *relative to* the extracellular side.

If we were to continue to record for a long time, the charge across the unstimulated membrane would remain much the same. The charge can change, given certain changes in the membrane, but at rest the difference in charge on the inside and outside of the membrane produces an electrical *potential*—the ability to use its stored power, analogous to a charged battery. The charge is thus a store of potential energy called the membrane's **resting potential**.

We might use the term *potential* in the same way to talk about the financial potential of someone who has money in the bank: the person can spend the money at some future time. The resting potential, then, is a store of energy that can be used later. Most of your body's cells have a resting potential, but it is not identical on every axon. Resting potentials vary from –40 to –90 mV, depending on neuronal type and animal species.

Four charged particles take part in producing the resting potential: ions of sodium ($Na^+$), potassium ($K^+$), chloride ($Cl^-$), and large negatively charged protein molecules ($A^-$). Recall from Section 4-1 that the positively charged ions are cations, and the negatively charged ions are anions. As **Figure 4-11** shows, these charged particles are distributed unequally across the axon's membrane, with more protein anions and potassium ions found in the intracellular fluid and more sodium and chloride ions present in the extracellular fluid. How do these unequal concentrations arise, and how does each contribute to the resting potential?

# Maintaining the Resting Potential

The cell membrane's channels, gates, and pumps collectively maintain the resting potential. **Figure 4-12**, which shows the resting membrane close up, details how these three features contribute to the cell membrane's resting charge:

1. Because the membrane is relatively impermeable to large molecules, the negatively charged proteins ($A^-$) remain inside the cell.

2. Ungated potassium channels, also known as *leak channels*, allow potassium ions ($K^+$) to pass through the membrane more freely. Ungated chloride channels also allow chloride ions ($Cl^-$) to pass, but gates on sodium channels keep out positively charged sodium ions ($Na^+$).

3. $Na^+$–$K^+$ pumps eject $Na^+$ from the intracellular fluid and draw in $K^+$.

## Inside the Cell

Large protein anions are manufactured inside cells. No membrane channels are large enough to allow these proteins to leave the cell, and their average negative charge alone is sufficient to produce transmembrane voltage, or a

$A^-$ ions and $K^+$ ions have higher concentration inside the axon relative to the outside,...

...whereas $Cl^-$ ions and $Na^+$ ions are more concentrated outside the axon.

Axon

$A^-$    $K^+$    $Na^+$    $Cl^-$

Intracellular

Extracellular

**FIGURE 4-11 Ion Distribution Across the Resting Membrane** The number of ions distributed across the resting cell membrane is unequal. Protein anions are represented by the label $A^-$.

Why zero? We are interested in the *relative difference*, not the actual charge.

Use this mnemonic to remember which ions are on which side: we put table salt—sodium chloride—on the outside of our food.

**resting potential** Electrical charge across the insulating cell membrane in the absence of stimulation; a store of potential energy produced by a greater negative charge on the intracellular side relative to the extracellular side.

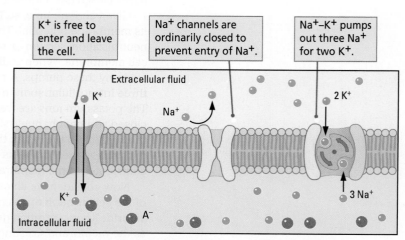

$K^+$ is free to enter and leave the cell.

$Na^+$ channels are ordinarily closed to prevent entry of $Na^+$.

$Na^+$–$K^+$ pumps out three $Na^+$ for two $K^+$.

Extracellular fluid

$K^+$    $Na^+$    $2 K^+$

$K^+$    $A^-$    $3 Na^+$

Intracellular fluid

**FIGURE 4-12 Maintaining the Resting Potential** Channels, gates, and pumps in the cell membrane contribute to the transmembrane charge.

resting potential. Because most cells in the body manufacture these large, negatively charged protein molecules, most cells have a charge across the cell membrane.

To balance the negative charge produced by large protein anions in the intracellular fluid, cells accumulate positively charged potassium ions to the extent that about 20 times as many potassium ions cluster inside the cell as outside it. Potassium ions cross the cell membrane through open potassium (or leak) channels, as shown in Figure 4-12. Given the high concentration of potassium ions inside the cell, however, the potassium concentration gradient across the membrane limits the number of potassium ions entering the cell. In other words, not all the potassium ions that could enter actually do enter. Because the internal concentration of potassium ions is much higher than the external potassium concentration, potassium ions are drawn out of the cell by the potassium concentration gradient.

A few residual potassium ions on the outside of the membrane are enough to contribute to the charge across the membrane. They add to the net negative charge on the intracellular side of the membrane relative to the extracellular side. You may be wondering whether you read the last sentence correctly. If there are 20 times as many potassium ions inside the cell as there are outside, why should the inside of the membrane have a negative charge? Shouldn't all those potassium ions in the intracellular fluid give the inside of the cell a positive charge instead? No, because not quite enough potassium ions are able to enter the cell to balance the negative charge of the protein anions.

Think of it this way: if the number of potassium ions that could accumulate on the intracellular side of the membrane were unrestricted, the positively charged potassium ions inside would exactly match the negative charges on the intracellular protein anions. There would be no charge across the membrane at all. But the number of potassium ions that accumulate inside the cell is limited because when the intracellular $K^+$ concentration becomes higher than the extracellular concentration, further potassium ion influx is opposed by its concentration gradient.

## Outside the Cell

The equilibrium of the potassium voltage and concentration gradients results in some potassium ions remaining outside the cell. Only a few positively charged potassium ions are needed outside the cell to maintain a negative charge inside the cell. As a result, potassium ions contribute to the charge across the membrane.

Sodium ($Na^+$) and chloride ($Cl^-$) ions also take part in producing the resting potential. If positively charged sodium ions were free to move across the membrane, they would diffuse into the cell and eliminate the transmembrane charge produced by the unequal distribution of potassium ions inside and outside the cell. This diffusion does not happen because a gate on the sodium ion channels in the cell membrane is ordinarily closed (see Figure 4-12, middle), blocking the entry of most sodium ions.

Given enough time, sufficient sodium ions could gain entry into the cell to neutralize its membrane potential. The cell membrane, however, has a mechanism to prevent this neutralization: *sodium–potassium pumps*, which are protein molecules embedded in the cell membrane. When sodium ions enter the neuron, they are immediately escorted out again by these pumps. A membrane's many thousands of pumps continually exchange three intracellular sodium ions for two potassium ions, as shown in Figure 4-12, right. The potassium ions are free to leave the cell through open potassium channels, but the closed sodium channels slow the reentry of the sodium ions. In this way, sodium ions are kept out to the extent that about 10 times as many sodium ions reside on the outside of the axon membrane as on its inside. This difference in sodium concentrations also contributes to the membrane's resting potential.

Now consider the chloride ions. Unlike sodium ions, chloride ions move in and out of the cell through open channels in the membrane. The equilibrium point, at which the chloride's concentration gradient equals its voltage gradient, is approximately the same as the membrane's resting potential, so chloride ions ordinarily contribute little to the resting potential. At this equilibrium point, there are about 12 times as many chloride ions outside the cell as inside it.

The cell membrane's semipermeability and the actions of its channels, gates, and pumps thus produce voltage across the cell membrane: its resting potential (**Figure 4-13**). The resting potential of the membrane is achieved by a balance of $Na^+$, $K^+$, $Cl^-$, and $A^-$ proteins that do not cross the cell membrane. Each of these ionic species has a differential distribution across the member and its own **equilibrium (reversal) potential** (see **Table 4-1**). The equilibrium potential of each ionic species is calculated using the **Nernst equation**, which takes into consideration the charge of the ion and its concentration gradient.

Notice that $Na^+$ and $Cl^-$ have opposing charges and are found on the outside of the cellular membrane in roughly the same proportion; thus, the overall charge from the combination of these ions is near zero. A formal presentation of the Nernst equation is beyond the scope of this text, but for our purposes, it is important to understand that a cell membrane's resting potential is closest to the equilibrium potential of $Cl^-$.

Unequal distribution of different ions causes the inside of the axon to be relatively negatively charged.

**FIGURE 4-13 Resting Transmembrane Charge**

# Graded Potentials

The resting potential provides an energy store that can be used somewhat like the water in a dam: small amounts can be released by opening gates for irrigation or to generate electricity. If the concentration of any of the ions across the unstimulated cell membrane changes, the membrane voltage changes. These small voltage fluctuations across the cell membrane are known as **graded potentials**.

Stimulating a membrane electrically through a microelectrode mimics the way the membrane's voltage changes to produce a graded potential in the living cell. If the voltage applied to the inside of the membrane is negative, the membrane potential increases in negative charge by a few millivolts. As illustrated in **Figure 4-14**A, it may change from a resting potential of −70 mV to a slightly greater potential of −73 mV.

This change is a **hyperpolarization** because the charge (polarity) of the membrane increases. Conversely, if positive voltage is applied inside the membrane, its potential decreases by a few millivolts. As illustrated in Figure 4-14B, it may change from, say, a resting potential of −70 mV to a slightly lower potential of −65 mV. This change is a **depolarization** because the membrane charge decreases. Graded potentials usually last only a few milliseconds.

Hyperpolarization and depolarization typically take place on neuronal dendrites and the soma (cell body) membrane. These areas contain gated channels that can open and close, thereby changing the membrane potential, as illustrated in Figure 4-14. Three channels—for potassium, chloride, and sodium ions—underlie graded potentials:

1. *Potassium ($K^+$) channels.* For the membrane to become hyperpolarized, its extracellular side must become more positive, which can be accomplished with an outward movement, or efflux, of potassium ions. But if potassium channels are ordinarily open, how can the efflux of potassium ions increase? Apparently, even though potassium channels are open, some resistance to the outward flow of potassium ions remains. Reducing this resistance enables hyperpolarization.

2. *Chloride ($Cl^-$) channels.* Even though chloride ions can pass through the membrane, more ions remain on the outside than on the inside, so an influx of chloride ions due to decreased resistance to $Cl^-$ flow can result in brief increases of $Cl^-$ inside the cell. Because the Nernst potential for $Cl^-$ is 64 mV and near the resting membrane potential, increased $Cl^-$ conductance has the effect of *stabilizing* (or "clamping") the membrane voltage, effectively preventing large depolarizations.

3. *Sodium ($Na^+$) channels.* Depolarization can be produced if normally closed sodium channel gates open to allow an influx of sodium ions.

Evidence that potassium channels have a role in hyperpolarization comes from the fact that the chemical tetraethylammonium (TEA), which blocks potassium channels, also blocks hyperpolarization. The involvement of sodium channels in depolarization is indicated by the fact that the chemical tetrodotoxin (TTX), which blocks sodium

**TABLE 4-1 Nernst Potentials for Each Ion**

| Ionic species | Intra-cellular concen-tration | Extra-cellular concen-tration | Equilib-rium potential |
|---|---|---|---|
| Sodium ($Na^+$) | 15 mM | 145 mM | +60.6 mV |
| Potassium ($K^+$) | 150 mM | 4 mM | −96.8 mV |
| Chloride ($Cl^-$) | 10 mM | 110 mM | −64.0 mV |

mM = millimolar (*milli-* is one thousandth); these units refer to the concentration of a chemical (ion, in this case) per unit volume of solution (in liters, L).

**equilibrium (reversal) potential** The membrane potential for an individual ion, at which there is no net (overall) flow of that particular ion from one side of the membrane to the other.

**Nernst equation** Calculates the equilibrium potential (also referred to as the *Nernst potential*) for an ion based on the charge on the ion (i.e., its valence) and its concentration gradient across the membrane.

**graded potential** A small voltage fluctuation across the cell membrane.

**hyperpolarization** Increase in electrical charge across a membrane, usually due to the inward flow of chloride ions or the outward flow of potassium ions.

**depolarization** Decrease in electrical charge across a membrane, usually due to the inward flow of sodium ions.

**FIGURE 4-14 Graded Potentials**
**(A)** Stimulation (S) that increases the relative membrane voltage produces a hyperpolarizing graded potential. **(B)** Stimulation that decreases the relative membrane voltage produces a depolarizing graded potential.

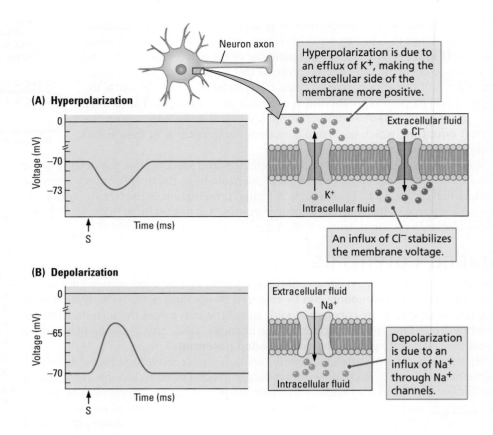

Neuron axon

**(A) Hyperpolarization**

Hyperpolarization is due to an efflux of $K^+$, making the extracellular side of the membrane more positive.

Extracellular fluid
$Cl^-$

$K^+$
Intracellular fluid

An influx of $Cl^-$ stabilizes the membrane voltage.

**(B) Depolarization**

Extracellular fluid
$Na^+$

Intracellular fluid

Depolarization is due to an influx of $Na^+$ through $Na^+$ channels.

The Photo Library - Sidney/Science Source

Puffer Fish

Table 6-2 lists a variety of neurotoxins and their sources and summarizes some of their effects.

channels, also blocks depolarization. The puffer fish, considered a delicacy in some countries, especially Japan, secretes TTX—a potentially deadly poison—to fend off would-be predators. Skill is required to prepare this fish for human consumption. It can be lethal to the guests of careless cooks because its toxin impedes the electrical activity of neurons.

# How Neurons Integrate Information

A neuron's extensive dendritic tree is covered with spines, and through them the neuron can establish more than 50,000 connections from other neurons. A neuron's body, which sits between its dendritic tree and axon, can also receive multiple connections. Nerve impulses traveling from other neurons to each of these synaptic locations bombard the receiving neuron with *excitatory inputs*, or depolarizations, and *inhibitory inputs*, or hyperpolarizations.

In the 1950s and 1960s, John C. Eccles (1965) and his students performed experiments that helped answer the question of how the neuron integrates such an enormous array of inputs into a nerve impulse. Rather than record from the giant axon of a squid, Eccles recorded from the cell bodies of large motor neurons in the vertebrate spinal cord. In doing so, he refined the electrical stimulating and recording techniques first developed for studying squid axons (see Section 4-1). Eccles received the Nobel Prize in Physiology or Medicine for his work.

Motor neurons, for example, receive input from multiple sources. A spinal cord motor neuron has an extensive dendritic tree with as many as 20 main branches that subdivide numerous times and are covered with dendritic spines. Input from the skin, joints, muscles, spinal cord, and brain make motor cells ideal for studying how a neuron responds to diverse inputs. Each motor neuron sends its axon directly to a muscle. The motor neuron is the final common pathway the nervous system uses to produce behavior.

# Excitatory and Inhibitory Postsynaptic Potentials

To study motor neuron activity, Eccles inserted a microelectrode into a vertebrate's spinal cord until the tip was in or right beside a motor neuron's cell body. He then placed stimulating electrodes on sensory nerve fiber axons entering the spinal cord. By teasing apart the many incoming sensory fibers, he was able to stimulate one nerve fiber at a time.

**Experiment 4-1** diagrams the experimental setup Eccles used. As shown at the left in the Procedures section, stimulating some incoming sensory fibers produced a depolarizing graded potential (reduced the charge) on the membrane of the motor neuron to which these fibers were connected. Eccles called these graded potentials **excitatory postsynaptic potentials (EPSPs)**. As shown in the graph on the left side of the Results section, EPSPs reduce (depolarize) the charge on the membrane. As we will explore in depth in Section 4-3, depolarizing the membrane moves the voltage on the membrane toward the threshold level for triggering an *action potential*.

**excitatory postsynaptic potential (EPSP)** Brief depolarization of a neuron membrane in response to stimulation, making the neuron more likely to produce an action potential.

Figure 2-31A diagrams the human spinal cord in cross section.

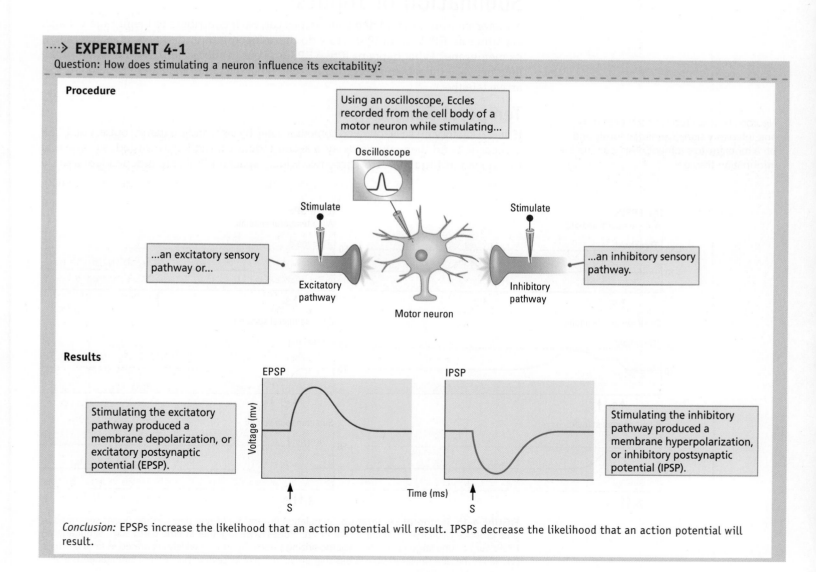

**····> EXPERIMENT 4-1**

Question: How does stimulating a neuron influence its excitability?

**Procedure**

Using an oscilloscope, Eccles recorded from the cell body of a motor neuron while stimulating...

Oscilloscope

Stimulate

Stimulate

...an excitatory sensory pathway or...

...an inhibitory sensory pathway.

Excitatory pathway

Inhibitory pathway

Motor neuron

**Results**

Stimulating the excitatory pathway produced a membrane depolarization, or excitatory postsynaptic potential (EPSP).

EPSP

IPSP

Stimulating the inhibitory pathway produced a membrane hyperpolarization, or inhibitory postsynaptic potential (IPSP).

Voltage (mv)

Time (ms)

S

S

*Conclusion:* EPSPs increase the likelihood that an action potential will result. IPSPs decrease the likelihood that an action potential will result.

**inhibitory postsynaptic potential (IPSP)** Brief hyperpolarization of a neuron membrane in response to stimulation, making the neuron less likely to produce an action potential.

**initial segment** Area near where the axon meets the cell body, which is rich in voltage-gated channels; these channels generate the action potential.

You can find several videos online that describe how the initial segment initiates an action potential.

Neurons typically receive both excitatory and inhibitory signals simultaneously and, on a moment-to-moment basis, sum up the information they get.

When Eccles stimulated other incoming sensory fibers, as graphed at the right of the Procedures section, he produced a hyperpolarizing graded potential (increased the charge) on the receiving motor neuron membrane. Eccles called these graded potentials **inhibitory postsynaptic potentials (IPSPs)**. As shown in the graph at the right in the Results section, IPSPs increase the negative charge on the membrane away from the threshold level and decrease the likelihood that an action potential will result.

Both EPSPs and IPSPs last only a few milliseconds before they decay and the neuron's resting potential is restored. EPSPs are associated with the opening of sodium channels, which allows an influx of sodium ions. IPSPs are typically associated with the opening of chloride channels, which allows an influx of chloride ions. They can also occur with the opening of potassium channels, which allows an efflux of potassium ions.

Although the size of a graded potential is proportional to the intensity of stimulation, an action potential is not produced on the motor neuron's cell body membrane even when an EPSP is strongly excitatory. The reason is simple: the cell body membrane of most neurons does not contain voltage-activated channels. The stimulation must reach the **initial segment**, which is found near or overlapping the axon hillock—an area rich in voltage-gated channels—for the action potential to begin (Bender & Trussel, 2012). We will return to this process in our discussion of the action potential in Section 4-3.

## Summation of Inputs

A motor neuron's myriad dendritic spines can each contribute to membrane voltage, via either an EPSP or an IPSP. How do these incoming graded potentials interact at its membrane? What happens if two EPSPs occur in succession? Does it matter if the time between them increases or decreases? What happens when an EPSP and an IPSP arrive together?

### Temporal Summation

If one excitatory pulse is followed sometime later by a second excitatory pulse, one EPSP is recorded and then, after a delay, a second identical EPSP is recorded, as shown at the top left in **Figure 4-15**. These two widely spaced EPSPs are independent and do

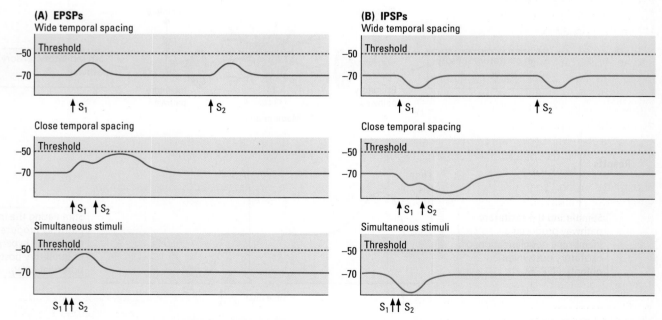

**FIGURE 4-15 Temporal Summation** Stimulation ($S_1$ and $S_2$) of two depolarizing pulses separated in time produce two EPSPs that are similar in size. Pulses close together in time partly sum. Simultaneous EPSPs sum as one large EPSP. Two hyperpolarizing pulses ($S_1$ and $S_2$) widely separated in time produce two IPSPs that are similar in size. Pulses that arrive in rapid succession partly sum. Simultaneous IPSPs sum as one large IPSP.

not interact. If the delay between them is shortened so that the two occur in rapid succession, however, a single large EPSP is produced, as shown in the left-center panel of Figure 4-15.

In this case, the two excitatory pulses at the same location are summed—added together to produce a larger depolarization of the membrane than either would induce alone. This relationship between two EPSPs occurring close together or even at the same time (bottom-left panel) is called **temporal summation**. The right side of Figure 4-15 illustrates that equivalent results are obtained with IPSPs. Therefore, temporal summation is a property of both EPSPs and IPSPs.

## Spatial Summation

How does physical spacing affect inputs to the cell body membrane? By using a recording electrode ($R_1$), we can see the effects of spatial relations on the summation of inputs.

If two EPSPs are evoked at the same time but on widely separated parts of the membrane (**Figure 4-16**A), they do not influence each other. If two EPSPs occurring close together in time are also close together on the membrane, however, they sum to form a larger EPSP (Figure 4-16B). This **spatial summation** occurs when two separate inputs are very close to each other both on the cell membrane and in time. Similarly, two IPSPs produced at the same time sum if they occur at approximately the same place and time on the cell body membrane, but not if they are widely separated.

## Role of Ions in Summation

Summation is a property of both EPSPs and IPSPs in any combination. These interactions make sense when you consider that ion influx and efflux are being summed. The influx of sodium ions accompanying one EPSP is added to the influx of sodium ions accompanying a second EPSP if the two occur close together in time and space. If the two influxes are remote in time or in space or in both, no summation is possible.

The same is true regarding influxes of chloride ions or effluxes of potassium ions. When they occur close together in time and space, they sum; when they are far apart in either or both ways, there is no summation. The patterns are identical for an EPSP and an IPSP. The influx of sodium ions associated with the EPSP is added to the influx of chloride ions or the efflux of potassium ions associated with the IPSP, and the difference between them is recorded as long as they are spatially and temporally close together. Conversely, if they are widely separated in time or in space, or in both, they do not interact and there is no summation.

A neuron with thousands of inputs responds no differently from one with only a few inputs; it sums all inputs that are close together in time and space. The cell body membrane, therefore, always indicates the summed influences of multiple temporal and spatial inputs. Therefore, a neuron can be said to analyze its inputs before deciding what to do. The ultimate decision is made at the initial segment, the region on the axon that initiates the action potential.

**(A)**

EPSPs produced at the same time, but on separate parts of the membrane, do not influence each other.

**(B)**

EPSPs produced at the same time, and close together, sum to form a larger EPSP.

**FIGURE 4-16 Spatial Summation** The process for IPSPs is equivalent to the process for EPSPs.

## 4-2 Review

Before you continue, check your understanding. Answers to Self-Tests appear at the back of the book.

1. The _____ results from the unequal distribution of _____ inside and outside the cell membrane.

2. Because it is _____, the cell membrane prevents the efflux of large protein anions and pumps sodium ions out of the cell to maintain a slightly _____ charge in the intracellular fluid relative to the extracellular fluid.

**temporal summation** Addition of graded potentials to each other, when the potentials occur close in time.

**spatial summation** Addition of graded potentials to each other, when the potentials occur close in space.

3. For a graded potential to arise, a membrane must be stimulated to the point that the transmembrane charge increases slightly to cause _____ or decreases slightly to cause _____.

4. Graded potentials that depolarize the cell membrane are called _____ because they increase the likelihood that an action potential will occur. Graded potentials that hyperpolarize the cell membrane are called _____ because they decrease the likelihood that an action potential will result.

5. Briefly explain spatial and temporal summation on the cell body membrane.

4-3

# Generation and Propagation of the Action Potential

Electrical stimulation of the cell membrane at resting potential produces local graded potentials (EPSPs and IPSPs). An **action potential**, in contrast, is a brief but very large reversal in an axon membrane's polarity (**Figure 4-17**A) that lasts about 1 ms. The voltage across the membrane suddenly reverses, making the intracellular side positive relative to the extracellular side, and then abruptly reverses again to restore the resting potential. Because the action potential is brief, hundreds of action potentials can occur within a second, as illustrated in Figures 4-17B and C, where the time scales are compressed.

## Triggering an Action Potential

An action potential occurs when a large concentration of first $Na^+$ and then $K^+$ crosses the membrane rapidly. The depolarizing phase of the action potential is due to $Na^+$ influx, and the hyperpolarizing phase is due to $K^+$ efflux. Sodium rushes in and then potassium rushes out. As shown in **Figure 4-18**, the *combined* flow of sodium and potassium ions underlies the action potential.

An action potential is triggered when the cell membrane is depolarized to about –50 mV. At this **threshold potential**, the membrane charge undergoes a remarkable change with no additional stimulation. The relative voltage of the membrane drops to zero and continues to depolarize toward the Nernst potential for sodium, until the charge on the inside of the membrane is as great as +30 mV—a total voltage change of 100 mV. At that point, the membrane potential reverses again, toward the Nernst potential for potassium, becoming slightly hyperpolarized—a reversal of a little more than 100 mV. After this second reversal, the membrane slowly returns to its resting potential at –70 mV.

## Learning Objectives

- Describe how a change in voltage across the initial segment of the membrane can trigger an action potential.
- Detail the phases of an action potential.
- Explain the role that the myelin sheath plays in the propagation of a nerve impulse.

**action potential**  Large, brief reversal in the polarity of an axon membrane.

**threshold potential**  Voltage of a neural membrane at which an action potential is triggered by the opening of sodium and potassium voltage-activated channels; about –50 mV relative to the extracellular surroundings. Also called *threshold limit*.

**FIGURE 4-17 Measuring Action Potentials (A)** Phases of a single action potential. The time scales on the horizontal axes are compressed to chart **(B)** each action potential as a discrete event, **(C)** the ability of a membrane to produce many action potentials in a short time, and **(D)** the series of action potentials over the course of 1 second (1000 ms).

FIGURE 4-18 **Triggering an Action Potential**

FIGURE 4-19 **Blocking an Action Potential**

FIGURE 4-20 **Voltage-Activated Potassium Channel**

The action potential normally consists of the summed current changes caused first by the inflow of sodium and then by the outflow of potassium on an axon. Experimental results have revealed that if an axon membrane is stimulated electrically while the solution surrounding the axon contains the chemical TEA (to block potassium channels), the result is a smaller-than-normal ion flow due entirely to an $Na^+$ influx. Similarly, if an axon's membrane is stimulated electrically while the solution surrounding the axon contains TTX (to block sodium channels), a slightly different ion flow, due entirely to the efflux of $K^+$, is recorded. **Figure 4-19** illustrates these experimental results, in which the graphs represent voltage change.

# Role of Voltage-Activated Ion Channels

What cellular mechanisms underlie the movement of sodium and potassium ions to produce an action potential? The answer reflects the behavior of a class of gated sodium and potassium channels that are sensitive to the membrane's voltage (**Figure 4-20**). These **voltage-activated channels** are closed when an axon's membrane is at its resting potential: ions cannot pass through them. When the membrane reaches the threshold voltage, however, the configuration of the voltage-activated channels changes: they open briefly, enabling ions to pass through, then close again to restrict ion flow. These channels, like those on the squid axon, open at a particular membrane voltage. The

**voltage-activated channel** Gated protein channel that opens or closes only at specific membrane voltages.

actual threshold voltage varies with the type of neuron, but to keep things simple, we will stick with a threshold level of –50 mV. The sequence of actions is as follows:

1. Both sodium and potassium voltage-activated channels are attuned to the threshold voltage of about –50 mV. If the cell membrane changes to reach this voltage, both types of channels open to allow ion flow across the membrane.

2. The voltage-activated sodium channels respond more quickly than the potassium channels do. As a result, the voltage change due to $Na^+$ influx takes place slightly before the voltage change due to $K^+$ efflux begins.

3. Sodium channels have two gates. Once the membrane depolarizes to about +30 mV, the second gate closes, inactivating the channel and preventing the flow of $Na^+$. Thus, $Na^+$ influx begins quickly and ends quickly.

4. The potassium channels open more slowly than the sodium channels, and they remain open longer. Thus, the efflux of $K^+$ reverses the depolarization produced by $Na^+$ influx and even hyperpolarizes the membrane.

## Voltage-Activated Channels and the Action Potential

Unlike the cell body membrane, the axon is rich in voltage-activated channels, beginning at the initial segment (**Figure 4-21**). To produce an action potential, the summed graded potentials—the IPSPs and EPSPs—on the cell body membrane must depolarize the membrane at the initial segment to –50 mV. If that threshold voltage is attained only briefly, voltage-activated channels open, and just one or a few action potentials may occur. If the threshold level is maintained for a longer period, however, action potentials will follow one another in rapid succession, just as quickly as the gates on the voltage-activated channels can reset. Each action potential is then propagated from the initial segment down the length of the axon.

Many neurons have extensive dendritic trees, but dendrites and dendritic branches do not have many voltage-activated channels and ordinarily do not produce action potentials. In addition, distant branches of dendrites may have less influence in producing action potentials initiated at the initial segment than do the more proximal branches of the dendrites. Consequently, inputs close to the initial segment are usually much more influential than those occurring some distance away, and those close to the initial segment are usually inhibitory, creating IPSPs. As in all governments, some inputs have more say than others (Höfflin et al., 2017).

## The Versatile Neuron

The preceding discussion described how dendrites collect information as graded potentials (EPSPs and IPSPs), and how the initial segment initiates discrete action potentials that are delivered to other target cells via the axon. However, some notable exceptions to this picture of how a neuron works exist. For example, some cells in the developing hippocampus can produce additional action potentials, called *giant depolarizing potentials*, when the cell would ordinarily be refractory. It is thought that giant depolarizing potentials aid in developing the brain's neural circuitry (Khalilov et al., 2015).

Because voltage-activated channels are located on the axon membrane and not the cell body membrane, a typical neuron does not initiate action potentials on its dendrites. In some neurons, however, voltage-activated channels on dendrites do enable action potentials. The reverse movement of an action potential from the initial segment into the dendritic field of a neuron is called **back propagation**. Back propagation, which signals to the dendritic field that the neuron is sending an action potential over its axon, may play a role in the plastic changes in the neuron that underlie learning. For example, back propagation may make the dendritic field refractory to incoming inputs, set the dendritic field to an electrically neutral baseline, or reinforce signals coming into certain dendrites (Schiess et al., 2016).

The neurons of some nonmammalian species have no dendritic branches. Also, some ion channels, rather than responding to voltage, respond to light by opening and

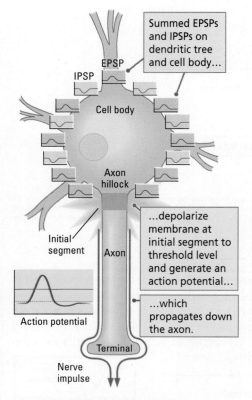

**FIGURE 4-21 How Summed Graded Potentials Trigger an Action Potential** If the summated graded potentials—the EPSPs and IPSPs—on the dendritic tree and cell body of a neuron charge the membrane to the threshold level at the initial segment, an action potential is initiated. This action potential then travels down the axon membrane.

**Principle 10:** Neuroplasticity is the hallmark of nervous system functioning.

We explore the neuronal basis of learning in Section 14-4.

**back propagation** Reverse movement of an action potential into the soma and dendritic field of a neuron; postulated to play a role in the plastic changes that underlie learning.

allowing ions to pass. The many differences among neurons suggest that the nervous system capitalizes on structural and functional modifications to produce adaptive behavior in each species. In research to determine the neuron's specific functions, neuroscientists have incorporated into certain types of neurons ion channels that respond to light, as described in Research Focus 4-2: Optogenetics and Light-Sensitive Ion Channels.

# Action Potentials and Refractory Periods

There is an upper limit to how frequently action potentials occur, and sodium and potassium channels are responsible for enforcing it. Stimulation of the membrane at the initial segment during the depolarizing phase of the action potential will not produce another action potential. Nor is the axon able to produce another action potential when it is repolarizing. During these times, the membrane is described as being **absolutely refractory**.

**optogenetics** Transgenic technique that combines genetics and light to excite or inhibit targeted cells in living tissue.

**absolutely refractory** The state of an axon in the repolarizing period, during which a new action potential cannot be elicited (with some exceptions) because gate 2 of the sodium channels, which are not voltage activated, is closed.

Exceptions do exist: some CNS neurons discharge during the repolarizing phase.

---

⊚ **RESEARCH FOCUS 4-2**

## Optogenetics and Light-Sensitive Ion Channels

Membrane channels that are responsive to light have been discovered in some nonmammalian animal species. Using the transgenic technique of **optogenetics**, researchers have also successfully introduced light-sensitive channels into a variety of species, including worms, fruit flies, and mice.

Optogenetics combines genetics and light to control targeted cells in living tissue. Here, we examine how introducing different light-sensitive channels into a species changes the organism's behavior with one wavelength and reverses them with another wavelength.

One class of light-activated ion channels in the green alga *Chlamydomonas reinhardtii* is called channelrhodopsin-2 (ChR2). The ChR2 light-activated channel absorbs blue light; in doing so, it opens briefly to allow the passage of Na$^+$ and K$^+$. The resulting depolarization excites the cell enough to generate action potentials.

Halorhodopsin (NpHR) is a light-driven ion pump, specific for chloride ions and found in phylogenetically ancient bacteria (archaea) known as halobacteria. When illuminated with green-yellow light, the NpHR pumps chloride anions into the cell, hyperpolarizing it and thereby inhibiting its activity.

In some studies, researchers have controlled the behavior of animals with genetically introduced light-sensitive channels by illuminating their nervous system cells with appropriate wavelengths of light. Using optogenetic techniques, light-sensitive channels can be incorporated into specific neural circuits so that light stimulation controls only a subset of neurons.

Stress has both behavioral and hormonal consequences for individuals, which can be transmitted socially to others. Using optogenetic techniques in mice, Sterley and colleagues (2018) *silenced* a specific collection of neurons in the hypothalamus during stress, thereby preventing changes to the brain that would normally occur after stress. They then took this research a step further and silenced the neurons in a partner mouse of a stressed individual, finding that the stress did not transfer to the partner. The group next performed the opposite experiment: in the absence of stress, they optogenetically *activated* the same hypothalamic neurons, causing the same changes in the brain as actual stress. They also observed that the partner mouse interacted with the light-activated–stressed individual in the same manner as they would approach a naturally stressed mouse (Sterley et al., 2018). This interaction is shown in the accompanying series of photos.

Optogenetics research has the potential to transform our understanding of the contributions of specific neuronal types to a behavior or disease state. But can optogenetics become a clinical tool to be used in people with a central nervous system (CNS) malady such as depression? One major hurdle is that specific viruses are used to transfer the light-activated channels to neurons in localized brain regions, and the usage of viruses in human populations is still fraught with difficulties. Some studies suggest that impaired vision due to the loss of the light-sensitive cells of the eye could be restored with light-activated channels in surviving retinal neurons (Pan et al., 2015). (For additional discussion of optogenetics and other experimental techniques, see Chapter 7.)

Courtesy of Toni-Lee Sterley and Jaideep Bains

**Light-Sensitive Channels**

**FIGURE 4-22 Phases of an Action Potential**
Initiated by changes in voltage-activated sodium and potassium channels, an action potential begins with a depolarization: gate 1 of the sodium channel opens, and then gate 2 closes, inactivating the channel. The slower-opening potassium channel gate contributes to repolarization and hyperpolarization until the resting membrane potential is restored.

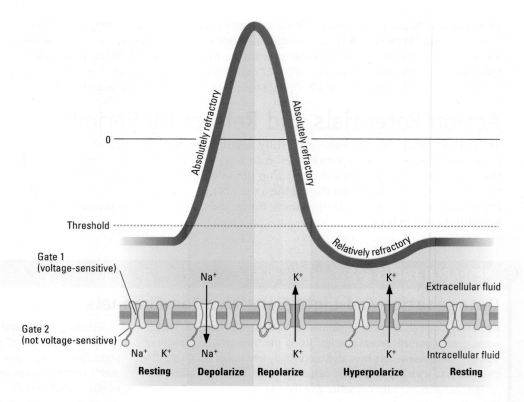

The second Na⁺ gate operates as a ball and chain mechanism (see Figure 4-22). The ball moves into the pore of the channel briefly inactivating the channel and preventing the influx of Na⁺.

**relatively refractory** The state of an axon in the later phase of an action potential, during which higher-intensity electrical current is required to produce another action potential; a phase during which potassium channels are still open.

In contrast, if the axon membrane is stimulated during hyperpolarization, another action potential can be induced, but the second stimulation must be more intense than the first. During this phase, the membrane is **relatively refractory**.

Refractory periods result from the way gates of the voltage-activated sodium and potassium channels open and close. A sodium channel has two gates, and a potassium channel has one gate. **Figure 4-22** illustrates the positions of these gates before, during, and after the phases of the action potential. Next, we describe changes first in the sodium channels and then in the potassium channels.

During the resting potential, gate 1 of the sodium channel depicted in Figure 4-22 is closed; only gate 2 is open. At the threshold level of stimulation, gate 1 also opens. Gate 2, however, closes very quickly, inactivating the channel, after gate 1 opens. This sequence produces a brief period during which both sodium gates are open. When both gates are open and when gate 2 is closed, the membrane is absolutely refractory.

The opening of the potassium channels repolarizes and eventually hyperpolarizes the cell membrane. The potassium channels open and close more slowly than the sodium channels do. The hyperpolarization produced by a continuing efflux of potassium ions makes it more difficult to depolarize the membrane to the threshold that reopens the gates underlying an action potential. While the membrane is hyperpolarizing, it is relatively refractory.

The changes in polarity that take place during an action potential are analogous to the action of a lever-activated toilet. Pushing the lever slightly produces a slight water flow that stops when the lever is released. This activity is analogous to a graded potential. A harder lever press brings the toilet to threshold and initiates flushing, a response that is out of all proportion to the lever press. This activity is analogous to the action potential.

During the flush, the toilet is absolutely refractory: another flush cannot be induced at this time. During the refilling of the bowl, in contrast, the toilet is relatively refractory, meaning that flushing again is possible but harder. Only after the cycle is over and the toilet is once again at rest can a full flush be produced again.

# Nerve Impulse

Suppose you place two recording electrodes at a distance from each other on an axon membrane and then electrically stimulate an area adjacent to one electrode. That electrode would immediately record an action potential. A similar recording would register on the second electrode in a flash. An action potential has arisen near this second electrode as well, even though it is located some distance away from the original point of stimulation.

Is this second action potential simply an echo of the first that passes down the axon? No, it cannot be because the action potential's size and shape are exactly the same at the two electrodes. The second is not just a faint, degraded version of the first, but rather is equal in magnitude. Somehow the full action potential has moved along the axon. This propagation of an action potential along an axon is called a **nerve impulse**.

Why does an action potential move? Recall that the total voltage change during an action potential is 100 mV, far beyond the 20-mV change needed to bring the membrane from its resting state of –70 mV to the action potential threshold level of –50 mV. Consequently, the voltage change on the part of the membrane where an action potential first occurs is large enough to bring adjacent parts of the membrane to a threshold of –50 mV.

When the membrane at an adjacent part of the axon reaches –50 mV, the voltage-activated channels at that location pop open to produce an action potential there as well. This second action potential, in turn, induces a change in the membrane voltage still farther along the axon, and so on and on, down the axon's length. **Figure 4-23** illustrates this process. The nerve impulse occurs because each action potential propagates another action potential on an adjacent part of the axon membrane. The word *propagate* means "to give birth," and that is exactly what happens. Each successive action potential gives birth to another down the length of the axon.

Because they are propagated by gated ion channels acting on the membrane in their own vicinity, action potentials on a nerve or tract are the same magnitude wherever they occur. An action potential depends on energy expended where it occurs, and the same amount of energy is typically expended at every site along the membrane as a nerve impulse is propagated.

As a result, action potentials do not dissipate: an action potential is either generated completely or not generated at all. Action potentials are all-or-none events. As the nerve's impulse, or message, the action potential maintains a constant size and arrives unchanged to every terminal on the nerve that receives it.

Think of the voltage-activated channels along the axon as a series of dominoes. When one falls, it knocks over its neighbor, and so on down the line. There is no decrement in the size of the fall. The last domino travels exactly the same distance and falls just as hard as the first one did.

Essentially, the domino effect happens when voltage-activated channels open. The opening of one channel produces a voltage change that triggers its neighbor to open, just as one domino knocks over the next. The channel-opening response does not grow any weaker as it moves along the axon, and the last channel opens exactly like the first, just as the domino action stays constant to the end of the line.

# Refractory Periods and Nerve Action

Refractory periods are determined by the positions of the gates that mediate ion flow in the voltage-activated channels. This limits the frequency of action potentials to about one every 5 ms. In consequence, the action potential's refractory phase has two practical uses for nerves that are conducting information.

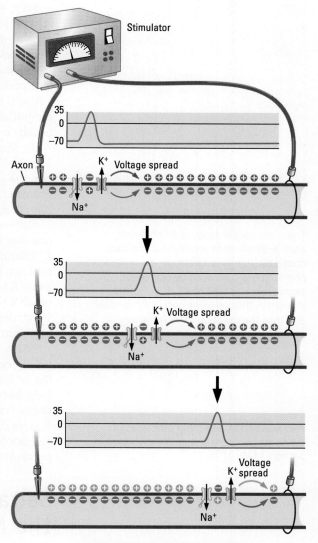

**FIGURE 4-23 Propagating an Action Potential** Voltage sufficient to open $Na^+$ and $K^+$ channels spreads to adjacent sites of the axon membrane, inducing voltage-activated gates to open. Here, voltage changes are shown on only one side of the membrane.

The Domino Effect

**nerve impulse** Propagation of an action potential on the membrane of an axon.

First, the maximum rate at which action potentials can occur is about 200 per second (1 s, or 1000 ms/5 ms limit = 200 action potentials in 1 s). The sensitivity of voltage-activated channels, which varies among kinds of neurons, likewise affects firing frequency.

Second, although an action potential can travel in either direction on an axon, refractory periods prevent it from reversing direction and returning to its point of origin. As a result, refractory periods produce a single, discrete impulse that travels away from the initial point of stimulation. When an action potential begins near the cell body, it usually travels down the axon to the terminals.

To return to our domino analogy, once a domino falls, setting it up again takes time. This is its refractory period. Because each domino falls as it knocks down its neighbor, the sequence cannot be reversed until the domino is set upright again: the dominos can fall in only one direction. The same principle determines the action potential's direction.

Different neurons perform somewhat different information-conducting roles, and one way that neurons can differ is in the sensitivity of their $K^+$ channels. Differences in $K^+$ channel sensitivity can affect the duration of the refractory periods, which in turn changes the rapidity with which a neuron can produce action potentials. For example, some $K^+$ channels open quickly, and the duration of the refractory period is shorter; other $K^+$ channels open slowly, and the duration of the refractory period is longer. Thus, depending on its set of $K^+$ channels, some neurons produce action potentials very frequently, whereas other neurons produce action potentials only infrequently.

Many different varieties of $K^+$ channels underlie the rich variation in action potentials generated by different neurons. This fact is important because it is not the size of the action potential that conveys variations in information, but rather the timing and frequency of action potentials that do so. For example, a small injury to the skin leads to only a few action potentials in injury-detecting neurons, resulting in a mild pain sensation. In contrast, a larger injury leads to more action potentials and a more severe pain sensation. The number of action potentials signals the degree of injury and leads to our perception of pain severity.

## Saltatory Conduction and the Myelin Sheath

Because the giant axons of squid are so large, they can transmit nerve impulses very quickly, much as a large-diameter pipe can rapidly deliver a lot of water. But large axons take up substantial space: a squid cannot accommodate many of them, or its body would be too bulky. For mammals, with our many axons innervating a substantial number of muscles, giant axons are out of the question. Instead, our axons must be extremely slender because our complex movements require a great many of them.

Our largest axons, which run to and from our muscles, are only about 30 μm wide, so the speed with which they convey information should not be especially fast. And yet, like most other vertebrate species, we humans are hardly sluggish creatures. We process information and generate responses with impressive speed. How do we manage this feat if our axons are so thin? In fact, the vertebrate nervous system has evolved a solution that has nothing to do with axon size.

Glial cells play a role in speeding nerve impulses in the vertebrate nervous system. Schwann cells in the peripheral nervous system and oligodendroglia in the central nervous system wrap around some axons, forming the myelin sheath that insulates them (**Figure 4-24**). Action potentials cannot occur where myelin is wrapped around an axon. For one thing, the myelin is an insulating barrier that blocks ionic current flow. For another, the axonal regions that lie under myelin have few channels through which ions can flow, and ion channels are essential to generating an action potential.

There are several types of $K^+$ channels, each with different sensitivities and each coded by slightly different genes. A neuron's phenotype is controlled by epigenetic expression of a type of $K^+$ channel that influences that neuron's overall $K^+$ sensitivity, and thus the duration of its refractory period.

Pain perception and other processes of the somatosensory system are discussed in Section 11-4.

**FIGURE 4-24 Myelination** An axon is insulated by **(A)** oligodendroglia in the CNS and **(B)** Schwann cells in the peripheral nervous system. Each glial cell is separated by a gap, or node of Ranvier.

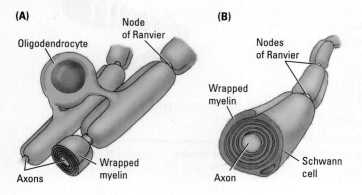

**(A)**
Oligodendrocyte
Node of Ranvier
Axons
Wrapped myelin

**(B)**
Nodes of Ranvier
Wrapped myelin
Axon
Schwann cell

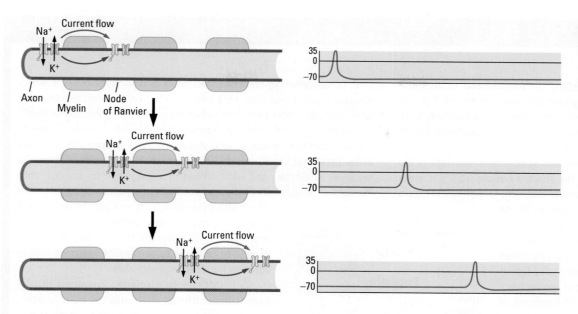

**FIGURE 4-25 Saltatory Conduction**
Myelinated stretches of axons are interrupted by nodes of Ranvier, which are rich in voltage-activated channels. In saltatory conduction, the action potential jumps rapidly from node to node.

But axons are not totally encased in myelin. Unmyelinated gaps between successive glial cell wrappings are richly endowed with voltage-activated channels. These tiny gaps in the myelin sheath, called the **nodes of Ranvier**, are sufficiently close to one another that an action potential at one node can open voltage-activated gates at an adjacent node. In this way, a relatively slow action potential jumps quickly from node to node, as shown in **Figure 4-25**. This flow of energy is called **saltatory conduction** (from the Latin verb *saltare*, meaning "to leap").

Myelin has two important consequences for propagating action potentials. First, propagation becomes energetically cheaper, since action potentials are regenerated only at the nodes of Ranvier, and not along the axon's entire length. Action potential conduction in unmyelinated axons, by contrast, carries a significant metabolic energy cost (Crotty et al., 2006). The second consequence is that myelin improves the action potential's conduction speed.

Jumping from node to node increases the speed at which an action potential can travel along an axon because the current flowing within the axon beneath the myelin sheath travels very fast. While the current moves speedily, the voltage drops quickly over distance. The nodes of Ranvier, however, are spaced ideally to ensure sufficient voltage at the next node will surpass the threshold potential and thus regenerate the action potential. On larger, myelinated mammalian axons, nerve impulses can travel as fast as 120 meters per second. On smaller, uninsulated axons, they travel at a speed of only about 30 meters per second.

Spectators at sporting events sometimes initiate a wave that travels around a stadium. Just as one person rises, the next person begins to rise, producing the wave effect. This human wave is like conduction along an unmyelinated axon. Now think of how much faster the wave would complete its circuit around the field if only spectators in the corners rose to produce it. This is analogous to a nerve impulse that travels by jumping from one node of Ranvier to the next. The quick reactions that humans and other mammals are capable of achieving are due in part to this saltatory conduction in their nervous system.

Neurons that send messages over long distances quickly, including sensory and motor neurons, are heavily myelinated. If this myelin becomes damaged, a neuron may be unable to send any messages over its axons. In **multiple sclerosis (MS)**, the myelin formed by oligodendroglia is damaged, which disrupts the functioning of neurons whose axons it encases. Clinical Focus 4-3: Multiple Sclerosis describes the course of the disease.

**node of Ranvier** The part of an axon that is not covered by myelin.

**saltatory conduction** Fast propagation of an action potential at successive nodes of Ranvier; *saltatory* means "leaping."

**multiple sclerosis (MS)** Nervous system disorder resulting from the loss of the myelin sheath around axons in the CNS.

## ◎ CLINICAL FOCUS 4-3

# Multiple Sclerosis

C. O. was a 20-year-old student finishing the requirements of her nursing degree when she noticed one day that the vision in her left eye was blurred. Three days later, she had complete vision loss in that eye. C. O. was experiencing *optic neuritis*, a potential indicator for multiple sclerosis (MS), and was referred to a neurologist.

MS results from a loss of myelin produced by oligodendroglia cells in the CNS (see the illustration). It disrupts the affected neurons' ability to propagate action potentials via saltatory conduction. This loss of myelin occurs in patches, and scarring frequently develops in the affected areas. Eventually, a hard scar, or *plaque*, forms at the site of myelin loss, which can be visualized with magnetic resonance imaging (MRI). (*Sclerosis* comes from the Greek word meaning "hardness.") The loss of myelin is associated with impairment of neuron function, which causes the characteristic MS symptoms of sensory loss and difficulty in moving. Fatigue, pain, and depression are common symptoms in people with MS, as are bladder dysfunction, constipation, and sexual dysfunction. The condition often takes a toll on the person's emotional, social, and vocational functioning.

MS is the most common of the nearly 80 **autoimmune diseases**, conditions in which the immune system makes antibodies to a person's own body (Rezania et al., 2012). The U.S. Food and Drug Administration (FDA) has approved 15 medications for modifying the progression of MS, but it is doubtful that the disease can be fully arrested with current therapies (Reich et al., 2018).

C. O.'s vision cleared after a few months, but later that year she developed numbness and tingling in the soles of her feet. MRI confirmed scarring on her spinal cord, so she began disease-modifying therapy with interferon beta-1a (Rebif), a medication that works by modulating the passage of certain immune cells into the CNS. C. O. describes a flu-like side effect that she calls "Rebif hangovers." Though she found it difficult to push through this downside of treatment while still a student, the side effect eventually eased after a few months (C. O., 2021).

Normal myelinated nerve fiber

Exposed fiber
Damaged myelin

Nerve affected by MS

C. O. has relapsing-remitting (RR) MS, a common type of MS in which symptoms occur and then fade over months, only to return sometime later. Four years after her initial symptoms and despite high doses of anti-inflammatory steroid treatment, she was forced to take a medical leave of absence from her job due to lack of sensation and weakness in her lower limbs. Later that same year, she lost most sensory and motor function in her lower extremities and was confined to a wheelchair for outings. With the help of an alternative disease-modifying therapy and diligent work with a physiotherapist, C. O. was able to walk with a cane and drive a car. New lesions have continued to appear, but C. O. is hopeful that her neurologist will be able to continue to personalize her treatment to adapt to her disease progression.

MS is difficult to diagnose. Symptoms usually appear in adulthood; their onset is quite sudden, and their effects can be swift. Initial symptoms may include loss of sensation in the face, limbs, or body; loss of control over movements; or loss of both sensation and control. Motor symptoms usually appear first in the hands or feet, but progress occurs rapidly over just a few years until the person is bedridden.

MS is most common in the northern-most and southern-most latitudes, so it may be related to a lack of vitamin D, which is produced by the action of sunlight on the skin. Many people with MS take vitamin $D_3$ and vitamin $B_{12}$ supplements. The disease may also be related to genetic susceptibility—C. O.'s mother and two of her aunts have also been diagnosed with MS, which is about twice as common in women as in men.

While MS is the most prevalent chronic inflammatory disease of the CNS, affecting more than 2 million people worldwide (Reich et al., 2018), the underlying cause of the inflammation and loss of myelin that characterize the disease course remains unknown. It has been suggested that MS may primarily be a degenerative disease that secondarily elicits an autoimmune response (Stys, 2013). Research aimed at solving this problem is important because the answer would likely influence therapeutic approaches.

---

## 4-3 Review

Before you continue, check your understanding. Answers to Self-Tests appear at the back of the book.

1. The membrane of the _____ does not contain voltage-activated ion channels, but if summed inputs excite the _____ to a threshold level, action potentials are triggered and then propagated as they travel along the cell's _____ as a nerve impulse.

2. The voltage change associated with a(n) _____ is sufficiently large to stimulate adjacent parts of the axon membrane to the threshold for propagating it along the length of an axon as a(n) _____.

3. An axon is unable to produce an action potential while it is repolarizing, during which the membrane is _____. However, an action potential can be induced while the axon is hyperpolarized, a state in which the membrane is _____.

4. Briefly explain why nerve impulses travel faster on myelinated axons than on unmyelinated axons.

5. Explain what happens during back propagation.

---

**autoimmune disease** Illness resulting from an abnormal immune response by the body against substances and tissues normally present in the body.

# Into the Nervous System and Back Out

The nervous system allows us to respond to afferent (incoming) sensory stimuli by detecting them and sending messages about them to the brain. The brain interprets the information, triggering efferent (outgoing) responses that contract muscles and produce behavior. Until now, we have been dealing only with the middle of this process—how neurons convey information to one another, integrate the information, and generate action potentials. Now we explore the beginning and end of the journey.

To fill in the missing pieces, we explain how a sensory stimulus initiates a nerve impulse and how a nerve impulse produces a muscular contraction. Once again, ion channels are vitally important, but, in muscles, the channels are different from those described so far.

## How Sensory Stimuli Produce Action Potentials

We receive information about the world through bodily sensations (touch and balance), auditory sensations (hearing), visual sensations (sight), and chemical sensations (taste and olfaction). Each sensory modality has one or more separate functions. In addition to touch, for example, the body senses include pressure, joint sense, pain, temperature, and itch. Receptors for audition and balance are modified touch receptors. The visual system has receptors for light and for colors. The taste and olfactory senses respond to a plethora of chemical compounds.

Processing all these varied sensory inputs requires a remarkable array of sensory receptors. But in all our sensory systems, the neurons related to these diverse receptors have one thing in common: conduction of information begins at ion channels. Ion channels initiate the chain of events that produces a nerve impulse.

An example is touch. Each hair on the human body allows an individual to detect even a very slight displacement. You can demonstrate this sensitivity yourself by selecting a single hair on your arm and bending it. If you are patient and precise in your experimentation, you will discover that some hairs are sensitive to displacement in one direction only, whereas others respond to displacement in any direction. What enables this finely tuned sensitivity?

The base of each hair is wrapped in a dendrite of a touch neuron. When you bend a hair or otherwise mechanically displace it, the encircling dendrite is stretched (**Figure 4-26**).

The displacement opens **stretch-activated channels** in the dendrite's membrane. When open, these channels allow an influx of sodium ions sufficient to depolarize the dendrite to threshold. When the threshold is reached, the voltage-activated sodium and potassium channels initiate a nerve impulse that conveys touch information to your brain.

Other kinds of sensory receptors have similar mechanisms for *transducing* (transforming) the energy of a sensory stimulus into nervous system activity. When displaced, the inner ear's *hair cell receptors*, which provide information about hearing and balance, likewise open stretch-activated channels. In the visual system, photons (light particles)

**Learning Objectives**
- Explain how the propagation of the action potential facilitates the communication of sensory information between neurons.
- Explain the similarities between the communication of sensory information and the generation of movement.

For details on how sensory receptors transduce external energy into action potentials:

Hearing, Section 10-1

Sensation and perception, Section 9-1

Smell and taste, Section 12-3

Touch, pain, and balance, Section 11-4

Vision, Section 9-2

**stretch-activated channel** Ion channel on a tactile sensory neuron that becomes activated in response to stretching of the membrane, initiating a nerve impulse.

**FIGURE 4-26 Tactile Stimulation** Activation of a hair's touch receptor by a feather results in a nerve impulse heading to the brain.

Feather

Displacement of hair...

...causes stretch-activated channels on dendrite to open, allowing an influx of Na⁺.

This Na⁺ influx causes voltage-activated Na⁺ and K⁺ channels to open, producing a nerve impulse.

Hair

Dendrite of sensory neuron wrapped around hair

Extracellular fluid

$Na^+$   Current flow

$Na^+$   Nerve impulse

$K^+$

Stretch-activated channel

Voltage-activated channels

Intracellular fluid

strike opsin proteins, resulting in a chemical change that opens ion channels within specialized cells (called *photoreceptors*) in the eye. An odorous molecule in the air that lands on an olfactory receptor and fits itself into a specially shaped compartment opens chemical-activated ion channels. When tissue is damaged, injured cells release chemicals that activate channels on a pain nerve. The point being made here is a simple one: ion channels are responsible for the conduction of information in all our sensory systems.

# How Nerve Impulses Produce Movement

What happens at the end of the neural journey? After sensory information has traveled to the brain and been interpreted, how does the brain generate output— muscular contractions—as a behavioral response? Behavior, after all, is movement, and for movement to take place, muscles must contract. Motor neurons in the spinal cord are responsible for activating muscles. Without them, movement becomes impossible and muscles atrophy, as described in Clinical Focus 4-4: ALS: Amyotrophic Lateral Sclerosis.

**Principle 9:** The nervous system produces movement in a perceptual world the brain constructs.

## ◉ CLINICAL FOCUS 4-4

# ALS: Amyotrophic Lateral Sclerosis

In 1869, French physician Jean-Martin Charcot first described ALS—that is, amyotrophic lateral sclerosis. *Amyotrophic* means "muscle weakness"; *lateral sclerosis* means "hardening of the lateral spinal cord."

In North America, ALS is also known as Lou Gehrig disease. A baseball legend who played for the New York Yankees from 1923 until 1939, Gehrig had set a host of individual records. He was an outstanding hitter, and his incredible durability earned him the nickname The Iron Horse. Gehrig played on many World Series championship teams, but ALS sapped his strength, forcing him to retire from baseball at age 36. His condition deteriorated rapidly, and he died just 2 years later.

ALS is due primarily to the death of spinal motor neurons, but it can affect brain neurons as well in some instances. It most commonly strikes people between ages 50 and 75, although its onset can be as early as the teenage years. Approximately 5000 new cases are reported in the United States each year, and roughly 10% of people with ALS have a family history of the disorder.

While death often occurs within 5 years of an ALS diagnosis, internationally renowned theoretical physicist and cosmologist Stephen Hawking was a notable exception. Diagnosed at age 21, Hawking had a rare early-onset, slowly progressing form of ALS. As a doctoral student at Oxford University, he grew increasingly clumsy, and his speech was slightly slurred. In his late twenties, he began to use crutches. In his thirties, his speech deteriorated to the point that only his family and close friends could understand him. In his seventies, and confined to a wheelchair, Hawking, pictured at right, was still able to communicate by using a single cheek muscle attached to a speech-generating device.

ALS typically begins with general weakness, at first in the throat or upper chest and in the arms and legs. Gradually, walking becomes difficult and falling common. ALS does not usually affect sensory systems, cognitive functions, bowel or bladder control, or even sexual function. Indeed, even as his motor neurons continued to die, Hawking's mind-blowing advancements continued to enrich our understanding of the universe. Sadly, the world lost Stephen Hawking in March 2018.

At present, no cure for ALS exists, although some individuals have been enrolled in clinical trials for cognitive neural prosthetics. With such a brain–machine interface, recordings can be made from microelectrode arrays in the cortex that are then transmitted wirelessly to external devices, such as robotic limbs. Alternatively, the arrays can be used for functional electrical stimulation of paralyzed limbs, wheelchair mobility, computer-assisted communication, environmental control (e.g., of a television or computer), and other applications. The original interfaces were invasive, relying on electrodes implanted in the brain. Today, ongoing trials are examining noninvasive interfaces such as scalp electrodes (EEG) and near-infrared spectroscopy (NIRS).

Tom Dymond/REX/Shutterstock

Motor neurons send nerve impulses to synapses on muscle cells. These synapses are instrumental in making the muscle contract. Each motor neuron axon contacts one or a few synapses on its target muscle (**Figure 4-27**A). The axon terminal contacts a specialized area of the muscle membrane called an **end plate**, where, in most animals, the axon terminal releases the chemical transmitter *acetylcholine*.

Acetylcholine does not actually enter the muscle, but rather attaches to **transmitter-activated channels** on the end plate (Figure 4-27B). When these channels open in response to acetylcholine's binding, they allow a flow of Na⁺ and K⁺ across the muscle membrane sufficient to depolarize the muscle to the threshold for its action potential. Yes, to contract, muscles generate action potentials. At this threshold, adjacent voltage-activated channels open. They in turn produce an action potential on the muscle fiber, just as they do in a neuron.

Three separate features ensure that synaptic communication is successful at the neuromuscular junction: (1) a very large number of vesicles containing acetylcholine are present in the motor neuron, (2) infoldings on the muscle side serve to increase the contact area, and (3) a high density of acetylcholine receptors are found on the end plates.

If the acetylcholine receptors on muscle end plates become blocked, acetylcholine released from the motor neuron cannot properly exert its depolarizing effect. This mechanism prevents muscular contraction in conditions such as the autoimmune disease *myasthenia gravis*. In affected individuals, the thymus—an immune system gland that normally produces antibodies that bind to foreign material such as viruses—makes antibodies that bind to the acetylcholine receptors on muscles, causing weakness and fatigue (see **Figure 4-28**).

Unlike MS, another autoimmune disease, myasthenia gravis is usually well controlled with treatment. Therapies for this disease include drugs that suppress the immune system or inhibit acetylcholine breakdown, thereby extending the time the transmitter can act. Removal of the thymus gland (thymectomy) is another treatment option.

The actions of membrane channels can explain a wide range of neural events. Some channels generate the transmembrane charge. Others mediate graded potentials. Still others trigger the action potential. Sensory stimuli activate channels on neurons to initiate a nerve impulse, and the nerve impulse eventually activates channels on motor neurons to produce muscle contractions.

The various channels and their different functions evolved over a long time as new species of animals and their behaviors evolved. We have not described all of the myriad ion channels that neural membranes possess, but you will learn about some additional ones in subsequent chapters.

# 4-4 Review

Before you continue, check your understanding. Answers to Self-Tests appear at the back of the book.

1. Across all sensory systems, the conduction of sensory information that occurs within the neuron begins at the _____.

2. A(n) _____ membrane contains a mechanism for transducing sensory energy into changes in ion channels. In turn, the channels allow ion flow to alter the membrane voltage to the point that _____ channels open, initiating a nerve impulse.

3. Sensory stimuli activate ion channels to initiate a nerve impulse, which then activates channels on _____ neurons, which in turn contract _____.

4. In myasthenia gravis, a(n) _____ disease, the thymus gland produces antibodies to _____ receptors on muscles, causing weakness and fatigue.

5. Why have so many kinds of ion channels evolved on cell membranes?

In some animals (such as crayfish and fruit flies), this process is mediated by the chemical transmitter glutamate rather than by acetylcholine.

Sections 5-2 and 5-3 describe the varieties of chemical transmitters and how they function.

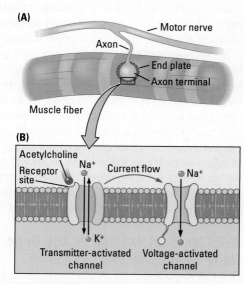

**(A)**

Motor nerve
Axon
End plate
Axon terminal
Muscle fiber

**(B)**

Acetylcholine
Receptor site
Na⁺
Current flow
Na⁺
K⁺
Transmitter-activated channel
Voltage-activated channel

**FIGURE 4-27 Muscle Contraction (A)** When a motor neuron's axon collaterals contact a muscle fiber end plate, **(B)** acetylcholine attaches to receptor sites on the end plate's transmitter-activated channels, opening them. These membrane channels allow simultaneous influx of Na⁺ and efflux of K⁺, generating current sufficient to activate voltage-activated channels, triggering action potentials, and causing the muscle to contract.

Courtesy of Y. Harati, M.D./Baylor College of Medicine, Houston, Texas

**FIGURE 4-28 Myasthenia Gravis** When this patient follows the direction to look up **(1)**, her eyelids quickly become fatigued and droop **(2, 3)**. After a few minutes of rest, her eyelids open normally **(4)**.

**end plate** On a muscle, the receptor–ion complex that is activated by the release of the neurotransmitter acetylcholine from the terminal of a motor neuron.

**transmitter-activated channel** Receptor complex that has both a receptor site for a chemical and a pore through which ions can flow.

# Summary

## 4-1 Searching for Electrical Activity in the Nervous System

Electrical stimulation studies dating as far back as the eighteenth century showed that stimulating a nerve with electrical current induces a muscle contraction. More recent recording studies, in which the brain's electrical current is measured using an oscilloscope, have shown that electrical activity in the nervous system is continuous.

In the twentieth century, researchers used giant axons of the squid to measure the electrical activity of a single neuron. Using microelectrodes that they could place on or in the cell, they recorded small, rapid electrical changes with an oscilloscope. Today, digital oscilloscopes and computers are used to record these measurements.

A neuron's electrical activity is generated by ions flowing across the cell membrane. Ions flow down a concentration gradient (from an area of relatively high concentration to an area of lower concentration) as well as down a voltage gradient (from an area of relatively high voltage to an area of lower voltage). The opening, closing, and pumping of ion channels in neural cell membranes also affect ion distribution.

## 4-2 Electrical Activity at the Dendritic and Cell Body Membrane

Unequal ion distribution on the two sides of a cell membrane generates the neuron's resting potential. At rest, the intracellular membrane registers about −70 mV relative to the extracellular side. Negatively charged protein anions are too large to leave the neuron, and the cell membrane actively pumps out positively charged sodium ions. Unequal distributions of potassium cations and chloride anions contribute to the resting potential as well.

Graded potentials, which are short-lived, small increases or decreases in transmembrane voltage, result when the neuron is stimulated. Voltage changes affect the membrane's ion channels and in turn change the cross-membrane ion distribution. An increase in transmembrane voltage causes hyperpolarization; a decrease causes depolarization.

Inputs to neurons from other cells can produce both excitatory postsynaptic potentials and inhibitory postsynaptic potentials. The membrane sums their voltages both temporally and spatially to integrate the incoming information. If the summed EPSPs and IPSPs move the membrane voltage at the initial segment to threshold, the axon generates an action potential.

## 4-3 Generation and Propagation of the Action Potential

An action potential is a brief but large change in axon membrane polarity triggered when the transmembrane voltage drops to a threshold level of about −50 mV. During an action potential, transmembrane voltage suddenly reverses—the intracellular side becomes positive relative to the extracellular side—and then abruptly reverses again. Gradually, the resting potential is restored. These membrane changes result from voltage-activated channels—sodium and potassium channels sensitive to the membrane's voltage.

When an action potential is triggered at the initial segment, it can propagate along the axon as a nerve impulse. Nerve impulses travel more rapidly on myelinated axons because of saltatory conduction: the action potentials leap rapidly between the nodes separating the glial cells that form the axon's myelin sheath.

The neuron is a versatile kind of cell. Some species' ion channels respond to light rather than to voltage changes, an attribute that genetic engineers are exploiting. Most of our neurons do not initiate action potentials on the cell body because the cell body membrane does not contain voltage-activated channels. However, some voltage-activated channels on dendrites do enable action potentials. Back propagation—the reverse movement of an action potential from the initial segment into the dendritic field of a neuron—may play a role in the plastic changes that underlie learning.

## 4-4 Into the Nervous System and Back Out

Sensory receptor cells convert sensory energy to graded potentials. These changes, in turn, alter transmembrane voltage to trigger an action potential and propagate a nerve impulse that transmits sensory information to relevant parts of the nervous system.

Ion channels come into play to activate muscles as well because the chemical transmitter acetylcholine, released at the axon terminal of a motor neuron, activates channels on the end plate of a muscle cell membrane. The subsequent ion flow depolarizes the muscle cell membrane to the threshold for its action potential. In turn, this depolarization opens voltage-activated channels, producing an action potential on the muscle fiber—hence the muscle contractions that enable movement. In myasthenia gravis, antibodies to the acetylcholine receptor prevent muscle depolarization, leading to the weakness and fatigue that characterize this disease.

# Key Terms

absolutely refractory, p. 131

action potential, p. 128

autoimmune disease, p. 136

back propagation, p. 130

concentration gradient, p. 118

depolarization, p. 123

diffusion, p. 118

electrical stimulation, p. 113

electroencephalogram (EEG), p. 115

electrographic seizures, p. 112

end plate, p. 139

equilibrium (reversal) potential, p. 123

excitatory postsynaptic potential (EPSP), p. 125

graded potential, p. 123

hyperpolarization, p. 123

inhibitory postsynaptic potential (IPSP), p. 126

initial segment, p. 126

microelectrode, p. 117

multiple sclerosis (MS), p. 135

Nernst equation, p. 123

nerve impulse, p. 133

node of Ranvier, p. 135

optogenetics, p. 131

oscilloscope, p. 117

relatively refractory, p. 132

resting potential, p. 121

saltatory conduction, p. 135

spatial summation, p. 127

stretch-activated channel, p. 137

temporal summation, p. 127

threshold potential, p. 128

transmitter-activated channel, p. 139

voltage-activated channel, p. 129

voltage gradient, p. 119

voltmeter, p. 116

# Selected Resources from

**Neuroscience in Action:** Neuronal Activity: Understanding Potential

**Neuroscience in Action:** Neural Integration: Sending Signals

**Concept Practice:** Action Potentials

**Concept Practice:** Resting Membrane Potential

**Videos**

Ion Flow

Signal Transmission

**LearningCurve**

**Practice Quiz**

# 5 How Do Neurons Communicate and Adapt?

## ◎ RESEARCH FOCUS 5-1

# The Basis of Neural Communication in a Heartbeat

Discoveries about how neurons communicate stem from experiments designed to study what controls an animal's heart rate. As happens with any animal, your heartbeat quickens if you are excited or exercising; it then slows as you rest. Heart rate changes to match energy expenditure—that is, to meet the body's nutrient and oxygen needs.

Your heartbeat undergoes a dramatic change when you dive beneath water: it slows almost to stopping. This drastic slowing, called diving *bradycardia*, conserves the body's oxygen when you are not breathing. Bradycardia (*brady*, meaning "slow," and *cardia*, meaning "heart") is a useful survival strategy. This energy-conserving response under water is common to many animals. But what controls your heartbeat?

Otto Loewi, a great storyteller, recounted that his classic experiment, which earned him a Nobel Prize in 1936, came to him in a dream. As shown in the Procedure section of Experiment 5-1, Loewi first maintained a frog's heart in a mild saline bath, then electrically stimulated the vagus nerve—the tenth cranial nerve that leads from the brain to the heart. At the same time, he channeled some of the fluid bath from the vessel containing the stimulated heart through a tube to another vessel in which a second heart was immersed but not electrically stimulated.

Loewi recorded both heart rates. His findings are represented in the Results section of Experiment 5-1. The electrical stimulation decreased the rate of the first heart, but more important, the second heartbeat also slowed. This result indicated that the fluid transferred from the first container to the second container carried instructions to slow down.

Where did the message come from originally? Loewi reasoned that a chemical released from the stimulated vagus nerve must have diffused into the fluid bath to influence the second heart. His experiment therefore demonstrated that the vagus nerve contains a chemical that tells the heart to slow its rate.

Loewi subsequently identified the messenger chemical. Later, he also showed that another chemical tells the heart to speed up. The heart adjusts its rate in response to at least two different messages: an excitatory message that says "speed up" and an inhibitory message that says "slow down."

Puffins fish by diving underwater, propelling themselves by flapping their short, stubby wings as if flying. During these dives, their heart displays the diving bradycardia response, just as the human heart does.

Chris Gomersall/Alamy

---

In Chapter 4, we learned how neurons transmit information as electrical signals: first an action potential is generated, and then that impulse flows down an axon to the synapse. In this chapter, first we explain how neurons communicate with one another using excitatory and inhibitory signals. Next, we describe how chemicals carried by one neuron signal receptors on receiving neurons to produce a response. We conclude by exploring hormones: we discuss how they are regulated within the body, their types, and their function.

The vagus nerve influences the heart and other internal body processes; see Figure 2-29.

## 5-1

# A Chemical Message

Otto Loewi's successful heartbeat experiment, discussed in Research Focus 5-1, The Basis of Neural Communication in a Heartbeat and diagrammed in Experiment 5-1, marked the beginning of research into how chemicals carry information from one neuron to another in the nervous system. Loewi was the first person to isolate a chemical messenger. We now know that chemical as **acetylcholine (ACh)**, the same transmitter that activates skeletal muscles, as described in Section 4-4. Yet in Loewi's experiment, ACh acts to *inhibit* the heartbeat—that is, to slow it down. In fact, ACh excites skeletal muscles in the somatic nervous system, causing them to contract, and it may either excite or inhibit various internal organs in the autonomic system. How can the same chemical messenger do both? It turns out that the ion channel and its associated receptor, rather than the molecule itself, determine whether the messenger will be excitatory or inhibitory—a process that we explore in Section 5-2. And, yes, acetylcholine is the chemical messenger associated with the slowed heartbeat in diving bradycardia.

### Learning Objectives

- Explain how Loewi's experiments contributed to our understanding of chemical transmission of messages in the central nervous system.
- Summarize the process of neurotransmission, listing the key synaptic structures involved.
- Differentiate between chemical and electrical synapses.

**acetylcholine (ACh)** First neurotransmitter discovered in the PNS and CNS; activates skeletal muscles in the SNS; either excites or inhibits internal organs in the ANS.

**epinephrine (EP)** Chemical messenger that acts as a neurotransmitter in the CNS and as a hormone to mobilize the body for fight or flight during times of stress; also known as *adrenaline*.

**norepinephrine (NE)** Neurotransmitter that accelerates heart rate in mammals; found in the brain and in the sympathetic division of the ANS; also known as *noradrenaline*.

**neurotransmitter** Chemical with an excitatory or inhibitory effect when released by a neuron onto a target.

····> **EXPERIMENT 5-1**

Question: How does a neuron pass on a message?

**Procedure**

Stimulating device

Recording device

**1** Vagus nerve of frog heart 1 is stimulated.

**2** Fluid is transferred from first to second container.

Vagus nerve

Fluid transfer

**Results**

Frog heart 1

Frog heart 2

Rate of heartbeats

Stimulation

**3** Recording from frog heart 1 shows decreased rate of beating after stimulation,...

**4** ...as does the recording from frog heart 2 after the fluid transfer.

*Conclusion*: The message is a chemical released by the nerve.

Jōkichi Takamine

In further experiments modeled on his procedure described in Experiment 5-1, Loewi stimulated another nerve to the heart, the accelerator nerve, and heart rate increased. The fluid that bathed the accelerated heart also accelerated the beat of a second heart that was not electrically stimulated. The chemical that carries the message to speed up heart rate in frogs, which was later isolated and purified by Jōkichi Takamine, is **epinephrine** (EP; *epi-*, "above," and *nephron*, "kidney"), also known as *adrenaline*. Adrenaline (Latin) and epinephrine (Greek) are the same substance, which is produced by the adrenal glands (located atop the kidneys). Adrenaline is the name more people know, in part because a drug company used it as a trade name, but epinephrine is common parlance in the science community.

The results of Loewi's complementary experiments showed that acetylcholine from the vagus nerve inhibits heartbeat, whereas epinephrine from the accelerator nerve excites it. Further experimentation eventually demonstrated that in mammals, the chemical that accelerates heart rate is **norepinephrine** (NE; also called *noradrenaline*), a chemical closely related to epinephrine.

Through these experiments, Loewi revealed the role of this new class of chemical messengers, which eventually became known as **neurotransmitters**, a name reflecting their function in the synaptic transmission. Neurotransmitters can have either excitatory or inhibitory activity and can carry messages between neurons, but they can also interact with organs and muscles.

Neurotransmitters are frequently known by their abbreviations, and neurons are often named after the type of chemical neurotransmitter they release. For example, neurons that secrete acetylcholine are called *cholinergic neurons*, those that secrete epinephrine are known as *adrenergic neurons*, and those that secrete norepinephrine are called *noradrenergic (NA) neurons*. The ACh, EP, and NE molecules differ from each other structurally, as can be seen in **Figure 5-1**, which allows each to interact with a specific receptor.

Outside the central nervous system, many of the same chemical messengers circulate in the bloodstream as *hormones*. Under the control of the hypothalamus, the pituitary gland releases its hormones into the bloodstream to excite or inhibit targets, such as the organs and glands in the autonomic and enteric nervous systems. In part because hormones travel throughout the body to distant targets, their actions are slower than those of the central nervous system (CNS) neurotransmitters prodded by the lightning-quick nerve impulses.

Neurotransmitters are released from neurons to act locally and hormones are released from neurons or other tissues and travel greater distances within the body, but they can be chemically identical. For example, when epinephrine is synthesized by a neuron and influences another neuron, it is called a neurotransmitter; in contrast, when it is synthesized by the adrenal gland and increases heart rate, it is called a hormone. The difference between neurotransmitters and hormones lies in the distances they travel from their release point to the receptor with which they interact. We explore hormones and their function in detail in Section 5-4.

Loewi's discoveries led to the search for more neurotransmitters and their functions. The actual number of these transmitters is an open question, with 200 posited as the maximum. The confirmed number is 60, with most of the work being done by 10 of them. Whether a chemical is accepted as a neurotransmitter depends on the extent to which it meets certain criteria. As this chapter unfolds, you will about learn those criteria, along with the names and functions of many neurotransmitters. You will also learn how groups of neurons form neurotransmitter systems throughout the brain that act to modulate, or temper, aspects of behavior. The three Clinical Focus boxes in this chapter tell the fascinating story of how one such neurotransmitter, dopamine, has yielded deep insights into brain function. When depleted in a particular brain area, dopamine is associated with a specific neurological disorder. The story begins with Clinical Focus 5-2, Parkinson Disease.

**Acetylcholine (ACh)**

**Epinephrine (EP)**    **Norepinephrine (NE)**

**FIGURE 5-1 ACh, EP, and NE** Three-dimensional space-filling models contrast the molecular structure of ACh, which inhibits heartbeat, with the structures of EP and NE, which excite the heart in frogs and humans, respectively.

# Structure of Synapses

Loewi's discovery about the chemical messengers that regulate heart rate was the first of two seminal findings that form the foundation for our current understanding of how neurons communicate. The second discovery had to wait until the invention of the electron microscope nearly 30 years later, which allowed researchers to determine that neurotransmitters are packaged into vesicles at the end terminals of axons. When tissue is stained with a substance that reflects electrons, ultrastructural details emerge.

## Chemical Synapses

Synaptic structure was first revealed in the 1950s, using electron microscopy. In the center of the micrograph in **Figure 5-2**A, the upper part of the synapse is the axon terminal, or end foot; the lower part is the receiving dendrite. The round granular substances in the terminal are the **synaptic vesicles**, which contain neurotransmitter molecules.

The dark patches visible on the axon terminal membrane are proteins that serve largely as ion channels to signal the release of the transmitters or as pumps to recapture the transmitter after its release. The dark patches on the dendrite consist mainly of receptor molecules, which are also made up of proteins that receive chemical messages. The terminal and the dendrite are separated by a small space, the **synaptic cleft**. The

**synaptic vesicle** Membranous compartment that encloses a fixed number (a *quantum*) of neurotransmitter molecules.

**synaptic cleft** Gap separating the neuronal presynaptic membrane from the postsynaptic membrane.

**(A)**

Axon
Presynaptic terminal
Presynaptic membrane
Synaptic vesicles
Synaptic cleft
Postsynaptic membrane
Dendritic spine
Astrocyte

Joseph F. Gennaro Jr/Science Source

**(B)**

Presynaptic neuron

Dendrite of postsynaptic neuron

**Microtubule:** Transport structure that carries substances to the axon terminal.

**Mitochondrion:** Organelle that provides the cell with energy.

**Synaptic vesicle:** Round granule that contains neurotransmitter.

**Storage granule:** Large compartment that holds synaptic vesicles.

**Presynaptic membrane:** Encloses molecules that transmit chemical messages.

**Synaptic cleft:** Small space separating presynaptic terminal and postsynaptic dendritic spine.

**Postsynaptic membrane:** Contains receptor molecules that receive chemical messages.

Presynaptic terminal

Neurotransmitter

Channel

Dendritic spine

**Postsynaptic receptor:** Site to which a neurotransmitter molecule binds.

**FIGURE 5-2 Chemical Synapse**
**(A)** Surrounding the central synapse in this electron micrograph are astrocytes (a type of glial cell), axons, dendrites, other synapses, and a synaptic cleft. **(B)** Within a chemical synapse, storage granules hold vesicles containing neurotransmitter; these vesicles travel to the presynaptic membrane in preparation for release. There, the neurotransmitter is expelled into the synaptic cleft by exocytosis, crosses the cleft, and binds to receptor proteins on the postsynaptic membrane.

The main classes of transmitters are small-molecule, peptide, lipid, gaseous, and ion. We describe each in Section 5-2.

**tripartite synapse** Functional integration and physical proximity of the presynaptic membrane, postsynaptic membrane, and their intimate association with surrounding astrocytes.

**chemical synapse** Junction at which messenger molecules are released when stimulated by an action potential.

**presynaptic membrane** Axon terminal membrane on the transmitter, or output, side of a synapse.

**postsynaptic membrane** Membrane on the transmitter, or input, side of a synapse.

**storage granule** Membranous compartment that holds several vesicles containing a neurotransmitter.

**anterograde synaptic transmission** Process that occurs when a neurotransmitter is released from a presynaptic neuron and binds to a receptor on the postsynaptic neuron.

synaptic cleft is central to synapse function because neurotransmitter chemicals must bridge this gap to carry a message from one neuron to the next.

As you can also see in the micrograph, the synapse is surrounded by many structures, including an astrocyte, other axons and dendritic processes, and other synapses. The surrounding astrocyte contributes to chemical neurotransmission in several ways—by, for example, supplying the building blocks for neurotransmitter synthesis, confining the movement of neurotransmitters to the synapse, and mopping up excess neurotransmitter molecules. This functional integration and physical proximity of the presynaptic membrane, postsynaptic membrane, and their intimate association with surrounding astrocytes make up what is known as the **tripartite synapse**.

Figure 5-2B details the process of neurotransmission at a **chemical synapse**, the junction where messenger molecules are released from one neuron to interact with the next neuron. Here, the **presynaptic membrane** forms the axon terminal, the **postsynaptic membrane** forms the dendritic spine, and the space between the two is the synaptic cleft. Within the axon terminal are specialized structures, including mitochondria, the organelles that supply the cell's energy needs; **storage granules**, large compartments that hold several synaptic vesicles; and microtubules, which transport substances, including neurotransmitter, to the terminal.

# Neurotransmission in Five Steps

**Anterograde synaptic transmission** is the five-step process of transmitting information across a chemical synapse from the presynaptic side to the postsynaptic neuron (see **Figure 5-3**). In brief:

1. The neurotransmitter is synthesized somewhere inside the neuron.

2. It is packaged and stored within vesicles at the axon terminal.

## ◎ CLINICAL FOCUS 5-2

# Parkinson Disease

Case VI: The gentleman . . . is seventy-two years of age. . . . About eleven or twelve, or perhaps more, years ago, he first perceived weakness in the left hand and arm, and soon after found the trembling to commence. In about three years afterwards, the right arm became affected in a similar manner: and soon afterwards the convulsive motions affected the whole body and began to interrupt speech. In about three years from that time the legs became affected. (James Parkinson, 1817)

In the 1817 essay from which this case study is taken, British physician James Parkinson reported similar symptoms in six patients, some of whom he had observed only in the streets near his clinic. Shaking was usually the first symptom, and it typically began in a hand. Over a span of years, the shaking spread to include the arm and then other parts of the body.

As the disease progressed, patients had a propensity to lean forward and walk on the balls of their feet. They also tended to run forward to prevent themselves from falling. In the later stages, patients had difficulty eating and swallowing. They drooled, and their bowel movements slowed. Eventually, the patients lost all muscular control and were unable to sleep because of the disruptive tremors.

More than 50 years after James Parkinson's descriptions, French neurologist Jean-Martin Charcot named the condition Parkinson's disease, known today as **Parkinson disease**. Three findings have helped researchers understand its neural basis:

Joy Milne

1. In 1919, Constantin Tréatikoff (1974) studied the brains of nine patients with Parkinson disease on autopsy and found that the *substantia nigra*, a small midbrain nucleus, had degenerated. In the brain of one patient who had Parkinson-like symptoms on only one side of the body, the substantia nigra had degenerated on the side opposite to that showing the symptoms.

2. Chemical examination of the brains of patients with Parkinson disease showed that symptoms appeared when the level of **dopamine (DA)**, then a proposed neurotransmitter, was reduced to less than 10% of normal in the basal ganglia (Ehringer & Hornykiewicz, 1960/1974).

3. In 1971, Urban Ungerstedt found that injecting a neurotoxin called 6-hydroxydopamine into rats selectively destroyed these dopamine-containing neurons and produced symptoms of Parkinson disease, thus confirming the role of dopamine in a neural pathway connecting the substantia nigra to the basal ganglia.

Loss of dopamine-containing substantia nigra neurons has been linked to environmental factors such as insecticides, herbicides, fungicides, flu virus, and toxic drugs. About 10% of people with Parkinson disease have a mutation in one of several specific genes, and people who are susceptible to environmental influences may also have a genetic predisposition to this disease.

Dopamine in other brain areas has been linked not only to motor behavior but also to some forms of learning and to neural structures that mediate

reward and addiction. Some people with Parkinson disease who receive dopaminergic drugs as therapy have become shopaholics or compulsive gamblers, despite having shown no such tendencies before treatment.

Treatments for neurological diseases are usually much more effective the earlier they are started, so early detection is important. Joy Milne, a nurse, has an incredible sense of smell that can recognize Parkinson disease on the human body (Morgan, 2016). She first noticed that her partner, Les, developed an "overpowering sort of nasty yeast smell" at age 31. Fourteen years later, Les was diagnosed with Parkinson disease. When they attended a support group for people with Parkinson disease, Joy noticed the same smell as soon as she entered the room.

Joy and Les approached a Parkinson researcher to test Joy's abilities. In a randomized and blinded experiment, she was asked to score T-shirts worn by people with Parkinson disease and a control group. She was incredibly accurate and made only one mistake, identifying a man in the control group as a person with Parkinson disease. However, many months later that man was also diagnosed with Parkinson disease—giving Joy a perfect record.

Joy's superior smelling abilities led to research into odors as a means of diagnosing Parkinson disease, resulting in the identification of several Parkinson-related compounds (Trivedi et al., 2019). This powerful tool combined with potential therapies may help to mitigate or even prevent Parkinson disease.

3. It is transported to the presynaptic membrane and released into the synaptic cleft in response to an action potential.

4. It binds to and activates receptors on the postsynaptic membrane.

5. It is degraded or removed, so it will not continue to interact with a receptor and work indefinitely.

**Parkinson disease** Motor system disorder correlated with dopamine loss in the substantia nigra; characterized by tremors, muscular rigidity, and reduction in voluntary movement.

**dopamine (DA)** Amine neurotransmitter involved in coordinating movement, attention, learning, and reinforcing behaviors.

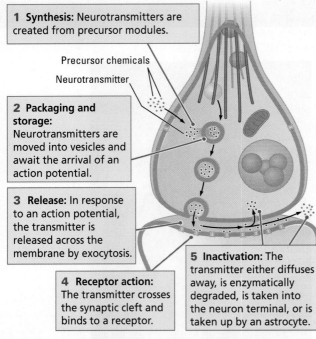

**1 Synthesis:** Neurotransmitters are created from precursor modules.

Precursor chemicals

Neurotransmitter

**2 Packaging and storage:** Neurotransmitters are moved into vesicles and await the arrival of an action potential.

**3 Release:** In response to an action potential, the transmitter is released across the membrane by exocytosis.

**4 Receptor action:** The transmitter crosses the synaptic cleft and binds to a receptor.

**5 Inactivation:** The transmitter either diffuses away, is enzymatically degraded, is taken into the neuron terminal, or is taken up by an astrocyte.

**FIGURE 5-3 Anterograde Synaptic Transmission**

For a refresher on protein export, review Figure 3-17.

**transporter** Protein molecule that pumps substances across a membrane.

**exocytosis** An active process by which chemical substances are carried in vesicles to the outer cell membrane, fuse with it, and release their contents.

**FIGURE 5-4 Neurotransmitter Release**

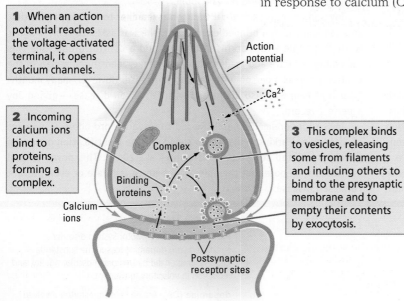

**1** When an action potential reaches the voltage-activated terminal, it opens calcium channels.

**2** Incoming calcium ions bind to proteins, forming a complex.

Complex

Binding proteins

Calcium ions

Action potential

Ca²⁺

**3** This complex binds to vesicles, releasing some from filaments and inducing others to bind to the presynaptic membrane and to empty their contents by exocytosis.

Postsynaptic receptor sites

# Steps 1 and 2: Neurotransmitter Synthesis, Packaging, and Storage

Several main classes of transmitters exist, which are derived in different ways. The *small-molecule* transmitters are synthesized in the axon terminal from building blocks that are often obtained from food. **Transporters** are protein molecules that move substances across cell membranes; they are responsible for packaging some neurotransmitter classes into vesicles. Mitochondria in the axon terminal provide the energy needed both to synthesize precursor chemicals into the transmitter and to power transporters.

*Peptide* transmitters are synthesized in the cell body according to instructions in the neuron's DNA, packaged in membranes on the Golgi bodies, and transported on microtubules to the axon terminal. Peptide transmitters may also be manufactured within the presynaptic terminal by ribosomes using mRNA transported to the terminal.

*Lipid* transmitters cannot be packaged and stored in vesicles, which are composed of lipids. Instead, they are synthesized "on demand" when an action potential reaches the axon terminal.

*Gaseous* transmitters are also generated within the cells by enzymes, but they differ from classical signaling molecules in many ways. Although their production is regulated, gaseous transmitters are able to permeate cell membranes. Given this ability, they are not stored within the cell.

*Ion* transmitters are not biochemically synthesized. Instead, like all other atoms heavier than helium, they are made in the hearts of dying stars. Within the body, ion transmitters can be packaged and stored in vesicles, usually along with other transmitter types, and then released into the synaptic cleft.

Regardless of their origin, neurotransmitters that are packaged into vesicles can be found in three locations at the axon terminal. Some vesicles are warehoused in granules, some are attached to microfilaments (a type of microtubule; see Figure 5-2B) in the terminal, and still others are attached to the presynaptic membrane. These sites correspond to the steps by which a transmitter is transported from a granule to the membrane, the site from which it is released into the synaptic cleft.

# Step 3: Neurotransmitter Release

Synaptic vesicles loaded with neurotransmitters must dock near release sites on the presynaptic membrane. There, the vesicles are primed to prepare them to fuse rapidly in response to calcium (Ca²⁺) influx. When an action potential reaches the presynaptic membrane, voltage changes on the membrane set the release process in motion. Calcium cations play a critical role in this process. The presynaptic membrane is rich in voltage-activated calcium channels, and the surrounding extracellular fluid is rich in Ca²⁺. As illustrated in **Figure 5-4**, the action potential's arrival opens these calcium channels, allowing an influx of calcium ions into the axon terminal.

Primed vesicles quickly fuse with the presynaptic membrane in response to the calcium influx and empty their contents into the synaptic cleft by **exocytosis**. The vesicles from storage granules and on filaments then move up to replace the vesicles that just emptied their contents.

# Step 4: Receptor-Site Activation

After its release from vesicles on the presynaptic membrane, the neurotransmitter diffuses across the synaptic cleft and binds to specialized protein molecules embedded in the postsynaptic membrane. These **transmitter-activated receptors** have binding sites for the transmitter, which we elaborate on in Section 5-3. The properties of the receptors on the postsynaptic membrane determine the effect on the postsynaptic cell.

**Ionotropic receptors** are associated with pores that can open to allow ions to pass through the membrane, rapidly changing the membrane voltage in one of two possible ways. These ion channels may allow $Na^+$ to enter the neuron, depolarizing the postsynaptic membrane, and so have an excitatory action on the postsynaptic neuron. Alternatively, the ion channels may allow $K^+$ to leave the neuron or $Cl^-$ to enter the neuron, which typically results in an inhibitory action on the postsynaptic neuron.

When bound by a transmitter, a second type of receptor, called a **metabotropic receptor**, may activate intracellular messenger systems. This action, in turn, may open an ion channel, thereby modulating either excitation or inhibition or influencing other functions of the receiving neuron. (This process is discussed in more detail in Section 5-2.)

In addition to interacting with the postsynaptic membrane's receptors, a neurotransmitter may interact with receptors on the presynaptic membrane. By doing so, it may influence the cell that just released it. Specifically, a neurotransmitter may activate presynaptic receptors called **autoreceptors** (self-receptors) to receive messages from their own axon terminals. Autoreceptors serve a critical function as part of a negative feedback loop, providing information about whether adjustments to synaptic communication should be made.

How much neurotransmitter is needed to send a message? Bernard Katz was awarded a Nobel Prize in 1970 for providing an answer to this question. While recording electrical activity from the postsynaptic membranes of muscles, he detected small, spontaneous depolarizations now called *miniature postsynaptic potentials*. The potentials varied in size, but each size appeared to be a multiple of the smallest potential.

Katz concluded that the smallest postsynaptic potential is produced by the release of the contents of just one synaptic vesicle. This number of neurotransmitter molecules is called a **quantum** (pl. **quanta**). Producing a postsynaptic potential large enough to initiate a postsynaptic action potential requires the simultaneous release of many quanta from the presynaptic cell.

The results of subsequent experiments showed that the number of quanta released from the presynaptic membrane in response to a single action potential depends on two factors: (1) the amount of $Ca^{2+}$ that enters the axon terminal in response to the action potential and (2) the number of vesicles docked at the membrane, waiting to be released. Both factors are relevant to synaptic activity that facilitates learning, a topic we consider in Section 14-4.

## Step 5: Neurotransmitter Inactivation

Chemical transmission would not be an effective messenger system if a neurotransmitter lingered within the synaptic cleft, continuing to occupy and stimulate receptors. If this happened, the postsynaptic cell could not respond to other messages sent by the presynaptic neuron. Thus, after a neurotransmitter has done its work, it is quickly removed from the receptor sites and from the synaptic cleft. Inactivation is accomplished in at least four ways:

1. *Diffusion*. Some of the neurotransmitter simply diffuses away from the synaptic cleft and is no longer available to bind to receptors.

2. *Degradation*. Enzymes in the synaptic cleft break down the transmitter.

3. *Reuptake*. Membrane transporters specific to that transmitter may bring it back into the presynaptic axon terminal for reuse. The by-products of degradation by enzymes also may be taken back into the terminal to be reused in the cell.

Review the actions of voltage-activated channels in Section 4-3.

**transmitter-activated receptor** Protein that has a binding site for a specific neurotransmitter and is embedded in the membrane of a cell.

**ionotropic receptor** Embedded membrane protein; acts as (1) a binding site for a neurotransmitter and (2) a pore that regulates ion flow to directly and rapidly change membrane voltage.

**metabotropic receptor** Embedded membrane protein with a binding site for a neurotransmitter linked to a G protein; can affect other receptors or act with second messengers to affect other cellular processes, including opening a pore.

**autoreceptor** Self-receptor in a neuronal membrane, which responds to the same transmitter released by the neuron; part of a negative feedback loop allowing the neuron to adjust its output.

**quantum** (pl. **quanta**) Number of neurotransmitter molecules, equivalent to the content of a single synaptic vesicle, that produces a just-observable change in the depolarizations of the postsynaptic terminal.

Table 3-1 describes astrocytes and other types of glial cells and their functions.

**4.** *Astrocyte uptake.* Some neurotransmitters are taken up by neighboring astrocytes. Astrocytes can also store certain transmitters for re-export to the axon terminal.

Chemical mechanisms within an axon terminal enable it to respond to the frequency of its own use—evidence of the flexibility of synaptic function. If the terminal is very active, the amount of neurotransmitter made and stored there may increase, more $Ca^{2+}$ may be available to stimulate transmitter release, or more $Ca^{2+}$ channels may be available to allow $Ca^{2+}$ entry. In contrast, if the terminal is rarely used, enzymes within the terminal buttons may break down excess transmitter. The by-products are then reused or excreted from the neuron. Axon terminals may even send messages to the neuron's cell body, stimulating an increase in the supply of the neurotransmitter or the molecules from which it is constructed.

# Varieties of Synapses

So far, we have considered a generic chemical synapse, with features possessed by most synapses. In reality, synapses vary widely in the nervous system. Each type is specialized in terms of its location, structure, function, and target. **Figure 5-5** illustrates this diversity on a single hypothetical neuron.

Figure 4-27 shows a schematic view of an axomuscular synapse.

You have already encountered two kinds of chemical synapses. First, in the *axomuscular synapse*, an axon synapses with a muscle end plate, releasing acetylcholine. Second, in the *axodendritic synapse*, detailed in Figure 5-2B, the axon terminal of a neuron synapses with a dendrite or dendritic spine of another neuron.

Figure 5-5 diagrams axon terminals at the axodendritic synapse, as well as the *axosomatic synapse*, at a cell body; the *axoaxonic synapse*, on another axon; and the *axosynaptic synapse*, on another presynaptic terminal (i.e., at the synapse between some other axon and its target). *Axoextracellular synapses* have no specific targets, but instead secrete their transmitter chemicals into the extracellular fluid. In the

**FIGURE 5-5 The Versatile Synapse**

*axosecretory synapse*, a terminal synapses with a tiny blood vessel (a capillary) and secretes its transmitter directly into the blood. Finally, synapses are not limited to axon terminals: dendrites also may send messages to other dendrites through *dendrodendritic synapses*.

This wide variety of connections makes the synapse a versatile chemical delivery system. Synapses can deliver transmitters to highly specific sites or diffuse locales. Through connections to the dendrites, cell body, or axon of a neuron, transmitters can control the neuron's actions in different ways, thus giving rise to the vast array of behaviors and functions.

Through axosynaptic connections, synapses can also exert precise control over another neuron's input to a cell. By excreting transmitters into extracellular fluid or into the blood, axoextracellular and axosecretory synapses can modulate the function of large areas of tissue or even the entire body. Many transmitters secreted by neurons act as hormones; circulating in the blood, they have widespread influences on the brain and body, as we will see in Section 5-4.

## Electrical Synapses

Chemical synapses are the most common synapses in mammalian nervous systems, but they are not the only kind of synapse. Some neurons influence each other electrically through an *electrical synapse*, or gap junction, where two neurons' intracellular fluids or cytoplasm can come into direct contact (see **Figure 5-6**). A **gap junction** is formed when connexin proteins in one cell membrane create a *hemichannel* that connects to a hemichannel in an adjacent cell's membrane, allowing ions to pass from one neuron to the other in both directions. Gap junctions constitute a regulated gate between cells because they can be either open or closed.

Gap junctions eliminate the brief delay in information flow—about 5 milliseconds per synapse—that occurs during chemical transmission (note the space between the presynaptic terminal and the dendritic spine in Figure 5-2B compared with Figure 5-6). For example, the crayfish's gap junctions activate its tail flick, a response that enables it to make a quick escape from a predator. The gap junctions found in some regions of the mammalian brain allow groups of interneurons to synchronize their firing rhythmically. Gap junctions also allow glial cells and neurons to exchange substances (Dere & Zlomuzica, 2012).

Gap junctions vary in other ways, too. Different connexin subunits give rise to different pore sizes, which allows selectivity for specific small molecules. Large biomolecules such as nucleic acids and proteins cannot fit through gap junctions.

Notably, gap junctions further increase the signaling diversity between neurons. Such interneuronal communication may occur via dendrodendritic and axoaxonic gap junctions. Interestingly, gap junctions at axon terminals synapsing on dendrites and cell bodies allow for dual chemical and electrical synaptic transmission. These "mixed synapses" have only recently been discovered, and their functional properties are still being determined in the mammalian CNS (Nagy et al., 2017).

If chemical synapses transmit messages more slowly, why do mammals rely more heavily on them than on gap junctions? The answer is that chemical synapses can show plasticity; they can amplify or diminish a signal sent from one neuron to the next; and they can change with experience to alter their signals and thus mediate learning. By comparison, gap junctions do not allow such plasticity—they are built for speed and efficient communication—but they can aid in binding neurons together functionally, as might be required for some forms of memory and other functions (Totland et al., 2019).

## Excitatory and Inhibitory Messages

As you have seen, a neurotransmitter can influence a neuron's functioning through a remarkable variety of mechanisms. In its direct actions in influencing a neuron's electrical activity, however, a neurotransmitter acting through its receptors has only one

**FIGURE 5-6 Gap Junction** The connexin proteins on adjacent cell membranes connect to form hemichannels, which allow ions to pass between the two neurons.

**gap junction** Area of contact between adjacent cells in which connexin proteins in each cell form connecting hemichannels; when open, the hemichannels allow ions to pass between the two cells. Also called an *electrical synapse*.

Each neuron receives thousands of excitatory and inhibitory signals every second. As indicated in **Principle 7:** The nervous system works by juxtaposing excitation and inhibition.

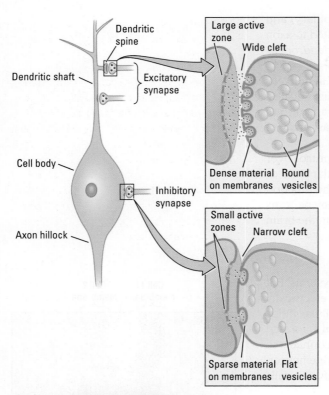

**FIGURE 5-7 Excitatory and Inhibitory Zones**
Excitatory synapses typically occupy spines and dendritic shafts on a neuron. Inhibitory synapses are typically found on the cell body.

Figure 4-2 illustrates the key components of a neuron involved in the generation of an action potential.

Behaviors are lost when a disorder prevents excitatory instructions, and they are uncontrollably expressed, or "released," when a disorder prevents inhibitory instructions.

of two immediate effects: it influences transmembrane ion flow either to increase or to decrease the likelihood that the cell with which it comes in contact will produce an action potential. Thus, despite the diversity of synapses, they all convey only excitatory or inhibitory messages. To be precise, neurotransmitters themselves do not determine excitation or inhibition. As noted at the beginning of this section, the ion channel associated with the receptor makes the call.

Excitatory and inhibitory synapses differ in their appearance and are generally located on different parts of the neuron. As shown in **Figure 5-7**, excitatory synapses are typically found on the shafts or spines of dendrites, whereas inhibitory synapses more frequently occur on the cell body. Excitatory synapses have round synaptic vesicles; the vesicles in inhibitory synapses are flattened. The material on the presynaptic and postsynaptic membranes is denser in an excitatory synapse than it is in an inhibitory synapse, and the excitatory synaptic cleft is wider. Finally, the active zone on an excitatory synapse is larger than that on an inhibitory synapse.

The differing locations of excitatory and inhibitory synapses divide a neuron into two zones: an excitatory dendritic tree and an inhibitory cell body. Think of excitatory and inhibitory messages as interacting from these two different perspectives. Viewed from an inhibitory perspective, you can picture excitation coming in over the dendrites and spreading past the axon hillock to trigger an action potential at the initial segment. If the message must be stopped, it is best halted by inhibiting the cell body close to the initial segment. In this model of excitatory–inhibitory interaction, inhibition blocks excitation by using a "cut 'em off at the pass" strategy.

Another way to conceptualize excitatory–inhibitory interaction is to picture excitation overcoming inhibition. In fact, excitatory synaptic inputs that are farther away from the soma are larger, to counteract the loss of signal that occurs over distance (Magee & Cook, 2000). If the cell body is typically in an inhibited state, the only way to generate an action potential is to reduce cell body inhibition. In this "open the gates" strategy, the excitatory message is like a racehorse that is ready to run down the track, but first the inhibitory starting gate must be removed. Research Focus 5-3, Dendritic Spines: Small but Mighty explains how continuous structural changes in dendritic spines, including the formation of new synapses, facilitates learning and behavior.

## Evolution of Complex Neurotransmission Systems

Considering all the biochemical steps required to get a message across a synapse and the variety of synapses, you might well wonder why—and how—such a complex communication system ever evolved. How did chemical transmitters originate?

To make the origin of chemical secretions for neuronal communication easier to imagine, think about the feeding behaviors of simple single-celled creatures. The earliest unicellular creatures secreted juices onto bacteria to immobilize and prepare them for ingestion. These digestive juices were probably expelled from the cell body by exocytosis: a vacuole or vesicle attached itself to the cell membrane and then opened into the extracellular fluid to discharge its contents. The prey, once immobilized, was captured through the reverse process of *endocytosis*.

The exocytosis mechanism for digestion in a single-celled organism parallels the release of a neurotransmitter for communication in more complex creatures. Quite possibly, evolution long ago adapted these primordial digestive processes into processes of neural communication in more complex organisms.

## ◎ RESEARCH FOCUS 5-3

# Dendritic Spines: Small but Mighty

Dendritic spines, which protrude from the dendrite's shaft, measure about 1 to 3 micrometers (μm, one-millionth of a meter) long and less than 1 μm in diameter. Each neuron can have many thousands of spines. The number of dendritic spines in the human cerebral cortex is estimated at $10^{14}$.

Dendritic spines originate in filopodia (from the Latin *file*, for "thread," and the Greek *podium*, for "foot") that bud out of neurons, especially at dendrites. Microscopic observation of dendrites shows that filopodia are constantly emerging and retracting over several seconds.

This budding of filopodia is much more pronounced in developing neurons and in the developing brain (this growth process is illustrated in Figure 8-13). Because filopodia can grow into dendritic spines, their budding suggests that they are searching for contacts from axon terminals with which to form synapses. Some of the new synapses formed when contact is made may have only a short life; others endure for longer periods.

Permanent dendritic spines tend to have large, mushroom-shaped heads, giving them a large contact area with a terminal button, and long stems, giving them an identity apart from the dendrite. The heads of spines and the terminals of presynaptic connections form functional compartments that can generate huge electrical potentials, thereby influencing the neuron's electrical messages.

Examination of dendritic spines in the nervous system shows that some are simple and others complex. The cellular mechanisms that allow synapses to appear on spines and to change shape include microfilaments linked to the membrane receptors, protein transport from the cell body, and the incorporation of nutrients from the extracellular space. All this activity changes the appearance of both presynaptic and postsynaptic structures. Why? Dendritic spines mediate learning, and in order to mediate learning, each spine must be able to act independently, undergoing changes that its neighbors do not undergo. The illustration summarizes the synaptic structures related to learning and behavior and the structural changes that may underlie learning.

Dendritic spines provide the structural basis for our behavior, skills, and memories (Chidambaram et al., 2019). Impairments in forming spines characterize some kinds of mental disability, and the loss of spines is associated with the dementia of Alzheimer disease.

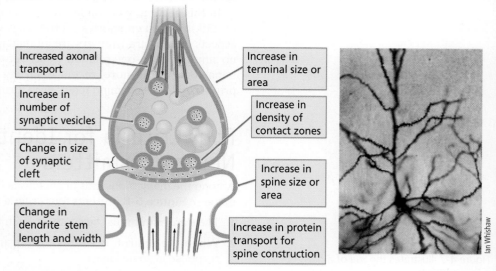

Synaptic structures that may underlie learning.

# 5-1 Review

Before you continue, check your understanding. Answers to Self-Test appear at the back of the book.

1. In mammals, the principal form of communication between neurons occurs via _____, even though this structure is slower and more complex than the fused _____.

2. The principal benefit of chemical synapses over electrical synapses is that they can change with _____ to alter their signals and so mediate _____.

3. The nervous system has evolved a variety of synapses:
   _____ between axon terminals and dendrites,
   _____ between axon terminals and cell bodies,
   _____ between axon terminals and muscles,
   _____ between axon terminals and other axons, and
   _____ between axon terminals and other synapses.
   A(n) _____ synapse releases chemical transmitters into extracellular fluid, a(n) _____ synapse releases transmitter into the bloodstream as hormones, and a(n) _____ synapse connects dendrites to other dendrites.

4. Excitatory synapses are usually located on a(n) _____, whereas inhibitory synapses are usually found on a(n) _____.

5. Describe the five steps in chemical neurotransmission.

# Varieties of Neurotransmitters and Receptors

Subsequent to Otto Loewi's 1921 discovery that excitatory and inhibitory chemicals control heart rate, many researchers thought that the brain must work under much the same type of dual control. Specifically, they reasoned that norepinephrine and acetylcholine were the transmitters through which excitatory and inhibitory brain cells worked. They did not imagine what we know today: the human brain employs a dazzling variety of neurotransmitters and receptors. The neurotransmitters operate in even more versatile ways: some may be excitatory at one location and inhibitory at another site, for example, and two or more may team up in a single synapse so that one makes the other more potent. Moreover, each neurotransmitter may interact with several varieties of receptors, each having a somewhat different function.

In this section, you will learn how neurotransmitters are identified and how they fit within broad categories on the basis of their chemical structure. The functional aspects of neurotransmitters are intimately intertwined and highly intricate, such that no simple one-to-one relation exists between a single neurotransmitter and a single behavior. Furthermore, receptor variety is achieved by the unique combination of protein molecules coming together to form a functional receptor.

## Four Criteria for Identifying Neurotransmitters

Among the many thousands of chemicals in the nervous system, which are neurotransmitters? **Figure 5-8** presents four criteria used to identify these molecules:

1. The transmitter must be synthesized in the neuron or otherwise be present in it.

2. When the neuron is excited, the transmitter must be released and produce a response in some target.

3. The same response must be obtained when the transmitter is experimentally placed on the target.

4. A mechanism must exist for removing the transmitter from its site of action after its work is done.

These criteria are fairly easy to apply when examining the somatic nervous system, especially at an accessible nerve–muscle junction with only one main neurotransmitter, acetylcholine. But identifying chemical transmitters in the CNS is not so easy. In the brain and spinal cord, thousands of synapses are packed around every neuron, preventing easy access to any single synapse and its activities. Consequently, researchers employ multiple techniques, including staining, stimulating, and collecting, to identify substances thought to be CNS neurotransmitters. A suspect chemical that has not yet been shown to meet all four of the identifying criteria is called a *putative* (supposed) *transmitter*.

Researchers trying to identify new CNS neurotransmitters can use microelectrodes to stimulate and record responses from single neurons. A glass microelectrode is small enough to be placed on specific neuronal targets. It can be filled with a chemical of interest, and then a current passed through the electrode, ejecting the chemical into or onto the neuron to mimic neurotransmitter release onto the cell.

Many staining techniques can identify specific chemicals inside the cell. Methods have also been developed for preserving nervous system tissue in a saline bath while experimenters determine how the neurons in the tissue communicate. The use of such living tissue slices simplifies the investigation

Figure 4-7 illustrates the use of a glass microelectrode.

**FIGURE 5-8 Criteria for Identifying Neurotransmitters**

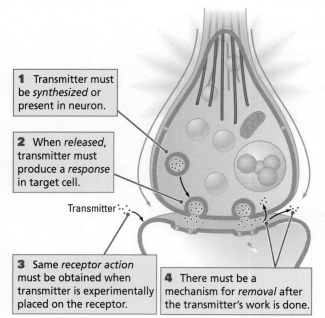

**1** Transmitter must be *synthesized* or present in neuron.

**2** When *released*, transmitter must produce a *response* in target cell.

Transmitter

**3** Same *receptor action* must be obtained when transmitter is experimentally placed on the receptor.

**4** There must be a mechanism for *removal* after the transmitter's work is done.

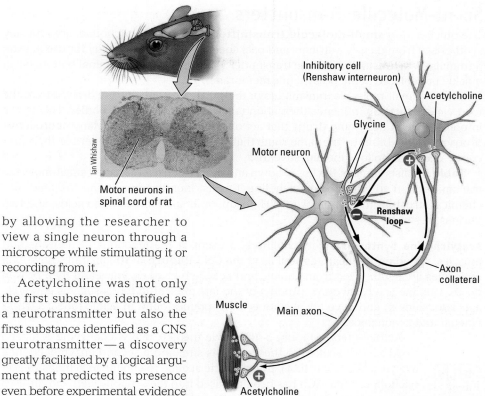

Ian Whishaw

Motor neurons in spinal cord of rat

**FIGURE 5-9 Renshaw Loop** *Left*: Some spinal cord motor neurons project to the rat's forelimb muscles. *Right*: In a Renshaw loop, the main motor axon (green) projects to a muscle, and its axon collateral remains in the spinal cord to synapse with a Renshaw interneuron (red). The Renshaw interneuron contains the inhibitory transmitter glycine, which acts to prevent motor neuron overexcitation. Both the main motor axon and its collateral terminals contain acetylcholine. When the motor neuron is highly excited, it can modulate its activity level through the Renshaw loop (plus and minus signs).

by allowing the researcher to view a single neuron through a microscope while stimulating it or recording from it.

Acetylcholine was not only the first substance identified as a neurotransmitter but also the first substance identified as a CNS neurotransmitter—a discovery greatly facilitated by a logical argument that predicted its presence even before experimental evidence was gathered. All motor neuron axons leaving the spinal cord use acetylcholine as a transmitter. Each axon has an axon collateral within the spinal cord that synapses on a nearby CNS interneuron. The interneuron, in turn, synapses on the motor neuron's cell body. **Figure 5-9** depicts this circular set of connections, called a *Renshaw loop* (after the researcher who first described it).

Because the main axon to the muscle releases acetylcholine, investigators suspected that its axon collateral also might release acetylcholine. For two terminals of the same axon to use different transmitters seemed unlikely. Knowing which chemical to look for made it easier to find and obtain the required evidence that acetylcholine is, in fact, a neurotransmitter in both locations.

The loop made by the axon collateral and the interneuron in the spinal cord forms a feedback circuit that enables the motor neuron to inhibit itself from overexcitation, should it receive a great many excitatory inputs from other parts of the CNS. Follow the positive and negative signs in Figure 5-9 to see how the Renshaw loop works. If the loop becomes blocked, such as with the toxin strychnine, motor neurons become over-active, producing convulsions that can choke off respiration and so cause death.

The term *neurotransmitter* is used much more broadly now than it was when researchers began to identify these chemicals. Today, the term applies to chemicals that have the following functions:

- Carry a message from the presynaptic membrane of one neuron to another by influencing the postsynaptic membrane's voltage.

- Change the structure of a synapse.

- Communicate by sending messages in the opposite direction. These *retrograde (reverse-direction) messages* influence the release or **reuptake** of transmitters on the presynaptic side.

**reuptake** Inactivation of a neurotransmitter when membrane transporter proteins bring the transmitter back into the presynaptic axon terminal for reuse.

## Classes of Neurotransmitters

We can impose some order on the diversity of neurotransmitters by classifying them into groups based on their chemical composition: small-molecule transmitters, peptide transmitters, lipid transmitters, gaseous transmitters, and the ion transmitter.

Taking drugs orally is easy and comparatively safe, but not all drugs can traverse the digestive tract. The various routes of drug administration are explained in Section 6-1.

**TABLE 5-1** Best-Known and Well-Studied Small-Molecule Neurotransmitters

| Acetylcholine (ACh) |
| --- |
| **Amines** |
| Dopamine (DA) |
| Histamine (H) |
| Norepinephrine (NE, *or* noradrenaline [NA]) |
| Epinephrine (EP, *or* adrenaline) |
| Serotonin (5-HT) |
| **Amino acids** |
| Gamma-aminobutyric acid (GABA) |
| Glutamate (Glu) |
| Glycine (Gly) |
| **Purines** |
| Adenosine |
| Adenosine triphosphate (ATP) |

**small-molecule transmitter** Quick-acting neurotransmitter synthesized in the axon terminal from products derived from the diet.

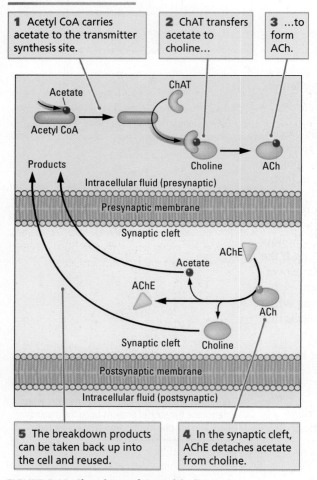

**1** Acetyl CoA carries acetate to the transmitter synthesis site.

**2** ChAT transfers acetate to choline...

**3** ...to form ACh.

**5** The breakdown products can be taken back up into the cell and reused.

**4** In the synaptic cleft, AChE detaches acetate from choline.

**FIGURE 5-10 Chemistry of Acetylcholine**
Two enzymes combine the dietary precursors of ACh within the cell, and a third breaks them down in the synapse for reuptake.

# Small-Molecule Transmitters

The quick-acting **small-molecule transmitters**, such as acetylcholine, are typically synthesized from dietary nutrients and packaged so that they are ready for use in axon terminals. When a small-molecule transmitter is released from a terminal button, it can quickly be replaced at the presynaptic membrane.

Because small-molecule transmitters or their main components are derived from the food we eat, diet can influence their abundance and activity in our bodies. This fact is important when designing drugs that act on the nervous system. Many neuroactive drugs reach the brain by the same route that small-molecule transmitters or their precursor chemicals follow: the digestive tract.

**Table 5-1** lists some of the best-known and most extensively studied small-molecule transmitters. In addition to acetylcholine, this list includes five amines (related by a chemical structure that contains an NH group, or *amine*), three amino acids, and two purines.

**Acetylcholine Synthesis** Acetylcholine is present at the junctions of neurons and muscles, including the heart, as well as in the CNS. **Figure 5-10** illustrates how ACh molecules are synthesized from choline and acetate by two enzymes and then broken down. Choline is a breakdown product of the fats present in foods such as egg yolk, avocado, salmon, and olive oil; acetate is a compound found in acidic foods, such as vinegar and lemon juice.

As depicted in Figure 5-10, inside the cell, acetyl coenzyme A (acetyl CoA) carries acetate to the synthesis site, and a second enzyme, choline acetyltransferase (ChAT), transfers the acetate to choline to synthesize acetylcholine. After ACh has been released into the synaptic cleft and diffuses to receptor sites on the postsynaptic membrane, a third enzyme, acetylcholinesterase (AChE), reverses the process, breaking down the transmitter by detaching acetate from choline. The breakdown products can then be taken back into the presynaptic terminal for reuse.

**Amine Synthesis** Some transmitters grouped together in Table 5-1 have common biochemical pathways to synthesis and, therefore, are related. You are already familiar with the amines dopamine (DA), norepinephrine (NE), and epinephrine (EP). To review, DA loss figures in Parkinson disease, EP is the excitatory transmitter within the amphibian heart, and NE is the excitatory transmitter within the mammalian heart.

**Figure 5-11** charts the biochemical sequence in which these amines are synthesized. The precursor chemical is tyrosine, an amino acid abundant in food. (Hard cheese and bananas are good sources.) The enzyme tyrosine hydroxylase (enzyme 1 in Figure 5-11) changes tyrosine into L-dopa, which other enzymes convert first into dopamine, then into norepinephrine, and finally into epinephrine.

Interestingly, the supply of the enzyme tyrosine hydroxylase is limited. Consequently, so is the rate at which dopamine, norepinephrine, and epinephrine can be produced, regardless of how much tyrosine is present or ingested. This **rate-limiting factor** can be bypassed by the oral administration of L-dopa, which is why this medication is used to treat Parkinson disease, as described in Clinical Focus 5-4, Awakening with L-Dopa.

*Histidine* is an amino acid that serves as the primary biological source of the transmitter **histamine (H)**. Histidine is converted by the enzyme histidine decarboxylase into histamine. Its many functions in the brain include control of arousal and of waking, but histamine can also cause the constriction of smooth muscles. This chemical plays an important role in the regulation of several essential events in the immune response. However, when activated in allergic reactions, histamine contributes to asthma, a constriction of the airways. You are probably familiar with antihistamine drugs used to treat allergies.

| Enzyme 1 | Enzyme 2 | Enzyme 3 | Enzyme 4 |
|---|---|---|---|

Tyrosine → L-Dopa → Dopamine → Norepinephrine → Epinephrine

**FIGURE 5-11 Sequential Synthesis of Three Amines** A different enzyme is responsible for each successive molecular modification in this biochemical sequence of amine neurotransmitters.

**Serotonin Synthesis** The amine transmitter **serotonin (5-HT**, for 5-hydroxytryptamine) is synthesized from the amino acid L-tryptophan. Tryptophan is abundant in pork, turkey, milk, and bananas, among other foods. Serotonin plays a role in regulating mood and aggression, appetite and arousal, respiration, and pain perception.

**Amino Acid Synthesis** Two amino acid transmitters, **glutamate (Glu)** and **gamma-aminobutyric acid (GABA)**, are closely related. GABA is formed by a simple modification of the glutamate molecule, as shown in **Figure 5-12**. These two transmitters are considered the workhorses of the brain because so many synapses use them.

In the forebrain and cerebellum, glutamate is the main excitatory transmitter and GABA is the main inhibitory transmitter. Thus, glutamate is a neurotransmitter in excitatory synapses, whereas GABA is a neurotransmitter in inhibitory synapses. Interestingly, glutamate is widely distributed in CNS neurons, but it becomes a neurotransmitter only if it is appropriately packaged in vesicles in the axon terminal. The amino acid transmitter glycine (Gly) is a much more common inhibitory transmitter in the brainstem and spinal cord, where it acts within the Renshaw loop, for example (review Figure 5-9).

Drugs to block the reuptake of serotonin, called selective serotonin reuptake inhibitors (SSRIs), are used to treat depression, and are discussed in Section 6-2.

**rate-limiting factor** Any chemical in limited supply that restricts the pace at which another chemical can be synthesized.

**histamine (H)** Neurotransmitter that controls arousal and waking; important in immune response, but can cause the constriction of smooth muscles; when activated in allergic reactions, constricts airway and contributes to asthma.

**serotonin (5-HT)** Amine neurotransmitter; helps to regulate mood and aggression, appetite and arousal, perception of pain, and respiration.

**glutamate (Glu)** Amino acid neurotransmitter; typically opens Na$^+$ and Ca$^{2+}$ channels and therefore excites neurons.

**gamma-aminobutyric acid (GABA)** Amino acid neurotransmitter; typically opens Cl$^-$ channels and therefore inhibits neurons.

## ◉ CLINICAL FOCUS 5-4

# Awakening with L-Dopa

He was started on L-dopa in March 1969. The dose was slowly raised to 4.0 mg a day over a period of three weeks without apparently producing any effect. I first discovered that Mr. E. was responding to L-dopa by accident, chancing to go past his room at an unaccustomed time and hearing regular footsteps inside the room. I went in and found Mr. E., who had been chair bound since 1966, walking up and down his room, swinging his arms with considerable vigor, and showing erectness of posture and a brightness of expression completely new to him. When I asked him about the effect, he said with some embarrassment: "Yes! I felt the L-dopa beginning to work three days ago—it was like a wave of energy and strength sweeping through me. I found I could stand and walk by myself, and that I could do everything I needed for myself—but I was afraid that you would see how well I was and discharge me from the hospital." (Sacks, 1976)

In this case history, neurologist and author Oliver Sacks describes administering L-dopa to a patient who had acquired Parkinsonism as an aftereffect of severe influenza in the 1920s. The relationship between the influenza and the Parkinsonlike symptoms suggests that the flu virus had entered the person's brain and selectively attacked dopamine neurons in his substantia nigra. By increasing the amount of DA in remaining synapses, L-dopa relieved their symptoms.

Two separate groups of investigators independently gave L-dopa to people with Parkinson disease beginning in 1961 (Barbeau et al., 1961; Birkmayer & Hornykiewicz, 1961). Both research teams knew that the chemical is catalyzed into dopamine at DA synapses (see Figure 5-11). The L-dopa, it turned out, reduced their muscular rigidity.

This work provided the first demonstration that a neurological condition can be relieved by a drug that aids in increasing the amount of a neurotransmitter. L-Dopa has since become a standard treatment for Parkinson disease. Its effects have been improved by the administration of drugs that prevent L-dopa from being converted to dopamine in the body before it passes through the blood–brain barrier and gets to dopamine neurons in the brain.

L-Dopa is not a cure, however. Parkinson disease still progresses during treatment, and as more and more dopamine synapses are lost, the treatment becomes increasingly less effective. L-Dopa can also produce *dyskinesias* — involuntary, unwanted movements, such as ballistic (throwinglike) or choreic (dancelike) movements. When these side effects eventually become severe, the treatment must be discontinued.

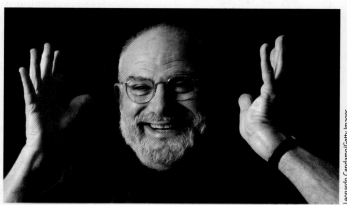

Oliver Sacks

Leonardo Cendamo/Getty Images

**Purines** The purines are synthesized as nucleotides—the kind of molecules that make up DNA and RNA. The purine *adenosine triphosphate* (*ATP*) consists of a molecule of adenine attached to a ribose sugar molecule and three phosphate groups. Removal of the three phosphate groups leaves adenosine, a neurotransmitter that plays a central role in promoting sleep, suppressing arousal, and regulating blood flow to various organs through *vasodilation* (the dilation of blood vessels).

## Peptide Transmitters

More than 50 short amino acid chains of various lengths (fewer than 100 amino acids) form the families of peptide transmitters, or **neuropeptides**, listed in **Table 5-2**. Synthesized through the translation of mRNA from instructions contained in the neuron's DNA, neuropeptides are multifunctional chains of amino acids that act as neurotransmitters.

**TABLE 5-2** Peptide Neurotransmitters

| Family | Examples |
| --- | --- |
| Opioids | Met-enkephalin, dynorphin, beta-endorphin |
| Neurohypophyseals | Vasopressin, oxytocin |
| Secretins | Secretin, motilin, glucagon, growth hormone–releasing factor |
| Insulins | Insulin, insulin growth factors |
| Gastrins | Gastrin, cholecystokinin |
| Somatostatins | Somatostatin |
| Tachykinins | Neurokinin A, neurokinin B, substance P |

In some neurons, peptide transmitters are made in the axon terminal, but most are assembled on the neuron's ribosomes, packaged in a membrane by Golgi bodies, and transported by the microtubules to the axon terminals. The entire process of neuropeptide synthesis and transport is relatively slow compared with the nearly ready-made small-molecule neurotransmitters at axon terminals. Consequently, peptide transmitters act slowly and are not replaced quickly.

Neuropeptides, however, perform an enormous range of functions in the nervous system, as might be expected from their large numbers. They act as hormones that respond to stress, enable a mother to bond with her infant, regulate eating and drinking and pleasure and pain, and probably contribute to learning.

Opium, morphine, and related synthetic chemicals such as heroin—long known both to produce euphoria and to reduce pain—mimic the actions of endogenous brain opioid neuropeptides: enkephalins, dynorphins, and endorphins. (The term *enkephalin* derives from the phrase "in the cephalon," meaning "in the brain or head," whereas the term *endorphin* is a shortened form of "endogenous morphine.") A part of the amino acid chain in each of these naturally occurring opioid peptides is structurally similar to the others, as illustrated for two of them in **Figure 5-13**. Morphine mimics this part of the chain. Synthetic opioids, such as fentanyl, have a similar action, but are much more potent and fast acting, putting the individuals who use these drugs at much greater risk of overdose.

The discovery of naturally occurring morphine-like neuropeptides suggested that one or more of them might have analgesic properties and play a role in pain perception. It turns out that beta-endorphin, a neurotransmitter released in response to exercise and thought to be responsible for the "runner's high," has many times the analgesic potency of morphine.

Some CNS peptides take part in specific periodic behaviors, each month or each year perhaps. For instance, in a female deer, neuropeptide transmitters act as hormones (luteinizing hormone) that prepare her for the fall mating season. Come winter, a different set of biochemicals facilitates the developing deer fetus. When the doe gives birth in the spring, still other highly specific neuropeptide hormones—such as

---

COOH
|
CH₂
|
CH₂
|
H₂N—CH
|
COOH

→

COOH
|
CH₂
|
CH₂
|
H₂N—CH₂

Glutamate        GABA

**FIGURE 5-12 Amino Acid Transmitters** *Top*: Removal of a carboxyl (COOH) group from the bottom of the glutamate molecule produces GABA. *Bottom*: Their different shapes, illustrated by three-dimensional space-filling models, allow these amino acid transmitters to bind to different receptors.

Section 3-2 includes a detailed description of DNA and RNA and the process of protein synthesis. Figure 3-15 diagrams peptide bonding, and Figure 3-17 diagrams protein export.

Met-enkephalin

( Tyr )( Gly )( Gly )( Phe )( Met )

Leu-enkephalin

( Tyr )( Gly )( Gly )( Phe )( Leu )

**FIGURE 5-13 Opioid Peptides** Parts of the amino acid chains of some neuropeptides that act on the brain centers for pleasure and pain are structurally similar and also share similarities to drugs such as morphine, which mimic their functions (see Section 6-2).

**neuropeptide** Short, multifunctional amino acid chain (fewer than 100 amino acids); acts as a neurotransmitter and can act as a hormone; may contribute to learning.

oxytocin, which enables the mother to bond to her fawn, and prolactin, which enables her to nurse—take control. The same neuropeptides serve similar specific hormonal functions in humans. Others, such as neuropeptide growth hormones, perform far more general functions in regulating growth.

Unlike many transmitters that bind to receptors associated with ion channels, neuropeptides are metabotropic and have no direct effects on the postsynaptic membrane's voltage. Instead, peptide transmitters activate synaptic receptors that indirectly influence cell structure and function. Digestive processes degrade neuropeptide amino acid chains, so they generally cannot be taken orally as drugs, whereas some small-molecule transmitters can.

## Lipid Transmitters

Predominant among the lipid neurotransmitters are the **endocannabinoids** (endogenous cannabinoids), a class of lipid neurotransmitters synthesized at the postsynaptic membrane to act on receptors at the presynaptic membrane. The endocannabinoids include anandamide (AEA) and 2-AG (2-arachidonoylglycerol), both of which are derived from arachidonic acid, an unsaturated fatty acid. Poultry and eggs are especially good sources of arachidonic acid. Endocannabinoids participate in a diverse set of physiological and psychological processes that affect appetite, pain, sleep, mood, memory, anxiety, and the stress response. Their scientific history is brief but illustrates how science can progress, punctuated by short steps.

Because endocannabinoids are lipophilic (fat-loving) molecules, they are not soluble in water and are not stored in vesicles. Rather, investigators hypothesize that endocannabinoids are synthesized on demand after a neuron has depolarized and calcium has entered the cell. Calcium activates the enzyme transacylase, the first step in producing anandamide. Once anandamide or 2-AG is synthesized, it diffuses across the synaptic cleft and interacts with its receptor on the presynaptic membrane. Thus, both molecules act as retrograde neurotransmitters, for a time reducing the amount of small-molecule transmitter being released. In this way, the postsynaptic neuron reduces the amount of incoming neural signal.

The $CB_1$ receptor is the target of all cannabinoids, whether generated by animals (endocannabinoids), plants (phytocannabinoids), or synthetically. **Figure 5-14** illustrates the structural similarities between anandamide and tetrahydrocannabinol (THC), which allows both to interact with $CB_1$ receptors. Yes, your body is teeming with weed receptors (Scudellari, 2017). $CB_1$ receptors are found at both glutamate and GABA synapses, so cannabinoids act as neuromodulators to inhibit release of glutamate and GABA. Consequently, cannabinoids dampen both neuronal excitation and inhibition.

Phytocannabinoids are obtained from the hemp plants *Cannabis sativa* and *Cannabis indica*. These plants have been used medically and recreationally for thousands of years, but only recently was an extract from cannabis synthesized. Early in the twentieth century, many constituents of cannabis, including THC and cannabidiol (CBD), were isolated and their chemical structure determined. In 1967, Raphael Mechoulam and Yehiel Gaoni reported the structure of the THC molecule, the main psychoactive constituent in cannabis. Next, investigators determined how THC is metabolized. (The process is quite slow, which explains why THC can be detected in urine for weeks after cannabis use.)

Research on the physiological and psychological effects of THC in animals and people, which began after its isolation and purification, is ongoing. Twenty-four years after the structure of the THC molecule was determined, the first cannabinoid receptor ($CB_1$) was found. Typically, receptors are activated by endogenous molecules, which motivated researchers to look for endogenous cannabinoids. In 1992, anandamide was finally isolated and its structure determined, but it took a few more decades to figure out that endocannabinoids act as retrograde transmitters (Mechoulam et al., 2014).

## Gaseous Transmitters

The gaseous transmitters further expand the repertoire of biochemical strategies demonstrated by transmitters. As water-soluble gases, they are neither stored in

Sections 12-2 and 12-6 explain hormonal influence on humans' motivated and emotional behavior.

The name *anandamide* comes from the Sanskrit word *ananda*, meaning "joy" or "bliss." Its action is mimicked by the major psychoactive compound tetrahydrocannabinol (THC), found in the *Cannabis* plant, as discussed in Section 6-2.

The fatty acid molecules that contribute to forming the cell membrane are also hydrophobic. See Figure 3-11.

Drug | Brain's Chemical

THC | Anandamide

**FIGURE 5-14 Anandamide Molecule and THC Molecule** The similarities in the structures of anandamide and THC show why both interact with the $CB_1$ receptor.

**endocannabinoid** Class of lipid neurotransmitters, including anandamide and 2-AG, synthesized at the postsynaptic membrane to act on receptors at the presynaptic membrane; affects appetite, pain, sleep, mood, memory, anxiety, and the stress response.

**nitric oxide (NO)** Gaseous neurotransmitter; acts, for example, to dilate blood vessels, aid digestion, and activate cellular metabolism.

**carbon monoxide (CO)** Gaseous neurotransmitter; activates cellular metabolism.

**hydrogen sulfide (H₂S)** Gaseous neurotransmitter; slows cellular metabolism.

**zinc** Ion transmitter that is packaged and stored in vesicles and when released, interacts with several receptors.

**G protein** Guanyl nucleotide–binding protein coupled to a metabotropic receptor; when activated, binds to other proteins.

**subunit** Protein molecule that assembles with other protein molecules.

synaptic vesicles nor released from them; instead, the cell synthesizes them on demand. After its synthesis, each gas diffuses away, easily crossing the cell membrane and immediately becoming active. Both **nitric oxide (NO)** and **carbon monoxide (CO)** activate metabolic (energy-expending) processes in cells, including processes modulating the production of other neurotransmitters. **Hydrogen sulfide (H₂S)** prevents oxygen from binding in the mitochondria, thereby slowing down metabolism.

All three gaseous transmitters serve as chemical messengers in many parts of the body. NO and H₂S control the intestinal wall muscles and dilate blood vessels in active brain regions, allowing these regions to receive more blood. Because NO and H₂S also dilate blood vessels in the sexual organs, both have an active role in producing penile erections. Drugs used to treat erectile dysfunction in men, such as Viagra (sildenafil) and Cialis (tadalafil), act by enhancing the chemical pathways influenced by NO. H₂S has several other functions, including protecting neurons from stress, enhancing calcium transport in the nerve membrane, and relaxing smooth muscles.

## Ion Transmitter

Recent evidence has led researchers to classify **zinc** ($Zn^{2+}$) as a transmitter. As a charged atom, zinc is not biologically synthesized; instead, like all other atoms, it was formed by fusion reactions in stars. Zinc is actively transported, packaged into vesicles (usually with another transmitter such as glutamate), and released into the synaptic cleft (Upmanyu et al., 2021). There, it interacts with several different receptors to cause biological change. When imbalances in vesicular zinc levels occur, individuals experience the cognitive declines associated with age and Alzheimer disease. In contrast, maintaining zinc homeostasis or correcting it with drug treatment protects cognitive ability (McAllister & Dyck, 2017).

# Varieties of Receptors

Each of the two general classes of receptor proteins produces a different effect: one class directly changes the postsynaptic membrane's electrical potential, whereas the other induces cellular change indirectly. A dazzling array of receptor subtypes allows for subtle differences in receptor function.

## Two Classes of Receptors

When a neurotransmitter is released from any of the many varieties of synapses onto the vast array of targets, as illustrated in Figure 5-6, it crosses the synaptic cleft and binds to a receptor. What happens next depends on the receptor type.

Ionotropic receptors allow ions such as $Na^+$, $K^+$, $Cl^-$, and $Ca^{2+}$ to move across a membrane (the suffix *-tropic* means "moving toward"). As **Figure 5-15** illustrates, an ionotropic receptor has two parts: (1) a binding site for a neurotransmitter and (2) a pore, or channel. When the neurotransmitter attaches to the binding site, the receptor quickly changes shape, either opening the pore and allowing ions to flow through it or closing the pore and blocking the ion flow. Thus, ionotropic receptors bring about rapid changes in membrane voltage and are usually excitatory: they trigger an action potential.

In contrast, a metabotropic receptor has a binding site for a neurotransmitter but lacks its own pore through which ions can flow. Through a series of steps, activated metabotropic receptors indirectly produce changes in nearby membrane-bound ion channels or in the cell's metabolic activity. **Figure 5-16**A shows the first of these two indirect effects. The metabotropic receptor consists of a single protein that spans the cell membrane, with its binding site facing the synaptic cleft. Each receptor is coupled to one of a family of guanyl nucleotide–binding proteins, called **G proteins** for short, shown on the inner side of the cell membrane in Figure 5-16A. When activated, a G protein binds to other proteins.

A G protein consists of three subunits: alpha, beta, and gamma. (A **subunit** is a protein that assembles with other proteins.) The alpha subunit detaches when a

Structurally, ionotropic receptors resemble voltage-activated channels, which propagate the action potential. See Figure 4-20.

**FIGURE 5-15 Ionotropic Receptor** When activated, embedded transmitter proteins bring about direct, rapid changes in membrane voltage.

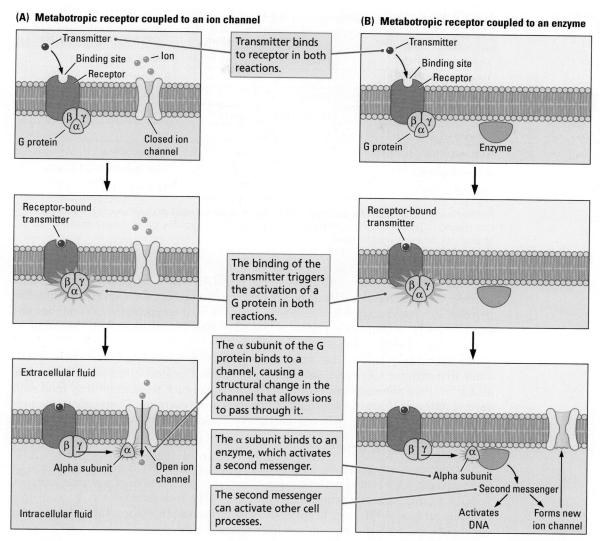

**(A) Metabotropic receptor coupled to an ion channel**

Transmitter
Binding site
Ion
Receptor
G protein
β γ α
Closed ion channel

Transmitter binds to receptor in both reactions.

Receptor-bound transmitter
β γ α

The binding of the transmitter triggers the activation of a G protein in both reactions.

Extracellular fluid
β γ α
Alpha subunit
Open ion channel
Intracellular fluid

The α subunit of the G protein binds to a channel, causing a structural change in the channel that allows ions to pass through it.

The α subunit binds to an enzyme, which activates a second messenger.

The second messenger can activate other cell processes.

**(B) Metabotropic receptor coupled to an enzyme**

Transmitter
Binding site
Receptor
G protein
β γ α
Enzyme

Receptor-bound transmitter
β γ α

β γ α
Alpha subunit
Second messenger
Activates DNA
Forms new ion channel

**FIGURE 5-16 Metabotropic Receptors**
When activated by a neurotransmitter, embedded membrane receptor proteins trigger associated G proteins, which exert indirect effects **(A)** on nearby ion channels or **(B)** in the cell's metabolic activity.

neurotransmitter binds to the G protein's associated metabotropic receptor. The detached alpha subunit can then bind to other proteins within the cell's membrane or its intracellular fluid. If the alpha subunit binds to a nearby ion channel in the membrane, as shown at the bottom of Figure 5-16A, the channel structure changes, modifying the flow of ions through it. If the channel is open, the alpha subunit may close it; alternatively, if the channel is closed, it may open. Changes in the channel and the ion flow across the membrane influence the membrane's electrical potential.

The binding of a neurotransmitter to a metabotropic receptor can also trigger more complicated cellular reactions, summarized in Figure 5-16B. These reactions begin when the detached alpha subunit binds to an enzyme. That enzyme, in turn, activates a **second messenger** (the neurotransmitter is the first messenger), which carries instructions to other cellular structures. As illustrated at the bottom of Figure 5-16B, the second messenger can perform one of several actions:

- It can bind to a membrane-bound channel, changing the channel's structure and altering ion flow through the membrane.

- It can initiate a reaction that incorporates intracellular (within the cell) protein molecules into the cell membrane, resulting, for example, in the formation of new ion channels.

- It can bind to sites on the cell's DNA to initiate or terminate the production of specific proteins.

**second messenger** Chemical that initiates a biochemical process when activated by a neurotransmitter (the first messenger).

**TABLE 5-3** Small-Molecule Transmitter Receptors

| Neurotransmitter | Ionotropic receptors | Metabotropic receptors |
| --- | --- | --- |
| Acetylcholine (ACh) | Nicotinic | 5 muscarinic* |
| Dopamine (DA) | — | 5 dopamine |
| GABA | GABA$_A$ | GABA$_B$ |
| Glutamate (Glu) | NMDA, AMPA, kainate | 7 mGluRs, NMDA |
| Glycine (Gly) | Glycine, NMDA | — |
| Histamine (H) | — | 3 histamine |
| Norepinephrine (NE) | — | 8 NE alpha and 3 NE beta |
| Serotonin (5-HT) | 5-HT$_3$ | 12 5-HT |

Peptide neurotransmitters and the lipid neurotransmitters anandamide and 2-AG have specific metabotropic-class receptors. Gaseous neurotransmitters do not have a specific receptor. The ion neurotransmitter zinc has binding sites on several receptor types.
*All metabotropic cholinergic receptors are muscarinic.

Metabotropic receptors also allow for the possibility that a single neurotransmitter's binding to a receptor can activate an escalating sequence of events called an *amplification cascade*. The cascade effect results in many downstream proteins (second messengers, channels, or both) being either activated or deactivated. Ionotropic receptors do not have such a widespread amplifying effect.

Recall that acetylcholine has an excitatory effect on skeletal muscles, where it activates an ionotropic receptor. Conversely, ACh has an inhibitory effect on the heart rate, as it activates a metabotropic receptor. Furthermore, each transmitter may bind with several different kinds of ionotropic or metabotropic receptors. Elsewhere in the nervous system, for example, ACh activates a wide variety of receptors of either type.

## Receptor Subtypes

While receptors are generally classified into just two groups, as either ionotropic or metabotropic, each neurotransmitter may interact with a number of receptor subtypes specific to that neurotransmitter. Serotonin (5-HT), for instance, has 1 ionotropic receptor subtype (5-HT$_3$) and 12 subtypes of metabotropic receptors. **Table 5-3** lists the variety of small-molecule neurotransmitter receptor subtypes.

How is this variety achieved? Alternative forms of each subunit can assemble in unique combinations to make a functional receptor. For instance, the functional NMDA receptor, which can act as an ionotropic receptor for glutamate, is always composed of 4 subunits, but a total of 12 distinct subunits are available to come together in various combinations to form the functional receptor. The NMDA receptor can also act as a metabotropic receptor, further broadening its function (Weilinger et al., 2016).

Figure 14-17 diagrams how glutamate and the NMDA receptor function in associative learning.

Why does the brain contain so many receptor subtypes for each neurotransmitter? The answer seems to be that each subtype has slightly different properties, which lead to different activities. These variations can include the presence or absence of binding sites for other molecules, how long a channel remains open or closed, and the ability to interact with intracellular signaling molecules.

It should not be surprising that a brain such as ours, with its incredible complexity, is built from a vast array of units, including copious neurotransmitter types and even more receptor types. All this, and more, allows the human brain to function successfully.

## 5-2 Review

Before you continue, check your understanding. Answers to Self-Test appear at the back of the book.

1. Neurotransmitters are identified using four experimental criteria: _____, _____, _____, and _____.

2. The broad classes of chemically related neurotransmitters are _____, _____, _____, _____, and _____.

3. Acetylcholine is composed of _____ and _____. After release into the synaptic cleft, ACh is broken down by _____, and the products can be recycled.

4. Endocannabinoids are _____ neurotransmitters, made on demand and released from the _____ membrane.

5. Contrast the major characteristics of ionotropic and metabotropic receptors.

# Neurotransmitter Systems and Behavior

**Learning Objectives**
- Summarize the role that neurotransmitters play in mediating behavior in the somatic, autonomic, and enteric nervous systems.
- List the four activating systems of the central nervous system and describe the behaviors associated with each.

When researchers began to study neurotransmission, some reasoned that any given neuron would contain only one transmitter at all its axon terminals. Newer methods of analysis have revealed that this hypothesis is not strictly accurate. A single neuron may use one transmitter at one synapse and a different transmitter at another synapse. Moreover, different transmitters may coexist in the same terminal or synapse. Neuropeptides have been found to coexist in terminals with small-molecule transmitters, and more than one small-molecule transmitter may be found in a single synapse. In some cases, more than one transmitter is packaged within a single vesicle.

Collectively, these findings allow for multiple combinations of neurotransmitters and receptors for them. Researchers also caution against assuming a simple cause-and-effect relation between a neurotransmitter and a behavior. What are the functions of so many combinations? The answer will likely vary, depending on the behavior being controlled. Historically, researchers have focused on the most abundant transmitter within any given axon terminal and then associated that neurotransmitter with a function or behavior.

We now consider some links between neurotransmitters and behavior. We begin by exploring the three peripheral nervous system divisions: somatic, autonomic, and enteric. Then we investigate neurotransmission in the central nervous system.

## Neurotransmission in the Somatic Nervous System (SNS)

Motor neurons in the brain and spinal cord send their axons to the body's skeletal muscles, including the muscles of the eyes and face, trunk, limbs, fingers, and toes. Without these SNS neurons, movement would not be possible. Motor neurons are also called **cholinergic neurons** because acetylcholine is their main neurotransmitter. At a skeletal muscle, cholinergic neurons are excitatory, producing muscular contractions.

Just as a single main neurotransmitter serves the SNS, so does a single main receptor: a transmitter-activated ionotropic channel called a *nicotinic acetylcholine receptor* (*nAChr*). As shown in **Figure 5-17**, when ACh binds to this receptor, its pore opens to permit ion flow, thus depolarizing the muscle fiber. The nicotinic receptor pore is large enough to permit the simultaneous efflux of $K^+$ and influx of $Na^+$. The molecular structure of nicotine, a chemical found in tobacco, activates the nAChr in the same way that ACh does, which is how this receptor got its name. The molecular structure of nicotine is sufficiently similar to that of ACh that nicotine acts as a mimic, fitting into acetylcholine receptors' binding sites.

Acetylcholine is the primary neurotransmitter at skeletal muscles, but other neurotransmitters also occupy these cholinergic axon terminals and are released onto the muscle along with ACh. For example, the neuropeptide called calcitonin gene–related peptide (CGRP) acts through CGRP metabotropic receptors to increase the force with which a muscle contracts.

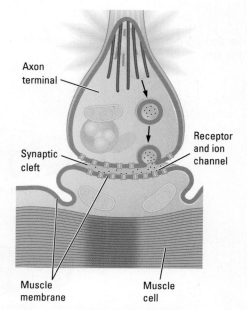

**FIGURE 5-17 Nicotinic ACh Receptor**

Labels: Axon terminal; Receptor and ion channel; Synaptic cleft; Muscle membrane; Muscle cell

**cholinergic neuron** Neuron that uses acetylcholine as its main neurotransmitter; *cholinergic* applies to any neuron that uses ACh as its main transmitter.

# Dual Activating Systems of the Autonomic Nervous System (ANS)

The complementary ANS divisions, sympathetic and parasympathetic, regulate the body's internal environment. The sympathetic division rouses the body for action, producing the fight-or-flight response. In this response, the heart rate ramps up, and digestive functions ramp down. The parasympathetic division calms the body down, producing the essentially opposite rest-and-digest response. In this state, digestive functions ramp up, heart rate ramps down, and the body is ready to relax.

*Preganglionic* refers to nerve fibers that run from the CNS to the ganglion. They are all cholinergic and myelinated. *Postganglionic* refers to nerve fibers that run from the ganglion to the effector organs. In the parasympathetic division, nerve fibers use acetylcholine; sympathetic nerve fibers use norepinephrine.

**Figure 5-18** shows the neurochemical organization of the ANS. Both divisions are controlled by preganglion cholinergic neurons that project from the CNS at two levels of the spinal cord. The CNS neurons synapse with parasympathetic postganglion neurons that also contain acetylcholine and with sympathetic postganglion neurons that contain norepinephrine. In other words, preganglion cholinergic neurons in the CNS synapse with sympathetic postganglion NE neurons to prepare the body's organs for fight or flight. Preganglion cholinergic neurons in the CNS synapse with autonomic postganglion ACh neurons in the parasympathetic division to prepare the body's organs to rest and digest.

Which type of synapse is excitatory and which is inhibitory depends on the particular body organ's receptors. During sympathetic arousal, norepinephrine turns up the heart rate and turns down the digestive functions because NE receptors on the heart are excitatory, whereas NE receptors on the gut are inhibitory. Similarly, acetylcholine turns down the heart rate and turns up the digestive functions because its receptors on these organs are reversed: on the heart, inhibitory; on the gut, excitatory. Neurotransmitter activity, by having excitatory effects in one location and inhibitory effects in another, mediates the sympathetic and parasympathetic divisions, forming a complementary autonomic regulating system that maintains the body's internal environment under dynamic circumstances.

# Enteric Nervous System (ENS) Autonomy

The ENS can act without input from the CNS, which is why it has been called the second brain. It uses the main classes of neurotransmitters—more than 30 transmitters in total. Most of these neurotransmitters are identical to those employed by the CNS. Chief among the small-molecule neurotransmitters used by the enteric nervous system are serotonin and dopamine.

Section 2-5 provides a detailed discussion of the ENS.

**FIGURE 5-18 Controlling Biological Functions in the Autonomic Nervous System** The neurotransmitter in all the preganglion neurons leaving the spinal cord is acetylcholine (ACh). Top: In the sympathetic division, ACh neurons activate autonomic norepinephrine (NE) neurons in the sympathetic postganglion neurons. NE stimulates organs required for the fight-or-flight response and suppresses activity in organs used in the rest-and-digest response. Bottom: In the parasympathetic division, preganglion ACh neurons from the spinal cord activate ACh neurons in the postganglion parasympathetic neurons near their target organs to suppress activity in the organs used for fight or flight and to stimulate the organs used to rest and digest. To review the ANS divisions and connections in detail, see Figure 2-32.

Sensory ENS neurons detect both mechanical and chemical conditions in the gastrointestinal system. Via the intestinal muscles, motor neurons in the ENS control the mixing of intestinal contents. Secretion of digestive enzymes is also under ENS control.

**Principle 2:** Sensory and motor divisions pervade the nervous system.

# Four Activating Systems in the Central Nervous System

Just as there is an organization to the neurochemical systems of the PNS, there is an organization of neurochemical systems in the CNS. These systems are remarkably similar across a wide range of animal species, allowing for their identification first in the rat brain and then in the human brain (Hamilton et al., 2010).

For each of the four **activating systems** described here, a relatively small number of neurons grouped together in one or a few brainstem nuclei send axons to widespread CNS regions, suggesting that these nuclei and their terminals help synchronize activity throughout the brain and spinal cord. You can envision an activating system as being analogous to the power supply in a house. The fuse box or breaker box is the source of the power, and transmission lines branch out from it to each room.

Just as in the ANS, the precise action of the CNS transmitter depends on which brain region is innervated and which types of receptors the transmitter acts on at that region. To continue with our analogy, the precise activating effect of the power in each room depends on the electrical devices present in that room.

Four neural activating systems have been identified, each named for the type of small-molecule transmitter present in that system: cholinergic, dopaminergic, noradrenergic, and serotonergic. **Figure 5-19** locates each system's nuclei, with arrow shafts mapping the axon pathways and arrowheads indicating axon terminal locales.

As summarized on the right in Figure 5-19, each CNS activating system is associated with numerous behaviors. Note, however, the lack of a one-to-one association between an activating system and the various behaviors and brain disorders. All of these relations are the subject of ongoing research. Making definitive correlations between activating systems and behavior or activating systems and a disorder is difficult because the axons of these systems connect to almost every part of the brain and spinal cord. Each system likely has both specific functions and modulatory roles. We detail some of the documented relationships between these systems and specific behaviors and disorders here and in many subsequent chapters.

## Cholinergic System

**Figure 5-20** shows in cross section a rat brain stained for the enzyme acetylcholinesterase (AChE), which breaks down ACh in synapses, as diagrammed earlier in Figure 5-10. The darkly stained areas contain high AChE concentrations, indicating the presence of cholinergic terminals. AChE permeates the cortex and is especially dense in the basal ganglia. Many of these cholinergic synapses are connections from ACh nuclei in the brainstem, as illustrated in the top panel of Figure 5-19.

The cholinergic system participates in typical waking behavior, attention, and memory. For example, cholinergic neurons take part in producing one form of waking activity that can be recorded by electroencephalography (EEG). People affected by the degenerative **Alzheimer disease**, which begins with minor forgetfulness, progresses to major memory dysfunction, and later develops into generalized dementia, show a profound loss of cholinergic neurons at autopsy. Two current treatment strategies for Alzheimer disease focus on the use of drugs that either inhibit the enzyme acetylcholinesterase, thereby elevating levels of ACh, or raise the number of nicotinic receptors (Anand et al., 2017). Recall that ACh is synthesized from nutrients in food; thus, the role of diet in maintaining acetylcholine levels is being investigated as well.

The brain abnormalities associated with Alzheimer disease are not limited to the cholinergic neurons, however. Autopsies of individuals with this disease also reveal extensive damage to the neocortex and other brain regions. Thus, what role, if any, the cholinergic neurons play in the progress of the disorder is not yet clear. Perhaps their destruction triggers degeneration of the cortex, or perhaps the cause-and-effect

The EEG detects electrical signals the brain emits during various conscious states; see Sections 7-2 and 13-3.

Clinical Focus 14-3 details research on Alzheimer disease. Section 16-3 reviews various causes of and treatments for neurocognitive disorders.

**activating system** Neural pathways that coordinate brain activity through a single neurotransmitter. Its cell bodies lie in a brainstem nucleus; axons are distributed through a wide CNS region.

**Alzheimer disease** Degenerative brain disorder related to aging; first appears as progressive memory loss and later develops into generalized dementia.

**FIGURE 5-19 Major Activating Systems**
Each system's cell bodies are gathered into nuclei (shown as ovals) in the brainstem. Their axons project diffusely through the CNS and synapse on target structures. Each activating system is associated with one or more behaviors or diseases.

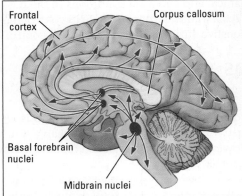

**Cholinergic system** (acetylcholine)
- Active in maintaining attention and waking EEG pattern.
- Thought to play a role in memory by maintaining neuron excitability.
- Death of cholinergic neurons and decrease in ACh in the neocortex are thought to be related to Alzheimer disease.

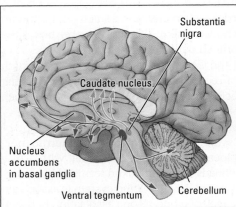

**Dopaminergic system** (dopamine)
*Nigrostriatal pathways* (orange projections)
- Active in maintaining normal motor behavior.
- Loss of DA is related to muscle rigidity and dyskinesia in Parkinson disease.

*Mesolimbic pathways* (purple projections)
- Dopamine release causes repetition of behaviors.
- Thought to be the neurotransmitter system most affected by addictive drugs and behavioral addictions.
- Increases in DA activity may be related to schizophrenia.
- Decreases in DA activity may be related to deficits of attention.

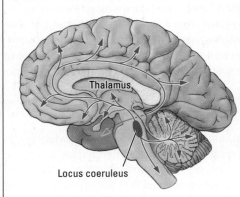

**Noradrenergic system** (norepinephrine)
- Active in maintaining emotional tone.
- Decreases in NE activity are thought to be related to depression.
- Increases in NE are thought to be related to mania (overexcited behavior).
- Decreased NE activity is associated with hyperactivity and attention-deficit/hyperactivity disorder.

**Serotonergic system** (serotonin)
- Active in maintaining waking EEG pattern.
- Changes in serotonin activity are related to obsessive-compulsive disorder, tics, and schizophrenia.
- Decreases in serotonin activity are related to depression.
- Abnormalities in brainstem 5-HT neurons are linked to disorders such as sleep apnea and SIDS.

relation is the other way around, with cortical degeneration causing cholinergic cell death. Moreover, the loss of cholinergic neurons is just one of the many neural symptoms of Alzheimer disease. In consequence, drug treatments that prevent cell death are also being developed in an effort to slow the progression of Alzheimer disease (Anand et al., 2017).

## Dopaminergic System

Figure 5-19 maps the dopaminergic activating system's two distinct pathways. The *nigrostriatal dopaminergic system* plays a major role in coordinating movement. As described throughout this chapter in relation to Parkinsonism, when most of the dopamine neurons in the substantia nigra are lost, the result is extreme muscular rigidity. Opposing muscles contract at the same time, making it difficult for an affected person to move.

People with Parkinson disease also exhibit rhythmic tremors, especially of the limbs, which signals a release of formerly inhibited movement. Although the causes of this disease are not fully known, it can actually be triggered by the ingestion of certain toxic drugs, as described in Clinical Focus 5-5, The Case of the Frozen Addict. Those drugs may act as selective neurotoxins that specifically kill dopamine neurons in the substantia nigra.

Dopamine in the *mesolimbic dopaminergic system* is the neurotransmitter most affected in addiction—to food, to drugs, and to other behaviors that involve a loss of impulse control. A common feature of addictive behaviors is that stimulating the mesolimbic dopaminergic system enhances responses to environmental stimuli, thus making those stimuli attractive and rewarding. Indeed, some people with Parkinson disease who take dopamine receptor agonists as medication show a loss of impulse control that manifests in such behaviors as pathological gambling, hypersexuality, and compulsive shopping (Moore et al., 2014).

Excessive mesolimbic dopaminergic activity has also been proposed to play a role in **schizophrenia**, a behavioral disorder characterized by delusions, hallucinations, disorganized speech, blunted emotion, agitation or immobility, and a host of associated symptoms. Blocking the dopamine system reduces the symptoms of schizophrenia; however, other neurotransmitter activity involving glutamate and GABA is also altered. Schizophrenia is one of the most common and most debilitating psychiatric disorders, affecting about 1 in 100 people.

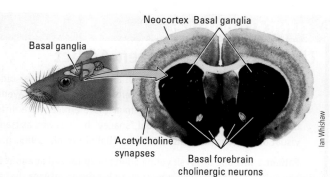

**FIGURE 5-20 Cholinergic Activation** The drawing at left shows the cortical location of the micrograph at right, stained to reveal acetylcholinesterase (AChE). Cholinergic neurons in the rat's basal forebrain project to the neocortex, and the darkly stained bands in the cortex show areas rich in cholinergic synapses. The darker central parts of the section, also rich in cholinergic neurons, are the basal ganglia.

Rhythmic movement helps people with Parkinson disease restore the balance between neural excitation and inhibition—between the loss and the release of behavior. Some patients, including those shown here along with family members, participate in a specially designed dance class for people with Parkinson disease. Participants enjoy the activity and report several benefits from it.

Sections 6-3, 6-4, and 12-1 describe drug effects on the mesolimbic DA system. Sections 6-2 and 7-4 discuss possible causes of schizophrenia, and Section 16-2 discusses its neurobiology.

## Noradrenergic System

Norepinephrine (noradrenaline) may play a part in learning by stimulating neurons to change their structure. This neurotransmitter may also facilitate healthy brain development and contribute to organizing movements. A neuron that uses norepinephrine as its transmitter is termed a **noradrenergic neuron** (derived from *adrenaline,* the Latin name for epinephrine).

Behaviors and disorders related to the noradrenergic system involve emotions. Some symptoms of **major depression**—a mood disorder characterized by prolonged feelings of worthlessness and guilt, the disruption of typical eating habits, sleep disturbances, a general slowing of behavior, and frequent thoughts of suicide—may be related to decreased activity of noradrenergic neurons. Conversely, some symptoms

**schizophrenia** Behavioral disorder characterized by delusions, hallucinations, disorganized speech, blunted emotion, agitation or immobility, and a host of associated symptoms.

**noradrenergic neuron** From *adrenaline,* Latin for *epinephrine;* a neuron containing norepinephrine.

**major depression** Mood disorder characterized by prolonged feelings of worthlessness and guilt, the disruption of normal eating habits, sleep disturbances, a general slowing of behavior, and frequent thoughts of suicide.

## ◎ CLINICAL FOCUS 5-5

# The Case of the Frozen Addict

Patient 1: During the first 4 days of July 1982, a 42-year-old man used 4½ grams of a "new synthetic heroin" . . . injected intravenously three or four times daily. . . . The immediate effects were different from heroin, producing an unusual "spacey" high as well as transient visual distortions and hallucinations. (Ballard et al., 1985, p. 949)

Patient 1 was one of seven young adults hospitalized at about the same time in California. All showed symptoms of Parkinson disease that appeared very suddenly after drug injection. They would awake to find themselves "frozen"—only able to move in "slow motion." According to Patient 1, he had to deliberately think through every movement, and described himself as stiff, slow, almost mute, and catatonic. These symptoms are extremely unusual in this age group. All who were affected reportedly injected a "new synthetic heroin" that was being sold on the streets in the summer of 1982.

J. William Langston and Jon Palfreman (2014) have recounted when they and colleagues found that the "synthetic heroin" contained a contaminant called MPTP (1-methyl-4-phenyl-1,2,3,6-tetrahydropyridine), whose presence resulted from poor technique during the drug's synthesis. Results of experimental studies in rodents showed that MPTP was not itself responsible for the symptoms, but rather was metabolized into MPP⁺ (1-methyl-4-phenylpyridinium), a neurotoxin.

The autopsy of one individual who was suspected of having died of MPTP poisoning showed that the brain had selectively lost dopamine neurons in the substantia nigra. The rest of the brain appeared healthy. Injecting MPTP into monkeys, rats, and mice produced similar symptoms and a similar selective loss of dopaminergic neurons in the substantia nigra. Thus, the combined clinical and experimental evidence indicates that a toxin can selectively kill dopamine neurons and that the die-off can induce Parkinson disease.

In 1988, Patient 1 received an experimental treatment at University Hospital in Lund, Sweden. Living dopamine neurons taken from human fetal brains at autopsy were implanted into the caudate nucleus and putamen (Widner et al., 1992). Extensive work with rodents and nonhuman primates in a number of laboratories had demonstrated that fetal neurons, before they develop dendrites and axons, can survive transplantation, mature, and secrete neurotransmitters.

Patient 1 had no serious postoperative complications and was much improved 24 months after the surgery. He could dress and feed himself, visit the bathroom with help, and make trips outside his home. He also responded much better to medication. The accompanying diagrams contrast DA levels in the brain of a patient with Parkinson disease before (left) and 2 years, 4 months after implantation of dopamine neurons (right).

Transplantation of fetal neurons to treat Parkinson disease typically does not work. Unlike in the case of the frozen addict, Parkinson disease is associated with a continuing, active process that destroys dopaminergic neurons, including transplanted neurons, in the substantia nigra. Parkinson disease affects as many as 20 people per 100,000, so the need for effective therapies is pressing. New approaches to transplantation are directed toward engineering the entire nigrostriatal pathway, of which dopamine neurons are a part, and then grafting the circuit (Harris et al., 2020). This new field, called *regenerative medicine*, uses cell replacement strategies and tissue engineering to promote regeneration and restoration of function.

As a footnote, Palfreman, one of the researchers in Patient 1's story, subsequently developed Parkinson disease—an experience that he details from a personal, historical, and clinical perspective in his book (Palfreman, 2015).

DA levels before fetal DA cell implantation          DA production at 2 years, 4 months after implantation

These diagrams represent positron emission tomography (PET) scans that contrast DA levels in the brain of a person with Parkinson disease before and 28 months after implantation of fetal neurons. Research from Widner et al. (1992).

---

**mania** Disordered mental state of extreme excitement.

The structural basis for memory and learning, including the role of serotonin, are detailed in Section 14-4.

The influences of norepinephrine and serotonin in a variety of disorders, including depression, anxiety, and schizophrenia, are detailed in Section 16-2.

of **mania** (excessive excitability) may be related to increased activity of these same neurons. Decreased NE activity has also been associated with both hyperactivity and attention-deficit/hyperactivity disorder (ADHD).

## Serotonergic System

The serotonergic activating system maintains waking activity (measurable via EEG) in the forebrain when we move; thus, it participates in wakefulness, as does the cholinergic system. Like norepinephrine, serotonin plays a role in learning. Some symptoms of depression may be related to decreased activity in serotonin neurons, and drugs commonly used to treat depression act on 5-HT neurons. Consequently, two forms of depression may exist, one related to norepinephrine and another related to serotonin.

Likewise, some research shows that various symptoms of schizophrenia may be related to increases in serotonin activity, which implies that different forms of schizophrenia may exist. Decreased serotonergic activity is related to symptoms observed in **obsessive-compulsive disorder (OCD)**, in which a person has repetitive and often unpleasant thoughts (obsessions) and compulsively repeats acts (such as hand washing). Evidence also points to a link between abnormalities in serotonergic nuclei and conditions such as *sleep apnea* and *sudden infant death syndrome* (*SIDS*).

## Neuromodulation

The neurotransmitters that facilitate each of these four activating systems are collectively referred to as **neuromodulators**—a group that also includes histamine, several of the neuropeptides, and the endocannabinoids. These chemical messengers are released from a neuron and act on receptors distributed over some region of the brain, in contrast to neurotransmitters, which act on adjacent postsynaptic receptors. As with neurotransmitters and hormones, the distinction made between neurotransmitters and neuromodulators reflects the distance they travel from their release point.

Recall that glutamatergic and GABAergic neurons make up most of the synaptic connections in the brain. Neuromodulators interact with metabotropic (G-protein coupled) receptors to initiate a second messenger signaling cascade that induces a long-lasting signal. This signal lasts between hundreds of milliseconds to several minutes and can alter the firing characteristics and plasticity of glutamatergic, GABAergic, and other neurons.

## 5-3 Review

Before you continue, check your understanding. Answers to Self-Test appear at the back of the book.

1. In the peripheral nervous system, the neurotransmitter at somatic muscles is _____; in the autonomic nervous system, preganglionic _____ neurons from the spinal cord connect with postganglionic _____ neurons for parasympathetic activity and with postganglionic _____ neurons for sympathetic activity.

2. The two principal small-molecule transmitters used by the enteric nervous system are _____ and _____.

3. The four main activating systems of the CNS are _____, _____, _____, and _____.

4. How would you respond to the comment that a behavior is caused solely by a chemical imbalance in the brain?

Consult the index of disorders inside the book's front cover for more information on major depression, mania, ADHD, OCD, sleep apnea, and SIDS.

**obsessive-compulsive disorder (OCD)** Behavior characterized by compulsively repeated acts (such as hand washing) and repetitive, often unpleasant, thoughts (obsessions).

**neuromodulators** Neurotransmitters that alter the firing and synaptic characteristics of other neurons typically over an extended period.

To refresh your understanding of metabotropic receptors, review Figure 5-16.

## 5-4

# Hormones

Many of the principles related to neurotransmitters also apply to the hormones that act on neuronal receptors. Hormones are secreted by glands in the body and by the brain. Interacting brain and body hormones form feedback loops that regulate their activity. Hormonal influences change across the life span, influencing development and body and brain function (McEwen, 2019). In many respects, hormone systems are like long-distance neurotransmitter-activating systems, except that hormones use the bloodstream as a conveyance. Indeed, many hormones act as neurotransmitters, and many neurotransmitters act as hormones.

**Learning Objectives**
- Explain the role that hormones play in mediating behavior and regulating function.
- Describe the four classes of hormones.
- Define homeostasis and describe the function that hormones play in this process.
- Summarize the body's stress response and explain how hormones function to stimulate and end this process.

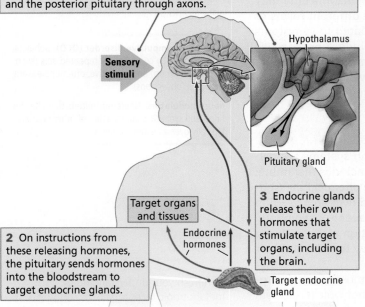

**1** In response to sensory stimuli and cognitive activity, the hypothalamus produces neurohormones that enter the anterior pituitary through veins and the posterior pituitary through axons.

Sensory stimuli

Hypothalamus

Pituitary gland

Target organs and tissues

**2** On instructions from these releasing hormones, the pituitary sends hormones into the bloodstream to target endocrine glands.

Endocrine hormones

**3** Endocrine glands release their own hormones that stimulate target organs, including the brain.

Target endocrine gland

**FIGURE 5-21 Hormonal Hierarchy**

The role of hormones in the regulation of behavior is explored further in Section 12-4.

We detail the role of melatonin in regulating the body's biological clock in Section 13-2.

**peptide hormone** Chemical messenger translated from cellular RNA; a short string of amino acids.

**amino acid hormone** Chemical messenger derived from amino acid, most commonly tyrosine.

**lipid hormone** Chemical messenger derived from lipids such as arachidonic acid, which acts on membrane receptors; also known as eicosanoids.

**steroid hormone** Fat-soluble chemical messenger synthesized from cholesterol.

# Hierarchical Control of Hormones

Many hormones operate in a feedback system that includes the brain and the body. **Figure 5-21** shows how the hypothalamus produces neurohormones that stimulate the pituitary gland to secrete releasing hormones into the circulatory system. These pituitary hormones, in turn, influence the remaining endocrine glands to release appropriate hormones into the bloodstream to act on various targets in the body and send feedback to the brain about the need for more or less hormone release.

Hormones not only affect body organs but also target virtually all aspects of brain function. Almost every neuron in the brain contains receptors on which various hormones can act. In addition to influencing sex organs and physical appearance, hormones affect neurotransmitter function, especially in neurons that influence sexual development and behavior (Barth et al., 2015). These substances can influence gene expression by binding to special receptors on or in the cell and then being transported to the nucleus to influence gene transcription. Transcription, in turn, influences the synthesis of proteins needed for a variety of cellular processes. Thus, hormones influence brain and body structure and behavior.

As with neurotransmitters in the CNS activating systems, many questions remain about how hormones produce or contribute to complex behavior. The diversity of their functions, however, clarifies *why* the body uses hormones as messengers: their targets are so widespread that the best possible way of reaching all of them is to travel in the bloodstream, which goes everywhere in the body.

# Classes and Functions of Hormones

Hormones can be used to treat or prevent disease. For example, people take synthetic hormones as replacement therapy if the glands that produce those hormones are removed or malfunction. Other people take hormones, especially sex hormones, to counteract the effects of aging, to increase physical strength and endurance, and to gain an advantage in sports. As many as 100 hormones are present in the human body, which are classified chemically as either peptides, amino acids, lipids, or steroids.

**Peptide hormones**, such as insulin, growth hormone, and endorphins, are made by cellular DNA in the same way that other proteins are made. They influence their target cell's activity by binding to metabotropic receptors on the cell membrane, generating a second messenger that affects the cell's physiology or gene transcription.

**Amino acid hormones**, such as melatonin and thyroxine, are derived from amino acids. Melatonin is primarily released by the pineal gland at night and has been associated with the sleep–wake cycle. Thyroxine, which is produced by the thyroid gland, is responsible for the regulation of metabolism.

**Lipid hormones**, also known as *eicosanoids*, are hydrophobic (water hating) and therefore lipophilic (fat loving). They include prostaglandins and thromboxanes. Prostaglandins play a major role in inhibiting blood clots, regulating blood flow, and both promoting and counteracting inflammation. Thromboxane acts in opposition to prostaglandin by facilitating blood clotting.

**Steroid hormones**, such as testosterone and cortisol, are synthesized from cholesterol and are lipid (fat) soluble. Steroids diffuse away from their sites of synthesis in glands, including the gonads, adrenal cortex, and thyroid. They bind to steroid receptors on the cell membrane or in the cell and frequently act on cellular DNA to influence gene transcription.

Steroid and peptide hormones fall into one of three main functional groups with respect to behavior, and they may be classified as members of more than one group:

1. **Homeostatic hormones** maintain a state of internal metabolic balance and regulate physiological systems. Mineralocorticoids (e.g., aldosterone) control both the concentration of water in blood and cells and the levels of sodium, potassium, and calcium in the body. In addition, they promote digestive functions.

2. **Gonadal (sex) hormones** control reproductive functions. They instruct the body to develop as male (testosterone) or female (estrogen); influence sexual behavior and conception; and, in women, control the menstrual cycle (estrogen and progesterone), labor and delivery of babies, and release of breast milk (prolactin, oxytocin). These hormones, especially oxytocin, influence mother–infant bonding and, in some species, including sheep, are essential for bonding to occur.

3. **Glucocorticoids** (e.g., cortisol and corticosterone), a group of steroid hormones secreted in times of stress, are important in protein and carbohydrate metabolism, as well as in controlling blood sugar levels and cellular absorption of sugar. Hormones activated in psychologically challenging events or emergencies prepare the body to cope by fighting or fleeing.

# Homeostatic Hormones

Homeostatic hormones are essential to the maintenance of life. The body's internal environment must remain within relatively constant parameters for us to function, regardless of a person's age, activities, or conscious state. Whether as children or adults, at rest or in strenuous work, when we have overeaten or when we are hungry, to survive we need a relatively constant internal environment. An appropriate balance of sugars, proteins, carbohydrates, salts, and water is necessary in the blood, in the extracellular compartments of muscles, in the brain and other body structures, and in all cells.

A typical homeostatic function is controlling blood sugar level. After a meal, digestive processes result in increased glucose in the blood. One group of cells in the pancreas releases insulin, a homeostatic hormone that instructs the enzyme glycogen synthase in liver and muscle cells to start storing glucose in the form of glycogen. The resulting decrease in glucose decreases the stimulation of pancreatic cells so that they stop producing insulin, and glycogen storage stops. When the body needs glucose for energy, another hormone in the liver, glucagon, acts as a countersignal to insulin. Glucagon stimulates yet another enzyme, glycogen phosphorylase, to initiate glucose release from its glycogen storage site.

*Diabetes mellitus* is a disorder caused by a failure of the pancreatic cells to secrete any or enough insulin. As a result, blood sugar levels can rise (hyperglycemia) or fall (hypoglycemia). In hyperglycemia, blood glucose levels rise because insulin does not instruct body cells to take up glucose. Consequently, cell function, including neuronal function, can fail through glucose starvation, even in the presence of high glucose levels in the blood. Chronic high blood glucose levels cause damage to the eyes, kidneys, nerves, heart, and blood vessels. In hypoglycemia, inappropriate diet can lead to low blood sugar severe enough to cause fainting. Insulin resistance in brain cells may be related to Alzheimer disease (Kellar & Craft, 2020).

Hunger and eating are influenced by a number of homeostatic hormones, including leptin and ghrelin. Leptin (from the Greek word for "thin"), secreted by adipose (animal fat) tissue, inhibits hunger—hence its nickname, the *satiety hormone*. Ghrelin (from the Indio-European *gher*, meaning "to grow"), secreted by the gastrointestinal tract, regulates growth hormones and energy use. Ghrelin also induces hunger. It is secreted when the stomach is empty; secretion stops when the stomach is full. Leptin and ghrelin act on receptors on the same neurons of the arcuate nucleus of the hypothalamus. Together, they contribute to energy homeostasis by managing eating.

The word *homeostasis* comes from the Greek words *stasis* ("standing") and *homeo* ("in the same place"). The homeostatic mechanisms that control regulated behavior are discussed in detail in Section 12-3.

Normal glucose concentration in the bloodstream varies between 80 and 130 mg per 100 milliliters (about 3.3 oz) of blood.

Consult the entry "hormonal disorders" in the index of disorders found inside the book's front cover.

**homeostatic hormone** One of a group of hormones that maintain internal metabolic balance and regulate physiological systems in an organism.

**gonadal (sex) hormone** One of a group of hormones, such as testosterone, that control reproductive functions and strongly influence sexual appearance as male or female.

**glucocorticoid** One of a group of steroid hormones, such as cortisol, secreted in times of stress; important in protein and carbohydrate metabolism.

# Anabolic–Androgenic Steroids

The members of a class of synthetic hormones related to *testosterone*, the sex hormone secreted by the testes and ovaries that is responsible for the distinguishing characteristics of the male, have both muscle-building (anabolic) and masculinizing (androgenic) effects. Anabolic–androgenic steroids, commonly known simply as **anabolic steroids**, were synthesized originally to build body mass and enhance endurance. Weight lifters were the first to use these substances, in 1952, as a means to enhance performance and win international competitions.

Synthetic steroid use rapidly spread to other sports, eventually leading to bans on their use in track and field and then in many other sports, enforced by drug testing. Anabolic steroids were at the center of scandals in Major League Baseball in the 1990s and 2000s and have been a focal point of efforts to eliminate "performance-enhancing drugs" from a wide variety of professional and amateur sports leagues. The testing policies implemented by sports organizations have led to a cat-and-mouse game in which unscrupulous individuals continually devise new anabolic steroids and new ways of taking them and masking them in an effort to evade detection by the tests.

Today, the use of anabolic steroids is about equal among athletes and nonathletes. More than 1 million people in the United States have used anabolic steroids not only to enhance athletic performance but also to enhance physique and appearance. The rates of anabolic steroid use in high schools may be as high as 7% for men and 3% for women.

The use of anabolic steroids carries health risks. Their administration results in the body reducing its own manufacture of testosterone, which in turn reduces fertility and spermatogenesis in men. Muscle bulk is increased, but so is aggression. Cardiovascular effects include increased risk of heart attack and stroke. Liver and kidney function may be compromised, and the risk of tumors may increase. Male-pattern baldness may be enhanced. Women may develop an enlarged clitoris, acne, increased body hair, and a deepened voice.

Anabolic steroids do have some approved clinical uses. For example, testosterone replacement is a treatment for hypogonadal men. It is also useful for treating muscle loss subsequent to trauma and for the recovery of muscle mass in malnourished people. In women, anabolic steroids are used to treat endometriosis and fibrocystic disease of the breast.

# Glucocorticoids and Stress

*Stress* is a term borrowed from engineering to describe a process in which an agent exerts a force on an object. Applied to humans and other animals, a stressor is a stimulus that challenges the body's homeostasis and triggers arousal. Stress responses—comprising behavioral as well as physiological changes—include both arousal and attempts to reduce stress. A stress response can outlast a stress-inducing incident and may even occur in the absence of an obvious stressor. Living with constant stress can be debilitating.

## Activating a Stress Response

Surprisingly, the body's response to stress is the same whether the stressor is exciting, sad, or frightening. Robert Sapolsky (2004) uses the vivid image of a hungry lion chasing down a zebra to illustrate the stress response. The chase elicits divergent behavior in the two animals, but their physiological responses are identical. The stress response begins when the body is subjected to a stressor and especially when the brain perceives a stressor and responds with arousal, directed from the brain by the hypothalamus. The response consists of two separate sequences, one fast and the other slow.

**The Fast Response** Shown at left in **Figure 5-22**, the sympathetic division of the ANS is activated to prepare the body and its organs for fight or flight. During the fast response,

The effects of sex hormones on the brain are detailed in Section 12-5.

**anabolic steroid** Class of synthetic hormones related to testosterone that have both muscle-building (anabolic) and masculinizing (androgenic) effects; also called *anabolic–androgenic steroid*.

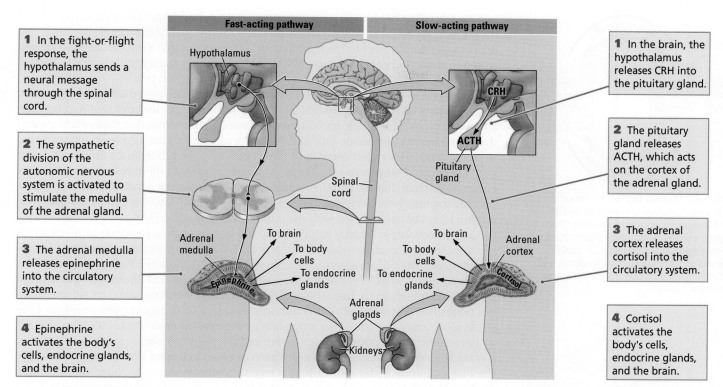

**Fast-acting pathway**

**1** In the fight-or-flight response, the hypothalamus sends a neural message through the spinal cord.

**2** The sympathetic division of the autonomic nervous system is activated to stimulate the medulla of the adrenal gland.

**3** The adrenal medulla releases epinephrine into the circulatory system.

**4** Epinephrine activates the body's cells, endocrine glands, and the brain.

**Slow-acting pathway**

**1** In the brain, the hypothalamus releases CRH into the pituitary gland.

**2** The pituitary gland releases ACTH, which acts on the cortex of the adrenal gland.

**3** The adrenal cortex releases cortisol into the circulatory system.

**4** Cortisol activates the body's cells, endocrine glands, and the brain.

Hypothalamus — Spinal cord — Pituitary gland — CRH — ACTH — Adrenal medulla — Epinephrine — Adrenal cortex — Cortisol — To brain — To body cells — To endocrine glands — Adrenal glands — Kidneys

**FIGURE 5-22 Activating a Stress Response** Two pathways to the adrenal gland control the body's stress response. The fast-acting pathway primes the body immediately for fight or flight. The slow-acting pathway both mobilizes the body's resources to confront a stressor and repairs stress-related damage. ACTH, adrenocorticotropic hormone; CRH, corticotropin-releasing hormone.

**Principle 3:** The CNS functions on multiple levels and is organized hierarchically and in parallel.

the parasympathetic division that governs the rest-and-digest response is turned off. The sympathetic division stimulates the medulla on the interior of the adrenal gland to release epinephrine. The subsequent epinephrine surge (often called the *adrenaline surge,* after epinephrine's original name) prepares the body for a sudden burst of activity. Among its many functions, epinephrine stimulates cell metabolism, readying the body's cells for action.

**The Slow Response** As shown at right in Figure 5-22, the slow response is controlled by the steroid cortisol, a glucocorticoid released from the outer layer (cortex) of the adrenal gland. Activating the cortisol pathway takes anywhere from minutes to hours. Cortisol has wide-ranging functions, including turning off all bodily systems not immediately required to deal with a stressor. For example, cortisol turns off insulin production so that the liver starts releasing glucose, thus temporarily increasing the body's energy supply. It also shuts down reproductive functions and inhibits the production of growth hormone. In this way, it concentrates the body's energy on dealing with the stress.

# Ending a Stress Response

Normally, stress responses are brief. The body mobilizes its resources, deals with the challenge physiologically and behaviorally, and shuts down the stress response. Just as the brain is responsible for turning on the stress reaction, it is also responsible for turning it off. But consider what can happen if the stress response is *not* shut down:

- The body continues to mobilize energy at the cost of energy storage.
- Proteins are used up, resulting in muscle wasting and fatigue.
- Growth hormone is inhibited, so the body cannot grow.
- The gastrointestinal system remains shut down, reducing the intake and processing of nutrients to replace used resources.
- Reproductive functions are inhibited.
- The immune system is suppressed, contributing to the possibility of infection or disease.

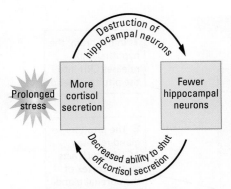

**FIGURE 5-23 Vicious Circle** Unrelieved stress promotes excessive release of cortisol, which damages hippocampal neurons. The damaged neurons cannot detect cortisol and therefore cannot signal the adrenal gland to stop producing it. The resulting feedback loop enhances cortisol secretion, further damaging hippocampal neurons.

PTSD is among the anxiety disorders detailed in Section 12-6. Research Focus 16-1 and Section 16-2 consider treatments.

Sapolsky (2005) argues that the hippocampus plays an important role in turning off the stress response. The hippocampus contains a high density of cortisol receptors, and it has axons that project to the hypothalamus. Consequently, the hippocampus is well suited to detecting cortisol in the blood and instructing the hypothalamus to reduce blood cortisol levels.

Nevertheless, a more insidious relationship may exist between the hippocampus and blood cortisol levels. Sapolsky observed wild-born vervet monkeys that had become agricultural pests in Kenya, and that were consequently trapped and caged. He found that some monkeys became sick and died of a syndrome that appeared to be related to stress. Those that died seemed to have been socially subordinate animals housed with particularly aggressive monkeys. Autopsies showed high rates of gastric ulcers, enlarged adrenal glands, and pronounced hippocampal degeneration. The hippocampal damage may have been due to prolonged high cortisol levels produced by the unremitting stress of being caged with the aggressive monkeys.

Cortisol levels are usually regulated by the hippocampus. However, if these levels remain elevated because of a perpetually stress-inducing situation, cortisol eventually damages the hippocampus, reducing its size. The damaged hippocampus is then unable to do its work of reducing the cortisol level. Thus, a vicious circle emerges in which the hippocampus undergoes progressive degeneration and cortisol levels are not controlled (**Figure 5-23**). Interestingly, research with rats suggests that ongoing stress also causes the size of the amygdala to increase (Bourgin et al., 2015).

Because stress response circuits in rats and monkeys are similar to those in humans, it is possible that excessive stress in humans can lead to similar brain changes. Because the hippocampus is thought to play a role in memory, stress-induced hippocampal damage is postulated to result in impaired memory. Because the amygdala is thought to play a role in emotion, stress-induced changes are postulated to result in increased emotional responses. This pattern of behavioral changes resembles posttraumatic stress disorder (PTSD). People with PTSD feel as if they are reliving the trauma, and the accompanying physiological arousal enhances their belief that danger is imminent.

Research has not yet determined whether the cumulative effects of stress can damage the human hippocampus. For example, research on women who were sexually abused in childhood and were diagnosed with PTSD has yielded some reports of changes in memory or in hippocampal volume, as measured with brain-imaging techniques. Other studies have failed to find any differences in individuals who experienced abuse versus those who did not (Landré et al., 2010). The fact that such apparently similar studies can produce different results can be explained in several ways.

First, the amount of damage to the hippocampus that must occur to produce a stress syndrome is not certain. Second, brain-imaging techniques may not be sensitive to subtle changes in hippocampal cell function or to moderate cell loss. Third, wide individual and environmental differences influence how people respond to stress. Fourth, neonatal stress can influence hippocampal neurogenesis (Lajud & Torner, 2015). The long-term consequence is a smaller hippocampus and increased susceptibility to stress. Finally, humans are long lived and gather many life experiences that complicate simple extrapolations from a single stressful event.

Nevertheless, Patrick McGowan and his colleagues (2009) report that the density of glucocorticoid receptors in the hippocampus of people who committed suicide and had been sexually abused as children was lower than that of both controls and suicide victims who had not been abused. The decrease in receptors and in glucocorticoid mRNA suggests that childhood abuse induces epigenetic changes in the expression of glucocorticoid genes. The decrease in glucocorticoid receptors presumably renders the hippocampus less able to mitigate stress responses. The most important outcome of the McGowan study is its suggestion of a mechanism through which stress can influence hippocampal function without necessarily being associated with a decrease in hippocampal volume. This study further underscores the point that stress likely produces many changes in many brain regions. It is unlikely that the full scope of these changes has been described or is understood as yet (Clauss et al., 2015).

# 5-4 Review

Before you continue, check your understanding. Answers to Self-Test appear at the back of the book.

1. The hypothalamus produces _____, which stimulate the _____ to secrete _____ into the circulatory system. Hormone levels circulating in the bloodstream send feedback to the _____.

2. Hormones are classified chemically as _____, _____, _____, or _____.

3. Broadly speaking, _____ hormones regulate metabolic balance, _____ hormones regulate reproduction, and _____ regulate stress.

4. One class of synthetic hormones is _____, which increase _____ and have _____ effects.

5. The stress response has a fast-acting pathway mediated by the release of _____ and a slow-acting pathway mediated by the release of _____.

6. Describe the proposed relationship among stress, cortisol, and the hippocampus.

7. What is the key characteristic that distinguishes neurotransmitters, neuromodulators, and hormones?

# Summary

## 5-1 A Chemical Message

In the 1920s, Otto Loewi suspected that nerves to the heart secrete a chemical that regulates the heart rate. His subsequent experiments with frogs showed that acetylcholine slows this rate, whereas epinephrine increases it. This observation proved key to understanding the basis of chemical neurotransmission.

The systems for chemically synthesizing excitatory and inhibitory neurotransmitters are found in the presynaptic neuron's axon terminal or its soma, whereas the systems for neurotransmitter storage are in its axon terminal. The receptor systems on which a neurotransmitter acts typically reside on the postsynaptic membrane. In turn, anterograde chemical neurotransmission is the dominant mechanism in the human nervous system. Nevertheless, neurons may also make direct connections with each other through gap junctions, channel-forming proteins that allow direct sharing of ions or nutrients.

The five major stages in the life of a neurotransmitter are (1) synthesis, (2) packaging and storage, (3) release from the axon terminal, (4) action on postsynaptic receptors, and (5) inactivation. After synthesis, the neurotransmitter is transported into synaptic vesicles that are stored near the axon terminal. When an action potential is propagated on the presynaptic membrane, voltage changes set in motion the vesicles' attachment to the presynaptic membrane and neurotransmitter release by exocytosis.

One synaptic vesicle releases a quantum of neurotransmitter into the synaptic cleft, producing a miniature potential on the postsynaptic membrane. Generating an action potential on the postsynaptic cell requires simultaneous release of many quanta of transmitter. After a transmitter has done its work, it is inactivated by such processes as diffusion out of the synaptic cleft, breakdown by enzymes, and reuptake of the transmitter or its components into the axon terminal (or sometimes uptake into astrocytes).

## 5-2 Varieties of Neurotransmitters and Receptors

Small-molecule transmitters, peptide transmitters, lipid transmitters, gaseous transmitters, and ion transmitters are broad classes proposed as a means of organizing the roughly 100 neurotransmitters that investigators suspect might exist. Neurons containing these transmitters make a variety of connections with other neurons, as well as with muscles, blood vessels, and extracellular fluid.

Functionally, neurons can be both excitatory and inhibitory, and they can participate in local circuits or in general brain networks. Excitatory synapses are usually on a dendritic tree, whereas inhibitory synapses are usually on a cell body.

Some neurotransmitters are associated with both ionotropic and metabotropic receptors. An ionotropic receptor quickly and directly induces voltage changes on the postsynaptic cell membrane. Slower-acting metabotropic receptors activate second messengers to indirectly produce changes in the cell's function and structure. A plethora of receptors, formed from combinations of multiple types of proteins called subunits, exist for most transmitters.

## 5-3 Neurotransmitter Systems and Behavior

Because neurotransmitters are multifunctional chemicals, scientists find it impossible to isolate relationships between a single neurotransmitter and a single behavior. Rather, activating systems of neurons that employ the same principal neurotransmitter influence various general aspects of behavior. For instance, acetylcholine, the main neurotransmitter in the SNS, controls movement of the skeletal muscles, whereas acetylcholine and norepinephrine, the main neurotransmitters in the ANS, control the body's internal organs. In the ENS, dopamine and serotonin serve as the main neurotransmitters that regulate the gut's functioning.

The CNS contains not only widely dispersed glutamate and GABA neurons—its main neurotransmitters—but also neural activating systems that employ acetylcholine, norepinephrine, dopamine, or serotonin. Collectively, these systems ensure that wide areas of the brain act in concert, and each is associated with various classes of behaviors and disorders.

## 5-4 Hormones

Hormones are produced by endocrine glands and the brain and circulate in the bloodstream, which enables them to affect a wide variety of targets. To regulate hormone levels, a hierarchy of sensory stimuli and cognitive activity in the brain stimulates the pituitary gland through the hypothalamus. The pituitary then either stimulates or inhibits the endocrine glands, which send feedback to the brain via other hormones.

Homeostatic hormones regulate the balance of sugars, proteins, carbohydrates, salts, and other substances in the body. Glucocorticoids are steroid hormones that regulate the body's ability to cope with stress—that is, with arousing and challenging situations.

The hippocampus plays an important role in ending the stress response. Failure to turn off stress responses after a stressor has passed can contribute to susceptibility to PTSD and other psychological and physical diseases. Stress may activate epigenetic changes that modify the expression of genes regulating hormonal responses to stress and may produce brain changes that persist long after the stress-provoking incident has passed.

Synthetic anabolic steroids are substances used by athletes and nonathletes alike. They mimic the effects of testosterone and so increase muscle bulk, stamina, and aggression, but can also have deleterious side effects.

# Key Terms

acetylcholine (ACh), p. 143
activating system, p. 165
Alzheimer disease, p. 165
amino acid hormone, p. 170
anabolic steroid, p. 172
anterograde synaptic transmission, p. 146
autoreceptor, p. 149
carbon monoxide (CO), p. 160
chemical synapse, p. 146
cholinergic neuron, p. 163
dopamine (DA), p. 147
endocannabinoid, p. 159
epinephrine (EP), p. 144
exocytosis, p. 148

G protein, p. 160
gamma-aminobutyric acid (GABA), p. 157
gap junction, p. 151
glucocorticoid, p. 171
glutamate (Glu), p. 157
gonadal (sex) hormone, p. 171
histamine (H), p. 156
homeostatic hormone, p. 171
hydrogen sulfide ($H_2S$), p. 160
ionotropic receptor, p. 149
lipid hormone, p. 170
major depression, p. 167
mania, p. 168
metabotropic receptor, p. 149

neuromodulators, p. 169
neuropeptide, p. 158
neurotransmitter, p. 144
nitric oxide (NO), p. 160
noradrenergic neuron, p. 167
norepinephrine (NE), p. 144
obsessive-compulsive disorder (OCD), p. 169
Parkinson disease, p. 147
peptide hormone, p. 170
postsynaptic membrane, p. 146
presynaptic membrane, p. 146
quantum (pl. quanta), p. 149
rate-limiting factor, p. 156
reuptake, p. 155

schizophrenia, p. 167
second messenger, p. 161
serotonin (5-HT), p. 157
small-molecule transmitter, p. 156
steroid hormone, p. 170
storage granule, p. 146
subunit, p. 160
synaptic cleft, p. 145
synaptic vesicle, p. 145
transmitter-activated receptor, p. 149
transporter, p. 148
tripartite synapse, p. 146
zinc, p. 160

# Selected Resources from  Achieve

**Neuroscience in Action:** Neurotransmission: Bridging the Divide

**Neuroscience in Action:** Getting to Know Your Neurotransmitters

**Concept Practice:** Structures of a Synapse

**Videos**

How Neurons Work

A Synaptic Activity

Parkinson: A Case Study

**LearningCurve**

**Practice Quiz**

# How Do Drugs Influence Brain and Behavior?

# 6

## ◎ CLINICAL FOCUS 6-1

# Cognitive Enhancement?

Some university and college students take certain psychoactive drugs without a prescription — for example, Adderall obtained through friends or family — or for uses other than as prescribed, such as to remain alert and focused for extended periods while studying for exams. Indeed, the number of prescriptions for Adderall has fallen, yet medical problems related to Adderall misuse have increased because the drug is being used in ways other than as legitimately prescribed. Many college students think stimulants like Adderall and Ritalin are harmless study aids, but misuse can carry serious health risks, including mental health problems, depression, bipolar disorder, incidents of aggressive or hostile behavior, and addiction (Han et al., 2016). More recently, students have been using modafinil (marketed under the brand name Provigil) — a nonamphetamine that has a modulatory effect on a wide range of neurotransmitter systems and is mainly prescribed for sleep disorders — as a cognitive enhancer (Sousa & Dinis-Oliveira, 2020).

Both Adderall (mainly dextroamphetamine) and Ritalin (methylphenidate) are prescribed as a treatment for **attention-deficit/hyperactivity disorder (ADHD)**, a developmental disorder characterized by core behaviors including impulsivity, hyperactivity, and/or inattention. Methylphenidate and dextroamphetamine are Schedule II drugs, signifying that they carry the potential for misuse and require a prescription when used medically. Their main illicit source is through falsified prescriptions or purchase from someone who has a prescription. Both drugs share the pharmacological properties of amphetamine: they prolong and increase levels of dopamine in the synapse by reversing its transporter (see Section 6-2 for details on this interaction).

The use of cognitive enhancers is not new. In his classic paper on cocaine, psychoanalyst Sigmund Freud stated in 1884, "The main use of coca [cocaine] will undoubtedly remain that which the Indians [of Peru] have made of it for centuries . . . to increase the physical capacity of the body." Freud later withdrew his endorsement when he realized that cocaine is addictive.

In 1937, an article in the *American Journal of Psychiatry* reported that a form of amphetamine called Benzedrine improved performance on mental efficiency tests (Bradley, 1937). This information was quickly disseminated among students, who began using the drug as a study aid for examinations. In the 1950s, dextroamphetamine, marketed as Dexedrine, was similarly prescribed for narcolepsy, a sleep disorder, and used illicitly by students as a study aid.

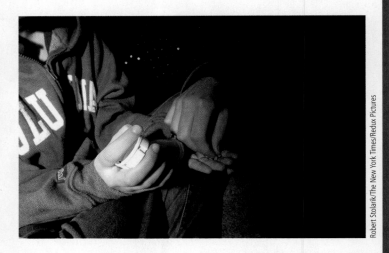

Robert Stolarik/The New York Times/Redux Pictures

The complex neural effects of amphetamine and other stimulants center on changes at the synapse by means of tolerance (weakened response to a stimulus) and sensitization (strengthened response to a stimulus). With repeated use for nonmedicinal purposes, the drugs can also begin to produce side effects, including sleep disruption, loss of appetite, and headaches. Some people develop cardiovascular abnormalities and/or become addicted to amphetamine.

Treatment of ADHD with prescription drugs and their long-term effectiveness is controversial, despite their widespread use for this purpose (Cortese, 2019). Data collected from more than 150 million individuals across the globe showed an increase in the prevalence of ADHD medications use over the past 15 years in all countries examined, though with large variations being seen across countries (Raman et al., 2018). Today, groups including the American Academy of Pediatrics recommend that children younger than age 5 start behavioral treatment for ADHD prior to the use of medication, and that anyone age 6 and older begin medication only after formal diagnosis of this disorder.

Despite the contention that stimulant drugs can improve school and work performance by improving brain function in otherwise healthy individuals, evidence for their effectiveness, other than a transient improvement in motivation, is weak.

---

**attention-deficit/hyperactivity disorder (ADHD)** Developmental disorder characterized by core behavioral symptoms including impulsivity, hyperactivity, and/or inattention.

**psychopharmacology** Study of how drugs affect the nervous system and behavior.

**substance use disorder (SUD)** A diagnostic term for a pattern of drug use in which people rely on a drug chronically and excessively, allowing it to occupy a central place in their life.

**Psychopharmacology**, the study of how drugs affect the nervous system and behavior, is the subject of this chapter. We begin by looking at the most common ways drugs are administered, the routes they take to reach the central nervous system (CNS), and how they are eliminated from the body. We then examine psychoactive drugs based on the primary neurotransmitter system with which they interact. Next, we consider why different people may respond differently to the same dose of a drug and why some people manifest a **substance use disorder (SUD)**. We also deal with the neurological basis of addiction. Note that, despite its widespread use, the term *addiction* has a specific scientific definition (presented in Section 6-3) that is quite different from the imprecise colloquial use.

Before we examine how drugs produce their effects on the brain for good or for ill, we must raise a caution: the sheer number of neurotransmitters, receptors, and possible sites of drug action is astounding. Every drug acts at many sites in the body and brain and affects more than one neurotransmitter system. In other words, every drug has a primary or intended action as well as secondary or unintended actions. Moreover, individual differences—genetic makeup, adverse childhood experiences, sex, age, height, and weight—all influence how drugs affect people. Considering all the variables, psychopharmacological research has made important advances in understanding drugs' actions, but neuroscientists do not know everything there is to know about every drug.

**psychoactive drug** Substance that acts to alter mood, thought, or behavior; is used to manage neuropsychological illness; and often is taken recreationally.

## 6-1

# Principles of Psychopharmacology

Drugs are simply chemical compounds, also known as *substances*, that are administered to bring about some desired change in the body and brain. Drugs are typically used to diagnose, treat, or prevent illness; to relieve mental or physical pain and suffering; or to improve some adverse physiological condition. In this chapter, we focus on **psychoactive drugs**—substances that alter mood, thought, or behavior. Psychoactive drugs are used to treat neuropsychological illness and may be taken recreationally. We also consider psychoactive drugs that, depending on their dose and repeated usage, can act as toxins, producing alterations in behavior, brain damage, or even death.

## Drug Routes into the Nervous System

To be effective, a psychoactive drug must reach its target in the nervous system. The way a drug enters and passes through the body to reach its target is called its *route of administration*. Drugs can be administered orally, inhaled into the lungs, administered rectally in a suppository, absorbed from patches applied to the skin or mucous membranes, or injected into the bloodstream, into a muscle, or even directly into the brain. **Figure 6-1** illustrates some of these routes of drug administration and summarizes the characteristics of drugs that allow them to pass through various barriers to reach their targets.

Oral administration of drugs is easy and convenient but is nonetheless a complex route. To reach the bloodstream, an ingested drug must first be absorbed through the lining of the stomach or small intestine. Drugs in liquid form are absorbed more readily. In contrast, drugs taken in solid form are not absorbed unless the stomach's gastric juices can dissolve them. Some drugs may be destroyed or altered by enzymes in the gastrointestinal tract's microbiome. Whether a drug is an acid or a base also influences its absorption.

Once absorbed by the stomach or intestine, the drug must enter the bloodstream. This leg of the journey requires that the drug have additional properties. Because blood has a high water concentration, the drug must be water-soluble. It is then diluted by the approximately 6 liters of blood that circulate through an adult body. When the drug leaves the bloodstream, the body's roughly 35 liters of extracellular fluid further dilute it.

Our largest organ, the skin, has three cell layers designed to be a protective body coat. Some small-molecule drugs (e.g., nicotine in a patch) easily penetrate the skin barrier.

Drugs administered as gases or aerosols penetrate the cell linings of the respiratory tract very easily and are absorbed across these membranes into the bloodstream almost immediately after they are inhaled. Thus, they reach the bloodstream by circumventing the barriers in the digestive system or skin. When administered as a gas or in smoke, drugs such as nicotine, cocaine, and tetrahydrocannabinol (THC), are similarly absorbed.

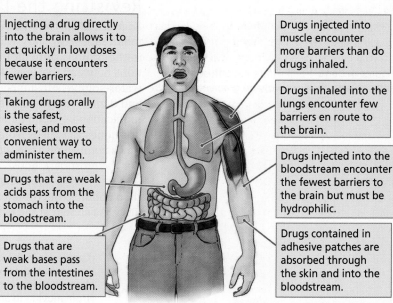

Injecting a drug directly into the brain allows it to act quickly in low doses because it encounters fewer barriers.

Taking drugs orally is the safest, easiest, and most convenient way to administer them.

Drugs that are weak acids pass from the stomach into the bloodstream.

Drugs that are weak bases pass from the intestines to the bloodstream.

Drugs injected into muscle encounter more barriers than do drugs inhaled.

Drugs inhaled into the lungs encounter few barriers en route to the brain.

Drugs injected into the bloodstream encounter the fewest barriers to the brain but must be hydrophilic.

Drugs contained in adhesive patches are absorbed through the skin and into the bloodstream.

**FIGURE 6-1 Routes of Drug Administration**

Still fewer obstacles confront a drug destined for the brain if that drug is injected directly into the bloodstream. And the fewest obstacles are encountered if a psychoactive drug is injected directly into the brain. In most cases, drugs are given by this route of administration only by medical professionals in a sterile setting.

With each obstacle eliminated en route to the brain, a drug's dosage can be reduced by a factor of 10. For example, 1 milligram or 1000 micrograms ($\mu$g; 1 $\mu$g is equal to one-thousandth of a milligram) of amphetamine, a psychomotor stimulant and major component of the drugs described in Clinical Focus 6-1: Cognitive Enhancement?, produces a noticeable behavioral change when ingested orally. If inhaled into the lungs or injected into the blood, thereby circumventing the stomach, a dose of just 100 $\mu$g yields the same result. If amphetamine is injected into the cerebrospinal fluid, bypassing both the stomach and the blood, 10 $\mu$g is enough to produce an identical outcome, as is a mere 1 $\mu$g if, rather than being diluted in the cerebrospinal fluid, the drug is applied directly to target neurons.

On the one hand, drugs that are prepared for inhalation or intravenous injection are much cheaper per dose because the amount required is so much smaller than that needed for an effective oral dose. On the other hand, increased risks are associated with intravenous injections and direct brain applications under nonsterile conditions, as happens when needles are shared among people injecting drugs, because small amounts of blood potentially containing viruses and microorganisms can be passed from one person to another. With the elimination of each protective barrier, the individual also faces an increased risk of overdosing (as progressively smaller amounts are needed to produce the same effect), given that it is nearly impossible to assess the quantity and purity of a drug in a nonmedical setting.

## Revisiting the Blood–Brain Barrier

Numerous barriers to the internal movement of drugs are present in the body: cell membranes, capillary walls, and the placenta. The passage of drugs across capillaries in the brain is difficult because the *blood–brain barrier*, consisting of the tight junctions between the cells of blood vessels found in the brain, blocks the passage of most water-soluble substances. The blood–brain barrier protects the brain's ionic balance and denies many neurochemicals passage into the brain, where they can disrupt communication between neurons. It protects the brain from the effects of many circulating hormones as well as from toxic and infectious substances. Injury or disease can sometimes compromise the integrity of the blood–brain barrier, letting pathogens through. For the most part, however, the brain remains protected from harmful substances.

The brain is supplied by a rich capillary network. None of its neurons is farther than about 50 micrometers ($\mu$m; 1 $\mu$m is equal to one-millionth of a meter) from a capillary. As shown at the left in **Figure 6-2**, brain capillaries (like all other capillaries) are

**1000 $\mu$g = 1 mg (milligram)**

Figures 4-7 and 4-8 illustrate ion diffusion and concentration and voltage gradients.

Capillaries in the brain form tight junctions and are covered with astrocyte feet. These properties prevent materials from moving in and out easily.

Small, uncharged molecules are able to pass through the endothelial membrane.

Certain other molecules are carried across the membrane by active transport.

Astrocyte feet

Capillaries in the body have few tight junctions. Materials can move in and out quite easily.

Endothelial cells

$CO_2$   $O_2$   Amino acids   Glucose   Fats

Transporter

$CO_2$   $O_2$

Capillary

Astrocyte feet   Tight junction

Large and electrically charged molecules are unable to pass out of the capillary.

**FIGURE 6-2 Blood–Brain Barrier** Capillaries in most of the body allow for substances to pass between capillary cell membranes. In contrast, the capillaries in the brain form the tight junctions of the blood–brain barrier.

composed of a single layer of *endothelial cells*. In most parts of the body, endothelial cells in capillary walls are not joined, so substances can pass through the clefts between the cells. In most parts of the brain, by contrast, endothelial cell membranes are fused to form tight junctions, so molecules of most substances cannot squeeze between them.

Figure 6-2 also shows that the endothelial cells of brain capillaries are surrounded by the end feet of astrocytes attached to and covering most of the capillary wall. Astrocytes provide a route for the exchange of food and waste between capillaries and the brain's extracellular fluid, as well as from there to other cells, shown at the right in Figure 6-2.

The cells of capillary walls in three brain regions, shown in **Figure 6-3**, lack a blood–brain barrier. The pituitary is a source of many hormones secreted into the blood, and their release is triggered in part by other hormones carried to the pituitary by the blood. The absence of a blood–brain barrier in the brainstem's area postrema allows toxic substances in the blood to enter that area and be detected by those neurons, which triggers vomiting to expel any ingested toxins that remain in the stomach. The pineal gland also lacks a blood–brain barrier, enabling hormones to reach it and modulate the day–night cycles it controls.

To carry out its work, the brain needs, among other substances, oxygen and glucose for fuel and amino acids to build proteins. Fuel molecules reach brain cells from the blood, just as carbon dioxide and other waste products are excreted from brain cells and are carried away by the blood. Molecules of these vital substances cross the blood–brain barrier in two ways:

1. Small molecules, such as oxygen and carbon dioxide, and lipid-soluble molecules can pass through the endothelial membranes.

2. Complex molecules of glucose, amino acids, and other food components are carried across the membrane by active transport systems or ion pumps (transporter proteins specialized to convey a particular substance).

A few psychoactive drug molecules are sufficiently small or have the correct chemical structure to gain access to the CNS. An important property possessed by those few drugs that have CNS effects, then, is an ability to cross the blood–brain barrier.

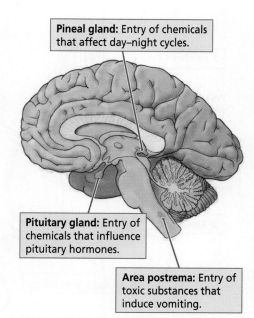

Pineal gland: Entry of chemicals that affect day–night cycles.

Pituitary gland: Entry of chemicals that influence pituitary hormones.

Area postrema: Entry of toxic substances that induce vomiting.

**FIGURE 6-3 Barrier-Free Brain Sites** The pituitary gland is a target for many blood-borne hormones. The pineal gland is a target for hormones that affect circadian rhythms. The area postrema detects and initiates vomiting of noxious substances.

Section 13-2 details the pineal gland's pacemaking function.

## How the Body Eliminates Drugs

Drugs developed for therapeutic purposes are usually designed not only to have an increased chance of reaching their targets, but also to remain active in the body for an extended time. Once a drug is diluted in the bloodstream, it becomes distributed throughout the body. In some cases, a drug then becomes sequestered in fat cells, from which it is released slowly. After a drug is administered, the body begins to break it down through *catabolism*, a process that takes place in several areas of the body, including the kidneys, liver, and the intestines. The body excretes drugs and their metabolites in urine, feces, sweat, breast milk, and exhaled air.

The function of the liver is to convert certain lipid-soluble molecules into a water-soluble form. To that end, the liver houses a family of drug-catabolizing enzymes, called the *cytochrome P450 enzyme family* (some of which are also present in the gastrointestinal tract microbiome), which break down many different drugs into forms more easily excreted from the body. Substances that cannot be catabolized or excreted can build up in the body and become toxic. The metal mercury, for instance, is not easily eliminated and can produce severe neurological effects when it lingers in the body. Current research into mercury poisoning treatment is therefore focused on methods to assist in its elimination while minimizing its harmful effects (Bjørklund et al., 2017).

Humans living in modern, industrialized societies consume a large number and enormous quantities of active drugs, which are eliminated from the body, along with their metabolites, and discharged into the environment, usually into water. This situation is highly problematic, as these substances are often reingested by many other animals, including other humans (Brown et al., 2015). Reingestion of some of these substances has been linked to adverse effects on fertility, development in high-risk groups (including embryos and juveniles), and even the physiology and behavior of adult organisms. A major focus of industrial and civil engineering in recent years has been

*Catabolic* processes break down; *anabolic* processes build up.

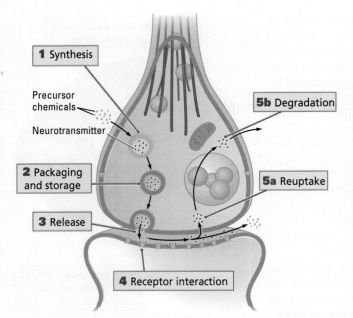

**1** Synthesis

Precursor chemicals

Neurotransmitter

**2** Packaging and storage

**3** Release

**5b** Degradation

**5a** Reuptake

**4** Receptor interaction

**FIGURE 6-4 Points of Influence** In principle, a drug can modify major chemical processes, any of which result in enhanced or reduced synaptic transmission, depending on the drug's action as an agonist or antagonist.

**agonist** Substance that enhances neurotransmitter function.

**antagonist** Substance that blocks neurotransmitter function.

the redesign of waste management systems to remove by-products eliminated by humans as well as by other animals (Meyer et al., 2019).

# Drug Action at Synapses: Agonists and Antagonists

Most drugs that produce psychoactive effects work by influencing chemical reactions at synapses. To understand how drugs work, we must explore the ways they modify synaptic actions. **Figure 6-4** summarizes the major steps in neurotransmission at a synapse—each a potential site of drug action:

1. *Synthesis* of the neurotransmitter in the cell body, the axon, or the terminal
2. *Packaging* and *storage* of the neurotransmitter in vesicles
3. *Release* of the transmitter from the terminal's presynaptic membrane into the synapse
4. *Receptor interaction* in the postsynaptic membrane, as the transmitter acts on an embedded receptor

**5a.** Inactivation by *reuptake* into the presynaptic terminal for reuse OR

**b.** Inactivation by enzymatic *degradation* of excess neurotransmitter

Ultimately, a drug that affects any of these synaptic functions either increases or diminishes neurotransmission. Drugs that increase neurotransmission are classified as **agonists**; drugs that decrease neurotransmission are classified as **antagonists**. To illustrate, consider a typical synapse: the acetylcholine synapse between motor neurons and muscles.

# An Acetylcholine Synapse: Examples of Drug Action

All synapses on muscles are cholinergic—that is, they use acetylcholine (ACh) as their neurotransmitter. Synapses on the heart are inhibitory, and synapses on somatic muscles are excitatory. **Figure 6-5** shows how some drugs and toxins act as agonists or antagonists at the ACh synapse on skeletal muscles. ACh agonists excite muscles,

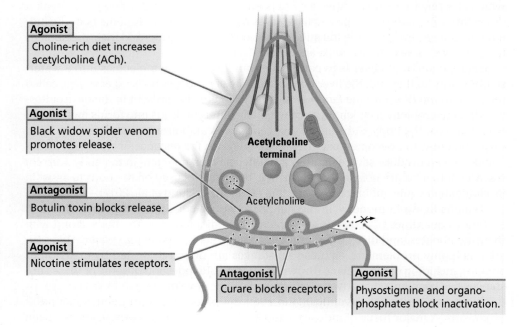

**Agonist**
Choline-rich diet increases acetylcholine (ACh).

**Agonist**
Black widow spider venom promotes release.

**Antagonist**
Botulin toxin blocks release.

**Agonist**
Nicotine stimulates receptors.

Acetylcholine terminal

Acetylcholine

**Antagonist**
Curare blocks receptors.

**Agonist**
Physostigmine and organo-phosphates block inactivation.

**FIGURE 6-5 Acetylcholine Agonists and Antagonists** Drugs and nutrients can affect ACh transmission by altering its synthesis or release or by binding to the postsynaptic receptor and affecting its breakdown or inactivation.

increasing muscle tone, whereas ACh antagonists inhibit muscles, decreasing muscle tone. Some of these substances may be new to you, but you have probably heard of others. By learning their effects at the ACh synapse, you can understand the relationships between these substances' neurochemical actions and their behavioral effects.

Figure 6-5 includes two toxins that influence ACh release from the axon terminal. Black widow spider venom acts as an agonist by promoting release of excessive amounts of ACh. The excitation caused by excess ACh is sufficient to induce paralysis and death in the black widow's insect prey, but the bite does not contain enough toxin to paralyze a human, though a bite victim may feel some muscle weakness.

Botulinum toxin, or botulin, is a poisonous agent found in improperly processed canned goods. An antagonist, it blocks ACh release, and the effect can last for weeks to months. Severe poisoning can paralyze both movement and breathing, thereby causing death. Botulin has medical uses, however. When injected into a muscle, it can selectively paralyze the muscle, making it useful for blocking excessive and enduring muscular twitches or contractions, including the spasms that make movement difficult—such as in people with cerebral palsy. Under the trade name Botox, botulin is also used cosmetically to paralyze facial muscles that cause wrinkling. In addition, Botox is used medically to prevent migraine headaches (Herd et al., 2018).

Figure 6-5 also shows two drugs that act on ACh receptors. Nicotine, a chemical found in cigarette smoke, acts as an agonist to stimulate cholinergic receptors. Nicotine's molecular structure is similar enough to that of ACh to allow nicotine to fit into ACh receptors' binding sites, where it causes the associated ion channel to open. Nicotine very often results in a substance use disorder, and smoking is linked to many negative effects, as we discuss in Section 6-2. Curare acts as an ACh antagonist: it occupies cholinergic receptors but does not cause the ion channel to open, so it prevents ACh from binding to the receptor. Once introduced into the body, curare acts quickly and is cleared from the body in a few minutes. Large doses, however, arrest movement and breathing for a period sufficient to result in death.

Early European explorers of South America discovered that the indigenous peoples living along the Amazon River killed small animals using arrowheads coated with curare prepared from the seeds of a plant. The hunters did not poison themselves when eating the animals because ingested curare cannot pass from the gut into the body. Since those early discoveries, many curare-like drugs have been synthesized. Some are used to briefly paralyze large animals for examination or tagging for identification; you have probably seen these drugs in action in wildlife videos. Skeletal muscles are more sensitive to curare-like drugs than are respiratory muscles, so an appropriate dose paralyzes an animal's movement temporarily but allows it to breathe.

The final drug action shown in Figure 6-5 is that of physostigmine and organophosphate agonists that inhibit acetylcholinesterase (AChE), the enzyme that breaks down ACh, thereby increasing the amount available in the synapse. Physostigmine, obtained from an African bean, is also used as a poison by hunters.

Large doses of physostigmine can be toxic because they produce excessive excitation of the neuromuscular synapse, disrupting movement and breathing. In small doses, however, physostigmine is used to treat *myasthenia gravis*, a condition of muscular weakness in which muscle receptors are less responsive to ACh because the person's antibodies are restricting access of ACh to its receptor.

Organophosphates bind irreversibly to AChE, allowing ACh to build up to toxic levels in the synaptic cleft. Many insecticides and chemical weapons are organophosphates. Insects use glutamate as a neurotransmitter at the nerve–muscle junction, but elsewhere in their nervous system, they have nicotinic receptors. Thus, organophosphates poison insects by acting centrally, but they poison chordates by acting peripherally as well. The Chemical Weapons Convention of 1993 banned one potent organophosphate agent, the lethal nerve gas sarin. That international ban, however, did not restrain the government of Syria, in 2013 and again in 2017, from using sarin against its own citizens.

Does a drug or toxin that affects neuromuscular synapses also affect ACh synapses in the brain? The answer to this question depends on whether the substance

Figure 4-27 details the structure and action of ACh at a neuromuscular synapse.

Clinical Focus 11-2 describes the causes and range of outcomes for cerebral palsy.

As illustrated in Section 5-3, a single main receptor serves the sympathetic nervous system: the nicotinic ACh receptor (nAChR).

Figure 5-10 illustrates ACh's synthesis and its breakdown by AChE.

In myasthenia gravis, muscle receptors lose their sensitivity to motor neuron messages, as illustrated in Section 4-4.

The Basics: Classification of Life in Section 1-3 charts nervous system evolution in the animal kingdom.

**tolerance** Decrease in response to a drug with the passage of time.

The concept of *tolerance* comes from the discipline of pharmacology and is similar to the concept of *habituation*, which comes from the discipline of learning; both terms indicate that the response to a drug or stimulus becomes weaker with repeated presentations (see Experiment 14-2).

can cross the blood–brain barrier. Physostigmine and nicotine readily pass the barrier; curare cannot. Nicotine's actions on the brain account for its addictive properties (see Section 6-4). Physostigmine-like drugs reportedly have some beneficial effects for memory disorders.

# Tolerance

**Tolerance** is a decreased response to a drug with repeated exposure. Harris Isbell and colleagues (1955) conducted an experiment that, while unethical by today's standards, did suggest how tolerance comes about. The researchers gave volunteers in a prison enough alcohol to initially induce a state of intoxication, and then administered additional doses daily over a 13-week period. The participants did not remain drunk for that entire period, however, but had to have their dosage increased to produce the same state of intoxication.

When the experiment began, the participants showed rapidly rising blood alcohol levels and behavioral signs of intoxication, as shown in the Results section of **Experiment 6-1**. Between the twelfth and twentieth days of alcohol consumption, however, their blood alcohol and the signs of intoxication fell, even though the participants increased their alcohol intake. Thereafter, their blood alcohol levels and signs of intoxication fluctuated; one did not always correspond to the other. A relatively high blood alcohol level was sometimes associated with a low outward appearance of intoxication. Why?

The three results were the products of three kinds of tolerance, each of which was much more likely to develop with repeated drug use:

1. In *metabolic tolerance*, the number of enzymes needed to break down alcohol in the liver, blood, and brain increases. As a result, any alcohol consumed is metabolized more quickly, so blood alcohol levels fall.

2. In *cellular tolerance*, brain cell activities adjust to minimize the effects of alcohol in the blood. Cellular tolerance can help explain why the behavioral signs of intoxication may be so low despite a relatively high blood alcohol level.

3. *Learned tolerance* explains a drop in outward signs of intoxication. As people learn to cope with the demands of living under the influence of alcohol, they may no longer appear intoxicated.

Does it surprise you that learning plays a role in alcohol tolerance? It has been confirmed in many studies, with a description of the effect first being reported by John Wenger and his colleagues (1981). These researchers trained rats to prevent electric foot shocks as they walked on a narrow conveyor belt sliding over an electrified grid. One group of rats received alcohol after training in walking the belt; another group received alcohol before training. A third group received training only, and a fourth group received alcohol only.

After several days' exposure to their respective conditions, all groups received alcohol before a walking test. The rats that had received alcohol before

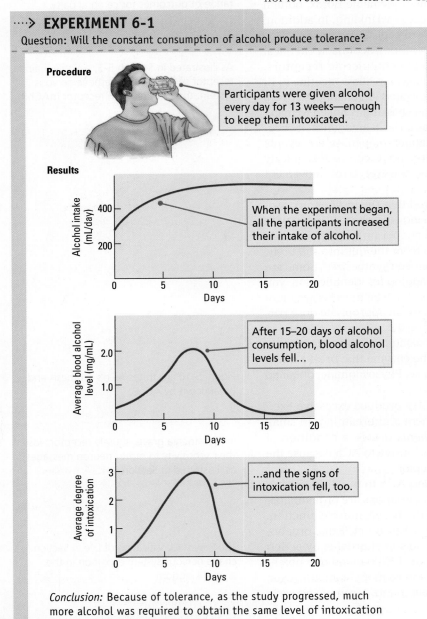

**EXPERIMENT 6-1**

Question: Will the constant consumption of alcohol produce tolerance?

**Procedure**

Participants were given alcohol every day for 13 weeks—enough to keep them intoxicated.

**Results**

When the experiment began, all the participants increased their intake of alcohol.

After 15–20 days of alcohol consumption, blood alcohol levels fell...

...and the signs of intoxication fell, too.

*Conclusion:* Because of tolerance, as the study progressed, much more alcohol was required to obtain the same level of intoxication that was produced at the beginning.

training performed well, whereas those that had received training and alcohol separately performed just as poorly as those that had never had alcohol or those that had not been trained. Despite alcohol intoxication, then, animals can acquire the motor skills needed to balance on a narrow belt. With motor experience, they can learn to compensate for being intoxicated.

With repeated administration, the effects of many psychoactive drugs may progressively diminish due to tolerance. A dose of 100 mg of morphine is sufficient to cause profound sedation—even death—in someone taking the drug for the first time, but people who have developed tolerance to the drug have been known to take up to 4000 mg without adverse effects. Similarly, someone who has been using amphetamine over an extended time may need to take doses 100 or more times as great as those they took initially to produce the same behavioral effect.

# Sensitization

Drug tolerance is much more likely to develop with repeated use than with intermittent use, but tolerance does not always follow repeated exposure to a drug. In fact, a drug may produce the opposite reaction, **sensitization**—that is, increased responsiveness to successive equal doses. Whereas tolerance generally develops with repeated drug use, sensitization is much more likely to develop with intermittent use.

To demonstrate drug sensitization, Terry Robinson and Jill Becker (1986) isolated rats in observation boxes and recorded their reactions to an injection of amphetamine, which is a dopaminergic agonist. Every 3 or 4 days, the investigators injected the rats. They noted that the rats' motor activities—sniffing, rearing, and walking—became more vigorous with each administration of the same drug dose, as graphed in Results 1 of **Experiment 6-2**.

The increased motor activity on successive tests was not due to the animals becoming comfortable with the test situation. Control animals that received no drug failed to display a similar escalation. Administering the drug to rats in their home cages did not affect activity in subsequent tests, either. Moreover, the sensitization to amphetamine was enduring. Even when two injections were administered months apart, the animals still showed an escalation of motor behavior. Even a single exposure to amphetamine produced sensitization.

The neural basis of sensitization lies in part in changes at the synapse. Studies on the dopamine synapse after sensitization to amphetamine show more dopamine is present in the synaptic cleft in sensitized animals. Sensitization can be associated with increases in the number of receptors on the postsynaptic membrane, decreases in the rate of transmitter metabolism in the synaptic space, decreases in transmitter reuptake by the presynaptic membrane, and increases in the number and size of synapses.

Sensitization is long-lasting because it is accompanied by long-lasting structural changes in the brain. **Figure 6-6** summarizes the results from a series of rat studies comparing the effects of amphetamine and saline treatments on cells in the nucleus accumbens, part of the subcortical basal ganglia, weeks after drug exposure was completed. Neurons in the amphetamine-treated brains had more dendritic branches and an increased number of spines compared with those in the saline-treated brains. These plastic changes were not found throughout the brain, but rather were limited to regions that received a large dopamine projection. This finding is important because the experiment clearly shows that drug use affects neuronal structure long after drug taking has ceased.

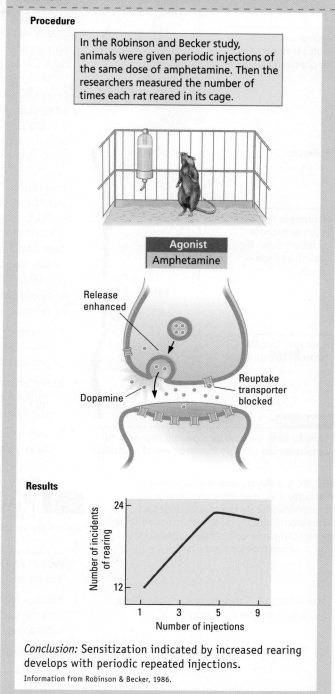

**EXPERIMENT 6-2**

Question: Does the injection of a drug always produce the same behavior?

**Procedure**

In the Robinson and Becker study, animals were given periodic injections of the same dose of amphetamine. Then the researchers measured the number of times each rat reared in its cage.

Agonist
Amphetamine

Release enhanced

Dopamine

Reuptake transporter blocked

**Results**

Number of incidents of rearing (y-axis: 12 to 24)
Number of injections (x-axis: 1, 3, 5, 9)

*Conclusion:* Sensitization indicated by increased rearing develops with periodic repeated injections.

Information from Robinson & Becker, 1986.

Experiment 14-3 describes sensitization at the level of neurons and synapses. Section 14-4 relates sensitization to neuroplasticity and learned addictions.

**sensitization** A process in which repeated administration of a stimulus results in the progressive amplification of a response.

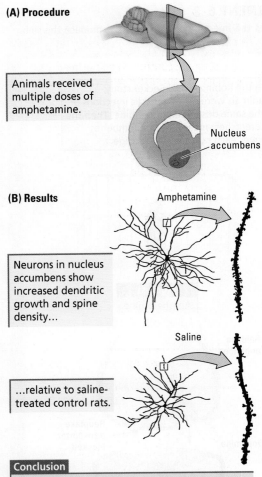

**(A) Procedure**

Animals received multiple doses of amphetamine.

Nucleus accumbens

**(B) Results**

Amphetamine

Neurons in nucleus accumbens show increased dendritic growth and spine density...

Saline

...relative to saline-treated control rats.

**Conclusion**

Sensitization induced by repeated exposure to amphetamine changes the structure of neurons.

**FIGURE 6-6 Psychoactive Drugs and Plasticity** Rats that show sensitization to amphetamine (or to cocaine) undergo increased dendritic growth and increased spine density compared with saline-treated control rats. Data from Robinson & Kolb, 1997.

Clinical Focus 8-5 relates the possible origin of schizophrenia and its progress.

Sensitization occurs not only to drugs but also to stress. The body's response to stress, which may include increased heart rate, respiration, and perspiration, can increase with each stress exposure. As sensitization progresses, a mild stressor can be associated with a strong stress response. Evidence also suggests that sensitization to stress and to stimulant drugs is interchangeable: someone who has experienced stress will be more responsive to stimulant drugs, and vice versa. Furthermore, sensitization to stress is proposed to contribute to depression and other clinical disorders (Stroud et al., 2011).

Sensitization can also have a learned basis. Animals show a change in learned responses to environmental cues as sensitization progresses. Consequently, sensitization is difficult to achieve in an animal tested in its home cage. In one study, Sabina Fraioli and her coworkers (1999) gave amphetamine to two groups of rats and recorded the behavioral responses to successive injections. One group of rats lived in the test apparatus, so for that group, home was the test box. The other group was taken out of their home cage and placed in the test box for each day's experimentation. The home group showed no sensitization to amphetamine, whereas the out group displayed robust sensitization.

At least part of the explanation of the home–out effect is that the animals are accustomed to engaging in a certain behavioral repertoire in their home environment, so it is difficult to get them to change their response to home cues even when influenced by a drug. In contrast, when subjects are away from home, they receive novel out cues, which favor conditioning of new responses.

Sensitization is relevant to understanding some psychopharmacological effects of drugs:

1. Many drug therapies, including those for schizophrenia, a psychiatric disorder, must be taken for several weeks before they produce beneficial effects. Possibly sensitization underlies the development of these beneficial effects.

2. Sensitization is related to the development of a substance use disorder in that the individual must be sensitized by numerous experiences with the drug away from the home environment.

3. Life experiences, especially stressful ones, can produce effects resembling sensitization that prime the nervous system for addiction (Roberts et al., 2015).

# 6-1 Review

Before you continue, check your understanding. Answers to Self-Test appear at the back of the book.

1. _____ are substances that produce changes in behavior by acting on the nervous system and are one subject of _____, the study of how drugs affect the nervous system and behavior.

2. Perhaps the most important obstacle on a psychoactive drug's journey between its entry into the body and its action at a target is the _____, which generally allows only substances needed for nourishment to pass from the capillaries into the _____.

3. Most drugs that have psychoactive effects influence chemical reactions at neuronal _____. Drugs that influence communication between neurons do so by acting either as _____ (increasing the effectiveness of neurotransmission) or as _____ (decreasing the effectiveness of neurotransmission).

4. Behavior may change with the repeated use of a psychoactive drug. These changes may include _____ and _____, in which the effect of the drug decreases or increases, respectively, with repeated use.

5. The body eliminates drugs through _____, _____, _____, _____, and _____.

6. Describe briefly how tolerance and sensitization might affect someone who uses cognitive enhancers occasionally (a) at home or (b) at work.

# Psychoactive Drugs

People have been using drugs for therapeutic and recreational reasons likely for as long as there have been, well, people. In fact, our closest relatives, including common chimpanzees, bonobos, and gorillas, appear to select and ingest, or topically apply, substances to prevent or reduce the harmful effects of pathogens and toxins—a behavior known as **zoopharmacognosy** (for "animal" + "drug" + "knowing") (Kapadia et al., 2014). Humans have taken this practice a step further by cultivating particular plants and fungi, then extracting, purifying, studying, and synthesizing their psychoactive ingredients—and making a great deal of profit from the enterprise. Over time, we have amassed an enormous catalogue of psychoactive drugs, and there is no question that the templates for these drugs come from the natural world (Campbell, 1996).

Finding a universally acceptable scheme for grouping the psychoactive drugs is virtually impossible. Any system will have a unique set of limitations because drugs with similar chemical structure can have different effects, while drugs with different structure can have similar effects. Furthermore, a single drug acts on many neurochemical systems and has many effects.

A full appreciation of any drug's action requires a multifaceted description, such as can be found in medical compendia. Behavioral descriptions undergo constant review, as illustrated by continuing revisions of the *Diagnostic and Statistical Manual of Mental Disorders* (DSM). Published by the American Psychiatric Association and currently in its fifth edition, text revision, the DSM offers a classification system for diagnosing neurological and behavioral disorders, including substance use disorders caused by drug use. For our purposes, we group psychoactive drugs based on the primary neurotransmitter system that they are known to affect, similarly to the way we organized transmitter systems in Chapter 5. Of course, our grouping system also has limitations. The vast majority of medically prescribed drugs were not created to act on specific neurotransmitter systems; rather, drugs were tested on different patient groups, and specific uses in medical treatments were approved based on analysis of their effectiveness.

**Table 6-1** categorizes psychoactive drugs based on their primary neurotransmitter system of action. Each category may contain a few to thousands of chemicals in its subcategories. In the following sections, we highlight drug actions, both on neurochemical systems in the brain and on synaptic function, and provide some examples. Note that many medically prescribed psychoactive drugs are also used and misused recreationally.

Most psychoactive drugs have three names: chemical, generic, and brand. The chemical name describes a drug's structure; the generic name is nonproprietary and is spelled lowercase; and the proprietary, or brand, name, which is selected by the pharmaceutical company that sells the drug, is capitalized. Some psychoactive drugs also sport street or club names.

## Adenosinergic

We begin with the world's most widely consumed psychoactive drug: caffeine. Caffeine-containing drinks, such as coffee, tea, soft drinks, and "energy drinks," are consumed daily by nearly 85% of adults in the United States. A cup of coffee contains about 100 mg of caffeine; many soft drinks contain almost as much; and some energy drinks pack as much as 500 mg.

### Learning Objectives

- List the categories of psychoactive drugs according to the primary neurotransmitter systems on which they act.
- Describe each of the transmitter systems' responses to various agonist and antagonist drugs.
- Summarize the dopamine hypothesis of schizophrenia.
- Explain how selective serotonin reuptake inhibitors can be used to treat major depression.

The DSM and other systems for classifying disorders are discussed in Section 16-1.

**zoopharmacognosy** Behavior in which nonhuman animals self-medicate.

**TABLE 6-1** Psychoactive Drugs

| Primary transmitter system | Recreationally used | Medically prescribed (for psychoactive conditions) |
|---|---|---|
| Adenosinergic antagonist | caffeine | |
| Cholinergic agonist | nicotine | tacrine (Cognex) |
| GABAergic agonists | alcohol | diazepam (Valium), alprazolam (Xanax), clonazepam (Klonopin) |
| Glutamatergic antagonists | phencyclidine/PCP (angel dust), ketamine (Special K) | memantine (Namenda) |
| Dopaminergic agonists | cocaine, amphetamine, methamphetamine | dextroamphetamine (Adderall), methylphenidate (Ritalin), L-dopa |
| Dopaminergic antagonists | | phenothiazines: chlorpromazine (Thorazine); butyrophenones: haloperidol (Haldol) clozapine (Clozaril), aripiprazole (Abilify, Aripiprex) |
| Serotonergic agonists | mescaline (peyote), DMT, psilocybin, lysergic acid diethylamide (LSD), MDMA (Ecstasy) | sertraline (Zoloft), fluoxetine (Prozac), imipramine (Tofranil) |
| Opioidergic agonists | opium, morphine, heroin | morphine, codeine, oxycodone (Percocet), fentanyl, methadone |
| Cannabinergic agonists | tetrahydrocannabinol (THC) | THC (Sativex) |

High levels of caffeine can also be found in foods such as chocolate, and may be added to pharmaceuticals to speed their delivery to their targets by raising the user's heart rate. Given the many substances in which this psychoactive drug is found, you may be consuming more caffeine than you realize.

Caffeine has a very similar structure to adenosine. It binds to adenosine receptors without activating them, thereby blocking the effect of adenosine; in other words, it acts as an adenosine antagonist. Endogenous adenosine induces drowsiness, and caffeine works in opposition to this effect, making us feel more alert and peppy. Excessive levels can lead to the jitters.

But caffeine has other mechanisms of action as well. For example, it inhibits an enzyme that ordinarily breaks down the second messenger, cyclic adenosine monophosphate (cAMP). The resulting increase in cAMP leads to increased glucose production, making more energy available and allowing higher rates of cellular activity. Caffeine also promotes the release of other neurotransmitters, such as dopamine and acetylcholine, which endows caffeine with its stimulant effects that improve reaction time, wakefulness, concentration, and motor coordination (Nehlig, 2010).

Repeated daily intake of caffeine results in tolerance and when discontinued, can result in withdrawal symptoms, such as sleepiness, headache, and irritability. These withdrawal symptoms can be avoided with continued daily consumption of caffeine but will fade with time (about 4 to 7 days) if the individual gives up caffeine altogether.

The most well-known source of caffeine is the coffee seed (not a bean) of *Coffea* plants. But caffeine is also found in the seeds, nuts, leaves, and nectar of a number of other plants native to East Asia and South America.

Why do some plants incorporate caffeine into their tissues? To properly answer this question, we need to consider life from the plants' perspective. Plants face several challenges, such as herbivores, pathogens (such as fungi), and attracting pollinators. All of these selective forces, and many others, have shaped plant adaptations; one such adaptation is incorporating toxins such as caffeine into the plant's tissues. Caffeine acts as a natural pesticide, discouraging or killing herbivorous insects and inhibiting the invasion and colonization of pathogenic fungi. Nectar containing caffeine may have especially rewarding properties for pollinators, such as honeybees, leading to improved distribution of the plant's pollen (Wright et al., 2013). We humans have contributed massively to the success of coffee and tea plants by distributing them widely over our planet, at the expense of native plant and animal species and the local ecology.

## Cholinergic

Nicotine is found in the leaves of the tobacco plant, *Nicotiana tabacum*. Like caffeine, it functions as an antiherbivore chemical and was at one time widely used as an insecticide. Nicotine is also found in small amounts in potatoes, tomatoes, and eggplant.

Nicotine's mood-altering effects are unusual in comparison to most drugs. At low doses, nicotine is a stimulant, but at very high doses, it dampens neuronal activity (Wadgave & Nagesh, 2016). Tobacco smokers report feelings of relaxation, sharpness, calmness, and alertness. When smoke from a tobacco cigarette is inhaled, within a few seconds nicotine stimulates acetylcholine nicotinic receptors (nAChr), which then indirectly cause the release of acetylcholine and several other neurotransmitters, including norepinephrine, epinephrine, arginine, vasopressin, serotonin, endorphins, and dopamine. It is the release of dopamine that provides the reinforcing aspect of nicotine. Nicotine use results in both psychological and physical changes in the person who consumes it. Smoking cessation leads to heightened anxiety, irritability, craving, inability to feel pleasure, and tremors.

This land near the La Tigra Rainforest Lodge in Costa Rica's San Carlos region is one of many examples of former coffee bean plantations that have been reforested.

Dirk Eisermann/laif/Redux

Nicotine is a potentially lethal poison; the total amount of nicotine in one cigarette, if injected, can be lethal to an inexperienced person. Tolerance develops rapidly, however, and people with a history of taking nicotine can withstand much higher levels. Respiratory diseases, lung cancer, and related negative effects are caused by the harmful chemicals found in tobacco smoke rather than by nicotine itself. This fact has propelled the popularity of vaping, in which nicotine can be inhaled without tobacco smoke. However, vaping can also lead to serious health consequences due to contaminants and the vaping solvent itself (Cherian et al., 2020).

While smoking is a risk factor for Alzheimer disease, cholinergic agonists are medically prescribed to treat it. Acetylcholinesterase inhibitors, such as tacrine (Cognex), raise ACh levels and may provide a small benefit for people with this disease (Birks et al., 2015). Nevertheless, no medication has been clearly shown to delay or halt the progression of Alzheimer disease.

# GABAergic

At low doses, GABAergic agonists reduce anxiety; at medium doses, they sedate; at high doses, they anesthetize or induce coma. At very high doses, they can kill (**Figure 6-7**).

To understand how GABAergic agonists work, we must consider the binding sites and channel associated with the GABA$_A$ receptor complex. The GABA$_A$ receptor, illustrated in **Figure 6-8**, contains a site where GABA binds, another separate site where alcohol binds, and still another site where benzodiazepines bind, as well as a chloride ion (Cl⁻) channel.

Excitation of the GABA$_A$ receptor produces an influx of Cl⁻ through its pore. An influx of Cl⁻ increases the concentration of negative charges inside the cell membrane, hyperpolarizing it and making it less likely to propagate an action potential. Thus, GABA produces its inhibitory effect by decreasing a neuron's firing rate. Widespread reduction of neuronal firing underlies the behavioral effects of drugs that affect the GABA$_A$ synapse.

Benzodiazepines are a class of chemicals that include diazepam (Valium), alprazolam (Xanax), and clonazepam (Klonopin) and are medically prescribed to reduce anxiety. Benzodiazepines are often used by people who are having trouble coping with significant physical or mental stress, such as a traumatic accident or a death in the family. They are also used as presurgical relaxation agents and can terminate seizures.

Because the GABA$_A$ receptor has different binding sites for GABA, alcohol, and benzodiazepines, activation of each site promotes an influx of Cl⁻, but in different ways. The effects of actions at these three sites summate, which is why alcohol and benzodiazepine drugs should not be consumed together. In the United States, combined doses

E-cigarettes are a chemical delivery system. When the user inhales, a heater turns some of the liquid into an aerosol that is taken into the lungs.

*Effect of drug* →

Death
Coma
General anesthesia
Sleep
Sedation
Disinhibition
Relief from anxiety
Normal

Increasing dose ⟶

**FIGURE 6-7 Behavioral Continuum of Sedation** Increasing doses of GABAergic agonists affect behavior: low doses reduce anxiety, and very high doses result in death.

**Principle 7:** The nervous system works by juxtaposing excitation and inhibition.

GABA is an amino acid. Figure 5-12 shows its chemical structure.

Sedative-hypnotic drugs (alcohol) increase GABA binding, thereby maximizing the time the pore is open.

Antianxiety drugs (benzodiazepines) influence the frequency of pore opening.

Because their different actions summate, these drugs should not be taken together.

**FIGURE 6-8 Drug Effects at the GABA$_A$ Receptor** These receptors have a binding site for alcohol (*left*) and a different binding site for benzodiazepines (*center*). When taken together (*right*), these two types of drugs can be lethal.

of these drugs reportedly contribute to as many deaths as occur annually from automobile accidents (Cho et al., 2020).

A characteristic feature of benzodiazepine drugs is that an individual who takes repeated doses develops a tolerance for them. A larger dose is then required to attain the drug's initial effect. Cross-tolerance results when the tolerance for one drug, such as a benzodiazepine, is carried over to a different member of the drug group. Cross-tolerance also suggests that benzodiazepines and alcohol act on the nervous system in similar ways.

Alcohol (ethyl alcohol, or ethanol) is present in alcoholic beverages and is an extraordinarily popular psychoactive and recreational drug, particularly among college-age students (see Section 6-3). The fermentation of sugar into alcohol was one of humanity's earliest biotechnologies, dating back at least 9000 years. Alcohol consumption has short-term psychological and physiological effects that depend on several factors, including the amount and concentration of alcohol, the duration over which it is consumed, the amount of food eaten, and the consumer's weight and experience with alcohol. Small amounts of alcohol typically cause an overall improvement in mood and possibly euphoria, increased self-confidence and sociability, decreased anxiety, impaired judgment and fine muscle coordination, and a flushing of the face. Medium doses result in lethargy, sedation, balance problems, and blurred vision. High doses lead to profound confusion, slurred speech ("Wats da proplem, ossifer?"), staggering, dizziness, and vomiting—an adaptive response to poisoning. Very high doses cause stupor, memory loss, unconsciousness, life-threatening respiratory depression, and inhalation of vomit.

The long-term and frequent consumption of alcohol can lead to increased risk of alcoholism, a condition ruinous to individuals and families, as well as an enormous economic burden; alcoholism costs $249 billion each year in the United States alone (Sacks et al., 2015). In the United States, approximately 8% of men and 4% of women met criteria for alcoholism in 2015 (Substance Abuse and Mental Health Services Administration, 2015). Individuals with alcohol use disorder often are malnourished and typically have elevated levels of chronic pancreatitis, liver disease, and cancer. Alcoholism results in damage to the central and peripheral nervous systems, as well as nearly every other system and organ in the body.

Drugs that act on GABA receptors also affect brain development because GABA is one of the substances that regulate brain development. Clinical Focus 6-2: Fetal Alcohol Spectrum Disorder explores the devastating effects of alcohol on developing fetuses.

## Glutamatergic

The glutamatergic system has several receptors, such as NMDA, AMPA, and kainate (see Table 5-3). Antagonists to the NMDA receptor, such as phencyclidine (PCP, or angel dust) and ketamine (Special K), can produce hallucinations and out-of-body experiences. Research indicates that PCP inhibits nicotinic acetylcholine receptors as well as dopamine reuptake; therefore, PCP is also a dopaminergic agonist, which may account for some of its psychoactive effects. Both PCP and ketamine are also known as *dissociative anesthetics*, compounds that produce feelings of detachment—dissociation—from the environment and self because they distort perceptions of sight and sound.

Ketamine is currently medically prescribed for starting and maintaining anesthesia. It induces a trance-like state while providing pain relief, sedation, and memory loss. Subanesthetic ketamine infusions have been shown to have promising antidepressant effects in people with depression who do not respond to the standard treatments, and this therapy is generally well tolerated, with minimal negative effects. Findings from 10 systematic reviews and randomized controlled trials indicated ratings of depression severity decreased both within one day and over several weeks in individuals receiving ketamine. Large, randomized controlled trials are needed to determine the longer-term efficacy, tolerance, and potential addictiveness of ketamine infusions (Lent et al., 2019). Ketamine's mechanism of action, as a glutamatergic antagonist, is very different from

The effects of preconception experience on prenatal development are discussed further in Section 8-5.

Glutamate is the main excitatory neurotransmitter in the forebrain and cerebellum. Section 6-4 describes the brain damage caused by the use of a variety of drugs. Section 14-4 describes how glutamate and NMDA receptors affect long-term learning.

## ⊚ CLINICAL FOCUS 6-2

# Fetal Alcohol Spectrum Disorder

The term *fetal alcohol syndrome* (*FAS*) was coined in 1973 to describe a pattern of physical malformation and intellectual disability observed in some children who had high levels of alcohol exposure during gestation. This condition is now called **fetal alcohol spectrum disorder (FASD)** to acknowledge the range of its effects. Children with FASD may have abnormal facial features, such as unusually wide spacing between the eyes. Their brains also display a range of abnormalities, from small size with abnormal gyri to abnormal clusters of cells and misaligned cells in the cortex.

Related to these brain abnormalities are certain behavioral symptoms that children with FASD tend to have in common. They display varying degrees of learning disabilities and low intelligence test scores, as well as hyperactivity and other social problems. Individuals with FASD are 19 times as likely to be incarcerated as those without it (Popova et al., 2011).

About 1 in 100 newborns in the United States has FASD (Mead & Sarkar, 2014). An especially high incidence in marginalized groups and among prison populations shows that these are at-risk populations, but these estimates are likely not generalizable to all communities.

Women who are most at risk for bearing babies with FASD are economically and educationally disadvantaged, have had issues with alcohol consumption that predate their pregnancy, and have little access to prenatal care. The absence of adequate prenatal health care often makes it difficult to inform potential parents about the dangers that alcohol poses to a fetus and the importance of abstaining from drinking alcohol before and during pregnancy.

Alcohol-induced abnormalities in children with FASD can vary from hardly noticeable physical and psychological effects to the full-blown range of symptoms. The severity of effects is related to when, how much, and how frequently alcohol is consumed over the course of pregnancy. The effects are worse if alcohol is consumed in the first trimester, a time of organogenesis and the highest levels of DNA synthesis. The risks are exacerbated at this stage of gestation, because many women may not realize yet that they are pregnant.

Severe FASD is also more likely to coincide with binge drinking, which produces high blood alcohol levels. Other factors related to severe outcomes include poor nutritional health of the mother and the mother's use of other drugs, including nicotine. In addition, alcohol use by mothers and fathers *before* conception can change the methylation status of some genes that contribute to disabilities found on the spectrum (Lee et al., 2015).

A major question related to FASD is how much alcohol is too much to drink during pregnancy. To be completely safe, it is best not to drink alcohol at all in the months preceding as well as during pregnancy. This conclusion is supported by findings that as little as a single drink of alcohol per day during pregnancy can lead to a decrease in children's intelligence test scores. This advice applies to men as well as women, because it is likely that if a man consumes alcohol, his partner does, too. In addition, use of alcohol by men may produce epigenetic changes in sperm that subsequently affect fetal development (Day et al., 2016).

The proposed mechanism by which alcohol produces the characteristic effects of FASD also includes general effects on cell division and maturation as well as epigenetic effects. Alcohol has an inhibitory effect on potassium channels, which suggests that their dysregulation contributes to development of FASD and that restoration of channels during development or shortly after birth may lessen symptoms (Mohammad et al., 2020).

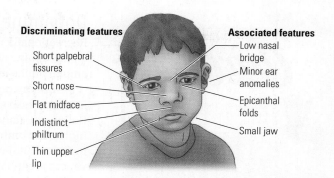

Discriminating features — Short palpebral fissures, Short nose, Flat midface, Indistinct philtrum, Thin upper lip

Associated features — Low nasal bridge, Minor ear anomalies, Epicanthal folds, Small jaw

Courtesy of Sterling K. Clarren, M.D., Professor of Pediatrics, University of British Columbia Faculty of Medicine.

(*Top*) Characteristic facial features that indicate FASD. Effects are not merely physical; many children endure severe intellectual disabilities. (*Bottom*) The convolutions characteristic of the brain of a healthy child at age 6 weeks (*left*) are grossly underdeveloped in the brain of a child with FASD (*right*).

---

those of most modern drugs prescribed to reduce depression, which operate on serotonin and norepinephrine targets (see the "Serotonergic" section later in this chapter).

Memantine (Namenda) is an NMDA antagonist that is prescribed in the treatment of Alzheimer disease to prevent neuronal loss.

# Dopaminergic

We first consider dopamine agonists that are used recreationally, such as cocaine, amphetamine, and methamphetamine, and agonists that are medically prescribed for attention-deficit/hyperactivity disorder (ADHD), such as dextroamphetamine (Adderall)

**fetal alcohol spectrum disorder (FASD)** Range of physical and intellectual impairments observed in some children born following significant alcohol exposure during gestation.

**FIGURE 6-9 Behavioral Stimulant** Cocaine (*left*) is obtained from the leaves of the coca plant (*center*). Crack cocaine (*right*) is chemically altered to form rocks that vaporize when heated at low temperatures.

GeniusKp/iStock/Getty Images Plus/Getty Images

Gregory G. Dimijian, M.D./Science Source

Tek Image/Science Source

GRANGER-Historical Picture Archive

**FIGURE 6-10 Warning Label** Cocaine was once an ingredient in such invigorating beverages as Coca-Cola.

**amphetamine** Synthetic compound that increases the neurotransmitter dopamine in the synaptic cleft by reversing the dopamine transporter.

Section 5-1 describes experiments performed by Otto Loewi that ultimately led to the identification of epinephrine, or adrenaline. Section 7-8 details symptoms and outcomes of ADHD and the search for an animal model of the disease.

and methylphenidate (Ritalin), and for Parkinsonian symptoms, such as L-dopa. We then consider dopamine antagonists that are medically prescribed for schizophrenia and drug-induced psychosis, including chlorpromazine (Thorazine), haloperidol (Haldol), clozapine (Clozaril), and aripiprazole (Abilify, Aripiprex).

## Dopamine Agonists

Recreationally used dopaminergic agonists include cocaine, amphetamine, and methamphetamine. Cocaine is purified from leaves of the coca plant (**Figure 6-9**), whereas amphetamine and methamphetamine are synthetically produced.

For many generations, the indigenous people of Peru have chewed coca leaves to increase their stamina in the harsh environment and high elevations where they live. Refined cocaine powder can either be sniffed (snorted) or injected. *Crack*, a potent, highly concentrated form of cocaine, can be sniffed or smoked. Crack (shown at right in Figure 6-9) is chemically altered so that it vaporizes at low temperatures, and the vapors are inhaled.

Sigmund Freud (1974) popularized cocaine in the late 1800s as an antidepressant. It was once widely used in soft drinks and wine mixtures promoted as invigorating tonics. It is the origin of the trade name Coca-Cola; at one time, this beverage contained cocaine (**Figure 6-10**). Cocaine's addictive properties soon became apparent, however, and it was replaced in these products with caffeine—a substance that can also lead to psychological and physical changes, but that produces less severe adverse effects relative to cocaine.

Freud also recommended that cocaine be used as a local anesthetic. Cocaine did prove valuable for this purpose, and many cocaine derivatives, such as xylocaine (often called Novocain), continue to be used today. These local anesthetic agents reduce a cell's permeability to sodium ions, thereby diminishing nerve conduction.

As **Figure 6-11** shows, the synthetic compound **amphetamine**—like cocaine—is a dopamine agonist that allows dopamine to continue to interact with postsynaptic D$_2$ receptors. Unlike cocaine, which blocks the dopamine reuptake transporter, amphetamine prevents dopamine reuptake by reversing the direction of the transporter that typically packages dopamine into vesicles, thereby removing dopamine that was already packaged and increasing its abundance in the synaptic terminal. The transporter found on the synaptic terminal then pumps the dopamine previously packaged in vesicles into the synaptic cleft. Thus, amphetamine acts in two different ways to increase the amount of dopamine in synapses, which stimulates dopamine receptors.

Amphetamine was discovered during attempts to synthesize the CNS neurotransmitter epinephrine, which also acts as a hormone to mobilize the body for fight or flight in times of stress (see Figure 5-18 in Section 5-3). As noted in Clinical Focus 6-1, amphetamine-based drugs are widely prescribed to treat ADHD.

Benzedrine, a form of amphetamine, was originally used to treat asthma and was sold in inhalers as a nonprescription drug through the 1940s. Soon people discovered that they could open the container and ingest its contents to obtain an energizing effect. Amphetamine was widely used in World War II to help troops and pilots stay alert, increase confidence and aggression, and boost morale—a practice that continues today. It was also used among the civilian population to improve wartime workers' productivity. Today, amphetamine is used as a popular weight-loss aid. Many over-the-counter compounds marketed as stimulants or weight-loss aids have amphetamine-like pharmacological actions.

Methamphetamine (also known as meth, speed, crank, smoke, and crystal ice) is a widely used, illegal amphetamine derivative. Lifetime prevalence of methamphetamine use in the U.S. population (defined as the percentage of the population who have used the drug at least once in their lives) was once estimated to be as high as 6.5% (Durell et al., 2008). The popularity of this drug is related to both its ease of manufacture in illicit laboratories and its potency, which combine to make it a relatively inexpensive, yet potentially devastating drug. The process of illicit manufacture makes it difficult to draw conclusions about the effects of methamphetamines compared to the effects of legally synthesized amphetamines.

Amphetamine (Adderall) and methylphenidate (Ritalin) are medically prescribed to treat ADHD. This disorder is characterized by excessive activity and difficulty controlling behavior or paying attention, though many people with ADHD have very long attention spans for tasks they find interesting. The neurobiological basis of ADHD and its treatment are detailed in Research Focus 6-3: Attention-Deficit/Hyperactivity Disorder.

The recreational dosage of amphetamine and methylphenidate is about 50 times higher than the medically prescribed dosage. Chronic recreational use can lead to *psychosis,* an umbrella term for behavioral disorders characterized by hallucinations (false sensory perceptions), delusions (false beliefs), paranoia, and disordered thoughts, among a host of other symptoms. These symptoms are also observed in individuals diagnosed with *schizophrenia.*

**Agonist**
**Amphetamine** and **cocaine** block the reuptake of dopamine.

**Agonist**
**Amphetamine** promotes the release of dopamine.

Dopamine terminal

Dopamine

Chlorpromazine  $D_2$ receptor

**Antagonist**
**Chlorpromazine** occupies the dopamine site on the $D_2$ receptor, preventing receptor activation.

**FIGURE 6-11 Drug Effects at $D_2$ Receptors** The antipsychotic agent chlorpromazine (Thorazine) can lessen schizophrenia symptoms, and amphetamine or cocaine use can produce them. This suggests that schizophrenia may be related, at least in part, to excessive activity at the $D_2$ receptor.

## ⊚ RESEARCH FOCUS 6-3

# Attention-Deficit/Hyperactivity Disorder

Taken together, attention-deficit/hyperactivity disorder (ADHD) and attention-deficit disorder (ADD) are probably the most common disorders of brain and behavior in children, with an incidence of 9.4% of school-aged children in the United States. Although it often goes unrecognized, an estimated 50% of children with ADHD still show symptoms in adulthood, when these behaviors may be associated with family breakups, substance use disorder, and driving accidents.

The neurobiological basis of ADHD and ADD is generally believed to be a dysfunction in the noradrenergic or dopaminergic activating system, especially in the prefrontal cortex and basal ganglia circuitry. Psychomotor stimulants such as Ritalin (methylphenidate) and Adderall (mainly dextroamphetamine) act to increase brain levels of noradrenaline and dopamine and are widely used for treating ADHD. Approximately 70% of children show improvement of attention and hyperactivity symptoms with treatment, but there is little evidence that drugs directly improve academic achievement. This point is important because an estimated 40% of children with ADHD fail to get a high-school diploma, even though many receive special education for their condition.

Stephen Faraone and coworkers (Lecendreux et al., 2015) have challenged the common view that ADHD is a cultural phenomenon reflecting parents' and teachers' intolerance of children's behavior. These investigators conclude that the prevalence of ADHD worldwide is remarkably similar when the same rating criteria are used. Little is known about incidence in developing countries, however. It is entirely possible that the incidence may actually be higher in developing countries, given that the learning environment for children is likely to be less structured than that found in developed nations.

The cause of ADHD is unknown but probably involves dopamine receptors in the forebrain. The areas most likely affected are the frontal lobe and subcortical basal ganglia. Evidence of reduced brain volumes in these regions in people with ADHD is growing, as is evidence of an increased level of the dopamine transporter protein. A dopamine transporter increase would mean that dopamine reuptake into the presynaptic neuron occurs faster than it does in the brains of people without ADHD, resulting in a relative decrease in dopamine levels. Ritalin works by blocking dopamine reuptake.

ADHD is believed to be highly heritable, a conclusion supported by twin studies showing a concordance of approximately 75% in identical twins. Molecular genetic studies have identified at least seven candidate genes, and several of them are related to the dopamine synapse—in particular, to the $D_4$ receptor gene.

## Dopamine Antagonists

The **dopamine hypothesis of schizophrenia** holds that some forms of this disease may be related to excessive dopamine activity—especially in the frontal lobes. If excessive dopamine is a consequence of drug-induced psychosis and some forms of naturally occurring schizophrenia, then dopamine antagonists should ameliorate the symptomology (see Figure 6-11). In fact, the use of dopamine antagonist drugs that preferentially bind to $D_2$ receptors has improved the functioning of people with schizophrenia. Since 1955, when dopaminergic antagonists (antipsychotic agents, or antipsychotics) were introduced into widespread therapeutic use, resident populations with schizophrenia in state and municipal mental hospitals in the United States have decreased dramatically.

The incidence of schizophrenia is about 7 people in every 1000, with slightly more males than females being affected (Charlson et al., 2018). Given the relatively high incidence of schizophrenia, the success of dopamine antagonists represents an important therapeutic achievement. Although using dopamine antagonists to treat psychosis makes these mental disorders manageable, it does not constitute a cure. In fact, according to findings from a recent meta-analysis of studies of the prevalence of schizophrenia and psychotic disorders among homeless individuals in developed and developing countries, more than 21% were diagnosed with psychosis, more than 16% with schizophrenia or a related disorder, and 9% with an unspecified psychotic disorder (Ayano et al., 2019).

Dopamine antagonists have been widely used to treat psychosis since the mid-1950s, beginning with the development of the first-generation antipsychotics (FGAs). These agents include the drug classes phenothiazines (e.g., chlorpromazine [Thorazine]) and butyrophenones (haloperidol [Haldol]). FGAs act mainly by blocking the dopamine $D_2$ receptor, which immediately reduces motor activity and alleviates the excessive agitation of some people with schizophrenia. But because schizophrenia involves more than just $D_2$ receptors, changes in dopamine synapses do not completely explain the disorder or the effects of dopaminergic antagonists. Beginning in the 1980s, newer drugs such as clozapine (Clozaril) and several other compounds emerged as second-generation antipsychotics (SGAs). SGAs block not only dopamine $D_2$ receptors but also serotonin $5\text{-}HT_2$ receptors.

The therapeutic actions of $D_2$ antagonists are not fully understood, and long-term use of these drugs can produce many unwanted side effects, including *tardive dyskinesia (TD)*. TD is a movement disorder that results in involuntary, repetitive body movements such as grimacing, sticking out the tongue, or smacking the lips, as well as rapid jerking movements or slow writhing movements. Recall that dopamine agonists, such as L-dopa, boost dopamine levels to restore movements in people with Parkinson disease. Thus, dopamine plays a central role in normal movement and mental health, as discussed in Section 6-3.

# Serotonergic

We now consider the serotonergic agonists. Keep in mind, however, that most serotonergic agonists also have adrenergic activity.

Serotonergic agonists are well known for altering perceptions of one's surroundings, feelings, sensations, and images (visual hallucinations), producing what are known as "trips." They were part of the counterculture movement of the 1960s and continue to be used recreationally and spiritually. Some serotonergic agonists, such as mescaline (peyote; 3,4,5-trimethoxyphenethylamine), DMT (*N,N*-dimethyltryptamine), and psilocybin, are found in plants and mushrooms. Others, such as lysergic acid diethylamide (LSD) and MDMA (Ecstasy, XTC; 3,4-methylenedioxymethamphetamine), are produced synthetically.

Beginning in the twentieth century, strong advocates for serotonergic agonists in the United States have promoted their use for "mind expansion and personal truth." Mescaline, obtained from the peyote cactus, is legal in the United States for

Psychosis and schizophrenia are described in detail in Section 16-2.

Tardive dyskinesia is discussed further in Section 16-3.

**dopamine hypothesis of schizophrenia** Idea that excess dopamine activity causes symptoms of schizophrenia.

use by Native Americans for spiritual practices. Serotonergic agonists can produce trips that are pleasurable and associated with feelings of joy or euphoria (referred to as a "rush"), disconnection from reality, decreased inhibitions, and the belief that one has extreme mental clarity or superpowers. Negative experiences, however, can also be associated with trips, inducing irrational fears, panic attacks, paranoia, rapid mood swings, intrusive thoughts of hopelessness, wanting to harm others, and suicidal ideation. Repeated use can lead to problems with sleep, mood, memory, and attention.

Although these drugs are currently illegal for prescription and for recreational use, increased awareness of the massive unmet mental health burden, coupled with a scarcity of breakthrough treatments, has led to a resurgence of research into the potential use of psychedelics as treatments for a wide range of serious disorders, including depression and addiction (for a review, see Nutt et al., 2020). A growing body of evidence supports the safety and efficacy of psychedelics in medical settings and suggests that the potential for addictive misuse is limited. Physiologically, psychedelics have novel, multilevel mechanisms of action that recent research suggests may lead to rapid and enduring relief of symptoms (Nutt, 2019).

The finding that an antagonist for the serotonin 2A receptor (5-HT$_{2A}$) fully blocks the psychedelic effects contributed to our understanding that psychedelic drugs are agonists for that receptor, making it a key target for these drugs (Preller et al., 2018). Psilocybin stimulates 5-HT$_{2A}$ receptors on pyramidal cells in neocortical layer 5. This activity leads to massive depolarization of the neurons and their rapid and repeated firing. Since these neurons are responsible for organizing cross-cortical integration, this activity results in a profound alteration of cortical signaling. Electroencephalography (EEG) recordings reveal a shift of typical rhythmical activity to desynchronization following administration of psilocybin, an effect that may contribute to the sense among people who frequently take these drugs of having new insights into past behavior, memories, actions, feelings, and beliefs. While research into the mechanisms and effects of psychedelics represents an exciting frontier in treatment, carefully controlled research on safety and efficacy remains to be done.

Other serotonergic agonists are currently medically prescribed for the treatment of **major depression**, a mood disorder characterized by prolonged feelings of worthlessness and guilt, disruption of normal eating habits, sleep disturbances such as insomnia, a general slowing of behavior, and frequent thoughts of suicide. At any given time, approximately 6% of the adult U.S. population has major depression, and in the course of a lifetime, 30% may have at least one episode that lasts for months or longer. Major depression is diagnosed in twice as many women as men.

Inadequate nutrition, stress from difficult life conditions, acute changes in neuronal function, and damage to brain neurons are among the factors implicated in depression. These factors may be related: nutritional deficiencies may increase vulnerability to stress; stress may change neuronal function; and if unrelieved, altered neuronal function may lead to neuron damage. Not surprisingly, a number of pharmacological approaches to depression are available, including normalizing stress hormones, modifying neuronal responses, and stimulating neuronal repair.

## Medications Used to Treat Depression

Three different types of serotonergic agonist drugs are prescribed for depression: the **monoamine oxidase (MAO) inhibitors**; the **tricyclics**, so called because of their three-ring chemical structure; and the **selective serotonin reuptake inhibitors (SSRIs)**. The SSRIs lack a three-ring structure but do share some similarities to the tricyclics in their actions.

Drugs prescribed for depression are thought to act by improving chemical neurotransmission at serotonin, noradrenaline (norepinephrine), histamine, and acetylcholine synapses, and perhaps at dopamine synapses as well. **Figure 6-12** shows the actions of MAO inhibitors, tricyclics, and SSRIs at a 5-HT synapse, on which most research is focused. These three classes of drugs act as agonists, but they have different mechanisms for increasing serotonin availability.

**major depression** Mood disorder characterized by prolonged feelings of worthlessness and guilt, disruption of normal eating habits, insomnia, a general slowing of behavior, and frequent thoughts of suicide.

**monoamine oxidase (MAO) inhibitor** Drug that blocks the enzyme monoamine oxidase from degrading such neurotransmitters as 5-HT, NE, and DA.

**tricyclic** Drug, characterized by its three-ring chemical structure, that blocks 5-HT reuptake transporter proteins.

**selective serotonin reuptake inhibitor (SSRI)** Drug that blocks 5-HT reuptake into the presynaptic terminal; most commonly used to treat depression.

Section 5-4 offers more information on stress and stress hormones. Section 12-4 explores the neural control of emotions and emotional disorders such as depression, and Section 16-2 focuses on the neurobiology and treatments for such disorders.

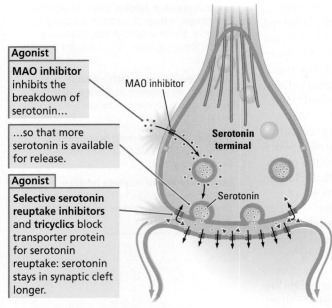

**Agonist**

**MAO inhibitor** inhibits the breakdown of serotonin...

...so that more serotonin is available for release.

**Agonist**

**Selective serotonin reuptake inhibitors** and **tricyclics** block transporter protein for serotonin reuptake: serotonin stays in synaptic cleft longer.

**FIGURE 6-12 Drug Effects at 5-HT Receptors** Different drugs prescribed to treat depression act on the serotonin synapse in different ways to increase its availability.

Reuptake is part of transmitter inactivation, the last of the five steps of neurotransmission (see Figure 5-3).

MAO inhibitors provide for more serotonin release with each action potential by inhibiting monoamine oxidase, an enzyme that breaks down serotonin in the axon terminal. In contrast, the tricyclics and SSRIs block the reuptake transporter that takes serotonin back into the axon terminal. Because the transporter is blocked, serotonin remains in the synaptic cleft, prolonging its action on postsynaptic receptors.

Although these drugs begin to affect synapses very quickly, their antidepressant actions take weeks to develop. One explanation for this delayed action is that these drugs, especially SSRIs, stimulate second messengers in neurons to activate the repair of neurons damaged by stress. Of interest in this respect, one particular SSRI, fluoxetine (Prozac), increases the production of new neurons in the hippocampus, a limbic structure in the temporal lobes. As detailed in Section 5-4, the hippocampus is vulnerable to stress-induced damage, and its restoration by fluoxetine is proposed to underlie one of the drug's antidepressant effects (Yamada et al., 2020).

Most people recover from depression within a year of its onset. If depression is left untreated, however, the incidence of suicide among depressed individuals is high, as described in Clinical Focus 6-4: Major Depression. Of all psychological disorders, major depression is one of the most treatable. Cognitive-behavioral therapies are most effective when combined with drug therapies (Comer & Comer, 2021).

Despite these successes, approximately 20% of patients with depression fail to respond to antidepressant drugs. Depression can have many causes, including dysfunction in other transmitter systems and even brain damage, such as frontal lobe damage—many of which are not treatable by serotonin agonists. In addition, some people have difficulty tolerating the side effects of antidepressants, which can include increased anxiety, sexual dysfunction, sedation, dry mouth, blurred vision, and memory impairment.

# Opioidergic

An *opioid* is any endogenous or exogenous compound that binds to opioid receptors to produce morphine-like effects. These psychoactive compounds have sleep-inducing

---

## Major Depression

P. H. was a 53-year-old high school teacher who, although popular with his students, was deriving less and less satisfaction from his work. His marriage was foundering because he was growing apathetic and no longer wanted to socialize or go on vacations. He was having difficulty getting up in the morning and arriving at school on time.

P. H. eventually consulted a physician, complaining of severe chest pains, which he feared signaled an impending heart attack. He informed his doctor that a heart attack would be a welcome relief because it would end his problems. The physician concluded that P. H. had depression and referred him to a psychiatrist.

Since the 1950s, depression has been treated with serotonergic drugs, a variety of *cognitive-behavioral therapies* (*CBTs*), and, when pharmacological approaches fail, electroconvulsive therapy (ECT), in which electrical current is briefly passed through one hemisphere of the brain. The risk of suicide and self-injurious behaviors is high in people with major depression, especially among depressive adolescents who are resistant to treatment with SSRIs (Asarnow et al., 2011). Even for those individuals who do respond

positively to SSRI treatment, the benefits are usually not observed for the first few weeks of treatment.

The glutamate antagonist ketamine, when given in smaller-than-anesthetic doses, can produce rapid beneficial effects that last for weeks, even in people who are resistant to SSRI medication (Reinstatler & Youssef, 2015). Ketamine has been proposed to be useful as an acute treatment for people with either major depression or bipolar depression who are at risk for suicide.

Prompted by complaints from family members that antidepressant drug treatments have caused suicide, especially in children, the U.S. Food and Drug Administration (FDA) has advised physicians to monitor the side effects of SSRIs, including fluoxetine (Prozac), sertraline (Zoloft), and paroxetine (Paxil, Seroxat). Findings from several studies show no difference in the suicide rate between children and adolescents who receive SSRIs and a placebo; in addition, the incidence of suicide after prescriptions were curtailed subsequent to the FDA warning actually increased after the warning was issued (Isacsson & Rich, 2014).

(narcotic) and pain-relieving (analgesic) properties. There are three sources of opioids: isolated (morphine, codeine), altered (heroin, oxycodone), and synthetic (fentanyl, methadone).

Research has identified five classes of opioid peptides: dynorphins, enkephalins, endorphins, endomorphins, and nociceptin. The four receptors to which each opioid peptide binds are the *delta, kappa, mu*, and nociceptin receptors. All opioid peptides and their receptors occur in many regions of the CNS, as well as in other areas of the body, including the enteric nervous system (ENS). Morphine most closely mimics the endomorphins and binds most selectively to the *mu* receptors.

*Opium* is a white, milky latex extracted from the seed pods of the opium poppy, *Papaver somniferum*, shown at top in **Figure 6-13**. Opium, whose primary active ingredient is morphine, has been used for thousands of years to produce euphoria, analgesia, sleep, and relief from diarrhea and coughing. In 1805, chemist Friedrich Sertürner isolated two chemicals from opium: codeine and morphine. Codeine is often an ingredient in prescription cough medicine and pain relievers. The liver has an enzyme that converts it to morphine, although some people with blond-haired and blue-eyed phenotypes lack this enzyme. Morphine, shown at center in Figure 6-13 and named for Morpheus, the Greek god of dreams, alters the perception of pain.

In addition to the natural opioids, semi-synthetic opioids, such as heroin and oxycodone, affect *mu* receptors. Heroin, shown at bottom in Figure 6-13, is altered from morphine. More potent and more fat-soluble than morphine, it also penetrates the blood–brain barrier more quickly, allowing it to produce very rapid but shorter-acting psychoactive affects. Heroin is a legal drug in some countries but remains illegal in others, including the United States.

Synthetic opioids, such as fentanyl, are prescribed for clinical use in pain management. Fentanyl is up to 100 times more potent than morphine, which contributes to the frequency with which it produces overdose-related deaths. All opioids are potently addictive, and misuse of medically prescribed opioids has reached a crisis point worldwide, as detailed in Clinical Focus 6-5: The Opioid Overdose Death Epidemic. Opioids also may be illegally modified, manufactured, and distributed. People who use opioids can develop opioid use disorder (OUD); some obtain multiple prescriptions and sell them illicitly.

Opioid ingestion produces wide-ranging physiological changes in addition to altering pain perception, including relaxation and sleep, euphoria, and constipation. (And, yes, the use of laxatives to reverse constipation is also on the rise in tandem with the opioid epidemic.) Other effects include respiratory depression, which is the primary cause of death of people with OUD, decreased blood pressure, pupil constriction, hypothermia, drying of secretions (e.g., dry mouth), reduced sex drive, and flushed, warm skin.

Repeated opioid use produces tolerance such that within a few weeks, the effective dose may increase 10-fold. Thereafter, many desired effects no longer occur. A person with an OUD cannot simply stop using the drug without adverse effects: severe withdrawal symptoms, physiologically and behaviorally opposite to those produced by the drug, result if drug use is abruptly stopped.

Drugs such as *naloxone* (Narcan, Nalone) act as antagonists at opioid receptors. Naloxone is a **competitive inhibitor**: it competes with opioids for neuronal receptors. Because they can enter the brain quickly, competitive inhibitors rapidly block the actions of opioids; thus, they are essential aids in treating opioid overdoses. Many people who misuse opioids or who work with at-risk populations routinely carry a competitive inhibitor as a treatment for overdosing. Because they can also be long-acting, competitive inhibitors can be used to treat opioid addiction after the individual has recovered from withdrawal symptoms.

Researchers have extensively studied whether opioid peptides produced in the brain can be used as drugs to relieve pain without addictive effects. The answer so far is uncertain, and producing an analgesic that does not produce addiction, which is one of the objectives of pain research, may be difficult to realize. The development of non-opioid pain medications remains an important avenue of research.

AtWaG/E+/Getty Images

DEA/Science Source

Bonnie Kamin/PhotoEdit

**FIGURE 6-13 Potent Poppy** Opium is obtained from the seed pods of the opium poppy (*top*). Morphine (*center*) is extracted from opium, and heroin (*bottom*) is in turn altered from morphine.

The term "cold turkey" is a reference to the cold skin that accompanies opioid withdrawal, as the hair stands up and looks like turkey skin. This effect is the opposite of the warm skin experienced after opioid use.

**competitive inhibitor** Drug used to treat overdoses and opioid use disorder; an example is naloxone, which acts quickly to block opioid action by competing with the opioid for binding sites.

## ◎ CLINICAL FOCUS 6-5

# The Opioid Overdose Death Epidemic

Before it was overtaken by COVID-19, drug overdose was for many years the leading cause of death in the United States and Canada in people younger than 50 years of age, and it will likely return to the top spot as the uptake of COVID-19 vaccines reduces this disease's death toll. Tragically, the COVID-19 pandemic also intensified the addiction crisis, leading to an estimated 74% increase in the number of opioid overdose deaths in North America in 2020 compared to 2019 (United Nations, 2021).

The opioid overdose epidemic in the United States can be broken into three waves. The first wave was tied to an increase in the number of prescription opioids available, which occurred in the 1990s. The second wave began in 2010, with rapid increases in deaths due to heroin usage, particularly associated with the unreliability of appropriate information on the drug's purity. The third wave began in 2013, with large increases in the illicit manufacture and use of highly potent and potentially lethal synthetic opioids, such as fentanyl (O'Donnell et al., 2017). Many opioid-involved overdose deaths also occur in conjunction with the use of other drugs, such as cocaine and methamphetamine.

The overwhelming majority of people who have died from an opioid-related overdose first became addicted through the use of physician-prescribed opioids (e.g., Demerol, Oxycodone, and Vicodin) for treatment of chronic pain after trauma or surgery. Opioids are relatively inexpensive, costing significantly less than alternative interventions, such as physical therapy. Indeed, much of the culpability for the opioid epidemic can be assigned to the over-prescription of opioids by physicians, and to the pharmaceutical industry's failure to properly represent the dangers of their opioid products and their public policy tactics that led administrators to pressure doctors to prescribe them (McGreal, 2018).

Several major U.S. court cases have resulted in substantial financial settlements related to the opioid epidemic in recent years. One of the first came in 2015, when Purdue Pharma pled guilty to criminal charges over how it misled the public about the addictiveness of its product OxyContin; the company agreed to pay the state of Kentucky $24 million. Since then, a long list of drug companies and distributers have agreed to pay billions of dollars in settlements to the U.S. Department of Justice, states, and municipalities. In July 2021, a group of state attorneys-general unveiled a proposal for a landmark settlement in which three large drug companies implicated in this epidemic would pay $21 billion — the second largest settlement in U.S. history — with

Health care providers prepare a patient with opioid use disorder for focused ultrasound to the nucleus accumbens while inducing drug cravings with visual images of drug use and drug paraphernalia, in an effort to weaken those associations.

the money expected to be used for addiction treatment, family support, education and other social programs.

Some countries, including Australia and Japan, have avoided public issues with opioids altogether by simply not treating chronic pain with opioids. In these countries and others, chronic pain is typically treated with anti-inflammatory agents such as ibuprofen and naproxen. Non-opioid drugs, including cannabis and cannabinoids, are also being used with increased frequency to help manage pain by promoting sleep.

Innovative treatments for opioid use disorder also offer hope in addressing this crisis. In 2021, West Virginia University's Rockefeller Neuroscience Institute launched a clinical trial to investigate the use of focused ultrasound. During a 30-minute procedure, ultrasound waves were focused on the nucleus accumbens of patients with opioid use disorder while drug cravings were induced with visuals of drug use and drug paraphernalia. Preliminary findings indicate the treatment led to a reduction in cravings and addictive behaviors, though the trial is ongoing. Other innovative addiction treatments being explored involve the use of wearable devices, artificial intelligence, transcranial magnetic stimulation, and deep brain stimulation.

# Cannabinergic

Tetrahydrocannabinol (THC) is one of 84 cannabinoids and the main psychoactive constituent in cannabis (inappropriately referred to as marijuana), a substance obtained from several species of *Cannabis* plants, shown in **Figure 6-14**. THC alters mood primarily by interacting with the cannabidiol 1 (CB1) receptor found on neurons; it also binds with the CB2 receptors found on glial cells and in other body tissues. Cannabis has extremely low toxicity—no one has *ever* died of an overdose—but may have a detrimental effect on mood and memory as well as a positive effect on mental overload.

The human body produces two endogenous molecules that bind to CB1 and CB2 receptors: anandamide and 2-AG. Results from numerous lines of research suggest that anandamide reduces anxiety and enhances forgetting. Anandamide may prevent the brain's memory systems from being overwhelmed by all the information to which we are exposed each day.

Cannabis can relieve nausea and emesis (vomiting) in patients undergoing cancer chemotherapy who are not helped by other treatments, and can stimulate the appetite in patients with anorexia–cachexia (wasting) syndrome. It has been found to be helpful for treating chronic pain through mechanisms that appear to be different from those of the opioids. In fact, cannabis reduces the dose of opioids needed in the treatment of pain.

Cannabis has also proved useful for treating glaucoma (increased pressure in the eye), spastic disorders such as multiple sclerosis, and disorders associated with spinal cord injury. In addition, it may have some neuroprotective properties. Many people self-prescribe cannabis for a wide range of ailments, including posttraumatic stress disorder (Roitman et al., 2014).

Not all cannabinoids produce psychoactive effects, because not all interact with the CB1 receptor. For example, some studies have shown that the compound cannabidiol (CBD) has neuroprotective properties because it reduces inflammation, but does not produce the mood-altering effects associated with other cannabinoids. CBD is under investigation for its benefit in a variety of neuropsychiatric disorders, including autism spectrum disorder, anxiety, psychosis, neuropathic pain, cancer pain, human immunodeficiency virus (HIV) infection, migraine, multiple sclerosis, Alzheimer disease, Parkinson disease, Huntington disease, hypoxic–ischemic injury, and epilepsy (Cristino et al., 2020). Many reports attest that some ingredients in cannabis, including CBD, reduce the frequency and severity of epileptic seizures. An oil-containing CBD, from a company named Charlotte's Web (after the first child who used it), is reported to be effective in treating certain childhood epilepsy syndromes (Robson, 2014).

Synthetic and derived forms of THC were developed in part to circumvent legal restrictions on its use. There is hope that the removal of legal restrictions against cannabis in Canada and an increasing number of U.S. states will lead to more scientific investigations into its useful medicinal effects in the coming years.

**FIGURE 6-14** *Cannabis sativa* The hemp plant, an annual herb, grows over a wide range of altitudes, climates, and soils. Hemp has myriad uses, including in manufacturing rope, cloth, and paper; tetrahydrocannabinol (THC) is the main psychoactive constituent in cannabis.

*Marijuana*, a Mexican Spanish term with obscure roots, rose in popularity in the early 1900s. The term made the plant sound scary and strange to White Americans at the time, which fed into a growing racism and xenophobia against Mexicans.

Anandamide (from Sanskrit, meaning "joy" or "bliss") acts on the CB1 receptor that naturally inhibits adenyl cyclase, part of a second messenger system active in sensitization (see Section 14-4).

## 6-2 Review

Before you continue, check your understanding. Answers to Self-Test appear at the back of the book.

1. _____, the world's most widely consumed psychoactive drug, binds to _____ receptors but also has other mechanisms of action.

2. Drugs that reduce anxiety and can induce sedation primarily exert their action on the _____ receptor, which hyperpolarizes neurons through the influx of _____.

3. Drugs prescribed for depression primarily exert their effect on the _____ergic system.

4. Opioids mimic the action of _____ by binding to the same receptors.

5. Amphetamine stimulates dopamine _____, and cocaine blocks dopamine _____, at the _____ synapse.

6. On which neurotransmitter systems do drugs that produce psychotropic effects act?

## 6-3

# Factors Influencing Individual Responses to Drugs

Specific behaviors often trigger predictable results. You strike the same piano key repeatedly and hear the same note each time. You flick a light switch today, and the bulb glows exactly as it did yesterday. This cause-and-effect consistency does not extend to the effects of psychoactive drugs: individuals may respond to these drugs in remarkably different ways at different times.

**Learning Objectives**

- Explain how the concept of learning can be applied to an individual's response to a psychoactive drug.
- Explain the relationship between tolerance, withdrawal, and addiction.
- Explain how adverse childhood experiences and individual and sex differences can contribute to person-to-person variations in responses to drugs.

Every psychoactive drug has variable effects, depending on the circumstances under which it is administered. Physical differences—in body weight, sex, age, or genetic makeup—influence a given drug's effect on an individual, as do learned behaviors and cultural and environmental contexts. Furthermore, potentially anyone can develop a substance use disorder to a given drug, because we all have receptors for neurotransmitters and hormones that influence our motivations and behaviors, and drugs interact with those same receptor systems. We begin by considering the drug alcohol before moving to a more general discussion of substance use disorder, addiction, and withdrawal.

# Behavior on Alcohol

Why do people do things while using alcohol that they never would do when sober? Risky behavior associated with alcohol use is costly both to individuals and to society. A vast number of negative behaviors are associated with excessive alcohol consumption, including unsafe sexual activity, impaired driving, violence including sexual assault, spousal and child abuse, and other forms of aggression.

In this section, we discuss some of the leading explanations for the effects of alcohol—namely, disinhibition, learning, and behavioral myopia. In addition, we consider some risk factors associated with individual outcomes of drug use and misuse.

## Disinhibition and Impulse Control

An early and still widely held explanation of alcohol's effects is **disinhibition theory**. This theory holds that alcohol has a selective depressant effect on the cortical brain region that controls judgment, while sparing subcortical structures that are responsible for more innate (unlearned) behaviors, such as desire. Stated differently, alcohol depresses learned inhibitions based on reasoning and judgment while releasing the "beast" within. A variation of disinhibition theory argues that the frontal lobes check impulsive behavior. According to this idea, impulse control is impaired after drinking alcohol because of a higher relative sensitivity of the frontal lobes to alcohol, leaving a person prone to engage in risky behavior (Hardee et al., 2014).

Proponents of disinhibition theories often excuse alcohol-related behavior, saying, for example, "They were too drunk to know better" or "They had a few too many and got carried away."

## Learning

If disinhibition theory is correct, then a person's behavior would be the same on each occasion where they consume alcohol, but this is not necessarily the case. Craig MacAndrew and Robert Edgerton (1969) question disinhibition theory along just these lines in their book *Drunken Comportment*. They cite many instances in which behavior under the influence of alcohol changes from one context to another. People who engage in polite social activity at home when consuming alcohol, for example, may become unruly and violent when drinking in a bar.

Even behavior at the bar may be inconsistent. You may know someone who, while drinking one night at a bar, might act obnoxiously and get into a fight. On another occasion, they might be charming and witty, even preventing a fight between two friends. On a third occasion, they become depressed and consumed with worries about personal problems. MacAndrew and Edgerton cite contrasting examples of cultures in which people are disinhibited when sober, only to become inhibited after consuming alcohol, as well as cultures in which people are inhibited when sober, but then become more inhibited when drinking. In cultures in which alcohol is used to facilitate social interactions, behavior while intoxicated represents a "learned time-out" from more conservative social rules.

The contextual cues associated with drug taking and a drug's nonspecific reinforcing qualities may explain some behavior under the influence, such as the violent and risky behavior associated with alcohol use. When a drug has a reinforcing effect, a wide variety of stimuli with which a person has become familiar (other than those directly related

**disinhibition theory** Explanation holding that alcohol has a selective depressant effect on the brain's frontal cortex, which controls judgment, while sparing subcortical structures responsible for more innate behaviors, such as desire.

to the drug) may also become more salient. A person may show increased responsiveness to cues with a positive valence. Accordingly, the increased salience of cues may lead a person who has been drinking, for example, to engage in violent or risky behavior, such as driving or engaging in unsafe sex, if the opportunity arises.

A person may also show increased responsiveness to cues that have a negative valence, such as those associated with disgust and fear. For example, after drinking, a person may display heightened fear in response to stimuli or events that ordinarily would produce only moderate anxiety. A person may even show heightened mixed responses, such as attraction and fearfulness at the same time (Berridge, 2018).

## Behavioral Myopia

A third explanation for alcohol-related lapses in judgment, **behavioral myopia** (nearsightedness), describes the tendency for people under the influence of certain drugs to respond to a restricted set of immediate and prominent cues while ignoring more remote cues and possible consequences. Immediate and prominent cues are very strong, obvious, and close at hand (Griffin et al., 2010). In an altercation, a person with behavioral myopia will be quicker than usual to throw a punch because the fight cue is so strong and immediate. At a raucous party, the myopic drinker will be more eager than usual to join in because the immediate cue of boisterous fun dominates their view.

Behavioral myopia can explain many lapses in judgment that lead to risky behavior—such as violence, sexual assault, or reckless driving while intoxicated. Individuals who have been drinking may also have poor insight into their level of intoxication: they may believe that they are less impaired than they actually are (Sevincer & Oettingen, 2014).

## Substance Use Disorder, Withdrawal, and Addiction

B. G. started smoking at 13 years old and has attempted to quit many times without success. After successfully abstaining from cigarettes for more than 6 months using a nicotine patch, B. G. began smoking again. Because the university where B. G. works has a no-smoking policy, B. G. has to leave campus and stand across the street to smoke. B. G.'s voice has developed a rasping sound, almost like having a chronic "cold." B. G. used to enjoy smoking but no longer does. Concern about quitting dominates B. G.'s thoughts.

B. G. has a *substance use disorder* (SUD), as do many of the approximately 15% of North Americans who smoke. SUD describes a pattern of drug use in which the individual relies on a drug chronically and excessively, allowing it to occupy a central place in their life. Like B. G., most smokers with an SUD realize that it is a health hazard, have experienced unpleasant side effects from it, and have attempted to quit but find it hard to do so.

Substance use disorder is a diagnostic term encompassing four categories: impaired control, social impairment, risky use, and pharmacological indicators (see **Table 6-2**). When an individual has two or three symptoms, they are considered to have a mild SUD; four to five symptoms is moderate SUD; and six or more symptoms is severe SUD. We introduced this language earlier in the chapter, but here we define these terms in the context of behavioral symptoms.

As discussed earlier, tolerance occurs with the repeated use of a drug, prompting a person to increase their consumption of the drug to achieve the same effect. What happens when drug use is discontinued? Following a period of nonuse, a person with an SUD will experience psychological and/or physical **withdrawal symptoms**. The psychological symptoms

**behavioral myopia** "Nearsighted" behavior displayed under the influence of alcohol, wherein local and immediate cues become prominent; remote cues and consequences are ignored.

**withdrawal symptom** Any of the physical and psychological behaviors displayed by when drug use ends.

**TABLE 6-2 DSM Criteria for Substance Use Disorder**

| Impaired control |
|---|
| A. Use for longer periods of time or in larger amounts than intended |
| B. Unsuccessful reduction in use |
| C. Excess time spent in getting, using, and recovering from the drug |
| D. Intense cravings that dominate thoughts |

| Social impairment |
|---|
| E. Continued use of drug despite negative impact on work, school, family, and social obligations |
| F. Continued use despite interpersonal problems caused by use |
| G. Abandonment of or reduction in meaningful social and recreational activities because of substance use |

| Risky use |
|---|
| H. Repeated use of substance in physically dangerous situations |
| I. Continued use of substance despite awareness of physical and psychological damage caused by use |

| Pharmacological indicators |
|---|
| J. Tolerance: Need for greater amounts of substance to produce an effect |
| K. Withdrawal: Physical response to the abrupt cessation of a drug |

**addiction** A complex brain disorder characterized by escalation, compulsive drug taking, and relapse.

**psychomotor activation** Increased behavioral and cognitive activity such that at certain levels of consumption, the person using the drug feels energetic and in control.

associated with withdrawal can include cravings, fatigue, anxiety and/or depression, insomnia, changes in appetite, and irritability; physical symptoms can be dangerous and include muscle aches and cramps, headache, sweating, nausea, and, for some drugs, convulsions and death. Symptoms of alcohol or morphine withdrawal, for example, can begin within hours of the last dose and tend to intensify over several days before they subside. Individuals with SUD will often continue taking the drug simply to prevent these unpleasant withdrawal symptoms.

In a more advanced state associated with SUD, clinically known as **addiction**, people exhibit three more characteristics: escalation, compulsive drug taking, and relapse. *Escalation* refers to increased drug consumption through increased dose or dosing frequency (Kenny, 2007). Tolerance to the psychoactive effects of the drug *cannot* explain escalation. Instead, escalation reflects a pathological increase in the motivation to consume a drug (Oleson & Roberts, 2009). Escalation of drug use is a critical factor in the transition from sporadic use to the compulsive and relapsing drug use that characterizes addiction.

*Compulsive drug taking* is defined as repetitive and persistent drug administration despite negative consequences. It is related to the inability to completely cease taking the drug. *Relapse* involves the recurrence of compulsive drug use after a period of abstinence. Addictive drug use is marked by inordinate time spent seeking, preparing, and consuming drugs, at the expense of everyday responsibilities, as well as numerous failed attempts at abstinence (Koob et al., 2014). Individuals who are addicted to drugs often experience very intense withdrawal symptoms, likely due to the higher level and more frequent usage of the substance that came with their addiction.

Many addictive drugs—particularly the dopaminergics, GABAergics, and opioidergics—have a common property: they produce **psychomotor activation** in some part of their dose range. That is, at certain levels of consumption, these drugs make the person using them feel energetic and in control. This commonly seen effect has led to the hypothesis that all addictive drugs may act on the same target in the brain: the dopaminergic pathway from the ventral tegmental area to the nucleus accumbens. These drugs increase dopamine activity in the nucleus accumbens, either directly or indirectly, whereas drugs that blunt use and addiction decrease dopamine activity in the nucleus accumbens.

## Risk Factors for Severe Substance Use Disorder

A number of environmental factors, called *adverse childhood experiences* (*ACEs*), are associated with an increased risk of substance initiation and SUD. ACEs include emotional, physical, and sexual abuse; emotional and physical neglect; mental illness of a household member; witnessing violence against one's mother; SUD by a household member; parental separation or divorce; and incarceration of a household member. Each ACE increases the likelihood for early drug initiation by a factor of 2 to 4. Compared to people with zero ACEs, people with five or more ACEs have been found to be 7 to 10 times more likely to report substance use disorder (see **Figure 6-15**).

Data collected over four generations provide evidence that the effects of these ACEs cannot be accounted for by increased availability of drugs, changes in social attitudes toward drugs, or recent massive expenditures and public information campaigns to prevent drug use (Dube et al., 2003). There is some good news here: if you examine Figure 6-15, you will also see that the vast majority (90%) of individuals who have experienced five or more ACEs have not developed a severe SUD.

Substance use disorders are also influenced by adult life experiences, such as the availability of addicting substances and individual circumstances that might lead to the use of a specific drug. For example, as detailed in Clinical Focus 6-5, the ease of availability of prescription opioids has fueled the recent surge in opioid use disorder.

**FIGURE 6-15 Adverse Childhood Experiences and Severe Substance Use Disorder** The percentage of individuals with a reported severe substance use disorder increases significantly with the addition of each ACE. Data from Dube et al., 2003.

# Individual and Sex Differences in Substance Use Disorder

The vast differences among individual responses to drugs are due to differences in age, body size, metabolism, and sensitivity to a particular substance. Larger people, for instance, are generally less sensitive to most drugs than smaller people are: the greater volume of body fluids in a larger individual dilutes drugs more than the smaller volume in the smaller person. Women are, on average, about twice as sensitive to drugs as are men, due in part to their relatively smaller body size. People with more adipose tissue absorb and retain more lipophilic drugs. Older people (typically aged 60 years and older) may be twice as sensitive to drugs as younger people. Those who are elderly often have less-effective barriers to drug absorption and less-effective processes for metabolizing and eliminating drugs from their bodies.

In the past, the general assumption that men are more likely to develop an SUD than are women led investigators to neglect research on drug use and misuse in women. Recent research has shown that women are less likely to develop an SUD than are men, but they are catching up and, for some drugs, surpassing men in terms of incidence of SUD (Becker & Chartoff, 2019).

Although the general pattern of drug use is similar in men and women, women are more likely than men to develop an SUD involving nicotine, alcohol, cocaine, amphetamine, opioids, cannabinoids, caffeine, and phencyclidine. Women begin to regularly self-administer licit and illicit drugs at lower doses than do men, and their use escalates more rapidly: in addition, compared to men, women are at greater risk for relapse after abstinence.

## 6-3 Review

Before you continue, check your understanding. Answers to Self-Test appear at the back of the book.

1. _____ is the tendency for people under the influence of a drug to respond to a restricted set of immediate and prominent cues while ignoring more remote cues and possible consequences.

2. _____ is a diagnosis ranging in severity from mild to moderate to severe, which is given when someone exhibits a variety of behavioral and physical symptoms as a result of drug use; _____ is more advanced condition that includes characteristics of escalation, compulsive drug taking, and relapse.

3. The evidence that many addictive drugs produce _____, which makes the person using the drug feel energetic and in control, suggests that activation in the _____ plays a role in drug misuse and addiction.

4. Common wisdom is incorrect in suggesting that _____ are less likely to misuse drugs than are _____.

5. Why can alcohol-related behavior vary widely in a single individual from time to time?

## 6-4

# Explaining Substance Use and Misuse

Why do people develop a substance use disorder? Early neuropsychological explanations centered on the pleasure associated with natural experiences surrounding sex, chocolate, and catching a fish, as well as the euphoria produced by psychoactive drugs. The pleasurable "rush" would supposedly lead to a variety of impulse control disorders, such as overeating, gambling, and repeated drug taking. But this explanation, known as the *hedonia hypothesis,* has a central problem: the initial pleasurable experience wears off with repeated drug taking and can become quite aversive, yet the person continues to take the drug. (Most of us have witnessed habitual smokers out in the

**Learning Objectives**
- Summarize the steps leading to addiction as explained by wanting-and-liking theory.
- Describe some of the legal and social challenges in the treatment of substance use disorder.
- Describe some of the ways in which drug use can damage the brain.

wind and cold having a cigarette.) In other words, over repeated drug exposure, the pleasurable or hedonic experience becomes dissociated from the drug taking. More recent work has shown that there are separate brain circuits for pleasure (liking) and for repeating behaviors (wanting).

## Wanting-and-Liking Theory

An early and popular explanation of addiction was the *hedonic theory of addiction* (also called the pleasure theory), which, simply put, postulated that a person takes a drug because they like it. But if someone with a severe SUD—such as B. G., described in Section 6-3—is asked whether they derive pleasure from the drug they are taking, they often say they do not. This seeming contradiction led researchers focusing on SUD to explore other explanations.

To account for the three components of addiction—escalation, compulsive drug taking, and relapse—Terry Robinson and Kent Berridge (2008) proposed the incentive sensitization theory, also called the **wanting-and-liking theory**, because wanting and liking are produced by different brain systems. Robinson and Berridge define *wanting* as craving, whereas *liking* is the pleasure the drug produces. With repeated use, tolerance for liking develops, and the expression of liking (pleasure) decreases as a consequence (**Figure 6-16**). In contrast, the system that mediates wanting becomes sensitized, and craving increases.

The first step on the proposed road to SUD is the initial experience, when the drug affects a neural system associated with pleasure. At this stage, the individual may like the substance—including liking to take it within a given social context. With repeated use, liking the drug may decline from its initial level. At this stage, the individual may also begin to show tolerance to the drug's effects and so may begin to increase the dosage to increase liking. Thus, according to wanting-and-liking theory, the pleasurable effect may initially mediate drug taking, but it is not the cause of substance use because pleasure decreases as SUD becomes more severe.

With each use, the person taking the drug increasingly associates the cues related to drug use—be it the paraphernalia used to take the drug (e.g., a hypodermic needle), the room in which the drug is taken, or the people with whom the drug is taken—with the drug-taking experience (Hodebourg et al., 2019). The person makes this association because the drug enhances classically conditioned cues associated with drug taking. Eventually, these cues come to possess incentive salience: they induce wanting, or craving, the drug-taking experience.

The neural basis of severe SUD is proposed to involve multiple brain systems. The decision to take a drug is made in the prefrontal cortex, an area that participates in most daily decisions. When a drug is taken, it activates endogenous opioid systems that are generally related to pleasurable experiences. In contrast, wanting drugs may spring from activity in the nucleus accumbens of the dopaminergic activating system.

**Figure 6-17** depicts an anatomical model of the relationship between the neural system for wanting and the neural system for liking. The neural system for wanting is the dopamine projection from midbrain dopamine neurons that project to the nucleus accumbens, the prefrontal cortex, the amygdala, and some other brainstem and forebrain regions. The neural system for liking consists of several small liking "hot spots" within the regions to which dopamine neurons project. These hot spots may consist of neurons that use endogenous opioids as neurotransmitters. The wanting-and-liking theory proposes that with initial drug use, the opioid hot spots and dopamine become activated. When drug takers encounter cues associated with drug taking, this system becomes active, releasing dopamine. Repeated use of a drug sensitizes (strengthens) the activity in the dopamine system, whereas drug activation of the opioid hot spots shows tolerance (weakens).

Another brain system may be responsible for conditioning drug-related cues to drug taking. Barry Everitt (2014) proposes that the repeated pairing of drug-related cues with drug taking creates neural associations, or learning, in the dorsal striatum, a region in the basal ganglia consisting of the caudate nucleus and putamen. When an individual repeatedly takes the drug, voluntary control gives way to unconscious

---

**wanting-and-liking theory** Explanation holding that when a drug is associated with certain cues, the cues themselves elicit desire for the drug; also called *incentive sensitization theory*.

In classical (Pavlovian) conditioning, learning to associate a formerly neutral stimulus (the sound of a bell) with a stimulus (food) elicits an involuntary response (salivation).

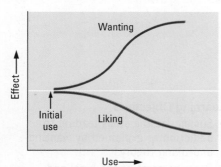

**FIGURE 6-16  Wanting-and-Liking Theory** With repeated drug use, wanting a drug increases (sensitization) while liking the drug decreases (tolerance). Wanting (craving) becomes more strongly associated with drug cues, such as lighting a cigarette.

processes—a habit. The result: someone engaged in habitual drug use loses control of decisions related to drug taking, and the wanting—the voluntary control over drug taking—gives way to the craving of addiction.

The findings from multiple research studies align with the wanting-and-liking explanation of severe SUD. Ample evidence confirms that drugs and the context in which they are taken initially have a pleasurable effect, and that people who take drugs habitually continue using their drug of choice even when taking it no longer produces any pleasure. Individuals addicted to heroin sometimes report that they are miserable: their lives are in ruins, and the drug no longer gives them pleasure. But they still want it, and they still take it. What is more, desire for the drug often is greatest just when the substance user is maximally high, not during withdrawal. Finally, cues associated with drug taking—the social situation, the sight of the drug, and drug paraphernalia—strongly influence decisions to take, or continue taking, a drug.

Notwithstanding the support for the proposed dopamine basis for SUD, recent research demonstrates that there are multiple neural systems at play in SUD. Some rats become readily conditioned to cues associated with reinforcement—for example, a bar that delivers a reward when pressed. Other rats ignore the bar's incentive salience but are attracted to the location where they receive reinforcement. Rats that display the former behavior are termed *sign trackers*; those in the other group are called *goal trackers*. Sign trackers exposed to addictive drugs appear to attribute incentive salience to drug-associated cues. Their drug wanting is dependent on the brain's dopamine systems. Goal trackers may also become addicted, possibly via different neural systems. Such findings imply at least two types of addiction exist (Yager et al., 2015).

We can extend wanting-and-liking theory to many life situations. Cues related to sexual activity, food, and even participation in sports can induce wanting, sometimes in the absence of liking. We frequently eat when prompted by the cue of other people eating, even though we may not be hungry and may derive little pleasure from eating at that time. The similarities between exaggeration of normal behaviors and substance use behavior suggest that they depend on the same learning and brain mechanisms. For this reason, any substance use is extremely difficult to treat.

## Why Doesn't Everyone Develop a Substance Use Disorder?

Observing that some people are more prone than others to compulsive drug taking, scientists have investigated and found three lines of evidence suggesting a genetic contribution to differences in drug use. First, if a twin develops an alcohol use disorder, their identical twin (same genotype) is more likely to develop such a disorder than a fraternal twin (only some genes in common) would be. Second, people adopted shortly after birth are more likely to misuse alcohol if their biological parents misused alcohol, even though they have had almost no contact with those parents. Third, although most animals do not care for alcohol, selective breeding of mice, rats, and monkeys can produce strains that consume large quantities of it.

Each line of evidence presents problems, however. Perhaps identical twins show greater concordance rates (incidence of similar behavioral traits) for alcohol misuse because their environments are more similar than those of fraternal twins. And perhaps the link between alcoholism in adoptees and their biological parents has to do with nervous system changes due to prenatal exposure to the drug. Finally, the fact that

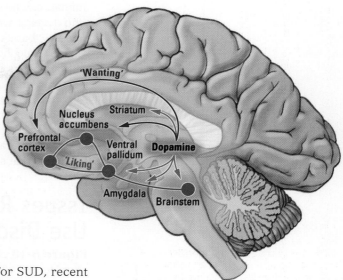

**FIGURE 6-17 Brain Systems for Wanting Versus Liking** The large dopamine projection from the midbrain to the forebrain (blue) mediates wanting, and the smaller widely distributed hot spots (red), which are perhaps neurons with opioid receptors, are responsible for liking.

When a rat is placed in an environment where it anticipates a favored food or sex, investigators record dopamine increases in the striatum (see Section 7-5).

People who enjoy high-risk adventures, such as the base jumpers pictured here, may be genetically predisposed to experiment with drugs, but people with no interest in risk taking are just as likely to use drugs.

Less-than-perfect concordance rates between identical twins for diseases ranging from schizophrenia to asthma point to epigenetic inheritance of behaviors by the next generation (see Section 3-3).

animals can be selectively bred for alcohol consumption does not mean that all human who develop an alcohol use disorder have a similar genetic makeup. The evidence for a genetic basis of alcoholism will become compelling only when a gene or set of genes related to alcoholism is found.

Epigenetics offers another complementary explanation of susceptibility to SUD (Hillemacher et al., 2015). Addictive drugs may reduce the transcriptional ability of genes related to voluntary control and increase the transcriptional ability of other genes related to behaviors susceptible to addiction. Epigenetic changes in an individual's gene expression may be relatively permanent and can be passed along, perhaps through the next few generations. For these reasons, epigenetics can account for both the enduring behaviors that support SUD and the tendency of the disorder to be inherited.

## Issues Related to Treating Substance Use Disorder

**Figure 6-18** charts the relative incidence of drug use in the United States among people aged 12 and older who reported using at least one psychoactive drug during the preceding year in the National Survey of Drug Use and Health conducted by the National Institute on Drug Abuse (2016). The two most commonly used drugs, alcohol and tobacco, are legal. The drugs that carry the harshest penalties, cocaine and heroin, are used by far fewer people. But criminalizing drugs clearly is not a solution to drug use or misuse, as illustrated by the widespread use of cannabis, the third most used drug on the chart. In response to its widespread use, several states and Canada have legalized cannabis to some degree, though it remains illegal under U.S. federal law.

Treating SUD is difficult in part because legal proscriptions are irrational. In the United States, the Harrison Narcotics Act of 1914 made heroin and a variety of other drugs illegal, and also made the treatment of people with SUD by physicians in their private offices illegal. The Drug Addiction Treatment Act of 2000 partly reversed this prohibition, allowing the treatment of patients, albeit with a number of restrictions. In addition, the legal consequences attending drug use vary greatly depending on the drug and the jurisdiction.

In its 2021 World Drug Report, the United Nations estimated that worldwide, 5.5% of people aged 15 to 64 used illicit drugs or misused prescription drugs at least once in the past year, and of those individuals, as many as 13% had an SUD (United Nations, 2021). While there was a sharp increase in drug use in 2020 and 2021, innovations in adaptive and flexible models of health-care delivery spurred by the COVID-19 pandemic may have implications for prevention and treatment of SUD in the future.

Decriminalizing drug use would allow for the promotion of safer drug use by decreasing the use of street drugs, for which ingredients are not known. It would also encourage the use of antidote medications such as naloxone, a drug that can quickly reverse the effects of an opioid overdose. Finally, it would improve access to drug treatment by lifting some of the barriers that prevent access, including the social stigma associated with SUD and addiction.

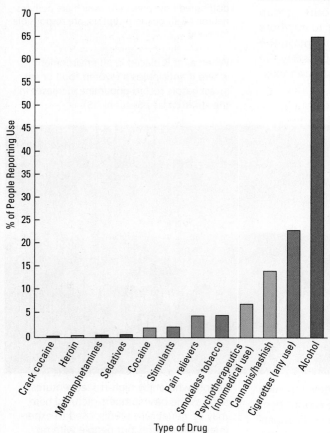

**FIGURE 6-18 Drug Use in the United States, 2016** Results from an annual national survey of Americans aged 12 and older who reported using at least one psychoactive drug during the past year. Percentages for alcohol, tobacco, and cannabis/hashish are rounded to the nearest whole numbers. Data from National Institute on Drug Abuse, 2016.

From a health standpoint, tobacco has much higher proven health risks than does cannabis. Moderate use of alcohol is likely benign. Moderate use of opioids is likely impossible. Social coercion and public policy can be useful in reducing tobacco use: witness the marked decline in smoking as a result of prohibitions against smoking in public places. Medical intervention is necessary for the treatment of dopaminergic, GABAergic, and opioid misuse.

The approaches to treating SUD vary depending on the drug. Online and in-person communities associated with self-help and professional groups address the treatment of specific drug addictions. Importantly, because SUD is influenced by conditioning to drug-related cues and by a variety of brain changes, recidivism remains an enduring risk for people who have apparently kicked their habit.

Neuroscience research will continue to lead to better understanding of the neural basis of drug use and to better treatment. The best approach to any drug treatment involves recognizing that SUD is a lifelong problem for most people. Thus, SUD must be treated in the same way as chronic behavioral addictions and medical problems—analogous to recognizing that controlling weight with appropriate diet and exercise is a lifelong struggle for many people.

Recently researchers and clinicians, and the authors of this book, have adopted language that eliminates or at least reduces stigma around drug use and misuse. The reason for this shift in language is that stigma itself harms individuals and can play a role in perpetuating the drug-taking cycle.

# Can Drugs Cause Brain Damage?

Many natural substances can act as neurotoxins; **Table 6-3** lists some of them. Ongoing investigations of the neurotoxicity of these substances and other drugs in animal models show that many cause brain damage. Certain drugs of misuse can cause brain damage in humans, though definitive proof is very difficult to obtain, for two reasons. First, it is difficult to parse other life experiences from drug taking. Second, it is difficult to obtain the brains of individuals with SUD for examination at autopsy. Nevertheless, evidence indicates that the developing brain can be particularly sensitive to drug effects, especially in adolescence—a time when drug experimentation is common (Teixeira-Gomes et al., 2015).

In the late 1960s, many reports linked monosodium glutamate (MSG), a salty-tasting, flavor-enhancing food additive, to headaches in some people. In investigating this effect, scientists placed large doses of MSG on cultured neurons, which died. Subsequently, they injected MSG into the brains of experimental animals, where it also killed neurons. This line of research led to the discovery that many glutamate-like substances, including domoic acid and kainic acid (both toxins in seaweed) and ibotenic acid (found in some poisonous mushrooms), similarly kill neurons (**Figure 6-19**).

Glutamate-like drugs are toxic because they act on glutamate receptors. Glutamate receptor activation results in an influx of $Ca^{2+}$ into the cell, which through second messenger activates a self-destruct gene leading to *apoptosis* (programmed cell death). This discovery shows that a drug might be toxic not only because of its general effect on cell function, but also as an epigenetic agent that activates normal cell processes related to apoptosis. It is now recognized that many types of injury, including concussion and stroke, might result in neuron death through excess glutamate release by synapses. We must add, though, that there is no evidence that moderate consumption of MSG is harmful.

**FIGURE 6-19 Neurotoxicity (A)** Domoic acid damage in this rat's hippocampus, and to a lesser extent in many other brain regions, is indicated by the darkest coloring. Domoic acid, a Glu analog and therefore a glutamatergic agonist, is the causative agent in amnesic shellfish poisoning, which can result in permanent short-term memory loss, brain damage, and, in severe cases, death. **(B)** As can be seen here, monosodium glutamate (MSG) and glutamate are nearly identical and have nearly identical properties.

**TABLE 6-3 Some Neurotoxins, Their Sources, and Their Actions**

| Substance | Origin | Action |
|---|---|---|
| Apamin | Bees and wasps | Blocks $Ca^{2+}$ channels |
| Botulin | Spoiled food | Blocks ACh release |
| Caffeine | Coffee seed | Blocks adenosine receptors, blocks $Ca^{2+}$ channels |
| Colchicine | Crocus plant | Blocks microtubules |
| Curare | Berry | Blocks ACh receptors |
| Domoic acid | Seaweed, shellfish | Mimics glutamate |
| Ibotenic acid | Mushroom | Mimics glutamate |
| Magnesium | Metallic element | Blocks $Ca^{2+}$ channels |
| Mercury | Metallic element | Blocks many brain enzymes |
| Rabies virus | Infected animal | Blocks ACh receptors |
| Reserpine | Shrub | Destroys storage granules |
| Spider venom | Black widow spider | Stimulates ACh release |
| Strychnine | Plant | Blocks glycine |
| Tetrodotoxin | Puffer fish | Blocks membrane permeability to $Na^+$ |

What about the many recreational drugs that affect the nervous system? Are any of them neurotoxic? Sorting out the effects of the drug itself from the effects of other factors related to taking the drug is a major problem. Chronic alcohol use, for instance, can be associated with damage to the thalamus and cortical areas, producing severe memory disorders. Alcohol does not directly cause this damage, though. People with alcohol abuse disorders typically consume low amounts of thiamine (vitamin $B_1$) in their diet, and alcohol interferes with the intestines' ability to absorb thiamine. Thiamine plays a vital role in maintaining cell membrane structure and a deficiency can result in severe memory impairment such as in Korsakoff syndrome (detailed in Clinical Focus 14-4).

Similarly, though many reports have cited people who developed a severe psychiatric disorder subsequent to misusing certain recreational drugs, in most cases determining whether the drug initiated the condition or aggravated an existing problem is difficult. Likewise, determining whether the drug itself or some contaminant in it caused a harmful outcome is difficult. With the increasing sensitivity of brain-imaging studies, however, evidence is increasing that glutamatergic and dopaminergic drugs used recreationally can cause brain damage and cognitive impairments, as discussed in Clinical Focus 6-6: Drug-Induced Psychosis.

Some addictive drugs do produce harmful effects on the brain (Urban et al., 2012). The strongest evidence for this relationship comes from the study of the synthetic amphetamine-like drug MDMA, also called Ecstasy and, in pure powdered form, Molly (Parrott, 2013). MDMA is often taken by people to enhance party experiences, such as at a rave (an all-night party featuring lights and music). Although MDMA is structurally related to amphetamine, it produces hallucinogenic effects; thus, it is called a hallucinogenic amphetamine. Findings from animal studies show that doses of MDMA approximating those taken by humans result in the degeneration of very fine serotonergic nerve terminals. In monkeys, significant terminal loss may be permanent. Memory impairments and damage in people who take MDMA (as revealed by brain imaging) may result from similar neuronal damage (Cowan et al., 2008). MDMA may also contain a contaminant called paramethoxymethamphetamine (PMMA). This notoriously toxic amphetamine is often called Dr. Death because the difference between a dose that causes behavioral effects and a dose that causes death

Clinical Focus 5-5 reports the chilling case of people who developed Parkinson disease after using synthetic heroin laced with a contaminant (MPTP).

---

## ⊙ CLINICAL FOCUS 6-6

## Drug-Induced Psychosis

L. V. is 22 years old and has been wandering the halls of a rehabilitation clinic for almost a year. At any given moment, he is either confused or hostile; he rarely has lucid moments. L. V. had been using crystal meth during his years as an undergraduate. Just before his final exams in his third year, he had a psychotic attack and since then has been continuously institutionalized.

L. V. grew up with an abusive father and a mother with an addiction to alcohol. As a child, he was artistic and sensitive, and he showed a quiet maturity beyond his years. He had a passion for science fiction and mathematics, and his friends thought he was fun to be around. During his high school years, his family noted long-lasting and recurring periods of silence during which he often withdrew from socialization. L. V. experimented with alcohol, tobacco, cannabis, mushrooms, and cocaine before he found crystal meth, which he would make by combining cold medication, Ritalin, fertilizer, drain cleaner, antifreeze, and Epsom salts.

In low doses, methamphetamine, the active ingredient in crystal meth, elevates mood; increases alertness, concentration, and energy; reduces appetite; and promotes weight loss. At higher doses, it induces psychosis in vulnerable individuals and can cause seizures and brain hemorrhage. Individuals who compulsively take methamphetamine, as L. V. did, display unpredictable and rapid mood swings, paranoia, hallucinations, delirium, and delusions, often accompanied by violent behavior.

Because methamphetamine is a dopaminergic agonist, it interacts directly with the nucleus accumbens, which can lead to compulsive drug use. Withdrawal symptoms during initial abstinence may persist for months beyond the typical withdrawal period observed for other drugs. Chronic methamphetamine use has a toxic effect on human midbrain dopaminergic neurons and serotonin neurons, leading to reductions in gray-matter volume in several brain regions and adverse changes in markers of metabolic integrity (Krasnova & Cadet, 2009).

A week before L. V.'s psychotic episode, he said he had not slept for 2 weeks, and his delusions had escalated. His dank apartment was strewn with drug paraphernalia, soiled bed sheets, and foul odors. There was no food in his apartment, and there had not been any there for some time.

Dopaminergic antagonists are used to treat psychosis, but they are not a cure. Despite treatment, L. V. continues to punch himself in the face, masturbate in public, yell obscenities, and make animal sounds. Doctors see little hope of recovery for him. Unfortunately, the medical profession continues to see young people who are aggressive and violent due to crystal meth.

is minuscule (Nicol et al., 2015). Contamination by unknown compounds can occur in any drug purchased on the street.

The psychoactive properties of cocaine are similar to those of amphetamine, so cocaine is also suspected to be linked to brain damage. Specifically, cocaine use has been connected to blockage of cerebral blood flow and other changes in blood circulation. Brain-imaging studies show that brain regions are reduced in size in people who regularly take cocaine, suggesting that cocaine use can be toxic to neurons (Reese et al., 2019).

THC may trigger psychosis in vulnerable individuals, but there is no evidence that this psychosis is a result of brain damage. Indeed, beyond the therapeutic applications of THC cited in Section 6-2, recent studies suggest that THC may have neuroprotective properties. It can aid brain healing after traumatic brain injury and slow the progression of diseases associated with brain degeneration, including Alzheimer disease and Huntington disease (Nguyen et al., 2014).

## 6-4 Review

Before you continue, check your understanding. Answers to Self-Test appear at the back of the book.

1. The wanting-and-liking theory of addiction suggests that with repeated use, _____ of the drug decreases as a result of _____, while _____ increases as a result of _____.

2. At the neural level, the decision to take a drug is made in the brain's _____. Once taken, the drug activates opioid systems related to pleasurable experiences in the _____. Drug cravings may originate in the _____, and the repeated pairing of drug-related cues and drug taking forms neural associations in the _____ that loosen voluntary control over drug taking.

3. As an alternative to explanations of susceptibility to addiction based on genetic inheritance, _____ can account for both the enduring behaviors that support substance use disorder and the tendency of the disorder to be inherited.

4. It is difficult to determine whether recreational drug use causes brain damage in humans because it is difficult to distinguish the effects of _____ from the effects of _____.

5. Briefly describe the basis for a reasonable approach to treating substance use disorder.

# Summary

## 6-1 Principles of Psychopharmacology

Psychoactive drugs—substances that alter mood, thought, or behavior—produce their effects by acting on neuronal receptors or on chemical processes in the nervous system, especially on neurotransmission at synapses. Drugs act either as agonists to stimulate neuronal activity or as antagonists to depress it. Psychopharmacology is the study of drug effects on the brain and behavior.

Drugs can be administered by mouth, by inhalation, by absorption through the skin, rectally by suppository, or by injection. To reach a nervous system target, a psychoactive drug must pass through numerous barriers posed by digestion and dilution, the blood–brain barrier, and cell membranes. Drugs are diluted by body fluids as they pass through successive barriers, are metabolized in the body, and are excreted through sweat glands and in feces, urine, breath, and breast milk.

A common misperception about psychoactive drugs is that they act specifically and consistently; in reality, experience and learning also affect individual responses to drugs. The body and brain may rapidly become tolerant to many drugs, so the dose must increase to produce a constant effect. Alternatively, people may become sensitized to a drug, in which case the same dose produces increasingly strong effects. These forms of learning also contribute to a person's behavior under a drug's influence.

## 6-2 Psychoactive Drugs

Psychoactive drugs can be organized according to the primary neurotransmitter system with which they interact, though all drugs interact with multiple receptor systems. Each group, summarized in Table 6-1 on page 187, contains recreational and medically prescribed drugs—all of which can be misused.

## 6-3 Factors Influencing Individual Responses to Drugs

A drug does not have a uniform action on every person. Physical differences—in body weight, sex, age, and genetic background—influence a given drug's effects on a given person, as do behaviors, such as learning, and cultural and environmental contexts.

The influence of drugs on behavior varies widely with the situation and as a person learns drug-related behaviors. Behavioral myopia, for example, can influence a person to focus primarily on prominent environmental cues. These cues may encourage the person to act in uncharacteristic ways.

Substance use disorder is a diagnosis that considers several behavioral and physical factors related to an individual's drug use. Risk factors for substance use disorder and addiction include emotional, physical, and sexual abuse; emotional and physical neglect; having a mentally ill household member; having witnessed violence against one's mother; substance misuse in the home; parental separation/divorce; and having an incarcerated household member. Women are more sensitive to drugs than men are, and may become addicted more quickly and to lower doses of drugs. The incidence of misuse of many kinds of drugs by women equals or exceeds the misuse of those drugs by men.

## 6-4 Explaining Substance Use and Misuse

Addiction is an advanced condition that includes three key components: escalation, compulsive drug taking, and relapse. The neural mechanisms implicated in addiction are the same neural systems responsible for wanting and liking more generally. Anyone has the potential to develop a substance use disorder or addiction.

Initially, drug taking produces pleasure (liking), but with repeated use the behavior becomes conditioned to associated objects, events, and places. Eventually, the conditioned cues motivate someone to seek them out (wanting), which leads to more drug taking. These subjective experiences become associated with prominent cues, and drug seeking promotes craving for the drug. As addiction proceeds, the subjective experience of liking decreases, while wanting increases.

Treatment for addiction varies with the drug. Whatever treatment approach is employed, success likely depends on permanent lifestyle changes. Considering how many people use tobacco, drink alcohol, use recreational drugs, or misuse prescription drugs, finding someone who has not used a drug when it was available is probably rare. Nevertheless, because of either genetic or epigenetic influences, some people do seem particularly vulnerable to drug misuse and addiction.

Excessive alcohol use can be associated with damage to the thalamus and hypothalamus, but the damage is caused by poor nutrition rather than the direct actions of alcohol. Cocaine can produce brain damage by reducing blood flow or by inducing bleeding within neural tissue. MDMA (Ecstasy) use can result in the loss of fine axon collaterals of serotonergic neurons and associated impairments in cognitive function.

Psychedelic drugs, such as methamphetamine and LSD, can be associated with psychotic behavior. Whether this behavior is due to the drugs' direct effects or to the aggravation of preexisting conditions is not clear.

## Key Terms

addiction, p. 202

agonist, p. 182

amphetamine, p. 192

antagonist, p. 182

attention-deficit/hyperactivity disorder (ADHD), p. 178

behavioral myopia, p. 201

competitive inhibitor, p. 197

disinhibition theory, p. 200

dopamine hypothesis of schizophrenia, p. 194

fetal alcohol spectrum disorder (FASD), p. 191

major depression, p. 195

monoamine oxidase (MAO) inhibitor, p. 195

psychoactive drug, p. 179

psychomotor activation, p. 202

psychopharmacology, p. 178

selective serotonin reuptake inhibitor (SSRI), p. 195

sensitization, p. 185

substance use disorder (SUD), p. 178

tolerance, p. 184

tricyclic, p. 195

wanting-and-liking theory, p. 204

withdrawal symptom, p. 201

zoopharmacognosy, p. 187

## Selected Resources from

**Neuroscience in Action:** Your Brain on Drugs: How Drugs Affect Behavior

**Videos**

Mental Health and Addiction

The Opioid Epidemic

Indigenous People Overrepresented in B. C. Overdose Deaths

TedEd: Is Marijuana Bad for Your Brain?

Can Cannabis Help Mental Illness?

Why are More Women Dying from Alcohol Use?

Psychedelic Drugs are Fueling a Mental Health Revolution

Compulsive Gambling and the Brain's Pleasure Center

**LearningCurve**

**Practice Quiz**

NEIL M. BORDEN/Science Source

# How Do We Study the Brain's Structures and Functions?

# 7

211

## RESEARCH FOCUS 7-1

# Tuning in to Language

The continuing search to understand the organization and operation of the human brain is driven largely by emerging technologies that can potentially enable us to answer questions that were previously impossible, impractical, or unethical (using older tools) to investigate. Over the past decades, neuroscience researchers have developed more accessible, high-resolution, noninvasive ways to image the brain's activity in people who are awake. One technique, **functional near-infrared spectroscopy (fNIRS)**, gathers light transmitted through cortical tissue to image oxygen consumption in the brain. fNIRS, a form of *optical tomography*, is detailed in Section 7-4.

fNIRS measures oxygen consumption as a surrogate marker of neuronal activity in relatively select cortical regions, even in newborn infants. Using fNIRS, investigators can answer the question: Do infants who can hear at birth respond preferentially to the language they were exposed to in utero? Ramírez and colleagues (2020) found that when newborns listened to a familiar language, their brains showed a generalized increase in oxygenated hemoglobin compared to conditions in which they listened either to their own language played backward or to an unfamiliar language. Newborns can distinguish relationships between sounds ("badada" versus "badaga") and whether sound relationships occur at the beginning or at the end of a sequence ("babada" versus "dababa"). They can also use *prosody* (tone of voice) to help discriminate sounds and to aid in learning two languages concurrently. This evidence suggests that at birth we are prepared to learn language and are actively engaged in doing so, a process that involves parental assistance.

Data from fNIRS provide a window into the brain that would not otherwise be accessible, but the technology does have limitations. For instance, only surface cortical activity can be sampled. In addition, the resolution is relatively low because the detectors are large—on the order of a centimeter. Nevertheless, fNIRS is relatively inexpensive and portable compared to other imaging techniques, and it can be used to address many basic neuropsychological puzzles, including clinically relevant questions about the effects of brain injury.

BSIP SA/Alamy Stock Photo

**fNIRS** Light injectors and detectors are distributed in an array across this infant's head.

---

The simple, noninvasive nature of fNIRS, described in Research Focus 7-1: Tuning in to Language, likely will yield new insights into not only brain development but also adult brain function. Over the coming decades, our understanding of the brain–behavior relationship will continue to be driven in large part by the introduction of new and better technologies, as well as by efforts to improve and cleverly exploit existing ones.

Scientists studying the brain prior to the advent of even rudimentary imaging techniques had two obvious choices. First, they could study the behaviors of people who had sustained brain injuries or had neurological impairment, and then examine their brains after their deaths to determine which parts were responsible for the deficits. Alternatively, they could purposely create lesions in animals and examine how their behaviors changed. Indeed, this was how the relationship between brain and behavior was studied well into the twentieth century. Today, we continue to observe and quantify behavior and aspects of brain function in people with neurological conditions and in a wide variety of animal models, but we also manipulate brain function by either increasing or decreasing activity in a highly specific and controlled fashion and then examining the effects of those changes in activity on behavior. Modern-day researchers seek to manipulate and measure the brain using a large array of tools, many of which are noninvasive and go right down to the molecular level.

Today, brain–behavior analyses combine the efforts of anatomists and geneticists, psychologists and physiologists, chemists and physicists, endocrinologists and neurologists, pharmacologists and psychiatrists, computer scientists and programmers, engineers, and biologists. The range of research methods available to the aspiring brain researcher is breathtaking.

We begin this chapter by reviewing how investigators measure behavior in both human and nonhuman subjects and how neuroscientists can manipulate behavior by

**functional near-infrared spectroscopy (fNIRS)**
Noninvasive technique that gathers light transmitted through cortical tissue to image oxygen consumption; a form of optical tomography.

perturbing the brain. Next, we consider and compare electrical techniques, including electroencephalography (EEG), for recording brain activity; noninvasive procedures, such as fNIRS, that image the brain; and chemical and genetic methods for both manipulating and measuring brain and behavior. We then explore computational neuroscience and deep learning, followed by a consideration of neuroethics as well as some issues surrounding the use of nonhuman animals in research.

**neuropsychology** Study of the relationships between brain function and behavior in humans.

Section 4-1 reviews how EEG enabled investigators to explain electrical activity in the nervous system.

## 7-1

# Measuring and Manipulating Brain and Behavior

During a lecture at a meeting of the Anthropological Society of Paris in 1861, physician Ernest Auburtin argued that language functions are located in the brain's frontal lobes. Five days later, a fellow physician, Paul Broca, observed a brain-injured patient who had lost his speech and was able to say only "tan" and utter a swear word. The patient soon died. Broca and Auburtin examined the man's brain and found the focus of his injury in the left frontal lobe.

By 1863, Broca had collected eight other similar cases and concluded that speech production is located in the third frontal convolution of the left frontal lobe—a region now called *Broca's area*. Broca's findings attracted others to study brain–behavior relationships in humans. The field that emerged from these research efforts is now called **neuropsychology**, the study of the relationships between brain function and behavior with a particular emphasis on humans. Today, techniques for measuring brain and behavior increasingly include noninvasive imaging, complex neuroanatomical measurement, and sophisticated behavioral analyses.

Section 10-4 explores the anatomy of language and music and describes Broca's contributions.

Compare Brodmann's map of the cortex, based on staining, shown in Figure 2-26.

## Early Origins of Behavioral Neuroscience

At the beginning of the twentieth century, the primary tools of neuroanatomy were *histological*: brains were sectioned postmortem, and the tissue (*histo-* in Greek) was stained with various dyes. As shown in **Figure 7-1**, there has been a progression in microscopy toward greater resolution and specificity and a movement from visualizing dead tissue to living tissue. Scientists can stain sections of brain tissue to identify cell bodies in the brain and view them with a light microscope (shown in panel A), and they can selectively stain individual neurons to reveal their complete structure (panel B). An electron microscope (panel C) makes it possible to view synapses in detail. Multiphoton imaging (panel D) can generate a three-dimensional image of living tissue.

By the dawn of the twentieth century, light microscopic techniques allowed researchers such as Korbinian Brodmann to divide the cerebral cortex into many distinct zones based on the characteristics of neurons in those zones. Investigators presumed that these cortical zones had specific functions. Early in

**(A) Light microscope, low magnification**

**(B) Light microscope, high magnification**

**(C) Electron microscope**

**(D) Multiphoton microscope**

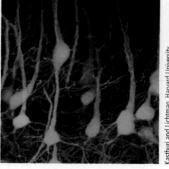

**FIGURE 7-1 Staining Cerebral Neurons** Viewed through a light microscope, **(A)** a Nissl-stained section of the parietal cortex shows all cell bodies but no cell processes (axons and dendrites). **(B)** At higher magnification, an individual Golgi-stained pyramidal cell from the parietal cortex is visible. The cell body (dark triangular shape at center) and spiny dendrites (A and B) are visible in detail at right. **(C)** The view through an electron microscope shows neuronal synapses in detail. **(D)** Multiple images from a multiphoton microscope are merged to generate a three-dimensional image of living tissue.

## RESEARCH FOCUS 7-2

### Brainbow: Rainbow Neurons

Were it not for the discovery of stains that can highlight brain cell features, their complexity and connections would remain unknown. Jean Livet (2007) and his colleagues at Harvard University developed a transgenic technique that involves labeling different neurons by highlighting them with distinct colors—a technique called *Brainbow*, a play on the word *rainbow*. (Transgenic techniques are a form of genetic engineering discussed in Section 3-3.)

To mimic the way a liquid crystal display (LCD) or light-emitting diode (LED) monitor produces the full range of colors that the human eye can see by mixing only red, green, and blue, the Brainbow scientists introduced genes that produce cyan (blue), green, and red fluorescent proteins into mice cells. The red gene is obtained from corals, and the blue and green genes are obtained from jellies. (The 2008 Nobel Prize in Chemistry was awarded to Roger Tsien, Osamu Shimomura, and Martin Chalfie for their discovery and development of fluorescent proteins in corals and jellies.)

The mice also received a bacterial gene called *Cre*, which activates the color genes inside each cell; due to chance factors, however, the extent to which each gene is activated varies. As the mice develop, the variable expression of the color-coding genes results in cells that fluoresce in at least 100 hues. When viewed through a fluorescent microscope sensitive to these wavelengths, individual brain cells and their connections can be visualized because they have slightly different hues, as illustrated in the accompanying micrographs.

Because individual cells can be visualized, Brainbow offers a way to describe where each neuron sends its processes and how it interconnects with other neurons. You have probably seen an electrical power cord in which the different wires have different colors (black, white, red) that signify what they do and how they should be connected. By visualizing living brain tissue in a dish, Brainbow provides a method for examining changes in neural circuits with the passage of time.

In the future, Brainbow will likely prove useful for examining populations of cells and their connections—such as which cells are implicated in specific brain diseases. In principle, Brainbow could be turned on at specific times—as an individual ages or solves problems, for example (Rojczyk-Gołębiewska et al., 2015). Recently, tissue-clearing techniques, which make a whole mouse brain optically transparent, have allowed for the visualization of deep brain structures without relying on histological sectioning. By coupling Brainbow and tissue-clearing techniques with light-sheet microscopy, which can construct 3D images of the whole mouse brain, researchers can trace the connections between neurons over time; these techniques can be applied to mouse models of neurodegenerative diseases (Parra-Damas & Saura, 2020).

**Cell Bodies**

**Axons**

**Terminals**

---

The hippocampus and dentate gyrus are illustrated in Figure 2-23.

**FIGURE 7-2 Miniscope**

the twenty-first century, dozens of techniques had developed for labeling neurons and their connections, as well as glial cells (for one colorful example, see Research Focus 7-2: Brainbow: Rainbow Neurons). Today, super-resolution microscopy is also being used to identify the locations of different receptors on the membranes of cells.

Contemporary techniques allow researchers to identify molecular, neurochemical, and morphological (structural) differences among neuronal types and ultimately to relate these characteristics to behavior. We even have miniaturized microscopes to the point where they can be mounted on the head of a mouse. These miniscopes, shown in **Figure 7-2**, can detect dozens to hundreds of neurons simultaneously by imaging a fluorescent signal activated by the neurons' calcium levels, which indicate their firing activity, while the mouse is navigating around an environment (Ghosh et al., 2011).

These techniques for visualizing neurons have played a key role in studying the connections between anatomy and behavior, as can be seen in studies of animals trained on various types of learning tasks, such as spatial mazes. Such learning can be correlated with a variety of neuroanatomical changes, such as modifications in the synaptic organization of cells in specific cortical regions—the visual cortex in animals trained in visually guided mazes is one example—or in the number of newly generated cells that survive in the dentate gyrus, a subregion of the hippocampus. Mammals require this hippocampal structure for remembering the context in which they encounter information.

Experimental evidence reveals that preventing the growth of new dentate gyrus neurons leads to certain kinds of memory deficits. To test the idea that neurons of the dentate gyrus contribute to object memory formation within a context, researchers tested healthy rats and ADX rats—that is, rats whose adrenal glands had been removed, thereby eliminating their ability to produce the hormone corticosterone. Without corticosterone, neurons in the dentate gyrus die.

Procedure 1 in Experiment 7-1 contrasts the appearance of a healthy rat dentate gyrus (left) and neuronal degeneration in an ADX rat after surgery (right). The behavior

Corticosterone, a steroid hormone secreted in times of stress, is important in protein and carbohydrate metabolism (see Section 5-4).

····> **EXPERIMENT 7-1**

Question: Do hippocampal neurons contribute to memory formation?

**Procedure 1**

Rat hippocampus before (left) and after (right) surgical removal of the adrenal glands. Note that there are fewer neurons in the after-surgery hippocampus, resulting from a lack of corticosterone.

Hippocampus

Healthy rat hippocampus

ADX-induced hippocampal degeneration

Courtesy of Dr. Simon Spanswick, Dept. of Psychology, University of Calgary.

**Procedure 2**

The behavior of healthy rats, ADX rats receiving no treatment, and ADX rats given treatments known to increase neuron generation in the dentate gyrus (enriched housing and exercise in running wheels) was studied in an object–context mismatch task in which two distinct contexts each contained a different type of object.

Training phase

During the training phase, each rat was placed in contexts A and B, each for 10 minutes on each of 2 days. Each context contained one type of object.

Context A    Context B

Testing phase

Contexts A and B with mismatched objects

OR

During the testing phase, each rat was placed either in context A or in context B, but with two *different* objects — one from that context and a second from the other context.

**Results**

Healthy rats investigate the mismatch object more than the object that is in context, but the nontreated ADX rats performed at the level of chance. The ADX rats given enriched housing and exercise in running wheels showed regeneration of dentate granule cells and performed like healthy rats.

The photo at right shows a rat hippocampus. A specific stain was used to identify new neurons in the dentate gyrus, which appear yellow.

*Conclusion:* Dentate gyrus neurons are necessary for contextual learning.

Information from Spanswick & Sutherland (2010) and Spanswick et al. (2011).

Courtesy Bryan of Kolb

**behavioral neuroscience** Study of the biological bases of behavior in animals, including humans.

of healthy and ADX rats was studied in the object–context mismatch task diagrammed in Procedure 2. During the training phase, the rats were placed in two distinct contexts, A and B, for 10 minutes on each of two days. Each context contained a different type of object. On the test day, the rats were placed in either context A or context B but with two different objects—one object from that context and a second object from the other context.

As noted in the Results section of Experiment 7-1, when healthy rats encountered objects in the correct context, they spent little time investigating them because the objects were familiar. If, however, they encountered an object in the wrong context, they were curious and spent about three-quarters of their time investigating it, essentially treating the mismatched object as new. In contrast, the ADX rats, which had fewer cells in their dentate gyrus, treated the mismatched and in-context objects in the same way, spending about half of their investigation time with each object.

Another group of ADX rats given a treatment known to increase neuron generation in the dentate gyrus—enriched housing and exercise in running wheels—was unimpaired at the object–context mismatch task. Experiment 7-1 concludes that cellular changes in the dentate gyrus and behavioral changes are closely linked: neurons of the dentate gyrus are necessary for contextual learning.

## Methods of Behavioral Neuroscience

**Behavioral neuroscience**—the study of the biological bases of behavior—seeks to understand the brain–behavior relationships in animals, including humans. The object–context mismatch task described in Experiment 7-1 is one of hundreds of different behavioral tests used by neuroscientists working in this area. In this section, we describe several neuropsychological tests for humans, as well as some spatial navigation and skilled reaching tasks, including one that involves an automated touchscreen apparatus used with rodents.

The field of neuropsychology, mentioned at the opening of this section, is a subdiscipline of behavioral neuroscience focusing largely on humans.

A major challenge for behavioral neuroscientists is developing methods for studying both typical and atypical behaviors. Techniques for measuring behavior in humans and laboratory animals differ in large part because humans can speak—so investigators can ask them directly about their symptoms or give them paper-and-pencil and computer-based tests to identify specific symptoms. By comparison, measuring behavior in laboratory animals is more complex. Researchers must learn to speak "ratese" with rat subjects or "monkeyese" with monkeys. In short, researchers must develop ways to enable the animals to "speak" to them and reveal their symptoms. The development of the fields of animal learning and *ethology*, the objective study of animal behavior, especially under natural conditions, provided the basis for modern behavioral neuroscience (see Whishaw & Kolb, 2005).

Table 7-3 summarizes selected brain measurement techniques, their goals, and examples.

## Neuropsychological Testing of Humans

*Neuropsychological testing* uses specifically designed tasks to measure brain functions known to be linked to a particular brain structure or pathway; it is typically applied to people who have sustained a brain injury. Neuropsychologists are health care workers who perform hands-on assessments of people in a medical setting.

The brain has exquisite control of an amazing array of functions, ranging from movement control and sensory perception to memory, emotion, and language. As a consequence, any analysis of behavior must be tailored to the particular function(s) under investigation. Consider the analysis of memory.

Memory is covered in more detail in Sections 14-1 through 14-3, including a discussion of dissociated memory circuits in Section 14-2.

People with damage to the temporal lobes often complain about disturbances to their memory. But memory is not a single function; rather, multiple, independent memory systems exist. We have memory for events, colors, names, places, and motor skills, among other categories, and each must be measured separately. It would be rare indeed for someone to be impaired in *all* forms of memory.

Neuropsychological tests of three distinct forms of memory are illustrated in **Figure 7-3**. The Corsi block-tapping test, shown in Figure 7-3A, requires

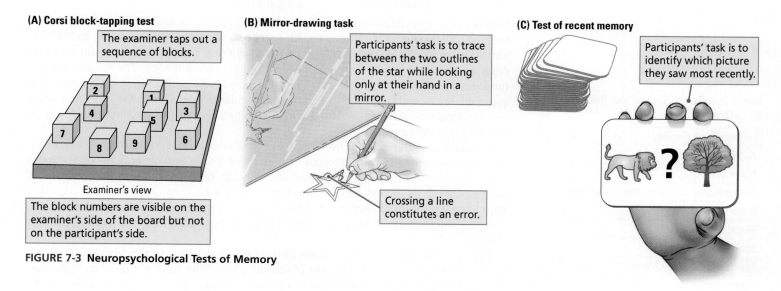

**(A) Corsi block-tapping test**

The examiner taps out a sequence of blocks.

Examiner's view

The block numbers are visible on the examiner's side of the board but not on the participant's side.

**(B) Mirror-drawing task**

Participants' task is to trace between the two outlines of the star while looking only at their hand in a mirror.

Crossing a line constitutes an error.

**(C) Test of recent memory**

Participants' task is to identify which picture they saw most recently.

**FIGURE 7-3 Neuropsychological Tests of Memory**

participants to observe an experimenter tap a sequence of blocks—blocks 4, 6, 1, 8, 3, for instance. The task is to repeat the sequence correctly. The participant does not see numbers on the blocks but rather must remember the locations of the tapped blocks.

The Corsi test provides a measure of short-term recall of spatial position, an ability we can call *block span*. The test can be made more difficult by determining the maximum block span of an individual participant (say, 6 blocks) and then adding one (span + 1). By definition, the participant will fail on the first presentation but, given the span + 1 sequence repeatedly, will eventually learn it.

Span + 1 identifies a different form of memory from block span. Different types of neurological dysfunction interfere differentially with tasks that superficially appear quite similar. Block span measures the short-term recall of information, whereas the span + 1 task reflects the learning and longer-term memory storage of information.

The *mirror-drawing task*, shown in Figure 7-3B, requires a person to trace a pathway, such as a star, by looking in a mirror. This motor task initially proves difficult because our movements appear backward in the mirror. With practice, participants learn how to accomplish the task accurately, and they show considerable recall of the skill when retested days later. Curiously, patients with certain types of memory problems have no recollection of learning the task on the previous day but nevertheless perform it flawlessly.

In the *recency memory task*, shown in Figure 7-3C, participants are shown a long series of cards, each bearing two stimulus items that are words or pictures. In some trials, a question mark appears between the items. The participants' task is to indicate whether they have seen the items before and, if so, which item they saw most recently. They might be able to recall that they have seen items before but may be unable to recall which was most recent. Conversely, they might not be able to identify the items as being familiar, but when forced to choose the most recent one, they may be able to identify it correctly.

The latter, counterintuitive result reflects the need for behavioral researchers to develop ingenious ways of identifying memory abilities. It is not enough simply to ask people to recall information verbally, although this, too, measures a form of memory.

In this book, we refer to healthy human volunteers in research studies as *participants* and to people who have a brain or behavioral impairment as *patients* or *subjects*.

Clinical Focus 15-3 traces the development of tests used in neuropsychological assessment.

## Behavioral Analysis of Rodents

More than 1.5 million animal species have been described, the vast majority of which demonstrate nervous system–generated behaviors. Researchers have used a large

**TABLE 7-1** Partial List of Rat Behaviors by Category

| Learning and memory |
| --- |
| Avoiding |
| Burying |
| Discrimination between sensory stimuli |
| Preferring places |
| Recognizing objects |
| Spatial navigating |
| **Species-typical behaviors** |
| Aggression |
| Caring of young |
| Circadian activity |
| Exploring and nose poking |
| Food hoarding |
| Food selection and foraging |
| Grooming and nail trimming |
| Nest building |
| Orienting |
| Playing |
| Sexual behavior |
| Social behavior |
| Vocalizing |
| **Locomotion** |
| Climbing |
| Jumping |
| Rearing |
| Swimming |
| Turning |
| Walking, trotting, and running |
| **Skilled movement** |
| Handling food |
| Pulling string |
| Walking on beams, posts, rotating rods, ladders |
| **Reflexes** |
| Placing and bracing |
| Posture and support |
| Righting |
| **Emotions** |
| Anxiety and fear |
| Depression |
| Responses to stress |

number of species from all major taxa in behavioral studies, and this rich diversity has been pivotal in driving our understanding of the relationship between brain and behavior (Miller et al., 2019). Yet despite the array of options, most research continues to be conducted using a small number of species, chiefly rats and mice. The reasons for the focus on these species are practical. Rats and mice breed prolifically and year-round in captivity. Furthermore, mice have proved particularly amenable to the most advanced gene-editing technologies, making them the single species most often used in research in the twenty-first century.

Researchers interested in the neural bases of sensation, cognition, memory, emotion, and movement have devised a vast array of mazes and other tests and tasks to determine the neural circuitry underlying specific behaviors in laboratory animals. Rats and mice have very large *behavioral repertoires,* meaning that they display a long list of capabilities that can be independently examined to understand the functional underpinnings of those behaviors; some of these capabilities are categorized in **Table 7-1**.

**Figure 7-4** illustrates three tests based on a navigation task devised by Richard Morris (1981). In this task, rats are placed in a large swimming pool with high slippery walls that do not allow them to escape. A hidden platform lies just below the water surface. Rats are terrific swimmers, and they quickly navigate around the pool until they bump into the platform. They learn that when they climb onto the platform, they are removed from the pool and returned to their home cage—their preferred place.

In one version of the task, called *place learning,* the rat must find the platform from a number of different starting locations in the pool (Figure 7-4A). The only cues available are outside the pool, so the rat must learn the relationship between several cues in the room and the platform's location.

In a second version of the task, called *matching-to-place learning,* the rat has already learned that a platform always lies somewhere in the pool, but the rat enters the pool from a different starting location every day. The rat is released and searches for the platform (Figure 7-4B). Once the rat finds the platform, the rat is removed from the pool and, after a brief delay (such as 10 seconds), is released again. The rat's task is to swim directly to the platform. The challenge for the rat in the matching-to-place test is to develop a strategy for finding the platform consistently: it is always in the same location on each trial each day, but each new day brings a new location.

In the *landmark* version of the task, the platform's location is identified by a cue on the pool wall (Figure 7-4C). The platform moves on every trial, but the relationship to the cue is constant. In this task, the brain is learning that the distant cues outside the pool are irrelevant; only the local cue is relevant. Rats with different neurological perturbations are selectively impaired in the three versions of the swimming pool task.

Another type of behavioral analysis in rats is related to movement. A major problem facing people with stroke is a deficit in controlling hand and limb movements. The prevalence of stroke has prompted considerable interest in devising ways to analyze such motor behaviors for the purpose of testing new therapies for facilitating recovery. In one test, rats are trained to reach through a slot to obtain a pellet of sweet food. The movements, which are remarkably similar to the movements people make in a similar task, can be broken down into segments. Investigators can score the segments separately, as they are differentially affected by different types of neurological perturbation.

The photo series in **Figure 7-5** details how a rat orients its body to the slot (shown in panel A), puts its hand through the slot (panel B), rotates the hand horizontally to grasp the food (panel C), and rotates the hand vertically and withdraws it to obtain the food (panel D). Primates are not the only animals to make fine digit movements, but because the rat's hand is small and moves so quickly, digit dexterity can be properly observed only during slow-motion video playback.

**FIGURE 7-4 Swimming Pool Tasks** General arrangement of the swimming pool used in three visuospatial learning tasks for rats. Red lines in parts A, B, and C mark the rat's swimming path during each trial (T). While Morris performed his swimming pool tasks with rats, mice are also used in similar experimental designs. **(A)** Information from Morris (1981). **(B)** Information from Whishaw (1989). **(C)** Information from Kolb & Walkey (1987).

Room cues

Submerged platform

**(A) Place-learning task**

Pool

Hidden platform

A rat placed in the pool at various starting locations must learn to find a hidden platform. The rat can do this only by considering the configuration of visual cues in the room—windows, wall decorations, potted plants, and the like.

**(B) Matching-to-place task**

The rat is again put into the pool at random locations, but the hidden platform is in a new location on each test day. The animal must learn that the location where it finds the platform on the first trial each day is its location for all trials on that day.

**(C) Landmark-learning task**

Cue (on wall of pool)

The rat must ignore the room cues and learn that only the cue on the wall of the pool signals the location of the platform. The platform and cue are moved on each trial, so the animal is penalized for using room cues to try to solve the problem.

Courtesy of Bryan Kolb

**FIGURE 7-5 Skilled Reaching in Rats** Movement series displayed by rats trained to reach through a narrow vertical slot to obtain a food pellet: **(A)** aim the hand, **(B)** reach over the food, **(C)** grasp the food, and **(D)** withdraw the hand and move food to the mouth.

**FIGURE 7-6 Automated Touchscreen Platform for Testing Rodents** Mice or rats are placed in the apparatus and receive a strawberry milkshake reward when they choose the correct visual image by touching the screen.

Tim Bussey, Lisa Saksida, and their colleagues have developed an automated touchscreen platform for cognitive and motivational testing of rodents (**Figure 7-6**). This innovation removes the variations and stress that humans introduce when testing animals. Moreover, it is possible to program the platform to deliver tests that are highly similar to the touchscreen tasks used in human cognitive testing (Oomen et al., 2013; Phillips et al., 2018).

# Manipulating Brain–Behavior Interactions

The predominant strategy used for studying brain–behavior relationships is to manipulate some aspect of brain function and see how behavior changes. Investigators do so to develop hypotheses about how the brain affects behavior and to test those hypotheses.

A second reason to manipulate the brain is to develop animal models of neurological and psychiatric disorders. The general presumption in neurology and psychiatry is that it ought to be possible to restore at least some healthy functioning by implementing pharmacological, behavioral, or other interventions. A major hurdle for developing such treatments is that, like most other new medical treatments, they must be tested in nonhuman subjects first. (In Section 7-8, we take up scientific and ethical issues surrounding the use of animals in research.)

Table 7-2 summarizes selected brain manipulation techniques, their goals, and examples.

Brains can be manipulated in various ways, with the precise manner depending on the specific research question being asked. Researchers can manipulate the whole animal by exposing it to differing diets, social interactions, exercise, sensory stimulation, and a host of other experiences. For brain manipulation, the principal direct techniques are to inactivate the brain via lesions or with drugs, or to activate it with electrical stimulation, drugs, or light.

Behavioral neuroscientists make a manipulation and then measure brain function and behavioral performance. Because a large variety of manipulation techniques and measurement techniques are available to researchers, techniques from these two categories are often mixed and matched.

## Brain Lesions

The first—and the simplest—technique used for brain manipulation is to ablate (remove or destroy) tissue. Beginning in the 1920s, Karl Lashley, a pioneer of neuroscience research, used *ablation* in his studies; for the next 30 years, he tried to find the site of memory in the brain. He trained monkeys and rats on various mazes and motor tasks and then removed bits of cerebral cortex, with the goal of producing amnesia for specific memories.

To his chagrin, Lashley failed in his quest. He observed instead that memory loss was related to the *amount* of tissue he removed. The conclusion that Lashley reached was that memory is distributed throughout the brain and not located in any single place.

Subsequent research, however, has strongly indicated that specific brain functions and associated memories are indeed localized to specific brain regions.

Ironically, just as Lashley was retiring, William Scoville and Brenda Milner (1957) described a patient from whose brain Scoville had removed both hippocampi as a treatment for epilepsy. The surgery rendered this patient amnesic. During his ablation research, Lashley had never removed the hippocampi because he had no reason to believe these structures had any role in memory. And because the hippocampus is not accessible on the brain's surface, other techniques had to be developed before subcortical lesions could be used.

The solution to the challenge of accessing subcortical regions is to use a **stereotaxic apparatus**, a device that permits a researcher or a neurosurgeon to target a specific part of the brain for destruction, as shown in **Figure 7-7**. The head is held in a fixed position, and because the location of brain structures is fixed in relationship to the junction of the skull bones, it is possible to visualize a three-dimensional brain map. Atlases of the brains of humans and laboratory animals have been constructed from postmortem tissue and advanced imaging techniques so that the precise location of any structure can be specified in three-dimensional space.

Consider Parkinsonian tremor, in which the hands can shake so severely that the afflicted person cannot hold a glass of water. The most widely used surgical treatment today is to drill a hole in the skull and, using stereotaxic coordinates obtained for that patient through magnetic resonance imaging (MRI; described in detail in Section 7-3), target the globus pallidus. An electrode is then lowered into the globus pallidus, and current is passed through it to destroy the structure and relieve the patient of the tremor.

A new technique called *high-intensity focused ultrasound* (*HIFU*) can now achieve the same result while avoiding the invasive surgery (Quadri et al., 2018). Focused ultrasound uses many individual ultrasonic beams, all of which are pointed at the same spot in the brain. Each beam passes through tissue with little effect; at the convergent point where all the beams intersect, however, the energy heats the tissue. Lightly heating the tissue temporarily prevents that part of the brain from working properly, thereby informing the surgeons that their targeting is correct. The tissue heating can then continue until the target is permanently destroyed and the tremor is noninvasively eliminated.

The techniques described so far result in permanent brain damage. With time, the research subject will show **compensation**, the neuroplastic ability to modify behavior from that expressed prior to the damage. To avoid compensation following permanent lesions, researchers have also developed temporary and reversible lesion techniques such as *regional cooling*, which prevents synaptic transmission. In this technique, a hollow metal coil is placed next to a neural structure and chilled fluid is then passed through the coil, cooling the brain structure to about 18°C (Lomber & Payne, 1996). When the chilled fluid is removed from the coil, the brain structure quickly warms, and synaptic transmission is restored.

Another technique involves local administration of a gamma-aminobutyric acid (GABA) agonist, which increases local inhibition and in turn prevents the brain structure from communicating with other structures. Degradation of the GABA agonist reverses the local inhibition and restores function.

## Brain Stimulation

The brain operates on both electrical and chemical energy, so it is possible to selectively turn brain regions on or off by using electrical or chemical stimulation. Wilder Penfield, in the mid-twentieth century, was the first to use electrical stimulation directly on the surface of the human cerebral cortex during neurosurgery. Later researchers used stereotaxic instruments to place an electrode or a cannula in specific

Both Lashley's work and Scoville and Milner's iconic patient, H. M., are discussed further in Section 14-2.

**FIGURE 7-7 Stereotaxic Apparatus** This instrument allows the precise positioning of all brain regions relative to each other and to landmarks on the skull. Rostral–caudal (front-to-back) measurements correspond to the *y*-axis; dorsal–ventral (top-to-bottom) measurements, the *z*-axis, are made relative to the surface of the brain; medial–lateral measurements, the *x*-axis, are made relative to the midline junction of the cranial bones.

Review the brain's anatomical locations and orientations in The Basics in Section 2-1.

**Principle 10:** Neuroplasticity is the hallmark of nervous system functioning.

**Principle 7:** The nervous system works by juxtaposing excitation and inhibition.

**stereotaxic apparatus** Surgical instrument that permits a researcher or neurosurgeon to target a specific part of the brain.

**compensation** Following brain damage, the neuroplastic ability to modify behavior from that demonstrated prior to the damage.

Read more about Penfield's dramatic discoveries in Sections 10-4 and 11-2.

Figure 12-7 diagrams the hypothalamus's anatomy. Chapter 12 details its role in motivated, regulatory, sexual, and emotional behavior.

View DBS in place in Figure 1-3.

**deep-brain stimulation (DBS)** Neurosurgical technique in which electrodes implanted in the brain stimulate a targeted area with a low-voltage electrical current to produce or facilitate behavior or give relief from psychiatric conditions.

**transcranial magnetic stimulation (TMS)** Procedure in which a magnetic coil is placed over the skull to stimulate the underlying brain; used either to induce behavior or to disrupt ongoing behavior.

brain locations. The objective: enhancing or blocking neuronal activity and observing the behavioral effects.

Perhaps the most dramatic research example comes from stimulating specific regions of the hypothalamus. Rats with electrodes placed in the lateral hypothalamus will eat whenever the stimulation is turned on. If the animals have the opportunity to press a bar that briefly turns on the current, they quickly learn to press the bar to obtain the current, a behavior known as *electrical self-stimulation*. It appears that the stimulation is affecting a neural circuit that involves both eating and pleasure.

Brain stimulation can also be used as a therapy. When the intact cortex adjacent to cortex injured by a stroke is stimulated electrically, for example, it leads to improvement in motor behaviors such as those illustrated in Figure 7-5. Cam Teskey and his colleagues (Brown et al., 2011) successfully restored motor deficits in a rat model of Parkinson disease by electrically stimulating a specific brain nucleus.

**Deep-brain stimulation (DBS)** is a neurosurgical technique. Electrodes implanted in the brain stimulate a targeted area with continuous pulses of low-voltage electrical current to facilitate behavior. The stimulation can then be adapted according to feedback about the person's clinical state, such as the presence of a tremor, and underlying pathophysiology. One hypothesis driving this line of research is that DBS modulates abnormal circuits toward a more typical or healthy state. DBS is mostly used with subcortical structures; for example, DBS to the globus pallidus in the basal ganglia of individuals with Parkinson disease makes their movements smoother, and improves cognition and mood as well, often allowing these individuals to dramatically reduce their intake of medications (Little & Brown, 2020).

DBS using several neural targets is an approved treatment for essential tremor, dystonia, obsessive-compulsive disorder, and epilepsy (Lee et al., 2019). Experimental trials are under way to identify the brain regions in which DBS are best used as a treatment for intractable psychiatric disorders such as major depressive disorder and schizophrenia; this approach may also be used as a treatment for Tourette syndrome, obesity, anorexia nervosa, addiction, and pain, and to stimulate recovery from traumatic brain injury (TBI) (Lee et al., 2019).

Electrical stimulation of the brain is invasive: holes must be drilled in the skull and an electrode lowered into the brain. Researchers have taken advantage of the relationship between magnetism and electricity to develop a noninvasive technique called **transcranial magnetic stimulation (TMS)**. During a treatment session, a small wire coil is placed adjacent to the skull, as illustrated in **Figure 7-8**A. A high-voltage current pulsed through the coil produces a rapid increase and subsequent decrease in the magnetic field around the coil. The magnetic field easily passes through the skull and causes a population of neurons in the cerebral cortex to depolarize and fire (Figure 7-8B).

If the motor cortex is stimulated, movement is evoked; conversely, if a movement is in progress, it is disrupted. Similarly, if the visual cortex is stimulated, the participant

The TMS coil, shown here in a composite MRI and PET scan photograph, interferes with brain function in the adjacent area.

TMS COIL

**FIGURE 7-8 Transcranial Magnetic Stimulation (A)** When used in clinical therapy for depression, TMS influences neural activity in a localized region. **(B)** This composite photo shows how TMS works.

sees dots of light (*phosphenes*). The effects of brief pulses of TMS do not outlive the stimulation, but *repetitive TMS* (rTMS), or continuous stimulation for up to several minutes, produces more long-lasting effects, including changing function or temporarily inactivating tissue. Both TMS and rTMS can be used to study brain–behavior relationships in healthy participants, and rTMS has been tested as a potential treatment for a variety of behavioral disorders, including pain, stroke-induced impairments, movement disorders, and depression (Iglesias, 2020).

Research Focus 16-5 describes use of rTMS to treat depression and other behavioral disorders.

## Drug Manipulations

Brain activity can also be stimulated by administration of drugs that pass into the bloodstream and eventually enter the brain, or that are sent through an indwelling cannula (illustrated in Figure 7-23) to allow direct application of the drugs to specific brain structures. Drugs can influence the activity of specific neurons in specific brain regions. For example, the drug haloperidol, which is used to treat schizophrenia, reduces dopaminergic neuron function and makes healthy rats dopey and inactive (*hypokinetic*). In contrast, drugs that increase dopaminergic activity, such as amphetamine, produce *hyperkinetic rats*—rats that are hyperactive. The advantage of administering drugs as a research manipulation is that their effects wear off in time as the drugs are metabolized. As a result, researchers can study drug effects on learned behaviors, such as skilled reaching (see Figure 7-5), and then reexamine the behavior after the drug effect wears off.

Chapter 6 discusses the influence of drugs on behavior, and Section 6-2 specifically details the effects of the drugs described here, among others.

Claudia Gonzalez and her colleagues (2006) administered nicotine to rats as they learned a skilled reaching task, then studied their later acquisition of a new skilled reaching task. The researchers found that the earlier nicotine-enhanced motor learning impaired the later motor learning. This finding surprised the investigators, but it now appears that repeated exposure to psychomotor stimulants such as amphetamine, cocaine, and nicotine can produce long-term effects on the brain's later plasticity (its ability to change in response to experience), including learning specific tasks.

## Genetic Manipulations and Combinations with Light and Drugs

In the past two decades, **synthetic biology**—the design and construction of biological devices, systems, and machines not found in nature—has transformed how neuroscientists manipulate brain cells. Techniques include inserting or deleting a genetic sequence into the genome of a living organism.

A new technique called CRISPR-Cas9 (clustered regularly interspaced short palindromic repeats), one of the many CRISPR techniques available to researchers, was discovered during studies of bacteria for fighting viruses; it serves as an all-purpose tool for cutting the DNA of any cell. Scientists simply provide the bacteria's Cas9 protein with the RNA sequence corresponding to the length of DNA they would like to remove from the subject. When used in this way, the CRISPR system can be used to silence one or many genes by cutting out those regions in the DNA. Then the DNA's repair machinery can be harnessed to insert a new sequence that replaces the one that was removed.

The CRISPR-Cas9 technique is detailed in Section 3-3 and illustrated in Figure 3-24.

It is difficult to overestimate the potential impact of CRISPR in neuroscience. As an experimental tool, it can help answer a key question: What is the role of this gene or these genes in this behavior? As a therapeutic intervention, it could eventually lead to the elimination of many forms of inherited disease. It could also counter antibiotic-resistant microbes, disable parasites, and improve food security.

Another transgenic technique, **optogenetics**, combines genetics and light to control targeted cells in living tissue. A sequence that codes for a light-sensitive protein associated with an ion channel enables investigators to use light to change the shape (conformation) of the channel.

Optogenetics is based on the discovery that light can activate certain proteins that occur naturally and have been inserted into cells of model organisms. For example, *opsins*, proteins derived from microorganisms, combine a light-sensitive domain with an ion

Section 3-3 explores some techniques in genetic and transgenic engineering.

**synthetic biology** Design and construction of biological devices, systems, and machines that are not found in nature.

**optogenetics** Transgenic technique that combines genetics and light to control targeted cells in living tissue.

FIGURE 7-9 **Lighting up Neurons** Optogenetics allows precise temporal control of cell firing and is rapidly reversible. Specific wavelengths activate light-sensitive proteins expressed in neurons. At bottom left, when blue light illuminates a cell in which ChR2 has been incorporated, its firing rate increases dramatically. At right, when green-yellow light illuminates a cell in which NpHR is incorporated, its firing rate decreases dramatically.

Figure 2-21 diagrams the relative location of the amygdala.

**chemogenetics** Transgenic technique that combines genetics and synthetic drugs to activate targeted cells in living tissue.

FIGURE 7-10 **GRAB Technology** The cannabinoid 1 receptor (CB1R) has a circular-permutated fluorescent protein (cpEGFP) that is inactive until the endocannabinoids (2-AG and AEA) interact with the receptor, which causes the circular-permutated protein to fluoresce. A microscope captures the fluorescent signal as the endocannabinoids interact with the CB1R.

channel, as shown in **Figure 7-9**. The first opsin used for the optogenetic technique was channelrhodopsin-2 (ChR2). When ChR2 is expressed in neurons and exposed to blue light, the ion channel opens and immediately depolarizes the neuron, causing excitation. In contrast, stimulation of halorhodopsin (NpHR) with a green-yellow light activates a chloride pump, hyperpolarizing the neuron and causing inhibition. A fiber-optic light can be delivered to selective brain regions so that all genetically modified neurons exposed to the light respond immediately (Haubensak et al., 2010).

Optogenetics has tremendous potential as a research tool. Investigators can insert light-sensitive proteins into specific neuron types, such as pyramidal cells of the CA1 region of the hippocampus, and use light to selectively activate just that cell type. Researchers hail optogenetics for its high spatial and temporal (time) resolution. Ion channels can be placed into specific cell lines and turned on and off on millisecond time scales. Optogenetics has also found application in behavioral studies. For example, the amygdala is a key structure in generating fear in animals; if it is targeted with opsins and then exposed to an inhibitory light, rats immediately show no fear and wander about in a novel open space. As soon as the light is turned off, they scamper back to a safe hiding place.

In the transgenic technique called **chemogenetics**, the inserted synthetic genetic sequence codes for a G protein–coupled receptor engineered to respond exclusively to a synthetic small-molecule "designer drug." Chemogenetics is best known by the acronym *DREADD* (designer receptor exclusively activated by designer drugs). Its principal advantage is that the drug activates only the genetically modified receptors, and the receptors are activated only by the designer drug, not by endogenous molecules (Wess et al., 2013). Thus, specificity is high, but temporal resolution is much lower than with optogenetics because the receptors are activated by drugs rather than by light.

What if you wanted to visualize and quantify a neurotransmitter interacting with its receptor? In the past, researchers' ability to describe the dynamics of neurotransmitter interactions was limited by their reliance on approaches that offered low spatial and temporal resolution, and in which animals had to be sacrificed, a structure removed, and then biochemical analysis performed. Now *GRAB technology* allows us to perform analysis with high spatial and temporal resolution in living mice, observed under a microscope, by making use of genetically encoded tools for sensing neurotransmitters as they interact with G protein–coupled receptors (GPCR) tagged with fluorescent proteins (Dong et al., 2020). This process is illustrated in **Figure 7-10**.

In one recent advance, a novel GPCR activation-based (GRAB) endocannabinoid sensor was utilized to track the kinetics of endocannabinoid release during physiological and pathological activities in the hippocampus. When Farrell and colleagues (2021) measured the endocannabinoid 2-AG in mice trained to run on a treadmill, they found that 2-AG interacting with the CB1 receptor is dynamically coupled to the activity of individual hippocampal neurons. Moreover, they determined that seizures resulted in 2-AG levels that were orders of magnitude larger than the physiological levels. The increased 2-AG levels were expressed in two separate waves. The first wave was observed during the seizure and is likely responsible for terminating the seizure. The second larger, longer-lasting wave appeared a short time later and initiated a stroke-like event in those brain areas that participated in the seizure (Farrell et al., 2016). Thus, the new GRAB technology revealed for the first time that 2-AG has two roles, one positive and one negative, in the pathogenesis of epilepsy—a discovery that could lead to effective treatments to prevent the adverse effects that come with seizures. GRAB technology has been applied to many neurotransmitter systems, giving researchers unprecedented insights into transmitter–receptor interactions under a wide range of experimental conditions.

Another innovative and highly promising transgenic technique is described in Clinical Focus 7-3: Brain Organoids and Personalized Medicine.

## ⦿ CLINICAL FOCUS 7-3

# Brain Organoids and Personalized Medicine

What if we had the capability to grow human tissue from an individual for use in lab studies? As it turns out, we do. **Organoids** are three-dimensional, artificially grown, miniature and simplified versions of parts of organs, including brains. Brain organoids of the midbrain, hypothalamus, and neocortex can serve as model systems for pathological conditions that affect the proper functioning of real human brains (Agboola et al., 2021).

The first step in the production of any organoid involves harvesting cells by taking either a hair follicle, blood, or urine sample from a willing donor. Four specific genes are then introduced into the cells that convert them into **induced pluripotent stem cells (iPSCs)**, which can differentiate under the proper conditions into nearly all cell types found in the body. These iPSCs are grown in a bioreactor with liquid media and particular growth factors that cause the cells to self-organize into sophisticated tissue structures, much as they would during typical uterine development.

As brain organoids develop, they show a great diversity of cell types, including astrocytes, oligodendrocytes, microglia, and vascular cells, as well as excitatory and inhibitory neurons that generate graded potentials and action potentials. Moreover, in a similar fashion to the developing neocortex, the developing cortical organoid develops deep- and superficial-layer neurons with an ordered geometry of multilayered groupings. This process is illustrated in the accompanying figure.

Once the cells have differentiated, the organoid is ready for scientific investigations of cell-to-cell interactions, use in modeling diseases, or even harvesting as a potential source of tissue for organ repair. What if a person had a disorder with a genetic component and their attending physician needed to determine which one of several drugs would work best for that individual? The trial-and-error practice of cycling through various drugs to find one that is effective for an individual can be inefficient and stressful for the patient (and potentially unethical). Organoids grown from that individual's own cells, however, could be used to screen the drugs for maximum efficacy before introducing them into the person. Thus, organoids can serve as vehicles for **personalized medicine:** treatments can be

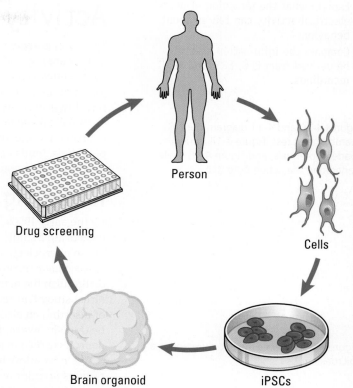

Creation and use of organoids for personalized medicine.

specifically tailored to an individual based on their predicted response from organoids built from their own cells. The use of brain organoids holds promise for a variety of neurodevelopmental disorders, such as autism spectrum disorders, several syndromes, and neurodegenerative diseases such as Alzheimer and Parkinson diseases.

# 7-1 Review

Before you continue, check your understanding. Answers to Self-Test appear at the back of the book.

1. Behavioral neuroscience is the study of relationships between _____ and _____; _____ is a subfield of behavioral neuroscience that focuses largely on humans.

2. Anatomical studies rely on techniques such as _____ and _____ tissue postmortem or visualizing living tissue using _____.

3. A recent innovation in behavioral testing in rodents uses automated _____, which removes the variation and stress that humans introduce when testing animals.

4. GRAB technology, a recent innovation, allows researchers to actually see the neurotransmitter–receptor interactions by genetically encoding _____ with fluorescent proteins.

5. Outline the various brain-stimulation methods that either activate or inhibit neural activity.

---

**organoid** Artificially grown, simplified, three-dimensional, miniature versions of organ parts, including brain tissue.

**induced pluripotent stem cells (iPSCs)** Cells created from the body's tissues that can differentiate into nearly all cell types found in the body.

**personalized medicine** A medical model whereby treatments can be tailored to the individual.

Figures 4-10 and 4-11 diagram the cell membrane at rest, Figure 4-14 during graded potentials, and Figure 4-18 while generating the action potential.

Figure 4-7 illustrates the structure and use of microelectrodes.

See, for example, "Seeing Shape" and "Seeing Color" in Section 9-4 and "Processing Language" in Section 10-4.

Place cells are part of the brain's navigation system, and the means by which animals orient themselves and navigate their environment. They are described in Section 14-3; their activity in the process of neural replay and memory storage during sleep is detailed in Section 13-4.

**place cells** Neurons maximally responsive to specific locations in the world.

**electrocorticography (ECoG)** Graded potentials recorded with electrodes placed directly on the surface of the brain.

## 7-2

# Measuring the Brain's Electrical Activity

The brain is always electrically active, even when we sleep. Electrical measures of brain activity are important for studying brain function, for medical diagnosis, and for monitoring the effectiveness of therapies used to treat brain disorders. The four major techniques for tracking the brain's electrical activity are single-cell recording, electroencephalography (EEG), event-related potentials (ERPs), and magnetoencephalography (MEG).

In part, these techniques are used to record electrical activity from different parts of neurons. The electrical behavior of cell bodies and dendrites, which give rise to graded potentials, tends to be much more varied and slower than the behavior of axons, which conduct action potentials.

## Recording Action Potentials from Single Cells

By the early 1950s, it was becoming possible to record the activity of individual cells by measuring a single neuron's action potentials with fine electrodes inserted into the brain. These microelectrodes can be placed next to cells (*extracellular recording*) or inside cells (*intracellular recording*). Modern extracellular recording techniques make it possible to distinguish the activity of as many as 40 neurons at once. Intracellular recording allows direct study and recording of a single neuron's electrical activity. The two disadvantages of inserting an electrode into a cell are that (1) it eventually kills the cell and (2) it cannot be done in awake, freely moving animals. Single-cell recording is therefore confined to neurons grown in a dish or, for short periods (hours), to neurons in living brain slices.

We now know from extracellular recordings that cells in the brain's various sensory regions are highly sensitive to specific stimuli. Some cells in the visual system fire vigorously in response to specific wavelengths of light (a color) or to specific orientations of bars of light (vertical, for example). Other cells in this region respond to more complex patterns, such as faces or hands. Similarly, cells in the auditory system respond to specific sound frequencies (a low or high pitch) or to more complex sound combinations, such as speech (the syllable *ba*, for example).

But certain cells respond to inputs that are rich in information—a fact that reveals much about brain–behavior relationships. John O'Keefe and his colleagues (O'Keefe & Dostrovsky, 1971) showed that neurons in the rat and mouse hippocampus fire vigorously when an animal is in a specific place in the environment. These **place cells**, illustrated in **Figure 7-11**, code the spatial location of the animal and contribute to a spatial map of the world in the brain. In 2014, John O'Keefe, May-Britt Moser, and Edvard I. Moser were awarded the Nobel Prize in Physiology or Medicine "for their discoveries of cells that constitute a positioning system in the brain."

O'Keefe's group (Cacucci et al., 2008) also demonstrated that, in mice with a genetically engineered mutation that produces deficits in spatial memory, place cells lack specificity: the cells fire in response to a very broad region of their world. As a result, these mice have difficulty finding their way around, much as people with dementia tend to get lost. One reason for this effect may be that a change similar to the engineered mutation in mice takes place in human brain cells.

## EEG: Recording Graded Potentials from Thousands of Cells

In the early 1930s, Hans Berger discovered that the brain's electrical activity could be recorded simply by placing electrodes on the scalp. In Berger's words, recording these "brain waves" produces an "electrical record from the head"—an electroencephalogram. The EEG measures the summed graded potentials from many thousands of neurons. EEG waves, shown in **Figure 7-12**, are recorded by a computer. In **electrocorticography (ECoG)**, a method used during neurosurgery, electrodes are placed directly on surface of the cerebral cortex. Electrodes can also be placed deeper

**FIGURE 7-11 Classes of Spatially Related Cells in the Hippocampal Formation (A and B)** Place cells discharge when a rat is at a spatial location, regardless of its orientation. **(C)** Head-direction cells discharge to indicate where the rat's head points, regardless of its location. **(D)** Grid cells discharge at many locations, forming a virtual grid that is invariant in the face of changes in the rat's direction, movement, or speed. At right in each part, *xy* coordinates indicate the directional selectivity of the cell recorded at left.

Courtesy of John O'Keefe

into human brain tissue to record local field potentials. This procedure is typically done in candidates for surgical resection of epileptic tissue, with the recordings being used to localize the brain area where seizures are started—the seizure *focus*.

EEGs reveal some remarkable features of the brain's electrical activity. The EEG recordings in **Figure 7-13** illustrate three of them:

1. EEG changes as behavior changes.

2. An EEG recorded from the cortex displays an array of patterns, some rhythmical.

3. The living brain's electrical activity is never silent, even when a person is asleep or comatose.

When a person is aroused, excited, or even just alert, the EEG pattern has a low amplitude and a fast frequency, as shown in Figure 7-13A. This pattern is typical of an EEG taken from anywhere on the skull of an alert subject—not only humans, but other animals, too. In contrast, when a participant is calm and quietly relaxed, especially with eyes closed, the rhythmical brain waves shown in Figure 7-13B often emerge. These **alpha rhythms** are extremely regular, with a frequency of approximately 11 cycles per second and amplitudes that wax and wane as the pattern is recorded. (*Amplitude* is a recorded brain wave's height. *Frequency* is the number of brain waves recorded per second.) In humans, alpha rhythms are generated in the region of the visual cortex at the back of the brain. If a relaxed person is disturbed, performs mental arithmetic, or opens their eyes, the alpha rhythms abruptly stop.

Roman Zaiets/Shutterstock

Southern Illinois University/Science Source

**1** Electrodes attached to the scalp correspond to specific brain areas...

**2** ...to record their electrical activity. This EEG indicates a relaxed person.

**FIGURE 7-12 Recording EEG Waves** EEG is a simple, noninvasive method for recording the brain's electrical activity. EEG waves recorded via computer (see Figure 4-6) can match wave activity to specific brain regions.

Clinical Focus 4-1 details epilepsy diagnoses, and Section 16-3 explores treatments.

**alpha rhythm** Regular wave pattern in an electroencephalogram; found in most people when they are relaxed with eyes closed.

**(A) Awake or excited**

**(B) Relaxed, eyes closed, alpha rhythms generated**

**(C) Drowsy — slowed frequency, increased-amplitude waves**

**(D) Asleep — slower, higher-amplitude waves**

**(E) Deep sleep — even slower and higher-amplitude waves**

Time (s)

**(F) Coma — further slowing**

Time (s)

**FIGURE 7-13 Characteristic EEG Recordings** Brain-wave patterns reflect different states of consciousness in humans. Data from Penfield & Jasper (1954).

Section 13-3 describes how EEG measures sleep and dreaming.

**event-related potential (ERP)** Complex electroencephalographic waveform related in time to a specific sensory event.

**FIGURE 7-14 Detecting ERPs** In the averaging process for an auditory ERP, a tone is presented at time 0, and EEG activity in response is recorded. After many successive presentations of the tone, the EEG wave sequence develops a distinctive shape that becomes extremely clear after 100 responses are averaged (bottom panel). Positive and negative waves that appear at different times after the stimulus presentation are used for analysis.

EEG is a sensitive indicator of behaviors beyond simple arousal and relaxation. Parts C, D, and E of Figure 7-13 illustrate EEG changes as a person moves from drowsiness to sleep and finally into deep sleep. Note how the EEG rhythms become progressively slower and larger in amplitude. Still slower waves appear during anesthesia, after brain trauma, or when a person is in a coma (shown in Figure 7-13F). Only in brain death does the EEG permanently become a flat line.

These distinctive brain-wave patterns make EEG a reliable tool for monitoring sleep stages, estimating the depth of anesthesia, evaluating the severity of head injury, and searching for brain abnormalities. In persons with epilepsy, for example, brief periods of impaired awareness or unresponsiveness and involuntary movements associated with spiking patterns in the EEG characterize electrographic seizures. EEG is an essential tool in the diagnosis of epilepsy and in determining the kind of epilepsy and seizures a person has.

The important point here is that EEG recordings provide a useful tool both for research and for diagnosing brain dysfunction. EEG can also be used in combination with the brain-imaging techniques described in Sections 7-3 and 7-4 to provide more accurate identification of the source of the large and highly synchronized EEG waves in epilepsy.

# Mapping Brain Function with Event-Related Potentials

Brief changes in an EEG signal in response to a discrete sensory stimulus produce complex electroencephalographic waveforms called **event-related potentials (ERPs)**. ERPs are largely the graded potentials on dendrites that a sensory stimulus triggers. You might think that they should be easy to detect, but they are not.

ERPs are mixed in with so many other electrical signals in the brain that they are difficult to spot just by visually inspecting an EEG record. One way to detect ERPs is to produce the stimulus repeatedly and average the recorded responses. Averaging tends to cancel out any irregular and unrelated electrical activity, leaving in the EEG record only the potentials the stimulus generated.

**Figure 7-14** shows an ERP record (top) that results when a person hears a tone. The EEG record is highly irregular when the tone is first presented. But by averaging more than 100 stimulus presentations, a distinctive wave pattern appears, as shown in the bottom panel of Figure 7-14. This ERP pattern consists of a number of negative (N) and positive (P) waves that occur within a few hundred milliseconds after the stimulus.

The waves are numbered in time sequence. For instance, in Figure 7-14, $N_1$ is a negative wave occurring about 100 milliseconds after the stimulus, whereas $P_2$ is a positive wave occurring about 200 milliseconds after the stimulus. (These waves may also be labeled N100 and P200, respectively.) Not all of these waves are unique to this particular stimulus: some are common to any auditory stimulus. Other waves, however, correspond to important differences in specific tone. ERPs to spoken words even contain distinctive peaks and patterns that differentiate such similar-sounding words as *cat* and *rat*.

Among the many practical reasons for using ERPs to study the brain is that this EEG technique is noninvasive and inexpensive. Electrodes are placed on the scalp, not in the brain. Therefore, ERPs can be used to study humans, including those most frequently used research participants—college students.

**Figure 7-15** shows a multiple-recording method that uses 128 electrodes simultaneously to detect ERPs at many cortical sites. Computed averaging techniques reduce the masses of information obtained to simpler comparisons between electrode sites. For example, if the focus of interest is $P_3$, a positive wave occurring about 300 milliseconds after the stimulus, the computer can display a graph of the skull showing only the amplitude of $P_3$. A computer can also convert the averages at different sites into a color code, graphically representing those brain regions most responsive to the signal. In addition to detecting which brain areas are processing particular stimuli, ERPs can be used to study the order in which different regions participate—an important use because we want to know which route the information takes as it travels through the brain.

# Magnetoencephalography

Passing a magnetic field across a wire induces an electrical current in the wire. Conversely, current flowing along a wire induces a magnetic field around the wire. The same is true in the brain: neural activity, by generating an electrical field, produces a magnetic field. Although the magnetic field produced by a single neuron is vanishingly small, the field produced by many neurons is sufficiently strong to be recorded on the scalp. The record of this phenomenon, a **magnetoencephalogram (MEG)**, is the magnetic counterpart of the EEG or ERP.

Calculations based on MEG measurements not only describe the electrical activity of neuronal groups, but also localize the cell groups generating the measured field in three dimensions. Magnetic waves conducted through living tissue undergo less distortion than electrical signals do, so an MEG can yield a higher resolution than an ERP. A major advantage of MEG over EEG and ERP, then, is the ability of MEG to more precisely identify the source of the activity being recorded. For example, MEG has proved useful in locating the source of epileptic discharges. The disadvantage of MEG is its very high cost in comparison with the apparatus used to produce EEGs and ERPs.

## 7-2 Review

Before you continue, check your understanding. Answers to Self-Test appear at the back of the book.

1. The four major techniques for tracking the brain's electrical activity are _____, _____, _____, and _____.

2. Single-cell recording measures _____ potentials from a single neuron.

3. EEG measures _____ potentials from very large numbers of neurons.

4. Magnetoencephalography measures the _____ activity of many neurons and also provides a three-dimensional localization of the _____ generating the measured field.

5. What is the key advantage of EEG techniques over MEG?

## 7-3

# Anatomical Imaging Techniques: CT and MRI

For much of the twentieth century, the only way to actually image the living brain was by using X-rays, which produce static images of brain anatomy from one angle. The modern era of brain imaging began in the early 1970s, when Allan Cormack and Godfrey Hounsfield independently developed an X-ray approach now called **computed tomography (CT)**, or *CT scan*. Cormack and Hounsfield both recognized that a narrow X-ray beam could be passed through the same object at many angles, creating many images; the images could then be combined with the use of computing and mathematical techniques to produce a three-dimensional image of the brain. *Tomo-* comes from the Greek word for "section," indicating that tomography yields a picture through a single brain slice.

The CT method resembles the way in which our two eyes (and our brain) work in concert to perceive depth and distance to locate an object in space. The CT scan, however, coordinates many more than two images—roughly analogous to our walking to several vantage points to obtain multiple views of an object. X-ray absorption varies with tissue density. High-density tissue, such as bone, absorbs a lot of radiation. Low-density material, such as ventricular fluid or blood, absorbs little. Neural tissue absorption lies between these extremes. CT scanning software translates these differences in absorption into a brain image in which dark colors indicate low-density regions and light colors indicate high-density regions.

Electrodes attached to the scalp of a research subject are connected to...

Electrodes in geodesic sensor net

...a computer display of electrical activity, showing a large positive (P₃) wave at the posterior right side of the head.

P₃

This electrical activity can be converted into a color representation showing the hot spot for the visual stimulus.

Resting    300 ms after viewing

**FIGURE 7-15  Using ERPs to Image Brain Activity**

### Learning Objective

- Compare and contrast the benefits and disadvantages of anatomical imaging techniques: CT, MRI, DTI, and MRS.

**magnetoencephalogram (MEG)** Magnetic potentials recorded from detectors placed outside the skull.

**computed tomography (CT)** X-ray technique that produces a static three-dimensional image (called a CT scan) of the brain in cross section.

**FIGURE 7-16 CT Scan and Brain Reconstruction (A)** Dorsal view of a horizontal CT scan of a subject with Broca's aphasia. The dark region at the left anterior is the area of the lesion. **(B)** A schematic representation of the horizontal section, with the area of the lesion shown in blue. **(C)** A reconstruction of the brain, showing a lateral view of the left hemisphere with the lesion shown in blue. Research from Damasio & Damasio (1989).

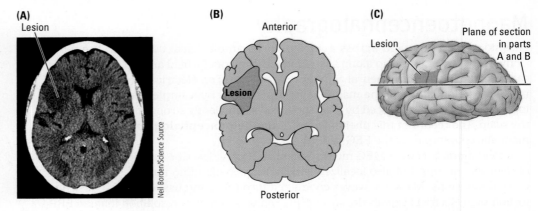

Section 10-4 delves into aphasias that result from damaged speech areas.

**magnetic resonance imaging (MRI)** Technique that produces a static three-dimensional brain image by passing a strong magnetic field through the brain, followed by a radio wave, then measuring a radiofrequency signal emitted from hydrogen atoms.

**diffusion tensor imaging (DTI)** Magnetic resonance imaging method that can image fiber pathways in the brain by detecting the directional movements of water molecules.

**Figure 7-16**A shows a typical CT scan. The dense skull forms a white border. The brain's gray-matter density does not differ sufficiently from that of white matter for a CT scan to distinguish between the two clearly, so the cortex and its underlying white matter show up as a more or less homogeneous gray. Ventricles can be visualized, however, because the fluid they contain is far less dense: they, as well as some major fissures in the cortex, are rendered darker in the CT scan. Each point on the image in Figure 7-16A represents about a 1-millimeter-diameter circle of tissue, a resolution sufficient to distinguish two objects about 5 millimeters apart and appropriate for localizing brain tumors and lesions.

The lesion revealed in Figure 7-16A is a damaged region where the presence of fewer neurons and more fluid produces a contrast that appears as a dark area in the CT scan. This person presented with symptoms of *Broca aphasia*, the inability to speak fluently despite having average comprehension and intact vocal mechanisms. The location of the lesion, in the left frontal cortex (adjacent to the butterfly-shaped lateral ventricles), confirms this diagnosis. Figure 7-16B, a drawing of the same horizontal section, uses color to portray the lesion. Figure 7-16C is a lateral view of the left hemisphere reconstructed from a series of horizontal CT scans and showing the extent of the lesion.

An anatomical alternative to the CT scan, **magnetic resonance imaging (MRI)** is based on the principle that hydrogen atoms behave like spinning bar magnets in the presence of a magnetic field. The MRI procedure is illustrated in **Figure 7-17**. The dorsal view of the brain portrays density differences among the hydrogen atoms in different neural regions as lighter or darker, depending on their density, on the horizontal slice through the head.

Normally, hydrogen atoms point randomly in different directions. When placed in a large, static magnetic field, however, they line up in parallel as they orient themselves with respect to the static field's lines of force. In an MRI scanner, radio pulses are applied to a brain whose atoms have been aligned in this manner, and each radio pulse forms a second magnetic field. The second field causes the spinning atoms to deviate from the parallel orientation caused by the static magnetic field to a new orientation.

As each radio pulse ends and the hydrogen atoms realign with the static field, they emit a tiny amount of energy, and a coil detects this realignment. Based on the signals from the coil, a computer re-creates the position of the hydrogen nuclei, producing an image. Thus, magnetic resonance images are based on the density of the hydrogen atoms in different brain regions. Areas with high water ($H_2O$) content (cell body–rich areas), for example, stand out from areas with lower water content (axon-rich areas). Figure 7-17C shows such an image.

**Diffusion tensor imaging (DTI)** is an MRI method that detects the directional movements of water molecules as a means of imaging nerve fiber pathways in the brain. Water can move relatively freely along the axons but less freely across cell membranes. The direction of this water movement is detected by a coil and interpreted by a computer. DTIs can delineate abnormalities in neural pathways. They are also used

**(A)**

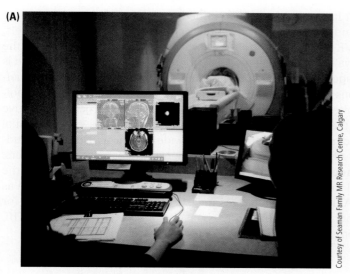

Courtesy of Seaman Family MR Research Centre, Calgary

**(B)**

Hollow
tube

Magnetic
coils

**(C)**

Brain
tissue

Skull

Roxana Wegner/Getty Images

**FIGURE 7-17 Magnetic Resonance Imaging (A and B)** The subject is placed in a long metal cylinder that has two sets of magnetic coils arranged at right angles. An additional radiofrequency coil (not shown) surrounds the head, perturbing the static magnetic fields to produce an image of a horizontal section through the head, shown in dorsal view. Electrical currents emitted by wobbling atoms are recorded by MRI to represent different types of tissue—cerebrospinal fluid, brain matter, and bone, for example—as lighter or darker, depending on the density of hydrogen atoms in the tissue, as seen in **(C)**.

to identify changes in fiber myelination, such as the damage that leads to myelin loss in multiple sclerosis.

Each scan in the series of DTIs shown in **Figure 7-18** represents a dorsal view at increasing depths through the brain. Although the images appear to show real fibers, DTIs are virtual and based on computer reconstructions of water movement along axons, which should correspond to actual fibers. Nonetheless, DTI easily detects abnormalities like those that occur in multiple sclerosis, stroke, or concussion, both in the imaged fiber pathways and in their myelin sheaths.

Clinical Focus 4-3 describes how myelin loss in multiple sclerosis disrupts neuronal function.

Zephyr/Science Source

**FIGURE 7-18 Diffusion Tensor Imaging** MRI can measure the diffusion of water molecules in white matter, allowing the visualization of nerve fiber tracts. The front of the brain is at the top in these scans of sections through a healthy brain. The axons are colored according to orientation: fibers running left–right are red, front–back are blue, and up–down are green. Section 15-3 outlines how DTI is helping researchers develop a *brain connectome* to map functional connections in the living brain.

The neurosurgeon shown here is using his hospital's surgical theater to perform complex brain procedures in virtual reality.

Recently, CT and DTI have been combined in dedicated virtual reality (VR) clinic rooms where patients and neurosurgeons can interact directly with 360° VR models. This innovative use of VR technology provides both surgeons and patients with the technological ability to walk into a virtual reconstruction of the patient's brain, which is viewable from any vantage point. In the surgical theater, the augmented reality visualization hub gives surgeons the ability to see anatomical and vascular structures, pathologies, and DTI white-matter tracts synchronized and aligned to the surgeon's operative view, while performing the surgery. Applications of VR technology have the potential to improve diagnosis and treatment of persons with a wide variety of disorders, including chronic pain, stroke, Alzheimer disease, and addiction and substance use disorders.

**Magnetic resonance spectroscopy (MRS)** is an MRI method that uses the hydrogen proton signal to determine the concentration of brain metabolites such as *N*-acetylaspartate (NAA) in brain tissue. This measurement is especially useful for detecting persistent abnormalities in brain metabolism in disorders such as mild TBI, also known as *concussion*.

## 7-3 Review

Before you continue, check your understanding. Answers to Self-Test appear at the back of the book.

1. The principal anatomical brain-imaging methods are _____ and _____.

2. Diffusion tensor imaging identifies _____, whereas magnetic resonance spectroscopy determines concentrations of _____.

3. In addition to imaging the density of different brain regions, CT and MRI can be used to assess _____.

4. Explain briefly the computed tomography (CT) method of brain imaging.

### 7-4

# Functional Brain Imaging

Advances in MRI and computing technologies led to a shift from purely anatomical imaging—which presented a static image of the tissue, as if it were not alive—to functional brain-imaging techniques, which allow investigators to measure the amount of blood flow, oxygen, and glucose usage in the brain as participants solve cognitive problems. When a brain region is active, the amount of blood, oxygen, and glucose flowing to the region increases. It is therefore possible to infer changes in brain activity by measuring either blood flow or levels of the blood's constituents, such as oxygen, glucose, and iron. Three techniques developed from this logic are functional MRI, optical tomography, and positron emission tomography.

## Functional Magnetic Resonance Imaging

As neurons become active, they use more oxygen, resulting in a temporary dip in the blood oxygen level. At the same time, active neurons increase blood carbon dioxide levels, which signal blood vessels to dilate, increasing blood flow and bringing more oxygen to the area. Peter Fox and colleagues (Fox & Raichle, 1986) discovered that when human brain activity increases, the extra oxygen produced by increased blood flow actually exceeds the tissue's needs. As a result, the amount of oxygen in an activated brain area increases.

In the body, oxygen is carried on the hemoglobin molecule in red blood cells. Changes in the ratio of oxygen-rich hemoglobin to oxygen-poor hemoglobin alter the blood's magnetic properties because oxygen-rich hemoglobin is less magnetic than oxygen-poor hemoglobin. In 1990, Segi Ogawa and his colleagues showed that MRI could accurately match these changes in magnetic properties to specific brain locations (Ogawa et al., 1990). This process, called **functional magnetic resonance imaging (fMRI)**, reveals which areas are displaying changes in activity.

**Learning Objective**

• Compare and contrast the benefits and disadvantages of functional imaging techniques: fMRI, rs-fMRI, fNIRS, and PET.

**magnetic resonance spectroscopy (MRS)** Magnetic resonance imaging method that uses the hydrogen proton signal to determine the concentration of brain metabolites.

**functional magnetic resonance imaging (fMRI)** Magnetic resonance imaging technique that measures brain activity indirectly by detecting changes associated with the ratio of oxygenated and deoxygenated blood; often used to measure cerebral blood flow during cognitive testing or resting.

**Figure 7-19** shows changes in the fMRI signal in the visual cortex of a person who is being stimulated with light. When the light is turned on, the visual cortex (bottom of the brain images) becomes more active than during baseline (no light). In other words, functional changes in the brain are inferred from increases and decreases in the MRI signal produced by changes in oxygen levels.

When superimposed on MRI-produced anatomical brain images, fMRI changes in activity can be attributed to particular structures. The dense blood vessel supply to the cerebral cortex allows for a spatial resolution of fMRI on the order of 1 millimeter, affording good spatial resolution of the brain activity's source. Unfortunately, because changes in blood flow take as long as one-third of a second to occur, the temporal resolution of fMRI is not as precise as that obtained with EEG recordings and ERPs.

Another disadvantage of fMRI is that persons undergoing this imaging must lie motionless in a long, noisy tube—an experience that can provoke claustrophobia. The confined space and lack of mobility also restrict the types of behavioral experiments that can be performed. Nonetheless, fMRI is a major tool in cognitive neuroscience.

The living brain is always active, and researchers have succeeded in inferring brain function and connectivity by studying fMRI signals when participants are resting—that is, not engaged in any specific task. This signal, called **resting-state fMRI (rs-fMRI)**, is collected when participants have their eyes closed or are asked to look at a fixation cross and to keep their eyes open.

The resting brain, however, is not *uniformly* active; rather, various brain regions share correlated activity from time to time. This finding has led to the description of several brain networks, one of which is the *default mode network* (DMN). The picture constructed from fMRI signals reveals that when the brain is at rest, such as when a person is musing or daydreaming, some regions of the brain remain relatively active, whereas other regions are less active. When a person engages in a cognitive task, the pattern of activity changes. This information provides evidence that during "rest," the DMN maintains brain consciousness, whereas during cognitive tasks, other neural networks involved in the specific task become active.

An MRI scanner collects data on brain activity, typically for at least 4-minute blocks. Researchers are attempting to shorten this period by increasing the strength of the static

**resting-state fMRI (rs-fMRI)** Magnetic resonance imaging method that measures changes in oxygenation levels when the individual is resting (not engaged in a specific task).

Figure 2-7 diagrams the extent of the major cerebral arteries.

The default mode network is diagrammed in Figure 8-19.

**FIGURE 7-19 Imaging Changes in Brain Activity** A functional MRI sequence of a horizontal section at the mid-occipital lobe (bottom of each image) in a normal human brain during visual stimulation. A baseline acquired in darkness (far left) was subtracted from the subsequent images. The participant wore tightly fitting goggles containing light-emitting diodes that were turned on and off as a rapid sequence of scans was obtained over a period of 270 seconds. Note the prominent activity in the visual cortex when the light is on and the rapid cessation of activity when the light is off, all measured in the graph of signal intensity below the images.

"Dynamic Magnetic Resonance Imaging of Human Brain Activity During Primary Sensory Stimulation," by K. K. Kwong et al., 1992, Proceedings of the National Academy of Sciences (USA), 89, 5678.

**FIGURE 7-20 How fNIRS Works** Light injected through the scalp and skull penetrates the brain to a depth of about 2 centimeters. A small fraction of the light is reflected and captured by a detector on the scalp surface. Light is reflected from as deep as 2 centimeters but also from the tissue above it, as illustrated by the banana shape of the curves. The photo in Research Focus 7-1 shows fNIRS affixed to an infant. Information from Spinney (2005).

When tagged to a glucose molecule, fluorine-18 ($^{18}$F) acts as a marker for metabolism. The $^{18}$F and $^{15}$O methods are essentially the same.

**positron emission tomography (PET)** Imaging technique that detects changes in blood flow by measuring changes in the uptake of compounds such as oxygen or glucose; used to analyze the metabolic activity of neurons.

magnetic field and developing more sensitive coils. Statistical analysis of the data entails correlating activity in different brain regions over time. Although rs-fMRI is still in its growth phase, investigators have already identified many consistent networks of brain activity and abnormalities in disease states such as schizophrenia (Forlim et al., 2020).

## Optical Tomography

Research Focus 7-1: Tuning in to Language describes a brain-imaging study that used functional near-infrared spectroscopy (fNIRS) to investigate newborns' responses to language. fNIRS is a form of *optical tomography*, a functional imaging technique that operates on the principle that an object can be reconstructed by gathering light transmitted through it. One requirement for using this approach is that the object must at least partially transmit light. Thus, optical tomography can image soft body tissues, such as those in the breast or the brain.

In fNIRS, reflected infrared light is used to determine blood flow because oxygen-rich hemoglobin and oxygen-poor hemoglobin differ in their absorption spectra. By measuring the blood's light absorption, it becomes possible to measure the brain's average oxygen consumption. In essence, then, fNIRS and fMRI measure the same thing but with different tools. In fNIRS, an array of optical transmitter and receiver pairs are fitted across the scalp, as illustrated in **Figure 7-20**.

The obvious advantage of fNIRS is that it is portable, movement tolerant, and safe, allowing the brain activity of participants to be repeatedly recorded over short periods, from infancy to senescence. The disadvantage is that the light does not penetrate far into the brain, so researchers are restricted to measuring cortical activity. The spatial resolution is also not as good as with other noninvasive methods, although fNIRS equipment can now use more than 100 light detectors on the scalp, which allows acceptable spatial resolution in the resulting image. The fNIRS technique can shed light on several aspects of cognition in the developing brain, including object, face, and language processing and functional specialization within the visual, auditory, and sensorimotor systems. Moreover, studies of atypical development using fNIRS, with a focus on executive dysfunction in neurodevelopmental disorders such as autism and attention-deficit/hyperactivity disorder, are providing insights into neurocognitive functions in individuals with these disorders (Pinti et al., 2020).

## Positron Emission Tomography

Researchers use **positron emission tomography (PET)** to study the metabolic activity of brain cells engaged in processing brain functions such as language. PET imaging detects changes in the brain's blood flow by measuring changes in the uptake of compounds such as oxygen and glucose (Posner & Raichle, 1997). A PET camera, like the one shown in **Figure 7-21**, comprises a doughnut-shaped array of radiation detectors that encircles a person's head. A small amount of water labeled with radioactive molecules is injected into the person's bloodstream. These molecules, which include the radioactive isotope oxygen-15 ($^{15}$O), do not pose any danger to the participant because they are very unstable. They break down in just a few minutes and are quickly eliminated from the body. (Most of the oxygen in air we breathe is the stable $^{16}$O molecule.)

Radioactive $^{15}$O molecules release tiny positively charged subatomic particles known as positrons (electrons carrying a positive charge). Positrons are emitted from an unstable atom because the atom is deficient in neutrons. The positrons are attracted to the negatively charged electrons in the brain, and the collision of the two particles leads to annihilation of both, which produces energy.

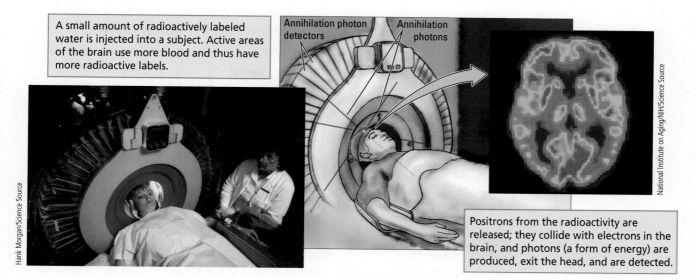

A small amount of radioactively labeled water is injected into a subject. Active areas of the brain use more blood and thus have more radioactive labels.

Annihilation photon detectors

Annihilation photons

Positrons from the radioactivity are released; they collide with electrons in the brain, and photons (a form of energy) are produced, exit the head, and are detected.

**FIGURE 7-21 PET Scanner and Image** The photo on the left shows a participant lying in a PET scanner, whose design is illustrated in the drawing. In the scan to the right, the bright red and yellow areas are regions of high blood flow.

This energy, in the form of two photons (a unit of light energy), leaves the person's head at the speed of light and is detected by the PET camera. The photons leave the head in exactly opposite directions from the site of positron–electron annihilation, so annihilation photon detectors can detect their source, as illustrated in Figure 7-21. A computer identifies the coincident photons and locates the annihilation source to generate the PET image.

The PET system enables the measurement of blood flow in the brain because the unstable radioactive molecules accumulate there in direct proportion to the rate of local blood flow. Local blood flow, in turn, is related to neural activity because potassium ions released from stimulated neurons dilate adjacent blood vessels. The higher the blood flow is, the higher the radiation counts recorded by the PET camera will be.

PET researchers who are studying the link between blood flow and mental activity use a *subtraction procedure*. That is, they subtract the blood-flow pattern when the brain is in a carefully selected control state from the pattern of blood flow imaged when the participant is engaged in the task under study, as illustrated in the top row of **Figure 7-22**. This subtraction process images the change in blood flow between the two states. The change can be averaged across participants (middle row) to yield a representative average image difference that reveals which brain areas are selectively active during the task (bottom). PET does not measure local neural activity directly, but rather infers activity on the assumption that blood flow increases where neuron activity increases.

A significant limitation of PET is that the radiochemicals used in this imaging, including the so-called radiopharmaceuticals used in diagnosing humans, must be prepared in a cyclotron quite close to the scanner because their half-lives are so short that transportation time is a severely limiting factor. Generating these materials is very expensive. Despite the expense, PET has important advantages over other imaging methods:

- PET can detect the decay of hundreds of radiochemicals, which allows the mapping of a wide range of brain changes and conditions, including changes in pH, glucose, oxygen, amino acids, neurotransmitters, and proteins.

- PET can detect relative amounts of a given neurotransmitter, the density of neurotransmitter receptors, and metabolic activities associated with learning, brain poisoning, and degenerative processes that might be related to aging.

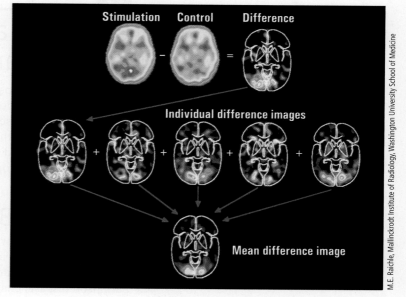

Stimulation    Control    Difference

Individual difference images

Mean difference image

**FIGURE 7-22 The Procedure of Subtraction** In the upper row of scans, the control condition, resting while looking at a static fixation point (control), is subtracted from the experimental condition, looking at a flickering checkerboard (stimulation). The subtraction produces a different scan for each of five experimental participants, shown in the middle row, but all show increased blood flow in the occipital region. The difference scans are averaged to produce the representative image at the bottom.

- PET has been widely used to study cognitive function with great success. For example, PET has confirmed that various brain regions perform different functions.

A variety of hybrid scanners are also available for diagnostic imaging, which come in different combinations—for example, PET with CT, PET with MRI, and PET with MRI and EEG. The advantage of these hybrid scanners is that they can acquire high-quality anatomical images and then overlay the functional/metabolic image information, allowing for precise localization that was not available before—all within a single examination.

Studies of metabolic and functional processes based on brain imaging have led to the construction of detailed brain atlases and extensive data sets. Brain-imaging atlases can represent neural structures and their pathways, neurochemistry, and even active genes. Today, hundreds of data sets compiled from imaging studies are available for use as reference and research sources.

## 7-4 Review

**Before you continue, check your understanding. Answers to Self-Test appear at the back of the book.**

1. The principal methods of functional brain imaging are _____, _____, and _____.

2. PET uses _____ to measure brain processes and to identify _____ changes in the brain.

3. fMRI and optical imaging measure changes in _____.

4. Why are resting-state measurements useful to researchers?

## 7-5

# Chemical and Genetic Measures of Brain and Behavior

**Learning Objectives**
- Explain the benefits of microdialysis and cerebral voltammetry techniques.
- Describe the role of twin studies in research into the genetic components of behavior.
- Define epigenetics, and explain how the study of its effects can inform our understanding of behavior.

Our focus so far has been on how neuroscientists study the individual and collective activity of neurons and how neuronal activity relates to behavior. Neurons are regulated by *genes*, DNA segments that encode the synthesis of particular proteins within cells. Genes control the production of chemicals in a cell, so it is possible to relate behavior to genes and to chemicals inside and outside the cell. Chemical and genetic approaches require sophisticated technologies that have seen major advances in the past two decades.

## Measuring Brain Chemistry

The brain contains a wide mixture of chemicals, ranging from neurotransmitters and hormones to glucose and gases, among many others. Abnormalities in the amounts of these chemicals can cause serious disruptions in behavior. Prime examples are Parkinson disease, characterized by low dopamine levels in the substantia nigra, and depression, correlated with low serotonin and/or noradrenaline production. The simplest way to measure brain chemistry in such diseases is to extract tissue postmortem from affected humans or laboratory animals and undertake traditional biochemical techniques, such as high-performance liquid chromatography (HPLC), to measure specific chemical levels.

Fluctuations in brain chemistry are associated not only with behavioral dysfunction but also with ongoing healthy behavior. For example, research over the past few decades shows that dopamine levels fluctuate in the nucleus accumbens (a structure in the subcortical basal ganglia) in association with stimuli related to rewarding behaviors

Section 3-1 investigates how neurons function. Section 3-3 relates genes to cell function, genetic engineering, and epigenetic mechanisms.

Section 12-7 explores the neural effects of rewarding events.

such as food and sex. Changes in brain chemistry can be measured in freely moving animals using two methods: *cerebral microdialysis* and *cerebral voltammetry*.

**Microdialysis**, which can determine the chemical constituents of extracellular fluid, is widely used in the laboratory; it has also found clinical application over the past 20 years. In this technique, a catheter with a semipermeable membrane at its tip is placed in the brain, as illustrated in **Figure 7-23**. A fluid flows through the cannula and passes along the cell membrane. Simple diffusion drives extracellular molecules across the membrane along their concentration gradient.

Fluid containing the molecules from the brain exits through tubing to be collected for analysis. This fluid is removed at a constant rate so that changes in brain chemistry can be correlated with behavior. For example, if a rat is placed in an environment in which it anticipates sex or a favored food, microdialysis will record an increase in dopamine within the basal ganglia regions of the caudate nucleus and putamen, known as the **striatum**.

Microdialysis is used in some medical centers to monitor chemistry in the injured brain. For example, the effects of TBI or stroke can be worsened by secondary events such as a drastic increase in the neurotransmitter glutamate. Such biochemical changes can lead to irreversible cell damage or death. Physicians use microdialysis to monitor such changes, which can then be treated.

**Cerebral voltammetry** works on a different principle. A small carbon fiber electrode and a metal electrode are implanted in the brain, and a weak current is passed through the metal electrode. The current causes electrons to be added to or removed from the surrounding chemicals. Changes in extracellular levels of specific neurotransmitters can be measured as they occur.

Because different currents lead to changes in different compounds, it is possible to identify levels of different transmitters, such as serotonin or dopamine, and related chemicals. Voltammetry has the advantage of not requiring the chemical analysis of fluid removed from the brain, as microdialysis does, but it has the disadvantage of being destructive. That is, the chemical measurements require the degradation of one chemical into another, making the technology suitable only for scientific studies in nonhuman animals. As an example, Wheeler and colleagues used voltammetry to demonstrate that the stress hormone corticosterone induced an increase in the amount of dopamine as well as how long it was detected in the nucleus accumbens (Wheeler et al., 2017). This finding is important because it provides evidence that stress can potentiate the effect of reinforcers.

# Measuring Genes in Brain and Behavior

Most human behaviors cannot be explained by genetic inheritance alone, but variations in gene sequences do contribute significantly to brain organization. About 1 in 250 live births consists of identical twins, people who share an identical genome. Identical twins often have remarkably similar behavioral traits. For example, twin studies show strong concordance rates that support genetic contributions to drug addiction and other psychiatric disorders. But twin studies also show that environmental factors and life experience must be involved: concordance for most behavioral disorders, such as schizophrenia and depression, is far less than 100%. Life experiences act epigenetically to alter gene expression.

Genetic factors can also be studied by comparing people who were adopted early in life and usually would not have a close genetic relationship to their adoptive parents. Here, a high concordance rate for behavioral traits would imply a strong environmental influence on behavior. Ideally, an investigator would be able to study both the adoptive and biological parents to tease out the relative heritability of behavioral traits.

**FIGURE 7-23  Microdialysis**
Information from Tisdall & Smith (2006).

Section 4-1 explains diffusion and concentration gradients in detail.

Section 6-4 investigates why glutamate and similar chemicals can act as neurotoxins.

**microdialysis** Technique used to determine the chemical constituents of extracellular fluid in freely moving animals.

**striatum** Caudate nucleus and putamen of the basal ganglia.

**cerebral voltammetry** Technique used to identify the concentration of specific chemicals in the brains of animals.

Section 8-2 explains how neurotrophic factors (nourishing chemical compounds) support growth and differentiation in developing neurons.

**Principle 10:** Neuroplasticity is the hallmark of nervous system functioning.

Research Focus 6-3 gives another example of a common brain–behavior disorder, ADHD, with a genetic component.

Sections 2-6 and 5-3 introduce factors that contribute to neurocognitive disorders. Clinical Focus 14-3 describes research, and Section 16-3 examines treatments.

See "A Case of Inheriting Experience" in Section 3-3.

With the development of relatively inexpensive methods of identifying specific genes in people, it is now possible to relate the *alleles* (different forms) of specific genes to behaviors. A gene related to the production of a compound called brain-derived neurotrophic factor (BDNF) is representative. BDNF plays an important role in stimulating neural plasticity, and low levels of BDNF have been correlated with mood disorders such as depression. The two alleles of this gene are *BDNF Val 66Met* and *BDNF Val 66Val*.

Joshua Bueller and his colleagues (2006) showed that the *Met* allele is associated with an 11% reduction in hippocampal volume in healthy participants. Other studies have associated the *Met* allele with poor memory for specific events (*episodic memory*) and a high incidence of dementia later in life. However, the *Val* allele is by no means the preferable variant: although *Val* carriers have better episodic memory, they also have a higher incidence of neuroticism and anxiety disorders. The two alleles produce different phenotypes because they influence brain structure and functions differently. Other genes that were not measured also differed among Bueller's participants and may have contributed to the observed difference.

# Epigenetics: Measuring Gene Expression

An individual's genotype exists in an environmental context fundamental to *gene expression*, the way genes become active (or not). While epigenetic factors do not change the DNA sequence, the genes that are expressed can change dramatically in response to environment and experience. Epigenetic changes can persist throughout a lifetime and even across multiple generations.

Changes in gene expression can result from widely ranging experiences, including chronic stress, traumatic events, drugs, culture, and disease. A study by Mario Fraga and his colleagues (2005) offers a powerful example of gene–experience interactions. These investigators examined epigenetic patterns in 40 pairs of identical twins by measuring two molecular markers related to gene expression.

Although twins' patterns of gene expression were virtually identical when measured in childhood, 50-year-old twins exhibited differences so remarkable as to make them as different epigenetically as young non-twin siblings! The specific cause or causes of such differences are unknown but are thought to be related to lifestyle factors, such as smoking and exercise habits, diet, stressors, drug use, and education, as well as to social experiences, such as marriage and child rearing, among others. The epigenetic drift in the twins supports the findings of less than 100% concordance for diseases in identical twins.

The role of epigenetic differences can also be seen across populations. Moshe Szyf, Michael Meaney, and their colleagues have shown, for instance, that the amount of maternal attention mother rats give to their newborn pups alters the expression of certain genes in the adult hippocampus (Szyf et al., 2008). These genes are related to the infants' stress response when they are adults. (Maternal attention is measured as the amount and type of mother–infant contact; a difference of up to 6 hours per day can exist between attentive and inattentive mothers.)

A subsequent study by the same group (McGowan et al., 2009) examined epigenetic differences in hippocampal tissue obtained from two groups of humans: (1) people with histories of childhood abuse who subsequently died by suicide and (2) people with no childhood abuse who died by suicide or controls who died of other causes. The epigenetic changes found in the group who were abused and died by suicide parallel those found in the rats with inattentive mothers, again suggesting that early experiences can alter hippocampal organization and function via changes in gene expression.

Experience-dependent changes in gene expression are probably found not only in the hippocampus but throughout the brain as well. For example, Richelle Mychasiuk and colleagues (2011) found that stressing pregnant rats led to wide changes in gene expression in their offspring, in both the frontal cortex and the hippocampus. However, there was virtually no overlap in the altered genes in the two brain regions: the same experience changed different brain regions differently.

Epigenetic studies promise to revolutionize our understanding of gene–brain interactions in healthy brain development and brain function. They will also help researchers develop new treatments for neurological disorders. For example, specific epigenetic changes appear to be related to the ability to make a functional recovery after stroke.

The effects and treatments for stroke are discussed in Section 16-3.

## 7-5 Review

**Before you continue, check your understanding. Answers to Self-Test appear at the back of the book.**

1. Concentrations of different chemicals in the brain can be measured in postmortem tissue using a(n) _____ or in vivo using _____ or _____.

2. Gene–environment interactions can be investigated in human populations by comparing _____ of behavioral traits in identical twins and adopted children.

3. The study of genes and behavior focuses on individual differences in _____, whereas the study of epigenetics and behavior examines differences in _____.

4. Describe briefly how epigenetic studies have led to the recognition that life experiences and the environment can alter brain function.

## 7-6

# Comparing Neuroscience Research Methods

We have considered a wide range of research methods for manipulating and measuring brain–behavior interactions. **Tables 7-2** and **7-3** summarize these methods, including the goals and examples for each method. How do researchers choose among the various options? Their main consideration is their research question. Ultimately, that question is behavioral, but many steps lie along the route to understanding behavior.

**Learning Objective**
• Summarize some of the challenges in studying human behavior and the ways various methods of brain manipulation and imaging help overcome those challenges.

**TABLE 7-2** Manipulating Brain and Behavior

| Method | Experimental goal | Examples |
|---|---|---|
| Whole-animal manipulations (Section 7-1) | Determine how an environmental condition affects brain and behavior | Diet, exercise, social interactions, sensory stimulation, drug usage |
| Brain lesions, permanent (Section 7-1) | Remove or destroy neural tissue to observe behavioral changes | Knife cuts or aspirations, electrolytic lesions, neurotoxic lesions, high-intensity focused ultrasound |
| Brain lesions, temporary and reversible (Section 7-1) | Short-term silencing of neural tissue to observe behavioral changes | Regional cooling to arrest synaptic transmission, delivery of an agonist for GABA through a cannula to increase local inhibition |
| Genetic lesions (Section 3-3; Section 7-1) | Remove genetic material | Knockout technology, CRISPR |
| Genetic stimulation (Section 3-3) | Add genetic material | Knock-in technology |
| Drug manipulations (Section 7-1) | Determine receptor system's role in the central nervous system | Use drugs to activate (agonists) or inactivate (antagonists) a receptor system |
| Electrical and magnetic stimulation (Section 7-1) | Excite tissue activity | DBS, TMS |
| Optogenetics (Section 7-1) | Use light to activate specific ion channels and relate to behavior | Insertion of specific light-sensitive proteins (e.g., GRAB technology) |
| Chemogenetics (Section 7-1) | Use specific synthetic drugs to activate designer receptors | Insertion of specific G protein–coupled receptors |

**TABLE 7-3** Measuring Brain and Behavior

| Method | Experimental goal | Examples |
|---|---|---|
| Behavioral analysis (Section 7-1) | Observe behavior; generate tests to allow people and lab animals to demonstrate behavioral capacities | Naturalistic observation; tests, mazes; automated touchscreen platform |
| Tissue analysis (Section 7-1) | Identify cell types and connections; identify disease states | Stains |
| Record electrical and magnetic activity (Section 7-2) | Measure action potentials from individual neurons; measure graded potentials to assess the coordinated activity of thousands of neurons; measure magnetic fields | Single-cell recording; EEG, ERP; MEG |
| Anatomical brain imaging (Section 7-3) | Noninvasive examination of brain structures | X-ray; CT; MRI; DTI |
| Functional brain imaging (Section 7-4) | Measure brain activity as specific behaviors are performed | Miniscopes; fMRI; fNIRS; MRS; PET |
| In vivo chemistry (Section 7-5) | Relate fluctuations in transmitter release to behavior | HPLC; microdialysis, voltammetry |
| Genetics (Section 7-5) | Determine presence of a gene and its products | DNA, RNA, protein analysis |
| Epigenetics (Section 7-5) | Discover effect of experience on gene expression, brain, and behavior | Gene expression analysis |

Some researchers focus on *morphology* (structure) in postmortem tissue. This approach allows detailed analysis of both macro and micro structure, depending on the method chosen. Identifying brain pathology, as in Parkinson disease, can lead to insights about the causes and nature of a disorder.

Other investigators focus more on the ways neurons generate electrical activity in relation to behavior or on functional changes in brain activity during specific types of cognitive processing. Both approaches are legitimate: the goal is gaining an understanding of brain–behavior relationships.

But investigators must consider practical issues, too. Temporal resolution (how quickly the measurement or image is obtained), spatial resolution (the accuracy of localization in the brain), and the degree of invasiveness are all pertinent concerns. In addition, it is not feasible to consider MRI-based methods for studies of very young children because they have difficulty remaining absolutely still for long periods.

Similarly, studies of individuals with brain injuries must take into account factors such as the person's ability to maintain attention for long periods—during neuropsychological testing or imaging studies, for example. In addition, practical problems such as motor or language impairment may limit the types of methods that researchers can use.

Of course, cost is also an ever-present practical consideration. Studying brain and behavior linkages by perturbing the brain is generally less costly than some imaging methods, many of which require expensive machinery. EEG, ERP, and fNIRS are noninvasive and relatively inexpensive to set up (less than $100,000 each). MRI-based methods, MEG, and PET are considerably more expensive (more than $2 million each), so they are typically found only in large research centers or hospitals. Similarly, epigenetic studies can be very expensive if investigators consider the entire genome in a large number of biological samples.

## 7-6 Review

Before you continue, check your understanding. Answers to Self-Test appear at the back of the book.

1. Neuroscience measurements and imaging vary along the dimensions _____, _____, and _____.

2. Relative to the expense of fMRI and PET imaging, noninvasively perturbing the brain using methods such as _____ or administering neuropsychological testing is much less expensive.

3. A researcher is interested in the relationship between dopamine levels in the nucleus accumbens and drug taking. What method(s) could they use to determine this relationship?

**computational neuroscience** Quantitative approach using biologically plausible mathematical models to mimic the development, structure, physiology, and cognitive abilities of the nervous system in an effort to better understand them; also called *mathematical neuroscience*.

# Computational Neuroscience and Deep Learning

Practitioners in the field of **computational neuroscience** are interested in using biologically plausible mathematical models to understand the brain at different levels of organization—from single channels and single neurons to simple and complex circuits and entire structures to cognitive abilities. Computational neuroscience applies mathematical modeling and analysis to understand the principles that govern the development, structure, physiology, and cognitive abilities of the nervous system by mimicking its architecture. The term *mathematical neuroscience* is sometimes used synonymously with computational neuroscience, to stress the quantitative nature of this field.

Computational neuroscience integrates the seminal findings of several key figures from the past century. In the early twentieth century, Louis Lapicque introduced the simplistic "integrate and fire model" of neurons, whereby a neuron receives input from several other neurons and then creates an output. In the 1950s, Hodgkin and Huxley proposed their biophysical model, which described this output (the action potential) in mathematical terms. A decade later, Hubel and Wiesel proposed that each cortical neuron could be thought of as a feature detector that fires when its preferred feature (the stimulus) surpasses a given threshold. The specifics of the feature detected by each neuron are determined by the connectivity of earlier neurons in the circuit. When Hubel and Wiesel recorded signals from cells in the visual cortex, they found that the features detected became more complex as they moved synaptically farther away from the retina. Based on this observation, they postulated that there would be a cell in some area of your brain that would fire only to the specific visual representation of your grandmother—dubbed the "grandmother cell."

Shortly after Hubel and Wiesel introduced their innovative model of the action of neurons within a neural circuit, David Marr proposed a new computational approach for determining how functional groups of neurons within the hippocampus and neocortex interact to store, process, and transmit information. Computational models are used to frame hypotheses that can be directly tested with biological or psychological experiments, and in this way computational neuroscience and neuroscience can inform each other and grow as a result.

*Deep learning* is a subdiscipline of computational neuroscience based on artificial neural networks that can learn with training. Intelligent agents perceive their environment and move or communicate (that is, they act or behave) to maximize their chances of achieving their goals. *Natural intelligence* is displayed by animals based on their senses, neural circuitry, motor systems and plasticity. *Artificial intelligence* (AI), in contrast, is demonstrated by machines. **Figure 7-24** represents the hierarchy of this discipline.

The simple, classic architecture of intelligence is depicted in **Figure 7-25**. Three layers in this architecture loosely model neurons: an input layer (on the left), a hidden layer of neurons (middle), and an output layer (on the right). The input layers make synaptic connections with the hidden layer, and the weightings of those synaptic connections change as the network learns and the learning is fueled by data. Deep learning networks learn from their world in much the same way that infants do, so that they gradually acquire the skills needed to navigate novel environments.

Applications of deep learning have made possible innovations in self-driving cars, language translation, facial recognition, legal discovery, and cancer diagnosis. Deep learning models have also beaten the world's grand masters at strategy games such as Go, chess, and poker. Using multiple levels of neural networks, computers now have the capacity to see, learn, and react to complex situations as well or better than humans. Many businesses are already delivering new products and services based on deep learning and related technologies, and most industries will likely be impacted by deep learning in the years to come.

**Learning Objectives**
- Define computational neuroscience, and explain how models derived from computational techniques can be used to study neural systems.
- Describe some applications of deep learning and artificial intelligence and some of the concerns associated with this work.

**Principle 1:** Neuronal circuits are the functional units of the nervous system.

Hodgkin and Huxley's work is described in Section 4-1. Hubel and Wiesel's work is covered in Section 9-6.

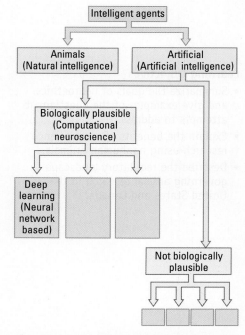

**FIGURE 7-24 Schema of Intelligent Agents** There are two categories of intelligent agents. Artificial intelligence is either biologically plausible or not. Deep learning is artificial but neural-network based and therefore biologically plausible. There are more non-biologically plausible than biologically plausible forms of artificial intelligence.

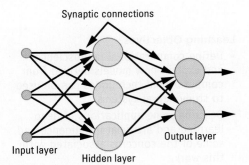

**FIGURE 7-25 Architecture of Deep Learning Intelligence** The basic architecture of a fully connected deep learning circuit has, at a minimum, an input layer, a hidden layer, and an output layer. As the network learns, the connection weights (represented there by arrow heads) change.

In his book *The Deep Learning Revolution*, Terrence J. Sejnowski (2018) expresses his desire to reverse-engineer the brain: "Nature may be cleverer than we are individually, but I see no reason why we, as a species, cannot someday solve the puzzle of intelligence" (p. 267). The evolution from the first organic compounds to intelligent humans took 3.5 billion of years; deep learning is on a trajectory measured in decades. However, there are risks to these advances: artificial neural nets are often so complex that we cannot understand their decisions in relatable terms and are therefore limited in our ability to control them, AI machines can be used to perpetuate discrimination if trained on biased data, and AI could be used for autonomous military applications.

In her book *Gods and Robots: Myths, Machines, and Ancient Dreams of Technology*, science historian Adrienne Mayor (2018) explains that over the last 2500 years people told tales of autonomous machines that could labor, entertain, kill, and seduce. Movies such as *Terminator, Blade Runner, The Matrix*, and *Ex Machina* present in dramatic terms similar stories of artificial life that threatens human existence. Of course, we humans have been harming ourselves without artificial help for a long time, and—at least so far—the benefits of deep learning appear to outweigh the risks.

## 7-7 Review

Before you continue, check your understanding. Answers to Self-Test appear at the back of the book.

1. There are two forms of intelligent agents: _____ and _____.

2. Computational neuroscience uses a quantitative approach with _____ plausible models that mimic the _____, _____, _____, and _____ of the nervous system in an effort to better understand them.

3. What are some potential applications of deep learning? What concerns might be related to these applications?

### Learning Objectives

- Summarize the goals of neuroethics, and give examples of the questions it attempts to address.
- Explain the benefits of neuroscience research using nonhuman animals.
- Describe the regulatory landscape governing animal research in the United States and Canada.

## 7-8

# Ethical Considerations

Before we conclude our discussion of the tools neuroscientists use to understand brain and behaviors, let's consider two areas of study that attempt to set the parameters for how we use those tools: neuroethics and the ethical treatment of nonhuman animals in research.

## Neuroethics

In this chapter, we have encountered some of the powerful technologies that have been developed to study brain and behavior. As technological progress allows us to develop increasingly more precise and predictive models to describe groups and individuals, we are faced with some important ethical considerations—questions such as "Should we predict who will develop autism, who will commit crimes, or who is lying?", "Should we influence and enhance a person's behavior, or even control it?", and "What are the neural substrates of sociality, morals, and values?"

**Neuroethics** is the branch of neuroscience that considers and researches these sorts of questions. It can be characterized as the study of the ethical issues arising from what we can do to the brain technologically and in a clinical setting and how we use what we have learned and know about the brain.

While many of the basic questions addressed by neuroethics are not new, formal research and published literature under the neuroethics umbrella generally extend over the last 15 years. Today, neuroethics courses are being taught at many universities and professional societies. Neuroethics is a recognized central aspect of neuroscience because it both anticipates and addresses ethical questions raised by emerging

**neuroethics** Discipline concerned with the ethics of medical and biological research, which also incorporates the meaning of being human from the perspective of philosophy of mind, psychology, theology, and law.

neuroscience developments, so it can be used to guide basic research and the translation and application of that research into the clinical setting.

# Using Nonhuman Species in Brain–Behavior Research

A complete understanding of brain–behavior relationships is limited in part by the ethical constraints placed on experimentation with both humans and nonhuman species. Most countries decide independently which experimental practices are acceptable for humans, for other vertebrates, and for invertebrate species. In general, fewer experimental methods are acceptable for use on humans than are employed on our most closely related primate relatives. Thus, as in most new treatments in medicine, a wide variety of nonhuman species are used to develop and test treatments for human neurological or psychiatric disorders before those interventions are tested on humans.

Although the human brain and the nonhuman brain have obvious differences with respect to language, the general organization of the brain across mammalian species is remarkably similar, and the functioning of basic neural circuits in nonhuman mammals appears to generalize to humans. Thus, neuroscientists use widely varying animal species to model human brain diseases as well as to infer typical human brain functioning.

Two important issues arise with use of animal models to develop treatments for brain and behavioral disorders. The first is whether animals actually display neurological diseases in ways similar to humans. The second involves the ethics of using animals in research. We consider each separately.

## Benefits of Animal Models of Disease

Some disorders—stroke, for example—seem relatively easy to model in laboratory animals because it is possible to interrupt blood supply to a brain area and induce injury and consequent behavioral change. However, it is far more difficult to determine whether human behavioral disorders can actually be induced in laboratory animals. Consider *attention-deficit/hyperactivity disorder* (*ADHD*), a developmental disorder characterized by the core behavioral symptoms of impulsivity, hyperactivity, and/or inattention. The most common issue for children with ADHD is problems at school. Lab animals such as rats and mice do not go to school, so how can researchers model ADHD in rodents?

ADHD has proved difficult to treat in children, and interest in developing an animal model is high. One way to proceed is to take advantage of the normal variance in the performance of rats on a variety of tests of working memory and cognitive functioning—tests that require attentional processes. The idea is that we can think of ADHD in people or in rats as one extreme on a spectrum of behaviors that are part of a normal distribution in the general population. Many studies show that treating rats with the dopaminergic agonist methylphenidate (Ritalin), a commonly used treatment for children diagnosed with ADHD, actually improves the performance of rats that do poorly on tests requiring attentional processes.

One rat strain, the Kyoto SHR rat, has proved an especially good model for ADHD and is widely used in the lab. This strain presents known abnormalities in prefrontal dopaminergic innervation that correlate with behavioral abnormalities such as hyperactivity. Dopaminergic abnormalities are believed to be one underlying symptom of ADHD in children. Methylphenidate can reverse behavioral abnormalities, both in children with ADHD and in the SHR rats.

## Animal Welfare and Scientific Experimentation

Use of nonhuman animals in scientific research has a long history, but only in the past century have ethical issues surrounding animal research drawn considerable attention and laws been instituted to limit such research. Just as the scientific community has

The National Institutes of Health's BRAIN Initiative is an ambitious funding project supporting hundreds of neuroscience research projects, including a number of complementary neuroethics research projects.

Clinical Focus 6-1 describes the illicit use of prescription ADHD medications to boost performance at school and at work. Section 15-2 explores the nature of attention and disorders that result in deficits of attention.

Many of the experiments presented in this text predate current ethical standards. Bartholow's brain stimulation (Section 4-1) and the volunteers in prison research (Experiment 6-1) are examples.

established ethical standards for research on humans, it has also developed regulations governing experimentation on animals. The governments of most developed nations regulate the use of animals in research; most states, territories, and provinces within a country have passed additional legislation dealing with this topic. Universities engaged in research have their own rules governing animal use, as do professional societies of scientists and the journals in which they publish.

Here are four principles used as guidelines in Canada for reviewing experimental and teaching protocols that will use animals:

1. The use of animals in research, teaching, and testing is acceptable only if it promises to contribute to the understanding of environmental principles or issues, fundamental biological principles, or development of knowledge that can reasonably be expected to benefit humans, animals, or the environment.

2. Optimal standards for animal health and care result in enhanced credibility and reproducibility of experimental results.

3. Acceptance of animal use in science critically depends on maintaining public confidence in the mechanisms and processes used to ensure necessary, humane, and justified animal use.

4. Animals are used only if the researcher's best efforts to find an alternative have failed. Researchers who use animals employ the most humane methods on the smallest number of appropriate animals required to obtain valid information.

Legislation concerning the care and use of laboratory animals in the United States is set forth in the Animal Welfare Act, which includes laws passed by Congress in 1966, 1970, 1976, and 1985. Legislation in other countries is similar to that of the United States, and in some European countries, it is much stricter. The U.S. act covers mammals, including rats, mice, cats, dogs, and primates, and birds, but excludes farm animals that are not used in research. The U.S. Department of Agriculture (USDA) administers the act through inspectors in the Animal Care section of the Animal and Plant Health Inspection Service.

In addition, the Office of Human Research Protections of the National Institutes of Health (NIH) administers the Health Research Extension Act (passed in 1986). This act covers all animal uses conducted or supported by the U.S. Public Health Service and applies to any live vertebrate animal used in research, training, or testing. Each institution must provide acceptable assurance that it meets all minimum regulations and conforms with *The Guide for the Care and Use of Laboratory Animals* (National Research Council, 2011) before conducting any activity that includes animals. The typical method for demonstrating conformance with the guide is to seek voluntary accreditation from the Association for Assessment and Accreditation of Laboratory Animal Care International, a private, nonprofit organization that promotes the humane treatment of animals.

All accredited U.S. and Canadian universities that receive government grant support are required to provide adequate treatment for all vertebrate animals. Reviews and specific protocols for vertebrates, including fish, amphibians, reptiles, birds, and mammals, to be used in research, teaching, or testing are administered through the same process. Anyone using animals in a U.S. or Canadian university must submit a protocol for the proposed research to the university's institutional animal care and use committee, which is composed of researchers, veterinarians, people who have some knowledge of science, and laypeople from the university and the community.

Companies that use animals for research are not required to follow this process. However, if they do not, they will be unable to publish the results of their research—because journals require that research conform to the national guidelines on animal care. In addition, discoveries made using animals will not be recognized by the government agencies that approve drugs for clinical trials with humans if the researchers do not follow the prescribed process in making those discoveries. To avoid these problems, companies can follow Good Laboratory Practice (GLP) standards, which are as rigorous as those used by government agencies.

Researchers are expected to consider alternatives to procedures that may cause more than momentary or slight pain or distress to animals. Most of the attention on alternatives has focused on the use of animals in testing and stems from high public awareness of some tests for pharmacological compounds, especially toxic compounds. In the United States, the National Institute of Environmental Health Sciences now regulates testing of such compounds.

Despite the legislation related to animal use, some controversy persists over the use of animals in scientific research. Advocates at one extreme approve of any usage, whereas those at the other extreme disapprove of using animals for any form of research. Most practitioners fall somewhere in between. This wide-ranging debate touches on issues of philosophy, law, morals, custom, and biology.

The issues in this debate are important to researchers in many branches of science who experiment with animals to understand the functions of the human and non-human body, brain, and behavior. They are also important to the human and veterinary medicine that can benefit from this research, as well as to people and other animals with diseases or damage to the nervous system. And they are important to those who are philosophically opposed to using animals for work or food. Finally, because you, as a student, will encounter many experiments on animals in this book, these issues are important to you as well.

## 7-8 Review

**Before you continue, check your understanding. Answers to Self-Test appear at the back of the book.**

1. _____ is a subdiscipline in neuroscience that explores ethical considerations related to research techniques, clinical practices, and the use of data and knowledge derived from neuroscience.

2. Laboratory animals can model some disorders, such as stroke, but are not as useful for modeling most _____ disorders, such as ADHD, because it is more difficult to re-create the human-specific conditions for these disorders.

3. Legislation governing the care and use of laboratory animals used in the United States was set forth in the _____.

4. List some of the reasons for conducting scientific research in animals.

5. What types of questions related to neuroscience research are addressed by neuroethics?

# Summary

## 7-1 Measuring and Manipulating Brain and Behavior

The brain's primary function is to produce behavior, so the fundamental research technique in behavioral neuroscience is to study the direct relationship between brain and behavior. Investigators study healthy humans and other animals as well as human patients and laboratory animals with neurological problems.

Initially, scientists simply observed behavior, but later they developed neuropsychological testing measures designed to study specific functions such as fine movements, memory, and emotion. Today, researchers correlate these behavioral outcomes with anatomical, physiological, chemical, genetic, and other molecular measures of brain organization.

Brain and behavioral relationships can be manipulated by altering brain function, either permanently or temporarily. Permanent changes involve damaging the brain directly by ablation or with neurotoxins that remove or destroy brain tissue. Transient changes in brain activity can be induced either by use of a mild electrical or magnetic current, as in DBS or TMS, or by administration of drugs. The synthetic biology technique CRISPR-Cas9 uses the Cas9 protein in bacteria to cut and replace a sequence of DNA of any cell. Optogenetics, a transgenic technique, employs light-activated ion channels to excite or inhibit targeted cells in living tissue. Chemogenetic stimulation combines designer receptors and synthetic drugs to excite targeted cells in living tissue.

## 7-2 Measuring the Brain's Electrical Activity

Recordings from single or multiple cells show that neurons fire in specific patterns and that cortical neurons are organized into functional groups that work as coordinated networks. Neurons in sensory areas respond to specific characteristics of stimuli, such as color or pitch. Other neurons, such as place cells in the hippocampal formation, can code for more complex information, such as an object's location in space.

Electroencephalographic or magnetoencephalographic recordings measure electrical or magnetic activity from thousands of neurons at once. EEG can reveal a gross relationship between brain and behavior, as when a person is alert and displays the beta-wave pattern versus when the person is resting or sleeping, indicated by the slower alpha-wave patterns. Event-related potentials tell us that even though the entire brain is active during waking, certain parts are momentarily much more active than others. ERP records how the location of increased activity changes as information moves from one brain area to another.

EEG and ERP are noninvasive methods that record information from electrodes on the scalp; in the case of MEG, magnetic detectors above the head are used. Electrocorticography, by contrast, records information via electrodes attached directly to the cortex. ECoG and single-cell recording techniques are invasive.

## 7-3 Anatomical Imaging Techniques: CT and MRI

Computed tomography (CT) and magnetic resonance imaging (MRI) are sensitive to the density of brain structures, ventricles, nuclei, and pathways. CT is a form of three-dimensional X-ray, whereas MRI works on the principle that hydrogen atoms behave like spinning bar magnets in the presence of a magnetic field.

Although CT scans are quicker and less expensive to perform, MRI provides exceptionally clear images, both of nuclei and of fiber pathways in the brain. MRI also indicates that people's brain structure varies widely. Both CT and MRI can be used to assess brain damage from neurological disease or injury, but MRI is more useful as a research tool.

Diffusion tensor imaging is a form of MRI that makes it possible to identify normal or abnormal fiber tracts and myelin in the brain. Magnetic resonance spectroscopy (MRS), another form of MRI, permits practitioners to detect brain metabolites, such as those produced following concussion.

## 7-4 Functional Brain Imaging

Metabolic imaging shows that any behavior requires the collaboration of widespread neural circuits. Positron emission tomography records blood-flow and other metabolic changes in periods measured in minutes; it requires complex subtraction procedures and the averaging of responses across multiple subjects. Records of blood flow obtained using functional magnetic resonance imaging can be combined with anatomical MRI images to locate changes in an individual brain and to complement ERP results. Resting-state fMRI allows investigators to measure connectivity across brain regions.

Functional near-infrared spectroscopy is the form of optical tomography typically used for functional brain-imaging studies. It works on the principle that an object, including brain tissue, can be reconstructed by gathering light transmitted through the object. fNIRS is much simpler to use than PET or fMRI, but because light does not penetrate very far into the brain, it can be used only to study cortical function.

## 7-5 Chemical and Genetic Measures of Brain and Behavior

Analysis of changes in both genes and neurochemicals provides insight into the molecular correlates of behavior. Although genes code all the information needed to construct and regulate cells, epigenetic research reveals that the environment and life experiences can modify gene expression. Even identical twins, who have an identical genome at birth, have widely differing patterns of gene expression and very different brains in adulthood.

## 7-6 Comparing Neuroscience Research Methods

The main consideration in neuroscience research is matching the question being posed with the appropriate methodologies to best answer that question. Whatever the approach, the goal is to understand brain–behavior relationships. Tables 7-2 and 7-3 on page 240 summarize the manipulations and measurements used in behavioral neuroscience. Among all the practical issues of measurement resolution and invasiveness, cost is often the ultimate consideration.

## 7-7 Computational Neuroscience and Deep Learning

Computational neuroscience uses a quantitative approach with biologically plausible models that mimic the development, structure, physiology, and cognitive abilities of the nervous system in an effort to better understand them. Deep learning is a subdiscipline of computational neuroscience based on artificial neural networks that can learn with training. Deep learning is behind self-driving cars, language translation, facial recognition, and cancer diagnosis innovations, and has been applied to beat the world's grand masters at strategy games such as Go, chess, and poker.

## 7-8 Ethical Considerations

Neuroethics is a discipline concerned with the ethics of medical and biological research, which also incorporates the meaning of being human from the perspective of philosophy of mind, psychology, theology, and law. Research aimed at better understanding function in both the healthy brain and the disordered brain often benefits from the use of animal models. Investigators can develop animal models to manipulate the brain, thereby determining how experiential factors and neurological treatments affect brain function.

Because animal subjects cannot protect themselves from abuse, governments and researchers have cooperated to develop ethical guidelines for the use of laboratory animals. These guidelines are designed to ensure that discomfort is minimized, as is the number of animals used for invasive procedures.

# Key Terms

alpha rhythm, p. 227

behavioral neuroscience, p. 216

cerebral voltammetry, p. 237

chemogenetics, p. 224

compensation, p. 221

computational neuroscience, p. 240

computed tomography (CT), p. 229

deep-brain stimulation (DBS), p. 222

diffusion tensor imaging (DTI), p. 230

electrocorticography (ECoG), p. 226

event-related potential (ERP), p. 228

functional magnetic resonance imaging (fMRI), p. 232

functional near-infrared spectroscopy (fNIRS), p. 212

induced pluripotent stem cells (iPSCs), p. 225

magnetic resonance imaging (MRI), p. 230

magnetic resonance spectroscopy (MRS), p. 232

magnetoencephalogram (MEG), p. 229

microdialysis, p. 237

neuroethics, p. 242

neuropsychology, p. 213

optogenetics, p. 223

organoid, p. 225

personalized medicine, p. 225

place cells, p. 226

positron emission tomography (PET), p. 234

resting-state fMRI (rs-fMRI), p. 233

stereotaxic apparatus, p. 221

striatum, p. 237

synthetic biology, p. 223

transcranial magnetic stimulation (TMS), p. 222

# Selected Resources from

**Neuroscience in Action:** Looking Inside: Techniques in Neuroscience

**Concept Practice:** Scanning the Brain

**Videos**

Neuroimaging Techniques

Functional Imaging Techniques

**LearningCurve**

**Practice Quiz**

# 8

# How Does the Nervous System Develop and Adapt?

Aynur_sib/Getty Images

## ⊙ RESEARCH FOCUS 8-1

# Linking Socioeconomic Status to Cortical Development

Nobel Prize–winning American economist James Heckman has argued passionately about one effective strategy for economic growth: investing as early as possible in families in low-income brackets promotes optimal development of young children at risk. Heckman notes that children from families in lower socioeconomic (SES) levels typically develop gaps in knowledge and ability relative to their peers from families with higher incomes.

These gaps influence health and prosperity, and they persist throughout life. Childhood SES correlates with cognitive development, language, memory, social and emotional processing, and ultimately income and health in adulthood. One reason for this linkage: early experiences related to SES influence children's cerebral development.

To examine cerebral development, neuroimaging studies visualize differences in brain development that relate to growing up in under-resourced environments. As the brain grows throughout childhood and adolescence, the cortical surface area expands before declining in adulthood (Schnack et al., 2014; also see Figure 8-14). Cortical surface area reflects the amount of neural tissue available for producing different behaviors and correlates positively with cognitive ability. It should be possible to estimate the effect of early experiences on brain and behavioral development by comparing the cortical surface area and cognitive abilities of people raised in lower- or higher-SES families.

Kimberly Noble and her colleagues (2015) used neuroimaging to investigate the relationship between SES and cortical surface area in more than 1000 participants ages 3 to 20. As shown in the illustration, lower family income, independent of race or sex, was associated with decreased cortical surface area in widespread regions of the frontal, temporal, and parietal lobes (the regions shown in red in the figure). A follow-up study by the same group found SES moderates patterns of age-related cortical thinning, especially in language-related cortical regions (Piccolo et al., 2016).

The investigators also measured participants' cognitive performance on tests of attention, memory, vocabulary, and reading. The larger the cortical surface area, the better the test outcomes were. The negative effects of low SES were especially dramatic at the lower end of the family income spectrum, in families with annual incomes less than $30,000. Follow-up studies by Noble's group have also shown that lower SES is associated with reduced white-matter volume and reduced cognitive flexibility, as well as age-related differences in cortical thickness (see the review by Noble & Giebler, 2020).

Patricia Kuhl (2011) has made the important point that SES itself is not the variable that drives the effects on language and brain development. Rather, SES is likely a proxy for the opportunity to learn language.

Low SES is associated with poor nutrition, high stress, and insufficient prenatal and infant care. According to Heckman's thesis, investing in educational opportunities for children from families with low incomes will increase societal health and prosperity because these children can optimize their brain development and realize their developmental potential. Policies aimed toward decreasing poverty and teaching parents how to improve language skills in their children can lead to clear improvements in children's cognitive and brain development (a benefit further detailed in Section 8-4).

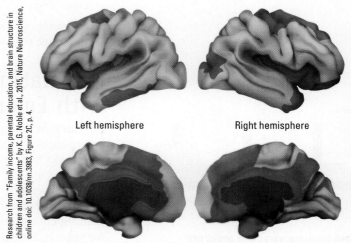

Research from "Family income, parental education, and brain structure in children and adolescents" by K. G. Noble et al., 2015, Nature Neuroscience, online doi: 10.1038/nn.3983, Figure 2C, p. 4.

Left hemisphere    Right hemisphere

After adjusting for age, sex, race, and parental education, Noble and colleagues (2015) associated family income with cortical surface area. Areal brain regions shown in red were significantly smaller in children from families in a low-SES bracket.

To see how scientists go about studying the interconnected processes of brain and behavioral development, think about all the architectural parallels between how the brain is constructed and how a house is built. House plans are drawn as blueprints; the plans for a brain are encoded in genes. Architects do not specify every detail in a blueprint, nor do genes include every instruction for brain assembly and wiring.

The brain is too complex to be encoded entirely and precisely in genes. This leaves the fate of billions of brain cells partly undecided, especially in regard to the massive undertaking of forming appropriate connections between cells.

If the structure and fate of each brain cell are not specified in advance, what controls brain development? Many factors are at work, and, as with house building, brain development is influenced by the environment during the course of the construction phase and by the quality of the materials. For example, as we saw in Research Focus 8-1, Linking Socioeconomic Status to Cortical Development, factors related to living in poverty can compromise children's brain development.

We can shed light on nervous system development by viewing its architecture from different vantage points—structural, functional, and environmental. In this chapter, we consider the neurobiology of development first, then explore behavioral correlates of developing brain functions next, and finally consider how experiences and environments influence neuroplasticity over the life span.

## 8-1

# Three Perspectives on Brain Development

Brain and behavior develop apace, a fact that has prompted scientists to reason that the two are closely linked. Events that alter behavioral development should similarly alter the brain's structural development, and vice versa. As the brain develops, neurons become ever more intricately connected, and these increasingly complex interconnections underlie increasingly complex behaviors. These observations enable neuroscientists to study the relationship between brain and behavioral development from three perspectives:

1. Structural development can be correlated with emerging behaviors.

2. Behavioral development can be predicted by the underlying circuitry that must be emerging.

3. Research can focus on factors such as hormones, injury, or variables related to socio-economic status (SES) that influence both brain structure and behavioral development.

## Correlating Emerging Brain Structures with Emerging Behaviors

We can look at the nervous system's structural development and correlate it with the emergence of specific behaviors. For example, the development of certain brain structures links to the motor development of, say, grasping or crawling in infants. As brain structures mature, their functions emerge and develop, as manifested in the behaviors we can observe.

Neural structures that develop quickly—the visual system, for instance—exhibit their functions sooner than do structures that develop more slowly, such as those used for speech. Because the human brain continues to develop well into adulthood, some abilities emerge or mature rather late. Some cognitive behaviors controlled by the frontal lobes are among the last to develop. One such behavior, the ability to plan efficiently, is a skill vital to many complexities of life, including organizing daily activities and making travel plans.

The Tower of Hanoi test, illustrated in **Figure 8-1**, shows how planning skills can be measured in the laboratory. In this test, the task is to plan how to move colored discs one by one, in the minimum number of moves, from one configuration to another. Most 10-year-olds can solve simple configurations, but more difficult versions of the task, such as that shown in Figure 8-1, cannot be performed efficiently until about age 15 to 17. No surprise, then, that adolescents often appear disorganized: their ability to plan has yet to mature.

Mature adults with acquired frontal lobe injuries also fail to perform well on the Tower of Hanoi test. Such evidence reinforces the idea that children are not miniature adults who simply need to learn the "rules" of adult behavior. A child's brain is vastly different from an adult's, and the brains of children at different ages are not really comparable to each other, either.

GOAL

Move discs on towers below one by one to match goal above.

**FIGURE 8-1 Testing Cognitive Development** The Tower of Hanoi is a mathematical puzzle consisting of three rods and several different-sized discs. The task is to match the goal in as few moves as possible, while obeying two rules: (1) only one disc may be moved at a time and (2) no disc may be placed on top of a smaller disc.

## Correlating Emerging Behaviors with Neural Maturation

We can turn our focus around and scrutinize behavior for the emergence of new abilities, from which we can then infer underlying neural maturation. For example, as language emerges in a young child, we would expect to find corresponding changes in the neural structures that control language. In fact, neuroscientists do find such changes.

At birth, children do not speak, and even extensive training would not enable them to do so because the neural structures that control language production are not yet ready to carry out this task. Thus, as spoken language emerges, the speech-related structures in the brain are undergoing the necessary maturation to support that behavior.

The same reasoning can be applied to frontal lobe development. As the frontal lobe structures mature through adolescence and into early adulthood, we look for related changes in behavior. We can also do the reverse: because we observe new abilities emerging in the teenage years and even later, we infer that they must be controlled by late-maturing neural structures and connections.

## Identifying Influences on Brain and Behavior

The third approach to developmental interrelations between brain and behavior is to identify and study factors that influence both. From this perspective, the mere emergence of a fully developed brain structure is not enough to explain the ensuing behaviors. That is, we must also know the events that shape how that structure functions and produces behaviors. Some events that influence brain function are sensory experience, injuries, the actions of hormones and genes, and factors related to SES.

Logically, if one factor influences behavior, then the brain structures changed by that factor are the ones responsible for the behavioral outcomes. For example, we might study how the atypical secretion of a hormone affects both a certain brain structure and a certain behavior. We can then infer that because the observed behavior results from the change in brain structure functioning, the structure must typically play some role in controlling the behavior. For example, the presence of testosterone in early development typically occurs only in males and results in changes in the organization and function of specific hypothalamic nuclei. But if the amount of testosterone release is low or if the release occurs at a different developmental time in males, or, alternatively, occurs in females, the structure of the hypothalamus may be altered. Consequently, sexual preference and perhaps gender identity may also be changed.

Language development is described in detail in Section 8-3; the anatomical structures related to language are detailed in Section 10-4.

Section 12-5 offers a detailed discussion of the mechanisms that control nonregulatory behavior, including sexual behavior.

## 8-1 Review

**Before you continue, check your understanding. Answers to the Self-Test appear at the back of the book.**

1. Structural brain development is correlated with the emergence of _____.

2. Behavioral development predicts the maturation of _____.

3. List three factors that influence brain function.

4. What important constraint determines when behaviors emerge?

## 8-2

# Neurobiology of Development

Some 2000 years ago, the Roman philosopher Seneca the Younger proposed that a human embryo is an adult in miniature, such that the task of development is simply to grow bigger. This idea of *preformation* was so appealing that it was widely believed for centuries. Even with the development of the microscope, the appeal of preformation proved so strong that biologists claimed to see microscopic horses in horse semen.

By the mid-1800s, preformation began to lose ground as people realized that embryos look nothing like the adults they become. In fact, it was obvious that embryos of different species more closely resemble one another than their respective parents. The top row of **Figure 8-2** shows the striking similarity among embryos of species as diverse as salamanders, chickens, and humans, each of which is shown in fetal form in the bottom row.

As embryos, all vertebrate species have a similar-looking primitive head, a region with bumps or folds, and a tail. Only as an embryo develops does it acquire the

**Learning Objectives**
- Summarize the major events in the development of the human nervous system.
- Identify the steps by which neurons and glia differentiate during development.
- Describe the seven major stages of brain growth and development.
- Explain the significance of the relatively slow frontal lobe development.

Salamander    Chick    Human

distinctive characteristics of its species. The similarity of young embryos is so great that many nineteenth-century biologists saw it as evidence for Darwin's view that all vertebrates arose from a common ancestor millions of years ago.

The embryonic nervous systems of vertebrates are as similar structurally as their bodies are. **Figure 8-3** details the three-chambered brain of a young vertebrate embryo: forebrain, midbrain, and hindbrain. The remaining neural tube forms the spinal cord. How do these three regions develop? We can trace the events as the embryo matures.

# Gross Development of the Human Nervous System

When a sperm fertilizes an egg, the resulting human zygote consists of just a single cell. But this cell soon begins to divide. By the fifteenth day after fertilization, the emerging embryo resembles a fried egg (**Figure 8-4**), a structure formed by several sheets of cells with a raised area in the middle called the *embryonic disc*—essentially the primitive body.

**FIGURE 8-2 Embryos and Evolution** The physical similarity of embryos of different species is striking in the earliest stages of development, as the salamander, chick, and human embryos in the top row show. This similarity led to the conclusion that embryos are not simply miniature versions of adults.

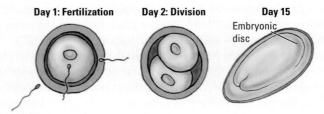

**FIGURE 8-4 From Fertilization to Embryo** Development begins at fertilization (day 1), with the formation of the zygote. On day 2, the zygote begins to divide. On day 15, the raised embryonic disc begins to form. Information from Moore, 1988.

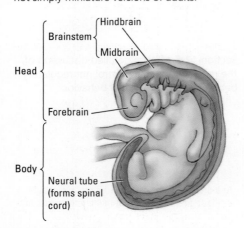

**FIGURE 8-3 Embryonic Vertebrate Nervous System** The forebrain, midbrain, and hindbrain are visible in the human embryo at about 28 days, as is the remaining neural tube, which will form the spinal cord.

By 3 weeks after conception, primitive neural tissue, known as the **neural plate**, occupies part of the outermost layer of embryonic cells. First, the neural plate folds to form the *neural groove*, detailed in **Figure 8-5**. The neural groove then curls to form the **neural tube**, much as you can curl a flat sheet of paper to make a cylinder.

**neural plate** Primitive neural tissue that gives rise to the neural tube.

**neural tube** Structure in the early stage of brain development from which the brain and spinal cord develop.

**FIGURE 8-5 Formation of the Neural Tube** A long depression, called the neural groove, first forms in the neural plate. By day 21, the primitive brain and neural groove are visible. On day 23, the neural tube is forming as the neural plate collapses inward along the length of the embryo's dorsal surface. The embryo is shown in a photograph at 24 days.

The cells that form the neural tube can be regarded as the nursery for the rest of the central nervous system. The open region in the tube's center remains open and matures into the brain's ventricles and the spinal canal. The micrographs in **Figure 8-6** show the neural tube closing in a mouse embryo.

The human body and nervous system change rapidly in the ensuing 3 weeks (**Figure 8-7**). By 7 weeks (49 days), the embryo begins to resemble a person. The brain looks distinctly human by about 100 days after conception, but it does not begin to form *gyri* and *sulci* until about 7 months. By the end of the ninth month, the fetal brain has the gross appearance of the adult human brain, although its cellular structure is different.

# Origins of Neurons and Glia

As we have noted, the neural tube is the brain's nursery. The **neural stem cells** lining the neural tube have an extensive capacity for self-renewal. When a stem cell divides, it produces two stem cells; one dies and the other lives to divide again. This process repeats again and again throughout life. In an adult human, neural stem cells line the ventricles, forming the **subventricular zone**.

If neural stem cells' only function throughout the decades of a human life were to line the ventricles, they would seem very odd cells to possess. But neural stem cells have a function beyond self-renewal: they give rise to **progenitor cells (precursor cells)**, which also can divide. As shown in **Figure 8-8**, progenitor cells eventually produce nondividing cells known as **neuroblasts** and **glioblasts**. In turn, neuroblasts and glioblasts mature into neurons and glia. Neural stem cells, then, are *multipotent*: they give rise to all of the many specialized cell types in the central nervous system (CNS).

Sam Weiss and his colleagues (1996) discovered that stem cells remain capable of producing neurons and glia not just into early adulthood, but even in the aging brain. This important discovery implies that any neurons that die in an adult brain should be replaceable. Indeed, neurogenesis beyond early development can be altered by growth factors, pharmacologic treatments, and environmental exposures, thus holding out the possibility that we might be able to manage neurologic diseases in the future (see the review by Jurkowski et al., 2020).

**(A) Day 9**    **(B) Day 10**    **(C) Day 11**

**FIGURE 8-6 Neural Tube Development**
Scanning electron micrographs show the neural tube closing in a mouse embryo. Reproduced with the permission of Prof. Dr. R. E. Poelmann, Department of Cardiology, Leiden University Medical Center, Institute of Biology, University of Leiden, Leiden, the Netherlands.

Gyri and sulci are introduced in Section 2-1.

The adult stem cells that line the subventricular zone can also be found in the hippocampus, spinal cord, and retina.

| Prenatal Stages | |
|---|---|
| Zygote | Fertilization to 2 weeks |
| Embryo | 2 to 8 weeks |
| Fetus | 9 weeks to birth |

4 weeks    5 weeks    6 weeks    7 weeks    14 weeks

20 weeks    24 weeks    28 weeks    32 weeks

36 weeks

☐ Forebrain
☐ Midbrain
☐ Hindbrain
☐ Neural tube (forms spinal cord)

**neural stem cell**  Self-renewing multipotential cell that gives rise to any of the different types of neurons and glia in the nervous system.

**subventricular zone**  Lining of neural stem cells surrounding the ventricles in adults.

**progenitor cell (precursor cell)**  Cell derived from a stem cell that migrates and produces a neuron or a glial cell.

**neuroblast**  Product of a progenitor cell that gives rise to any of the different types of neurons.

**glioblast**  Product of a progenitor cell that gives rise to different types of glial cells.

**FIGURE 8-7 Prenatal Brain Development**
The developing human brain undergoes a series of embryonic and fetal stages. You can identify the forebrain, midbrain, and hindbrain by color (review Figure 8-3) as they develop in the course of gestation. At 6 months, the developing forebrain has enveloped the midbrain structures. Research from Cowan, 1979.

| Cell type | Process | |
|---|---|---|
| Stem | Self-renewal | |
| Progenitor | Progenitor produced | |
| Blast | Neuroblasts and glioblasts produced | Neural / Glial |
| Specialized | Neurons and glia differentiate | Interneuron / Pyramidal neuron / Oligodendroglia / Astrocyte |

**FIGURE 8-8 Origin of Brain Cells** Cells in the brain begin as multipotential stem cells, develop into precursor cells, and then produce blasts that finally develop into specialized neurons or glia.

One potential avenue for managing these diseases is to make use of signals that the brain typically uses to control stem cell production in adults. For example, the level of the neuropeptide *prolactin* increases when female mice are pregnant and stimulates the fetal brain to produce more neurons. These naturally occurring hormonal signals have been shown to replace lost neurons in brain-injured laboratory animals (see the reviews by Bond et al., 2015, and Faiz & Morshead, 2018).

How does a stem cell know to become a neuron rather than a skin cell? In each cell, certain genes are expressed (turned on) by a signal, and those genes then produce a particular cell type. *Gene expression* is the process whereby information from a gene is used in the synthesis of a gene product, such as a protein. You can easily imagine that certain proteins produce skin cells, whereas other proteins produce neurons. Similarly, certain proteins produce one type of neuron, such as pyramidal cells, whereas others might produce granule cells.

The specific signals for gene expression are largely unknown but are probably chemical, and they form the basis of epigenetics. A common epigenetic mechanism that suppresses gene expression during development is *gene methylation*, or *DNA methylation*. In this process, a methyl group ($CH_3$) attaches to the nucleotide base cytosine lying next to guanine on the DNA sequence. It is relatively simple to quantify gene methylation in different phenotypes, reflecting either an increase or a decrease in overall gene expression.

Methylation alters gene expression dramatically during development. For example, prenatal stress can reduce gene methylation by 10%—which means that prenatally stressed infants express 2000 more genes (of the more than 20,000 in the human genome) than unstressed infants (Mychasiuk et al., 2011). Other epigenetic mechanisms, such as histone modification and mRNA modification, can regulate gene expression, although their effects are more difficult to quantify.

Thus, the chemical environment of a brain cell differs from that of cells found elsewhere in the body: different genes in brain cells are activated, producing different proteins and different cell types. The chemical environments needed to trigger cellular differentiation could be produced by the activity of neighboring cells or by chemicals, such as hormones, that are transported in the bloodstream.

Protein synthesis is described in more detail in Section 3-2, and the epigenetic factors influencing gene expression are discussed in Section 3-3.

Figure 3-26 (excerpted here), which shows gene methylation, contrasts the mechanisms of histone and mRNA modification to DNA methylation.

Methyl groups (M) bind to CG base pairs to block transcription.

DNA

The differentiation of stem cells into neurons requires a series of gene-activating signals. A chemical signal must induce stem cells to produce progenitor cells; another chemical signal must induce the progenitor cells to produce either neuroblasts or glioblasts. Finally, a chemical signal—perhaps a set of signals—must induce the genes for neuroblasts to make a particular type of neuron.

Compounds that signal cells to develop in particular ways are called **neurotrophic factors** (*trophic* means "nourishing"). By removing stem cells from an animal's brain and placing those cells in solutions that keep them alive, researchers can study how neurotrophic factors function. One compound, *epidermal growth factor* (EGF), when added to the stem cell culture stimulates production of progenitor cells. Another compound, *basic fibroblast growth factor* (bFGF, or FGF-2), stimulates progenitor cells to produce neuroblasts.

At this point, the destiny of a given neuroblast is undetermined. The blast can become any type of neuron if it receives the right chemical signals. Thus, the body relies on a general-purpose neuron that matures into a specific cell type in a particular location when exposed to certain neurotrophic factors.

This flexibility makes brain development simpler than it would be if each particular cell type, as well as the number of cells of each type, had to be specified precisely in an organism's genes. In the same way, building a house from all-purpose two-by-fours that can be cut to any length as needed is easier than specifying in a blueprint a precise number of precut pieces of lumber that can be used only in a certain location.

**neurotrophic factor** Chemical compound that supports growth and differentiation in developing neurons and may act to keep certain neurons alive in adulthood.

Therapies for brain injury, including the use of trophic factors to stimulate neurogenesis, in adult brains are discussed in Section 14-5.

# Neuronal Growth and Development

The human brain requires approximately 10 billion ($10^{10}$) cells to form just the cortex that blankets a single hemisphere. This means it must produce about 250,000 neurons per minute at the peak of prenatal brain development. But as **Table 8-1** shows, this rapid formation of neurons (neurogenesis) and glia (gliogenesis) is just the first step in brain growth. These new cells must travel to the correct destination (*migration*), they must differentiate into the right type of neuron or glial cell, and the neurons must then grow dendrites and axons and form synapses.

The brain also prunes unnecessary cells and connections, sculpting itself according to the particular person's experiences and needs. We consider these stages in brain development next. We focus our discussion on cortical development, because neuroscientists know more about development of the cortex than of any other area of the human brain. The principles derived from our examination of the cortex, however, apply to neural growth and development in other brain regions as well.

## Neuronal Generation, Migration, and Differentiation

**Figure 8-9** shows that neurogenesis is largely complete after about 25 weeks' gestation. (Some growth continues until about 5 years of age.) An important exception is the hippocampus, where new neurons continue to develop throughout life.

In Research Focus 8-1, investigators used cortical development as a measure of the effects of SES.

**TABLE 8-1 Stages of Brain Development**

| |
| --- |
| 1. Cell birth (neurogenesis; gliogenesis) |
| 2. Neural migration |
| 3. Cell differentiation |
| 4. Neural maturation (dendrite and axon growth) |
| 5. Synaptogenesis (formation of synapses) |
| 6. Cell death and synaptic pruning |
| 7. Myelogenesis (formation of myelin) |

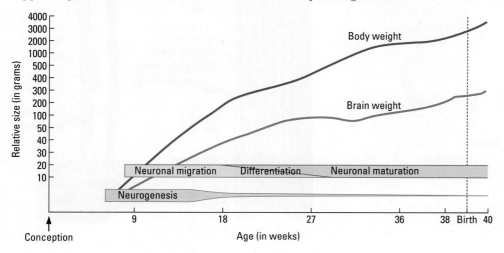

**FIGURE 8-9 Prenatal Development of the Human Cerebral Cortex** Brain weight and body weight increase rapidly and in proportion. The cortex begins to form about 6 weeks after conception, with neurogenesis largely being complete by 25 weeks. Neural migration and cell differentiation begin at about 8 weeks and are largely complete by about 29 weeks. Neuron maturation, including axon and dendrite growth, begins at about 20 weeks and continues until well after birth. Information from Marin-Padilla, 1993.

**radial glial cell** Path-making cell that a migrating neuron follows to its appropriate destination.

Clinical Focus 11-2 describes outcomes resulting from cerebral palsy, caused by brain trauma acquired perinatally.

The hippocampus (see Figure 2-23) is critical to memory (Section 14-3) and vulnerable to stress (Section 5-4).

Section 2-3 details the brain's structural organization, including the neocortical layers and lobes.

Figure 2-25 contrasts the sensory and motor cortices' six distinct layers and their functions.

Until after full-term birth, the fetal brain is especially delicate and extremely vulnerable to injury, *teratogens* (chemicals that cause malformations), and trauma. Apparently, the developing brain can more easily cope with injury earlier, during neurogenesis, than it can during the later stages of cell migration or cell differentiation, when cell maturation begins (see Table 8-1). One reason may be that once neurogenesis has slowed, it is very hard to start this process up again. If neurogenesis is still progressing at a high rate, more neurons can be made to replace injured ones, or perhaps existing neurons can be allocated differently.

Cell migration begins shortly after the first neurons are generated and continues for about 6 weeks in the cerebral cortex (and throughout life in the hippocampus). Cell differentiation, in which neuroblasts become specific types of neurons, follows migration. Cell differentiation is essentially complete at birth, although neuron maturation, which includes the growth of dendrites, axons, and synapses, goes on for years and in some parts of the brain may continue throughout adulthood.

The cortex is organized into layers distinctly different from one another in their cellular makeup. How does this arrangement of differentiated areas occur? Neuroscientist Pasko Rakic and his colleagues (e.g., Geschwind & Rakic, 2013) have been investigating this question for more than four decades. Their work shows that the subventricular zone contains a primitive cortical map, which predisposes cells formed in a certain ventricular region to migrate to a certain cortical location. One subventricular region may produce cells destined to migrate to the visual cortex; another might produce cells destined to migrate to the frontal lobes, for example.

How do the migrating cells know where to find these different parts of the cortex? They follow a path formed by **radial glial cells**. A glial fiber from each of these path-making cells extends from the subventricular zone to the cortical surface, as illustrated in **Figure 8-10**A. The close-up views in Figures 8-10B and C show that neural cells from a given subventricular region need only follow the glial road to end up in the correct location.

As the brain grows, the glial fibers stretch but still go to the same place. Figure 8-10B also shows a cell moving across the radial glial fibers. Although most cortical neurons follow the radial glial fibers, a small number appear to migrate by seeking out some type of chemical signal.

Cortical layers develop from the inside out, much like adding floors to a house. The neurons of the innermost layer (VI) migrate to their locations first, followed by those destined for layer V, and so on, as successive waves of neurons pass

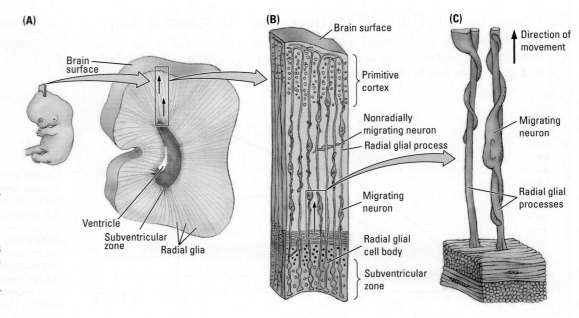

**FIGURE 8-10 Neuronal Migration (A)** Neuroscientists hypothesize that the cortical map is represented in the subventricular zone. **(B)** Radial glial fibers extend from the subventricular zone to the cortical surface. **(C)** Neurons migrate along the radial glial fibers that take them from the protomap in the subventricular zone to the corresponding region in the cortex. Information from Rakic, 1974.

earlier-arriving neurons and move to progressively more exterior positions in the cortex. And, as with building a house from the ground up, where materials needed to build higher floors must pass through lower floors to get to their destinations, the new cells must also migrate through the lower layers.

To facilitate house construction, each new story has a blueprint-specified dimension, such as 10 feet high. How do neurons determine how thick a cortical layer should be? This is a tough question, especially when you consider that the cortical layers are not all the same thickness.

Local environmental signals—chemicals produced by other cells—likely influence the way cells form layers in the cortex. These intercellular signals progressively restrict the choice of traits a cell can express, as illustrated in **Figure 8-11**. Thus, the emergence of distinct cell types in the brain results not from the unfolding of a specific genetic program but rather from the interaction of genetic instructions, timing, and signals from other cells in the local environment.

## Neuronal Maturation

After neurons migrate to their destination and differentiate, they begin to mature by first growing dendrites to provide surface area for synapses with other cells. They then extend their axons to appropriate targets to initiate synapse formation.

Two events take place in dendrite development: dendritic arborization (branching) and the growth of dendritic spines. As illustrated in **Figure 8-12**, dendrites in newborn babies begin as individual processes protruding from the cell body. In the first 2 years of life, dendrites undergo arborization: they develop increasingly complex extensions that look much like leafless tree branches. The dendritic branches then begin to form spines, where most synapses on dendrites are located.

Although dendritic development begins prenatally in humans, it continues for a long time after birth, as Figure 8-12 shows. Dendritic growth proceeds at a slow rate, on the order of microns ($\mu$m, millionths of a meter) per day. Contrast this with the development of axons, which grow on the order of a millimeter per day—about a thousand times faster.

The disparate developmental rates of axons and dendrites are important because the faster-growing axon can reach its target cell before the cell's dendrites are

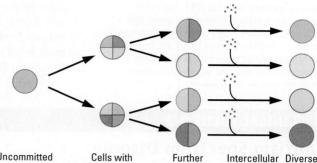

Uncommitted precursor | Cells with some segregation of determinants | Further segregation of determinants | Intercellular environment | Diverse cells

**FIGURE 8-11  Cellular Commitment** As also shown in Figure 8-8, precursor cells have unlimited possibilities. However, as they develop, interacting genetic, maturational, and environmental influences increasingly steer them toward developing into a particular cell type.

Recall from Section 3-1 that dendrites collect information and that axons transmit information to other neurons.

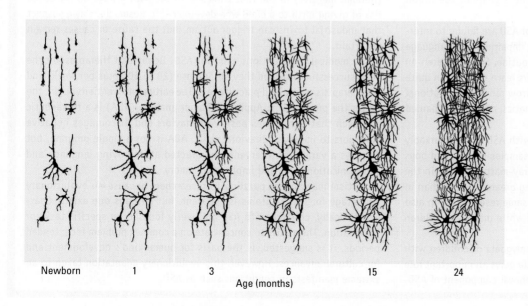

Newborn   1   3   6   15   24
Age (months)

**FIGURE 8-12  Neuronal Maturation in Cortical Language Areas** In postnatal cortical differentiation—shown here around Broca's area, which controls speech—neurons begin with simple dendritic fields that become progressively more complex until a child reaches about 2 years old. Brain maturation thus parallels a behavioral development: the emergence of language. Book: Eric H. Lenneberg, Biological Foundations of Language, New York: Wiley, 1967, pp. 160–161.

**autism spectrum disorder (ASD)** The range of cognitive symptoms, from mild to severe, that characterize autism; severe symptoms include greatly impaired social interaction, a bizarre and narrow range of interests, marked abnormalities in language and communication, and fixed, repetitive movements.

completely formed. Thus, the axon may play a role in dendritic differentiation and ultimately in neuron function—for example, as part of the brain's visual, motor, or language circuitry. Abnormalities in neuronal maturation rate can produce abnormalities in patterns of neural connectivity, as explained in Clinical Focus 8-2, Autism Spectrum Disorder.

## CLINICAL FOCUS 8-2

# Autism Spectrum Disorder

In the 1940s, Leo Kanner and Hans Asperger first used the term *autism* (from the Greek *autos*, meaning "self") to describe children who seem to live in their own world. Some of these children were classified at the time as intellectually disabled; others seemed to function well intellectually.

The contemporary term **autism spectrum disorder (ASD)** accommodates this behavioral range, as it includes children with mild to severe symptoms. Severe symptoms include greatly impaired social interaction, a bizarre and narrow range of interests, marked abnormalities in language and communication, and fixed, repetitive movements.

The autism spectrum includes classic autism and related disorders. *Asperger syndrome*, for example, is distinguished by an obsessive interest in a single topic or object to the exclusion of nearly any other. Children with Asperger syndrome are socially awkward and usually have delayed motor skill development. Although not formally recognized as a form of autism, *Rett syndrome* is characterized by poor expressive language and clumsy hand use, which are autism-like symptoms. It almost exclusively affects girls.

The rate of ASD has been rising over the past four decades, from fewer than 1 person in 2000 in 1980 to the 2020 estimate by the Centers for Disease Control and Prevention that as many as 1 in 54 children have been identified with ASD. The cause of this increased incidence is uncertain. Suggestions include changes in diagnostic criteria, diagnosis of children at a younger age, and epigenetic influences. Although it knows neither racial nor ethnic nor social boundaries, ASD is four times as prevalent in boys as in girls.

The behavior of many children with ASD is noticeable from birth. To avoid physical contact, these babies arch their backs and pull away from caregivers or grow limp when held. Approximately one-third of children develop typically until somewhere between 1 and 3 years of age, when symptoms of autism emerge.

Perhaps the most recognized characteristics of ASD are failure to interact socially, repetitive rocking or hand flapping, impairments in language development, and resistance to any change in routine. Some children on the autism spectrum are severely impaired; others learn to function quite well. Still others display *savant syndrome*, a narrow range of exceptional abilities in areas such as in music, art, or mathematics, often accompanied by severe cognitive deficits.

Although the brains of children diagnosed with ASD look remarkably typical by most measures, MRI studies of large samples of girls and boys from age 2 to 13 years have revealed greater gray-matter volume in the brains of children with ASD, with the effect being greater in boys than in girls (Lee et al., 2020). A parallel study by the same research group also showed an atypical developmental trajectory of white matter in children with ASD (Andrews et al., 2021).

Excessive brain volume is also clear in the amygdala of children with ASD (Hessl et al., 2021). The subcortical amygdala plays an important role in generating fear, anxiety, and the social withdrawal component of ASD,

Longitudinal trajectories of gray-matter volume in early childhood in girls (red) and boys (blue) with ASD versus typically developing (TD) children. Note that the curves for the girls converge by 80 months (approximately 7 years), whereas the curves for the boys do not converge by 180 months (approximately 15 years). Research from Lee et al., 2020.

and variations in the severity of anxiety in children with ASD are related to differences in the size of the amygdala.

Accelerated brain growth associated with enlarged regions of the brain suggests that connections between cerebral regions are atypical, which would in turn produce atypical functioning. What leads to such brain development? More than 100 genetic differences have been described in children with ASD, so it is clear that no single "autism gene" is at work.

The mechanism that translates genetic irregularities into the autistic brain is unknown but likely includes epigenetic factors that could occur prenatally, postnatally, or both. Women who have been exposed to rubella (German measles) in the first trimester of pregnancy have an increased risk of giving birth to a child who develops ASD. Researchers also suspect that industrial toxins can trigger autism, but the cause or causes remain uncertain.

No medical interventions exist for ASD. Behavioral therapies are the most successful, provided they are intense (20 to 40 hours per week) and the therapists are trained practitioners. The earlier interventions begin, the better the prognosis is. Applied behavior analysis (ABA) is a therapeutic approach that encourages positive behaviors and discourages negative behaviors to improve behavioral skills. ABA is not a single program, but employs a variety of interventions directed at improving language and communication skills and improving memory.

Autism may appear puzzling to researchers because no evolutionary advantage for its symptoms is apparent, but perhaps one exists. Characteristically, children with ASD are overly focused on specific tasks or information. The ability to concentrate on a complex problem for extended periods, it is suggested, is the basis for humankind's development and for cultural advances. However, this evolutionary adaptation taken to an extreme manifests in conditions such as ASD.

**(A)**

Growth cone    Axon

Filopodia

Courtesy of Dennis Bray

**(B)**

Target cell    Growth cone

Filopodia

◄— Increasing concentration of chemical —►

**FIGURE 8-13 Seeking a Path (A)** At the tip of this axon, which was nurtured in a culture, a growth cone sends out filopodia seeking specific molecules to guide the axon's direction of growth. **(B)** Filopodia guide the growth cone toward a target cell that is releasing cell adhesion or tropic molecules, represented in the drawing by red dots.

Axon connections present a significant engineering problem for the developing brain. An axon might connect to a cell that is millimeters or even a meter away in the developing brain, and the axon must find its way through complex cellular terrain to get there. Genetic–environmental interaction is at work again, as various molecules that attract or repel the approaching axon tip guide the formation of axonic connections.

A century ago, Santiago Ramón y Cajal became the first scientist to describe this developmental process. He called the growing tips of axons **growth cones**. **Figure 8-13**A shows that as growth cones extend, they send out shoots, analogous to fingers reaching out to find a pen on a cluttered desk. When one shoot, known as a **filopod** (pl. **filopodia**), reaches an appropriate target, the others follow.

Growth cones are responsive to cues from two types of molecules (Figure 8-13B):

- **Cell adhesion molecules (CAMs)** are cell-manufactured molecules that either lie on the target cell's surface or are secreted into the intercellular space. Some provide a surface to which growth cones can adhere—hence the name cellular adhesion molecule; others serve to attract or repel growth cones.

- **Tropic molecules**, which are produced by the targets that the axons' growth cones are seeking (*tropic* means "moving toward"; pronounced as in *trope*, not *tropical*), essentially tell growth cones, "Come over here" (chemoattractive). They likely also tell other growth cones seeking different targets, "Keep away" (chemorepulsive).

Although Ramón y Cajal predicted their existence more than 100 years ago, tropic molecules have proved difficult to find. The best-understood chemoattractive molecules are the **netrins** (from Sanskrit, meaning "to guide"). But the guidance of axon growth also entails telling axons where *not* to go. One class of these chemorepulsive molecules, called the **semaphorins** (Greek for "signal"), act to prevent axon extension in their vicinity.

## Synaptic Development

The number of synapses in the human cerebral cortex is staggering, on the order of $10^{14}$, or 100,000 trillion. A genetic program that assigns each synapse a specific location could not possibly determine each spot for this huge number of connections. As with all other stages of brain development, only the general outlines of neuronal connections in the brain are likely to be genetically predetermined. The vast array of specific synaptic contacts is then guided into place by a variety of local environmental cues and signals.

A human fetus displays simple synaptic contacts in the fifth gestational month. By the seventh gestational month, synaptic development on the deepest cortical neurons is extensive. After birth, synapse numbers increase rapidly. In the visual cortex, synaptic density almost doubles between ages 2 months and 4 months and then continues to increase until age 1 year. Not all synapses in the developing visual cortex are visually related, however. This leads to a phenomenon called *synesthesia*, the ability to perceive a sensation of one sense as a sensation of another sense, as when sound leads to a sensation of color (see Section 15-5 for a more detailed discussion of this phenomenon).

Do not confuse the *tropic* (guiding) molecules with the *trophic* (nourishing) molecules, discussed earlier, which support neuronal growth.

**growth cone** Growing tip of an axon.

**filopod (pl. filopodia)** Process at the end of a developing axon that reaches out to search for a potential target or to sample the intercellular environment.

**cell adhesion molecule (CAM)** Chemical molecule to which specific cells can adhere, thus aiding in migration.

**tropic molecule** Signaling molecule that attracts or repels growth cones.

**netrin** Chemoattractive tropic molecule that guides axon growth.

**semaphorins** Class of chemorepulsive molecules that deflect axons from inappropriate regions.

**FIGURE 8-14 Progressive Changes in Cortical Thickness** MRI scans track the maturation of gray matter in typical development, revealing the length and pattern of maturation from the back of the cortex to the front. Cortical thinning and increased surface area progress together. Courtesy Paul M Thompson/Laboratory of Neuro Imaging, Keck School of Medicine of USC

# Cell Death and Synaptic Pruning

To carve statues, sculptors begin with blocks of stone and chisel away the unwanted pieces. The brain does something similar during cell death and synaptic pruning. The chisel in the brain could be a genetic signal, an experience, reproductive hormones, stress, or even SES. The effects of these chisels can be seen in changes in cortical thickness over time, as illustrated in **Figure 8-14**, an atlas of brain images. The cortex actually becomes measurably thinner in a caudal–rostral (back-to-front) gradient, a process that is probably due both to synaptic pruning and to white-matter expansion. This expansion stretches the cortex, leading to increased surface area, as illustrated in Research Focus 8-1.

The graph in **Figure 8-15** plots this rise and fall in synaptic density. Pasko Rakic (1974) estimated that at the peak of synapse loss, a person may lose as many as 100,000 synapses per second. Synapse elimination is extensive and prolonged. Peter Huttenlocher (1994) estimated that the process affects 42% of synapses in the human cortex and, in the prefrontal cortex, it continues into an individual's thirties. We can only wonder what the behavioral consequences of this rapid synaptic loss might be. It is probably no coincidence that children, especially toddlers and adolescents, seem to change moods and behaviors quickly.

How does the brain eliminate excess neurons? The simplest explanation is competition, sometimes referred to as **neural Darwinism**. Charles Darwin believed that one key to evolution is the variation it produces in the traits possessed by a species. Those organisms whose traits are best suited to the local environment are most likely to survive. From a Darwinian perspective, then, more animals are born than can survive to adulthood, and environmental pressures weed out the less fit ones. Similar pressures cause neural Darwinism.

What, exactly, causes this cellular weeding out in the brain? It turns out that when neurons form synapses, they become somewhat dependent on their targets for survival. In fact, when deprived of synaptic targets, neurons eventually die. They die because target cells produce neurotrophic (nourishing) factors absorbed by the axon terminals that function to regulate neuronal survival. *Nerve growth factor* (NGF), for example, is manufactured by cortical cells and absorbed by cholinergic neurons in the basal forebrain.

If many neurons compete for a limited amount of a neurotrophic factor, only some can survive. The death of neurons deprived of a neurotrophic factor is different from the cell death caused by injury or disease. When neurons are deprived of a neurotrophic factor, certain genes seem to be expressed, resulting in a message for the cell to die. This programmed process is called **apoptosis**.

Apoptosis accounts for the death of overabundant neurons, but it does not account for the synaptic pruning from cells that survive. In 1976, French neurobiologist Jean-Pierre Changeux proposed a theory for synapse loss that also takes competition into account (Changeux & Danchin, 1976). According to Changeux, synapses persist into adulthood only if they have become members of functional neural networks. If not, they are eventually eliminated from the brain. We can speculate that environmental factors such as hormones, drugs, and experiences may influence active neural circuit formation and, in turn, influence synapse stabilization and pruning.

In addition to outright errors in synapse formation that give rise to synaptic pruning, subtler changes in neural circuits may trigger the same process. One such change accounts for the findings of Janet Werker and Richard Tees (1992), who studied the ability of infants to discriminate speech sounds taken from widely disparate languages, such as English, Hindi (from India), and Salish (a Native American language). Their results show that young infants can discriminate speech

**neural Darwinism** Hypothesis that the processes of cell death and synaptic pruning are, like natural selection in species, the outcome of competition among neurons for connections and metabolic resources in a neural environment.

**apoptosis** Genetically programmed cell death.

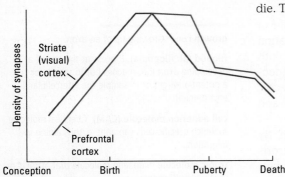

**FIGURE 8-15 Synapse Formation and Pruning** Changes in the relative density of synapses in the human visual cortex and prefrontal cortex (its frontmost part) as a function of age. Data from Bourgeois, 2001.

Left    Right

Language-related regions thicken

Visual cortex thins

**FIGURE 8-16 Gray-Matter Thickness** Brain maps showing the statistical significance of yearly change in cortical thickness measures taken from MRIs. Shading represents increasing (white) or decreasing (red) cortical thickness. Research from Sowell, Thompson, & Toga, 2004.

sounds of different languages without previous experience, but their ability to do so declines in the first year of life. An explanation for this declining ability is that synapses encoding speech sounds not typically encountered in an infant's daily environment are not active simultaneously with other speech-related synapses. As a result, they are eliminated.

Synaptic pruning may also allow the brain to adapt more flexibly to environmental demands. Human culture is probably the most diverse and complex environment with which any animal must cope. Perhaps the flexibility in cortical organization achieved by the mechanism of selective synaptic pruning is a necessary precondition for successful development in a cultural environment.

Synaptic pruning may also be a precursor related to different perceptions that people develop about the world. Consider, for example, the obvious differences in Eastern and Western philosophies about life, religion, and culture. Given the cultural differences to which people in the East and West are exposed as their brains develop, imagine how different their individual perceptions and cognitions may be. Considered together as a species, however, we humans are far more alike than we are different.

An important and unique characteristic common to all humans is language. As illustrated in Figure 8-14, the cortex generally thins from ages 2–5 to age 20. The sole exception is that major language regions of the cortex actually show an *increase* in gray matter. **Figure 8-16** contrasts the thinning of other cortical regions with the thickening of language-related regions (O'Hare & Sowell, 2008). A different pattern of development for brain regions critical in language processing makes sense, given language's unique role in cognition and the long learning time.

# Glial Development

*Astrocytes* and *oligodendrocytes* begin to develop after most neurogenesis is complete, and continue to develop throughout life. Radial glial cells form during embryonic development, and most of them differentiate into astrocytes once neural migration along them is complete. Others remain in the subventricular zone and later can give rise to neurons, oligodendrocytes, and more astrocytes (for a review, see Arai & Lo, 2017). Astrocytes play a key role in synaptic pruning during development and contribute to plasticity throughout life (for a review, see Zuchero & Barres, 2015). Oligodendrocytes myelinate axons, which increases the efficiency of axonal function. Consequently, myelination is a useful rough index of cerebral maturation.

In the early 1920s, Paul Flechsig noticed that cortical myelination begins just after birth and continues until at least 18 years of age. He also noticed that some cortical regions were myelinated by age 3 to 4 years, whereas others showed virtually no myelination at that time. **Figure 8-17** shows one of Flechsig's cortical maps with areas shaded according to earlier or later myelination.

Flechsig hypothesized that the earliest-myelinating areas control simple movements or sensory analyses, whereas the latest-myelinating areas control the highest mental functions. Magnetic resonance imaging (MRI) analyses of myelin development in the cortex show that the thickness of white matter largely does correspond to

Astrocytes nourish and support neurons; oligodendroglia form myelin in the CNS (see Table 3-1).

Light-colored zones myelinate last.

**FIGURE 8-17 Progress of Myelination** The fact that the light-colored zones are very late to myelinate led Flechsig to propose that they are qualitatively different in function from those that mature earlier.

**FIGURE 8-18 Sex Differences in Brain Development** Mean brain volume by age in years for males (green) and females (brown). Arrows above the curves indicate that females show more rapid growth than males, reaching maximum overall volume **(A)** and gray-matter volume **(B)** sooner. Decreasing gray matter corresponds to cell and synaptic loss. Increasing white-matter volume **(C)** largely corresponds to myelin development. Information from Lenroot et al., 2007.

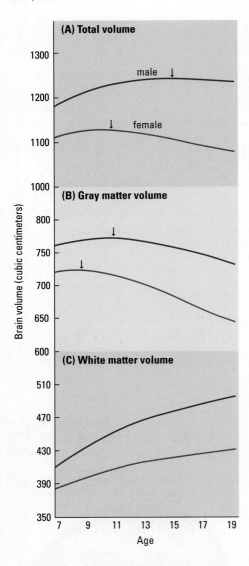

the progress of myelination, confirming Flechsig's ideas. Myelination continues until at least 20 years of age, as illustrated in **Figure 8-18**, which contrasts total brain volume, gray-matter volume, and white-matter volume during brain development in females and males.

## Neurogenesis in the Adult Brain

For most of the twentieth century, it was believed that neurogenesis in humans ended in infancy, but over the past 50 years it has become increasingly evident that the adult mammalian brain retains the capacity to generate new neurons (Jurkowski et al., 2020). Adult neurogenesis is not ubiquitous in the brain, however: animal studies so far have reported new neuron growth only in the hippocampus, subventricular zone, hypothalamus, striatum, substantia nigra, neocortex, and amygdala. In humans, the most studied region—and the most controversial—has been the hippocampus. Peter Eriksson and colleagues (1998) examined the postmortem brains of human cancer patients who had been injected with the neuronal neurogenesis marker Bromo-D-oxy-Uridine (BrdU) to estimate proliferation of tumor cells during their cancer treatments. The authors subsequently identified BrdU-labeled cells in the dentate gyrus of the hippocampus—an unexpected finding that suggested neurogenesis continues in the hippocampus of adult humans, albeit likely at a slower rate than in adult rodents (Snyder, 2019). The author's finding stimulated dozens of follow-up studies by laboratories worldwide, and their conclusion of continuing neurogenesis remains controversial.

Two papers published simultaneously in 2021 elegantly examine the data to date and reach different conclusions: Moreno-Jimenez and colleagues (2021) argued that there is significant adult neurogenesis in the hippocampus, whereas Sorrells and colleagues (2021) argued that there is little, if any. The discrepancies between these studies are related to variations in the methods the researchers used to preserve postmortem brain tissue (a process called *fixation*), and in the technical challenges in using antibodies to stain the "fixed" tissue. As yet, there is no resolution of these methodological difficulties, but given that adult neurogenesis in the hippocampus has been shown to occur in many other species—and considering the hippocampus's role in memory—it would be odd if this neurogenesis did not take place in humans as well.

One important point is that, as observed in animal studies, the properties of new neurons in the dentate gyrus change with age: the neurons formed in adulthood mature and form new synapses more slowly than those born earlier in life. We can speculate that the neurons formed in adulthood may have unique functions, and the need for new neurons may decline later in life, making it more difficult to identify them in older human brains (Seki, 2020). Given the importance of determining whether neurogenesis occurs in adult humans and what its role in memory might be, we can be sure that this will remain an important active area of investigation for some time to come.

## Unique Aspects of Frontal Lobe Development

The imaging atlas in Figure 8-14 confirms that the frontal lobe is the last brain region to mature. Since the atlas was compiled, neuroscientists have confirmed that frontal lobe maturation extends far beyond its age 20 boundary, including in the **dorsolateral prefrontal cortex (dlPFC)**. The dlPFC, which comprises Brodmann areas 9 and 46, makes reciprocal connections with the posterior parietal cortex and the superior temporal sulcus: it selects behavior and movement with respect to temporal memory.

Zdravko Petanjek and colleagues (2011) analyzed synaptic spine density in the dlPFC in a large sample of human brains ranging in age at death from newborn to 91 years. Their analysis confirms that dendritic spine density—which is a good measure of the number of excitatory synapses—is two to three times greater in children than in adults and that spine density begins to decrease during puberty. Their analysis also shows

**dorsolateral prefrontal cortex (dlPFC)** Brodmann areas 9 and 46; makes reciprocal connections with the posterior parietal cortex and superior temporal sulcus; responsible for selecting behavior and movement with respect to temporal memory.

**Left lateral view**
Prefrontal cortex
Inferior parietal lobule

**Left medial view**
Posterior cingulate/ retrosplenial cortex
Dorsomedial prefrontal cortex
Extended hippocampal formation
Ventromedial prefrontal cortex

**FIGURE 8-19 The Default Network** These regions of the cerebral cortex, which show increased connectivity related to intelligence, form the default network. Data after Sherman et al., 2014.

that dendritic spines continue to be eliminated well beyond age 20, stabilizing at the adult level around age 30.

Two important correlates attend slow frontal lobe development:

1. *The frontal lobe is especially sensitive to epigenetic influences* (Kolb et al., 2012). In a study of more than 170,000 people, Robert Anda and colleagues (Anda et al., 2006) showed that *aversive childhood experiences* (ACEs), such as verbal or physical abuse, a family member's addiction, or loss of a parent, are predictive of physical and mental health in middle age. People with two or more ACEs, for example, are 50 times more likely to acquire addictions or attempt suicide and are more likely to be victims of sexual assault. We hypothesize that early aversive experiences promote ACE-related susceptibilities by compromising frontal lobe development.

2. *The trajectory of frontal lobe development correlates with adult intelligence.* Two important features of frontal lobe development are (a) the reduction in cortical thickness and (b) the increase in connectivity between the medial regions of the frontal lobe, the posterior regions of the cingulate cortex, and the lateral regions of the parietal lobe, which together are referred to as the **default network** (**Figure 8-19**). The trajectory of change in cortical thickness, which continues until late adolescence, and the increased connectivity in the default network, which appears adult-like by approximately age 13, is related to scores on intelligence tests. Thus, children who score highest in intelligence show the greatest plastic changes in the frontal lobe over time.

Three-dimensional atlases guide researchers to the precise locations of various brain regions (Section 7-1). See Sections 12-4 and 15-3 for more on how the dlPFC functions.

The Adverse Childhood Experience (ACE) Questionnaire is available online, where you can view and answer the questions.

**default network** Brain network of interacting regions of the frontal and parietal lobes that have highly correlated activity.

# 8-2 Review

Before you continue, check your understanding. Answers to the Self-Test appear at the back of the book.

1. The central nervous system begins as a sheet of cells, which folds inward to form the _____.

2. The growth of neurons is referred to as _____, whereas formation of glial cells is known as _____.

3. Growth cones are responsive to two types of cues: _____ and _____.

4. Erickson and colleagues' studies of postmortem cancer patients suggested that neurogenesis continues in the _____ in adulthood.

5. What is the functional significance of the prolonged development of the frontal lobe?

# Using Emerging Behaviors to Infer Neural Maturation

**Learning Objectives**
- Explain how the development of specific motor behaviors relates to brain development.
- Correlate the development of language capabilities to brain development.
- Describe Piaget's stages of cognitive development.

As brain areas mature, a person's behaviors correspond to the functions of the maturing areas. Stated differently, behaviors cannot emerge until the requisite neural machinery to support them has developed. When that machinery is in place, however, related behaviors develop quickly through stages and are shaped significantly by epigenetic factors.

Researchers have studied these interacting changes in the brain and behavior. Their pattern manifests in a wide variety of behaviors, and is especially evident in the emergence of motor skills, language, and problem solving in children. We now explore development in these three areas.

## Motor Behaviors

Developing locomotion skills are easy to observe in human infants. At first, babies cannot move about independently, but eventually, they roll over, then crawl, then walk.

Other motor skills develop in less obvious, but no less systematic ways. Shortly after birth, infants are capable of flexing their arms in such a way that they can scoop something toward their body, and they can direct a hand, as toward a breast when suckling. Between 1 and 3 months of age, babies also begin to make spontaneous hand and digit movements consisting of almost all the skilled finger movements they will make as an adult—a kind of motor babbling.

These movements at first are directed toward handling parts of their body and their clothes (Wallace & Whishaw, 2003). Only then are reaching movements directed toward objects in space. Tom Twitchell (1965) studied and described how the ability to reach for objects and grasp them progresses in stages, illustrated in **Figure 8-20**.

Between 8 and 11 months, infants' grasping becomes more sophisticated as the pincer grasp, created by employing the index finger and the thumb, develops. The pincer grasp is significant developmentally: it allows babies to make the very precise finger movements needed to manipulate small objects, and it continues to mature until age 3. What we see, then, is a sequence in the development of grasping: first scooping, then grasping with all the fingers, then grasping with independent finger movements.

If increasingly well-coordinated grasping depends on the emergence of certain neural machinery, anatomical changes in the brain should accompany the emergence of these motor behaviors. Such changes do take place, especially in the development of dendritic arborizations and in fiber connections between the neocortex and spinal cord. Likewise, a correlation has been found between myelin formation and the ability to grasp (Yakovlev & Lecours, 1967).

In particular, a group of axons from the motor cortex neurons myelinate at about the same time that whole-hand reaching and grasping develop. Another group of motor cortex neurons known to control finger movements myelinates at about the time that the pincer grasp develops. MRI studies of changes in cortical thickness show that increased motor dexterity is associated with decreased cortical thickness in the hand region of the left motor cortex of right-handed individuals (**Figure 8-21**A). It might seem odd that both cortical thinning and thickening can be associated with improved performance, but the reason is straightforward: thinning partly reflects the pruning of neurons and synapses throughout development, whereas thickening reflects the addition of synapses, along with associated astrocytes and blood vessels related to learning.

| 2 months | 4 months | 10 months |
|---|---|---|

| Orients hand toward an object and gropes to hold it. | Grasps appropriately shaped object with entire hand. | Uses pincer grasp with thumb and index finger opposed. |
|---|---|---|

**FIGURE 8-20 Development of the Grasping Response of Infants** Information from Twitchell, 1965.

A classic symptom of motor cortex damage, detailed in Section 11-1, is permanent loss of the pincer grasp.

**Principle 3:** The CNS functions on multiple levels and is organized hierarchically and in parallel.

**(A)**    **(B)**    **(C)**

**FIGURE 8-21 Correlations Between Gray Matter Thickness and Behavior (A)** Red shading corresponds to regions showing significant cortical thinning correlated with improved motor skills. **(B)** White shading corresponds to regions showing significant cortical thickening correlated with improved language skills. **(C)** Red shading shows regions of decreased cortical thickness correlated with improved vocabulary scores. (A) and (B): Research from Lu et al., 2007; (C): Research from Sowell et al., 2004.

We can now make a simple prediction. If specific motor cortex neurons are essential for adult-like grasping movements to emerge, then removing those neurons should make an adult's grasping ability similar to a young infant's. That is, in fact, what happens.

# Language Development

According to Eric Lenneberg (1967), children reach certain important speech milestones in a fixed sequence and at constant chronological ages. Children start to form a vocabulary by 12 months. Their 5- to 10-word repertoire typically doubles over the next 6 months. By age 2 years, their vocabulary will range from 200 to 300 words, which mostly name everyday objects. In another year, vocabulary approaches 1000 words and begins to include simple sentences. At age 6 years, children boast a vocabulary of about 2500 words and can understand more than 20,000 words; they are en route to an adult vocabulary of more than 50,000 words. The speed of language development is influenced by a wealth of environmental variables, including those associated with socioeconomic status, as noted in Research Focus 8-1; we will return to this point in Section 8-4.

Although language skills and motor skills generally develop in parallel, the capacity for language depends on more than just the ability to make controlled movements of the mouth, lips, and tongue. Precise movements of the muscles controlling these body parts develop well before children can speak. Furthermore, even when children have sufficient motor skills to articulate most words, their vocabulary does not rocket ahead but rather progresses gradually.

A small proportion of children (approximately 1%) have typical intelligence and motor skills development, yet their speech acquisition is markedly delayed. Such children might not begin to speak in phrases until after age 4, despite an apparently healthy environment and the absence of any obvious neurological signs of brain damage. Because the timing of speech onset appears universal in the remaining 99% of children across all cultures, something different has likely taken place in the brain maturation of a child with late language acquisition. The difficulty comes in specifying that difference.

Because the age of language onset is usually between 1 and 2 years and language acquisition is largely complete by age 12, the best strategy for determining the reasons for these differences is to consider how the cortex differs before and after these two milestones. By age 2, cell division and migration are complete in the language zones of the cerebral cortex. The major changes that take place from ages 2 to 12 occur in neuronal connectivity and myelination of the speech zones.

Changes in dendritic complexity in speech zones are among the most impressive in the brain. Recall from Figure 8-12 that the axons and dendrites of the speech zone called Broca's area are simple at birth but grow dramatically denser at age 15 to 24 months. This neuronal development correlates with an equally dramatic change in language ability, given that a baby's vocabulary starts to expand rapidly at about age 2.

We can therefore infer that language development may be constrained, at least in part, by the maturing language areas in the cortex. Individual differences in the speed of language acquisition may reflect differences in this neural development. Children with early language ability may have an early-maturing speech zone, whereas this zone may develop later in children with delayed language onset.

Results of MRI studies of the language-related cortex show that, in contrast to the thinning of motor cortex associated with enhanced dexterity shown in Figure 8-21A, there is a *thickening* of the left inferior frontal cortex areas associated with enhanced phonological processing (understanding speech sounds), as shown in Figure 8-21B. The unique association between cortical thickening and phonological processing is not due to a general relationship between all language functions and cortical thickening, however. Figure 8-21C shows significant thinning of diffuse cortical regions associated with better vocabulary—regions outside the language areas—and vocabulary is one of the best predictors of general intelligence.

Research Focus 7-1 describes research on newborns' reactions to language.

## Development of Problem-Solving Ability

The first researcher to try to identify discrete stages of cognitive development was psychologist Jean Piaget (1952). He realized that he could infer children's understanding of the world by observing their behavior. For example, a baby who lifts a cloth to retrieve a hidden toy shows an understanding that objects continue to exist even when out of sight. This understanding of *object permanence* is revealed by the behavior of the infant in the top row of photographs in **Figure 8-22**.

An absence of understanding also can be seen in children's behavior, as shown by the actions of the 5-year-old girl in the bottom row of photographs in Figure 8-22. She was shown two identical beakers with identical volumes of liquid, then watched as one beaker's liquid was poured into a shorter, wider beaker. When asked which beaker contained more liquid, she pointed to the taller beaker, not understanding that the amount of liquid remains constant despite the difference in appearance. Children display an understanding of this principle, the *conservation of liquid volume*, at about age 7.

By studying children engaged in such tasks, Piaget concluded that cognitive development is a continuous process. Children's strategies for exploring the world and their understanding of it are constantly changing. These changes are not simply the result of acquiring specific pieces of new knowledge. Instead, at certain points in development,

**FIGURE 8-22 Two Stages of Cognitive Development** The infant shows that she understands object permanence—that things continue to exist when they are out of sight (*top*). The young girl does not yet understand the principle of conservation of liquid volume. Beakers with identical volumes but different shapes seem to her to hold different amounts of liquid (*bottom*).

Doug Goodman/Science Source

© Macmillan, photo by Ellie Miller

fundamental changes take place in the organization of a child's strategies for learning about the world and for solving problems. With these developing strategies comes new understanding.

Piaget identified four major stages of cognitive development, which are summarized in **Table 8-2**:

- Stage I is the *sensorimotor* period, from birth to about 18 to 24 months of age. During this time, babies learn to differentiate themselves from the external world, come to realize that objects exist even when out of sight, and gain some understanding of cause and effect.

- Stage II, the *preoperational* period, takes place at ages 2 to 6 years. Children gain the ability to form mental representations of things in their world and to represent those things in words and drawings.

- Stage III, the period of *concrete operations*, typically occurs around 7 to 11 years. Children learn to mentally manipulate ideas about material (concrete) things such as volumes of liquid, dimensions of objects, and arithmetic problems.

- Stage IV, the period of *formal operations*, is attained sometime after age 11. Children are now able to reason in the abstract, not just in concrete terms.

Although there have been many revisions to Piaget's stage theory in the nearly 70 years since it was first proposed, we can still take Piaget's stages as rough approximations of qualitative changes that take place in children's thinking as they grow older, and we can ask which neural changes might underlie them. One place to look for brain changes is in the relative rate of brain growth.

After birth, brain and body do not grow uniformly but rather during irregularly occurring periods commonly called **growth spurts**. In his analysis of ratios of brain weight to body weight, Herman Epstein (1979) found consistent spurts in brain growth between 3 and 10 months (accounting for an increase of 30% in brain weight by age 18 months), as well as during ages 2 to 4, 6 to 8, 10 to 12, and 14 to 16+ years. Brain weight increased in increments of approximately 5% to 10% in each of these 2-year periods.

Brain growth takes place without a concurrent increase in the number of neurons, so it is most likely due to the growth of glial cells, blood vessels, myelin, and synapses. Although synapses themselves would be unlikely to add much weight to the brain, their growth is accompanied by increased metabolic demands that cause neurons to become larger, new blood vessels to form, and new astrocytes to be produced for neuronal support and nourishment.

We would expect such an increase in cortical complexity to generate more complex behaviors, so we might predict significant, perhaps qualitative, changes in cognitive function during each growth spurt. The first four brain growth spurts Epstein identified

**TABLE 8-2** Piaget's Stages of Cognitive Development

| Approximate typical age range (years) | Description of stage | Developmental phenomena |
|---|---|---|
| 0–2 | *I: Sensorimotor*<br>Experiences the world through senses and actions (looking, touching, mouthing) | Object permanence<br>Stranger anxiety |
| 2–6 | *II: Preoperational*<br>Represents things with words and images but lacks logical reasoning | Pretend play<br>Egocentrism<br>Language development |
| 7–11 | *III: Concrete operational*<br>Thinks logically about concrete events; grasps concrete analogies and performs arithmetical operations | Conservation<br>Mathematical transformations |
| 12+ | *IV: Formal operational*<br>Reasons abstractly | Abstract logic<br>Potential for mature moral reasoning |

Data from Myers, 2015.

**growth spurt** Sporadic period of sudden growth that lasts for a finite time.

····> **EXPERIMENT 8-1**

Question: In what sequence do the forebrain structures required for learning and memory mature?

**Procedure**

I. Displacement task

II. Nonmatching-to-sample learning task

Participant is shown object that can be displaced for a food reward (+).

Preceding object and new object are presented.

Displacement of new object is rewarded with food.

III. Concurrent-discrimination learning task

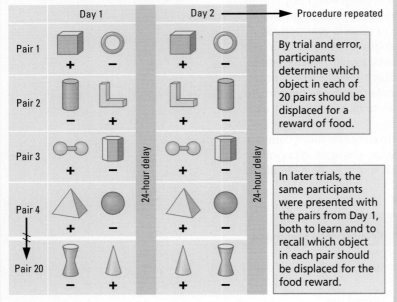

By trial and error, participants determine which object in each of 20 pairs should be displaced for a reward of food.

In later trials, the same participants were presented with the pairs from Day 1, both to learn and to recall which object in each pair should be displaced for the food reward.

**Results**

Both human and monkey infants learn the concurrent-discrimination task at a younger age than they learn the nonmatching-to-sample task.

*Conclusion:* Neural structures underlying the concurrent-discrimination task mature sooner than those underlying the nonmatching-to-sample task.

Research from Overman et al., 1992.

---

coincide nicely with the four main stages of cognitive development Piaget described. Such correspondence suggests significant alterations in neural functioning with the onset of each cognitive stage.

At the same time, differences in the rate of brain development, or perhaps in the rate at which specific groups of neurons mature, may account for individual differences in the age at which the various cognitive advances identified by Piaget emerge. Although Piaget did not identify a fifth stage of cognitive development in later adolescence, a growth spurt that occurs during this period implies one exists.

Growth spurts are superficial measures of changes taking place in the brain. To link them to cognitive development, we need to know at a deeper level which neural events are contributing to brain growth and where they are taking place. One way to find out is to observe healthy children's attempts to solve specific problems that are diagnostic of damage to discrete brain regions in adults. If children perform a particular task poorly, then whatever brain region regulates that task must not be mature as yet. Similarly, if children can perform one task but not another, the tasks apparently require different brain structures, and these structures must mature at different rates.

William Overman and Jocelyne Bachevalier (Overman et al., 1996) used this logic to study the development of forebrain structures required for learning and memory in young children and in monkeys. The Procedure section of **Experiment 8-1** shows the three test items they presented to their participants. The first task was simply to learn to displace an object to obtain a food reward. When participants had learned the *displacement* task, they were trained in two more tasks believed to measure temporal lobe and basal ganglia functioning, respectively.

In the *nonmatching-to-sample* task, participants were shown an object they could displace to receive a food reward. After a brief (15-second) delay, two objects were presented: the first object and a novel object. The participants then had to displace the novel object to obtain the food reward. The nonmatching-to-sample task is thought to measure object recognition, which is a temporal lobe function. The participant can find the food only by recognizing the original object and not choosing it.

In the third task, *concurrent discrimination*, participants were presented with a pair of objects and had to learn that one object in that pair was always associated with a food reward, whereas the other object was never rewarded. The task was made more difficult by sequentially giving participants 20 different object pairs. Each day, they were presented with one trial per pair. Concurrent discrimination is thought to measure trial-and-error learning of specific object information, a function of the basal ganglia.

Healthy adults easily solve both the nonmatching and the concurrent tasks but report that the concurrent task is more difficult because it requires remembering far more information. The key question developmentally is whether there is a difference in the ages at which children (or monkeys) can solve these two tasks.

It turns out that children can solve the concurrent task by about 12 months of age, but not until about 18 months can they solve what most adults believe to be the easier nonmatching task. These results imply that the basal ganglia, the critical area for the concurrent discrimination task, mature more quickly than the temporal lobe, the critical region for the nonmatching-to-sample task.

## A Caution about Linking Correlation to Causation

Throughout this section, we have described research results implying that changes in the brain cause changes in behavior. Neuroscientists assert that by looking at behavioral development and brain development in parallel, they can make some inferences regarding the causes of behavior. Bear in mind, however, that the fact that two things correlate (take place together) does not prove that one of them *causes* the other.

Changes in behavior and in the brain are likely to interact such that neither directly causes the other. Consider a study by Fengji Geng and colleagues (2021), which followed the development of *source memory* (the ability to remember the origin of a memory—that is, the memory of how we came to have a given memory) in children over a 3-year period lasting from ages 4 to 6. After administering memory tasks, the researchers imaged each child's brain using resting-state functional MRI (rs-fMRI). Given that the hippocampus is a key structure in the control of source memory, the research team predicted a relationship between the development of memory and the development of the hippocampus. Specifically, the investigators asked: (1) Does improvement in memory over time stimulate changes in hippocampal connectivity? and (2) Can maturation of the hippocampal circuits predict memory improvement in the future? The results indicated the answer was "yes" to both questions: improved memory over time predicted later changes in functional connectivity, and changes in functional connectivity in the hippocampus predicted later memory improvement.

Overall, Geng and his team concluded that not only does behavioral experience (in this case, the memory tasks) change the brain, but changes in the brain also shape changes in behavior (the later memory changes). In other words, the development of cognitive functions interacts with the development of brain connectivity in a two-way process: experience shapes future changes in the brain, and the brain shapes future changes in behavior. This conclusion is important because it demonstrates that there is no simple, direct causal relationship between behavior and brain development.

## 8-3 Review

**Before you continue, check your understanding. Answers to the Self-Test appear at the back of the book.**

1. The last stage in motor development in infants is the ability to make _____.

2. Language development is correlated with cortical thinning related to _____ and cortical thickening related to _____.

3. _____ are irregularly occurring periods of brain growth that can be correlated to major stages of development.

4. The nonmatching-to-sample task is believed to measure the function of the _____; the concurrent-discrimination learning task is believed to measure the function of the

   _____.

5. Describe a major challenge in inferring changes in brain development from the emergence of behaviors.

## Learning Objectives

- Explain how experience can influence cortical organization, neural connections, and neural structure.
- Describe the impact that environmental conditions can have on brain maturation and plasticity.
- Explain the role that critical periods play in brain development.
- Describe the role of gonadal hormones in brain development.
- Describe the role of gut bacteria and brain development.

**Principle 10:** Neuroplasticity is the hallmark of nervous system functioning.

Section 1-5 summarizes humanity's acquisition of culture. Section 15-3 discusses the emerging field of social neuroscience.

The Hebb synapse, described in Section 15-1, illustrates Hebb's predictions about synaptic plasticity. Section 14-4 elaborates his contributions to learning theory.

**FIGURE 8-23 Hebb–Williams Maze** In this version of the maze, a rat is placed in the start box (S) and must learn to find the food in the goal box (G). Investigators can reconfigure the walls of the maze to set new problems. Rats raised in complex environments solve such mazes much faster than do rats raised in standard laboratory cages.

### 8-4

# Brain Development and the Environment

Developing behaviors are shaped not only by the maturation of brain structures, but also by each person's environment and experience. Neuroplasticity suggests that the brain can be molded, at least at the microscopic level. Brains exposed to different environmental experiences are molded in different ways. For example, culture is an important aspect of the human environment, so culture must help shape the human brain. We would therefore expect people raised in widely differing cultures to acquire brain structure differences that have lifelong effects on their behavior.

The brain is plastic not only in response to external events, but also in response to events within a person's body, including the effects of hormones, injury, and genetic mutations. The developing brain early in life is especially responsive to these internal factors, which in turn alter how the brain responds to external experiences. In this section, we explore a whole range of external and internal environmental influences on brain development. We start with a question: Exactly how does experience alter brain structure?

## Experience and Cortical Organization

Researchers can study the effects of experience on the brain and behavior by placing laboratory animals in different environments and observing the results. In one of the earliest such studies, Donald Hebb (1947) took a group of young laboratory rats home and let them grow up in his kitchen. A control group grew up in standard laboratory cages at McGill University.

The home-reared rats had many experiences that the caged rats did not, including being chased with a broom by Hebb's less-than-enthusiastic wife. Subsequently, Hebb gave both groups a rat-specific intelligence test that consisted of learning to solve a series of mazes, collectively known as Hebb–Williams mazes. **Figure 8-23** shows a sample maze. Home-reared rats performed far better on these tasks than caged rats did. Hebb therefore concluded that experience must influence intelligence.

On the basis of his research, Hebb reasoned that people reared in a stimulating environment will maximize their intellectual development, whereas people raised in impoverished or under-resourced environments, such as those described in the SES study in Research Focus 8-1, will struggle to reach their intellectual potential. Although a generalization, Hebb's reasoning seems logical. But how do we define an environment as stimulating or impoverished?

On the one hand, people living in poverty typically have few formal educational resources—decidedly not an enriched setting—but that does not mean that their environment offers no cognitive stimulation or challenge. On the contrary, people raised in impoverished neighborhoods are better adapted for survival in those settings than are people raised in upper-class homes. Does this adaptability make them more intelligent in a certain way? Could it make them more resilient?

On the other hand, variables associated with poverty can negatively impact development, leading to challenges in future academic achievement. This is probably closer to what Hebb had in mind when he referred to an impoverished environment as limiting intellectual potential. Indeed, Hebb's logic influenced the development of television programs for preschool-age children, such as *Sesame Street*, that offer enrichment for children who would otherwise have little exposure to reading prior to entering school.

At 36 months of age, on average, the vocabulary of children from a low-SES environment is less than one-third that of high-SES children (400 versus 1200 words). This difference grows wider as children develop. It is hypothesized to result from less direct conversation with caregivers and less reading to the children by caregivers. Estimates suggest that by age 4, children from low-SES families have been exposed to about 30 million fewer words than children from high-SES families.

Note that the SES/verbal ability relationship is not mediated by the sheer number of words to which the children are exposed, but rather by the number of "conversational turns" (the back-and-forth dialog between child and adult). Rachel Romeo and colleagues (2018a) used fMRI to show that 4- to 6-year-old children who experienced more conversational turns exhibited greater activation of their left inferior frontal regions (i.e., Broca's area) during language processing. A parallel study by Romeo and another research group (2018b) also showed that the number of conversational turns is related to the amount of white-matter connectivity in language-related tracts to and from Broca's area, but not to other white-matter tracts. It is likely that conversational turns provide increased opportunities for children to practice language. Thus, interventions aimed at increasing children's conversational exposure may ameliorate some of the disadvantages associated with low-SES environments by capitalizing on the early brain plasticity underlying cognitive development.

Seven decades ago, Hebb's studies used complex stimulating environments, but much simpler experiences can also influence brain development. Tactile stimulation of human infants—such as being held closely, massaged, or stroked—is important not only for bonding with caregivers but also for stimulating brain development. For example, tactile stimulation of premature infants in incubators speeds their growth and allows for their quicker release from the hospital. Laboratory studies show that brushing infant rats for 15 minutes 3 times per day for the first 3 weeks of life also speeds up growth and development. Such rats show enhanced motor and cognitive skills in adulthood as well. Tactile stimulation also dramatically improves recovery from brain injury incurred early in development.

The idea that early experiences can affect later behaviors seems sensible enough, but we are left to question why such experiences should make such a difference. One reason is that experience changes neuronal structure, which is especially evident in the cortex, as seen in the Romeo study. Neurons in the brains of animals raised in complex environments, such as that shown in **Figure 8-24**A, are larger and richer in synapses than are those of animals reared in barren cages. Compare the neurons shown in Figure 8-24B. Similarly, 3 weeks of tactile stimulation in infancy increases synapse numbers all over the cortex in adulthood.

Presumably, increased synapse numbers result from increased sensory processing in a complex and stimulating environment. The brains of animals raised in complex settings also display more (and larger) astrocytes. Although complex-rearing studies do not address the effects of human culture directly, making predictions about human development on the basis of their findings is easy. We know that experience can modify the brain, so we can predict that different experiences might modify the brain differently. Musical training is an example, as Research Focus 8-3, Keeping Brains Young by Making Music, explains.

**(A)**                    **(B)**

Laboratory housed          Complex-environment housed

**FIGURE 8-24 Enriched Environment, Enhanced Development (A)** A complex environment for a group of about six rats allows the animals to move about and to interact with one another and with toys that are changed weekly. **(B)** Representative neurons from the parietal cortex of a laboratory-caged rat and a complex-environment–housed rat; the latter has about 25% more dendritic space for synapses.

Research Focus 5-3 describes some structural changes that neurons undergo as a result of learning.

## RESEARCH FOCUS 8-3

### Keeping Brains Young by Making Music

Music is a widespread leisure activity that is known to increase brain plasticity and can lead to a wide range of benefits, including enhanced motor skills, increased intelligence, and increased verbal skills—especially when music training begins in childhood. Music is also known to have beneficial rehabilitative effects in stroke patients and individuals with Parkinson disease. In addition, data suggest that musical training is beneficial in forestalling the effects of aging on the brain (see the review by Herholz & Zatorre, 2012). For example, musical practice reduces age-related declines in a variety of cognitive processes, including nonverbal memory and frontal lobe functions.

Lars Rogenmoser and colleagues (2018) used a novel MRI-based procedure known as *BrainAGE* to investigate the impact of musical training on brain maturation. *BrainAGE* is based on a database of structural MRI data that aggregates brain structure across the whole brain to one single value—the estimated brain age. Rogenmoser and colleagues found that, compared to amateur or professional musicians, non-musicians exhibited higher *BrainAGE* scores, even in relatively young participants (mean ages of approximately 25 years). Thus, making music early in life appears to modulate the effects of aging on the brain.

The *BrainAGE* procedure has applications beyond music. Using this procedure, Katje Franke and colleagues have shown, in a series of papers, that older estimated brain age is predictive of dementia (Franke et al., 2014; Franke & Gaser, 2019). Incidentally, premature-born adults also demonstrated elevated *BrainAGE*, suggesting an increased risk for accelerated aging from human prematurity (Hedderich et al., 2021).

Not only does early musical training keep the brain young, but music can also be used as a therapy to help old brains act like younger brains.

You may have noticed that young children often spontaneously begin to dance when they hear music. The ability of music to stimulate movement has been used as a therapy to restore behaviors such as walking in patients with Parkinson disease. By hearing, or even mentally remembering, the tune of songs, such patients can move with the music rather than being frozen in place and unable to move.

**Depiction of the *BrainAGE* Concept** MRI scans of healthy brains at different ages provides a model of normal age-related changes. This graph compares the new brains with the archived brains to get an estimate of individual brain ages.

Figure 15-12 shows enhanced nerve tract connectivity in people with perfect pitch.

Like early exposure to language during development, early exposure to music alters the brain. Perfect (absolute) pitch, or the ability to re-create a musical note without external reference, is believed to require musical training during an early period, when brain development is most sensitive to this experience. Similarly, adults exposed only to Western music since childhood usually find Eastern music peculiar, even nonmusical, on first encountering it. Not only does early musical training alter brain development, but it also acts to enhance healthy brain aging, much like learning a second language early in life.

Such loss of plasticity does not mean that the adult human brain becomes fixed and unchangeable. Adults' brains are influenced by exposure to new environments and experiences, albeit more slowly and less extensively than children's brains are. In fact, evidence reveals that experience affects the brain well into old age—good news for those of us who are no longer children (Kolb et al., 2003). We will return to the impacts of experience and environment in the context of abnormal brain development in the Section 8-5.

## Environmental Influences on the Pace of Brain Development

As demonstrated by the work of Hebb and Romero (and in the work of Heckman and Noble, covered in Research Focus 8-1), variables associated with SES have a significant influence on brain development. But SES is associated not only with outcome; it is also associated with the pace of brain development (see the review by Tooley et al., 2021).

As described in Section 8-2, cortical thickness increases until about age 2, after which widespread thinning begins between 2 and 5 years of age; this thinning then continues through adolescence and into early adulthood.

Children living in high-SES environments generally have a thicker cortex after about age 4 compared to children living in lower-SES environments, but the difference varies with brain region and age. As detailed in Research Focus 8-1, there is a negative relationship between low SES and cortical thickness in the frontal lobe, and a positive relationship between high SES and cortical thickness in the posterior cortex. The primary sensory and association cortexes display a similar pattern, as seen in **Figure 8-25:** compared to children in high-SES environments, the peak of cortical thickness is reached earlier and pruning begins sooner in the brains of children in low-SES environments. Furthermore, there is a smaller overall decline in the brains of children from high-SES environments. Results from studies such as these have led researchers to associate higher SES with protracted development.

**FIGURE 8-25 Socioeconomic Status and Cortical Thickness** The trajectories shown in the graph are conceptual, based on findings across multiple studies. In the illustration, the brain regions shown in green indicate negative relationships between SES and cortical thickness, and those shown in purple indicate positive relationships between SES and cortical thickness. Research from Tooley et al., 2021.

Imaging studies have also shown differences in the maturation of functional networks such as the default network. Early in their development, all children show extensive connectivity. However, as the brain continues to develop, those connections begin to segregate into networks characteristic of the adult brain. Children from high-SES backgrounds show a slower segregation, which leaves their brains plastic for a longer period of time. Faster development in children from low-SES backgrounds is seen not just in the brain, but in other aspects of development, such as the onset of puberty. Researchers hypothesize that this effect is driven by early stressors.

Several explanations have been proposed for why stress might accelerate brain development (Tooley et al., 2021). Repeated use of stress-detection and stress-regulation brain circuits may lead to faster maturation of the circuitry. Another suggestion is that stressors increase glucocorticoid levels (see Section 14-4), thereby promoting inflammatory processes and causing faster aging across the entire body, including the brain. A third possibility is that children are sensitive to a perceived lack of protection by caregivers, an experience more common among children in less stable environments; this then leads to accelerated development as a means of self-protection and preservation. It follows that higher parental investment associated with higher-SES families would be associated with slower maturation, which appears to the case.

Hebb's experiments with rats demonstrated that an enriched environment provides benefits for brain development. In human studies, this outcome is often referred to as *cognitive enrichment,* such as when children are exposed to more complex and stimulating environments that offer a wide range of learning opportunities. Just as stress accelerates development and shortens the period for developmental plasticity, cognitive enrichment slows development and extends the period of plasticity, which in turn is advantageous for the development of more complex cortical networks. Tooley and colleagues (2021) have proposed the integrative theory, illustrated in **Figure 8-26**, to describe this relationship. In this model, experiences that are negative and repetitive encourage faster maturation, thus potentially restricting plasticity, whereas experiences that are rare and positive are

**Principle 1:** Neural circuits are the functional units of the nervous system.

**FIGURE 8-26 Integrative Theory** In this model, repetitive and negative experiences are associated with accelerated maturation and shortened plasticity periods (*top left* quadrant), and rare and positive experiences are associated with slower maturation and extended plasticity (*bottom right* quadrant). Experiences in the other two quadrants are not predicted to have significant effects on brain maturation. Data from Tooley et al., 2021.

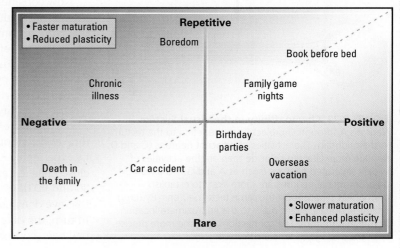

**Principle 10:** Neuroplasticity is the hallmark of nervous system functioning.

**chemoaffinity hypothesis** Proposal that neurons or their axons and dendrites are drawn toward a signaling chemical that indicates the correct pathway.

**amblyopia** Condition in which vision in one eye is reduced as a result of disuse; usually caused by a failure of the two eyes to look in the same direction.

Section 9-2 describes the visual system's anatomy. Figure 2-18 details the midbrain structures.

**FIGURE 8-27 Chemoaffinity in the Visual System**
Neurons A through G project from the retina to the tectum in the midbrain. The activities of adjacent neurons (C and D, say) are more likely to coincide than are the activities of widely separated neurons (such as A and G). As a result, adjacent retinal neurons are more likely to establish permanent synapses on the same tectal neurons. By using chemical signals, axons grow to the approximate location in the tectum (*top*). The connections become more precise with the passage of time (*bottom*).

associated with signals that delay maturation and enhance plasticity. Experiences that are rare and negative or repetitive and positive are predicted to have smaller effects on the pace of maturation. This novel and stimulating model is likely to generate further research in the coming years.

# Experience and Neural Connectivity

We just saw how environment can impact brain development in early childhood, but experience can actually sculpt the brain prenatally, as studies of the developing visual system show quite clearly. A simple analogy will illustrate the anatomical challenge of connecting the visual receptors in the eyes to the rest of the visual system. Imagine that students in a large lecture hall are each viewing the front of the room (the visual field) through a small cardboard tube, such as an empty paper towel roll. If each student looks directly ahead, he or she will see only a small bit of the total visual field.

Essentially, this is how the photoreceptor neurons in the eyes act. Each cell sees only a small bit of the visual field. The problem lies in putting all of the bits together to form a complete picture. To do so, analogously to students sitting side by side, receptors that see adjacent views must send their information to adjacent regions in the various parts of the brain's visual system, such as the midbrain. How do they accomplish this feat?

Roger Sperry (1963) suggested the **chemoaffinity hypothesis**, the idea that specific molecules in different cells in various midbrain regions give each cell a distinctive chemical identity. Each cell has an identifiable biochemical label. Presumably, incoming axons seek out a specific chemical, such as the tropic factors discussed in Section 8-2, and consequently land in the correct general midbrain region.

Many experiments have shown that this process takes place prenatally, as the eye and brain are developing. But the problem is that chemical affinity directs incoming axons only to a general location. To return to our two adjacent retinal cells, how do they now place themselves in precisely the correct position?

Here is where postnatal experience comes in: fine-tuning of neural placement is believed to be dependent on the neurons' activity. Because adjacent receptors tend to be activated at the same time, they tend to form synapses on the same neurons in the midbrain after chemoaffinity has drawn them to a general midbrain region. **Figure 8-27** illustrates this process. Neurons A and G are unlikely to be activated by the same stimulus, so they seldom fire synchronously. Neurons A and B, in contrast, are apt to be activated by the same stimuli, as are B and C. Through this simultaneous activity and with the passage of time, cells eventually line up correctly in the connections they form.

Now consider what happens to axons coming from different eyes. Although the neural inputs from the two eyes may be active simultaneously, neurons in the same eye are more likely to be active together than are cells in different eyes. The net effect is that inputs from the two eyes tend to organize themselves into neural bands, called *columns*, that represent the same region of space in each eye, as shown on the left in **Figure 8-28**. Formation of these segregated cortical columns therefore depends on the patterns of coinciding electrical activity on the incoming axons.

If experience is abnormal—for example, if one eye is covered during a crucial time in development—the neural connections will not be guided appropriately by experience. As shown at the right in Figure 8-28, the effect of suturing one eye closed has the most disruptive effect on cortical organization in kittens between 30 and 60 days after birth. In a child who has a "lazy eye," visual input from that eye does not contribute to fine-tuning the neural connections as it should. In turn, the details of those connections develop abnormally, much as if the eye had been covered. The resulting loss of sharpness in vision is called **amblyopia**.

To summarize, an organism's genetic blueprint is vague in regard to exactly which connections in the brain go to exactly which neurons. Experience fine-tunes neural connectivity by modifying those details.

# Critical Periods for Experience and Brain Development

The preceding examples of perfect pitch, plasticity, and visual connectivity show that for healthy development, specific sensory experiences occurring at particular times are especially important. A time during which brain development is most sensitive to a specific experience is called either a **critical period** or a *sensitive period*.

A lack of appropriate sensory experience during a critical period may result in abnormal brain development, leading to abnormal behavior that endures even into adulthood. Our colleague Richard Tees offered an analogy to help explain the concept. He pictured the developing animal as a little train traveling past an environmental setting, perhaps the Rocky Mountains. All the windows are closed at the beginning of the journey (prenatal development), but at particular stages of the trip, the windows in certain cars open, exposing the occupants (different parts of the brain) to the outside world. Some windows open to expose the brain to specific sounds, others to certain smells, others to particular sights, and so on.

This exposure affects the brain's development, and the absence of any exposure through an open window severely disturbs that development. As the journey continues, the windows become harder to open, and finally they close permanently. This does not mean that the brain can no longer change, but rather that changes become much harder to induce.

Now imagine two different trains, one headed through the Rocky Mountains and another traveling across Eastern Europe. The views from the windows are very different, and the effects on the brain are correspondingly different. In other words, not only is the brain altered by the experiences it has during a critical period, but the particular kinds of experiences encountered matter, too.

An extensively studied example of a behavior occurring during a critical period is the phenomenon of **imprinting**, whereby an animal learns to restrict its social preferences to a specific class of objects, usually the members of its own species. In birds, such as chickens and waterfowl, the critical period for imprinting often comes shortly after hatching. Typically, the first moving object a young hatchling sees is a parent or sibling, so the hatchling's brain appropriately imprints to its own species.

Appropriate imprinting is not inevitable, however. Konrad Lorenz (1970) demonstrated that if the first animal or object that baby goslings encounter is a person, the goslings imprint to that person as though he or she were their mother. **Figure 8-29** shows a flock of goslings that imprinted to Lorenz and followed him wherever he went. Incorrect imprinting has long-term consequences for the hatchlings. They often direct their subsequent sexual behavior toward humans. A Barbary dove that had become imprinted to Lorenz directed its courtship toward his hand and even tried to copulate with the hand if it was held in a certain orientation.

This quick acquisition and its permanent behavioral consequences suggest that during imprinting, the brain makes a rapid change of some kind, probably a structural change, given the permanence of the new behavior. Indeed, such a change does happen. Gabriel Horn and his colleagues at Cambridge University (1985) showed that synapses in a specific forebrain region enlarge with imprinting. Thus, imprinting seems a good model for studying brain plasticity during development, in part because the changes are rapid, related to specific experience, and localized in the brain.

But why do critical periods end? Takao Hensch (2018) hypothesizes that two types of *molecular brakes* act in tandem to terminate critical periods. One type of

**critical period** Developmental window during which some event has a long-lasting influence on the brain; also called *sensitive period*.

**imprinting** Formation of an attachment by an animal to one or more objects or animals at a critical period in development.

In infancy, the projections from the two eyes overlap.

In adulthood, a nonoverlapping pattern of terminal arborizations from each eye is normal.

If one eyelid of a kitten is occluded during a critical week of development, the terminations from that eye retract and those from the open eye expand.

**FIGURE 8-28 Ocular Dominance Columns** Typically in the postnatal development of the cat brain, axons from each eye enter the cortex, where they grow large terminal arborizations. (L, left eye; R, right eye.)

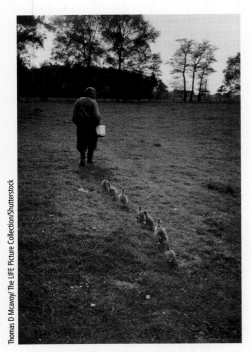

**FIGURE 8-29 Strength of Imprinting**
Ethologist Konrad Lorenz followed by goslings that imprinted on him. He was the first object that the geese encountered after hatching, so he became their "mother."

The perineuronal net, depicted here, covers PV neurons and limits plasticity.

brake is epigenetic and leads to increased expression of certain genes during development, which act to limit plasticity. The second type of brake involves *perineuronal nets*, which are specialized structures in the extracellular matrix that act as a molecular lattice-work over a neuron (much like the netting that surrounds neuronal cell bodies), such as GABAergic interneurons containing the calcium-binding protein *parvalbumin* (known as PV cells). Perineuronal nets reach maturity at the end of the critical period and can act as a physical barrier to morphological plasticity by blocking the generation of new synapses. A growing body of evidence shows that disruption of perineuronal nets in adulthood can allow a reopening of critical periods. Temporarily removing perineuronal nets on PV cells may provide a promising avenue for the development of brain therapies.

Our earlier discussion of the effect of SES on language development is clearly related to the idea of critical periods. The influence of SES is especially important to language and brain development in the first 3 years after birth, so these years represent a critical period in language development. As with Lorenz's goslings, later similar experiences do not have the same impact. Hensch's general mechanisms for closing critical periods may well be applicable in the context of SES and language development, as it is known that early experiences can have large effects on gene expression.

## The Adolescent Brain as a Critical Period

There is a growing consensus that adolescence is a period of heightened neural plasticity relative to the juvenile and adult brains (e.g., Fuhrmann et al., 2015). The onset of enhanced plasticity likely coincides with the release of gonadal hormones (discussed later), but the timing of the reduction in plasticity at the end of adolescence has not been well studied. Several brain changes clearly occur during adolescence, including increased production of astrocytes and myelin, decreased cortical thickness, and, most importantly, active changes in connectivity. Connections with the amygdala, striatum, hippocampus, and prefrontal cortex are changing throughout this period. Casey and colleagues (2015) provided an oversimplified illustration (presented in **Figure 8-30**) of the types of changes in prefrontal-subcortical circuitry: the interconnections and their relative strength change with development, providing insights into the emotional, social, and other nonemotional behaviors of adolescents. These studies support the important principle that changes in connectivity must be precise enough for an altered circuit to process information differently and carry out the altered (or new) function.

The dramatic changes that characterize adolescence allow for a high degree of adaptability, a crucial fact at a time when individuals are essentially inventing themselves (Blakemore, 2018). But enhanced plasticity also renders the brain vulnerable to a wide range of experiences, such as stress, psychoactive drugs, brain trauma (e.g., concussion), and harmful peer relationships, which influence brain organization and function differently in adolescents than in adults. It is no accident that many forms of mental illness become apparent in adolescence (e.g., Tottenham & Galvan, 2016).

**FIGURE 8-30 Changes in Prefrontal-Subcortical Circuitry** Simplistic illustration of hierarchical age-related changes in connectivity from subcortico-subcortical to cortico-subcortical circuits. Regional changes in connectivity are indicated with dotted and bolded lines. The relative strength of the connections is indicated by the dashed lines (weaker), solid lines (stronger), and bold lines (strongest). Color indicates areas of more intense change at each stage, with yellow indicating less intense change and red indicating more. Abbreviations: Amy: amygdala; IPFC: lateral prefrontal cortex; mPFC: medial prefrontal cortex; OFC: orbitofrontal cortex; VS: ventral striatum; VTA: ventral tegmental area. Research from Casey et al., 2015.

## Gonadal Hormones and Brain Development

Gonadal (sex) hormones—particularly testosterone and estrogen—play a key role in brain changes during adolescence, but they are also central to brain development prenatally. In humans, the genitals begin to form in the seventh week after conception, but they appear identical in the two sexes at this early stage. At this point in embryonic development, no *sexual dimorphism*—that is, structural differences related to the influence of sex hormones—yet exists. The Y chromosome in males controls the process by which an undifferentiated, primitive gonad develops into testes. The testes subsequently secrete the sex hormone **testosterone**, the best-known **androgen** (the class of hormones that stimulates or controls masculine characteristics), which stimulates development of male reproductive organs and, in puberty, the appearance of male secondary sexual characteristics such as facial hair and deepening of the voice. This process is termed **masculinization**. **Estrogens**, the variety of sex hormones responsible for the female's distinguishing characteristics, play a similar role in the development of female sexual and reproductive organs, among other characteristics.

Gonadal hormones, including both testosterone and estrogen, change the genetic activity of certain cells. Most obviously, they influence the cells that form the genitals, but neural cells also respond to them. For example, as testosterone secretion begins (about 60 days after conception), regions of the embryonic brain typically begin to show sexual dimorphism. Throughout prenatal development, the presence of testosterone affects the number of neurons formed in certain brain areas, reduces the number of neurons that die, increases cell growth, increases or reduces dendritic branching and synaptic growth, and regulates synaptic activity, among other effects.

Jill Goldstein and her colleagues found sex differences in the volume of cortical regions known to have differential levels of receptors for testosterone (androgen receptors) and estrogen, respectively, as shown in **Figure 8-31** (Goldstein et al., 2001). Orange areas in the figure are larger in females, and green areas are larger in males. Clearly, a male brain and a female brain are not the same. Hormones alter brain development, and clear sex differences appear in the rate of brain development (see Figure 8-18).

Although postnatal experiences may influence sex differences in the brain, an MRI study of the brains of newborns conducted by Douglas Dean and his colleagues (2018) showed that sex differences in brain structure exist at 1 month of life. This finding suggests that the sex differences emerge in the prenatal period and in the first month of life.

In recent years, many assumptions about gonadal hormones and their role in development have been overturned. For example, it was once thought that testosterone played no important role in brain development. Another recently overturned assumption is that the major effects of testosterone on the brain are found only in males. Tiffany Ho and colleagues (2020) found in a study using diffusion tensor imaging (DTI) of adolescent brains that testosterone levels in females, but not in males, were positively related to changes in white matter in the corpus callosum and other cortical tracts.

## Gut Bacteria and Brain Development

We have emphasized factors that affect CNS development directly, but a less direct route involves the enteric nervous system (ENS). The ENS sends information to the brain that affects our mental state. The brain, in turn, can modify gut function.

An important component of the ENS is the *microbiome*, the bacteria in the gut with which the ENS interacts. Approximately $10^{14}$ microbiota populate the adult gut, which means that the microbiota outnumber the host body cells by a factor of 10. In utero, however, the fetus's gut is sterile. It is only at birth that trillions of microbes from the mother's vaginal and anal fluids, and later from her skin, invade the baby's body and start to grow. The mode of delivery (vaginal versus cesarean delivery), breastfeeding

**testosterone** Sex hormone secreted by the testes and responsible for the emergence of typically masculine characteristics.

**androgen** Class of hormones that stimulates or controls masculine characteristics.

**masculinization** Process by which exposure to androgens (male sex hormones) alters the brain and stimulates an individual to develop male reproductive organs and secondary sexual characteristics (e.g., facial hair and deepening of the voice).

**estrogen** Variety of sex hormones responsible for the distinguishing female characteristics.

Section 12-5 details the actions of gonadal hormones on brain, sex, and cognitive behavior.

Lateral view          Medial view

**FIGURE 8-31 Sex Differences in Brain Volume** Cerebral areas related to sex differences in the distribution of estrogen (orange) and androgen (green) receptors in the developing brain correspond to areas of relatively larger cerebral volumes in adult women and men. Information from Goldstein et al., 2001.

Sex differences in brain organization are described further in Section 12-5.

Section 2-5 introduces the ENS and microbiome.

**FIGURE 8-32  PGN Path to the Brain** Gut bacteria can access the brain via the blood circulation. Bacterial peptidoglycans (PGN) leave the gut, enter the bloodstream, and cross the blood–brain barrier to interact with neurons. Research from Gonzalez-Santana & Diaz-Heijtz, 2020.

**psychobiotics** Treatment that uses live bacteria (probiotics) or compounds to enhance the growth of gut bacteria (prebiotics).

practices (formula versus breast milk), and antibiotic use influence the growth of the microbiome. But in addition, many other factors, such as length of gestation (e.g., full term versus preterm), nutritional status, and genetics, can profoundly alter colonization of the microbiome. The fact that gut microbiome maturation occurs in parallel with brain development has led some researchers to propose that the early postnatal period is a critical time-window for microbiota–brain interactions, and is a key determinant of health later in life (see the reviews by Cussotto et al., 2019, and Gonzalez-Santana & Diaz-Heijtz, 2020).

The precise mechanisms of the gut–brain interactions have not yet been clearly defined, but we do know of multiple direct and indirect pathways for these interactions. For example, it appears that bacteria-derived products such as peptidoglycans (PGNs) might directly affect the brain by activating the pattern-recognition receptors (PRRs) of the immune system, as illustrated in **Figure 8-32**. PGNs derive from the plasma membrane of bacteria. They are present in circulating blood and can cross the blood–brain barrier to affect pattern-recognition receptors.

Indeed, many neurodevelopmental disorders, including autism, may be related to an atypical microbiome early in life (e.g., Gonzalez-Santana & Diaz-Heijtz, 2020; Kelly et al., 2017). One preventive measure is to intervene to alter the microbiome. Such interventions are known as **psychobiotics**, referring to their use of live bacteria (probiotics) or compounds that enhance the growth of gut bacteria (prebiotics) to confer mental health benefits. Although relatively few human clinical trials of psychobiotics have been published, animal laboratory studies have proven encouraging (Bastiaanssen & Cryan, 2021). For example, a series of studies using a rodent model of early-life stress showed that untreated stressed animals exhibited cognitive deficits in adulthood, whereas animals whose mothers received a probiotic formulation in their drinking water while the pups were nursing displayed no such effects in adulthood (e.g., Cowan et al., 2016). Other studies have shown that certain bacteria can enhance emotional learning and reduce anxiety and the effects of stress. These same bacteria may play an important role in the neurodevelopment and programming of social behaviors across diverse animal species (Sherwin et al., 2019).

## 8-4 Review

Before you continue, check your understanding. Answers to the Self-Test appear at the back of the book.

1. The idea that specific molecules in different cells in various midbrain regions give each cell a distinctive chemical identity is known as the _____.

2. Exposure to environmental stress early in life can _____ brain development and _____ the period for developmental plasticity.

3. During brain development, the hormone _____ influences the development of masculine characteristics, and _____ are responsible for the development of female characteristics.

4. The brain's sensitivity to experience is highest during _____.

5. Why do so many mental disorders appear during adolescence?

**Learning Objectives**

- Describe how prenatal and postnatal aversive experiences can affect brain development.
- Define time-dependent effects and explain their relationship to brain injury and subsequent development.
- Explain the role of neuroplasticity in our ability to overcome minor deviations in brain development.

## 8-5

# Abnormal Experience and Brain Development

As we have shown, both prenatal and postnatal experience and environment play a significant role in modifying brain development. In this section, we discuss how aversive experiences, injury, and other factors can lead to abnormal brain development and neurodevelopmental disorders.

# Aversive Experience and Brain Development

In Section 8-4, we saw how brain development is affected by a range of environmental stimuli, but not all experiences benefit brain development. If complex or enriched experiences early in life can stimulate brain growth and influence later behavior, then it seems likely that severely restricted experiences early in life would delay both brain growth and behavior. To study the effects of such restrictions, Donald Hebb and his colleagues (Clarke et al., 1951) placed young Scottish terriers in the dark with as little stimulation as possible and compared their behavior to that of dogs raised in a typical environment.

When the dogs raised in the barren environment (an approach that would obviously be considered unethical by today's standards) were later removed from it, their behavior was highly unusual. They showed virtually no reaction to people or other dogs and appeared to have lost any pain sensation. Even sticking pins in them (also unethical) produced no response. When given a dog version of the Hebb–Williams intelligence test for rats, these dogs performed terribly and were unable to learn tasks that dogs raised in more stimulating settings learned easily.

Results of subsequent studies show that depriving young animals of visual input or of maternal contact, specifically, has devastating consequences for their behavioral development and presumably for their brain development. Austin Riesen (1982) and his colleagues extensively studied animals raised in the dark. They found that after early visual deprivation, even though the animals' eyes still work, they may be functionally blind. An absence of visual stimulation results in the atrophy of dendrites on cortical neurons—essentially the opposite of the results observed in the brains of animals raised in complex and stimulating environments.

Not only does the absence of specific sensory inputs adversely affect brain development; so, too, does the absence of more complex typical experiences. In the 1950s, Harry Harlow (1971) began the first systematic laboratory studies of analogous deprivation in laboratory animals. Harlow showed that infant monkeys raised without maternal (or paternal) contact develop grossly atypical intellectual and social behaviors in adulthood.

Guided in part by studies of human orphanages, which mistakenly concluded that minimal maternal contact would benefit development and reduce infant mortality, Harlow separated baby monkeys from their mothers shortly after birth and raised them in individual cages (for an engaging account of the orphanage studies, see Blum, 2002). The effects were very different from Harlow's expectations. Perhaps the most stunning effect occurred in adulthood, when these animals were totally unable to establish normal relations with other animals. Unfortunately, Harlow did not analyze the deprived monkeys' brains. We would predict atrophy of cortical neurons, especially in the frontal lobe regions related to social behavior. Harlow's student Stephen Suomi has found a wide variety of hormonal and neurological abnormalities among motherless monkeys, including epigenetic changes (see the review by Dettmer & Suomi, 2014).

Children who are raised in a barren environment or are abused or neglected are at a serious disadvantage later in life. In Section 8-4, we discussed the impact of an impoverished environment on the brain development of children. Proof of this impact is also evident in the hampered intellectual and motor development displayed by children raised in dreadful circumstances, such as those described in Clinical Focus 8-4, Romanian Orphans. Adverse developmental experiences, particularly those that are severe or extreme, can clearly alter the brain irrevocably. Future success in school and in life is not simply a matter of individual willpower, but rather depends on effective interventions. As a society, we cannot ignore the effects of the environment to which our children are exposed.

Early exposure to stress, including prenatally, also has major effects on a child's later behavior. Stress can alter the expression of certain genes, such as those related to serotonin (5-hydroxytryptamine, or 5-HT) reuptake. Early alteration in serotonin activity can severely alter how the brain responds to stressful experiences later in life.

Section 7-8 details current guidelines for the ethical treatment of non-human animals in brain-behavior research.

## ◉ CLINICAL FOCUS 8-4

# Romanian Orphans

In the 1970s, Romania's Communist regime outlawed all forms of birth control and abortion. The natural result: more than 100,000 unwanted children in state-run orphanages.

The conditions in these institutions were appalling. The children were housed and clothed, but given virtually no environmental stimulation. Mostly they were confined to cots with few, if any, playthings and virtually no personal interaction with their overworked caregivers, who looked after 20 to 25 children at once. Bathing often consisted of being hosed down with cold water.

After the Communist government fell, the outside world intervened. Hundreds of these children were placed in adoptive homes throughout the world, especially in the United States, Canada, and the United Kingdom. Studies of these severely deprived children on arrival in their new homes document malnourishment, chronic respiratory and intestinal infections, and severe developmental impairments.

A British study by Michael Rutter (1998) and his colleagues assessed the orphans as being 2 standard deviations below age-matched children in terms of weight, height, and head circumference (taken as a very rough measure of brain size). The application of scales of motor and cognitive development showed that most of the children placed in the impaired range.

The improvement these children showed in the first 2 years after placement in their adoptive homes was nothing short of spectacular. Average height and weight advanced to nearly normal, although head circumference remained below normal. Many tested in the normal range of motor and cognitive development. But a significant number were still considered intellectually impaired. What caused these individual differences in recovery from the past deprivation?

The key factor was age at adoption. Children adopted before 6 months of age did significantly better than those adopted later. In a Canadian study by Elinor Ames (1997), Romanian orphans who were adopted before 4 months of age and then tested at 4½ years of age had an average Stanford–Binet IQ score of 98. Age-matched Canadian controls had an average score of 109. Brain-imaging studies showed that children adopted at an older age had smaller brains than normal.

Charles Nelson and his colleagues (Berens & Nelson, 2015; Nelson et al., 2007; Nelson et al., 2019) analyzed cognitive and social development as well as event-related potential (ERP) measures in a group of children who had remained in Romania. Whether these children had moved to foster homes or remained in institutions, the studies reveal severe abnormalities at about 4 years of age. The age at adoption was again important, but in

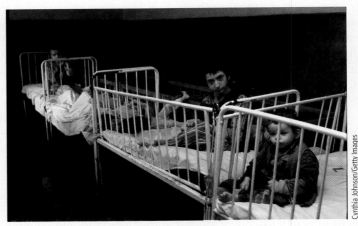

Romanian orphans warehoused in the 1970s and 1980s endured the conditions shown in this photograph. The utter absence of stimuli hampered their normal brain development.

the Nelson studies the critical age appears to be before 24 months rather than 6 months, as in the earlier studies.

The extent of early deprivation was extreme in the Romanian study, but analysis of children who experienced less extreme periods of institutionalization and subsequent adoption have also shown significant changes in the volume of cerebral structures, especially in the frontal lobe, hippocampus, and amygdala. For example, Hodel et al. (2015) studied a diverse group of post-institutionalized children (ages 12–14) who had entered the United States predominately from China, Eastern Europe/Russia, and India. These children had been living with their adopted families for an average of about 12 years, but they still exhibited abnormal development of the prefrontal cortex. Hodel's study showed that the prefrontal cortex may be particularly vulnerable to early life adversity.

The inescapable conclusion is that the human brain may be able to recover from a brief period of extreme deprivation in early infancy, but periods of deprivation longer than 24 months produce significant developmental abnormalities that cannot be rehabilitated completely. The studies of Romanian and other orphans make it clear that the developing brain requires stimulation for healthy development. Although the brain may be able to catch up after brief deprivation, severe deprivation lasting many months results in a small brain and associated behavioral abnormalities, especially in terms of cognitive and social skills.

Stress early in life may predispose people to develop behavioral disorders, such as depression (Tottenham, 2014). Michelle VanTieghem and colleagues (2021) performed repeated structural MRIs on children from ages 4 to 20 years who had been institutionalized during the first 3 years of life, and found a lasting imprint on brain structure. The amygdala was enlarged in early life, but by 9 years, it was reduced to below-average size compared to the amygdala in the non-institutionalized comparison group. In addition, the hippocampus remained small throughout life relative to the comparison group, even though the institutionalized children had been adopted into stable homes by around age 3. Other studies have found changes in frontal lobe anatomy associated with the development of depressive and anxiety disorders in adopted children that may be linked to the epigenetic effects described in Section 8-2.

Section 5-4 explains the neurobiology of the stress response. Section 16-2 connects mood and reactivity to stress.

Cynthia Johnson/Getty Images

## Effects of Adverse Experience on Prenatal Development

As noted in Section 8-4, brain development can be affected by either parent's experiences before conception or the experiences of the mother or fetus during gestation. Because developmental events change so dramatically and quickly in utero, we should not be surprised that the effects of fetal experiences vary with the precise developmental stage. As a rule, the CNS is especially sensitive during gestational weeks 4 to 8, as the neural tube forms. It remains sensitive through the period of cerebral neurogenesis, which continues until the end of the second trimester. In the previous section, we presented evidence showing how environmental influences can impact an animal's neuronal structure. Work by Robbin Gibb and her colleagues (2014) has also shown that housing pregnant rats in complex environments, like that depicted in Figure 8-24A, results in the offspring showing increased dendritic spine density in the cortex, as though the animals had been placed in the environment in adulthood.

As noted earlier, prenatal experiences also can lead to abnormal behavior in children and adults. The consensus is that perinatal adversity, such as gestational stress at or near birth, is a significant risk factor for later behavioral disorders (Bock et al., 2014). Even events such as stress or drug use that occur *before* conception can lead to epigenetic effects in offspring. Although such effects are usually presumed to come from maternal exposure before conception, increasing evidence from research on humans points to paternal preconception experience also modifying children's brain development, perhaps including acquisition of fetal alcohol spectrum disorder (FASD) (e.g., Zuccolo et al., 2016). Similarly, studies using laboratory animals have shown that preconception stress in either females or males alters brain and behavior in their offspring (e.g., Harker et al., 2015; Jenkins et al., 2018).

In fact, evidence from studies of laboratory animals suggests that the effects of preconception experiences are greater from the father than from the mother (e.g., Dias & Ressler, 2014). One explanation is that the preconceptual experiences in males may change the *germline*, the genetic material of cells that is passed through successive generations. For example, the genetic material in the sperm or egg is part of the germline. The egg cells of adults are not easily changed by experiences because they are formed early in body development in females. In contrast, sperm are constantly being renewed, so gene expression in sperm is more likely to be altered by males' experience and passed on to their progeny. Meanwhile, maternal experience before conception can affect offspring directly by changing the stress response of the mother, which could in turn alter the offspring's brain development, or by changing the mother's behavior toward her infant(s).

Clinical Focus 6-2 details FASD.

## Injury and Brain Development

Into the late 1800s, infants and children were generally believed to show better recovery from brain injury than did adults. In the 1930s, Donald Hebb studied children with major birth-related injuries to the frontal lobes and found them to have severe and permanent behavioral abnormalities in adulthood. He concluded that brain damage early in life can alter the brain's subsequent development and actually may be worse than injury later in life.

Have other studies confirmed Hebb's conclusion? Few anatomical studies of humans with early brain injuries exist, but we can make some general predictions from studying laboratory animals. In general, early brain injuries do produce atypical brains, especially when those injuries occur at certain critical periods in development.

For humans, the worst time for a brain injury appears to be in the last half of the intrauterine period and the first couple of months after birth. Rats and cats that are injured at a comparable time have a significantly smaller brain than average, and their cortical neurons show general atrophy relative to healthy brains, as illustrated on the left in **Figure 8-33**. Behaviorally, these animals appear cognitively deficient over a wide range of skills.

**FIGURE 8-33 Time-Dependent Effects**
Damage to the rat's frontal cortex on the day of birth leads to cortical neurons with simple dendritic fields and sparse growth of spines in the adult (*left*). In contrast, damage to the frontal cortex at 10 days of age leads to cortical neurons with expanded dendritic fields and denser spines than normal in adults (*right*). Information from Kolb & Gibb, 1993.

Injury to the developing brain is not always devastating, however. For example, researchers have known for more than 100 years that children who have brain injuries in the first couple of years after birth almost never have the severe language disturbances common to adults with equivalent injuries. Animal studies help explain why.

Whereas damage to the rat brain in the developmental period comparable to the last few months of gestation in humans produces widespread cortical atrophy, damage at a time in rat brain development roughly comparable to ages 6 months to 2 years in humans actually produces more dendritic development in rats (Figure 8-33, right). Furthermore, these animals show dramatic recovery of functions, which implies that during development the brain has a capacity to compensate for injury. Parallel studies in cats have shown extensive reorganization of cortex-to-cortex connections after early injury to the visual cortex (see the review by Payne & Lomber, 2001; for a review of critical periods in recovery from brain injury during development, see Kolb, 2021).

# Other Sources of Abnormal Brain Development

The nervous system need not be damaged by external forces to develop abnormally. Many genetic aberrations are believed to result in abnormalities in brain development and ultimately brain structure. *Spina bifida*, in which the genetic blueprint goes awry and the neural tube does not close completely, leads to an incompletely formed spinal cord. After birth, unless they are treated with folic acid, children with spina bifida usually have serious motor problems.

Imagine what happens if some genetic aberration causes improper closure of the front end of the neural tube. Because the front end of the neural tube forms the brain (see Figure 8-5), this failure results in gross abnormalities in brain development known as **anencephaly**. Affected infants die soon after birth.

Atypical brain development can be much subtler than anencephaly. For example, if cells do not migrate to their correct locations, and if these mispositioned cells do not subsequently die, they can disrupt brain function and may lead to disorders ranging from seizures to schizophrenia (see the review by Guerrini et al., 2007). In a variety of conditions, neurons fail to differentiate normally. In certain cases, neurons fail to produce long dendrites or spines, which results in abnormal brain connectivity and developmental disabilities.

The opposite condition also is possible: neurons may continue to make dendrites and form connections with other cells until the neurons reach an extraordinarily large size. The functional consequences of all these newly formed connections can be devastating. Excitatory synapses in the wrong location effectively short-circuit a neuron's function.

Subtle abnormal events also can be devastating—and even terminal. **Sudden infant death syndrome (SIDS)**, the unexplained death while asleep of a seemingly healthy infant less than 1 year old, kills approximately 2500 babies each year in the United States alone. Postmortem studies reveal that SIDS victims are more likely than other babies to have a particular gene variation that makes the serotonin transporter unusually efficient. Normally, the serotoninergic system helps stimulate a respiratory mechanism that responds to high carbon dioxide levels in the blood and acts to expel the gas.

In babies who die of SIDS, serotonin is cleared from the synapse more rapidly than normal. This action makes 5-HT less effective in regulating life-threatening events such as carbon dioxide buildup during sleep. Babies can breathe in excessive levels of carbon dioxide when this gas is trapped in their bedding, for example, and suffocate.

In addition to the serotonin transporter abnormality, David Paterson and his colleagues (2006) found an abnormally low occurrence of 5-HT$_{1A}$ receptors in SIDS victims' brains. These researchers found that boys have significantly fewer 5-HT$_{1A}$ receptors than do females, a result consistent with the higher SIDS mortality noted in boys. Hannah Kinney (2009) speculates that the primary defect is increased numbers of

**anencephaly** Failure of the forebrain to develop.

**sudden infant death syndrome (SIDS)** Unexplained death while asleep of a seemingly healthy infant less than 1 year old.

5-HT cells, possibly arising during fetal development and owing to unknown causes, but augmented by adverse prenatal exposure to alcohol, nicotine, and/or other factors. This defect leads to the changes in 5-HT$_{1A}$ receptors.

A curious consequence of abnormal brain development is that behavioral effects may emerge only as the brain matures and the maturing regions begin to play a greater role in behavior. This consequence is especially evident with frontal lobe injuries. The frontal lobes continue to develop into early adulthood, and often not until adolescence do the effects of frontal lobe abnormalities become noticeable.

Schizophrenia is a disease characterized by slow development, usually not becoming obvious until late adolescence. Clinical Focus 8-5, Schizophrenia, relates the disease's progress to its possible origin.

Section 16-2 describes the schizophrenic brain, and Section 5-3 explores schizophrenia's possible relation to excessive DA or 5-HT activity in that brain.

## ◉ CLINICAL FOCUS 8-5

# Schizophrenia

When Mrs. T. was 16 years old, she began to experience her first symptom of schizophrenia: a profound feeling that people were staring at her. These bouts of self-consciousness soon forced her to end her public piano performances. Her self-consciousness led to withdrawal, then to fearful delusions that others were speaking about her behind her back, and finally to suspicions that they were plotting to harm her.

At first Mrs. T.'s illness was intermittent, and the return of her intelligence, warmth, and ambition between episodes allowed her to complete several years of college, to marry, and to rear three children. She had to enter a hospital for her illness for the first time at age 28, after the birth of her third child, when she began to hallucinate.

Now, at 45, Mrs. T. is never entirely well. She has seen dinosaurs on the street and live animals in her refrigerator. While hallucinating, she speaks and writes in an incoherent, but almost poetic way. At other times, she is more lucid, but even then the voices she hears sometimes lead her to do dangerous things, such as driving very fast down the highway in the middle of the night, dressed only in a nightgown. . . . At other times and without any apparent stimulus, Mrs. T. has bizarre visual hallucinations. For example, she saw cherubs in the grocery store. These experiences leave her preoccupied, confused, and frightened, unable to perform such everyday tasks as cooking or playing the piano. (Gershon & Rieder, 1992, p. 127)

It has always been easier to identify schizophrenic behavior than to define schizophrenia. Perhaps the one universally accepted criterion for its diagnosis is the absence of other neurological disturbances or affective (mood) disorders that could cause a person to lose touch with reality—a definition by default.

Schizophrenia is generally considered to be a developmental disorder because symptoms usually emerge in adolescence and early adulthood. These symptoms are believed to be a consequence of events occurring early in development and reflect a combination of genetic and environmental effects on brain development. It has been proposed that multiple genes trigger a cascade of neuropathological events, which begin during gestation and progress during adolescence and adulthood, as they are influenced by environmental factors (see the review by Rapoport et al., 2012).

Symptoms of schizophrenia vary, suggesting that biological abnormalities also vary from person to person. Most patients appear to stay at a fairly stable level after the first few years of symptoms, with little evidence of a decline in neuropsychological functioning. Symptoms come and go, much as they did for Mrs. T., but the severity is relatively constant after the first few episodes.

Numerous studies have investigated the brains of schizophrenia patients, both through MRI and computed tomography (CT) scans and in autopsies. Although the results vary, most neuroscientists agree that brains affected by schizophrenia weigh less than normal and have enlarged ventricles. Research findings also suggest that brains affected by schizophrenia have smaller frontal lobes (or at least a reduction in the number of neurons in the prefrontal cortex) and thinner parahippocampal gyri. Furthermore, the onset of symptoms appears to be associated with progressive gray-matter abnormalities, especially during the early stages of the illness (for a review, see Dietsche et al., 2017).

Joyce Kovelman and Arnold Scheibel (1984) found abnormalities in the orientation of hippocampal neurons in people with schizophrenia. Rather than the consistently parallel orientation of neurons in this region characteristic of healthy brains, brains affected by schizophrenia have a more haphazard organization, as shown in the accompanying drawings.

**Hippocampus**

Pyramidal cell orientation in the hippocampus of **(A)** a healthy brain and **(B)** a brain affected by schizophrenia. Research from Kovelman & Scheibel, 1984.

**(A)** Organized (healthy) pyramidal neurons

**(B)** Disorganized (schizophrenic) pyramidal neurons

# Developmental Disability

Impaired cognitive functioning accompanies abnormal brain development. Impairment may range from mild, allowing the individual to have an almost normal lifestyle, to severe, with the individual requiring constant care. As summarized in **Table 8-3**, such developmental disability can result from chronic malnutrition, genetic abnormalities such as Down syndrome, hormonal abnormalities, brain injury, or neurological disease. Different causes produce different abnormalities in brain organization, but all types of developmental disability share one critical similarity: the brain is not normal.

Dominique Purpura (1974) conducted one of the few systematic investigations of the brains of children with developmental disabilities. Purpura used Golgi staining to examine the neurons of children who had died of accidents or diseases unrelated to the nervous system. When he examined the brains of children with various forms of intellectual disability, he found that dendrite growth was stunted and the spines were very sparse relative to the dendrites from children of typical intelligence, as illustrated in **Figure 8-34**.

The simpler neuronal structure probably indicates a marked reduction in the number of brain connections, which presumably caused the developmental disability. Variation in both the nature and the extent of neuronal abnormality in different children would lead to different behavioral syndromes. In addition, an abnormality in one system during development can interact with other systems, thereby producing new abnormalities. For example, children with recurrent ear infections often have delayed hearing development, which in turn can slow language development. Similarly, early stress can alter brain development, which in turn can render the brain sensitive to stressors in adolescence.

# How Do Any of Us Develop a Normal Brain?

When we consider the brain's complexity, the less-than-precise process of brain development, and the myriad factors—from SES to gut bacteria—that can influence this development, we are left to marvel at how so many of us end up with brains that pass for normal. We all must have had neurons that migrated to wrong locations, made incorrect connections, and were exposed to viruses or other harmful substances. If the brain were as fragile as it might seem, to end up with a normal brain would seem to be an unusual outcome.

Apparently, animals have evolved a substantial capacity to repair minor abnormalities in brain development. Most people have developed in the range that we call normal because the human brain's plasticity and regenerative powers overcome minor

Figure 3-22 illustrates trisomy, the chromosomal abnormality that causes Down syndrome.

**FIGURE 8-34 Neuronal Contrast** Representative dendritic branches from cortical neurons in a child of typical intelligence (*left*) and a child with developmental disabilities (*right*), whose neurons are thinner and have far fewer spines. Information from Purpura, 1974.

Typical child    Child with Developmental disabilities

**TABLE 8-3** Causes of Developmental Disability

| Cause | Example mechanism | Example condition |
|---|---|---|
| Abnormal embryonic development | Exposure to a toxin | Fetal alcohol spectrum disorder (FASD) |
| Birth trauma | Anoxia (oxygen deprivation) | Cerebral palsy |
| Chronic malnutrition | Abnormal brain development | Kwashiorkor |
| Drugs (e.g., valproate) | Neural tube defects | Spina bifida Autism spectrum disorder (ASD) |
| Environmental abnormality | Sensory deprivation | Growth and developmental deficits |
| Genetic abnormality | Error of metabolism Chromosomal abnormality | Phenylketonuria Down syndrome |
| Prenatal disease | Infection (e.g., Rubella, or German measles) | ASD Developmental delays |

developmental deviations. By initially overproducing neurons and synapses, the brain gains the capacity to correct errors that might have arisen accidentally.

These same plastic properties later allow us to cope with the ravages of aging. Neurons are continually dying throughout our lifetime. By age 60, investigators ought to see significant effects from all this cell loss, especially considering the cumulative results of exposure to environmental toxins, drugs, traumatic brain injuries, and other neural perturbations. But this is not what happens.

Although some teenagers may not believe it, relatively few 60-year-olds have dementia. By most criteria, the 60-year-old who has been intellectually active throughout adulthood is likely to be much wiser than the 18-year-old whose brain has lost relatively fewer neurons. A 60-year-old chess player will have a record of many more chess matches from which to draw game strategies than would an 18-year-old, for example. Recall, too, that early music or second language experience appears to partly protect the brain from degenerative neural diseases such as dementia.

Clearly, some mechanism must enable us to compensate for loss and minor injury to our brain cells. This capacity for plasticity and change, for learning and adapting, is arguably the most important characteristic of the human brain during development and throughout life.

We return to learning, memory, and neuroplasticity in Chapter 14.

## 8-5 Review

Before you continue, check your understanding. Answers to the Self-Test appear at the back of the book.

1. Brain injuries have an increased potential to produce atypical brains if they occur during _____ periods in development.

2. Postmortem studies have revealed that _____, which is the unexplained death of a sleeping infant, may be linked to a gene variation that makes the serotonin transporter unusually efficient.

3. Riesen's studies on animals raised in the dark show that an absence of _____ stimulation can affect brain development.

4. Explain why, despite the fact that neurons are dying throughout our lifetimes, researchers do not see significant effects from cell loss in the brains of individuals in their fifties and sixties.

5. Why might the effects of preconception experiences from the father have a greater impact on the offspring than those from the mother?

## Summary

### 8-1 Three Perspectives on Brain Development

Nervous system development entails more than just the unfolding of a genetic blueprint. Development is a complex dance of genetic and environmental events that interact to sculpt the brain to fit within a particular cultural and environmental context. We can approach this dance from three perspectives: (1) by correlating emerging brain structures with emerging behaviors, (2) by correlating new behaviors with neural maturation, and (3) by identifying influences on brain and behavior.

### 8-2 Neurobiology of Development

Human brain maturation is a long process, lasting as late as age 30. Neurons, the units of brain function, develop a phenotype, migrate, and, as their processes elaborate, establish connections with other neurons even before birth. The developing brain produces many more neurons and connections than it needs and then prunes them back in toddlerhood, and again in adolescence and early adulthood, to a stable level maintained by some neurogenesis throughout the life span. Experiences throughout development can trigger epigenetic mechanisms, such as gene methylation, that alter gene expression.

### 8-3 Using Emerging Behaviors to Infer Neural Maturation

Throughout the world, across the cultural spectrum, and from newborn to adult, we all develop through similar behavioral stages. As infants develop physically, motor behaviors emerge in a predictable sequence from gross, poorly directed movements toward objects to controlled pincer grasps to pick up objects as small as pencils by about

11 months. Cognitive behaviors also develop through stages of logic and problem solving. Beginning with Jean Piaget, researchers have identified and characterized four or more distinct stages of cognitive development. Each stage can be identified by specific behavioral tests.

Behaviors emerge as the neural systems that produce them develop. Matching the median timetables of neurodevelopment with observed behavior infers the hierarchical relationship between brain structure and brain function. Motor behaviors emerge in synchrony with maturating motor circuits in the cerebral cortex, basal ganglia, and cerebellum, as well as with the connections from these areas to the spinal cord. Similar correlations between emerging behaviors and neuronal development accompany the maturation of cognitive behavior as neural circuits in the frontal and temporal lobes mature in early adulthood.

## 8-4 Brain Development and the Environment

The brain is most plastic during its development, and neuronal structures and their connections can be molded by various factors throughout development. The brain's sensitivity to factors such as external events, quality of the environment, tactile stimulation, drugs, gonadal hormones, stress, and injury varies over time. At critical periods in the course of development, beginning prenatally, different brain regions are particularly sensitive to different events.

## 8-5 Abnormal Experience and Brain Development

Adverse prenatal and early childhood experiences can have profound effects on brain development and behavior. Prenatal and early life stress can predispose people to develop behavioral disorders, as well as leave a lasting imprint on brain structure. Even parental stress before conception can result in epigenetic effects in the fetus.

Brain perturbations in the course of development from, say, anoxia, trauma, or toxins can alter brain development significantly; can result in severe behavioral abnormalities, including intellectual disability; and may be related to such disorders as ASD or SIDS. Other behavioral disorders emerge in adolescence, a time of prolonged frontal lobe change. Abnormalities affecting one brain system during development can interact with other systems to produce new abnormalities.

The brain has a substantial capacity to repair or correct minor abnormalities, allowing most people to develop normal behavioral repertoires and to maintain brain function throughout life.

## Key Terms

amblyopia, p. 274

androgen, p. 277

anencephaly, p. 282

apoptosis, p. 260

autism spectrum disorder (ASD), p. 258

cell adhesion molecule (CAM), p. 259

chemoaffinity hypothesis, p. 274

critical period, p. 275

default network, p. 263

dorsolateral prefrontal cortex (dlPFC), p. 262

estrogen, p. 277

filopod (pl. filopodia), p. 259

glioblast, p. 253

growth cone, p. 259

growth spurt, p. 267

imprinting, p. 275

masculinization, p. 277

netrin, p. 259

neural Darwinism, p. 260

neural plate, p. 252

neural stem cell, p. 253

neural tube, p. 252

neuroblast, p. 253

neurotrophic factor, p. 255

progenitor cell (precursor cell), p. 253

psychobiotics, p. 278

radial glial cell, p. 256

semaphorin, p. 259

subventricular zone, p. 253

sudden infant death syndrome (SIDS), p. 282

testosterone, p. 277

tropic molecule, p. 259

## Selected Resources from  Achie√e

**Neuroscience in Action:** How Our Brains Grow

**Videos**

Correlation and Causation

Brain Plasticity: Rewiring the Visual Cortex

Childhood Trauma

Can Trauma be Inherited?

Childhood Trauma Impacts Millions of Americans

Epigenetics and the Curious Journey into Education

**LearningCurve**

**Practice Quiz**

Science Photo Library/Alamy

# How Do We Sense, Perceive, and See the World?

# 9

## ◎ CLINICAL FOCUS 9-1

# Migraines and a Case of Blindsight

D. B.'s recurring headaches began at about age 14. A visual aura warned of a headache's approach: an oval area of flashing (scintillating) light would appear just left of center in his field of vision. Over the next few minutes, the oval would enlarge. After approximately 15 minutes, the flashing light would vanish, and D. B. would be left temporarily blind in the region of the oval.

D. B. described the oval as an opaque white area surrounded by a rim of color. A headache on the right side of his head followed its appearance, and could persist for as long as 48 hours. D. B. usually fell asleep before that much time elapsed. When he awakened, the headache was gone, and his vision was normal again.

The recurrent headaches from which D. B. suffered are called migraines, and they were caused by the dilation of cerebral blood vessels that occurs during an aura. Auras may be auditory, tactile, or visual, and they may result in an inability to move or talk. And just as an aura is usually limited to one side of the visual field, as in D. B.'s case, migraines are usually limited to one side of the head.

Migraines vary in severity, frequency, and duration. Left untreated, some may last for hours or even days. They are often accompanied by nausea, vomiting, and severe head pain. Migraine is perhaps the most common of all neurological disorders, affecting some 5% to 20% of the population at some time in their lives.

D. B.'s attacks continued at intervals of about 6 weeks for 10 years. After one attack, he was left with a small blind spot, or *scotoma*, illustrated in the accompanying photographs. When D. B. was 26 years old, a neurologist found that a collection of abnormal blood vessels at the back of his right occipital lobe was causing the migraine attacks—a most unusual cause, because an obvious vascular abnormality is only rarely seen in people with migraine.

By the time D. B. was 30, the migraines had begun to interfere with his family life, social life, and job. No drug treatment was effective, so D. B. had the malformed blood vessels surgically removed. The operation relieved his pain and generally improved his life, but a part of his right occipital lobe, deprived of blood, had died. D. B. was blind in the left half of his visual field: as he looks at the world through either eye, he is unable to see anything left of the midline.

Lawrence Weizkrantz (1986) made a remarkable discovery about D. B.'s blindness. D. B. could not identify objects in his blind area but could very accurately tell whether a light had blinked on there and even where the light source was. Apparently, D. B.'s brain knew when a light blinked and where it appeared—a phenomenon called *blindsight*, in which his brain knew more than he was aware of consciously. D. B.'s case provides an excellent example of the parallel streams of visual processing in the cortex. His system for processing objects was impaired, but his system for locating objects in space was not.

A similar conclusion comes from the study of patient T. N., who had suffered strokes in each visual cortex, leaving him with clinical blindness over his whole visual field (de Gelder et al., 2008). Like D. B., he retained some unconscious visual abilities, the most impressive being that T. N. could successfully navigate down a long corridor obstructed with objects (a video clip accompanying the de Gelder paper demonstrates this ability). He claimed not to be aware of the objects and believed he had walked in a straight path down the hallway.

The source of the severe head pain has long been a mystery, but the 2021 Brain Prize (awarded for outstanding contributions to neuroscience) was bestowed on Lars Edvinsson, Peter Goadsby, Jes Olesen, and Michael Moskowitz for their discovery that migraine pain is caused by calcitonin gene–related peptide (CGRP), which can stimulate receptors on the trigeminal nerve fibers that wrap around cranial blood vessels. Pharmaceutical companies are now developing medications such as *ubrogepant*, which blocks CGRP receptors, for the treatment of acute migraines.

Tyler Olson/Shutterstock.com

**X** = Fixation point

As a typical migraine scotoma develops, a person looking at the small white X in the photograph at the far left first sees a small patch of lines. This striped area continues growing outward, leaving an opaque area (scotoma) where the stripes were, almost completely blocking the visual field within 15 to 20 minutes. Normal vision returns shortly thereafter.

As you look at the photographs in Clinical Focus 9-1: Migraines and a Case of Blindsight, you see three people—two women and a man—who appear to be walking and talking on a warm summer day. Trees appear in the background, clearly behind the people. It is tempting to believe that this visual image is transferred whole to the brain, where we see it.

But how could the nervous system do this? There is no viewing screen in the brain. Instead, the nervous system must construct the image from bits of information, such as shape and color. Then the brain must put all of these pieces together to form what we perceive as a complete image. The neural reconstruction is not a passive image such as a screen projects. Rather, the brain continuously employs memories, both to interpret moment-to-moment sensory information and to predict the immediate future.

D. B.'s case demonstrates that we are consciously aware of only part of the visual information our brain is processing. This *selective awareness* is an important working principle that underlies human sensation and perception. Weizkrantz, a world-renowned visual neuroscientist at Oxford University, detected it in the visual system only because of D. B.'s injury.

The ability to lose conscious visual perception while retaining unconscious vision, as D. B. did, leads us to this chapter's central question: How do we see the world? We remain blissfully unaware of much of the sensory processing that takes place in the neural pathways for vision, hearing, touch, taste, and smell. All of our senses convert energy into neural activity that has meaning for us. We begin this chapter with a general summary of sensation and perception that explores how this energy conversion takes place. We next look at visual system anatomy and consider the connections between the eyes and the sections of the brain that process visual information.

Turning to the perceptual experience of sight, we focus on how neurons respond to visual input and enable the brain to perceive features such as color, shape, and movement. At the chapter's end, we explore vision's culmination: understanding what we see. How do we infuse light energy with meaning to grasp the content of written words or to see the beauty in a painting? Read on.

Vision is this chapter's main topic; hearing is Chapter 10's focus. Section 11-4 covers body senses and balance. Section 12-3 explains smell and taste.

## 9-1

# Nature of Sensation and Perception

We naturally presume that our sensory experiences tell us what is "real" in our environment, but our sensory experience can deceive us; two people looking at the same image can see very different things. We may believe that we see, hear, touch, smell, and taste real things in a real world. In fact, the only input our brain receives from the "real" world is a series of action potentials that originate from energy that is transduced by our sensory receptors and passed along to the neurons that form our various sensory pathways.

Although we experience visual and body sensations as fundamentally different from one another, the action potentials produced in these two sensory systems are similar, as are the neurons themselves. Neuroscientists understand how neurons can turn energy, such as light waves, into nerve impulses. They have also identified the pathways those nerve impulses travel to reach the brain. But they do not know how we end up perceiving one set of nerve impulses as what the world looks like and another set as what we are hearing.

Our sensory systems appear to be extremely diverse: vision, audition, touch, balance, taste, and olfaction seem at first to have little in common. Although our perceptions and behaviors in relation to them differ, each sensory system is organized on a similar hierarchical plan. We now consider the features common to the sensory systems—receptors, neural relays between receptor and neocortex, sensory coding and representation, and perception.

## Sensory Receptors

Sensory receptor neurons are specialized to transduce (convert) environmental energy—light, for example—into neural activity. If we put flour into a sieve and shake it, the more finely milled particles fall through the holes, whereas the coarser particles and lumps get left behind in the sieve. Sensory receptors are designed to respond only to a narrow band of energy—analogous to particles of certain sizes—such as the specific wavelengths of electromagnetic energy that form the basis of our vision. Each sensory system's receptors are specialized to filter a different form of energy:

- For vision, the photoreceptors in the retina (shown in **Figure 9-1**) convert light energy into chemical energy, which is in turn converted into action potentials. (Section 4-3 gives a detailed discussion of action potentials.)

### Learning Objectives

- Explain the role of sensory receptors in the nervous system.
- Explain how the qualities of density and sensitivity relate to sensory receptor function.
- Contrast the processes of sensation and perception.

**FIGURE 9-1 Photo Receptor Cells** Vision begins in the photoreceptor cells, the rods and cones shown here. Section 9-2 details how they work.

**receptive field** Region of sensory space (e.g., skin surface) in which a stimulus modifies a receptor's activity.

### Functional Anatomy of the Sensory Systems

| Visual | Section 9-2 |
|---|---|
| Auditory | Section 10-2 |
| Somatosensory | Section 11-4 |
| Taste and olfaction | Section 12-3 |

An animal's perception of the world depends on its nervous system's complexity and organization. Section 1-3 gives an overview of the development of nervous system complexity across animal species.

**Principle 9:** The nervous system produces movement in a perceptual world the brain constructs.

Section 10-4 explains how we process music.

- In the auditory system, air pressure waves are first converted into mechanical energy, which activates the auditory receptors that produce action potentials in auditory receptor neurons.

- In the somatosensory system, mechanical energy activates receptors sensitive to touch, pressure, or pain. These somatosensory receptors in turn generate action potentials in somatosensory receptor neurons.

- For taste and olfaction, various chemical molecules in the air or in food fit themselves into receptors of various shapes to activate action potentials in the respective receptor neurons.

Were our visual receptors somewhat different, we would be able to see in the ultraviolet range as well as the visible parts of the electromagnetic spectrum, as honeybees and butterflies can. The same can be said of our other sensory receptors: receptors in the human ear respond to a wide range of sound waves, but elephants and bats can hear and produce sounds far below and above, respectively, the range humans can hear. Different species are specialized to respond to different aspects of sensory inputs.

In a sense, our pet dogs have "superhuman" powers: they can detect trace odors; hear low-range sounds, as elephants do; and see in the dark. But compared to many other animal species, including dogs, we have our own "super" powers: like most other primates, we have superior color vision. In a way, the dog world is olfactory, and the human world is color. Thus, for each species and its individual members, sensory systems filter the inputs to produce an idiosyncratic representation of reality.

## Receptive Fields

Every sensory receptor organ and cell has a **receptive field**, a specific part of the world to which it responds. If you fix your eyes on a point directly in front of you, for example, what you see of the world is the scope of your eyes' receptive field. If you close one eye, the visual world shrinks. What the open eye sees is the receptive field for that eye.

Each photoreceptor cell (out of about 120 million) in the eye points in a slightly different direction and so has a unique receptive field. You can grasp the conceptual utility of the receptive field by considering that the brain uses information from each sensory receptor's receptive field not only to identify sensory information but also to contrast the information each receptor field is providing.

Receptive fields not only sample sensory information but also help locate events in space. Because adjacent receptive fields may overlap, the contrast between their responses to events help us localize sensations. This spatial dimension of sensory information produces cortical patterns and maps that form each person's sensory reality.

## Receptor Density and Sensitivity

Sensory receptors are not evenly distributed across the body or its organs. For example, visual receptors are more numerous in the center of our visual field than toward the edges. This difference explains why our vision is sharper in the center than at the periphery. Similarly, tactile receptors on the fingers are more numerous compared with those on the arm; as a result, fingers can discriminate touch remarkably well, whereas the arm cannot. Thus, the density of receptors is related to sensory sensitivity—in other words, acuity.

In addition to the density of our receptors, our sensory systems use different types of receptors to enhance our perceptual experience. For instance, the visual system uses different sets of receptors to respond to light and color. Color photoreceptors are small and densely packed, which enables us to make sensitive color discriminations in bright light. Receptors for black–white vision are larger and more scattered, but their sensitivity to light—say, a lighted match at a distance of 2 miles on a dark night—is truly remarkable. (We return to the discussion of visual receptors and receptive fields in Section 9-4.)

Differences in the density and sensitivity of sensory receptors determine many animals' special abilities—dogs' excellent olfactory ability and the excellent tactile ability of raccoons' digits. Variations in receptor density in the human auditory receptor organ, for example, may explain such abilities as the perfect pitch displayed by some musicians.

# Neural Relays

All receptors connect to the cortex through a sequence of intervening neurons. The number of these neural relays varies across different sensory systems. For example, one route for vision passes from the retina to the thalamus to the first area of the visual cortex (called V1), and then to other visual cortical regions. For audition, input from the auditory receptors in the ear goes to the hindbrain, the midbrain, the thalamus, and finally the cortex. **Figure 9-2** illustrates a simplified flowchart for three major sensory systems.

Sensory information is modified at each stage in the relay, allowing each region to construct different aspects of the sensory experience. In the visual system, each of our two eyes has a separate view of the world. The information from the two views is combined in the thalamus such that the input from the left side or right side of each field is superimposed to produce two visual fields, one for the left and one for the right. At the next stage in the relay (V1), the brain begins to separate different aspects of the visual input such as shape and color. There is also a second visual pathway that goes from the retina to the superior colliculus and then to the thalamus and cortex. This pathway is involved in the perception of movement. (In Section 9-2, we provide a detailed description of the visual pathways and the role of V1.)

Neural relays also allow sensory systems to interact. One dramatic effect of sensory interaction is the visual modification of sound. If a person hears a speech syllable such as *ba* while observing someone who is articulating *ga,* the listener hears not the actual sound *ba* but a hybrid sound, *da.* The viewed lip movements modify the listener's auditory perception.

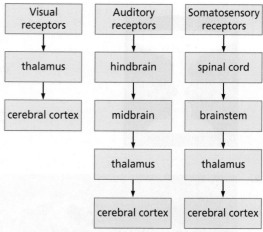

**FIGURE 9-2 Simplified Sensory Pathways to the Cerebral Cortex**

**topographic map** Spatially organized neural representation of the external world.

# Sensory Coding and Representation

After it has been transduced, all information from all sensory systems is encoded by action potentials that travel along nerves until they enter the spinal cord or brain. From there, the action potentials travel on nerve tracts within the central nervous system. Every bundle carries the same kind of signal. But how do action potentials encode different sensations? (How does vision differ from touch?) And how do they encode the features of particular sensations? (How does purple differ from blue?)

Parts of these questions seem easy to answer; others pose a fundamental challenge to neuroscience. The presence of a stimulus can be encoded by an increase or a decrease in a neuron's discharge rate, and the amount of increase or decrease can encode stimulus intensity. As detailed in Section 9-4, qualitative visual changes, such as from red to green, can be encoded by activity in different neurons or even by different levels of discharge in the same neuron. For example, more activity might signify redder, while less activity might signify greener.

What is less clear is how we perceive such sensations as vision, touch, sound, and smell as different from one another. Part of the explanation is that each sensation is processed in its own distinct cortical region. Also, we learn through experience to distinguish them. In addition, each sensory system has a preferential link with certain movements, constituting a separate wiring that helps keep each system distinct at all levels of neural organization. For instance, the sudden appearance of an object, such as a ball, produces withdrawal responses to avoid being struck, even though we may not know what we are avoiding until other regions can analyze the details.

The distinctions among the sensory systems, however, are not always clear: some people hear in color or identify smells by how the smells sound to them. This mixing of the senses is called *synesthesia.* Anyone who has shivered when hearing a piece of music or cringed at the noise fingernails make when scraping a blackboard has "felt" sound.

In most mammals, the neocortex represents the sensory field of each modality—vision, hearing, touch, smell, or taste—as a spatially organized neural representation of the external world. This **topographic map** is a neural–spatial representation of the body or of the areas of the sensory world perceived by a sensory organ (a model based on such a map appears in **Figure 9-3**). All mammals have at least one primary

**Principle 3:** The CNS functions on multiple levels and is organized hierarchically and in parallel.

The process by which sensory information produces action potentials is described in Section 4-4.

Section 15-5 details synesthesia.

**FIGURE 9-3 Topographic Model** This curious figure (referred to as a *homunculus*) reflects the topographic map in the sensorimotor cortex. Disproportionately large areas control the body parts we use to make the most-skilled movements. See Sections 11-2 and 11-5.

**(A)**

**(B)**

© Gerry Lemmo

**FIGURE 9-4 Perceptual Illusions (A)** Edgar Rubin's ambiguous reversible image can be perceived as a vase or as two faces. **(B)** In this photo, each cheetah's head can be perceived as belonging to either cheetah's body.

**sensation** Registration by the sensory organs of physical stimuli from the environment.

**perception** Subjective interpretation of sensations by the brain.

**Learning Objectives**

- Describe the structure of the fovea and retina and explain the different functions of photoreceptors and retinal ganglion cells in conveying visual information to the brain.
- Trace the three routes that visual information takes from the eye through to the cortex.
- Explain the distinct roles of the dorsal and ventral streams in processing visual input, and how information from both streams is assembled in the occipital cortex.

cortical area for each sensory system, such as V1. Additional areas are usually referred to as *secondary* because most of the information that reaches these areas is relayed through the primary area. Each additional representation is probably dedicated to encoding one specific aspect of the sensory modality. For vision, different additional representational areas may take part in perceiving color, movement, and form.

## Perception

Compared with the richness of actual sensation, our description of sensory neuroanatomy and function is bound to seem sterile. **Sensation** is far more than the simple registration of physical stimuli from the environment by the sensory organs. Our sensory impressions are affected by the context in which they take place, by our emotional state, and by our past. All of these factors contribute to **perception**, the subjective experience of sensation—how we interpret what we sense.

That perception is more than sensation is evidenced by the fact that different people transform the same sensory stimulation into totally different perceptions. A classic demonstration of this fact uses an ambiguous image such as the well-known Rubin's vase shown in **Figure 9-4**A. This image may be perceived either as a vase or as two faces. If you fix your eyes on the center of the picture, the two perceptions may alternate, even though the sensory stimulation remains constant.

Similarly, the photograph of two cheetahs in Figure 9-4B is ambiguous. Which head goes with which cheetah? As with the Rubin's vase, the two perceptions may alternate. Such ambiguous images and illusions demonstrate the workings of complex perceptual phenomena and enlighten our insight into our cognitive processes.

## 9-1 Review

Before you continue, check your understanding. Answers to Self-Test appear at the back of the book.

1. _____ are energy filters that transduce incoming physical energy into neural activity.

2. _____ fields locate sensory events. Receptor _____ determines acuity to sensory stimulation.

3. We distinguish one sensory modality from another by its target in the _____ and _____ in the brain.

4. Sensation registers physical stimuli from the environment received by the sensory organs. Perception is the _____ experience of sensation.

5. How is the anatomical organization similar for each sense?

### 9-2

# The Visual System's Functional Anatomy

Our primary sensory experience is visual. Indeed, far more of the human brain is dedicated to vision than to any other sense. Understanding the visual system's organization, then, is key to understanding human brain function. To build this understanding, we begin by following the routes that visual information takes into and within the brain. This exercise is a bit like traveling a road to discover where it goes.

# Structure of the Retina

Light energy travels from the outside world through the pupil and into the eye, where it strikes a light-sensitive surface, the **retina**, at the back of the eye (**Figure 9-5**). From this stimulation of **photoreceptor** cells on the retina, we begin to construct a visual world. (With the exception of the photoreceptors, all retinal neurons are insensitive to light, so they are unaffected by light passing through them en route to the light-sensitive photoreceptors.) If you are familiar with the properties of the electromagnetic spectrum and with the structure of the eye, read on. To refresh your knowledge of these topics, read The Basics: Visible Light and the Structure of the Eye before you continue.

**Figure 9-6** includes a photograph of the retina, which is composed of photoreceptors beneath a layer of other neurons connected to them. These other neurons lie in front of the photoreceptor cells, but they do not prevent incoming light from being absorbed by those receptors because the neurons are transparent and the photoreceptors are extremely sensitive to light.

Together, the photoreceptor cells and the retinal neurons perform some amazing functions. They translate light into action potentials, discriminate wavelengths so that we can distinguish colors, and work in a range of light intensities from bright to dim. These cells afford visual precision sufficient for us to see a human hair lying on the page of this book from a distance of 18 inches.

As in a camera, the image of objects projected onto the retina is upside down and backward. This flip-flopped orientation poses no problem for the brain. Remember that the brain is constructing the outside world, so it does not really care how the image is oriented initially. In fact, the brain can make adjustments regardless of the orientation of the images that it receives.

If for several days you were to wear glasses that invert visual images, the world would first appear upside down but then would suddenly appear right side up again because your brain would correct the distortion (Held, 1968). Curiously, upon removing the glasses, the world would temporarily seem upside down once again because your brain at first would be unaware that you had tricked it again. Eventually, your brain would solve this puzzle, too, and the world would flip back to the correct orientation.

## Fovea

Try this experiment. Focus on the print at the left edge of this page (if you are using the online version of this text, you can use any page with print text). The words will be clearly legible. Now, while holding your eyes still, try to read the words on the right side of the page. It will be very difficult, and perhaps even impossible, even though you can see that words are there.

The lesson is that our vision is better in the center of the visual field than at the margins, or *periphery*. Letters at the periphery must be much larger than those in the center for us to see them as well. **Figure 9-7** shows how much larger. The difference is partly due to the fact that photoreceptors are more densely packed at the center of the retina, in a region known as the **fovea**. As shown in Figure 9-6, the retinal surface is depressed at the fovea. This depression forms because many optic nerve fibers skirt the fovea to facilitate light access to its receptors.

## Blind Spot

Now try another experiment. Stand with your head over a tabletop and hold a pencil in your hand. Close one eye. Stare at the edge of the tabletop nearest you. Now hold the pencil in a horizontal position with the eraser on the table. Beginning at a point

**retina** Light-sensitive surface at the back of the eye consisting of neurons and photoreceptor cells.

**photoreceptor** Specialized retinal neuron that transduces light into neural activity.

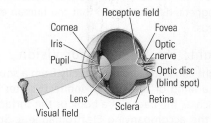

**FIGURE 9-5 Anatomy of the Eye** Light reflected from an object is focused by the lens on the fovea of the retina.

**(A) Retina**

**(B) SEM of fovea**

**FIGURE 9-6 The Fovea** This cross section through the retina **(A)** shows the depression at the fovea (with its densely packed cones)—also shown in the scanning electron micrograph **(B)**—where photoreceptors are packed most densely and where our vision is clearest.

## ◎ THE BASICS

# Visible Light and the Structure of the Eye

The brain's visual system analyzes visible light—the part of the electromagnetic (EM) spectrum that the human eye evolved to capture and focus.

## Light: The Stimulus for Vision

Light can enter the eye directly from a source that produces it (such as a lamp or the sun) or indirectly after reflecting from a surface (such as the pages of a book or the surface of water). As illustrated in the accompanying Electromagnetic Spectrum diagram, not all light waves are the same length, and only a sliver of the EM spectrum is visible to us. If our photoreceptors could detect light in the shorter ultraviolet or longer infrared wavelengths, we would see additional colors.

## Structure of the Eye

The range of light visible to humans is constrained not by the properties of light waves, but rather by the properties of our visual receptors. How do photoreceptor cells in the retina absorb light energy and initiate the processes leading to vision? The diagram How the Eye Works illustrates the eye's structure and shows how its design captures and focuses light.

## Optical Errors of Refraction

A web of muscles adjusts the shape of the eye's lens to bend light to greater or lesser degrees, which allows near or far images to be focused on the retina. When images are not properly focused, we need corrective lenses.

The eye, like a camera, works correctly only when sufficient light passes through the lens and is focused on the receptor surface—the retina in the eye or the light-sensitive material in the camera. If the focal point of the light falls slightly in front of the receptor surface or slightly behind it, a refractive error causes objects to appear blurry. Refractive errors in the eye are of two basic types, as illustrated in the Refractive Errors diagram.

Myopia (nearsightedness) afflicts about 50% of young people in the developed world. Hyperopia (farsightedness) is a less common refractive error, but as people age, the lens loses its elasticity and consequently becomes unable to refract light from nearby objects correctly. This form of hyperopia, called presbyopia (old-sightedness), is so common that you rarely find people older than 50 who do not need glasses to see up close, especially for reading.

It is also common to see young children wearing corrective lenses. The incidence of myopia in the United States has doubled in the past 40 years, to about 42%. It is even higher in Northern Europe (50%) and Asia (50% to 80%). Two factors probably account for this increase. First, more young people are attending school for longer periods of time and thus are doing more close-up work, especially reading, which strains the eye muscles. Today's close-up work typically involves prolonged use of computer monitors or LED lights, both of which tend to be bright. Second, people are spending less and less time outdoors in natural bright light. Bright light makes the pupil contract, which improves visual depth of field; your eyes focus better. Children should probably spend at least 2 hours each day outside in bright light. Consider that myopia is less common in countries such as Australia (17%), where bright light is plentiful.

### Electromagnetic Spectrum

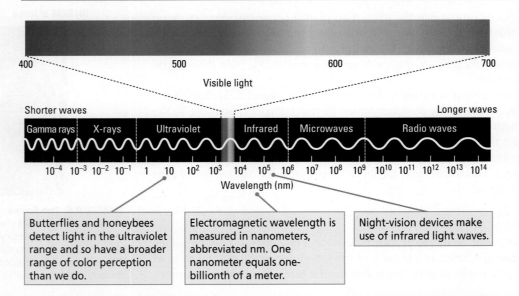

The electromagnetic energy visible to humans varies in wavelength from about 400 to 700 nanometers. We perceive the shortest visible wavelengths as deep purple. As wavelength increases, perceived color morphs from violet to blue to green to yellow, orange, and red: the colors of the rainbow.

Butterflies and honeybees detect light in the ultraviolet range and so have a broader range of color perception than we do.

Electromagnetic wavelength is measured in nanometers, abbreviated nm. One nanometer equals one-billionth of a meter.

Night-vision devices make use of infrared light waves.

## How the Eye Works

The *sclera* forms the eyeball, the white of the eye. The *cornea* is the eye's clear outer covering. The colored *iris* opens and closes to allow more or less light through a hole, the *pupil*. The *lens* focuses light.

In the *retina*, light energy initiates neural activity. At the center of the retina, the *fovea* is the region of sharpest vision and has the densest distribution of photoreceptors specialized for color.

A photograph of the retina's surface shows blood vessels emerging from the blind spot and their near absence around the fovea.

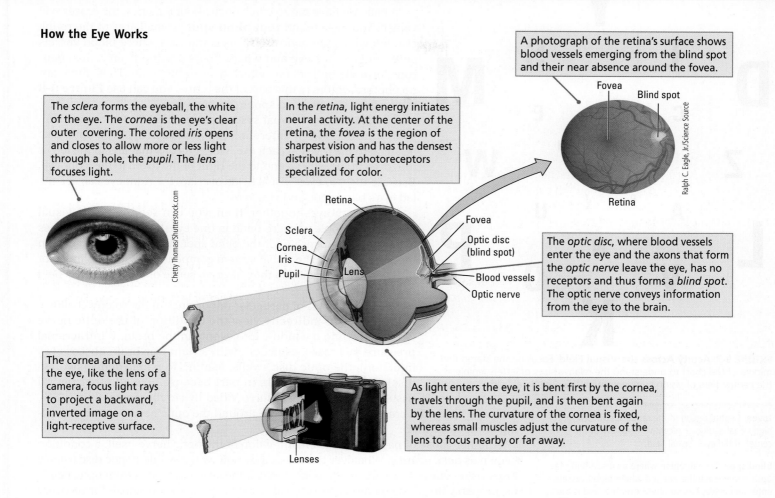

Fovea

Blind spot

Retina

Ralph C. Eagle, Jr./Science Source

Chetty Thomas/Shutterstock.com

Retina
Sclera
Cornea
Iris
Pupil
Lens
Fovea
Optic disc (blind spot)
Blood vessels
Optic nerve

The *optic disc*, where blood vessels enter the eye and the axons that form the *optic nerve* leave the eye, has no receptors and thus forms a *blind spot*. The optic nerve conveys information from the eye to the brain.

The cornea and lens of the eye, like the lens of a camera, focus light rays to project a backward, inverted image on a light-receptive surface.

As light enters the eye, it is bent first by the cornea, travels through the pupil, and is then bent again by the lens. The curvature of the cornea is fixed, whereas small muscles adjust the curvature of the lens to focus nearby or far away.

Lenses

## Refractive Errors

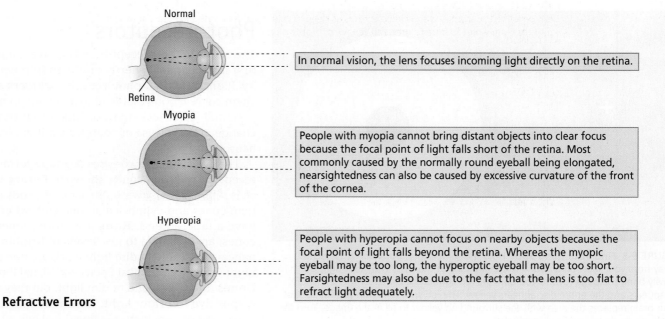

Normal

Retina

In normal vision, the lens focuses incoming light directly on the retina.

Myopia

People with myopia cannot bring distant objects into clear focus because the focal point of light falls short of the retina. Most commonly caused by the normally round eyeball being elongated, nearsightedness can also be caused by excessive curvature of the front of the cornea.

Hyperopia

People with hyperopia cannot focus on nearby objects because the focal point of light falls beyond the retina. Whereas the myopic eyeball may be too long, the hyperoptic eyeball may be too short. Farsightedness may also be due to the fact that the lens is too flat to refract light adequately.

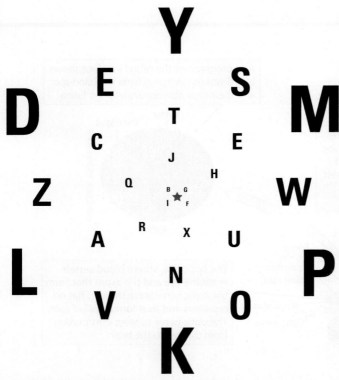

**FIGURE 9-7 Acuity Across the Visual Field** Focus on the star in the middle of the chart to understand the relative sizes of letters legible in the central field of vision compared with the peripheral field.

**fovea** Central region of the retina specialized for high visual acuity; its receptive fields are at the center of the eye's visual field.

**blind spot** Retinal region where axons forming the optic nerve leave the eye and where blood vessels enter and leave; has no photoreceptors and is thus said to be blind.

approximately below your nose, move the pencil slowly along the table in the direction of the open eye.

When you have moved the pencil about 6 inches, the eraser will vanish. You have found your **blind spot**, a small area of the retina also known as the *optic disc*. This is the area where blood vessels enter and exit the eye and where fibers leading from retinal neurons form the optic nerve, which goes to the brain. Thus, there are no photoreceptors in this part of the retina. You can use **Figure 9-8** to demonstrate the blind spot in another way.

Fortunately, your visual system solves the blind spot problem: your optic disc is in a different location in each eye. The optic disc is lateral to the fovea in each eye, which means that it is to the left of the fovea in the left eye and to the right of the fovea in the right eye. Because the two eyes' visual fields overlap, the right eye can see the left eye's blind spot, and vice versa.

Using both eyes together, then, you can see the whole visual world. For people who are blind in one eye, however, the sightless eye cannot compensate for the blind spot in the functioning eye. In these individuals, the visual system compensates for the blind spot in several other ways, so they have no sense of a hole in their field of vision.

The blind spot is of particular importance in neurology. It allows neurologists to indirectly view the condition of the optic nerve while providing a window into events in the brain. If intracranial pressure increases, as occurs with a tumor or brain abscess (an infection), the optic disc swells, leading to *papilledema* (swollen disc). The swelling occurs in part because, like all other neural tissue, the optic nerve is surrounded by cerebrospinal fluid (CSF). Pressure inside the cranium can displace CSF around the optic nerve, causing swelling at the optic disc.

Another cause of papilledema is inflammation of the optic nerve itself, a condition known as *optic neuritis*. Whatever the cause, a person with a swollen optic disc usually loses vision due to pressure on the optic nerve. If the swelling results from optic neuritis, probably the most common neurological visual disorder, the prognosis for recovery is good.

**FIGURE 9-8 Find Your Blind Spot** Hold this (or another) book about 12 inches away from your face. Shut your left eye and look at the cross with your right eye. Slowly bring the page toward you until the red spot in the center of the yellow disc disappears and the entire disc appears yellow. The red spot is now in your blind spot. Your brain replaces the area with the surrounding yellow to fill in the image. Turn the book upside down to test your left eye.

## Photoreceptors

The retina's photoreceptor cells convert light energy first into chemical energy and then into neural activity. Light striking a photoreceptor triggers a series of chemical reactions that lead to a change in membrane potential (electrical charge), which in turn leads to a change in the release of neurotransmitters onto nearby neurons.

The eye contains two types of image-forming photoreceptors: rods and cones, shown in **Figure 9-9**. These cells differ in many ways. Structurally, rods are longer than cones and cylindrical at one end, whereas cones have a tapered end. **Rods** are more numerous than cones; are sensitive to low levels of brightness (luminance), especially in dim light; and function mainly for night vision (see Clinical Focus 9-2: Visual Illuminance). **Cones** do not respond to dim light, but they are highly responsive to bright light. Cones mediate both color vision and our ability to see fine detail (visual acuity).

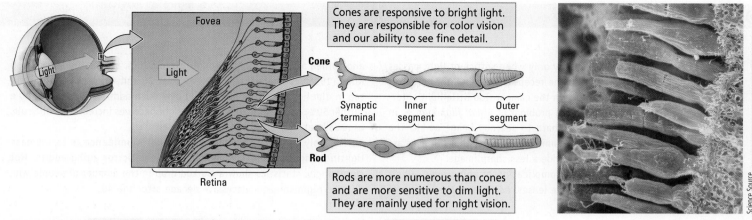

**FIGURE 9-9 Photoreceptor Cells** Rods and cones are tubelike structures, as the scanning electron micrograph at right shows. They differ especially in the outer segment that contains the light-absorbing visual pigment. Rods are highly sensitive to broad-spectrum luminance, whereas cones are sensitive to particular wavelengths of light.

Rods and cones are unevenly distributed over the retina. The fovea has only cones, but their density drops dramatically beyond the fovea, where both rods and cones are intermixed (see Figures 9-6 and 9-9). For this reason, our vision is not so sharp at the edges of the visual field, as demonstrated in Figure 9-7.

A final difference between rods and cones relates to their light-absorbing pigments. All rods have the same pigment, whereas each cone has one of three pigments. These four pigments—one in the rods and three in the cones—form the basis for our vision.

As shown on the spectrum in **Figure 9-10**, the three cone pigments absorb light across a range of visible frequencies, but each is most responsive to a small range of wavelengths—short (bluish light), medium (greenish light), and long (reddish light). As you can see on the background spectrum in Figure 9-10, however, if you were to look at lights with wavelengths of 419, 531, and 559 nanometers (nm), they would not appear blue, green, and red but rather blue–green, yellow–green, and orange. Remember, though, that you are looking at the lights with all three of your cone types and that each cone pigment responds to light across a range of frequencies, not just to its frequency of maximum absorption.

Both the presence of the three types of cone receptors and their relative numbers and distribution across the fovea contribute to our perception of color. As **Figure 9-11** shows, the three cone types are distributed more or less randomly across the retina, making our ability to perceive different colors fairly constant across the visual field. The numbers of red and green cones are approximately equal, but both outnumber the blue cones. As a result, we are not as sensitive to wavelengths in the blue part of the visible spectrum as we are to red and green wavelengths.

Other species that have color vision similar to humans' also have three types of cones with three color pigments. Because of slight variations in these pigments, however, the exact frequencies of maximum absorption differ among species. For humans, the exact frequencies are not identical with the numbers given earlier, which are an average across mammals. They are actually 426 and 530 nm for the blue and green cones, respectively, and 552 or 557 nm for the red cone. The two peak sensitivity levels of red cones represent the two variants that humans have evolved. The difference in these two red cones appears minuscule, but it does make a functional difference in some human females' color perception.

**rod** Photoreceptor specialized for functioning at low light levels.

**cone** Photoreceptor specialized for color and high visual acuity.

A nanometer (nm) is one-billionth of a meter.

**FIGURE 9-10 Range and Peak Sensitivity Averaged Across Mammals** Our color perception corresponds to the summed activity of the three types of cones: S cones, M cones, and L cones (for short, medium, and long wavelengths). Each type is most sensitive to a narrow range of the visible spectrum. Rods (white curve) prefer a range of wavelengths centered on 496 nm but do not contribute to our color perception. Rod activity is not summed with the cones in the color vision system.

## ◉ CLINICAL FOCUS 9-2

### Visual Illuminance

The eye, like a camera, works correctly only when sufficient light passes through the lens and is focused on the receptor surface—the retina of the eye or the light-sensitive surface in the camera. Too little light entering the eye or the camera produces a problem of *visual illuminance*, in which objects are too dim and it is hard to see any image at all. The reason objects appear blurry in low illuminance is likely that our eyes are mostly relying on the rods, which provide a less sharp image.

Visual illuminance is typically a complication of aging eyes, albeit one that cannot be cured by corrective lenses. As we age, the eye's lens

and cornea allow less light through, so less light strikes the retina. Don Kline (1994) estimated that between ages 20 and 40, people's ability to see in dim light drops by 50%—and over each additional 20 years, by a further 50%. As a result, seeing in dim light becomes increasingly difficult, especially at night.

The only way to compensate for visual illuminance is to increase lighting. Night vision is especially problematic for aging adults. Not surprisingly, statistics show a marked drop in the number of people who drive at night in each successive decade after age 40.

*Photo Courtesy of Dr. Donald Kline, University of Calgary*

These photographs represent the typical drop in luminance between age 20 (*left*) and age 60 (*right*).

**FIGURE 9-11 Retinal Receptors** The retinal mosaic of rods and three cone types. This diagram represents the distribution near the fovea, where cones outnumber rods. Red and green cones outnumber blue ones.

The gene for the red cone is carried on the X chromosome. Males have only one X chromosome, so they have only one of these genes and only one type of red cone. The situation is more complicated for females, who possess two X chromosomes. Although most women have only one type of red cone, those who have both are more sensitive than the rest of us to color differences at the red end of the spectrum. We could say that women who have both red cone types have a slightly rosier view of the world: their color receptors construct a world with a richer range of red experiences. But they also have to contend with seemingly peculiar color coordination by others.

## Types of Retinal Neurons

Photoreceptors are connected to two layers of retinal neurons. In the progression from the rods and cones toward the brain shown in **Figure 9-12**, the first layer contains three cell types: *bipolar, horizontal,* and *amacrine*. Horizontal cells link photoreceptors with bipolar cells, whereas amacrine cells link bipolar cells with cells in the second neural layer, the **retinal ganglion cells (RGCs)**. RGC axons cluster together in a bundle at the optic disc and leave the eye to form the optic nerve. RGCs are especially sensitive to increased intraocular pressure, which can lead to blindness (see Clinical Focus 9-3: Glaucoma).

Retinal ganglion cells can be classified into two major categories, which are called M and P cells in the primate retina. These designations derive from the distinctly different cell populations in the visual thalamus to which these two classes

**retinal ganglion cell (RGC)** One of a group of retinal neurons with axons that give rise to the optic nerve.

**FIGURE 9-12 Retinal Cells** Neurons in the retina—bipolar, horizontal, amacrine, and ganglion cells—form two layers moving outward from the rods and cones at the retinal surface. Light must pass through both transparent neuron layers to reach the photoreceptors. Müller cells run from the front of the retina to the back.

of RGCs send their axons. As shown in **Figure 9-13**, one population consists of **magnocellular cells** (hence M); the other consists of **parvocellular cells** (hence P). The larger M cells receive their input primarily from rods and so are sensitive to light but not to color; the smaller P cells receive their input primarily from cones and so are sensitive to color.

M cells are found throughout the retina, including the periphery, where our eyes are sensitive to movement but not to color or fine detail. P cells are found largely in the region of the fovea, where our eyes are sensitive to color and fine details. As we follow the ganglion cell axons into the brain, these two categories of RGCs maintain their distinctiveness throughout the visual pathways.

The retina also contains special glial cells called *Müller cells* that span from the retina's inner membrane at the front to the photoreceptors at the back. These cells act as optical fibers, channeling light to the buried photoreceptors (see Figure 9-12).

Although the primary function of the eye is to form images, it also collects information on ambient light intensity. A tiny subset of retinal ganglion cells (around 1%) contain melanopsin, a light-sensitive protein, and thus form a third type of photoreceptor in the eye. These photoreceptors function to synchronize circadian rhythms, regulate pupil size, and regulate the release of melatonin, a hormone associated with regulation of the sleep–wake cycle.

**magnocellular (M) cell** Large visual system neuron sensitive to moving stimuli.

**parvocellular (P) cell** Small visual system neuron sensitive to differences in form and color.

In Latin, *magno* means "large," and *parvo* means "small."

The role of melatonin in regulating our daily and seasonal biorhythms is discussed in Section 13-2.

**FIGURE 9-13 Visual Thalamus** The optic nerves connect with the lateral geniculate nucleus of the thalamus. The LGN has six layers: two magnocellular layers, which receive input mainly from rods, and four parvocellular layers, which receive input mainly from cones.

## Glaucoma

Glaucoma—a group of eye diseases that damage the optic nerve—is the most common cause of irreversible blindness and a prime target for research to restore vision. The optic nerve, which conveys information from the eye to the brain, begins with the axons of the retinal ganglion cells (RGCs). If the RCGs are dead or dysfunctional, vision is impossible. Thus, the clinical goal with glaucoma is to repair or replace RGCs after injury. One proposed strategy is to transplant healthy RGCs from recently deceased donors to patients with glaucoma or to transplant RGC precursors isolated from developing retinas—this option is currently being tested on mice in the lab (see Oswald et al., 2021). Another strategy is to stimulate nonhuman embryonic stem cells to generate RGCs in vivo. These efforts are complicated by the existence of approximately 40 different types of RGCs that differ in their physiological functionality and regenerative potential.

**Allogeneic transplantation**
RGCs from healthy eyes into host eyes may represent a viable strategy for curing irreversible forms of blindness

Site of optic nerve damage

Transplanted donor RGCs → Intrinsic signals drive initial neurite and axonal outgrowth → Complete integration into retina and axon grows into optic nerve

**Potential Treatment to Restore Vision** Healthy RGCs can be injected into a damaged eye to potentially restore lost vision. Republished with permission of American Association for the Advancement of Science, from Bireswar Laha, Ben K. Stafford, Andrew D. Huberman, "Regenerating optic pathways from the eye to the brain." Science, 2017, June 9;356(6342):1031–1034, Figure 3. Permission conveyed through Copyright Clearance Center, Inc.

Once the RGCs are generated, the next task is to regenerate the axon. RGC axons do not spontaneously regenerate after injury, so their restoration requires stimulation of either the genetic expression of transcription factors or the signaling pathways (see the review by Yuan et al., 2021). Andrew Huberman and his colleagues (Lim et al., 2016) used both genetic and visual stimulation to enhance neural activity in the RGCs of mice with severed RGC axons. These researchers activated a common growth-inducing mechanism in cells, called the *mTOR signaling pathway*, while repeatedly exposing the eye to high-contrast black-and-white images. This procedure stimulated the RGCs to reestablish many of the lost connections to their correct targets and achieved a partial restoration of vision. The authors believe that the next step is to increase neural activity in the RGCs in additional ways to enhance regeneration and restore more visual capacity. Indeed, given the importance of restoring vision in disorders such as glaucoma, researchers are optimistic that these efforts to regenerate RGCs and their axons may also lead to the restoration of sight in patients with other types of blindness.

Not all blindness originating in the eye is related directly to lost or damaged RGCs, however. If photoreceptors are dysfunctional or dying, as happens in *retinitis pigmentosa* (RP), patients will also develop blindness. Several possible therapies are under active investigation. One approach seeks to implant prosthetic devices into the eye to convert light into electrical signals and then pass these signals on to RGCs. Another option is to introduce light-sensitive ion-gated channels to repair the receptors. Preliminary results in humans and nonhuman primates suggest that this strategy can stimulate recovery of the ability to read words.

Another possibility is based on independent parallel work by two different research groups on mouse models of RP. In this line of research, experimenters used CRISPR to reprogram genes expressed in rods, leading to an increase in conelike cells, with restoration of visual function (Quinn et al., 2021). Taken together, these reparative strategies alone or in combination offer a realistic possibility for visual restoration (see the review by Laha et al., 2017).

## Visual Pathways

RGCs form the optic nerve, the road into the brain. This road is not a single, straight path, but rather forks off to several places. The destinations of these branches give us clues to what the brain is doing with visual input and how the brain constructs our visual world.

## Crossing the Optic Chiasm

The optic chiasm gets its name from the shape of the Greek letter chi (χ, pronounced "kai").

We begin with the optic nerves, one of which exits from each eye. Just before entering the brain, the optic nerves partly cross, forming the **optic chiasm**.

About half the fibers from each eye cross in such a way that the left half of each optic nerve goes to the left side of the brain, and the right half goes to the brain's right side, as diagrammed in **Figure 9-14**. The medial path of each retina, the *nasal retina,*

**optic chiasm** Junction of the optic nerves, one from each eye, at which the axons from the nasal halves of the retinas cross to the brain's opposite side.

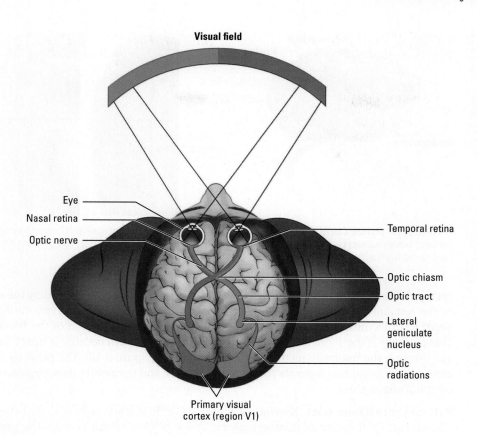

**Visual field**

Eye
Nasal retina
Optic nerve

Temporal retina

Optic chiasm

Optic tract

Lateral geniculate nucleus

Optic radiations

Primary visual cortex (region V1)

**FIGURE 9-14 Crossing the Optic Chiasm**
This dorsal view shows the visual pathway from each eye to the primary visual cortex of each hemisphere. Information from the right side of the visual field (blue) moves from the two left halves of the retinas, ending in the left hemisphere. Information from the left side of the visual field (red) hits the right halves of the retinas and travels to the right side of the brain.

crosses to the opposite side; the lateral path, the *temporal retina*, travels straight back on the same side. Because light that falls on the right half of each retina actually comes from the left side of the visual field, information from the left visual field goes to the brain's right hemisphere, and information from the right visual field goes to the left hemisphere. Thus, half of each retina's visual field is represented on each side of the brain.

By connecting both eyes with both hemispheres, our visual system represents the world seen through two eyes as a single perception.

**Principle 4:** Many brain circuits are crossed.

## Three Routes to the Visual Brain

On entering the brain, the RGC axons separate, forming two distinct pathways, as shown in **Figure 9-15**. These two main pathways lead to the visual cortical regions: the geniculostriate pathway for processing the object's image and the tectopulvinar pathway for directing rapid eye movements and detecting movement and location. A third, smaller pathway tracks into the hypothalamus.

**Geniculostriate System**  All of the P ganglion axons and some of the M ganglion axons form a pathway called the **geniculostriate system**. This pathway goes from the retina to the lateral geniculate nucleus (LGN) of the thalamus and then to layer IV of the primary visual cortex in the occipital lobe.

When stained, the *primary visual cortex* shows a broad stripe across it in layer IV; for this reason, it is also known as the **striate (striped) cortex** (**Figure 9-16**). The geniculostriate system therefore bridges the thalamus (geniculate) and the striate cortex. From the striate cortex, the axon pathway divides. One route goes to vision-related regions of the parietal lobe, and another route goes to vision-related regions of the temporal lobe.

**geniculostriate system**  Projections from the retina to the lateral geniculate nucleus to the visual cortex.

**striate (striped) cortex**  Primary visual cortex (V1) in the occipital lobe; shows stripes (striations) on staining.

**FIGURE 9-15 Main Visual Pathways into the Brain**  The optic nerve follows (1) the geniculostriate path to the primary visual cortex and (2) the tectopulvinar path to the temporal and parietal lobes. (The LGN of the thalamus is part of the diencephalon, shown in Figure 2-19; the superior colliculus in the tectum is part of the midbrain, shown in Figure 2-18.)

**tectopulvinar system** Projections from the retina to the superior colliculus to the pulvinar (thalamus) to the parietal and temporal visual areas.

**retinohypothalamic tract** Neural route formed by axons of photosensitive retinal ganglion cells (pRGCs) from the retina to the suprachiasmatic nucleus; allows light to entrain the suprachiasmatic nucleus's rhythmic activity.

**ventral stream** Visual processing pathway from region V1 to the temporal lobe for object identification and perceiving related movements.

**dorsal stream** Visual processing pathway from region V1 to the parietal lobe; guides movements relative to objects.

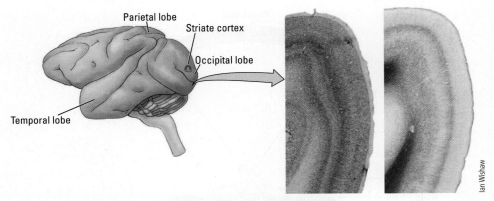

**FIGURE 9-16 Striate Cortex** Area V1 is also called the *striate cortex* because sections appear striated (striped) when stained with either a cell body stain (*left*) or a myelin stain (*right*). The sections shown here come from a rhesus monkey's brain.

**Tectopulvinar System** The second pathway leading from the eye is formed by the axons of the remaining M ganglion cells. The axons of these cells project to the midbrain's superior colliculus, which sends connections to the pulvinar region of the thalamus. This pathway is therefore known as the **tectopulvinar system** because it runs from the eye through the midbrain tectum to the pulvinar (see Figure 9-15). The pulvinar sends connections along two separate routes to the parietal and temporal lobes, bypassing the occipital visual areas.

**Retinohypothalamic Tract** Between 1% and 3% of RGCs are unique in that they are *photosensitive*: they act as photoreceptors. These *pRGCs*, which contain the pigment melanopsin, absorb blue light at a wavelength (between 460 and 480 nm) different from the wavelengths of rods or cones (see Figure 9-9). Axons of pRGCs form a small third visual pathway, the **retinohypothalamic tract**.

Figure 13-7 maps the retinohypothalamic tract into the SCN.

**Principle 8:** The brain divides sensory input for object recognition and movement.

The retinohypothalamic tract synapses in the tiny suprachiasmatic nucleus (SCN) in the hypothalamus, next to the optic chiasm. Photosensitive RGCs participate both in regulating circadian rhythms and in the pupillary reflex that expands and contracts the pupil in response to the amount of light falling on the retina.

## Dorsal and Ventral Visual Streams

The geniculostriate and tectopulvinar pathways extend into the visual brain. Separate routes along each pathway eventually lead to either the parietal lobe or the temporal lobe. Our next task is to determine the role each lobe plays in building our visual world. When we look at the photographs in Clinical Focus 9-1, we can identify objects and we can point to them. Identifying and pointing are different functions.

Having identified the temporal lobe and parietal lobe visual pathways, researchers went looking for their possible functions. Why would evolution produce two different destinations for these neural pathways? Each route must produce visual knowledge for a different purpose.

David Milner and Mel Goodale (2006) proposed that these two purposes are to identify a stimulus (the *what* function) and to control movement to or away from the stimulus (the *how* function). This *what–how* distinction came from an analysis of the routes that visual information takes when it leaves the striate cortex. **Figure 9-17**A shows the two distinct visual pathways that originate in the striate cortex, one progressing to the temporal lobe and the other to the parietal lobe. The pathway to the temporal lobe is the **ventral stream**, whereas the pathway to the parietal lobe is the **dorsal stream**.

In humans, the ventral stream appears to have expanded to form a third stream that travels to the regions referred to as the temporal–parietal junction

**FIGURE 9-17 Visual Streaming** Information travels from the occipital visual areas to the parietal and temporal lobes, forming the dorsal (*how*) and ventral (*what*) streams, respectively.

(TPJ) and superior temporal sulcus (STS) (Haak & Beckmann, 2018; Patel et al., 2019). This third stream is proposed to be involved in language (e.g., reading), tool use, face-emotion processing, and "theory of mind" operations (i.e., the ability to attribute mental states to others).

Read more about theory of mind in Section 15-3.

Both the geniculostriate and the tectopulvinar pathways contribute to the dorsal and ventral streams. To understand how the two streams function, we return to the details of how visual input from the eyes contributes to them.

## Geniculostriate Pathway

The RGC fibers from the two eyes distribute their connections to the two lateral geniculate nuclei (left and right) of the thalamus. At first glance, this appears to be an unusual arrangement. As shown in Figure 9-14, the fibers from the left half of each retina go to the left LGN; those from the right half of each retina go to the right LGN. But the fibers from each eye do not go to exactly the same LGN location.

Figure 2-25 maps layers I through VI in the primary motor and sensory cortices.

Each LGN has six layers, and the projections from the two eyes go to different layers, as illustrated in anatomical context in Figure 9-13 and diagrammed in **Figure 9-18**. Layers 2, 3, and 5 receive fibers from the ipsilateral eye (the eye on the same side), whereas layers 1, 4, and 6 receive fibers from the contralateral eye (the eye on the opposite side). This arrangement allows the information from the two eyes to be combined, but also makes it possible to segregate the information from the P and M ganglion cells.

Axons from the P cells go only to layers 3 through 6 (the parvocellular layers), whereas axons from the M cells go only to layers 1 and 2 (the magnocellular layers). Because the P cells are responsive to color and fine detail, LGN layers 3 through 6 must be processing information about color and form. In contrast, the M cells mostly process information about movement, so layers 1 and 2 must deal with movement.

As illustrated in **Figure 9-19**, input from the two eyes also remains separated in the cortex. The input from the ipsilaterally and contralaterally connected parts of the LGN go to adjacent strips of occipital cortex. These strips, which are about 0.5 mm across, are known as **cortical columns**.

In summary, P and M retinal ganglion cells send separate pathways to the thalamus, and this segregation continues in the striate cortex. The left and right eyes also send separate pathways to the thalamus; these pathways, too, remain segregated in the striate cortex.

Information travels from the right side of each retina to the right LGN.

Left eye (contralateral)　Right eye (ipsilateral)

Nasal projection　Temporal projection

Information from the contralateral side goes to layers 1, 4, and 6.

Information from the ipsilateral side goes to layers 2, 3, and 5.

Layers of LGN

Left LGN　Right LGN

Layers 1 and 2 receive input from the magnocellular pathway.

Layers 3 through 6 receive input from the parvocellular pathway.

**FIGURE 9-18 Geniculostriate Pathway**

## Tectopulvinar Pathway

To review, magnocellular (M) RGCs found throughout the retina receive input primarily from the rods and so are sensitive to light but not to color. M cells in the periphery of the retina are sensitive to movement but not to color or fine details. In the brain, some M cells join P cells to form the geniculostriate pathway; the tectopulvinar pathway is formed by the axons of the remaining M cells.

**cortical column** Anatomic organization that represents a functional unit six cortical layers deep and approximately 0.5 mm square, perpendicular to the cortical surface.

These M cells send their axons to the superior colliculus in the midbrain's tectum. One function of the tectum is to produce orienting movements—to detect stimuli and shift the eyes toward them. The superior colliculus sends connections to the pulvinar region of the thalamus. The medial pulvinar sends connections to the parietal lobe (related to eye movements), and the lateral pulvinar sends connections to the temporal lobe (related to movement detection). One type of information that these connections are conveying is related to *where*. *Where* is important in both the *what* and *how* visual streams.

The *where* function of the tectopulvinar system is useful in understanding D. B.'s blindsight, described in Clinical Focus 9-1. His geniculostriate system was disrupted by surgery, but his tectopulvinar system was not, which allowed him to identify the location of stimuli (*where*) that he could not identify (*what*).

Many textbooks emphasize the *how* pathway as a *where* function. Because *where* is both a property of *what* a stimulus is and a cue for *how* to control movement, we use Milner and Goodale's *what–how* distinction.

**FIGURE 9-19 Maintaining Separate Visual Input** *Left*: Information from the eyes is segregated by layers in the LGN, which maintains this segregation in its projections from the thalamus to the primary visual cortex. Information from each eye travels to adjacent regions in cortical layer IV. *Right*: A horizontal plane through striate cortex shows a zebralike effect of alternating left and right eye regions.

Every mammal has at least one primary cortical area for each sensory system. The primary area relays most of the information that reaches the secondary areas.

**primary visual cortex (V1)** Striate cortex in the occipital lobe that receives input from the lateral geniculate nucleus.

**extrastriate (secondary visual) cortex (V2–V5)** Visual cortical areas in the occipital lobe outside the striate cortex.

**blob** Region in area V1 that contains color-sensitive neurons, as revealed by staining for cytochrome oxidase.

# Occipital Cortex

Our route down the visual pathways has led us from the retina all the way back to the occipital lobe and into the parietal and temporal lobes. Now we explore how visual information proceeds from the striate cortex through the rest of the occipital lobe to the dorsal and ventral streams.

As shown in **Figure 9-20**, the occipital lobe is composed of at least six visual regions: V1, V2, V3, V3A, V4, and V5. As noted earlier, V1 is the striate cortex; it is the **primary visual cortex**. The remaining occipital visual areas form the **extrastriate (secondary visual) cortex**, with each region processing specific features of visual information. Because each occipital region has a unique cytoarchitecture (cellular structure) and unique inputs and outputs, we can infer that each must be doing something different from the others.

As shown in Figures 9-16 and 9-19, a remarkable feature of region V1 is its striations—its distinctly visible layers. When Margaret Wong-Riley and her colleagues (1993) stained region VI to identify the locations of the enzyme cytochrome oxidase, which has a role in cell metabolism, they found an unexpected heterogeneity. So they sectioned the V1 layers in such a way that each cortical layer was in one plane of section, much like peeling off the layers of an onion and laying them flat on a table. The surface of each flattened layer could then be viewed from above. When layers are viewed in this way, the heterogeneous cytochrome staining appears as random blobs in the V1 layers, as diagrammed in **Figure 9-21**. These darkened regions have since become known as **blobs**, and the less-dark regions separating them are called *interblobs*. Blobs and interblobs serve different functions. Neurons in the blobs take part in color perception; neurons in the interblobs participate in perception of form and motion. Within region V1, then, input arriving from the P cell and M cell pathways of the geniculostriate system is segregated into three separate types of information: color, form, and motion.

All three types of information move from region V1 to the adjoining region V2. Here, the color, form, and motion inputs remain segregated, as can again be seen through the pattern of cytochrome oxidase staining. But as Figure 9-21 shows, the staining pattern in region V2 differs from that in region V1. Region V2 has a pattern of thick and thin stripes intermixed with pale zones. The thick stripes receive input from the movement-sensitive neurons in region V1; the thin stripes receive input from V1's color-sensitive neurons; and the pale zones receive input from V1's form-sensitive neurons.

As charted in **Figure 9-22**, the visual pathways proceed from region V2 to the other occipital regions and then to the parietal and temporal lobes, forming the dorsal and ventral streams. Although many parietal and temporal regions take part, the major ones are region G in the parietal lobe (thus called region PG) and region E in the temporal lobe (thus called region TE).

**(A) Medial view of functional areas**

**(B) Lateral view of functional areas**

V1 = Primary visual cortex
V2–V5 = Extrastriate cortex

**FIGURE 9-20 Visual Regions of the Occipital Lobe**

The simple records of color, form, and motion from the occipital regions are assembled in the dorsal and ventral streams to produce a rich, unified visual world of complex objects (such as faces and paintings) and complex skills (such as bike riding and ball catching). We can think of the complex representations of the dorsal and ventral streams as consisting of *how* functions and *what* functions. *How* is looking at, reaching for, and grasping; *what* is the object, such as a spoon.

The visual system's functional anatomy is summarized in **Figure 9-23**, which shows how the dorsal and ventral pathways have evolved to use vision in two distinctly different ways: the dorsal stream for guiding movements and the ventral stream for identifying objects. Damage to either of these systems will produce distinctly different visual syndromes, several of which we discuss in Section 9-5.

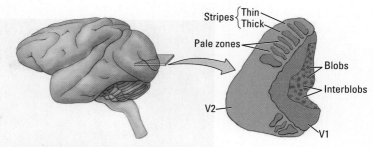

**FIGURE 9-21 Heterogeneous Layering** Blobs in region V1 and stripes in region V2 are illustrated in this drawing of a flattened section through the visual cortex of a monkey. The blobs and stripes are revealed by a special stain for cytochrome oxidase, a marker for mitochondria, the organelles in cells that gather, store, and release energy.

## Vision Beyond the Occipital Cortex

Visual processing that begins in the occipital cortex continues via the ventral and dorsal streams into the temporal and parietal visual cortex. Each region contains multiple

**FIGURE 9-22 Charting the Visual Streams** The dorsal stream, which controls visual action (*top*), begins in region V1 and flows through V2 to the other occipital areas and finally to the parietal cortex, ending in area PG. The ventral stream, which controls object recognition (*bottom*), begins in region V1 and flows through V2 to the other occipital areas and finally to the temporal cortex, ending in area TE. Information from the blobs and interblobs in V1 flows to the thick, thin, and pale zones of V2 and then to regions V3 and V4 to form the ventral stream. Information in the thick and pale zones goes to regions V3A and V5 to form the dorsal stream.

**FIGURE 9-23 Functional Anatomy of the Visual System**

**FIGURE 9-24 Vision Beyond the Occipital Cortex (A)** In the temporal lobe, the fusiform face area (FFA) processes faces, and the parahippocampal place area (PPA) processes scenes. **(B)** In the parietal lobe, the lateral intraparietal area (LIP) contributes to eye movements; the anterior intraparietal area (AIP) is involved in visual control of grasping; and the parietal reach region (PRR) participates in visually guided reaching. Republished with permission of American Association for the Advancement of Science, from Hasson, U., Y. Nir, I. Levy, G. Fuhrmann, and R. Malach. "Intersubject synchronization of cortical activity during natural vision." Science 303, 5664 (2004): pp.1634–1640, Figure 3. Permission conveyed through Copyright Clearance Center, Inc.

areas specialized for specific visual functions. For example, **Figure 9-24**A shows two regions on the ventral surface of the temporal lobes. One is specialized for recognizing faces (the fusiform face area [FFA]) and the other for analyzing landmarks such as buildings or trees (the parahippocampal place area [PPA]). As we gaze at the photographs in Clinical Focus 9-1, then, the three faces activate the FFA, and the trees engage the PPA. Figure 9-24B shows three regions in the parietal lobe related to eye movements (the lateral intraparietal area [LIP]) and visual control of grasping (the anterior intraparietal area [AIP]). The parietal reach region (PRR) has a role in visually guiding our reaching movements.

*Agnosia* means "not knowing." Section 15-7 ties conditions such as agnosia to the search for a neural basis of consciousness.

Damage to these regions can produce surprisingly specific deficits. For example, damage to the FFA leads to **facial agnosia**, also called *prosopagnosia*, a condition in which an individual cannot recognize faces. We saw one patient with prosopagnosia so severe that she could not recognize her identical twin sister's face, and presumably could recognize her own face in the mirror only because she knew it had to be herself (her other visual functions seemed to be normal). Curiously, most individuals with prosopagnosia can distinguish human facial expressions and can distinguish human faces from nonhuman ones. When they do recognize faces, it is based on distinguishing information, such as a birthmark, facial hair, or unique hair style.

## 9-2 Review

Before you continue, check your understanding. Answers to Self-Test appear at the back of the book.

1. Neurons that project into the brain from the retina and form the optic nerve are called _____.

2. _____ retinal ganglion cells receive input mostly from cones and carry information about color and fine detail, whereas _____ retinal ganglion cells receive input mostly from rods and carry information about light but not color.

3. The two major pathways from the retina into the brain are _____ and _____.

4. Damage to the fusiform face area in the temporal lobe can produce _____.

5. Contrast the paths and functions of the dorsal and ventral streams.

**facial agnosia** Face blindness; the inability to recognize faces. Also called *prosopagnosia*.

# 9-3

# Location in the Visual World

As we move about from place to place, we encounter objects in specific locations. If we had no awareness of location, the world would be a bewildering mass of visual information. The next leg of our journey down the neural roads traces how the brain constructs a spatial map. In Clinical Focus 9-1, each of the photographs has a left and a right, an up and a down. All these elements must be coded separately in the brain.

Neural coding of location begins in the retina and is maintained throughout all visual pathways. To understand how this spatial coding is accomplished, imagine your visual world as seen by your two eyes. Imagine the large red and blue rectangles in **Figure 9-25** as a wall. Focus your gaze on the black cross in the middle of the wall.

The part of the wall that you can see without moving your head is your **visual field**. It can be divided into two halves, the left and right visual fields, by drawing a vertical line through the middle of the black cross. Now recall from Figure 9-14 that the left half of each retina looks at the right side of the visual field, whereas the right half of each retina looks at the visual field's left side. Thus, input from the right visual field goes to the left hemisphere, and input from the left visual field goes to the right hemisphere.

Therefore, the brain can easily determine whether visual information lies to the left or right of center. If input goes to the left hemisphere, the source must be in the right visual field; if input goes to the right hemisphere, the source must be in the left visual field. This arrangement tells you nothing about the precise location of an object in the left or right side of the visual field, however. To understand how precise spatial localization is accomplished, we must return to the retinal ganglion cells.

## Coding Location in the Retina

Look again at Figure 9-12, and you can see that each RGC receives input through bipolar cells from several photoreceptors. In the 1950s, Stephen Kuffler, a pioneer in visual system physiology, made an important discovery about how photoreceptors and retinal ganglion cells are linked (Kuffler, 1952). By shining small spots of light on the receptors, he found that each ganglion cell responds to stimulation on just a small circular patch of the retina—the ganglion cell's receptive field.

A ganglion cell's receptive field is therefore the retinal region on which it is possible to influence that cell's firing. Stated differently, the receptive field represents the outer world as seen by a single cell. Each RGC sees only a small bit of the world, much as you would if you looked through a narrow cardboard tube. The visual field is composed of thousands of such receptive fields.

Now let us consider how receptive fields enable the visual system to interpret an object's location. Imagine that the retina is flattened like a piece of paper. When a tiny light shines on different parts of the retina, different ganglion cells respond. For example, when a light shines on the top-left corner of the flattened retina, a particular RGC responds because that light is in its receptive field. Similarly, when a light shines on the top-right corner, a different RGC responds.

By applying this principle, we can determine the location of a light on the retina by the ganglion cell it activates. Another location device determines where the light must be originating to hit a particular place on the retina. Light coming from above hits the bottom of the retina after passing through the eye's lens, and light from below hits the top of the retina. Information at the top of the visual field stimulates ganglion cells on the bottom of the retina; information at the bottom of the field stimulates ganglion cells on the top of the retina.

**Principle 9:** The nervous system produces movement in a perceptual world the brain constructs.

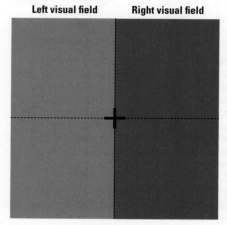

Left visual field    Right visual field

**FIGURE 9-25 Visual-Field Demonstration** As you focus on the cross at center, information to the left of this focal point forms the left visual field (red) and travels to the right hemisphere. Information to the right of the focal point forms the right visual field (blue) and travels to the left hemisphere. The visual field can be split horizontally as well: information above the focal point is in the upper visual field, and information below the focal point is in the lower visual field.

Like a camera lens, the lens in the eye focuses light rays to project a backward, inverted image onto a light-receptive surface (see the diagram How the Eye Works in The Basics: Visible Light and the Structure of the Eye).

**visual field** Region of the visual world seen by the eyes.

**FIGURE 9-26 Receptive-Field Projection**
Information from a receptive field in the retina retains its spatial relation when sent to the lateral geniculate nucleus. Information at the top of the visual field goes to the top of the LGN; information from the bottom of the visual field goes to the bottom of the LGN; and information from the left or right goes to the left or right of the LGN, respectively.

In Figure 1-14, we apply Jerison's ideas to relative differences in overall brain size across mammals.

**FIGURE 9-27 Topographic Organization of Region V1** The fovea sends information to a disproportionately large part of the occipital cortex, which is why visual acuity is best in the central part of the visual field.

# Location in the Lateral Geniculate Nucleus and Region V1

Now consider the connection from the retinal ganglion cells to the lateral geniculate nucleus. In contrast to the retina, the LGN is not a thin sheet; it is shaped more like a sausage. We can compare it to a stack of sausage slices, with each slice representing a layer of cells.

**Figure 9-26** shows how the connections from the retina to the LGN can represent location. A retinal ganglion cell that responds to light in the top-left region of the retina connects to the left side of the first slice. A retinal ganglion cell that responds to light in the bottom-right region of the retina connects to the right side of the last slice. In this way, the location of left–right and top–bottom information is maintained in the LGN.

Like the ganglion cells, each LGN cell has a receptive field—the region of the retina that influences its activity. If two adjacent retinal ganglion cells synapse on a single LGN cell, the receptive field of that LGN cell will be the sum of the two ganglion cells' receptive fields. As a result, the receptive fields of LGN cells are bigger than those of RGCs.

The LGN projection to the striate cortex (region V1) also maintains spatial information. As each LGN cell, representing a particular place, projects to region V1, the cells collectively produce a spatially organized neural representation—a topographic map—in the cortex. As illustrated in **Figure 9-27**, this representation is essentially a map of the visual world.

The central part of the visual field is represented at the back of the brain, whereas the periphery is represented more anteriorly. The upper part of the visual field is represented at the bottom of region V1 and the lower part at the top of V1. The other regions of the visual cortex (such as V3, V4, and V5) have topographic maps similar to that of V1. Thus, the V1 neurons must project to the other regions in an orderly manner, just as the LGN neurons project to region V1 in an orderly way.

Within each visual cortical area, each neuron's receptive field corresponds to the part of the retina to which the neuron is connected. As a rule of thumb, cells in the cortex have much larger receptive fields than do RGCs. This large field size means that the receptive field of a cortical neuron must be composed of the receptive fields of many RGCs, as illustrated in **Figure 9-28**.

One additional wrinkle pertains to the organization of the topographic maps in the cortex. Harry Jerison (1973) proposed the *principle of proper mass*, which states that the amount of neural tissue responsible for a particular function is proportional to the amount of neural processing that function requires. The more complex a function is, the larger a specific region performing that function must be. The visual cortex provides some good examples.

As you can see in Figure 9-27, not all parts of the visual field are equally represented in region V1. The small central part

The central part of the visual field is represented at the back of the brain.

The peripheral areas of the visual field are located more anteriorly.

The top part of the visual field is represented in the lower part of the occipital lobe.

of the visual field seen by the fovea is represented by a larger area in the cortex than is the visual field's periphery, even though the periphery covers a much larger area. In accord with Jerison's principle, we would predict more processing of foveal information than of peripheral information in region V1. This prediction makes intuitive sense because we can see more clearly in the center of the visual field than at the periphery (see Figure 9-7). In other words, sensory areas that have more cortical representation provide a more detailed construct of the external world.

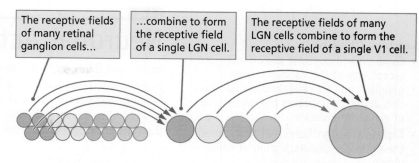

The receptive fields of many retinal ganglion cells...

...combine to form the receptive field of a single LGN cell.

The receptive fields of many LGN cells combine to form the receptive field of a single V1 cell.

**FIGURE 9-28 Receptive-Field Hierarchy**

## Visual Corpus Callosum

Topographic mapping based on neuronal receptive fields is an effective way for the brain to code object location. But if the left visual field is represented in the right cerebral hemisphere and the right visual field is represented in the left cerebral hemisphere, how are the two halves of the visual field ultimately merged into a unified representation? After all, we have the subjective impression not of two independent visual fields, but rather of a single, continuous field of vision.

The answer to how this unity is accomplished lies in the corpus callosum (shown in **Figure 9-29**A), which binds the two sides of the visual field together at the midline. Until the 1950s, the function of the corpus callosum was largely a mystery. Physicians would occasionally cut the corpus callosum to control severe epilepsy or to reach a very deep tumor, but patients did not appear much affected by this surgery. The corpus callosum clearly linked the two hemispheres of the brain, but exactly which parts were connected was not yet known.

We now realize that the corpus callosum connects only certain brain structures. As shown in Figure 9-29B, the frontal lobes have many callosal connections, but the occipital lobes have almost none. If you think about it, there is no reason for a neuron in the visual cortex that is looking at one place in the visual field to be concerned with what another neuron in the opposite hemisphere is looking at in another part of the visual field.

Cells that lie along the midline of the visual field are an exception, however. These cells look at adjacent places in the visual field, one slightly to the left of center and one slightly to the right. Callosal connections between such cells zip the two visual fields together by combining their receptive fields to overlap at the midline. In this way, the two fields become one.

Section 15-4 describes the revelations learned from studying split-brain patients, whose corpus callosa have been severed.

**(A) Human**

Corpus callosum

**(B) Rhesus monkey**

Most of the two frontal lobes have callosal connections,...

...whereas the occipital lobes have almost no connections.

Parietal lobe

Frontal lobe

Occipital lobe

Temporal lobe

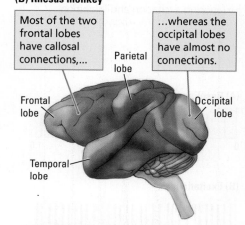

**FIGURE 9-29 Callosal Connections**
**(A)** Corpus callosum in the human brain.
**(B)** Darker areas show regions of the rhesus monkey cortex that receive projections from the opposite hemisphere through the corpus callosum. As similar pattern of projections connects the two hemispheres of the human brain.

## 9-3 Review

Before you continue, check your understanding. Answers to Self-Test appear at the back of the book.

1. The visual field is composed of thousands of small _____ of the retinal ganglion cells.

2. Light stimulates _____ cells in the retina, which in turn stimulate _____ cells, the axons of which form the optic nerve. The optic nerve connects to cells in the _____, where this visual information is processed to represent location.

3. Inputs to different parts of cortical region V1 from different parts of the retina essentially form a(n) _____ of the visual world within the brain.

4. The two sides of the visual world are bound together as one perception by the _____.

5. How does Jerison's principle of proper mass apply to the visual system?

## Learning Objectives

- Compare and contrast the on–off receptivity of the various retinal ganglion and V1 cells, and explain how this activity facilitates the processing of visual information.
- Explain the significance of trichromatic theory in our understanding of color vision.
- Explain how opponent-process pairing of the retinal ganglion and V1 cells allows us to distinguish color.

The process by which microelectrodes can be used to record information from a neuron is described in Section 4-1; Figure 4-4 illustrates how we measure the flow of electrical activity across neurons and Figure 4-7 diagrams how microelectrodes work.

**Principle 7:** The nervous system works by juxtaposing excitation and inhibition.

**(A) Baseline (12 per second)**

**(B) Excitation**

**(C) Inhibition**

**FIGURE 9-30 Recording Neuronal Stimulation** Each action potential is represented by a spike. **(A)** In a 1-second period at this neuron's baseline firing rate, 12 spikes were recorded. **(B)** A firing rate greater than the baseline signals excitation. **(C)** A firing rate less than the baseline signals inhibition.

## 9-4

# Neuronal Activity

Individual neurons make up the visual system pathways. By studying how these cells behave when their receptive fields are stimulated, we can begin to understand how the brain processes the features of the visual world beyond the location of a light. We first examine how neurons in the ventral stream respond to objects' shapes and colors. We then briefly consider how neurons in the dorsal stream direct vision for action.

## Seeing Shape

Imagine a microelectrode placed near a neuron somewhere in the visual pathway from retina to cortex. The microelectrode is recording changes in the neuron's firing rate. This cell occasionally fires spontaneously, producing action potentials with each discharge. Assume that the neuron discharges, on average, once every 0.08 second. Each action potential is brief, on the order of 1 millisecond.

If we plot action potentials spanning 1 second, we see only spikes in the record because the action potentials are so brief. **Figure 9-30**A is a single-cell recording of 12 spikes in the span of 1 second. If the firing rate of this cell increases, we see more spikes (Figure 9-30B). If the firing rate decreases, we see fewer spikes (Figure 9-30C). The increase in firing results from neuronal excitation, whereas the decrease indicates inhibition. Excitation and inhibition, of course, are the principal mechanisms by which information transfer occurs in the nervous system.

Now suppose we present a stimulus to the neuron by illuminating its receptive field in the retina, perhaps by shining a light on a blank screen within the cell's visual field. We might place before the eye a straight line positioned at a 45° angle. The cell could respond to this stimulus by either increasing or decreasing its firing rate. In each case, we would conclude that the cell is generating information about the line.

The same cell could show excitation to one stimulus, inhibition to another stimulus, and no reaction at all to a third. The cell could be excited by lines oriented 45° to the left and inhibited by lines oriented 45° to the right. Similarly, the cell could be excited by stimulation in one part of its receptive field (such as the center) and inhibited by stimulation in another part (such as the periphery).

Finally, we might find that the cell's response to a particular stimulus is selective. Such a cell would indicate the importance of the stimulus to the animal. For instance, the cell might be excited when a stimulus is presented with food, but inhibited when the same stimulus is presented alone. In each case, the cell is selectively sensitive to characteristics in the visual world.

Neurons at each level of the visual system have distinctly different characteristics and functions. Our goal is not to look at each neuron type, but rather to consider generally how some typical neurons at each level differ from one another in their contributions to processing shape. We focus on neurons in three areas: the ganglion cell layer of the retina, the primary visual cortex, and the temporal cortex.

## Processing in RGCs

The receptive fields of ganglion cells in the retina are minuscule dots. Each retinal ganglion cell responds only to the presence or absence of light in its receptive field, not to shape. Thus, these cells do not detect shape. Instead, shape is constructed by processes in the cortex from the information that those ganglion cells pass on about events in their receptive fields.

The receptive field of a ganglion cell has a concentric circle arrangement, as illustrated in **Figure 9-31**A. A spot of light falling in the receptive field's central circle excites some of these cells, whereas a spot of light falling in the receptive field's surrounding area (periphery) inhibits the cell. A spot of light falling across the entire receptive field weakly increases the cell's firing rate.

This type of neuron is called an *on-center cell*. Other RGCs, called *off-center cells*, have the opposite arrangement—that is, light in the center of the receptive field inhibits

**(A) On-center cell's receptive field**

Response of cell to stimulus at left

Light strikes center

0    1   Excitation   2    3
Time (seconds)

Light strikes surround

0    1   Inhibition   2    3
Time (seconds)

**(B) Off-center cell's receptive field**

Light strikes center

0    1   Inhibition   2    3
Time (seconds)

Light strikes surround

0    1   Excitation   2    3
Time (seconds)

the cell, light in the surrounding area excites the cell, and light across the entire field produces weak inhibition of the cell (Figure 9-31B). The on–off arrangement of RGC receptive fields makes these cells especially responsive to tiny spots of light.

This description of ganglion cell receptive fields might mislead you into thinking that they form a mosaic of discrete little circles on the retina. In fact, neighboring retinal ganglion cells receive their inputs from an overlapping set of photoreceptors. As a result, their receptive fields overlap, as illustrated in **Figure 9-32**. In this way, a small spot of light shining on the retina is likely to produce activity in both on-center and off-center RGCs.

How can on-center and off-center ganglion cells tell the brain anything about shape? The answer is that a ganglion cell tells the brain about the amount of light hitting a certain spot on the retina compared with the average amount of light falling on the surrounding retinal region. This comparison is known as **luminance contrast**. *Luminance* is the amount of visible light reflected to the eye from a surface, and *contrast* is the difference in luminance between adjacent parts of that surface. The photographs in Clinical Focus 9-1 show us two clear differences in luminance contrast. On the left, the woman's pink top contrasts sharply with her black slacks, but the sleeve on the right contrasts far less with the background. It does not appear as bright.

To understand how luminance contrast tells the brain about shape, consider the hypothetical population of on-center ganglion cells represented in **Figure 9-33**. Their receptive fields are distributed across the retinal image of a light–dark edge. Some of the ganglion cells' receptive fields are in the dark area, others are in the light area, and still others' fields straddle the edge of the light.

**FIGURE 9-31 On–Off Receptivity (A)** In the receptive field of an RGC with an on-center and an off-surround, a spot of light shining on the center excites the neuron, whereas a spot of light in the surround inhibits it. When the light in the surround is turned off, the firing rate increases briefly—an offset response. A light shining in both the center and the surround (periphery) would produce a weak increase in firing. **(B)** In the receptive field of an RGC with an off-center and an on-surround, light in the center produces inhibition, light on the surround produces excitation, and light across the entire field produces weak inhibition.

**luminance contrast** Amount of light an object reflects relative to its surroundings.

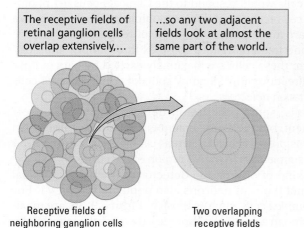

The receptive fields of retinal ganglion cells overlap extensively,...

...so any two adjacent fields look at almost the same part of the world.

Receptive fields of neighboring ganglion cells

Two overlapping receptive fields

**FIGURE 9-32 Overlapping Receptive Fields**

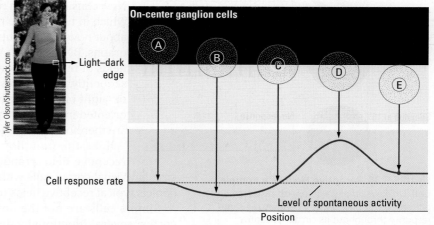

Tyler Olson/Shutterstock.com

Light–dark edge

On-center ganglion cells

Cell response rate

Level of spontaneous activity

Position

**FIGURE 9-33 Activity at the Margins** Responses of a hypothetical population of on-center ganglion cells whose receptive fields (A–E) are distributed across a light–dark edge. The activity of the cells along the edge is most affected relative to those away from the edge. Information from Purves et al., 1997.

**(A) Horizontally aligned preferred orientation**

No stimulus

Simple cell's receptive field

OFF
ON
OFF

Baseline response

Light

OFF
ON
OFF

Strong response

OFF
ON
OFF

No response

Light

**(B) Oblique preferred orientation**

No stimulus

OFF
ON
OFF

Baseline response

Light

OFF
ON
OFF

No response

OFF
ON
OFF

Strong response

Light

**FIGURE 9-34 Typical Receptive Fields for Simple V1 Cells** Simple cells respond to a bar of light in a particular orientation, such as **(A)** horizontal or **(B)** oblique. The position of the bar in the visual field is important because the cell either responds (ON) or does not respond (OFF) to light in adjacent visual field regions.

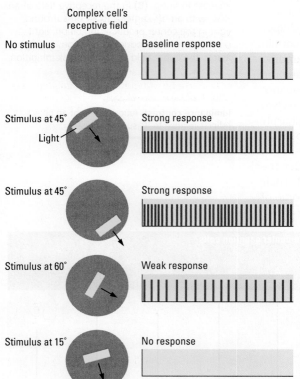

**FIGURE 9-35 Receptive Field of a Complex Cell** Unlike a simple cell's on–off response pattern, a complex cell in V1 shows the same response throughout its circular receptive field, responding best to bars of light moving at a particular angle. The response is reduced or absent with the bar of light at other orientations.

The ganglion cells with receptive fields in the dark or light areas are least affected because they receive either no stimulation or stimulation of both the excitatory and inhibitory regions of their receptive fields. The ganglion cells most affected by the stimulus are those lying along the edge. Ganglion cell B is inhibited because the light falls mostly on its inhibitory surrounding area; ganglion cell D is excited because its entire excitatory center is stimulated, but only part of its inhibitory surround is.

Consequently, information transmitted from retinal ganglion cells to the visual areas in the brain does not give equal weight to all visual field regions. Instead, it emphasizes those regions containing differences in luminance—areas along the edges. In essence, RGCs send signals about edges, and edges form shapes.

## Processing Shape in the Primary Visual Cortex

Now consider cells in region V1 that receive their visual inputs from LGN cells, which in turn receive theirs from retinal ganglion cells. As you read on, think about how these cortical cells would respond to the Clinical Focus 9-1 photographs. Because each V1 cell receives input from multiple RGCs, the receptive fields of the V1 neurons are much larger than those of retinal neurons. Consequently, V1 cells respond to stimuli more complex than simply "light on" or "light off." In particular, these cells are maximally excited by bars of light oriented in a particular direction rather than by spots of light. These V1 cells are therefore called *orientation detectors*.

Like the ganglion cells, some orientation detectors have an on–off receptive-field arrangement, but the arrangement is rectangular rather than circular. Visual cortex cells with this property are known as *simple cells*. **Figure 9-34** depicts typical receptive fields for simple cells in the V1 region of the cortex.

Simple cells are not the only kind of orientation detector in the primary visual cortex; several functionally distinct types of neurons also populate region V1. For instance, the receptive fields of *complex cells*, such as those in **Figure 9-35**, are maximally excited by bars of light moving in a particular direction through the visual field. A *hypercomplex cell*, like a complex cell, is maximally responsive to moving bars but also has a strong inhibitory area at one end of its receptive field. As illustrated in **Figure 9-36**, a bar of light landing on the right side of the hypercomplex cell's receptive field excites the cell. However, if the bar lands mainly on the inhibitory area to the left in this example, the cell's firing is inhibited.

Each class of V1 neurons responds to bars of light in some way, yet this response results from input originating in retinal ganglion cells that respond maximally not to bars but to spots of light. How does this conversion from responding to spots to responding to bars take place? An example will help explain the process.

Imagine a thin bar of light falls on the retinal photoreceptors, striking the receptive fields of perhaps dozens of retinal ganglion cells. The input to a V1 neuron comes from a group of ganglion cells that happen to be aligned in a row, as in **Figure 9-37**. That V1 neuron is activated (or inhibited) only when a bar of light hitting the retina strikes that particular row of ganglion cells. If the bar of light shines at a slightly different angle, only some of the retinal ganglion cells in the row are activated, in which case the V1 neuron is excited only weakly.

Figure 9-37 illustrates the connection between light striking the retina in a certain pattern and the activation of a simple cell in the primary visual cortex, one that responds to a bar of light in a particular orientation. Using the same logic, we can also diagram the retinal receptive fields of complex or hypercomplex V1 neurons.

A characteristic of cortical structure is that the neurons are organized into *functional columns*. The connectivity pattern in a column is vertical: inputs arrive

**FIGURE 9-36 Receptive Field of a Hypercomplex Cell** A hypercomplex cell in V1 responds to a moving bar of light in a particular orientation (e.g., horizontal) anywhere in the excitatory (ON) part of its receptive field. If most of the bar extends into the inhibitory area (OFF), however, the response is inhibited.

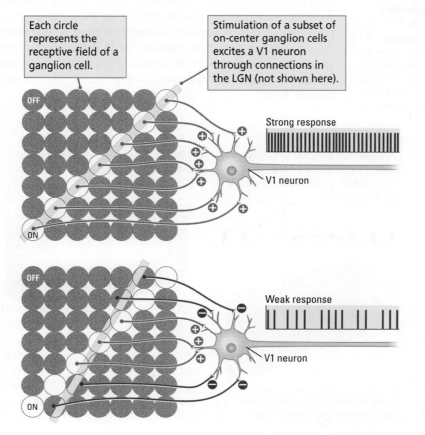

Each circle represents the receptive field of a ganglion cell.

Stimulation of a subset of on-center ganglion cells excites a V1 neuron through connections in the LGN (not shown here).

**FIGURE 9-37 V1 Receptivity** A V1 cell responds to a row of ganglion cells in a particular orientation on the retina. The bar of light strongly activates a row of ganglion cells, each connected through the LGN to a V1 neuron. The activity of this V1 neuron is most affected by a bar of light at a 45° angle.

Visual cortex

Vertical column

Stellate cells

Pyramidal cell

Output        Input destined for layer IV

**FIGURE 9-38 Neural Circuit in a Column in the Visual Cortex** In this three-dimensional view, sensory inputs enter the cortical column at layer VI (bottom) and terminate on stellate cells in layer IV that synapse with pyramidal cells in layers III and V. The information flow is vertical. Axons of the pyramidal cells leave the column to join other columns or structures. Information from Szentagothai, 1975.

**ocular dominance column** Functional column in the visual cortex that is maximally responsive to information coming from one eye.

in layer IV and then connect with cells in the other layers. **Figure 9-38** shows such a column, a 0.5-mm-diameter strip of cortex that includes representative neurons and their connections.

Neurons within a cortical column have similar functions. For example, **Figure 9-39**A shows that neurons within the same column respond to lines oriented in the same direction. Adjacent columns house cells that are responsive to different line orientations. Figure 9-39B shows the cortical columns of input coming from each eye, as discussed earlier, called **ocular dominance columns**. Thus, V1 has orientation columns housing neurons of similar sensitivity, as well as ocular dominance columns that contain input from one eye or the other.

## Processing Shape in the Temporal Cortex

Consider neurons along the ventral stream in temporal lobe region TE. Rather than being responsive to spots or bars of light, TE neurons are maximally excited by complex visual stimuli, such as faces (recall Figure 9-24A) or hands, and can be remarkably specific in their responsiveness. They may be responsive to particular faces seen head-on, to faces viewed in profile, to the posture of the head, or even to particular facial expressions.

How far does this specialized responsiveness extend? Would it be practical to have visual neurons in the temporal cortex specialized to respond to every conceivable feature of objects? Keiji Tanaka (1993) approached this question by presenting monkeys with many three-dimensional representations of animals and plants in an effort to find stimuli that are effective in activating particular neurons of the inferior temporal cortex.

Having identified stimuli that were especially effective, such as faces or hands, he then wondered which specific features of those stimuli are critical to stimulating the neurons. When Tanaka inserted electrodes in area TE to record the neural activity, he found that most of these neurons require rather complex features for their activation. These features include a combination of characteristics such as orientation, size, color, and texture. Furthermore, neurons with similar but not identical responsiveness to particular features tend to cluster in columns, as shown in **Figure 9-40**.

**(A)**

Adjacent columns house neurons that are responsive to slightly different line orientations, forming an array of 180°.

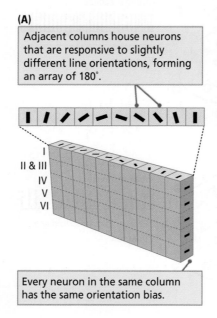

Every neuron in the same column has the same orientation bias.

**(B)**

Ocular dominance columns receive input from the right or left eye.

**FIGURE 9-39 Organization of Functional Columns in Area V1**

Based on Tanaka's findings and subsequent studies, it seems an object is represented not by the activity of a single neuron, but rather by the activity of many neurons with slightly varying stimulus specificities. These neurons are grouped in a column. This finding is important because it provides an explanation for *stimulus equivalence*—recognizing an object as remaining the same despite being viewed from different orientations.

Think of how the representation of objects by multiple neurons in a column can produce stimulus equivalence. If each neuron in the column module varies slightly in regard to the features to which it responds but the effective stimuli largely overlap, the effects of small changes in incoming visual images will be minimized, and we will continue to perceive an object as itself.

The stimulus specificity of neurons in the inferior temporal cortex in monkeys shows remarkable neuroplasticity. If monkeys are trained to discriminate particular shapes to obtain a food reward, not only do they improve their discriminatory ability, but neurons in the temporal lobe also modify their preferred stimuli to fire maximally to some of the stimuli used in training. This result shows that the temporal lobe's role in visual processing is not determined genetically, but instead is subject to experience, even in adults.

We can speculate that this neuroplastic characteristic evolved because it allows the visual system to adapt to a changing visual environment. Think of how different the demands on your visual recognition abilities are when you move from a dense forest to a treeless plain to a city street. The visual neurons of your temporal cortex can adapt to these differences (Tanaka, 1993). In addition, experience-dependent visual neurons ensure that people can identify visual stimuli that were never encountered as the human brain evolved. We will return to the topic of neuroplasticity in visual processing in Section 9-6.

The preferred stimuli of neurons in the primary visual cortex are not modified by experience. Their static nature implies that the stimulus preferences of V1 neurons are genetically programmed. Regardless, the functions of the V1 neurons underlie the more complex and flexible characteristics of the inferior temporal cortex neurons.

# Seeing Color

Scientists have long wondered why—and how—we see a world so rich in color. One hypothesis on the *why* is that color vision evolved first in the great apes, specifically in apes that eat fruit. Chimpanzees and humans are members of this family. Over their evolution, both species have faced plentiful competition for ripe fruits—from other animals, insects, and each other. Scientists suspect that color vision gave the great apes a competitive evolutionary advantage.

Our explanation of how color vision works has its roots in the Renaissance, a period of rich cultural development that occurred 600 years ago in Italy. Painters of the time discovered that they could obtain the entire range of colors in the visual world by mixing only three colors of paint (red, blue, and yellow). This process of *subtractive color mixing* is shown in **Figure 9-41**A.

We now know that such trichromatic color mixing is a property of the cones in the retina. Subtractive color mixing works by removing light from the mix. It is why matte black surfaces reflect no light: the darker the color, the less light it contains.

Conversely, *additive color mixing* increases light to make color (Figure 9-41B). The lighter the color, the more light it contains, which is why a white surface reflects the entire visible spectrum. In contrast to the primary paint colors of red, blue, and yellow, the primary colors of light are red,

Neurons in the temporal lobe form columns that respond to categories of shapes.

Temporal lobe

I
II & III
IV
V
VI

**FIGURE 9-40  Columnar Organization of Area TE** Neurons with similar but slightly different pattern selectivity cluster in vertical columns, perpendicular to the cortical surface.

**Principle 10:** Neuroplasticity is the hallmark of nervous system functioning.

Section 1-4 recounts several ideas on how the primate lifestyle, including diet, encouraged the evolution of complex nervous systems.

**FIGURE 9-41  Color Mixing (A)** Subtractive color mixing absorbs light waves that we see as red, blue, or yellow. When all visible wavelengths are absorbed, we see black. **(B)** Additive color mixing reflects light waves that we see as red, blue, and green. When all visible wavelengths are reflected, we see white.

(A)

(B)

Changes in a neuron's preferred stimulus reflect changes in its sensitivity to particular features.

blue, and green. Light of different wavelengths stimulates the three cone receptor types in different ways. It is the ratio of activity of these three receptor types that forms our impressions of colors.

## Trichromatic Theory

According to the **trichromatic theory**, the color we see—say, blue at short 400-nm wavelengths, green at medium 500-nm wavelengths, and red at long 600-nm wavelengths—is determined by the relative responses of the corresponding cone types (see Figure 9-9). If all three types are equally active, we see white.

Trichromatic theory predicts that if we lack one type of cone receptor, we cannot process as many colors as we could with all three types. This is exactly what happens when a person is born with only two cone types. The colors this person cannot perceive depend on which receptor type is missing, as illustrated in Research Focus 9-4: Color-Deficient Vision.

The mere presence of cones in an animal's retina does not mean that the animal has color vision as we know it. Instead, it simply means that the animal has photoreceptors that are particularly sensitive to light. Many animals lack color vision as we know it, but the only animal with eyes known to have no cones at all is a type of fish called a skate. A key feature of primate color vision is the processing of color in V1 and V4.

**trichromatic theory** Explanation of color vision based on the coding of three primary colors: red, green, and blue.

---

◉ **RESEARCH FOCUS 9-4**

## Color-Deficient Vision

Most people's retinas contain three types of cones; these people have trichromatic vision. But some people are missing one or more cone types. These individuals are often mistakenly said to be color-blind — mistakenly because people who have two types of cones can still distinguish lots of colors, though not as many as people with all three types of cones.

To have no color vision at all, someone would have to have only one type of photoreceptor — that is, just rods. This is a rare occurrence, but we do have a friend who has no concept of color. It has led to a lifetime of practical jokes because others (especially his wife) must choose properly color-coordinated clothes for him to wear.

A complete lack of red cones leads to a condition called *protanopia*; a lack of green cones produces *deuteranopia*; a lack of blue cones results

in *tritanopia*. The frequency of each condition is about 1% in men and 0.01% in women. Having fewer cones of one type, most commonly the green cones, is also possible. This condition affects about 5% of men and 0.4% of women.

The accompanying illustration provides a simple approximation of what people with protanopia (center) or deuteranopia (right) see, compared with what trichromats (left) see. Individuals with protanopia and deuteranopia still see plenty of color, but that color is significantly different from the color that trichromats see. Many domestic animals (dogs, cats, and horses among them) have deuteranopia, which actually gives them an advantage in seeing objects that would appear camouflaged to trichromats. In fact, military forces often use humans with deuteranopia to help see through camouflage.

Image as viewed by a trichromat observer

Protanopia: image as viewed by an observer lacking red cones

Deuteranopia: image as viewed by an observer lacking green cones

Dr. Terrace L. Waggoner/www.ColorVisionTesting.com

**FIGURE 9-42 Demonstrating Opposing Color Pairs** Stare at the rectangle on the left for about 30 seconds. Then stare at the white box on the right. You will see an afterimage of green on the red side and of yellow on the blue side.

## Opponent Processes

Although the beginning of color perception in the cones follows the trichromatic model, succeeding levels of color processing use a different strategy. Try staring first at the red and blue box in **Figure 9-42** for about 30 seconds and then at the white box next to it. When you shift your gaze to the white surface, you will see an afterimage in the colors opposite to red and blue — green and yellow. Conversely, if you stare at a green and yellow box and then shift to white, you will see a red and blue afterimage. Such afterimages lead to the sense that there are actually four basic colors (red, green, yellow, and blue).

A characteristic of RGCs explains the two opposing pairs of four basic colors. Recall that RGCs have an on–off and center–surround organization. Stimulation to the center of the cell's receptive field is either excitatory (in some cells) or inhibitory (in other cells), whereas stimulation to the periphery of the receptive field has the opposite effect (see Figure 9-31).

This arrangement can be adapted to produce color-opponent cells. If one wavelength of light produced excitation and another inhibition, cells would evolve that are excited by red and inhibited by green (or vice versa), as would cells that are excited by blue and inhibited by yellow (or vice versa). Red–green and blue–yellow would therefore be linked to each other as color opposites, or opponents.

In fact, about 60% of human retinal ganglion cells are color-sensitive in this way, with the center being responsive to one wavelength and the surrounding area to another. The most common **opponent-process** pairing, shown in **Figure 9-43**, is medium wavelength (green) versus long wavelength (red), but we also have blue-versus-yellow RGCs. Most likely, opponent-process cells evolved to enhance the relatively small differences in spectral absorption among the three cone types.

Cortical neurons in region V1 also respond to color in an opponent-process manner reminiscent of retinal ganglion cells. Recall that color inputs in the primary visual cortex go to the blobs that appear in sections stained for cytochrome oxidase (see Figure 9-21). These blobs are where the color-sensitive cells are located.

**Figure 9-44** models how the color-sensitive cells in the blobs are inserted amid the orientation-sensitive and ocular dominance columns. In this model, the primary visual cortex appears to be organized into modules that include ocular dominance and orientation-sensitive columns as well as blobs. Think of V1 as being composed of several thousand modules, each analyzing color and contour for a particular visual region. This organization allows the primary visual cortex to perform several functions concurrently.

How do neurons in the visual system beyond V1 process color? You have already learned that cells in region V4 respond to color, but in contrast to the cells in region V1, these V4 cells do not respond to particular wavelengths. Rather, they are responsive to different perceived colors, with the center of the field being excited by a certain color and the surrounding area being inhibited.

**(A) White light** — Baseline response

**(B) Red light** — Strong response

Green light — Strong response

**(C) Green light** — Weak response

**(D) Red and green light** — Very strong response

**(E) Green and red light** — No response

**FIGURE 9-43 Opponent-Color Contrast Response (A)** A red–green color-sensitive RGC responds weakly to white light on its center and surround because red and green cones absorb white light to similar extents, so their inputs cancel out. **(B)** The cell responds strongly to a spot of red light in its center as well as to the red light's paired wavelength, green, in the surround. **(C)** The cell is strongly inhibited by a small spot of green in its center. **(D)** The RGC responds very strongly to simultaneous illumination of the center with red and the surround with green. **(E)** It is completely inhibited by the simultaneous illumination of the center with green and the surround with red.

**opponent process** Explanation of color vision that emphasizes the importance of the apparently opposing color pairs: red versus green and blue versus yellow.

**color constancy** Phenomenon whereby an object's perceived color tends to remain constant relative to other colors, regardless of changes in illumination.

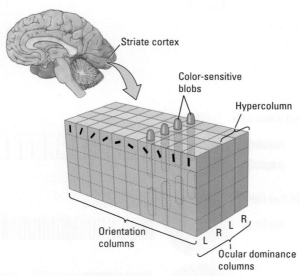

FIGURE 9-44 **V1 Modules** A model of striate cortex showing the orientation-sensitive columns, ocular dominance columns, and color-sensitive blobs as composed of two hypercolumns. Each consists of a full set (red and blue) of orientation-sensitive columns spanning 180° of the preferred angle as well as a pair of blobs. All cells in the hypercolumn share the same receptive field.

FIGURE 9-45 **Color Constancy** Depending on the viewer, the dress in the center photo will be perceived as either white and gold or blue and black. The image has been color-balanced, at left, to show the dress as white and gold; at right, it appears blue and black. What color is the original?

The blue-and-black dress at right is the original.

Speculation continues to swirl about the function of these V4 cells. One idea is that they are important for **color constancy**, the property of perception whereby colors appear to remain the same relative to one another despite changes in light. For instance, imagine you looked at a bowl of fruit through light-green glasses: the fruit would take on a greenish tinge, but bananas would still look yellow relative to red apples. If you removed all the fruit except the bananas and looked at them through the tinted glasses, the bananas would appear green because the color you perceive is isolated relative to any other. Evidence for this theory about V4 cells' function includes the finding that monkeys with V4 lesions lose color constancy, though they can discriminate different color wavelengths.

In February 2015, Celia Bleasdale took a cell phone photo of the black-and-blue dress she intended to wear to her daughter's wedding. The image, popularly referred to as "The Dress," was posted online and immediately went viral because different observers expressed radically different opinions of the color scheme (see **Figure 9-45**). Pascal Wallisch (2017) studied this phenomenon by surveying about 13,000 online observers. He found that observers' unconscious assumptions about the source of the illumination of the dress influenced their color perception. People who believed the dress to be illuminated with artificial incandescent light saw the dress as blue, whereas people who believed the dress was photographed in daylight saw the dress as gold. Our assumptions are a necessary component of the human visual system's color constancy. "The Dress" not only provides an example of color constancy, but also shows how our color perception is idiosyncratic.

# Neuronal Activity in the Dorsal Stream

A striking characteristic of many cells in the visual areas of the parietal cortex is that they are virtually silent to visual stimulation when a person is under anesthesia. This is true of neurons in the posterior parietal regions of the dorsal stream. In contrast, cells in the visual temporal cortex do respond to visual stimulation when a person is anesthetized.

The silence on the part of neurons in the posterior parietal cortex under anesthesia makes sense if their role is to process visual information for action. An unconscious person is unable to perform actions, so there is no need for these neurons to process visual information. Hence, the cells remain inactive.

Many types of cells can be found in the dorsal stream, their details varying with the nature of the movement in which a particular cell takes part. One interesting category of cells processes the visual appearance of an object to be grasped. If a monkey is going to pick up an apple, for instance, these cells respond even when the monkey is simply looking at the apple. The cells do not respond when the monkey encounters the same apple if no movement will be made.

These dorsal stream cells also respond if the monkey merely watches another monkey making movements to pick up the apple. Apparently, the cells have some understanding of what is happening in the external world. That understanding, however, is always related to action performed with respect to visually perceived objects. These cells led David Milner and Mel Goodale (2006) to conclude that the dorsal stream is a *how* visual system, as described in Section 9-3.

But the dorsal stream may actually have a greater role in shape perception than previously thought. Recent functional magnetic resonance imaging (fMRI) studies have shown that the dorsal pathway can also perceive and process objects, although studies of patients show that this function is not possible without the presence of the ventral stream (Freud et al., 2017). It is still not known exactly what role the dorsal stream plays in object perception, but research results suggest that shape processing may be more distributed in an extensive visual network than was previously believed (Garcea et al., 2018).

## 9-4 Review

**Before you continue, check your understanding. Answers to Self-Test appear at the back of the book.**

1. Neurons in the primary visual cortex respond to properties of shapes, especially to _____ oriented in a certain direction.

2. Recognition of complex visual stimuli such as faces is completed in the _____ lobe.

3. The idea that the color we see is determined by the relative responses of the three types of cones in the retina is called _____.

4. Retinal ganglion cells mediate color vision by _____ processes.

5. Describe the opponent process in the retinal ganglion cells.

6. What do the differing responses to "The Dress" say about the way we perceive color?

## 9-5

# The Visual Brain in Action

Anatomical and physiological studies of brain systems leave one key question unanswered: How do all of the cells in these systems act together to produce a particular function? One way to answer this question is to evaluate what happens when parts of the visual system are dysfunctional. Then we can see how these parts contribute to the workings of the whole. We use this strategy to examine the neuropsychology of vision—the study of the visual brain in action.

## Injury to the Visual Pathway Leading to the Cortex

What happens when parts of the visual pathway leading from the eye to the cortex are injured? For instance, destruction of the retina or optic nerve of one eye produces *monocular blindness*, the loss of sight in that eye. Partial destruction of the retina or optic nerve produces a partial loss of sight in one eye, restricted to the visual field region that has severed connections to the brain.

Injuries to the visual pathway beyond the eye also produce blindness. For example, complete cuts of the optic tract, the LGN, or cortical region V1 result in **homonymous hemianopia**, blindness of one entire side of the visual field, as shown in **Figure 9-46**A. We encountered this syndrome in Clinical Focus 9-1, the story of D. B.'s lesion in region V1. A partial lesion in one of these areas—which is often the case—leads to **quadrantanopia**, destruction of only a part of the visual field, illustrated in Figure 9-46B. Note that injuries affecting vision are rarely localized to gray matter but also include white matter, leading to disconnection of different brain regions.

Figure 9-46C shows that small lesions in V1 often produce small blind spots, or **scotomas**, in the visual field. As noted in Clinical Focus 9-1, scotomas can be a warning symptom for individuals who experience migraines. In contrast, people with brain injuries are often totally unaware of them. One reason is that the eyes are usually moving.

Our eyes make tiny, involuntary movements almost constantly. Because of this usually constant eye motion, called *nystagmus*, a scotoma moves about the visual field, allowing the intact brain regions to perceive all the information in that field. If the eyes are temporarily held still, the visual system actually compensates for a scotoma through pattern completion—filling in the hole, so to speak—so that the people and objects in the visual world are perceived as whole. The result: a seemingly normal set of perceptions.

The visual system may cover up a scotoma so successfully that its presence can be demonstrated to the patient only by tricking the visual system. The test for this condition is to place an object entirely within the scotoma and, without allowing the patient to shift gaze, asking what the object is. If the patient reports seeing nothing, to confirm the existence of a blind area, the examiner moves the object out of the scotoma so that it suddenly appears in the intact region of the visual field.

### Learning Objectives

- Describe some of the conditions that can result from injury to the visual pathway to the cortex.
- Explain how damage to the *what* and *how* pathways in the cortex can differentially affect visual processing and movement.

---

**homonymous hemianopia** Blindness of the entire left or right visual field.

**quadrantanopia** Blindness of one quadrant of the visual field.

**scotoma** Small blind spot in the visual field caused by migraine or by a small lesion of the visual cortex.

Left visual cortex

Calcarine fissure

**(A) Hemianopia**

Left visual field    Right visual field

Injury

**(B) Quadrantanopia**

Injury

**(C) Scotoma**

Injury

Glowimages/Getty Images

**FIGURE 9-46 Consequences of Lesions in Region V1** The shaded areas indicate regions of visual loss. **(A)** A complete lesion of V1 in the left hemisphere results in hemianopia affecting the right visual field. **(B)** A large lesion of the lower lip of the calcarine fissure produces quadrantanopia that affects most of the upper right visual quadrant. **(C)** A smaller lesion of the lower lip of the calcarine fissure results in a smaller scotoma.

**visual-form agnosia** Inability to recognize objects or drawings of objects.

This technique is similar to demonstrating the presence of the blind spot created by the optic disc (as in Figure 9-8). When a person is looking at an object with only one eye, the brain compensates for the scotoma in the same way as it does for the optic disc's blind spot. As a result, the person does not notice the scotoma.

Thus, the type of blindness offers clues about the location of the problem in the visual pathway. If the loss of vision affects one eye only, the problem must lie in that eye or its optic nerve; if the vision loss affects both eyes, the problem most likely resides in the brain. Many people have difficulty understanding why a person with damage to the visual cortex has difficulty with both eyes. They fail to realize that the visual field, not the eye, is represented in the brain.

Beyond region V1, the nature of visual loss caused by injury is considerably more complex. It also differs in significant ways in the ventral versus dorsal streams. We therefore look at each pathway separately.

## Injury to the *What* Pathway

We have encountered an example of damage to the *what* pathway: the case of D. B. in Clinical Focus 9-1. He appeared to be blind in his affected visual field but could point to the location of blinking lights in that field, suggesting that some part of his visual system was working. An even more dramatic example of ventral stream injury comes from the case of D. F., a 35-year-old woman who, while taking a shower, was poisoned by carbon monoxide (CO) from a faulty gas-fueled water heater. The length of her exposure was unclear, but when her roommate found her, the shower was running cold. CO poisoning can cause several kinds of neurological damage, and the result for D. F. was an extensive lesion of the lateral occipital region, including cortical tissue in the ventral visual pathway.

D. F.'s principal deficit was **visual-form agnosia**, an inability to recognize objects, real or drawn (see Farah, 1990). Not only was D. F. unable to recognize objects, especially line drawings of objects, but she could neither estimate their size and orientation nor draw copies of them. Likewise, as **Figure 9-47** illustrates, patient J. W., who suffered occipital damage similar to that experienced by D. F., was unable to recognize or copy simple drawings.

Clearly, D. F.'s lesion interfered with her ventral stream *what* pathway. Remarkably, despite her inability to identify objects or to estimate their size and orientation, D. F. retained the capacity, illustrated in **Figure 9-48**, to appropriately shape her hand when reaching out to grasp something. Goodale, Milner, and their research colleagues (1991) studied D. F. extensively for years and devised a way to demonstrate D. F.'s skill at reaching for objects.

The middle column in **Figure 9-49** shows the grasp patterns of a control participant (S. H.) when she picked up something irregularly shaped. S. H. grasped the object along whichever of the two axes makes it easier to pick up. When D. F. was presented with the same task, shown in the left-hand column, she was as good as S. H. at placing her index finger and thumb on appropriately opposed grasp points.

Clearly, D. F. remained able to use the structural features of objects to control her visually guided grasping movements, even though she was unable to interpret these same features. This result demonstrates once more that we are consciously aware of only a small part of the sensory processing that goes on in the brain. Furthermore, D. F.'s ability to use structural features of objects for guiding movement, but not for perceiving shapes, again shows us that the brain has separate systems for each type of visual operation.

D. F.'s lesion was located quite far back in the ventral visual pathway. More anterior lesions produce other deficits, depending on the exact location. For example, J. I., described by Oliver Sacks and Robert Wasserman (1987), was an artist who developed complete color deficiency due to a cortical lesion presumed to be in region V4. His principal symptom was *achromatopsia,* or color agnosia. He saw the world in black and white, but despite his inability to distinguish any colors whatsoever, J. I.'s vision appeared otherwise unaffected.

Similarly, L. M., a woman described by Josef Zihl and his colleagues (1983), lost her ability to detect movement after suffering a bilateral lesion presumed to be in region V5. In her case, objects either vanished when they moved or appeared frozen despite their movement. L. M. had particular difficulty pouring tea into a cup because the fluid appeared to be frozen in midair. Yet she could read, write, and recognize objects, and she appeared to have normal form vision—until objects moved.

These varied cases demonstrate that cortical injuries in the ventral stream all somehow interfere with determining what things are or are like or are doing. In each case, the symptoms are somewhat different, which is thought to reflect damage to different subregions or substreams of the ventral visual pathway.

# Injury to the *How* Pathway

Early in the twentieth century, R. Bálint (1909) described a rather peculiar set of visual symptoms associated with a bilateral parietal lesion. The patient had full visual fields and could recognize, use, and name objects, pictures, and colors normally. But he had a severe deficit in visually guided reaching, even though he could still make accurate movements directed toward his own body (presumably guided by tactile feedback from his joints). Bálint called this syndrome **optic ataxia**.

Since Bálint's time, many descriptions of optic ataxia associated with parietal injury have been recorded. Goodale has studied several such patients, one of whom is a woman identified as R. V. (Milner & Goodale, 2006). In contrast to patient D. F.'s visual form agnosia, R. V.'s perception of drawings and objects was normal, but she could not guide her hand to reach for objects.

The rightmost column in Figure 9-49 shows that, when asked to pick up the same irregularly shaped objects that D. F. could grasp normally, R. V. often failed to place her fingers on the appropriate grasp points, even though she could distinguish the objects

Section 9-2 describes damage to the temporal lobe area that causes facial agnosia.

**FIGURE 9-47 Injury to the Ventral Stream** J. W. survived a severe heart attack while exercising. As a result, he suffered anoxia (loss of oxygen) and ensuing occipital damage. Subsequently, he was unable to recognize the simple line drawings on the left and copied them poorly (right). Marlene Behrmann, Director Cognitive Neuroscience Lab, Carnegie Mellon University

Section 11-4 details the somatic senses, including *proprioception,* or body awareness.

**optic ataxia** Deficit in the visual control of reaching and other movements.

**FIGURE 9-48 Visual Guidance** You may consciously reach for an object such as a pen or a mug, but your hand forms the appropriate posture automatically, without your conscious awareness. Figure 11-1 details this type of sequentially organized movement.

Each line passes through the points where the index finger and thumb first contacted the perimeter of the shape on individual trials in which the subjects and the control were instructed to pick up the shape.

**2** ...but she and S. H. both place finger and thumb on appropriately opposed points on either side of the shapes.

**3** R. V., whose object recognition is unimpaired, chooses unstable grasp points that often do not pass through the object's center of mass.

**1** D. F. cannot recognize these shapes,...

D. F.
(ventral-stream deficit)

S. H.
(control)

R. V.
(dorsal-stream deficit)

**FIGURE 9-49 Grasp Patterns** The Milner–Goodale experiments confirm that the brain has different systems for visual object recognition and visual guidance of movement. Information from Milner & Goodale, 2006.

easily. In other words, although R. V.'s perception of an object's features was normal for the task of describing that object, her perception was not normal for the task of visually guiding her hand to reach for the object.

To summarize, people with damage to the parietal cortex in the dorsal visual stream can see perfectly well, but cannot accurately guide their movements on the basis of visual information. This relationship illustrates that the dorsal stream functions to guide movement. In contrast, people with damage to the ventral stream cannot perceive objects because object perception is a ventral stream function. Yet these same people can guide their movements to objects on the basis of visual information.

Patients with dorsal stream damage, like R. V., have intact ventral streams that analyze the visual characteristics of objects. Patients with ventral stream damage, like D. F., have intact dorsal streams that visually direct movements. Comparing the two types of cases enables us to infer the visual functions of the dorsal and ventral streams.

## 9-5 Review

Before you continue, check your understanding. Answers to Self-Test appear at the back of the book.

1. Complete cuts of the optic tract, LGN, or V1 produce _____.

2. Small lesions of V1 produce small blind spots called _____.

3. Destruction of the retina or the optic nerve of one eye produces _____.

4. The effect of severe deficits in visually guided reaching is called _____.

5. Contrast the effects of injury to the dorsal stream with the effects of injury to the ventral stream.

### 9-6

# Plasticity in the Visual Pathways

**Learning Objective**
• Explain how our visual systems can adapt to experience and injury.

The pioneering work of Torsten Wiesel and David Hubel (1965) showed that depriving one eye of visual information in kittens led to shrinkage of cortical areas that receive input from the deprived eye, resulting in poor vision in the deprived eye (a condition known as *amblyopia*). However, this deprivation also led to an expansion of cortical areas related to the non-deprived eye. Wiesel and Hubel's work led to dozens of studies in rats, cats, and monkeys showing that manipulation of visual experience in the young brain chronically alters visual perception. For example, fitting kittens with goggles that allow vision only of lines of a single orientation leads to deficits in perceiving lines of other orientations (see Tanaka et al., 2020, for details and additional examples).

Injury can also prompt more radical changes to sensory systems. Individuals who have had strokes involving the occipital cortex often have severe visual impairments immediately after the event, but over the ensuing weeks or months will show significant recovery as the brain changes to accommodate to the injury. These individuals often respond well to rehabilitation even when it is initiated long after the injury occurred (Shibuki et al., 2020).

Injury to the occipital cortex early in life can result in extensive rewiring of visual pathways, as in the case of B. I., described by Inaki-Carril Mundinano and colleagues (2019). A genetic enzyme disorder resulted in a bilateral occipital-lobe injury in the first 2 weeks of B. I.'s life. Investigation at age 6 revealed that despite extensive occipital lobe damage, B. I. had surprisingly good conscious visual abilities, such that he could recognize facial expressions and colors, and visually navigate around his environment. Magnetic resonance imaging (MRI) tractography revealed an expanded pulvinar–V5 pathway and LGN–V5 pathway that were likely supporting his visual abilities (see **Figure 9-50**).

Another example of visual system plasticity is seen in blind people who have learned to use *echolocation* (the ability to

Control      Patient B.I.

Plm-MT
**LGN-MT**
LGN-V1

Inaki-Carril Mundinano, Juan Chen, Mitchell de Souza, Marc G Sarossy, Marc F Joanisse, Melvyn A Goodale, James A Bourne, Monash University.

**FIGURE 9-50 Diffusion Tractography Results** Connections from LGN to V1 are shown in blue and are absent in B. I.'s brain. Connections from the pulvinar to middle temporal (MT) area are shown in red, and those from the LGN to MT in yellow.

perceive objects by the sound reflecting from them) to safely navigate about the world. Liam Norman and Lore Thaler (2019) used MRI to identify regions of the occipital cortex that were active when participants were echolocating a nearby object. Remarkably, the MRI results suggested the presence of spatial maps from auditory inputs in the visual cortex (see **Figure 9-51**).

What role does experience play in "normal" vision? From the moment it begins to develop, our visual system has a lot to learn about things in the environment. Neurons in the ventral stream could not possibly be selective for all unique stimuli that we encounter, but with experience, these neurons can improve their selectivity to identify novel objects, which presumably improves our visual abilities. Recall Tanaka's work (1993) on shape processing in the ventral stream (area TE) of monkeys, described in Section 9-4, in which monkeys were trained to discriminate different shapes. Among trained monkeys, 39% of the TE neurons sampled gave a maximum response to specific stimuli used in training, compared to only 9% of the neurons in untrained animals. Thus, experience changed the tuning of these TE neurons—and presumably the animals' ability to discriminate the stimuli. The changes not only affected neurons in the TE, but also involved an interplay between the frontal and temporal cortex (see the review by Lehky & Tanaka, 2016), suggesting that an object is represented by a network of many cells within TE and beyond. In sum, our visual abilities are not solely genetically determined, but rather are modified significantly by our experiences. This fact is true not only of the visual system, but also of our other sensory systems.

Chapter 10 explores the role of experience in the development of the auditory system, as applied to language and music. Research Focus 10-4 discusses echolocation.

Echo sound maps in expert echolocators

Stimulus spatial position

L40°  L20°  L10°  L05°    R05°  R10°  R20°  R40°

Norman, L.J., & Thaler, L. (2019) Retinotopicike maps of spatial sound in primary 'visual' cortex of blind human echolocators. Proceedings of the Royal Society, Biological Sciences, 286, 10.1098/rspb.2019.1910.

**FIGURE 9-51  Hearing in the Visual Cortex**
MRI-derived maps for echo sounds in the primary "visual" cortex of blind expert echolocators. These representative pairs of images show the left- and right-hemisphere visual cortex for the participants. The color-coded legend for spatial position is shown in the bottom right.

## 9-6 Review

Before you continue, check your understanding. Answers to Self-Test appear at the back of the book.

1. Blocking visual input to one eye during development leads to _____.

2. Neurons in the _____ lobe of monkeys can be trained to alter their visual specificities.

3. _____, the process of using auditory clues to navigate around the world, makes use of spatial maps derived from _____ inputs in the visual cortex.

4. Describe how experience, such as injury, can alter the development of our visual system.

# Summary

### 9-1 Nature of Sensation and Perception

Sensory systems allow animals, including ourselves, to adapt to the world around them. Animals adapted to different environments vary widely in their sensory abilities. What is distinctive about humans is the extent to which we can transform sensations into perceptual information to mediate aspects of language, music, and culture. For each sense, mammals represent the world in topographic maps that form neural–spatial representations in the cortex.

### 9-2 The Visual System's Functional Anatomy

Like all other sensory systems, vision begins with receptor neurons. The visual photoreceptors (rods and cones) at the back of the eye in the retina transduce the physical energy of light waves into neural activity.

Rods are sensitive to dim light. Cones, which are sensitive to bright light, mediate color vision. Each of the three cone types is maximally sensitive to a different wavelength—short, medium, or long. We see these wavelengths as the colors blue, green, or red, respectively; thus the short, medium, and long cone receptors often are referred to as blue, green, and red receptors.

Retinal ganglion cells receive input from photoreceptors through bipolar cells and send out their axons from the retinas to form the optic nerve. P ganglion cells receive input mostly from cones and convey information about color and fine detail. M cells receive input from rods and convey information about luminance and movement but not color.

The optic nerve forms two distinct major routes into the brain. The geniculostriate pathway synapses first in the thalamic LGN nucleus and then in region V1. The tectopulvinar pathway synapses first in the midbrain's tectum (superior colliculus), then in the pulvinar of the thalamus, and finally in the temporal and parietal visual cortex areas. A few optic nerve fibers also form the retinohypothalamic tract, which functions in part to control circadian rhythms.

Among the visual regions in the occipital cortex, V1 and V2 carry out multiple functions; the remaining regions (V3, V3A, V4, and V5) have specialized functions. Visual information flows from the thalamus to V1 and V2, and then divides to form the visual stream pathways. The unconscious dorsal stream aids in guiding movements visually, whereas the conscious ventral stream aids in visual object perception.

### 9-3 Location in the Visual World

At each step along the visual pathways, neuronal activities are distinctly different; it is the summed neural activity in all regions that produces our visual experience. Each functional column in the cortical visual regions is approximately 0.5 mm in diameter and extends to the depth of the cortex. The visual system cortical columns are specialized for processes such as analyzing line orientation or comparing similar shapes as complex as faces.

## 9-4 Neuronal Activity

Neurons in the ventral stream are selective for aspects of shape. Those in the visual cortex are maximally responsive to lines of different orientations. Upstream, cells in the inferior temporal cortex are responsive to shapes—some abstract—and to concrete forms as complex as hands or faces.

Cones in the retina are maximally responsive to different light wavelengths, roughly corresponding to colors we perceive as green, blue, and red. At the next level, RGCs' center-surround organization facilitates their opponent-process function. Specifically, the cells are excited by one hue and inhibited by another—for example, red versus green or blue versus yellow.

Color-sensitive cells in V1, located in the blobs, also have opponent-process properties. Cells in region V4 respond to colors that we perceive rather than to particular visible light wavelengths. Both the luminance and the color of nearby objects influence the colors we perceive.

## 9-5 The Visual Brain in Action

Upon entering the brain, information from the left and right visual fields proceeds via the optic nerve to the brain's right and left sides, respectively. As a result of these contralateral connections, damage to the visual areas on one side of the brain results in visual disturbance in both eyes because half of each retina's visual field is represented on each side of the brain.

Specific visual functions are localized to different brain regions, so local damage results in the loss of a particular function. Damage to region V4 produces a loss of color constancy, for example; damage to regions in the parietal cortex inhibits the contralateral hand's grasping ability.

## 9-6 Plasticity in the Visual Pathways

Although the anatomical organization of visual pathways reflects the unfolding of a genetic blueprint, the visual system is remarkably plastic. Manipulation of visual experiences during prenatal and early development and beyond can have profound effects on our visual perception. People can show remarkable plasticity after injury to, or even complete loss of, the visual pathways. An example is the ability of blind individuals to echolocate, which is correlated with the emergence of auditory spatial maps in the occipital cortex.

# Key Terms

blind spot, p. 296
blob, p. 304
color constancy, p. 318
cone, p. 297
cortical column, p. 303
dorsal stream, p. 302
extrastriate (secondary visual) cortex (V2–V5), p. 304
facial agnosia, p. 306
fovea, p. 296

geniculostriate system, p. 301
homonymous hemianopia, p. 319
luminance contrast, p. 311
magnocellular (M) cell, p. 299
ocular dominance column, p. 314
opponent process, p. 317
optic ataxia, p. 321
optic chiasm, p. 300
parvocellular (P) cell, p. 299

perception, p. 292
photoreceptor, p. 293
primary visual cortex (V1), p. 304
quadrantanopia, p. 319
receptive field, p. 290
retina, p. 293
retinal ganglion cell (RGC), p. 298
retinohypothalamic tract, p. 302

rod, p. 297
scotoma, p. 319
sensation, p. 292
striate (striped) cortex, p. 301
tectopulvinar system, p. 302
topographic map, p. 291
trichromatic theory, p. 316
ventral stream, p. 302
visual field, p. 307
visual-form agnosia, p. 320

# Selected Resources from  Achieve

**Neuroscience in Action:** Visual Pathways: The What and the How

**Concept Practice:**

Structures of the Eye

**Videos**

"Blindsight": Seeing Without Awareness

Vision: How We See

Our Senses

Brain Plasticity: Rewiring the Visual Cortex

Face Blindness and How Our Minds Process What We See

**LearningCurve**

**Practice Quiz**

# How Do We Hear, Speak, and Make Music?

# 10

## RESEARCH FOCUS 10-1

# Evolution of Music and Language

We have unambiguous evidence that about 40,000 years ago modern humans (*Homo sapiens*) created musical instruments, and that the creation of these instruments would have required large investments in time, energy, skill, and resources (an example of an early flute is shown here). The finding that humans from this period made music using instruments that they fashioned implies that music mattered to them. Investigations of other animals suggests that rhythmic and melodious vocalizations evolved much earlier in our lineage than did the use of instruments.

Given the biological continuity between modern humans and their hominin and primate ancestors, music likely evolved from earlier communication systems. Nonhuman animals have communication systems that appear analogous to human music—for example, the songs produced by birds and mammals, such as whales, seals, and other primates. Thomas Geissmann (2001) noted that among most of the 26 species of singing primates, males and females sing duets. Furthermore, all singing primates are monogamous, suggesting that singing may somehow relate to sexual behaviors and may also play a role in parenting behaviors. Additional evidence of an innate and inherited predisposition toward music comes from the observations that very young human infants respond strongly to music and that caregivers use both music and speech to communicate emotionally with preverbal infants.

As hominin brain size increased dramatically over the last million years, larynges also moved lower in the throat, increasing the vocal range and accommodating a greater diversity of sounds produced. As a result, our human ancestors became more verbally communicative. Over time, the neural and anatomic mechanisms underlying auditory perception became more finely tuned, especially with respect to hearing hominin voices (Purves, 2017). In this context, music may have served as a protolanguage for our hominin ancestors, helping to strengthen social cohesion—one can easily imagine hominin kin groups gathering around fires in the evenings, dancing, gesturing, and vocalizing.

While hominin vocalizations are likely built on an acoustic and emotional foundation shared with other primates, vocal learning in modern humans appears to be the output of highly structured neural systems for complex signaling that includes song without words (music), speech (language), and the combination of the two. The modern human brain is specialized for analyzing certain aspects of music in the right temporal lobe, which complements the left temporal lobe's specialization for analyzing aspects of speech.

It seems likely that the cognitive mechanisms underpinning rhythmic vocalizations and song production resemble music rather than language in its present form, so these mechanisms may have evolved earlier. Music is appreciated over longer time scales compared to spoken language and may have emerged to sustain and foster emotion-based social interactions while also communicating other aspects of human experience. Language came later, to fulfill defining, directing, and problem-solving functions with an immediate effect on shorter time scales.

**Paleolithic Flute** The bone flute pictured here, discovered in northern Europe in 2008 and dated to approximately 35,000 years ago, provides evidence of the production of instruments specifically for the creation of music by our human ancestors.

Figure 1-11 charts the steady increase in brain size across the most recent hominin species leading up to our own.

Language and music are universal among humans. The oral language of every known culture follows similar basic structural rules, and people in all cultures make and enjoy music. Music and language allow us both to organize and to interact socially. Like music, language probably improves parenting (the relationship between music and infant care is described in Research Focus 10-1: Evolution of Music and Language). People who can communicate their intentions to one another and to their children presumably are better parents.

Language is the use of complex systems of communication and includes syntax (innate grammar). Although the processing and production of certain forms of language may involve specific sensory and motor systems for input and output, language itself is independent of the route of sensory input and structures of motor output. For instance, sign language uses visual input and motor output using the hands and arms, whereas spoken language uses auditory input and motor output using the vocal cords. In this chapter, we focus on *vocalization* (spoken language or speech) and *audition* (perceiving sounds).

Humans' capacities for spoken language and music are linked conceptually because both are based on sound. Understanding how and why we engage in speech and music is this chapter's goal. We first examine the physical energy that we perceive as sound, and then we consider how the human ear and nervous system detect and interpret sound. We next examine the complementary, yet specialized, neuroanatomy of human language and music processing. Finally, we investigate how two other species, birds and whales, produce and listen to songs.

**sound wave** Mechanical displacement of molecules caused by changing pressure that possesses the physical properties of frequency and amplitude, and their complex interaction; also referred to as a *compression wave*.

## 10-1

# Sound Waves: Stimulus for Audition

Just as what we experience as seeing is the brain's construct, so is what we experience as hearing. Without a brain, vision and hearing would not exist. When you strike a tuning fork, the energy of its vibrating prongs displaces adjacent air molecules. **Figure 10-1** shows how, as one prong moves to the left, air molecules to the left compress (grow more dense) and air molecules to the right become more rarefied (grow less dense). The opposite happens when the prong moves to the right. The undulating energy generated by this displacement of molecules causes *compression waves* of changing air pressure to emanate from the tuning fork. These **sound waves** move through compressible media—air, water, ground—but not through the vacuum of outer space.

The top graph in **Figure 10-2** represents the waves of changing air pressure emanating from a tuning fork by plotting air molecule density against time at a single point. The bottom graph shows how the energy from the right-hand prong of the tuning fork moves to create the air pressure changes associated with a single cycle. A *cycle* is one complete peak and valley on the graph—the change from one maximum or minimum air pressure level of the sound wave to the next maximum or minimum level, respectively.

## Physical Properties of Sound Waves

Light is electromagnetic energy we see; sound is mechanical energy we hear. Sound wave energy has two physical attributes—*frequency* and *amplitude*—that are produced by the displacement of air molecules; the combination of these qualities produces *complexity*. These three properties are summarized in **Figure 10-3**. The auditory system analyzes each property separately—just as the visual system analyzes color and form separately—to give us three perceptions: pitch, loudness, and timbre.

## Sound Wave Frequency

Sound waves travel at a fixed speed of 1100 feet (343 meters) per second in air, and more than four times faster in water, but sound energy varies in wavelength.

**Learning Objectives**
- Describe the physical properties of sound, frequency, and amplitude, and how they interact to produce complexity.
- Explain how the properties of sound function in language and music.

**Principle 9:** The nervous system produces movement in a perceptual world the brain constructs.

Section 9-4 explains how we see shapes and colors.

**FIGURE 10-2 Visualizing a Sound Wave** Air molecule density plotted against time at a single point relative to the tuning fork's right prong. Physicists call the resulting cyclical waves *sine waves*.

**FIGURE 10-1 How a Tuning Fork Produces Sound Waves (A)** The fork is still, and air molecules are distributed randomly. **(B)** When struck, the fork's right arm moves to the left; air on the leading edge compresses, and air on the trailing edge rarefies. **(C)** As the arm rebounds, air to the right compresses, and air to the left rarefies.

**FIGURE 10-3 Physical Dimensions of Sound Waves** The frequency, amplitude, and complexity of sound wave sensations correspond to the perceptual dimensions of pitch, loudness, and timbre, respectively.

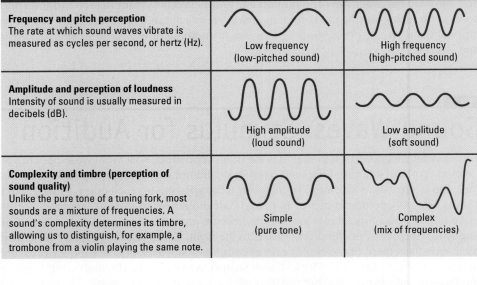

| Properties of Sound Waves | | |
|---|---|---|
| **Frequency and pitch perception** The rate at which sound waves vibrate is measured as cycles per second, or hertz (Hz). | Low frequency (low-pitched sound) | High frequency (high-pitched sound) |
| **Amplitude and perception of loudness** Intensity of sound is usually measured in decibels (dB). | High amplitude (loud sound) | Low amplitude (soft sound) |
| **Complexity and timbre (perception of sound quality)** Unlike the pure tone of a tuning fork, most sounds are a mixture of frequencies. A sound's complexity determines its timbre, allowing us to distinguish, for example, a trombone from a violin playing the same note. | Simple (pure tone) | Complex (mix of frequencies) |

**frequency** Number of cycles a wave completes in a given time.

**hertz (Hz)** Measure of sound wave frequency (repetition rate); 1 hertz equals 1 cycle per second.

**amplitude** Stimulus intensity; in audition, roughly equivalent to loudness, graphed by the increasing height of a sound wave.

Section 8-4 suggests there is a critical period in brain development when we are most sensitive to musical training. Figure 15-12 shows the enhanced connectivity noted in people with perfect pitch.

**Frequency** is the number of cycles a wave completes in a given amount of time. Sound wave frequencies are measured in cycles per second, a unit called **hertz (Hz)**, in honor of physicist Heinrich Rudolph Hertz. One hertz is 1 cycle per second, 50 hertz is 50 cycles per second, 6000 hertz is 6000 cycles per second, and so on. Sounds we perceive as low pitched have fewer wave frequencies (fewer cycles per second), whereas sounds that we perceive as high pitched have more wave frequencies (many cycles per second), as shown in the top panel of Figure 10-3.

Just as we can perceive light only at visible wavelengths, we can perceive sound waves only in the limited range of frequencies plotted in **Figure 10-4**. Healthy young adult humans' hearing range is from about 20 to 20,000 hertz. Many animals communicate with sound, with their auditory system being designed to interpret their species-typical sounds. After all, what is the point in making complicated songs or calls if other members of your species cannot hear and interpret them?

The range of sound wave frequencies heard by different species varies extensively. Some (such as frogs and birds) have a rather narrow hearing range; others (such as dogs, elephants, whales, and humans) have a broad range. Some species use extremely high frequencies (bats go as high as 115 kilohertz, as indicated in Figure 10-4); others (fish, for example) use the low range.

The auditory systems of whales and dolphins are responsive to a remarkably wide range of sound waves. Characteristics at the extremes of these frequencies allow marine mammals to use them in different ways. Very low-frequency sound waves travel long distances in water. Whales produce them for underwater communication over hundreds of miles. High-frequency sound waves echo and form the basis of sonar. Dolphins produce them in bursts and listen for the echoes that bounce back from objects. These echoes help the dolphins to navigate and locate prey.

Differences in sound wave frequencies become differences in pitch when heard. Each note in a musical scale must have a different frequency because each has a different pitch. Middle C on the piano, for instance, has a frequency of 264 hertz.

Most people can discriminate between one musical note and another, but some can actually name any note they hear (A, B flat, C sharp, and so forth). This ability, which is known as *perfect* (or *absolute*) *pitch*, runs in families, suggesting a genetic influence is involved. On the side of experience, most people who develop perfect pitch also receive musical training in matching pitch to note from an early age.

## Sound Wave Amplitude

Sound waves vary not only in frequency, which causes differences in perceived pitch, but also in **amplitude** (strength), which causes differences in perceived *intensity,* or *loudness.* If you hit a tuning fork lightly, it produces a tone with a frequency of, say,

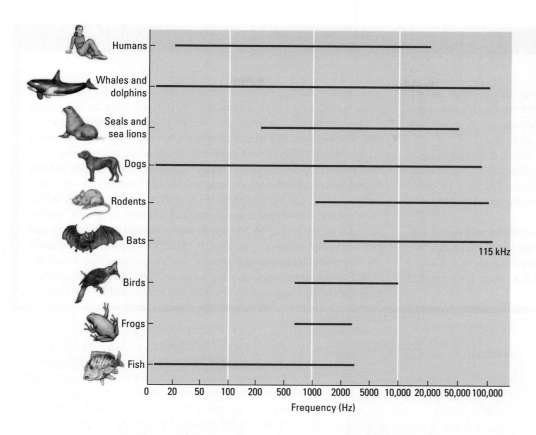

**FIGURE 10-4 Hearing Ranges among Animals** Frogs and birds hear a relatively narrow range of frequencies; the ranges for whales and dolphins are extensive, as is that for dogs. Humans' hearing range is broad, yet we do not perceive many sound frequencies at both the extreme upper and extreme lower ranges that other animals can both make and hear.

264 hertz (middle C). If you hit it harder, the frequency remains 264 hertz, but you also transfer more energy into the vibrating prong, increasing its amplitude. The fork now moves farther left and right but at the same frequency. Increased air molecule compression intensifies the energy in a sound wave, which amplifies the sound (makes it louder). Differences in amplitude are graphed by increasing the height of a sound wave, as shown in the middle panel of Figure 10-3.

Sound wave amplitude is usually measured in **decibels (dB)**, a unit indicating the strength of a sound relative to the threshold of human hearing as a standard, pegged at 0 decibels (**Figure 10-5**). Typical speech sounds, for example, measure about 40 decibels. Sounds that register more than about 70 decibels we perceive as loud; those of less than about 20 decibels we perceive as soft, or quiet, such as a person whispering.

The human nervous system evolved to be sensitive to soft sounds, so it is actually blown away by extremely loud ones. People regularly damage their hearing through exposure to very loud sounds (such as rifle fire at close range) or even by prolonged exposure to sounds that are only relatively loud (such as at a live concert). Prolonged exposure to sounds louder than 100 decibels is likely to damage our hearing. Clinical Focus 10-2: Tinnitus describes a common condition that may result from such damage.

Loud bands routinely play music that registers higher than 120 decibels and sometimes as high as 135 decibels. Adrian Drake-Lee (1992) found that rock musicians had

**decibel (dB)** Measure of the relative physical intensity of sounds.

**FIGURE 10-5 Sound Intensity**

## CLINICAL FOCUS 10-2

### Tinnitus

As a young man, J. E. spent a great deal of time at the rifle range. In fact, he fired 200 rounds a month for years. He did not wear appropriate noise attenuators to dampen the sound. Now in his seventies, J. E. experiences *tinnitus*—ringing in the ears—and has for the past 15 years.

Tinnitus is described as a ringing, whining, whistling, clicking, hissing, or roaring, and it may be soft or loud, low pitched or high pitched. Tinnitus can be intermittent or it can be continuous, as in J. E.'s case. Tinnitus is estimated to affect about 10% to 15% of people younger than the age of 40 worldwide; its prevalence doubles with advanced age.

Two broad categories of tinnitus are distinguished: objective and subjective. *Objective tinnitus* may be the result of actual sound produced within the ear. For instance, muscle spasms around the middle ear or blood flow can cause sounds that some individuals can detect, which they report as an annoying tinnitus.

*Subjective tinnitus*, the more common form, is a condition of hearing a sound in the absence of an external auditory stimulus. There are many causes of subjective tinnitus. The most common is noise-induced damage to inner hair cells, which explains why rates of tinnitus are very high among those who work in high-intensity sound environments such as war zones, certain heavy industries, and music production. Other causes include ear infections, head and neck injuries, and exposure to certain drugs. More than 260 medications—including aspirin—have been reported to cause intermittent tinnitus as a side effect.

At present, no medications provide effective treatment for tinnitus, and prevention is recommended. The best way to prevent tinnitus is to avoid prolonged exposure to high-intensity sound levels of 70 decibels or higher (in other words, *turn down your music*) and to wear ear plugs when those situations are unavoidable.

J. E. enjoys listening to classical music and finds that auditory distractions are the best way to help him with the annoying effects of tinnitus.

**FIGURE 10-6 Breaking Down a Complex Tone** The waveform of a single note (*top*) from Don Byron's clarinet and the simple sound waves—the fundamental frequency (*middle*) and overtones (*bottom*)—that make up the complex tone.

a significant loss of sensitivity to sound waves, especially at about 6000 hertz. After a typical 90-minute concert, this loss was temporarily far worse; as much as a 40-fold increase in sound pressure was needed to reach a musician's hearing threshold. But rock concerts are not the only music venues that can damage hearing. Some reports indicate that symphony orchestras also produce dangerously high sound levels and that hearing loss is common among symphony musicians (Teie, 1998). Similarly, prolonged listening through headphones or earbuds to music played loudly on personal music players is responsible for significant hearing loss in many young people (Daniel, 2007). In 2018, the World Health Organization estimated that by 2050 some 900 million people around the world will have a disabling hearing loss—93% more than those who do today—in part because of damaging levels of sound from personal audio devices. Noise-canceling headphones minimize extraneous noises, allowing listeners to play their music at a lower intensity and thereby helping to preserve their hearing.

## Sound Wave Complexity

Sounds with a single frequency wave are *pure tones*, much like those that emanate from a tuning fork or pitch pipe. Most sounds, however, mix wave frequencies and their amplitudes together in combinations called *complex tones*. To better understand the blended nature of a complex tone, picture a clarinetist, such as Don Byron in **Figure 10-6**, playing a steady note. The upper graph in Figure 10-6 represents the sound wave a clarinet produces.

The waveform pattern is more complex than the simple, regular waves visualized in Figures 10-2 or 10-3. Even when a musician plays a single note, the instrument is making a complex tone. Using a mathematical technique known as Fourier analysis, we can break down this complex tone into its many component pure tones, depicted as the numbered waves traced at the bottom of Figure 10-6.

The *fundamental frequency* (wave 1) is the rate at which the complex waveform pattern repeats. Waves 2 through 20 are *overtones*, a set of higher-frequency sound waves that vibrate at whole-number (integer) multiples of the fundamental frequency. Different musical instruments sound unique because they produce overtones of different amplitudes. Among the clarinet's overtones, represented by the heights of the blue waves in Figure 10-6, wave 5 is low amplitude, whereas wave 2 is high amplitude.

Just as primary colors can be blended to create a nearly infinite variety of colors, so pure tones can be blended to form complex tones. Complex tones emanate from musical instruments, from the human voice, from birdsong, and from machines or repetitive mechanisms that make rhythmic buzzing or humming sounds. A key feature of complex tones, besides being made up of two or more pure tones, is *periodicity*: the fundamental frequency repeats at regular intervals. Sounds that are aperiodic, or random, we call *noise*.

## Perception of Sound

Visualize what happens when you toss a pebble into a pond. Waves of water emanate from the point where the pebble enters the water. These waves produce no audible sound. But if your skin were able to convert the water wave energy (sensation) into neural activity that stimulated your auditory system, you would hear the waves when you placed your hand in the rippling water (perception). When you removed your hand, the sound would stop.

The pebble hitting the water is much like a tree falling to the ground, and the waves that emanate from the pebble's entry point are like the air pressure waves that emanate from the place where the tree strikes the ground. The frequency of the waves determines the pitch of the sound heard by the brain, whereas the height (amplitude) of the waves determines the sound's loudness.

Our sensitivity to sound waves is extraordinary. At the threshold of human hearing, we can detect the displacement of air molecules of about 10 picometers in size. We are rarely in an environment where we can detect such a small air pressure change: there is usually too much background noise. A quiet, rural setting is probably as close as we ever get to an environment suitable for testing the acuteness of our hearing. The next time you visit the countryside, take note of the sounds you can hear. If there is no sound competition, you can often hear a single car engine miles away.

In addition to detecting minute changes in air pressure, the auditory system is adept at simultaneously perceiving different sounds. As you read this chapter, you can differentiate all sorts of sounds around you—traffic on the street, people talking next door, your air conditioner humming, footsteps in the hall. As you listen to music, you detect the sounds of different instruments and voices.

You can perceive more than one sound simultaneously because each frequency of change in air pressure (each different sound wave) stimulates different neurons in your auditory system. Sound perception is only the beginning of your auditory experience. Your brain interprets sounds to obtain information about events in your environment, and it analyzes a sound's meaning. Your use of sound to communicate with other people through both spoken language and music clearly illustrates these processes.

1 picometer = one-trillionth of a meter.

## Properties of Spoken Language and Music as Sounds

Language and music differ from other auditory sensations in fundamental ways. For example, both convey meaning and evoke emotion. Analyzing meaning in sound is a considerably more complex behavior than simply detecting a sound and identifying it. The brain has evolved systems that analyze sounds for meaning: speech in the left temporal lobe and music in the right.

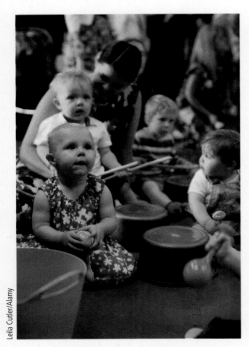

Leila Cutler/Alamy

Music classes for infants have been shown to benefit their development.

Auditory constancy is reminiscent of the visual system's capacity for color constancy; see Section 9-4.

Infants are receptive to speech and musical cues before those sounds have any obvious utility, which suggests both the innate presence of these skills and the effects of prenatal experiences (see Research Focus 10-1). Humans have an amazing capacity for learning and remembering linguistic and musical information. In fact, comprehensive oral histories in some cultures are expressed as songs, as they were for millennia before the advent of writing, though this tradition is being lost to modern technology. We are capable of learning a vocabulary of tens of thousands of words, often in many spoken languages, and have a capacity for recognizing thousands of songs.

Language both facilitates and expands communication. We can organize our complex perceptual worlds by categorizing information with words. We can tell others what we think and know and imagine. Imagine the efficiency that gestures and language added to the cooperative food hunting and gathering behaviors of early humans.

All these benefits of language seem obvious, but the benefits of music may seem less straightforward. In fact, music helps us to regulate our own emotions and to affect the emotions of others. After all, when do people most commonly make music? We sing and play music to communicate with infants and put children to sleep. We play music to enhance social interactions and gatherings and romance. We use music to console ourselves or to express complex emotions in times of strife. We use music to bolster group identification — school songs and national anthems are examples. Music as we know it might be unique to humans.

Another characteristic that distinguishes speech and musical sounds from other auditory inputs is their delivery speed. Nonspeech and nonmusical noise produced at a rate of about 5 segments per second is perceived as a buzz. (A sound segment is a distinct unit of sound.) Normal speed for speech is on the order of 8 to 10 segments per second, and we are capable of understanding speech at nearly 30 segments per second. Speech perception at these higher rates is astounding because the input speed far exceeds the auditory system's ability to transmit all the speech segments as separate pieces of information.

Next, we will look at some unique properties of language and music. In Section 10-4, we delve into the neural structures involved in our processing of these sounds.

## Properties of Language

Experience listening to a particular language helps the brain analyze rapid speech, which is one reason people who are speaking languages unfamiliar to you often seem to be talking incredibly fast. Your brain does not know where the foreign words end and begin, so they seem to run together in a rapid-fire stream.

A unique characteristic of our perception of speech sounds is our tendency to hear variations of a sound as if they were identical, even though the sound varies considerably from one context to another. For instance, the English letter *d* is pronounced differently in the words *deep*, *deck*, and *duke*, yet a listener perceives the pronunciations to be the same *d* sound.

The auditory system must therefore have a mechanism for categorizing sounds as being the same despite small differences in pronunciation. Experience must affect this mechanism because different languages categorize speech sounds differently. A major obstacle to mastering a distinctly different language after age 10 is the difficulty of learning which sound categories are treated as equivalent.

## Properties of Music

As with other sounds, the subjective properties that people perceive in musical sounds differ from one another. One subjective property is *loudness*, the magnitude of a sound as judged by a person. Loudness is related to the amplitude of a sound wave measured in decibels, but loudness is also subjective. What is very loud music for one person may be only moderately loud for another, whereas music that seems soft to one listener may not seem at all soft to someone else. Your perception of loudness also changes with context. After you've slowed down from driving fast on a highway, for example, your car's music system seems louder. The reduction in road noise alters your perception of the music's loudness.

Another subjective property of musical sounds is *pitch*, the position of each tone on a musical scale, as judged by the listener. Although pitch is clearly related to sound wave frequency, there is more to it than that. Consider the note middle C as played on a piano. This note can be described as a pattern of sound frequencies, like the clarinet note in Figure 10-6.

Like the note played on the piano, any musical note is defined by its fundamental frequency—the lowest frequency of the sound wave pattern, or the rate at which the overall pattern repeats. For middle C, the fundamental frequency is 264 hertz. The sound waves for notes C, E, and G, as measured by a spectrograph, are shown in **Figure 10-7**. Notice that by convention, sound wave spectrographs are measured in kilohertz (kHz), or thousands of hertz. Thus, if we look at the fundamental frequency for middle C, it is the first large wave on the left, at 0.264 kilohertz. The fundamental frequencies for E and G are 0.330 and 0.392 kilohertz, respectively.

An important feature of the human brain's analysis of music is that any pure note, such as middle C, is perceived as being the same note whether it is played on a piano or on a guitar, even though the sounds of these instruments differ widely. The right temporal lobe extracts pitch from sound, whether the sound is speech or music. In speech, pitch contributes to the perceived melodic tone of a voice, or **prosody**.

A final property of musical sound is *quality*, or *timbre* (pronounced "TAM-ber"), the perceived complexity that distinguishes a particular sound from all others of similar pitch and loudness. We can easily distinguish the timbre of a violin from that of a trombone, even if both instruments are playing the same note at the same loudness. The complexity of their sounds differs.

# 10-1 Review

**Before you continue, check your understanding. Answers to Self-Test appear at the back of the book.**

1. The physical stimulus for audition, produced by changes in _____, is a form of mechanical energy converted in the ear to neural activity.

2. Sound waves have two properties: the physical attributes of _____ and _____. These two properties interact to produce _____.

3. Four properties of musical sounds are _____, _____, _____, and _____.

4. Sound is processed in the _____ lobes.

5. What distinguishes speech and musical sounds from other auditory inputs?

## 10-2

# Functional Anatomy of the Auditory System

To understand how the nervous system analyzes sound waves, we begin by tracing the pathway sound energy takes to and through the brain. The ear collects sound waves from the surrounding air and converts their mechanical energy to electrochemical neural energy, which kicks off a long route through the brainstem to the auditory cortex.

Before we can trace the journey from ear to cortex, we must ask what the auditory system is designed to do. Because sound waves have the physical properties of frequency and amplitude, we can predict that the auditory system is structured to decode these properties. In addition, most animals can tell where a sound comes from, so there must be some mechanism that can locate sound waves in space. Finally, many animals, including humans, not only analyze sounds for meaning but also make sounds. Because the properties of the sounds an animal produces fall within the range of the ones that it hears, we can infer that the neural systems for sound production and sound analysis must be closely related.

**prosody** Melodic tone of the speaking voice.

**FIGURE 10-7 Fundamental Frequencies of Piano Notes** Waveforms of the notes C, E, and G, as played on a piano and recorded on a spectrograph. The first wave in each graph is the fundamental frequency; the secondary waves are the overtones.

**Learning Objectives**

- Explain how sound waves are translated into neural impulses.
- Describe the major anatomical features of the human ear.
- Chart the path that sound takes through the ear and into the auditory cortex.
- Describe the asymmetrical organization and function of the auditory cortex.

In humans, the evolution of sound-processing systems for both language and music was accompanied by enhancement of specialized cortical regions, especially in the temporal lobes. In fact, a major difference between the human cortex and the monkey cortex is a marked expansion of auditory areas in humans.

## Structure of the Ear

The ear is a biological masterpiece in three acts: outer ear, middle ear, and inner ear. All of these structures are illustrated in **Figure 10-8**.

### Processing Sound Waves

Both the *pinna*, the funnel-like external structure of the outer ear, and the external ear canal, which extends a short distance from the pinna inside the head, are made of cartilage and flesh. The pinna is designed to catch sound waves in the surrounding environment and deflect them into the external ear canal. This observation explains why animals that rely on acute hearing have large ears relative to the rest of their heads, and why we often cup a hand around our pinna to enhance sound detection when we want to hear better.

Because it narrows from the pinna, the external canal amplifies sound waves and directs them to the *eardrum* at its inner end. When sound waves strike the eardrum, it vibrates, with the rate of vibration varying with the frequency of the waves. On the inner side of the eardrum, as depicted in Figure 10-8, is the middle ear, an air-filled chamber that contains the three smallest bones in the human body, connected in a series.

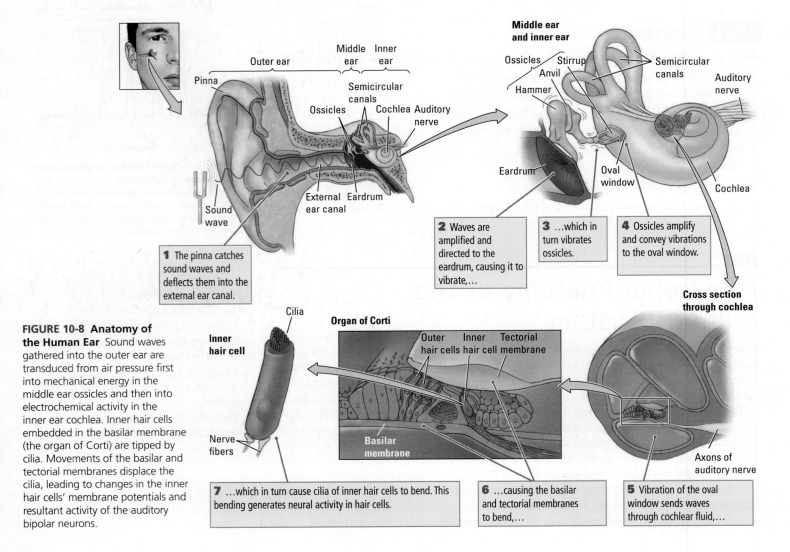

**FIGURE 10-8 Anatomy of the Human Ear** Sound waves gathered into the outer ear are transduced from air pressure first into mechanical energy in the middle ear ossicles and then into electrochemical activity in the inner ear cochlea. Inner hair cells embedded in the basilar membrane (the organ of Corti) are tipped by cilia. Movements of the basilar and tectorial membranes displace the cilia, leading to changes in the inner hair cells' membrane potentials and resultant activity of the auditory bipolar neurons.

**1** The pinna catches sound waves and deflects them into the external ear canal.

**2** Waves are amplified and directed to the eardrum, causing it to vibrate,…

**3** …which in turn vibrates ossicles.

**4** Ossicles amplify and convey vibrations to the oval window.

**5** Vibration of the oval window sends waves through cochlear fluid,…

**6** …causing the basilar and tectorial membranes to bend,…

**7** …which in turn cause cilia of inner hair cells to bend. This bending generates neural activity in hair cells.

These three **ossicles** are called the *hammer,* the *anvil,* and the *stirrup* because of their distinctive shapes. The ossicles attach the eardrum to the *oval window,* an opening in the bony casing of the **cochlea**, the inner ear structure that contains the auditory receptor cells.

When sound waves cause the eardrum to vibrate, the vibrations are transmitted to the ossicles. The leverlike action of the ossicles amplifies the vibrations and conveys them to the membrane that covers the cochlea's oval window. As Figure 10-8 shows, the cochlea coils around itself and looks a bit like a snail shell. Inside its bony exterior, the cochlea is hollow, as the cross-sectional drawing reveals. Pressure from the stirrup on the oval window makes the cochlear fluid move because a second membranous window in the cochlea (the *round window*) bulges outward as the stirrup presses inward on the oval window.

The *organ of Corti* is the receptor organ for hearing. It is composed of a strip of endothelial cells that sits on the **basilar membrane** (the word "basilar" derives from *base*). This organ contains one row of inner hair cells and three rows of outer hair cells, as shown in Figure 10-8. Hair-like organelles called *cilia* protrude from each **hair cell**. The cilia loosely contact another membrane, the *tectorial* (roof) *membrane,* which is located just above the cilia. In a chain reaction, the waves traveling through the cochlear fluid bend the basilar and tectorial membranes. The opposing movements of these two membranes bend the cilia of the hair cells. In turn, this bending of the cilia activates stretch-sensitive ion channels in the inner hair cell to generate a graded potential, which induces an action potential in an auditory nerve cell. The potentials from the auditory nerve are the electrical signals that we ultimately experience as hearing.

## Transducing Sound Waves into Neural Impulses

How does the conversion of sound waves into neural activity code the various properties of sound that we perceive? In the late 1800s, Hermann von Helmholtz proposed that sound waves of different frequencies cause different parts of the basilar membrane to resonate. Von Helmholtz was partly correct. Actually, all parts of the basilar membrane bend in response to incoming waves of any frequency. The key is *where* the peak displacement takes place **(Figure 10-9)**.

The solution to this coding puzzle was discovered in 1960, when George von Békésy observed the basilar membrane directly. He saw a traveling wave moving along the membrane all the way from the oval window to the membrane's apex. The coiled cochlea in Figure 10-9A maps the frequencies to which each part of the basilar membrane is most responsive. When the oval window vibrates in response to the vibrations of the ossicles, shown beside the uncoiled membrane in Figure 10-9B, it generates waves that travel through the cochlear fluid. Békésy placed little grains of silver along the basilar membrane and watched them jump in different places to different frequencies of incoming waves. Higher wave frequencies caused maximum peaks of displacement near the base of the basilar membrane; lower wave frequencies caused maximum displacement peaks near the membrane's apex.

As a rough analogy, consider what happens when you shake a rope. If you shake it quickly, the waves in the rope are small and short, and the peak of activity remains close to the base—the hand holding the rope. But if you shake the rope slowly, with a broader

**ossicles** Bones of the middle ear: the hammer, anvil, and stirrup.

**cochlea** Inner ear structure containing the auditory receptor cells.

**basilar membrane** Receptor surface in the cochlea that transduces sound waves into neural activity.

**hair cell** Specialized neurons in the cochlea tipped by cilia; when stimulated by waves in the cochlear fluid, the cilia bend and generate graded potentials in inner hair cells, the auditory receptor cells.

*Cochlea* actually means "snail shell" in Latin.

**FIGURE 10-9 Anatomy of the Cochlea (A)** The basilar membrane is maximally responsive to frequencies mapped as the cochlea uncoils. **(B)** Sound waves of different frequencies produce maximal displacement of the basilar membrane (shown uncoiled) at different locations.

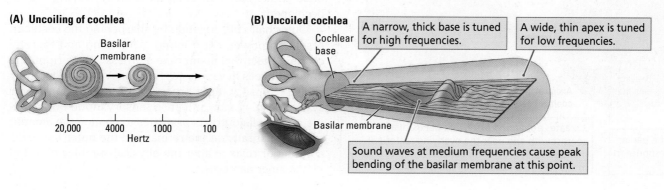

**(A) Uncoiling of cochlea**

Basilar membrane

20,000  4000  1000  100
Hertz

**(B) Uncoiled cochlea**

Cochlear base

A narrow, thick base is tuned for high frequencies.

A wide, thin apex is tuned for low frequencies.

Basilar membrane

Sound waves at medium frequencies cause peak bending of the basilar membrane at this point.

movement, the longer waves reach their peak farther along the rope—toward the apex. Thus, although both rapid and slow shakes produce movement along the entire length of the rope, the point of maximum displacement depends on whether the wave movements are rapid or slow.

The same response pattern holds for the basilar membrane and sound wave frequency. All sound waves cause some displacement along the entire length of the membrane, but the amount of displacement at any point varies with the frequency of the sound wave. In the human cochlea, shown uncoiling in Figure 10-9A, the basilar membrane near the oval window is maximally affected by frequencies as high as about 20,000 hertz, the upper limit of our hearing range. The most effective frequencies at the membrane's apex register less than 100 hertz, closer to our lower limit of about 20 hertz (see Figure 10-4).

Intermediate frequencies maximally displace points on the basilar membrane between its ends, as shown in Figure 10-9B. When a wave of a certain frequency travels down the basilar membrane, hair cells at the point of peak displacement are stimulated, resulting in a maximal neural response in those cells. An incoming signal composed of many frequencies causes several points along the basilar membrane to vibrate, exciting hair cells at all these points.

Not surprisingly, the basilar membrane is much more sensitive to changes in frequency than is the rope in our analogy, because this membrane varies in width and thickness along its entire length. It is narrow and thick at the base, near the oval window, and wider and thinner at its tightly coiled apex. The combination of varying width and thickness enhances the effect of small frequency differences. As a result, the cochlear receptors can code small differences in sound wave frequency as neural impulses.

# Auditory Receptors

Two kinds of hair cells with very different functions transform sound waves into neural activity. Figure 10-8 (bottom left) shows the anatomy of the inner hair cells; **Figure 10-10** illustrates how sound waves stimulate them. A young person's cochlea has approximately 12,000 outer and 3500 inner hair cells; these numbers fall off with age. Only the inner hair cells act as auditory receptors, and their numbers are small, considering how many different sounds we can hear. As diagrammed in Figure 10-10, both outer and inner hair cells are anchored in the basilar membrane. The tips of the cilia of outer hair cells are attached to the overlying tectorial membrane, but the cilia of the inner hair cells only loosely touch that membrane. Nevertheless, the movement of the basilar and tectorial membranes causes the cochlear fluid to flow past the cilia of the inner hair cells, bending them back and forth.

Animals with intact outer hair cells but no inner hair cells are completely deaf. That is, they can perceive only very loud, low-frequency sounds via the somatosensory system. You may have experienced this feeling when a subwoofer or a passing truck caused vibrations in your chest. Inner hair cells can be destroyed by prolonged exposure to intense sound pressure waves, infections, diseases, or certain chemicals and drugs. Inner hair cells do not regenerate in mammals; thus, once your inner hair cells have died, hearing loss is permanent.

Outer hair cells function by sharpening the cochlea's resolving power, contracting or relaxing and thereby changing tectorial membrane stiffness. That's right: the outer hair cells have a motor function. While we typically think of sensory input preceding motor output, motor systems can, in fact, influence sensory input. For example, the pupil contracts or dilates to change the amount of light that falls on the retina, and the outer hair cells contract or relax to alter the physical stimulus detected by the inner hair cells.

**FIGURE 10-10 Transducing Waves into Neural Activity** Movement of the basilar membrane produces a shearing force in the cochlear fluid that bends the cilia, leading to the opening or closing of calcium channels in the outer hair cells. An influx of calcium ions leads the inner hair cells to release neurotransmitter, stimulating increased action potentials in the auditory neurons.

Cochlea

Tectorial membrane
Inner hair cell
Outer hair cells
Basilar membrane
Axons of cochlear nerve
Displacement

Movement of the basilar membrane in response to sound waves…

…creates a shearing force that bends cilia in contact with and near the overlying tectorial membrane. This bending generates neural activity in the hair cells from which the cilia extend.

How this outer hair cell function is controlled is puzzling. What stimulates these cells to contract or relax? The answer seems to be that through connections with axons in the auditory nerve, the outer hair cells send a message to the brainstem auditory areas and receive a reply that causes the cells to alter the tension on the tectorial membrane. In this way, the brain helps the hair cells construct an auditory world. The outer cells are also part of a mechanism that modulates auditory nerve firing, especially in response to intense sound pressure waves, which offers some protection against their damaging effects.

A final question remains: How does movement of the inner hair cell cilia alter neural activity? The neurons of the auditory nerve have a spontaneous baseline rate of firing action potentials, and this rate is changed by the amount of neurotransmitter the hair cells release. It turns out that movement of the cilia changes the inner hair cell's polarization and its rate of neurotransmitter release. Inner hair cells continuously leak calcium, and this leakage causes a small but steady amount of neurotransmitter release into the synapse. Movement of the cilia in one direction results in depolarization: calcium channels open and release more neurotransmitter onto the dendrites of the cells that form the auditory nerve, generating more nerve impulses. Movement of the cilia in the other direction hyperpolarizes the cell membrane, so that transmitter release decreases, thereby decreasing the activity in auditory neurons.

Inner hair cells are amazingly sensitive to the movement of their cilia. A movement of only about 0.3 nm is sufficient to allow sound wave detection—that's about the diameter of a large atom! Such sensitivity helps to explain why our hearing is so incredibly sensitive. Research Focus 10-3: Otoacoustic Emissions describes a consequence of cochlear function.

## Pathways to the Auditory Cortex

Inner hair cells in the organ of Corti synapse with neighboring bipolar cells, the axons that form the auditory (cochlear) nerve. The auditory nerve, in turn, forms part of the eighth cranial nerve—that is, the auditory vestibular nerve, which governs hearing and balance. Whereas ganglion cells in the eye receive inputs from many receptor cells, bipolar cells in the ear receive input from but a single inner hair cell receptor.

Cochlear-nerve axons enter the brainstem at the level of the medulla and synapse in the cochlear nucleus, which has ventral and dorsal subdivisions. Two nearby structures in the hindbrain (brainstem), the superior olive (a nucleus in the olivary complex) and the trapezoid body, receive connections from the cochlear nucleus, as

**Principle 2:** Sensory and motor divisions permeate the nervous system.

Section 4-3 reviews phases of the action potential and its propagation as a nerve impulse.

Figure 2-29 lists and locates the cranial nerves, and in its caption is a mnemonic for remembering them in order.

**otoacoustic emissions** Spontaneous or evoked sound waves produced within the ear by the cochlea that escape from the ear.

---

### ⊚ RESEARCH FOCUS 10-3

## Otoacoustic Emissions

While the ear is exquisitely designed to amplify and convert sound waves into action potentials, it is unique among the sensory organs: the ear actually *produces* the physical stimulus it is designed to detect! A healthy cochlea produces sound waves called **otoacoustic emissions.**

The cochlea acts as an amplifier. The outer hair cells amplify sound waves, providing an energy source that enhances cochlear sensitivity and frequency selectivity. Not all of the energy that the cochlea generates is dissipated within it. Some escapes toward the middle ear, which works efficiently in both directions, thus setting the eardrum in motion. The eardrum then acts as a loudspeaker, radiating sound waves—the otoacoustic emissions—out of the ear.

Sensitive microphones placed in the external ear canal can detect both types of otoacoustic emissions: spontaneous and evoked. As the name implies, *spontaneous otoacoustic emissions* occur without external

stimulation. *Evoked otoacoustic emissions* are generated in response to sound waves, and they are useful for assessing hearing impairments.

A simple, noninvasive test can detect and evaluate evoked otoacoustic emissions, and this test is particularly useful with newborns and children who are too young to take conventional hearing tests. A small speaker and microphone are inserted into the ear. The speaker emits a click sound, and the microphone detects the resulting evoked emission without damaging the delicate workings of the inner ear. Missing or abnormal evoked emissions predict a hearing deficit. Many countries now sponsor universal programs to test the hearing of all newborn babies using otoacoustic emissions.

Otoacoustic emissions serve a useful purpose, yet they play no direct role in hearing. They are considered an *epiphenomenon*—a secondary phenomenon that occurs in parallel with or above (*epi*) a primary phenomenon.

**FIGURE 10-11 Auditory Pathways** Auditory inputs cross to the hemisphere opposite the ear in the hindbrain and midbrain, then recross in the thalamus. In this way, the information from each ear reaches both hemispheres. Multiple nuclei process inputs en route to the auditory cortex, charted here for the left ear.

Figure 9-17 maps the *what* and *how* visual streams through the brain.

**Principle 5:** The brain is symmetrical and asymmetrical.

---

**medial geniculate nucleus** Major thalamic region concerned with audition.

**primary auditory cortex (area A1)** Asymmetrical structures within Heschl's gyrus in the temporal lobes; receives input from the ventral region of the medial geniculate nucleus.

**Wernicke's area** Secondary auditory cortex (planum temporale) lying behind Heschl's gyrus at the rear of the left temporal lobe; regulates language comprehension. Also known as the *posterior speech zone.*

**lateralization** Localization of function primarily on one side of the brain.

shown in **Figure 10-11**. Projections from the cochlear nucleus connect with cells on the same side of the brain, as well as with cells on the opposite side. This arrangement mixes the inputs from the two ears to form a single sound perception.

Both the cochlear nucleus and the superior olive send projections to the inferior colliculus in the dorsal midbrain. Two distinct pathways emerge from the inferior colliculus, coursing to the **medial geniculate nucleus** in the thalamus. The ventral region of the medial geniculate nucleus projects to the **primary auditory cortex (area A1)**, whereas the dorsal region projects to the auditory cortical regions adjacent to area A1.

Analogous to the two visual pathways—the ventral stream for object recognition and the dorsal stream for visual control of movement—a similar distinction exists in the auditory cortex (Romanski et al., 1999). Just as we can identify objects by their sound characteristics, so we can direct our movements by the sound we hear. The role of sound in guiding movement is less familiar to sight-dominated people than it is to individuals who are blind. Nevertheless, the ability exists in us all. Imagine waking up in the dark and reaching to pick up your phone to turn off the alarm. Your hand automatically forms the appropriate shape in response to the sound you have heard. That sound guides your movements much as visual images can guide them.

Relatively little is known about the what–how auditory pathways in the cortex. One auditory pathway appears to continue through the temporal lobe, much like the ventral visual pathway, and plays a role in identifying auditory stimuli. A second auditory pathway apparently goes to the posterior parietal region, where it forms a dorsal route for the auditory control of movement. It also appears that auditory information can gain access to the visual cortex, as described in Research Focus 10-4: Seeing with Sound.

## Auditory Cortex

In humans, the primary auditory cortex (A1) lies within Heschl's gyrus, which is surrounded by secondary cortical areas (A2), as shown in **Figure 10-12**A. The secondary cortex lying behind Heschl's gyrus is called the *planum temporale* (Latin for "temporal plane").

In right-handed people, the planum temporale is larger on the left side of the brain than it is on the right side, whereas Heschl's gyrus is larger on the right side than on the left. The cortex of the left planum forms a speech zone known as **Wernicke's area** (the posterior speech zone), whereas the cortex of the larger right-hemisphere Heschl's gyrus has a special role in analyzing music.

These hemispheric differences mean that the auditory cortex is anatomically and functionally asymmetrical. Although cerebral asymmetry is not unique to the auditory system, it is most obvious here because auditory analysis of speech takes place only in the left hemisphere of right-handed people. Approximately 70% of left-handed people have the same anatomical asymmetries as right-handers, an indication that speech organization is not strictly related to hand preference. Language, including speech and other functions such as reading and writing, is asymmetrical as well, although the right hemisphere also contributes to these broader functions.

The remaining 30% of left-handers fall into two distinct groups. The organization in about half of these people is opposite to that in right-handers. The other half have some idiosyncratic bilateral speech representation. That is, approximately 15% of all left-handed people have some speech functions in one hemisphere and some in the other hemisphere.

Localization of language on one side of the brain is an example of **lateralization**. Note that in neuroanatomy, if one hemisphere is specialized for one type of analysis, the other hemisphere has a complementary function. For example, the left hemisphere is specialized for language, and the right hemisphere appears to be lateralized for music.

## ⊙ RESEARCH FOCUS 10-4

# Seeing with Sound

**Echolocation**—the ability to use sound to locate objects in space—has been extensively studied in species such as bats and dolphins. It was also reported more than 50 years ago that some blind people echolocate.

More recently, anecdotal reports have surfaced of blind people around the world navigating using clicks made with their tongues and mouths and then listening to the returning echoes. Congenitally blind people can ride a bicycle down a street filled with silent obstacles such as parked cars. But how do they do this, and what part of the brain enables it?

Behavioral studies of blind people reveal that echolocators make short, spectrally broad clicks by moving the tongue backward and downward from the roof of the mouth directly behind the teeth. Skilled echolocators can identify properties of objects such as position, distance, size, shape, and texture (Teng & Whitney, 2011).

Thaler and colleagues (2011) used functional magnetic resonance imaging (fMRI) to investigate the neural basis of this ability. They studied two blind echolocation experts who used echolocation to perceive the shape, motion, and even identity of objects. The researchers then compared the two experts' brain activity following sounds that contained the self-produced clicks and returning echoes with the brain activity generated by control sounds that did not contain the echoes but were otherwise acoustically matched (same intensities and frequencies). The researchers found similar activity in the auditory cortex in both experts: as expected, they were hearing sounds using their auditory cortex.

However, when the blind echolocators listened to recordings of their echolocation clicks and the reflected echoes, their primary visual cortex *also* showed enhanced activity. Sighted controls showed enhanced activation only in the auditory cortex with no enhanced visual cortex activity. Furthermore, as illustrated in the figure, the blind echolocators showed activity only

in the visual cortex when sounds with and without echoes were compared (subtracted). This finding indicates that the echolocators were *seeing* the echoes. Sighted controls (findings not indicated in the figure) showed no activity in either the visual or auditory cortex in this comparison.

These results provide evidence that blind echolocation experts process click–echo information using brain regions typically devoted to vision. Thaler and his colleagues propose that the primary visual cortex is performing a spatial computation using information from the auditory cortex.

In a follow-up study, Thaler and colleagues (2018) found that echolocators make adjustments to the intensity and number of clicks based on environmental conditions—strategies similar to those employed by other echolocating animals. More immediately, these studies provide hope that echolocation could be taught to blind and visually impaired people to provide them increased independence in their daily lives (to learn about the results of one such training program, see Norman et al., 2021).

**Seeing with Sound** When cortical activation for sound with and without echoes is imaged in a blind echolocator, only the visual cortex shows activation (*left*) relative to the auditory cortex (*right*). Research from Thaler, L., Arnott, S.R., & Goodale, M.A. (2011) Neural correlates of Natural Human echolocation in Early and Late Blind Echolocation Experts. PLoS ONE, 6, (5)e20162. doi:10.1371/journal.pone.0020162.

**FIGURE 10-12 Human Auditory Cortex (A)** The left hemisphere, showing the lateral fissure retracted to reveal the primary auditory cortex buried within Heschl's gyrus, and the adjacent secondary auditory regions. In cross section, the posterior speech zone (Wernicke's area) is larger on the left, and Heschl's gyrus is larger in the right hemisphere. **(B)** Frontal view showing the extent of the multifunctional insular cortex buried in the lateral fissure.

**echolocation** The ability to use sound to locate objects in space.

**insula** Multifunctional cortical tissue located within the lateral fissure; contains language- and taste perception-related regions and neural structures underlying social cognition.

**tonotopic representation** In audition, structural organization for processing of sound waves from lower to higher frequencies.

The temporal lobe sulci enfold a volume of cortical tissue far more extensive than the auditory cortex (Figure 10-12B). Buried in the lateral fissure, cortical tissue called the **insula** contains not only lateralized regions related to language but also areas controlling taste perception (the gustatory cortex) and areas linked to the neural structures underlying social cognition. As you might expect, injury to the insula can produce such diverse deficits as disturbance of both language and taste.

## 10-2 Review

Before you continue, check your understanding. Answers to Self-Test appear at the back of the book.

1. Incoming sound wave energy causes the eardrum to vibrate, which in turn vibrates the _____.

2. The auditory receptors are the _____, found in the _____.

3. The motion of cochlear fluid causes displacement of the _____ and _____ membranes.

4. The axons of bipolar cells from the cochlea form the _____ nerve, which is part of the _____ cranial nerve.

5. The auditory nerve originating in the cochlea projects to various nuclei in the brainstem; then it projects to the _____ in the midbrain and the _____ in the thalamus.

6. Describe the asymmetrical structure and functions of the auditory cortex.

### 10-3

# Neural Activity and Hearing

We now turn to the neuronal activity in the auditory system that produces our perception of sound. Neurons at different levels in this system serve different functions. To get an idea of what individual hair cells and cortical neurons do, we consider how the auditory system codes sound wave energy so that we perceive pitch, loudness, location, and pattern.

## Hearing Pitch

Recall that perception of pitch corresponds to the frequency (repetition rate) of sound waves, which is measured in hertz (cycles per second). Hair cells in the cochlea code frequency as a function of their location on the basilar membrane. In this **tonotopic representation**, hair cell cilia at the base of the cochlea are maximally displaced by high-frequency waves, which we hear as high-pitched sounds; those at the apex are displaced the most by low-frequency waves, which we hear as low-pitched sounds. Because each bipolar cell axon that forms the cochlear nerve is connected to only one inner hair cell, the bipolar cells convey information about the spot on the basilar membrane, from apex to base, that is being stimulated.

Recordings from single fibers in the cochlear nerve reveal that although each axon transmits information about only a small part of the auditory spectrum, each cell does respond to a range of sound wave frequencies—if the wave is sufficiently loud. That is, each hair cell is maximally responsive to a particular frequency and also responds to nearby frequencies, but the sound wave's amplitude must be greater (louder) for those nearby frequencies to excite the receptor's membrane potential.

We can plot this range of hair cell responses to different frequencies at different amplitudes as a tuning curve. As graphed in **Figure 10-13**, each hair cell receptor is maximally sensitive to a particular wavelength but still responds somewhat to nearby wavelengths.

Bipolar cell axons in the cochlea project to the cochlear nucleus in an orderly manner (see Figure 10-11). Axons entering from the base of the cochlea connect with one location; those entering from the middle connect to another location; and those entering from the apex connect to yet another site. Thus, the basilar membrane's tonotopic representation is reproduced in the hindbrain cochlear nucleus.

### Learning Objectives

- Explain how the anatomical structure of the cochlea facilitates our ability to hear pitch and frequency.
- Describe the anatomical features and neural pathways that allow us to detect loudness and location.
- Summarize the role of the dorsal and ventral auditory pathways in the recognition of sound patterns.

*Tonotopic* literally means "of a tone place."

Individual hair cells and photoreceptors (see Figure 9-9) maximally respond to their preferred frequency, but also respond to a range of frequencies within their sensory domains.

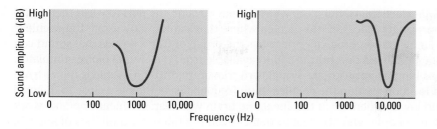

**FIGURE 10-13 Tuning Curves** Graphs plotted for the sound wave frequency and amplitude energy required to increase the firing rates of two axons in the cochlear nerve. The lowest point on each tuning curve is the frequency to which that hair cell is most sensitive. The curve at left is centered on a frequency of 1000 Hz, the midrange of human hearing; the curve at right is centered on a frequency of 10,000 Hz, in the high range.

This systematic representation is maintained throughout the auditory pathways and into the primary auditory cortex. **Figure 10-14** shows the distribution of projections from the base and apex of the cochlea across area A1. Similar tonotopic maps can be constructed for each level of the auditory system.

This systematic auditory organization has enabled the development of **cochlear implants**—cranial nerve stimulators, consisting of electronic devices with wires surgically inserted in the inner ear—that serve as prostheses to allow deaf people to hear (Naples & Ruckenstein, 2020). Cochlear implants are not a cure for deafness, but rather serve as a hearing substitute. As shown in **Figure 10-15**, a miniature microphone-like processor, magnetically secured to a port, detects the component frequencies and amplitudes of incoming sound waves. The sound waves are converted to

**cochlear implant** Electronic device with wires that is implanted surgically into the inner ear; the wires carry transduced sound waves that directly excite the cranial nerve, allowing a deaf person to hear.

**FIGURE 10-14 Tonotopic Representation of Area A1** A retractor holds the lateral fissure open to reveal the underlying primary auditory cortex. The anterior end of area A1 corresponds to the apex of the cochlea, and hence to low frequencies. The posterior end corresponds to the base of the cochlea, and hence to high frequencies.

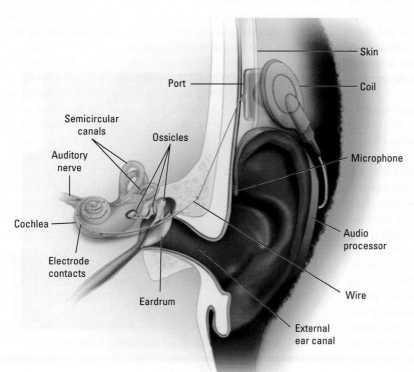

**FIGURE 10-15 Tonotopic Technology** A cochlear implant captures incoming sound wave stimulation via a microphone worn behind the ear. An audio processor converts the frequencies and amplitudes into electric current and stimulates the cochlear nerve at the correct locations in the cochlea.

battery-driven electrical stimulation, which is sent through the port to wires that terminate on appropriate places in the cochlea where they can directly excite the cochlear nerve. The implantation procedure destroys the organ of Corti, so external sound can no longer be perceived beyond the sound available from the cranial nerve stimulator. However, as long as appropriate signals are transmitted to the cochlear nerve from the correct locations within the cochlea (high frequencies at the base close to the oval window and low frequencies at the apex), the brain will hear. Cochlear implants work well, allowing people who are deaf to detect even the fluctuating pitches of speech. The success of this revolutionary device corroborates the tonotopic representation of pitch in the basilar membrane, and its medical and societal impact cannot be understated. The story of one child who received cochlear implants is recounted in Clinical Focus 10-5: Cochlear Implant in a Deaf Child.

Even so, the quality of sound that cochlear implants create is low relative to natural hearing. Adults who lose their hearing and then get cochlear implants describe the sounds as "computerized" and "weird" and find music unpleasant and difficult to listen to. However, this reaction doesn't seem to be true for deaf children, who have limited or no natural hearing experience to use for comparison.

Graeme Clark (2015) developed a prototype for a high-fidelity cochlear implant with 50 electrodes (typically, these devices have 22 electrodes) to increase basilar membrane

## CLINICAL FOCUS 10-5

# Cochlear Implant in a Deaf Child

G. D. was born to first-time parents without incident and appeared healthy and typical. Her parents noticed that G. D. did not respond to the loud barking of the family dog, so they took her to their family doctor, who also observed that G. D. did not respond to sound. Otoacoustic emissions tests and brainstem auditory evoked responses (BAER) were performed at a nearby clinic, and both results came back negative, indicating a problem (recall the discussion of otoacoustic emissions in Research Focus 10-3). G. D. was referred to the local children's hospital for further tests, and her results indicated that she was profoundly deaf, with her hearing on the right side being worse than that on the left. Hearing aids were fitted, and for some time she was able to respond to spoken words and react to sounds. However, her hearing slowly deteriorated. G. D.'s family was hopeful that she would be able to communicate with spoken language, enjoy music, and be mainstreamed at school, and a cochlear implant was an attractive option for meeting these goals.

Deafness in children has many causes, including genetic mutation (approximately 50% of cases) and a variety of infections, such as toxoplasmosis, syphilis, rubella, cytomegalovirus, and herpesvirus (Kenna, 2015). Most deaf children, like G. D., have hearing parents.

G. D. underwent a full genome screen, and a novel mutation in her *SOX10* gene was determined to be the culprit for her deafness. She is a *heterozygote*, meaning she has one typical copy and one mutated copy of the gene. Because the *SOX10* mutation is dominant, it was likely not inherited from a parent (otherwise, that parent would have also been deaf). Thus, the mutation appeared *de novo* (spontaneously) in G. D.

Five days after her first birthday, G. D. received a cochlear implant on her right side. After a one-month waiting period to allow healing following destruction of the organ of Corti, the implant was turned on for the first time. G. D. responded well. In fact, the next day she made comments about the birds chirping in the trees and airplanes flying overhead — her family was overjoyed at her response to these previously unknown sounds. The implant's external processors are easily removed for bathing, sleeping, and battery recharge.

G. D. received speech therapy and had her implant tested regularly. However, her speech therapists recommended only a minimal amount of sign language learning so as not to interfere with G. D.'s learning of spoken language, a much more difficult skill to acquire. Although she tested well above her age group for spoken language comprehension, hearing on her left side continued to deteriorate, and 2 years after her right-side implant, G. D. received a cochlear implant on the left side. Three months after the left implant was turned on, G. D. began to localize sounds in her environment (discussed in Section 10-3), a skill that was new for her and something most people take for granted.

External cochlear implant device in a 1-year-old child.

stimulation. His goal is to achieve better music perception and enhanced ability to discern specific voices in noisy rooms. No matter what the person's age, a shorter time span between the hearing loss and treatment can lead to better hearing: early intervention can lead to better results.

One minor difficulty with frequency detection is that the human cochlea does not respond in a tonotopic manner to frequencies below about 200 hertz, yet we can hear frequencies as low as 20 hertz. At its apex, all the cells respond to movement of the basilar membrane, but they do so in proportion to the frequency of the incoming wave (see Figure 10-9B). Higher rates of bipolar cell firing signal a higher frequency, whereas lower rates of firing signal a lower frequency.

Why the cochlea uses a different system to distinguish pitch within this range of very low-frequency sound waves is not clear. It probably has to do with the physical limitations of the basilar membrane. Discriminating among low-frequency sound waves is vital to animals such as elephants and whales, which depend on these frequencies to communicate. These species most likely have more neurons at the apex of the basilar membrane than we humans have.

## Detecting Loudness

The simplest way for cochlear (bipolar) cells to indicate sound wave intensity is to fire at a higher rate when amplitude is greater, which is exactly what happens. More intense air pressure changes produce more intense basilar membrane vibrations and, therefore, greater shearing of the cilia. Increased shearing leads to more neurotransmitter being released onto bipolar cells. As a result, the bipolar axons fire more frequently, telling the auditory system that the sound is getting louder.

## Detecting Location

Psychologist Albert Bregman devised a visual analogy to describe what the auditory system is doing when it detects sound location:

> Imagine a game played at the side of a lake. Two small channels are dug, side by side, leading away from the lake, and the lake water is allowed to fill them up. Partway up each channel, a cork floats, moving up and down with the waves. You stand with your back to the lake and are allowed to look only at the two floating corks. Then you are asked questions about what is happening on the lake. Are there two motorboats on the lake or only one? Is the nearer one going from left to right or right to left? Is the wind blowing? Did something heavy fall into the water? You must answer these questions just by looking at the two corks. This would seem to be an impossible task. Yet consider an exactly analogous problem. As you sit in a room, a lake of air surrounds you. Running off this lake, into your head, are two small channels—your ear canals. At the end of each is a membrane (the ear drum) that acts like the floating corks in the channels running off the lake, moving in and out with the sound waves that hit it. Just as the game at the lakeside offered no information about the happenings on the lake except for the movements of the corks, the sound-producing events in the room can be known by your brain only through the vibrations of your two eardrums. (Bregman, 2005, p. 35)

We estimate the location of a sound both by taking cues derived from one ear and by comparing cues received at both ears. The fact that each cochlear nerve synapses on both sides of the brain provides mechanisms for locating a sound source. In one mechanism, neurons in the brainstem compute the difference in a sound wave's arrival time at each ear—the *interaural time difference* (*ITD*). Differences in arrival time need not be large to be detected. If two sounds presented through earphones are separated in time by as little as 10 microseconds, the listener will perceive that a single sound came from the leading ear.

This computation of left-ear–right-ear arrival times is carried out in the medial part of the superior olivary complex (see Figure 10-11). Because these hindbrain cells receive inputs from each ear, they can compare exactly when the signal from each ear reaches them.

**Figure 10-16** shows how sound waves originating on the left reach the left ear slightly before they reach the right ear. As the sound source moves from the side of

Extra distance that sound must travel to reach the right ear.

**FIGURE 10-16 Locating a Sound** Compression waves originating on the left side of the body reach the left ear slightly before reaching the right. The ITD is small, but the auditory system can discriminate it and fuse the dual stimuli so that we perceive a single, clear sound coming from the left. Horizontal orienting is called *azimuth detection*; vertical orienting is called *elevation detection*.

the head toward the middle, a person has greater and greater difficulty locating it: the ITD becomes smaller and smaller, until there is no difference at all. When we detect no difference, we infer that the sound is either directly in front of us or directly behind us. To locate it, we turn our head, making the sound waves strike one ear sooner. We have a similar problem distinguishing between sounds directly above and below us. Again, we solve the problem by tilting our head, thus causing the sound waves to strike one ear before the other.

Another mechanism used by the auditory system to detect the source of a sound is the sound's relative loudness on the left and the right—the *interaural intensity difference* (*IID*). The head acts as an obstacle to higher-frequency sound waves, which do not easily bend around the head. As a result, higher-frequency waves on one side of the head are louder than on the other side. The lateral part of the superior olive and the trapezoid body detect this difference. Again, sound waves coming from directly in front or behind or from directly above or below require the same solution: tilting or turning the head.

Head tilting and turning take time, which is important for animals, such as owls, that hunt using sound. Owls need to know the location of a sound simultaneously in at least two directions—right or left and above or below. Owls, like humans, can orient themselves in the horizontal plane to sound waves by using ITD. In addition, the owl's ears have evolved to detect the relative loudness of sound waves in the vertical plane. As diagrammed in **Figure 10-17**, owls' ears are slightly displaced vertically. This solution allows owls to hunt entirely by sound in the dark—bad news for mice.

# Detecting Patterns in Sound

Perceiving sound wave patterns as meaningful units, such as units of music and speech, is fundamental to human auditory analysis. Because music perception and language perception are lateralized in the right and left temporal lobes, respectively, we can guess that neurons in the right and left temporal cortex take part in pattern recognition and analysis of both auditory experiences. Studying the activities of individual auditory neurons in humans is not easy, however, because there is no noninvasive way to do so.

Most of what neuroscientists know comes from studies of how individual neurons respond in nonhuman primates. Both human and nonhuman primates have a ventral and dorsal cortical pathway for audition. Neurons in the ventral pathway decode spectrally complex sounds, a process some investigators refer to as *auditory object recognition*. This process facilitates both the decoding of the meaning of speech sounds for people and the decoding of meaning of species-typical vocalizations in monkeys (for a review, see Rauschecker, 2012). Less is known about the properties of neurons in the dorsal auditory stream, but this path clearly has a role in integrating auditory and

Facial ruff

Ear-canal opening

Ear opening

Ear opening

**FIGURE 10-17 Hunting by Ear** *Left*: In the dark, a saw-whet owl aligns its talons with the body axis of the mouse it is about to catch. *Center*: The owl's facial ruff collects and funnels sound waves into ear canal openings through tightly feathered troughs above and below the eyes. The owl's left ear is more sensitive to sound waves from the left and below because the ear canal is higher on the left side, and the trough is tilted down. The right-side ear canal is lower, and the trough tilts up, making the right ear more sensitive to sound waves from the right and above. *Right*: The owl's asymmetric skull produces a similar auditory asymmetry. Information from Knudsen (1981).

somatosensory information to control speech production—a process called *audition for action*.

Audition for action parallels unconscious, visually guided movements by the dorsal stream; see Figure 9-22.

## 10-3 Review

Before you continue, check your understanding. Answers to Self-Test appear at the back of the book.

1. Bipolar neurons in the cochlea form _____ representations that code sound wave frequencies.

2. Loudness is indicated by the firing rate of cells in the _____.

3. Detecting the location of a sound is a function of neurons in the _____ and _____ of the brainstem.

4. The function of the dorsal auditory pathway can be described as _____.

5. Explain how the brain detects a sound's location.

6. Explain how cochlear implants facilitate hearing in the absence of the organ of Corti.

## 10-4

# Anatomy of Language and Music

This chapter began by exploring the evolutionary implications of discovering a flute made by our ancestors 35,000 years ago (see Research Focus 10-1). That modern humans made flutes so long ago implies not only that they made music, but also that they processed musical sound wave patterns. In the human brain, musical ability is generally a right-hemisphere specialization complementary to language ability, which is lateralized to the left hemisphere in most people.

No one knows whether these complementary systems evolved together in the hominid brain, but it is likely that music evolved first. Language and music abilities are highly developed in the modern human brain. Although little is known about how each is processed at the cellular level, electrical stimulation and recording as well as blood-flow imaging studies yield important insights into the cortical regions that process them. We investigate such studies next, focusing first on how the brain processes language.

## Processing Language

An estimated 5000 to 7000 human languages are spoken in the world today, and many more have gone extinct in past millennia. Researchers have wondered whether the brain has a single system for understanding and producing any language, regardless of its structure, or whether disparate languages, such as English and Japanese, are processed differently. To answer this question, it helps to analyze languages to determine just how fundamentally similar they are, despite their obvious differences.

### Uniformity of Language Structure

Most languages seem impossibly complex to those who do not speak them. Their sounds alone may seem odd and difficult to make. To a native English speaker, for instance, certain languages, such as Japanese, probably sound especially melodic and almost without obvious consonants, whereas Germanic languages may sound heavily guttural with many consonants.

Even within such related languages as Spanish, Italian, and French, marked differences can make learning one of them challenging, even if the student already knows another. Yet as real as all these linguistic differences may be, they are superficial. The similarities among human languages, although not immediately apparent, are actually far more fundamental than their differences.

Noam Chomsky (1965) is usually credited as the first linguist to stress similarities in human language structure over differences—a decidedly scientific approach to

---

**Learning Objectives**

- Explain how similarities in language structure influence our understanding of the genetic basis for language.

- Describe the function of Broca's area and Wernicke's area in language processing, and describe aphasias associated with each.

- Summarize the process by which Penfield mapped the auditory and speech zones.

- Describe the cortical structures associated with music processing.

Section 7-4 surveys functional brain-imaging methods; Section 7-2 reviews methods for measuring the brain's electrical activity.

linguistic study. In a series of books and papers written over more than a half-century, Chomsky has articulated a sweeping claim, as have researchers such as Steven Pinker (1997). They argue that all languages have common structural characteristics stemming from a genetically determined constraint, and these common characteristics form the basis of universal grammar theory. Humans, apparently, have a built-in capacity for learning and using language, just as we have for walking upright.

Chomsky's theory was greeted with deep skepticism when he first proposed this idea in the 1960s, but it has since become clear that the capacity for human language is, indeed, genetic. An obvious piece of evidence: language is universal in human populations. All people everywhere use language.

The complexity of a language is unrelated to its culture's technological complexity. The languages of technologically unsophisticated peoples are every bit as complex and elegant as the languages of postindustrial cultures. The English of Shakespeare's time is neither inferior nor superior to today's English; it is just different.

Another piece of evidence that Chomsky adherents cite for the genetic basis of human language is that humans learn language early in life and seemingly without effort. By about 12 months of age, children everywhere have started to speak words. By 18 months, they are combining words, and by age 3 years, they have a rich language capability.

Perhaps the most amazing thing about language development is that children are not formally taught the structure of their language, just as they are not taught to crawl or walk. They just do it. As toddlers, they are not painstakingly instructed in the rules of grammar. In fact, their early errors—sentences such as "I goed to the zoo"—are seldom even corrected by adults. Yet children master language rapidly. They also acquire language through a series of stages that are remarkably similar across cultures. Indeed, the process of language acquisition plays an important role in Chomsky's theory of its innateness—which is not to say that language development is not influenced by experience.

At the most basic level, children learn the language or languages that they hear spoken. In an English household, they learn English; in a Japanese home, they learn Japanese. They also pick up the language structure—the vocabulary and grammar—of the people around them, even though that structure can vary from one speaker to another. Children go through a sensitive period for language acquisition, probably from about 1 to 6 years of age. If they are not exposed to language throughout this critical period, their language skills are severely compromised. If children learn two languages simultaneously, the two share the same part of Broca's area. In fact, their neural representations overlap (Kim et al., 1997).

Both its universality and natural acquisition favor the theory asserting a genetic basis of human language. A third piece of evidence is the many basic structural elements common to all languages. Granted, every language has its own particular grammatical rules that specify exactly how various parts of speech are positioned in a sentence (syntax), how words are inflected to convey different meanings, and so forth. Nevertheless, an overarching set of rules also applies to all human languages, and the first rule is that there *are* rules.

For instance, all languages employ parts of speech that we call subjects, verbs, and direct objects. Consider the sentence *Jane ate the apple. Jane* is the subject, *ate* is the verb, and *apple* is the direct object. Syntax is not specified by any universal rule but rather is a characteristic of the particular language. In English, syntactical order (usually) is subject, verb, object; in Japanese, the order is subject, object, verb; in Gaelic, the order is verb, subject, object. Nonetheless, all these languages have both syntax and grammar.

The existence of these two structural pillars of all human languages is seen in the phenomenon of *creolization*—the development of a new language from what was formerly a rudimentary language, or *pidgin language,* formed when two or more unrelated languages merge. In one example of creolization from Queensland in northeastern Australia, Pacific Islanders speaking numerous different languages were sent to work together on plantations. These laborers began to develop a pidgin, drawing

A 1-year-old child's 5- to 10-word vocabulary doubles in the next 6 months and by 36 months mushrooms to 1000 words; see Section 8-3.

Section 15-1 discusses the connection between language and human thought, and Section 15-4 explores the areas of the brain involved in language processing.

vocabulary primarily from English but also from German, Malay, Portuguese, and their own Austronesian languages.

This English-based pidgin evolved into Tok Pisin, which is now one of the three official languages of Papua New Guinea, is spoken by 6 million people, and is crowding out other languages in that region. The original pidgin had a crude syntax (word order) but lacked a formal grammatical structure. The children of the laborers who invented this pidgin grew up with caretakers who spoke only pidgin to them. Yet within a generation, these children had developed their own *creole*, a language complete with a formal syntax and grammar.

Clearly, the pidgin invented of necessity by adults was not a learnable language for children. Instead, their innate biology shaped a new language, one that was similar in basic structure to all other human languages. Creolized languages seem to evolve in a similar way, even though the base languages are different. This phenomenon is possible only because there is an innate biological component to language development.

## Localizing Language in the Brain

By the mid-1800s, it had become clear that language functions were at least partly localized not just within the left hemisphere, but to specific areas there. The clues that led to this conclusion began to emerge in the early nineteenth century, when neurologists observed patients with frontal lobe injuries who had language difficulties.

Then, in 1861, physician Paul Broca confirmed that certain language functions are localized in the left hemisphere. Broca concluded, on the basis of several postmortem examinations, that language is localized in the left frontal lobe, in a region just anterior to the central fissure. A person with damage in this area is unable to speak despite having both an intact vocal apparatus and normal language comprehension. The confirmation of **Broca's area** was significant because it led to the idea that the left and right hemispheres might have different functions.

Other neurologists of the time thought that Broca's area might be only one of several left-hemisphere regions that control language. In particular, they suspected a relationship existed between hearing and speech. Proving this suspicion correct, Karl Wernicke later described patients who had difficulty comprehending language after injury to the posterior region of the left temporal lobe, identified as Wernicke's area in **Figure 10-18**.

In Section 10-2, we identified Wernicke's area as a speech zone (see Figure 10-12A). Damage to any speech area produces some form of **aphasia**, the general term for any inability to comprehend or produce language, despite the presence of otherwise normal comprehension and intact vocal mechanisms. At one extreme, people

**Broca's area** Anterior left-hemisphere speech area that functions with the motor cortex to produce the movements needed for speaking.

**aphasia** Inability to speak or comprehend language despite the presence of normal comprehension and intact vocal mechanisms. *Broca's aphasia* is the inability to speak fluently despite the presence of normal comprehension and intact vocal mechanisms. *Wernicke's aphasia* is the inability to understand or to produce meaningful language even though word production remains intact.

**Principle 5:** Brain functions are localized and distributed.

Section 7-1 links Broca's observations to his contributions to neuropsychology.

**FIGURE 10-18 Neurology of Language**
**(A)** In Wernicke's model of speech recognition, stored sound images are matched to spoken words in the left posterior temporal cortex, shown in red. **(B)** Speech is produced through the connection that the arcuate fasciculus makes between Wernicke's area and Broca's area.

who suffer *Wernicke's aphasia* can speak fluently, but their language is confused and makes little sense, as if they have no idea what they are saying. At the other extreme, a person with *Broca's aphasia* cannot speak despite having normal comprehension and intact physiology.

Wernicke went on to propose a model for how the two language areas of the left hemisphere interact to produce speech. He theorized that images of words are encoded by their sounds and stored in the left posterior temporal cortex. When we hear a word that matches one of those sound images, we recognize it, which is how Wernicke's area contributes to speech comprehension (see Figure 10-18A).

To *speak* words, Broca's area in the left frontal lobe must come into play because the motor program to produce each word is stored in this area. Messages travel to Broca's area from Wernicke's area through the *arcuate fasciculus,* a fiber pathway that connects the two regions. Broca's area, in turn, controls articulation of words by the vocal apparatus, as diagrammed in Figure 10-18B.

Wernicke's model provided a simple explanation for both the existence of two major language areas in the brain and the contribution that each area makes to the control of language. But the model was based on postmortem examinations of patients with brain lesions, which were often extensive in nature. Not until neurosurgeon Wilder Penfield's pioneering brain stimulation studies, beginning in the 1930s, were the left-hemisphere language areas clearly and accurately mapped.

## Auditory and Speech Zones Mapped Using Brain Stimulation

Among Penfield's discoveries are that Broca's area is not the independent site of speech production, and Wernicke's area is not the independent site of language comprehension. Instead, he found, electrical stimulation of either region disrupts both processes.

Penfield took advantage of the chance to map the brain's auditory and language areas when he operated on patients undergoing elective surgery to treat epilepsy that was unresponsive to antiseizure medication. The goal of this surgery is to remove tissues where the abnormal discharges are initiated without damaging the areas responsible for linguistic ability or vital sensory or motor functioning. To determine the locations of these critical regions, Penfield used a weak electrical current to stimulate the brain surface. By monitoring the patient's responses during stimulation in different locations, Penfield could map brain functions over the entire exposed cortex.

Section 7-1 describes brain stimulation techniques used in neuroscience research.

Typically, two neurosurgeons perform the operation after local anesthesia is applied to the patient's skin, skull, and dura mater, as a neurologist analyzes the electroencephalogram (EEG) in an adjacent room. Patients, who are awake throughout the surgery, are asked to contribute during the procedure, and the effects of brain stimulation in specific regions can be determined in detail and mapped. Penfield (shown operating in **Figure 10-19**A) placed tiny numbered tickets on different parts of the brain's surface where the patient noted that stimulation had produced some noticeable sensation or effect, and he eventually produced the cortical map shown in Figure 10-19B.

When Penfield stimulated the auditory cortex, patients often reported hearing such sounds as a ringing that sounded like a doorbell, a buzzing noise, or a sound like birds chirping. This result is consistent with later single-cell recordings from the auditory cortex in nonhuman primates. Findings in these later studies showed that the auditory cortex participates in pattern recognition.

Penfield also found that stimulation in area A1 seemed to produce simple tones — ringing sounds, and so forth — whereas stimulation in the adjacent auditory cortex (Wernicke's area) was more apt to cause some interpretation of a sound — ascription of a buzzing sound to a familiar source such as a cricket, for instance. There was no difference in the effects of stimulation of the left or right auditory cortex, and the patients heard no words when the brain was stimulated.

Sometimes, however, stimulation of the auditory cortex produced effects other than sound perceptions. Stimulation of one area, for example, might cause a patient to

**(A)**

**(B)**

Central sulcus

Lateral fissure

**FIGURE 10-19 Mapping Cortical Functions (A)** Neurosurgery for eligible patients with epilepsy who failed to respond to antiseizure medications. The patient is fully conscious, lying on his right side, and kept comfortable with local anesthesia. Wilder Penfield stimulates discrete cortical areas in the patient's exposed left hemisphere. In the background, a neurologist monitors an EEG recorded from each stimulated area to help identify the epileptogenic focus. The anesthetist (seated) observes the patient's responses to the cortical stimulation. **(B)** A drawing overlies a photograph of the patient's exposed brain. The numbered tickets identify points Penfield stimulated to map the cortex in this patient's brain. At points 26, 27, and 28, a stimulating electrode disrupted speech. Point 26 presumably is in Broca's area, 27 is the motor cortex facial control area, and 28 is in Wernicke's area.

experience a complete absence of sound, whereas stimulation of another area might produce a distortion of sounds actually being heard. As one patient exclaimed after a certain region had been stimulated, "Everything you said was mixed up!"

Penfield was most interested in the effects of brain stimulation not on simple sound wave processing, but on language. He and later researchers used electrical stimulation to identify four important cortical regions that underlie speech production and comprehension. The two classic regions—Broca's area and Wernicke's area—are left-hemisphere regions. Located on both sides of the brain are the other two major language-use regions: the dorsal area of the frontal lobes and the areas of the motor and somatosensory cortex that control facial, tongue, and throat muscles and sensations. Although the effects on speech vary depending on the region, stimulating any one region disrupts speech in some way.

Clearly, much of the left hemisphere takes part in audition. **Figure 10-20** shows the areas that Penfield found engaged in some way in processing language. In fact, Penfield mapped cortical language areas in two ways, first by disrupting speech and then by eliciting speech. Not surprisingly, damage to any speech area produces some form of aphasia.

**Disrupting Speech** Penfield expected that electrical current might disrupt ongoing speech by effectively short-circuiting the brain. To test his hypothesis, he stimulated different cortical regions while the patient was speaking. In fact, the speech disruptions took several forms, including slurring, word confusion, and difficulty finding the right word.

Electrical stimulation of the **supplementary speech area** on the dorsal surface of the frontal lobe (shown in Figure 10-20) can even stop ongoing speech completely, a reaction that Penfield called *speech arrest*. Stimulation of other cortical regions far removed from the temporal and frontal speech areas has no effect on ongoing speech, with the exception of the motor cortex regions (shown in Figure 10-20) that control facial movements. This exception makes sense because talking requires movement of the facial, tongue, and throat muscles.

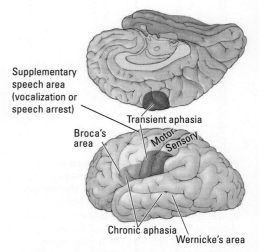

Supplementary speech area (vocalization or speech arrest)

Transient aphasia

Broca's area

Motor

Sensory

Chronic aphasia

Wernicke's area

**FIGURE 10-20 Speech Interference** Regions where electrical stimulation has been shown to affect speech. Damage to areas around Broca's and Wernicke's areas is proposed to produce chronic aphasia, whereas damage to sensory and motor regions is proposed to produce transient (temporary) aphasia. Damage outside these areas does not produce aphasia.

**supplementary speech area** Speech production region on the left frontal lobe dorsal surface.

**Eliciting Speech** The second way Penfield mapped language areas was to stimulate the cortex when a patient was not speaking. Here, the goal was to see if stimulation caused the person to utter a speech sound. Penfield did not expect to trigger coherent speech; cortical electrical stimulation is not physiological, so he anticipated that it probably would not produce actual words or word combinations. His expectation was borne out, likely because the stimulation applied was too short in duration and excited too large of an area.

Stimulation of regions on both sides of the brain—for example, the supplementary speech areas—produces a sustained vowel cry, such as *Oooh* or *Eee*. Stimulation of the facial areas in the motor and somatosensory cortices produces some vocalization related to mouth and tongue movements. Stimulation outside these speech-related zones produces no such effects.

## Auditory Cortex Mapped by Positron Emission Tomography

Section 7-4 details the procedure used to obtain a PET scan.

To study the metabolic activity of brain cells engaged in tasks such as processing language, researchers use positron emission tomography (PET), a brain-imaging technique that detects changes in brain blood flow. Robert Zatorre and his colleagues (1992, 1994) hypothesized that simple auditory stimulation, such as bursts of noise, are analyzed by area A1, whereas more complex auditory stimulation, such as speech syllables, are analyzed in adjacent secondary auditory areas.

Zatorre's research team also hypothesized that performing a discrimination task for speech sounds would selectively activate left-hemisphere regions. Indeed, this selective activation is exactly what they found. **Figure 10-21**A shows increased activity in the primary auditory cortex in response to bursts of noise, whereas secondary auditory areas are activated by speech syllables (Figure 10-21B and C).

Both types of stimuli produced responses in both hemispheres but with greater activation of the left hemisphere being noted for the speech syllables. These results imply that area A1 analyzes all incoming auditory signals, speech and nonspeech, whereas the secondary auditory areas are responsible for some higher-order signal processing required for analyzing language sound patterns.

As Figure 10-21C shows, the speech sound discrimination task yielded an intriguing additional result: Broca's area in the left hemisphere was also activated. The involvement of this frontal lobe region during auditory analysis may seem surprising. In Wernicke's model, Broca's area is considered the storage area for the motor programs needed to produce words. It is not usually a region thought of as a site of speech sound discrimination.

A possible explanation is that to determine that the *g* in *bag* and the *g* in *pig* are the same speech sound, the auditory stimulus must be related to how the sound is actually articulated. That is, speech sound perception requires a match with the motor behaviors associated with making the sound.

This role for Broca's area in speech analysis is confirmed further when investigators ask people to determine whether a stimulus is a word or a nonword (e.g., *tid* versus *tin* or *gan* versus *tan*). In this type of study, information about how the words are articulated is irrelevant, and Broca's area need not be recruited. Imaging reveals that, in fact, Broca's area is not activated during this task.

**FIGURE 10-21 Cortical Activation in Language-Related Tasks (A)** Passively listening to noise bursts activates the primary auditory cortex. **(B)** Listening to words activates the posterior speech zone, including Wernicke's area. **(C)** Making a phonetic discrimination activates the frontal region, including Broca's area.

**(A) Listening to bursts of noise**

Area A1

**(B) Listening to words**

Wernicke's area

**(C) Discriminating speech sounds**

Broca's area

# Processing Music

Although Penfield did not study the effect of brain stimulation on musical analysis, many researchers study musical processing in brain-damaged patients. Collectively, the results of these studies confirm that musical processing is largely a right-hemisphere specialization, just as language processing is largely a left-hemisphere one.

## Localizing Music in the Brain

A famous patient, the composer Maurice Ravel (1875–1937), provides an excellent example of right-hemisphere predominance for music processing. *Boléro* is perhaps Ravel's best-known work. At the peak of his career, Ravel developed aphasia as a result of a previously undiagnosed degenerative brain disorder exacerbated by a severe blow to the head, followed a few months later by a left-hemisphere stroke. Yet many of his musical skills remained intact after his stroke because they were localized to the right hemisphere. Ravel could still recognize melodies, pick up tiny mistakes in music he heard, and even judge the tuning of pianos. His music perception was largely intact.

Skills that had to do with producing music, however, were among those destroyed. Ravel could no longer recognize written music, play the piano, or compose. This dissociation of music perception and music production may parallel the dissociation of speech comprehension and speech production in language. Apparently, the left hemisphere plays at least some role in certain aspects of music processing, especially those that have to do with making music.

To find out more about how the brain carries out the perceptual side of music processing, Zatorre and his colleagues (1994) conducted PET studies. When participants listened to bursts of noise, Heschl's gyrus became activated (**Figure 10-22**A); in contrast, perception of melody triggered major activation in the right-hemisphere auditory cortex lying in front of Heschl's gyrus (Figure 10-22B), as well as minor activation in the same left-hemisphere region (not shown).

In another test, participants listened to the same melodies. The investigators asked them to indicate whether the pitch of the second note was higher or lower than that of the first note. During this task, which requires short-term memory of what was just heard, blood flow in the right frontal lobe increased (Figure 10-22C). As with language, then, the frontal lobe plays a role in auditory analysis when short-term memory is required. People with enhanced or impaired musical abilities show differences in frontal lobe organization, as described in Research Focus 10-6: The Brain's Music System.

As noted earlier, the capacity for language is innate. Sandra Trehub and her colleagues (1999) showed that music may be innate as well, as we hypothesized at the beginning of the chapter. Trehub found that infants show learning preferences for musical scales versus random notes. Like adults, children are sensitive to musical errors, presumably because they are biased for perceiving regularity in rhythms. Thus, it appears that the brain is prepared at birth for hearing both music and language, and presumably it selectively attends to these auditory signals.

In addition to its impact on his musical abilities, Ravel's left-hemisphere dysfunction affected his speech and writing, as is typical of damage to this hemisphere. Neurologist Théophile Alajouanine, who specialized in aphasia, treated Ravel and wrote a famous case study tracking the development of his condition.

The brain may be tuned prenatally to the language it will hear at birth; see Research Focus 7-1.

**FIGURE 10-22 Cortical Activation in Music-Related Tasks (A)** Passively listening to bursts of noise activates Heschl's gyrus. **(B)** Listening to a melody activates the secondary auditory cortex. **(C)** Making relative pitch judgments about two notes in each melody activates a right frontal lobe area.

**(A) Listening to bursts of noise**

Heschl's gyrus

**(B) Listening to melodies**

A2

**(C) Comparing pitches**

Frontal lobe

## The Brain's Music System

Nonmusicians often enjoy music and have musical ability. Musicians show an enormous range of ability: some have perfect pitch and some do not, for example. Approximately 4% of the population, however, is tone deaf. Their difficulties—characterized as **amusia**, an inability to distinguish between musical notes—are lifelong.

Robert Zatorre and his colleagues (Bermudez et al., 2009; Hyde et al., 2007) used magnetic resonance imaging (MRI) to look at differences among the brains of musicians, nonmusicians, and amusics. MRIs of the left and right hemispheres show that the cortical thickness is greater in dorsolateral frontal and superior temporal regions in musicians than in nonmusicians. Curiously, musicians with perfect pitch have a thinner cortex in the posterior part of the dorsolateral frontal lobe. Thinner appears to be better for some music skills.

Compared to nonmusicians, then, musicians with a thicker-than-normal cortex must have enhanced neural networks in the right-hemisphere frontal-temporal system linked to performing musical tasks. A thicker-than-normal cortex, however, can bestow both advantages and impairments.

Analysis of the brains of participants with amusia showed that they had a thicker cortex in the right frontal area and in the right auditory cortex

regions. Some abnormality in neuronal migration during brain development is likely to have led to an excess of neurons in the right frontal-temporal music pathway of the amusics, resulting in their impaired music cognition.

**Right hemisphere**

**Left hemisphere**

Compared to nonmusicians and amusics, musicians' thicker cortex, shown in the green, yellow, and red areas, contributes to performance. Research Focus 14-5 describes how playing music can affect sensorimotor maps in the cortex. Research from Bermudez et al. (2009).

---

**amusia** Tone deafness; inability to distinguish between musical notes.

Individuals with Parkinson disease step to the beat of music to improve their gait length and walking speed.

Sections 16-1 and 16-3 revisit music therapy.

## Music as Therapy

The power of music to engage the brain has led to its use as a therapeutic tool for individuals with brain dysfunctions. The best evidence of its effectiveness has been obtained in studies of motor disorders such as stroke and Parkinson disease (Pereira et al., 2019). Listening to rhythm activates the motor and premotor cortex and can improve gait and arm training in individuals who experience a stroke. Musical experience reportedly also enhances the ability to discriminate speech sounds and to distinguish speech from background noise in persons with aphasia.

Music therapy also appears to be a useful complement to more traditional therapies, especially when the person has problems with mood, such as in depression or brain injury. This may prove important in the treatment of stroke and traumatic brain injury, as depression is a common complication in recovery from these conditions. Music therapy also has positive effects following major surgery, in both adults and children, by reducing both their pain perception and the amount of pain medication they use (Sunitha Suresh et al., 2015). With all these applications, perhaps researchers will decide to use noninvasive imaging to determine which brain areas music therapy recruits.

## 10-4 Review

Before you continue, check your understanding. Answers to Self-Test appear at the back of the book.

1. The human auditory system has complementary specialization for the perception of sounds: left for _____ and right for _____.

2. The three frontal lobe regions that participate in producing language are _____, _____, and _____.

3. _____ area identifies speech syllables and words and stores their representations in that location.

4. _____ area matches speech sounds to the motor programs necessary to articulate them.

5. At one end of the spectrum for musical ability are people with _____, and at the other end are people with _____.

6. What evidence supports the idea that language is innate?

# Auditory Communication in Nonhuman Species

**Learning Objective**
- Explain the significance of birdsong and whale songs in our understanding of the biological and evolutionary basis for auditory processing in humans.

Sound has survival value. You will appreciate this if you've ever narrowly escaped becoming an accident statistic when crossing a busy intersection on foot while listening to music or looking at your phone. Audition is as important a sense to many other animals as vision is to humans. In addition, humans and many other animals communicate with members of their species by using sound.

Here, we consider just two types of auditory communication in nonhumans: birdsong and whale songs. Each provides a model for understanding different aspects of brain–behavior relations in which the auditory system plays a role.

## Birdsong

About half of the nearly 8500 living bird species are considered songbirds. Birdsong has many functions, including attracting mates (usually employed by males), demarcating territories, and announcing location or even just presence.

### Parallels Between Birdsong and Language

**Figure 10-23** shows sound wave spectrograms for the songs of male white-crowned sparrows that live in three localities near San Francisco. These songs differ markedly from region to region, much as dialects of the same human language vary. The differences stem from the fact that song development in young birds is influenced not just by genes but also by early experience and learning. Young birds that have good tutors can acquire more elaborate songs than can other members of their species (Bertram et al., 2020).

These gene–experience interactions are the result of epigenetic mechanisms. For example, brain areas that control singing in adult song sparrows show altered gene expression in spring as the breeding—and singing—season begins (Thompson et al., 2012).

Birdsong and human language have broad similarities beyond regional variation. Both appear to be innate, yet are sculpted by experience. Humans seem to have a basic template for language that is programmed into the brain, and experience adds a variety of specific structural forms to this template. If a young bird is not exposed to song until it is a juvenile and then listens to recordings of birdsongs of various species, the young bird shows a general preference for its own species' song. This preference must mean that each bird has a species-specific song template in the brain. As with human language, experience modifies the details of this birdsong template.

Another broad similarity between birdsong and human language is the great diversity. Among birds, diversity is apparent in the sheer number of songs that some species possess. Though species such as the white-crowned sparrow have but a single song, others, like the marsh wren, can have as many as 150.

White-crowned sparrow

**FIGURE 10-23 Birdsong Dialects** The songs of male white-crowned sparrows recorded in three locales around San Francisco Bay are similar, but sound wave spectrograms reveal that the dialects differ. Like humans, birds acquire regional dialects. Information from Marler (1991).

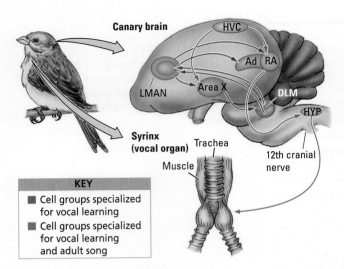

**FIGURE 10-24 Avian Neuroanatomy** This lateral view of the canary brain shows several left-hemisphere nuclei that control song learning. Two that are necessary both for adult singing and for learning the song are the higher vocal control center (HVC) and the nucleus robustus archistriatalis (RA). Other regions necessary for learning the song during development but not required for adult singing include the dorsal archistriatum (Ad), the lateral magnocellular nucleus of the anterior neostriatum (LMAN), area X of the avian striatum, and the medial dorsolateral nucleus of the thalamus (DLM).

Studies of sex differences in behavior and structural anatomy in canaries (top) and zebra finches (bottom) have been essential to our understanding of the neurological basis of song learning and production. Males and females of both species are shown here.

The number of syllables in birdsong also varies greatly, ranging from 30 for the canary to approximately 2000 for the brown thrasher. Similarly, modern human languages vary significantly in the type and number of elements they employ. The number of meaningful patterns in speech sounds in human languages ranges from about 15 for some Polynesian languages to about 100 for some dialects spoken in the Caucasus Mountains. English has 24 such patterns.

A final broad similarity between birdsong and human language lies in how they develop. In many bird species, song development is heavily influenced by experience during a critical period, just as language development is in humans. Birds also go through stages in song development, just as humans go through stages in language development. Hatchlings make noises that attract their parents' attention, usually for feeding, and human babies emit cries to signal hunger, among other things. (For more on critical periods, see Section 8-4.)

The fledgling begins to make noises that Charles Darwin compared to the prespeech babbling of human infants. These noises, called *subsong*, vary in structure, are low in volume, and are often produced as the bird appears to doze. Presumably, subsong, like human babbling, is practice for the later development of adult communication after the bird has left the nest.

As a young bird matures, it starts to produce sound wave patterns that contain recognizable bits of the adult song. Finally, the adult song emerges. In most species, the adult song remains remarkably stable, although a few species, such as canaries, can develop a new song every year to replace the previous year's song.

## Neurobiology of Birdsong

The neurobiology of birdsong is a topic of intense research, partly because it provides an excellent model of brain changes that accompany learning and partly because it offers insight into how sex hormones influence behavior. In the 1970s, Fernando Nottebohm and his colleagues first identified the major structures controlling birdsong, illustrated in **Figure 10-24** (Nottebohm & Arnold, 1976). The largest structures are the higher vocal control center (HVC) and the nucleus *robustus archistriatalis* (RA). The axons of the HVC connect to the RA, which in turn sends axons to the twelfth cranial nerve. This nerve controls the muscles of the *syrinx*, the structure that actually produces the song.

The HVC and RA have several important characteristics, including some that are similar to auditory functions in humans:

- The structures are asymmetrical in some bird species, with those in the left hemisphere being larger than those in the right hemisphere. In many cases, this asymmetry is similar to the lateralized control of language in humans: if the left-hemisphere pathways are damaged, the bird stops singing, but similar injury in the right hemisphere has no effect on song.

- Birdsong structures are sexually dimorphic: they are much larger in males than in females. In male canaries, the structures are five times as large as in the female. This sex difference is due to the hormone testosterone in males. Injection of testosterone into female birds causes the song-controlling nuclei to increase in size.

- The size of the birdsong-controlling nuclei is related to singing skill. Unusually talented singers among male canaries tend to have larger HVCs and RAs than do less gifted singers.

- The HVC and RA contain cells that produce birdsong as well as cells responsive to hearing song, especially the song of a bird's own species.

The same structures therefore play a role in both song production and song perception. This avian neural anatomy is comparable to the overlapping roles of Broca's and Wernicke's areas in language perception and production in humans.

# Whale Songs

Analog radio stations transmit their signals in one of two forms: amplitude modulation (AM) or frequency modulation (FM). Both forms transmit information as variations in electromagnetic waves, but AM works by varying the amplitude (intensity) of the signal, whereas FM works by varying the frequency (pitch). Each system has pros and cons. AM, which was first successfully carried out in the mid-1870s, is cheaper and can be transmitted over longer distances. FM, developed in the 1930s, is less prone to interference than AM, but is impacted by physical barriers, such as mountains and buildings.

Variations in amplitude and frequency are not just the tools of radio broadcast. Humans use them in normal speech, as do other vocalizing animals. Cetaceans (whales, dolphins, and porpoises) have also evolved to use a variety of AM and FM sounds for several different communication purposes.

Living in the oceans presents certain challenges. For instance, vision and smell are limited—suspended particulates scatter light and odorous molecules diffuse more slowly than they would in air. But water also presents an advantage: sound travels more than four times faster in water than in air.

The humpbacked whale's songs are composed of a set of predictable and regular sounds that bear striking similarities to human musical traditions. They have been described as being probably the most complex songs in the animal kingdom. Whale songs may aid in mate selection, social bonding, navigation, and individual identification. Researchers wonder if whales sometimes sing purely for aesthetic enjoyment.

Whale songs follow a distinct hierarchical structure, like a set of nested matryoshka dolls. Base units are composed of single uninterrupted emissions that last for a few seconds and contain frequency or amplitude modulation. Frequencies vary from 20 hertz to 24 kilohertz, and a spectrogram representation reveals the pulsed nature of the FM sounds, as seen in **Figure 10-25**. A collection of base units makes up a phrase, and when a phrase is repeated over and over, it becomes a theme. A set of themes constitutes a song, and a song can last up to half an hour. This length of song is impressive and is likely related to cetaceans' extraordinary ability to remember long strings of information—strings about 10 times longer than the average human can remember.

**FIGURE 10-25 Spectrogram Representation of Humpback Whale Song** This spectrogram (a representation of a spectrum of sound) shows the frequency (*top*) and amplitude (*bottom*) of a humpback whale's (pictured) song. Both the frequency and amplitude indicate the pulsed nature of the song, as phrases are repeated over and over.

Whales sharing an area that can be as large as an entire ocean basin sing virtually the same song. The song itself constantly changes over time, and it appears that old combinations are not reused. Whale songs are no longer being transmitted as far as they once were, due to the increase in ambient noise pollution that humans are creating with large-scale ocean shipping; this interference is fracturing the whale communities that share the same song.

## 10-5 Review

Before you continue, check your understanding. Answers to Self-Test appear at the back of the book.

1. Song development in young birds is influenced both by genes and by early experience and learning, interactions indicative of _____ mechanisms.

2. In many bird species, the control of song in the brain is lateralized to the _____ hemisphere.

3. A(n) _____ representation can display the pulsed nature of whale songs.

4. What does the presence of dialects in birdsong in the same species demonstrate?

5. What does the suggestion that whales sing in part for enjoyment say about our own relationship to and appreciate for music, as demonstrated by our paleolithic ancestors and as explored throughout this chapter?

# Summary

Although we often take language and music for granted, both play central roles in our mental lives and in our social lives. Language and music provide ways to communicate with other people—and with ourselves. They facilitate social identification, parenting, and cultural transmission.

## 10-1 Sound Waves: Stimulus for Audition
The stimulus for the auditory system is the mechanical energy of sound waves that results from changes in air pressure. The ear transduces two fundamental physical qualities of sound wave energy: frequency (repetition rate) and amplitude (size), which combine to produce complexity. Perceptually, neural networks translate these energies into the pitch, loudness, and timbre of the sounds we hear.

## 10-2 Functional Anatomy of the Auditory System
Beginning in the ear, mechanical and electrochemical systems combine to transform sound waves into auditory perceptions—what we hear. Changes in air pressure are conveyed in a mechanical chain reaction from the eardrum to the bones of the middle ear to the oval window of the cochlea and the cochlear fluid that lies behind it in the inner ear. Movements of the cochlear fluid produce movements in specific regions of the basilar membrane, leading to changes in the electrochemical activity of the auditory receptors, the inner hair cells on the basilar membrane that send neural impulses through the auditory nerve into the brain.

## 10-3 Neural Activity and Hearing
The basilar membrane has a tonotopic organization. High-frequency sound waves maximally stimulate hair cells at the base, whereas low-frequency sound waves maximally stimulate hair cells at the apex, enabling cochlear neurons to code sound frequencies.

Tonotopic organization analyzes sound waves at all levels of the auditory system, which also detects both amplitude and location. The firing rate of cochlear neurons codes for sound amplitude, with louder sounds producing higher firing rates than softer sounds do. Location is detected by structures in the brainstem that compute differences in the arrival times and loudness of a sound in the two ears.

Cochlear hair cells synapse with bipolar neurons that form the cochlear nerve, which in turn forms part of the eighth cranial nerve. The cochlear nerve transmits auditory information to three structures in the hindbrain: the cochlear nucleus, the superior olive, and the trapezoid body. Cells in these areas are sensitive to differences in both sound wave intensity and arrival times at the two ears. In this way, they enable the brain to locate a sound. Cochlear implants transduce sound from the environment into electrical impulses that directly stimulate the cochlear nerve.

The auditory pathway continues from the hindbrain areas to the inferior colliculus of the midbrain, then to the medial geniculate nucleus in the thalamus, and finally to the auditory cortex. As is the case for vision, both dorsal and ventral pathways exist in the auditory cortex: one for pattern recognition and the other for controlling movements in auditory space. Cells in the cortex are responsive to specific sound categories, such as species-specific communication.

## 10-4 Anatomy of Language and Music
Despite differences in the patterns and structures of speech sounds, all human languages have the same basic foundation: syntax and grammar. This commonality implies that humans must have an innate template for creating language. Auditory areas of the left-hemisphere cortex play a special role in analyzing language-related information, whereas those in the right hemisphere play a special role in analyzing music-related information. The right temporal lobe also analyzes prosody, the melodic qualities of speech.

As one of several left-hemisphere language-processing areas, Wernicke's area identifies speech syllables and words and so is critically engaged in speech comprehension. Broca's area matches speech sound patterns to the motor behaviors necessary to make them; thus, it plays a major role in speech production. Broca's area also discriminates between closely related speech sounds. Aphasia is an inability to speak (Broca's aphasia) or to comprehend language (Wernicke's aphasia), despite the presence of normal cognition and intact vocal mechanisms.

Auditory analysis of music draws more on right-hemisphere activity than on the left-hemisphere activity. In addition, music production is not localized to the right hemisphere; it recruits the left hemisphere as well. Music perception engages both the right temporal and frontal regions.

The power of music to engage both right- and left-hemisphere activity makes it a powerful tool for engaging an injured or dysfunctioning brain. Music therapy is playing an increasingly important role in treatment of these conditions.

## 10-5 Auditory Communication in Nonhuman Species

Nonhuman animals have evolved specialized auditory structures and behaviors. Regions of songbirds' brains are specialized for producing and comprehending song. In many species, these regions are lateralized to the left hemisphere, analogous to how language areas are lateralized to the left hemisphere in most humans. Similarities in the development of song in birds and the development of music and language in humans, as well as similarities in the neural mechanisms underlying both the production and the perception of birdsong and language, are striking. Whales sing by modulating both amplitude and frequency, much as human do in vocal communication.

# Key Terms

amplitude, p. 328

amusia, p. 352

aphasia, p. 347

basilar membrane, p. 335

Broca's area, p. 347

cochlea, p. 335

cochlear implant, p. 341

decibel (dB), p. 329

echolocation, p. 340

frequency, p. 328

hair cell, p. 335

hertz (Hz), p. 328

insula, p. 340

lateralization, p. 338

medial geniculate nucleus, p. 338

ossicle, p. 335

otoacoustic emissions, p. 337

primary auditory cortex (area A1), p. 338

prosody, p. 333

sound wave, p. 327

supplementary speech area, p. 349

tonotopic representation, p. 340

Wernicke's area, p. 338

# Selected Resources from  Achieve

**Neuroscience in Action:** Auditory System: How the Ears Process Sound

**Concept Practice**

Language Areas in the Brain

**Videos**

Hearing: From Vibration to Sound

How Do We Hear?

Sound and Sound Localization

Sound and the Cochlea

**LearningCurve**

**Practice Quiz**

Tim Gainey/Alamy Stock Photo

## 11 How Does the Nervous System Respond to Stimulation and Produce Movement?

## ⊙ RESEARCH FOCUS 11-1

# Neuroprosthetics

Most of us seamlessly control the approximately 650 muscles that move our bodies. But if the motor neurons that control those muscles no longer connect to them, as happens in amyotrophic lateral sclerosis (ALS, also called Lou Gehrig disease), then movement becomes impossible, and eventually even breathing may cease.

This happened to Scott Mackler, a neuroscientist and marathon runner, who developed ALS in his late 30s. Dependent on a respirator to breathe, he developed *locked-in syndrome*: Mackler lost virtually all ability to communicate.

ALS has no cure, and death often occurs within 5 years of diagnosis. Yet Mackler beat the odds: he survived for 17 years before he died in 2013, at age 55. Mackler was a pioneer in using *brain–computer interface* (*BCI*) technology, which employs the brain's electrical signals to direct computer-controlled devices. Mackler learned to translate his mental activity into movement. He returned to work at the University of Pennsylvania, stayed in touch with family and friends, and even gave an interview to CBS's *60 Minutes* in 2008.

**Neuroprosthetics** is a field that focuses on development of three types of computer-assisted devices to replace lost biological function. BCI uses brain signals to instruct a computer, *computer–brain interface* (*CBI*) employs electrical signals from a computer to instruct the brain, and *brain–computer–brain interface* (*BCBIs*) combines the BCI and CBI approaches, enabling the brain to command robotic devices that provide sensory feedback to the brain (Kawala-Sterniuk et al., 2021).

BCIs can be made that use any signal from the body, including muscle activity, signals in peripheral nerves, and any signal collected from the brain including EEG, blood flow, and single-cell activity. BCIs were initially slow—for example, BCI-aided speech originally required words to be spelled out letter-by-letter. But through advances in signal processing and the use of artificial intelligence (AI), speech can now be produced word-by-word at normal speeds; future devices may be able to process more complex instructions.

Brain–computer–brain interfaces such as the robotic limb shown here enable the brain to command robotic devices that provide sensory feedback.

Despite these advances, BCBI devices still have drawbacks: body/brain signals have relatively low resolution, the devices usually require daily recalibration, and the process of attaching a device to the body may require assistance for some individuals. Nevertheless, BCBIs have enabled a wide range of motion and control that would not have been possible just a few years ago. For example, BCBIs can command robotic hands to grasp objects while tactile receptors on the robot deliver touch and other sensory information to the user. BCBIs can also control exoskeletal devices that reach and walk and return touch, body position, and balance information to guide movement. In addition, BCBIs are being developed to command almost any daily function, including digital game playing.

---

Movement is a defining feature of animals, and this chapter explores how the nervous system produces movement. The somatosensory system, which includes fine touch, pressure, pain, temperature, and balance, is closely related to movement, which is why we describe both movement and body senses in this chapter.

At the level of the spinal cord, somatosensory information contributes to motor reflexes. In the brainstem, somatosensation contributes to movement timing and control. In the cerebrum, somatosensation contributes to complex voluntary movements. Indeed, for many functions, the other senses work through the somatosensory system to produce movement. In essence, if the motor system is a vehicle and the somatosensory system is the driver, the other sensory systems act like backseat drivers. A brief summary of the interactions between the motor system and somatosensation is given in The Basics: Relating the Somatosensory and Motor Systems on pages 362–363.

**neuroprosthetics** Field that develops computer-assisted devices to replace lost biological function.

Section 1-1 offers a simple definition of behavior: any movement in a living organism.

In this chapter, we begin with movement and end with sensation. Section 4-4 begins with sensation and ends with movement.

### Learning Objectives

- Summarize the steps performed by the different cortical regions when initiating a motor sequence.
- Explain the role of the brainstem in facilitating species-typical behavior.
- Explain the spinal cord's role in executing movement, and describe the conditions that can result from injury to the spinal cord.

## 11-1

# Hierarchical and Parallel Movement Control

Getting from decisions to movements requires the participation of most of our nervous system. **Figure 11-1** illustrates the stepwise sequence your central nervous system (CNS) performs in the seemingly simple act of directing your hand to pick up a cup.

**FIGURE 11-1 Sequentially Organized Movement**

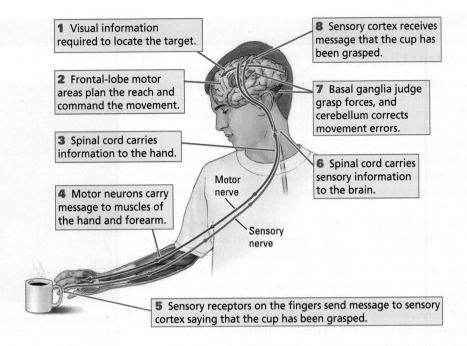

**1** Visual information required to locate the target.

**2** Frontal-lobe motor areas plan the reach and command the movement.

**3** Spinal cord carries information to the hand.

**4** Motor neurons carry message to muscles of the hand and forearm.

**8** Sensory cortex receives message that the cup has been grasped.

**7** Basal ganglia judge grasp forces, and cerebellum corrects movement errors.

**6** Spinal cord carries sensory information to the brain.

Motor nerve

Sensory nerve

**5** Sensory receptors on the fingers send message to sensory cortex saying that the cup has been grasped.

The nature of consciousness is the subject of Section 15-7.

**Principle 9:** The nervous system produces movement in a perceptual world the brain constructs.

For now, remember that the entire sensorimotor system is organized hierarchically. When you reach the chapter's end, review Figure 11-1 to reinforce what you have learned.

Your decision to pick up the cup is conscious. When you visually inspect the cup to determine what part to grasp, this visual information directs the somatosensory regions to the motor regions to initiate the movement, and these regions instruct to the spinal cord segments to move the arm and hand muscles to grasp the cup. Reaching is done relatively automatically, without much conscious monitoring.

As you grasp the cup's handle, the nervous system engages in further relatively automatic functions. Information transmitted from sensory receptors in your fingers aids in adjusting your grip; information is then sent back through the spinal cord and from there to a number of brain regions, signaling that the cup is secured. These brain regions include the subcortical basal ganglia, which determines the appropriate force for grasping the cup handle; the cerebellum, which regulates the movement's timing and accuracy; and, of course, the cortex, which makes the conscious decision about whether to drink from the cup. The brain's role in both the conscious decisions and the relatively unconscious execution of those decisions are the key principles incorporated into neuroprosthetic devices, as described in Research Focus 11-1.

The important feature in the controlled process of picking up of a cup is the hierarchical arrangement of the brain regions that control the movement. Forebrain areas involved in the decision to pick up the cup must act through lower functional areas, the brainstem and spinal cord. There must also be parallel organization within these brain areas because you can do other things, such as speaking or singing, at the same time that you pick up a cup. In addition, these brain regions must function independently. Once you have made the decision to pick up the cup, most of the movement happens without conscious control. Unless you have studied motor control, you can't actually describe the sequence of actions or produce an accurate pantomime of the movements needed to actually grasp a cup despite having performed the action thousands of times.

The hierarchical control of movement was illustrated in an experiment by Liu and colleagues (2020). These researchers imaged the brains of control participants who performed actions using their hands and experimental participants born without upper limbs (so they had no experience of using hands) who performed the same actions using their toes—a demonstration of *motor equivalence* (the ability to use different body parts to accomplish the same task). Results showed similar activity in the same region of the motor cortex of both groups, suggesting cortical organization based on abstract action as well as activity in the portions of the brain needed to carry out the specific action. This study demonstrates that the mental representation of an action, such as signing your name, does not exist in a single point of your brain, but instead involves a circuit that includes the cortex, basal ganglia, and cerebellum, which can then execute the action through a hand or toe as the situation requires.

# Forebrain: Organizing Movement

Complex movements consist of many acts. Consider playing basketball. At every moment, players must make decisions and perform actions. *Dribble, pass,* and *shoot* are different movement categories, and each can be performed in many ways. Skilled players choose among these categories effortlessly and blend them together seemingly without thought. Indeed, someone who is seemingly unable to miss a shot during a game is often described as being "unconscious."

An early explanation for the control of such complex movements centered on feedback: after we act, we wait for feedback about how well the action has succeeded, and only then make the next movement. The pioneering neuroscience researcher Karl Lashley (1951), in the article "The Problem of Serial Order in Behavior," found fault with this explanation. Lashley realized that we perform skilled movements too quickly to rely on feedback about one movement before shaping the next. The time required to receive feedback about the first movement combined with the time needed to develop a plan for the subsequent movement and send a corresponding message to muscles is simply too long for effective action. Lashley argued that movements must be performed as **motor sequences**, with the next sequence held in readiness while the ongoing one is under way.

All complex behaviors—for example, speaking, playing the piano, and playing basketball—require selecting and executing movements as sequences. Indeed, most of our motor learning involves mastering sequences of action. As one sequence is being executed, the next sequence is being prepared to follow the first smoothly. The act of speaking illustrates this activity. When people use complex rather than simple word sequences, they are more likely to pause and make *umm* and *ahh* sounds, suggesting that it is taking them more time than usual to organize their speech sequences.

## The Anatomy of Cortical Motor Systems

Each frontal lobe is divided into several regions, including the three illustrated in **Figure 11-2**. These regions are further subdivided into many more regions. For now, we will just consider (from front to back in the frontal lobe) the prefrontal cortex, premotor cortex, and primary motor cortex. An early understanding of the relationships among these regions posited that the prefrontal cortex sends instructions to the premotor cortex, which in turn instructs the motor cortex. As we will learn later in this chapter, each of these regions can produce behavior on its own and each can receive instructions from the posterior cortex, especially the parietal cortex.

**Prefrontal Cortex** The prefrontal cortex (PFC) plans our behavior, a role also described as *executive function*. Deciding to get up at a certain hour to arrive at work on time, choosing to stop at the library to return a book, and even identifying whether a behavior is right or wrong and whether it should be performed at all are examples of complex acts ascribed to PFC functions. The PFC does not specify the precise movements to be made, but simply makes a decision about which goal to select. Humans with PFC injury often break social and legal rules not because they do not know the rules or the consequences of breaking them, but because their decision making is faulty.

**Premotor Cortex** The premotor cortex produces movements that involve the coordination of many body parts, such as walking, jumping, and climbing. If the premotor cortex becomes damaged, movement involving many body parts cannot be accomplished. For

**Principle 3:** The CNS functions on multiple levels and is organized hierarchically and in parallel.

Lashley also experimented for three decades to find the location of memory in the brain. He failed.

**2** Premotor cortex organizes movement sequences.

**3** Motor cortex produces specific movements.

**1** Prefrontal cortex plans movements.

| Prefrontal cortex plans | → | Premotor cortex sequences | → | Motor cortex executes actions |

**FIGURE 11-2 Initiating a Motor Sequence**

Section 15-2 continues the discussion of executive function.

Sections 12-6 and 15-2 explore cognitive deficits caused by frontal lobe injury.

**motor sequence** Movement modules preprogrammed by the brain and produced as a unit.

## ◎ THE BASICS

# Relating the Somatosensory and Motor Systems

The intimate relationship between the motor and somatosensory systems is apparent in their close anatomical relationships. *Afferent* somatosensory information travels from the body inward via the somatic nervous system. Movement information travels out of the central nervous system via a parallel *efferent* motor system.

As diagrammed in the accompanying Information Flow figure, when you step on a tack, the sensory signals transmitted by the SNS from the body through the spinal cord and into the brain are afferent. Efferent signals from the CNS trigger a motor response: you lift your foot.

The spinal cord connects the somatosensory and motor systems throughout the CNS. The Connections Between the Nerves and the Spine figure shows the spinal cord in cross section. In the outer part, which consists of white matter, posterior tracts are sensory and anterior tracts are motor, with some exceptions. The butterfly-shaped inner cord is gray matter composed largely of cell bodies.

SNS nerves entering the spinal cord's posterior side carry information inward from the body's sensory receptors and merge into a posterior root as the fibers enter a spinal cord segment of the CNS. Fibers leaving the spinal cord's anterior side carry information out from the spinal cord

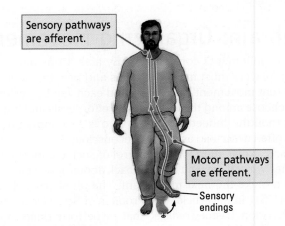

**Information Flow**

to the muscles. They, too, bundle together as the fibers exit the spinal cord, forming an *anterior root*. (Bundles of nerve fibers within the CNS are called tracts; outside the CNS they are called *nerves*. Anterior and

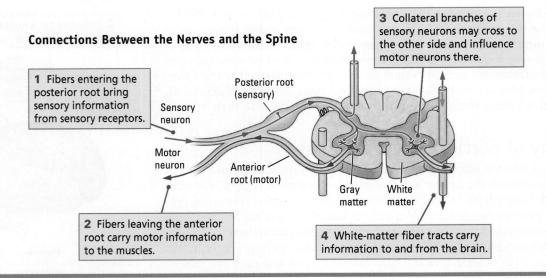

**Connections Between the Nerves and the Spine**

**1** Fibers entering the posterior root bring sensory information from sensory receptors.

**2** Fibers leaving the anterior root carry motor information to the muscles.

**3** Collateral branches of sensory neurons may cross to the other side and influence motor neurons there.

**4** White-matter fiber tracts carry information to and from the brain.

example, the monkey on the right in **Figure 11-3** has a lesion in the dorsal premotor cortex. This monkey has been given the task of extracting a piece of food wedged in a hole in a table (Brinkman, 1984). It simply pushes the food with a finger; the food drops to the floor and is lost. To succeed at the task, the monkey should catch the food by holding a palm beneath the hole as the food is being pushed out. Because of its brain injury, however, the animal is unable to make the two complementary movements together. It can push the food with a finger or extend an open palm, but it cannot coordinate the actions of its two hands, as the healthy monkey on the left can.

**Primary Motor Cortex** The primary motor cortex (area M1) specializes in producing focal skilled movements, such as those involving our arms, hands, and mouth. To understand its role, consider the rich array of movements we can use to grasp objects. For example, we can hold an object in one hand, with two hands, or between a hand and another part of the body.

*posterior* are applied in reference to the human standing body position; the same roots are called *dorsal* and *ventral*, respectively, in quadrupeds).

The spinal cord lies within a series of small bones called *vertebrae*, which are categorized into the five anatomical regions diagrammed in the Spinal Segments and Dermatomes figure. Each spinal segment corresponds to a region of body surface called a *dermatome* (literally, "skin cut"), shown on the right. From top to bottom, the cervical, thoracic, lumbar, sacral, and coccygeal regions are identified by spinal segment number: C5 (cervical segment 5) at the base of the neck, for example, and L2 (lumbar segment 2) in the lower back.

The Layering in the Neocortex diagram plumbs the depths of the primary motor cortex (shown in blue) and the adjacent sensory (red) cortical regions. Viewed through a microscope, the six cortical layers differ in appearance, characteristics, and functions. Layer IV is relatively thick in the sensory cortex but relatively thin in the motor cortex. Layer V is relatively thick in the motor cortex and relatively thin in the sensory cortex. Cortical layer IV is afferent and layer V is efferent, and this makes sense: sensory regions have a large input layer, and motor regions have a large output layer.

**Spinal Segments and Dermatomes**

The motor cortex lies in the frontal lobe just anterior to the brain's central fissure.

The sensory cortex lies posterior to the central fissure and extends into the parietal lobe.

**Layering in the Neocortex**

**FIGURE 11-3 Premotor Control** On a task requiring both hands, the healthy monkey can push the peanut out of a hole with one hand and catch it in the other, but 5 months after receiving a lesion of the premotor cortex, the brain-injured monkey cannot do this.

**(A) Pincer grip**

**(B) Whole-hand grip**

Ian Whishaw

**FIGURE 11-4 Getting a Grip** In a pincer grip **(A)**, an object is held between the thumb and index finger. In a power, or whole-hand, grip **(B)**, the entire hand holds the object. Figure 8-20 illustrates the development of grasping responses in infants, from the whole-hand grip to the pincer grip.

Section 7-4 describes imaging methods that record and measure blood flow in the brain.

Section 1-5 introduces species-typical behavior, noting that evolutionary principles apply *across* species but not to individuals *within* a species.

In using the pincer grip (**Figure 11-4**A), we hold an object between the thumb and index finger. We can also perform many precision grips using the thumb and one or more of our other fingers in opposition. Precision grips not only enable us to pick up small objects easily but also allow us to use the objects with skill. In contrast, when using a whole-hand grip, also called a power grip (Figure 11-4B), we hold an object with all our fingers and with more power but less precision.

People with damage to area M1 have difficulty performing reaching movements and shaping their fingers correctly to perform various hand grasps. They also have difficulty enunciating words and performing many skilled hand, arm, and trunk movements, such as bringing their hand to their mouth to feed themselves.

## Cortical Contributions to Movement

As noted earlier, each frontal lobe region involved in movement can act with some independence, depending on the nature of the task. The primary roles of different regions of the frontal cortex can be illustrated by imaging either blood flow or metabolic activity during behavior. **Figure 11-5** shows the brain regions that were active as the participants in one study performed various tasks (Roland, 1993).

As the participants use a finger to push a lever, increased blood flow occurs in the primary somatosensory and primary motor cortex (Figure 11-5A). As they execute a sequence of finger movements, blood flow also increases in the premotor cortex (Figure 11-5B). And as the participants use a finger to trace their way through a maze, a task that requires coordinated movements in relationship to a goal, blood flow increases in the prefrontal cortex as well (Figure 11-5C). As the study participants performed these tasks, relative blood flow increased most in those regions taking part in the required movements rather than throughout the frontal lobe.

## Brainstem: Species-Typical Movement

Walter Hess (1957) was awarded the 1949 Nobel Prize for his studies that demonstrated *species-typical behaviors*—that is, the characteristic actions displayed by every member of a species, such as the fearful arched back movements of a cat withdrawing from a dog or the predatory crouch of a cat hunting a mouse—can be elicited by brainstem electrical stimulation. Hess developed the technique of fixing electrodes to the brains of cats and other animals by cementing to the skull a wire that formed the electrode. These electrodes could then be attached to stimulating leads in the freely moving animal without causing it much discomfort.

By stimulating the brainstem, Hess elicited most of the movements that the animal might be expected to make. A resting cat could be induced to suddenly leap up with

**(A) Simple movement**

Blood flow increases in hand area of primary somatosensory and primary motor cortex when participants use a finger to push a lever.

Motor cortex | Sensory cortex

**(B) Movement sequence**

Blood flow increases in premotor cortex when participants perform a sequence of movements.

Dorsal premotor cortex

**(C) Complex movement**

When participants use a finger to find a route through a maze, blood flow also increases in prefrontal, temporal, and parietal cortex.

**FIGURE 11-5 Movement Control in the Brain** Research from Roland (1993).

an arched back and erect hair as though frightened, for example. The elicited movements began abruptly when the stimulating current was turned on and ended equally abruptly when it was turned off. An animal performed such species-typical behaviors in a subdued manner when the stimulating current was low, but displayed increased vigor as the stimulating current was turned up.

The actions varied depending on the brainstem site that was stimulated. Stimulating some sites produced head turning; others, walking or running; and still others, displays of aggression or fear. The animal's response to a particular stimulus could be modified accordingly. For instance, when shown a stuffed toy, a cat responded to electrical stimulation of some brainstem sites by stalking it and responded to stimulation of other sites by showing fear and withdrawing. Hess's experiments demonstrate that although decisions about engaging in a behavior may be made in the cortex, the production of the movement also requires the participation of the brainstem.

For brainstem stimulation to produce adaptive species-typical behavior, all regions of the motor system, including the cortex and spinal cord, must be recruited. **Experiment 11-1** shows the effects of brainstem stimulation on a chicken under various conditions (von Holst, 1973). Notice the effect of context—how the stimulated neural site interacts both with the object presented and with the stimulation's duration.

With stimulation at a certain site alone, the chicken displays only restless behavior. When a fist is displayed, the same stimulation elicits slightly threatening behavior. When the display switches from a fist to a stuffed polecat, the chicken responds with vigorous threats. Finally, with continued stimulation in the presence of the polecat, the chicken flees, screeching.

Such experiments show that producing complex patterns of adaptive behavior is an important brainstem function. These adaptive patterns include movements used in eating and drinking and in sexual behavior. Animals can be induced to display survival-related behaviors when certain brainstem areas are stimulated. An animal can even be induced to eat nonfood objects, such as chips of wood, if the part of the brainstem that triggers chewing is stimulated.

As one example, grooming illustrates how the brainstem coordinates complex action patterns (Kalueff et al., 2016). A grooming rat sits back on its haunches, licks its paws, wipes its nose with its paws, wipes its paws across its face, and finally turns to lick the fur on its body. These movements are always performed in the same order, from the face to the shoulders and then toward the rear of the body. The next time you dry off after a shower or swimming, note the grooming sequence you use. Humans' grooming pattern is very similar to the one rats use. In addition to controlling grooming, the brainstem is important for maintaining posture, standing upright, coordinating limb movements, swimming and walking, and making nests.

····▷ **EXPERIMENT 11-1**

Question: What are the effects of brainstem stimulation under different conditions?

**Procedures**

Electrical stimulation alone produces restless behavior.

Electrical stimulation in the presence of a fist produces slight threats.

Electrical stimulation in the presence of a stuffed polecat (a type of weasel) produces vigorous threats.

Continued electrical stimulation in the presence of the stuffed polecat produces flight and screeching.

**Results** — Stimulating electrode in brainstem

*Conclusion:* Stimulation of some brainstem sites produces behavior that depends on context, suggesting that an important function of the brainstem is to activate appropriate species-typical behavior.

Information from von Holst (1973).

**cerebral palsy (CP)** Group of disorders that result from brain damage acquired perinatally (at or near birth).

The effects of brainstem damage on behavior can be seen in **cerebral palsy (CP)**, a disorder primarily of motor function. In individuals with CP, making voluntary movements becomes difficult, yet many aspects of conscious behavior controlled by the cortex may remain intact. CP is often caused by brainstem trauma before or shortly after birth. As described in Clinical Focus 11-2: Cerebral Palsy, trauma leading to cerebral palsy can sometimes happen in early infancy as well.

# Spinal Cord: Executing Movement

The late actor Christopher Reeve, who portrayed Superman in three 1980s films, was thrown from a horse during a riding competition in 1995. Other than head movements and slight movement in his shoulders, Reeve's body was completely paralyzed. He was even unable to breathe without assistance. Each year, more than 17,800 new cases of spinal cord injury occur in the United States (National Spinal Cord Injury Statistics Center, 2020). Nearly 80% of the people affected by such injuries are male, and most of the injuries are the result of vehicular accidents (nearly 39%), falls (32%), and violence (14%). In most cases, the injury is "incomplete," meaning some communication continues to occur from the brain to the body via the spinal cord, including some sensation and movement below the site of the injury, though this movement and sensation are greatly impaired.

## ◎ CLINICAL FOCUS 11-2

### Cerebral Palsy

When he was about 6 months old, E. S. had a cold and infection. Subsequently, he had great difficulty coordinating his movements. As he grew up, his hands and legs were almost useless, and his speech was extremely difficult to understand. E. S. was considered intellectually disabled and spent most of his childhood in a custodial school.

When E. S. was 13 years old, the school bought a computer. One teacher attempted to teach E. S. to use it by pushing the keys with a pencil held in his mouth. Within a few weeks, the teacher realized that E. S. could communicate and complete school assignments on the computer. He eventually received a motorized wheelchair that he could control with finger movements of his right hand.

Assisted by the computer and the wheelchair, E. S. attended college, where he became a student leader. He graduated with a degree in psychology, became a social worker, and now works with children with cerebral palsy.

William Little, an English physician, first noticed in 1853 that difficult or abnormal births could lead to later motor difficulties in children. The condition that Little described was cerebral palsy (also called *Little disease*), a group of disorders that result from brain damage acquired perinatally (at or near birth). Cerebral palsy is a relatively common disorder, whose incidence is estimated to be 1.5 in every 1000 births. Among babies who weigh less than 2.5 kilograms (5.5 pounds) at birth, the incidence is higher—about 10 in 1000.

The most common causes of cerebral palsy are birth injury, especially due to *anoxia* (lack of oxygen), and genetic defects. Anoxia may result from a defect in the placenta, the organ that allows oxygen and nutrients to pass from mother to child in utero, or it may be caused by a tangled umbilical cord that reduces the oxygen supply to the infant during birth. Other causes include infections, hydrocephalus, seizures, and prematurity. All of these causes may produce a defect in the immature brain before, during, or just after birth.

Children with cerebral palsy may appear healthy in the first few months of life, but as their nervous system develops, motor disturbances become noticeable. Commonly seen symptoms include spasticity, an exaggerated contraction of muscles when they are stretched; dyskinesia, involuntary extraneous movements such as tremors and uncontrollable jerky twists (athetoid movements); and rigidity, or resistance to passive movement. The affected person may be confined to a wheelchair.

To examine the relationship between brain development and susceptibility to brain injury, investigators can use an MRI-derived baby connectome that maps a baby's changing brain connections during development. This connectome provides a comprehensive map of the structural connectivity (the physical wiring) of the baby's brain. The baby connectome can reveal developmental abnormalities in brain connections, such as those indicative of cerebral palsy, at very early ages, which in turn expands the window of time for initiating therapeutic strategies (Stewart et al., 2021).

Courtesy of The Medical University of South Carolina

Many people with cerebral palsy have successful professional careers, including pediatrician Dr. John Melville, who operates his wheelchair with finger movements of his right hand.

Reeve's spinal cord was completely severed near its upper end, at the C1–C2 level (see the Spinal Segments and Dermatomes figure in The Basics). This injury rendered him **quadriplegic** (also referred to as *tetraplegic*), without sensation or movement in his arms and legs. Injury at this level of the spinal cord leaves the brain and remaining spinal cord intact and functioning, but the brain and spinal cord are no longer connected. If the cut occurs below the cervical nerves, **paraplegia** results: paralysis and loss of sensation are confined to the legs and lower body.

Spinal cord injury is usually due to trauma that results in severing of the spinal cord plus secondary degenerative processes that increase the size of the lesion. Thereafter, the formation of scar tissue, a cavity, and cysts block communication between the two severed sides. Before recent innovations in medical intervention, a complete cut through the spinal cord would have been fatal, but modern and timely medical treatment has helped many people survive their initial injury.

Far from being only a system for relaying messages between the body and the brain, the spinal cord contains complex motor programs. Indeed, many people with spinal cord injury are able to make stepping movements when their body is supported using handrails or by water in a swimming pool. A person with a spinal cord injury may walk on a conveyor belt if the body is supported. When their leg is moved backward on a conveyor belt, causing the foot to lose support, the limb reflexively lifts off the belt and swings forward underneath the body. As the foot touches the surface of the belt again, tactile receptors initiate the reflex that causes the foot to push against the surface and support the body's weight. In this way, several spinal reflexes work together to facilitate the complex movement of walking. Walking's reflexive organization can even be achieved in a premature or newborn baby: when held upright, the baby will perform stepping movements. One of the goals of prosthetic limb technology is to build these reflexive movements into the limbs so that commands from the brain to move the limb need only be concerned with the intention of the movement.

Among the complex reflexes observed in other vertebrates is the **scratch reflex**, in which an animal reflexively scratches a part of its body in response to a stimulus from the body surface. The complexity of the scratch reflex is revealed in the movement's accuracy. Absent the brain's direction, the tip of a limb (usually a hind limb in a quadruped) can be correctly directed to the irritated body part. Typically, itching is the sensation that elicits scratching; it is likely that the sensory receptors on the skin that produce itches evolved for detecting parasites and other foreign objects. We return to itching sensations in Section 11-4.

In humans and other animals whose spinal cord is severed, spinal reflexes continue to function. As a result, the paralyzed limbs may display spontaneous movements or spasms. The brain can no longer guide the timing of these movements, however. In addition, reflexes related to bladder and bowel control may have to be artificially stimulated by caregivers. One treatment for spinal cord injury involves electrically stimulating the endogenous sensory and motor circuits of the spinal cord through implanted electrodes to aid in bladder and bowel control and to facilitate walking therapy (McHugh et al., 2021).

Restoring function by replacing the connections across the site of injury presents researchers with a conceptually simple but so far intractable problem—and one for which a remarkable number of solutions have been proposed. In particular, *nanotechnology*, the science of making and using molecular-sized tools, holds promise for decreasing the acute effects of spinal injury and restoring function. Nanotechnology works with substances between 1 and 100 nanometers (nm) in size. (A nanometer is one-billionth, or $10^{-9}$, of a meter.)

Nanotubes or nanovesicles can be engineered to transport drugs, RNA, or new stem cells into the area of injury, where they can arrest degenerative changes and help form neural bridges across the injury. Nanotubes that can carry chemicals or conduct electrical impulses can be threaded into the injury through blood vessels, and then into the very small capillaries within the spinal cord. They can also be injected as molecules that self-assemble into scaffolding or tubes when they reach a target area.

Rick Hansen suffered a spinal cord injury in 1973 at the age of 15. In 1985, Hansen wheeled his chair around the world in the Man in Motion Tour to raise money for spinal cord injury research. He subsequently started the Rick Hansen Foundation and contributed to the Blusson Spinal Cord Center in Vancouver, Canada.

Scratch reflex

**quadriplegia** Paralysis of the legs and arms due to spinal cord injury; also referred to as *tetraplegia*.

**paraplegia** Paralysis of the legs due to spinal cord injury.

**scratch reflex** Automatic response in which an animal's hind limb reaches to remove a stimulus from the surface of its body.

Nanomedicinal substances, because of their small size, can interact with spinal cord cells on both sides of an injury (Shahsavani et al., 2021). Nanoscaffolding, when introduced into the injury to form a bridge, can aid the regrowth of axons across the injury. Nanoaxons can be introduced into the region of injury to synapse with neurons on both sides of the injury and to carry messages across the injury. Nanovesicles—small capsules that contain drugs such as nerve growth factors—can be injected into sites of injury to promote cell growth. Although specific applications are still being tested and refined, advances in *nanomedicine* have clearly demonstrated the potential to revolutionize treatment and rehabilitation practices, such as for individuals with spinal cord injury, as well as in other areas of medical and neurological practice, including diagnosis, imaging, and drug delivery. This will be an interesting area to watch in the coming years.

## 11-1 Review

**Before you continue, check your understanding. Answers to Self-Test appear at the back of the book.**

1. The CNS regions and pathways involved in motor control display both a(n) _____ and a(n) _____ arrangement.

2. The frontal cortex consists of three regions, the _____ , _____ , and _____ cortices.

3. The _____ is responsible for species-typical movements, for survival-related actions, and for posture and walking.

4. In addition to serving as a pathway between the brain and the rest of the body, the _____ independently produces reflexive movements.

5. Describe two kinds of impairments related to severing of the spinal cord at different levels.

6. What specific contributions do the forebrain, brainstem, and spinal cord make to movement?

## 11-2

# Motor System Organization

In the previous section, we described some of the contributions of the cortex, brainstem, and spinal cord to movement. In this section, we examine first the organization of the motor cortex, and then the descending pathways from the motor cortex to the brainstem and spinal cord, and finally the motor neurons that in turn connect with the body's muscles.

## Motor Cortex

In 1870, two physicians, Gustav Fritsch and Eduard Hitzig, discovered that they could electrically stimulate the neocortex of an anesthetized dog to produce movements of the mouth, limbs, and paws on the opposite side of the dog's body. Their work provided the first direct evidence that the neocortex controls movement. Later researchers confirmed this finding with a variety of animal subjects, including rats, monkeys, and apes. Subsequent researchers also developed two types of maps to summarize their results, *body maps* and *action maps*. A body map shows which part of a neural area is related to a particular body part, whereas an action map shows the function that a neural area mediates. We will clarify the utility of these two kinds of maps in the following sections.

## Mapping the Motor Cortex

Beginning in the 1930s, Wilder Penfield (Penfield & Boldrey, 1937) used electrical stimulation and the effects it produced to map the cortices of conscious human patients who were about to undergo elective neurosurgery. Penfield used his stimulation results to

---

**Learning Objectives**

- Contrast body maps and action maps in the nervous system, and explain how these two maps interact to facilitate movement.
- Explain how the on–off responses of motor cortex neurons produce skilled movements.
- Describe the motor tract organization by charting the motor neurons through the lateral and ventral pathways of the corticospinal tracts from the brainstem to the spinal cord and out to the muscles.

Section 4-1 describes the milestones that led to our understanding of how the nervous system uses electrical charge to convey information.

assist in surgery, but because he was stimulating a patient's brain, he kept the intensity and duration of the stimulation to a minimum; consequently, the movements that he produced in his patients were mainly brief twitches. In Section 10-4, we discussed Penfield's work identifying the auditory and speech zones in the cortex.

Penfield summarized his results by drawing body maps, in the form of cartoons of body parts that represented the areas of the motor cortex that produce movement in those parts. A **body map**, formerly called a *homunculus* (pl. *homunculi*; Latin for "little person"), can be identified across the primary motor cortex, as illustrated in **Figure 11-6**. Because the body is symmetrical, an equivalent body map is discernible in the primary motor cortex of each hemisphere, and each motor cortex mainly controls movement in the opposite side of the body. Penfield also identified another, smaller body map in the dorsal premotor area of each frontal lobe, a region sometimes referred to as the *supplementary motor cortex*.

The striking feature of the body maps shown in **Figure 11-7** is the relative sizes of the brain regions associated with specific body parts compared with the sizes of actual parts of the human body. The body map has huge hands with an especially large thumb and large lips and tongue. By contrast, the trunk, arms, and legs—most of the area of a real body—are small. These distortions illustrate that extensive areas of M1 allow precise regulation of the hands, fingers, lips, and tongue (see Figure 11-6). By comparison, body areas over which we have relatively little motor control, such as the trunk, have a much smaller representation in the motor cortex.

The body map as laid out across the motor cortex is discontinuous—that is, it is arranged differently from the actual body. The cortical area that produces eye movements is located in the front of the head on the motor cortex (see the top drawing in Figure 11-6), and the head is oriented with the chin up and the forehead down (bottom drawing). The tongue is below the forehead. This map shows at a glance that relatively large areas of the brain control the body parts we use to make the most skilled movements—our hands, mouth, and eyes—making it useful for understanding M1's **topographic organization** (functional layout). Indeed, considerable research has explored how the motor areas represented by Penfield's body map might produce movement.

One early idea in this line of research proposed that each part of the map controls muscles in that part of the body. Information from other cortical regions could be sent to the map, and neurons in the appropriate part of the map could then activate the body muscles required for producing the movement. If you wanted to pick up a coin, for example, the executive region of the prefrontal cortex could send a message to the M1 finger area to instruct the fingers. The brain's role in movement control was thus analogous to playing a piano: decision-making areas of the brain press the keys or combinations of keys in the body map to produce movements.

When Michael Graziano and his coworkers administered longer durations of electrical stimulation than those used by Penfield, lasting approximately 2 seconds, they found that the motor

Figure 10-19 shows Penfield using brain stimulation to map the cortex.

**body map** Representation of the human body in the sensory or motor cortex; also, any topographical representation of the body by a neural area.

**topographic organization** Neural spatial representation of the body or areas of the sensory world perceived by a sensory organ.

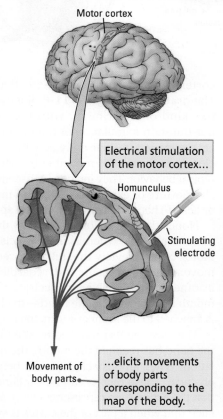

**FIGURE 11-6 Penfield's Body Maps**
Movements are topographically organized in M1. Stimulation of dorsal medial regions produces movements in the lower limbs. Stimulation of ventral regions of the cortex produces movements in the upper body, hands, and face.

*Motor cortex*

*Electrical stimulation of the motor cortex...*

*Homunculus*

*Stimulating electrode*

*Movement of body parts*

*...elicits movements of body parts corresponding to the map of the body.*

© Natural History Museum, London/Bridgeman Images

**FIGURE 11-7 Homuncular Human**
An artist's representation illustrates the disproportionate areas of the sensory and motor cortices that control different body parts.

**FIGURE 11-8 Natural Movement Categories**
Movement categories evoked by electrical stimulation of the monkey cortex and the primary motor and premotor regions from which the categories were elicited. Research from Aflalo & Graziano (2007).

**action map**  Representation of the body performing actions in the sensory or motor cortex; also, any topographical representation of the body in action by a neural area.

**position-point theory**  Idea that the motor cortex allows an appropriate body part to be moved to a point in space.

cortex can also represent actions that form movement categories (Graziano, 2009). The drawings in **Figure 11-8** illustrate the **action map** that can be produced with this kind of experiment, with the main movement categories produced by longer-duration stimulation of the motor cortex of a macaque monkey. Studies of monkeys engaged in their daily activities show that the actions produced by stimulation closely resemble the movements used by the monkeys during spontaneous species-typical behavior. They include (A) ascend, descend, or jump; (B) reach to grasp; (C) defensive posture or expression; (D) hand movement toward the mouth; (E) masticate (chew) or lick; (F) hand movement in central space; and (G) hand movement in distal space.

Notice that the action maps show that whole-body movements are elicited from the premotor cortex, whereas more precise hand and mouth movements are elicited from motor cortex (review the initiating sequence described in Figure 11-2). Each elicited movement has the same end, regardless of the starting location of a monkey's limb or its other ongoing behavior. Electrical stimulation that results in the hand coming to the mouth always recruits the hand—the hand's starting point is not important. If a weight is attached to the monkey's arm, the evoked movement compensates for the added load.

The movements produced by stimulation are inflexible. If stimulation continues after the hand has reached the mouth, the hand remains there for the duration of the stimulation. When an obstacle is placed between the hand and the mouth, the hand hits the obstacle. These results can be explained by the **position-point theory**, which states that the action map represents where a part of the body must be in body-relative space, such that when a part of the cortex is stimulated, the associated part of the body moves to the appropriate spatial position, regardless of its starting position.

Magnetic resonance imaging (MRI) studies on human subjects suggest that the human motor cortex, like the monkey motor cortex shown in Figure 11-8, is also organized in terms of action maps. For example, Huber and colleagues (2020) recorded blood flow with functional MRI (fMRI) from Penfield's hand region of the motor cortex as participants tapped with different fingers. They found two hand representations featuring each of the fingers, and these dual finger representations occurred in both the sensory and motor cortices. When participants were asked to make complex movements that involved all fingers simultaneously, either grasping or releasing an object, one of the hand representations was active when the participants grasped and the other representation was active when they released the object. The results from this experiment suggest that other action maps of the fingers may be found that represent other types of complex finger use.

Huber's experiment is consistent with the understanding that the motor cortex encodes not just muscle twitches, but a lexicon, or dictionary, of movements. As with words and sentences, only a few movements used in different combinations can produce all the movements you are capable of making, even in activities as complex as playing basketball.

## Motor Cortex and Skilled Movement

In a study designed to investigate how neurons in the motor cortex control movement, Edward Evarts (1968) used the simple procedure illustrated in **Experiment 11-2**. Evarts trained a monkey to flex its wrist to move a bar. Different weights could be attached to the bar. An electrode implanted in the wrist region of the monkey's motor cortex recorded the activity of neurons there.

Evarts discovered that the neurons began to discharge even before the monkey began the movement, as shown in the Results section of Experiment 11-2. In other words, these neurons took part in planning the movement as well as initiating it. The neurons continued to discharge as the wrist moved, confirming that they also played a role in *producing* the movement. Finally, the neurons discharged at a higher rate when the bar was loaded with a weight. This finding shows that motor cortex neurons plan and execute movements and increase a movement's force by increasing their firing rate and its duration, as stated in the experiment's Conclusion. Recall (from Figure 11-5) that simple movements, such as using a finger to push a lever, correlate to blood flow specifically to the primary motor cortex in humans.

Evarts's findings also reveal that the motor cortex has a role in specifying the end point of a movement. Motor cortex neurons in the wrist might have discharged when the monkey flexed its wrist inward but not when the wrist was extended back to its starting position. These on–off neuronal responses are a simple way of coding a desired final position of a movement. In short, not only does Evarts's experiment support the position-point theory, but it also shows that movements made to a point in space take into account environmental contingencies, such as whether the limb has to move a load in getting to its destination.

The activity of motor neurons in freely moving monkeys suggests that the neurons, depending on their location, move the body or parts of the body to specific positions (Aflalo & Graziano, 2007). For example, if some neurons are very active when a hand is moved to a specific location, they become progressively less active when the hand is moved away from that position. Thus, the neurons in the motor cortex regions illustrated in Figure 11-8 are responsible for configuring movements that achieve the same end point obtained when those same neurons are electrically stimulated.

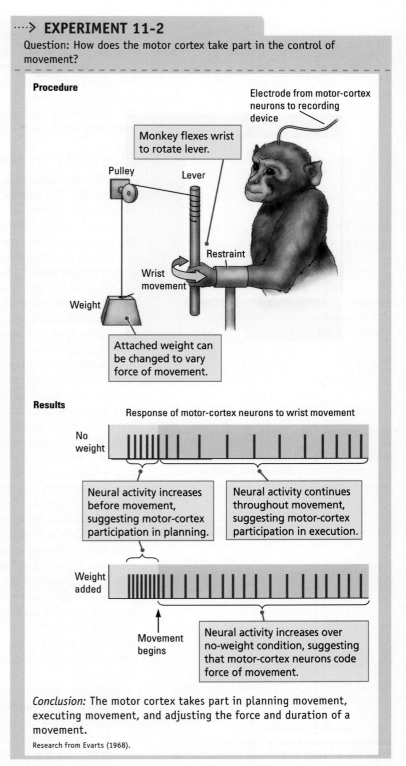

···> **EXPERIMENT 11-2**

Question: How does the motor cortex take part in the control of movement?

**Procedure**

Electrode from motor-cortex neurons to recording device

Monkey flexes wrist to rotate lever.

Pulley

Lever

Restraint

Wrist movement

Weight

Attached weight can be changed to vary force of movement.

**Results**

Response of motor-cortex neurons to wrist movement

No weight

Neural activity increases before movement, suggesting motor-cortex participation in planning.

Neural activity continues throughout movement, suggesting motor-cortex participation in execution.

Weight added

Movement begins

Neural activity increases over no-weight condition, suggesting that motor-cortex neurons code force of movement.

*Conclusion:* The motor cortex takes part in planning movement, executing movement, and adjusting the force and duration of a movement.

Research from Evarts (1968).

Section 4-4 details the process by which neural activity produces movement.

Further evidence that motor cortex neurons may be involved in planning movements comes from research showing that motor neurons can display subthreshold activity—that is, activity that resembles movement-related activity, but is not strong enough to produce a movement. Findings by Schieber (2011) suggests that this subthreshold activity may be involved in planning a movement and may also be responsible for mental imagery of that movement. Subthreshold activity has been harnessed to allow motor cortex neurons to control brain–computer interfaces while not producing overt movement in the patient (see Research Focus 11-1).

## Plasticity in the Motor Cortex

An intimate relationship connects the activity of motor cortex neurons with movement of the body. The studies just described show that flexibility is part of this relationship. Flexibility underlies another property of the motor cortex: its plasticity, which contributes both to motor learning and to recovery after the motor cortex is damaged, as the following example explains.

Section 14-4 explores how motor maps change in response to learning.

A study by Randy Nudo and his coworkers (1996), summarized in the Procedure section of **Experiment 11-3**, illustrates changes due to cortical damage. These researchers mapped the motor cortices of monkeys to identify the hand and digit areas. They then surgically removed a small part of the cortex representing the digit area. After undergoing this electrolytic lesion, the monkeys used the affected hand much less, relying mainly on the unaffected hand.

Section 7-1 describes ablation techniques that neuroscience researchers use to manipulate the brain.

When the researchers stimulated the cortex of the monkeys 3 months later, the animals were unable to produce many hand–arm movements—including movements of the wrist, hand, and digits—that they had produced prior to the lesion. Much of the area representing the hand and lower arm had disappeared from the animals' cortical maps. The shoulder, upper arm, and elbow areas had spread out to take up what had formerly been space representing the hand and digits. The Results section of Experiment 11-3 shows this topographic change.

Clinical Focus 2-3 describes motor disruptions that stroke causes; Section 16-3 reviews stroke treatments.

The researchers wondered whether the change could have been prevented had they forced the monkeys to use the affected arm. To find out, they used the same procedure on other monkeys, except that during the postsurgery period, they forced the animals to rely on the affected arm by binding the unaffected arm in a sling. When the researchers reexamined these monkeys' motor maps 3 months later, they found that the hand and digit area retained its original size. Even though no neural activity occurred in the spot with the lesion, the monkeys had gained some function in the digits that were previously connected to the damaged spot. Apparently, the remaining cortical digit area was now controlling the movement of these fingers.

Most likely, plasticity is involved in the formation of new connections and the strengthening of existing connections among different parts of the body map. Humans who have experienced a stroke to the motor cortex also display plasticity-mediated recovery. Immediately after the stroke, they may be completely unable to use their contralateral forelimb, but with time and practice, they may recover a great deal of movement.

Section 16-3 discusses constraint-induced therapy as a treatment for stroke.

As Nudo's monkey experiment illustrates, one way to enhance recovery is to restrain the good limb. **Constraint-induced therapy**, which forces a person to use the affected limb, is an important therapy for individuals with stroke-induced limb paralysis. Its effectiveness depends on frustration of the unaffected limb, which promotes a concerted effort to use the impaired limb and promotes neural plasticity (Rocha et al., 2021).

## Corticospinal Tracts

A conventional description of the motor cortex, derived from the dye staining of neurons, proposes that it has six layers, with layer V, its largest layer, projecting via the **corticospinal tracts** to the motor neurons of the spinal cord to produce movement. As part of its initial objective, the BRAIN Initiative Cell Census Network (2021) study—the

**constraint-induced therapy** Procedure in which restraint of a healthy limb forces a person to use an impaired limb to enhance recovery of function.

**corticospinal tract** Bundle of nerve fibers that directly connects the cerebral cortex to the spinal cord; it branches at the brainstem into an opposite-side lateral tract, which informs movement of limbs and digits, and a same-side anterior tract, which informs movement of the trunk; also called *pyramidal tract*.

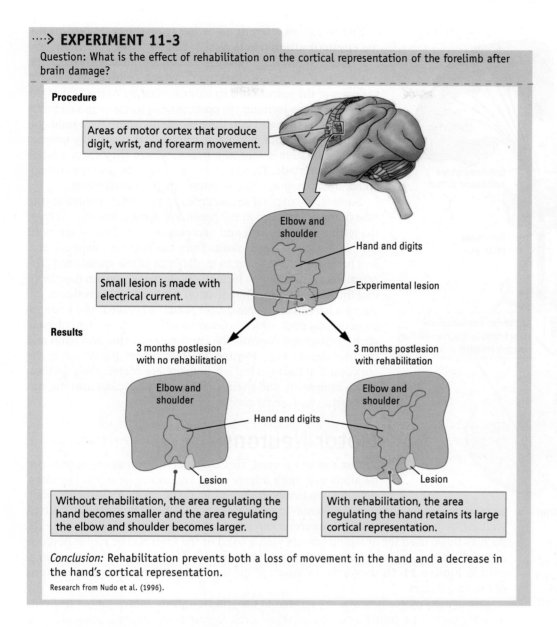

····> **EXPERIMENT 11-3**

Question: What is the effect of rehabilitation on the cortical representation of the forelimb after brain damage?

**Procedure**

Areas of motor cortex that produce digit, wrist, and forearm movement.

Elbow and shoulder

Hand and digits

Small lesion is made with electrical current.

Experimental lesion

**Results**

3 months postlesion with no rehabilitation

3 months postlesion with rehabilitation

Elbow and shoulder

Hand and digits

Elbow and shoulder

Lesion

Lesion

Without rehabilitation, the area regulating the hand becomes smaller and the area regulating the elbow and shoulder becomes larger.

With rehabilitation, the area regulating the hand retains its large cortical representation.

*Conclusion:* Rehabilitation prevents both a loss of movement in the hand and a decrease in the hand's cortical representation.

Research from Nudo et al. (1996).

U.S.-based part of an international initiative to create an atlas of the more than 1,000 neuron types found in mouse, marmoset, and human brains—showed that the motor cortex is more complex than this conventional description.

The method used in the BRAIN analysis describes the electrical activity of each neuron, its neurotransmitter grouping, its connections with other neurons and brain areas, and its RNA and epigenetic expression. Initial results suggest that the mouse motor cortex can be divided into 11 layers, and its more than 100 different types of neurons project more than 100 targets, including targets in the ipsilateral hemisphere, the contralateral hemisphere, the thalamus and basal ganglia, the brainstem, and the spinal cord. Each neuron makes contact with many cells in multiple target regions, and it receives projection back from those targets. The marmoset and human motor cortex are similar to that of the mouse, but even more complex.

This analysis suggests that in addition to sending instructions to the spinal cord, the motor cortex communicates its message to much of the rest of the brain, and the rest of the brain communicates back. This communication is similar to what we do when we copy a large group of people on a digital message and each person in the group responds. Despite this complexity, the motor cortex is hierarchically organized, allowing us to focus on the function of its major targets in the brainstem and spinal cord.

**Principle 3:** The CNS functions on multiple levels and is organized hierarchically and in parallel.

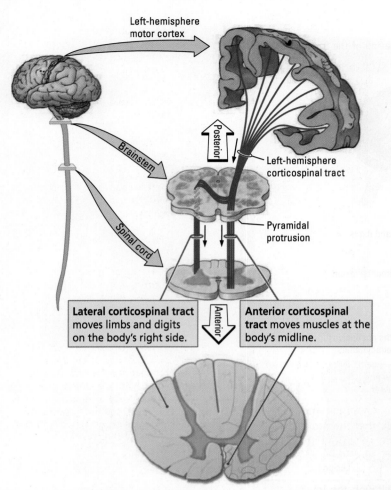

Left-hemisphere motor cortex

Brainstem

Spinal cord

Posterior

Left-hemisphere corticospinal tract

Pyramidal protrusion

Anterior

**Lateral corticospinal tract** moves limbs and digits on the body's right side.

**Anterior corticospinal tract** moves muscles at the body's midline.

**FIGURE 11-9 Left-Hemisphere Corticospinal Tract** Nerve fibers descend from the left-hemisphere motor cortex to the brainstem, where the tract branches into the spinal cord. The lateral tract crosses the brainstem's midline, descending into the right side of the spinal cord to move limb and digit muscles on the body's right side. The anterior tract remains on the left side to move muscles at the body's midline.

**corticobulbar tract** Bundle of nerve fibers that directly connects the cerebral cortex to the brainstem nuclei that control facial muscles.

If you are right-handed, the neurons your brain is using to carry out this task are the same neurons that you are tracing.

The two main efferent pathways from the motor cortex are the **corticobulbar tracts**, which project to the brainstem cranial nuclei to produce movements of head muscles (except the eyes), and the corticospinal tracts, which connect with motor neurons of the spinal cord to control muscles in the rest of the body. The axons forming the corticospinal tracts originate in the motor cortex, descend into the brainstem, where they send collaterals to numerous brainstem nuclei, and eventually emerge on the brainstem's ventral surface, where they form a large bump on each side. These bumps, or pyramids, give the corticospinal tracts their alternative name, the *pyramidal tracts*.

Some corticospinal axons cross to the other (contralateral) side of the spinal cord at the pyramids. Axons descending from the left hemisphere arm and hand areas cross over to the right side of the spinal cord; axons from the right hemisphere arm and hand areas cross over to the left side of the spinal cord. The remaining axons, which form the body trunk, stay on their original (ipsilateral) side. This division produces two corticospinal tracts: a *lateral corticospinal tract*, which is crossed, and a *ventral corticospinal tract*, which is uncrossed. Thus, the motor cortex in each hemisphere controls the contralateral arms and hand and the ipsilateral trunk. **Figure 11-9** illustrates the origin of the corticospinal tracts in the left-hemisphere cortex, their division in the brainstem, and their routes as they descend into the spinal cord as two spinal cord tracts.

## Motor Neurons

Within the spinal cord, corticospinal fibers make synaptic connections with both interneurons and motor neurons. The interneurons are involved in organizing complex movements, such as movements involving many joints. In addition to whole-body movements such as walking or jumping, the motor neurons can produce more fractionated movements, such as those used for grasping objects with a hand or the fingers. The motor neurons carry all nervous system commands out to the muscles. The cross section of a spinal cord in **Figure 11-10** shows the locations of the interneurons and the motor neurons of the spinal cord.

Spinal cord motor neurons are located in the anterior horns, which jut out from the anterior part of the spinal cord. The anterior horns contain both interneurons and motor neurons. Interneurons lie just medial to the motor neurons and project onto them, and the motor neurons send their axons to the body muscles. The fibers from the corticospinal tracts make synaptic connections with both the interneurons and the motor neurons, but the motor neurons carry all nervous system commands to the muscles.

Figure 11-10 is a map of the body as represented in the spinal cord. The more lateral motor neurons project to muscles that control the fingers and hands, whereas intermediate motor neurons project to muscles that control the arms. The most medial motor neurons project to muscles that control the body's shoulders and trunk. Axons of the lateral corticospinal tract connect mainly with the lateral interneurons and motor neurons, and axons of the anterior corticospinal tract connect mainly to the medial interneurons and motor neurons.

To visualize how the cortical body map relates to the spinal cord body map, look again at Figure 11-9. Place your finger on the index finger region of the cortical body map on the left side of the brain. If you trace the axons of the cortical neurons downward, your route takes you through the brainstem, across its midline, and down the right lateral corticospinal tract. The journey ends at the interneurons and motor neurons in the most lateral region of the spinal cord's right anterior horn—the horn on the opposite (contralateral) side of the nervous system from which you began. Following the axons of these motor neurons, you will find that they synapse on muscles that move the right index finger.

If you repeat the procedure by tracing the pathway from the trunk area of the cortical body map, near the top on the left side of the brain, you will follow the same route through the upper part of the brainstem. You do not cross over to the opposite side, however. Instead, you descend into the spinal cord on the left side—the same (ipsilateral) side of the nervous system on which you began—and eventually end up in the most medial interneurons and motor neurons of the left side's anterior horn. (At this point, some of these axons also cross over to the other side of the spinal cord.) Thus, if you follow these motor neuron axons, you will end up at their synapses with the muscles that move the trunk on both sides of the body.

This visualization can help you remember the routes taken by motor system axons. The limb regions of the cortical body map contribute most of their fibers to the lateral corticospinal tract, the fibers that cross over to the opposite side of the spinal cord. They activate motor circuits that move the arm, hand, leg, and foot on the opposite side of the body. In contrast, the trunk regions of the cortical body map contribute their fibers to the anterior corticospinal tract. Only a few of these fibers cross, close to their termination in the spinal cord; most control the trunk and limbs on the same side of the body.

Remember that the motor cortex is organized in terms of functional movement categories, such as reaching or climbing (see Figure 11-8). It is likely that the motor neurons of the spinal cord have a similar action map to ensure that instructions from the motor cortex are reproduced. Presumably, lateral interneurons produce acts of reaching or bringing the hand to the mouth, and the medial interneurons and motor neurons produce whole-body movements, including walking. Recall that a spinal cord isolated from the brain by a cut is still capable of many kinds of movements, and it is able to do so because the movements are organized by its interneurons and motor neurons. This anatomical organization is likely the reason that electrical stimulation of the spinal cord has been reported to facilitate movement in people with spinal cord injury (Inanici et al., 2021).

In addition to the corticospinal pathways, 24 other pathways from the brainstem to the spinal cord are believed to carry instructions, such as information related to posture and balance (see Section 11-4). These pathways also control the enteric nervous system as well as portions of the sympathetic nervous system (SNS) division of the autonomic nervous system (ANS). For all these functions, the motor neurons are the final common path.

## Control of Muscles

Spinal cord motor neurons synapse on the muscles that control body movements. For example, the biceps and triceps of the upper arm control movement of the lower arm. These muscles are arranged in pairs, as shown in **Figure 11-11**, as are most of the body's muscles. One member of a pair, the *extensor*, moves (extends) the limb away from the trunk. The other member of the pair, the *flexor*, moves (flexes) the limb in toward the trunk. Experiment 11-2 demonstrates

Anterior horn of spinal cord

Fingers
Arms
Shoulders
Trunk

**Lateral corticospinal tract** synapses with interneurons and motor neurons that innervate muscles of the limbs and digits.

Interneurons project to motor neurons.

Motor neurons project to muscles of the body.

**Anterior corticospinal tract** synapses with interneurons and motor neurons that innervate the trunk (midline of the body).

The interneurons and motor neurons of the spinal cord are envisioned as a homunculus representing the muscles that they innervate.

**FIGURE 11-10  Motor Tract Organization** Interneurons and motor neurons in the left and right anterior part of the spinal cord are topographically arranged: the more lateral neurons innervate more distal parts of the limbs (the hands and fingers), and the more medial neurons innervate more proximal body muscles (the arms, shoulders, and trunk).

**FIGURE 11-11  Coordinating Muscle Movement**

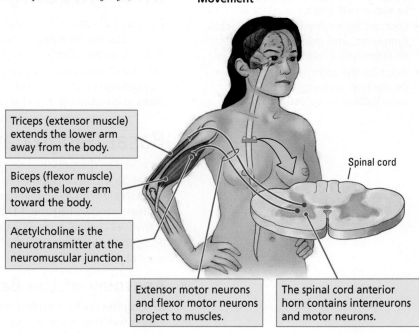

Triceps (extensor muscle) extends the lower arm away from the body.

Biceps (flexor muscle) moves the lower arm toward the body.

Acetylcholine is the neurotransmitter at the neuromuscular junction.

Spinal cord

Extensor motor neurons and flexor motor neurons project to muscles.

The spinal cord anterior horn contains interneurons and motor neurons.

Figure 4-27 illustrates ACh action at a motor neuron–muscle junction.

the on–off responses of cortical motor neurons, depending on whether the flexor or extensor muscle is being used.

Connections between spinal cord interneurons and motor neurons ensure that the muscles work together so that when one muscle contracts, the other relaxes. Thus, the spinal cord interneurons and motor neurons not only relay instructions from the brain but also, through their connections, cooperatively organize the movement of many muscles. As you know, the neurotransmitter at the motor neuron–muscle junction is acetylcholine.

## 11-2 Review

Before you continue, check your understanding. Answers to Self-Test appear at the back of the book.

1. The organization of the motor cortex is described by _____ maps and _____ maps.

2. _____ theory states that the motor cortex has a map of where body parts can be in space, such that when a part of the cortex is stimulated, the associated body part moves to an appropriate special position.

3. Many corticospinal-tract fibers cross to the opposite side of the spinal cord to form the _____ tracts; some stay on the same side to form the _____ tracts.

4. The anterior corticospinal tracts carry instructions for _____ movements, whereas the lateral corticospinal tracts carry instructions for _____ movements.

5. Motor neuron axons in the spinal cord carry instructions to _____ that are arranged in pairs. One _____ a limb; the other _____ the limb.

6. In what way is the action map of the motor cortex different from the body maps?

7. Why might electrical stimulation of the spinal cord aid recovery after spinal cord injury?

## 11-3

# Basal Ganglia, Cerebellum, and Movement

### Learning Objectives
- Describe the anatomy of the basal ganglia, and explain their contribution to movement force.
- Contrast hyperkinetic and hypokinetic symptoms, and give examples of disorders associated with each.
- Describe the anatomy of the cerebellum, and explain its contribution to guided movement.

The main evidence that the basal ganglia and the cerebellum perform motor functions is that damage to either structure impairs movement. Both have extensive connections with the motor cortex, as might be expected. This section provides an overview of each structure's anatomy, before detailing some symptoms that arise after damage to the basal ganglia or the cerebellum. It concludes by taking a look at the roles each structure plays in controlling movement.

## Basal Ganglia and the Force of Movement

As noted in the previous section, a complex network of pathways connects the motor cortex to other regions of the brain and to the spinal cord. The neocortex connects extensively with the basal ganglia, a collection of nuclei lying just beneath the cortex, as illustrated in **Figure 11-12**. One function of the basal ganglia is to modulate the activity of cortical motor systems. In doing so, they participate in a wide range of functions, including association or habit learning, motivation, and emotion, as well as motor control.

## Anatomy of the Basal Ganglia

Among the nuclei forming the basal ganglia are the *caudate nucleus* and the *putamen*, which together form the *striatum* (meaning "striped body" and named for the fibers, including corticospinal fibers, running through it), and the subthalamic nucleus and globus pallidus. As shown in Figure 11-12, the striatum extends as a tail (*caudate* means "having a tail") into the temporal lobe, ending in the amygdala. With respect to functions of the neocortex, there are three main basal ganglia connections:

1. All areas of the neocortex project to the basal ganglia.

2. The basal ganglia project to the motor cortex via relays in the thalamus.

3. The basal ganglia receive connections from the dopamine cells of the midbrain substantia nigra over the nigrostriatal pathway and also project to the substantia nigra.

Through these connections, the basal ganglia form reciprocal circuits, or loops, connecting all cortical regions to the motor cortex. Other loops connect the basal ganglia and substantia nigra, allowing the substantia nigra to modulate the subcortical–motor cortex loops. Separate loops likely participate in selecting and producing skilled movements for learned actions and emotional expression. The functions of some of these loops have been revealed through the behavioral deficits that follow damage to the basal ganglia.

## How the Basal Ganglia Control Movement Force

Two types of movement disorders—in many ways opposites—result from basal ganglia damage. If cells of the caudate putamen are damaged, a person will exhibit unwanted writhing and twitching movements called *dyskinesias*. For example, in Huntington disease, striatal cells are destroyed; thus, this disease is characterized by involuntary, exaggerated, and disjointed movements. Other involuntary movements related to striatal damage include the unwanted tics and vocalizations associated with Tourette syndrome (see Clinical Focus 11-3: Tourette Syndrome).

In addition to causing involuntary movements—called **hyperkinetic symptoms**—basal ganglia damage can result in a loss of control over motor ability. The **hypokinetic symptoms** resulting from such damage are characterized by rigidity and difficulty initiating and producing voluntary movements. People with Parkinson disease, for example, develop hypokinetic symptoms owing to the loss of dopamine cells in the substantia nigra that project into the basal ganglia.

The fact that either hyperkinetic or hypokinetic symptoms arise after to basal ganglia damage suggests that one function of these nuclei is regulating movement force. The underlying idea is that hyperkinetic disorders, such as Huntington disease, result from errors of too much force and so result in excessive movement. Conversely, hypokinetic disorders, such as Parkinson disease, result from errors of too little force and so result in insufficient movement.

Which features of the reciprocal basal ganglia loops allow for selecting movements or modulating movement force? The *volume control theory* holds that the basal ganglia can influence whether movement occurs. As illustrated in **Figure 11-13**, a pathway (green) from the thalamus to the cortex to the spinal cord produces movement. The globus pallidus (red) can inhibit this pathway at the level of the thalamus.

The globus pallidus is controlled by two basal ganglia pathways, one indirect and one direct. If the globus pallidus is excited, it in turn inhibits the thalamus and blocks movement. If it is inhibited, motor cortex circuits that include the thalamus are able to produce movement. Thus, the globus pallidus acts like a volume control. If it is turned down, movement can occur; if it is turned up, movement is blocked. This model proposes that diseases of the basal ganglia affecting its "volume control" function impair movement, causing it to be either excessive or slowed. The model also suggests that we make choices by manipulating this volume control mechanism, selecting goals that we think may benefit us while rejecting less optimal options (Park et al., 2020).

The idea that the globus pallidus acts like a volume control has led to the development of several treatments for Parkinson disease. Consistent with the volume control theory,

**FIGURE 11-12 Basal Ganglia Connections** The caudate putamen in the basal ganglia connects to the amygdala through the tail of the caudate nucleus. The lateral see-through view shows the basal ganglia relative to surrounding structures, including the substantia nigra, with which it shares reciprocal connections. The basal ganglia receive input from most regions of the cortex and send input into the frontal lobes through the subthalamic nucleus.

Figure 5-19 traces the nigrostriatal pathways in the dopaminergic activating system and highlights their importance for maintaining healthy motor behavior.

Clinical Focus 3-3 describes the genetic basis of Huntington disease.

Detailed coverage of Parkinson disease and its treatment appears in Chapters 5, 7, and 16.

**hyperkinetic symptom** Excessive involuntary movement, as seen in Tourette syndrome.

**hypokinetic symptom** Paucity of movement, as seen in Parkinson disease.

## ◎ CLINICAL FOCUS 11-3

# Tourette Syndrome

The neurological disorder Tourette syndrome (TS) was first identified in 1885 by Georges Gilles de la Tourette, a French neurologist, who described the symptoms as they appeared in one of his patients. When she was 7, Miss D. was afflicted with convulsive movements of the hands and arms. These abnormal tics frequently occurred when she tried to write, causing her to make poorly formed letters. After a tic, her movements were well controlled until another convulsive movement occurred. At first, Miss D. was thought to be acting out, and she was reprimanded. Eventually, it became clear that the movements were involuntary. The movements involved the shoulders and the neck and were accompanied by facial grimaces. By the time Miss D. was 26, the tics began to include her speech, and she made strange cries and said words that made no sense.

The statistical incidence of TS is about 1 in 1000 people. This disorder affects all racial groups and seems to be hereditary, and the age range of its onset is 2 to 25 years. The most frequently observed symptoms are involuntary tics and complex movements, such as hitting, lunging, or jumping. People with TS may also emit sudden cries and other vocalizations or may inexplicably utter words that do not make sense in the context, including *coprolalia* (uttering vulgar words) and swearing.

Tourette syndrome is thought to reflect an abnormality of the basal ganglia, especially in the right hemisphere. Its symptoms can be controlled with haloperidol, an antipsychotic drug that blocks dopamine synapses in the basal ganglia. Understanding the neural cause is difficult because the condition may be part of a group of disorders that include tics and hyperactivity and that vary widely in their symptoms (Black et al., 2021).

The urge to make involuntary movements and vocalizations may be similar to behaviors that have an urge-to-action feature, such as the contagious yawning and stretching that often occur after others are observed to display the same behavior. Much of our learning occurs as a result of copying others; frequently, speech habits, mannerisms, and the styles of others can be quickly and unconsciously adopted. This idea has led researchers to suggest that the compulsion associated with conditions such as TS results from activity in brain systems that mediate normal learning by imitation (Quadrelli et al., 2021).

We frequently yawn after we see others yawn. The urge-to-action featured in contagious yawning may reflect the activity of neural systems normally devoted to learning by imitation. The urge-to-action symptoms associated with Tourette syndrome may reflect abnormal activity in these neural systems that likely include the basal ganglia.

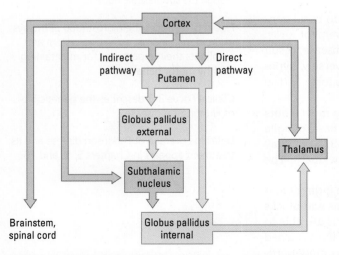

**FIGURE 11-13 Regulating Movement Force** Two pathways in the basal ganglia modulate movements produced in the cortex. Green pathways are excitatory; red are inhibitory. The indirect pathway excites the globus pallidus internal, whereas the direct pathway has an inhibitory effect. If activity in the indirect pathway dominates, the thalamus shuts down, and the cortex is unable to produce movement. If direct-pathway activity dominates, the thalamus can become overactive, amplifying movement. Information from Alexander & Crutcher (1990).

recordings made from globus pallidus cells of people with Parkinson disease shows that their activity is excessive, and likely accounts for their difficulty in moving. If the globus pallidus or the subthalamic nucleus (a relay in the indirect pathway) is partially surgically destroyed in these individuals, their muscular rigidity is reduced and their normal movement is improved. Similarly, deep brain stimulation (DBS) of the globus pallidus inactivates it, allowing the person to move more freely.

Interestingly, impairments in the application of force may underlie motor disorders of skilled movements such as writer's cramp, drumming cramp, and gaming keyboard cramp. These kinds of hand movement impairments, called *selective dystonias*, stem from engaging in repetitive tasks. Another such impairment, the *yips*, involves distorted execution of skilled movements by professional athletes. For example, the yips may end the career of a professional golfer by ruining the player's putting swing.

Everyday errors, called *action slips*, occur when we, for example, accidentally drive past our intended destination or grab a fork to eat our cereal instead of a spoon. These impairments may be related to errors in decision-making control mediated by the globus pallidus (Mylopoulos, 2021).

The nucleus accumbens, another structure in the basal ganglia, is also called the ventral striatum because it is the most ventral basal ganglia nucleus. The nucleus accumbens receives projections from dopamine cells of the ventral tegmental area, a nucleus just medial to the substantia nigra in the midbrain. The resulting mesolimbic dopamine (DA) pathway (see **Figure 11-14**) is part of a loop that aids our perception of cues signaling reward and is related to drug addiction, a topic discussed in Chapter 6. An error in accurately evaluating a cue may prompt us to place either too much emphasis on it (such that a cue might create an urge to take a drug), or no emphasis on it, as can occur with the apathy associated with some forms of depression.

# Cerebellum and Movement Skill

Musicians have a saying: "Miss a day of practice and you're okay, miss two days and you notice, miss three days and the world notices." Apparently, changes take place in the brain when we practice—or neglect to practice—a motor skill, and the cerebellum may be the affected component of the motor system. Whether the skill is playing a musical instrument, pitching a baseball, or texting, the cerebellum is critical for acquiring and maintaining motor skills.

## Anatomy of the Cerebellum

The cerebellum sits atop the brainstem, clearly visible just behind the cerebrum. Like the cerebrum, it is divided into two hemispheres (**Figure 11-15**). A small lobe, the flocculus, projects from its ventral, or inferior, surface. The cerebellum makes up approximately 10% of the mammalian brain, and in primates it contains about four times as many neurons as does the cortex and is distinctive in having many more folds than does the cerebral cortex. Just as the neocortex of humans has increased in size as the human brain has increased in size relative to other primates, the cerebellum shares the same proportional increase. This increase suggests that the cerebellum is involved in all sensory, motor, and cognitive functions of the neocortex (Sereno et al., 2021).

As Figure 11-15 shows, the cerebellum can be divided into several regions, each specialized for an aspect of motor control. At its base, the flocculus receives projections from the inner ear vestibular system (described in Section 11-4) and takes part in controlling balance. Many projections from the flocculus go to the spinal cord and to the motor nuclei that control eye movements.

Clinical Focus 6-5 describes an innovative treatment for opioid use disorder that uses ultrasound stimulation of the nucleus accumbens while cravings are induced through visual cues.

Frontal cortex

Nucleus accumbens of basal ganglia

Hippocampus (part of limbic system)    Ventral tegmental area of midbrain

**FIGURE 11-14 Mesolimbic Dopamine Pathway** The mesolimbic DA pathway (purple projections from the ventral tegmentum) is a substrate of not only reward but also addictive behavior. See Section 6-4.

The elephant's cerebellum, in contrast to that of primates, contains 97.5% of the elephant's neurons. Details can be found in Comparative Focus 1-3.

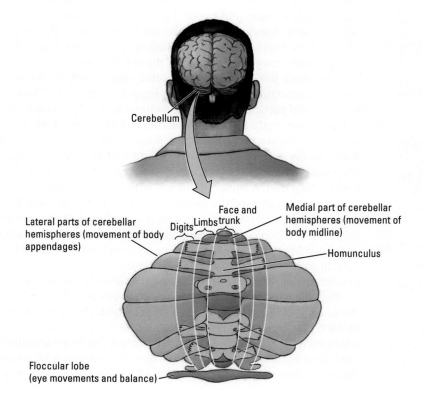

Cerebellum

Lateral parts of cerebellar hemispheres (movement of body appendages)

Digits    Limbs

Face and trunk

Medial part of cerebellar hemispheres (movement of body midline)

Homunculus

Floccular lobe (eye movements and balance)

**FIGURE 11-15 Cerebellar Body Map** The cerebellar hemispheres control body movements, and the flocculus controls eye movements and balance. In the cerebellum's body map organization, relatively medial parts represent the body's midline, and relatively lateral parts represent the limbs and digits.

Ramón y Cajal's drawing of a Purkinje cell, circa 1900.

····> **EXPERIMENT 11-4**

Question: Does the cerebellum help make adjustments required to keep movements accurate?

**(A) Procedure**

Prism glasses

Person throws dart at target

Person wears prisms that divert gaze

Prisms removed, person adapts, or not.

**(B) Results—Control participant**

Distance from target (to the right) / (to the left)

Initial throws | With prisms | Prisms removed

Trials

**(C) Results—Patient with damage to cerebellum**

Distance from target (to the right) / (to the left)

Initial throws | With prisms | Prisms removed

Trials

*Conclusion:* Many movements we make depend on moment-to-moment learning and adjustments made by the cerebellum.

Information from Thach et al. (1992).

Just as the motor cortex has a body map organization, the cerebellar hemispheres have at least two body maps, as shown in Figure 11-15. The medial part of each map controls the face and the body's midline. The more lateral parts of each map connect to motor cortex areas associated with movements of the limbs, hands, feet, and digits. Pathways from the cerebellar hemispheres project to nuclei at the interface of the cerebellum and spinal cord. These nuclei, in turn, project to other brain regions, including the motor cortex, such that the cortical body maps and the cerebellar body maps are aligned.

To summarize the cerebellum's topographic organization, the trunk of the body is represented in the central part of the body map; the limbs and digits are represented in the map's lateral parts. Tumors or damage to midline areas of the cerebellum disrupt balance, eye movement, upright posture, and walking, but do not substantially disrupt other movements, such as reaching, grasping, and using the fingers. A person with medial damage to the cerebellum may, when lying down, show few symptoms. Damage to lateral parts of the cerebellum disrupts arm, hand, and finger movements much more than movements of the body's trunk.

The arrangement and connections of the cerebellum are built to a common plan. The cerebellar cortex consists of three layers of cells, with the distinctive Purkinje cells forming the second layer. Purkinje cells (shown in the illustration in the margin) are the output cells of the cerebellum. This plan suggests that every region of the cerebellum processes information in much the same way with respect to its control over other motor system regions of the brain.

## How the Cerebellum Improves Movement Control

Attempts to understand how the cerebellum controls movement have focused on movement timing. The cerebellum can time movement through its connections with each region of the neocortex, such that different regions of the cerebellum participate in the timing of different behaviors. Humans have a great deal of difficulty producing two different movements at the same time—for example, tapping our head with one hand and making a circular movement on the chest with the other hand. If we synchronize the rhythm of the two movements, the action is much easier. Such synchronization of the timing of movements may be a function of the cerebellum.

Tom Thach (2007), in an informative experiment, illustrated how the cerebellum times movements to keep them accurate. Control participants and participants with cerebellar damage threw darts at a target, as shown in the Procedure section of **Experiment 11-4**. After a number of throws that allowed them to become reasonably accurate, both groups donned glasses containing wedge-shaped prisms that displaced the apparent location of the target to the left. Now when they threw a dart, it landed to the left of the intended target.

Both groups showed the same initial distortion in their aim. But then came an important difference, graphed in the Results section of Experiment 11-4. When controls saw the dart miss the mark, they adjusted each successive throw until they once again achieved reasonable accuracy. In contrast, subjects with cerebellar damage could not correct for this error. Time after time, they missed the target far to the left.

Next, the controls removed the prism glasses and threw a few more darts. Again, a significant difference emerged. The first dart thrown by each participant was much too far to the right (due to the previous adjustment they had learned to make), but soon each one adjusted once again until accuracy was regained. In contrast, subjects with damage to the cerebellum showed no aftereffects of wearing the prisms; they had never compensated for the glasses to begin with. This experiment suggests that many movements we make—whether throwing a dart, organizing a movement sequence to shoot a basketball, or even timing our social and emotional behaviors—depend on moment-to-moment adjustments made by the cerebellum (Fleury et al., 2021).

To better understand how the cerebellum improves motor skills by timing movements, consider the model shown in **Figure 11-16**. Imagine throwing a dart. You aim at the bull's-eye, throw the dart, and find that it misses the board completely. You aim again, this time adjusting your throw to correct for the original error. As the model illustrates, you track two versions of your action: (1) the movement you intended to make and (2) the actual movement, as recorded by sensory receptors in your arm and shoulder. If you carry out the intended movement successfully, you need make no correction on your next try. But if you miss, and you frequently will, you make an adjustment for the next throw.

This model illustrates that the cortex sends instructions to the spinal cord to throw a dart at the target. A copy of the same instructions is sent to the cerebellum through the *inferior olive*, a nucleus in the brainstem that projects to the cerebellum. Then, when you throw the dart, the sensory receptors in your arm and shoulder code the actual movement you make and send a message about it back to the cerebellum through the spinocerebellar tract. The cerebellum now has information about both versions of the movement—what you intended to do and what you actually did—and can calculate the error and inform the cortex about how to correct the next attempt. When you next throw a dart, you incorporate the correction into your throw. If the cerebellum is damaged, however, the ability to correct errors by comparing intended and actual movements is impaired (Morelli & Hoch, 2020).

*Predictive processing theory* argues that all of our behavior, including our social behavior, involves a learning process that is similar to dart throwing. We predict the effect of our actions on others and, depending on the outcome, we modify our future behavior. In a practical application of this theory, we can see that the impairments in social skills seen in persons with autism spectrum disorder may be related to their reduced experimentation with social skills (Bukhari et al., 2021).

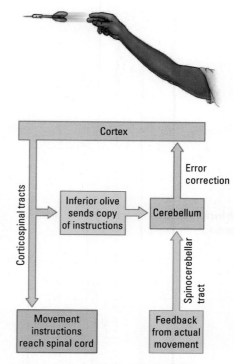

**FIGURE 11-16 Intention, Action, and Feedback** By comparing the message for the intended movement with the movement that was actually performed, the cerebellum sends an error message to the cortex to improve the accuracy of a subsequent movement.

## 11-3 Review

Before you continue, check your understanding. Answers to Self-Test appear at the back of the book.

1. The _____ contribute(s) to motor control by adjusting the _____ associated with a movement.

2. Damage to the basal ganglia results either in unwanted involuntary _____ movements (too much force exerted) or in such _____ rigidity that movements are difficult to perform (too little force exerted).

3. The cerebellum contributes to motor control by correcting for _____ associated with movements.

4. Why do Huntington disease and Parkinson disease seem to be polar opposites?

5. Why has the cerebellum expanded in size along with the neocortex in humans?

## 11-4

# Somatosensory System Receptors and Pathways

Although the motor system produces movement, without sensation, any semblance of controlled, purposeful movement would be impossible. The somatosensory system is indispensable for providing this guidance. The body senses tell us where the parts of our body are, what they are doing, and how they are interacting with the world around

**Learning Objectives**

- Describe the three functional classes of somatosensory receptors.
- Contrast slowly and rapidly adapting receptors, and give examples of each.
- Chart the pathway by which the posterior root ganglion neurons convey somatosensory information from the body to through brain.
- Distinguish central and referred pain; summarize the pain gate theory of pain perception.
- Describe the mechanism by which the vestibular system produces a sense of balance.

them. The neural systems that control our somatic sensations likely remember past movements, help plan future movements, and provide movement-related information to our other senses. For example, basketball players may spend hours practicing a particular shot so they can execute it during a game, but can also adjust their movements to the conditions specific to the moment in the game when they take the shot.

*Somatic sensation* is unique among the sensory systems. It is distributed throughout the body rather than being localized in the head, as are vision, hearing, taste, and smell. Only one part of the system is confined to a single organ: the inner ear houses the vestibular system, which contributes to our sensations of balance and head movement.

In our exploration of the motor system, we started at the cortex and followed the motor pathways out to the spinal cord (review Figures 11-9 and 11-10). This efferent route follows the outward flow of neural instructions regarding movement. As we explore the somatosensory system, we will proceed in the opposite direction because afferent sensory information flows inward, from the body's sensory receptors through sensory pathways in the spinal cord to the cortex.

**Principle 2:** Sensory and motor divisions pervade the nervous system.

# Somatosensory Receptors and Perception

Our body is covered with somatosensory receptors. For example, each of our body hairs is attached to the dendrites of sensory neurons. Different receptor types are embedded in surface skin, in deeper layers of the skin, and in muscles, tendons, and joints. Some receptors consist simply of a sensory neuron dendrite. Others are specialized capsules or connective tissue surrounding a dendrite, and still others include a dendrite attached to the base of a hair.

The density of somatosensory receptors varies greatly throughout the body and determines sensitivity to stimulation. Body parts that are highly sensitive to touch—including the hands, feet, lips, and tongue—have far more sensory receptors than less sensitive body parts—the arms, back, and legs.

Humans have two kinds of skin: hairy skin and glabrous skin. **Glabrous skin** covers the body parts that we use to explore objects, such as the lips, tongue, and palms of the hands and feet. It is hairless and exquisitely sensitive to a wide range of stimuli.

The skin's touch sensitivity can be measured with a two-point sensitivity test. By touching the skin with two sharp points simultaneously, we can observe how close together the points can be placed while still being detected by the participant as two points rather than one. On glabrous skin, we can detect the two points when they are as close as 3 millimeters apart.

Two-Point Sensitivity Test

On hairy skin, two-point sensitivity is weaker by a factor of about 10. The two points seem to merge into one below a separation distance ranging from 2 to 5 cm, depending on the exact body part tested. You can confirm these differences in sensitivity on your own body by touching two sharp pencil points to a palm and to a forearm, varying the distances between the two points. Be sure not to look as you touch each surface.

## Classifying Somatosensory Receptors

There may be 20 or more types of somatosensory receptors in the human body, but they can all be classified into the three perceptual groupings, illustrated in **Figure 11-17**: irritation (nociception), pressure (hapsis), and movement (proprioception).

**Irritation** **Nociception** is the perception of pain, temperature, and itch. Most nociceptors are free nerve endings, consisting of the tips of sensory neuron dendrites, as diagrammed at the top of Figure 11-17. When damaged or irritated, these endings secrete chemicals, usually peptides, that stimulate the nerve to produce an action potential. The action potential then conveys a message about pain, temperature, or itch to the central nervous system.

**Pressure** **Hapsis** (from the Greek for "touch") is the ability to discriminate objects on the basis of contact. Haptic receptors enable us to perceive fine touch and pressure and to identify objects that we touch and grasp. These receptors occupy both superficial and deep skin layers and are attached to body hairs as well.

**glabrous skin** Skin that does not have hair follicles but contains larger numbers of sensory receptors than do hairy skin areas.

**nociception** Perception of pain, temperature, and itch.

**hapsis** Perceptual ability to discriminate objects on the basis of touch or contact.

| Nociception (pain, temperature, itch) | Adaptation | Damage or irritation to the dendrite or to surrounding cells releases chemicals that stimulate the dendrite to produce action potentials. |
|---|---|---|
| Free nerve endings for pain (sharp pain and dull pain) | Slow | |
| Free nerve endings for temperature (heat or coldness) | Slow | |

| Hapsis (fine touch and pressure) | Adaptation | Pressure on the various types of tissue capsules mechanically stimulates the dendrites within them to produce action potentials. |
|---|---|---|
| Meissner corpuscle (touch) | Rapid | |
| Pacinian corpuscle (flutter) | Rapid | |
| Ruffini corpuscle (indentation) | Slow | |
| Merkel disc (steady skin indentation) | Slow | |
| Hair receptors (flutter or steady skin indentation) | Slow | |

| Proprioception (body awareness) | Adaptation | Movements stretch the receptors to mechanically stimulate the dendrites within them to produce action potentials. |
|---|---|---|
| Muscle spindles (muscle stretch) | Rapid | |
| Golgi tendon organs (tendon stretch) | Rapid | |
| Joint receptors (joint movement) | Rapid | |

Hair

**FIGURE 11-17 Somatosensory Receptors**
Perceptions derived from the body senses of nociception, hapsis, and proprioception depend on various receptors in various parts of the skin, muscles, joints, and tendons.

As diagrammed in the center of Figure 11-17, haptic receptors consist of a dendrite attached to a hair, to connective tissue, or to a dendrite encased in a capsule of tissue. Mechanical stimulation of the hair, tissue, or capsule activates touch-sensitive $Na^+$ ion channels on the dendrite, which in turn initiate an action potential. Differences in the tissue forming the capsule determine the kinds of mechanical energy transduced by the haptic receptor to the nerve. For example, pressure that squeezes the capsule of a Pacinian corpuscle is the necessary stimulus for initiating an action potential conveying pressure information. Displacement of a hair is a necessary stimulus for initiating action potentials that convey some other types of directional touch information.

**Movement Proprioception**, or body awareness, is the perception of body location and movement. Proprioceptors are encapsulated nerve endings that are sensitive to the stretch of muscles and tendons and the movement of joints. In the Golgi tendon organ shown at the bottom of Figure 11-17, for instance, an action potential is triggered when the tendon moves, stretching the receptor attached to it.

Figure 4-26 illustrates the cellular processes at work in a sensory neuron dendrite when a hapsis receptor is activated.

## Duration of Receptor Response

Somatosensory receptors are specialized to tell us when a sensory event occurs, when it stops occurring, and whether it is still occurring. Information about when a stimulus occurs is conveyed mainly by **rapidly adapting receptors**, which activate neurons when stimulation begins and when it ends. In contrast, **slowly adapting receptors** continue to activate neurons as long as a sensory event is present: they detect whether a stimulus is still occurring. For instance, after you have put on an article of clothing and become accustomed to how it feels, only the slowly adapting haptic receptors remain active. The difference between a rapidly adapting receptor and a slowly adapting receptor rests on three factors: the structure of the receptor, how the receptor is stimulated, and how the ion channels in its dendrite membrane respond to mechanical stimulation.

**proprioception** Perception of the position and movement of the body, limbs, and head.

**rapidly adapting receptor** Body sensory receptor that responds briefly to the onset of a stimulus on the body.

**slowly adapting receptor** Body sensory receptor that responds as long as a sensory stimulus is on the body.

As shown in Figure 11-17, four types of haptic receptors respond to different aspects of touch. Two types of receptors are located near the skin surface: slowly adapting *Merkel discs* respond to light touch on hairy skin and rapidly adapting *Meissner corpuscles* respond to rapid vibrations on glabrous skin. Two additional types of receptors are located deeper within the skin: *Pacinian corpuscles* respond to rapid vibrations and deep pressure and *Ruffini endings* respond to slow stretch. As their functions suggest, the former is a rapidly adapting receptor and the latter is a slowly adapting receptor. As their locations suggest, the two surface receptors are responsive to gentle touch and are used in making fine-grained discriminations, whereas the two receptors located deeper within the skin are less sensitive to detail and more sensitive to force and displacement.

## Posterior Root Ganglion Neurons

The dendrites that carry somatosensory information into the CNS belong to neurons whose cell body is just outside the spinal cord in posterior root ganglia. Their axons enter the spinal cord. As illustrated in **Figure 11-18**, such a posterior root ganglion neuron contains a single long dendrite. Only the tip is responsive to sensory stimulation. This dendrite is continuous with the neuron's axon, which enters the spinal cord. The somatosensory cell body sits to one side of this long pathway.

Every spinal cord segment is flanked by a posterior root ganglion that contains many types of neurons. Each neuron type responds to a particular kind of somatosensory information. Within the spinal cord, the axons of posterior root ganglion neurons may synapse with other neurons, continue to the brain, or do both.

The axons of posterior root ganglion neurons vary in diameter and myelination. These structural features are related to the kind of information the neurons carry. Proprioceptive information (location and movement) and haptic information (touch and pressure) are carried by posterior root ganglion neurons that have large, well-myelinated axons. Nociceptive information (pain, temperature, itch) is mainly carried by posterior root ganglion neurons that have smaller axons with little or no myelin.

Because of their size and myelination, the larger neurons carry information faster than the smaller neurons do. One possible reason proprioceptive and haptic neurons are designed to carry messages quickly is that their information requires a rapid response. Imagine that you've touched a hot stove. A myelinated pain fiber activates and instructs the hand to withdraw quickly. A nonmyelinated pain fiber, which acts in a less hurried manner, will let you know for some time afterward that your finger has been burned.

Myelin is the fatty coating around axons, formed by glial cells, that speeds neurotransmission. See Section 3-1.

**FIGURE 11-18 Haptic Neuron of the Posterior Root Ganglion** The dendrite and axon of this neuron of the posterior root ganglion, which are contiguous, carry sensory information from the skin to the CNS. These large, myelinated ganglionic axons travel up the spinal cord to the brain in the posterior column, whereas the small axons synapse with neurons whose axons cross the spinal cord and ascend on the other side (shown in Figure 11-19).

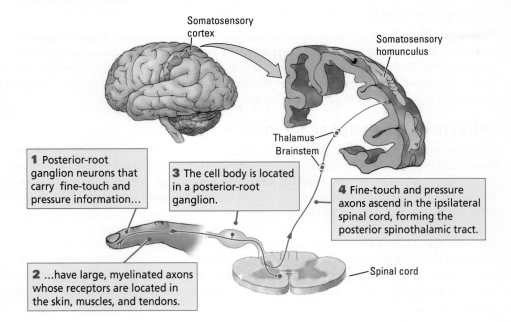

**1** Posterior-root ganglion neurons that carry fine-touch and pressure information...

**2** ...have large, myelinated axons whose receptors are located in the skin, muscles, and tendons.

**3** The cell body is located in a posterior-root ganglion.

**4** Fine-touch and pressure axons ascend in the ipsilateral spinal cord, forming the posterior spinothalamic tract.

Somatosensory cortex

Somatosensory homunculus

Thalamus
Brainstem

Spinal cord

## Disruption of Posterior Root Ganglion Function

We can support the claim that somatosensory information is essential for movement by describing what happens when posterior root ganglion cells do not function. A clue comes from a visit to the dentist. If you have ever had the area around a tooth numbed for dental work, you have felt the strange effect of losing sensation on one side of your face. Not only do you lose pain perception, but you also seem to lose the ability to move your facial muscles properly, making it awkward to talk and smile and downright dangerous to chew. Similarly, if your mouth or hands become terribly cold, which disrupts receptor function there, talking or making hand movements becomes difficult. So even though only the sensory nerves are blocked, movement is affected as well.

In much the same way, sensory nerve damage affects both somatosensory perceptions and motor abilities. John Rothwell and his colleagues (1982) described a patient, G. O., who had undergone **deafferentation** (had lost afferent sensory fibers) because of a disease that destroyed his somatosensory posterior root ganglion neurons. G. O. received no sensory input from his hands. He could not, for example, feel when his hand was holding something.

Even so, G. O. could still accurately produce a range of finger movements, and he could outline figures in the air even with his eyes closed. He could also move his thumb accurately through different distances and at different speeds, judge weights, and match movement force. Nevertheless, his hands were relatively useless to him in daily life. Although G. O. could drive his old car, he was unable to learn to drive a new one. He was also unable to write, fasten his shirt buttons, or hold a cup.

G. O. began movements quite normally, but as he proceeded, the movement patterns gradually fell apart, ending in failure. Part of G. O.'s difficulties lay in maintaining muscle force for any time. When he tried to carry a suitcase, he would quickly drop it unless he continually looked down to confirm that he was carrying it. Clearly, although only G. O.'s somatosensory neurons were damaged, he also had severe motor disability, including cognitive disability in learning new motor skills.

## Disruption of Body Awareness

Movement abnormalities may also result from more selective damage to neurons that carry proprioceptive information about body location and movement. Neurologist Oliver Sacks (1998) gives a dramatic example in his description of a patient, Christina, whose proprioceptive sensory fibers throughout her body were damaged after she took megadoses of vitamin $B_6$. Christina was left with little ability to control her movements and spent most of each day lying prone. Here is how she describes what a loss of proprioception means:

> "What I must do then," she said slowly, "is use vision, use my eyes, in every situation where I used—what do you call it?—proprioception before. I've already noticed," she added, musingly, "that I may lose my arms. I think they are in one place, and I find they're in another. This proprioception is like the eyes of the body, the way the body sees itself. And if it goes, as it's gone with me, it's like the body's blind. My body can't see itself if it's lost its eyes, right? So I have to watch it—be its eyes." (Sacks, 1998, p. 46)

Clearly, Christina's motor system is intact, but with no sense of where in space her body is and what it is doing, she is almost completely immobilized.

Jonathan Cole (1995) described the now classic case of Ian Waterman, who lost proprioception after a presumed viral infection at age 19. He is the only person with this disability to have learned how to move again, and this relearning took years. All his regained movement was mediated by vision; if he lost focus or closed his eyes, he would collapse. He managed to replace the "eyes of his body" with visual control of his movements.

# Somatosensory Pathways to the Brain

As the axons of somatosensory neurons enter the CNS in the spinal cord, they divide, forming two pathways to the brain. The haptic-proprioceptive axons for touch and body awareness ascend the spinal cord ipsilaterally, whereas the nociceptive (pain, temperature, itch) nerve fibers synapse with neurons whose axons cross immediately

Oliver Sacks's research informed scientific understanding of conditions as diverse as Parkinson disease (Clinical Focus 5-4 and Section 16-3) and ventral visual stream injury (Section 9-5).

---

**deafferentation** Loss of incoming sensory input, usually due to damage to sensory fibers; also loss of any afferent input to a structure.

Primary somatosensory cortex

**6** Afferent somatosensory information arrives in the primary somatosensory cortex (areas 3-1-2).

**5** The ventrolateral area of the thalamus relays sensory information to the primary somatosensory cortex.

**4** In the brainstem, posterior spinothalamic neurons cross to the contralateral pathway, where axons of the medial lemniscus carry information from posterior and anterior tracts to the ventrolateral thalamus.

**3** Posterior column nuclei that relay haptic-proprioceptive sensations ascend the dorsal spinothalamic tract ipsilaterally.

**1** Posterior root ganglion neurons respond to fine touch and pressure; joint, tendon, and muscle change; pain, temperature, and itch.

**2** After crossing to the contralateral side of the spinal cord, nociceptive nuclei form the anterior spinothalamic tract, which joins the medial lemniscus pathway.

Thalamus

Medial lemniscus

Brainstem

Posterior root ganglion

Spinal cord

**FIGURE 11-19 Dual Somatosensory Pathways to the Brain** As neurons from the posterior root ganglia enter the spinal cord, the two somatosensory pathways to the brain diverge.

**Principle 4:** Many brain circuits are crossed.

to the contralateral side of the spinal cord before ascending to the brain. Ipsilateral connections lie on the side of the body on which they enter; contralateral connections lie on the side opposite.

**Figure 11-19** shows these two routes through the spinal cord. The posterior haptic-proprioceptive pathway is shown as a solid red line and the anterior nociceptive pathway as a dashed red line.

## The Posterior Spinothalamic Tract

Haptic-proprioceptive axons, which are found in the posterior portion of the spinal cord, form the **posterior spinothalamic tract**. These axons for fine touch and pressure synapse in the posterior column nuclei at the base of the brain. As shown in Figure 11-19, axons of neurons in the posterior column nuclei cross to the other side of the brainstem and ascend as part of a pathway called the medial lemniscus (*lemniscus* is Greek for "ribbon" or "band").

The posterior column axons synapse in the **ventrolateral thalamus**, the part of the thalamus that sends afferent information about body senses on to the somatosensory cortex. Although ventrolateral thalamic neurons send most of their axons to the somatosensory cortex, some do go to the motor cortex.

Thus, three relay neurons are required to carry haptic-proprioceptive information from a receptor to the cortex: posterior root ganglia neurons, posterior column nuclei neurons, and thalamic neurons. Because the posterior column neurons cross to the opposite hemisphere, each hemisphere perceives the opposite side of the somatosensory world.

## The Anterior Spinothalamic Tract

Most nociceptive axons take a different route to the brain. As shown in Figure 11-19, they first synapse with neurons in the anterior part of the spinal cord's gray matter; in turn, these neurons send their axons across to the other side of the spinal cord. There, these axons form the **anterior spinothalamic tract**, which carries afferent

**posterior spinothalamic tract** Pathway that carries fine-touch and pressure fibers toward the brain.

**ventrolateral thalamus** Part of the thalamus that carries information about body senses to the somatosensory cortex.

**anterior spinothalamic tract** Pathway from the spinal cord to the thalamus that carries information about pain and temperature toward the brain.

information about pain, temperature, and itch to the thalamus. This tract joins the medial lemniscus in the brainstem, and both continue on to the ventrolateral thalamus. The thalamic neurons project to the somatosensory cortex. So again, conveying information from a pain or temperature receptor to the cortex requires three groups of relay neurons: posterior root neurons, spinal cord gray matter neurons, and ventrolateral thalamic neurons.

## Effects of Unilateral Somatosensory System Damage

Unilateral damage dissociates the functions of the two somatosensory pathways—haptic-proprioceptive and nociceptive. Because these pathways enter the spinal cord together, separate in the spinal cord, and finally join up again in the brainstem, unilateral damage to this system results in distinctive sensory losses, depending on the site of injury.

Damage to the posterior roots produces global somatosensory deficits in a particular part of the body. In contrast, as illustrated in **Figure 11-20**, after unilateral spinal cord injury, loss of hapsis and proprioception occur unilaterally, to the side of the body below where the damage occurred. Loss of nociception also occurs unilaterally, but to the opposite side of the body, below where the damage occurred. Unilateral damage at the points where the pathways merge in the brainstem, thalamus, and cortex affects all three of these types of perception—hapsis, proprioception, and nociception—with all symptoms occurring on the opposite side of the body.

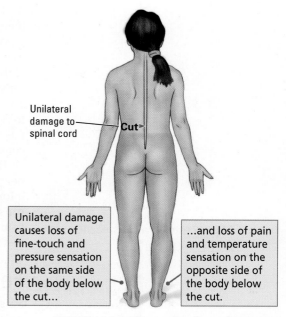

Unilateral damage to spinal cord

**Cut**

Unilateral damage causes loss of fine-touch and pressure sensation on the same side of the body below the cut...

...and loss of pain and temperature sensation on the opposite side of the body below the cut.

**FIGURE 11-20 Effects of Unilateral Damage to the Somatosensory System**

## Spinal Reflexes

Not only do somatosensory nerve fibers convey information to the cortex, but they also participate in behaviors mediated by the spinal cord and brainstem. Spinal cord somatosensory axons—even those ascending the posterior columns—give off axon collaterals, with each somatosensory neuron making synapses with interneurons and motor neurons on both sides of the spinal cord. The circuits made between sensory neurons and muscles through these connections mediate the spinal reflexes.

The simplest spinal reflex is formed by a single synapse between a somatosensory neuron and a motor neuron. **Figure 11-21** illustrates such a **monosynaptic reflex,**

**monosynaptic reflex** Reflex requiring one synapse between sensory input and movement.

**FIGURE 11-21 Monosynaptic Reflex**

**1** A tap on the patellar tendon stretches the quadriceps muscle.

**2** The sensory nerve responds to the muscle stretch...

**3** ...by sending a signal to the spinal cord, where it connects to a motor neuron through a single synapse.

Spinal cord

Sensory neuron

Quadriceps muscle

**4** The motor neuron stimulates the quadriceps muscle to contract and reduce the stretch.

**5** The quadriceps contracts, extending the lower leg.

Extension

the knee jerk. It affects the quadriceps muscle of the thigh, which is anchored to the leg bone by the patellar tendon.

When the lower leg hangs free and this tendon is tapped with a small hammer, the quadriceps muscle is stretched, activating the stretch-sensitive sensory receptors embedded in it. The sensory receptors then send a signal to the spinal cord through sensory neurons that synapse with motor neurons projecting to the same thigh muscle. The discharge from the motor neurons stimulates the muscle, causing it to contract to resist the stretch. Because the tap is brief, the stimulation is over before the motor message arrives, and the muscle contracts even though it is no longer stretched. This contraction pulls the leg up, producing the knee jerk reflex.

This simplest of reflexes entails monosynaptic connections between single sensory neurons and single motor neurons. By comparison, somatosensory neurons receiving information from the skin make much more complex connections with both interneurons and motor neurons. These polysynaptic connections are responsible for more complex spinal movements, such as those involved in standing and walking, actions that require the actions of many muscles on both sides of the body.

Figure 2-34 demonstrates a polysynaptic circuit at work.

# Feeling and Treating Pain

Most visits to physicians are for ailments associated with some kind of pain. For many people, pain is a constant companion, and the incidence of pain increases as people age. People may have pain as a result of acute injuries such as broken bones, chronic conditions such as cancer and arthritis, internal ailments (in the case of stomach or chest pains), and, for women, during menstruation, pregnancy, and childbirth.

## Perceiving Pain

One function of pain is to indicate a body part that is suffering an ailment. We can also experience pain in a part of the body that is not obviously injured, such as occurs in cases of *referred pain*, in which a pain on the body surface indicates a body organ ailment (e.g., pain in the back due to a kidney stone). Another kind of pain is *central pain*, the experience of pain in the absence of an ongoing ailment in a body part. *Phantom limb pain*, a type of central pain in which phantom sensations are felt in a limb that has been lost, is described in Research Focus 11-4: Phantom Limb Pain.

Although people in pain would happily dispense with it, pain is actually necessary. The rare person born without pain receptors develops body deformities because of failure to adjust posture and may receive acute injuries because of failure to avoid harm.

Pain perception results from the synthesis of a plethora of somatosensory information. As many as eight kinds of pain fibers may be found in the body, judging from the peptides and other chemicals released by these nerves when irritated or damaged. Some of these chemicals irritate surrounding tissues, stimulating them to release other chemicals to stimulate blood flow and to stimulate the pain fibers themselves. These reactions contribute to pain, redness, and swelling at the site of an injury.

Consider itch. We may feel itchy and consequently scratch a foreign object on our body. We also frequently feel itch in the absence of an obvious stimulus. Some drugs, including opioids, enhance itch sensations in the absence of a physical stimulus at the itchy body part.

Haptic information also contributes to pain perception. For example, people can accurately report the location and characteristics of various kinds of pain, but in the absence of fine-touch and pressure information, pain becomes more difficult to identify and localize.

The anterior spinothalamic tract, illustrated in Figure 11-19, is the main pain pathway to the brain, but as many as four other pathways may carry pain information from the spinal cord to the brain. These pathways are both crossed and uncrossed. They project to the reticular formation of the midbrain, where they produce arousal; to the amygdala, where they produce emotional responses typically associated with pain; and to the hypothalamus, where they activate hormonal and cardiovascular responses related to coping with pain.

## ◉ RESEARCH FOCUS 11-4

# Phantom Limb Pain

As many as 80% of people who have had a limb amputated subsequently experience phantom limb phenomena, including pain and other sensations and motor phantoms, such as phantom movement and cramps (Stankevicius et al., 2021). Phantom sensations and movements are illusions that originate in the brain.

Various techniques are used to minimize phantom limb pain, including drug-based pain management with opioids and the injection of pain medications into the spinal cord. An innovative method devised by V. S. Ramachandran and D. Rogers-Ramachandran (1996) assists the patient in setting up a counter-illusion that the limb is intact and is providing normal sensory input to the brain.

Ramachandran devised a mirror box into which a person who has lost an arm inserts the intact arm and then observes its reflection in the mirror. The reflection suggests that the missing arm is present and can be controlled, as shown in the illustration. (Note that the walls of the box in this illustration have been removed to show the hidden arm.) The perception of the limb as intact counteracts phantom pain and cramps.

Inspired by Ramachandran's mirror box, researchers have developed other illusions to suggest that a missing limb is present and can be controlled. One method involves using virtual reality goggles. Another uses the so-called rubber limb phenomenon to produce the illusion that a missing limb is present. To induce this phenomenon, the stump of the amputated limb is stimulated tactually while the participant observes a prosthetic limb being touched. Using similar logic, Granata and associates (2020) showed that using neuroprosthetic limbs after amputation reduces phantom pain in the amputated limbs. All of these counter-illusions lessen phantom limb pain and cramps by suggesting that a normal limb is present.

There are at least two explanations of phantom limb pain, both related to cortical maps. The first explanation is based on the finding that when a limb is amputated, the map representation of that limb in the cortex shrinks and the adjacent regions of the cortex expand their map representation at the expense of the missing limb. Abnormalities related to this cortical organization — perhaps from the intact adjacent body maps — are proposed to be the cause of the phantom pain.

The second explanation is that the missing limb's map representation in the cortex remains intact in some form following injury and continues activating muscle activity via residual motor projections that have retargeted muscles adjacent to the missing limb. This explanation posits that these signals are related to the phantom pain (Therrien et al., 2021). Both explanations suggest that plastic changes within either the brain or the peripheral nervous system are in some way related to phantom pain, but neither provides a good reason why pain sensations should arise from these plastic changes. Future research may reveal this piece of the phantom pain puzzle.

Mirror Box Therapy

The likelihood that each pain pathway has its own function — either for sensation, arousal, emotional responses, or other physiological responses — complicates the treatment of chronic pain. Any treatment for one pathway may not be effective for the others. Even selectively cutting the pain fibers before or after they enter the spinal cord — a radical procedure that is used to control debilitating chronic pain — is not always effective.

## The Pain Gate

The puzzling responses to pain, which vary from person to person, complicate most attempts to provide a comprehensive theory of pain. For example, someone stepping on a sharp object while walking barefoot might feel the pain immediately, but someone engaged in combat or intense athletic competition may receive a serious physical injury but start to feel the pain only much later.

A friend of ours (F. V.) was attacked by a grizzly bear while hiking and required 200 stitches to close his wounds. When friends asked if it hurt to be bitten by a grizzly bear, he surprisingly answered no, explaining, "I had read the week before about someone who was killed and eaten by a grizzly bear. So I was thinking that this bear was going to eat me unless I got away. I did not have time for pain. I was fighting for my life. It was not until the next day that I started feeling pain."

The primacy of F. V.'s fear over his pain was related to the stress he was under. Not feeling pain in a fight-or-flight situation is obviously adaptive, as this story illustrates, and may be related to the activation of endogenous opioid peptides. Treatments for pain include opioid drugs (such as morphine), acupuncture (which entails the rapid vibration of needles embedded in the skin), and simply rubbing the area surrounding the injury. Psychological factors interact with pain treatments, and most studies on pain management have found that placebos can be as effective as actual treatments.

Section 6-2 notes similarities between the brain's endogenous opioids and opioid analgesic drugs.

To explain both the perception of pain and how it can be suppressed in so many ways, Ronald Melzack and Patrick Wall (1965) proposed the *gate theory of pain*, which has had enduring appeal. According to this theory, activities in different sensory pathways play off against each other, thereby determining whether and how much pain is perceived as a result of an injury.

According to gate theory, haptic-proprioceptive stimulation can reduce pain perception, whereas the absence of such stimulation can increase pain perception through interactions at a pain gate. A **pain gate**, illustrated in **Figure 11-22**, consists of a haptic-proprioceptive fiber that conveys fine touch and pressure information and a nociceptive fiber that conducts pain information. Each fiber synapses with the same interneuron. Collaterals from the haptic-proprioceptive pathway excite the interneuron, whereas collaterals from the nociceptive pathway inhibit it. The interneuron, in turn, inhibits a neuron that relays pain information from the spinal cord to the brain. Consequently, when the haptic-proprioceptive pathway is active, the interneuron is stimulated, inhibiting the secondary pain neuron, and the interneuron acts as a gate, reducing the pain sensation.

**FIGURE 11-22 Pain Gate** A spinal cord interneuron receives excitatory input (plus signs) from the fine-touch and pressure pathway; it receives inhibitory input (minus signs) from the pain and temperature pathway. The interneuron's relative activity then determines whether pain and temperature information ascends to the brain. Information from Melzack (1973).

Although the proposed anatomy of the pain gate in the spinal cord has come under question, this theory endures as an explanatory principle. The correct anatomy remains to be found.

## Treating Pain

Gate theory helps explain how many pain treatments work (Foster et al., 2015). When you stub your toe, for instance, you feel pain because the pain pathway to the brain is open. If you then rub your toe, pain is reduced. Rubbing activates the haptic-proprioceptive pathway and reduces the information flow in the pain pathway because the pain gate partly closes, relieving the pain by crowding it out.

Similarly, a variety of pain treatments, including massage, warm water immersion, and acupuncture, may produce pain-relieving effects by selectively activating haptic and proprioceptive fibers relative to pain fibers, thus closing the pain gate. With acupuncture, vibrating needles on different body points presumably activate fine-touch and pressure fibers. The pain gate model may also explain why opioid drugs influence pain. The interneuron that is the gate uses an endogenous opioid as an inhibitory neurotransmitter. Thus, opioids relieve pain by mimicking the actions of the endogenous opioid neurotransmitter of the interneuron.

Figure 2-4 diagrams the triple-layered meninges encasing the brain and spinal cord.

One of the most successful pain treatments involves the injection of small amounts of morphine under the dura mater of the spinal cord, the outer layer of the meninges. This epidural anesthesia is mediated by the action of morphine on interneurons in the spinal cord. Although morphine is a highly useful pain treatment, its effects lessen with continued use. Such tolerance may be related to changes that take place on the postsynaptic receptors of pain neurons in the spinal cord and brain.

**pain gate** Hypothetical neural circuit in which activity in fine-touch and pressure pathways diminishes the activity in pain and temperature pathways.

Gate theory also suggests an explanation for the pins-and-needles effect we feel after sitting too long in one position. Loss of oxygen from reduced blood flow first deactivates the large myelinated axons that carry touch and pressure information, leaving the small unmyelinated fibers that carry pain and temperature messages unaffected.

As a result, ungated sensory information flows in the pain and temperature pathway, leading to the pins-and-needles sensation.

Neural circuits resembling pain gates may be located in the brainstem and cortex as well as the spinal cord. These gates help explain how cognition and emotion influence pain and how other approaches to pain relief work. For example, researchers have found that feelings of severe pain can be lessened when people can shift their attention from the pain to other stimuli. Dentists have long used this technique by giving their patients something soothing to watch or listen to during procedures, or by talking to their patients throughout the entire time.

The brain can also influence the pain signal it receives from the spinal cord. The cell bodies of **periaqueductal gray matter (PAG)** neurons, shown in **Figure 11-23**, surround the cerebral aqueduct connecting the third and fourth ventricles. Electrical stimulation of the PAG is effective in suppressing pain. Neurons in the PAG produce their pain-suppressing effect by exciting pathways (including serotonergic and noradrenergic pathways) in the brainstem that project to the spinal cord. There, they inhibit the neurons that form the ascending pain pathways. Activation of these inhibitory circuits in part explains why pain sensation and perception ease during sleep. Deep brain stimulation (DBS) of the PAG through implanted microelectrodes is one way of treating pain that is resistant to all other therapies, including treatment with opioid drugs.

Many internal organs, including the heart, kidneys, and blood vessels, have pain receptors, but the ganglion neurons carrying information from these receptors do not have their own pathway to the brain. Instead, they synapse with spinal cord neurons that receive nociceptive information from the body's surface. Consequently, the spinal cord neurons that relay pain and temperature messages to the brain receive two sets of signals: one from the body's surface and the other from the internal organs.

These spinal cord neurons cannot distinguish between the two sets of signals—nor can we. As a result, pain in body organs is felt as **referred pain** coming from the body surface. For example, pain in the heart associated with a heart attack may be felt as pain in the left shoulder and upper arm (**Figure 11-24**). Pain in the stomach is felt as pain in the midline of the trunk; pain in the kidneys is felt as pain in the lower back. Pain in the blood vessels in the head is felt as diffuse pain, which we call a headache. (Remember that the brain has no pain receptors.)

Adding to the complexity are sex differences in pain perception, which may be related to sociocultural factors, hormonal factors, or differences in biological and neural mechanisms. For example, when they experience acute myocardial infarction (commonly called a "heart attack"), women are significantly more likely to report neck, back, and jaw pain, as well as nausea, whereas men are more likely to display shoulder pain and sweating. As this example suggests, recognizing such sex differences is important to the diagnosis and treatment of pain.

# Vestibular System and Balance

The only localized part of the somatosensory system, the **vestibular system**, consists of two organs, one in each inner ear. As **Figure 11-25**A shows, each vestibular organ consists of two groups of receptors: the three semicircular canals form one group, and the otolith organs—the utricle and the saccule—form the other group. These vestibular receptors do two jobs: (1) the semicircular canals detect head rotatory movements and (2) the otoliths sense the body's relationship to gravity and linear acceleration.

In Figure 11-25A, the semicircular canals are oriented in three planes that correspond to the three dimensions in which we move through space. Each canal furnishes information about movement in its particular plane. The semicircular canals are filled with a fluid called endolymph; immersed in the endolymph is a set of hair cells.

When the head moves, the endolymph also moves, pushing against the hair cells and bending the cilia at their tips. The force of the bending is converted into receptor potentials in the hair cells, which send action potentials over auditory vestibular nerve axons to the brain. These axons are normally quite active: bending the cilia in one

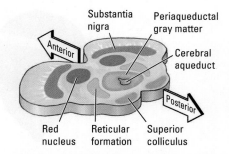

**FIGURE 11-23 Periaqueductal Gray Matter** The PAG is one nucleus in the midbrain's tegmentum (floor), shown here in cross section.

Figure 1-3 depicts DBS.

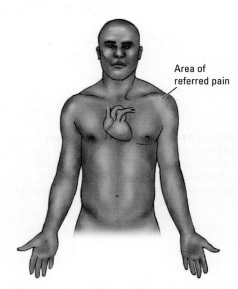

**FIGURE 11-24 Referred Pain** During a heart attack, pain from receptors in the heart is commonly felt in the left shoulder and upper arm, especially in men, or as pain in the jaw or back, especially in women.

Vestibular hair cells work on the same principles as cochlear inner hair cells, which mediate hearing. See Section 10-2.

Cranial nerve 8 conveys both hearing and balance information to the brain. See Figure 2-29.

**periaqueductal gray matter (PAG)** Nuclei in the midbrain that surround the cerebral aqueduct joining the third and fourth ventricles; PAG neurons contain circuits for species-typical behaviors (e.g., female sexual behavior) and play an important role in the modulation of pain.

**referred pain** Pain that arises in one of the internal organs but is felt on the surface of the body.

**vestibular system** Somatosensory system comprising a set of receptors in each inner ear that respond to body position and to movement of the head.

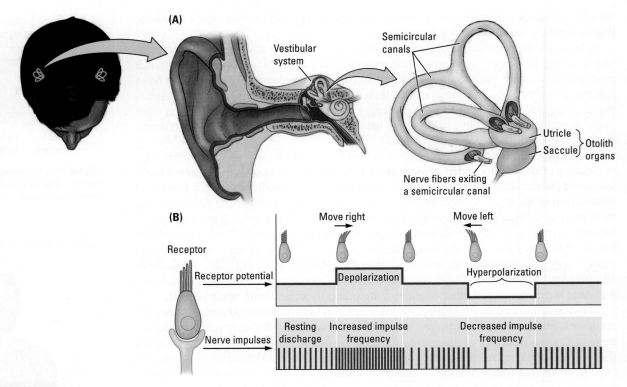

**FIGURE 11-25 The Vestibular System**
**(A)** The vestibular organs in each inner ear contain hair cells that are sensitive to head movement and to gravity. **(B)** A vestibular neuron is normally active. Its activity increases if the cilia at the tips of its hair cell receptors bend in one direction, but activity decreases if the receptors bend in the opposite direction.

direction increases receptor potentials, consequently increasing vestibular nerve axon activity; bending them in the other direction decreases vestibular afferent axon activity. These responses are diagrammed in Figure 11-25B. Typically, when the head turns in one direction, the receptor message on that side of the body increases neuronal firing. The message on the body's opposite side leads to decreased firing.

The utricle and saccule lie stacked just beneath the semicircular canals, as shown at the right in Figure 11-25A. These organs also contain hair cells, but the receptors are embedded in a gelatinous substance that contains otoconia (sing. *otoconium*), small crystals of the salt calcium carbonate. When you tilt your head, the gelatin and otoconia press against the hair cells, bending them. The mechanical action of the hair bending modulates the rate of action potentials in vestibular afferent axons that convey messages about the head's position in three-dimensional space.

The receptors in the vestibular system tell us about our location relative to gravity, about acceleration and deceleration of our movements, and about changes in movement direction. They also allow us to ignore the otherwise destabilizing influence that our movements might have on us. When you are standing on a moving bus, for example, even slight movements of the vehicle could potentially throw you off balance, but they do not. Similarly, when you move, you easily avoid tipping over, despite the constant shifting of your body weight. Your vestibular system enables your stability.

To demonstrate the role of vestibular receptors in helping you compensate for your own movements, try this experiment. Hold your hand in front of your eyes and shake it. Your hand appears blurry. Now shake your head instead of your hand, and the hand remains in focus. Compensatory signals from your vestibular system allow you to see the hand as stable, even though you are moving around.

*Vertigo* (from the Latin for "spinning"), a sensation of spinning when the person is not actually moving, is a dysfunction of the inner ear that can be accompanied by nausea as well as difficulty maintaining balance while walking. A common way to induce vertigo is to spin, as children do when playing. Vertigo can also occur when looking down from a height or looking up at a tall object, or even when a person is simply standing up or sitting down. One intoxicating effect of alcohol is vertigo.

**Ménière disease**, named after a French physician, is a disorder resulting in vertigo and loss of balance that may be related to changing pressure of the fluid in the inner ear (Xie et al., 2021).

**Ménière disease** Disorder of the inner ear resulting in vertigo and loss of balance.

## 11-4 Review

Before you continue, check your understanding. Answers to Self-Test appear at the back of the book.

1. Body senses contribute three types of perception: _____ (touch and pressure), _____ (location and movement), and _____ (temperature, pain, itch).

2. Haptic-proprioceptive information is carried into the CNS by the _____ spinothalamic tract; nociceptive information is carried in by the _____ spinothalamic tract.

3. The two tracts interact in the spinal cord to regulate pain perception via a hypothetical _____.

4. In the midbrain, the _____ suppresses pain by activating neuromodulatory circuits that inhibit pain pathways.

5. The only localized somatosensory system is the _____ system, which helps us maintain _____ by transmitting information about the head's position and our movement through space.

6. What are the possible sources of phantom limb pain?

7. Explain how proprioception acts as the "eyes of the body."

## 11-5

# Exploring the Somatosensory Cortex

Somatosensory neurons do more than convey sensation to the brain: the information they process enables us to perceive things that we describe as pleasant or unpleasant, determine the shape and texture of objects, assess the effort required to complete tasks, and even navigate our spatial environment. They also play a central role in movement. **Figure 11-26** illustrates the two main somatosensory areas in the cortex.

The primary somatosensory cortex, which receives projections from the thalamus, consists of Brodmann areas 3-1-2 (shaded red in Figure 11-26). The primary somatosensory cortex begins to construct perceptions from somatosensory information. It mainly consists of the postcentral gyrus in the parietal lobe, which is located just behind the central fissure. Thus, the primary somatosensory cortex lies adjacent to the primary motor cortex, on the other side of the central fissure in the frontal lobe.

The secondary somatosensory cortex (Brodmann areas 5 and 7, shaded green and purple in Figure 11-26) is located in the parietal lobe just behind the primary somatosensory cortex. It is involved in combining the somatosensory information from primary somatosensory cortex with information from the visual and auditory systems, and thus plays a role in the multisensory control of movement.

**Learning Objectives**

- Summarize the function of the primary somatosensory cortex as outlined by the two models covered in this section.
- Explain how somatosensory information is processed through the primary and secondary somatosensory cortexes.

Korbinian Brodmann numbered these areas more than a century ago on his map of the cortex (see Figure 2-26).

Primary somatosensory cortex (3-1-2) receives sensory information from the body.

Secondary somatosensory cortex (5, 7) receives sensory information from the primary somatosensory cortex.

**FIGURE 11-26 Somatosensory Cortex** Stimulation of the primary somatosensory cortex in the parietal lobe produces sensations that are referred to appropriate body parts. Information from the primary somatosensory cortex travels to the secondary somatosensory cortex for further perceptual analysis.

# Somatosensory Body Map

In his studies of human patients undergoing brain surgery, Wilder Penfield electrically stimulated the somatosensory cortex and recorded patients' responses. Stimulation at sites mainly in the primary somatosensory cortex (S1) elicited sensations in the foot; stimulation of other sites produced sensations in a hand, the trunk, or the face. By mapping these responses, Penfield was able to construct a sensory body map in the cortex, shown in **Figure 11-27**A. The sensory body map looks nearly identical to Penfield's motor body map shown in Figure 11-6, in that the most sensitive areas of the body are accorded relatively large cortical areas.

Using smaller electrodes and more precise recording techniques in monkeys, Jon Kaas (1987) found that Penfield's sensory body map could be subdivided into a series of thinner body maps. When Kaas stimulated sensory receptors on the body and recorded the activity of cells in the sensory cortex, he found that a somatosensory cortex comprises four body maps, each associated with a different class of sensory receptors.

The progression of these representations from front to back across the primary somatosensory cortex is shown in Figure 11-27B. Area 3a cells are responsive to muscle receptors; area 3b cells are responsive to slowly responding skin receptors. Area 1 cells are responsive to rapidly adapting skin receptors, and area 2 cells are responsive to deep tissue pressure and joint receptors. In another study, Hiroshi Asanuma (1989) and his coworkers found a fifth body map in the motor cortex (area 4), in which cells respond to muscle and joint receptors.

Perceptions constructed from elementary sensations depend on combining the sensations. This combination process takes place as areas 3a and 3b project onto area 1, which in turn projects onto area 2. Whereas a cell in area 3a or 3b may respond to activity in only a certain area on a certain finger, for example, cells in area 1 may respond to similar information from a number of fingers.

*See Section 9-1 for more information on receptive fields.*

At the next level of synthesis, cells in area 2 respond to stimulation in a number of locations on a number of fingers, as well as to stimulation from different kinds of

**(B) Four-homunculus model**

Primary somatosensory cortex

S1 is organized into four separate homunculi consisting of areas 3a, 3b, 1, and 2. Information is passed from other areas into area 2, which is responsive to combined somatosensory information.

3a  3b  1  2

Muscles    Skin (slow)    Skin (fast)    Joints, pressure

**(A) Penfield's single-homunculus model**

Primary somatosensory cortex

S1 is organized as a single homunculus with large areas representing body parts that are very sensitive to sensory stimulation.

**FIGURE 11-27 Two Models of the Primary Somatosensory Cortex**

## Tickling

Everyone knows the effects and consequences of tickling. This perception is a curious mixture of pleasant and unpleasant sensations. The two kinds of tickling are *kinismesis*, the sensation from a light caress, and *gargalesis*, the pleasurable effect of hard rhythmic probing.

The tickle sensation is experienced not only by humans but also by other primates and by cats, rats, and probably most other mammals. Play in rats is associated with 50-kilohertz vocalizations, and tickling body regions that are targets of the rats' own play also elicits 50-kilohertz vocalizations (LaFollette et al., 2017).

The fact that people and animals solicit tickles from others suggests that tickling is rewarding. Humans and other animals even enjoy observing others being tickled.

Using a robot and brain imaging techniques, Sarah Blakemore and her colleagues (1998) explained why we cannot tickle ourselves. Blakemore had participants deliver two kinds of identical tactile stimuli to the palms of their hand. In one condition, the stimulus was predictable; in the other, a robot introduced an unpredictable delay in the stimulus. Only the unpredictable stimulus was perceived as a tickle. Thus, it is not the stimulation itself but its unpredictability that contributes to the tickle perception. This is why we cannot tickle ourselves: we know what we are doing. Windt and associates (2015), using a self-report method, found that during lucid dreams, the self–other distinction is absent: people do dream that they tickle themselves.

One interesting feature of tickling is the distinctive laughter it evokes. This laughter can be identified by sonograms (sound analysis), and people can distinguish tickle-related laughter from other forms of laughter. In mother–child interactions, tickling laughter may serve to strengthen social bonds. Species comparisons suggest that chimpanzee and human laughter have many similarities. Tickling, play, and laughter are shared by many animal species and should be considered a form of animal communication (Winkler & Bryant, 2021).

somatosensory receptors. Thus, area 2 contains multimodal neurons responsive to force, orientation, and direction of movement. We perceive all these properties when we hold an object in our hands and manipulate it.

With each successive information relay, both the size of the pertinent receptive fields and the synthesis of somatosensory modalities increase. The segregation of sensory neuron types at the level of the cortex is likely the basis for our ability to distinguish among different kinds of sensory stimuli coming from different sources. For example, we can distinguish between tactile stimulation on the surface of the skin, which is usually produced by some external agent, and stimulation coming from muscles, tendons, and joints, which is usually produced by our own movements.

At the same time, we perceive the combined sensory properties of a stimulus. For instance, when we manipulate an object, we know the object both by its sensory properties, such as temperature and texture, and by the movements we make as we handle it. Thus, the primary somatosensory cortex provides for somatosensory synthesis, too. The tickle sensation seems rooted in an other-versus-us somatosensory distinction, as described in Research Focus 11-5: Tickling.

Research by Vernon Mountcastle (1978) showed that cells in the primary somatosensory cortex are arranged in functional columns running from layer I to layer VI, similar to the functional columns found in the visual cortex. Every cell in a functional somatosensory cortical column responds to a single class of receptors. Some columns are activated by rapidly adapting skin receptors, others by slowly adapting skin receptors, still others by pressure receptors, and so forth. All neurons in a functional column receive information from the same local skin area. In this way, neurons lying within a column seem to be the elementary functional unit of the somatosensory cortex.

Figure 9-38 shows the functional column organization in V1.

# Secondary Somatosensory Cortex

The secondary somatosensory cortex receives not only somatosensory information from the primary somatosensory cortex, but also information from the visual cortex and auditory cortex. In studies using monkeys, electrical stimulation of the secondary

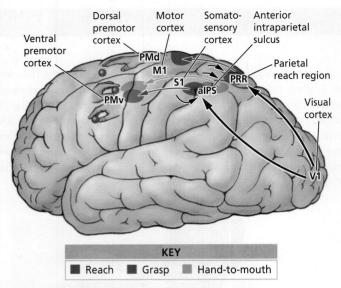

**KEY**

■ Reach ■ Grasp ■ Hand-to-mouth

**FIGURE 11-28 Multiple Channels for Eating** Eating a food item such as a grape requires three channels: a reach channel (red) takes the hand to the grape, a grasp channel (purple) shapes the fingers to grasp the grape, and a hand-to-mouth channel (orange) brings the grape to the mouth. The reach and grasp actions are performed under visual guidance.

somatosensory cortex has been shown to produce action movements that resemble the action movements produced by electrical stimulation of the motor cortex. Stimulation of the more dorsal regions of the secondary somatosensory cortex produces whole-body movements resembling jumping and climbing; stimulation of the more ventral regions produces movements of reaching to points around the body or to the mouth. This action map arrangement of movement in the somatosensory cortex is not only similar to the action map of movement in the motor cortex, but its associated anatomy indicates that neural connections between the functional zones represent the same categories of movement in both the somatosensory and motor cortices.

The connections between the action maps of the somatosensory cortex and the motor cortex show that these two regions share control of movement. But what is the precise contribution of the somatosensory cortex? One explanation is that maps of visual and auditory cortices identify the spatial locations of objects in our surroundings with which we might interact. This information is sent to the somatosensory parietal cortex, which identifies the body part that we might use to interact with objects at that location. (e.g., we can use our arm and hand to reach for that grape or swat that mosquito.) Information specifying location and body part is then sent to the motor cortex, which performs the movement.

An example of this type of movement arrangement is illustrated in **Figure 11-28**. This figure shows three pathways, or channels: a dorsal channel for reaching, a ventral channel for grasping, and, between the two, a channel for bringing the hand to the mouth. The channels for reaching and grasping receive connections from the visual cortex; the channel for hand-to-mouth movement does not. When we reach for a food item such as a grape, the reach channel directs our hand to the spatial location of the grape, the grasp channel shapes our fingers to appropriately grasp it, and the hand-to-mouth channel brings it to our mouth. The hand-to-mouth channel does not require visual information because our somatosensory system can identify that we are holding a grape, it knows where the mouth is, and it can arrange transport of the grape to our mouth (Karl et al., 2018). As this example demonstrates, our movements are synthetized using a smaller number of building-block movements, such as those illustrated in Figure 11-8. These building blocks are like words that can be arranged in different ways to produce different movement sentences.

## Effects of Somatosensory Cortex Damage

Damage to the primary somatosensory cortex impairs the ability to make even simple sensory discriminations and movements. Suzanne Corkin and her coworkers (1970) demonstrated this effect by examining patients with cortical lesions that included most of areas 3-1-2 in one hemisphere. The researchers mapped the primary sensory cortex of each of these patients before they underwent elective surgery for removal of a carefully defined piece of that cortex, including the hand area.

The patients' sensory and motor skills in both hands were tested on three occasions: before the surgery, shortly after the surgery, and almost a year afterward. The tests included pressure sensitivity, two-point touch discrimination, position sense (reporting the direction in which a finger was being moved), and haptic sense (using touch to identify objects, such as a pencil, a coin, eyeglasses, and so forth). For all the sensory abilities tested, the surgical lesions produced a severe and seemingly permanent deficit in the contralateral hand. Sensory thresholds, proprioception, and hapsis were all greatly impaired.

Nevertheless, like the motor cortex, the somatosensory cortex is plastic. Plasticity is illustrated by the reorganization of the somatosensory cortex after deafferentation. Tim Pons and his coworkers (1991) reported a dramatic change in the somatosensory maps of monkeys in which the ganglion cells projecting to the spinal cord for one arm

**(A) Control monkey**

This area of the somatosensory cortex represents the arm and face.

Leg
Trunk
Arm

Face

This normal pattern is illustrated by a normal face.

**FIGURE 11-29 Somatosensory Plasticity**
Information from Pons et al. (1991).

**(B) Deafferentated monkey**

The area of the somatosensory cortex that formerly represented the arm has been taken over by expansion of the face area.

Leg
Trunk

Face

This expansion is illustrated by an elongated face.

had been cut, deafferentating the limb, a number of years earlier. The researchers had wanted to develop an animal model of damage to sensory nerves that could offer insight into human injuries, but they were interrupted by a legal dispute with an animal advocacy group. Years later, as the health of the animals declined, a court injunction allowed the mapping experiment to be conducted.

Pons and his coworkers discovered that the area of somatosensory cortex that had formerly represented the arm no longer did so. Light touches on a monkey's lower face now activated cells in what had formerly been the cortical arm region. As illustrated in **Figure 11-29**, the cortical facial area had expanded by as much as 10 to 14 millimeters, virtually doubling its original size by entering the arm area.

This massive change was completely unexpected. The stimulus–response patterns associated with the expanded facial area of the cortex appeared indistinguishable from those associated with the original facial area. Furthermore, the trunk area, which bounded the other side of the cortical arm area, did not expand into the vacated arm area. A possible explanation of the expansion of the face area is that this monkey began to use its mouth to compensate for many of the movements that were the responsibility of its hand before deafferentation. Although the monkeys in Pons's research had been deafferented years before the recording study was performed, more recent work suggests that changes in cortical reorganization begin almost immediately after injury (Bao et al., 2021).

Section 7-8 considers debates over using laboratory animals in brain–behavior research.

Figure 14-22 diagrams the phenomenon of coritcal reorganization.

# Somatosensory Cortex and the Hierarchy and Parallel Control of Movement

We began this chapter by describing the motor system as hierarchical but with a parallel organization. Damage to the secondary somatosensory cortex does not disrupt the plans for making movements, but it does disrupt how the movements are performed,

The term *apraxia* is derived from the Greek words for "no" and "action."

---

**apraxia** Inability to make voluntary movements in the absence of paralysis or other motor or sensory impairment, especially an inability to make proper use of an object.

---

leaving their execution fragmented and confused. This inability to complete a plan of action accurately—to make a voluntary movement—is called **apraxia**. The following case highlights its symptoms:

> A woman with a biparietal lesion [damage on the left- and right-hemisphere secondary somatosensory cortex] had worked for years as a fish-filleter. With the development of her symptoms, she began to experience difficulty in carrying on with her job. She did not seem to know what to do with her knife. She would stick the point in the head of a fish, start the first stroke, and then come to a stop. In her own mind she knew how to fillet fish, but yet she could not execute the maneuver. The foreman accused her of being drunk and sent her home for mutilating fish.
>
> The same patient also showed another unusual phenomenon that might possibly be apraxic in nature. She could never finish an undertaking. She would begin a job, drop it, start another, abandon that one, and within a short while would have four or five uncompleted tasks on her hands. This would cause her to do such inappropriate actions as putting the sugar bowl in the refrigerator, and the coffeepot inside the oven. (Critchley, 1953, pp. 158–159)

The somatosensory cortex contributes to movement by participating in both the dorsal and ventral visual streams. The dorsal action stream works without conscious awareness, so that we automatically shape a hand as we reach to grasp a cup (recall Figure 11-1). Within this stream, the action map of the secondary parietal cortex describes the categories of movements that we can make. We make specific movements as required by the current situation, but with little awareness of how we perform them.

As **Figure 11-30** illustrates, the dorsal stream projects to the secondary somatosensory cortex and then to the frontal cortex. In this way, it integrates visual information with somatosensory information to produce movements appropriately to targets, as in reaching for a cup.

The ventral stream, in contrast, works with conscious awareness for perception—that an object is a cup, it contains water, and it has a use when we are thirsty. The secondary somatosensory area contributes perceptual information to the ventral stream by providing information about categories of movement that can be selected from the action map in the somatosensory cortex. This information is then sent to the frontal cortex, which can imagine the consequence of a movement and select the actions that appropriately follow from those already completed—for example, to reach or not to reach.

The different contributions of the dorsal stream and the ventral stream to movement are illustrated in the differences in movements displayed by people when they make a real action of reaching for a food item to eat it compared to when they pantomime the same movement. The pantomime movement is not as precise as the real movement, but its communicative value is just as accurate: observers understand what people mean when they pantomime a reaching-to-eat movement (van Nispen et al., 2018).

Information from the secondary somatosensory cortex contributes to the dorsal stream by specifying the movement used for grasping a target.

Information from the secondary somatosensory cortex contributes to the ventral stream by providing information about objects' size, shape, and texture.

**FIGURE 11-30 Visual Aid** Section 9-5 explains how visual information from the dorsal and ventral streams contributes to movement.

## 11-5 Review

Before you continue, check your understanding. Answers to Self-Test appear at the back of the book.

1. The primary somatosensory cortex is arranged as a series of _____ maps.

2. The secondary somatosensory cortex is arranged as a(n) _____ map.

3. Damage to the secondary somatosensory cortex produces _____, an inability to complete a series of movements.

4. The somatosensory cortex provides information to the _____ stream to produce unconscious movements and also provides information to the _____ stream for conscious recognition of objects.

5. Explain briefly why we can't tickle ourselves.

6. Should play, tickling, and laughter be considered a part of language?

# Summary

The somatosensory and motor systems are interrelated at all levels. Throughout the body, sensory receptors from a body part acquire signals relevant to the muscles of that body part. At the level of the spinal cord, sensory information contributes to motor reflexes of that body part; in the brainstem, sensory information contributes to complex regulatory movements. At the level of the neocortex, sensory information represents the sizes, shapes, positions, and values of objects relevant to movement. Just as the activation of sensory receptors leads to movement, movement in turn leads to activation of sensory receptors.

## 11-1 Hierarchical and Parallel Movement Control

Movement is organized hierarchically and in parallel throughout the nervous system (review Figure 11-1). The forebrain plans, organizes, and initiates movements, whereas the brainstem coordinates regulatory functions, such as eating and drinking, and controls neural mechanisms that maintain posture and produce locomotion. The spinal cord's neurons serve as the final common path through which the brain produces movement. Throughout this hierarchy, parallel pathways are responsible for different movements.

## 11-2 Motor System Organization

The results of electrical stimulation of the motor cortex are summarized using two types of maps. Brief electrical stimulation shows that the motor and premotor cortices have a topographic organization as a homunculus, a body map that is distorted so that the most dexterous parts of the body are accorded the largest representation. Longer-duration stimulation reveals that the motor cortex can be represented as an action map, with each region of the motor cortex representing an adaptive movement category. Recordings from individual motor cortex neurons reveal that these regions plan movement, initiate movement, produce movement, and control movement force and direction. Disuse of a limb, such as might result from a motor cortex injury, results in shrinkage of the limb's cortical representation. This shrinkage can be prevented, however, if the limb can be forced into use, as in constraint-induced therapy.

Two corticospinal pathways emerge from the motor cortex to the spinal cord. Lateral corticospinal axons projecting from the arm and hand/finger cortical areas cross in the brainstem to control contralateral arm and hand movements. Anterior corticospinal tract axons projecting from the trunk and shoulder cortical motor regions continue on the same side of the brainstem and spinal cord to produce whole-body movements. The lateral corticospinal tract synapses with interneurons and motor neurons located laterally in the spinal cord; the anterior corticospinal tract synapses with interneurons and motor neurons located medially and ipsilaterally in the spinal cord. Lateral motor neurons project to digit, hand, and arm muscles to produce arm and hand movements, and medial motor neurons project to trunk muscles and mediate whole-body movements, including locomotion.

## 11-3 Basal Ganglia, Cerebellum, and Movement

Both the basal ganglia and the cerebellum participate in the control of movement by modulating the movements initiated by the cortex. The basal ganglia regulate movement force. Damage to the basal ganglia is associated with diseases in which unwanted movements occur, such as Huntington disease, or in which affected individuals have difficulty making movements, such as Parkinson disease. The cerebellum has evolved in size in parallel with the neocortex. It participates in movement, motivation, and cognition by timing behavior and ensuring that a movement to be made is the desired movement.

## 11-4 Somatosensory System Receptors and Pathways

Distributed throughout the body, the somatosensory system consists of more than 20 types of specialized sensory neurons and receptors, each sensitive to a particular form of mechanical or chemical energy. Each receptor has a specialized projection through the posterior dorsal root ganglia into the spinal cord and to the brain.

Neurons carrying proprioceptive (location and movement) information and haptic (touch and pressure) information have large, myelinated axons that ascend the spinal cord as the posterior spinothalamic tract. These fibers synapse in the posterior column nuclei at the base of the brain. From there, axons cross to the other side of the brainstem to form the medial lemniscus, which ascends to the ventrolateral thalamus. Most of the ventrolateral thalamus cells project to the somatosensory cortex.

Nociceptive (pain, temperature, and itch) posterior root ganglion neurons are small and unmyelinated; they synapse on entering the spinal cord. Their relay neurons cross the spinal cord to ascend to the thalamus as the anterior spinothalamic tract.

Because the two somatosensory pathways take somewhat different routes, unilateral spinal cord damage impairs proprioception and hapsis ipsilaterally, below the site of injury, and impairs nociception contralaterally below the site.

## 11-5 Exploring the Somatosensory Cortex

The somatosensory system is represented by several body maps in parietal areas 3-1-2, with different maps representing different sensory receptor types. The most sensitive body parts are accorded the largest regions in these body maps, as befits the body parts most capable of fine movements. If sensory input from anywhere in the body is cut off from the cortex by damage to sensory fibers, adjacent positions of the body maps can expand into the now-unoccupied region.

The body maps of the primary somatosensory cortex project to the secondary somatosensory cortex, which represents information in the form of an action map. Categories of movements in the somatosensory action map project to the same part of the motor cortex action map.

The dorsal stream projects through the somatosensory cortex to the motor cortex to represent movements that are performed online. The ventral stream projects through the somatosensory cortex to the temporal cortex and then to the frontal cortex to control conscious movement in relation to perception and executive control.

# Key Terms

# Selected Resources from  Achieve

JGI/Jamie Grill/Getty Images

# What Causes Emotional and Motivated Behavior?

# 12

# The Pain of Rejection

We often use words like *sorrow*, *grief*, and *heartbreak* to describe a loss. Loss evokes painful feelings, and the loss or absence of contact that comes with social rejection leads to hurt feelings. Several investigators have attempted to discover whether physically painful and emotionally hurtful feelings are manifested in the same neural regions.

Physical pain (say, a hot or cold stimulus) is easy to inflict, but inducing equivalently severe emotional, or *affective*, pain is more difficult. Ethan Kross and colleagues (2011) performed an experiment that may have succeeded in balancing participants' degree of emotional and physical pain. Using fMRI, they scanned 40 people who had recently gone through an unwanted breakup. To compare brain activation, the participants viewed two photographs: one of their ex-partner, to evoke negative emotion, and the other of a same-gender friend with whom the participant shared a pleasant time at about the time of the breakup. The picture order was randomized across participants.

Emotional cue phrases associated with each photograph directed the participants to focus on a specific experience they shared with each person. In a separate session, researchers employed a physical stimulus in the form of either painful hot or painless warm stimulation of participants' forearms.

The research question is, Do physical pain and social pain have a common neuroanatomical basis? The results from Kross's experiment and similar studies reveal that two regions in particular respond to both types of pain: the insula and the dorsal anterior cingulate cortex (dACC) (see also Eisenberger, 2012) (see illustration). Their conclusion: social rejection hurts in much the same way that physical pain hurts. If this finding is true, then we would expect that treatments to reduce physical pain, such as the use of anti-inflammatories, might also reduce social pain. In fact, they do. People experiencing social pain report reduced pain sensation when given acetaminophen (an analgesic typically used to treat minor aches and fever) compared to a placebo, and this result correlates with reduced activity in the anterior cingulate cortex and insula (De Wall et al., 2010; see also the review by Eisenberger & Moieni, 2020).

Although it appears that social and physical pain overlap in the brain, we obviously can distinguish between our own experiences of social and physical pain, suggesting that the two experiences are mediated by different systems. There is also a difference in the phenomenology of

**Physical and Social Pain** Both the anterior insula (AI) and the dorsal anterior cingulate cortex (dACC) are implicated in the responses to both physical pain and the pain of social rejection. (Research from Kross et al., 2011.)

the two pains. Thus, we can re-experience or "relive" feelings of social pain, even when the painful episode has long passed; feelings of physical pain are not so easily relived. Meghan Meyer and colleagues (2015) have also found that reliving social pain activates the dorsolateral prefrontal cortex, whereas reliving physical pain activates the somatosensory cortex. A more recent study found that social rejection also activates the default network, which extends far beyond the anterior cingulate and insular areas (Mwilambwe-Tshilobo & Spreng, 2021).

The images obtained by Kross and colleagues and others suggest that the brain systems underlying emotional reactions to social rejection may have developed by co-opting brain circuits that support the affective (emotional) component of physical pain. We hasten to point out, however, that the overlapping activity in brain regions does not rule out unique neural components of emotional experiences. Certainly, our subjective experiences are unique (e.g., Kragel et al., 2018).

Another insight from this body of evidence is that normalizing the activity of these brain regions probably provides a basis for both physical and mental restorative processes. Seeing the similarity in brain activation during social pain and physical pain helps us understand why social support can reduce physical pain, much as it soothes emotional pain.

---

Knowing that the brain has a real sensation of emotional experience—more than a mere metaphorical experience of *hurt* or *pain*—as we learned from Research Focus 12-1, how do we incorporate our thoughts and reasons for behaving as we do? Clearly, our subjective feelings and thoughts influence our actions. The cognitive interpretations of subjective experiences are **emotions**—anger, fear, sadness, jealousy, embarrassment, joy. These interpretations can operate outside our immediate awareness.

This chapter begins by exploring the causes of behavior, which include sensory stimulation, neural circuits, hormones, and reward. We focus both on emotion and on the underlying reasons for behaviors that seem purposeful and goal directed (in other words, "motivated"). Like emotion, motivated behavior is both inferred and subjective, and it can occur without awareness or intent. It includes both regulatory behaviors (such as eating), which are essential for survival, and nonregulatory behaviors (such as curiosity), which are not required to meet an animal's basic needs.

---

**emotion** Cognitive interpretation of subjective experiences that can influence thought and behavior.

Research on the neuroanatomy responsible for emotional and motivated behavior focuses on a neural circuit formed by the hypothalamus, the frontal lobes, and the structures associated with the limbic system. But behavior is influenced as much by the interaction of our social and natural environments and by evolution as it is by our individual biological makeup, which is indicated by our genotypes and phenotypes. To explain how all these interactions affect the brain's control of behavior, we will concentrate on two specific examples: eating and sexual activity. Our exploration leads us to revisit the idea of reward, which is key to explaining emotional and motivated behaviors.

We first encountered the idea of reward in our discussion of wanting-and-liking theory in Section 6-4.

12-1

# Identifying the Causes of Behavior

We may think that the most obvious explanation for our behavior is simply that we act in a state of free will: we do what we want to, and we always have a choice. But in reality, free will is not a likely cause of behavior.

Consider Roger. We first met 25-year-old Roger in the admissions ward of a large mental hospital when he approached us and asked if we had any snacks. We had chewing gum, which he accepted eagerly. We thought little about this encounter until 10 minutes later, when we noticed Roger eating the flowers from the stems in a vase on a table. A nurse took the vase away but said little to Roger.

Later, as we wandered about the ward, we encountered a worker replacing linoleum floor tiles. Roger was watching the worker, and as he did, he dipped his finger into the pot of gluing compound and licked the glue from his finger, as if he were sampling honey from a jar. When we asked Roger what he was doing, he said that he was really hungry and that this stuff was not too bad. It reminded him of peanut butter. One of us tasted the glue and concluded that it did not taste like peanut butter—it tasted awful. Roger was undeterred. We alerted a nurse, who quickly removed him from the glue. Later, we saw him eating flowers from another bouquet.

Neurological testing revealed that a tumor had invaded Roger's hypothalamus at the base of his brain. He was indeed hungry all the time, and in all likelihood would consume more than 20,000 calories a day if allowed to do so.

Would you say that Roger was exercising free will regarding his appetite and food preferences? Probably not. Roger seemed compelled to eat whatever he could find, driven by a ravenous hunger. His nervous system—not an act of free will—produced this behavior. Undoubtedly, it produces many other behaviors for both Roger and the rest of us.

If free will does not adequately explain why we act as we do, what does? One obvious answer is that we do things that we find rewarding. That is, rewarding experiences must activate brain circuits that make us feel good. Consider domestic cats' propensity to stalk and kill prey.

One frustrating thing about being a cat owner is that even well-fed cats kill small animals, such as birds and mice. Most people are not much bothered when their cats kill mice: they view mice as a nuisance. But birds are different. People enjoy watching birds in their yard and garden. Many cat owners wonder why their pets keep killing birds.

To provide an answer, we look to the activities of neural circuits. Cats must have a brain circuit that controls prey killing. When this circuit is active, a cat makes an "appropriate" kill. Viewed in an evolutionary context, it makes sense for cats to have such a circuit: in the days when doting humans did not keep cats as pets, cats did not have food dishes that were regularly filled.

Why does this prey-killing circuit become active when a cat does not need food? One explanation is that, to ensure animals' survival, the activity of circuits like the prey-killing circuit is in some way rewarding—it makes the cat feel good. As a result, the cat will engage often in the pleasure-producing behavior. This helps to guarantee that the cat will usually not go hungry.

**Learning Objectives**
- Identify those behaviors useful for brain maintenance.
- Describe how neural circuits for behavior can be modified.
- Summarize the evolutionary influences on behavior.

Many people find watching and sharing cute cat videos rewarding: it makes them feel good, and they do it often. How could this behavior be explained evolutionarily?

In the wild, after all, a cat that did not like killing would probably be dead. In the 1960s, Steve Glickman and Bernard Schiff (1967) first proposed the idea that behaviors such as prey killing are rewarding. We return to reward in Section 12-7 because it is important in understanding the causes of behavior.

## Behavior for Brain Maintenance

Some experiences are rewarding. Others are aversive, again because brain circuits are activated to produce behaviors that reduce the aversive experience. One example is the brain's inherent need for stimulation.

Psychologists Robert Butler and Harry Harlow (1954) conducted a series of studies in which they placed rhesus monkeys in a dimly lit room with a small door that could be opened to view an adjoining room. As shown in **Figure 12-1**, the researchers could vary the stimuli in the adjoining room so that the monkeys could view different objects or animals each time they opened the door.

The monkeys in these studies spent a lot of time opening the door and viewing whatever was on display, such as toy trains circling a track. The monkeys were even willing to perform various tasks just for an opportunity to look through the door. The longer they were deprived of a chance to look, the more time they spent looking when finally given the opportunity. These experiments show that in the absence of stimulation, the brain will seek it out.

**FIGURE 12-1 Brain Maintenance** Monkeys quickly learn to solve puzzles or perform other tricks to gain access to a door that looks out from their dimly lit quarters into an adjacent room. A toy train is a strong visual incentive for the monkey peeking through the door; a bowl of fruit is less rewarding. University of Wisconsin; "Persistence of Visual Exploration in Monkeys," by R. A. Butler and H. F. Harlow, 1954, *Journal of Comparative and Physiological Psychology*, 47, p. 260.

## Neural Circuits and Behavior

Researchers have identified brain circuits associated with the "reward" sensation; they have also discovered that these circuits can modulate to increase or decrease activity. Researchers studying the rewarding properties of sexual activity in males, for example, found that a man's frequency of copulation correlates with his levels of **androgens** (hormones related to masculine characteristics). Unusually high androgen levels are related to ultrahigh sexual interest; abnormally low androgen levels are linked to low sexual interest or perhaps no interest at all. The brain circuits are more difficult to activate in the absence of androgens.

Another way to modulate reward circuits involves our chemical senses—that is, smell and taste. The odor of a mouse can stimulate hunting in cats, whereas the odor of a cat will drive mice into hiding. Similarly, the smell from a bakery can make us hungry, whereas foul odors can reduce the rewarding value of our favorite foods. Although we tend to view the chemical senses as relatively minor influences in our daily lives, they are central to motivated and emotional behavior.

Understanding the neural basis for motivated behavior has wide application. For instance, we can say that Roger had a voracious and indiscriminate appetite either because the brain circuits that initiate eating were excessively active or because the circuits that terminate eating were inactive. Similarly, we can say that Harlow and Butler's monkeys were interested in opening the door because the neural circuits that respond to sensory inputs were abnormally underactive. So, the main reason for a particular thought, feeling, or action lies in what is happening in the brain circuits.

**androgens** Hormones that are related to masculine characteristics and that play a role in levels of sexual interest in humans.

**innate releasing mechanism (IRM)** Hypothetical mechanism that detects specific sensory stimuli and directs an organism to take a particular action.

## Evolutionary Influences on Behavior

An understanding of brain circuits can help us understand the causes of behavior, but we are still left with a question: Why? One evolutionary explanation of behavior hinges on the concept of **innate releasing mechanisms (IRMs)**, activators of inborn adaptive responses that aid an animal's survival. IRMs help an animal to feed, reproduce, and escape predators. This concept is best understood by analyzing its parts.

As the term *innate* implies, IRMs are present from birth rather than being acquired through experience. These mechanisms have proved adaptive and, therefore, have been maintained in the genome of the species. The term *releasing* indicates that IRMs act as triggers for behaviors set in motion by internal programs.

Let us return to prey killing by cats. The cat's brain must have a built-in mechanism that triggers stalking and killing in response to a stimulus such as a bird or a mouse. A cat must also have a built-in mechanism that triggers mating behavior in the presence of a suitable cat of the opposite sex. Not all cat behaviors are due to IRMs, but you probably can think of other IRMs that cats possess—arching and hissing upon encountering a threat, for example. For all these mechanisms, the animal's brain must have a set of norms against which it can match stimuli to trigger an appropriate response.

An experiment by Bryan Kolb and Arthur Nonneman (1975) suggests the existence of such innate, internalized norms. These researchers allowed a litter of 6-week-old kittens to play in a room and become familiar with it. After this adjustment period, they introduced a two-dimensional image of an adult cat in a Halloween posture, as shown in **Figure 12-2**A, and a "Picasso" control version, as shown in Figure 12-2B.

The kittens responded to the Halloween cat image with raised fur, arched backs, and bared teeth—all signs of being threatened by the image of the adult cat. Some even hissed at the model. These kittens had no experience with any adult cat except their mother, and there was no reason to believe that she had ever shown them this behavior. The Picasso cat evoked no response. Some sort of template of this posture must be prewired in the kitten brain, such that seeing the model that matched this preexisting template automatically triggered a threat response. This innate trigger is an IRM.

The IRM concept also applies to humans. In one study, Tiffany Field and her colleagues (1982) asked an adult to display to young infants various exaggerated facial expressions, such as happiness, sadness, and surprise. As **Figure 12-3** shows, the babies responded with very much the same expressions the adults displayed. These newborns were too young to be imitating the adult faces intentionally. Rather, babies must innately match these facial expressions to their internal templates, which in turn triggers some prewired program to reproduce the expressions in their own faces. Evidence for a prewired motor program related to facial expressions also comes from studies of congenitally blind children, who spontaneously produce the very same facial expressions that sighted people do, even though they have never seen them in others. Such an IRM would have adaptive value if these facial expressions serve as important social signals for humans.

Although IRMs are prewired into the brain, experience can modify them. For example, our cat Hunter's stalking skills were not inherited fully developed at birth but rather matured functionally as she grew older. The same is true of many human IRMs, such as those for responding to sexually arousing stimuli. Indeed, we find that different cultures emphasize different stimuli as arousing. Even within a single culture, what different people find sexually stimulating varies. Nonetheless, some human attributes are universally sexually arousing. For most human males, an example is the hip-to-waist ratio of human females: women with a hip-to-waist ratio of .70 are curvy and considered ideal across cultures, though there is considerable variation in this preference across males. Our perception of facial attractiveness provides another example: both women and men rate as more attractive those faces that are symmetrical and average, where averageness refers to how closely a face resembles the majority of faces in a given population (Little et al., 2011).

**(A)**

**(B)**

*Courtesy of Arthur Nonneman and Bryan Kolb*

**FIGURE 12-2 Innate Releasing Mechanism in Cats (A)** Displaying the Halloween cat image stimulates defensive responses in cats—raised fur, arched backs, and bared teeth. This behavior appears at about 6 weeks of age in kittens who have never seen such a posture before. **(B)** The scrambled "Picasso cat" evokes no response at all.

**FIGURE 12-3 Innate Releasing Mechanism in Humans** Facial expressions made by young infants in response to expressions made by the experimenter. Republished with permission of the American Association for the Advancement of Science, from M Field, R Woodson, R Greenberg, D Cohen, "Discrimination and imitation of facial expression by neonates", Science 8 October 1982: Vol. 218 no. 4568 pp.179-181, Figure 1. Permission conveyed through Copyright Clearance Center, Inc.

Section 1-2 reviews Darwin's theory, materialism, and contemporary perspectives on brain and behavior.

The IRM concept can also be related to the Darwinian view of nervous system evolution. Natural selection favors behaviors that prove adaptive for an organism, and these behaviors are passed on to future generations. Because behavior patterns are produced by the activity of neurons in the brain, the natural selection of specific behaviors is really the selection of particular brain circuits.

Animals that survive long enough to reproduce and have healthy offspring are more likely to pass on their brain circuit genes than are animals with traits that make them less likely to survive and successfully reproduce. Thus, feral cats adept at stalking prey or responding fiercely to threats are more likely to survive and produce many offspring, passing on their adaptive brain circuits and behaviors to their young. In humans, the ideal hip-to-waist ratio in women appears to be an indicator of health and fertility and is likely related to longevity and increased fecundity. In this way, evolution slowly selects traits that become widespread in the species over time.

The Darwinian view seems straightforward when we consider how cats evolved brain circuits for stalking prey or responding to threats. Similarly, the connection between hip-to-waist ratio and successful child rearing may appear sensible for humans, but the evolutionary influence is less obvious when applied to complex human behaviors. Why, for instance, have humans evolved the behavior of killing other humans? At first glance, it seems counterproductive to the survival of the human species. Why has it endured? For an answer, we turn to **evolutionary psychology**, the field that applies principles of natural selection to explain human behaviors.

Evolutionary psychologists assume that any behavior, including homicide, occurs because natural selection has favored the neural circuits that produce it. When two people fight a duel, one commonsense explanation might be that they are fighting over grievances. But evolutionary psychologists would instead ask: Why is a behavior pattern that risks people's lives sustained in a population? Their answer: fights are about social status.

Historically, men who fought and won duels passed on their genes to future generations. Through time, therefore, the traits associated with successful dueling—strength, aggression, agility—became more prevalent among humans, as did dueling. Martin Daly and Margot Wilson (1988) extended this evolutionary analysis to account for homicide: homicide may endure in our society, despite severe punishments for engaging in it, because it is related to behaviors that were adaptive in the human past.

David Buss (2014) has examined patterns of mate selection across thousands of participants from 37 cultures, seeking to identify factors beyond culture that influence mate selection. His conclusions after nearly 30 years of study are that women tend to value dependability, stability, education, and intelligence in a long-term mate more than men do. Men, by contrast, tend to value good looks, health, and a desire for home and children more than women do.

Section 15-5 posits a genetic explanation for the evolution of sex-related cognitive differences.

Older men and younger women are most likely to exhibit a mutually desired set of traits, which leads to a universal tendency for age differences between mates. On average, older men are more stable, dependable, and educated than younger men are, and younger women are healthier and able to have more children than older women are. Although the idea is controversial, Buss argues that these preferences are a product of natural selection in a Stone Age environment, when women and men would have faced different daily problems and, in turn, would have developed separate adaptations related to mating.

Evolutionary theory cannot account for all human behavior, and perhaps not even homicide or mate selection. By adopting an evolutionary perspective on the neurological bases of behavior, though, evolutionary psychologists can generate intriguing hypotheses about how natural selection might have shaped the brain and behavior.

# Environmental Influences on Behavior

Many psychologists have emphasized learning as a cause of behavior. No one would question that we modify our behavior as we learn, but the noted behaviorist B. F. Skinner (1938) went much further, suggesting that behaviors are actually selected by environmental factors.

**evolutionary psychology** Discipline that seeks to apply the principles of natural selection to understand the causes of human behavior.

Skinner's argument is simple. Certain events function as rewards, or **reinforcers**. When a reinforcing event follows a particular response, similar responses are more likely to occur. Skinner argued that reinforcement can be manipulated to encourage the display of complex behaviors.

The power of experience to shape behavior by pairing stimuli and rewards is typified by one of Skinner's experiments. A pigeon is placed in a box that has a small disc (the stimulus) on one wall. If the pigeon pecks at the disc (the response), a food tray opens, and the pigeon can feed (the reinforcement or reward). The pigeon quickly learns the association between the stimulus and the response, especially if the disc has a small spot on it. It pecks at the spot, and within minutes it has mastered the response needed to receive a reward.

Now the response requirement can be made more complex. For example, the pigeon might be required to turn 360 degrees before pecking the disc to gain the reward. The pigeon can learn this response, too. Other contingencies might then be added, making the response requirements even more complex. For instance, the pigeon might be trained to turn in a clockwise circle if the disc is green, to turn in a counterclockwise circle if the disc is red, and to scratch at the floor if the disc is yellow.

Skinner box

If you suddenly came across this complex behavior in a pigeon, you would probably be astounded. But if you understood the experience that had shaped the bird's behavior, you would understand its cause. The rewards offered to the pigeon altered its behavior: its responses were controlled by the color of the disc on the wall.

Skinner extended behavioral analysis to include actions of all sorts—behaviors that at first do not appear easily explained. For instance, he argued that understanding a person's reinforcement history could account for various phobias. Someone who has a terrifying, turbulent plane ride thereafter avoids air travel and manifests a phobia of flying. The avoidance of flying is rewarding because it lowers the person's anxiety level, which then maintains the phobic behavior.

Skinner also argued against the commonly held view that much of human behavior is under our own control. From Skinner's perspective, free will is an illusion because behavior is controlled not by the organism, but rather by the environment, through experience. Yet what is the experience actually doing? Increasing evidence suggests that epigenetic changes regulate changes in memory circuits. Skinner did not study the brain directly, but subsequent research has shown that epigenetics supports his perspective. We learn many complex behaviors through changes in memory-related genes that act to modify neural circuits (see the review by Collins et al., 2019).

Epigenetic mechanisms mediate synaptic plasticity, especially in learning and memory. For a more detailed discussion, see Section 14-4.

The environment does not always change the brain. To see this, we again turn to our pigeons. A pigeon in a Skinner box can quickly learn to peck a disc to receive a bit of food, but it cannot learn to peck a disc to escape from a mild electric shock to its feet. Why not? Although the same simple pecking behavior is being rewarded, apparently the pigeon's brain is not prewired for this second kind of association. The bird is prepared genetically to make the first association, for food, but is not prepared to make the second association, for pain. This makes adaptive sense: typically, a pigeon flies away from noxious situations.

John Garcia and R. A. Koelling (1966) were the first psychologists to demonstrate the specific nature of this range of behavior–consequence associations that animals are able to learn. Garcia observed that farmers in the western United States are constantly shooting at coyotes for attacking lambs, yet despite the painful consequences, the coyotes never seem to learn to stop killing lambs in favor of safer prey. The reason, Garcia speculated, is that a coyote's brain is not prewired to make this kind of association.

To deter coyotes from killing lambs, Garcia proposed an alternative—an association that a coyote's brain is prepared to make: the connection between eating something that makes one sick and avoiding that food in the future. Garcia gave the coyotes a poisoned lamb carcass, which sickened but did not kill them. With only one pairing of lamb and illness, most coyotes learned not to eat sheep for the rest of their lives.

Many humans have similarly acquired food aversions because a certain food's taste—especially a novel taste—was subsequently paired with illness. This **learned taste aversion** is acquired even when the food eaten is, in fact, unrelated to

**reinforcer** In operant conditioning, any event that strengthens the behavior it follows.

**learned taste aversion** Acquired association between a specific taste or odor and illness; leads to an aversion to foods that have the taste or odor.

Section 14-4 has more information on how our brains are wired to link unrelated stimuli.

the later illness. As long as the taste and the nausea are paired in time, the brain is pre-wired to connect them.

One of us ate his first Caesar salad the night before coming down with a stomach flu. A year later, he was offered another Caesar salad and, to his amazement, felt ill just at the smell of it. Even though he knew that the salad had not caused his earlier illness, he nonetheless had formed an association between the novel flavor and the illness. This strong and rapid *associative learning* makes adaptive sense. Having a brain that is pre-pared to make a connection between a novel taste and subsequent illness helps an ani-mal avoid poisonous foods and so aids in its survival. A curious aspect of taste aversion learning is that we are unaware of having formed the association until we encounter the taste and/or smell again.

The fact that the nervous system is often prewired to make some associations but not others has led to the concept of **preparedness** in learning theories. Preparedness can help account for some complex behaviors. For example, if two rats are paired in a small box and exposed to a mild electric shock, they will immediately fight with each other, even though neither was responsible for the shock. Apparently, the rat brain is predisposed to associate injury with nearby objects or other animals. The extent to which we might adapt this idea to explain such human behaviors as bigotry and racism is an interesting topic to ponder. Although only a few studies have directly addressed this idea, findings suggest that social factors, including learning (in the form of stereotypes and prior experience) play a role in our perception of both racial in-groups and out-groups (e.g., Dunsmoor et al., 2016). Further study may help to explain the persistence of these behaviors.

## 12-1 Review

Before you continue, check your understanding. Answers to Self-Test appear at the back of the book.

1. Glickman and Schiff first proposed the idea that animals engage in prey-killing behaviors, such as when a cat kills a bird, because these behaviors are _____.

2. Studies by Butler and Harlow suggest the reason animals get bored and seek out new activities is to maintain brain _____.

3. A man's frequency of copulation correlates with his _____ levels.

4. The brain of a species is prewired to produce _____ to specific sensory stimuli selected by evolution to prompt certain associations between events.

5. Why is free will inadequate to explain why we do the things we do?

### 12-2
# Neuroanatomy of Motivated Behavior

**Learning Objectives**
- Distinguish between regulatory behavior and nonregulatory behavior.
- Describe the primary activities of the hypothalamic circuit.

**Principle 3:** The CNS functions on multiple levels and is organized hierarchically and in parallel.

**preparedness** Predisposition to respond to certain stimuli differently from other stimuli.

**motivation** Internal state of an organism that acts to initiate or energize behavior; from the Latin *motivus*, meaning "a moving cause."

**Motivation** refers to an internal state that acts to initiate or energize behavior (from the Latin *motivus*, meaning "a moving cause"). The neural circuits that control motivated behavior encompass regions at all levels of the brain, but the critical neural structure in producing motivated behavior is the hypothalamus. The hypothalamus receives pro-jections from all major subdivisions of the nervous system and functions to integrate diverse adaptive behaviors. It is not an individual brain region, but rather is composed of smaller neural units devoted to specific functions.

In his epic review of motivated behavior, Larry Swanson (2000) concluded that the hypothalamus is an integrative center of a larger "behavioral control column" (or net-work) controlled by the cerebral hemispheres. This behavioral column is composed of a rostral brainstem region devoted to social (including reproductive and defen-sive) behaviors and ingestion (eating and drinking), as well as a more caudal region extending into other brainstem areas related to exploration and foraging behaviors, such as the substantia nigra and ventral tegmentum. These functions are modulated by the cerebral hemispheres through descending pathways from the cerebral cortex, striatum, and pallidum. The hypothalamus acts to organize these cerebral inputs and produce feedback loops that regulate cerebral information to orchestrate homeostasis and motivated behaviors; it also ensures that the cerebral regions are aroused and online when needed. In addition, outputs from the hypothalamus project to the pituitary to control the release of a broad range of hormones.

In **Figure 12-4**, the neck of the funnel represents the hypothalamus, and the cerebral hemispheres form the funnel's rim. To produce behavior, the hypothalamus sends axons to other brainstem circuits—but not all behavior is controlled via the funnel to the hypothalamus. Many other routes to the brainstem and spinal cord bypass the hypothalamus, among them projections from the motor cortex to the brainstem and spinal cord. Thus, it is primarily motivated behaviors that require hypothalamic involvement.

# Regulatory and Nonregulatory Behavior

Brain activity prompts animals to seek out mates, food, or sensory stimulation, yet we talk about such behavior as being motivated. Motivations, however, are not components or processes that we can point to in the brain. Rather, motivations are inferences we make about why animals, including humans, engage in particular behaviors. Motivated behaviors fall into two general classes: regulatory and nonregulatory. In this section, we explore both categories before delving into the neuroanatomy of motivation.

## Regulatory Behaviors

**Regulatory behaviors** are those behaviors motivated by an organism's survival (see **Table 12-1**); they are controlled by **homeostatic mechanisms**. By analogy, consider a house whose thermostat is set at 18°C. When the temperature falls below a certain tolerable range (say, to 16°C), the thermostat turns on the furnace. When the temperature rises above a certain tolerable level (say, 20°C), the thermostat turns on the air conditioner.

Human body temperature is controlled in a somewhat similar manner by a thermostat in the hypothalamus that holds the internal temperature at about 37°C, a temperature referred to as a *set point*. Even slight variations in the internal temperature cause us to engage in various behaviors to regain the set point. For example, when body temperature drops slightly, neural circuits that increase body temperature turn on. These neural circuits might induce an involuntary response such as shivering or a seemingly voluntary behavior such as moving closer to a heat source. Conversely, if body temperature rises slightly, we sweat or move to a cooler place.

Similar mechanisms control many other homeostatic processes, including the amount of water in the body, the balance of dietary nutrients, and the blood sugar level. The control of many such homeostatic systems is quite complex, requiring both neural and hormonal mechanisms. In some way, however, all of the body's homeostatic systems involve hypothalamic activity.

Imagine that specific cells are especially sensitive to temperature. When they are cool, they become very active; when they are warm, they become less active. These cells could function as a thermostat, telling the body when it is too cool or too warm. A similar set of cells could serve as a glucostat, controlling the level of sugar in the blood, or as a hydrostat, controlling the amount of water in the body. Although the body's real homeostatic mechanisms are slightly more complex than this imagined one, they work on the same general principle.

Mechanisms to hold constant various conditions such as temperature have evolved because the body, including the brain, is a chemical soup in which thousands of reactions are taking place all the time. Maintaining constant temperature is critical. When temperature changes, even by as little as 2°C, the rates at which chemical reactions take place change. Such fluctuations might be tolerable, within certain limits, if all the reaction times changed to the same extent. But they do not. Consequently, an increase of 2°C might increase one reaction by 10% and another by only 2%. Such uneven changes would wreak havoc on finely tuned body processes such as metabolism and the workings of neurons.

A similar logic applies to maintaining homeostasis in other body systems. For instance, cells require certain concentrations of water, salt, and glucose to

Section 5-4 explores hormonal regulation of homeostatic mechanisms.

**FIGURE 12-4 Funneling Signals** In this model, many inputs from the cerebral hemispheres funnel through the hypothalamus, which sends its axons to control brainstem circuits that produce motivated behaviors.

**TABLE 12-1 Categories of Motivated Behavior**

| Some regulatory behaviors |
|---|
| Internal body temperature maintenance |
| Eating and drinking |
| Salt consumption |
| Waste elimination |
| **Some nonregulatory behaviors** |
| Sex |
| Parenting |
| Aggressive acts |
| Preferential eating (e.g., eating sweets) |
| Curiosity |
| Reading |

**regulatory behavior** Behavior motivated to meet an animal's survival needs.

**homeostatic mechanism** Process that maintains critical body functions within a narrow, fixed range.

**nonregulatory behavior** Behavior unnecessary to an animal's basic survival needs.

**pituitary gland** Endocrine gland attached to the bottom of the hypothalamus; its secretions control the activities of many other endocrine glands; associated with biological rhythms.

Figure 2-32 diagrams ANS pathways and connections.

Sections 6-2 and 6-4 elaborate on dopamine's importance in experiences related to drug use.

function properly. Wild fluctuations in the concentrations cause a gross disturbance of metabolic balance and eventually biological disaster.

## Nonregulatory Behaviors

Unlike regulatory behaviors, such as eating or drinking, **nonregulatory behaviors** are neither required to meet the animal's basic survival needs nor controlled by homeostatic mechanisms (see Table 12-1). Thus, nonregulatory behaviors include everything else we do—from sexual intercourse to parenting to such curiosity-driven activities as conducting psychology experiments.

Some nonregulatory behaviors, such as sexual intercourse, do involve the hypothalamus, but most of them probably do not. Rather, such behaviors rely on a variety of forebrain structures, especially the frontal lobes. Presumably, as the forebrain evolved and enlarged, so did our range of nonregulatory behaviors.

# Activities of the Hypothalamic Circuit

The hypothalamus maintains homeostasis by acting on both the endocrine system and the autonomic nervous system (ANS) to regulate our internal environment. The hypothalamus also influences the behaviors selected by the rest of the brain, especially by the cerebral hemispheres. Although it constitutes less than 1% of the human brain's volume, the hypothalamus controls an amazing variety of motivated behaviors, ranging from heart rate to eating and sexual activity.

## Hypothalamic Involvement in Hormone Secretions

A principal function of the hypothalamus is to control the **pituitary gland**, which is attached to this brain structure by a stalk (**Figure 12-5**A). Figure 12-5B diagrams the anatomic location of the hypothalamus in each hemisphere, with the thalamus above it and the optic tracts just lateral to it.

**FIGURE 12-5 Nuclei and Regions of the Hypothalamus (A)** Medial view shows the relationship between the hypothalamic nuclei and the rest of the brain. **(B)** Frontal view shows the relative positions of the hypothalamus, thalamus, and—in the midline between the left and right hemispheres—the third ventricle. Note the three principal hypothalamic regions: periventricular, lateral, and medial.

We can divide the hypothalamus into three regions: lateral, medial, and periventricular (see the frontal view in Figure 12-5B). The lateral hypothalamus, which is composed of both nuclei and nerve tracts running up and down the brain, connects the lower brainstem to the forebrain. The principal tract, shown in **Figure 12-6**, is the **medial forebrain bundle (MFB)**.

The MFB connects brainstem structures with various parts of the limbic system and forms the activating projections that run from the brainstem to the basal ganglia and frontal cortex. Fibers that ascend from the dopamine- and noradrenaline-containing cells of the lower brainstem form a significant part of the MFB. The dopamine-containing MFB fibers contribute to the control of many motivated behaviors, including eating and sex. They also contribute to pathological behaviors, such as addiction and impulsivity.

Each hypothalamic nucleus is anatomically distinct, and most have multiple functions, in part because the cells in each nucleus contain a different mix of peptide neurotransmitters. Each peptide participates in different behaviors. For instance, transmitters in the cells in the paraventricular nucleus may consist of vasopressin, oxytocin, or various combinations of other peptides (such as enkephalin and neurotensin). When peptide neurotransmitters act, we may experience a range of feelings such as well-being (endorphins) or attachment (oxytocin and vasopressin). For example, oxytocin is released during intimate moments such as nurturing behavior, hugging, or sex, so it is sometimes known as the bonding hormone.

The production of various neuropeptides hints at the special relationship between the hypothalamus and the pituitary. The pituitary consists of distinct anterior and posterior glands, as shown in **Figure 12-7**. The posterior pituitary is composed of neural tissue and is essentially a continuation of the hypothalamus.

Neurons in the hypothalamus make peptides (e.g., oxytocin and vasopressin) that are transported down their axons to terminals lying in the posterior pituitary. When these neurons become active, they send action potentials to the terminals to release

**FIGURE 12-6  Medial Forebrain Bundle**
The activating projections that run from the brainstem to the basal ganglia and frontal cortex are major components of the medial forebrain bundle (MFB), a primary pathway for fibers connecting various parts of the limbic system with the brainstem.

Section 5-2 reviews the structures and functions of peptide neurotransmitters.

**medial forebrain bundle (MFB)**  Tract that connects brainstem structures with various parts of the limbic system; forms the activating projections that run from the brainstem to the basal ganglia and frontal cortex.

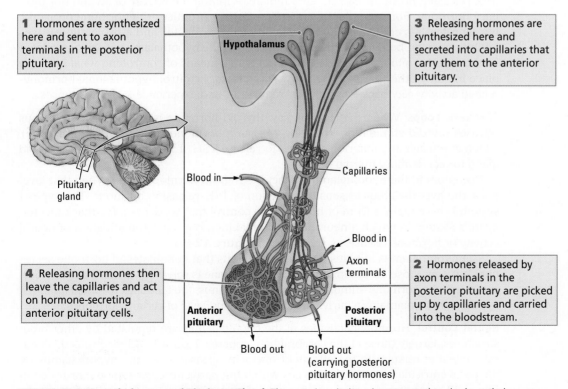

**1** Hormones are synthesized here and sent to axon terminals in the posterior pituitary.

**3** Releasing hormones are synthesized here and secreted into capillaries that carry them to the anterior pituitary.

Hypothalamus

Pituitary gland

Blood in → Capillaries

Blood in

Axon terminals

**4** Releasing hormones then leave the capillaries and act on hormone-secreting anterior pituitary cells.

**2** Hormones released by axon terminals in the posterior pituitary are picked up by capillaries and carried into the bloodstream.

**Anterior pituitary**        **Posterior pituitary**

Blood out        Blood out (carrying posterior pituitary hormones)

**FIGURE 12-7  Hypothalamus and Pituitary Gland**  The anterior pituitary is connected to the hypothalamus by a system of blood vessels that carry hormones from the hypothalamus to the pituitary. The posterior pituitary receives input from axons of hypothalamic neurons. Both regions respond to hypothalamic input by producing hormones that travel in the bloodstream to stimulate target organs.

**TABLE 12-2** Major Hormones Produced by the Anterior Pituitary

| Hormone | Function |
| --- | --- |
| Adrenocorticotrophic hormone (ACTH) | Controls secretions of the adrenal cortex |
| Thyroid-stimulating hormone (TSH) | Controls secretions of the thyroid gland |
| Follicle-stimulating hormone (FSH) | Controls secretions of the gonads |
| Luteinizing hormone (LH) | Controls secretions of the gonads |
| Prolactin | Controls secretions of the mammary glands |
| Growth hormone (GH) | Promotes growth throughout the body |

the peptides stored there. But rather than these peptides affecting another neuron, as occurs at most synapses, capillaries (tiny blood vessels) in the posterior pituitary's rich vascular bed pick them up. The peptides then enter the bloodstream, which carries them to distant targets throughout the body, where they exert their effects. Vasopressin, for example, affects water resorption by the kidneys, and oxytocin controls both uterine contractions and the ejection of milk by mammary glands in the breasts.

Peptides can have multiple functions, depending on where their receptors are. Thus, oxytocin not only controls milk ejection in females, but also performs a more general role in several forms of affiliative behavior, including parental care, grooming, and sexual behavior in both men and women (Insel & Fernald, 2004).

The glandular tissue of the anterior pituitary, by contrast, synthesizes various hormones. The major hormones and their functions are listed in **Table 12-2**. The hypothalamus controls the release of these anterior pituitary hormones by producing **releasing hormones**, peptides that act to increase or decrease hormone release. Releasing hormones, which are produced by hypothalamic cell bodies, are secreted into capillaries, which then transport them to the anterior pituitary, as shown in Figure 12-7.

A releasing hormone can either stimulate or inhibit the release of an anterior pituitary hormone. For example, the anterior pituitary produces the hormone prolactin, but its release is controlled by a prolactin-releasing factor and a prolactin release–inhibiting factor, both of which are synthesized in the hypothalamus. Hormone release by the anterior pituitary provides the brain with a means of controlling what is taking place in many other parts of the body. Three factors control hypothalamic hormone-related activity: feedback loops, neural regulation, and experience-based responses.

**Feedback Loops** When the level of, say, thyroid hormone is low, the hypothalamus releases thyroid-stimulating hormone–releasing hormone (TSH-releasing hormone), which stimulates the anterior pituitary to release TSH. TSH then acts on the thyroid gland to secrete more thyroid hormone.

Receptors in the hypothalamus detect the thyroid hormone level. When that level rises, the hypothalamus lessens its secretion of TSH-releasing hormone. This type of system is essentially a form of homeostatic control that works as a feedback mechanism, a system in which a neural or hormonal loop regulates the initiation of neural activity or hormone release, as illustrated in **Figure 12-8**A.

The hypothalamus initiates a cascade of events that culminates in hormone secretion, but pays close attention to how much hormone is released. When a certain level is reached, its hormone-stimulating signals stop. Thus, the feedback mechanism in the hypothalamus maintains a fairly constant circulating level of certain hormones.

**Neural Control** Hormonal activities of the hypothalamus are regulated by other brain structures, largely those in the cerebral hemispheres. Figure 12-8B diagrams this neural control in relation to the effects of oxytocin released from the hypothalamus by the paraventricular nucleus, which lies within the periventricular region (illustrated in Figure 12-5). As stated earlier, one function of oxytocin is to stimulate cells of the mammary glands to release milk. As shown in Figure 12-8B, when an infant suckles the mother's breast, the tactile stimulation causes hypothalamic cells to release oxytocin, which

Thyroid gland

**releasing hormone** Peptide released by the hypothalamus that increases or decreases hormone release from the anterior pituitary.

**FIGURE 12-8 Hypothalamic Controls**
**(A)** Releasing hormones from the hypothalamus stimulate the anterior pituitary to release hormones. The pituitary hormones stimulate target organs, such as the thyroid and adrenal glands, to release their hormones. In the feedback loop, those hormones in turn influence the hypothalamus to decrease its secretion of the releasing hormones. **(B)** In the milk letdown response, oxytocin released from the hypothalamus stimulates the mammary glands to release milk. Milk letdown is enhanced by infant-related stimuli and inhibited by maternal anxiety.

then stimulates milk letdown. In this way, the oxytocin cells participate in a fairly simple reflex that is both neural and hormonal.

Other stimuli can also influence oxytocin release, however, which is where control by other brain structures comes in. For example, the sight, sound, or even thought of her baby can trigger the breast of a lactating mother to eject milk. Conversely, as diagrammed in Figure 12-8B, feelings of anxiety in a lactating woman can inhibit milk ejection. These excitatory and inhibitory influences exerted by cognitive activity imply that the cortex can influence neurons in the periventricular region. It is likely that projections from the frontal lobes to the hypothalamus perform this role.

**Experiential Responses** A third factor controlling the hormonal activities of the hypothalamus is the brain's responses to experience: neurons in the hypothalamus undergo structural and biochemical changes, just as cells in other brain regions do. In other words, hypothalamic neurons are like neurons elsewhere in the brain in that they can be changed by heavy demands on them.

Such changes in hypothalamic neurons can affect hormone output. For instance, when a woman is lactating, the cells producing oxytocin increase in size to promote oxytocin release and meet the increasing demands of a growing infant for more milk. Through this control, which is mediated by experience, a mother provides her baby with sufficient milk over time. Thus, we can see that both the neural regulation and the environmental demands can influence a single system (in this case, oxytocin and milk letdown) in different ways.

**Principle 10:** Neuroplasticity is the hallmark of nervous system functioning.

## Hypothalamic Involvement in Generating Behavior

Not only does the hypothalamus control hormone systems, but it also play a central role in generating behavior. This function was first demonstrated by studies in which stimulating electrodes were placed in the hypothalamus of various animals, ranging from chickens to rats and cats. When a small electric current was delivered through a wire electrode, the animal suddenly engaged in some complex behavior—eating, drinking, or digging; displaying fear, attack, predatory, or reproductive behavior. The specific behavior exhibited depended on which site was stimulated. All of the behaviors were smooth, well integrated, and indistinguishable from typically occurring ones. Furthermore, all were goal directed.

The onset and termination of these behaviors depended entirely on hypothalamic stimulation. For example, if an electrode in a certain location elicited eating behavior, the animal ate as soon as the stimulation was turned on and continued to eat until the stimulation was turned off. If the food was removed, however, the animal would not eat but might engage in other behaviors, such as drinking. Recall that Roger, profiled in Section 12-1, ate continuously if food-like materials were present, corresponding to the continuous hypothalamic activity caused by a tumor.

**FIGURE 12-9 Generating Behavior** When rats receive electrical stimulation to the hypothalamus, they produce goal-directed behaviors. This rat is stimulated to dig when and only when the electricity is on and when sawdust is present. If the sawdust is removed (not shown), there is no digging.

**Figure 12-9** illustrates the effect of stimulation at a site that elicits digging. When no current is delivered, the animal sits quietly. When the current is turned on, the animal vigorously digs in the sawdust. When the current is turned off, the animal stops digging. If the sawdust is removed, the animal does not dig.

Behaviors generated by hypothalamic stimulation are related to two characteristics: (1) survival and (2) reward. Regulatory behaviors are required for survival, but animals apparently also find the stimulation of these behaviors pleasant, as suggested by the fact that they willingly expend effort, such as pressing a bar, to trigger the stimulation. Recall that cats kill birds and mice because the act of stalking and killing prey is rewarding to them. Similarly, we can hypothesize that animals eat because eating is rewarding, drink because drinking is rewarding, and mate because mating is rewarding.

Up to this point, we have ignored the role of chemical senses (olfaction and taste) in motivating behavior, but these senses can modulate the hypothalamic control of behavior. Next, we explore how chemical senses function and influence behavior.

## 12-2 Review

Before you continue, check your understanding. Answers to Self-Test appear at the back of the book.

1. Motivated behaviors can be divided into two categories: _____ behaviors, which maintain homeostasis, and _____ behaviors, encompassing basically all other behaviors.

2. The brain's homeostat for many functions is found in the _____.

3. The hypothalamus controls the _____, an endocrine gland that secretes hormones that control the activities of other endocrine glands throughout the body.

4. Explain how the hypothalamus acts as an integrative center for the behavioral control column.

### 12-3

**Learning Objectives**

- Explain the role of cognitive appraisal in olfaction and taste.
- Describe the organization and function of the olfactory system.
- Describe the organization and function of the gustatory system.

# The Role of the Chemical Senses in Motivated Behavior

Chemical reactions are central to nervous system activity, and *chemosignals* (chemical signals) play a central role in motivated and emotional behavior. For example, mammals identify group members by odor; mark their territory with urine and other odorants; identify favorite and forbidden foods by taste; and form associations among odors, tastes, and emotional events. But animals also make cognitive appraisals related to the chemical senses, such as when a dog evokes a taste aversion or turns away food that smells spoilt.

Humans apply terms such as "disgusting" to refer to bad odors or tastes, but we also use similar suggestive terms in cognitive appraisals of complex actions, such as the unfair treatment of others. Therefore, it is not surprising to discover that chemical disgust, social disgust, and other cognitive appraisals related to disgust involve overlapping neural representations in brain structures including the insular cortex.

Paul Rozin and colleagues (2009) noted that a neural system that has evolved for one purpose can later be used for another purpose. (We encountered an example of this in Research Focus 12-1, where the social pain system co-opted the physical pain system.) Rozin's idea is that evolution created a disgust behavior system that would protect individuals from sickness, but this system was without a disgust evaluation component. At some point in human evolution, the disgust behavior system was harnessed to a disgust evaluation system that responded initially to more cognitively elaborated appraisals (e.g., the feeling of disgust at seeing a cockroach near food), but later was enlarged to more abstract things, such as specific people, social groups, or even culture. In addition, the original physiological expression (e.g., nausea) and behavioral expression (e.g., withdrawal) expanded to include both verbal and nonverbal behaviors. Rozin and others have proposed that the disgust evaluation system became further extended to include a range of moral offenses, such as violations of fairness and justice, as well as "divinity violations," which include violations of food and sex taboos (Rozin et al., 2009).

Curtis and de Barra (2018) have suggested that moral disgust may have arisen as an extension of *hygiene disgust,* the system that causes someone to distance themself from those who represent a possible source of infection. This system could, for example, be activated when someone distances themself from individuals who perpetrate social infractions. In a sense, sensations of disgust to tastes and smells evolved into sensations related to morals.

The development and expansion of the disgust system illustrates how the chemical senses play both direct and indirect roles in controlling behavior. To get a broader understanding of how chemical senses can influence motivated behavior, we first need to briefly describe their organization and operation before considering their role in motivated behavior.

# Olfaction

Olfaction is the most puzzling sensory system. We can discriminate thousands of odors and, as we have just seen, attach appraisals to them, yet we have great difficulty finding words to describe what we smell. We may like or dislike smells or compare one smell to another, but we lack a vocabulary for olfactory perceptions.

Wine experts rely on olfaction to tell them about wines, but they must learn to use smell to do so. Training courses in wine sniffing typically run a full day each week for a year, and most participants have great difficulty passing the final test. This degree of difficulty contrasts with those attached to vision and audition—senses designed to analyze the specific qualities of sensory input, such as pitch in audition or color in vision. Olfaction seems designed to discriminate whether information is safe or familiar (Is the smell from an edible food? from a friend or a stranger?) or to identify a signal, perhaps from a receptive mate.

## Receptors for Smell

Conceptually, identifying chemosignals is similar to identifying other sensory stimuli (light, sound, touch), but rather than converting physical energy such as light or sound waves into receptor potentials, scent interacts with chemical receptors. This constant chemical interaction must be tough on the receptors: in contrast to the receptors for light, sound, and touch, chemical receptors are constantly being replaced. The life of an olfactory receptor neuron is about 60 days.

Figure 5-16A illustrates activity in such a metabotropic receptor.

The receptor surface for olfaction, illustrated in **Figure 12-10**, is the *olfactory epithelium* in the nasal cavity. The epithelium is composed of receptor cells and support cells. Each receptor cell sends a process ending in 10 to 20 cilia into a mucous layer, the *olfactory mucosa.* Chemicals in the air we breathe are absorbed in the mucosa, where

**FIGURE 12-10 Olfactory Epithelium** Air carrying odorant molecules enters the nasal pathway and makes contact with the epithelium, where the molecules dissolve into the mucosa. If an olfactory chemosignal affects the receptors within the mucosa, proteins within the receptor are activated, opening sodium channels and sending signals through the glomeruli and mitral cells in the olfactory bulb and on to the forebrain.

they interact with the cilia. If an olfactory chemosignal affects the receptors, metabotropic activation of a specific G protein leads to an opening of sodium channels and a change in membrane potential.

The epithelial receptor surface varies widely across species. In humans, this area is estimated to range from 2 to 4 square centimeters; in dogs, it is approximately 18 square centimeters; and in cats, it is about 21 square centimeters. No wonder our sensitivity to odors is less acute than that of dogs and cats: they have 10 times as much receptor area as humans have! Roughly analogous to the tuning characteristics of cells in the auditory system, olfactory receptor neurons in vertebrates do not respond to specific odors but rather to a range of odors.

How are we able to detect so many different odors despite having a small number of receptor types? The simplest explanation is that any given odorant stimulates a unique pattern of receptors, and the summed activity or pattern of activity produces our perception of a particular odor. Analogously, the visual system enables us to identify several million colors despite having only three receptor types in the retina; the summed activity of the three cones leads to our richly colored life.

A fundamental difference, however, is that the olfactory system is estimated to contain about 400 kinds of receptors, compared with just 4 types (rods plus the cones) in the visual system. Some researchers have proposed that humans can discriminate as many as 1 trillion smells. At present, the true number is unknown but is likely more than commonly believed (Gerkin & Castro, 2015).

## Olfactory Pathways

Olfactory receptor cells project to the olfactory bulb, ending in ball-like tufts of dendrites—the *glomeruli* shown in Figure 12-10—where they form synapses with the dendrites of *mitral cells*. Mitral cells send their axons from the olfactory bulb to the broad range of forebrain areas summarized in **Figure 12-11**. Many olfactory targets, such as the amygdala and pyriform cortex, have no connection *through* the thalamus, as do other sensory systems. However, a thalamic connection (to the dorsomedial nucleus) does project to the **orbitofrontal cortex (OFC)**, the prefrontal area behind the eye sockets (the orbits).

## Accessory Olfactory System

One unique class of odorants is the **pheromones**, biochemicals released by one animal that act as chemosignals and can affect the physiology or behavior of another animal of the same species. In most mammals (though perhaps not in humans), pheromones are detected by a special olfactory receptor system, the *vomeronasal organ*, which is made

---

The process by which the activity of visual receptors allows us to see color is detailed in Section 9-4.

In Section 12-6, we explain the central role of the OFC in emotional behaviors.

**orbitofrontal cortex (OFC)** Prefrontal cortex behind the eye sockets (the *orbits*); receives projections from the dorsomedial nucleus of the thalamus; central to a variety of emotional and social behaviors, including eating; also called *orbital frontal cortex*.

**pheromone** Odorant biochemical released by one animal that acts as a chemosignal and can affect the physiology or behavior of another animal.

up of a small group of sensory receptors connected by a duct to the nasal passage. The receptor cells in the vomeronasal organ send their axons to the accessory olfactory bulb, which lies adjacent to the main olfactory bulb; this connects primarily with the amygdala and hypothalamus, through which it probably plays a role in reproductive and social behavior.

The vomeronasal organ likely participates in the analysis of pheromones, such as those in urine or sweat. You may have seen horses or cats engage in a behavior known as *flehmen*, illustrated in **Figure 12-12**. When exposed to novel urine from a cat or human, cats raise their upper lip to close off the nasal passages and suck air into the mouth. The air flows through the duct on the roof of the mouth en route to the vomeronasal organ.

## Human Olfactory Processing

Our ability to distinguish a surprisingly large number of odors upends the common misperception that humans have a miserable sense of smell relative to other mammals. Still, our threshold for detecting many smells is certainly inferior to that of our pet dogs, cats, and horses, to name just a few examples. Yet humans have a surprisingly acute sensitivity to behaviorally significant smells. As discussed in the introduction to this section, evidence from a variety of sources indicate a vital link between human olfaction and many socially and culturally relevant behaviors, as well as our cognitive appraisals of many odors.

The compound delta 4,16-androstadien-3-one (*androstadienone*), a natural component of human sweat, plays a unique role in communication between humans. A growing body of evidence indicates that people can identify their own odor, the odor of kin versus not-kin, and the odor of friends versus strangers with an accuracy significantly greater than chance (e.g., Olsson et al., 2006). Yet humans do not appear to possess a functional vomeronasal organ. So how are these social odors perceived? Tom Hummer and colleagues (2017) used functional magnetic resonance imaging (fMRI) to examine the effect of androstadienone on the brain's response to emotional images (relative to neutral images) of participants who were exposed to the odor versus no odor. They found increased activity in the right dorsolateral prefrontal and orbital prefrontal regions, especially when the images were positive. Another study found that smelling a stranger's odor activates the amygdala and insular cortex, similar to the activation observed for fearsome visual stimuli, such as masked or scary faces (Lundstrom et al., 2008).

## Gustation

Research has revealed significant differences in taste preferences both between and within species. Humans and rats like sucrose and saccharin solutions, but dogs reject saccharin, and cats are indifferent to both, inasmuch as they do not detect sweetness at all. The failure of cats to taste sweetness may not be surprising: they are pure carnivores, and nothing that they normally eat is sweet.

Among humans, individual differences in taste thresholds and preferences are quite obvious. An example is the preference for or dislike of bitter tastes—the flavor of brussels sprouts, for instance. People tend to love them or hate them. Linda Bartoshuk (2000) showed absolute differences among adults: some perceive certain tastes as very bitter, whereas others are indifferent to them. Presumably, the latter group is more tolerant of brussels sprouts.

**FIGURE 12-11 Olfactory Pathways**

To thalamus and orbitofrontal cortex

To hypothalamus

Olfactory bulb

To amygdala

Pyriform and entorhinal cortex

The insular cortex contains regions related to language, taste perception, and social cognition.

**FIGURE 12-12 Response to Pheromones**
*Left*: A cat sniffs a urine-soaked cotton ball. Center: It raises its upper lip to close off the nasal passages. *Right*: It follows with the full gape response characteristic of flehmen, a behavior mediated by the accessory olfactory system.

Courtesy Arthur Nonneman and Bryan Kolb

Sensitivity to bitterness is related to genetic differences in the ability to detect a specific bitter chemical, 6-*n*-propylthiouracil (PROP). PROP bitterness is associated with allelic variation in the taste receptor gene *TAS2R38*. People who are able to detect minute quantities of PROP find the taste extremely bitter; they are sometimes called *supertasters*. Those who do not taste PROP as very bitter are called *nontasters*. The advantage of being a supertaster is that many bitter "foods" are poisonous. The disadvantage is that supertasters avoid many nutritious fruits and vegetables, such as grapefruit, that they find too bitter.

Differences in taste thresholds also emerge as we age. Children are much more responsive to taste than adults are and are often intolerant of spicy foods because they have more taste receptors than adults have. It is estimated that by age 20, humans have lost at least 50% of their taste receptors. No wonder children and adults have different food preferences.

Ethnic differences in taste perception also exist. In one study, participants identifying as Hispanic or African American rated taste sensations as being stronger than did non-Hispanic Whites. The researchers proposed that such differences in ratings may reflect differences in diet between ethnic groups related to variations in experiences with types or spiciness of foods, or it may reflect a physiological difference, such as the density of taste receptors (Williams et al., 2016).

## Receptors for Taste

Taste receptors are found in taste buds on the tongue, under the tongue, on the soft palate on the roof of the mouth, on the sides of the mouth, and at the back of the mouth on the nasopharynx. Each of the five taste receptor types responds to a different chemical component in food. The four most familiar types are sweet, sour, salty, and bitter. The fifth type, called the *umami* (meaning "savory" in Japanese) receptor, is especially sensitive to glutamate. Although it was once widely believed that different regions of the tongue are responsible for each of the five basic tastes, we now know that the five taste receptors are found all over the tongue.

Taste receptors are grouped into taste buds, each containing several, if not all, receptor types, as illustrated in **Figure 12-13**. Gustatory stimuli interact with the receptor tips, the *microvilli*, to open ion channels, leading to changes in the membrane potential. At its base, the taste bud contacts the branches of afferent cranial nerve 7 (facial), 9 (glossopharyngeal), or 10 (vagus).

## Gustatory Pathways

Cranial nerves 7, 9, and 10 form the main gustatory nerve, which becomes the *solitary tract* once it enters the CNS. On entering the brainstem, this tract splits, as illustrated in **Figure 12-14**. One route (traced in red) travels through the posterior medulla to the ventroposterior medial nucleus of the thalamus. This nucleus, in turn, sends out two pathways: one to the primary somatosensory cortex (SI) and the other to the primary gustatory cortex of the insula, a region just rostral to the secondary somatosensory cortex (SII).

The gustatory region in the insula is dedicated to taste, whereas SI is also responsive to tactile information and is probably responsible for our reactions to a food's texture. The gustatory cortex sends a projection to the orbital frontal cortex. Neuroimaging studies suggest that the mixture of olfactory and gustatory inputs in the orbital cortex gives rise to our perception of flavor. It is believed that the insula identifies the nature and intensity of flavors, whereas the orbital frontal cortex evaluates the affective properties of tastes. Ambience, including music and light, also affects this region of orbital cortex, increasing blood flow and thereby enhancing our experience of flavor. The involvement of the orbital cortex may be related to the cognitive appraisal of odors, as discussed in the section opening.

The second pathway from the gustatory nerve (shown in blue in Figure 12-14) projects via the nucleus of the solitary tract in the brainstem to the hypothalamus and amygdala. Researchers hypothesize that these inputs somehow play a part in eating, possibly by enabling us to evaluate the pleasantness and strength of flavors.

Tongue    Taste pore    Microvilli

- Bitter receptor
- Sweet receptor
- Sour receptor
- Umami receptor
- Salt receptor

Processes of cranial nerves 7, 9, 10

**FIGURE 12-13 Anatomy of a Taste Bud** Information from Smith & Shepherd (2003).

Ventral posteromedial nucleus of thalamus    Primary gustatory cortex (insula)    Primary somatosensory cortex

Lateral hypothalamus    Amygdala    Nucleus of solitary tract    Cranial nerves 7, 9, 10

**FIGURE 12-14 Gustatory Pathways**

# Impairments in the Chemical Senses and Behavior

Although impairments in vision and hearing can certainly produce major disruptions in our daily lives, impairments in the chemical senses can also have profound, if more subtle, impacts. Impairments in olfactory function are related to many behaviors, including an increased incidence of depression, decreased enjoyment of eating and drinking, and decreased sexual satisfaction in both women and men. A loss of smell is also related to deficits in personal hygiene because unpleasant smells, such as body odor, go undetected. In addition, loss of olfactory and gustatory functions (referred to as *anosmia* and *ageusia*, respectively) is an early biomarker of both Parkinson disease and dementia, often preceding the emergence of motor or cognitive symptoms (Adams et al., 2018; Eliyan et al., 2021; Melis et al., 2021; Siegel et al., 2021). More recently, anosmia and ageusia have been identified as early and prominent symptoms of COVID-19 infection, often slowly abating only after respiratory issues associated with this disease are resolved (Rouadi et al., 2021).

The loss of taste and olfaction in many disorders results in a lack of interest in food, which can be tasteless; when eating is an unrewarding experience, it may in turn lead to a reduction in food consumption. This change is associated with significant detrimental health effects, such as malnutrition, especially among elderly individuals (Meunier et al., 2021). Additionally, deficits in these chemical senses can lead to a failure to activate the disgust system that protects individuals from eating unsafe or rotten food, potentially leading to food poisoning.

In Section 12-4, we explore some of the neural structures related to the control of eating and drinking, and review some of the eating disorders that correspond to damage to these structures.

## 12-3 Review

Before you continue, check your understanding. Answers to Self-Test appear at the back of the book.

1. The receptor surface for olfaction is the _____.

2. Olfactory and gustatory pathways pass through the thalamus and merge in an area behind the eye sockets known as the _____.

3. The perception of bitterness is related to both the _____ and the number of _____.

4. Three disorders associated with a loss of smell and taste are _____, _____, and _____.

5. Explain how our ability to make abstract evaluations, such as in cases involving fairness and morality, may have arisen out of a neural system for making cognitive appraisals based on chemical senses.

6. What role does olfactory processing play in humans' social behavior?

## 12-4

# Control of Regulatory Behavior

The two distinctly different types of motivated behaviors described in Section 12-2 are *regulatory* behaviors, which maintain vital body system balance, or homeostasis; and *nonregulatory* behaviors, which are not controlled by a homeostatic mechanism and encompass basically all other behaviors. We focus here on the control of two regulatory behaviors in humans—eating and fluid intake. In the next section, we explore control of human sexual behavior, a nonregulatory behavior that is of enormous significance to humans.

**Learning Objectives**
- Identify the neural mechanisms that control eating.
- Identify the types of thirst and their mechanisms.

# Controlling Eating

Eating entails far more than sustenance alone. We must eat and drink to live, but we also derive great pleasure from these acts. For many people, eating is a focus of daily life, not just for survival, but also for its centrality to social activities such as get-togethers with family and friends or business meetings, and even to group identification (gourmet, vegetarian, snack food junkie, dieter, and so on).

Control over our eating is a source of frustration and even grief for many people in the developed world. According to the World Health Organization (2021), rates of **obesity**—the excessive accumulation of body fat—have nearly tripled worldwide since 1975; this condition now affects more than 13% of the world's adult population and 6% to 8% of children ages 5 to 19. In the United States, the proportion of people who are obese increased from approximately 30% of the population in 1999–2000 to more than 40% in 2017–2018, according to the Centers for Disease Control and Prevention. This upward trend accelerated during the pandemic in 2020, particularly among children ages 5 to 11 (Woolford et al., 2021). In a shift from previous decades, high rates of obesity and overweight among children are now being seen not only in high-income communities but across socioeconomic lines—they are truly a universal concern. Many lower-income communities face the combined burden of obesity and malnutrition because their access to foods is largely limited to those that are simultaneously high in fat, sugar, and salt but poor in nutrients, particularly in prenatal, infant, and young-child diets.

The increasing numbers of overweight and obese children and adults persist despite a substantial decrease in fat intake in American diets. Which behaviors might cause persistent weight gain in the postindustrial world? One clue is found in history. Until the mid-twentieth century, much of our food was only seasonally available. In an environment with uncertain food availability, it makes sense for the body to store excess calories in the form of fat to be used later, when food is scarce. Throughout history, and in many cultures today, plumpness was and is desirable as a standard of beauty and a sign of health and wealth.

In postindustrial societies, people often eat as though food will be scarce, even though it is continuously and easily available. The failure to burn off the extra calories by exercising results in weight gain and health risks. Compounding the problem, the ubiquity of digital media and computer-based work over the past half-century has led to a more sedentary lifestyle than was common in previous generations.

The human control system for eating has multiple neurobiological inputs, including cognitive factors such as thinking about food and the association between environmental cues and the act of eating. The constant pairing of such cues with eating—for example, snacking paired with studying or television viewing—can result in the cues alone becoming a motivation, an incentive to eat. We return to this phenomenon in the discussion of reward and addiction in Section 12-7.

Eating disorders entail being either overweight or underweight. **Anorexia nervosa** is an eating disorder with a huge cognitive component—namely, self-image. A person's body image is highly distorted in anorexia. This misperception leads to an exaggerated concern with being overweight. That concern spirals into excessive dieting, compulsive exercising, and severe, potentially life-threatening weight loss. Anorexia is especially prevalent among adolescent girls.

The neurobiological control of eating behavior in humans is not a simple process. The multiple inputs to the human control system for eating come from three major sources: the cognitive factors already introduced, the hypothalamus, and the digestive system.

## Digestive System and Control of Eating

Digestion is controlled by the enteric nervous system (ENS). As illustrated in **Figure 12-15**, the digestive tract begins in the mouth and ends at the anus. As food travels through the tract, the digestive system extracts three types of nutrients: lipids (fats), amino acids (the building blocks of proteins), and glucose (sugar). Each nutrient

**obesity** Excessive accumulation of body fat.

**anorexia nervosa** An eating disorder characterized by exaggerated concern with being overweight that leads to inadequate food intake and often excessive exercising; can lead to severe weight loss and even starvation.

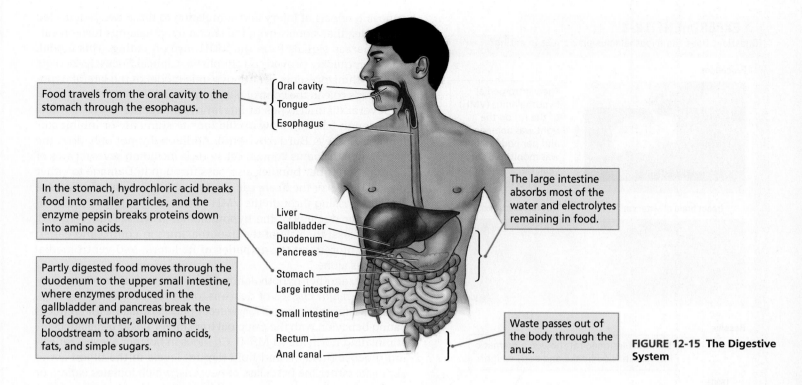

Food travels from the oral cavity to the stomach through the esophagus.

In the stomach, hydrochloric acid breaks food into smaller particles, and the enzyme pepsin breaks proteins down into amino acids.

Partly digested food moves through the duodenum to the upper small intestine, where enzymes produced in the gallbladder and pancreas break the food down further, allowing the bloodstream to absorb amino acids, fats, and simple sugars.

Oral cavity
Tongue
Esophagus

Liver
Gallbladder
Duodenum
Pancreas
Stomach
Large intestine
Small intestine
Rectum
Anal canal

The large intestine absorbs most of the water and electrolytes remaining in food.

Waste passes out of the body through the anus.

**FIGURE 12-15  The Digestive System**

is a specialized energy reserve. Because we require varying amounts of these reserves depending on what we are doing at any given moment, the body has detector cells to keep track of the level of each nutrient in the bloodstream.

Glucose is the body's primary fuel and virtually the only energy source for the brain. Because the brain requires glucose even when the digestive tract is empty, the liver acts as a short-term reservoir of glycogen, a starch that acts as an inert form of glucose. When blood sugar levels fall, such as when we are sleeping, detector cells tell the liver to convert glycogen into glucose for release into the bloodstream.

Thus, the digestive system functions mainly to break down food, and the body needs to be apprised of how this breakdown is proceeding. Feedback mechanisms provide such information. When food reaches the intestines, it interacts with receptors in the ENS to trigger the release of at least 10 different peptide hormones, including cholecystokinin (CCK), glucagonlike peptide 1 (GLP-1), and peptide YY (PYY). Each peptide hormone, by virtue of its release as food is absorbed, acts as a satiation (or satiety) signal that inhibits food intake. For example, when CCK is infused into an animal's hypothalamus, the animal's appetite diminishes.

## Hypothalamus and Control of Eating

Eating is influenced by multiple hormones, including insulin, growth hormone, and sex steroids, that stimulate and inhibit eating and also aid in converting first nutrients into fat, and then fat into glucose. The hypothalamus, which controls hormone systems, is the key brain structure in eating as well as in satiety.

Investigation into how the hypothalamus controls eating began in the early 1950s, when researchers discovered that damage to the lateral hypothalamus in rats caused the animals to stop eating, a symptom known as **aphagia** (in Greek, *phagein* means "to eat"). In contrast, damage to the ventromedial hypothalamus (VMH) caused the animals to overeat—thus displaying **hyperphagia**. A VMH-lesioned rat that overate to the point of obesity is shown in the Procedure section of **Experiment 12-1**. The Results section reveals that the VMH-lesioned rat weighed more than 1 kilogram, three times the weight of her healthy sister, at 340 grams.

Researchers also found that electrical stimulation of the lateral hypothalamus elicits eating, whereas stimulation of the ventromedial hypothalamus inhibits eating. The

Figure 2-33 diagrams the inner workings of the ENS and Section 5-3 describes the main neurotransmitters it employs.

Section 5-4 reviews the major categories of hormones and discusses how they work.

**aphagia**  Failure to eat; may be due to an unwillingness to eat or to motor difficulties, especially with swallowing.

**hyperphagia**  Overeating that leads to significant weight gain.

## ⋯⋯> EXPERIMENT 12-1

Question: Does the hypothalamus play a role in eating?

**Procedure**

The ventromedial hypothalamus (VMH) of the rat on the right was damaged, and her body weight was monitored for a year. Her sister on the left is normal.

Ian Whishaw/Bryan Kolb

Intact brain of sister rat

Rat brain with lesion

Ian Whishaw/Bryan Kolb

Lesion

**Results**

The VMH-lesioned rat showed a dramatic increase in food intake and body weight.

Lesioned rat

Control rat

Body weight (g) vs Time (months)

*Conclusion:* The VMH plays a role in controlling the cessation of eating. Damage to the VMH results in prolonged and dramatic weight gain.

**FIGURE 12-16 Modeling Control of Eating**

opposing effects of injury and stimulation to these two regions led to the idea that signals from the lateral hypothalamus turn on eating, whereas signals from the VMH turn off eating. This model, however, quickly proved too simplistic. Clinical Focus 12-2: Diets and Rhythms presents a more dynamic model of the lateral hypothalamus's role in the control of eating.

Several distinct types of lateral hypothalamic neurons interact through fast and slow oscillations to stimulate or inhibit eating (see Kosse & Burdakov, 2018). Additionally, not only does the lateral hypothalamus contain cell bodies, including several types of neurons, but fiber bundles also pass through it. Damage to either the cell bodies or the fibers can produce aphagia. Similarly, damage to fibers passing through the VMH often causes injury to the paraventricular nucleus of the hypothalamus (review Figure 12-5A). Nevertheless, the role of the hypothalamus in controlling eating involves more than the activities of its lateral and ventromedial structures alone.

In fact, another hypothalamic region, the arcuate nucleus, contains two major classes of neurons, one that initiates eating (e.g., neurons expressing genes for neuropeptide Y) and one that reduces eating behavior, with the principal transmitter being $\alpha$-melanocyte–stimulating hormone ($\alpha$-MSH). Changes in hormone levels reflecting glucose (insulin) and lipid (leptin) levels in the blood act to stimulate either the first class of neurons, which initiates eating, or the second class, which acts to inhibit eating. Neurons of the arcuate nucleus also connect to the paraventricular nucleus. Damage to this region produces hyperphagia, like that experienced by Roger and described at the beginning of this chapter.

The summed activity of all such hypothalamic neurons constitutes a complex homeostat that controls eating. As shown in **Figure 12-16**, this homeostat receives inputs from three sources: the ENS (such as information about blood glucose levels), the hormone systems (such as information about the level of appetite-diminishing CCK), and parts of the brain that process cognitive factors. We describe these cognitive factors next.

## Cognitive Control of Eating

Pleasure and its absence are cognitive factors in controlling eating. Just thinking about a favorite food can make many of us feel hungry. The cognitive aspect of eating includes not only images of food that we pull from memory but also external sensations, especially food-related sights and smells. Learned associations, such as the taste aversions discussed in Section 12-1, and the cognitive appraisals discussed in Section 12-3 are also related to eating.

Neural control of the cognitive factors important for controlling eating in humans probably originates in multiple brain regions. Two structures are clearly important: the amygdala and the orbital prefrontal cortex (PFC). Damage to the amygdala alters food preferences and abolishes taste aversion learning. These effects are probably related to the amygdala's efferent connections to the hypothalamus.

The amygdala's role in regulating species-typical behaviors is well established, but the role of the orbital PFC has proved more difficult to pin down. Rats and monkeys with damage to the orbital cortex lose weight, in part because they eat less. Humans with orbital injuries are invariably slim, but we know of no formal studies on their eating habits. The orbital PFC receives projections from the olfactory bulb, and cells in this region respond to smells. Because odors influence the taste of foods, it is likely that damage to the orbital cortex decreases eating due to diminished sensory responses to food odor and perhaps to taste.

## Diets and Rhythms

Despite the wide range of diets and weight-loss strategies on the market, none has stopped the obesity epidemic facing the developed world. Overall, studies of the effectiveness of different diets show that although people generally lose weight in the first months or year, they usually gain it back, and in many cases their weight increases over the baseline (see Harvard Medical School's *The Diet Review,* 2020, for a comparison of diets). The failure of diets to control weight suggests that we may need a different approach to weight control.

One challenge in developing obesity interventions is that little is known about the cognitive regulation of eating-related behaviors. Much is known about the role of molecules, cells, and even brain areas in the control of eating, but it is not yet clear how these elements all work together. Over the past decade, however, researchers have shown that rhythms in brain activity (known as oscillations) act to integrate diverse brain regions (see, for example, Buzaki, 2011). These oscillations can be measured at many levels, ranging from membrane potentials to electroencephalography (EEG) tracings. Diffuse brain circuits can work together to produce behavior simply by being in phase and oscillating at the same rhythms.

Marta Carus-Cadavieco and colleagues (2017) asked whether the dissociation between food-seeking behavior and metabolic needs leading to obesity could be related to brain oscillations in a diffuse eating system. Using an impressive range of electrophysiological, optogenetic, and molecular techniques in mice, they were able to show that a gamma rhythm (30–80 Hz) originating in the prefrontal cortex tied together the lateral septum and the lateral hypothalamus to direct food seeking and eating. Optogenetic stimulation could either drive or reduce food-seeking behavior through effects on neurons in the lateral hypothalamus (see accompanying figure).

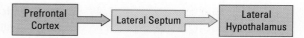

The prefrontal cortex sends projections to the lateral septum, which sends inhibitory inputs to eating-related neurons in the lateral hypothalamus. This pathway interacts via gamma rhythms to modulate eating. Research from Narayanan & DiLeone, 2017.

This work demonstrates a mechanism whereby cognitive activity can control eating. Although prefrontal rhythms are well known to synchronize cortical networks in humans, it was not known that they could also affect subcortical networks. Because gamma activity can be measured by scalp EEG, it may be possible to monitor how modulation of the prefrontal-driven oscillatory rhythms coordinate the eating network, which could lead to direct interventions to regulate body weight.

---

An additional cognitive factor in the control of eating is the pleasure we derive from it, especially from eating foods with certain tastes—think chocolate. What pleasure is and how the brain produces it are discussed in Section 12-7 in the context of reward.

Randy Seeley and Stephen Woods (2003) noted that in spite of contemporary problems with weight gain, adult mammals usually do a masterful job of matching their caloric intake to their caloric expenditure. Even so, a growing body of evidence suggests that an individual's specific intake of macronutrients (e.g., carbohydrates, proteins, lipids), together with gut microbiota composition and genetic makeup, can modulate their body's ability to control weight and store the energy surplus that drives weight gain (see the review by San-Cristobal et al., 2020). Thus, advice on individual dietary strategies should be based on each individual's own precise nutrition criteria.

## Controlling Drinking

The human body is 70% water; dissolved in that water are chemicals that participate in the hundreds of reactions necessary for bodily functions. Essential homeostatic mechanisms control water levels (and hence chemical concentrations) within rather narrow limits. The rate of a chemical reaction is partly determined by the concentration of the participating chemicals.

As with eating, we drink for many reasons. We consume certain beverages—such as coffee, wine, beer, or juice—for an energy boost or to relax, as part of social activities, or just because they taste good. We drink water for its health benefits, to help wash down a meal, or to intensify the flavor of dry foods. On a hot day, we drink water because we are thirsty, presumably because we become dehydrated through sweating and evaporation.

These examples illustrate the two kinds of thirst. **Osmotic thirst** results from increased concentrations of dissolved chemicals, known as solutes, in the body fluids. **Hypovolemic thirst** results from a loss of overall fluid volume from the body.

**osmotic thirst** Thirst that results from a high concentration of dissolved chemicals, or *solutes*, in body fluids.

**hypovolemic thirst** Thirst produced by a loss of overall fluid volume from the body.

## Osmotic Thirst

Solutes inside and outside cells are ideally concentrated for the body's chemical reactions. Maintaining this concentration requires a kind of homeostat, much like the mechanism that controls body temperature. Deviations from the ideal solute concentration activate systems to reestablish it.

When we eat salty foods, such as potato chips, the salt (NaCl) spreads through the blood and enters the extracellular fluid between our cells. This shifts the solute concentration away from the ideal. Receptors in the hypothalamus along the third ventricle detect the altered solute concentration and relay the message "too salty" to various hypothalamic areas, which in turn stimulate us to drink. Other messages are sent to the kidneys to reduce water excretion.

**Water Intoxication**  Eating too much leads to obesity. But what happens when we drink too much water? Our kidneys are efficient at processing water, but if we drink a large volume all at once, the kidneys cannot keep up. The result is a condition called water intoxication. Body tissues swell with the excess fluid, essentially drowning the cells in fresh water. At the same time, the relative concentration of sodium drops, leading to an electrolyte imbalance.

Water intoxication can produce a wide range of symptoms, from irregular heartbeat to headache. In severe cases, people may show motor disorganization, as though they are drunk. The most likely way for an adult to develop water intoxication is to sweat heavily, while running a marathon in hot weather, for example, and then drink too much water without added electrolytes.

## Hypovolemic Thirst

Unlike osmotic thirst, hypovolemic thirst arises when the total volume of body fluids declines, motivating us to drink more and replenish those fluids. In contrast to osmotic thirst, however, hypovolemic thirst encourages us to choose something other than water because water would dilute the solute concentration in the blood. Rather, we prefer to drink flavored beverages that contain salts and other nutrients, such as fruit juices or milk.

Hypovolemic thirst and its satiation are controlled by a different hypothalamic circuit than the one that controls osmotic thirst. When fluid volume drops, the kidneys send a hormone signal (angiotensin) that stimulates midline hypothalamic neurons. These neurons, in turn, stimulate drinking.

Turning to sugar-sweetened beverages to quench thirst from eating salty foods increases the likelihood of weight gain.

## 12-4 Review

Before you continue, check your understanding. Answers to Self-Test appear at the back of the book.

1. The three main hypothalamic regions that control eating are the _____, _____, and _____.

2. Digestion is controlled by the _____ nervous system.

3. _____ thirst results from an increase in the concentration of dissolved chemicals; _____ thirst results from a decline in the total volume of body fluids.

4. Describe the cognitive factors in the control of eating.

**Learning Objectives**
- Describe sexual differentiation of the brain.
- Identify the effects of sex hormones on the brain.
- Summarize the neural control of and cognitive influences on sexual behavior.
- Describe neural correlates of sexual orientation.

## 12-5

# Sexual Differences and Sexual Behavior

Individuals must eat and drink continually to survive—that is the essence of regulatory behavior. But although procreation is certainly essential to the survival of the species, sexual behavior is nonregulatory; it is not essential for an individual organism's survival. This fact does nothing to diminish the importance of sexual behavior. But before we discuss sexual behavior, we first look at sexual differentiation.

Margaret McCarthy and colleagues (2017) have identified 10 concepts that are consistent with the established evidence and form the foundation for our understanding of sexual differentiation (see **Table 12-3**). We summarize these 10 concepts next and recommend the McCarthy et al. (2017) review for an in-depth discussion.

# Sexual Differentiation of the Brain

Charles Phoenix and colleagues (1959) first showed that hormones have two general effects on brain organization: during development gonadal hormones *organize* the brain, and in adulthood they *activate* many sex-specific behaviors, such as mating behaviors. We return to this concept in more detail later, but first we note that many other behaviors show sex differences as well (for a more extensive discussion, see Kolb & Whishaw, 2021). Perhaps the best-known sex difference in humans is the female advantage in verbal fluency, which is apparent in young children. When asked to write down words beginning with a particular letter in five minutes, females typically produce at least 10% more words than males. Karson Kung and colleagues (2016) found that higher levels of salivary testosterone at 1–3 months are related to a smaller expressive vocabulary measured at 18–30 months.

Perhaps the clearest example of sex differences involves spatial behavior (see Section 15-5 for a more extensive discussion). A male advantage in spatial navigation is found not only in humans but also in most other mammals that have been studied. Male rodents typically can navigate larger territories and are better at solving problems, such as the Morris Swimming Pool Task (see Figure 7-4A), in which the solution requires the mental construction of a configuration of the room cues. But if room cues must be ignored, such as in the landmark task (see Figure 7-4C), females perform better. Therefore, differences in task performance are rooted in the *strategy* used by each sex rather than the spatial cognitive *ability* of each sex. This strategy difference alerts us to the fact that sex differences are context dependent. In another example, the wording of instructions on a test can influence the outcome by altering the strategy typically used by one sex or the other.

Sex differences in behavior are not absolute; the differences tend to be about 1 standard deviation apart. Thus, when male rats solve the Morris Swimming Pool Task faster than females, it is not because females are unable to do the task; rather, females learn the correct strategy more slowly—and vice versa for the landmark task.

Sex differences in physiology can also be seen in statistics for neurological diseases, and especially for neurodevelopmental disorders, which are more common in boys. This male bias is striking because these early-onset disorders are less likely to have experiential causes but rather tend to reflect prenatal or postnatal differences in brain development. For adult-onset disorders, sex differences vary by disease. For example,

**TABLE 12-3** Ten Things We Know about Sexual Differentiation

| |
|---|
| 1. Hormones cause sex differences by acting during development as well as in adulthood. |
| 2. There are sex differences in behavior. |
| 3. There are sex differences in physiology. |
| 4. There are sex differences in disease susceptibility. |
| 5. There are sex differences in neural and glial structure and neural connectivity. |
| 6. There are sex differences in neurochemistry. |
| 7. Androgens and estrogens play a role in sexual differentiation in the brain. |
| 8. The sex chromosome complement contributes to sexual differentiation. |
| 9. Sex differences are context dependent. |
| 10. Sexual differentiation depends on four key processes: neurogenesis, cell migration, cell death, and the differentiation of neural circuits. |

*Data Source:* McCarthy et al., 2017.

See Section 15-5 for further discussion of sex differences in cognitive organization.

females have a higher incidence of Alzheimer disease (1.5 to 3 times greater), after accounting for the sex difference in life expectancy, whereas males have a higher incidence of Parkinson disease (1.5 times greater).

Sex differences in behavior, physiology, and neurological disorders likely reflect sex differences in the brain. An extensive literature highlights sex differences in brain structure—both in the size of different brain regions and in the structure of neurons, glia, and connections—as well as in the details of neurochemistry (see Kolb & Whishaw, 2021; McCarthy et al., 2017; Ritchie et al., 2018). For example, the amygdala is larger in males, and the language areas are larger in females. Differences in connectivity are reflected in the observation that females have greater interhemispheric connections and males have greater intrahemispheric connections. Finally, sex differences in neurotransmitter and neurotransmitter receptor expression are seen throughout the brain. Although we tend to view female and male as binary, Research Focus 12-3: The Brain Gender Continuum illustrates that despite identifiable differences in the female and male brain, things are a bit more complex.

Sexual differentiation is also directly related to sex chromosomes. This can be seen most clearly in females, who typically have two X chromosomes. Normally, one of the X chromosomes is largely silenced, but approximately 15% of the genes escape inactivation. Therefore, female cells have a double dose of some genes, which creates epigenetic effects that influence gene expression (see Arnold et al., 2016, for a review).

---

## ◉ RESEARCH FOCUS 12-3

# The Brain Gender Continuum

Although biological sex organs can be described using the binary terms "female" and "male," it is difficult to identify a "female" or "male" brain. Although anatomical and magnetic resonance imaging (MRI) studies have shown sex differences in brain structure, it is unclear how these differences relate to the femaleness or maleness of a brain. A study by Zhiguo Luo and colleagues (2019) used machine learning to investigate sex differences of cortical morphology in more than 1000 brains from the Human Connectome Project. Their system had an accuracy of 96.77% in sex classification using morphological features. But do these anatomical differences necessarily suggest functional differences between the brains of females and males?

Susanne Weis and her colleagues (2020) used a different machine learning system to determine how accurately the resting state MRI (rsMRI) could predict sex from another sample of 1000 brains from the Connectome Project. Their program was approximately 75% accurate, which is well above chance, but 25% of the brains were identified as neither female nor male. Following this result, Yi Zhang and colleagues (2021) used rsMRI to compare nearly 10,000 brains ranging in age from 17 to 78 years. Much as in the Luo study, these authors found an accuracy of nearly 77.75% for their program, but the Zhang system also rated the brains on a continuum, with female brains being toward one end of the continuum (0) and male brains toward the other end (1). As can be seen in the accompanying graph, a large group accounting for roughly 25% of brains could not be assigned to a specific sex (shown in purple), leading the authors to propose the novel hypothesis of a neuroimaging concept of androgyny.

Based on earlier research, the Zhang group hypothesized that a corresponding androgenous gender role would lead to higher self-esteem and better mental health because individuals identifying as androgenous would be free to act in both masculine and feminine ways without the cultural constraints of gender appropriateness. When the authors obtained

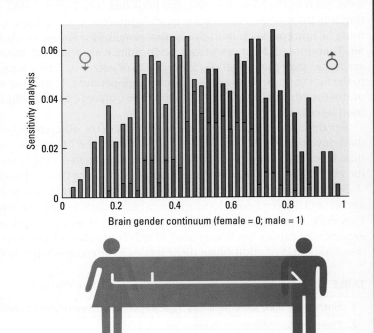

Overview of the study in which there were four analyses of the rsMRI data classifier. A brain gender continuum was built that classified a value closer to 1 as a male brain and a value closer to 0 as a female brain.
Research from Zhang et al., 2021.

participants' self-reports of internalizing problems (e.g., depression, anxiety, somatic complaints, withdrawal), they found fewer internalizing symptoms in the androgenous group (a result similar to that found in earlier studies); they interpreted this state as better mental health, especially in males.

Finally, McCarthy and her colleagues note that sexual differentiation of any trait must be due to effects on the basic processes of brain development (see Table 8-1)—namely, neurogenesis, cell migration, cell death, and the differentiation of neural circuits by neuronal differentiation and maturation. Determining how hormonal or genetic factors differentially affect these processes in what we consider to be female or male brains has proved difficult because of the complexity involved (see McCarthy et al., 2017, for an extensive discussion). Despite this complexity, we will discuss brain differences in terms of "female" or "male" for the sake of simplicity.

# Effects of Sex Hormones on the Brain

With McCarthy and colleagues's foundational concepts in mind, we now consider the relationship between hormones and sex-related behavior. During the fetal stage of pre-natal development, a male's Y chromosome controls the differentiation of embryonic gonad tissue into testes, which secrete testosterone. This process is an organizing effect of gonadal hormones. Testosterone masculinizes both the sex organs and the brain during development. A major organizing effect of gonadal hormones on the brain occurs in the hypothalamus, especially the preoptic area of the medial hypothalamus. Organizing effects also operate in other nervous system regions, especially the amyg-dala, the prefrontal cortex, and the spinal cord.

Gonadal hormones produce the enzymes necessary for epigenetic changes such as gene methylation. One action of steroid hormones is to methylate brain regions. For example, estrogen methylates the preoptic area of females, leading to the suppression of male characteristics. Increased environmental levels of some compounds, such as agricultural pesticides, can interfere with hormone activity, resulting in multigenera-tional epigenetic effects (see, for example, McCarthy et al., 2009). These effects may be linked to anxiety levels and obesity and possibly to the organizational effects of gonadal hormones.

The case study in Section 3-3 describes such epigenetic inheritance.

Sex-related differences in the nervous system make sense from a behavioral per-spective. After all, animal courtship rituals differ between the sexes, as do copulatory behaviors, with females typically engaging in sexually receptive responses and males in mounting ones. Producing these sex differences in behaviors depends on the action of gonadal hormones on the brain during development and in adulthood.

Hormonal actions on the adult brain are referred to as **activating effects**, in con-trast to developmental **organizing effects**. Next we consider both types of effects.

Section 8-4 explains organizing influences of gonadal hormones and critical periods in brain development.

# Organizing Effects of Sex Hormones

During fetal development, a male's testes produce male hormones, the *androgens*. In the developing rat, androgens are produced during the last week of fetal development and the first week after birth. The androgens produced at this time greatly alter both neural structures and later behavior. For example, a male rat's hypothalamus and prefrontal cortex differ structurally from those of both female rats and male rats that were not exposed to androgens during development.

Male rats that have little exposure to the androgen testosterone during development behave like genetically female rats in adulthood. If given estrogen and progesterone, they become sexually receptive and display typical female behaviors when mounted by males. Male rats castrated in adulthood do not act in this way.

**Sexual dimorphism**, the differential development of brain areas in the two sexes, arises from a complex series of steps. Cells in the brain produce *aromatase*, an enzyme that converts testosterone into *estradiol*, one of the class of female sex hormones called *estrogens*. That is, when males produce testosterone, the brain converts it to an estrogen. Thus, a female hormone, estradiol, actually masculinizes the male brain.

Females are not masculinized by the presence of estrogens because fetuses of both sexes produce a liver enzyme (alpha fetoprotein) that binds to estrogen, rendering it incapable of entering neurons. Testosterone is unaffected by alpha fetoprotein: it enters neurons and is converted into estradiol.

---

**activating effects** Hormonal actions that influence activities in the adult brain.

**organizing effects** Hormonal actions that influence the organizational development of the fetal brain.

**sexual dimorphism** Differential development of brain areas in the two sexes.

The organizing effects of testosterone are clearly illustrated in the preoptic area of the hypothalamus (see Figure 12-5A), which plays a critical role in male rats' copulatory behavior. Comparing this area in males and females, Roger Gorski (1984) and his colleagues found a nucleus about five times as large in males as in females. Significantly, manipulating gonadal hormones during development can alter the sexual dimorphism of the preoptic area. Castrating male rats at birth leads to a smaller preoptic area; treating infant females with testosterone enlarges it.

The organizing effects of gonadal hormones are more difficult to study in humans. Alpha fetoprotein, a fetal protein, is known to be less effective in blocking estrogen in humans, so human fetuses of both sexes are exposed to estrogen. This finding suggests that androgens may play a more central role in sexual differentiation in humans. The direct role of androgens can be seen in the studies by John Money and Anke Ehrhardt (1972). Clinical Focus 12-4: Androgen Insensitivity Syndrome and Androgenital Syndrome describes this role.

## Activating Effects of Sex Hormones

The sexual behavior of both males and females depends on the actions of gonadal hormones on the adult brain. In most vertebrate species, female sexual behavior varies in the course of an estrous cycle, during which the levels of ovarian hormones fluctuate. The rat's estrous cycle is about 4 days long, with sexual receptivity occurring only in the few hours during which the production of the ovarian hormones estrogen and progesterone peaks. These ovarian hormones alter brain activity, which in turn alters

---

### ⊚ CLINICAL FOCUS 12-4

## Androgen Insensitivity Syndrome and Androgenital Syndrome

After the testes have formed in a male fetus, sexual development depends on the actions of testicular hormones. Studying people with *androgen insensitivity syndrome* makes this dependence crystal clear. In this syndrome, an XY (genetic male) fetus produces androgens, but the body cannot respond to them.

Because androgen insensitivity syndrome does not affect estrogen receptors, affected individuals are still responsive to estrogen produced by both the adrenal glands and the testes. As a result, they develop female secondary sexual characteristics during puberty, even without additional hormone treatment. A person with androgen insensitivity syndrome is therefore a genetic male who develops a female phenotype — that is, appears to be female, as shown in the photograph on the left.

If no Y chromosome is present to induce the growth of testes, an XX (genetic female) fetus develops ovaries and becomes a female. If the adrenal glands of either the mother or the infant produce an excessive amount of androgens, however, exposure of the female fetus to these hormones produces *androgenital syndrome* (*congenital adrenal hyperplasia*).

The effects vary, depending on when the androgens are produced and on the level of exposure. In extreme cases, the clitoris enlarges until it can be mistaken for a small penis, as shown in the photograph on the right.

In less severe cases, no gross change in genital structure develops, but there is a behavioral effect: in early childhood, these girls tend to identify with boys and prefer boys' clothes, toys, and games. One explanation for this behavioral effect is that the developing brain is masculinized, which changes later behavior.

*Left*: In androgen insensitivity syndrome, a genetic male (XY) is insensitive to gonadal androgens but remains sensitive to estrogens, which leads to the development of a female phenotype. *Right*: In congenital adrenal hyperplasia, a genetic female (XX) is exposed to androgens produced by the adrenal gland embryonically, which leads to the partial development of male external genitalia. Reprinted from Man and Woman, Boy and Girl by John Money and Anke A. Ehrhardt (1972)/John's Hopkin's University Press, Baltimore

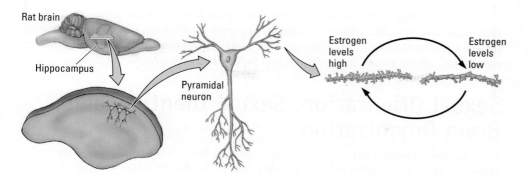

**FIGURE 12-17 Hormonal Effects** A comparison of the dendrites of hippocampal pyramidal neurons at high and low levels of estrogen in the rat's (4-day) estrous cycle reveals far fewer dendritic spines in the low period. Information from Woolley and colleagues (1990).

behavior. In female rats, various chemicals released after mating inhibit further mating behavior.

The activating effect of ovarian hormones can be seen clearly in hippocampal cells. **Figure 12-17** compares hippocampal pyramidal neurons taken from female rats at two points in the estrous cycle: when estrogen levels are high and when they are low. When estrogen levels are high, more dendritic spines and presumably more synapses emerge. These neural differences during the estrous cycle are all the more remarkable when we consider that cells in the female hippocampus continually change their connections to other cells every 4 days throughout the animal's adulthood.

In males, testosterone activates sexual behavior in two distinct ways. First, testosterone's actions on the amygdala are related to the motivation to seek sexual activity. Second, the actions of testosterone on the hypothalamus are needed to produce copulatory behavior. We look at both processes next.

# Neural Control of Sexual Behavior

The hypothalamus is the critical structure involved in controlling copulatory behaviors in both male and female mammals. The ventromedial hypothalamus controls the female mating posture, which in quadrupedal animals is called *lordosis*—that is, arching the back and elevating the rump while the female otherwise remains quite still. Damage to the VMH abolishes lordosis. The role of the VMH is probably twofold: it controls the neural circuit that produces lordosis, and it influences hormonal changes in the female during coitus.

In males, neural control of sexual behavior is somewhat more complex. The medial preoptic area, which is larger in males than in females, controls copulation. Damage to this area greatly disrupts mating performance, whereas its electrical stimulation activates mating, provided that testosterone is circulating in the male's bloodstream. Curiously, although destruction of the medial preoptic area stops male mammals from mating, they continue to show interest in receptive females. For instance, monkeys with lesions in the medial preoptic area will not mate with receptive females, but they will masturbate while watching females from across the room.

Barry Everitt (1990) designed an ingenious apparatus that allows male rats to press a bar to obtain access to receptive females. After males were trained to use this apparatus, shown in **Figure 12-18**, lesions were made in their medial preoptic areas. Immediately, their sexual behavior changed: they would still press the bar to obtain access to females, but would no longer mate with them.

Apparently, the medial preoptic area controls mating but not sexual motivation. The brain structure responsible for motivation appears to be the amygdala. When Everitt trained male rats in use of the apparatus and then lesioned their amygdala, they would no longer press the bar to gain access to receptive females, but would mate with receptive females provided to them.

It is not practical to discriminate small hypothalamic nuclei in fMRI studies of humans. Studies have shown a bilateral increase in hypothalamic activity when men view erotic video clips but not when they view sports video clips. The degree of sexual arousal is related to the increase in hypothalamic activity (e.g., Brunetti et al., 2008).

Typical posture

Lordosis

**FIGURE 12-18 Studying Sexual Motivation and Mating** In this experiment, a male rat must press the bar 10 times to gain access to a receptive female, who drops in through a trapdoor. The copulatory behavior of the male rat illustrates mating behavior, whereas the bar pressing for access to a female rat illustrates sexual motivation. Barry J. Everitt, Department of Experimental Psychology and the MRC-Wellcome Behavioural and Clinical Neuroscience Institute, University of Cambridge

In summary, the hypothalamus controls copulatory behavior in both male and female mammals. In males, the amygdala influences sexual motivation. Likewise, it probably plays a key role in female sexual motivation, especially among females of species, such as humans, whose sexual activity is not tied to fluctuations in ovarian hormones.

# Sexual Orientation, Sexual Identity, and Brain Organization

Does **sexual orientation**—a person's sexual attraction to the opposite sex or to the same sex or to both sexes—have a neural basis? Sexual orientation appears to be determined during early development, influenced by genetics and by epigenetic factors during prenatal brain development. No solid evidence points to any postnatal experience directing sexual orientation.

Indeed, it appears virtually impossible to change a person's sexual orientation. Both lesbian and gay couples commonly rear children who identify as heterosexual, and no evidence supports the notion that homosexuality is a lifestyle choice or that it stems from social learning (Bao & Swaab, 2011). The place to look for differences, therefore, is in the brains of people who identify themselves as heterosexual or homosexual.

Like rats, humans have sex-related differences in the structure of the hypothalamus and amygdala. Several hypothalamic nuclei are two to three times larger in males than in females (for a review, see McCarthy et al., 2017). Sexual differentiation of the brain results from the effect of testosterone and is complete by birth.

But sex differences in the brain are not simply a matter of hormones. Epigenetics plays a role, too, beginning early in development. In females, for example, one of the two X chromosomes is largely silenced, but not all its genes are silenced, thereby providing a basis for sex differences. Furthermore, emerging evidence suggests that sex differences in the hypothalamus result from differences in gene methylation (again, see McCarthy et al., 2017).

Among gay males and lesbians, variations in epigenetic effects could lead to differences in the architecture and function of the hypothalamus. Differences in the hypothalamus of heterosexual and homosexual men suggest that homosexual men form, in effect, a third sex because their hypothalamus differs from that of both females and heterosexual males.

Researchers have also identified differences in cerebral thickness and connectivity between heterosexual and homosexual brains. Amirhossein Manzouri and Ivanka Savic (2018) showed a sex difference in the functional connections in the default network of heterosexual brains (with greater connectivity observed in males), but not in homosexual male and female brains, which displayed values in between those of heterosexual males and females. With regard to cortical thickness, the homosexual males had thicker midline cortical layers relative to heterosexual males, heterosexual females, and homosexual females. Thus, although homosexual brains differed from heterosexual brains, male and female homosexual brains differed in how they compared to heterosexual brains.

Architectural and functional differences in the hypothalamus may form a basis for the spectrum of **gender identity**—a person's concept of self as male, female, both, or neither. Gender identity is a core aspect of self-identity and is usually concordant with birth-assigned sex. People who view themselves as **transgender**, whose personal characteristics transcend traditional gender boundaries and corresponding sexual norms, identify with a gender different from that expected based on the sex assigned at birth. The principal feature of the transgender condition is a strong perception of incongruence between one's sense of self and one's body, and a feeling of estrangement from one's physical sex (Cohen-Kettenis & Pfafflin, 2010). Transgender individuals may choose to undergo gender transition to align themselves more closely with their internal sense of gender, either through social conventions (e.g., the use of different names or pronouns and changes in dress) or medical intervention.

**sexual orientation** A person's pattern of sexual attraction—to the opposite sex, to the same sex, or to both sexes.

**gender identity** An individual's concept of self as male, female, neither, or both.

**transgender** Possessing personal characteristics that transcend traditional gender boundaries and corresponding sexual norms; identification with a gender different from that expected based on the sex assigned at birth.

Several biological factors could influence the likelihood of transgender identity—chromosomal differences, polymorphisms of the genes for the estrogen and androgen receptors, atypical gonadal hormone levels, prenatal exposure to certain anticonvulsants, and immune system activity directed toward the Y chromosome. These factors are hypothesized to lead to differences in the architecture and function of certain brain structures.

Many structural differences have been noted between cisgender (having a gender identity aligned with one's birth-assigned sex) and transgender individuals, including a larger hippocampus and caudate volume in cisgender women, a larger putamen and amygdala volume in cisgender men, and greater cortical thickness in cisgender women. More recent fMRI data have shown that transgender persons have a different pattern of cerebral networks mediating self-body perception from cisgender individuals (Manzouri & Savic, 2019). These networks are incorporated into the *default network*, which is a network of highly correlated interacting regions of the prefrontal, medial temporal, posterior parietal, and posterior cingulate cortex. Although the name "default network" derives from the original belief that this network reflected a resting state of the brain, it proved to be a misnomer; this network is now known to be active and involved in a range of cognitive activities, such as thinking about one's past (autobiographical memory), thinking about the future, and perception of one's own body.

Behzad Khorashad and colleagues (2021) proposed that there are cerebral differences in the own-body processing networks in both transgender females and males compared to cisgender individuals, and that these differences may be related to a person's sense of body congruence. Using MRI, these researchers scanned participants in their study before and after hormone treatment. They found differences between cisgender and transgender individuals in the "before" scan, but functional processing differences in the default network and related structures disappeared in both transgender women and men in the "after" scan. This functional change was correlated with an increase in perceptual accuracy in body self-perception. These results strongly suggest that transgenderism is related to cerebral networks underlying self-body perception.

It is important to distinguish between the nonbinary anatomical differences that characterize intersex individuals, described in Clinical Focus 12-4, from the gender identity differences that characterize transgender individuals.

The prefix *cis* means "on this side of."

The default network is illustrated in Figure 8-19.

## Cognitive Influences on Sexual Behavior

People think about sex, dream about sex, make plans about sex. These behaviors may reflect activity in the amygdala or the hypothalamus, but they must certainly also depend on the cortex. For instance, imagery about sexual activity must include activity in the cortical ventral visual pathway. In contrast, thinking about sexual activity and planning for it must require frontal lobe participation.

As you might expect, these aspects of sexual behavior are not easily studied in rats, and they remain uncharted waters in research on humans. However, changes in the sexual behavior of people with frontal lobe injury are well documented. For example, when a man had a small tumor removed from his medial frontal region, 5 years later his wife reported that since the operation, she and her husband had not had any sexual contact whatever. He was simply not interested, even though both were still in their twenties. The husband said that he no longer had sexual fantasies or sexual dreams, and although he still loved his wife, he did not have any sexual urges toward her or anyone else. Such cases clearly indicate that the human cortex is important in controlling sexual behaviors. The exact nature of its role remains poorly understood.

## 12-5 Review

Before you continue, check your understanding. Answers to Self-Test appear at the back of the book.

1. The key brain structures in the control of sexual behavior are the _____ and the _____.

2. The two types of effects that hormones exert on the brain are _____ and _____.

3. The brain structure responsible for mating in males is the _____, whereas the structure responsible for sexual motivation is _____.

4. MRI studies have implicated the _____ network in own-body perception in both transgender and cisgender individuals.

5. Describe why sex differences in the brain are not simply a matter of hormones.

## 12-6

# The Neural Control of Emotion

The clinical study of emotion dates back to the late nineteenth century, but little consensus has been reached regarding exactly how to define emotion (see the reviews by Kringelbach & Phillips, 2014; Levenson et al., 2017). Opposing theoretical positions hinder agreement on even basic concepts, such as whether emotions are discrete (anger, love, sadness, and so on) or dimensional (positive to negative). Most people can agree that emotions are central to human life, yet we must acknowledge that emotions are not restricted to humans (see the review by Anderson & Adolphs, 2014). A horse that is expecting alfalfa for dinner will turn up its nose at grass hay and may stomp its front feet and toss its head. Two dogs that are in competition for attention may snap at each other. In fact, it has even been proposed that flies show emotion.

Many neuroscientists are moving to the position that rational decision making depends on accurate emotional processing. Patients who have neurological conditions that render them unable to process emotional information are characterized by poor judgment in a variety of situations (see Bechara, 2017). It is becoming clear that the control of emotions includes more than just the brainstem; specifically, activity in both the cortical and subcortical regions plays a role in their processing.

Emotion, like motivation, is intangible: it is an inferred state. But the importance of emotion to our everyday lives is hard to exaggerate. Emotion can motivate us. In some people, it inspires artistic expressions ranging from poetry to filmmaking to painting. Many people enjoy the arts simply because they evoke emotions. And while people find certain emotions pleasant, severe and prolonged negative emotions, especially anxiety and depression, can develop into clinical disorders.

To explore the neural basis of emotions, we must first specify the three types of behavior we want to explain. Think of a recent emotional experience. Perhaps you had a serious disagreement with a close friend or recently entered a romantic relationship. These experiences often include autonomic responses such as rapid breathing, sweating, and dry mouth. Emotions may also entail strong subjective feelings that we label as anger, fear, or love, among others. Finally, emotions typically encompass thoughts or plans related to the experience itself and may take the form of replaying conversations and events in your mind, anticipating what you might say or do differently in the future.

These three forms of emotional experience suggest the influence of different neural systems. The autonomic component must include the hypothalamus and associated structures, as well as the ENS (the neurons in the gut). The components affecting subjective feelings are more difficult to localize but clearly include the amygdala and probably parts of the frontal lobes. Meanwhile, thoughts and plans are likely to have a cortical origin.

A major challenge in identifying the neural correlates of emotion lies with the problem that emotion words, such as *anger* or *love*, are not the emotion. In a thoughtful review, Kagan (2018) notes that just because many languages contain words that are approximate synonyms of the English terms *happy*, *surprise*, *anger*, *fear*, *disgust*, *sad*, and so on, it does not mean that these named states are related to specific brain activity. Emotions occur in context, and brain activity is strongly influenced by context. To further complicate our understanding, measures of brain activity related to emotion are typically made using fMRI—and this is most certainly not a normal context for having emotional experiences. Consequently, there is little evidence that individual categories of emotion can be consistently localized to specific brain regions (see Barrett et al., 2019). Research does suggest, however, that emotions are likely to be related to diffuse networks (see Dubois et al., 2017, for more on this relationship). Before considering where these networks might be found, we look briefly at theories of emotion.

See Section 7-4 for a description of the setting in which fMRI and other brain scanning techniques are practiced.

## Theories of Emotion

Three general theoretical models have emerged over the past century. The first model, labeled *constructivist theory,* suggests that the brain interprets physiological changes (such as trembling and rapid heartbeat) as an emotion. This perspective implies that the brain (most likely the cortex) produces a cognitive response to autonomic information. That response varies with the context in which the autonomic arousal occurs, including the effects on the gut via the ENS. In cases of extreme autonomic activity, serotonin release surges in the gut, which can lead to diarrhea and cramping. If we are frightened by a movie, we feel a weaker, shorter-lived emotion than if we are frightened by a real-life encounter with a gang of muggers. Variations of this perspective have gone by many terms, beginning with the *James–Lange theory,* named for its nineteenth-century originators. However, all assume that the brain concocts a story to explain bodily reactions.

A modern view of constructed emotion posits that the primary role of the brain in emotional behavior is to integrate all of the body's resources to meet the organism's imminent needs for action in the short term and for growth, survival, and reproduction in the long term (see Friedman et al., 2019). To meet these various needs, the brain must anticipate them; to do so, it constructs an internal predictive model of the world and of the body. Certain animals, such as species of mammals and birds, do not like surprises and thus strive to reduce the uncertainty of future outcomes. In the face of a real or perceived threat, the body generates both behavioral and physiological responses to reduce the resulting stress. Constructivist researchers propose that brain structures—including the anterior cingulate cortex, ventromedial PFC, insula, amygdala, and ventral striatum—receive inputs from the periphery (e.g., skin, ANS, and other body organs) to generate affective (i.e., emotional) feelings.

The second type of emotional theory is *appraisal theory* (for a review, see Scherer & Moors, 2019). Its general idea is that emotional episodes comprise several components, including an appraisal of the situation, preparation for both mental and physical reactions, physiological responses, expressive behavior, and subjective feelings (see **Figure 12-19**). Emotions are elicited either by external events or objects or by internal processes, such as imagination and memory. Our appraisal leads to the process of *differentiation,* which encompasses action tendencies (preparation for both mental and physical actions), physiological responses (e.g., changes in blood pressure or heart rate), and motor expression (e.g., facial expression). These events are theorized to interact in the brain to induce nonverbal feelings, which are then categorized and labeled with emotional terms (such as good or bad feelings). These components then form the representation of the emotional event.

Finally, some theories of emotion are informally grouped together and labeled *neuropsychological theories.* In the 1930s, clinicians noticed that patients with large left and right hemisphere injuries suffered starkly different changes in emotional behavior. Typically, left hemisphere lesions produce fearfulness and depression, and right hemisphere lesions are associated with emotional indifference. Given that a patient with a large left-hemisphere injury presumably has an intact right hemisphere, researchers reasoned that the observed behaviors of such a person must reflect the activity of the right hemisphere. This observation led to the conclusion that the right hemisphere plays a major role in producing strong emotions, especially emotions regarded as negative, such as fear and anger. Because the left hemisphere has a major role in language, it has been suggested that cognitive appraisals involve the left hemisphere, whereas the right hemisphere's role is more automatic. In other words, the right hemisphere *generates* emotional feelings, and the left hemisphere *interprets* those feelings.

After Christopher Reeve's spinal cord was severed at the cervical level (high), his emotions may have been blunted, but his motivation clearly remained intact. See Section 11-1.

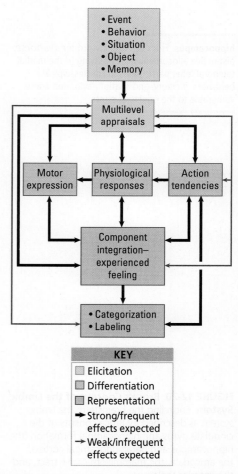

**FIGURE 12-19 A Multicomponent Emotion Process Model**  This model reflects a widely held view that emotion episodes are elicited by a cognitive evaluation or appraisal of events, which produces synchronized changes in several components of the emotion system. The model includes considerable feedback between the differentiation components and experience feeling, leading to categorization and labeling of the emotional response (the representation). Research from Scherer & Moors (2019).

Cerebral asymmetry in cognitive functions is discussed in Section 15-4.

The limbic circuit derives its name from the Latin *limbus*, meaning "border."

The allocortex is found in the brains of mammals and other chordates, especially birds and reptiles. See Section 2-3 for more details.

**hippocampus** From the Greek word for *seahorse*; distinctive allocortical structure lying in the medial temporal lobe; participates in species-typical behaviors, memory, and spatial navigation and is vulnerable to the effects of stress.

Although considerable evidence supports this theory of asymmetric control of emotional behavior, there is a danger in overemphasizing laterality at the expense of diminishing the bilateral roles of regions such as the prefrontal cortex, anterior cingulate cortex, and amygdala (for an extensive review, see Kolb & Whishaw, 2021). In many ways, the role of the cerebral *site* (e.g., the PFC) is far greater than that of the cerebral *side*. Unfortunately, popular psychology has tended to overgeneralize and oversimplify this asymmetry, implying the existence of "right brain" and "left brain" thinking.

# Emotion and the Limbic Circuit

It was not until the early twentieth century that physiologists began to study the relationship among autonomic, endocrine, and hormonal factors and inferred emotional states. Paul Broca, impressed by the development of brain structures that seemed to form a ring around the brainstem in amphibians and reptiles, described these structures as the *limbic lobe*.

Although the limbic lobe concept is vague, the idea continues to have heuristic value. Today it is referred to as the *limbic system*, though it is not actually a single system. The structures are formed from a three- and four-layered cortex (known as the allocortex), which lies adjacent to the six-layered neocortex. In mammals, the allocortex encompasses the cingulate (meaning "girdle") gyrus and the hippocampal formation, as shown in **Figure 12-20**. The hippocampal formation includes the **hippocampus**—an allocortical structure important in species-typical behaviors, memory, and spatial navigation and vulnerable to the effects of stress—and the *parahippocampal cortex* adjacent to it.

## Organization of the Limbic Circuit

As anatomists began to study the limbic structures, connections to the hypothalamus became evident. It also became apparent that the limbic system has a role in emotion. For instance, in the 1930s, James Papez observed that people with rabies display radically abnormal emotional behavior, and postmortem examinations showed that the rabies virus had selectively attacked the hippocampus. (Even today, obtaining definitive proof of rabies still requires postmortem hippocampal examination.)

Papez concluded from his observations that the limbic lobe and its associated subcortical structures provide the neural basis of emotion. He proposed a neural circuit, traced in **Figure 12-21**A and now known as the *Papez circuit*, whereby emotion could reach consciousness, which was presumed at that time to reside in the cerebral cortex. In 1949, Paul MacLean expanded Papez's concept of the limbic circuit to include the amygdala and prefrontal cortex. Figures 12-20 and 12-21A show the amygdala lying adjacent to the hippocampus in the temporal lobe, with the prefrontal cortex lying just anterior.

**FIGURE 12-20 Broca's Concept of the Limbic System** Encircling the brainstem, the limbic system as described by Broca consists of the cingulate gyrus and hippocampal formation (the hippocampus and parahippocampal cortex), the amygdala, the mammillothalamic tract, and the anterior thalamus.

Figure 12-21B charts the limbic circuit schematically. The hippocampus, amygdala, and prefrontal cortex all connect with the hypothalamus. The mammillary nucleus of the hypothalamus connects to the anterior thalamus, which in turn connects with the cingulate cortex. The cingulate cortex completes the circuit by connecting with the hippocampal formation, amygdala, and prefrontal cortex. This anatomical arrangement can be compared to the funnel in Figure 12-21C, which shows the hypothalamus as the spout leading to motivated and emotional behavior.

Scientists now have little doubt that most structures associated with the concept of a limbic system, especially the amygdala and hypothalamus, take part in emotional behaviors, as detailed later in this section. But most limbic structures perform important roles in various motivated behaviors as well, especially in motivating species-typical behaviors such as eating and sexual activity.

## Amygdala

Named for the Greek word for "almond" because of its shape, the **amygdala** consists of three principal subdivisions: the corticomedial area, the basolateral area, and the central area. Like the hypothalamus, the amygdala receives inputs from all sensory systems. But in contrast to the hypothalamic neurons, more complex stimuli are necessary to excite amygdalar neurons. Indeed, many amygdalar neurons are *multimodal*: they respond to more than one sensory modality. In fact, some respond to the entire sensory array—sight, sound, touch, taste, and smell. These amygdalar cells must shape a rather complex image of the sensory world.

The amygdala sends connections primarily to the hypothalamus and the brainstem, where it influences neural activity associated with emotions and species-typical behavior. For example, when the amygdala of a person with epilepsy is electrically stimulated before brain surgery, that person becomes fearful and anxious. We observed a woman who responded with increased respiration and heart rate, saying that she felt as if something bad was going to happen, although she could not specify what.

Amygdala stimulation can also induce eating and drinking. We observed a man who drank water every time the stimulation was turned on. (There happened to be a pitcher of water on the table next to him.) Within 20 minutes, he had consumed about 2 liters of water. When asked if he was thirsty, he said, "No, not really. I just feel like drinking."

The role of the amygdala in emotion can be seen most clearly in monkeys whose amygdalae have been removed. In 1939, Heinrich Klüver and Paul Bucy reported an extraordinary result, now known as **Klüver–Bucy syndrome**, that followed removal of the amygdala and anterior temporal cortex of monkeys. The principal symptoms included the following:

1. Tameness and loss of fear

2. Indiscriminate dietary behavior (eating many types of formerly rejected foods)

3. Greatly increased autoerotic and sexual activity with inappropriate object choice (e.g., the sexual mounting of chairs)

4. Tendency to attend to and react to every visual stimulus

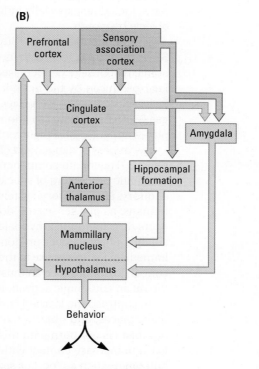

**FIGURE 12-21 Limbic System (A)** In this contemporary conception of the limbic system, an interconnected network of structures—the Papez circuit—controls emotional expression. **(B)** A schematic representation, coded to the brain areas shown in part A by color, charts the limbic system's major connections. **(C)** Parts A and B can be conceptualized as part of a funnel rim of outputs that, through the hypothalamus, produce emotional and motivated behavior.

Section 15-2 elaborates on multisensory integration and the binding problem.

**amygdala** The part of the brain that participates in species-typical behaviors, emotion, and emotional memory; from the Greek word for *almond*, reflecting the general shape in the medial temporal lobe.

**Klüver–Bucy syndrome** Behavioral syndrome, characterized especially by hypersexuality, that results from bilateral injury to the temporal lobe.

5. Tendency to examine all objects by mouth

6. Visual agnosia, an inability to recognize objects or drawings of objects

Chapter 9 describes varieties of visual-form agnosia in a range of case studies.

The visual agnosia results from damage to the ventral visual stream in the temporal lobe, but the other symptoms are related to the amygdalectomy. The tameness and loss of fear observed in the monkeys with Klüver–Bucy syndrome are especially striking. Monkeys that normally show a strong aversion to stimuli such as snakes show no fear of them whatsoever. In fact, amygdalectomized monkeys may pick up live snakes and even put them in their mouths.

Clinical Focus 2-2 examines some causes and symptoms of encephalitis.

Although Klüver–Bucy syndrome is not common in humans—because bilateral temporal lobectomies are rare—its symptoms can be seen in people with certain forms of encephalitis, a brain infection. In some cases, encephalitis centered on the base of the brain can damage both temporal lobes and produce many Klüver–Bucy symptoms, including especially indiscriminate sexual behavior and the tendency to examine objects by mouth.

The amygdala's role in Klüver–Bucy syndrome points to its central role in emotion. So do the effects seen with its electrical stimulation: such a stimulus produces an autonomic response (e.g., increased blood pressure and arousal) as well as a feeling of fear. Fear produced by the brain in the absence of an obvious threat might seem odd, but fear is basic to species' survival. To improve their chances of surviving, most organisms use fear as a stimulus to minimize their contact with dangerous animals, objects, and places and maximize their contact with safe things.

Awareness of danger and of safety has both an innate component and a learned component. The innate component, much as in the IRMs described in Section 12-1, is the automatic processing of species-relevant sensory information—inputs from the visual, auditory, and olfactory systems. The importance of olfactory inputs is not obvious to humans, as our senses are dominated by vision. Even so, olfactory information connects directly to the amygdala in the human brain (see Figure 12-20). For many other animals, olfactory cues predominate. A rat that has never encountered a ferret shows an immediate fear response to the odor of ferret. Other novel odors (such as peppermint or coffee) do not produce an innate fear reaction in the rat. The innate response triggers in the rat an autonomic activation that stimulates conscious awareness of danger.

In contrast, the learned component of fear consists of the avoidance of specific animals, places, and objects that the organism has come to associate with danger. The organism is not born with this avoidance behavior prewired. In a similar way, animals learn to increase contact with environmental stimuli that they associate with positive outcomes, such as food or sexual activity or, in the laboratory, drugs. Damage to the amygdala interferes with all these behaviors. With such an injury, the animal loses not only its innate fears but also its acquired fears of and preferences for certain environmental stimuli.

*Prefrontal* literally means "in front of the front."

To summarize, the survival of a species requires a functioning amygdala. The amygdala influences autonomic and hormonal responses through its connections to the hypothalamus. It influences our conscious awareness of the positive and negative consequences of events and objects through its connections to the prefrontal cortex.

## Prefrontal Cortex

Figure 11-2 charts the hierarchy of frontal lobe regions with regard to movement. Section 11-2 discusses the functions of the motor and premotor regions.

The prefrontal cortex is a large area of the brain that is made up of several functionally distinct regions, mapped in **Figure 12-22**A. The general areas of the prefrontal cortex are the dorsolateral region; the orbitofrontal cortex (OFC), also shown from a ventral aspect in Figure 12-22B; and the ventromedial PFC. The anterior cingulate cortex (ACC), shown in Figure 12-22C, is closely associated with the PFC albeit not strictly part of it.

Like the amygdala, the frontal lobes receive highly processed information from all sensory areas, and many neurons in the PFC, like those in the amygdala, are multimodal. As shown in **Figure 12-23**, the PFC receives input via connections from the amygdala, dorsomedial thalamus, sensory association cortex, posterior parietal cortex, and dopaminergic cells of the ventral tegmental area. Dopaminergic input is

**(A) Lateral view**

Dorsolateral prefrontal cortex · Premotor cortex · Motor cortex · Central sulcus

Prefrontal cortex

Orbitofrontal cortex

**(B) Ventral view**

Ventromedial prefrontal cortex · Orbitofrontal cortex

**(C) Medial view**

Dorsomedial prefrontal cortex

Anterior cingulate cortex

Ventromedial prefrontal cortex

**FIGURE 12-22 Gross Subdivisions of the Frontal Lobe and Prefrontal Cortex**

Section 16-2 elaborates on the causes of and treatments for schizophrenia.

important for regulating how prefrontal neurons react to stimuli, including emotional ones. Abnormalities in this dopaminergic projection may account for some disorders, including schizophrenia, in which people evince little emotional reaction to typically arousing stimuli.

Figure 12-23 also shows the areas to which the PFC sends connections—that is, its output. The inferior prefrontal region projects axons to the amygdala and the hypothalamus in particular. These PFC axons provide a route for influencing the ANS and ENS, which control changes in blood pressure, respiration, and other internal processes, especially those related to emotions. The dorsolateral prefrontal region sends its connections primarily to the sensory association cortex, posterior parietal cortex, cingulate cortex, basal ganglia, and premotor cortex; it plays a larger role in cognitive behaviors than in emotional behaviors.

Section 15-2 expands on the role of prefrontal regions in cognition.

PFC output influences movement (Section 11-1), memory (Section 14-1), and cognition (Section 15-2).

One overall function of the PFC is to select behaviors appropriate to the particular time and place, cued by either internal information or the environmental context. Disruption of this selection function can be seen in people who experience injury to the dorsolateral frontal lobe (see Figure 12-22A). These individuals become overly dependent on environmental cues to determine their behavior. Like small children, they can be easily distracted by what they see or hear. We have all experienced a loss of concentration to some extent, but for a patient with frontal lobe damage, the problem is both exaggerated and persistent. Because the person becomes so absorbed in irrelevant stimuli, he or she cannot act on internalized information most of the time.

A good example is J. C., who sustained bilateral damage to the dorsolateral PFC from having a tumor removed. J. C. would lie in bed most of the day, fixated on

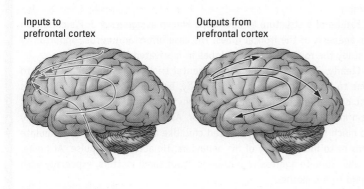

Inputs to prefrontal cortex

Outputs from prefrontal cortex

**FIGURE 12-23 Prefrontal Connections** The PFC receives inputs (red arrows in the anatomical illustration) and sends outputs (blue arrows in the illustration) to the areas charted on the diagram to the right.

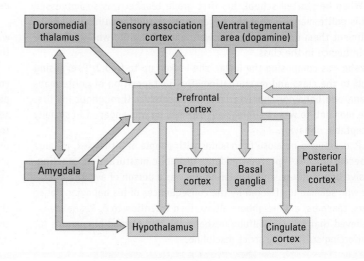

Dorsomedial thalamus · Sensory association cortex · Ventral tegmental area (dopamine)

Prefrontal cortex

Amygdala

Premotor cortex · Basal ganglia · Posterior parietal cortex

Hypothalamus · Cingulate cortex

television programs. He was aware of his wife's negative opinion of this behavior, but only the sound of the garage door opening when she returned home from work in the evening would stimulate him into action. Getting out of bed was controlled by this specific environmental cue; without it, he seemed to lack motivation. Television completely distracted him from acting on internal knowledge of things that he could or should do.

Adapting behavior appropriately to the environmental context also is a PFC function. Most people readily change their behavior to match the situation at hand. We behave one way with our parents, another with our friends, another with our children, and yet another with our coworkers. Each set of people constitutes a different context, and we alter our behaviors accordingly. Our tone of voice, our use of slang or profanity, and the content of our conversations are quite different in different contexts. Even among our peers we act differently, depending on who is present. We may be relaxed in the presence of some people and ill at ease with others. It is therefore no accident that the size of the frontal lobes is related to species' sociability. Social behavior is extremely rich in contextual information, and humans are highly social animals.

Controlling behavior in context requires detailed sensory information, which is conveyed from all sensory regions of the body to the frontal lobes. This sensory input includes not only information from the external world but also internal information from the ANS. People with damage to the orbital PFC, as is common in traumatic brain injuries (TBIs), have difficulty adapting their behavior to the context, especially the social context. Consequently, they often make social gaffes.

In summary, the role of the frontal lobes in selecting behaviors is important for considering what causes behavior. The frontal lobes act much like a composer, but instead of selecting notes and instruments, they select our actions. Not surprisingly, the frontal lobes are sometimes described as housing the brain's executive functions. To grasp the full extent of frontal lobe control of behavior, see Clinical Focus 12-5: Agenesis of the Frontal Lobe.

Clinical Focus 1-1 and Section 1-1 recount behavioral effects of TBI; Section 14-5 details recovery from such an injury; Section 16-3 explores TBI symptoms and treatments.

Section 15-2 considers the frontal lobes and the executive function of planning.

---

◉ **CLINICAL FOCUS 12-5**

# Agenesis of the Frontal Lobes

The role of the frontal lobes in motivated behavior is perhaps best understood by looking at J. P.'s case, described in detail by Stafford Ackerly (1964). Born in December 1914, J. P. was a problem child. Early on, he became a wanderer. Police officers would find him miles from home, as he had no fear of being lost. Severe whippings by his father did not deter him.

J. P.'s behavioral problems continued and expanded as he grew older, and by adolescence, he was constantly in trouble. Yet J. P. also had a positive side. When he started school, his first-grade teacher was so impressed with his polite manners that she began writing a letter to his parents to compliment them on having such a well-mannered child who was such a good influence in the class.

As she was composing the letter, she looked up to find J. P. exposing himself to the class and masturbating. This juxtaposition of polite manners and odd behavior characterized J. P.'s conduct throughout his life. At one moment he was charming; at the next, he was engaged in socially unacceptable behavior.

J. P. developed no close friendships with people of either sex, in large part because of his repeated incidents of public masturbation, stealing, excessive boastfulness, and wandering. He was a person of average intelligence who seemed unaffected by the consequences of his behavior. Police officers, teachers, and neighbors all ascribed intention to J. P.'s behavior: all believed that he was willfully misbehaving and blamed his parents for not enforcing sufficiently strict discipline.

Perhaps as a result, not until he was 19 years old was J. P.'s true condition detected. To prevent him from serving a prison term for repeated automobile theft, a lawyer suggested that J. P. undergo psychiatric evaluation. The psychiatrist who examined him ordered an X-ray (the only brain scan available at the time). The image revealed that J. P. lacked a right frontal lobe, and his left frontal lobe was about 50% the normal size. It is almost certain that his frontal lobes simply failed to develop.

Failure of a structure to develop is known as *agenesis*; J. P.'s condition was agenesis of the frontal lobes. His case offers an unusual opportunity to study the role of the frontal lobes in motivated behavior.

Clearly, J. P. lacked the bag of mental tricks that most people use to come to terms with the world. Normally, behavior is affected by both its past consequences and the current environmental input. J. P. did not seem much influenced by either factor. As a result, the world was simply too much for him. He always acted childlike and was unable to formulate plans or to inhibit many of his behaviors. He acted on impulse. At home, he was prone to aggressive outbursts about small matters, especially with regard to his mother.

Curiously, J. P. seemed completely unaware of his life situation. Even though the rest of his brain was working fairly well—his IQ score was in the normal range, and his language skills were very good—the rest of his brain was unable to compensate for the absence of frontal lobes.

# Prefrontal Cortex and Emotional Behavior

At about the same time that Klüver and Bucy began studying their monkeys, Carlyle Jacobsen was investigating the effects of frontal lobotomy on the cognitive capacities of two chimpanzees. A frontal lobotomy, which involves inserting a sharp instrument into the frontal lobes and moving it back and forth to disconnect the lobes from the rest of the brain, destroys substantial brain tissue.

In 1936, Jacobsen reported that one of the chimps was particularly neurotic before being subjected to this procedure. She became more relaxed afterward. Incredibly, a leading neurologist of the time, Egas Moniz, seized on this observation as the basis for treating behavioral disorders in humans and began performing frontal lobotomies in his patients. Frontal lobotomy was the first technique of **psychosurgery**, or neurosurgery intended to alter behavior. It was later refined by Walter Freeman to become the transorbital leukotomy illustrated in **Figure 12-24**.

**FIGURE 12-24 Transorbital Leukotomy** In this procedure, a leukotome is inserted through the bone of the eye socket to disconnect the orbitofrontal cortex from the rest of the brain.

The use of psychosurgery grew rapidly in the 1950s. In North America alone, nearly 40,000 people received frontal lobotomies as a treatment for psychiatric disorders. Not until the 1960s was any systematic research conducted into the effects of frontal lesions on social and emotional behavior. By that time, the frontal lobotomy had virtually vanished as a "treatment." We now know that prefrontal lesions in various species, including humans, severely impact social and emotional behavior.

Agnes is a case in point. We met Agnes at the same psychiatric hospital where we met Roger (whose indiscriminate eating we described in Section 12-1). At the time, Agnes, a 57-year-old woman, was visiting one of the nurses. In the past, she had been a patient there.

The first thing we noticed about Agnes was that she exhibited no outward sign of emotion and showed almost no facial expression. Agnes had been subjected to a procedure known as a *frontal leukotomy* because her husband, an oil tycoon, felt that she was too gregarious. Evidently, he felt that her "loose lips" were a detriment to his business dealings. He convinced two psychiatrists that she would benefit from psychosurgery, and her life was changed forever.

To perform a leukotomy, as illustrated in Figure 12-24, a surgeon uses a special knife called a leukotome to sever the connections of a region of the orbitofrontal cortex (see Figure 12-22). In our conversations with Agnes, we quickly discovered her considerable insight into the changes brought about by her leukotomy. In particular, she indicated that she no longer had any feelings about things or most people, although, curiously, she was attached to her dog. She said that she often just felt empty and much like a zombie.

Agnes's only moment of real happiness in the 30 years since her operation was the sudden death of her husband, whom she blamed for ruining her life. Unfortunately, Agnes squandered her dead husband's considerable wealth as a consequence of her inability to plan or organize. This inability, we have seen, is another symptom of prefrontal injury.

The orbitofrontal area has direct connections with the amygdala and hypothalamus. Stimulating it can produce autonomic responses, and, as we saw in Agnes, damage to the orbital region can produce severe personality changes characterized by apathy and loss of initiative or drive. The orbital cortex is probably responsible for the conscious awareness of emotional states produced by the rest of the limbic system, especially the amygdala.

Agnes's lack of facial expression is also typical of frontal lobe damage. In fact, people with frontal lobe injuries and people who have schizophrenia or autism spectrum disorder (ASD) are usually impaired at both producing and perceiving facial expressions, including a wide range of expressions found in all human cultures—happiness, sadness, fear, anger, disgust, and surprise. As with J. P.'s frontal lobe agenesis, described in Clinical Focus 12-5, it is difficult to imagine how such people can function effectively in our highly social world without being able to express their own emotions or to recognize those of others.

ASD is the topic of Clinical Focus 8-2; schizophrenia is the topic of Clinical Focus 8-5.

While facial expression is a key to recognizing emotion, so is tone of voice, or *prosody*. Patients with damage to the frontal lobe are devoid of prosody, both in producing their own speech and in understanding the prosody of others. The lost ability to comprehend or produce emotional expression in both faces and language

**psychosurgery** Any neurosurgical technique intended to alter behavior.

The vmPFC is illustrated in Figure 12-22B.

The insular cortex is diagrammed in Figure 10-12B.

partly explains those patients' apathy. In some ways, they are similar to patients with spinal cord injuries who have lost autonomic feedback and so can no longer feel the arousal associated with emotion. These patients can no longer either read emotion in other people's faces and voices or express it in their own.

As noted earlier, a growing body of evidence indicates that emotion is linked to decision making, and the ventromedial prefrontal cortex (vmPFC) plays a key role in that process. Patients with damage to the vmPFC develop severe deficits in personal and social decision making, despite having largely preserved intellectual abilities (see Bechara, 2017). It is hypothesized that the vmPFC has a role in accessing visceral (internal) information that is related to the value (e.g., pleasant versus unpleasant) of objects in the world. Noninvasive imaging studies (fMRI) have also shown that changes in the activity of the vmPFC result in changes in the subjective pleasantness of experiences involving food, drugs, music, and sexual activity (see Berridge & Kringelbach, 2015). Notably, however, imaging studies also reveal the presence of a more extensive network of increased activity, including in the anterior cingulate cortex, the insular cortex, and subcortical regions such as the amygdala and striatum. We return to these regions in our discussion of reward in Section 12-7.

## 12-6 Review

Before you continue, check your understanding. Answers to Self-Test appear at the back of the book.

1. The three types of theories of emotion are _____, _____, and _____.

2. List three key brain regions involved in emotions: _____, _____, and _____.

3. Which factors complicate the study of anatomical correlates to human emotions?

4. Describe the symptoms of Klüver–Bucy syndrome.

### 12-7

# Reward

**Learning Objectives**
- Identify the reward system and give the major structures associated with it.
- Map pleasure in the brain.

**Principle 1:** Neuronal circuits are the functional units of the nervous system.

Throughout this chapter, we have concluded repeatedly that animals engage in a wide range of voluntary behaviors because those behaviors are rewarding and avoid behaviors that are not rewarding. That is, these behaviors increase the activity in neural circuits that function to maintain an animal's contact with certain environmental stimuli, either in the present or in the future. Presumably, the animal perceives the activity of these circuits as pleasant. This conclusion would explain why reward can help maintain not only adaptive behaviors, such as eating and sexual activity, but also potentially nonadaptive behaviors, such as drug addiction. After all, evolution would not have prepared the brain specifically for the eventual development of psychoactive drugs.

## The Reward System

To understand the neural circuitry of pleasure and reward, we should recognize that rewards are not a single thing but rather involve several different components. The English word *hedonic,* derived from the Greek word for "pleasure," can refer to many types of pleasure, including sensory, cognitive, social, aesthetic, and moral. *Anhedonia* refers to the lack of pleasure, which can result from a breakdown in the reward system. Kent Berridge and Terry Robinson (2003) emphasize that reward has three main components: (1) *learning* about rewards and the cues that predict their availability; (2) *motivation* for these rewards and the cues associated with them ("wanting" the reward); and (3) *affective* (hedonic) responses to the actual pleasure of rewards ("liking" the reward). A challenge for neuroscience is to understand how brain mechanisms generate each of these components. Consider why we increase contact with a stimulus such as chocolate. Three independent factors are at work: our knowledge of where the chocolate might be, our desire to eat the chocolate (wanting), and the pleasurable effect of eating the chocolate (liking). Where do these events occur in the brain?

The first clue to the presence of a reward system in the brain came with an accidental discovery by James Olds and Peter Milner in 1954. These researchers found that rats would perform behaviors such as pressing a bar to administer a brief burst of electrical stimulation to specific sites in their brain. This phenomenon is called *intracranial self-stimulation* or *brain stimulation reward*.

Typically, rats will press a lever hundreds or even thousands of times per hour to obtain this brain stimulation, stopping only when they are exhausted. Why would animals engage in such behavior when it has absolutely no survival value to them or to their species? The simplest explanation is that the brain stimulation is activating the system underlying reward. Stimulation along the MFB tract activates fibers that form the ascending pathways from dopamine-producing cells of the midbrain tegmentum, shown in **Figure 12-25**. This mesolimbic dopamine pathway sends terminals to sites that include, notably, the nucleus accumbens in the basal ganglia and the prefrontal cortex.

Many researchers initially hypothesized that the brain stimulation was activating the mesolimbic dopamine pathway, which sends terminals to sites that include the nucleus accumbens in the basal ganglia and the PFC. Blocking dopamine with drugs such as neuroleptics appear to take the pleasure out of normally rewarding events such as self-stimulation and amphetamine, leading Roy Wise (1980) to propose that dopamine synapses represent a place where sensory inputs are translated into hedonic messages that we experience as pleasure. Thus was born the well-known idea that dopamine is the pleasure transmitter. Unfortunately, this idea is wrong. Wise himself has since admitted as much, but the idea remains in the public's imagination.

Perhaps the first clear indication that dopamine is not the pleasure molecule came from earlier studies by Berridge and Robinson (1998). Berridge had been using facial expressions in rats and people to measure how pleasurable or unpleasurable tastes were. As shown in **Figure 12-26**, exposure to palatable tastes (chocolate) elicits hedonic reactions in humans, such as licking the fingers and lips. In contrast, exposure to unpleasant tastes such as something overly salty elicits negative reactions such as grimacing, spitting, or wiping the mouth with the back of the hand. Rats, too, show distinctive positive and negative responses to pleasant and unpleasant tastes.

Now consider rats with lesions of the ascending dopaminergic pathway to the forebrain. These rats do not eat. Is it simply that they do not desire to eat (a loss of wanting), or has food become aversive to them (a loss of liking)? By watching the facial expressions and body movements after food is squirted into the mouth of a rat that otherwise

Robinson and Berridge's wanting-and-liking theory of addiction includes a multipart reward system; see Section 6-4.

Section 7-1 describes how electrical stimulation works both as a treatment and as a research tool.

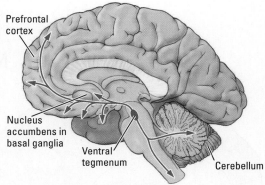

**FIGURE 12-25 Mesolimbic Dopamine System** Axons emanating from the ventral tegmentum (blue arrows) project diffusely through the brain. Dopamine release in these mesolimbic pathways has a role in feelings of reward and pleasure. The nucleus accumbens is a critical structure in this reward system.

**FIGURE 12-26 Human Reactions to Taste** Sucrose and other palatable tastes elicit positive (hedonic) reactions, including licking the fingers and the lips. Quinine and other unpleasant tastes elicit negative (aversive) reactions, including spitting, expressing distaste, and wiping the mouth with the back of the hand. Information from Berridge (1996).

refuses to eat, we can tell to what extent a loss of liking is a factor in the animal's food rejection. Interestingly, rats that do not eat after receiving lesions to the dopamine pathway act as though they still like food.

Next, consider a rat with a self-stimulation electrode in the lateral hypothalamus. This rat will often eat heartily while the stimulation is on. The obvious inference is that the food must taste good—presumably even better than usual. But what happens if we squirt food into the rat's mouth and observe its behavior when the stimulation is on versus when it is off?

If the brain stimulation primes eating by evoking pleasurable sensations, we would expect the animal to be more positive in its facial and body reactions to foods when the stimulation is turned on. In fact, the opposite occurs. During stimulation, rats react more aversively to tastes such as sugar and salt than when the stimulation is off. Apparently, the stimulation increases wanting but not liking.

Such experiments show that what appears to be a single event—reward—is actually composed of at least two independent processes. Just as our visual system independently processes *what* and *how* information in separate streams, our reward system appears to process wanting and liking independently. Reward is not a single phenomenon any more than perception or memory is.

## Mapping Pleasure in the Brain

Although the experiences of different pleasures (e.g., delicious foods, romantic gestures, listening to music) may seem very different from each other, neuroimaging studies suggest that they all activate surprisingly similar brain circuitry in regions of the prefrontal cortex, anterior cingulate cortex, and insula, as well as subcortical limbic structures such as the nucleus accumbens, ventral pallidum, and amygdala (for details, see Berridge & Kringelbach, 2015). Although the wanting and liking systems overlap to some extent, wanting is generated by a large distributed brain system dominated by dopamine projections, especially to the striatum and prefrontal cortex. In contrast, liking is generated by a smaller set of hedonic hot spots within the limbic circuitry, shown in **Figure 12-27**.

From this perspective, we can see that dopamine is the neurotransmitter related to wanting, but which neurotransmitter(s) are related to liking? Berridge and his colleagues have identified small regions in the nucleus accumbens and associated ventral pallidum and ventromedial orbitofrontal cortex and insula, as well as a site in the hindbrain dorsal pons, that contribute to hedonic functions and are known to contribute to taste and pain. Each of these hot spots uses opioid (natural heroinlike) neurotransmitters and endocannabinoid (natural marijuana-type) neurotransmitters—but never dopamine—to amplify liking (pleasure) reactions. These hedonic hot spots are relatively small in each region, but they appear to act together as a unified system to enhance pleasure. The intensity of pleasure is believed to be related to the number of regions that are simultaneously activated.

**FIGURE 12-27 Liking and Wanting Systems in the Brain** Wanting is mediated by an extensive brain system including dopamine projections (the blue arrows), whereas liking is mediated by a more restricted brain system of small hedonic hot spots (red). Research from Berridge & Robinson (2016).

## Pleasure Electrodes?

Pleasure is not merely a sensation or thought, but instead is best conceived of as an additional "hedonic gloss," which creates the pleasure-versus-displeasure affect (see the review by Kringelbach & Berridge, 2017). The hedonic gloss of objects or events is generated in the brain by activity in networks of hedonic hot spots (pleasure) or cold spots (displeasure). Berridge and his colleagues have identified these regions in the rodent nucleus accumbens and ventral pallidum, the adjacent insula in the cortex, and the orbitofrontal cortex through direct neurochemical or optogenetic manipulation generating positive or negative changes in "liking" reactions to tastes (see the details in Berridge & Kringelbach, 2015).

Recall that the active search for a pleasure center in the brain was initiated, at least in part, by Olds and Milner's discovery that rats would press a bar to get an electrical current to the brain. Although we now know that the current was evoking wanting, not pleasure, the question remains: Could stimulation of hedonic hot spots actually induce pleasure? More importantly, could stimulation be used to reverse states of *anhedonia*, such as depression? In the 1970s, studies involving deep brain stimulation in humans purportedly produced feelings of pleasure in the participants, but a review of this work by Berridge and Kringelbach (2015) suggests that there is no evidence that patients actually acknowledged this effect.

Nonetheless, in the past decade deep brain stimulation has been utilized as a therapeutic technique for a wide range of conditions, including chronic pain, depression, and Parkinson disease. Stimulation of the nucleus accumbens of humans has been reported to induce sudden feelings of "wanting" to do something, but as yet there is no convincing evidence that such stimulation can produce "liking" (pleasure). In addition, there are clearly technical issues to be resolved: electrodes would need to be targeted at a hot spot without also stimulating an adjacent cold spot, which would produce a mixed response. Nevertheless, evidence suggests that stimulation of the nucleus accumbens or prefrontal cortex can provide relief from anxiety or depression, which can have a significant positive impact on people's lives.

Major depression, described in Clinical Focus 6-4, is among the most treatable psychological disorders. Cognitive and intrapersonal therapies are as effective as drugs. See Sections 16-2 and 16-3.

## 12-7 Review

Before you continue, check your understanding. Answers to Self-Test appear at the back of the book.

1. Animals prefer to engage in many voluntary behaviors because the behaviors are _____.

2. Neural circuits maintain contact with rewarding environmental stimuli in the present or in the future through _____ and _____ subsystems.

3. The neurotransmitter hypothesized to be related to reward is _____, and the neurotransmitters hypothesized to be related to liking are _____ and _____.

4. What is intracranial self-stimulation, and what does it tell us about the brain's reward system?

# Summary

## 12-1 Identifying the Causes of Behavior

Our inner subjective feelings (emotions) and goal-directed thoughts (motivations) influence how we behave and adapt as individuals and as a species. Emotion and motivation are inferred states that can escape conscious awareness or intent and that make the case for free will difficult to argue.

Biologically, reward motivates animals to engage in behavior. Aversive circumstances prompt brain circuits to produce behaviors that will reduce those circumstances. The brain inherently needs stimulation. In its absence, the brain will seek it out.

Sensory stimulation leads both to hormone activity and to dopamine activity in the brainstem. Neural circuits organized in the brainstem control species-typical behaviors, such as prey killing by cats and singing by birds. These brainstem circuits manifest their evolutionary advantage: they are rewarding. Rewarding behavior motivates living beings. When animals disengage from behaviors that motivate their species, they go extinct.

Behavior is controlled by its consequences as well as by its biology. Consequences may affect the evolution of a species or the behavior of an individual. Behaviors selected by evolution are often triggered by innate releasing mechanisms (IRMs). Behaviors selected only in an individual animal are shaped by that animal's environment and are learned.

## 12-2 Neuroanatomy of Motivated Behavior

The neural structures that initiate emotional and motivated behaviors are the hypothalamus, pituitary gland, amygdala, dopaminergic and noradrenergic activating pathways from nuclei in the lower brainstem, and frontal lobes.

The experience of both emotion and motivation is controlled by activity in the autonomic nervous system, hypothalamus, and forebrain, especially the amygdala and frontal cortex. Emotional and motivated behavior may be unconscious responses to internal or external stimuli that are controlled either by the activity of innate releasing mechanisms or by cognitive responses to events or thoughts.

## 12-3 The Role of the Chemical Senses in Motivated Behavior

Animals make cognitive appraisals related to their chemical senses. Researchers propose that the system for cognitive appraisal was adapted to the appraisal of more abstract things, such as people, groups, and actions, as well as to the appraisal of the treatment of others and questions of morality.

In the olfactory and gustatory senses, chemical neuroreceptors in the nose and tongue, respectively, interact with chemosignals, leading to neural activity in cranial nerve 1 for olfaction and cranial nerves 7, 9, and 10 for taste. The cranial nerves enter the brainstem and, through a series of synapses, pass into the forebrain. Smell and taste inputs merge in the orbitofrontal cortex to produce our perception of flavor. Impairments to the chemical senses can have profound, if subtle, impacts, and have been linked to conditions such as depression, decreased enjoyment of food and drink, and decreased sexual satisfaction.

## 12-4 Control of Regulatory Behavior

The two distinctly different types of motivated behaviors are (1) regulatory (homeostatic) behaviors, which maintain balance of the vital body systems, and (2) nonregulatory behaviors, which include basically all nonreflexive behaviors and behaviors not controlled by a homeostatic mechanism. Eating and drinking are regulatory behaviors controlled by the interaction of the digestive and hormonal systems, the enteric nervous system, and the hypothalamic and cortical circuits. Osmotic thirst results from increased concentrations of dissolved chemicals, known as solutes, in the body fluids. Hypovolemic thirst results from a loss of overall fluid volume from the body.

## 12-5 Sexual Differences and Sexual Behavior

Sexual differentiation results from an organizing effect of gonadal hormones and sex chromosomes during fetal development. Sexual differentiation results in sexually dimorphic brain structures and behavior, although in humans the male/female distinction in the brain can be blurred. Gonadal hormones also affect brain and behavior through activating effects later in life. Sexual orientation, including homosexuality and transgender, is related to differences in brain organization.

Copulatory behavior is controlled by the hypothalamus (the ventromedial hypothalamus in females and the preoptic area in males). Sexual activity is a nonregulatory behavior motivated by the amygdala.

Sexual orientation (a person's attraction to the opposite or same sex, or both) and gender identity (a person's feeling of being male, female, both, or neither) are related to the organization of the hypothalamus. Differences in hypothalamic organization are likely related to epigenetic effects in early development.

## 12-6 The Neural Control of Emotion

Emotion is an inferred state that is difficult to define. We consider three models of emotion. Constructivist theories argue that the brain produces a cognitive response to autonomic states. Appraisal theories define emotional episodes as processes rather than states. According to these theories, emotions result from an evaluation of context, including somatic components, which lead to a subjective feeling. Neuropsychological theories emphasize asymmetrical cerebral control of emotions.

Emotions are not found in a single place in the brain but rather are distributed in limbic and frontal lobe structures, especially the amygdala and prefrontal cortex.

## 12-7 Reward

Survival depends on maximizing contact with some environmental stimuli and minimizing contact with others. The reward mechanism controls this differential. Two independent features of reward are wanting and liking. The wanting component is thought to be controlled by dopaminergic activating systems, whereas the liking component is thought to be controlled by opioid and endocannabinoid systems. The wanting system is generated by a large distributed brain system dominated by dopamine projections found especially in striatal and prefrontal regions. The liking system is distributed by a smaller localized set of hedonic hot spots in the striatum and brainstem.

# Key Terms

activating effects, p. 427

amygdala, p. 435

androgens, p. 404

anorexia nervosa, p. 420

aphagia, p. 421

emotion, p. 402

evolutionary psychology, p. 406

gender identity, p. 430

hippocampus, p. 434

homeostatic mechanism, p. 409

hyperphagia, p. 421

hypovolemic thirst, p. 423

innate releasing mechanism (IRM), p. 404

Klüver–Bucy syndrome, p. 435

learned taste aversion, p. 407

medial forebrain bundle (MFB), p. 411

motivation, p. 408

nonregulatory behavior, p. 410

obesity, p. 420

orbitofrontal cortex (OFC), p. 416

organizing effects, p. 427

osmotic thirst, p. 423

pheromone, p. 416

pituitary gland, p. 410

preparedness, p. 408

psychosurgery, p. 439

regulatory behavior, p. 409

reinforcer, p. 407

releasing hormone, p. 412

sexual dimorphism, p. 427

sexual orientation, p. 430

transgender, p. 430

# Selected Resources from  Achieve

**Neuroscience in Action:** Hypothalamic Circuit: Feedback and Regulation

**Neuroscience in Action:** The Reward System: Wanting and Liking

**Concept Practice:**

The Limbic System

**Videos**

Hunger and Eating

What is Emotion?

**LearningCurve**

**Practice Quiz**

# Why Do We Sleep and Dream?

## 13

Ashima Narain/Getty Images

## CLINICAL FOCUS 13-1

### Doing the Right Thing at the Right Time

We have all heard this advice: Maintaining regular sleeping and eating habits contributes to good health. Scientific evidence supports this good advice.

We humans are **diurnal animals** (from the Latin *dies*, meaning "day"): we are active and eat during daylight, and we sleep when it is dark. This day-and-night rhythm is our **circadian rhythm**, and it regulates not only our sleep but other behaviors such as eating times. Most organisms have a circadian rhythm.

Today our environment allows us to intrude on our circadian rhythm in two ways. First, artificial lighting allows us to extend our waking hours well into the night and into sleep time. Second, handy food sources — often easily metabolized high-calorie foods — allow us to eat whenever we want. Together these intrusions into our natural circadian rhythm contribute to a combination of medical disorders, known as **metabolic syndrome**, that collectively increase the risk of developing sleep disorders, cardiovascular disease, and diabetes (Spiesshoefer et al., 2019).

The roots of metabolic syndrome may lie in disruptions of our **biological clocks**, the neural systems that regulate our circadian behavior. We likely have two clocks: one that controls sleep–waking and another that controls the functioning of body organs related to feeding, such as the liver, pancreas, and gut. The clock that controls sleep–waking responds to light, whereas the clock that controls feeding responds to eating. The activities of these two clocks are reciprocal: disrupting one disrupts the other.

Irregular sleep and meal schedules change the synchrony of our biological clocks. Metabolic rate, plasma glucose, and pancreatic insulin secretion can slow down or speed up at inappropriate times, contributing to obesity and diabetes. Prevention and treatment of obesity and diabetes can include doing the right thing at the right time when it comes to sleep schedules and mealtimes.

Marcus Chung /Getty Images

---

**diurnal animal** Organism that is active chiefly during daylight.

**circadian rhythm** Day–night rhythm.

**metabolic syndrome** Combinations of medical disorders, including obesity and insulin abnormalities, that collectively increase the risk of developing cardiovascular disease and diabetes.

**biological clock** Neural system that times behavior by producing biorhythms.

**biorhythm** A natural rhythm in behavior or bodily process.

**period** Time required to complete an activity cycle.

---

### Learning Objectives

- Describe the various biorhythms, including free-running rhythms.
- Explain how Zeitgebers work to set our biological clocks.
- Explain how entrainment can work to counter the effects of light pollution and other disruptive factors.

Our daily rhythms of sleeping and waking, feeding, exercising, and social interaction are rhythmical over days and years. Other animals share these daily activities and also migrate, hibernate, and shed or grow feathers or fur as the seasons change. In this chapter, we answer questions related to these daily and seasonal rhythms, including how the brain produces biological rhythms, why sleep evolved, and which neural mechanisms regulate sleeping, waking, and sleep-related disorders.

## 13-1

# A Clock for All Seasons

We first consider biological rhythms and then present evidence that some rhythms are produced by a biological clock. Because environmental cues are not always consistent, we examine how our biological clock helps us interpret environmental cues in an adaptive way. We also consider evidence for the health consequences that arise when behavior conflicts with our biological clock.

## Biological Rhythms

**Biorhythms** are cyclical changes in behavior or bodily functions. They have their origins in the first unicellular organisms and are a feature of all living organisms today. Every cyclical activity has a **period**, the time required to complete one cycle of activity. Biorhythms are defined by their periods. Biorhythms and their periods are controlled by genes, so genetic regulation also factors into our discussion of biological rhythms.

A variety of biorhythms regulate an organism's behaviors and functions. *Circannual rhythms* have a period of about a year. Many animals' migratory and mating cycles are circannual. *Infradian rhythms* have monthly or seasonal periods greater than a day

**TABLE 13-1** Types of Biorhythms

| Biological rhythm | Time frame | Example |
|---|---|---|
| Circannual | Yearly | Migratory cycles of birds |
| Infradian | More than a day | Human menstrual cycle |
| Circadian | Daily | Human sleep–wake cycle |
| Ultradian | Less than a day | Human eating cycles |

but less than a year. The menstrual cycle and associated hormonal changes of human females, with an average period of about 28 days, is an infradian biorhythm. The menstrual cycle is linked to the cycle of the moon, so it is also referred to as a *circalunar cycle* (Helfrich-Förster et al., 2021). *Circadian rhythms* have a daily period, as exemplified by the human sleep–waking cycle; many other biological functions share this rhythm. *Ultradian rhythms* have a period of less than a day. Our eating behavior, which takes place about every 90 minutes to 2 hours, including snacking, is one example. These different biorhythms are summarized in **Table 13-1**.

*Circadian* comes from the Latin *circa*, meaning "around," and *diem*, meaning "day."

## The Origin of Biorhythms

Biorhythms help living things adapt to the cyclical changes that take place in the environment as a result of Earth's rotation and orbit in relation to the sun. The energy provided by the sun is essential to the biology of most animal species, and the genes that regulate biorhythms evolved to optimize the energy that it provides.

Because the Earth's axis is tilted slightly, as our planet makes its annual orbit around the sun, the North and South Poles incline toward the sun for part of the year and away from it for the rest of the year (see **Figure 13-1**). Regions near the equator experience little change in day and night length over the course of a year, but the magnitude of the day–night change increases as distance from the equator increases. As the Southern Hemisphere inclines toward the sun, its inhabitants experience longer days and shorter nights; conversely, inhabitants in the Northern Hemisphere experience shorter days and longer nights. This relationship reverses as the year progresses.

A circadian biorhythm allows an organism to make adjustments to day-to-night changes and to the relative lengthening and shortening of day and night at the latitude at which it lives. A circannual biorhythm helps an animal adapt to the environmental changes that occur over a year, especially if it lives in northern and southern climates. Migration allows an organism to optimize light, climate, and food availability.

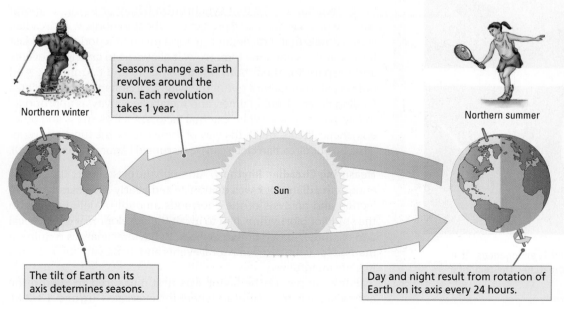

Northern winter

Seasons change as Earth revolves around the sun. Each revolution takes 1 year.

Sun

Northern summer

The tilt of Earth on its axis determines seasons.

Day and night result from rotation of Earth on its axis every 24 hours.

**FIGURE 13-1 Origins of Biorhythms** Each point on Earth between the Arctic and Antarctic Circles faces the sun for part of its daily rotation cycle (daytime) and faces away from the sun for the other part (nighttime). Seasonal changes in temperature and in the amount of daylight result from the tilt of Earth's axis during its annual revolution around the sun.

In the following sections, we first describe how some biorhythms help us adapt to daily changes, and then consider how the same biorhythms interact with other, shorter and longer biorhythms.

## Circadian Rhythms

Just as waking and sleep behavior have a circadian rhythm, so too do pulse rate, blood pressure, body temperature, rate of cell division, blood cell count, alertness, urine composition, metabolic rate, sexual drive, feeding behavior, responsiveness to medications, cognitive ability, and emotions.

Circadian rhythms are not unique to animals. Plants display rhythmic behavior exemplified by species whose leaves or flowers open during the day and close at night. Even unicellular algae and fungi display rhythmic behaviors related to the passage of the day. Some animals, including lizards and crabs, change color in a rhythmic pattern. The Florida chameleon, for example, turns green at night, whereas its coloration matches its environment during the day. In short, almost every living organism and every living cell displays circadian rhythms.

**The Endogenous Origin of Circadian Rhythms** Circadian rhythms are produced by an endogenous (internal) mechanism referred to as a biological clock. The existence of a biological clock was first recognized in 1729 by the geologist Jean Jacques d'Ortous de Mairan (see Raven et al., 1992). In an experiment similar to the one illustrated in the Procedure section of **Experiment 13-1**, de Mairan isolated a plant from daily light, dark, and temperature cues. He noted that the rhythmic movements of its leaves seen over a light–dark cycle continued when it was isolated, as graphed in the Results section of the experiment.

What concerned investigators who came after de Mairan was the possibility that some undetected external cue stimulates the plant's rhythmic behavior. Such cues could include changes in temperature, in electromagnetic fields, and even in the intensity of cosmic rays from outer space. But further experiments showed that daily fluctuations are *endogenous*—they come from within the plant. Thus, the plant must have a biological clock.

Similar experiments have revealed that almost all organisms have circadian clocks that synchronize behavior to the temporal passage of a day and make predictions about tomorrow. A circadian clock signals that if daylight lasts for a given time today, it will last for about the same time tomorrow. It allows us to anticipate events and prepare for them both physiologically and cognitively. And unless external factors get in the way, a circadian clock regulates feeding times, sleeping times, and metabolic activity as appropriate to day–night cycles. When external factors, such as stress and other epigenetic effects, get in the way of these cycles, the functions regulated by our circadian clock can be disrupted (Agorastos et al., 2020).

**Measuring Circadian Rhythms** Although the existence of the endogenous circadian clock was demonstrated nearly 300 years ago, collection and analysis of the enormous amount of data entailed in the study of biorhythms had to await the development of electrical and computer-based timing devices. Behavioral analysis requires a method for counting behavioral events and displaying those events in a meaningful way.

For example, rat behavior was first measured by giving the animal access to a running wheel for exercise (**Figure 13-2**A).

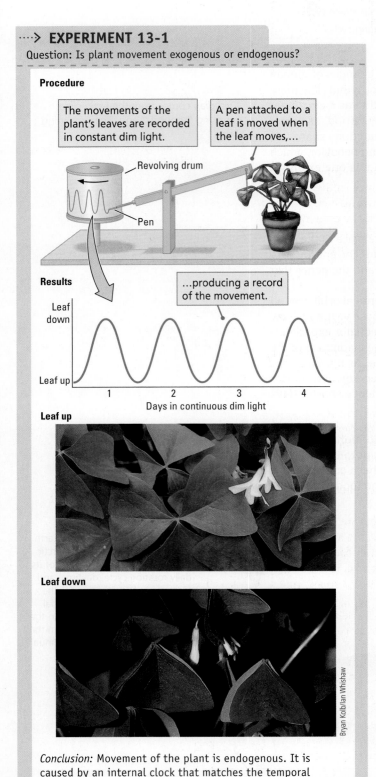

### ⋯⟶ EXPERIMENT 13-1

Question: Is plant movement exogenous or endogenous?

**Procedure**

The movements of the plant's leaves are recorded in constant dim light.

A pen attached to a leaf is moved when the leaf moves,...

Revolving drum

Pen

**Results**

...producing a record of the movement.

Leaf down

Leaf up

1    2    3    4
Days in continuous dim light

**Leaf up**

**Leaf down**

Bryan Kolb/Ian Whishaw

*Conclusion:* Movement of the plant is endogenous. It is caused by an internal clock that matches the temporal passage of a real day.

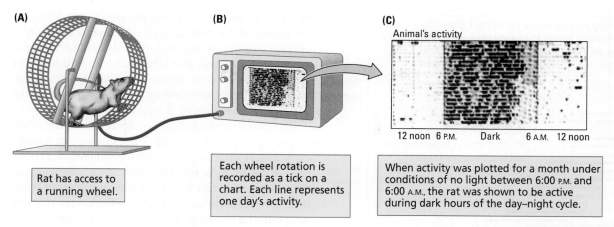

**(A)** Rat has access to a running wheel.

**(B)** Each wheel rotation is recorded as a tick on a chart. Each line represents one day's activity.

**(C)** Animal's activity

12 noon  6 P.M.    Dark    6 A.M.   12 noon

When activity was plotted for a month under conditions of no light between 6:00 P.M. and 6:00 A.M., the rat was shown to be active during dark hours of the day–night cycle.

**FIGURE 13-2 Recording the Daily Activity Cycle of a Rat** Data from Richter (1965).

A computer records each turn of the wheel and displays the result (Figure 13-2B). Because rats are nocturnal, sleeping during light hours and becoming active during dark hours, their wheel running takes place in the dark. If each day's activity is plotted under the preceding day's activity in a column, a cycle of activity over time is revealed—a record of when the animal is active (Figure 13-2C). Electronic innovations that place movement sensors in smart watches and smartphones are now used to measure the circadian activity of human participants.

## Free-Running Rhythms

The fact that a behavior appears to be rhythmic does not mean that it is ruled solely by a biological clock. In reality, animals adjust their circadian activities in response to the availability of food, the presence of predators, and competition from other members of their own species. For example, animals may postpone migrations when food supplies remain abundant. We humans obviously change our daily activities in response to seasonal changes, work schedules, and play opportunities.

Whether a rhythmic behavior is produced by a biological clock and the extent to which it is controlled by a biological clock can be demonstrated experimentally. When investigating these questions, researchers conduct a number of tests in which they manipulate test conditions. A test may be given (1) in continuous light; (2) in light of varying brightness; (3) in continuous darkness; (4) by light choice of the participant; or (5) with eating, activity, and sleep times all regulated. Each treatment yields a slightly different insight into that period of the biological clock.

Aschoff (1978) first demonstrated that the human sleep–waking rhythm is governed by a biological clock that has a preferred period. He and his coworkers allowed participants to select their light–dark cycle and studied them in an underground bunker, where no cues signaled when day began or ended. The participants selected the periods when they were active and when they slept, and they turned the lights on and off at will. In short, they selected the length of their own day and night.

Measures of ongoing behavior and recording of sleep periods with sensors on the beds revealed that the participants continued to show daily sleep–activity rhythms, confirming an endogenous biological clock that governs sleep–waking behavior. As shown in **Figure 13-3**, however, their biorhythms under the experimental condition differed from their biorhythms before and after isolation. Specifically, the period of the participants' sleep–wake cycles approximated 24 hours before and after the test. During the test, the cycles lengthened to about 25 to 27 hours, depending on the person. The participants chose to go to bed 1 to 2 hours later every "night." Soon they were getting up at about the time the experimenters outside the bunker were going to bed. The participants' individual cycles are called their **free-running rhythms**. For each individual, the free-running rhythm has a period of the body's own devising.

Subsequent research suggested that the human free-running rhythm is not as long as the rhythm described by Aschoff. Because the participants controlled the lights

**free-running rhythm** Rhythm of the body's own devising in the absence of all external cues.

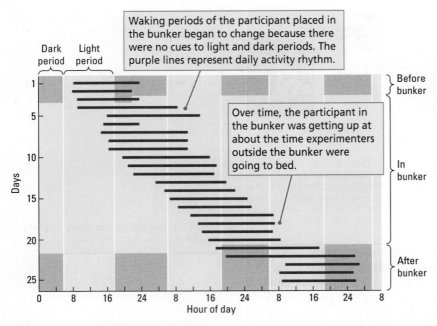

**FIGURE 13-3 Free-Running Rhythm in a Human** The record for days 1 through 3 shows the daily sleep period under typical day–night conditions. The record for days 4 through 20 shows the free-running rhythm that developed while this participant was isolated in a bunker and allowed to control day and night lengths. The daily activity period shifts from 24 hours to 25.9 hours. On days 21 through 25, the period returns to 24 hours as the participant is again exposed to a natural light–dark cycle. Data from Hobson (1989).

**FIGURE 13-4 Free-Running Rhythms of a Diurnal Animal** Data from Binkley (1990).

in their environment, the light affected the apparent phase of their rhythm by advancing the length of time they stayed up each day. When light, eating times, temperature, and sleep times are added into the experiment to more closely regulate behavior, the average human free-running period is about 24.1 to 24.2 hours (Phillips et al., 2011).

The period of free-running rhythms also depends on the light-related biology of a species. When hamsters, a nocturnal species, are tested in constant darkness, their free-running periods are a little shorter than 24 hours; when they are tested in constant light, their free-running periods are a little longer than 24 hours. In the constant-darkness test with two closely related species, rats have a cycle that expands slightly, whereas mice have a cycle that contracts slightly. As **Figure 13-4** shows, the opposite free-running periods can be found in some diurnal animals (Binkley, 1990). When sparrows (which are diurnal birds) are tested in constant darkness, their free-running periods are a little longer than 24 hours; when they are tested in constant light, their free-running periods are a little shorter than 24 hours. Thus, period length for any species or condition requires explicit experimental verification (An et al., 2021).

# Zeitgebers

Because the daily cycle of light and dark varies both with latitude and with the seasons, a biological clock must keep to a time that predicts actual changes in the day–night cycle. If free-running rhythms are not exactly 24 hours, how does a biological clock keep accurate time? The free-running period suggests that the biological clock is like a slightly defective clock—over time, it becomes useless.

If we reset an errant clock each day, however—say, when we awaken—it provides useful information. Aschoff realized that when the participants in the bunker were again exposed to regular light cues, their circadian period was reset. A clock-setting cue is called a **Zeitgeber** (for the German *Zeitgeber* for "time giver").

## Entraining a Circadian Rhythm

When a Zeitgeber resets a biorhythm, the rhythm is said to be **entrained**. Clinical Focus 13-2: Seasonal Affective Disorder explains light's importance in entraining circadian rhythms. When its biological clock is entrained, an animal is able to organize its daily schedule, including when it eats, exercises, and sleeps. For some animals that live in polar regions, the constant light of summer and the constant dark of winter exceed their clock's capacity to adjust; for those animals, the clock turns off. The light Zeitgeber that is most effective for humans is sunrise (Khodasevich et al., 2021). Humans respond to many nonphotic Zeitgebers, however, including ambient temperature, activity, mealtimes, work, and social events that can in some circumstances entrain the circadian rhythm if the event occurs at the same time each day.

**Disrupting the Circadian Rhythm** When we stay up late in artificial light, sleep late on some days, and get up early by using an alarm clock on other days, we disrupt our circadian rhythm. *Anthropogenic lighting*, the light caused by humans, can also result in **light pollution** that floods our workplaces, homes, and environment, disrupting our circadian rhythm.

Disruptions of the circadian rhythm account for some inconsistent behaviors associated with accidents, daytime fatigue, alterations in emotional states, obesity, diabetes, and other disorders characteristic of *metabolic syndrome*, described in Clinical Focus 13-1: Doing the Right Thing at the Right Time. The extent to which humans

**Zeitgeber** Environmental event that entrains biological rhythms; German for "time giver."

**entrain** To determine or modify the period of a biorhythm.

**light pollution** Exposure to artificial light that changes activity patterns and so disrupts circadian rhythms.

---

◎ **CLINICAL FOCUS 13-2**

## Seasonal Affective Disorder

The symptoms of many psychiatric diseases may display seasonal occurrence (Zhang et al., 2021). One example is *seasonal affective disorder* (*SAD*), a seasonal form of depression that occurs in winter in as many as 10% of people who live in northern latitudes. Women are five times more likely to be affected by SAD compared to men.

One explanation for the development of SAD is that the low levels of sunlight in winter do not entrain the circadian rhythm. Because people vary in the duration of their free-running rhythms, lack of entrainment affects individuals differently. Some people are phase-retarded, with desired sleep time coming earlier each day; some are phase-advanced, with desired sleep time coming later each day.

Because a class of retinal ganglion cells that express a photosensitive pigment called *melanopsin* are responsive to blue light (see Section 13-2), it has been proposed that exposure to bright white light that contains this blue frequency can reset the circadian clock and ameliorate depression. This treatment, called *phototherapy* or *light therapy*, seeks to increase the short winter photoperiod by exposing a person to special artificial bright light in the morning or in both morning and evening (Bais et al., 2021). Typical room lighting is not bright enough.

A word of caution, however: decreased exposure to sunlight in winter can result in vitamin D deficiency, which may also contribute to depression. Other changes associated with winter, including changes in diet, exercise, and social events may affect mood, further complicating the study of SAD.

Because cause–effect relationships between mood and seasons are difficult to study in humans, researchers often develop animal models

During the polar night in northern Europe, people take light treatment to combat SAD.

(Shankar & Williams, 2021), though this presents several research challenges. Researcher must find an animal that is diurnal (Mongolian gerbils and Degus and Nile grass rats are among the rodent species typically used) and displays a behavior analogous to human depression (social tests, responses to open areas, and receptivity to sweet substances are often used). The researcher's task is then to identify which of the many brain changes—including changes in gene expression, brain regions, and neurochemical systems—are important contributors to SAD.

display many of these same symptoms in coping with changes in their biological clocks brought on by the extreme day–night cycles found at more northern and southern latitudes is an area of active research (Sivertsen et al., 2021).

Entrainment works best if the adjustment made to the biological clock is not too large. People who work night shifts are often subject to huge adjustments, especially when they work the graveyard shift (typically 11:00 P.M. to 7:00 A.M.), the period when they would normally sleep. Adapting to such a change is difficult and stressful, and it increases susceptibility to disease by altering immune system rhythms (Hulsegge et al., 2021). Compared with people who have a regular daytime work schedule, people who work night shifts and switch between work and nonwork schedules have a higher incidence of metabolic syndrome. Thus, shift workers can benefit from vigilance in maintaining good sleep habits and diet and in exercising to minimize other risk factors for metabolic syndrome. In particular, individuals trying to adapt to shift work fare better if they first work the swing shift (typically 3:00 P.M. to 11:00 P.M.) for a time before beginning the graveyard shift.

Long-distance air travel — say, from North America to Europe or Asia — demands large and difficult time adjustments. For example, travelers flying east from New York to Paris begin their first day in Europe just when their biological clock is signaling that it is time for sleep (**Figure 13-5**). The difference between a person's circadian rhythm

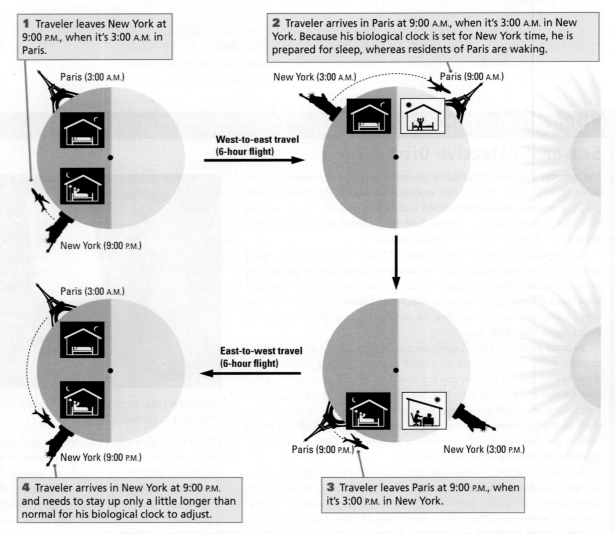

**1** Traveler leaves New York at 9:00 P.M., when it's 3:00 A.M. in Paris.

**2** Traveler arrives in Paris at 9:00 A.M., when it's 3:00 A.M. in New York. Because his biological clock is set for New York time, he is prepared for sleep, whereas residents of Paris are waking.

Paris (3:00 A.M.)

New York (9:00 P.M.)

New York (3:00 A.M.)   Paris (9:00 A.M.)

**West-to-east travel (6-hour flight)**

Paris (3:00 A.M.)

New York (9:00 P.M.)

**East-to-west travel (6-hour flight)**

Paris (9:00 P.M.)   New York (3:00 P.M.)

**4** Traveler arrives in New York at 9:00 P.M. and needs to stay up only a little longer than normal for his biological clock to adjust.

**3** Traveler leaves Paris at 9:00 P.M., when it's 3:00 P.M. in New York.

**FIGURE 13-5 Jet Lag** Disruption in the entrainment of a person's biological clock is undoubtedly more pronounced in west-to-east jet travel because the disruption in the person's circadian rhythm is dramatic. On the return journey, the traveler's biological clock has a much easier adjustment to make.

and the daylight cycle in a new environment can produce the disorientation and fatigue associated with **jet lag**.

The west-to-east traveler has a more difficult adjustment than does the east-to-west traveler, who needs to stay up only a little longer than usual. The occasional traveler may cope with jet lag well, by managing jet lag with sleep on arrival or shortly after. The brain's biological clock resets in a day, and other body organs follow after about a week. For frequent travelers and flight crews, resetting the internal clock is not so easy. Persistent asynchronous rhythms generated by jet lag are associated with altered sleep and temperature rhythms, fatigue, stress, and even reduced success by sports teams—one study estimates that for every 500 miles an National Basketball Association (NBA) team travels, their chances of winning the game are reduced by 4% (Charest et al., 2021).

**jet lag** Fatigue and disorientation resulting from rapid travel through time zones and exposure to a changed light–dark cycle.

## 13-1 Review

Before you continue, check your understanding. Answers to Self-Test appear at the back of the book.

1. Many behaviors occur in a rhythmic pattern in relationship to time. Biorhythms that display a daily cycle are _____ and those that display a yearly cycle are _____.

2. Although biological clocks keep fairly good time, their _____ rhythms may be slightly shorter or longer than 24.

3. An event that resets a biological clock is called a _____.

4. The brain's main biological clock receives light information primarily from _____.

5. What is the most effective influence in resetting the human biological clock and why?

## 13-2

# The Suprachiasmatic Biological Clock

In a series of studies conducted in the 1930s, Curt Richter located biological clocks in the brain. He captured wild rats and found that they ate, and drank, and ran in activity wheels when the lights were off and were quiescent when the lights were on. After an electric current was used to damage their hypothalamus, the animals lost their circadian rhythm (Richter, 1965). Subsequently, by making much more discrete lesions, experimenters found that a region of the hypothalamus, the suprachiasmatic nucleus (SCN), acts as the master biological clock (Buijs et al., 2021). The SCN is named for its location just above (*supra-*) the optic chiasm, where the optic tracts cross at the base of the hypothalamus, as shown in **Figure 13-6**.

## Suprachiasmatic Rhythms

Evidence for the SCN's role as the master biological clock for the central nervous system (CNS) comes from many sources, but other brain structures, including the intergeniculate leaflet and the pineal gland, have a clocklike role in controlling behavior.

Evidence supporting the idea that something other than the SCN can act as a clock includes the observation that feeding behavior in rats follows a timed pattern after removal of their SCN. Animals without an SCN can still display anticipatory behavior—becoming active in relation to scheduled mealtimes—and can organize related behaviors, including memory for food locations, in relationship to mealtimes. In addition, scheduled feeding activity can act as a Zeitgeber for the main SCN clock. That is, a regular feeding schedule can entrain the SCN clock and many other body organs and cells, and an irregular feeding schedule can be disruptive to their rhythms. This food-related rhythm may be timed by a clock in the liver (McCommis & Butler, 2021). In all other respects, the SCN acts as the master clock, setting the time for all the other clocks.

**Learning Objectives**
- Summarize the anatomical components of the retinohypothalamic tract and the SCN.
- Describe the role that the SCN plays in maintaining our circadian and circannual rhythms.
- Explain the relationship between circadian rhythms and our cognitive and emotional behavior.

Richter's discovery of the SCN's role in timekeeping was the first in a series of findings that revealed how a specialized system in the brain controls a specific behavior.

Optic    Suprachiasmatic    Hypothalamus
chiasm    nucleus

Ian Whishaw

**FIGURE 13-6 Suprachiasmatic Nucleus in a Rat Brain**

Section 9-2 traces the three main routes from the retina to the visual brain and details the roles of rods, cones, and retinal ganglion cells. Figures 9-9 and 9-12 diagram the retina's cellular structure.

Glutamate is the main excitatory neurotransmitter in the CNS.

# Keeping Time

If SCN neurons are isolated from one another, each remains rhythmic, as do all of the body's cells. Thus, although rhythmic activity is a property of SCN cells, the timing of the rhythm must depend on groups of cells that synchronize their activity in relationship to each other. Their entrainment depends on external inputs, the most important of which is light.

The SCN receives information about light through a dedicated pathway, the retinohypothalamic (retina-to-hypothalamus) tract, which extends from the retina to the SCN (**Figure 13-7**). The retinohypothalamic tract signal does not rely on input from the rods and cones, but rather from specialized retinal ganglion cells called *intrinsically photosensitive retinal ganglion cells* (ipRGCs). These ipRGCs contain *melanopsin*, an *opsin* (photosensitive pigment) that is sensitive to wavelengths of blue light (about 460 to 480 nm). This specific sensitivity of ipRGCs explains why blue light is the central stimulus for entraining—and for disrupting—circadian rhythms.

The existence of ipRGCs involved in entraining the circadian rhythm explains the continued presence of an entrained rhythm in people who are blind as a result of retinal degeneration that destroys the rods and cones (Zaidi et al., 2007). In addition, ipRGCs receive inputs from cones and rods. Cones can influence the activity of ipRGCs in bright daylight, and rods can influence their activity in dim light.

The ipRGC are distributed across the retina, and in humans they make up between 1% and 3% of all retinal ganglion cells. Their axons innervate the SCN bilaterally. Melanopsin-containing ganglion cells use glutamate as their primary neurotransmitter but also contain two co-transmitters: substance P and pituitary adenylate cyclase–activating polypeptide (PACAP). When stimulated by light, ipRGCs are excited, and in turn they excite cells in the SCN.

As illustrated in Figure 13-7, the SCN consists of two parts: a ventrally located *core* and a dorsally located *shell*. The retinohypothalamic tract activates the core cells. Core neurons are not rhythmic, but they entrain the shell neurons, which are rhythmic.

In addition to receiving retinohypothalamic input, the SCN receives projections from other brain regions, including the intergeniculate leaflet in the thalamus and the raphe nucleus, which is the nonspecific serotonergic-activating system of the brainstem. The terminal regions of these inputs to the SCN display variations, suggesting that different portions of the shell and the core have somewhat different functions.

**FIGURE 13-7 The Retinohypothalamic Tract and the SCN**

Retina

Retinohypothalamic tract

Optic chiasm

Suprachiasmic nucleus { Core — Shell

Other input and output

Third ventricle

Slave oscillators

Photosensitive retinal ganglion cells respond to blue light.

Retinohypothalamic tract carries information about light changes to core cells in the SCN.

Signal from SCN core neurons entrains shell neurons.

SCN drives slave oscillators (diagrammed in Figure 13-9) and receives signals from other brain and body areas.

As described earlier, the SCN's circadian rhythm is usually entrained by morning and evening light, but it can also be entrained or disrupted by sudden changes in lighting, by arousal, by moving about, and by feeding. These influences differ from the light entrainment provided over the retinohypothalamic tract. The intergeniculate leaflet and the raphe nucleus are pathways through which nonphotic events can influence the SCN rhythm (Cain et al., 2007).

Nevertheless, light is the main influence on the SCN. Anthropogenic light can disrupt SCN activity. Because artificial light from light-emitting diode (LED) lights has a stronger blue-light component than older lights (e.g., incandescent light bulbs), LED light is a potent source of light pollution. Because of its relative affordability, LED lighting is growing in popularity worldwide. In turn, an estimated 80% to 90% of people now live in light-polluted environments, largely driven by increases in LED use, and the amount of land polluted by light is growing. Light pollution not only affects the health of humans, but also disrupts the sexual, migratory, and other behaviors of many other animal species. Solutions to light pollution include fitting LED bulbs with filters that remove blue light, attaching dimming systems to LED lights, and providing public education to raise awareness of the adverse effects of light pollution and ways to prevent it (Pothukuchi, 2021). The International Dark Sky Association works to protect the night sky and offers awards for projects that modify lighting.

## Immortal Time

The endogenous rhythm of SCN cells is not learned. Indeed, when animals are raised in constant darkness, their behavior is still rhythmic. In experiments in which animals have been maintained without entraining cues for a number of generations, each generation continues to display rhythmic behavior. Even if the mother has received an SCN lesion so that her behavior is not rhythmic, her offspring's behavior is rhythmic.

Evidence supporting the idea that suprachiasmatic cells are genetically programmed for rhythmicity comes from studies performed by Martin Ralph and his colleagues, which relied on the use of transplantation techniques (Ralph & Lehman, 1991). **Figure 13-8** illustrates the experiment.

As reflected in the top chart, in these studies, hamsters were tested in constant dim light or in constant darkness to establish their free-running rhythms. They then received a suprachiasmatic lesion, which was followed by another test to show that the lesion had abolished their rhythmicity (center chart). Finally, the hamsters received transplants of new suprachiasmatic cells obtained from hamster embryos. About 60 days later, the hamsters again showed rhythmic activity, demonstrating that the transplanted cells had been integrated into the host brain and had reestablished rhythmic behavior (bottom chart). Follow-up studies showed that the rhythms of many, but not all, body organs also showed restored rhythmic activity following the suprachiasmatic transplant.

## What Ticks?

Molecular research shows that the circadian rhythm involves a feedback loop. First, two different proteins are made from DNA instructions. Next, these proteins combine. The combined protein, called a **dimer** ("two parts," for the two proteins), then inhibits the genes that made its original constituent proteins. Finally, the dimer degrades, and the process begins anew. Research Focus 13-3: Synchronizing Biorhythms at the Molecular Level describes this feedback loop in mammals. Just as the back-and-forth swing of a pendulum makes a grandfather clock tick, the increase and decrease in protein synthesis once each day produce the cellular rhythm.

## Pacemaking Circadian Rhythms

The SCN itself is not directly responsible for producing behavior. After it has been damaged, drinking and eating, sleeping, and wakefulness still occur—though they no longer occur at appropriate times.

An explanation for how the SCN controls biological rhythms is illustrated in **Figure 13-9**. Light entrains the SCN, and the SCN in turn drives a number of slave oscillators. Each slave oscillator is responsible for the rhythmic occurrence of one activity. In other words, drinking, eating, body temperature, and sleeping are each influenced by a separate slave oscillator.

The SCN clock entrains slave oscillators through a remarkable array of pathways. For example, SCN neurons send axonal connections to nuclei close by in the hypothalamus and thalamus. In addition, the SCN connects with pituitary endocrine neurons. The SCN also sends indirect messages to autonomic neurons in the spinal cord to inhibit the pineal gland from producing the hormone **melatonin**, which influences daily and seasonal biorhythms. SCN cells themselves release hormones. Thus, through multiple pathways, the SCN exerts its control on the entire body. This wide distribution

**Healthy** — Normal free-running rhythm in constant darkness

**Suprachiasmatic lesion** — Absence of circadian rhythm in a light–dark environment

**Suprachiasmatic transplant** — Normal free-running rhythm in constant darkness restored by transplant

0    Time (hours)    24

**FIGURE 13-8 Circadian Rhythms Restored by Neural Transplantation** Information from Ralph & Lehman (1991).

Figure 3-13 diagrams the process of protein synthesis.

Figure 12-7 diagrams how the pituitary gland works.

**dimer** Two proteins combined into one.

**melatonin** Hormone secreted by the pineal gland during the dark phase of the day–night cycle; influences daily and seasonal biorhythms.

## RESEARCH FOCUS 13-3

# Synchronizing Biorhythms at the Molecular Level

In 2017, Jeffrey C. Hall, Michael Rosbash, and Michael W. Young were awarded the Nobel Prize in Physiology or Medicine for their contributions to our understanding of the human biological clock and their description of the molecular changes through which the clock keeps time and regulates our circadian rhythm.

The timing mechanism in the suprachiasmatic nucleus (SCN), the brain's master clock, resides in each individual cell that has a circadian rhythm. The cell's main clock mechanism is a *transcription–translation–inhibition–feedback loop* that paces the clock over a 24-hour period. The complete clockwork in the feedback loop involves as many as 10 genes and their protein products. Its sequence, mapped in the illustration, follows:

**STEP 1: TRANSCRIPTION** In the cell nucleus, one of three *Period* genes (*Per1,*\* *Per2, Per3*) and one of two *Cryptochrome* genes (*Cry1, Cry2*) are transcribed into the appropriate *Per* or *Cry* mRNA.

**STEP 2: TRANSLATION** Ribosomes in the endoplasmic reticulum translate these mRNAs into the appropriate PER[†] and CRY proteins. In the extranuclear fluid, the two proteins come together to form a dimer, or two-protein combination of PERCRY.

**STEP 3: INHIBITION** The PERCRY dimer enters the cell nucleus, where it binds to and inhibits the Enhancer box (Ebox), a part of the DNA that activates transcription of the *Period* and *Cryptochrome* genes. The result of this inhibition is that *Per* and *Cry* are no longer produced.

**STEP 4: DECAY** After it plays its inhibitory role, the PERCRY dimer decays. When this occurs, the *Per* and *Cry* genes resume expression, and the 24-hour cycle begins anew.

\**Gene* and *mRNA* names are italicized.
[†]PROTEIN names are capitalized.

This sequence of gene turn-on followed by gene turn-off occurs in an inexorable daily loop.

The SCN clock mechanism is influenced by light through a number of SCN biochemical pathways and, depending on the animal species, is particularly sensitive to light presented around the beginning or the end of the dark period, such as sunrises and sunsets (Alzate-Correa et al., 2021). Mutations in any circadian gene can lead to circadian alterations, including absence of a biorhythm or an altered biorhythm. For example, alleles of the *Period 1* and *Period 2* genes determine chronotype — whether an individual will be early to bed and early to rise or late to bed and late to rise. The search for therapies for clock disorders includes looking for small molecules that can act as drugs to reset biorhythms disrupted by jet lag, shift work, and epigenetic and inherited gene irregularities.

**Main SCN Clock Mechanism**

system explains why disruption of the SCN clock can have widespread disruptive effects on many behaviors and can even have transgenerational consequences (Nesan et al., 2021).

The SCN's widespread effects can be seen in its control of two hormones, melatonin and glucocorticoids. The SCN controls the release of melatonin from the pineal gland so that this hormone circulates during the dark phase of the circadian cycle. It also

**FIGURE 13-9 Circadian Timing System Organization**

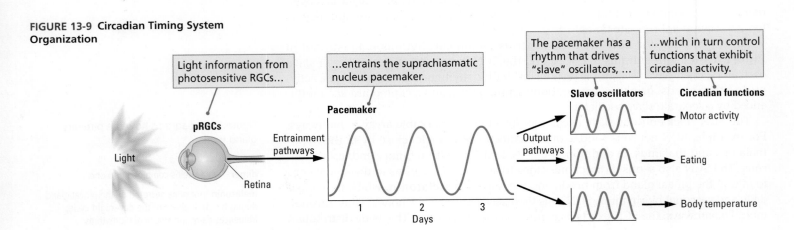

controls the release of glucocorticoids from the adrenal glands so that they circulate during the light phase of the circadian cycle.

Melatonin promotes sleep and activates the parasympathetic rest-and-digest system, as well downregulates (suppresses) other physiological events in the body. Glucocorticoids mobilize glucose for cellular activity to support arousal responses in the sympathetic system. These two hormones will entrain body organs that have receptors for them—and most organs do. Thus, melatonin promotes rest activities during the dark portion of the circadian cycle, and glucocorticoids promote arousal activities during the light portions of the circadian cycle. Their actions explain in part why it is difficult to sleep during the day and difficult to stay awake at night. The role of melatonin as a slave oscillator in part explains its use as a drug for regulating sleep (Fatemeh et al., 2021).

Figure 2-32 diagrams the autonomic nervous system. Section 5-4 describes how glucocorticoids affect the body and brain.

## Pacemaking Circannual Rhythms

The suprachiasmatic nucleus controls circannual rhythms as well. Russel Reiter (1980) first illustrated this form of pacemaking in hamsters. Hamsters are summertime (long-day) breeders. As the days lengthen in springtime, the gonads of male hamsters grow and release hormones that stimulate sexual behavior. Later, as the days shorten in the winter, the gonads shrink, the amount of the hormones they produce decreases, and the males lose interest in sex.

During the dark phase of the day–night cycle, the hamster's pineal gland secretes melatonin; during the light phase, it does not. **Figure 13-10** shows that when a male hamster's melatonin level is low, the gonads enlarge, and when the level is high, the gonads shrink. The SCN thus controls the pineal gland's sway over the gonads.

During the long daylight period of the circadian cycle, the SCN inhibits melatonin secretion by the pineal gland. As the days become shorter, the melatonin release increases. When the daylight period is shorter than 12 hours, melatonin release time becomes sufficient to inhibit the hamster's gonads, and they shrink.

Melatonin also influences the testes of short-day breeders, such as sheep and deer, that mate in the fall and early winter. Melatonin's effect on reproductive behavior in these species is the reverse of that in the hamster: reproductive activities begin as melatonin release increases. There is no evidence that a melatonin cycle influences the gonads of human males.

In his classic book *Biological Clocks in Medicine and Psychiatry*, Curt Richter (1965) hypothesized that many physical and behavioral disorders might be caused by shocks, either physical or environmental, that upset the timing of the biological clock. For example, the record of psychotic episodes experienced by the English writer

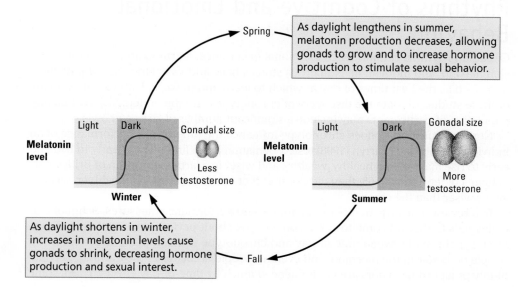

Spring

As daylight lengthens in summer, melatonin production decreases, allowing gonads to grow and to increase hormone production to stimulate sexual behavior.

Light Dark Gonadal size
Melatonin level
Less testosterone
Winter

Light Dark Gonadal size
Melatonin level
More testosterone
Summer

As daylight shortens in winter, increases in melatonin levels cause gonads to shrink, decreasing hormone production and sexual interest.

Fall

**FIGURE 13-10 Hamster's Circannual Pacemaker** Information from Reiter (1980).

**FIGURE 13-11 Dysfunctional Clock?** Attacks of mental illness displayed by the English writer Mary Lamb through her adult life appear to have had a cyclical component. Such observations would be difficult to obtain today because the drugs used to treat psychiatric disorders can mask disordered biorhythms.
Information from Richter (1965).

Mary Lamb (1764–1847), illustrated in **Figure 13-11**, is one of many rhythmic records that Richter thought represented the action of an abnormally functioning biological clock. Richter noted that because many disorders are now treated, often with drugs, rhythmic patterns may be muted and so are more difficult to detect.

## Chronotypes

Across human populations, and within other animal species, individuals show variation in their circadian activities. These distinctive patterns of behavior are referred to as **chronotypes** ("time types"). Some people are early to bed and early to rise and are energetic in the morning. Other people are late to rise and late to bed and are energetic in the evening. These "lark" and "owl" chronotypes are produced by differences in SCN neurons and the genes that influence the clock in those neurons. A large number of genes contribute to the function of the mammalian biological clock, and alleles of these genes are associated with chronotypes. In hamsters and mice, mutant gene variations produce chronotypes with circadian periods as varied as 24, 20, or 17 hours (Monecke et al., 2011).

Comparative studies of the free-running rhythms of African Americans and European Americans show that the former have shorter free-running periods. Genetic studies suggest that small changes in about 10 genes influence the chronotypes of these populations (Putilov et al., 2017). Presumably, these genetic differences allowed the clocks of the ancestral African populations living closer to the equator to synchronize with the more equal day–night lengths. Similar genetic forces allowed the ancestral European populations in northern latitudes to synchronize with the more variable day–night lengths. As genetic analysis becomes less expensive, the study of the genes underlying chronotypes is providing new insights into individual differences in our biological clocks and into the relationships between chronotypes and disease.

Chronotype also changes with age. Younger people, for example, are more likely to be owls, whereas older people are more likely to be larks. Chronotype can also vary with emotional conditions and disease. These changes are likely mediated by gene expression in the biological clock, which then has widespread influences on the brain. For example, one estimate suggests more than 1000 gene differences related to chronotype can be found in the frontal cortex (Chen et al., 2016).

## Rhythms of Cognitive and Emotional Behavior

Circadian rhythms can influence emotional experience, learning and retention, decision making, and motivation. Numerous studies have addressed the *time-of-day* question, such as the best times of day at which to learn and to work. Unfortunately, many of these studies predate the discovery of chronotypes and the understanding that any population of participants may include a significant number of larks and owls.

Now the question is, does chronotype influence the time-of-day performance of an individual? Gale and Martyn (1998) tested Benjamin Franklin's maxim "early to bed and early to rise make a man healthy, wealthy, and wise" in a large population of British participants older than age 65; they did not find that one group was any healthier, wealthier, or wiser than the other.

In a review of a large number of cognitive and performance measures, Schmidt and colleagues (2012) did come to some conclusions about performance and time of day. First, synchrony between time of day and chronotype is a dominant effect: morning people do better in the morning, and evening people do better in the evening. Second, highly practiced behaviors are not influenced much by time-of-day effects. Third, some

**chronotype** Time type; individual variations in circadian activity.

large differences between young and old people related to performance and time of day are likely related to chronotype. Finally, a weakness of studies of time-of-day effects is that they depend on self-reports of chronotype. More rigorous studies will depend on determining *chronogenotype*—that is, which chronotype allele people have.

A different question related to time of day and learning is *time stamping*: Is memory for learned items better when the test–retest assessments occur at the same time of the circadian cycle? Much of everyday behavior is synchronized with the circadian period. Animals have a variety of needs for food, water, and sleep, and it is adaptive for them to know when these resources become available. If food is available on a schedule, animals display anticipatory behaviors—becoming active as the feeding time arrives, for example. Other anticipatory events include salivation, intestinal activity, and sensations of hunger. Anticipatory activity might also include recalling events related to the timing of feeding and food location.

In athletics, a strong home advantage is noted in many sports, and it is likely that this advantage stems from a time-of-day effect in which competition fits into athletes' home daily schedule better than in their away schedule. Studies have also found that the circadian period influences emotional behavior. A time-of-day effect may account for some of our emotional responses to daily events, independent of the events themselves (Bolsius et al., 2021).

## 13-2 Review

**Before you continue, check your understanding. Answers to Self-Test appear at the back of the book.**

1. Biological rhythms are timed by internal biological clocks. The master clock is the
_____.

2. Light cues entrain the suprachiasmatic nucleus to control daily rhythms via the
_____ tract.

3. The cells that receive blue light information in the retina are called _____.

4. Pacemaking is produced by the SCN oscillator, which in turn times _____ oscillators.

5. Why should mealtimes occur at the same time of day each day?

6. Why might oversleeping be detrimental to circadian entrainment?

## 13-3

# Sleep Stages and Dreaming

We all intuitively understand what *sleep* is, but it is a difficult concept to define. A witty definition focuses on what sleep is not: the absence of waking or the absence of consciousness. The challenge in defining sleep is that its events are as complex as are waking events.

The two-process theory defines sleep by it by its two constituent processes: a sleep–wake dependent Process S that produces sleep and a circadian Process C that generates sleep's timing. We described the circadian processes in Section 13-2. In this section, we describe the brain events associated with producing sleep.

## Measuring How Long We Sleep

A popular adage suggests that the optimal sleep time is 7 to 8 hours per night, but many exceptions to this rule of thumb exist. People sleep more when they are young, after engaging in physical activity, or when pregnant. Some people are long sleepers; some are short sleepers. Numerous genetic mutations have been identified in people displaying very short sleep durations—as short as 1 hour. Some people nap for a brief period in the daytime; others never nap. Variations in sleeping times are normal, but

**Learning Objectives**

- Summarize the various methods used to measure sleep.
- Chart the sleep cycle and describe the behaviors associated with each stage of waking and sleeping.
- Explain the possible function of dreaming, as proposed by the activation-synthesis and coping hypotheses.

**TABLE 13-2 Recommended Sleep Duration by Age**

| Age | Sleep time (hours) |
|---|---|
| Newborn up to 3 months | 14–17 |
| Infant younger than 1 year | 12–15 |
| Toddler up to 3 years | 11–14 |
| Preschool (3–5 years) | 10–13 |
| Elementary-school age (6–13 years) | 9–11 |
| Adolescent (14–17 years) | 8–10 |
| Adult (18–64 years) | 7–9 |
| Adult 65 years and older | 7–8 |

*Source:* Information from the Sleep Foundation.

**polysomnography (PSG)** Sleep measurement method that combines measures of multiple sleep events including brain activity, muscle activity, and ocular activity to give a representation of an individual's sleep patterns.

napping normally is best if it is short in duration (less than 20 minutes), happens earlier in the day to avoid disrupting nighttime sleep, and occurs at scheduled times of day. **Table 13-2** lists the suggested sleep duration for various age ranges, but note that the hours listed do not account for many of the variations we've just described.

# Measuring Sleep

The standard method of measuring sleep is **polysomnography (PSG)**, which graphs multiple sleep events concurrently, including brain activity (EEG), muscle activity (EMG), and eye or ocular activity (EOG). PSG measures are recorded in a laboratory, usually from one individual at a time. This method is expensive in terms of both time demands on researchers and the costs of maintaining a suitable laboratory.

PSG requires recording at least three electrical body signals: brain activity, muscle activity, and eye movement. These measures are made from standard locations on the body and are interpreted using standard definitions. Electrodes pasted onto standard locations on the skull's surface yield an electroencephalogram (EEG), a record of brainwave activity. Electrodes placed on neck muscles provide an electromyogram (EMG), a record of muscle activity. Electrodes located near the eyes provide an electrooculogram (EOG), a record of eye movements. Taken together, these measures are used to define sleep. **Figure 13-12** illustrates a typical setup in a sleep laboratory. Other measures that can be recorded include heart rate, body temperature, skin conductance, circulating hormones, blood glucose levels, and other physiological events. Laboratory sleep studies using PSG allow researchers to measure sleep accurately and to record physiological changes associated with sleep.

The advent of wearable technology has facilitated some new approaches to measuring sleep. Wearable devices are commercially available, are relatively inexpensive, and afford many do-it-yourself possibilities. First-generation wearable devices measured a single target, such as activity obtained from a sensor worn on the wrist. Second-generation wearables can measure multiple targets, with the aim of approximating the utility of laboratory PSG.

**FIGURE 13-12 Polysomnography Setup** Electronic equipment records readouts from electrodes attached to the sleeper. **(A)** EEG made from a point on the skull relative to a neutral point on the ear. **(B)** EMG made between two muscles, such as those on the chin and throat. **(C)** EOG made between the eye and a neutral point on the ear.

**(A) Electroencephalogram (EEG)**

**(B) Electromyogram (EMG)**

**(C) Electrooculogram (EOG)**

Philippe Garo/Science Source

When compared against commercial wearable technologies on measures of *reliability* (how accurately a measure is made) and *validity* (whether the measure is recording what it is designed to measure), laboratory-based PSG remains the gold standard for sleep assessment. Although wearable technologies provide a clear benefit to personal sleep assessment, expert reviews suggest that it still has growing pains. Sleep is a complex phenomenon, and wearable technology is often insensitive to that complexity. Furthermore, sleep measurements produce a lot of data and sophisticated big-data methods are required to interpret it—methods that are beyond the average person's reach. Hannah Scott and colleagues (2020) provide a useful and accessible review of many issues related to laboratory PSG and the use of wearable technology.

## Stages of Waking and Sleeping

Sleep, like waking, is not a unitary state, but rather encompasses a number of stages. The EEG recording shows distinct patterns of brain-wave activity for states categorized as awake, relaxed, drowsy, sleep, deep sleep, and dreaming (see **Figure 13-13**). Sleep consists of periods when a sleeper is relatively still as well as periods when the mouth, fingers, and toes twitch. Twitching can be readily observed in household pets and bed partners. In 1955, Eugene Aserinsky and Nathaniel Kleitman (Lamberg, 2003) observed that this twitching is periodic and is also associated with rapid eye movements (REMs) and an awake pattern in the EEG record. Since their report, the conventional classification has been to refer to this state of sleep as **REM sleep (R-sleep)**, in recognition of the presence of these eye movements, and to refer to other sleep states as **non-REM (NREM) sleep (N-sleep)**. Consistent with this designation, the American Association of Sleep Medicine provides a five-point classification of sleep based on EEG patterns that incorporates the R-sleep/N-sleep distinction:

- W—Waking
- N1—NREM stage 1
- N2—NREM stage 2
- N3—NREM stage 3
- R—REM

## W (Waking) State

The W state represents behavior varying from alert wakefulness to drowsiness. When a person is awake, the EEG pattern consists of small-amplitude (height) waves with a fast frequency (repetition period). This pattern, called the **beta rhythm**, is defined by a frequency of 15 to 30 Hz (times per second). It is also called *fast-wave activity-activated EEG*, or *waking EEG*. In the waking state, the EMG is active and the EOG indicates that the eyes move.

When awake people relax and close their eyes, they may produce the **alpha rhythm** (see the associated marginal traces). These large, regular brain waves have a frequency ranging from 7 to 11 Hz. Humans generate alpha rhythms in the region of the visual cortex at the back of the brain, and the rhythms abruptly stop if a relaxed person is disturbed or opens their eyes. Not everyone displays alpha rhythms, and some people display them much more strongly than others.

## N1 Sleep

The behavioral state of a person in N1 is sleep onset. The EEG indicates that beta-wave activity gives way to low-amplitude, mixed-frequency activity, including slower 4- to 11-Hz waves, called **theta-wave** activity. Concurrently, the EMG remains somewhat active, as the muscles have tone, and the EOG typically indicates that the eyes can be rolling.

**REM sleep (R-sleep)** Faster brain-wave pattern displayed by the neocortical EEG record during sleep.

**non-REM (NREM) sleep (N-sleep)** Slow-wave sleep associated with rhythms having slower waves with larger amplitude.

**beta rhythm** Fast brain-wave activity pattern associated with a waking EEG.

**alpha rhythm** Brain waves with a frequency ranging from 7 to 11 Hz.

**theta wave** Brain waves with a frequency ranging from 4 to 11 Hz.

Figure 7-12 shows EEG patterns that reflect a range of sleep–week states in humans.

Excited–beta rhythm

Relaxed, eyes closed–alpha rhythm

Deep sleep–delta rhythm

1    2    3
Time (s)

**FIGURE 13-13 EEG sleep patterns** The EEG patterns of the neocortex are the basis for defining stages of waking and sleep. Information modified from Kelley (1991).

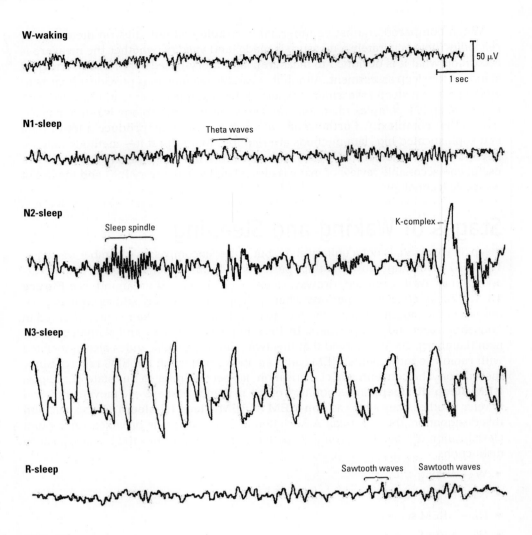

## N2 Sleep

A person in N2 is asleep. In this behavioral state, a person continues to produce theta waves but also produces periodic *sleep spindles* (brief runs of 11- to 16-Hz rhythmic waves) and *K-complexes,* well-defined sharp waves followed by slow waves, all lasting for about a half-second. Sleep spindles, which are proposed to be a sign of a healthy and mature cortex, may contribute to memory formation during sleep (Farhadian et al., 2021). The K-complex is described as one of the largest slow waves produced by the cortex, and is proposed to play a role in the maintenance of sleep, arousal from sleep, and the balancing of activity across the cortex (Gandhi & Emmady, 2021).

## N3 Sleep

N3 is deep sleep. A person in this behavioral state is difficult to arouse, groggy when aroused, and quick to go back to sleep when undisturbed. The EEG is characterized by larger-amplitude, slow (1–3 Hz) EEG waves called **delta rhythms**. Still, the EMG indicates muscle activity, signifying that the muscles retain tone, although the EOG indicates that the eyes do not move.

## R-Sleep (REM)

R-sleep consists of periods when a sleeper is relatively still with no muscle activity, with this quiescent state interrupted by bursts of activity, including REMs, as indicated by the EOG. In short, during R-sleep, the mouth, fingers, and toes twitch and the eyes move. Other than these movements, the EMG indicates that muscles are inactive, a condition termed **atonia** (Greek via Latin, meaning "without tone"). The EEG displays a beta rhythm similar to that displayed in the W stage and N1 stage.

**delta rhythm** Brain-wave activity pattern of 1–3 Hz.

**atonia** Reduced muscle tone; a condition of maximally low muscle inactivity produced by motor neuron inhibition.

In summary, W is associated with active EEG recordings, muscle tone, and eye movement; the three phases of N-sleep are associated with slower EEG recordings, muscle tone, and no eye movement; and R-sleep is associated with active EEG recordings, eye movement, and no muscle tone (outside of periodic twitching). The utility of the combined PSG measures is that they provide an objective measure of waking and sleep states. Note that someone pretending to be asleep could fool an observer, but not PSG—which is why it is the gold standard for waking/sleep measurement.

## Other Sleep-Related and Waking-Related Activities

Although PSG defines sleep stages, many other bodily and physiological events are associated with waking and sleep stages. Measures of metabolic activity such as body temperature, breathing, and heart rate decline during sleep. The sleeper's behaviors—tossing and turning, moaning, and laughing—also occur during specific sleep stages. Taken together, these measures yield insights into the many causes and symptoms of normal sleep and disturbed sleep.

## A Typical Night's Sleep

**Figure 13-14** illustrates a hypnogram (sleep graph, also called a *somnogram*) of one participant cycling through the various sleep stages in the course of a night's sleep. Notice that the depth of sleep, as indicated by a progression from N1 through N3, changes several times through the night and that each of these progressions is followed by an R-sleep stage. This N–R sequence lasts approximately 90 minutes and occurs about five times in the course of a participant's sleep period. The labels indicating R-sleep in Figure 13-14 tell us that the sleep stage durations roughly divide sleep into two parts: the first is dominated by N-sleep and the second dominated by R-sleep.

A person's duration of R-sleep changes dramatically over the life span. Periods of R-sleep are long in infancy; they increase during growth spurts, in conjunction with physical exertion, and during pregnancy. **Figure 13-15** shows that most people sleep less as they grow older. In the first 2 years of life, R-sleep makes up nearly half of sleep time, but it declines proportionately until in middle age it constitutes little more than 10% of sleep time.

## Contrasting N-Sleep and R-Sleep

Although sleep seems like an inactive period, a remarkable range of activity takes place during sleep. N-sleep and R-sleep differ not only in their physiological measures, but also in the occurrence of such behavioral events as cognition, memory storage, and sleep disorders.

During N-sleep, body temperature declines, heart rate and blood flow decrease, body weight decreases from water loss through perspiration, and growth hormone levels increase. N-sleep is also the time when we toss and turn in bed, pull on the covers, and engage in other movements. If we talk in our sleep or grind our teeth, we do so during N-sleep. If we flail about, banging an arm or kicking a foot, we usually do so in N-sleep. Some people even get up and walk around, and this sleepwalking takes place during N-sleep. We maintain muscle tone during N-sleep and can sleep in a variety of postures, including standing up, sitting (as might occur during a nap in a lecture), or in any of several reclining positions.

R-sleep is no less eventful than N-sleep. During R-sleep, mechanisms that regulate body temperature stop working. You may wake up from R-sleep feeling cold or hot (because you *are* cold or hot), depending on the temperature of the room, because your body has drifted toward room temperature during an R-sleep period. During portions of R-sleep, eyes move; toes, fingers, and mouths twitch; and genitals display signs of sexual arousal (regardless of whether an accompanying dream has sexual content). Even so, we are paralyzed, as indicated by atonia. This absence of muscle tone is the result of inhibitory signals sent from the brainstem to motor neurons in the spinal cord that command movement. In the sleep lab, atonia is recorded on an electromyogram as the absence of muscle activity (see Figure 13-12B).

**FIGURE 13-14  A Hypnogram** Over a typical night's sleep, a person undergoes several sleep state changes in roughly 90-minute periods. N-sleep dominates the early sleep periods, and R-sleep dominates later sleep. The duration of each sleep stage is reflected in the thickness of each bar, which is color-coded to the corresponding stage. The depth of each stage is graphed as the relative height of the bar. Information from Kelley (1991).

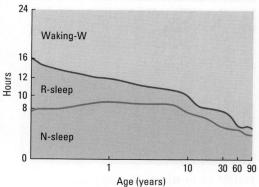

**FIGURE 13-15  Sleeping and Waking over the Life Span** The amount of time humans spend sleeping decreases with age. The proportion of R-sleep is especially high in the first few years of life. Information from Roffward et al. (1966).

Courtesy of Ian Whishaw

**FIGURE 13-16 Nap Time** Horses usually seek open, sunny areas for a brief sleep. I. Q. W.'s horse Lady Jones illustrates three sleep postures. *Top*: N-sleep, standing with legs locked and head down. *Center*: N-sleep, lying down with head up. *Bottom*: R-sleep, in which all postural and muscle tone is lost.

Posture is lost during R-sleep. As it enters R-sleep, an animal subsides into a sprawled position as muscle paralysis sets in. **Figure 13-16** illustrates the sleep postures of a horse. Horses remain standing in N-sleep, by locking their knee joints, or lie down with their head held slightly up. When completely sprawled out, they are in R-sleep.

One explanation for the twitching of eyes, face, and distal parts of the limbs in R-sleep is that such movements help to maintain blood flow in those parts of the body. Another explanation is that the brain is developing coordinated movements and tuning the neural circuits that support those movements—an activity especially important to infants, who have not yet developed full motor control (Blumberg, 2015).

# Dreaming

In 1957, William Dement and Nathaniel Kleitman discovered that vivid dreaming occurs during R-sleep (Dement, 1972). PSG measures taken from sleeping participants in a sleep laboratory made it possible to identify sleep states and any associated dreaming. When participants were awakened from R-sleep, they reported that they had been having vivid dreams. In contrast, participants who were aroused from N-sleep were less likely to report that they had been dreaming, and the dreams they did report were less vivid.

People's reports on their dreaming once suggested that some people dream and other don't. Studies in which participants were awakened during R-sleep periods, however, showed that everyone dreams several times each night, and that dreams last longer as a sleep session progresses. Those who claimed not to dream have merely forgotten their dreams by the time they wake—perhaps because they do not wake up during a dream or immediately afterward, which allows subsequent N-sleep activity to erase the memory of the dream. It could also be that the neural systems that store memories are not fully active during R-sleep. Or perhaps, just as we don't remember much of each day's waking events because they are not important, we conclude that some dreams are not worth remembering. As far as anyone has been able to tell, there is no deleterious consequence for not remembering dreams.

Common wisdom once suggested that dreams last but an instant. By waking people up at different intervals after the onset of R-sleep and matching the reported dream content to the previous duration of R-sleep, research has shown that dreams take place in real time. An action that a person performs in a dream lasts about as long as it would take to perform while awake. So why does it sometimes appear that a dream takes place in a moment? It is likely that time shrinking is a product of remembering a dream, just as time shrinking is a feature of our recall of other memories.

# What We Dream about

Past explanations of dreaming have ranged from messages from the gods to indigestion. The first modern treatment of dreams was undertaken by the founder of psychoanalysis, Sigmund Freud, in *The Interpretation of Dreams*, published in 1900. In Freud's report, and others like it, dreams are selected for discussion because they have interesting features. There is, however, no way to know that this method of selecting dreams is representative of the range of dreams that a person may have.

We consider Freud's theory because it remains popular in psychoanalysis and in the arts and is representative of other psychoanalytical theories of dreams. Freud suggested that the function of dreams is the symbolic fulfillment of unconscious wishes—specifically, sexual wishes. He further proposed that dreams have two levels of meaning. The *manifest content* of a dream is a series of often bizarre, loosely connected images and actions. The *latent content* of the dream contains its true meaning. Certain images, such as oblong and round objects, called *phallic symbols*, and their actions reflect sexual events. As interpreted by a psychoanalyst, the symbolic events of a dream provide a coherent account of the dreamer's unconscious wishes.

Freud provided a method for interpreting manifest symbols and reconstructing the latent content of dreams. For example, he pointed out that a dream usually begins with an incident from the previous day, incorporates childhood experiences, and includes ongoing unfulfilled wishes. He also identified several types of dreams—those that deal with childhood events, anxiety, and wish fulfillment. The latent content of the dream was important to Freud and other psychoanalysts in clinical practice because interpretation of dreams was proposed to offer insight into a patient's problems.

Other psychoanalysts, unhappy with Freud's emphasis on sex, developed their own dream interpretation systems. The psychoanalyst Carl Jung, a contemporary of Freud, proposed that dream symbolism signifies distant human memories long since lost to conscious awareness. Jung proposed that dreams allow the dreamer to relive the history of the human race—our "collective unconscious." As new theories were advanced, a shared central weakness became apparent: there is no way to know which interpretation is correct.

Calvin Hall and his colleagues (1982) documented more than 10,000 dreams of healthy people and found that more than 64% are associated with sadness, anxiety, or anger. Only about 18% are happy. Hostile acts against the dreamer outnumber friendly acts by more than 2 to 1. Freud's theory notwithstanding, only about 1% of dreams include content that seems related to sexual feelings or acts. Subsequent studies of the content of dreams have shown that approximately 80% are dreams about the recent past and only 20% reference events that are more than a year old. Dreams are also age-appropriate; for example, adolescent males tend to have dreams that include more aggression than older males—a tendency related to the increased hormonal activity in adolescent males.

Two contemporary explanations of dream content are polar opposites: one sees no meaning in dreams, while the other sees the content of dreams as reflecting biologically adaptive coping mechanisms. The first approach is *bottom-up:* the person has a dream, and then either the dreamer or a dream interpreter analyzes it. The second approach is *top-down:* the dreamer creates the dream.

## Dreams as Meaningless Brain Activity

The bottom-up approach is represented by J. Allan Hobson's (2004) *activation–synthesis theory,* which states that during a dream, the cortex is bombarded by signals from the brainstem, and these signals produce the pattern of a waking EEG. In response to this excitation, some parts of the cortex generate images, actions, and emotions from personal memory stores. In the absence of external verification, these dream events are fragmented and bizarre and reveal nothing more than that the cortex is activated.

Hobson proposes, on the basis of positron emission tomography (PET) imaging, that part of the frontal cortex is less active in dreaming than in waking. The frontal cortex controls working memory for recent events and attention. The dreamer thus cannot remember and link dream events as they take place because monitoring by the frontal cortex is required for these functions. On waking, the dreamer may attempt to come up with a story line for these fragmented, meaningless images. In Hobson's theory, dreams are personal, in that memories and experiences are activated, but they have no intrinsic meaning.

Chapter 14 describes the extent of frontal cortex involvement in memory. Attention is discussed in detail in Section 15-2.

## Dreams as a Coping Strategy

Anttio Revonsuo uses content analysis to argue that dreams are biologically adaptive, in that they lead to enhanced coping strategies for threatening life events (Valli & Revonsuo, 2009). The evolutionary aspect of this top-down approach (also called *coping theory*) is that enhanced performance is especially important for people whose environment typically includes dangerous events that constitute extreme threats to reproductive success. Dreams provide the dreamer with strategies for dealing with problems, even without the dreamer having to remember the dream. Revonsuo notes people seldom dream about reading, writing, and calculating. Dream threats are the same events that are threatening in waking life (**Figure 13-17**). For example, animals and strange men who could be characterized as enemies figure prominently in dreams. A study of the dreams of participants isolated due to the COVID-19 pandemic found that they had

**FIGURE 13-17 Dream Content** Terrifying visions that may persist even after awakening from a frightening dream as represented in *The Night*, by Swiss painter Ferdinand Hodler (1853–1918). Oil on canvas 116 × 299 cm. Kunstmuseum, Bern, Switzerland.

more vivid dreams related to being in crowded places where they could catch the virus, illustrating how dreams were part of their coping strategy (Scarpelli et al., 2021).

Malcolm-Smith and her colleagues (2012) report that approach behavior occurs more frequently in dreams than does avoidance behavior. They therefore suggest that reward-seeking behavior is as likely to represent a dream's latent content as avoidance behavior is.

A summary of the top-down approach to dream interpretation is that people are problem solvers when awake, and problem solving continues during sleep. Have you ever been advised to "sleep on it"—and did that prove to be good advice?

## Lucid Dreams

Dreams that occur during N-sleep are not as vivid as those in R-sleep. We can have dreamlike experiences just as we drop off to sleep, as our ongoing thoughts seem to disintegrate into hallucinations. Sometimes we are aware of these dreams as we dream, a phenomenon called *lucid dreaming*. Not only is the lucid dreamer conscious of the content of the dream, but they may actually direct the dream. For many individuals, lucid dreams occur infrequently; by contrast, a small number of people may experience lucid dreams several times a week.

One explanation of lucid dreaming stems from a two-system theory of consciousness proposed by Gerald Edelman (1989), who won the 1972 Nobel Prize for his work on the immune system. A *core consciousness system* mediates much the conscious behavior of most vertebrates—for example, our cats, our horses, and ourselves. In the case of humans, however, language and long-term memory systems provide an additional *global consciousness*, which can monitor core consciousness. Ordinarily, both consciousness systems sleep together, but occasionally the global consciousness system awakens and becomes an observer of the dream produced by the core consciousness system. The contrasting states of these two consciousness systems are experienced as lucid dreaming.

Theories of consciousness are discussed further in Section 15-7.

People who have vivid dreamlike experiences when awake are said to be hallucinating. And, of course, we daydream when awake. Eric Klinger (1990) argues that daydreams are ordinary and often fun, featuring little of the turmoil encountered in sleep dreams.

## 13-3 Review

Before you continue, check your understanding. Answers to Self-Test appear at the back of the book.

1. The multipronged measurement of sleep that serves as the gold standard for sleep assessment is called _____.

2. The classification of sleep based on EEG divides sleep into _____ and _____.

3. PSG can be used to record three common measures of sleep: _____, _____, and _____.

4. Sleepers experience about _____ R-sleep periods each night, with the duration of each period getting _____ as sleep progresses.

5. What factors makes interpreting dreams difficult?

6. What are some of the strengths and weakness of wearable devices for sleep measurement?

## 13-4

# What Does Sleep Accomplish?

**Learning Objectives**
- Explain how biological adaptation accounts for sleep.
- Explain how sleep and deprivation studies contribute to our understanding of sleep as a restorative process.
- Explain the role of sleep in the storage of explicit and implicit memory.
- Summarize sleep memory storage theory and synaptic homeostasis memory theory.

We all sleep, but differences in the manner and duration of sleep are striking. Some people sleep on beds with mattresses, some sleep on pallets, some in hammocks. Some people sleep clothed, others naked. Some people sleep with bed covers, others without. Some people sleep with their babies, children, and pets, and some people sleep alone. Some people segment their day with a single time for sleep, and others break up their days with naps or siestas. Some people value sleep, and others see it as an intrusion on other activities.

Variety in sleep behavior is not just individual but also cultural. In North America, reduced sleep time is associated with metabolic disease and reduced life spans, whereas in Japan, reduced sleep time is associated with health and longevity (Cheung et al., 2021).

All of this variation can seem bewildering. Here, we approach the variations in sleep by considering three explanations for the necessity of sleep: as adaptive, as restorative, and as supportive of brain health and memory.

## Sleep as a Biological Adaptation

Sleep serves as an energy-conserving strategy. The brain is a major user of the body's energy supply, so decreasing brain activity during sleep—especially N-sleep—conserves energy. The decline in body temperature during sleep decreases the body's metabolism, as exemplified by animals that display extreme decreases in body temperature characteristic of hibernation.

If the food that a species eats has a high nutrient value, that species can spend less time foraging and more time sleeping. Whether a species is predator or prey also influences sleep. A predator can sleep at its ease; the prey's sleep time is reduced because it must remain alert and ready to fight or flee at unpredictable times (**Figure 13-18**). Strictly nocturnal or diurnal animals are likely to sleep when they cannot travel easily. Dement (1972) proposed this colloquially: "We sleep to keep from bumping into things in the dark."

**Figure 13-19** charts the average sleep times of some common mammals. Herbivores, including donkeys, horses, and cows, spend a long time collecting enough food to sustain themselves. Long awake time and relatively short sleep time for them is adaptive. Because they are also prey, long awake time and less sleep time is also adaptive, as they watch for predators. Carnivores, including domestic cats and dogs, eat nutrient-rich foods and consume most of a day's or even a week's food at a single meal. Because they do not need to eat constantly, because they can conserve energy by resting, and because they are not at great risk of predation, a lifestyle with a great deal of sleep is adaptive for these animals.

The behavior of some animals does appear odd, however, so understanding any animal's sleep behavior requires understanding its natural history. Opossums, which spend much of their time asleep, may have specialized in energy conservation as a survival strategy.

We humans are average among species in terms of our sleep time. As we are omnivores and not subject to overwhelming predation, our sleep is intermediate between that of herbivores and carnivores.

**FIGURE 13-18 Do Not Disturb** Biological theories of sleep suggest that it is an energy-conserving strategy that serves other functions as well, such as staying safe through the night.

Lynn Hoffman/Science Source

**FIGURE 13-19 Average Sleep Time** Sleep time is affected both by the amount of time different species require to obtain food and by the risk of predation.

## The Basic Rest–Activity Cycle

Kleitman suggested that animals have a **basic rest–activity cycle (BRAC)**; for humans, this cycle lasts about 90 minutes (see Dement, 1972). Kleitman based his theory on the observation that human infants have frequent feeding periods between which they sleep.

As illustrated in **Figure 13-20**, the behavior of adult humans suggests that activity and rest are organized into 90-minute temporal packets. School classes, work periods, exercise sessions, mealtimes, coffee breaks, and snack times appear to be divided into intervals of 90 minutes or so. The discovery that R-sleep occurs at intervals of about 90 minutes suggests that it, too, can be considered a continuation into sleep of the 90-minute BRAC rhythm.

Kleitman proposed that the BRAC rhythm is so fundamental that it cannot be turned off. Accordingly, to ensure a night's sleep is uninterrupted by periodic waking (and perhaps snacking), the body is paralyzed and only the brain is active. An analogy: rather than turning off a fuel-powered car's engine when stopped at a red light, you apply the brakes to keep the idling car from moving. For R-sleep, the atonia that paralyzes movement is the brakes.

## Sleep as a Restorative Process

In Macbeth's description of sleep, Shakespeare illustrates in words the idea that sleep has restorative properties:

*Sleep that knits up the ravell'd sleave of care,*
*The death of each day's life, sore labour's bath,*
*Balm of hurt minds, great nature's second course,*
*Chief nourisher in life's feast.*
*—Act II, Scene 2*

## Sleep Deprivation Studies

To evaluate whether sleep is essential for bodily processes, investigators have conducted sleep deprivation studies. These studies have not clearly identified any essential function for sleep, but rather point to multiple physiological and cognitive functions altered by various degrees of sleep deprivation (Hanson & Huecker, 2021).

Sleep researcher William Dement participated as an observer in one case study on sleep deprivation that illustrates this point. In 1965, as part of a science fair project, a high school student named Randy Gardner planned to break the Guinness World Record of 260 hours (almost 11 days) of consecutive wakefulness with the help of two classmates who would keep him awake. Gardner did break the record, and then he slept for 14 hours and reported no ill effects. Dement reported that Gardner hallucinated and had cognitive and memory lapses during his period of sleep deprivation. These negative effects did not last. Reviews of sleep deprivation research are consistent in concluding that limited periods of sleep deprivation do not produce prolonged physiological alterations. Nevertheless, because of concerns about individual differences

**basic rest–activity cycle (BRAC)** Recurring cycle of temporal packets (about 90-minute periods in humans), during which an animal's level of arousal waxes and wanes.

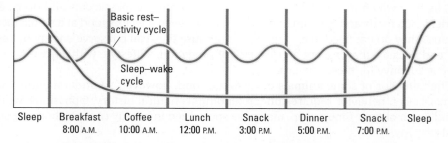

**FIGURE 13-20 Behavioral Rhythms** Our behavior is dominated by a basic rest–activity cycle (red), through which our activity levels change in the course of the day, and by an N-sleep–R-sleep cycle (purple) during the night.

in the short-term negative consequences of sleep deprivation, the Guinness World Records no longer records wakefulness records.

Recurring periods of brief sleep deprivation and irregular sleep do have adverse physiological consequences, however, in that they are associated with poorer health and cognitive performance. Performance on tasks that require attention declines as a function of hours of sleep deprivation. Sleep deprivation figures into accidents both at work and on the road. Sleep deprivation deficit does not manifest itself in an inability to do a task, because sleep-deprived participants can perform even very complex tasks; rather, the deficit affects the ability to maintain sustained attention. Irregular sleep can also contribute to metabolic syndrome, described in Clinical Focus 13-1.

A confounding factor in evaluating sleep deprivation is that people can engage in **microsleeps**, brief sleep periods lasting up to a few seconds. During microsleep, participants may remain sitting or standing, but their eyelids droop briefly, and they become less responsive to external stimuli. If you have driven a car while tired, you may have had a microsleep and awakened just in time to prevent yourself from driving off the road—or worse.

## R-Sleep Deprivation

Some studies have focused on the selective benefits of R-sleep. To deprive a participant of R-sleep, researchers allow participants to sleep but awaken them as R-sleep begins. R-sleep deprivation has two effects. First, participants show an increased tendency to enter R-sleep in subsequent sleep sessions, so awakenings must become more and more frequent. Second, after R-sleep deprivation, participants experience R-sleep rebound, showing more than the usual amount of R-sleep in the first available sleep session.

Because most sleep studies are of relatively brief duration, capturing potential long-term physiological changes that may take place during or after sleep deprivation remains elusive. Nevertheless, in humans, sleep deprivation impairs many functions, but recovery after restored sleep is substantial (Yamazaki et al., 2021).

# Sleep for Memory Storage

The suggestion that sleep plays a role in memory dates back more than a century. We know that memory storage takes time because memories are best acquired after repeated practice with intervals between the practice. We also rehearse memories by frequently recalling them. It therefore makes sense that the time spent in sleep affords the opportunity for rehearsal, contributing to memory retention. Here we describe two formative studies showing that the events of a day are replayed during sleep.

Section 14-1 expands on the processes of encoding and recall of memories.

## N-Sleep and Explicit Memory

Hippocampal **place cells** are proposed to be the basis of *spatial explicit memory*—that is, memory of location that can be easily recalled and used. When a rat is searching for food in a certain location, many hippocampal place cells fire. These cells are relatively inactive until the rat passes through that place again, when they become reactivated—activity taken to indicate the rat remembers the location.

Based on this understanding, Gerrard and colleagues (2008) took recordings from as many as 100 cells under three conditions—during N-sleep prior to food search, during a food search task, and during N-sleep after a food search. Their findings showed that during the food search, the activity of some place cells becomes correlated, suggesting that these cells form a representation of the specific spatial location. During the rats' subsequent periods of N-sleep, the correlations recur (**Figure 13-21**). This result suggests that the memory of the previous food-searching experience is being replayed and thus stored during N-sleep.

Figure 7-11 shows the classes of place cells and their directional selectivity. Section 14-3 describes the relationship between the hippocampus and spatial memory, including the role of place cells.

## R-Sleep and Implicit Memory

To determine whether humans' dreams are related to memory, Pierre Maquet and his coworkers in Belgium (2000) trained participants on a serial reaction task. In this task

**microsleep** Brief sleep period lasting a second or so.

**place cell** Hippocampal neuron maximally responsive to specific locations in the world.

**FIGURE 13-21 Neural Replay?** Hippocampal cell activity suggests that rats dream about their experiences. Dots on the periphery of the circles represent the activity of 42 hippocampal cells recorded at the same time during (*left*) N-sleep before a food-searching task, (*center*) the food-searching task, and (*right*) N-sleep after the task. No strong correlations among cells emerged during the N-sleep that preceded the food search, but correlations were strong among cells during the food search and during the subsequent slow-wave sleep. Information from Wilson and McNaughton (1994).

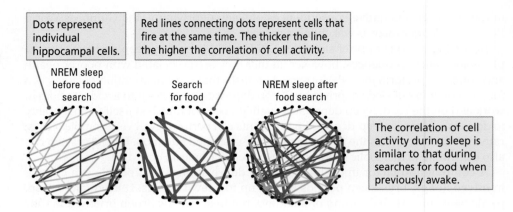

Chapter 14 details our understanding of implicit and explicit memory and their anatomical correlates.

of *implicit* (or unconscious) *motor memory,* a participant learns through repetition to make a quick response to a cue. The investigators observed regional blood flow in the brain with PET scans during training and during R-sleep on the subsequent night. The participants faced a computer screen displaying six positional markers and were instructed to push one of six keys when a corresponding positional marker was illuminated. They did not know that the illumination sequence was predetermined.

As training progressed, the investigators could tell that participants were learning because their reaction times improved during trials in which a positional marker was correlated with a preceding marker. On PET scan measures of brain activation, a similar pattern of neocortical activation appeared during task acquisition and during R-sleep (**Figure 13-22**). On the basis of this result, Maquet and coworkers suggested that the participants were dreaming about their learning experience, and that replay during R-sleep strengthened the task memory. Thus, the conclusion is that rule learning in both motor and cognitive domains is strengthened during sleep, including R-sleep.

# Brain Events During Sleep Memory Storage

Two theories describe how memories are reactivated and stored during sleep. *Sleep memory storage theory* proposes that the brain makes a rendition of a memory that is replayed during sleep. According to this theory, recording the brain's electrical events will reveal when memory replay is occurring. The *synaptic homeostasis memory theory of sleep* proposes that the brain undergoes global changes during sleep that allow the biochemical events associated with memory storage to occur. We describe each of these theories in turn, but note that the theories are not mutually exclusive, as replay and homeostasis could occur together.

## Sleep Memory Storage Theory

Sleep memory storage theory suggests that the replay of a memory during sleep contributes to the way that memory is stored. Replay has an effect similar to the repetition involved in school learning, learning to play a skilled sport, or running through an event over and over in our minds. Replay not only stores a memory, but also distributes that memory to relevant brain structures, where it is integrated with previously acquired information.

**FIGURE 13-22 Do We Store Implicit Memories During R-Sleep?** Information from Maquet et al. (2000).

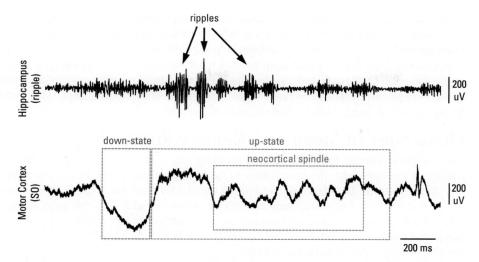

**FIGURE 13-23 N-Sleep Activity** EEG ripples occur in the hippocampus and slow oscillations (SO) occur in the neocortex. The activity of neurons during these waveforms may encode memory in compressed form. The repetition of the waves may be the signature of memory replay and the transfer of memory between forebrain structures. (Research from Javad Karimi Abadchi.)

EEG recordings show that specific patterns of activity, shown in **Figure 13-23**, become more frequent during the sleep that follows a learning session (Schreiner et al., 2021). The hippocampus displays brief *ripples* consisting of a short burst of 80 to 100-Hz waves, the neocortex displays an up–down pattern of *slow oscillations* (SO) at a maximum frequency of 0.75 Hz, and the thalamus displays *spindles* with a waxing and waning pattern of 12 to 16 Hz.

Many thousands of neurons may be active during each of these slow-wave electrical events. Accordingly, these EEG patterns may represent the replay, transfer, and storage of memory encoded in their neuronal activity. For example, hippocampal ripples are brief, lasting less than a second, and are suggested to be the electrical signature of memory replayed in a compressed form, analogous to a video played in fast forward. The memory encoded in a hippocampal ripple may be recoded in a thalamic spindle so that a memory can be distributed to the neocortex through thalamic projections, where it is integrated with other memories. Neurons in the neocortex are active during the up (depolarizing) phase of the SO and inactive during the down (hyperpolarizing) phase. When a thalamic spindle and neocortical SO occur together, a memory could then be integrated and stored in various neocortical locations (see Figure 13-23).

## The Synaptic Homeostasis Theory of Sleep and Memory

The synaptic homeostasis memory theory of sleep is both a theory of why we sleep and a theory of how we store memory. It is based on the idea that sleep allows synapses that have been active during waking to return to their resting state during sleep (Tononi & Cirelli, 2016). Synaptic activity is the major consumer of the brain's energy, and synaptic activity (firing rate) is high during waking activities (Lucas et al., 2018). Not only do daytime events call upon a lot of synaptic activity, but all this activity also changes synapses and begins to use up their plasticity—their ability to undergo further change. During sleep, the slow electrical waves, especially the 4- to 7-Hz theta waves of N1-sleep and N2-sleep, allow synaptic activity to shift to a resting or homeostatic energy-conserving state. Thus, synapses can return to a state in which they are more plastic and so are available to be engaged during the next waking period.

As an analogy, consider your own working space. During the day, you take out books, move papers around, and perhaps even accumulate some dishes or wrappings from snacks. If left in this condition each day, your working space would quickly become unusable. But if you clean up after each working day, it is ready to be used the next day. According to the synaptic homeostasis memory theory, this is what the brain is doing during sleep: cleaning up.

How do firing rates and plasticity relate to memory storage? The homeostasis theory proposes that some synapses, especially those that have recently been involved in a new learning experience, are more metabolically active than other synapses and take

**Principle 10:** Neuroplasticity is the hallmark of nervous system functioning.

longer to return to a resting state. Because these synapses are more active than surrounding synapses in N-sleep, they are in an optimal condition to undergo structural changes without interference. It is these structural changes that represent new memory. To investigate the idea that sleep returns neurons to an optimal firing rate, Pacheco and colleagues (2021) used patches to deprive rats of vision in one eye. The deprivation caused visual cortex cells to increase their firing rates. After the rats slept, however, the firing rate of the visual cortex cells returned to normal.

## Challenges in Sleep and Memory Research

The central challenge for sleep-related memory research lies in associating the complexity of memory with the complexity of neuronal activity in the brain. Memory for any daily event can be substantial and much may be remembered without sleep, so any added contribution from sleep may be difficult to detect. Adding to this complexity, the roles of various brain regions in memory are not a settled issue. Finally, experiments on sleep and memory are often not replicable (Cordi & Rasch, 2021). It is best to think of the sleep-memory field as being in its infancy.

## 13-4 Review

Before you continue, check your understanding. Answers to Self-Test appear at the back of the book.

1. Three possible purposes for sleep discussed in this section are _____, _____, and _____.

2. A theory associated with the function of sleep based on restoring synapses to a functional balance is called _____.

3. In rats performing a spatial task, correlations develop between the firing of _____ cells in the hippocampus and the replay of location memory during _____ sleep.

4. When you are sleep deprived, you are more likely to slip into a(n) _____ for a few seconds.

5. EEG wave patterns that replay memory in a compressed form are called _____.

6. What does multiple process theory suggest about the relationship between sleep and memory?

7. What was the significance of Randy Gardner's record-setting sleep deprivation experiment?

## 13-5

**Learning Objectives**
- Describe the anatomical components of the RAS.
- Summarize the role the RAS system plays in producing and maintaining sleeping and waking states.
- Explain how the peribrachial area and MPRF contribute to R-sleep activities.

# The Neural Bases of Sleep

One plausible explanation for sleep is that the brain contains a sleep-inducing substance that causes the cortex to sleep. After all, many chemical substances, including sleep-inducing drugs, can put us to sleep and stimulants can keep us awake. The hormone melatonin, secreted from the pineal gland during the dark phase of the light–dark cycle, promotes sleepiness and may contribute to falling asleep. A synthetic form of this hormone can even be taken as a sleep aid. Nevertheless, melatonin is not the body's sleep-producing chemical because sleep survives the removal of the pineal gland. A more recent idea is that sleep is necessary for DNA repair and that a protein Parp1 senses DNA damage and facilitates sleep so that DNA can be repaired (Zada et al., 2021). Nevertheless, Parp1, like melatonin, may promote sleep, but not cause it.

Our understanding of circadian rhythms and brain mechanisms suggests that human sleep–wake cycles are the result of contributions made by many neural regions, neurochemicals and hormones, and the metabolic activity of most of the body's cells. In this section, we consider the neural mechanisms that regulate sleep. We look at evidence that brainstem nuclei control the various events associated with sleep, with different nuclei being linked to N-sleep versus R-sleep.

# Reticular Activating System and Sleep

A pioneering experiment by Giuseppe Moruzzi and Horace Magoun (1949) began to answer the question of which brain areas regulate sleep. Their research suggested that an extensive region forming the core of the brainstem from the posterior hypothalamus through the midbrain and into the hindbrain could constitute the sleep–wake system. They named this brainstem area, diagrammed in **Figure 13-24**, the **reticular activating system (RAS)**.

The experiment performed by Moruzzi and Magoun (1949) involved cortical EEG recordings taken from anesthetized cats while their brainstems were electrically stimulated. The researchers were surprised to find that, in response to the electrical stimulation, large, slow waves typical of anesthesia and sleep were replaced by the low-voltage fast-wave beta EEG typical of waking. The waking EEG activity outlasted the stimulation period, demonstrating that the effect was not due to the online activity of neurons in the region of the stimulating electrode, but could be maintained by these neurons independent of the stimulation. During the "waking period," an anesthetized cat did not become behaviorally aroused, but its cortical EEG appeared to indicate that it was awake. In a normally sleeping cat, the same stimulation did lead to waking. When the RAS was isolated from sensory input from the body and head, electrical stimulation still produced a waking cortical EEG, indicating that the RSA was not simply relaying arousing sensory information from the body.

Subsequent research has shown that the RAS is complex and may feature as many as 100 different regions or nuclei. To explain the activating properties of the RAS, researchers initially directed their attention to the nonspecific noradrenergic (NE), cholinergic (ACh) and serotonergic (5-HT) systems of the brain (described in Section 5-3). These systems consist of nuclei in the RAS that project indirectly and directly to the neocortex. These projections were initially proposed to be the pathway through which the RSA could activate the cortex, but later research implicated other nonspecific systems in this activation process. For example, the histamine and orexin systems similarly have cell bodies in the RAS that influence the cortex. Activation of the cell bodies of one or another of these systems via circadian influences (e.g., sunlight), electrical stimulation, or the actions of drugs could produce the electrical events in the cortex and the behaviors associated with waking.

Studies of these ascending projections from the RAS to the cortex suggest that they form two general pathways, a dorsal pathway and a ventral pathway (charted in Figure 13-24). The dorsal pathway projects through the medial nuclei of the thalamus and is proposed to be responsible for arousal; the ventral pathway projects through the hypothalamus and basal forebrain and is proposed to be responsible for awareness. Several lines of evidence support the differential roles of these pathways in arousal and awareness.

## The RAS Dorsal Pathway

**Coma** can result from many kinds of brain injury and is usually associated with diffuse brain damage to cells and fibers in a number of brain regions. One of these regions is located in the posterior portion of the RAS just below the cerebellum, with the left side of the brainstem making a larger contribution to coma than the right side does (Fischer et al., 2016). Coma can also result from damage to the dorsal thalamic projections of the RAS, even when the RAS itself is undamaged.

In one highly publicized case, after taking a minor tranquilizer and having a few drinks at a birthday party, a 21-year-old woman named Karen Ann Quinlan sustained brain damage that left her comatose (Quinlan & Quinlan, 1977). She was hospitalized, placed on a respirator to support breathing, and fed by tubes. Her family fought a protracted legal battle to have her removed from life support, a battle they finally won before the Supreme Court of New Jersey. Even after she was removed from the respirator, however, Karen Ann lived in a perpetual coma, aided by artificial feeding, for 10 more years. Postmortem inspection of her brain showed that neither the cortex nor the RAS had suffered much damage, but the thalamus, especially its midline nuclei, was

**FIGURE 13-24 Sleep–Wake Controller** The reticular activating system (RAS), a region at the center of the brainstem, contains a mixture of cell bodies and fiber pathways extending to various cortical regions. The RAS influences the cortex to produce arousal through the dorsal pathway and awareness through the ventral pathway.

Chapter 1 discusses the role of arousal and awareness in consciousness.

**reticular activating system (RAS)** Large reticulum (mixture of cell nuclei and nerve fibers) that runs through the core of the brainstem; associated with sleep–wake behavior and behavioral arousal; also called the *reticular formation*.

**coma** Prolonged state of deep unconsciousness resembling sleep.

extensively damaged. Thus, projections from the RAS through the thalamus may have contributed to the almost complete absence of arousal that characterized her coma (Kinney et al., 1994).

## The RAS Ventral Pathway

Another line of investigation has associated the RAS ventral pathway through the basal forebrain with a loss of awareness in the absence of coma. Vanderwolf (2002) used EEG recordings of rats to show that at least two brainstem systems project via the ventral pathway to influence the activation of the cortex (see **Figure 13-25**). Each pathway is associated with a different aspect of awareness.

The basal forebrain contains large cholinergic cells that receive extensive projections from cholinergic cell groups of the RAS, as well as other RAS nuclei. These basal forebrain cholinergic cells project to the cortex and secrete acetylcholine (ACh) from their terminals onto cortical neurons to stimulate a waking beta-rhythm EEG. Beta EEG activity of these cholinergic cells is associated with alert but immobile behavior, such as when attention is directed to something. The median raphe nuclei of the midbrain RSA contain serotonin (5-HT) neurons, whose axons also project diffusely to the cortex; they, too, stimulate cortical cells to produce a beta EEG. This serotonergic beta EEG is associated with overt movement, such as walking.

If the activity of the cholinergic projection is blocked by drugs or disrupted by lesions to the cholinergic cells of the basal forebrain, the waking EEG normally recorded from an immobile rat is replaced by EEG activity resembling that occurring in N-sleep, even though the animal is not behaviorally asleep. If the rat walks or is otherwise active, a waking EEG due to serotonergic activity is obtained from the cortex. These findings, graphed in Figure 13-25, suggest that the cholinergic EEG is responsible for waking associated with being alert yet still, whereas the serotonergic activation is responsible for the waking EEG associated with movement.

Neither the basal forebrain system nor the median raphe system is responsible for overt behavior. In fact, if both structures are pharmacologically or surgically destroyed, a rat can still stand and walk around. Its EEG, however, permanently resembles that of a sleeping animal. In addition, so long as one activating system is producing a waking EEG, rats can learn simple tasks. But if both systems are destroyed, an animal, while still able to walk around, is no longer able to learn or display intelligent behavior. In a sense, the cortex is like a house in which the lights are powered by two separate sources: both must fail for the house to be left in darkness, but if at least one source is operating, at least some lights stay on.

Taken together, case studies of people with coma and animal experiments with EEG suggest that the projections of RAS contribute to arousal and awareness via different neural pathways to the cortex. Presumably in N-sleep, both pathways turn off and we lose both arousal and awareness. We now turn to the contributions of RAS systems to R-sleep.

## Neural Basis of R-Sleep

N-sleep is characterized by a loss of both arousal and awareness. The cortex of someone in R-sleep, however, displays waking beta activity in the absence of arousal. What are the neural mechanisms that produce this state?

Barbara Jones (1993) and her colleagues describe a group of cholinergic neurons, collectively known as the **peribrachial area**, that contribute to R-sleep. This area, which is part of the RAS, is located in the dorsal brainstem just anterior to the cerebellum (**Figure 13-26**). Jones selectively destroyed peribrachial cells in rats by spraying them with the neurotoxin kainic acid. She found that R-sleep was drastically reduced. This result suggests that the peribrachial area contributes to R-sleep and R-sleep–related behaviors.

The peribrachial area projects into a more ventrally located nucleus called the **medial pontine reticular formation (MPRF)**, also shown in Figure 13-26. Lesions of

Figure 5-19 summarizes the major neural activating systems and their functions.

Figure 6-5 shows agonist action at the ACh synapse.

**FIGURE 13-25 Brain Activators** Basal forebrain ACh neurons produce an activated EEG pattern when a rat is alert but immobile. The 5-HT raphe neurons of the midbrain produce an activated EEG pattern when the rat moves.

**FIGURE 13-26 Brainstem Nuclei Responsible for R-Sleep** Damage to either the peribrachial area or the medial pontine formation reduces or abolishes R-sleep.

**Principle 7:** The nervous system works by juxtaposing excitation and inhibition.

**peribrachial area** Cholinergic nucleus in the dorsal brainstem having a role in R-sleep behaviors; part of the RAS, which projects to medial pontine reticular formation.

**medial pontine reticular formation (MPRF)** Nucleus in the pons that participates in R-sleep.

the MPRF also abolish R-sleep, and injections of cholinergic agonists (drugs that act like ACh) into this region induce R-sleep.

If both the peribrachial area and the MPRF take part in producing R-sleep, how do other events related to R-sleep—including a waking EEG, REMs, and atonia—take place? **Figure 13-27** charts an explanation, showing how other R-sleep–related activities are induced:

- The peribrachial area initiates R-sleep by activating the MPRF.

- The MPRF sends projections to excite basal forebrain cholinergic neurons, which in turn produce the activity seen on the EEG recorded from the cortex.

- The MPRF also excites brainstem motor nuclei to produce REMs and other twitches.

- The atonia of R-sleep is produced by the MPRF through a pathway that sends input to the subcoerulear nucleus located just behind it.

- The subcoerulear nucleus excites the magnocellular nucleus of the medulla, which sends projections to the spinal motor neurons to inhibit them so that paralysis is achieved during the R-sleep period. Uchida and colleagues (2021) showed that blocking the glycine projection from the subcoerulear nucleus to the motor neurons of the spinal cord inhibits these neurons, thereby blocking movement.

**FIGURE 13-27 Neural Control of R-Sleep**

## 13-5 Review

Before you continue, check your understanding. Answers to Self-Test appear at the back of the book.

1. The _____ in the core region of the brainstem is associated with sleepwalking behavior.

2. Sleep mechanisms regulate two aspects of consciousness: _____, which involves the medial nuclei of the thalamus, and _____, which involves the basal forebrain.

3. Destruction of cells in the _____ results in drastically reduced R-sleep.

4. If you nod off to sleep at an inappropriate or inconvenient time, why does moving awaken you?

5. Why does an attempt to explain sleep in relation of a single brain system fail?

## 13-6

# Disorders of Sleep

Occasional sleep disturbances are annoying and may impair performance the following day. Continuing sleep problems, by comparison, can contribute to long-term health problems. Sleep disorders are also a symptom of many other conditions, including anxiety, depression, schizophrenia, and dementia.

The *International Classification of Sleep Disorders* lists six categories of sleep disorders (Sateia, 2014). The following sections describe five of these categories: insomnia, hypersomnia, breathing disorders, parasomnias, and sleep-related movement disorders. A sixth category, circadian-rhythm sleep disorder, includes disorders related to sleep time, shift work, and jet lag; these disorders were described in Section 13-1.

## Insomnia: Inability to Sleep

**Insomnia** is a descriptive term for the inability to fall asleep, stay asleep, or experience satisfactory sleep. Our understanding of insomnia is complicated by the wide variation among people in how much time they spend asleep (Kay & Buysse, 2017). Insomnia is diagnosed when a person experiences difficult sleep for at least three nights a week over a period lasting at least 3 months. It is the most common sleep disorder, affecting

**Learning Objective**

- Summarize the behaviors associated with various sleep disorders, including insomnia, hypersomnia, breathing disorders, parasomnias, cataplexy, and movement disorders.

**insomnia** Symptom of a number of disorders characterized by an inability to fall asleep, stay asleep, or experience satisfactory sleep.

**hypersomnia** Disorder of falling asleep at inappropriate times, or a difficulty staying awake.

**sleeping beauty syndrome** A rare condition in which the affected individual has recurring bouts of excessive sleeping.

**sleep apnea** Inability to breathe during sleep, causing a sleeper to wake up to breathe.

Section 6-1 presents theories of drug tolerance.

For more about prion disorders, see Section 16-3.

an estimated 14% of people (Dopheide, 2020). Anxiety and depression co-occur in approximately 35% of insomnia cases. The most at-risk group for insomnia is women older than age 60, with risk factors including preexisting health disorders, chronic stress, and an irregular schedule. Anyone displaying one of these risk factors can suffer from insomnia.

Insomnia can be treated with sedative-hypnotic drugs, including barbiturates, sodium amytal, and many other tranquilizers. The term "sleeping pill" is typically applied to any drug with sedative-hypnotic properties. One drawback of regular use of sleep medication is that it can leave a person feeling groggy the next day, defeating the purpose of taking the drug. A second, more significant drawback is that people may develop tolerance to the medications, become dependent on them, and display rebound insomnia when they stop taking them. A person then may increase the dose each time the drug fails in an effort to produce the desired effect. The syndrome in which patients unsuccessfully attempt to sleep by increasing their drug dosage is called *drug dependence insomnia*. Finally, although sleeping pills promote N-sleep, they deprive the user of R-sleep. The most successful nondrug treatment of insomnia consists of training in sleep hygiene and behavioral therapy.

*Fatal familial insomnia* is an almost complete inability to sleep. As its name implies, this condition contributes to death within months. The onset of this rare disease occurs in midlife. It is caused by a mutation of the *PrP* gene on chromosome 20, which expresses the protein that is, or becomes, a causative prion. The normal *PrP* gene may have a role in protecting the cell membrane, but the mutation causes a misfolding of the protein, resulting in cascading effects that include brain cell death. Fatal familial insomnia is associated with panic attacks, paranoia, phobias, weight loss, and eventual dementia. Although there is no treatment, a mouse model of the condition has been created to study the disease and search for treatments.

## Hypersomnia: Inability to Stay Awake

From time to time, we all suffer from daytime sleepiness and will occasionally fall asleep during the day. **Hypersomnia** is diagnosed if a person sleeps more than 9 hours at night but is still tired, frequently feels groggy and tired, and tends to fall asleep during the day, with the condition persisting for at least 3 months. Though it is thought to be rare, incidence of hypersomnia is difficult to determine because it is associated with other sleep-related problems, such as the sleep-related breathing problems described next.

**Sleeping beauty syndrome**, also called *Kleine–Levin syndrome*, is a very rare condition in which the person has recurring bouts of excessive sleeping. A single sleep episode may last from 15 hours to more than 20 hours. Periods of excessive sleeping may last for a week or more, interspersed with periods in which sleep has a more normal duration. Some individuals may experience an increased urge to eat and hypersexuality when awake. Sleeping beauty syndrome usually affects adolescent males. There is no obvious cause for this condition and no effective treatment.

## Breathing Disorders

Sleep clinic studies of people with excessive daytime sleepiness have resulted in a surprising discovery concerning one cause of this condition: **sleep apnea**, an inability to breathe during sleep. Although other breathing-related sleep disorders exist, including chronic snoring and catathrenia (abnormal breathing and vocalizations), sleep apnea is one of the more common and potentially harmful due to its effects on sleep and on oxygen and carbon dioxide levels in the blood. Being overweight is one factor contributing to sleep apnea, as the respiratory pathway may be constricted in such individuals. Sleep apnea can also have central causes in the neural circuits that regulate respiration.

Sleep apnea may be produced by a CNS problem, such as weak neural command to the respiratory muscles in the case of *central sleep apnea*, or it may be caused by collapse or blockage of the upper airway, as in the case of *obstructive sleep apnea*. When people with sleep apnea stop breathing, either they wake up completely and have

*Apnea* come from the Latin *a*, meaning "not," and *pnea*, meaning "breathing."

difficulty getting back to sleep or they partially awaken repeatedly throughout the night to gasp for breath. **Figure 13-28** shows recordings of the irregular breathing rate and blood oxygen levels of someone with sleep apnea.

Sleep apnea affects people of all ages and both sexes, and as many as 30% of individuals older than 65 may have some form of it. Sleep apnea can even occur in children; it may be related to some cases of *sudden infant death syndrome* (*SIDS*), or crib death, in which otherwise healthy infants inexplicably die in their sleep. Obstructive sleep apnea is more common among people who are overweight and those who snore—two conditions in which airflow is restricted.

Treatments for sleep apnea include weight loss, a face mask to deliver negative pressure to open the airway, an appliance to expand the upper airway, and, as a last resort, surgery. Untreated sleep apnea can cause high blood pressure and other cardiovascular disease, memory problems, weight gain, impotence, headaches, and brain damage due to oxygen insufficiency (Corrêa et al., 2015).

**FIGURE 13-28 Sleep Apnea** Breathing rate and blood oxygen level recorded during R-sleep, when muscle tone is ordinarily low, from a person with sleep apnea. Notice that blood oxygen increased after each breath and then continued to fall until another breath was taken. This person inhaled only four times in the 6-minute period; a healthy sleeper would breathe more than 60 times in the same interval.

# Parasomnias

**Parasomnias** are unusual and unwanted behaviors that disrupt sleep. They can occur at any point in the sleep cycle, including just before falling asleep, during N-sleep or R-sleep, or just as a sleeper wakes up. They disrupt sleep by delaying sleep onset and by causing a sleeping person to wake up. They can also disrupt the sleep of bed partners.

Parasomnias are grouped as N-parasomnias and R-parasomnias according to their respective disruptive symptoms. Because N-sleep is the first stage of sleep, *N-parasomnias* interfere with sleep onset or occur early in a sleeping period. *R-parasomnias* appear as elements of R-sleep that can occur alone and at other times but can also occur together.

## Sleep Terrors

As many as 6 in 100 children experience brief frightening dreams called *sleep terrors* or *night terrors*. Night terrors are N-parasomnias that may involve intense screaming, crying, thrashing, or fear that occurs again and again over the course of successive nights' sleep. Generally, the experience is not recalled after waking. Children who suffer from night terrors often also display sleepwalking, restless legs syndrome, and sleep-related breathing disorder. This parasomnia tends to run in families, suggesting that there may be a genetic basis to this disorder.

## Sleepwalking

**Sleepwalking**, also called *somnambulism,* is an N-parasomnia that involves getting up and walking about. It more commonly occurs in children but can occur in adults. A sleepwalker may get up and walk, or just sit up in bed in a dazed condition. They may not respond to others and may be difficult to wake up. They will be confused when awoken and have no memory of the episode. In extreme cases, the individual may engage in various activities such as cooking, leaving the house, and even driving a car. Sleepwalking is not treated unless it frequently recurs, extends into adulthood, or becomes dangerous.

## Sleep-Related Eating Disorders

There are several sleep-related eating disorders in which individuals will eat instead of going to bed. Consequently, an individual gains weight despite displaying typical eating habits during the day. This behavior is not common, but affected individuals are typically female, and the median age of onset is younger than 40. Most individuals display a triad of nocturnal *hyperphagia* (excessive hunger and eating), insomnia, and morning anorexia. Individuals usually consume high-calorie foods, such that 25% of their daily caloric intake occurs during their sleep-related eating binge. The frequency of episodes varies, but sleep-related eating is associated with stressful life events. Individuals are frequently depressed and suffering from anxiety. This N-parasomnia disorder is treated with education in sleep hygiene and cognitive therapy.

**parasomnia** Unusual or unwanted behaviors that disrupt sleep.

**sleepwalking** N-parasomnia in which the person may sit up, walk around, and, in some extreme cases, perform complex activities, such as cooking or driving; also called *somnambulism*.

**sleep paralysis** Atonia and dreaming that occur when a person is awake, usually when just falling asleep or waking up.

**cataplexy** State of atonia, as in R-sleep, occurring while a person is awake and active; linked to strong emotional stimulation.

# Nightmare Disorder

*Nightmares* are vivid dreams marked by intense feelings of dread or terror that awaken the individual. These well-remembered dreams usually involve threats to survival, security, or physical integrity. On waking from a nightmare, the individual becomes alert quickly, and may not want to go back to sleep for fear of reoccurring episodes. When asked about this phenomenon, approximately 86% of people report at least one incident in the past year, making nightmare disorder among the most common of parasomnias. As many as 2% to 6% of people, however, report nightmares as a weekly event. People who have repeated nightmares may also have *nightmare distress*, daytime worry and anxiety related to their nightmares (Allen et al., 2021).

Nightmares are particularly common in children but may also occur in adults. In one case, a 4-year-old child suddenly woke up screaming that she was covered in ants. It took hours for her father to convince her that her experience was not real. Only reassurance from a sleep expert later convinced the father that nothing was amiss with his daughter and that nightmares are common among young children (Carter et al., 2014).

Nightmares occur during R-sleep, and especially in the second half of R-sleep, a period called *deep sleep*. The incidence of nightmares tends to increase as a result of sleep deprivation, anxiety, or a recent traumatic event. Recommended treatments include adopting regular sleep habits and cognitive-behavioral therapy.

# Sleep Paralysis

In the R-parasomnia known as **sleep paralysis**, a person is conscious but has a loss of muscle tone and is paralyzed. This condition occurs most frequently upon waking, either just after falling asleep or after a night's sleep. In informal class surveys, almost one-third of students report having had such an experience. A likely explanation is that the person is experiencing the atonia of R-sleep either as they wake up or as they go to sleep.

# Sleep-Related Hallucinations

A person experiencing *sleep-related hallucinations* sees imaginary creatures or hears imaginary voices while conscious and in an atonic or sleep paralysis condition. The hallucinations are often accompanied by emotional experiences, including fear and dread. People displaying sleep-related hallucinations may also be in a state of sleep paralysis or cataplexy. Sleep-related hallucinations give every appearance of R-sleep dreaming, albeit in the absence of other features of R-sleep, such as loss of consciousness.

# R-Sleep Behavioral Disorder

Michel Jouvet (1972) observed that cats with lesions in the subcoerulear nucleus display a remarkable behavior when they enter R-sleep. Rather than stretching out in the atonia that typically accompanies R-sleep, the cats stand up, look around, and make movements of catching an imaginary mouse or running from an imaginary threat. Apparently, if cats with damage to this brain region dream about catching mice or escaping from a threat, they act out their dreams.

Humans display a condition similar to the one Jouvet observed in cats, called *R-sleep behavioral disorder* (R-sleep without atonia). People with this disorder behave as though they are acting out their dreams (Matar et al., 2021). For example, someone may dream that they are being shot at and awaken to find themselves crouched behind their bed with their arms positioned as if aiming a rifle (Schenck et al., 1986). The cause may be either genetic or neurological, related to aging. R-sleep behavioral disorder is often associated with early symptoms of Parkinson disease and may be brought on by the same α-synuclein prions that are implicated in Parkinson disease.

# Cataplexy

**Cataplexy** is atonia that occurs when a person is awake and active. The person loses muscle tone and collapses, atonic but still conscious. Episodes can occur gradually or so suddenly that injury is a risk and can be accompanied by sleep-related hallucinations. Cataplexy can be triggered by excitement or laughing.

*Cataplexy* comes from the Greek word *kataplessein*, meaning "to strike down."

Cataplexy can have a genetic basis. In 1970, William Dement was given a litter of Doberman Pinscher dogs, all of which displayed cataplexy. This disease is transmitted as a recessive trait: to develop it, a dog must inherit the gene from both its mother and its father. The descendants of those dogs, and others that have been found to have the condition, provide animal models for investigating the neural basis of the disease as well as its treatment.

When Jerome Siegel (2004) investigated the cause of catalepsy in these dogs, he found that during attacks, neurons in the subcoerulear nucleus of the brainstem become inactive and neurons in the magnocellular nucleus of the medulla become active, just as they do during R-sleep. Anatomical examinations of the brains of affected dogs also revealed neuronal loss in the hypothalamus and amygdala.

This line of investigation led to the discovery that a subset of these affected neurons produce a peptide neurotransmitter called *orexin* (also called *hypocretin*), which serves as a signaling molecule to maintain wakefulness (see Research Focus 13-4: Orexin). Orexin cells are located in the hypothalamus and send projections to many other brain regions, including the hypothalamus and the nonspecific activating acetylcholine and serotonin systems. Thus, orexin cells play a role in maintaining waking.

To test the idea that orexin loss is related to cataplexy, investigators have developed mice that lack the gene related to orexin production. When these mice become active, such as at feeding time, they collapse into cataplexy, supporting the idea that an orexin system contributes to maintaining waking behavior (Rosenberg et al., 2021).

Figure 3-21 explains inheritance patterns for genetic disorders.

Section 3-3 investigates knockout technology and other genetic engineering techniques.

# Sleep-Related Movement Disorders

People can display a variety of *sleep-related movement disorders,* including *bruxism* (teeth clenching or grinding), arm or leg flailing, periodic leg movements, periodic leg cramps, and restless legs. People may also display sudden convulsive movements called

---

## ◉ RESEARCH FOCUS 13-4

### Orexin

In 1998, a research group identified two neuropeptides in the hypothalamus that appeared to be new neurotransmitter substances (Azeez et al., 2021). Because both neuropeptides were found in the hypothalamus and appeared structurally similar to the neuropeptide *secretin,* the group named them *hypocretins* (hypocretin-1 and hypocretin-2). At about the same time, a separate research group identified the same substances and found they induced eating when injected into the hypothalamus. This second group called these substances *orexins* (orexin-A and orexin-B), from the Greek word for "appetite."

Neurons that produce orexin are found in the lateral hypothalamus. Their axons have a wide distribution, innervating a number of brainstem and basal forebrain regions (see the figure). Multiple lines of evidence implicate orexins as having a role in sleep: damage to the posterior hypothalamus produces a transitory coma; orexin axons innervate the serotonergic and cholinergic nuclei of the brainstem that produce waking EEGs; and dogs that display catalepsy have featured a loss of orexin neurons (Tisdale et al., 2021).

Because the activity of the orexin systems is associated with arousal, orexins are proposed to be "waking" neurotransmitters and to contribute to cognitive function, sensory processes, and motivation. Because orexins are also associated with eating, they are proposed to play a role in reward, addiction, and metabolic disease as well. The activity of the orexin system may be timed by circadian pacemakers (de Lecea, 2021).

Orexins are associated with a variety of sleep disorders. Insomnia and hypersomnia, for example, may be related to decreased and increased activity

Projections from orexin-producing neurons influence the hypothalamus and acetylcholine and serotonin pathways. They play a role in various activities related to arousal/wakefulness, appetite, and reward.

of orexins, respectively. The association between insomnia and eating characteristic of sleep-related eating disorders may reflect the shared orexin function in controlling waking and eating. The loss of orexin neurons is associated with catalepsy in certain genetic lines of dogs and with genetic models of catalepsy in mice. It is also likely that loss of orexin neurons is related to R-sleep behavioral disorder.

*hypnic jerks*, which can involve the whole body or body parts such as the face. These movements can hamper sleep onset, induce waking, and impair the sleep of bed partners.

Clinical Focus 5-4 describes the treatment of Parkinson patients with L-Dopa.

*Restless legs syndrome* (RLS) is a movement disorder in which people experience unpleasant sensations in the legs, described as creeping, crawling, tingling, pulling, or painful, often accompanied by periodic leg movements. One or both legs may be affected, and sometimes the arms may also be affected. RLS affects from 2% to 5% of the population, and is more common in women than in men. In mild cases, massage, exercise, stretching, and hot baths may be helpful. For more severe cases, patients can restrict their intake of caffeine and take benzodiazepines to help them get to sleep. L-Dopa, a drug used to treat Parkinson disease, and alpha$_2$-delta ligands, which enhance the function of calcium channels, are other pharmaceutical treatments. RLS has been associated with poor iron uptake, especially in the substantia nigra, and some people have been helped by iron supplements. (See Silber et al., 2021, for a summary of RLS treatments.)

## 13-6 Review

Before you continue, check your understanding. Answers to Self-Test appear at the back of the book.

1. Sleep disorders include _____, in which a person has difficulty falling asleep at night, and _____, in which a person falls asleep involuntarily in the daytime.

2. Treating insomnia with sleeping pills, usually sedative-hypnotics, may cause _____, in which progressively higher doses must be taken to achieve sleep.

3. Parasomnias include disorders related to _____ and _____.

4. People who act out their dreams, a condition termed _____, may have damage to the _____ nucleus.

5. Explain the role that orexin cells play in maintaining activity during waking.

6. It is notoriously difficult to obtain an accurate count of how many people have a given sleep disorder. Based on your understanding of sleep disorders, why is this so?

### Learning Objective

- Explain what the study of sleep and waking states can tell us about consciousness.

## 13-7

# What Does Sleep Tell Us about the Brain?

Sleep gives us remarkable insights into the organization of the brain. The two-process theory, described in the opening section, defines sleep as consisting of Process S, a sleep–wake process that produces the various aspects of sleep, and Process C, a circadian process that generates sleep's timing. Both processes are controlled by a large number of interacting brain regions.

As described throughout this chapter, our sleep–wake cycle is controlled by circadian processes whose timing is affected by the rhythm of day and night. What we colloquially refer to as waking comprises at least three states, each associated with a different neurotransmitter system. First, alert consciousness without accompanying movement is associated with cholinergic system activity. Second, consciousness with movement is associated with additional serotonergic system activity. Third, the peptide orexin plays a role in maintaining waking activity in response to circadian influences.

Similarly, sleep consists of N-sleep and R-sleep phases. N-sleep entails three stages, indicated by characteristic features on an EEG (see Figure 13-12A). R-sleep periods consist of at least two stages, one in which small twitching movements and REMs occur and intervening periods in which twitching and REMs are absent.

R-sleep neurobehavioral events can also occur relatively independently. Sleepers may awake to find themselves in the midst of sleep paralysis, during which they experience the hallucinations and fear that are common in dreams. People who are awake may fall into a state of cataplexy: they are conscious of being awake during the atonia and visual and emotional features of dreams. In both of these conditions, neural centers in the brainstem produce loss of muscle tone in the absence of a sleep state.

Sleep researcher J. Allan Hobson (2002) reported his peculiar symptoms after he experienced a brainstem stroke. For the first 10 days after the stroke, he had complete insomnia, experiencing neither N-sleep nor R-sleep. Whenever he closed his eyes, however, he did have visual hallucinations that had a dreamlike quality. This experience suggested that eye closure is sufficient to produce the visual components of R-sleep but with neither loss of consciousness nor atonia. Hobson eventually recovered typical sleeping patterns, and the hallucinations stopped.

Beyond teaching us that the neural basis of sleep is complex, the study of sleep states and dreaming may help explain some psychiatric and drug-induced conditions. Disruption of circadian rhythms can result in many unhealthy habits and metabolic disease. Outside the context of sleep, the visual and auditory hallucinations associated with dreams are among the symptoms of schizophrenia. Are these hallucinations actually dream events that occur unexpectedly during waking? Many people who take hallucinogenic drugs, such as LSD, report experiencing visual hallucinations. Does the drug initiate visual features of dreams? People who have panic attacks suffer from very real fright that has no obvious cause. Are they experiencing the fear attacks that commonly occur during sleep paralysis and cataplexy related to R-sleep?

The study of sleep tells us that a remarkable number of variations of sleep–wake states exist. René Descartes conceived his idea of a mind through a lucid dream, one in which a person has some consciousness and can report on, or even direct, the events of a dream. Descartes dreamed that he was interpreting the dream as it occurred. Later, when awake, he reasoned that if he could think and analyze a dream while asleep, his mind must function during both waking and sleeping. He proposed that the mind must therefore be independent of the body that undergoes sleeping and waking transitions, an idea taken up by Endelman in his two-system theory of consciousness, described in Section 13-3. Some states are associated with what we usually term waking and sleeping, and these variations can mix together in unusual ways to produce a range of odd conditions. Clearly, there is far more to sleeping and waking than just sleeping and waking.

Section 1-2 recounts Descartes's search for the seat of the mind.

# Summary

### 13-1 A Clock for All Seasons
Biorhythms are cyclical behavior patterns of varying length displayed by animals, plants, and even single-celled organisms. Biorhythms displayed by mammals include, among others, circadian (daily) rhythms and circannual (yearly) rhythms. In the absence of environmental cues, circadian rhythms are free-running, lasting a little more or a little less than their usual period of about 24 hours, depending on the individual organism or the environmental conditions. Cues called Zeitgebers reset biological clocks to a 24-hour rhythm. Circadian rhythms allow us to synchronize our behavior with our body's metabolic processes—so that we are hungry at optimal times. Environmental intrusions into our natural circadian rhythm, from artificial lighting to jet lag, contribute to metabolic syndrome. Biological clocks produce epigenetic effects: they regulate gene expression in every cell in the body.

### 13-2 The Suprachiasmatic Biological Clock
A biological clock is a neural structure responsible for producing rhythmic behavior. Our master biological clock is the suprachiasmatic nucleus (SCN). The SCN is responsible for circadian rhythms; it has its own free-running rhythm with a period of a little more than 24 hours. Stimuli from the environment, especially sunrise and sunset, as well as meals or exercise, entrain the free-running rhythm and keep its period near 24 hours. Across human populations, and within other animal species, individuals show variation in their circadian activities; these distinctive patterns are referred to as chronotypes.

SCN neurons are active in the daytime and inactive at night. These neurons retain their rhythmicity when disconnected from other brain structures, when removed from the brain and cultured in a dish, and after culture in a dish for many generations. When reimplanted in a brain without an SCN, they restore the animal's circadian rhythms. Aspects of neuronal circadian rhythms, including their period, are under genetic and epigenetic control.

### 13-3 Sleep Stages and Dreaming
Sleep events are measured by recording the brain's activity to produce an electroencephalogram (EEG), muscular activity to produce an

electromyogram (EMG), and eye movements to produce an electrooculogram (EOG).

A typical night's sleep, as indicated by physiological measures, consists of stages that take place in cycles over the course of the night. During R-sleep (the "R" stands for rapid eye movement [REM] sleep), the EEG displays a waking pattern, and the sleeper displays rapid eye movements. Sleep stages in which the EEG has a slower rhythm are called N-sleep (the "N" stands for non-REM [NREM] sleep) stages. Intervals of N-sleep and R-sleep alternate four or five times each night. The duration of N-sleep periods is longer earlier in sleep, whereas the duration of R-sleep periods is longer in the later part of sleep. These intervals also vary with age. A sleeper in N-sleep has muscle tone, may toss and turn, and has dreams that are not especially vivid. A sleeper in R-sleep has vivid dreams in real time but has no muscle tone and so is paralyzed. Dream duration coincides with the duration of the R-period.

The activation–synthesis hypothesis proposes that dreams are not meaningful but are merely a by-product of the brain's state of excitation during R-sleep. The coping hypothesis suggests that dreaming evolved as a mechanism to deal with challenges and fears posed by life.

## 13-4 What Does Sleep Accomplish?

Several theories of sleep have been advanced, but the main proposition is that sleep is a biological adaptation that conserves energy. Sleep is suggested to serve as a restorative process that fixes wear and tear in the brain and body, including synapses, and also organizes and stores memories.

## 13-5 The Neural Bases of Sleep

Separate neural regions are responsible for N-sleep and R-sleep. The reticular activating system (RAS), located in the central brainstem, is responsible for N-sleep. If the RAS is stimulated, a sleeper awakes; if it is damaged, a person may enter a coma. The peribrachial area and the medial pontine reticular formation in the brainstem are responsible for R-sleep. If these areas are damaged, R-sleep may no longer occur. Pathways projecting from these areas to the cortex produce the cortical activation of R-sleep, and those projecting to the brainstem produce the muscular paralysis of R-sleep.

## 13-6 Disorders of Sleep

Disorders of sleep include insomnia, hypersomnia, breathing disorders, parasomnias, sleep-related movement disorders, and circadian-rhythm disorders. Sleep disorders are symptoms of many other conditions, including anxiety and depression, schizophrenia, dementia, and brain trauma and injury. They can be treated with stimulants to enhance waking and sleeping pills to initiate sleep. Sleep hygiene and cognitive therapy are the most effective nonpharmacological treatments.

## 13-7 What Does Sleep Tell Us about the Brain?

Sleep research provides insights into brain function by revealing many kinds of waking and sleeping. Just as the events of wakefulness intrude into sleep, so the events of sleep can intrude into wakefulness. The study of sleep also reveals how different interacting neural structures are responsible for the sleep timing provided by circadian rhythms and the orderly procession of NREM and REM sleep.

# Key Terms

alpha rhythm, p. 461

atonia, p. 462

basic rest–activity cycle (BRAC), p. 468

beta rhythm, p. 461

biological clock, p. 446

biorhythm, p. 446

cataplexy, p. 478

chronotype, p. 458

circadian rhythm, p. 446

coma, p. 473

delta rhythm, p. 462

dimer, p. 455

diurnal animal, p. 446

entrain, p. 451

free-running rhythm, p. 449

hypersomnia, p. 476

insomnia, p. 475

jet lag, p. 453

light pollution, p. 451

medial pontine reticular formation (MPRF), p. 474

melatonin, p. 455

metabolic syndrome, p. 446

microsleep, p. 469

non-REM sleep (N-sleep), p. 461

parasomnia, p. 477

peribrachial area, p. 474

period, p. 446

place cell, p. 469

polysomnography (PSG), p. 460

REM sleep (R-sleep), p. 461

reticular activating system (RAS), p. 473

sleep apnea, p. 476

sleep paralysis, p. 478

sleeping beauty syndrome, p. 476

sleepwalking, p. 477

theta wave, p. 461

Zeitgeber, p. 451

# Selected Resources from  Achieve

**Neuroscience in Action:** The Neuroscience of Sleep

**Concept Practice:** Stages of Sleep

**Videos**

Sleep: Why We Sleep

Sleep and the Immune System

The Health Impact of Taking a Nap

**LearningCurve**

**Practice Quiz**

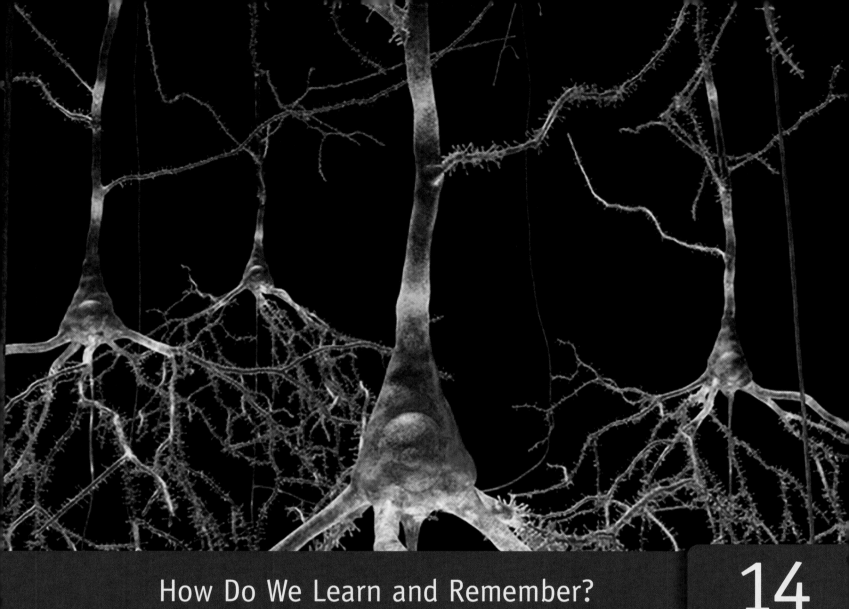

Russell Kightley/Science Source

# How Do We Learn and Remember?

# 14

## ◎ CLINICAL FOCUS 14-1

# Remediating Dyslexia

**Dyslexia**, impairment in learning to read and write, may be the most common learning disability. Children with dyslexia (a term derived from Greek words suggesting "bad" and "reading") have difficulties in reading, writing, spelling, and phonological processing, which is the discrimination of *phonemes* (units of sound in speech) in language. These learning difficulties are not accounted for by mental age, sight defects, or insufficient schooling. Estimates of the prevalence of dyslexia in the United States range from 5% to 17%, making it a common problem.

Dyslexia is not a single disorder, but rather varies with language orthography — that is, the set of conventions, including spelling norms, for a written language. Some languages (especially English) are considered to have deep orthography because of the inherent difficulty in mapping sounds (phonemes) to the written words (graphemes). The phoneme/grapheme match in other languages (such as Italian, Dutch, German, and Swedish) is more obvious (i.e., words are generally spelled the way they sound); thus, these languages have shallow orthographies. In people with dyslexia, persistently slow word recognition is evident in all orthographies, whereas inaccurate mapping of phonemes to graphemes is observed only in deep orthographies. Variations in behavioral manifestations across languages suggest different cognitive dysfunctions are associated with different forms of dyslexia (Richlan, 2020).

For many years, the general consensus was that dyslexia is chiefly a phonological deficit, which led researchers to focus on auditory processing and the auditory system, especially the thalamus and auditory cortex. Over the past decade, however, a shift toward viewing developmental disorders as multidimensional has led to growing interest in the role of extended cortical networks and cortical connectivity (see, for example, Kronbichler & Kronbichler, 2018).

Brain-imaging studies have shown that, relative to the brains of healthy participants, activity in the brains of people with dyslexia is reduced in the left temporoparietal, occipitotemporal, and inferior frontal cortex, as illustrated in the figure (see the review by Martin et al., 2016). The reduced temporoparietal activity is associated with deficits in auditory processing. The reduced occipitotemporal activity occurs largely in the visual word-form area (VWFA), which is believed to be responsible for rapid word recognition. The reduced inferior frontal activity occurs in the inferior frontal gyrus, a large region that includes the anterior speech zone known as Broca's area.

As shown in the illustration, the brain activity patterns differ in dyslexia associated with deep versus shallow orthographies, which reflects the different behavioral manifestations. In a meta-review of studies addressing gray matter volume in people with dyslexia, Fabio Richlan (2020) concluded that there is reduced gray matter volume in the left superior temporal sulcus and right superior temporal gyrus across orthographies, which might exist even before the onset of formal reading instruction. The right temporal abnormality was not anticipated, given that language is largely controlled in the left hemisphere, and a right hemisphere abnormality has not been seen in all studies. The left temporal abnormality was expected and is consistent with postmortem studies done in the 1980s (e.g., Galaburda et al., 1985). Recent fMRI studies have also shown reduced functional connectivity between the medial geniculate nucleus and auditory cortex in individuals with dyslexia (Tsechentscher et al., 2019).

The reduced activity in these brain regions results in inconsistent neural processing of sounds, which is hypothesized to reflect the large variability in auditory processing common in children with dyslexia (Tallal, 2012). Children who perform most poorly on auditory discrimination tasks tend to develop poor reading skills. A variety of training programs have been devised to stimulate plasticity in the reading-related brain systems, and many have proved effective in improving attention, listening, and reading skills. These programs range from musical training and neuroplasticity-based auditory training designed to improve dynamic auditory processing, to the use of speech that has been computer modified to enhance the various aspects of the rapidly changing acoustic components of ongoing speech. For example, Jane Hornickel and colleagues (2012) used assistive listening devices with their study participants who had dyslexia for a year to enhance the subjects' acoustic clarity and attention. Their program reduced the variability of neurophysiological responses to sound — a result that has been linked to improved reading and phonological awareness.

(A)    (B)

Surface renderings illustrate under-activation (red) and over-activation (green) in deep orthographies **(A)** and under-activation (blue) and over-activation (yellow) in shallow orthographies **(B)**. Research from Martin et al. (2016).

---

**Principle 10:** Neuroplasticity is the hallmark of nervous system functioning.

The brain is plastic. It changes throughout life, allowing us to modify our behavior, to adapt and learn, and to remember. If we reflect on our own lives, we can easily compile a list of experiences that must change the brain: profound changes during development, acquisition of culture, learning a new language or a new game, and the ability to cope with the neurodegeneration of aging and to accommodate neurological injury or disease at any age.

Learning is common to all these experiences. Understanding how the brain supports learning is fundamental in neuroscience. At the level of the neuron, synapses change with experience — learning new information, for example. But how are learning-related changes organized in the brain to support memory? One research strategy is to

---

**dyslexia** Impairment in learning to read and write; probably the most common learning disability.

investigate neuronal changes that support the learning of specific types of information by describing changes in cells exposed to specific sensory experiences. Another strategy is to examine neural changes related to a range of experiences, including learning and memory, electrical brain stimulation, chemical influences, and brain injury. This chapter reviews both types of studies. First, however, we establish what we mean by learning and memory and how both are tested.

# Connecting Learning and Memory

**Learning** is a relatively permanent change in an organism's behavior as a result of experience that leads to the acquisition of new understanding, behaviors, knowledge, attitudes, and skills. **Memory** is the ability to recall or recognize previous experience. Memory thus implies a mental representation of a previous experience. This representation is thought to be the product of a physical trace, or *engram*, of the memory in the brain (for a history of the term *engram*, see Josselyn et al., 2017). Neuroscientists have shown that the engram results from physical changes in the brain, both at synapses and in the nucleus of neurons.

At the macro level, we infer what we know about learning and memory formation from behavioral changes, rather than by observing the brain directly. Studying learning and memory therefore requires behavioral measures that can help us evaluate how these changes come about. We begin here by reviewing how learning and memory researchers study animals in the laboratory. The results suggest, in a general way, how the brain organizes its learning and memory systems.

## Studying Learning and Memory in the Laboratory

A challenge for behavioral scientists when studying memory in laboratory animals (or people) is to get the subjects or participants to reveal what they remember. For humans, investigators tend to use either paper-and-pencil or computer-based tests. But because nonhuman laboratory animals do not speak or write, investigators must devise other ways for these subjects to show their knowledge. Different nonhuman species "talk" to us in different ways, so the test choice must match each species' capabilities.

Mazes or swimming pools are typically used to study rats because rats live in tunnels and near water. Monkey studies take advantage of monkeys' sharp vision and avid curiosity by requiring them to look under objects for food or to watch television monitors. With birds, natural behaviors such as singing are used.

Two classic traditions for training animals to "talk" to investigators emerged a century ago. These diverse approaches are based on the work of Edward Thorndike (1898) in the United States and on experiments conducted by Ivan Pavlov in Russia beginning in the 1890s.

## Pavlovian Conditioning

Early in the twentieth century, Ivan Pavlov, a Russian physiologist, discovered that when a food reward accompanies some stimulus, such as a tone, dogs learn to associate the stimulus with the food. Later, whenever they hear the tone, they salivate even though no food is present. This type of learning has many names, including **Pavlovian conditioning**, *respondent conditioning,* and *classical conditioning,* and many studies document its characteristics.

A key feature of Pavlovian conditioning is that animals learn to associate two stimuli (such as the presentation of the tone and the food) and to communicate to us that they have learned it by giving the same response (salivation) to both stimuli. Pet owners know that to a cat or dog, the sound of a can being opened is a clear stimulus for food.

---

**Learning Objectives**

- Describe how learning is studied in the laboratory.
- Describe two categories of memory.
- Identify how explicit, implicit, and emotional memory are different.
- Explain the unique role of episodic memory.

---

Figure 7-4 describes swimming pool tests for rats; Experiment 15-1, monkeys' perceptual threshold; and Clinical Focus 15-3, the tools used to assess the effects of brain injuries on humans' cognitive performance.

---

**learning** Relatively permanent change in an organism's behavior as a result of experience, leading to the acquisition of new understanding, behaviors, knowledge, attitudes, and skills.

**memory** Ability to recall or recognize previous experience.

**Pavlovian conditioning** Learning achieved when a neutral stimulus (such as a tone) comes to elicit a response after its repeated pairing with some event (such as delivery of food); also called *classical conditioning* or *respondent conditioning.*

**1** Headgear is arranged for eyeblink conditioning.

Electrodes

**2** Puff of air to eye causes eye to blink.

Air jet tube

Audio speaker

**3** After pairing air puff with tone, tone alone comes to elicit a blink.

**FIGURE 14-1 Eyeblink Conditioning**
Neural circuits in the cerebellum mediate this form of stimulus–response learning.

In the cerebellum, the flocculus controls eye movements; see Figure 11-15.

**eyeblink conditioning** Experimental technique in which subjects learn to pair a formerly neutral stimulus with a defensive blinking response.

**conditioned stimulus (CS)** In Pavlovian conditioning, an originally neutral stimulus that, after association with an unconditioned stimulus (UCS), triggers a conditioned response (CR).

**unconditioned stimulus (UCS)** A stimulus that naturally and automatically (unconditionally) triggers an unconditioned response (UCR).

**unconditioned response (UCR)** Unlearned, naturally occurring response to an unconditioned stimulus (UCS), such as salivation when food is in the mouth.

**conditioned response (CR)** In Pavlovian conditioning, the learned response to a formerly neutral conditioned stimulus (CS).

**fear conditioning** Conditioned emotional response between a neutral stimulus and an unpleasant event, such as a shock, that results in a learned association.

Two forms of Pavlovian conditioning are common in experiments today: eyeblink conditioning and fear conditioning. Each is associated with neural circuits in discrete brain regions; thus both are especially useful.

**Eyeblink conditioning** has been used to study Pavlovian learning in rabbits and people (**Figure 14-1**). In these studies, a tone (or some other stimulus) is associated with a painless puff of air to the participant's eye. The tone is the **conditioned stimulus (CS)** that comes to elicit a blink produced initially by the air puff. The air puff is the **unconditioned stimulus (UCS)** because blinking is the normal reaction—the **unconditioned response (UCR)**—to a puff of air. The participant communicates that it has learned that the signal stimulus predicts the puff by blinking in response to the signal (the CS) alone—a **conditioned response (CR)**. The circuits in the cerebellum that mediate such Pavlovian learning are designed to pair motor responses with environmental events. Eyeblink conditioning experiments take advantage of this biological predisposition.

In **fear conditioning**, an unpleasant but harmless stimulus is used to elicit an emotional response: fear. A rat or other animal is placed in a box. A mild but unpleasant electric current, approximating a spark of static electricity, can be passed through the grid floor. As shown in **Experiment 14-1**, a tone (the CS) is presented just before a brief, unexpected mild electric shock. When the tone is presented later without the shock, the animal acts afraid, becoming motionless and perhaps urinating in anticipation of the shock. A novel stimulus, perhaps a light, presented in the same environment has little effect. Thus, the animal communicates that it has learned the association between the tone and the shock.

Because the CR in this experiment is emotional, and because circuits of the amygdala rather than the cerebellum mediate fear conditioning, we conclude that the amygdala is involved in this CR. Although both eyeblink and fear conditioning are Pavlovian conditioning processes, different brain areas mediate the learning.

## Operant Conditioning

Edward Thorndike (1898), working in the United States, began a second tradition for studying learning and memory. Thorndike was interested in how animals solve problems. In one series of experiments, he placed a cat in a box with a plate of fish outside it (**Figure 14-2**). The only way for the hungry cat to get to the fish was to figure out how to get out of the box.

The solution was to press on a lever to activate a system of pulleys that opened the box door. The cat gradually learned that its actions had consequences: on the initial trial, the cat touched the releasing mechanism only by chance as it restlessly paced inside the box. The cat apparently learned that something it had done opened the door, and it tended to repeat its behaviors from just before the door opened. After a few trials, the cat took just seconds to get the door open to devour the fish.

Later studies by B. F. Skinner (e.g., 1938) used a similar strategy of *reinforcement* to train rats to press bars or pigeons to peck keys to obtain food. Just as Thorndike's cats

····▷ **EXPERIMENT 14-1**

Question: Does an animal learn the association between emotional experience and environmental stimuli?

**Procedure and Results**

Rat receives mild electrical shock in combination with tone.

Tone plus shock

Later →

If a light is presented alone later, rat ignores it.

Light only — no tone

Later →

Rat freezes in fear when tone alone sounds.

Tone only

*Conclusion:* The rat has learned an association between the tone and the shock, which produces a fear response. Circuits that include the amygdala take part in this learning process.

learned to escape his puzzle boxes, many animals learn to press the bar or peck the key simply if they are placed in the apparatus and allowed to discover the response that obtains the reward. Thorndike called this type of learning *instrumental conditioning*, but it is more commonly known as **operant conditioning**. The animal demonstrates that it has learned the association between its actions and the consequences by performing the task more frequently and sometimes more quickly.

The variety of operant associations is staggering: we learn constantly to associate our behavior with its consequences. It is no surprise, then, that operant learning is not localized to any particular brain circuit. Instead, the necessary circuits vary with the task requirements. For example, olfactory tasks involve olfactory-related structures such as the orbitofrontal cortex and amygdala, spatial tasks recruit the hippocampus, and motor tasks require the basal ganglia.

The cat is placed in the box with the food reward outside.

The hungry cat eventually learns that pressing on the lever will result in getting out of the box and getting to the food.

Pulley system

Lever

Food reward

**FIGURE 14-2 Thorndike's Puzzle Box**

## Two Categories of Memory

Humans present a distinct challenge to researchers who are studying memory because much of our learning is verbal. Psychologists have studied human memory since the mid-1800s, but only in the past few decades have cognitive psychologists developed sophisticated measures of learning and memory for neuropsychological investigations. Two such measures help distinguish between two categories of memory in humans.

In one kind of task, one group of participants reads a list of words, such as *spring, winter, car,* and *boat*. Another group reads a list consisting of the words *trip, tumble, run,* and *sun*. All the participants are then asked to define a series of words. One of these words is *fall*.

The word *fall* has multiple meanings, including the season and a tumble. People who have just read the word list containing names of seasons are likely to give the meaning as *autumn*; those who have read the second list, containing action words, typically give the meaning as *tumble*. Some form of unconscious (and unintentional) learning takes place as the participants read the word lists. This unconscious learning, known as **priming**, occurs when exposure to a stimulus influences a response to a later stimulus.

This task measures **implicit memory**; that is, participants demonstrate knowledge—a skill, conditioned response, or recall of events on prompting that is neither intentional nor premeditated. People with **amnesia**, a partial or total loss of memory, perform at normal levels on tests of implicit memory. A person with amnesia has no recollection of having read the word list, yet acts as though some neural circuit has been influenced by it. In amnesia, a *dissociation*—a disconnect—occurs between the memory of the unconscious (or implicit) learning and **explicit memory**, conscious recollections of training, such as the name of the person in charge of the training or the layout of the training room. People without amnesia can retrieve an explicit memory and indicate that they know the retrieved item is correct.

This implicit–explicit distinction is not restricted to verbal learning; it holds for visual learning and motor learning as well. For example, when people are shown the leftmost panel of the Gollin figure test in **Figure 14-3** and asked what it shows, they are

**operant conditioning** Learning procedure in which the consequences (such as obtaining a reward) of a particular behavior (such as pressing a bar) increase or decrease the probability of the behavior occurring again; also called *instrumental conditioning*.

**priming** Using a stimulus to sensitize the nervous system to a later presentation of the same or a similar stimulus.

**implicit memory** Unconscious memory: subjects can demonstrate knowledge, such as a skill, conditioned response, or recall of events on prompting that is not intentional.

**amnesia** Partial or total loss of memory.

**explicit memory** Conscious memory: subjects can retrieve an item and indicate that they know the retrieved item is the correct one.

**FIGURE 14-3 Gollin Figure Test** Participants are shown a series of drawings in sequence, from least to most clear, and asked to identify the image. Most people must see several panels before they can identify the image. On a retention test some time later, however, participants identify the image sooner than they did on the first test, indicating some form of memory for the image. Participants with amnesia also show improvement on this test, even though they do not recall having taken it.

**FIGURE 14-4 Pursuit-Rotor Task** The participant must keep the stylus in contact with a metal disc moving in a circular pattern on a turntable while also rotating in a circular pattern. Although the task is difficult, most people show significant improvement after brief training. Given a second test at some later time, both control participants and participants with amnesia show task retention, but typically those with amnesia do not recall having learned it before.

**TABLE 14-1 Differentiating Two Memory Categories**

| Terms that describe conscious memory | Terms that describe unconscious memory |
|---|---|
| Explicit | Implicit |
| Declarative | Nondeclarative |
| Fact | Skill |
| Memory | Habit |
| Knowing that | Knowing how |
| Locale | Taxon |
| Conscious recollection | Skills |
| Elaboration | Integration |
| Memory with record | Memory without record |
| Autobiographical | Perceptual |
| Representational | Dispositional |
| Episodic | Procedural |
| Semantic | Nonassociative |
| Working | Reference |

*Note:* This paired list of terms differentiates conscious from unconscious forms of memory. It will help you relate other memory discussions to the one in this book, which favors the explicit–implicit distinction.

**declarative memory** Ability to recount what one knows, to detail the time, place, and circumstances of events; often lost in amnesia.

**procedural memory** Ability to recall a movement sequence or how to perform some act or behavior.

**learning set** Rules of the game; implicit understanding of how a problem can be solved with a rule that can be applied in many different situations.

unlikely to identify an image. They are then presented with a succession of more nearly complete sketches until they can identify the picture. When control participants and participants with amnesia are later shown the same sketch, both groups identify the figure sooner than they could the first time. Even though the participants with amnesia may not recall having seen the sketches before, they behave as though they have.

To measure implicit motor skills learning, a person initially learns a skill, such as the pursuit rotor task shown in **Figure 14-4**. In this task, a small metal disc moves in a circular pattern on a turntable, which is also moving. The task is to hold a stylus on the small disc as it spins. This task is not as easy as it looks, especially when the turntable is moving quickly. Nonetheless, with an hour's practice, most people become reasonably proficient. Presented with the same task a week later, both controls and participants with amnesia take less time to perform it successfully. Here, too, those persons with amnesia fail to recall having performed the task before.

The distinction between tests of implicit memory and explicit memory is consistently observed in research studies, so it must offer a key to how the brain stores information. Some theorists make subtle distinctions between the implicit–explicit dichotomy we use and other terminologies for categorizing unconscious and conscious memory. For example, many researchers prefer to distinguish between **declarative memory**, the specific contents of specific experiences that can be verbally recalled (times, places, or circumstances), and **procedural memory**, the ability to perform a task. As applied to humans, there is little practical difference between these classifications.

**Table 14-1** lists commonly used dichotomies, with the general distinction being that one memory category requires recalling specific information, whereas the other refers to knowledge of which we are not consciously aware. We can include Pavlovian conditioning and Thorndike's and Skinner's operant learning in this analysis, too: all are forms of implicit learning.

Like humans, nonspeaking animals can display explicit memory. One of your authors owned a cat that loved to play with a little ball. One day, as the cat watched, the ball was temporarily put on a high shelf to keep it away from an inquisitive toddler. For weeks afterward, the cat sat and stared at the shelf where the ball had been placed, even though the ball was not visible — an example of explicit memory.

Animals also display explicit memory when they learn psychological tasks. Rats can be trained to find highly palatable food in a new location in a large compound each day. The task is to go to the most recent location. This piece of information is explicit and demonstrably can be forgotten. Suppose a rat trained to find food in a particular location in a small arena is given several trials with the food at a new location and then retested an hour, a day, 3 days, or a week later. The rat has no difficulty with an hour's delay or perhaps even a day's delay. Some rats are flawless at 3 days, but most have forgotten the location by the time a week has elapsed. Instead, they wander around looking for the food. This behavior illustrates their implicit memory of the **learning set**, the rules of the game — an implicit understanding of how a problem can be solved with a rule that can be applied in many situations — namely, that a desired food can be found with a certain search strategy.

# What Makes Explicit and Implicit Memory Different?

One reason explicit and implicit memories differ is that the set of neural structures that houses each type of memory is different. Another reason they differ is that the brain processes explicit and implicit information differently.

## Encoding and Processing Memories

Before information is processed, it must be changed into a form that can be stored in the brain, a process referred to as *encoding*. Many types of encoding may occur.

For example, visual encoding is the storage of visual sensory information, such as the position of an object in a room. *Semantic encoding* is the storage of input that has a particular meaning and becomes part of one's knowledge of the world, such as knowing that Tokyo is in Japan. The process of encoding is not yet well understood, but it appears to include modification of synapses, creation of new synapses, changes in gene expression, and modification of, or creation of, proteins.

Implicit information is encoded in much the same way it is perceived: this type of processing can be described as data driven or bottom up. The idea is that information enters the brain through sensory receptors and then is processed in a series of subcortical and cortical regions. For instance, visual information about an object moves from the photoreceptors (the bottom) to the thalamus, then to the occipital cortex, and finally through the ventral stream to the temporal lobe (the top), where the object is recognized.

Explicit memory, in contrast, depends on conceptually driven, or top-down, processing: the person reorganizes the data. If you were searching for a particular object—say, your keys—you would ignore other objects. This process is top down because circuits in the temporal lobe (the top) form an image (keys) that influences how incoming visual information (the bottom) is processed and, in turn, greatly influences information recall later.

Because people have a relatively passive role in encoding implicit memory, they have difficulty recalling the memory spontaneously but will recall it more easily with priming by the original stimulus or some feature of it. In contrast, because people play an active role in processing information explicitly, internal cues (such as related memories) used in processing can also be used to initiate spontaneous recall.

Findings from studies of eyewitness testimony demonstrate the active nature of explicit memory recall—as well as its fallibility (e.g., Loftus, 1997). In a typical experiment, participants view a video clip of an accident in which a car collides with another car stopped at an intersection. One group is asked to estimate how fast the moving car was going when it "smashed" into the other car. A second group is asked how fast the car was going when it "bumped" into the other car.

Later questioning reveals that the memory of how fast the moving car was going is biased by the instruction: participants looking at "smashing" cars estimate faster speeds than do participants looking at "bumping" cars. The instruction actually causes the information to be processed differently. In both cases, participants were certain their memories were accurate.

Other experiments show that implicit memory also is fallible. For example, participants are read the following list of words: *sweet, chocolate, shoe, table, candy, horse, car, cake, coffee, wall, book, cookie, hat*. After a few minutes' delay, they hear a second list of words that includes some from the first list and some that are new. Participants are asked to identify which words were included in the first list and to indicate how certain they are of the identification. This task tests implicit memory because the participant is unaware which of the original words will be included in the second list—their memory has to be prompted by the administrator.

One of the words in the second list is *sugar*. Most participants are certain that *sugar* was in the first list. Although other sweet things were included, *sugar* was not. This demonstration is intriguing because it shows how easily we can form false memories and defend their veracity with certainty.

Although we can distinguish memories generally as implicit or explicit, the brain does not process all implicit or all explicit memories in the same way. Memories can be divided according to categories that differ from those listed in Table 14-1. For instance, we can make a distinction between memories for different types of sensory information.

Different neural areas process visual and auditory information, so it is reasonable to assume that auditory memories are encoded in brain regions different from the regions in which visual memories are encoded. We can also make a distinction between information stored in *short-term memory* and information held in *long-term memory*, as illustrated in **Figure 14-5**. In short-term memory (sometimes referred to as *working*

**FIGURE 14-5 Multiple Memory Systems** The broadest classification of memory distinguishes transient *short-term memory* for recent sensory, motor, or cognitive information from relatively permanent *long-term memory*. Conscious, long-term memories may be *explicit*—events and facts that you can spontaneously recall—and either *episodic*, for personal experiences (your first day at school), or *semantic*, for facts (Kenya is in Africa). *Implicit*, nonconscious memories (say, riding a bicycle) consist of learned skills, conditioned responses, and unintentional storage of ongoing experiences. *Emotional memory* for the affective properties of stimuli or events (your first kiss) is vivid and has characteristics of implicit and explicit memories.

| Short-term memory |
| --- |
| Sensory, motor, cognitive |

| Long-term memory |
| --- |

| Explicit (conscious) | | Implicit (unconscious) | Emotional (conscious and unconscious) |
| --- | --- | --- | --- |
| Episodic: Personal Autobiographical | Semantic: Facts Knowledge | Skills Habits Priming Conditioning | Attraction Avoidance Fear |

*memory* or *temporal memory*), information—such as the final score of a playoff game or the combination of your friend's bike lock—is held in memory only briefly, for a few minutes at most, and then discarded. In long-term memory, information—such as your own bike lock's combination—is held in memory indefinitely, perhaps for a lifetime. Long-term memory is more complex and includes different types of explicit memory as well as implicit memory and emotional memory.

The frontal lobes are central in short-term memory, whereas the temporal lobe is central in long-term storage of verbal information. The crucial point is that no single place in the nervous system can be identified as *the* location for memory or learning. Virtually the entire nervous system can be changed by experience, but different parts of an experience change different parts of the nervous system. One challenge for the experimenter is to devise ways of manipulating experiences to demonstrate changes in different parts of the brain.

## Storing Memories

Over the past two decades, hundreds of noninvasive imaging studies have looked for the engram of semantic memories, which include our knowledge about the world. Jeffrey Binder and his colleagues (2009) performed a meta-analysis of 120 functional magnetic resonance imaging (fMRI) semantic memory studies. They found a distinct network comprising seven different left-hemisphere regions, including regions of the parietal lobe, temporal lobe, prefrontal cortex, and posterior cingulate cortex (see **Figure 14-6**). Not all regions are active at once when a semantic memory is stored, but subregions are likely to be relatively specialized for specific object characteristics (such as color or shape) or types of knowledge (such as names or places).

**FIGURE 14-6 Semantic Memory System** The various components of the semantic memory system found in the left hemisphere are shown in red. Research from Binder et al. (2009).

The default network is described in the context of sexual identity and orientation in Section 12-5.

This extensive network is similar to the *default network*—that is, the network of regions that is active when participants are resting rather than engaged in specific cognitive tasks. Given the similarity in the semantic memory and default network, it appears that semantic processing constitutes a large component of the cognitive activity that occurs during passive states. In the resting state, the semantic system is operating on the internal stores of knowledge to "make sense" of all the new information. Binder and his colleagues (2009) note that these regions are more extensive than those described for nonhuman primates and may explain uniquely human capacities to use language productively, plan, solve problems, and create technological and cultural artifacts.

# What Is Special about Personal Memories?

One aspect of explicit memory unique to each of us is our personal, or *autobiographical*, memory. This **episodic memory** includes not only a record of events (episodes) that have taken place but also a record of our presence and role in those events. Our personal experiences form the basis of who we are and the rules by which we live. That is, we have memories not only for events but also for their context at a particular time in a particular place. By imbuing our experiences with meaning, we gain a concept of time and a sense of our personal role in a changing world.

Questions have long been asked about how and where autobiographical memories are stored in the brain. The current consensus is that the key regions involved in this process are the ventromedial prefrontal cortex (vmPFC) and hippocampus, and the pathways between them. Heidi Bonnici and Eleanor Maguire conducted a series of clever fMRI studies to test this assumption. In the initial fMRI study, Bonnici and her colleagues (2012) asked participants to recall three personal episodes that were 2 weeks old and three personal episodes that were 10 years old. The goal was to determine whether the patterns of brain activity could be used to predict which memory was being recalled by the participant. The results showed that, although the discriminability in the hippocampus was similar for the old and new memories, discriminability in

**episodic memory** Autobiographical memory for events pegged to specific place and time contexts.

the prefrontal cortex was much poorer for the new memories; this suggested that the memories were not yet strongly represented there.

In the second study, conducted 2 years later, the authors tested the same participants on the same memories, which were now 2 and 12 years old (Bonnici & Maguire, 2018). There was no change in the hippocampal results, but the discriminability in the prefrontal activity was now similar for the newer and older memories, suggesting that the memory representations were now equally strong for both. Thus, there was a change in the engram in the prefrontal cortex over the 2 years, but the hippocampus remained stable.

Further studies by the Maguire group (e.g., McCormick et al., 2020) have shown that both the hippocampus and vmPFC are critical for retrieval of personal memories. The researchers propose that during the consolidation process, the vmPFC works with the hippocampus to integrate new personal memories into existing schemata. Over time, the hippocampus reconstructs the memories stored in the vmPFC to make them more distinctive. The amount of time required for this consolidation to occur remains unknown, but is likely less than the 2-year period that separated the first and second studies performed by Maguire's team.

## Loss of Personal Memories

Imagine what would happen if you lost your personal memories. You would still recall events but would be unable to see your role in them. People with frontal lobe injuries sometimes exhibit such symptoms, as illustrated in a case described by Endel Tulving (2002).

K. C. suffered a serious traumatic brain injury in a motorcycle accident that produced multiple cortical and subcortical lesions. Remarkably, K. C.'s cognitive abilities were intact and indistinguishable from those of most typical healthy adults. He played chess and the organ—skills he had acquired prior to the accident—and his short-term memory was intact. He knew who he was and when his birthday was, the names of schools he had attended, and the location of his family's cottage. Recalling facts, figures, dates, and times posed no difficulty for K. C.

What K. C. could no longer do was to recall any personally experienced events. This episodic autobiographical amnesia covered his entire life from birth. He knew facts about himself but had no memory for events that included him personally. For example, K. C. could recall going to school and the knowledge he had gained there, but he could not describe an event that took place in school that specifically included him.

Hippocampal injury is also associated with poor episodic memory. Cornelia McCormick and colleagues (2018) compared autobiographical memory and brain activity in people with temporal lobe epilepsy (including unilateral hippocampal injury) and in controls. The people with epilepsy showed reduced hippocampal activity during episodic memory retrieval, which was associated with impaired episodic memory. Curiously, they also showed increased vmPFC activity during memory retrieval, presumably as a result of partial compensation for the hippocampal dysfunction.

## Superior Autobiographical Memory

Whereas some people exhibit poor autobiographical memory, a rare group displays *highly superior autobiographical memory* (*HSAM*) (LePort et al., 2012). These people have virtually complete recall for events in their lives, usually beginning around age 10, and can often describe any episode, including the day of the week and date that it occurred. They can even recall the weather that day, as well as social and public events. Brain imaging of persons who display HSAM shows increased gray matter in the temporal and parietal lobes and increased size in the fiber projection between the temporal and frontal lobes.

Lawrence Patihis and colleagues (2013) wondered if individuals with HSAM might also be immune to memory distortion, such as the false memories described earlier. When they studied this issue, however, the investigators found that these individuals are as likely as other participants to develop false memories. Whatever the source of their extraordinary autobiographical memory is, it does not prevent the sort of memory distortions that the rest of us experience. The source of HSAM has only just begun to be explored but does not appear to reflect superior cognitive functioning. And though individuals with HSAM show superior personal memories, they do not show any signs of elevated performance in terms of their memory of personal memories described by other people. In other words, HSAM appears to require an experience that is part of the individual's personal narrative (LePort et al., 2017).

## 14-1 Review

Before you continue, check your understanding. Answers to Self-Test appear at the back of the book.

1. An organism learns that some stimulus is paired with a reward. This is _____ conditioning.

2. After learning that consequences follow its behavior, an organism modifies its behavior. This is _____ conditioning.

3. Information that is unconsciously learned forms _____ memory, whereas specific factual information forms _____ memory.

4. _____ memory is autobiographical and unique to each person.

5. Where is memory stored in the brain?

## 14-2

# Dissociating Memory Circuits

Beginning in the 1920s and continuing until the early 1950s, American psychologist Karl Lashley searched in vain for the neural circuits underlying memories. Lashley's working hypothesis was that memories must be represented in the perceptual and motor circuitry used in problem solving. To find that circuitry, he investigated the ways laboratory rats and monkeys learn specific tasks to obtain food rewards. He believed that if he either removed bits of this circuitry or disconnected it from the rest of the brain, amnesia should result.

In fact, neither ablation procedure produced amnesia. Lashley found instead that the severity of memory disturbance was related to the *size* of the lesion rather than to its location. After searching for 30 years, Lashley concluded that he had failed to find the location of a memory trace, although he believed that he knew where it was *not* located (Lashley, 1960).

## Disrupting Explicit Memory

Neurosurgeon William Scoville discovered serendipitously what Lashley's studies had not predicted. Scoville was attempting to rid people of seizures by removing the abnormal brain tissue that caused them. In August 1953, he performed a bilateral medial temporal lobe removal on a young man, Henry Molaison (H. M.), whose severe epilepsy could not be controlled by medication. H. M.'s seizures originated in the medial temporal lobe region, so Scoville bilaterally removed much of the hippocampal formation, along with some of the amygdala and adjacent neocortical structures. The procedure left the more lateral temporal lobe tissue intact. As shown in **Figure 14-7**, the tissue removed specifically included the anterior part of the hippocampus, the amygdala, and adjacent cortex.

The behavioral symptoms Scoville noted after the surgery were completely unexpected. He invited Brenda Milner (Milner et al., 1968) to study H. M. Milner had been studying memory difficulties in patients who underwent unilateral temporal lobe removals for the treatment of epilepsy. She and her colleagues worked with H. M. for more than 50 years, making his the most studied case in neuroscience (see, for example, Corkin, 2002). H. M. died in 2008. (For an engaging history of Case H. M., see Dittrich, 2016.)

### Learning Objectives

- Describe the effects of disruptions to explicit memory.
- Describe the effects of disruptions to implicit memory.

**Principle 1:** Neuronal circuits are the functional units of the nervous system.

Brain lesions are an ablation technique—the first and simplest brain manipulation; see Section 7-1.

As you've seen throughout this book, initials are typically used in case studies to protect the identity of patients. Though he was identified only as H. M. in the literature printed during his lifetime, Henry Molaison's name was revealed after his death.

H. M.'s most remarkable symptom was severe amnesia: he was unable to recall anything that had happened since his surgery in 1953. H. M. retained an above-average IQ score (118 on the Wechsler Adult Intelligence Scale; 100 is average), and he performed at normal levels on perceptual tests. His recall of events from his childhood and school days was intact. Socially, H. M. was well mannered, and he engaged in sophisticated conversations. He had, however, no recall for recent events. H. M. lacked any explicit memory.

In one study by Suzanne Corkin (2002), H. M. was given a tray of hospital food, which he ate. A few minutes later, he was given another tray. He did not recall having eaten the first meal and proceeded to eat the second meal. A third tray was brought, but this time he ate only the dessert, explaining that he did not seem to be very hungry.

To understand the implications and severity of H. M.'s condition, one need only consider a few events in his postsurgical life. His father died, but H. M. continued to ask where his father was, only to experience anew the grief of learning that his father had passed away. (Eventually, H. M. stopped asking about his father, suggesting that some type of learning had taken place.)

Similarly, in the hospital, he typically asked the nurses, with many apologies, to tell him where he was and how he had come to be there. He remarked on one occasion, "Every day is alone in itself, whatever enjoyment I've had and whatever sorrow I've had." He perceived his surroundings but could not comprehend his situation because he did not remember what had gone before.

Formal tests of H. M.'s memory showed, as you would expect, no recall for specific information just presented. In contrast, his implicit memory performance was nearly intact. He performed at normal levels on tests such as the incomplete figure and pursuit rotor tasks, illustrated in Figures 14-3 and 14-4, respectively. While his implicit memory system must have been intact, the systems crucial to explicit memory were missing or dysfunctional. Yet H. M. recognized faces, including his own, and he recognized that he aged. Face recognition depends on the parahippocampal gyrus, which was partly intact on H. M.'s right side. Clinical Focus 14-2: Patient Boswell's Amnesia describes a case similar to H. M.'s.

## Disrupting Implicit Memory

Among the reasons Lashley's research did not find a syndrome like that shown by H. M., two stand out as particularly important. First, Lashley did not damage the medial temporal regions of his animal subjects. Second, he did not use tests of explicit memory, so his subjects would not have shown H. M.'s deficits. Rather, Lashley's tests were mostly measures of implicit memory, with which H. M. had no problems.

The case of J. K. illustrates that Lashley probably should have been looking in the basal ganglia for the deficits that his implicit memory tests revealed. The basal ganglia play a central role in motor control. Among the compelling examples of implicit memory is motor learning—such as that related to driving and playing musical instruments or online games.

J. K. was above average in intelligence and worked as a petroleum engineer for 45 years. In his mid-seventies, he began to show symptoms of Parkinson disease, in which the projections from the dopaminergic cells of the brainstem to the basal ganglia die. At about age 78, J. K.'s memory difficulties started.

Curiously, his memory disturbance was related to tasks J. K. had performed his whole life. On one occasion, he stood at his bedroom door, frustrated by his inability to recall how to turn on the lights. "I must be crazy," he remarked. "I've done this all my life and now I can't remember how to do it!" On another occasion, he was seen trying

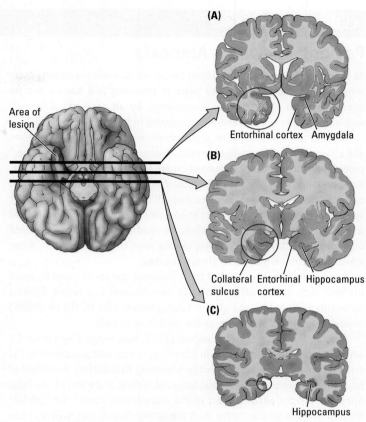

**FIGURE 14-7 Extent of H. M.'s Surgery** H. M.'s right-hemisphere lesion is highlighted in the brain viewed ventrally. The lesion runs along the wall of the medial temporal lobe. The left side of the brain has been left intact to show the relative location of the medial temporal structures. Parts A, B, and C, based on MRI scans, depict a series of coronal sections of H. M.'s brain. Research from Corkin et al. (1997).

Prosopagnosia, an inability to recognize faces, and other visual-form agnosias are discussed in Chapter 9.

Clinical Focus 5-2, 5-4, and 5-5 and Section 7-1 detail aspects of Parkinson disease. Section 16-3 reviews treatments for this disease.

## ⊙ CLINICAL FOCUS 14-2

# Patient Boswell's Amnesia

At the age of 48, Boswell developed herpes simplex encephalitis, a brain infection. He had completed 13 years of schooling and had worked for nearly 30 years in newspaper advertising. By all accounts a normal, well-adjusted person, Boswell was successful in his profession.

Boswell recovered from the acute symptoms, which included seizures and a 3-day coma. His intelligence post-disease was rated as "low average," probably due to neurological damage caused by the infection. Nonetheless, his speech and language remained typical in every respect, and he showed no perceptual or movement deficits. Boswell was left with a severe amnesic syndrome, however. If he listened to someone read a short paragraph and was asked to describe its main points, he routinely scored zero. He could only guess the day's date and was unable even to guess the year. When asked what city he was in, he simply guessed.

Boswell did know his place of birth, however, and could correctly recall his birth date about half the time. In sum, Boswell had severe amnesia for events both before and after his encephalitis. Like H. M., he showed implicit memory on tests such as the pursuit rotor task.

Antonio Damasio and his colleagues (1989) have investigated Boswell's amnesia extensively, and his brain pathology is now well documented. The critical damage, diagrammed in the adjoining illustration, consisted of bilateral destruction of the medial temporal regions and a loss of the basal forebrain and the posterior part of the orbitofrontal cortex. In addition, Boswell lost the insular cortex from the lateral fissure (not visible in the illustration).

Boswell's sensory and motor cortices are intact, as are his basal ganglia, but his injury is more extensive than H. M.'s. Like H. M., he has no new memories. Unlike H. M., he also has a severe loss of access to old

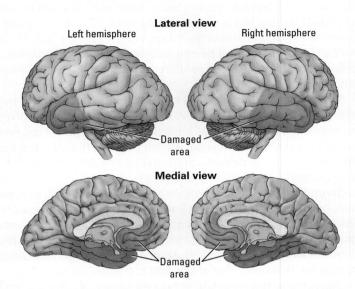

Since recovering from a herpes simplex encephalitis infection, patient Boswell has had great difficulty remembering events before and after his illness. Areas of damage in the medial temporal region, basal forebrain, and posterior orbitofrontal cortex are highlighted in red. Compare the figure above to Figure 14-6.

information, probably due to his insular and prefrontal injuries. Nonetheless, again like H. M.'s, Boswell's procedural memory is intact, illustrating the dissociation between the neural circuits underlying explicit and implicit forms of memory.

to turn off the radio with the television remote control. This time he explained, "I don't recall how to turn off the radio so I thought I would try this thing!"

J. K.'s clear implicit memory deficit contrasts sharply with his awareness of daily events. He recalled explicit events as well as most men his age and spoke intelligently on issues of the day that he had just read about. Once when two of us visited him, one of us entered the room first, and he immediately asked where the other was, even though it had been 2 weeks since we told him that we would be coming to visit.

The intact long-term memory displayed by J. K. was vastly different from H. M.'s situation: H. M. would not have remembered that anyone was coming even 5 minutes after being told of their expected arrival. Because Parkinson disease primarily affects the basal ganglia, J. K.'s deficit in implicit memory was probably related to his basal ganglia dysfunction.

## 14-2 Review

Before you continue, check your understanding. Answers to Self-Test appear at the back of the book.

1. Based on the case of H. M., we can conclude that the structures involved in explicit memory include the _____, the _____, and adjacent cortex.

2. Implicit memory deficits in patients with Parkinson disease demonstrate that a major structure in implicit memory is the _____.

3. What is the main difference between the Lashley and Milner studies?

# Neural Systems Underlying Explicit and Implicit Memories

Laboratory studies, conducted largely on rats and monkeys, have reproduced the symptoms of patients such as H. M. and J. K. by injuring the animals' medial temporal regions and basal ganglia, respectively. Other structures, most notably in the frontal and temporal lobes, also participate in certain types of explicit memory. We now consider the systems for explicit and implicit memory separately.

**Learning Objectives**
• Describe the neural circuits for explicit and implicit memories.
• Summarize the process of consolidation of explicit memories.
• Describe a neural circuit for emotional memories.

## Neural Circuit for Explicit Memories

The dramatic amnesic syndrome discovered in H. M. in the 1950s led investigators to focus on the hippocampus, which at the time was regarded as a large brain structure in search of a function. But H. M. had other damaged structures, too, and the initial focus on the hippocampus as the location of explicit memory processing turned out to be misguided.

After decades of anatomical and behavioral studies sorted out the complexities, consensus on the anatomy of explicit memory coalesced by the mid-1990s. The primary structures for explicit memory include the medial temporal region, the prefrontal cortex, and structures closely related to them.

The macaque monkey's medial temporal region shares many anatomical similarities with the same region in the human brain. In addition to the hippocampus and amygdala, three medial temporal areas, illustrated in **Figure 14-8**, take part in explicit memory: lying adjacent to the hippocampus are the **entorhinal cortex**, the **parahippocampal cortex**, and the **perirhinal cortex**. A sequential arrangement of two-way connections, charted in Figure 14-8, projects from the major cortical regions into the perirhinal and parahippocampal cortices, which in turn project to the entorhinal cortex and then to the hippocampus.

The prominent cortical input to the perirhinal region comes from the visual ventral stream coursing through the temporal lobe. The perirhinal region is thus a prime candidate location for visual object memory. Similarly, the parahippocampal cortex receives strong input from parietal regions believed to take part in visuospatial processing and likely participates in **visuospatial memory**—using visual information to recall an object's location in space.

The hippocampus participates in species-specific behaviors, spatial navigation, and memory; it is also vulnerable to stress. Figure 2-23 shows this structure.

If you consult sources published before 1995, you may find explanations for memory far different from those presented in this chapter (see Gazzaniga, 2000).

In Greek, *para* means "beside"; *rhino* means "nose." The perirhinal cortex lies beside the rhinal sulcus on the bottom of the brain.

Section 9-2 traces the visual pathways in detail.

**entorhinal cortex** Cortex located on the medial temporal lobe surface; provides a major route for neocortical input to the hippocampal formation; often degenerates in Alzheimer disease.

**parahippocampal cortex** Cortex located along the dorsal medial temporal lobe surface.

**perirhinal cortex** Cortex lying next to the rhinal fissure on the ventral surface of the brain.

**visuospatial memory** Use of visual information to recall an object's location in space.

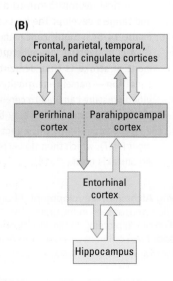

**(A)**

Perirhinal cortex
Parahippo-campal cortex
Entorhinal cortex
Amygdala
Hippocampus

**(B)**

Frontal, parietal, temporal, occipital, and cingulate cortices

Perirhinal cortex | Parahippocampal cortex

Entorhinal cortex

Hippocampus

**FIGURE 14-8 Medial Temporal Structures Participating in Memory in Monkeys (A)** Ventral view of the rhesus macaque monkey brain. Left side: The medial temporal regions. Each plays a distinct role in processing sensory information for memory storage. Right side: The hippocampus and amygdala are not directly visible from the brain surface; they lie within the cortical regions illustrated on the left. All these structures are present on both sides of the brain. **(B)** Flow of input from the sensory cortices: first to the parahippocampal and perirhinal regions, then to the entorhinal cortex, and finally to the hippocampus. The hippocampus feeds back to the medial temporal regions and then to the neocortical sensory regions.

Section 16-3 elaborates on Alzheimer disease, along with other neurocognitive disorders, and on prion theory.

---

**neuritic plaque** Area of incomplete necrosis (dead tissue) consisting of a central protein core (amyloid) surrounded by degenerative cellular fragments; often seen in the cortex of people with neurocognitive disorders such as Alzheimer disease.

---

Because both the perirhinal and the parahippocampal regions project to the entorhinal cortex, this region probably participates in more integrative memory functions. The entorhinal cortex is, in fact, the first area to show cell death in Alzheimer disease, a neurocognitive disorder characterized by severe deficits in explicit memory (see Clinical Focus 14-3: Alzheimer Disease).

One implication of the anatomical organization shown in Figure 14-8B is that the parahippocampal and perirhinal cortices act together as a gateway into the entorhinal cortex and hippocampus. Although this is a widely accepted perspective, it ignores the extensive connections between the prefrontal cortex and the hippocampus (for an extensive discussion, see Murray et al., 2017). We return to the prefrontal–hippocampal interaction in memory shortly.

---

◉ **CLINICAL FOCUS 14-3**

## Alzheimer Disease

In the 1880s, it was noted that the brain may undergo atrophy with aging, but the reason was not specifically described until the German physician Alois Alzheimer published a landmark study in 1906. Alzheimer described a set of behavioral symptoms and associated neuropathology in a 51-year-old woman who displayed symptoms of dementia. The cellular structure of her neocortex and allocortex showed various abnormalities.

An estimated 5.7 million people in the United States have Alzheimer disease, although the only test able to definitively confirm this diagnosis remains postmortem examination of cerebral tissue. The disease progresses slowly, and many people with Alzheimer disease often die of other causes before the cognitive symptoms incapacitate them.

We knew of a physics professor who continued to work until, when he was nearly 80, he died of a heart attack. Postmortem examination of his brain revealed significant Alzheimer pathology. The professor's colleagues had attributed the professor's slipping memory to "old-timer's" disease.

The cause of Alzheimer disease remains unknown, but has been variously attributed to genetic predisposition, abnormal levels of trace elements (e.g., aluminum), immune reactions, slow viruses, and *prions* (abnormal, infectious forms of proteins). Two principal neuronal changes take place in Alzheimer disease:

1. *Loss of cholinergic cells in the basal forebrain.* A proposed treatment for Alzheimer disease, therefore, is medication that increases acetylcholine levels in the forebrain. One such medication is Exelon, which is the trade name for rivastigmine, a cholinergic agonist that appears to provide temporary relief from the progression of the disease and is available both orally and as a skin patch.

2. *Development of neuritic plaques and tangles in the cerebral cortex.* Alzheimer disease is characterized by two misfolded proteins: amyloid-ß (Aß) and tau. Aß fragments accumulate extracellularly to form **neuritic plaques**; pathological tau deposits accumulate intracellularly as *neurofibrillary tangles* (NFT). The plaques are not distributed evenly throughout the cortex, but instead become mostly concentrated in the temporal lobe areas associated with memory, and particularly in the entorhinal cortex (see the accompanying graph). It is believed that neuritic plaques appear first, followed by an inflammatory process that is mediated mainly by microglia activation; this activation, in turn, facilitates the production of tau pathology (Avila & Perry, 2021). Researchers have established an association between Aß/NFT levels, though some people who are found to have high Aß/NFT levels postmortem have surprisingly few cognitive symptoms.

Cortical neurons begin to deteriorate as the cholinergic loss, plaques, and tangles develop. The first cells to die are in the entorhinal cortex (see Figure 14-8A). Significant memory disturbance ensues.

A controversial idea emerging from neurologists specializing in treatment of stroke is that dementia may reflect a chronic cerebrovascular condition — namely, marginally high blood pressure. Marginal elevations in blood pressure can lead to cerebral microbleeds, especially in white matter. Years or even decades of tiny bleeds may eventually lead to increasingly disturbed cognition. This effect might first appear as *mild cognitive impairment* (*MCI*), which then slowly progresses with cumulative microbleeds (see Arvanitakis et al., 2018).

**Cognition and Biomarkers During Alzheimer Development** About 20 years before cognitive symptoms are diagnosed, Aß aggregates can be detected, as seen in the graph. The Aß activates microglia cells that stimulate inflammation, leading the production of tau proteins. In the accompanying photo scan, the red area (bottom right) near the cell nucleus in this false-color brain cell from a person with Alzheimer disease represents a neurofibrillary tangle of misfolded tau proteins. Data from Avila, J., & Perry, G. (2021). A multilevel view of the development of Alzheimer's disease. *Neuroscience, 457,* 283–293.

**(A) Basic training**

A monkey is shown an object,...

...which it then displaces to obtain a food reward.

**(B) Visual-recognition task**

A monkey is trained to displace an object to obtain a food reward...

...then shown two objects. The task is to displace the *new* object to obtain the reward.

**(C) Object-position task**

The monkey is shown one object to displace for a food reward.

On the next trial, the monkey is shown two identical objects and must choose the one at the same location as in the initial presentation.

**FIGURE 14-9 Two Memory Tasks for Monkeys (A)** In "basic training," a monkey learns to displace an object to obtain a food reward. In **(B)** and **(C)**, the plus and minus signs indicate whether the object (1) is or (2) is not associated with food.

# The Hippocampus and Spatial Memory

We are left with a conundrum. If the hippocampus is not the key structure in explicit memory, even as it receives the entorhinal connections, what does it do? John O'Keefe and Lynn Nadel were the first to advance the idea, in 1978, that the hippocampus is probably engaged in the visuospatial memory processes required for memories related to places, such as recalling an object's location.

Certainly both laboratory animals and human patients with selective hippocampal injury have severe deficits in various forms of spatial memory. Similarly, monkeys with hippocampal lesions have difficulty learning the locations of objects (*visuospatial learning*), as can be demonstrated in tasks such as the ones illustrated in **Figure 14-9**.

In these types of experiments, monkeys are trained to displace objects to obtain a food reward (Figure 14-9A), then given one of two tasks. In the *visual-recognition task* (Figure 14-9B), the animal displaces a sample object for the food reward. After a short delay, the animal is presented with two objects, one of which is novel. The task is to learn to displace the novel object for the food reward. This task tests explicit visual object memory. Monkeys with perirhinal lesions find it difficult to complete this task successfully.

In the *object-position task* (Figure 14-9C) the monkey is shown one object to be displaced for a food reward. Then the monkey is shown the same object along with a second, identical one. The task is to learn to displace the object that is in the same position as it was in the initial presentation. Monkeys with hippocampal lesions are selectively impaired at this task.

From these results, we would predict that species with an especially good spatial memory should have bigger hippocampi than do species with a poorer spatial memory. David Sherry and his colleagues (1992) tested this hypothesis in birds.

Many species of birds are *cachers*: they harvest sunflower seeds and other favored foods and hide (cache) them to eat later. Some birds can find hundreds of items they have cached. To evaluate whether the hippocampus plays a role in this activity, Sherry and his coworkers measured hippocampal size in closely related bird species, only one of which was a food cacher. As shown in **Figure 14-10**, they found that the hippocampal formation is larger in birds that cache food than in birds that do not. In fact, the

**FIGURE 14-10 Inferring Spatial Memory** This graph relates hippocampal volume to forebrain volume in food-storing (*left*) and non-food-storing (*right*) families of songbirds. Birds that cache food, such as the black-capped chickadee, have hippocampi about twice as large as those of birds that are not cachers, such as the sparrow. Data from Sherry et al. (1992).

Section 1-4 explains the encephalization quotient (EQ), an index of ratios of brain to body size. EQs allow comparisons of the relative brain sizes of different species.

hippocampi of food-storing birds are more than twice as large as expected for birds of their brain size and body weight.

Sherry found a similar relationship when he compared different species of food-storing rodents. Merriam's kangaroo rats, rodents that store food throughout their territory, have larger hippocampi than do bannertail kangaroo rats, which store food only in their burrow. Thus, hippocampal size, both in birds and in mammals, appears to be related to the cognitive demands of two highly spatial activities: foraging for food and storing food.

One prediction we might make based on the Sherry experiments is that people who have a job with high spatial demands have large hippocampi. Taxi drivers in London fit this category. Successful candidates for a cab driver's license in London must demonstrate that they know the location of every street in that huge and ancient city. In a study using magnetic resonance imaging (MRI), Eleanor Maguire and her colleagues (2000) found the posterior region of the hippocampus in London taxi drivers to be significantly larger than the same region in the control participants. This finding presumably explains why only a select few pass a spatial memory test that most of us would fail miserably.

## Spatial Cells in the Hippocampal Formation

Given the role of the hippocampus in spatial behavior, we might predict that individual cells would code spatial information—and they do. Three classes of spatially related cells have been identified in the hippocampus and medial entorhinal cortex of rats and mice (**Figure 14-11**). That is, neurons vigorously fire when an animal is in a specific place in the environment. In 2014, John O'Keefe, Edvard Moser, and May-Britt Moser were awarded the Nobel Prize in Physiology or Medicine for this discovery.

*Place cells*, shown in Figure 14-11A and B, discharge when rats are in a spatial location, regardless of its orientation. *Head direction cells* (Figure 14-11C) discharge whenever a rat's head points in a particular direction. *Grid cells* (Figure 14-11D) discharge at many locations, forming a virtual grid that is invariant to changes in the rat's direction, movement, or speed.

These cells are not localized to the hippocampus, but rather are found within a network that includes the hippocampus as its central structure. Place cells and head direction cells are located in the hippocampus and closely related structures. Grid cells are found in the entorhinal cortex, a major afferent route into the hippocampus (see Figure 14-8B). Taken together, we can envision the place cell system as indicating where things are in the world, the grid system as indicating how big our present navigating environment is, and the head direction and grid systems as telling us where we ourselves are in the environment.

This integrated spatial system operates much like a type of GPS (global positioning system) for the brain, but the brain's GPS is a bit more interesting than the one used by your smartphone or car. Jorgen Sugar and May-Britt Moser (2019) have proposed that

**FIGURE 14-11 Classes of Spatially Related Cells in the Hippocampal Formation** At right in each part, the X–Y coordinates indicate the directional selectivity of the cell recorded at left. **(A and B)** Place cells discharge when a rat is at a spatial location, regardless of its orientation. **(C)** Head direction cells discharge when the rat's head points in a given direction, regardless of its location. **(D)** Grid cells discharge at many locations, forming a virtual grid that is invariant in the face of changes in the rat's direction, movement, or speed. Research from O'Keefe (2006).

**(A) Place cell**

**(B) Place-by-direction cell**

**(C) Head direction cell**

**(D) Grid cell**

Courtesy of John O'Keefe

the brain's positioning system is integrated into a larger network that not only codes "where," but also "when" and "what." *When* is recorded by hippocampal neurons that code the duration and sequence of specific events. *What* is derived from the activity of cells in the entorhinal cortex that are preferentially active when an animal is in close proximity to objects. The *where* system combines with the *when* and *what* neurons to form large ensembles that provide a basis for our memory of episodes—that is, our episodic memory (discussed in Section 14-1).

## Reciprocal Connections for Explicit Memory

The temporal lobe pathway of explicit memory is reciprocal: connections from the neocortex run to the entorhinal cortex, and then back to the neocortex (see Figure 14-8B). Reciprocal connections have two benefits:

1. Signals from the medial temporal regions back to the cortical sensory regions keep the sensory experience alive in the brain: the neural record of an experience outlasts the actual experience.

2. The pathway back to the neocortex keeps it apprised of information being processed in the medial temporal regions.

Although we have focused on the medial temporal regions, other structures are also important in explicit memory. People with frontal lobe injuries are not amnesic like H. M. or J. K., but they do have difficulties with memory for the temporal (time) order of events. Imagine being shown a series of photographs and asked to remember them. A few minutes later, you are asked whether you recognize two photographs and, if so, to indicate which one you saw first. H. M. would have no memory of ever seeing the photographs. People with frontal lobe injuries would recall having seen the photographs but would have difficulty recalling the order in which they were presented. The frontal lobe's role in explicit memory clearly is subtler than that of the medial temporal lobe.

**The Frontal Lobe and Short-Term Memory** All sensory systems in the brain send information to the frontal lobe, as do the medial temporal regions. This information is not used for direct sensory analysis, so it must have another purpose. In general, the frontal lobe appears to participate in many forms of short-term memory.

Joaquin Fuster (e.g., Fuster et al., 2000) studied single-cell activity in the frontal lobe during short-term memory tasks. For instance, if monkeys are shown an object that they must remember for a short time before being allowed to make a response, neurons in the prefrontal cortex show sustained firing during the delay between exposure and response. Consider the tests illustrated in **Figure 14-12**:

- In the general design for each test, a monkey is shown a light (the cue); after a delay, it must make a response to get a reward.

- In the *delayed-response task,* the monkey is shown two lights in the choice test and must choose the one that is in the same location as the cue.

- In the *delayed-alternation task,* the monkey is again shown two lights in the choice tests but now must choose the light that is *not* in the same location as the cue.

- In the *delayed matching-to-sample task,* the monkey is shown, say, a red light, and then, after a delay, a red light and a green light. The task is to choose the red light, regardless of its new location.

Fuster found that in each task, certain cells in the prefrontal cortex fire throughout the delay. Animals that have not learned the task show no such cell activity. Curiously, if a trained animal makes an error, its cellular activity shows a corresponding glitch—that is, the cells stop responding before the error occurs. They have "forgotten" the cue.

The basal ganglia systems that take part in implicit memory do not feed back to the cortex, which helps explain the unconscious nature of implicit memory.

In the following tests, a monkey is shown a light, which is the cue, and then it makes a response after a delay.

**Delayed-response task:** The monkey must choose the light that is in the same location as the cue.

**Delayed-alternation task:** The monkey must choose the light that is not in the same location as the cue.

**Delayed matching-to-sample task:** The monkey must choose the light that is the same color as the cue.

**FIGURE 14-12 Testing Short-Term Memory** A monkey performing a short-term memory task responds by pressing the disc to get a fruit juice reward (*top*). The correct disc varies, depending on the task requirements (*bottom*). (For each task, an arrowhead shows the correct choice.) Information from Fuster (1995).

The diencephalon is diagrammed in Figures 2-16 and 2-19.

**retrograde amnesia** Inability to remember events that took place before the onset of amnesia.

**anterograde amnesia** Inability to remember events subsequent to a disturbance of the brain such as head trauma, electroconvulsive shock, or neurodegenerative disease.

**Korsakoff syndrome** Permanent loss of the ability to learn new information (anterograde amnesia) and to retrieve old information (retrograde amnesia) caused by diencephalic damage resulting from chronic alcohol use disorder or malnutrition that produces a vitamin $B_1$ deficiency.

**Tracing the Explicit Memory Circuit** People who have chronically used alcohol can develop an explicit memory disturbance known as **Korsakoff syndrome**. In some cases, severe deficits in explicit memory extend to implicit memory as well. Korsakoff syndrome is caused by a thiamine (vitamin $B_1$) deficiency that kills cells in the medial part of the diencephalon, including the medial thalamus and mammillary bodies in the hypothalamus. In 80% of patients with Korsakoff syndrome, the frontal lobes show atrophy (loss of cells). The memory disturbance is probably so severe because the damage includes not only the forebrain but also brainstem structures (see Clinical Focus 14-4: Korsakoff Syndrome).

Mortimer Mishkin and his colleagues (Mishkin, 1982; Murray, 2000) proposed a neural circuit for explicit memory that incorporates the evidence from both humans and laboratory animals with injuries to the temporal and frontal lobes. **Figure 14-13** presents a modified version of the Mishkin model. Anatomically (Figure 14-13A), it includes not only the frontal and temporal lobes but also the medial thalamus, which is implicated in Korsakoff syndrome, and the basal forebrain–activating

---

## ◎ CLINICAL FOCUS 14-4

# Korsakoff Syndrome

Over the long term, alcohol use disorder, especially when accompanied by malnutrition, obliterates memory. When 62-year-old Joe R. was hospitalized, his family complained that his memory had become abysmal. His intelligence was in the average range, and he had no obvious sensory or motor difficulties. Nevertheless, he could not say why he was in the hospital and usually stated that he was actually in a hotel.

When asked what he had done the previous night, Joe R. typically said that he "went to the Legion for a few beers with the boys." Although he had, in fact, been in the hospital, it was a sensible response — because going to the Legion is what he had done on most nights in the preceding 30 years.

Joe R. was not certain what he had done for a living, but believed he had been a butcher. In fact, he had been a truck driver for a local delivery firm. His son was a butcher, however, so once again his story related to something in his life.

Joe's memory for immediate events was little better. On one occasion, we asked him to remember having met us; then we left the room. On our return 2 or 3 minutes later, he had no recollection of ever having met us or of having taken the psychological tests that we had administered.

Joe R. had Korsakoff syndrome. In the 1880s, Sergei Korsakoff, a Russian physician, became the first researcher to call attention to a syndrome that accompanies chronic alcoholism. The most obvious symptom is severe memory loss, including amnesia for both information learned in the past (**retrograde amnesia**) and information learned since the onset of the memory disturbance (**anterograde amnesia**).

One unique characteristic of the amnesic syndrome in people with Korsakoff syndrome is that they tend to make up stories about past events rather than admit that they do not remember. These stories are generally plausible, like those Joe R. told, because they are based on actual experiences.

Curiously, people with Korsakoff syndrome have little insight into their memory disturbance and are generally indifferent to suggestions that they have a memory problem. Such patients are generally apathetic to what's going on around them, too. Joe R., for example, was often seen watching television when the set was turned off.

The cause of Korsakoff syndrome is a thiamine (vitamin $B_1$) deficiency resulting from poor diet and prolonged intake of large quantities of alcohol. (In addition to having a "few beers with the boys," Joe R. had a long history of drinking a 26-ounce bottle of rum every day.) The thiamine deficiency results in the death of cells in the midline diencephalon, especially in the medial regions of the thalamus and the mammillary bodies of the hypothalamus.

Most people with Korsakoff syndrome also show cortical atrophy, especially in the frontal lobe. Once Korsakoff symptoms appear, which can happen suddenly, prognosis is poor. Only about 20% of people with Korsakoff syndrome show much recovery after a year on a vitamin $B_1$–enriched diet. Joe R. had shown no recovery after several years and spent the final 15 years of his life in a hospital setting.

Living Art Enterprises, LLC/Science Source

MRI scan from a patient with Korsakoff syndrome showing degeneration along the middle region of the diencephalon (light area). The figure on the left shows the associated memory impairments.

**FIGURE 14-13 Reciprocal Neural Circuit Proposed for Explicit Memory (A)** General neuroanatomical areas controlling explicit memory. **(B)** The information flow begins on the right with inputs from the sensory and motor systems, which are not considered part of the explicit memory circuit.

systems, which are implicated in Alzheimer disease. Figure 14-13B charts the information flow:

- Sensory and motor neocortical areas send their connections to the medial temporal regions, which are in turn connected to the medial thalamus and prefrontal cortex.

- Basal forebrain structures are hypothesized to play a role in maintaining appropriate activity levels in other forebrain structures so that they can process information.

- The temporal lobe structures and prefrontal cortex are hypothesized to be central to long-term explicit memory formation.

- The prefrontal cortex is central to maintaining temporary (short-term) explicit memories as well as memory for the recency (chronological order) of explicit events.

The brain's activating systems, shown in Figure 14-13, are described in detail in Section 13-5.

## Consolidation of Explicit Memories

Amnesia often appears to be time dependent. H. M. could not form new explicit memories but appeared to have had good recall of facts and events from periods long before his surgery, including his childhood. Such findings led to the idea that the medial temporal region could *not* be the ultimate storage site for long-term memories, but that the neocortex was the more likely site (for a review, see Squire et al., 2015).

This idea led to the hypothesis that the hippocampus *consolidates* new memories, a process that makes them permanent. In **consolidation**—that is, the process of stabilizing a memory trace after learning—memories move from the hippocampus to diffuse neocortical regions. Once they move to these sites, hippocampal involvement is no longer needed.

It is not clear how memories are moved, however, or how long it takes. Robert Sutherland and his colleagues (2010) have proposed a model of consolidation called the *distributed reinstatement theory*. In their model, a learning episode rapidly produces a stored memory representation that is strong in the hippocampus but weak elsewhere. This memory is replayed on a time scale of hours, days, or months after the learning, leading to enhanced representations outside the hippocampus. Each repetition of the learning—that is, each practice—progressively enhances the nonhippocampal memory representation, as we saw in the Maguire studies of spatial memory discussed earlier.

An extension of the distributed reinstatement model is the *trace transformation theory*, which proposes that perceptual features of events are richly represented in the posterior hippocampus. Over time, these details are shifted to the anterior hippocampus, which represents the *gist* (general outline) of the memory. The memory is then encoded in the medial prefrontal cortex, where similar memories are grouped together (Sekeres et al., 2018). The movement of memory traces throughout the brain suggests that our memory of an event is not constant over time, but rather is modified as it moves from one region to another.

**consolidation** Process of stabilizing a memory trace after learning.

**reconsolidation** Process of restabilizing a memory trace after the memory is revisited.

**emotional memory** Memory for the affective properties of stimuli or events.

Section 5-4 links stress-related hippocampal activity to PTSD, and Research Focus 16-1 covers treatments.

Another theory suggests that whenever we recall a specific memory—even if the associated memory trace is not active at the time—it is open to further consolidation, or **reconsolidation**, the process of restabilizing a memory trace after the memory is revisited. Researchers have shown intense interest in this idea. Although the final story is yet to be written, it appears that reconsolidation does occur, at least for some types of memories. Nevertheless, the process of reconsolidation does create a notable problem: memories can be altered if the context of the reconsolidation is changed. The technique of always using the same space when studying probably decreases the likelihood of memory changes in reconsolidation, which would likely improve later recall.

One way to think of the reconsolidation process is to see memory consolidation as never-ending: new information is constantly being integrated into existing memory networks. After all, we frequently recall memories, rehash them, and integrate them with new events. Our memories are not laid on a tabula rasa but instead must be interwoven into a lifetime of memories.

One implication of reconsolidation is that it suggests the possibility of erasing negative memories by using amnesic agents when the memory is revisited. This idea has important implications for reducing or eliminating the effects of strong emotional experiences, such as those seen in posttraumatic stress disorder (PTSD). One promising agent is the inert gas xenon, which has been used in humans as a fast-acting anesthetic and has been shown to erase memories during reconsolidation in a rat model of PTSD (Meloni et al., 2014), as well as in a case report of a human with PTSD (Dobrovolsky et al., 2019).

## Neural Circuit for Implicit Memories

Hypothesizing that the basal ganglia are central to implicit memory, Mishkin and his colleagues proposed a neural circuit for implicit memories (Mishkin, 1982; Mishkin et al., 1997). As **Figure 14-14** shows, the basal ganglia receive input from the entire neocortex and send projections first to the ventral thalamus and then to the premotor cortex. The basal ganglia also receive widely and densely distributed projections from dopamine-producing cells in the substantia nigra. Dopamine appears necessary for basal ganglia circuits to function and may indirectly participate in implicit memory formation.

The connection from the cortex to the basal ganglia in the implicit memory system flows in only one direction. Most of the neocortex receives no direct information regarding activities in the basal ganglia. Mishkin believes that this unidirectional flow accounts for the unconscious nature of implicit memories. For memories to be conscious, the neocortical regions involved must receive feedback, as they do in the explicit memory system that Mishkin and colleagues proposed (see Figure 14-13).

Mishkin's models show why people with basal ganglia dysfunction, like that seen in Parkinson disease, have implicit memory deficits. People with frontal or temporal lobe injuries, by contrast, have relatively good implicit memories, even though they may have profound explicit memory disturbances. Some people with Alzheimer disease can play games expertly, even with no recollection of having played them before. Daniel Schacter (1983) wrote of a golfer with Alzheimer disease whose medial temporal system was severely compromised by the disease but whose basal ganglia were unaffected. Despite this golfer's explicit knowledge impairment, as indexed by his inability to find balls he had hit or to remember how many strokes he had made on each hole, the man retained his ability to play the game.

**FIGURE 14-14 Unidirectional Neural Circuit Proposed for Implicit Memory**
**(A)** Anatomical areas controlling implicit memory. **(B)** Circuit diagram showing the one-way flow of implicit information, beginning with inputs from the sensory and motor systems not considered part of the memory circuit.

## Neural Circuit for Emotional Memories

Whether **emotional memory** for the affective properties of stimuli or events is implicit or explicit is not altogether clear. It is likely both. Certainly, people can react with fear to specific stimuli they can identify, and we have seen that they can also fear situations for which they do not seem to have specific memories. Panic disorder is a common pathology of emotional memory, as people may show marked anxiety but cannot identify a specific cause.

Emotional memory has been studied most thoroughly in fear conditioning by pairing unpleasant stimuli, such as a shock to the foot, with a tone. In fact, many studies have used fear conditioning to establish that emotional memory has a unique anatomical component, the amygdala; this structure mediates fear conditioning (see Experiment 14-1) and seems to evoke our feelings of anxiety toward stimuli that by themselves would not typically produce fear (e.g., Davis, 1992). The amygdala presents a complicating factor in establishing the relationship between emotional memory and implicit and explicit memory, as damage to the amygdala abolishes emotional memory but has little effect on implicit or explicit memory.

The amygdala has close connections with medial temporal cortical structures as well as with the rest of the cortex. It also sends projections to brainstem structures that control autonomic responses such as blood pressure and heart rate; to the hypothalamus, which controls hormonal systems; to the periaqueductal gray matter (PAG), which affects pain perception; and to the enteric nervous system (ENS). The amygdala hooks into the implicit memory system through its connections with the basal ganglia (**Figure 14-15**).

Fear is not the only aspect of emotional memory the amygdala codes, as was illustrated in a study of individuals with severe dementia carried out by Bob Sainsbury and Marjorie Coristine (1986). The study participants were believed to have severe cortical abnormalities but intact amygdalar functioning. The researchers first established that their ability to recognize photographs of close relatives was severely impaired. The participants were then shown four photographs, one depicting a relative (either a sibling or a child) who had visited in the past 2 weeks and the other three depicting complete strangers. The task was to identify the person whom they liked better than the other three. Although the subjects were unaware that they knew anyone depicted in the photographs, they consistently preferred pictures of their relatives. This result suggests that although the explicit, and probably the implicit, memory of the relative was gone, each patient's emotional memory guided their preference.

We tend to remember emotionally arousing experiences vividly, a fact confirmed by findings from both animal and human studies. James McGaugh (2004) concluded that emotionally significant experiences, both pleasant and unpleasant, must activate hormonal and brain systems that act to stamp these vivid memories in our brain. McGaugh noted that many neural systems probably take part in this process, but the basolateral part of the amygdala plays a critical role. The general idea is that emotionally driven hormonal and neurochemical activating systems (probably cholinergic and noradrenergic) stimulate the amygdala. The amygdala, in turn, modulates the laying down of emotional memory circuits in the rest of the brain, especially in the medial temporal and prefrontal regions and in the basal ganglia. We would not expect people with amygdala damage to have vivid memory for emotion-laden events, and they do not (Cahill et al., 1995).

## Evolution of Memory Systems

Elizabeth Murray, Steven Wise, and Kim Graham (2017) published a proposal on the organization of memory systems, which they call the *evolution accretion model of memory*, that differs dramatically from those described previously. These researchers suggest that several memory systems arose during evolution to exploit specific opportunities at particular times and places; they contend that this exploitation led to

The ANS monitors and controls life support functions (Figure 2-32); the ENS controls the gut (Figure 2-33). Section 11-4 reviews the PAG's role in pain perception.

Section 12-6 details the amygdala's influence on emotional behavior.

Figure 5-19 traces the neural activating system connections. Section 5-4 explains how hormones work.

**(A)**

**(B)**

Frontal, parietal, temporal, occipital, and cingulate cortices

Hypothalamus and PAG

Basal ganglia — Amygdala — Medial temporal cortex

Hypothalamus
Amygdala

**FIGURE 14-15 Neural Circuit Proposed for Emotional Memory (A)** The amygdala is the key structure in emotional memory. **(B)** Circuit diagram showing information flow in emotional memory.

Note that Figures 14-13 and 14-14 include boxes for the "Rest of neocortex" in the proposed neural circuit for explicit and implicit memory.

radical changes in cerebral anatomy and function. They further argue that virtually all cortical areas are involved in memory, with different regions using specialized neural networks. Their idea is not radically different from the theory that we discussed earlier (see Figure 14-8A, for example), but it does include more regions than are usually suggested. Murray and colleagues' more radical proposal is that owing to the large expansion of the human brain, and especially the prefrontal regions and the related connections with the hippocampal region, the human explicit memory system not only encodes experiences but embeds them in time and in our concept of self. Thus, we perceive ourselves to be participating in an ongoing chain of events, and when we retrieve memories, we experience them from the perspective of a participant or an observer. Murray, Wise, and Graham argue that this way of experiencing and encoding memory is *true explicit memory* and is unique to humans.

Over the course of human evolution, this significant change in cerebral anatomy resulted in the emergence of the many unique cognitive abilities that humans possess, including language. A full accounting of this proposal is beyond the scope of this chapter, but one can predict that over the next decade, it will generate considerable academic discussion and research. The authors foresee this in their statement: "Readers who view the cortex of other mammals as replicas in miniature or amalgams of primate areas will find our principal thesis unpalatable, to say the least" (Murray et al., 2017, pp. vii–viii).

## 14-3 Review

Before you continue, check your understanding. Answers to Self-Test appear at the back of the book.

1. The two key structures for explicit memory are the _____ and the _____.

2. A system consisting of the basal ganglia, substantia nigra, and neocortex forms the neural basis of the _____ memory system.

3. The _____ and associated structures form the neural basis for emotional memory.

4. The progressive stabilization of memories is known as _____.

5. Why do we remember emotionally arousing experiences so vividly?

6. Explain why the evolutionary explanation of memory proposed by Murray, Wise, and Graham represented a break from the established view as presented in this section.

### Learning Objectives

- Summarize the habituation and sensitization studies of *Aplysia*.
- Describe long-term potentiation.
- Explain how experience changes the brain.
- Describe how hormones, drugs, and trophic factors change the brain.
- Summarize guiding principles of brain plasticity.

## 14-4

# Structural Basis of Brain Plasticity

We have encountered three categories of memory—explicit, implicit, and emotional—and their underlying brain circuits. Next, we consider how the neurons in these circuits change to allow us to consolidate and store memories. The consensus among neuroscientists is that the changes take place at the synapse, in part simply because that is where neurons influence one another. This idea dates to 1928, when the Spanish anatomist Santiago Ramón y Cajal suggested that learning might produce prolonged morphological (structural) changes in the efficiency of synapses activated in the learning process. Cajal's idea turned out to be easier to propose than to study.

Researchers still encounter a major challenge as they investigate Cajal's suggestion because it is not clear where in the brain to look for synaptic changes that might correlate with memory for a specific stimulus. The task is formidable. Imagine trying to find the exact location of the neurons responsible for storing your grandmother's name. You would face a similar challenge in trying to pinpoint the neurons responsible for the memory of an object in a monkey's brain as the monkey performs the visual recognition task illustrated in Figure 14-9B.

One approach to finding memory's neuronal correlates aims first to determine that synaptic changes do correlate with memory in laboratory animals; second, to localize

Cajal's neuron theory—that the neuron is the nervous system's functional unit—is now universally accepted, including the idea that these discrete cells' interactions enable behavior. Cajal's work is discussed in detail in Section 3-1.

the synaptic changes to specific neural pathways; and third, to analyze the synaptic changes themselves. This section reviews studies that have begun to show how experience correlates with synaptic changes related to memory. We first consider a strategy based on neuronal physiology and experience in a relatively simple sea slug, *Aplysia*, which has about 20,000 neurons. Next, we review physiological and behavioral changes related to the hippocampus in a paradigm called *long-term potentiation*. We then look at gross neural changes that correlate with select experiences. These range from potentially good—living in enriched environments and learning specific tasks—to probably bad—chronic administration of trophic factors, hormones, and addictive drugs. These diverse experiences modify the brain's general synaptic organization in a strikingly similar manner.

# Habituation and Sensitization in *Aplysia*

*Aplysia* live in shallow tidal zones where they are constantly buffeted by the flow of waves against their bodies, but they learn that these waves are just background sensations in daily life. The process by which the response to a stimulus weakens with repeated exposure is called **habituation**. Although *Aplysia* habituate to the flow of waves, they remain sensitive to other novel touch sensations. When prodded with a novel object, *Aplysia* initially respond by withdrawing their siphon and gill. Repeated presentation of the prodding, however, leads again to habituation. Thus, it provides a useful model of learning, as illustrated in **Experiment 14-2**.

The Procedure section of Experiment 14-2 shows the setup for studying what happens to the withdrawal response of *Aplysia*'s gill after repeated stimulation. A gentle jet of water is sprayed on the siphon while gill movement is recorded. If the water jet is presented to *Aplysia*'s siphon as many as 10 times, the gill withdrawal response is weaker when the animal is retested some minutes later. The decrement in the strength of the withdrawal is attributable to habituation, which can last as long as 30 minutes in this case.

The Results section of Experiment 14-2 shows a simple representation of the pathway that mediates *Aplysia*'s gill withdrawal response. For purposes of illustration, only one sensory neuron, one motor neuron, and one synapse are shown; in actuality, nearly 300 neurons may take part in this response. The water jet stimulates the sensory neuron, which in turn stimulates the motor neuron responsible for the gill withdrawal. But where, exactly, do the changes associated with habituation take place? In the sensory neuron? In the motor neuron? In the synapse between the two?

Habituation does not result from an inability of either the sensory neuron or the motor neuron to produce action potentials—both the sensory neuron and the motor neuron retain this ability in response to direct electrical stimulation after habituation. Electrical recordings from the motor neuron, however, show that as habituation develops, the excitatory postsynaptic potentials (EPSPs) in the motor neuron become smaller. The most likely explanation for the decrease in the size of the EPSPs is that the motor neuron is *receiving* less neurotransmitter from the sensory neuron across the synapse, which suggests that the changes accompanying habituation must take place in the presynaptic axon terminal of the sensory neuron.

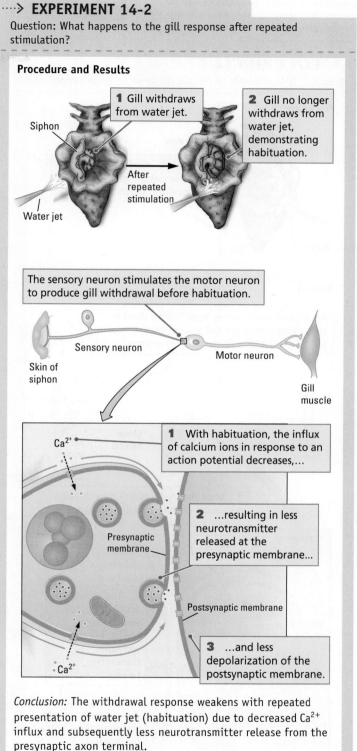

····> **EXPERIMENT 14-2**

Question: What happens to the gill response after repeated stimulation?

**Procedure and Results**

**1** Gill withdraws from water jet.

Siphon

After repeated stimulation

Water jet

**2** Gill no longer withdraws from water jet, demonstrating habituation.

The sensory neuron stimulates the motor neuron to produce gill withdrawal before habituation.

Sensory neuron

Skin of siphon

Motor neuron

Gill muscle

$Ca^{2+}$

**1** With habituation, the influx of calcium ions in response to an action potential decreases,...

Presynaptic membrane

**2** ...resulting in less neurotransmitter released at the presynaptic membrane...

Postsynaptic membrane

$Ca^{2+}$

**3** ...and less depolarization of the postsynaptic membrane.

*Conclusion:* The withdrawal response weakens with repeated presentation of water jet (habituation) due to decreased $Ca^{2+}$ influx and subsequently less neurotransmitter release from the presynaptic axon terminal.

**habituation** Learned behavior in which the response to a stimulus weakens with repeated presentations.

Refer to Sections 4-2 and 4-3 for a detailed explanation of the role of EPSPs in triggering of an action potential.

**sensitization** Learned behavior in which the response to a stimulus strengthens with repeated presentations.

···> **EXPERIMENT 14-3**

Question: What happens to the gill response in sensitization?

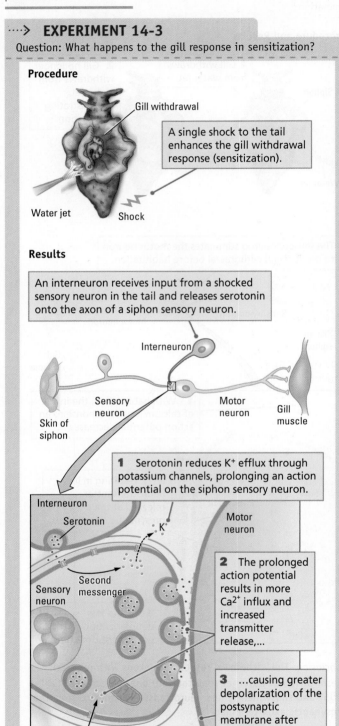

**Procedure**

Gill withdrawal

A single shock to the tail enhances the gill withdrawal response (sensitization).

Water jet    Shock

**Results**

An interneuron receives input from a shocked sensory neuron in the tail and releases serotonin onto the axon of a siphon sensory neuron.

Interneuron

Sensory neuron    Motor neuron    Gill muscle

Skin of siphon

**1** Serotonin reduces K⁺ efflux through potassium channels, prolonging an action potential on the siphon sensory neuron.

Interneuron

Serotonin

K⁺

Second messenger

Sensory neuron

**2** The prolonged action potential results in more Ca²⁺ influx and increased transmitter release,...

Motor neuron

**3** ...causing greater depolarization of the postsynaptic membrane after sensitization.

Ca²⁺

*Conclusion:* Enhancement of the withdrawal response after a shock (sensitization) is due to increased Ca²⁺ influx and subsequently more neurotransmitter release from the presynaptic axon terminal. Repeated exposure to the shock stimulus strengthens the withdrawal response.

## Reduced Sensitivity of Calcium Channels Underlies Habituation

Eric Kandel and his coworkers measured neurotransmitter output from a sensory neuron and verified that less neurotransmitter is, in fact, released from a habituated neuron than from a nonhabituated one (Bailey et al., 2015). Recall from Figure 5-4 that neurotransmitter release in response to an action potential requires an influx of calcium ions across the presynaptic membrane. As habituation takes place, that Ca²⁺ influx decreases in response to the voltage changes associated with an action potential. Presumably, with repeated use, voltage-activated calcium channels become less responsive to voltage changes and more resistant to the passage of calcium ions.

The neural basis of habituation lies in the change in presynaptic calcium channels. The underlying mechanism, which is summarized in the Results section of Experiment 14-2, is a reduced sensitivity of calcium channels and a consequent decrease in neurotransmitter release. Thus, habituation can be linked to a specific molecular change, as summarized in the experiment's Conclusion.

## Sensitization Response

**Sensitization**, defined as an enhanced response to some stimulus, is the opposite of habituation. In this process, the organism becomes hyperresponsive to a stimulus rather than accustomed to it. Sensitization occurs within a particular context. Sudden, novel stimulation heightens our general awareness and often results in larger-than-typical responses to all kinds of stimulation. If a loud noise startles you, for example, you become much more responsive to other stimuli in your surroundings, including some to which you previously were habituated.

We can observe this behavior in *Aplysia*. Sudden, novel stimuli can heighten the slug's responsiveness to familiar stimulation. When attacked by a predator, for example, the slug displays heightened responses to many other stimuli in its environment. In the laboratory, a small electric shock to *Aplysia*'s tail mimics a predatory attack and effects sensitization, as illustrated in the Procedure section of **Experiment 14-3**. A single electric shock to the slug's tail enhances its gill withdrawal response for a period that lasts for minutes to hours.

The neural circuits participating in sensitization differ from those that take part in a habituation response. The Results section of Experiment 14-3 shows the sensory and motor neurons that produce the gill withdrawal response and adds an interneuron that is responsible for sensitization. An interneuron that receives input from a sensory neuron in *Aplysia*'s tail (and so carries information about the shock) makes an *axoaxonic synapse* (a synapse between the axons of two neurons) with a sensory neuron in the siphon. The interneuron's axon terminal contains serotonin (5-HT). Consequently, in response to a tail shock, the tail's sensory neuron activates the interneuron, which in turn releases serotonin onto the axon of the siphon sensory neuron. Information from the siphon's sensory neuron continues to activate the motor neuron leading to the gill muscle, but the release of serotonin from the interneuron into the sensory neuron's presynaptic membrane amplifies the gill withdrawal response.

At the molecular level (shown close up in the Results section of Experiment 14-3), the serotonin released from the interneuron binds to a metabotropic serotonin receptor on the siphon's sensory neuron axon. This binding activates second messengers (cyclic adenosine monophosphate [cAMP]) in the sensory neuron.

Through several chemical reactions, cAMP attaches a phosphate molecule ($PO_4$) to potassium channels, rendering them less responsive. The close-up view in Experiment 14-3 sums it up. In response to an action potential traveling down the axon of the siphon's sensory neuron (such as an action potential generated by a touch to the siphon), the potassium ($K^+$) channels on that neuron are slower to open. Consequently, $K^+$ ions cannot repolarize the membrane as quickly as normal, so the action potential lasts longer than it usually would.

## Less-Responsive Potassium Channels Underlie Sensitization

The longer-lasting action potential that occurs because $K^+$ channels are slower to open prolongs the $Ca^{2+}$ inflow. $Ca^{2+}$ influx is necessary for neurotransmitter release. Thus, greater $Ca^{2+}$ influx results in more neurotransmitter being released from the sensory synapse onto the motor neuron. This increased neurotransmitter release produces greater activation of the motor neuron and, therefore, a larger-than-normal gill withdrawal response. During this process, more synaptic vesicles in the sensory neuron could be mobilized, making more neurotransmitter ready for release into the sensory-motor synapse, further enhancing the gill withdrawal response.

Sensitization, then, is the opposite of habituation at the molecular level as well as at the behavioral level. In sensitization, more $Ca^{2+}$ influx results in more transmitter being released, whereas in habituation, less $Ca^{2+}$ influx results in less neurotransmitter being released. The structural basis of cellular memory in these two forms of learning is different, however. In sensitization, the change takes place in the potassium channels, whereas in habituation, the change takes place in the calcium channels.

# Long-Term Potentiation

Demonstrations of habituation and sensitization in *Aplysia* show that physical changes in synapses do underlie learning. Adaptive synapses in the mammalian brain participate in **associative learning**, a response elicited by linking unrelated stimuli together—by learning that stimulus A goes with stimulus B.

Learned associations are a common type of explicit memory; examples include associating a face with a person, an odor with a food, or a sound with a musical instrument. The phenomenon underlying associative learning entails an enduring neural change in a postsynaptic cell after an EPSP from the presynaptic cell crosses the synaptic gap.

Both the relatively simple circuitry of the hippocampus and the ease of recording postsynaptic potentials there make this brain structure ideal for studying the neural basis of associative learning. In 1973, Timothy Bliss and Terje Lømø demonstrated that repeated electrical stimulation of the pathway entering the hippocampus progressively increases EPSP size as recorded from hippocampal cells. The enhancement in the size of these graded field potentials lasts several hours to weeks, and sometimes even longer. This long-lasting increase in synaptic effectiveness after high-frequency stimulation was termed **long-term potentiation (LTP)** by Bliss and Lømø.

**Figure 14-16**A illustrates the experimental procedure for obtaining LTP. The presynaptic neuron is stimulated electrically, and the electrical activity produced by this stimulation is recorded from the postsynaptic neuron. The readout in Figure 14-16A shows the EPSP produced by a single pulse of electrical stimulation. In a typical experiment, many test stimuli are given to estimate the size of the induced EPSP. Then a strong burst of stimulation, consisting of a few hundred pulses of electrical current per second, is administered (Figure 14-16B). The test pulse is then given again. The increased amplitude of the EPSP endures for as long as 90 minutes after the high-frequency burst: LTP has taken place. For the EPSP to increase in size, more neurotransmitter must be

Figure 5-16 summarizes the metabotropic receptors.

Kandel received the 2000 Nobel Prize in Physiology or Medicine for his *Aplysia* studies showing a physiological basis of memory.

Postsynaptic potentials may either increase (excitatory/EPSP) or decrease (inhibitory/IPSP) the probability that an action potential will occur. See Experiment 4-1.

**associative learning** Linkage of two or more unrelated stimuli to elicit a behavioral response.

**long-term potentiation (LTP)** Long-lasting increase in synaptic effectiveness after high-frequency stimulation.

**(A)**

**(B)**

Each dot represents EPSP amplitude in response to one weak test stimulation.

**FIGURE 14-16 Recording Long-Term Potentiation** **(A)** Experimenters stimulate the presynaptic neuron with a test pulse and record the EPSP from the postsynaptic neuron. **(B)** After an intense stimulation period, the amplitude of the EPSP produced by the test pulse increases: LTP has taken place.

Deep brain stimulation, when used as a treatment for severely depressed people, induces a change, similar to LTP, that appears to increase brain plasticity; see Section 16-3.

NMDA is shorthand for *N*-methyl-ᴅ-aspartate; AMPA stands for alpha-amino-3-hydroxy-5-methylisoxazole-4-propionic acid.

**long-term depression (LTD)** Long-lasting decrease in synaptic effectiveness after low-frequency electrical stimulation.

released from the presynaptic membrane, or the postsynaptic membrane must become more sensitive to the same amount of transmitter, or both changes must take place.

Increased transmitter release can result from enhanced $Ca^{2+}$ influx into the presynaptic terminal, which begins a chain of events leading to enhanced glutamate release. It can also be increased by the production of diffusible postsynaptic retrograde messengers that modify transmitter release. The precise mechanism of the retrograde messengering is not clear, but gases such as carbon monoxide and nitric oxide have been proposed as actors in this process. In addition, both ionotropic and metabotropic receptors at the presynaptic terminals can modulate LTP.

The discovery of LTP led to a revolution in thinking about how memories are stored. As investigators varied the stimulation that produced LTP, they discovered its opposite. In other words, instead of using high-frequency stimulation (e.g., 100 Hz), they used low-frequency stimulation (e.g., 5 Hz) and recorded a *decrease* in EPSP size, termed **long-term depression (LTD)**. If LTP is a mechanism for creating memories, perhaps LTD is a mechanism for clearing out old memories.

If LTP and LTD form the basis for understanding the synaptic changes underlying memory, two predictions follow. First, when animals learn to solve problems, we should see enhanced LTP in the recruited pathways. Second, LTP should produce enduring changes in synaptic morphology that resemble those seen in memory. Both predictions appear to be true.

The original studies of LTP concentrated on excitatory glutamate synapses. Glutamate is released from the presynaptic neuron and acts on two different types of receptors on the postsynaptic membrane, the NMDA and AMPA receptors, as shown in **Figure 14-17**A. AMPA receptors ordinarily mediate responses produced when glutamate is released from a presynaptic membrane. They allow sodium ions ($Na^+$) to enter, depolarizing and thus exciting the postsynaptic membrane. The initial amplitude of the EPSP in Figure 14-16A is produced by this AMPA receptor action.

NMDA receptors do not usually respond to glutamate because their pores are blocked by magnesium ions ($Mg^{2+}$). NMDA receptors are doubly gated ion channels that can open to allow the passage of $Ca^{2+}$ if two events take place at approximately the same time:

1. The postsynaptic membrane is depolarized, displacing the magnesium ion from the NMDA pore (Figure 14-17B). The strong electrical stimulation delivered by the experimenter serves as a way of displacing magnesium.

2. NMDA receptors are activated by glutamate from the presynaptic membrane (Figure 14-17C).

With the doubly gated NMDA channels open, calcium ions enter the postsynaptic neuron and act through second messengers to initiate the cascade of events associated with LTP. These events include increased responsiveness of AMPA receptors to glutamate, formation of new AMPA receptors, and even retrograde messages to the presynaptic terminal to enhance glutamate release. One or more of these actions produces the final EPSP amplitude in Figure 14-16B.

**(A) Weak electrical stimulation**

Because the NMDA receptor pore is blocked by a magnesium ion, release of glutamate by a weak electrical stimulation activates only the AMPA receptor.

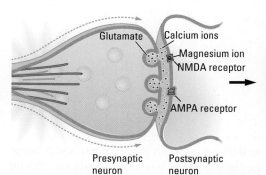

Glutamate    Calcium ions
            Magnesium ion
            NMDA receptor

            AMPA receptor

Presynaptic    Postsynaptic
neuron         neuron

**(B) Strong electrical stimulation (depolarizing EPSP)**

A strong electrical stimulation can depolarize the postsynaptic membrane sufficiently that the magnesium ion is removed from the NMDA receptor pore.

NMDA receptor

AMPA receptor

**(C) Weak electrical stimulation**

Now glutamate, released by weak stimulation, can activate the NMDA receptor to allow $Ca^{2+}$ influx, which, through a second messenger, increases the function or number of AMPA receptors or both.

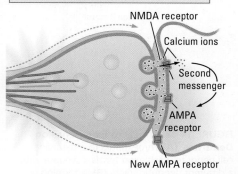

NMDA receptor

Calcium ions

Second messenger

AMPA receptor

New AMPA receptor

**FIGURE 14-17 Lasting Effects of Glutamate** Enhanced glutamate prompts a neurochemical cascade that underlies synaptic changes and LTP.

Although the studies generated by Bliss and Lømø's discoveries have focused on excitatory synapses, experiments on inhibitory GABA interneurons demonstrate phenomena similar to LTP and LTD, labeled *iLTP* and *iLTD*, respectively. This discovery was a surprise. At the time, it was generally believed that inhibitory neurons were not plastic, but we now know that they definitely are. It appears that the plasticity of GABAergic (inhibitory) synapses plays some fundamental role in modulating networks of excitatory neurons.

Studying LTP mechanisms highlights neuroscientists' uncertainty over where plastic changes are located. Our discussion emphasizes postsynaptic changes, but a strong case can be made that key presynaptic changes are at work, too (e.g., MacDougall & Fine, 2014). In general, plasticity likely requires change on both sides of the synapse. The presynaptic side, by virtue of being activated first, may prove key in the early phases of synaptic changes.

# Measuring Synaptic Change

In principle, experience could change the brain in either of two ways: by modifying existing circuitry or by creating novel circuitry. In actuality, the plastic brain uses both strategies.

## Modifying Existing Circuits

The simplest way to find synaptic change is to look for gross changes in the morphology of dendrites. Essentially, dendritic spines are extensions of the neuron membrane that allow more space for synapses: more dendrites mean more connections. Cells that have few or no dendrites have limited space for inputs. Cells with complex dendritic protrusions may have space for tens of thousands of inputs—in pyramidal cells, for example, 95% of excitatory synapses are on the dendrites. Change in dendritic structure, therefore, implies change in synaptic organization. Measuring the extent of dendritic changes allows us to infer synaptic change.

What do changes in dendritic morphology reveal? Consider a given neuron that generates more synaptic space. The new synapses can provide either additional points of contact between neurons that were already connected with that neuron or new contacts between neurons not formerly connected. **Figure 14-18** illustrates examples of these distinct synapse types.

New synapses can result either from the growth of new axon terminals or from the formation of synapses along axons as they pass by dendrites (Figure 14-18A and B). In both cases, the new synapses correspond to changes in local or regional circuitry

**(A) Before experience**

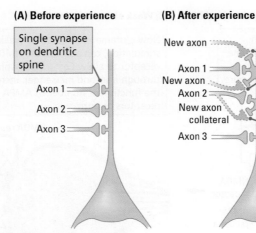

Single synapse on dendritic spine

Axon 1
Axon 2
Axon 3

**(B) After experience**

New axon
Axon 1
New axon
Axon 2
New axon collateral
Axon 3

Formation of new synapses from new axon terminals

Formation of new synapses from original terminals

**(C) Various observed shapes of new dendritic spines**

**FIGURE 14-18 Effects of Experience on Dendrites (A)** Three inputs to a pyramidal cell dendrite. Each axon forms a synapse with a different dendritic spine. **(B)** In forming multiple spine heads, either the original axons can divide and innervate two spine heads, or new axons or axon collaterals (dotted outlines) can innervate the new spine heads. **(C)** Single dendritic spines may sprout multiple synapses.

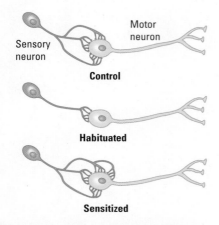

Sensory neuron

Motor neuron

**Control**

**Habituated**

**Sensitized**

**FIGURE 14-19 Physical Basis of Memory** Relative to a control neuronal connection (*top*), the number of synapses between *Aplysia*'s sensory neuron and a motor neuron decline as a result of habituation (*middle*) and increase as a result of sensitization (*bottom*). Such structural changes may underlie enduring memories.

Section 10-5 discusses the neurobiology of birdsong.

Experiment 7-1 confirms the hypothesis that hippocampal neurons contribute to memory formation.

rather than to the development of new connections between distant parts of the brain. Forming new connections between widely separated brain regions would be difficult in a fully developed brain: the dense plexus of cells, fibers, and blood vessels blocks the way.

Neurons change their synaptic structure in response to changing experiences, as illustrated again by *Aplysia*. Researchers working with Eric Kandel (Bailey et al., 2015) found that the number and size of sensory synapses change in well-trained, habituated, and sensitized *Aplysia*. Relative to a control neuron, the number and size of synapses decrease in habituated animals and increase in sensitized animals, as represented in **Figure 14-19**. Apparently, synaptic events associated with habituation and sensitization can also trigger processes in the sensory cell that result in the loss or formation of new synapses.

Tammy Ivanco and her colleagues (2000) similarly showed that LTP in the somatosensory cortex leads to increased dendritic length and spine density in cortical pyramidal neurons. Thus, we can see that learning, whether in simple animals such as *Aplysia* or in more complex animals such as rats, is consistently associated with changes in synapse numbers (see also Kolb et al., 2008).

## Creating Novel Circuits

Only 50 years ago, the general assumption was that the mammalian brain does not generate new neurons in adulthood. The unexpected discovery in the 1970s that the brains of songbirds such as canaries grow new neurons that allow them to produce songs in the mating season led researchers to reconsider this assumption. Ultimately, they found that the adult mammalian brain is also capable of generating new neurons.

This discovery emerged from directly injecting animals with a compound — bromodeoxyuridine (BrdU) — that is taken up by cells when they divide to produce new cells, including neurons. When the compound is injected into adult rats, dividing cells incorporate it into their DNA. In later analysis, a specific stain can identify the new neurons.

The BrdU technique has yielded considerable evidence that the mammalian brain, including the primate brain, can generate neurons destined for the olfactory bulb, the hippocampal formation, and possibly even the frontal and temporal lobe neocortex (Eriksson et al., 1998; Gould et al., 1999). The mechanism by which this occurs is not yet clear, but adult neurogenesis may enhance brain plasticity, particularly in regard to the processes underlying learning and memory. Elizabeth Gould and her colleagues (1999) showed, for example, that generation of new neurons in the hippocampus is enhanced when animals learn explicit memory tasks.

Experience appears to increase the generation of these new neurons. A fascinating demonstration of experience driving neurogenesis comes from a study by Katherine

Woollett and Eleanor Maguire (2011). As we noted in Section 14-3, London taxi drivers, who must learn the locations of and pass an exam on central London's roughly 25,000 irregular streets, have been shown to possess larger-than-normal volumes of neurons in their hippocampal posterior region. The investigators wanted to determine whether this large volume resulted from taking a 4-year course to pass the exam or was already present when the candidate drivers started the course.

Woollett and Maguire recorded structural MRIs from the would-be taxi drivers before and after training and then compared the trainees who passed the qualifying exam (*n* = 39) with those who failed it (*n* = 20). The MRIs showed that for the qualifiers, hippocampal volume increased over the pre-course measures; those who failed showed no changes. Woollett and Maguire later showed that when taxi drivers retired, their hippocampal volume decreased, indicating that the changes were related to use.

# Enriched Experience and Plasticity

One way to stimulate animals' brains is to house the animals in environments that provide sensory or motor experiences. Donald Hebb (1947, 1949) took laboratory rats home and gave them the run of his kitchen. After an interval, Hebb compared these "enriched" rats with a group that had remained caged in his laboratory at McGill University: he trained both groups to solve various mazes. The enriched animals performed better, and Hebb concluded that one effect of the enriched experience is to enhance later learning. This important conclusion laid the foundation for the U.S. Head Start programs, which provide healthy, enriched academic experiences for preschool-aged children living in under-resourced environments.

Subsequent investigators have opted for a more constrained enriched enclosure. For example, in our own studies, we place groups of about six rats in enclosures (see **Figure 14-20**). The enclosures give animals a rich social experience as well as extensive sensory and motor experiences. The most obvious consequence is increased brain weight—on the order of 10% relative to cage-reared animals—even though the "enriched" rats typically weigh less, in part because they get more exercise.

The key question is, What is responsible for the increased brain weight? A comprehensive series of studies by Anita Sirevaag and William Greenough (1988) used light- and electron-microscopic techniques to analyze 36 aspects of cortical synaptic, cellular, and vascular morphology in rats raised either in a cage or in a complex environment. The simple conclusion: in response to differential experiences, a coordinated change occurs not only in dendritic extent, but also in glial, vascular, and metabolic processes (**Figure 14-21**).

Animals with enriched experience have more synapses per neuron, as well as more astrocytes, more blood capillaries, and higher mitochondrial volumes. Clearly, when the brain changes in response to experiences, the expected neural changes take place, along with adjustments in the metabolic requirements of the now larger neurons.

Gerd Kempermann and his colleagues (1998) sought to determine whether experience actually alters the number of neurons in the brain. To test this idea, they compared neuronal generation in the hippocampi of mice housed in a complex environment with that of mice reared in a laboratory cage. They located the number of new neurons by injecting the animals with BrdU several times while they were living in complex housing. The new neurons generated in the brain during the experiment incorporated the BrdU.

When the researchers later looked at the hippocampi, they found more new neurons in the complex-housed rats than in the caged rats—a result that has been repeatedly confirmed (see the review by Kempermann, 2019). Although the investigators did not look in other parts of the brain, such as the olfactory bulb, we can reasonably expect that similar changes took place in other neural structures. This result is exciting because it implies that experience can not only alter existing circuitry but also influence neurogenesis and, therefore, new circuitry.

**FIGURE 14-20 Enriched Enclosure for Rats**

Section 8-4 details Hebb's first enrichment exercise—and his wife's reaction.

**FIGURE 14-21 Consequences of Enrichment** Cortical changes that occur in response to experience are found not only in neurons but also in astrocytes and vasculature. (Data from Kolb et al., 2003; Sirevaag & Greenough, 1987; and Turner & Greenough, 1985).

# Sensory or Motor Training and Plasticity

Studies showing neuronal changes in animals housed in a complex environment demonstrate that large areas of the brain can change with experience. This finding leads us to ask whether specific experiences might produce synaptic changes in localized cerebral regions. One way to approach this question is to give animals specific experiences and then see how their brains have changed. Another way is to look at the brains of people who have had a lifetime of some particular experience. In the following subsections, we consider each of these research strategies separately.

## Manipulating Experience Experimentally

Fen-Lei Chang and William Greenough (1982) conducted perhaps the most convincing manipulated-experience study. In doing so, they took advantage of the fact that the laboratory rat's visual pathways are approximately 90% crossed. That is, approximately 90% of the connections from the left eye to the cortex project through the right thalamus to the right hemisphere, and vice versa for the right eye. (In humans, only about half of the optic fibers cross—see Figure 9-14.)

Chang and Greenough placed a patch over one eye of each rat and then trained the animals in a maze. The visual cortex of only one eye received input about the maze, but the auditory, olfactory, tactile, and motor regions in both hemispheres were equally active as the animals explored. A comparison of the neurons in each hemisphere revealed that those in the visual cortex of the trained hemisphere had more extensive dendrites. Because the hemispheres did not differ in other respects, the researchers concluded that some feature associated with encoding, processing, or storage of visual input from training was responsible for forming new synapses.

Randy Nudo and his colleagues (1997) conducted complementary studies, mapping the motor cortex of monkeys. They noted striking individual differences in the topography. The investigators speculated that individual variability might be due to each monkey's experiences up to the time at which the cortical map was derived. To test this idea directly, Nudo and colleagues trained two groups of squirrel monkeys to retrieve banana-flavored food pellets from either a small food well or a large one. The monkeys from the first group were able to insert their entire hand into the large well, but the monkeys from the second group were able to fit only one or two fingers into the small well, as illustrated in the Procedures section of **Experiment 14-4**.

Researchers allowed the monkeys from each group to make the same number of finger flexions to retrieve the food. They charted each group's success over a 2-week period (after approximately 12,000 flexions in total). The monkeys trained on the small well improved with practice, making fewer finger flexions per food retrieval as training proceeded. When the researchers

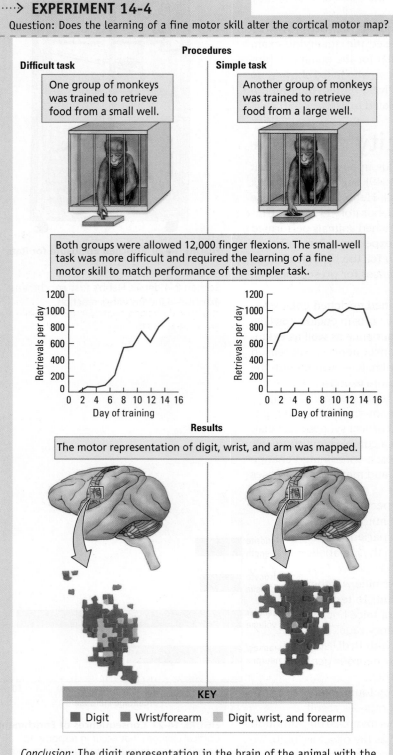

Information from Nudo et al. (1997).

····▸ **EXPERIMENT 14-4**

Question: Does the learning of a fine motor skill alter the cortical motor map?

**Procedures**

**Difficult task**

One group of monkeys was trained to retrieve food from a small well.

**Simple task**

Another group of monkeys was trained to retrieve food from a large well.

Both groups were allowed 12,000 finger flexions. The small-well task was more difficult and required the learning of a fine motor skill to match performance of the simpler task.

**Results**

The motor representation of digit, wrist, and arm was mapped.

**KEY**

■ Digit    ■ Wrist/forearm    ■ Digit, wrist, and forearm

*Conclusion:* The digit representation in the brain of the animal with the more difficult task is larger, corresponding to the neuronal changes necessary for the acquired skill.

used microelectrode stimulation of the cortex to create maps of the monkeys' forelimb movements (shown in the Results section), the maps showed systematic changes in the animals trained on the small well but not on the large well. Presumably, these changes resulted from the more demanding motor requirements of the small-well condition. The results from this study demonstrate that learning new motor skills, rather than simply repetitive motor use, shapes the functional topography of the motor cortex.

Most studies demonstrating plasticity in the motor cortex have been performed with laboratory animals whose cortex was mapped by microelectrode stimulation. More recently, imaging techniques such as transcranial magnetic stimulation (TMS) and fMRI have made it possible to show parallel results in humans who have special motor skills. For example, right-handed musicians who play stringed instruments show an increased cortical representation of the fingers of the left hand and Braille readers an increased cortical representation of the reading finger.

Thus, the functional organization of the motor cortex is altered by skilled use in humans. It can also be altered by chronic injury in humans and laboratory animals. Jon Kaas (2000) showed that when the sensory nerves in one limb are severed in monkeys, large-scale changes in their somatosensory maps ensue. In particular, in the absence of input, the relevant part of the cortex no longer responds to limb stimulation, which is not surprising. However, this cortex does not remain inactive. Rather, the deafferented cortex begins to respond to input from other body parts. For example, the region that formerly responded to hand stimulation now responds to stimulation on the face, a cortical area normally adjacent to the hand area.

Similar results can be found in the cortical maps of people who have had a limb amputated. For example, Vilayanur Ramachandran (1993) found that when a hand amputee's face is brushed lightly with a cotton swab, the person has a sensation of the amputated hand being touched. **Figure 14-22** illustrates the rough map of the hand that Ramachandran was actually able to chart on the face. The likely explanation for this finding is that the face area in the motor cortex has expanded to occupy the deafferented limb cortex, but the brain circuitry still responds to the cortical activity as representing input from the limb. This change may be related to the phantom limb pain often experienced by amputees. Researchers have shown that aberrant activity also occurs in the residual intact muscles in the leg when the phantom foot moves, and this sensation is related to the phantom limb pain (Therrien et al., 2021).

The idea that experience can alter cortical maps can be demonstrated with other experiences. For instance, if animals are trained to make certain digit movements over and over again, the cortical representation of those digits expands at the expense of the remaining motor areas. Similarly, if animals are trained extensively to discriminate among different sensory stimuli such as tones, the auditory cortical areas responding to those stimuli increase in size.

As described in Research Focus 14-5: Movement, Learning, and Neuroplasticity, one effect of musical training is to alter the motor representations of the digits used to play different instruments. We can speculate that musical training probably alters the auditory representations of specific sound frequencies as well. Both changes are essentially forms of memory, and the underlying synaptic changes likely take place on the appropriate sensory or motor cortical maps.

## Experience-Dependent Changes in the Human Brain

According to Ramachandran's amputee study, the human brain appears to change with altered experience. However, this study did not examine neuronal change directly, but rather inferred it from behavior. The only way to examine synaptic change directly is to look directly at brain tissue. In living humans, this is not an option, but the brains of

**(A)**

Cotton swab

**(B)**

Thumb

Ball of thumb

Index finger

Pinkie finger

**FIGURE 14-22 Cortical Reorganization** When a hand amputee's face is stroked lightly with a cotton swab **(A)**, the person experiences the stroke as a light touch on the missing hand **(B)** as well as a touch to the face. The deafferented cortex forms a representation of the amputated hand on the face. As in the normal somatosensory homunculus, the thumb is disproportionately large. Information from Ramachandran (1993).

Research Focus 11-4 recounts Ramachandran's therapy for minimizing phantom limb pain and describes some innovative treatments using neuroprosthetics and other techniques.

Section 10-4 discusses the benefits of music for the brain. Section 15-3 examines the neural basis for perfect pitch. Section 16-1 describes music as therapy for neurological disorders, including Parkinson disease.

## RESEARCH FOCUS 14-5

# Movement, Learning, and Neuroplasticity

Many lines of research show that practicing a motor skill — playing a musical instrument, for instance — induces changes in the cortical somatosensory and motor maps. The mental maps generally become larger, at least for the finger and hand representations.

Presumably, musical skill improves with practice, but are other abilities enhanced, too? Patrick Ragert and colleagues (2003) showed that professional pianists have not only better motor skills in their fingers but also enhanced somatosensory perception. When these researchers measured the ability to detect subtle sensory stimulation of the fingertips, they found that the pianists were more sensitive than controls. They also found that the enhanced tactile sensitivity was related to the number of hours per day that the musicians spent practicing.

The investigators then asked whether the enhanced perceptual ability precluded further improvement in the musicians. Surprisingly, when both the musicians and the controls were given a 3-hour training session designed to improve tactile sensitivity, the musicians showed more improvement than did the controls. Again, the extent of improvement correlated with daily practice time. This result implies that well-practiced musicians not only learn to play music but also develop a greater capacity for learning. Rather than use up all the available synapses, they gain the capacity to make even more.

Not all motor learning is good, however. Many musicians develop *focal hand dystonia* — abnormal finger and hand positions, cramps, and difficulty

emreogan/Getty Images

coordinating hand and finger movements. Dystonia can be so disabling that some musicians must give up their occupation.

Typically, dystonia afflicts musicians who practice trying to make perfect finger movements on their instruments. Musicians at high risk include string players, who receive vibratory stimulation at their fingertips. The constant practice has been suggested to lead to not only improved musical ability but also distorted or disordered cortical motor maps. Synchronous activation of the digits by the vibration leads to this unwanted side effect.

Victor Candia and colleagues (2003) reasoned that musicians' dystonia was probably an example of disordered learning and could be treated by retuning the motor map. The investigators used magnetoencephalography (MEG) to measure changes in sensory-evoked magnetic fields in the cortex.

At the beginning of the study, the musicians with dystonia had a disordered motor map: the finger areas overlapped one another. During the training, each particpcant used a hand splint tailored to their hand. The splint immobilized different fingers while the participants independently moved the others. After 8 days of training for about 2 hours per day, the participants showed marked alleviation in the dystonic symptoms, and the neuroimaging showed a normalization of the cortical map, with distinct finger areas. Thus, training reversed the learned changes in the motor map and treated the dystonia. The musicians had actually learned a disorder, and they were able to unlearn it.

---

people who have died of something other than neurological causes can be examined so that the structure of their cortical neurons can be related to their experiences.

One way to approach this idea is to look for a relationship between neuronal structure and education. Arnold Scheibel and his colleagues conducted many such studies in the 1990s (e.g., Jacobs & Scheibel, 1993; Jacobs et al., 1993). In one study, they found a relationship between dendrite size in Wernicke's area and level of education. In the brains of college-educated deceased people, the cortical neurons from this language area had more dendritic branches than did those from people with a high school education, which, in turn, had more dendritic material than did those from people with less education. The general conclusion is that education increases neuron complexity, but it is also possible that people who have more dendrites may be more likely to go to college — a hypothesis that is not easy to test.

Another way to look at the relationship between neurons in Wernicke's area and behavior is to take advantage of the now well-documented observation that, on average, females' verbal abilities are superior to those of males. When Scheibel and his colleagues examined the structure of neurons in Wernicke's area, they found that females do have more extensive dendritic branching there than males do.

Finally, these investigators took a slightly different approach to explore the link between experience and neuronal morphology. They began with two hypotheses.

First, they suggested a relationship between the complexity of dendritic branching and the nature of the computational tasks performed by a brain area. To test this

Wernicke's area contributes to speech and to language comprehension; see Figure 10-18.

Figure 15-20 diagrams tasks that consistently show, on average, that females' verbal fluency surpasses males', and that males outperform females on spatial reasoning tasks.

hypothesis, they examined the dendritic structure of neurons in different cortical regions that handle different computational tasks. For example, when they compared the structure of neurons corresponding to the somatosensory representation of the trunk with those for the fingers, they found that the latter have more complex cells (**Figure 14-23**). They reasoned that the somatosensory inputs from receptive fields on the chest wall would constitute less of a computational challenge to cortical neurons than would those from the fingers and that the neurons representing the chest would therefore be less complex.

The group's second hypothesis was that dendritic branching in all regions is subject to experience-dependent change (recall the changes in hippocampal volume for the taxi drivers noted earlier). The researchers hypothesized that predominant life experiences (e.g., occupation) should, as a result, alter dendritic structure. Although they did not test this hypothesis directly, they did make an interesting observation. In their study comparing cells in the trunk area, in the finger area, and in the supramarginal gyrus—a parietal lobe region associated with higher cognitive processes (thinking)—they found curious individual differences.

For instance, especially large differences in trunk and finger neurons appeared in the brains of people who had a high level of finger dexterity maintained over long periods (say, computer programmers or typists). In contrast, no difference between trunk and finger neurons was found in sales representatives. Remember that Scheibel and colleagues conducted their research before portable electronic devices entered the workplace; we would not expect a good deal of specialized finger use among sales representatives during that era and, therefore, would see less complex demands on their finger neurons.

In summary, although the studies showing a relationship between experience and neuronal structure in humans depend on correlations rather than actual experiments, their findings are consistent with those observed in experimental studies of other species. We are led to the general conclusion that specific experiences can produce localized changes in the synaptic organization of the brain and that such changes form the structural basis of memory.

**FIGURE 14-23 Experience and Neuronal Complexity** Confirmation of Scheibel's hypothesis that cell complexity is related to the computational demands required of the cell. Neurons that represent the body's trunk area have relatively less computational demands than do cells representing the finger region. In turn, cells engaged in higher cognitive functions (such as language, as in Wernicke's area) have greater computational demands than do those engaged in finger functions.

## Epigenetics of Memory

An enigma in the search for neural mechanisms underlying memory is the fact that whereas memories remain stable over time, all cells are constantly undergoing molecular turnover. The simplest explanation for this seeming contradiction is epigenetic: specific sites in the DNA of neurons involved in specific memories might exist in either a methylated or a nonmethylated state.

Courtney Miller and colleagues (2010) tested this idea directly by measuring methylation in the hippocampi of rats that underwent contextual fear conditioning (see Experiment 14-1). They showed that fear conditioning is associated with rapid methylation; in contrast, if they pharmacologically blocked methylation, there was no memory of the fear stimulus. The investigators concluded that epigenetic mechanisms mediate synaptic plasticity broadly—but especially in learning and memory. One implication of these results is that cognitive disorders, including memory defects, could result from aberrant epigenetic modifications (for a review, see Day et al., 2015).

Some evidence also indicates that memory-related epigenetic changes can be transmitted to later generations. Brian Dias and colleagues (2015) trained male mice in an olfactory fear conditioning paradigm in which a specific odor was paired with a mild shock to the foot. The mice with this training developed more olfactory neurons responsive to the odor and more axons into the olfactory glomeruli. The mice mated following the conditioning, and the changes in the olfactory bulb were observed in the future offspring and grand-offspring, even though the younger mice had never been conditioned. Inheritance was associated with decreased DNA methylation around the specific olfactory receptor gene in the sperm of the original males and their offspring. In a subsequent study, when Dias and his colleagues extinguished the learning in the male parent mice with repeated presentations of odor only, the subsequent offspring

Figure 3-26 illustrates two aspects of methylation: histone and DNA modification.

Figure 12-10 provides a refresher on the anatomy related to olfaction.

This transmission of epigenetic changes to offspring is also observed in the context of alcohol use by fathers prior to conception, with potential negative impacts on fetal development, as described in Clinical Focus 6-2.

Chapter 6 details the effects of a variety of drugs on our various neurotransmitter systems.

Section 5-4 explains the classes, functions, and control that hormones exert; Section 8-4, their organizing effects during development; and Section 12-5, their activating effects in adulthood.

did not show the changes in the olfactory bulb or the decreased methylation observed in prior generations (Aoued et al., 2019).

Other studies have shown that early traumatic stress alters small noncoding RNAs in sperm, and this effect is related to behavioral and metabolic alterations in offspring (see, for example, Gapp et al., 2014). Taken together, these studies suggest that epigenetic changes related to experiences may contribute to the inheritance of phenotypes across generations.

# Plasticity, Hormones, Trophic Factors, and Drugs

Historically, media reports have tended to emphasize the risks of brain damage from the use of psychoactive drugs, but the reality is a bit more complicated than that broad-brush presentation suggests. Some drugs certainly do act as toxins and can selectively kill brain regions, but a more accurate description of drugs' action is that they *change* the brain. Although not many studies have looked at drug-induced morphological changes, evidence reveals that some compounds can greatly change the brain's synaptic organization. These compounds include hormones, neurotrophic factors, and psychoactive drugs. We briefly consider each category.

## Hormones and Plasticity

Levels of circulating hormones are critical both in determining brain structure and in eliciting certain behaviors in adulthood. Although the structural effects of hormones were once believed to be expressed only in the course of development, current belief is that adult neurons also can respond to hormonal manipulations with dramatic structural changes. Here we consider the actions of gonadal hormones and stress hormones.

Research findings have established that structural differences in cortical neurons of male and female rats depend on gonadal hormones. More surprising, perhaps, is that gonadal hormones can influence cell structure and behavior in human females across the menstrual cycle, although the data are inconsistent and remain controversial (e.g., Le et al., 2020).

Changes in estrogen level appear to alter the structure of neurons and astrocytes in the neocortex and hippocampus, which would predict fluctuations in behavior over the menstrual cycle. **Figure 14-24** illustrates changes in dendritic spines in the hippocampal cells of female rats at different phases of their 4-day estrous cycle. As the estrogen level rises, the number of synapses rises; as the estrogen level drops, the number of synapses declines.

Curiously, estrogen's influence on cell structure may differ in the hippocampus and the neocortex. Jane Stewart found, for example, that when the ovaries of middle-aged female rats are removed, their estrogen levels drop sharply, producing increased numbers of spines on pyramidal cells throughout the neocortex but decreased spine density in the hippocampus (Stewart & Kolb, 1994). How these synaptic changes might influence processes such as memory is not immediately obvious, but the question is reasonable, especially because menopausal women also experience sharp drops in estrogen levels and a corresponding decline in verbal memory ability.

Estrogen levels high

Estrogen levels low

**FIGURE 14-24 Hormones and Neuroplasticity** Sections of dendrites from hippocampal cells during times of high and low estrogen levels during the rat's 4-day estrous cycle reveal many more dendritic spines when estrogen levels are high. Information from Woolley et al. (1990).

This question is also relevant to middle-aged men, who show a slow decline in testosterone levels that correlates with a drop in spatial ability. Rats that are gonadectomized in adulthood show increased cortical spine density, much like the ovariectomized females. Although we do not know how this change relates to spatial behavior, a reasonable supposition is that testosterone levels might influence spatial memory throughout life.

When the body is stressed, the pituitary gland produces adrenocorticotrophic hormone (ACTH), which stimulates the adrenal cortex to produce steroid hormones, known as *glucocorticoids*. Important in protein and carbohydrate metabolism, control of sugar levels in the blood, and absorption of sugar by cells, glucocorticoids have many actions on the body, including the brain. Robert Sapolsky (1992) proposed that glucocorticoids can sometimes be neurotoxic. In particular, he found that with prolonged stress, glucocorticoids appear to kill hippocampal cells.

Elizabeth Gould and her colleagues (1998) showed that even brief periods of stress can reduce the number of new granule cells produced in the hippocampi of monkeys, presumably through the actions of stress hormones. Neuron death and reduced neuron generation in the hippocampus has obvious implications for animal behavior, especially for processes such as spatial memory. Moreover, Richelle Mychasiuk and her colleagues (2016) showed that stress has contrasting epigenetic effects in the hippocampus and prefrontal cortex of rats, with virtually no overlap in which genes are expressed in these regions in males versus females.

In sum, hormones can alter the brain's synaptic organization and even the number of neurons in the brain. As yet, little is known about the behavioral consequences of such changes. It is likely that hormones can alter the course of plastic changes in the brain, possibly through epigenetic mechanisms.

## Neurotrophic Factors and Plasticity

*Neurotrophic factors,* chemical compounds that signal stem cells to develop into neurons or glia, also act to reorganize neural circuits. **Table 14-2** lists molecules that act as neurotrophic factors. The first, **nerve growth factor (NGF)**, was discovered in the peripheral nervous system more than a generation ago. NGF is trophic (nourishing) in the sense that it stimulates neurons to grow dendrites and synapses, and in some cases promotes neuronal survival.

Trophic factors produced in the brain by neurons and glia can affect neurons both through cell membrane receptors and by actually entering the neuron to act internally on its operation. Trophic factors may be released postsynaptically, for example, to act as signals that can influence the presynaptic cell. Experience stimulates their production, so neurotrophic factors have been proposed as agents of synaptic change. For example, levels of brain-derived neurotrophic factor (BDNF) increase when animals solve specific problems such as mazes. This finding has led to speculation that BDNF release may enhance such plastic changes as the growth of dendrites and synapses.

Although many researchers would like to conclude that BDNF has a role in learning, this conclusion does not necessarily follow. When animals solve mazes, their behavior differs from their behavior when they remain in cages. So, we must first demonstrate that changes in BDNF, NGF, or any trophic factor are actually related to forming new synapses. Nevertheless, if we assume that trophic factors do act as synaptic change agents, then we should be able to use increased trophic factor activity during learning as a marker for where to look for changed synapses associated with learning and memory.

## Psychoactive Drugs and Plasticity

Many people regularly use the stimulant caffeine, and some use more stimulating psychoactive drugs, such as nicotine, amphetamine, or cocaine. The long-term consequences of using certain psychoactive drugs, such as Ecstasy, are now well documented, but the question of *why* these drugs cause problems remains to be answered. One explanation for the behavioral changes associated with chronic psychoactive drug abuse is that the drugs change the brain.

One experimental demonstration of these changes relies on *drug-induced behavioral sensitization,* often referred to as simply **behavioral sensitization** and defined as the progressive increase in behavioral actions in response to repeated administration of a drug. Behaviors may increase even when the amount given in each dose does not change. Behavioral sensitization occurs with most psychoactive drugs, including amphetamine, cocaine, morphine, and nicotine.

As we saw in Experiment 14-3, the sea slug *Aplysia* becomes more sensitive to a stimulus after repeated exposure. Psychoactive drugs appear to have a parallel action: they lead to increased behavioral sensitivity to their actions. For example, a rat given a small dose of amphetamine may show increased activity. When the rat is given the

Figure 5-22 illustrates the body's stress response.

Section 8-2 explains how neurotrophic factors send these signals.

**TABLE 14-2** Molecules Exhibiting Neurotrophic Activity

| Proteins initially characterized as neurotrophic factors |
| --- |
| Nerve growth factor (NGF) |
| Brain-derived neurotrophic factor (BDNF) |
| Neurotrophin 3 (NT-3) |
| Ciliary neurotrophic factor (CNTF) |
| **Growth factors with neurotrophic activity** |
| Fibroblast growth factor, acidic (aFGF *or* FGF-1) |
| Fibroblast growth factor, basic (bFGF *or* FGF-2) |
| Epidermal growth factor (EGF) |
| Insulinlike growth factor (ILGF) |
| Transforming growth factor (TGF) |
| Lymphokines (interleukin 1, 3, 6 or IL-1, IL-3, IL-6) |
| Protease nexin I, II |
| Cholinergic neuronal differentiation factor |

The potentially damaging effects of specific psychoactive drugs are detailed in Section 6-4.

**nerve growth factor (NGF)** Neurotrophic factor that stimulates neurons to grow dendrites and synapses and in some cases promotes the survival of neurons.

**behavioral sensitization** Escalating behavioral response to the repeated administration of a psychomotor stimulant such as amphetamine, cocaine, or nicotine; also called *drug-induced behavioral sensitization* and sometimes simply *sensitization.*

···▷ **EXPERIMENT 14-5**

Question: What effect do repeated doses of amphetamine, a psychomotor stimulant, have on neurons?

**Procedure**

Animals received multiple doses of amphetamine. Neurons were drawn from nucleus accumbens.

**Results**

Amphetamine                     Saline

Nucleus accumbens

Rats that show sensitization to amphetamine have increased dendritic growth and spine density...

...relative to saline-treated rats that served as controls.

*Conclusion:* The sensitization induced by repeated exposure to amphetamine changes the structure of neurons in certain brain areas.

Information from Robinson & Kolb (1997).

Section 6-1 details the development of the contrasting processes of sensitization and tolerance to drugs.

same dose of amphetamine on subsequent occasions, the increase in activity is progressively larger. If no drug is given for weeks or even months and then amphetamine is given in the same dose as before, behavioral sensitization picks up where it left off and continues to progress. This suggests that some long-lasting change must have taken place in the brain in response to the drug. Drug-induced behavioral sensitization can therefore be viewed as a memory for a particular drug.

The parallel between drug-induced behavioral sensitization and other forms of memory leads us to ask if the changes in the brain after behavioral sensitization are similar to those found after other forms of learning. They are. For instance, researchers have found evidence of increased numbers of receptors at synapses and of more synapses in sensitized animals.

In a series of studies, Terry Robinson and his colleagues documented dramatic increases in dendritic growth and spine density in rats sensitized to amphetamine, cocaine, or nicotine relative to rats that received injections of a saline solution (Robinson & Kolb, 2004). **Experiment 14-5** compares the effects of amphetamine and saline treatments on cells in the nucleus accumbens in the basal ganglia. Neurons in amphetamine-treated brains have more dendritic branches and increased spine density, indicating that repeated exposure to psychoactive stimulants alters the structure of brain cells. These changes, in turn, may be related to learned addictions.

In Robinson and colleagues' studies, these plastic changes were not found throughout the brain, but rather were localized to regions such as the prefrontal cortex and nucleus accumbens that receive a large dopamine projection. (Recall from Section 6-4 that dopamine is believed to play a significant role in the "wanting" aspect of drug use.) Other psychoactive drugs also appear to alter neuronal structure. Notably, tetrahydrocannabinol (THC; an active component of cannabis), morphine, and certain antidepressants change dendritic length and spine density, albeit in ways different from those of stimulants. Morphine, for example, reduces dendritic length and spine density in the nucleus accumbens and prefrontal cortex (Robinson & Kolb, 2004).

What do drug-induced changes in synaptic organization mean for later experience-dependent plasticity? If rats are given amphetamine, cocaine, nicotine, or THC for 2 weeks before being placed in a complex environment, the expected increases in dendritic length and spine density in the cortex do not happen (see Kolb et al., 2003; Kolb et al., 2018). This is not because the brain can no longer change: giving the animals additional drug doses can still produce changes in its structures. Rather, something about the prior drug exposure alters the way in which the brain later responds to experience.

Why prior drug exposure alters how the brain changes with experience remains unknown, but obviously drug taking can have long-term effects on brain plasticity. One possible explanation is epigenetic. Giving animals repeated doses of amphetamine or nicotine decreases methylation in both the prefrontal cortex and the nucleus accumbens, and decreased methylation is related to drug- and region-specific increases in gene expression (Mychasiuk et al., 2013). These epigenetic changes may render the synapses less able to change in response to later experiences.

# Some Guiding Principles of Brain Plasticity

Brain plasticity will continue to be a fundamental concept underlying research into brain–behavior relationships during the coming decades. Some basic rules have emerged to guide this research (see Kolb & Gibb, 2014, for more details). Here we list seven.

## 1. Behavioral Change Reflects Brain Change

The brain's primary function is to produce behavior, but behavior is not static. We learn and remember, we think new thoughts or visualize new images, and we change throughout life. All these processes require changes in neural networks. Whenever neural networks change, behavior, including mental behavior, also changes. One corollary to this rule is especially important as neuroscientists search for treatments for brain injuries or behavioral disorders: *to change behavior, we must change the brain.*

## 2. All Nervous Systems Are Plastic in the Same General Way

Even the simplest animals, such as the roundworm *Caenorhabditis elegans,* can show simple learning that correlates with neuronal plasticity. The molecular details may differ between simple and complex systems, but the principles of neuroplasticity appear to be conserved across both simple and complex animals. This conservation allows more studies of neural plasticity among a wider range of animal species than is possible in most other areas of neuroscience.

Investigators study neuroplasticity in species ranging from worms and insects to fish, birds, and mammals.

## 3. Plastic Changes Are Age Specific

The brain responds to the same experiences differently at different ages—and especially during development. The prefrontal cortex is late to mature, for example, so the same experience affects this region differently in infancy than it does in adolescence and later throughout life.

Section 8-4 traces how brain organization details change rapidly—and sometimes critically—during development.

## 4. Prenatal Events Can Influence Brain Plasticity Throughout Life

Prenatal experiences can alter brain organization. Potentially negative experiences, such as prenatal exposure to recreational or prescription drugs, and positive experiences, such as tactile stimulation of the mother's skin, may alter gene expression or induce other epigenetic effects that produce enduring effects on brain organization. Even paternal or maternal experiences before conception can alter later offspring's brain development and organization.

Section 8-4 recounts the benefits of tactile stimulation; Clinical Focus 8-2, epigenetic factors' roles in the autism spectrum; and Clinical Focus 6-2, the tragedy of fetal alcohol spectrum disorder.

## 5. Plastic Changes Are Brain-Region Dependent

Although we are tempted to expect plastic changes in neuronal networks to be fairly general, it is becoming clear that many experience-dependent changes are highly specific. We saw this specificity in the effects of psychoactive drugs on the prefrontal cortex but not on other cortical regions. Not only do drugs selectively change the prefrontal cortex, but the dorsolateral and orbital prefrontal areas also show opposite changes. The precise changes vary with the particular drug. For example, stimulants such as amphetamine increase spine density in the dorsolateral region but decrease it in the orbital region.

Figure 12-23 diagrams these prefrontal regions.

## 6. Experience-Dependent Changes Interact

**Metaplasticity** is a property of a lifetime's interactions among the different plastic changes occurring in the brain. As an animal travels through life, infinite experiences can alter its brain organization. On occasion, these experiences interact. Housing animals in complex environments, for example, produces profound changes in their neural network organization, but prior exposure to psychoactive drugs completely blocks the enrichment effect. Conversely, although complex housing does not block drug effects, enrichment markedly attenuates them. Prenatal events can affect later drug effects: prenatal tactile stimulation of the mother, for example, reduces the later effects of psychoactive drugs on the offspring.

## 7. Plasticity Has Pros and Cons

We have mainly emphasized the neuroplastic changes that can support improved motor and cognitive function. But, as we noted in our discussion of the effects of psychoactive drugs, plastic changes in neural networks can also interfere with behavior.

**metaplasticity** Interaction among different plastic changes in the brain.

People who have developed an addiction to a drug, and whose prefrontal cortex has been subsequently altered, are prone to poor judgment in their personal life. People who have posttraumatic stress disorder show altered blood flow in the amygdala and cingulate cortex. That's the bad news.

The good news is that by encouraging plastic changes that reverse these prefrontal alterations, we can treat or even eliminate some prefrontal disorders. For instance, age-related neurocognitive disorder is related to synaptic loss that various forms of cognitive therapy can reverse (e.g., Mahncke et al., 2006).

## 14-4 Review

Before you continue, check your understanding. Answers to Self-Test appear at the back of the book.

1. *Aplysia*'s synaptic function mediates two basic forms of learning: _____ and _____.

2. Repeated high-frequency stimulation of excitatory neurons leads to the phenomenon of _____, whereas repeated low-frequency stimulation leads to _____.

3. iLTP and iLTD are found in _____ neurons.

4. Structural changes underlying memory include changes in both _____ and the _____.

5. Learning complex spatial information has been linked to increased gray matter in the _____.

6. The progressive increase in behavioral actions in response to repeated administration of a drug is called _____.

7. How can plastic changes in the brain produce adverse effects?

## 14-5

# Recovery from Brain Injury

**Learning Objective**
• Describe ways in which recovery from brain injury can be stimulated.

Traumatic brain injury, along with a variety of other neurological disorders and their treatments, are discussed in Section 16-3.

The nervous system appears conservative in its use of mechanisms related to behavioral change. If neuroscientists wish to change the brain, perhaps after injury or disease, then they should look for treatments that will produce plastic changes related to learning, memory, and other behaviors.

Recall that H. M. failed to recover his lost memory capacities, even after 55 years of practice in trying to remember information. Relearning simply was not possible for H. M., because he had lost the requisite neural structures. But other people do show some recovery from brain injury.

A common assumption might suggest that the recovery process after brain trauma requires the injured person to relearn lost skills, whether walking, talking, or using the fingers. But what exactly does recovery entail? Partial recovery of function is common after brain injury, but a person with brain trauma or brain disease has lost neurons. The brain may be missing structures critical for relearning or remembering.

## Donna's Experience with Traumatic Brain Injury

Donna started dancing when she was 4 years old, and she was a natural. By the time she finished high school, she had the training and skill necessary to apprentice with and later join a major dance company. Donna remembers vividly the day she was chosen to dance a leading role in *The Nutcracker*. She had marveled at the costumes as she watched the popular Christmas ballet as a child, and now she would dance in those costumes!

The births of two children interrupted her career as a dancer, but Donna never lost the interest. In 1968, when both her children were in school, she began dancing again with a local company. To her amazement, she could still perform most of the movements, although she was rusty on the choreography of the classical dances that she had once memorized so meticulously. Nonetheless, she quickly relearned. In retrospect, she should not have been so surprised because she had always had an excellent memory.

One evening in 1990, while she was on a bicycle ride, a drunk driver struck Donna. She was wearing a helmet but received a brain-damaging blow to the head—a *traumatic brain injury (TBI)*. Donna was comatose for several weeks. When she regained consciousness, she was confused and had difficulty talking to and understanding others. Her memory was very poor; spatial disorientation meant she often got lost; she endured various motor disturbances; and she had difficulty recognizing anyone except her family and closest friends.

Over the ensuing 10 months, Donna regained most of her motor abilities and language skills, and her spatial abilities improved significantly. Nonetheless, she was short-tempered and easily frustrated by the slowness of her recovery—symptoms typical of people with brain trauma. She suffered periods of depression.

Donna also found herself prone to inexplicable surges of panic when doing simple things. On one occasion early in her rehabilitation, she was shopping in a large supermarket and became overwhelmed by the number of salad dressing choices. She ran from the store, and only after she sat outside and calmed herself could she go back inside to continue shopping.

Two years later, Donna was dancing once again, but she found learning and remembering new steps difficult. Her emotions were still unstable, which put a strain on her family, but her episodes of frustration and temper outbursts grew far less frequent. A year later, they were gone, and her life was not obviously different from that of other middle-aged women.

Even so, some cognitive changes persisted. Donna seemed unable to remember the names or faces of new people she met. She lost concentration if background distractions such as a television or a radio playing intruded. She could not dance as she had before her injury, but she did work at it diligently. Maintaining her balance on sudden turns gave her the most difficulty. Rather than risk falling, she retired from her life's first love.

Donna's case demonstrates the human brain's capacity for continuously changing its structure and ultimately its function throughout a lifetime. From what we have explored in this chapter, we can identify three ways in which Donna could recover from her brain injury: she could learn new ways to solve problems, she could reorganize the brain to do more with less, and she could generate new neurons to produce new neural circuits. We briefly examine each possibility.

Clinical Focus 1-1 and Section 1-1 introduce the consequences of and treatments for TBI, which we elaborate here and in Section 16-3.

## Three-Legged Cat Solution

A cat that loses a leg quickly learns to compensate for the missing limb and once again become mobile. In essence, it shows recovery of function: the limb is gone, but the cat's behavior has changed to compensate for the loss. This simplest solution to recovery from brain injury is thus called the *three-legged cat solution*.

A similar explanation can account for many instances of apparent recovery of function after TBI. Imagine a right-handed person has a stroke that costs them the use of their right hand and arm. Unable to write with the affected limb, the person switches to their left hand. Such behavioral compensation presupposes that some nervous system changes underlie this new skill.

## New-Circuit Solution

A second way to recover from brain damage is for the brain to form new connections that allow it to do more with less. This change is most easily accomplished by processes similar to those we considered for other forms of plasticity. In this case, the brain changes its neural connections to overcome the loss.

Without some intervention, recovery from most brain injuries is relatively modest. Recovery can increase significantly if the person engages in behavioral, pharmacological, or brain-stimulation therapy that encourages the brain to make new connections.

Behavioral therapy—such as speech therapy, physiotherapy, and music therapy—presumably increases brain activity, which facilitates neural changes. In a pharmacological intervention, the patient takes a drug, such as NGF, that is known to influence brain plasticity.

The brains of these dancers change in response to new experiences and new abilities. After her accident, Donna's brain had to change to allow her to regain her lost abilities, but she never recovered the ability that these young women have to learn new dances.

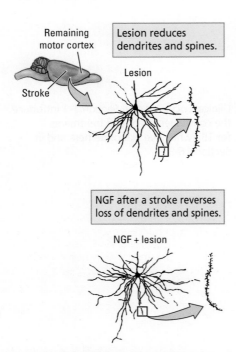

Remaining motor cortex

**Lesion reduces dendrites and spines.**

Stroke

Lesion

**NGF after a stroke reverses loss of dendrites and spines.**

NGF + lesion

**FIGURE 14-25 Dendritic Growth and NGF Treatment** Lesions caused by stroke reduce the number of dendrites and spines (*top*). Treatment with NGF reverses this reduction and promotes dendritic growth and spine density (*bottom*).

Clinical Focus 5-5 recounts a successful case of fetal stem cell transplantation.

The striatum, a region in the basal ganglia, includes the caudate nucleus and putamen.

Parmar, M., Grealish, S., & Henchcliffe, C. (2020). The future of stem cell therapies for Parkinson disease. *Nature Reviews Neuroscience, 21(2)*, 103-115.

Even in adults, neural stem cells line the subventricular zone, which is diagrammed in Figure 8-10A.

**epidermal growth factor (EGF)** Neurotrophic factor; stimulates the subventricular zone to generate cells that migrate into the striatum and eventually differentiate into neurons and glia.

When NGF is given to animals with stroke damage to the motor cortex, their motor functions improve. In a study carried out by the author, cortical strokes were induced in rats (Kolb et al., 1997). Some of the stroke-affected rats were given NGF treatment and tested against an untreated group and a healthy control group on tasks of skilled reaching. Both the healthy and NGF-treated groups showed improvement on repeated attempts; the untreated group showed no improvement. Postmortem analysis revealed that NGF stimulated dendritic growth and increased spine density in both of these groups (see **Figure 14-25**).

The behavioral changes displayed by the rats correlated with a dramatic increase in dendritic branching and spine density in the remaining intact motor regions, much as we saw in Experiment 14-5 with amphetamine exposure. The morphological changes correlated with improved motor functions, such as reaching with the forelimb to obtain food, as illustrated in Experiment 14-4 (Kolb et al., 1997). But because brain tissue was still missing, recovery was by no means complete.

In principle, we might expect that any drug that stimulates the growth of new connections would help people recover from brain injury. However, neural growth must occur in those brain regions that can influence a lost function. A drug that stimulates synaptic growth on cells in the visual cortex, for example, would not enhance recovery of hand use, because the visual neurons play no direct role in moving the hand.

A third strategy to generate new neural circuits is to use either deep brain stimulation (DBS) or direct electrical stimulation of perilesional regions. With DBS, the goal is to put the brain into a more plastic (trainable) state so that rehabilitation therapies work better. Electrical stimulation directly increases activity in the remaining parts of specific damaged neural networks. Both strategies are in preliminary clinical trials.

## Lost Neuron Replacement Solution

The third way a patient like Donna could pursue recovery is to generate new neurons to produce new neural circuits. The idea that brain tissue could be transplanted from one animal to another goes back a century. Tissue transplanted from fetal brains will grow and form some connections in the new brain, but in contrast to transplanted hearts or livers, the transplanted brain tissue functions poorly. This procedure seems best suited to conditions in which a small number of functional cells are required, as in the replacement of dopamine-producing cells in Parkinson disease or in the replacement of suprachiasmatic cells to restore circadian rhythms.

Today, dopamine-producing cells have been surgically transplanted into the striata of many people with Parkinson disease. Although the disease has not been reversed, some of these individuals, especially younger ones, have shown functional gains that justify the procedure. Nonetheless, ethical issues will remain as long as the tissue is taken from aborted human fetuses (Parmar et al., 2020).

Adult stem cells in the brain offer a second way to replace lost neurons. Investigators know that the brain is capable of making neurons in adulthood. The challenge is to get the brain to do so after an injury. Brent Reynolds and Sam Weiss (1992) made the first breakthrough in this line of research. In their studies, cells lining the ventricles of adult mice were removed and placed in a culture medium. The researchers demonstrated that if the correct trophic factors are added, the cells will begin to divide and can produce new neurons and glia. Furthermore, if trophic factors—particularly **epidermal growth factor (EGF)**—are infused into the ventricle of a living animal, the subventricular zone generates cells that migrate into the striatum and eventually differentiate into neurons and glia.

In principle, it ought to be possible to use trophic factors to stimulate the subventricular zone to generate new cells in the injured brain. If these new cells were to migrate to the site of injury and essentially regenerate the lost area, as shown in **Figure 14-26**, then it might be possible to restore at least some lost function. Not all lost behaviors could be restored, however, because the new neurons would have to establish the same connections with the rest of the brain that the lost neurons once had.

This task would be daunting: connections would have to be formed in an adult brain that already has billions of connections. Nonetheless, such a treatment might someday be feasible, and preclinical laboratory trials have yielded promising results. In previous research, cocktails of trophic factors have been shown to stimulate neurogenesis in the subventricular zone after brain injury. For example, as shown at left in Figure 14-26, animals first received ischemic injuries (strokes), then received intraventricular infusions of trophic factors for 14 days. New cells migrated to the site of injury, as shown at right in Figure 14-26, and many of them differentiated into immature neurons.

Although they did not integrate well into the existing brain, the new cells influenced behavior and led to functional improvement (Kolb et al., 2007). The mechanism by which this influence occurred remains poorly understood, however. The new neurons apparently had some trophic influence on the surrounding uninjured cortex. Preliminary clinical trials with humans are under way and so far show no ill effects in volunteers.

Another method of generating stem cells is to take advantage of *mesenchymal stem cells* (MSCs). This broad term encompasses many types of cells, but those most frequently used in research are derived from bone marrow. MSCs show promise for treating Parkinson-like diseases because they can be induced to differentiate into neuron-like cells and astrocytes. To date, applications of MSCs have shown promise in laboratory animal models (Liu & Cheung, 2020). Another type of stem cell that has shown promise in replacing neurons is the *pluripotent stem cell,* which can be generated directly from an adult somatic cell and can produce dopamine neurons in laboratory animals (see Sonntag et al., 2018).

**FIGURE 14-26  Stem Cells Do the Trick** *Left*: After cortical stroke (damage is visible at upper right), infusion of epidermal growth factor into a rat's lateral ventricle induced neurogenesis in the subventricular zone. *Right*: The stem cells migrated to the site of injury and filled in the damaged area. The cytological organization is, however, abnormal.

Bryan Kolb

## 14-5 Review

Before you continue, check your understanding. Answers to Self-Test appear at the back of the book.

1. Three ways to compensate for the loss of neurons are _____, _____, and _____.

2. Two methods of using electrical stimulation to enhance postinjury recovery are _____ and _____.

3. Endogenous stem cells can be recruited to enhance functional improvement by using _____ factors.

4. What is the lesson of the three-legged cat?

# Summary

## 14-1 Connecting Learning and Memory

Learning is a change in an organism's behavior as a result of experience. Memory is the ability to recall or recognize previous experience. For more than a century, laboratory studies using animals have uncovered two diverse types of learning: Pavlovian (or classical) and operant (or instrumental).

The two basic types of memory are implicit (unconscious) and explicit (conscious). Episodic memory includes not only a record of events (episodes) that occurred, but also our presence there and our role in those events. The frontal lobe likely plays a unique role in this autobiographical memory.

## 14-2 Dissociating Memory Circuits

Multiple subsystems control different aspects of memory within the explicit and implicit memory systems. People with damaged explicit memory circuits have impaired recall for facts and events. People with damaged implicit memory circuits have impaired recall and/or performance of skills and habits.

## 14-3 Neural Systems Underlying Explicit and Implicit Memories

The neural circuits underlying implicit and explicit memory are distinctly different: the reciprocal system for explicit memory includes medial temporal structures; the unidirectional system for implicit memory includes the basal ganglia. Emotional memory has characteristics of both implicit and explicit memory. Neural circuits for emotional memory also are unique in that they include the amygdala. Figure 14-5 summarizes broad categories within these multiple memory systems.

For memories to become established in the brain—a process known as consolidation—experiences must change neural connections, and these changes must become relatively permanent. When memories are revisited, neural connectivity can become less fixed, allowing for the neural networks and thus the memory to be modified, a process called reconsolidation.

## 14-4 Structural Basis of Brain Plasticity

The brain has the capacity for structural change, and structural change presumably underlies functional change. The brain's structure changes in two fundamental ways in response to experience.

First, existing neural circuits change largely by modifying synaptic connections. One proposed mechanism of synaptic change is long-term potentiation, which is reflected in the modification of excitatory postsynaptic potentials following learning.

Second, novel neural circuits form both by forging new connections among existing neurons and by generating new neurons. Generating new neurons in the hippocampus is one mechanism for establishing novel circuits. A likely mechanism for maintaining synaptic changes is epigenetic: specific sites in the neuronal DNA in modified circuits can exist in either methylated or unmethylated states.

Neuronal activity is key to brain plasticity: through it, synapses form and change. Neuronal activity can be induced by general or specific experiences as well as by electrical or chemical stimulation. Chemical stimulation may range from hormones and neurotrophic compounds to psychoactive drugs.

Much of the brain is capable of plastic change with experience. Different experiences lead to changes in different neural systems. The following table summarizes seven principles that guide research about brain plasticity and behavior.

### Some Guiding Principles of Brain Plasticity

| | |
|---|---|
| 1 | Behavioral change reflects brain change. |
| 2 | All nervous systems are plastic in the same general way. |
| 3 | Plastic changes are age specific. |
| 4 | Prenatal events can influence brain plasticity throughout life. |
| 5 | Plastic changes are brain-region dependent. |
| 6 | Experience-dependent changes interact. |
| 7 | Plasticity has pros and cons. |

## 14-5 Recovery from Brain Injury

Plastic changes after brain injury parallel those seen when the brain changes with experience. Changes related to recovery do not always occur spontaneously, but rather must be stimulated by behavioral training, by the effects of psychoactive drugs or neurotrophic factors, or by electrical brain stimulation. The key to stimulating recovery from brain injury is to increase the plastic changes underlying the recovery.

# Key Terms

# Selected Resources from

**Neuroscience in Action:** How Memory Works (and Doesn't Work)

**Concept Practice:**

Cognitive Influences Conditioning

How Reliable Is Your Memory?

**Videos:**

Classical Conditioning: Pavlov and His Legacy

Operant Conditioning: Learned Behaviors

Pavlov's Discovery of Classical Conditioning

A Pill for Forgetting

Memory and Alzheimer's Research

An Amazing Memory

App for Memory Loss

Enhancing Memory: The Role of Emotion

Daniel Schacter: The Seven Sins of Memory

How Exercise Can Improve Your Memory

How Reliable Is Your Memory?

Memory Retrieval

Models of Memory

Neuroscience Research with Sea Slugs

**LearningCurve**

**Practice Quiz**

# How Does the Brain Think? 15

Movus/Getty Images

## Split Brain

Epileptic seizures may begin in a restricted region of one brain hemisphere and spread through the fibers of the corpus callosum to the corresponding location in the opposite hemisphere. To prevent the spread of seizures that cannot be controlled through medication, neurosurgeons sometimes sever the 200 million nerve fibers of the corpus callosum. The procedure is medically beneficial for many people with epilepsy, leaving them virtually seizure free, with only minimal effects on their everyday behavior. In certain circumstances, however, the aftereffects of a severed corpus callosum become more readily apparent, as extensive psychological testing by Roger Sperry, Michael Gazzaniga, and their colleagues has demonstrated (Gazzaniga, 1970; Sperry, 1968). We note that although this procedure is seldom used today, the study of patients by these investigators has provided unique and important insights into brain function.

On close inspection, such split-brain patients reveal a unique behavioral syndrome that offers insights into the nature of cerebral asymmetry. Cortical asymmetry is essential for such integrative tasks as language and body control.

One split-brain participant was presented with several blocks. Each block had two red sides, two white sides, and two half-red and half-white sides, as illustrated. The task was to arrange the blocks to form patterns identical to those shown on cards.

When the participant used his right hand to perform the task, he had great difficulty. His movements were slow and hesitant. In contrast, when he performed the task with his left hand, his solutions were not only accurate but also quick and decisive.

Sample card

Blocks

Using his right hand, the participant is unable to duplicate the pattern...

...but with his left hand, the split-brain participant performs the task correctly.

In this experiment, a split-brain patient's task is to arrange a set of blocks to match the pattern shown on the card. Information from Gazzaniga et al. (1999).

Findings from studies of other split-brain patients have shown that, as tasks of this sort become more difficult, left-hand superiority increases. Participants whose brain is intact perform equally well with either hand, indicating the intact connection between the two hemispheres. But in split-brain participants, each hemisphere works on its own.

Apparently, the right hemisphere, which controls the left hand, has visuospatial capabilities that the left hemisphere does not.

---

**psychological construct** Idea or set of impressions that some mental ability exists as an entity; examples include memory, language, and emotion.

Studies of split-brain patients reveal that the left and right cerebral hemispheres process information—a key aspect in the act of thinking—in fundamentally different ways. Typically, however, we are unaware of these brain asymmetries. In this chapter, we examine the neural systems and subsystems that control thinking. In the mammalian brain, these systems are found in the cortex.

Our first task is to define the mental processes we wish to study by asking the question: What is the nature of thought? Then we consider the cortical regions—for vision, audition, movement, and associative function—that play major roles in thinking. We examine how these cortical connections are organized into systems and subsystems and how neuroscientists study them.

Next, we explore the brain's asymmetrical organization and delve deeper into split-brain phenomena. Another distinguishing feature of human thought is the different ways in which individual people think. We consider several sources of these differences, including those related to biological sex and to what we call intelligence. Finally, we address consciousness and how it may relate to the neural control of thought.

**Learning Objectives**
- Summarize the characteristics of human thought.
- Describe the neural units of thought.

**15-1**

# The Nature of Thought

Studying abstract mental processes such as thought, language, memory, emotion, and motivation can be tricky. These processes cannot be seen, but can only be inferred from behavior. They are best thought of as **psychological constructs**, ideas that result from a set of impressions. The mind constructs an idea as real, even though it is not tangible.

We run into trouble when we try to locate constructs such as thought or memory in the brain. The fact that we have words for these constructs does not mean that the brain is organized around them. Indeed, it is not. For instance, although people talk about memory as a unitary thing, as we saw in Chapter 14, the brain neither treats memory as unitary nor localizes it in one particular place. The many forms of memory are each treated differently by widely distributed brain circuits. The psychological construct of memory that we think of as being a single thing turns out not to be unitary at all.

To assume a neurological basis for psychological constructs such as memory and thought is risky, but we certainly should not give up searching for where and how the brain produces them. After all, thought, memory, emotion, motivation, and other such constructs are the most interesting activities the brain performs.

Psychologists typically use the term **cognition** (knowing) to describe thought processes—how we come to know about the world. For behavioral neuroscientists, cognition usually entails the ability to pay attention to stimuli (whether external or internal), to identify stimuli, and to plan meaningful responses to them. External stimuli cue neural activity in our sensory receptors. Internal stimuli can spring from the autonomic nervous system (ANS) as well as from neural processes—that is, from constructs such as memory and motivation.

> **Principle 5:** Brain functions are localized and distributed.

> Section 14-1 details types of memory; Section 14-4 describes how neuroplasticity contributes to memory processing and storage.

## Characteristics of Human Thought

Human cognition is widely believed to have unique characteristics. For one thing, human thought is both verbal and nonverbal, whereas the thought of other animals is only nonverbal. Language is presumed to give humans an edge in thinking, and in some ways it does:

- Language provides the brain with a means of categorizing information. It allows us to easily group together objects, actions, and events that have common factors.

- Language provides a means of organizing time, especially future time. It enables us to plan our behavior around time (say, Monday at 3 P.M.) in ways that nonverbal animals cannot.

- Perhaps most importantly, human language has **syntax**—sets of rules for putting together words to create meaningful utterances.

> For our discussion here, we use the term "verbal" to refer to human language systems—what would be considered syntactically structured, or *linguistic*.

Neuroscientists have generally assumed that modern language, guided by explicit principles and rules, is a recent phenomenon whose development was restricted to *Homo sapiens* beginning approximately 100,000 years ago (see Chomsky, 2010). Recently, evidence has emerged to suggest that Neanderthals also had language and that the common ancestor of modern humans and Neanderthals had this capacity some 500,000 years ago (Dediu & Levinson, 2013). If this view is correct, our present-day linguistic diversity could contain traces of the languages spoken by other human forms such as Neanderthals.

Linguists argue that although other nonhuman animals, such as chimpanzees, can use and recognize vocalizations (about three dozen for chimps), they do not rearrange these sounds to produce new meanings. Linguists maintain that this lack of syntax makes chimpanzee language literal and inflexible, although it can still be quite complex, as seen in the chimp Kanzi, discussed in Comparative Focus 1-2: The Speaking Brain. Human language, in contrast, has enormous flexibility that enables us to talk about virtually any topic, even highly abstract topics such as psychological constructs. In this way, our thinking is carried beyond the rigid here and now.

Language, including syntax, develops innately in children because the human brain is programmed to use words in a form of universal grammar. But in the absence of words—either spoken or signed—no grammar can develop. Without the linguistic flexibility that grammar allows, it is difficult for "higher-level" thought to emerge. Syntax, in other words, influences the very nature of our thinking. Even so, we would

> The appearance of human language correlates with a dramatic brain size increase; see Section 2-2. Section 10-4 explains the foundations underlying all languages.

> **cognition** Act or process of knowing or coming to know; in psychology, refers to thought processes; in behavioral neuroscience, refers to identification and planned response to stimuli.

> **syntax** Set of rules for putting together words; proposed to be unique to human language.

be remiss if we did not acknowledge that chimpanzees are capable of remarkable cognitive abilities (e.g., see Dolins et al., 2014).

In addition to arranging words in syntactical patterns, the human brain has a passion for stringing together events, movements, and thoughts. We combine musical notes into melodies, movements into dance, images into videos. We design elaborate rules for games and governments. It seems reasonable to conclude that the human brain is organized to chain together events, movements, and thoughts. Syntax is merely one example.

We do not know how this propensity to string things together evolved, but one possibility is natural selection: stringing movements together into sequences is highly adaptive. It would allow for building houses or weaving threads into cloth, for instance.

William Calvin (1996) proposed that the motor sequences most important to ancient humans were those used in hunting. Throwing a rock or a spear at a moving target is a complex act that requires much planning. Sudden ballistic movements, such as throwing, last less than one-eighth of a second and cannot be corrected by feedback. The brain has to plan every detail and then spit out the details as a smooth-flowing sequence.

Figure 11-2 diagrams the frontal lobe hierarchy that initiates motor sequences.

Today, a football quarterback does exactly this when throwing a football to a receiver running a zigzag pattern to elude a defender. A skilled quarterback can hit the target on almost every throw, stringing movements together rapidly in a continuous sequence, with no pauses or gaps. This skill is uniquely human. Chimpanzees can throw, but no chimpanzee could learn to throw a ball to hit a target moving in a zigzag pattern.

The human predisposition to sequence movements may have encouraged language development. Spoken language, after all, is a sequence of movements involving the throat, tongue, and mouth muscles. Viewed in this way, language is the by-product of a brain that was already predisposed to operate by stringing together movements, events, and even ideas.

A critical characteristic of human motor sequencing is our ability to create novel sequences with ease. We constantly produce new sentences. Composers and choreographers earn their living by making new music and dance sequences. Novel movement or thought sequences are a product of the frontal lobe. People with frontal lobe damage have difficulty generating novel solutions to problems; in turn, they are described as lacking imagination. The frontal lobes are critical not only for organizing behavior but also for organizing thinking. One major difference between the human brain and other primates' brains is the size of the frontal lobes.

## Neural Units of Thought

What goes on within the brain to produce what we call thinking? Is thought an attribute exclusive to humans? Before you answer these questions, consider the mental feats of Alex and Griffin, two grey parrots, profiled in Comparative Focus 15-2: Animal Intelligence.

The cognitive abilities of grey parrots are unexpected in a bird. Dating back to the mid-twentieth century, the intellectual capacities of chimpanzees and dolphins have provoked great interest, but Alex's mental life appears to have been just as rich as the mental life of those two large-brained mammals.

The fact that birds are capable of thought is a clue to the neural basis of thought. A logical presumption may be that thinking, at which humans excel, must be due to some special property of the massive human neocortex. But birds do not possess a neocortex. Rather, they evolved specific brain nuclei that function much as the layers of the human cortex do. This organizational difference in the forebrain of birds and mammals implies that thinking must be an activity of complex neural circuits, not of some particular brain region.

Seweryn Olkowicz and colleagues (2016) analyzed neuron counts and packing density in parrots and corvids (a family of birds that includes crows) and found that these species have higher proportions of brain neurons in the telencephalon than do either mammals (including primates) or other birds.

Cerebrum  Cerebellum  Cerebrum  Cerebellum

**Parrot**  **Human**

## ◉ COMPARATIVE FOCUS 15-2

# Animal Intelligence

Intelligent animals think. We all know that parrots can talk, but most of us assume that no real thought lies behind their words. An African grey parrot named Alex proved otherwise. Irene Pepperberg, pictured here with Alex, studied his ability to think and use language for more than three decades (Pepperberg, 1990, 1999, 2006).

A typical session with Alex and Pepperberg proceeded roughly as follows (Mukerjee, 1996). First, Pepperberg would show Alex a tray with four corks. "How many?" she would ask. "Four," Alex would reply. Then, she might show him a metal key and a green plastic one.

"What toy?"

"Key."

"How many?"

"Two."

"What's different?"

"Color."

Alex did not just have a vocabulary: words had meaning to him. He correctly applied English labels to numerous colors (red, green, blue, yellow, gray, purple, orange), shapes (two-, three-, four-, five-, six-cornered), and materials (cork, wood, rawhide, rock, paper, chalk, wool). He also labeled various items made of metal (chain, key, grate, tray, toy truck), wood (clothespin, block), and plastic or paper (cup, box).

Most surprisingly, Alex used words to identify, request, and refuse items. He responded to questions about abstract ideas, such as the color, shape, material, relative size, and quantity of more than 100 objects.

Alex's thinking was often quite complex. Presented with a tray that contained seven items—a circular rose-colored piece of rawhide, a piece of purple wool, a three-cornered purple key, a four-cornered yellow piece of rawhide, a five-cornered orange piece of rawhide, a six-cornered purple piece of rawhide, and a purple metal box—and then asked, "What shape is the purple hide?" Alex would answer correctly, "Six-corner."

To come up with this answer, Alex had to comprehend the question, locate the correct object of the correct color, determine the answer to the question about the object's shape, and encode his answer into an appropriate verbal response. This task was not easy. After all, four objects were pieces of rawhide, and three objects were purple.

Alex could not respond just to one attribute. Rather, he had to combine the concepts of rawhide and purple and find the object that possessed them both. Then he had to figure out the object's shape. Clearly, considerable

The African grey parrot Alex, shown here with Irene Pepperberg and a sampling of the items he could count, describe, and answer questions about. Alex died in 2007 at the age of 31.

*Jeff Topping/The New York Times/Redux*

mental processing was required, but Alex succeeded at such tasks time and again.

Alex also demonstrated that he understood what he said. If he requested one object and was presented with another, he was likely to say no and repeat his original request. In fact, when given incorrect objects on numerous occasions in formal testing, he said no and repeated his request 72% of the time, said no without repeating his request 18% of the time, and made a new request the other 10% of the time. These responses suggest that Alex's requests led to an expectation in his mind. He knew what he was asking for, and he expected to get it.

Although no other grey parrot yet has developed a vocabulary as extensive as that of Alex, another of Pepperberg's African grey parrots, Griffin, has a spoken vocabulary of 30 words and comprehends at least 40 words. Griffin's performance on tasks that demonstrate mental manipulation and visual working memory routinely exceeds that of humans aged 6–8 years—in fact, his performance on many tasks is equivalent to that of Harvard University undergraduates (Pailian et al., 2020).

Griffin, now 21 years old, has been with Pepperberg since he was about 8 weeks of age. With more training, his vocabulary likely to increase in the years to come.

---

Given their smaller brain size, this finding indicates that parrot and corvid neurons are tightly packed together into highly concentrated areas, which is likely the basis of avian intelligence.

The idea of neural circuits is the essence of Donald Hebb's (1949) theory that **cell assemblies** (networks of neurons) represent objects or ideas, and the interplay among the networks results in complex mental activity such as cognition. Connections among neurons are not random, but rather are organized into systems and subsystems. Thinking must result from the activity of these complex neural circuits. One way to identify their role is to consider how individual neurons respond during cognitive activity.

William Newsome and his colleagues (1995) took this approach in training monkeys to identify apparent motion in a set of moving dots on a television screen. The Procedure section of **Experiment 15-1** shows how the researchers varied the difficulty of

Measures of brain size, including brain cell counts and packing density, are detailed in Section 1-4.

**cell assembly** Hypothetical group of neurons that become functionally connected via common sensory inputs; proposed by Hebb to be the basis of perception, memory, and thought.

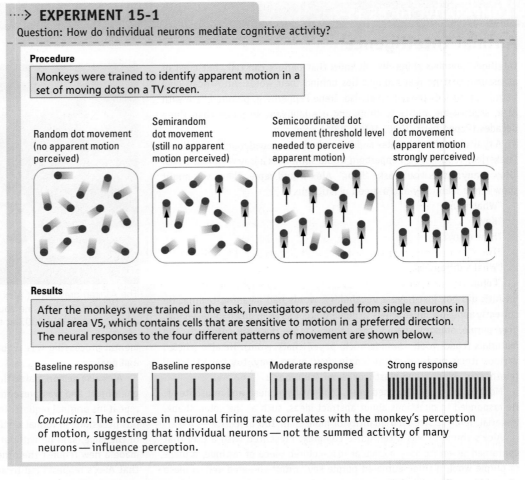

···> **EXPERIMENT 15-1**

Question: How do individual neurons mediate cognitive activity?

**Procedure**

Monkeys were trained to identify apparent motion in a set of moving dots on a TV screen.

Random dot movement (no apparent motion perceived)

Semirandom dot movement (still no apparent motion perceived)

Semicoordinated dot movement (threshold level needed to perceive apparent motion)

Coordinated dot movement (apparent motion strongly perceived)

**Results**

After the monkeys were trained in the task, investigators recorded from single neurons in visual area V5, which contains cells that are sensitive to motion in a preferred direction. The neural responses to the four different patterns of movement are shown below.

Baseline response   Baseline response   Moderate response   Strong response

*Conclusion*: The increase in neuronal firing rate correlates with the monkey's perception of motion, suggesting that individual neurons—not the summed activity of many neurons—influence perception.

Figure 9-20 locates visual regions V1 through V5 in the occipital lobe.

the task by manipulating the number of dots that moved in the same direction. If all the dots move in the same direction, perceiving the whole array as moving is very easy. If only a small percentage of the dots move in the same direction, however, perceiving apparent motion in that direction is much more difficult.

In fact, a threshold number of dots moving together is required to make directional motion apparent. If too few dots are moving in the same direction, the viewer gets an impression of random movement. Apparently, on the basis of the proportion of dots moving in the same direction, the brain concludes whether dots are moving in a consistent direction.

After the monkeys were trained in the task, the investigators recorded from single neurons in visual area V5, which contains cells sensitive to movement in a preferred direction. When vertical movement crosses its receptive field, a neuron that is sensitive to vertical motion responds with a vigorous burst of action potentials. But just as the observer has a threshold for perceiving coherent motion in one direction, so too does the neuron. If at some point the random activity of the dots increases to a level that obscures movement in a neuron's preferred direction, the neuron will stop responding because it does not detect any consistent pattern.

So how does the activity of any given neuron correlate with the perceptual threshold for apparent motion? On the one hand, if our perception of apparent motion results from the summed activity of many dozens or even thousands of neurons, little correlation would exist between the activity of any one neuron and the perception. On the other hand, if individual neurons influence our perception of apparent motion, then a strong correlation would exist between the activity of a single cell and the perception.

The results of Experiment 15-1 are unequivocal: the sensitivity of individual neurons is very similar to the perceptual sensitivity of the monkeys to apparent motion. As shown in the Results section, if individual neurons failed to respond to the stimulus, the monkeys behaved as if they did not perceive any apparent motion.

This finding is curious. Given the large number of V5 neurons, it seems logical that perceptual decisions are based on the responses of a large pool of neurons. The loss of a few neurons in V5 is unlikely to have much effect on the perception of movement, but recall the case of L. M. in Chapter 9, who had a large injury to V5 and lost her ability to see movement.

Still, Hebb's idea of a cell assembly—an ensemble of neurons that represents a complex concept (see **Figure 15-1**)—suggests a way of converging the inputs of individual neurons to arrive at a consensus (Hebb, 1949). Here, the neuronal ensemble represents a sensory event (apparent motion) that the activity of the ensemble detects. Cell assemblies could be distributed over fairly large regions of the brain, or they could be confined to smaller areas, such as cortical columns.

Using computer modeling, cognitive scientists have demonstrated the capacity of cell assembly circuits to perform sophisticated statistical computations. Other complex tasks, such as Alex the parrot's ability to detect the color of an object, are also believed to entail neuronal ensembles. Cell assemblies provide the basis for cognition. Different ensembles come together, much like words in language, to produce coherent thoughts.

What do individual neurons contribute to a cell assembly? Each acts as a computational unit. As Experiment 15-1 shows, even one solitary neuron can fire on its own if its summed inputs indicate that movement is taking place. Neurons are the only elements in the brain that combine evidence to generate knowledge; they are the foundation of cognitive processes and of thought. The combination of individual neurons into novel neural networks produces complex mental representations—ideas, for instance.

**FIGURE 15-1 Hebb's Cell Assembly** Hypothetical group of neurons that become functionally connected by firing together.

Figures 9-38 to 9-40 diagram functional columns in occipital and temporal cortices.

**Principle 1:** Neuronal circuits are the functional units of the nervous system.

## 15-1 Review

Before you continue, check your understanding. Answers to Self-Test appear at the back of the book.

1. Cognition, or thought, entails the abilities of _____, _____, and _____ stimuli.

2. Unlike other animals, humans have the added advantage of _____, which adds _____ to thought.

3. The _____ is the basic unit of thought production.

4. Describe the most important way in which human thought differs from thinking in other animals.

## 15-2

# Cognition and the Association Cortex

Altogether, the primary sensory and motor cortical regions occupy about one-third of the neocortex (**Figure 15-2**). The remaining two-thirds of the neocortex, located in the frontal, temporal, parietal, and occipital lobes, is referred to generally as the **association cortex**. It functions to produce cognition.

A fundamental difference between the association cortex and the primary sensory and motor areas is that the association cortex has a distinctive pattern of connections. A major source of input to all cortical areas is the thalamus, which rests atop the brainstem. The primary sensory cortex receives inputs from thalamic nuclei, which in turn receive information from the body's sense organs. In contrast, inputs to the association cortex come from other thalamic areas and other cortical regions. As a result, inputs to the association cortex are already highly processed—which means this information must be fundamentally different from the information reaching the primary sensory and motor cortex.

### Learning Objectives

- Locate the association cortex and describe its function.
- Describe the problem of sensory integration.
- Describe the types of spatial cognition.
- Identify the types of attention and deficits in attention.
- Describe executive function.
- Identify neural mechanisms of imitation and understanding.

**association cortex** Neocortex outside primary sensory and motor cortices functions to produce cognition.

**KEY (cortical areas)**

| | | |
|---|---|---|
| ■ Primary motor | ■ Primary visual | ■ Primary olfactory and taste |
| ■ Primary somatosensory | ■ Primary auditory | |

**FIGURE 15-2 Cortical Functions** Lateral view of the left hemisphere and medial view of the right hemisphere, showing the primary motor and sensory areas. All remaining cortical areas are collectively referred to as the association cortex, which functions in thinking.

Recall the case of L. M. (described in Section 9-5), who lost the ability to detect motion after damage to region V5.

The neural pathways associated with seeing shapes are described in Section 9-4.

Due to their close relationship with the visual and auditory sensory regions, the temporal association regions tend to produce cognition related to visual and auditory processing. Similarly, the parietal cortex is closely related to somatosensation and movement control. In contrast, the frontal cortex coordinates information coming from the parietal and temporal association regions, which receive information from subcortical regions.

As diagrammed in **Figure 15-3**, the multiple subdivisions of the *prefrontal cortex (PFC)* encompass its dorsal, lateral, orbital, and medial regions. Activity in each prefrontal region is associated with the types of cognitive processing that we describe throughout this chapter. An additional frontal lobe region, also shown in Figure 15-3, is the anterior cingulate cortex (ACC). Although the ACC was once believed to play a role only in emotion, it is becoming clear that it functions as an interface between emotion and cognition.

To understand the types of knowledge that the association areas contain, we next consider discrete cognitive behaviors and then trace these behaviors to different parts of the association cortex.

# Knowledge about Objects

Visualize a rectangular milk carton sitting on a counter directly in front of you. What do you see? Now imagine moving the carton a few inches off to one side as you continue to stare directly ahead. What do you see now? Next, imagine that you tilt the carton toward yourself at a 45° angle. Again, what do you see? Probably you answered that you saw the same thing in each situation: a rectangular box with lettering on it.

Intuitively, you feel that the brain must see the object much as you have perceived it. The brain's seeing, however, is more compartmentalized than are your perceptions. Compartmentalization is revealed in people with damage to various regions of the occipital cortex, many of whom lose one particular aspect of visual perception. For instance, persons with damage to visual area V4 can no longer perceive color, whereas those with damage to area V5 can no longer see movement (as the milk carton moves, e.g., it becomes invisible to them).

Moreover, your perception of the milk carton's consistently rectangular shape does not always match the forms that your visual system is processing. When you tip the carton toward you, you still perceive it as rectangular, even though it no longer presents a rectangular shape to your eyes. Your brain has somehow ignored the change in information about shape that your retinas have sent it and concluded that this object, no matter its apparent shape, remains the same milk carton.

**FIGURE 15-3 Prefrontal Association Cortex** Lateral view of the brain's left hemisphere **(A)** and medial view of the right hemisphere **(B)**. These depictions represent regions of the prefrontal cortex (PFC) in relationship to the associated anterior cingulate allocortex (ACC), shown in (B).

**(A) Lateral view**

Dorsolateral prefrontal cortex

Orbital prefrontal cortex

**(B) Medial view**

Dorsomedial prefrontal cortex

Anterior cingulate cortex

Ventromedial prefrontal cortex

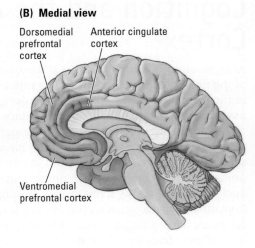

There is more to your conception of the milk carton than merely perceiving and processing its physical characteristics. You also know what a milk carton is, what it contains, and where you can get one. The knowledge about milk cartons that you have acquired is represented in the temporal association cortex, which forms the ventral stream of visual processing. If the temporal association regions are destroyed, a person loses visual knowledge not only about milk cartons but also about all other objects—that is, the person becomes *agnosic* (unknowing).

Knowledge about objects encompasses even more than how they look and what they are used for. It also includes what will be done with the information—how to pick up the milk carton, for example. Knowledge of *what* things are is largely stored in the temporal lobe; knowledge of *how* to grasp the object is largely stored in the parietal lobe (**Figure 15-4**).

**FIGURE 15-4 Streaming Visual Information** The dorsal visual stream mediates vision for action. The ventral stream mediates vision for object recognition.

The condition of facial agnosia is described in Section 9-2. Section 9-5 recounts cases illustrative of other visual-form agnosias.

**Principle 8:** The brain divides sensory input for object recognition and movement.

The sensations of smell and taste are integrated to produce the experience of flavor; see Section 12-3.

# Multisensory Integration

Our knowledge about the world comes through multisensory channels. When we look at a person's face, for example, the shape, color, and details about various features, such as the eyes and mouth, are combined to form a coherent image. How does the brain do this? As we saw in Section 9-2, the brain contains many visual areas, each of which is involved in analyzing different components of an object, such as a face, but not all of these regions are connected.

Philosophers, impressed with this integrative capacity, identified the **binding problem**, which asks how the brain ties its single and varied sensory and motor events together into a unified perception or behavior. It is gradually becoming clear how the brain binds up our perceptions and how this ability is gradually acquired in postnatal life (see the reviews by Stein & Rowland, 2011; Stein et al., 2020).

One solution to the sensory integration aspect of the binding problem lies in multimodal regions of the association cortex—that is, regions populated by neurons that respond to information from more than one sensory modality, as illustrated in **Figure 15-5**. Investigators presume that multimodal regions combine characteristics of stimuli across different senses when we encounter them either separately or together. For example, the fact that we can visually identify objects that we have only touched implies that a common perceptual system links the visual and somatic circuits. Section 15-5 describes the condition known as *synesthesia*, in which stimulation from one sensory modality (e.g., taste) concurrently induces the experience of a different modality (e.g., touch). Synesthesia can be seen as an exaggerated solution to the binding problem.

**FIGURE 15-5 Multisensory Areas in the Monkey Cortex** Color-coded areas represent regions where anatomical data and/or electrical stimulation demonstrate multisensory interactions. Dashed lines represent multimodal areas revealed when sulci are opened. Information from Ghanzanfar & Schroeder (2006).

# Spatial Cognition

*Spatial cognition* refers to our knowledge about the environment that allows us to determine where we and objects in our environment are, how to go from one place to another, how to interpret our spatial world, and how to communicate about space (for an extensive discussion, see Waller & Nadel, 2013). There are multiple ways to conceptualize space, including making distinctions between the body, grasping, distal, and cognitive space (see **Figure 15-6**A); allocentric (object-to-object) and egocentric (self-to-object) space (Figure 15-6B); and a more abstract cognitive space (Figure 15-6C).

Imagine going for a walk in an unfamiliar park. Rather than walking around in circles, you proceed in an organized, systematic way. You also need to find your way back. These abilities require a representation of the physical environment in your mind's eye.

At some point during the walk, suppose that you become uncertain of where you are—a common problem. One solution is to make a mental image of your route, complete with various landmarks and turns. It is a small step from mentally manipulating these kinds of navigational landmarks and movements to manipulating other kinds

**Principle 4:** The central nervous system functions on multiple levels.

**binding problem** Philosophical question focused on how the brain ties single and varied sensory and motor events together into a unified perception or behavior.

**(A)**

**(B)** Spatial Reference Frames

**(C)**

**FIGURE 15-6 Ways to Conceptualize Space** Space, both external and mental, can be related to the body (panel A; after Kolb & Whishaw, 2021). The locations of objects can be represented in egocentric and allocentric spatial reference frames (panel B; after Proulx et al., 2016). The same figure can be oriented differently in space (panel C).

Section 1-3 traces nervous system evolution across the animal kingdom.

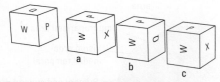

**FIGURE 15-7 Mental Manipulation** Try this sample test item used to measure spatial orientation. Compare the three cubes on the right with the cube on the left. No letter appears on more than one face of a given cube. Which cube—a, b, or c—could be a different view of the cube on the left? The correct answer appears at the bottom of the page.

The answer to the mental manipulation in Figure 15-7 is *a*.

of images in your mind. Thus, the ability to mentally manipulate visual images seems likely to have arisen in parallel with the ability to navigate in space.

The evolution of skill in mental manipulation is also closely tied to the evolution of physical movements. It is likely that animals first moved using whole-body movements (the swimming motion of a fish), then developed coordinated limb movements (quadrupedal walking), and finally mastered discrete limb movements (such as a human arm reaching out). As the guidance strategies for controlling movements became more sophisticated, cognitive abilities evolved to support the guidance systems.

It seems unlikely that more sophisticated cognitive abilities evolved on their own. Why would a fish, say, be able to manipulate an object in its mind that it could not manipulate in the real world? In contrast, a human, who can manipulate objects by hand, should be able to imagine such manipulations. Once the brain can manipulate objects that are physically present, it seems a small step to manipulating imagined objects—so as to solve problems like the one depicted in **Figure 15-7**. The ability to manipulate an object in the mind's eye probably flows from the ability to manipulate tangible objects with the hands.

Research findings provide clues about which brain regions participate in various aspects of spatial cognition. For instance, the dorsal stream in the parietal lobes is central in controlling vision for action. Humans make discrete limb movements to points in space, so a reasonable supposition is that the dorsal stream's evolutionary development provided a neural basis for such spatial cognitive skills as mentally rotating objects. By tracing the evolutionary development of the human brain, we find that the parietal association regions expanded considerably more in humans than in other primates. This expanded brain region functions in part to perform the complex spatial operations just discussed. Humans have a capacity for building that far exceeds that of our nearest relative, the chimpanzee. Perhaps our increased capacity for building and manipulating objects played heavily into the development of our cognitive spatial abilities.

## Deficits of Spatial Behavior

Evidence gathered since the early 1950s indicates that the posterior parietal cortex has a special role in spatial behavior, as individuals with right posterior parietal lesions show a variety of spatial deficits. One example is *topographic disorientation*, an inability to find one's way in relationship to salient environmental cues, even in familiar environments. Multiple forms of topographic disorientation exist, including *egocentric disorientation*, which is difficulty perceiving relative locations of objects with respect to the self. In his fascinating account of a Russian World War II soldier with a bullet wound to his parietal cortex, Alexander Luria (1972) describes how the man got off at a bus stop in sight of his apartment building but had to ask for directions to the building. Other individuals with such deficits have been reported to be unable to set a course to a specific location, even though they can recognize landmarks and their own location in relationship to landmarks. In essence, they have "no sense of direction." Further examples of spatial deficits include an inability to mentally manipulate objects, like those shown in Figures 15-6C and 15-7.

Deficits in spatial behavior are seen not only in individuals with posterior parietal lesions but also in those with damage to their posterior cingulate cortex and medial temporal regions (see Kolb & Whishaw, 2021, for details). Given that the parietal cortex forms the major component of the dorsal stream, it would not be surprising to discover that the dorsal stream is involved in many aspects of spatial cognition. Persons with bilateral injuries to the posterior parietal cortex may experience Bálint syndrome, a serious disturbance of spatial processing that includes deficits in directing eye gaze peripherally and in comprehending the spatial features of a familiar object. Such individuals are unable to judge the location of objects in space, estimate distance, discriminate length and size, evaluate depth and thickness, or pay attention to more than one object at a time. As a result, they run into objects when walking and have difficulty reading and counting scattered objects.

An extensive literature implicates the temporal cortex, and especially medial temporal regions, in spatial behavior. Both the dorsal and ventral streams converge on the hippocampus, and, as described in Section 14-3, several classes of spatially tuned cells are found in the hippocampal formation (see Figure 14-11). There is also a relationship between the size of the posterior hippocampal region and spatial navigation skills in humans. Taxi drivers in London, England, have larger posterior hippocampal regions than do bus drivers, who navigate a fixed route; and functional magnetic resonance imaging (fMRI) studies show greater activation of the posterior hippocampal region of taxi drivers when they play a video game in which they virtually navigate around London (see the review by Woollett et al., 2009). Curiously, when the taxi drivers retire, their hippocampi shrink over time, suggesting that navigation expertise results in structural changes that reverse with disuse.

Bálint syndrome, also called optic ataxia, is detailed in Section 9-5.

**Principle 10:** Neuroplasticity is the hallmark of nervous system functioning.

# Attention

Imagine that you're meeting some friends at a football game. You search for them as you meander through the crowd in the stadium. Suddenly, you hear one friend's distinctive laugh and turn to scan in that direction. You see your group and rush to join them.

This everyday experience demonstrates the nature of **attention**, defined as selective narrowing or focusing of awareness to part of the sensory environment or to a class of stimuli. Even as you are bombarded with a wealth of sounds, smells, feelings, and sights, you can still detect a familiar laugh or spot a familiar face: you can direct your attention. Thus, attention can enhance neural activity associated with the perception of specific information, such as visual and auditory cues associated with your friend. Conversely, attention can decrease neural activity associated with other, extraneous information, such as empty seats or the sound of the band playing at the game. We can attend selectively to thoughts as well as to sensory stimuli. Who hasn't, at some time, been so preoccupied with a thought as to exclude all else from mind?

**attention** Narrowing or focusing awareness to a part of the sensory environment or to a class of stimuli.

## Selective Attention

As is true with many other inferred mental processes, studying the neural basis of attention is challenging. Research with monkeys trained to attend to particular locations or visual stimuli, however, has identified neurons in the cortex and midbrain that show enhanced firing rates to particular locations or visual stimuli. Significantly, the same stimulus can activate a neuron at one time but not at another, depending on the monkey's learned focus of attention.

James Moran and Robert Desimone (1985) trained monkeys to hold a bar while gazing at a fixation point on a screen. A sample stimulus (a vertical red bar) appeared briefly at one location in the visual field, followed about 500 milliseconds later by a test stimulus at the same location (see **Figure 15-8**). When the test stimulus was

Fixation point    Stimulus

**FIGURE 15-8 Selective Attention**

**contralateral neglect** Ignoring a part of the body or world on the side opposite (contralateral to) that of a brain injury.

**extinction** In neurology, neglect of information on one side of the body when presented simultaneously with similar information on the other side of the body.

Clinical Focus 8-2 describes the excess focus associated with people who have autism spectrum disorder.

**When shown two identical objects**

Patient's right visual field

Patient's left visual field

Patient sees only the object in his right visual field.

**When shown two different objects**

Patient sees the object in both visual fields.

**When shown two kinds of an object**

Patient sees only the object in his right visual field.

**FIGURE 15-9 Testing for Extinction**
A person who has experienced a stroke and shows neglect for information presented to the left visual field responds differently depending on whether the objects in the left and right visual fields are similar or different.

The damage to the parietal association cortex described here differs from the loss of proprioception following damage to the neurons that carry sensory information to the cortex, as described in Section 11-4.

identical with the initial sample stimulus, an animal was rewarded if it immediately released the bar.

Each animal was trained to attend to stimuli presented in one particular area of the visual field and to ignore stimuli in any other area. In this way, the same visual stimulus could be presented to different regions of a neuron's receptive field to test whether the cell's response varied with stimulus location.

As the animals performed the task, the researchers recorded neurons firing in visual area V4. These neurons are sensitive to color and form, and different neurons respond to different combinations of the two variables (such as a red vertical bar or a green horizontal bar). Visual stimuli were presented either in the correct location for a reward or in an incorrect location for no reward.

Before training, the neurons responded to all stimuli regardless of location. The results of the experiment showed that after training, neurons responded only when a visual stimulus was in the reward location; the neurons would not respond when the same stimulus was presented in a no-reward location. This finding tells us that attending to specific parts of the sensory world is a property of single neurons—more evidence that the neuron is the computational unit of cognition.

## Deficits of Attention

Attention is probably a property of neurons throughout the brain, with some regions playing more prominent roles than others. The frontal lobes, for instance, are central in attention. People with frontal lobe injuries tend to become overly focused on environmental stimuli. They seem to selectively direct attention to an excessive degree or to have difficulty shifting attention. Studies of these people suggest that the frontal association cortex controls the ability to direct attention flexibly to where it is needed. Indeed, planning—a key frontal lobe function—requires this ability.

The point that the parietal association cortex is key in other aspects of attention is perhaps best illustrated by the attention deficit referred to as *neglect*. Neglect occurs when a person with brain injury ignores sensory information that should be considered important. Usually, this condition affects only one side of the body and, therefore, is called **contralateral neglect**. We observed a dog that had developed a right-hemisphere tumor and ate only the food on the right side of its dish, ignoring the food on the left side. Neglect is a fascinating symptom because it often occurs despite a lack of damage to the sensory pathways. That is, neglect is a failure of attention.

People with damage to the parietal association cortex of the right hemisphere may have particularly severe neglect of objects or events in the left side of their world. For example, one man dressed only the right side of his body, shaved only the right side of his face, and read only the right side of a page (if you can call that reading). He could move his left limbs spontaneously, but when asked to raise both arms, he would raise only the right. When pressed to do so, he could be induced to raise the left arm, but he quickly dropped it to his side again. When questioned about whether he had any difficulty engaging with the left side of his body or with the left side of the visual world, he answered that he was just fine—a response indicative of *anosognosia*, the neglect of illness.

As people with contralateral neglect begin to recover, they show another interesting symptom: they neglect information on one side of the body when it is simultaneously presented with similar information on the other side of the body. **Figure 15-9** shows a common clinical test for this symptom, called **extinction**.

In an extinction test, the person is asked to keep their eyes fixed on the examiner's face and to report objects presented in one or both sides of the visual field. When presented with a single object, such as a fork, to one side or the other, the person orients themselves toward the appropriate side of the visual field, so we know that they cannot be blind on either side. But now suppose that two forks are presented, one on the left and one on the right. The person ignores the fork on the left and reports the one on the right. When asked about the left side, the individual is quite certain that nothing appeared there and that only one fork was presented, on the right.

Perhaps the most curious aspect of neglect is that people who have it fail to pay attention not only to one side of the physical world around them but also to one side of the world represented in their mind. We studied one woman who had complete neglect for everything on her left side. She complained that she could not use her kitchen because she could never remember the location of anything on her left. We asked her to imagine standing at the kitchen door and to describe what was in the various drawers on her right and left. She could not recall anything on her left. We then asked her to imagine walking to the end of the kitchen and turning around. We again asked her what was on her right, the side of the kitchen that had previously been on her left. She broke into a big smile and tears ran down her face as she realized that she now knew what was on that side of the room. All she had to do was reorient her body in her mind's eye. She later wrote and thanked us for changing her life, because she was now able to cook again. Clearly, neglect can exist in the mind as well as in the physical world.

Although complete contralateral neglect is usually associated with parietal lobe injury, specific forms of neglect can arise from other injuries. Ralph Adolphs and his colleagues (2005) describe the case of S. M., a woman with bilateral amygdala damage who could not recognize fear in faces. On further study, the reason for this deficit was discovered: S. M. failed to look at the eyes when she looked at faces; instead, she looked at other facial features, such as the nose. Because fear is most clearly identified in the eyes, not the nose, she did not identify the emotion. When she was specifically instructed to look at the eyes, her recognition of fear became entirely normal. Thus, the amygdala plays a role in directing attention to the eyes to identify facial expressions. S. M.'s neglect of fear in the faces of others, however, was also associated with her inability to experience fear in situations that would induce fear in others, such as being held up at knifepoint and being nearly killed in an act of domestic violence (for a review of S. M.'s life, see Feinstein et al., 2016).

## Planning and Executive Function

In daily life, we constantly face changing circumstances that require the planning and generation of novel actions. Consider the following example. At noon on a Friday, a friend proposes that you both go to a nearby city for the weekend to attend a concert. The friend will pick you up at 6 P.M., and you will drive to the concert together. Because of the short notice, you must rush home after your 4 P.M. class to get ready. En route, you stop for fast food so that you won't be hungry on the 2-hour drive. You also need cash, so you head to the nearest ATM. When you get home, you grab various pieces of clothing appropriate for the concert and the trip. You also pack your toiletries. You somehow manage to get ready by 6 P.M., when your friend arrives.

The ability to perform planning and novel actions is often referred to as **executive function**. The definition of this term is rather vague, but executive functions are generally considered to encompass cognitive processes such as attentional control, planning, reasoning, working memory, problem solving, abstract thinking, and self-monitoring. Although executive function is often envisioned as solely a frontal lobe activity, it also includes other cortical regions such as the parietal cortex, which are connected with the prefrontal cortex through several networks.

People with frontal lobe injuries are often unable to organize their behavior, despite exhibiting normal or even superior cognitive skills, such as those related to memory and language. The Wisconsin Card Sorting Test may be used to demonstrate the deficits that frontal lobe injury causes. **Figure 15-10** shows the testing materials. The participant is presented with four stimulus cards bearing designs that differ in color, form, and number of elements, thus setting up three possible sorting categories. The participant must sort a deck of cards into piles in front of the various stimulus cards, depending on the sorting category called for. But the correct sorting category is never stated.

**executive function** Cognitive processes such as attentional control, planning, reasoning, working memory, problem solving, abstract thinking, and self-monitoring; associated primarily with the frontal lobe, but also involves other cortical regions such as posterior parietal cortex.

**FIGURE 15-10 Wisconsin Card Sorting Test** The participant receives a deck of cards containing multiple copies of those represented here, and is presented with a row of four cards selected from the deck. The task is to place each card in the pile under the appropriate card in the row, sorting by one of three possible categories. Participants are never explicitly told what the correct sorting category is—color, number, or form. They are told only whether their responses are correct or incorrect. After they have begun sorting by one category, the tester unexpectedly changes to another category.

**perseveration** Tendency to emit repeatedly the same verbal or motor response to varied stimuli.

**mirror neuron** Cell in the primate premotor and parietal cortex that fires when an individual observes an action taken by another individual.

The participant is simply told after placing each card whether the choice is correct or incorrect, and must figure out the new solution based only on this feedback.

In one trial, for example, the first correct sorting category is color. After the participant has sorted a number of cards by color, the correct solution switches, without warning, to form. When the participant has started to sort by form, the correct solution again changes unexpectedly, this time to the number of items on each card. The sorting rule later becomes color again, and so on, with each change in rule being unannounced.

Shifting response strategies is particularly difficult for people with frontal lobe lesions: they may continue responding to the original stimulus (color) for as many as 100 cards until the test ends. This pattern, known as **perseveration**, reflects the tendency to emit repeatedly the same verbal or motor response to varied stimuli. This tendency is also found in young children, likely due to the immature development of their prefrontal cortex.

Individuals with frontal lobe injury may even comment that they know that color is no longer the correct category, but they continue to sort by color. One stated: "Form is probably the correct solution now so this [sorting by color] will be wrong, and this will be wrong, and wrong again." Despite knowing the correct sorting category, the individual with frontal lobe damage cannot shift behavior in response to the new external information.

## Imitation and Understanding

In all communication—verbal and nonverbal—the sender and the receiver must share an understanding of what matters. If a person speaks a word or makes a gesture, another person will understand only if they interpret it correctly. To accomplish this coordination in communication, the processes of producing and perceiving a message must share a common representation in the sender's and the receiver's brains.

How do both sender and receiver of a potentially ambiguous gesture, such as a raised hand or a faint smile, achieve a common understanding? Giacomo Rizzolatti and his colleagues proposed an answer (see, e.g., Rizzolatti & Sinigaglia, 2016; Umiltà et al., 2001). In the course of recording single neurons on monkeys reaching for objects, they made the serendipitous discovery that a subset of neurons in the premotor cortex discharge not only when a monkey makes a movement, but also when watching other monkeys (or humans) make the same movements. Rizzolatti called these neurons **mirror neurons**, and the name stuck. Subsequent researchers have proposed that mirror neurons represent actions—one's own or those of others. Such neural representations could be used both for imitating others' actions and for understanding their meanings, thereby enabling appropriate responses. Thus, mirror neurons could provide the link between the sender and the receiver of a communication.

Mirror neurons have been the focus of intense research. A mirror neuron system (MNS) is now generally thought to be distributed within the brain, and to include cortical areas in the posterior parietal cortex, premotor cortex, inferior frontal gyrus, and superior temporal sulcus. As shown in **Figure 15-11**, these regions can be subdivided into areas related to different types of movements. Originally, mirror neurons were hypothesized to be the basis of *understanding* actions rather than merely recognizing them. This possibility had profound implications and led to propositions that mirror neurons form the basis of speech and language, empathy, social cognition, theory of mind—even civilization! Within a few years, however, cracks began to show in the mirror theory. Gregory Hickok (2014) has argued that mirror neurons do not make actions understandable, but do refine movement control. Hickok and others suggest that mirror neurons do not "understand" action, but rather their function arises from an association between executing an action and the self-observation of the action.

More recently, data accumulated from many brain mapping methods, including fMRI, positron emission tomography (PET), transcranial magnetic stimulation (TMS),

**FIGURE 15-11 Mirror Neuron System** The core mirror neuron system (yellow) is sensitive to transitive movements and comprises the inferior frontal cortex (IFG, or frontal gyrus), ventral premotor cortex (PMV), and inferior parietal cortex (IPL, inferior parietal lobule, and intraparietal sulcus (IPS). The distributed mirror neuron system in humans responds to hand movements (purple) in the dorsal premotor cortex (PMD) and superior parietal lobe (SPL); upper limb movements (blue) in a portion of the superior temporal sulcus (STS); tool use (orange); and intransitive movements in which no object is manipulated (green). Research from Cattaneo & Rizzolatti (2009).

magnetoencephalography (MEG), and neuronal recording, have revealed the complexity of the MNS. Findings from these imaging studies clearly show that during the observation of action, the strength of neuronal responses in the MNS is modulated by multiple factors. In an extensive review, David Kemmerer (2021) identified 22 distinct modulating factors involving the action, the actor, the observer, the relationship between the actor and observer, and the context. For example, the strength of neural activity related to the relationship between the actor and observer is mediated by racial and ethnic congruence as well as by interpersonal liking and eye contact. Although several theoretical models have been proposed to account for the actions of the MNS, Kemmerer concludes that none is as yet able to account for the full complexity of the system. Nonetheless, studies of the MNS demonstrate that the brain understands actions and facilitates making movements quickly and more accurately.

The concept of the MNS is already being applied to rehabilitation interventions. In action observation treatment (AOT), patients are asked to carefully watch a video and to imitate the actions seen. Rizzolatti and colleagues (2021) have collected evidence that AOT can aid in the recovery of impaired motor ability for a range of clinical conditions spanning from stroke to neurodegenerative diseases, such as Parkinson disease. In addition, AOT has been shown to improve precise motor control in neurologically normal participants (Mancuso et al., 2021).

## 15-2 Review

Before you continue, check your understanding. Answers to Self-Test appear at the back of the book.

1. Knowledge is stored in the _____ cortex, which functions to produce _____.

2. As a general rule, the _____ lobes processes information about objects, whereas the _____ lobes produce various forms of spatial cognition.

3. The frontal lobes function not only to make movements but also to _____ movements and to _____ behavior over time.

4. _____ neurons in the frontal and parietal lobes represent actions—one's own or those of others.

5. Describe the function of the multimodal cortex.

6. Explain how applications of the mirror neuron system can be used in the context of rehabilitation.

---

### 15-3

# Expanding Frontiers of Cognitive Neuroscience

Beginning in the late 1970s, sophisticated noninvasive stimulation and recording techniques were developed for measuring the brain's electrical (electroencephalography [EEG], event-related potential [ERP]), metabolic (PET), and vascular (magnetic resonance imaging [MRI], fMRI) activity related to behavior. These technical developments led to the emergence of a new field in studying brain and behavior: **cognitive neuroscience**, which focuses on the neural bases of cognition. The new imaging techniques can help cognitive neuroscientists map the human brain, allow social psychologists (social neuroscience) to explore how the brain mediates social interactions, and aid economists in discovering how the brain makes decisions, as discussed later in this section. Clinical Focus 15-3: Neuropsychological Assessment describes how neuroimaging techniques can be integrated with more traditional assessments.

**Learning Objectives**
- Explain what recent brain mapping techniques have revealed about cortical networks.
- Identify the cerebellum's role in cognition.
- Describe how the brain mediates social interactions, as explained by theories in social neuroscience.
- Summarize the goals of the discipline of neuroeconomics.

---

**cognitive neuroscience** Study of the neural bases of cognition.

## ◎ CLINICAL FOCUS 15-3

# Neuropsychological Assessment

*Neuropsychological assessment* is the systematic evaluation of cognitive function in an individual who may be suffering from neurological or psychological impairment. With the advent of functional imaging, neuropsychological assessment has moved beyond simply being the diagnostic tool that it was in the past, and now plays a key role in rehabilitation, especially in cases of chronic disease (e.g., stroke and traumatic brain injury), where neuroimaging often fails to identify brain changes. Even when brain pathology may be clear, however, there is large variability in the cognitive effects of neurological disease, in part because brains are not identical and in part because brain function does not occur in a vacuum. Cognitive functions are not only influenced by the nature of brain pathology or dysfunction, but also by psychological factors (including premorbid experiences, personality, and values) and by socioenvironmental factors (such as living arrangements, culture, finances, past and ongoing stressors, and stability of family and work relationships). Thus, an assessment must be done in a holistic context of a person's life (see Kolb & Whishaw, 2021, for more details).

Neuropsychological assessment evolved after World War II as many investigators began to study soldiers who had suffered brain injury. These investigations led to the development of broad standardized test batteries that were essentially paper-and-pencil tests, including tests of intelligence, memory, spatial and perceptual skills, among many others, normally conducted by psychologists with special training in neuropsychology. Although these test batteries have proved very useful, they have remained rather static for the past 30 years—a surprising fact given the advances in neuroscience that have occurred over the same span of time (Bilder & Reise, 2019).

The Cambridge Neuropsychological Test Battery (CANTAB) was developed in the 1990s and allows for tests to be administered via a touchscreen computer. Since its introduction, the success of the CANTAB has led to the development of about 20 other computerized batteries that will soon be integrated with neuroimaging results, including MRI, fMRI, and EEG, to provide deeper insights into the relationship between brain injury and cognitive function (see Sternin et al., 2019). In addition, new technologies that take advantage of online and mobile devices enable the acquisition of voice, facial expressions and other three-dimensional actions, and complex behaviors to provide information that cannot be collected using paper-and-pencil tests.

New statistical methods developed over the past few years are also changing the nature of neuropsychological assessment. One major advantage of the computerized batteries is that an individual's scores can be compared to a growing database of scores from thousands of people from diverse psychosocial backgrounds (e.g., in terms of ethnicity, race, education, and gender). The goal of computer-generated data analysis is to supplement—not replace—the work of trained neuropsychologists, who are still needed to consider biopsychosocial factors as well as qualitative impressions from these assessments and interviews.

# Mapping the Brain

**brain connectome** Map of the complete structural and functional fiber pathways of the human brain in vivo.

For more on the HCP, including connectome images, go to www.humanconnectome.org/.

Glasser's parcellation work, and the resulting FACT definition of the brain's functional areas, is discussed in Section 2-3.

Among the great scientific challenges of the twenty-first century, mapping the human **brain connectome** may be the most intriguing. Toward this end, the U.S. National Institutes of Health (NIH) awarded grants totaling $40 million to researchers seeking to map the complete structural and functional fiber pathway connections of the human brain in vivo. Researchers participating in the Human Connectome Project (HCP) are combining diffusion tensor imaging (DTI) and functional connectivity magnetic resonance imaging (fcMRI) to plot these connections in the living human brain. By the end of 2016, HCP investigators had completed scanning 1200 healthy adults' brains, including 300 twin pairs. The HCP continues with different research groups focusing on different populations; for example, one study in the United Kingdom aims to scan a total of 100,000 participants (for a thorough review, see Elam et al., 2021).

The first step in the HCP mapping was to identify an accurate parcellation of the cerebral cortex. Researchers have been constructing brain maps for more than 100 years, but the number of distinct areas in those maps varies from about 50 to 200, depending on the method of analysis. The HCP investigators used a machine learning classifier of more than 500 brains to parcel the cortex into 180 areas whose presence could be detected in about 97% of new participants in the HCP research (Glasser et al., 2016). This parcellation, shown in **Figure 15-12**A, is more complex than Brodmann's original cytoarchitectonic map, shown in Figure 2-26, but still derives from Brodmann's basic organization.

In addition to these efforts, a myriad of studies outside the HCP are seeking to describe specific processes and disorders using mapping technology. For example, age-related brain changes are an important topic due to the increasing life span and the size of elderly populations. Many reports have suggested that as people age, there is a reduction in functional connectivity (e.g., Sala-Llonch et al., 2015). However, growing

**FIGURE 15-12 Two Parcellations of Cerebral Cortical Networks** (A) The Human Connectome Project's multimodal parcellation map based on the FACT technique (Glasser et al., 2016). This technique identified 180 distinct regions. (B) An estimate of 17 cortical networks based on fcMRI data from 1000 participants. Each color represents a network. Some networks, such as the blue auditory areas in the temporal lobe, are localized; others are widely distributed, such as the yellow regions, which reveal prefrontal–posterior parietal connectivity. (A) Research from Glasser et al. (2016). (B) Republished with permission of the American Physiological Society from B. T. T. Yeo, F. M. Krienen, J. Sepulcre, M. R. Sabuncu, D. Lashkari, et al., "The Organization of the Human Cerebral Cortex Estimated by Intrinsic Functional Connectivity," 2011, *Journal of Neurophysiology, 106,* pp. 1125–1165. Permission conveyed through Copyright Clearance Center, Inc.

evidence indicates that though some brain networks show reduced connectivity, other networks (such as the default network) show increasing connectivity with greater age. This increased connectivity may provide the mechanism for maintaining healthy cognitive function as we age (Podgórski et al., 2021).

## Using fMRI in Brain Mapping

The functional connectivity MRI (fcMRI) technique uses resting-state fMRI (rs-fMRI) to measure intrinsic functional correlations between brain regions. Pooling fcMRI data across thousands of healthy young adults makes it possible to identify consistent patterns of connectivity, or nerve tracts, in the brain. Utilizing fcMRI data from 1000 participants, Thomas Yeo and colleagues (2011) parcellated the human cerebral cortex into the 17 networks illustrated in Figure 15-12B.

The cerebral cortex is made up of primary sensory and motor networks, as well as the multiple, large-scale networks that form the association cortex. The sensory and motor networks are largely local: adjacent areas tend to show strong functional coupling with one another. In Figure 15-12B, the turquoise and blue/gray regions in the somatosensory and motor cortex and the purple region in the visual cortex illustrate these couplings.

In contrast, the association networks include areas distributed throughout the prefrontal, parietal, anterior temporal, and midline regions. In Figure 15-12B, the distributed yellow regions show prefrontal–posterior parietal connectivity. Some distributed networks, shown in light red, include the temporal, posterior parietal, and prefrontal regions.

Another complex set of networks are related to the social brain. As illustrated in **Figure 15-13**, a large number of cortical regions are functionally connected into four distinct social networks. In addition, many other networks are related to functions such as memory, space, and vision (for more details, see Kolb & Whishaw, 2021).

The *default network* is a brain network involving regions of the frontal and parietal lobes (see Figure 8-19). Using higher-resolution imaging, researchers have shown that the default network is not a single network, but rather is composed of at least two parallel networks, including adjacent dorsal and ventral components (Braga et al., 2019). As Sangil Lee and colleagues (2021) demonstrated, these components can be

**FIGURE 15-13 Networks of the Social Brain** Four proposed social-brain networks. The red areas represent the amygdala network, light blue is the mentalizing network, dark blue is the empathy network, and green is the mirror/simulation/action-perception network. Research from Kennedy & Adolphs (2012).

Chapter 7 describes a variety of brain mapping and neuroimaging techniques. Section 7-7 introduces the field of computational neuroscience, which uses mathematical models to understand brain organization.

Research Focus 10-6 describes additional research into perfect pitch.

**hyperconnectivity** Increased local connections between two related brain regions.

**FIGURE 15-14 Tractography of Temporal Lobe Auditory Circuits** Color overlaid on DTI images demonstrates tracts between the superior temporal gyrus and middle temporal gyrus in three individuals. Participants A and B had more accurate and less accurate perfect pitch, respectively; participant C did not have perfect pitch. The tracts that connect the regions in the left hemisphere (orange) are larger in participants A and B than in participant C. Tracts colored purple connect the regions in the right hemisphere. Copyright © 2011, Massachusetts Institute of Technology. Loui, P., Li, H. C., Hohmann, A., & Schlaug, G. (2011). Enhanced Connectivity in Absolute Pitch Musicians: A model for local hyperconnectivity. *Journal of Cognitive Neuroscience, 23*(4), 1015–1026. Permission conveyed through Copyright Clearance Center, Inc.

functionally dissociated. Using fMRI, these researchers measured brain activity when participants imagined future events that varied in vividness and valence (affective quality) and showed that the ventral region responded to the vividness of the imagined events, whereas the dorsal region responded to their valence.

# Tractography Using Diffusion Tensor Imaging

DTI studies provide results, often called *tractography,* that complement the networks mapped by fcMRI. Tractography measures actual neuroanatomical pathways that can be related to specific traits. Traditionally, postmortem tract tracing was performed on single brains. Today, tractography can be performed quickly on many living brains, and measurements can be made simultaneously in the entire brain. This advance allows researchers to correlate specific behavioral traits with specific patterns of connectivity.

Psyche Loui and her colleagues (2011) were interested in the neural basis of perfect (or absolute) pitch—the ability not only to discriminate among musical notes but also to name any note heard. Perfect pitch is rare among humans but is shared by people with remarkable musical talents. (Think Mozart.) Development of perfect pitch is sensitive to early experiences, including musical training and exposure to tonal languages such as Japanese.

Loui's team studied musicians, with and without absolute pitch, who were matched in gender, age, handedness, ethnicity, IQ score, and years of musical training. Participants were given a test of pitch-labeling that allowed the researchers to place the musicians with absolute pitch into two categories: more accurate and less accurate. The less accurate group was superior to participants without absolute pitch, who could not accurately identify the note.

The investigators hypothesized that absolute pitch could be related to increased connectivity in brain regions that process sounds. They used DTI to reconstruct white-matter tracts connecting two temporal cortex regions involved in auditory processing, the superior and middle temporal gyri, and regions not involved in auditory processing (corticospinal tract). The results, reproduced in **Figure 15-14**, show that people with absolute pitch have greater connectivity in temporal lobe regions responsible for pitch perception than do people without it. The effect is largest in people in the more accurate group.

Although enhanced connectivity appeared in both hemispheres of the musicians, when the investigators correlated performance on a test of absolute pitch with tract volume, only left-hemisphere tract volume predicted performance. It appears that having more local connections, or **hyperconnectivity**, in the left hemisphere is responsible for absolute pitch.

It is tempting to speculate that other exceptional talents, such as creativity, might be related to hyperconnectivity in cerebral regions. For example, Matthew Sachs and colleagues (2016) showed that connectivity between auditory regions in the superior temporal gyrus and emotional processing in the medial prefrontal cortex and insula could explain individual differences in reward sensitivity to music. Conversely, we can speculate that reduced structural and functional connectivity is related to cognitive impairments acquired after brain injuries, neurodevelopmental and psychiatric disorders, or even degeneration associated with healthy aging.

**(A) More accurate perfect pitch**    **(B) Less accurate perfect pitch**    **(C) Lacking perfect pitch**

| Left | Right | Left | Right | Left | Right |
| hemisphere | hemisphere | hemisphere | hemisphere | hemisphere | hemisphere |

# Cognition and the Cerebellum

So far, we have emphasized the role of the neocortex in cognitive functions, in part because of its marked expansion in size and neuron numbers in primate brains. Yet the human cerebellum accounts for 80% of the brain's neurons. The cerebellum has long been known to play a central role in motor control and motor learning, but the concurrent evolution of neocortex, cerebellum, and cognitive complexity in primates suggests that the cerebellum may play a larger role in cognitive processes than investigators have appreciated.

The extensive neocortex–cerebellum interconnections include prefrontal cortex, Broca's area, and neocortical regions that have sensory or perceptual functions. Thus, the cerebellum appears to be critical in producing fine movements and perception, but some executive functions also may be associated with working memory, attention, language, music, social and emotional processing, mood, and decision-making processes (e.g., Adamaszek et al., 2017; Guell et al., 2018). Furthermore, rs-fMRI has identified cerebellar networks, shown in **Figure 15-15** (Van Overwalle et al., 2020), that are related to similar cortical networks (shown with the same color legend in Figure 15-12B). It is not yet clear how these cerebellar and cortical networks interact, but the coming decade will undoubtedly deliver an abundance of new information on this topic, likely allowing researchers to develop a model of cortical–cerebellar functions in cognition (see also Gatti et al., 2021).

# Social Neuroscience

By combining cognitive neuroscience tools, especially functional neuroimaging, with abstract constructs from social psychology, **social neuroscience** seeks to understand how the brain mediates social interactions. Matthew Lieberman (2007) identified broad themes that attempt to encompass all cognitive processes involved in understanding and interacting with others and in understanding ourselves.

## Understanding Others

Animals' minds and experiences are not open to direct inspection. In consequence, we must infer animals' minds in part by observing their behaviors and, in the case of humans, by listening to their words. In doing so, we may develop a **theory of mind (ToM)**, the attribution of mental states to others. Theory of mind includes an understanding that others may have feelings and beliefs different from our own.

The capacity to understand others can also be inferred from the presence of empathy. For example, when observers view others in pain, this experience induces feelings in the observers similar to those in the models—a phenomenon correlated with activation of an empathy network, described in Figure 15-13. The intensity of the empathy activation varies with several factors, including the relationship between the observer and the model. Silvio Ionta and colleagues (2020) analyzed fMRI data from participants who observed painful or tactile stimuli delivered to a human baby's hand, a human adult's hand, a puppy's paw, and a robotic hand. The intensity of the activation in the empathy network was greater for the adult and baby models than for the other models.

fMRI studies related to ToM have also revealed the presence of a network that is dissociable from the empathy network. This work suggests that the affective (empathy) and cognitive (ToM) systems are separate routes to understanding others (Tholen et al., 2020).

Although the original studies on ToM focused on humans, a growing literature suggests that many other animals may have a form of ToM, although this view has attracted some skeptics (e.g., see the review by Heyes, 2015). Nonetheless, experimental methods have been developed to examine the degree of understanding that one animal can gain by observing the intention, gaze, perspective, or knowledge of another. Some studies claim that apes and some monkeys show ToM, as do dogs and corvid birds (jays, crows, ravens) and parrots (e.g., Bugnar et al., 2016; Maginnity & Grace, 2014).

Research Focus 2-1 describes the effects of cerebellar agenesis.

- ■ Somatomotor network
- ■ Ventral attention network
- ■ Dorsal attention network
- □ Limbic network
- ▨ Frontoparietal network
- ■ Default mode network
- ■ Visual network

**FIGURE 15-15 Parcellation of Cerebellar Resting-State Networks** The networks are identified with the same colors as those for the cerebral cortex in Figure 15-12B. Van Overwalle, F., Manto, M., Cattaneo, Z. et al. Consensus Paper: Cerebellum and Social Cognition. Cerebellum 19, 833–868 (2020). https://doi.org/10.1007/s12311-020-01155-1, Figure 2a. CC BY 4.0 license.

**social neuroscience** Interdisciplinary field that seeks to understand how the brain mediates social interactions.

**theory of mind (ToM)** Ability to attribute mental states to others.

## Understanding Oneself

Not only are we humans aware of others' intentions, but we also have a sense of self. Humans, as well as some apes, dolphins, elephants, pigs, and magpies, have the ability to recognize themselves in a mirror; human infants demonstrate this ability by about 21 months of age. Studies using fMRI show that when we recognize our own face versus the faces of familiar others, brain activity increases in the right lateral prefrontal cortex and in the lateral parietal cortex. The parietal cortex activation is thought to reflect the body's recognition of what it feels like.

But self-recognition is only the beginning of understanding oneself. People also have a self-concept that includes beliefs about their own personal traits (such as kindness and intelligence). When participants are asked to determine whether trait words or sentences are self-descriptive, brain activity in the medial prefrontal regions increases.

## Self-Regulation

Self-regulation is the ability to control emotions and impulses as a means of achieving long-term goals. We may wish to yell at the professor because an exam was unfair, but most of us recognize that this action will not be productive. Dynamic imaging studies again reveal that prefrontal regions are critical in social cognition — in this case, in self-regulation.

Children are often poor self-regulators, which probably reflects slow development of the prefrontal regions responsible for impulse control. A uniquely human ability of self-regulation is the capacity to put feelings into words, a strategy that allows us to control emotional outbursts. Curiously, such verbal labeling is associated with increased activity in the right lateral prefrontal regions but *not* in the left regions.

Not only can humans control their emotions, but they also have expectations about how a stimulus might feel (e.g., an injection by syringe). Our expectations can alter the actual feeling of an event. It is common for people to say "ouch" when they do something like stub a toe, even if they actually feel no pain. Nobukatsu Sawamoto and colleagues (2000) found that when participants expect pain, activity increases in the anterior cingulate cortex (see Figure 15-3B), a region associated with pain perception, even if the stimulus turns out not to be painful. In a review of more than 10,000 fMRI studies, Matthew Lieberman and Naomi Eisenberger (2015) concluded that the best description of the function of the anterior cingulate cortex is related to pain processing.

## Living in a Social World: Social Cognition and Brain Activity

We spend much of our waking time interacting with others socially. In a sense, our understanding of our self and our social interactions link together into a single mental action. One important aspect of this behavior includes forming attitudes and beliefs about ourselves and about others. When we express attitudes (including prejudices) toward ideas or human groups, brain imaging shows activation in prefrontal, anterior cingulate, and temporoparietal junction (TPJ) regions.

Similarly, social cognitions that run the gamut from understanding ourselves to understanding others are clearly associated with activation of specific brain regions, especially medial prefrontal (mPFC) and TPJ regions. The obvious conclusion is that mPFC-TPJ activity produces our social cognitions, just as activity in visual regions produces our visual perceptions. Evidence suggests that during rest, mPFC-TPJ–correlated activity, along with activity in other regions in the default network, may serve to commit new social information to memory. Furthermore, high levels of activity in the default network are correlated with superior social cognition (forming a social impression) and social memory (Meyer et al., 2019).

Conclusions drawn from these studies tend to be controversial, because the ability to replicate findings is central to the scientific method, yet replication is rarely done in fMRI studies (see further discussion in Poldrack et al., 2017). However, in the past few

Section 8-2 describes unique aspects of frontal lobe development that extend beyond childhood — up to age 30.

Feeling and treating physical pain is the topic of Section 11-4. Research Focus 12-1 reports on emotional pain.

The role of sleep in memory storage is discussed in detail in Section 13-4.

years, several meta-analyses combining studies from many locations have enhanced the validity of these conclusions. As one example, consider the 10,000 pain and anterior cingulate studies reviewed by Lieberman and Eisenberger.

## Neuroeconomics

Historically, economics was a discipline based on the "rational actor," which involves the belief that people make rational decisions. In the real world, people often make decisions based on assumption or intuition, as is common in gambling. Why don't people always make rational decisions?

The cerebral processes underlying human decision making are not easily inferred from behavioral studies. Nevertheless, investigators in the field of **neuroeconomics**, which combines ideas from economics, psychology, and neuroscience, attempt to explain those processes by studying patterns of brain activity as people make decisions in real time. The general assumption among neuroeconomists is that two neural decision pathways influence our choices. One is deliberate, slow, rule-driven, and emotionally neutral; it acts as a *reflective system*. The other pathway—fast, automatic, emotionally biased—forms a *reflexive system*.

If people must make quick decisions that they believe will lead to immediate gains, widespread activity appears in the dopaminergic reward system. This system includes the ventromedial prefrontal cortex and ventral striatum (nucleus accumbens), which constitute the reflexive pathway. If slower, deliberative decisions are possible, activity is greater in the lateral prefrontal, medial temporal, and posterior parietal cortex, the areas that form the reflective pathway.

Neuroeconomists aim to identify patterns of neural activity in everyday decision making, patterns that may help account for how people make decisions about their finances, social relations, and other personal choices. Although most neuroeconomic studies to date have used fMRI, in principle these studies could use other noninvasive imaging technologies to obtain evidence. Epigenetic factors probably contribute to developing the balance between the reflective and reflexive systems in individuals. Epigenetic studies therefore may help explain why many people make decisions that are not in their long-term best interest.

Because of predictions that all mammals will be shown to have similar reflective and reflexive decision systems and because all animals make decisions, the neural bases of decision processes in nonhumans undoubtedly will receive more study in the future.

**neuroeconomics** Interdisciplinary field that seeks to understand how the brain makes decisions.

Leonard Mlodinow's wonderful book *The Drunkard's Walk: How Randomness Rules Our Lives*, published in 2009, offers many everyday examples.

Figure 6-17 maps the dopaminergic pathways associated with reward.

## 15-3 Review

Before you continue, check your understanding. Answers to Self-Test appear at the back of the book.

1. Noninvasive imaging techniques enable cognitive psychologists to investigate the neural bases of thought in the "normal" brain, leading to the field called _____.

2. By using imaging methods such as DTI and fcMRI, researchers are developing a _____, a map of the complete structural and functional fiber pathway connections in the living human brain.

3. The formerly unappreciated role of the _____ in cognition is now attracting researchers' attention.

4. Social neuroscience is an interdisciplinary field that seeks to understand how the brain mediates _____.

5. Our attribution of mental states to others is known as _____.

6. Neuroeconomics seeks to understand the neural bases of _____.

7. List four general themes of social neuroscience research.

# Cerebral Asymmetry in Thinking

Seizing on Sperry's findings, the 1980s saw an avalanche of self-help books about "left-brained" and "right-brained" people. The theories espoused in these books largely ignored functions shared by both hemispheres, and the novelty eventually wore off. Even so, the concept of cerebral asymmetry remains important to understanding how the human brain thinks.

**Principle 6:** The brain is symmetrical and asymmetrical.

Fundamental to behavioral neuroscience was the finding by Paul Broca and his contemporaries in the mid-1800s that language is lateralized to the brain's left hemisphere. But the implications of lateralized brain functions did not become fully understood until the 1960s, when Roger Sperry (1968) and his colleagues began to study people who, as described in Research Focus 15-1, had undergone surgical separation of the two hemispheres as a treatment for intractable epilepsy. It soon became apparent that the cerebral hemispheres are more functionally specialized than researchers had previously realized. Before considering how the brain's two sides cooperate in generating cognitive activity, we look at the anatomical differences between the left and right hemispheres. Note that although the cerebral asymmetry of most left-handers is similar to that of right-handers, about one-third have a somewhat different organization, which is beyond the scope of this discussion (for details see Kolb & Whishaw, 2021).

## Anatomical Asymmetry

Building on Broca's findings, investigators have learned how the language- and music-related areas of the left and right temporal lobes differ anatomically. In particular, the primary auditory area is larger on the right, whereas the secondary auditory areas are larger on the left in most people. Other brain regions also are asymmetrical.

**Figure 15-16** shows that the lateral fissure, which partly separates the temporal and parietal lobes, has a sharper upward course in the right hemisphere relative to the left. As a result, the posterior right temporal lobe is larger than the same region on the left, as is the left parietal lobe relative to the right.

Among the anatomical asymmetries in the frontal lobes, the region of sensorimotor cortex representing the face is larger in the left hemisphere than in the right, a difference that presumably corresponds to the left hemisphere's special role in talking. Broca's area is organized differently on the left and the right. The area visible on the brain's surface is about one-third larger on the right than on the left, whereas the cortical area buried in the sulci of Broca's area is larger on the left side than on the right.

Not only does the brain show these gross anatomical differences, but it also evidences hemispheric differences in the details of its cellular and neurochemical structures. For example, neurons in Broca's area on the left have larger dendritic fields than do corresponding neurons on the right. The discovery of structural asymmetries tells us little about why such differences exist, but there are clear correlations with differences in cognitive processing by the brain's two sides.

Although many anatomical asymmetries in the human brain are related to language, brain asymmetries are not unique to humans. The brains of most, if not all, mammals have asymmetries, as do the brains of many bird species. Thus, the functions of cerebral asymmetry cannot be limited to language processing. Instead, human language likely evolved after the brain became asymmetrical. Language simply took advantage of the processes, including the development of mirror neurons, that had already been lateralized by natural selection in earlier members of the human lineage.

Left hemisphere    Right hemisphere

**FIGURE 15-16 Cerebral Asymmetry** The lateral fissure takes a flatter course in the left hemisphere than in the right hemisphere. As a result, the posterior right temporal lobe is larger than the same region on the left side, and the inferior parietal region is larger on the left than on the right.

## Functional Asymmetry in Neurological Patients

The specialized functions of the cerebral hemispheres often become obvious in people with damage to the left or right side of the brain. To see these functional differences clearly, compare the cases of G. H. and M. M.

# Right Parietal Damage

When G. H. was 5 years old, as he was hiking with his family, a large rock rolled off an embankment and hit him on the head. He was unconscious for a few minutes and had a severe headache for a few days, but quickly recovered. Around age 18, however, he started having seizures. Neurosurgical investigation revealed that G. H. had suffered a right posterior parietal injury from the rock accident. **Figure 15-17**A shows the area affected. After surgery to remove this area, G. H. had weakness on the left side of his body and showed contralateral neglect. These symptoms lessened fairly quickly, however, and had completely cleared a month after the surgery.

Nevertheless, G. H. had chronic difficulties in copying drawings: four years after the surgery, he still performed this task at about the level of a 6-year-old. He also had trouble assembling puzzles, a pastime he had enjoyed before the surgery. When asked to perform mental manipulations like the one in Figure 15-7, he became very frustrated and refused to continue. G. H. also had difficulty finding his way around familiar places. The landmarks he had used to guide his travels before the surgery no longer worked for him. G. H. now has to learn street names and use a verbal strategy to go from one place to another.

# Left Parietal Damage

M. M.'s difficulties were quite different from those experienced by G. H. A meningioma had placed considerable pressure on the left parietal region in M. M.'s brain. This tumor, which was surgically removed when M. M. was 16 years old, was found to have damaged the area shown in Figure 15-17B.

After the surgery, M. M. had various problems, including *aphasia*, impaired language use. The condition lessened over time: a year after the surgery, M. M. spoke fluently. Unfortunately, other difficulties persisted. In solving arithmetic problems, in reading, and even in simply calling objects or animals by name, M. M. performed at about a 6-year-old level. She had no difficulty making movements spontaneously, but when asked to copy a series of arm movements, such as those diagrammed in **Figure 15-18**, she had great difficulty. She could not figure out how to make her arm move to match the example. A general impairment in making voluntary movements in the absence of paralysis or a muscular disorder is a symptom of *apraxia*, the inability to complete a plan of action accurately.

**(A) Participant G. H.**

Injury to this area of the right hemisphere caused difficulties in copying drawings, assembling puzzles, and finding the way around a familiar city.

**(B) Participant M. M.**

Injury to this area of the left hemisphere caused difficulties in language, copying movements, reading, and generating names of objects or animals.

**FIGURE 15-17 Contrasting Parietal Lobe Injuries**

An image of a meningioma appears in Clinical Focus 3-2.

Section 10-4 describes how left-hemisphere damage causes aphasias. Section 11-5 explains how somatosensory cortex damage contributes to apraxia.

**FIGURE 15-18 Two Arm Movement Series** Participants observe the tester perform each sequence and then copy it as accurately as they can. People with left-hemisphere injury, especially in the posterior parietal region, are impaired at copying such movements.

**Series 1**

**Series 2**

**dichotic listening** Experimental procedure for simultaneously presenting a different auditory input to each ear through stereophonic earphones.

## Lessons from Patients G. H. and M. M.

What can we learn about brain function by comparing G. H. and M. M.? Their lesions were in approximately the same location but in opposite hemispheres, and their symptoms were very different.

Judging from G. H.'s difficulties, the right hemisphere contributes to controlling spatial skills, such as drawing, assembling puzzles, and navigating in space. In contrast, M. M.'s condition reveals that the left hemisphere seems to contribute to controlling language functions and cognitive tasks related to schoolwork—namely, reading and arithmetic. In addition, the left hemisphere's role in controlling voluntary movement sequences differs from the right hemisphere's role.

To some extent, then, the left and right hemispheres think about different types of information. The question is whether these functional differences can be observed in a healthy brain.

## Functional Asymmetry in the Healthy Brain

In the course of studying the auditory capacity of people with temporal lobe lesions, Doreen Kimura (1967) found something unexpected. She presented her control participants with two strings of digits, one played into each ear; such a procedure is known as **dichotic listening**. The task was to recall as many digits as possible.

Kimura found that the controls recalled more digits presented to the right ear than to the left. This result is surprising because the auditory system crosses repeatedly, beginning in the midbrain. Nonetheless, information coming from the right ear seems to have preferential access to the left (speaking) hemisphere.

In a later study, Kimura (1973) played two pieces of music for participants, one to each ear. She then gave the participants a multiple-choice test, playing four bits from musical selections and asking the participants to pick out the bits they had heard before. In this test, participants were more likely to recall the music played to the left ear than to the right. This result implies that the left ear has preferential access to the right (musical) hemisphere.

The demonstration of this functional asymmetry in the healthy brain provoked much interest in the 1970s, leading to demonstrations of functional asymmetries in the visual and tactile systems as well. Consider the visual system. If we fixate on a target, such as a dot positioned straight ahead, all the information to the left of the dot goes to the right hemisphere, and all the information to the right of the dot goes to the left hemisphere, as shown in **Figure 15-19**.

If information is presented for a relatively long time—say, 1 second—we can easily report what appeared in each visual field. If, however, the presentation is brief—say, only 40 milliseconds—then the task is considerably harder. This situation reveals a brain asymmetry. Words presented briefly to the right visual field and hence sent to the left hemisphere are more easily reported than are words presented briefly to the left visual field. Similarly, if complex geometric patterns or faces are shown briefly, those presented to the left visual field and hence sent to the right hemisphere are more accurately reported than are those presented to the right visual field.

Apparently, the hemispheres not only think about different types of information, but also process information differently. The left hemisphere seems biased toward processing language-related information, whereas the right hemisphere seems biased toward processing nonverbal, and especially spatial, information.

Does asymmetry remain the same throughout our lifetime or does it change over the course of development? Although previous studies of anatomy and fMRI activation suggested a left lateralization for language at birth, an fMRI study by Olumide Olulade and colleagues (2020) showed that young children demonstrate extensive right hemisphere activation for language that declines through childhood. We can speculate that a similar pattern may exist for other functions, such as visuospatial processing, which shows considerable bilateral activation even in adults (Seydell-Greenwald et al., 2017).

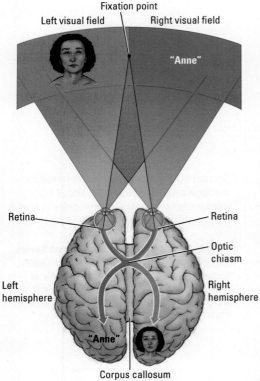

**FIGURE 15-19 Visual Pathways to the Hemispheres** When fixating at a point, each eye sees both visual fields but sends information about the right visual field only to the left hemisphere. Information about the left visual field proceeds only to the right hemisphere. In healthy participants given short exposures to stimuli (less than 1 second), the left hemisphere is more accurate at perceiving words, whereas the right hemisphere is more accurate at perceiving objects, including faces.

A word of caution: although asymmetry studies are fascinating, what they tell us about the differences between the hemispheres is not entirely clear. They tell us *something* is different, but it is a broad leap to conclude that the hemispheres house entirely different skill sets. The hemispheres have many functions in common, such as controlling movement in the contralateral hand and processing sensory information through the thalamus. Nevertheless, differences in the hemispheres' cognitive operations do exist. We can better understand these differences by studying split-brain patients, whose cerebral hemispheres have been surgically separated for medical treatment.

## Functional Asymmetry in the Split Brain

Before considering the details of split-brain studies, let us review what we already know about cerebral asymmetry. First, the left hemisphere talks; the right hemisphere does not. Second, as demonstrated in Research Focus 15-1, the right hemisphere performs better than the left on certain nonverbal tasks, especially those that engage visuospatial skills. (Organizational differences related to handedness are discussed in section 15-5.)

But how does a severed corpus callosum affect how the brain thinks? After the corpus callosum has been cut, the hemispheres have no way of communicating with each other. The left and right hemispheres, then, are free to think about different things. In a sense, a split-brain patient has two brains.

One method to test the hemispheres' cognitive functions in a split-brain patient takes advantage of the fact that, in a healthy brain, information in the left visual field goes to the right hemisphere, and information in the right field goes to the left hemisphere (see Figure 15-19). When the corpus callosum is cut, however, information presented to one side of the brain has no way of traveling to the other side. It can be processed only in the hemisphere that receives it.

**Experiments 15-2** and **15-3** show some basic testing procedures based on this dichotomy. The split-brain patient fixates on the dot in the center of the screen while information is presented to the left or right visual field. The person must respond with the left hand (controlled by the right hemisphere), with the right hand (controlled by the left hemisphere), or verbally (also a left-hemisphere function). In this way, researchers can observe what each hemisphere knows and what it is capable of doing.

As illustrated in Experiment 15-2, a picture—say, of a spoon—might be flashed and the patient asked to state what they see. If the picture is presented to the right visual field, the person will answer, "Spoon." If the picture is presented to the left visual field, however, the person will say, "I see nothing." The split-brain patient responds in this way for two reasons:

1. The right hemisphere (which receives the visual input) does not talk, so it cannot respond verbally, even though it sees the spoon in the left visual field.

2. The left hemisphere does talk, but it does not see the spoon, so it answers—quite correctly, from its own perspective—that nothing was presented.

····▷ **EXPERIMENT 15-2**

**Question:** Will severing the corpus callosum affect the way in which the brain responds?

**Procedure**

The split-brain patient fixates on the dot in the center of the screen while an image is projected to the left or right visual field. They are asked to identify verbally what they see.

Screen          Projector

**Results**

| If the spoon is presented to the right visual field, the patient answers, "Spoon." | If the spoon is presented to the left visual field, the patient answers, "I see nothing." |

Left visual field   Right visual field        Left visual field   Right visual field

Severed corpus callosum

*Conclusion:* When the left hemisphere, which can speak, sees the spoon in the right visual field, the patient responds correctly. When the right hemisphere, which cannot speak, sees the spoon in the left visual field, the patient does not respond.

Now suppose the task changes, as shown in Experiment 15-3A. If the picture of a spoon is still presented to the left visual field, but the split-brain patient now is asked to use the left hand to pick out the object shown on the screen, the left hand (controlled by the right hemisphere, which sees the spoon) readily picks out the correct object. Can the right hand also choose correctly? No, because it is controlled by the

···→ **EXPERIMENT 15-3**

**(A) Question:** How can the right hemisphere of a split-brain patient show that it knows information?

**(B) Question:** What happens if both hemispheres are asked to respond to competing information?

**Procedure**

The split-brain patient is asked to use their left hand to pick out the object shown on the screen to the left visual field (right hemisphere).

**Procedure**

Each visual field is shown a different object—a spoon to the left and a pencil to the right. The split-brain patient is asked to use both hands to pick up the object seen.

**Results**

The patient chooses the spoon with their left hand because the right hemisphere sees the spoon and controls the left hand. If the right hand is forced to choose, it will do so by chance because no stimulus is shown to the left hemisphere.

**Results**

In this case, the right and left hands do not agree. They may each pick up a different object, or the right hand may prevent the left hand from performing the task.

Left visual field  Right visual field

Severed
corpus callosum

Left visual field  Right visual field

Severed
corpus callosum

*Conclusion:* Each hemisphere is capable of responding independently. The left hemisphere may dominate in a competition, even if the response is not verbal.

left hemisphere, which cannot see the spoon. If the person in this situation is forced to select an object with the right hand, the left hemisphere does so at random.

Now let's consider an interesting twist (see Experiment 15-3B), in which each hemisphere is shown a different object—say, a spoon is presented to the right hemisphere and a pencil to the left. The split-brain patient is asked to use both hands to pick out "the object." The problem here is that the right and left hands do not agree. While the left hand tries to pick up the spoon, the right hand tries to pick up the pencil or tries to prevent the left hand from picking up the spoon.

This conflict between the hemispheres can be seen in the everyday behavior of some split-brain patients. One woman, P. O. V., reported frequent interhemispheric competition for at least 3 years after her surgery. "I open the closet door. I know what I want to wear. But as I reach for something with my right hand, my left comes up and takes something different. I can't put it down if it's in my left hand. I have to call my daughter."

We know from Experiment 15-2 that the left hemisphere is capable of using language, and Research Focus 15-1 reveals that the right hemisphere has visuospatial capabilities that the left hemisphere does not. Although findings from more than half a century of studying split-brain patients show that the hemispheres process information differently, another word of caution is needed: there is more functional overlap between the hemispheres than was at first suspected. The right hemisphere, for instance, does have some language functions, and the left hemisphere does have some spatial abilities. Nonetheless, the two undoubtedly are different.

# Explaining Cerebral Asymmetry

Various hypotheses have been proposed to explain hemispheric differences. One idea, that the left hemisphere is important in controlling fine movements, dates back a century. Recall M. M., the individual in whom removal of a meningioma left her with left parietal lobe damage and apraxia (see Figure 15-17B). Although the apraxia eventually subsided, she was left with chronic trouble copying movements.

Perhaps one reason that the left hemisphere has a role in language is that speaking requires fine motor movements of the mouth and tongue. Significantly, damage to the language-related areas of the left hemisphere almost always interferes with both language and movement, whether the person speaks or signs. The ability to read Braille, a tactile writing system that renders characters as combinations of small bumps, however, may not be so affected by left-hemisphere lesions. Most people prefer to use the left hand to read Braille, which essentially consists of spatial patterns, and processes related to reading Braille may therefore reside in the right hemisphere.

That said, another clue that the left hemisphere's specialization for language may be related to its special role in controlling fine movements comes from investigations of where the brain processes certain parts of speech. Recall that cognitive systems for representing abstract concepts likely are related to systems that produce more concrete behaviors. Consequently, we might expect that the left hemisphere would participate in forming concepts related to fine movements.

Concepts that describe movements are the parts of speech we call *verbs*. A fundamental difference between left- and right-hemisphere language abilities is that verbs seem to be processed only in the left hemisphere, whereas nouns are processed in both hemispheres. In other words, not only does the left hemisphere specialize in producing actions, but it also produces mental representations of actions in the form of words.

If the left hemisphere excels at language because it is better at controlling fine movements, what is the basis of the right hemisphere's abilities? One idea is that the right hemisphere specializes in controlling movements in space. In a sense, this role elaborates on the functions of the dorsal visual stream (diagrammed in Figure 15-4).

Once again, we can propose a link between movement at a concrete level and movement at a more abstract level. If the right hemisphere is producing movements

**Principle 9:** The nervous system produces movement in a perceptual world the brain constructs.

in space, then it is also likely to produce mental images of such movements. We would therefore predict that impairment of the right hemisphere would affect patients' abilities both to think about and to make spatially guided movements. In fact, such patients are impaired in these ways.

Bear in mind that theories about the reasons for hemispheric asymmetry remain highly speculative. The brain has evolved to produce movement and to construct a sensory reality, so the observed asymmetry must somehow relate to these overriding functions. By comparison, more recently evolved functions, such as language, likely are extensions of preexisting functions. Thus, the fact that language is represented asymmetrically does not mean that the brain is asymmetrical because of language. After all, other species that do not talk have asymmetrical brains.

## Left Hemisphere, Language, and Thought

As we end our examination of brain asymmetry, consider one more provocative idea. Michael Gazzaniga (1992) proposed that the left hemisphere's superior language skills are important for understanding the differences between humans' and other animals' thinking. He called the speaking hemisphere the *interpreter*. The following experiment, using split-brain patients, illustrates what Gazzaniga meant.

Each hemisphere is shown a picture of a match, followed by a picture of a piece of wood, for example. Another set of pictures is then shown. The task is to pick from this set a third picture that has an inferred relationship to the first two. In this example, the third related picture might be a bonfire. The right hemisphere is incapable of making the inference that a match struck and held to a piece of wood could start a bonfire, whereas the left hemisphere easily arrives at this interpretation.

An analogous task uses words. One hemisphere or the other might be shown the words *pin* and *finger* and then asked to pick out a third word related to the other two. In this case, the correct answer might be *bleed*. The right hemisphere cannot make this connection. Although it has enough language ability to pick out close synonyms for *pin* and *finger* (*needle* and *thumb*, respectively), it cannot make the inference that pricking a finger with a pin will result in bleeding.

Again, the left hemisphere has no difficulty with this task. Apparently, the left hemisphere's language capability gives it a capacity for interpretation that the right hemisphere lacks. One reason may be that language serves to label and express the computations of other cognitive systems.

Gazzaniga goes even further. He suggests that the evolution of left-hemisphere language abilities makes humans a "believing" species: humans can make inferences and have beliefs about sensory events. By contrast, Alex, the African grey parrot profiled in Comparative Focus 15-2, would not have been able to make inferences or hold beliefs because he did not have a system analogous to our left-hemisphere language system. Alex could use language but could not make inferences about sensory events with language.

Gazzaniga's idea is intriguing. It implies a fundamental difference in the nature of cerebral asymmetry—and therefore in the nature of cognition—that exists between humans and other animals because of the nature of human language. We return to this idea in Section 15-7.

## 15-4 Review

**Before you continue, check your understanding. Answers to Self-Test appear at the back of the book.**

1. The right hemisphere plays a role in _____ and _____.

2. The left hemisphere plays a role in _____ and _____.

3. The split brain results from severing the _____.

4. Why does it matter that the two cerebral hemispheres process information differently?

# Variations in Cognitive Organization

No two brains are identical. Some differences are genetically determined; others result from plastic changes caused, for example, by experience and learning or epigenetic factors. Some brain differences are idiosyncratic (unique to a particular person); many others are systematic and common to whole categories of people. In this section, we consider two systematic variations in brain organization—those related to sex and handedness—and one idiosyncratic variation, the fascinating sensory phenomenon called *synesthesia*.

## Sex Differences in Cognitive Organization

The idea that men and women think differently probably originated with the first men and women. Science backs it up. Multiple books, including one by Doreen Kimura (1999), present persuasive evidence for marked differences between men's and women's performance on many cognitive tests. As illustrated in **Figure 15-20**, paper-and-pencil tests consistently show that, on average, females have better verbal fluency than males, whereas males do better on tests of spatial reasoning. Our focus here is on how such differences relate to the brain.

**Learning Objectives**

- Describe sex differences in cognitive function.
- Identify some of the neural bases of sex differences.
- Explain what handedness might indicate about cognition.
- Define synesthesia and explain what it might reveal about cognition.

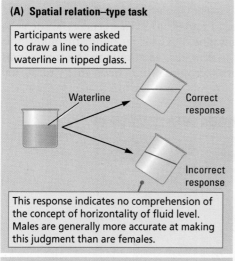

**(A) Spatial relation–type task**

Participants were asked to draw a line to indicate waterline in tipped glass.

Waterline — Correct response

Incorrect response

This response indicates no comprehension of the concept of horizontality of fluid level. Males are generally more accurate at making this judgment than are females.

**(B) Mental rotation–type task**

Participants were asked to choose the block that could be made from a plan.

Plan

a      b      c      d

Males are generally more accurate than females at this task.

**(C) Short-term-memory–type task**

Participants were asked to fill in the empty boxes with the appropriate symbols from the top row.

| 1 | 2 | 3 | 4 | 5 | 6 | 7 | 8 | 9 |
|---|---|---|---|---|---|---|---|---|
| ◯ | ⫽ | ▢ | △ | ✕ | ＞ | ∩ | ⬡ | ‖‖ |

| 2 | 8 | 3 | 2 | 1 | 4 | 2 | 3 | 5 | 9 | 2 | 1 | 7 | 3 | 6 |
|---|---|---|---|---|---|---|---|---|---|---|---|---|---|---|

| 9 | 7 | 2 | 3 | 1 | 4 | 6 | 1 | 9 | 7 | 4 | 3 | 1 | 6 | 8 |
|---|---|---|---|---|---|---|---|---|---|---|---|---|---|---|

When given a larger number of boxes to fill in and a time limit, females complete from 10% to 20% more items than males do.

**(D) Verbal fluency–type task**

Participants were asked to fill in each blank to form words that make a sentence.

1. F_____ M_____ A_____ J_____

2. C_____ B_____ E_____ S_____

3. D_____ I_____ J_____ K_____

Females are generally faster at this type of test than males are.

**FIGURE 15-20 Tasks That Reliably Show Sex-Related Cognitive Differences**

**Lateral view**

**Medial view**

**FIGURE 15-21 Sex Differences in Brain Volume** Women's brain volume in the prefrontal and medial paralimbic regions (orange) is significantly greater than men's brain volume in the same regions. Men have larger relative volumes in the medial and orbitofrontal cortex and the angular gyrus (green). Orange areas correspond to regions that have high levels of estrogen receptors during development, green to regions with high levels of androgen receptors during development. Information from Goldstein et al. (2001).

Research Focus 12-3 outlines several studies exploring brain–gender correlates.

# Neural Bases of Sex Differences

Considerable evidence points to sex differences both in the brain's gross cerebral structure and at a neuronal level. Jill Goldstein and her colleagues (2001) conducted a large MRI study of sexual dimorphism in the human brain. They found that women have larger volumes of dorsal prefrontal and associated paralimbic regions, whereas men have larger volumes of more ventral prefrontal regions (**Figure 15-21**). (Brain size is related to body size, and on average, male brains are bigger than female brains, so the investigators corrected for size.)

A more recent study of more than 5000 brains showed a fairly similar pattern of differences when corrected for brain size. In addition, this study demonstrated a striking difference in the pattern of intrahemispheric connections (Ritchie et al., 2018). Not only is the general pattern different, but women have more dispersed connections within their white matter than men do. Finally, the researchers found that for all measures, there was considerable overlap between the sexes (approximately 50%), and males had much higher variability.

Another way to measure sex differences is to assess cortical thickness, independent of volume. **Figure 15-22** shows that relative to men, women have increased cortical gray matter concentrations in many cortical regions. Men's gray matter concentrations, by contrast, are more uniform across the cortex. Collectively, the MRI studies represented in Figures 15-21 and 15-22 point to differences between men's and women's cortical organization.

Sex differences in neuronal structure also exist. Gonadal hormones influence the structure of neurons in the prefrontal cortices of rats (Kolb & Stewart, 1991). The cells in one prefrontal region, located along the midline, have larger dendritic fields (and presumably more synapses) in males than in females, as shown in the top row of **Figure 15-23**. In contrast, the cells in the orbitofrontal region have larger dendritic

Courtesy Dr. Arthur Toga, Laboratory of Neuro Imaging at USC

**Left hemisphere**

**FIGURE 15-22 Sex Differences in Gray-Matter Concentration** Women show increased gray-matter concentration in the cortical regions shown in color on this MRI. Gray-shaded regions are not statistically different in males and females. Courtesy of Dr. Arthur Toga, Laboratory of Neuro Imaging, University of Southern California.

**FIGURE 15-23 Sex Differences in Neuronal Architecture** In the frontal cortices of male and female rats, cells in the midline frontal region (*top two drawings*) are more complex in males than in females, whereas the opposite is true of the orbitofrontal region (*bottom two drawings*).

fields (and presumably more synapses) in females than in males, as shown in the bottom row. These sex differences are not found in rats that have had their testes or ovaries removed at birth. Presumably, sex hormones somehow change the brain's organization and, ultimately, its cognitive processing.

Stewart and Kolb (1994) found that the presence or absence of gonadal hormones affects the brain in adulthood as well as in early development. In their study, which focused on how hormones affect recovery from brain damage, the ovaries of middle-aged female rats were removed. When they examined the brains of these rats and those of control rats some months later, researchers observed that the cortical neurons of the rats whose ovaries had been removed—especially the prefrontal neurons—had undergone structural changes. The cells had grown 30% more dendrites, and their spine density increased compared with the control rats' cells. Clearly, gonadal hormones can affect the brain's neuronal structure at any point in an animal's life.

An additional way to consider the neural basis of sex differences is to look at the effects of cortical injury in men and women. If sex differences exist in the neural organization of cognitive processing, the effects of cortical injury in the two sexes should also differ. When Doreen Kimura (1999) conducted this kind of study, she found that the pattern of cerebral organization within each hemisphere may, in fact, differ between the sexes.

When investigating people who had a cortical stroke in adulthood, Kimura tried to match the location and extent of injury in her male and female study participants. She found that men and women were almost equally likely to be aphasic subsequent to left-hemisphere lesions of some kind. However, men were more likely to be aphasic and apraxic after damage to the left posterior cortex, whereas women were far more likely to be aphasic and apraxic after lesions to the left frontal cortex.

These results, summarized in **Figure 15-24**, suggest a sex difference in intrahemispheric organization—a conclusion supported by a later study (**Figure 15-25**) using diffusion tensor analysis of brain networks in more than 900 participants. In this population, which comprised nearly equal numbers of each sex, females had greater interhemispheric connectivity, whereas males had greater intrahemispheric connectivity (Ingalhalikar et al., 2014).

## Evolution of Sex-Related Cognitive Differences

Although gonadal hormones have taken center stage in explaining sex differences in cognitive function, we are still left with the question of how these differences arose. To answer this question, we must look back at human evolution. Mothers pass their genes to both sons and daughters, and fathers do the same. Ultimately, then, males and females of a species have virtually all their genes in common.

The only way a gene can affect one sex preferentially is for the animal's gonadal hormones to influence the gene's activities. Production of gonadal hormones is determined by the presence or absence of the Y chromosome, which carries a gene called the *testes-determining factor (TDF)*. TDF stimulates the body to produce testes, which then manufacture androgens, which in turn influence other genes' activities.

Like other body organs, the brain is a potential target of natural selection. We should therefore expect to find sex-related differences in the brain whenever the sexes differ in the adaptive problems they have faced in their species' evolution. Aggressive behavior is a good example. Males in most mammalian species typically are more physically aggressive than females. This trait presumably improves males' reproductive success by selecting against individuals with lesser aggressiveness. Higher levels of aggression are associated with higher androgen levels. We know from studies of nonhuman species that aggression is related directly to the presence of androgens and to their effects on gene expression, both during brain development and later in life. In this case, therefore, natural selection has worked on gonadal hormone levels to favor aggressiveness in males.

**FIGURE 15-24 Evidence for Sex Differences in Cortical Organization** Apraxia and aphasia are associated with frontal damage to the left hemisphere in women and with posterior damage in this hemisphere in men. Information from Kimura (1999).

(A) Male brain

(B) Female brain

**FIGURE 15-25 Sex Differences in the Connectome** DTI analysis of brain networks in these dorsal views reveals greater intrahemispheric connections in males **(A)** and greater interhemispheric connections in females **(B)**. Information from Ingalhalikar et al. (2014).

Explanations of sex-related differences in cognitive processes, such as language or spatial skills, are more speculative than explanations of sex-related differences in aggressive behavior. Nevertheless, some hypotheses come to mind. We can imagine, for instance, that in the history of mammalian evolution, males have tended to range over larger territories than have females. This behavior requires spatial abilities, so evolution would have favored these skills in males.

Support for this hypothesis comes from comparing spatial problem solving in males of closely related mammalian species—species in which the males range over large territories versus species in which the males' range is not as extensive. Pine voles, for example, have a restricted range and no sex-related difference in range, whereas meadow voles have a range about 20 times as large as that of pine voles, and male meadow voles range more widely than the females do.

Meadow voles display far superior spatial skills compared to pine voles. A sex difference in spatial ability among meadow voles favors males, but pine voles have no such sex difference. The hippocampus is implicated in spatial navigation skills. Significantly, the hippocampus is larger in meadow voles than in pine voles, and it is larger in male meadow voles than in females (Gaulin, 1992). A similar logic could help explain sex-related differences in spatial abilities between human males and females (see Figure 15-20).

Explanations of sex-related differences in language skills are also speculative. One hypothesis holds that if males were hunters and often away from home, home-based females formed social groups that were selectively favored to develop tools—language, for example—for social interactions. We might also argue that females with superior fine motor skills (such as foraging for food and making clothing and baskets) had a selective advantage. The relationship between language and fine motor skills may have favored enhanced language capacities in females.

Although such speculations are interesting, they are not testable. We will probably never know with certainty why sex-related differences in brain organization developed.

# Handedness and Cognitive Organization

Nearly everyone prefers one hand to the other for writing or throwing a ball. Most people prefer the right hand. In fact, left-handedness has historically been viewed as odd, though it is not actually rare. An estimated 10% of the human population worldwide is left-handed. This proportion represents only the number of people who write with the left hand. When broader criteria are used to determine left-handedness, estimates of its prevalence range from 10% to 30% of the population.

Because the left hemisphere controls the right hand, the general assumption is that right-handedness is somehow related to the presence of speech in the left hemisphere. If this were so, language would be located in the right hemisphere of left-handed people. This hypothesis is easily tested, and it turns out to be false.

In the course of preparing patients with epilepsy for surgery to remove the abnormal tissue causing their seizures, Ted Rasmussen and Brenda Milner (1977) injected the left or right hemisphere with sodium amobarbital. This drug produces a short-acting anesthesia of the entire hemisphere, making it possible to determine where speech originates. As described in Clinical Focus 15-4: Sodium Amobarbital Test, if a person becomes aphasic when the drug is injected into the left hemisphere but not when the drug is injected into the right hemisphere, then speech must reside in that person's left hemisphere.

Rasmussen and Milner found that in virtually all right-handed people, speech was localized in the left hemisphere, but the reverse was not true for left-handed people. Approximately 70% of left-handers also had speech in the left hemisphere. Of the remaining 30%, about half had speech in the right hemisphere and half had speech in both hemispheres. Findings from neuroanatomical studies have subsequently shown that left-handers with speech in the left hemisphere have asymmetries similar to those of right-handers. By contrast, in left-handers

## ◎ CLINICAL FOCUS 15-4

# Sodium Amobarbital Test

Guy, a 32-year-old lawyer, had a vascular malformation over the brain region corresponding to the posterior speech zone. This malformation was beginning to cause neurological symptoms, including seizures. The ideal surgical treatment was removal of the abnormal vessels.

The complication with this surgery is that removing vessels sitting over the posterior speech zone poses a serious risk of permanent aphasia. Because Guy was left-handed, his speech areas could be located in the right hemisphere of his brain. If so, the surgical risk would be much lower.

To achieve certainty in such doubtful cases, Jun Wada and Ted Rasmussen (1960) pioneered the technique of injecting sodium amobarbital, a barbiturate, into the carotid artery to briefly anesthetize the ipsilateral hemisphere. (Today, a catheter inserted into the femoral artery is more often used to deliver the medication.) This procedure enables an unequivocal localization of speech because injection into the speech hemisphere results in speech arrest lasting as long as several minutes. As speech returns, it is characterized by aphasic errors. Injection of sodium amobarbital into the nonspeaking hemisphere may produce no or only brief speech arrest.

This procedure allows each hemisphere to be studied separately in the functional absence of the other (anesthetized) hemisphere. Because the period of anesthesia lasts several minutes, a variety of functions, including memory and movement, can be studied to determine a hemisphere's capabilities.

The sodium amobarbital test is always performed bilaterally, with the second cerebral hemisphere being injected several days after the first

Left carotid artery

Sodium amobarbital

To avoid damaging speech zones in patients who are about to undergo brain surgery, surgeons inject sodium amobarbital into the carotid artery. This drug anesthetizes the hemisphere where it is injected (here, green), allowing the surgeon to determine whether that hemisphere is dominant for speech.

one to make sure no residual drug effect lingers. During the brief period of drug action, the patient is given a series of simple tasks requiring the use of language, memory, and object recognition. To test speech, the patient is asked to name some common objects presented in quick succession, to count, to recite the days of the week forward and backward, and to spell simple words.

If the injected hemisphere is nondominant for speech, the patient may continue to carry out the verbal tasks, although there is often a period as long as 30 seconds during which they appear confused and are silent but can resume speech with urging. When the injected hemisphere is dominant for speech, the patient typically stops talking and remains completely aphasic until recovery from the anesthesia occurs, somewhere in the range of 4 to 10 minutes.

Guy was found to have speech in the left hemisphere. During the test of his left hemisphere, he could not talk. Later, he said that when he was asked about a particular object, he wondered just what the question meant. When he finally had some vague idea of the question, he had no idea what the answer was or how to say anything. By then, he realized that he had been asked all sorts of other questions to which he had also not responded.

When asked which objects he had been shown, Guy said he had no idea. However, when given an array of objects and asked to choose them with his left hand, he identified the objects by pointing because his nonspeaking right hemisphere controlled that hand. In contrast, his speaking left hemisphere had no memory of the objects: it had been asleep.

with speech originating in the right hemisphere or in both hemispheres—known as **anomalous speech representation**—the anatomical symmetry is reversed or absent.

Sandra Witelson and Charlie Goldsmith (1991) examined whether any other gross differences in the brain structure of right- and left-handers might exist. One possibility is that the connectivity of the cerebral hemispheres may differ. To test this idea, the investigators studied the hand preference of terminally ill patients on a variety of one-handed tasks. They later performed postmortem studies of these patients' brains, paying particular attention to the size of the corpus callosum. They found that the callosal cross-sectional area was 11% larger in left-handed and ambidextrous (little or no hand preference) people than in right-handed people.

Eileen Luders and her colleagues (2010) noted that left-handed people tend to be less lateralized in their hand dominance than right-handed people. They proposed that callosal size is not related to handedness per se, but rather to the degree of handedness lateralization. In their study, which used both MRIs and handedness questionnaires, these authors found a negative correlation between callosal size and handedness laterality. Thus, the more lateralized the participants were, the smaller the callosum was, regardless of handedness.

**anomalous speech representation** Condition in which a person's speech zones are located in the right hemisphere or in both hemispheres.

**synesthesia** Ability to perceive a stimulus of one sense as the sensation of a different sense, as when sound produces a sensation of color; literally, *feeling together.*

Musician–composer Stevie Wonder is a synesthete, as were music legends Duke Ellington and Franz Liszt, Nobel Prize–winning physicist Richard Feynman, and novelist Vladimir Nabokov (and his son). Singers including Billy Joel, Beyoncé, and Billie Eilish have said that synesthesia inspires their creativity.

# Synesthesia

Some variations in brain organization are idiosyncratic, rather than systematic. **Synesthesia** is an individual's capacity to join sensory experiences across sensory modalities. Examples include the ability to hear colors or taste shapes. Edward Hubbard (2007) estimated the incidence of synesthesia at about 1 in 23 people, although for most this ability is likely limited in scope. Synesthesia can become more pronounced after brain injury, suggesting that new connections between sensory systems can occur as the brain compensates for injury (Yong et al., 2017).

Sensory blendings may be difficult to imagine. How can sounds or letters possibly produce colors? Studies of synesthetes show that the same stimuli always elicit the same experiences for them. The most common form of synesthesia is colored hearing. For many synesthetes, this means hearing both speech and music in color—perceiving a visual mélange of colored shapes, movement, and scintillation. The fact that colored hearing is more common than other types of synesthesia is curious.

The five primary senses (vision, hearing, touch, taste, and smell) all generate synesthetic pairings. Most, however, are in one direction. For instance, whereas synesthetes may see colors when they hear, they do not hear sounds in colors. Furthermore, some sensory combinations occur rarely, if at all. In particular, taste or smell rarely triggers a synesthetic response.

Because each case is idiosyncratic, synesthesia's neurological basis is difficult to investigate. Few studies have related it directly to brain function or brain organization, and different people may experience it for different reasons. Various hypotheses have been advanced to account for synesthesia, such as extraordinary neural connections between the sensory regions being related in a particular synesthete; increased activity in the frontal lobe multimodal cortex, which receives inputs from more than one sensory area; or particular sensory inputs that elicit unusual patterns of cerebral activation. This condition may at least partly be determined by genes influencing brain development. Whatever the explanation, when it comes to certain sensory inputs, the brain of a synesthete certainly works differently from other people's brains.

## 15-5 Review

Before you continue, check your understanding. Answers to Self-Test appear at the back of the book.

1. The two major contributors to organizational differences in individual brains are _____ and _____.

2. Differences in the cerebral organization of thinking are probably related to differences in the _____ that underlie different types of cognitive processing.

3. People who experience certain sensations in more than one sensory modality are said to have _____.

4. What roles do gonadal hormones play in brain organization and function?

## Learning Objectives

- Describe Spearman's idea of general intelligence.
- Contrast the concepts of divergent and convergent intelligence.
- Describe the genetic and experiential components of Hebb's intelligence A and intelligence B concepts.
- Explain the P-FIT and NNT models of intelligence.

### 15-6

# Intelligence

Intelligence exerts a major influence on anyone's thinking ability. It is easy to identify in people and even easy to observe in other animals. Yet intelligence is not at all easy to define. Despite more than a century of study, researchers have not yet reached agreement on what intelligence entails. We therefore begin this section by reviewing some hypotheses of intelligence.

## Concept of General Intelligence

In the 1920s, Charles Spearman proposed that although different kinds of intelligence may exist, humans also have an underlying general intelligence, which he called the *g* factor. Consider for a moment what a general intelligence factor might mean for the brain. Presumably, brains with high or low *g* would have some general difference in brain architecture—perhaps in gyral patterns, cytoarchitectonics, vascular patterns, or neurochemistry, for example.

The difference in *g* could not be something as simple as size, because human brain size (which varies from about 1000 to 2000 grams) correlates poorly with intelligence. Another possibility is that *g* is related to special cerebral connectivity or even to the ratio of neurons to glia. Still another possibility is that *g* is related to the activation of specific brain regions, possibly in the frontal lobe (Duncan et al., 2000; Gray & Thompson, 2004).

The results of preliminary studies of Albert Einstein's brain implied that cerebral connectivity and the ratio of glia to neurons may be important. Sandra Witelson and her colleagues (1999) found that although Einstein's brain was the same size and weight as the average male brain, its lateral fissure was short, and both the left and the right lateral fissures demonstrated a particularly striking upward deflection (**Figure 15-26**). This arrangement essentially fused the inferior parietal area with the posterior temporal area.

The inferior parietal cortex has a role in mathematical reasoning, so it is tempting to speculate that Einstein's mathematical abilities were related to neural rearrangements in this area. But another important difference may distinguish Einstein's brain. Marion Diamond and her colleagues (1985) looked at its glia-to-neuron ratio versus the mean for a control population. They found that Einstein's ratio in the inferior parietal cortex was higher than average: each neuron in this region had an unusually high number of glial cells supporting it.

The glia-to-neuron ratio was not unusually high in any other cortical areas of Einstein's brain measured by these researchers. Possibly, then, certain types of intelligence could be related to differences in cell structure in localized brain regions. But even if this hypothesis proves correct, it offers little neural evidence in favor of a general intelligence factor.

One possibility is that *g* is related to the brain's language processes, given that language ability qualitatively changes the nature of cognitive processing in humans. So perhaps people with very good language skills also have an advantage in general thinking ability. Or *g* could be an artifact of culture.

Many other hypotheses on intelligence have been proposed since Spearman's general intelligence theory was introduced, all following from the general idea that distinct forms of intelligence exist and should be dissociable. The idea of multiple human intelligences should not be surprising, given the varied cognitive operations the human brain can perform. To date, however, theories of intelligence have not considered the anatomy and function of the brain directly. Moreover, although they are often favored by educators, they have not been rigorously tested scientifically.

*Cytoarchitectonics* refers to brain cell organization, structure, and distribution.

Section 1-5 reveals fallacies inherent in correlating human brain size with intelligence.

**FIGURE 15-26 Einstein's Brain** The lateral fissure of Einstein's brain takes an exaggerated upward course relative to its course in typical brains, essentially fusing the posterior temporal regions with the inferior parietal regions (compare this image to the typical lateral fissure shown in Figure 15-16).

# Divergent and Convergent Intelligence

One clear difference between lesions in the parietal and temporal lobes and lesions in the frontal lobes is how they affect performance on standardized intelligence tests. Posterior lesions produce reliable and often large decreases in intelligence test scores, whereas frontal lesions do not. This is puzzling. If frontal lobe damage does not diminish a person's intelligence test score, why do people with this kind of damage often do irrational things, such as failing to go to work or keep appointments? The answer lies in the difference between two kinds of intelligence.

According to J. P. Guilford (1967), traditional intelligence tests measure **convergent thinking**—that is, the application of knowledge and reasoning skills to narrow the range of possible solutions to a problem and then zero in on one correct answer. Typical intelligence test items using vocabulary words, arithmetic problems, puzzles, block designs, and so forth all require convergent thinking. They demand a single correct answer that can be easily scored.

**convergent thinking** Form of thinking that searches for a single answer to a question (such as $2 + 2 = ?$); contrasts with divergent thinking.

**divergent thinking** Form of thinking that searches for multiple solutions to a problem (how many ways can a pen be used?); contrasts with convergent thinking.

**intelligence A** Hebb's term for innate intellectual potential, which is highly heritable and cannot be measured directly.

**intelligence B** Hebb's term for observed intelligence, which is influenced by experience and other factors in the course of development; measured by intelligence tests.

In contrast, **divergent thinking** reaches outward from conventional knowledge and reasoning skills to explore new, more unconventional solutions to problems. Divergent thinking assumes a variety of approaches and answers to a question are possible, rather than just a single "correct" solution. An example of a task that requires divergent thinking would be asking a person to list all the possible uses they can imagine for a coat hanger.

Clearly, a person who is very good at divergent thinking might not necessarily be good at convergent thinking, and vice versa. The distinction is useful because it helps us to understand the effects of brain injury on thought. Frontal lobe injury is believed to interfere with divergent thinking. The convergent thinking measured by standardized IQ tests is often impaired in people with damage to the temporal and parietal lobes.

Injury to the left parietal lobe in particular causes devastating impairment in the ability to perform cognitive processes related to academic work. People with this kind of injury may be aphasic, alexic (have difficulty understanding and processing written words), and apraxic. Many have severe deficits in arithmetic ability. All of these impairments would interfere with school performance and performance at most jobs.

Patient M. M., discussed in Section 15-4, had a left parietal lobe injury and was unable to return to school. In contrast to people like M. M., individuals with frontal lobe injuries that spare Broca's language area seldom have deficits in reading, writing, or arithmetic—tasks associated with convergent thinking. Likewise, they show no decrement in standardized IQ tests. C. C.'s case provides a good example.

C. C. had a meningioma along the midline between the frontal lobes. Extracting it required removal of brain tissue from both hemispheres. Before his surgery, C. C. was a prominent lawyer. Afterward, although he still had a superior IQ and superior memory, he was unable to work, in part because he no longer had any imagination. He could not generate the novel solutions to legal problems that had characterized his career before the surgery. Thus, both M. M. and C. C. had problems that prevented them from working, but their problems differed because their injuries affected different kinds of thinking.

# Intelligence, Heredity, Epigenetics, and the Synapse

Donald Hebb proposed another way to categorize human intelligence. Like Guilford, Hebb thought of people as having two forms of intelligence, which he called intelligence A and intelligence B. Unlike Guilford's convergent–divergent dichotomy, Hebb's **intelligence A** refers to innate intellectual potential, which is highly heritable: it has a strong genetic component. **Intelligence B** is observed intelligence, which is influenced by experience, including environmental conditions, as well as by other factors, such as disease, injury, or exposure to environmental toxins, especially during development.

Hebb (1980) understood that experience can significantly influence brain cell structure. In his view, experiences influence brain development, and thus observed intelligence, because they alter the brain's synaptic organization. It follows that appropriate postnatal experiences can enhance development of intelligence B in people with lower-than-average intelligence A, whereas an under-resourced environment can hinder the development of intelligence B in people with higher-than-average intelligence A. The task is to identify an enriched environment and a deprived environment so as to stimulate people to reach their highest potential intelligence.

Research Focus 8-1 explores the link between socioeconomic factors and cortical development. Section 8-4 recounts Hebb's pioneering work on the importance of enriched environments in early childhood education.

One implication of Hebb's view is that the brain's synaptic organization plays a key role in producing intelligence. Synaptic organization is partly directed by a person's genes, but is also affected by epigenetic factors. Variations in the experiences to which people are exposed, coupled with variations in genetic patterns, undoubtedly contribute to the individual differences in intelligence that we observe—both quantitative (as measured by IQ tests) and qualitative (as seen in special abilities such as mathematics).

# How Smart Brains Differ

A seminal review by Rex Jung and Richard Haier (2007) compared 37 neuroimaging studies of intelligence and concluded that differences in intelligence are linked to structural and functional variations in the lateral prefrontal cortex, medial prefrontal cortex, posterior parietal cortex, and sensory areas in the occipital and temporal lobes. The authors recognized that these regions are connected by white-matter tracts and proposed that these regions form a network that underlies intelligence—an idea that they called the parieto-frontal integration theory of intelligence (P-FIT) model. In the 15 years since Jung and Haier introduced their proposal, significant methodological improvements in imaging technology have occurred, but the general consensus remains that a parieto-frontal network forms the basis of intelligence and that individual differences in intelligence are related to structural and functional differences in these regions (for a review, see Haier, 2017).

Ulrike Basten and colleagues (2015) have modified the P-FIT model to differentiate between functional (brain activation in fMRI) and structural (amount of gray matter in MRI) correlates of intelligence. Their new version of the theory also identifies both positive and negative associations between intelligence and brain activation. Thus, higher intelligence is associated with increased activation in some regions and reduced activation in others (see **Figure 15-27**). Furthermore, these authors' analysis extends the network to include insular cortex, posterior cingulate cortex, and subcortical structures. They note, however, that we do not yet know how differences in intelligence arise from these anatomical differences, nor can we be certain that the differences between brains appear *because* of differences in intelligence rather being the cause of the differences.

Differences in regions in the P-FIT model can also be seen at the microstructural level. In a recent study, Erhan Genç and colleagues (2018) combined an advanced DTI method with a culturally neutral reasoning test. They measured all 180 areas identified in the HCP research and confirmed the positive association between intelligence and the volume of cerebral cortex. In addition, they found that specific microstructural properties are associated with intelligence, especially the cortical regions in the parietal–frontal network. Cortical gray matter is mostly composed of neurites (dendrites and axons); because these structures restrict the movement of water molecules, it is possible to estimate neurite density and orientation.

The results from Genç and colleagues' (2018) study showed that neurite density is negatively correlated with intelligence (see **Figure 15-28**). At first glance, this appears counterintuitive because it means that less is better. However, recall that during brain maturation, synapses are overproduced and then pruned, making the brain more efficient. Conditions in which pruning is reduced, such as Down syndrome, result in less efficient cerebral processing and lower intelligence. Thus, this study shows that human intelligence is related to brain structure in two different ways. First, bigger brains with more neurons are associated with higher intelligence. Second, higher intelligence is associated with sparsely and well-organized dendritic arbor, which increases processing speed and network efficiency.

Aron Barbey (2018) proposed a parallel theory, the network neuroscience theory (NNT), which states that there are different brain networks for *crystallized intelligence* (acquired knowledge) and *fluid intelligence* (problem solving). General intelligence (Spearman's *g*) is the combination of these two forms of intelligence. According to NNT, crystallized intelligence is heavily dependent on the default network, which is an integrated subsystem. Fluid intelligence, in contrast, is based on activity in two networks—a network joining the frontal and parietal cortex (frontoparietal) and a network joining the anterior cingulate cortex with the operculum (the cortex covering the insula). These two networks are considered segregated subsystems.

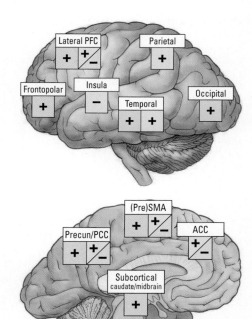

**FIGURE 15-27 The Brain Bases of Intelligence** A meta-analysis of structural MRIs (pink) and fMRIs (gray/yellow) collected during cognitive tasks found clusters of regions showing positive (+) or negative (–) associations between intelligence and brain activation.

**FIGURE 15-28 Neurite Density** Panel A shows the high neurite density and dendritic arborization correlated with lower intelligence. Panel B shows the comparatively lower density and arborization correlated with higher intelligence. Higher-intelligence individuals have a larger cortical volume and more neurons, as indicated by the dotted line.

**(A)**

**(B)**

Resting brains show a balanced state between integrated and segregated networks, which enables the brain to flexibly switch task states to match varying task demands (see Wang et al., 2021, for details). Integrated networks are proposed to underlie general cognitive ability, whereas segregated networks underlie crystallized intelligence and processing speed. This balance is not perfect, however: resting brains tending toward greater segregation may be more efficient in switching task states that need higher segregation, and vice versa for tasks needing higher integration. Such differences can provide a basis for differences in cognitive abilities across individuals. The capacity to flexibly transition between these network states provides the basis of general intelligence and may be related to sparsely and well-organized dendritic arbor discussed above.

## 15-6 Review

Before you continue, check your understanding. Answers to Self-Test appear at the back of the book.

1. Different concepts of intelligence include Spearman's _____, Guilford's concepts of _____ and _____ thinking, Hebb's _____ and _____, the _____ theory of intelligence, and the _____ neuroscience theory.

2. Intelligence is likely related to the brain's _____ organization as well as to its _____ efficiency.

3. Evidence that Hebb's intelligence A can be altered by experience to produce intelligence B demonstrates _____ influences on brain organization.

4. How might intelligence be related to brain organization and function?

### 15-7

# Consciousness

Our conscious experience is familiar and intimate, yet remains largely a mysterious product of the brain. Everyone has an idea of what it means to be conscious, but like thinking and intelligence, consciousness is easier to identify than it is to define. Definitions range from a mere manifestation of complex thought processes to more slippery notions that see it as the subjective experience of awareness, or the "inner self."

Despite the difficulty of defining consciousness, scientists generally agree that it is a process—not a thing—that emerges as information is sorted out. For example, vision involves the interplay among sensory receptors, pathways to the brainstem and cortex, and processing in multiple brain regions. Our visual experience is not the result of any specific region, but rather an emergent property that gives us an integrated percept. Consciousness allows us to combine integrated information from multiple brain systems, such as those associated with sensory perception, emotion, thinking, and so on.

## Why Are We Conscious?

Countless people, including neuroscience researchers, have wondered why we experience **consciousness**, the mind's level of responsiveness to impressions made by the senses. The simplest explanation is that consciousness provides an adaptive advantage. Either our construct of the sensory world or our selection of behavior is enhanced by being conscious. Consider visual consciousness.

According to Francis Crick and Christof Koch (1998), an animal such as a frog acts a bit like a zombie when it responds to visual input. Frogs respond to small, preylike objects by snapping and to large, looming objects by jumping away. These responses are controlled by different visual systems and are best thought of as reflexive rather than conscious. Such visual systems work well for the frog, so why would humans need to add consciousness? Crick and Koch suggest that reflexive systems are fine when their number is limited, but as their numbers grow, reflexive arrangements become inefficient, especially when two or more systems conflict. As the amount of information

**consciousness** The mind's level of responsiveness to impressions made by the senses.

about an event increases, it becomes advantageous to produce a single complex representation and make it available for a sufficient time to the parts of the brain—such as the frontal lobes—that choose among many possible action plans. This sustained, complex representation is consciousness.

Of course, to survive, we must retain the ability to respond quickly and unconsciously when we need to. This reflexive ability exists alongside our ability to process information consciously. The ventral visual stream is conscious, but the dorsal stream, which acts more rapidly, is not. Athletes model the unconscious action of the online dorsal stream. To hit a baseball or tennis ball traveling at more than 100 miles per hour requires athletes to swing before they are consciously aware of actually seeing the ball. Conscious awareness of the ball comes just after hitting it.

In a series of experiments, Marc Jeannerod and his colleagues (Castiello et al., 1991) found a similar dissociation between behavior and awareness in healthy volunteers as they made grasping movements. **Experiment 15-4** illustrates a representative experiment. Participants were required to grasp one of three rods as quickly as possible. A light on a rod indicated it to be the correct target rod on any given trial.

On some trials, unknown to the participants, the light jumped from one target to another. Participants were asked to report whether such a jump had occurred. As shown in the Results section of the experiment, although participants were able to make the trajectory correction, they were sometimes actually grasping the correct target before they were aware the light had changed.

On some trials, the extent of dissociation between motor and vocal responses was so great that, to their surprise, participants grasped the target some 300 milliseconds before they emitted the vocal response. As with baseball players, their conscious awareness of the stimulus event occurred only after their movements took place. No thought was required to make the movement, just as frogs catch flies without having to think about it.

Unconscious movements differ from those consciously directed toward a specific object, as when we reach into a bowl of jellybeans to select a candy of a certain color. In this case, we must be aware of all the different colors surrounding the color we want. The conscious ventral stream is needed to discriminate among these particular stimuli and respond differentially to them. Consciousness, then, allows us to select behaviors that correspond to an understanding of the nuances of sensory inputs.

## What Is the Neural Basis of Consciousness?

Consciousness must be related in some way to neural system activity, particularly in the forebrain. One way to investigate these systems is to contrast two kinds of neurological conditions. In the first condition, a person lacks conscious awareness of some subset of information, even though the person processes that information unconsciously. Examples include blindsight, visual form agnosia, implicit learning in amnesia, and contralateral neglect (discussed in Section 15-2). Another example is obsessive-compulsive disorder, in which people persist in some checking behavior—for example, confirming that the stove is off or the door is locked—even though they have already checked many times.

All these phenomena show that stimuli can be highly processed by the brain without entering conscious awareness. This is quite different from the second neurological condition, in which people are consciously aware of stimuli that are not actually there. Examples of such stimuli include phantom limbs and the hallucinations of schizophrenia. In both of these cases, consciousness of specific events, such as pain in a missing limb or hearing voices, exists even though these events clearly are not "real."

We can draw two conclusions from these contrasting conditions. First, the representation of a visual object or event is likely to be distributed over many parts of the visual system and probably over parts of the frontal lobes as well. Damage to different areas not only

An anatomical description of the dorsal and ventral visual streams is given in Section 9-2 and a functional description is given in Section 9-5.

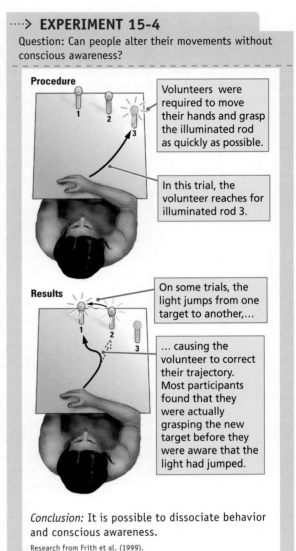

····> **EXPERIMENT 15-4**

Question: Can people alter their movements without conscious awareness?

**Procedure**

Volunteers were required to move their hands and grasp the illuminated rod as quickly as possible.

In this trial, the volunteer reaches for illuminated rod 3.

**Results**

On some trials, the light jumps from one target to another,...

... causing the volunteer to correct their trajectory. Most participants found that they were actually grasping the new target before they were aware that the light had jumped.

*Conclusion:* It is possible to dissociate behavior and conscious awareness.

Research from Frith et al. (1999).

Clinical Focus 9-1 describes blindsight, Sections 9-2 and 9-5 discuss visual agnosias, Section 14-2 explores implicit learning in amnesia, and Section 16-3 focuses on obsessive-compulsive disorder.

Research Focus 11-5 outlines phantom limb pain, Figure 14-22 shows how amputation remaps the cortex, and Clinical Focus 8-5 discusses brain abnormalities in schizophrenia.

produces different specific symptoms, such as agnosia or neglect, but can also produce a specific loss of visual consciousness. Disordered functioning can induce faulty consciousness, such as hallucinations. Second, because visual consciousness can be lost, it follows that parts of the neural circuit must produce this awareness. But how does this work? Over the past decade, several theories of the neural basis of consciousness have been proposed. We will briefly consider three of these theories here to give a flavor of their nature.

The general consensus among neuroscience researchers holds that the neural basis of consciousness has two distinct features: (1) the level of consciousness (arousal/wakefulness), which is related to the activity of ascending activating systems of the brainstem, and (2) the content of consciousness, which is related to the connections between the thalamus and the cortex (the thalamocortical system). Our focus here is on the *content* of consciousness because, although arousal is necessary for consciousness, it is not sufficient. Patients with brain injuries who survive in a "vegetative" state, for example, may exhibit unresponsive wakefulness for years, with no obvious signs of conscious content. We will also restrict our discussion here to the mammalian brain, but recognize that other animals (especially birds) are likely to have these two features of consciousness.

The first theory we will discuss is Antonio Damasio's (2012) proposed *evolutionary theory*. Damasio argues that early organisms were simple, without a real nervous system. As organisms became more complex, with more and more cells, a nervous system developed to coordinate the cells' activity. Neurons emerged and came to be responsible for the organization of the other cells, followed by the emergence of a sense of internal state, or *interoception,* and a sense of external state, or *exteroception.* As nervous systems became more complex to meet the needs of increasingly complex organisms, incentives arose—namely, the ability to choose advantageous opportunities. A reward system evolved to maximize incentives, as did an alerting system (the reticular activating system) to activate other systems.

This development led to the evolution of emotions, again to maximize opportunities for survival. Sensory systems became more complex, and as the cerebral cortex evolved and expanded in mammals, the number of cerebral maps of the external world expanded—again to maximize incentives. Damasio posits that "mind" emerged from the expansion of maps, which again was advantageous, and that maps began to "feel" like something with a representation of the physical and social environments that an individual inhabited. This mind led to a sense of "self," which Damasio proposes as the emergence of consciousness.

Over the past decade, two other theories have emerged, both of which have independently gained substantial empirical support (Melloni et al., 2021). One problem is that these two theories make diverging claims and predictions that cannot be simultaneously true.

The *global neuronal workspace theory* (GNWT) proposes that consciousness is instantiated by the amplification of information across an interconnected network of sensory cortical areas and prefrontal–parietal networks (see **Figure 15-29**). Information is received and processed by sensory regions in encapsulated modules and remains unconscious until the executive process in the frontal–parietal networks integrate the information and distribute it widely across the brain, leading to consciousness (Mashour et al., 2020).

In contrast, the *information integration theory* (IIT) defines consciousness as the ability to integrate information that is generated by cortical sensory modules (Boly et al., 2017; Tonini, 2012). IIT proposes that consciousness reflects the amount of maximally irreducible integrated information generated by regions of the posterior cortex. The details of this theory are mathematically complex and beyond this discussion, but the basic idea is that consciousness emerges from a neural network that perpetuates itself for as long as the experience exists.

Thus, according to IIT, consciousness manifests in integrated information in the posterior cortex; in contrast, GNWT asserts that consciousness manifests in a message that is broadcast globally. Furthermore, the prefrontal cortex is not involved in this process, according to IIT, but according to GNWT, the prefrontal cortex is essential.

The neural bases of sleep and wakefulness, including the reticular activating system, are discussed in Section 13-5.

● Prefrontal cortex
● High-level visual areas
● Early visual areas
● GNWT
○ IIT
— Synchronization GNWT
— Synchronization IIT

**FIGURE 15-29 GNWT and IIT** A comparison of key brain regions in the global neuronal workspace theory (GNWT) and the integrated information theory (IIT). Note the overlapping regions in the temporal lobe.

A consortium called the Collaboration on GNW and IIT: Testing Alternative Theories of Experience is currently collecting data to compare the two theories (see https://osf.io/mbcfy). A variety of experiments are being independently carried out across six laboratories to test and compare the predictions made by IIT versus GNWT. In one experiment, a participant engages in a video game with seen and unseen stimuli in the background to investigate whether neural correlates of the visual experience are present irrespective of the task. In another experiment, stimuli are shown for variable durations to investigate for how long the neural correlate of the visual experience exists. In both cases, neuronal activity in human participants is measured using several noninvasive methodologies (e.g., fMRI, MEG, and EEG). The results are likely to show that neither theory is completely correct, but regardless of the outcome, these investigations will be a step toward understanding the neural basis of consciousness.

## 15-7 Review

**Before you continue, check your understanding. Answers to Self-Test appear at the back of the book.**

1. _____ is the mind's level of responsiveness to impressions made by the senses.

2. The slow-acting _____ stream is conscious, but the _____ stream, which acts more rapidly, is not.

3. Briefly describe the three theories of the neural basis of consciousness covered in this section.

# Summary

### 15-1 The Nature of Thought

The complex processes we call thinking, or cognition, are products of both human and nonhuman brain activity. We use such words as *language* and *memory* to describe cognitive operations, but these concepts are abstract psychological constructs—merely inferred and not found in discrete places in the brain. They exist but have no physical form.

The brain carries out multiple cognitive operations—perception, action for perception, imagery, planning, spatial cognition, and attention. Each requires widespread activity in many cortical areas. The basic unit of cognition, however, is the neuron.

### 15-2 Cognition and the Association Cortex

The brain's association cortex includes medial, dorsal, and orbital subdivisions of the prefrontal cortex, the posterior parietal cortex, and anterior regions of the temporal lobe. Cell assemblies in the association cortex specifically take part in most forms of cognition.

The frontal lobes not only plan, organize, and initiate movements, but also organize our behavior over time (temporally). As a general rule, the temporal lobes generate knowledge about objects, whereas the parietal lobes produce varied forms of spatial cognition. Neurons in both the temporal lobes and the parietal lobes contribute to our ability to selectively attend to sensory information.

Regions in the frontal and parietal lobes contain mirror neurons that represent actions—one's own or those of others. Such neural representations could be used both for imitating others' actions and for moving more quickly and more accurately. A significant area of the cortex is considered multisensory, allowing the brain to combine characteristics of stimuli across sensory modalities, whether we encounter the stimuli together or separately.

### 15-3 Expanding Frontiers of Cognitive Neuroscience

Neuropsychological studies that began in the late 1800s to examine the behavioral capacities of people and laboratory animals with localized brain injuries did not allow investigators to study "normal" brains. Today, noninvasive brain recording systems and imaging techniques are enabling significant advances to be made in the field of cognitive neuroscience, which studies the neural basis of cognition by measuring brain activity while healthy participants engage in cognitive tasks.

An important step in identifying the neural bases of cognition is mapping cortical connections for the brain connectome. Two promising imaging tools are functional connectivity magnetic resonance imaging and tractography using diffusion tensor imaging.

The cerebellum, which houses 80% of the human brain's neurons, was long believed to have primarily motor functions. Emerging data, however, have revealed cerebellar involvement in a wide range of cognitive functions as well.

Social neuroscience—a field that combines cognitive neuroscience with social psychology—explores how we understand others' intentions by constructing a theory of mind. It also investigates how we develop attitudes, beliefs, and a sense of self. Using noninvasive imaging techniques such as fMRI, researchers have shown that social cognition primarily involves activity in the prefrontal cortex.

Neuroeconomics combines psychology, neuroscience, and economics in seeking to understand human decision making. fMRI studies have revealed that two decision-making pathways exist. One is slow and reflective, involving diffuse regions of association cortex. The other is quick and reflexive, involving the dopaminergic reward system.

## 15-4 Cerebral Asymmetry in Thinking

Cognitive operations are organized asymmetrically in the left and right cerebral hemispheres: the two hemispheres carry out complementary functions. The most obvious functional difference is in language, which is typically housed in the left hemisphere.

Cerebral asymmetry, manifested in anatomical differences between the two hemispheres, can be inferred from the differential effects of injury to opposite sides of the brain. Asymmetry can also be seen in the healthy brain and in the brain that is surgically split to relieve intractable epilepsy. Various syndromes result from association cortex injury, among them agnosia, apraxia, aphasia, and amnesia. Each includes the loss or disturbance of some cognitive function.

## 15-5 Variations in Cognitive Organization

Unique brains produce unique thought patterns. Marked variations in brain organization among individuals are exhibited in idiosyncratic capacities such as synesthesia. Systematic differences in cognition exist as well, manifested in the performance of females and males on cognitive tests, especially on tests of spatial and verbal behavior.

Sex differences in cognition result from the action of gonadal hormones on cortical organization, possibly on the architecture of cortical neurons, and ultimately on neural networks. Female and male cerebral hemispheres exhibit marked differences in anatomical organization.

Right- and left-handers also differ in hemispheric organization. Left-handers constitute at least three distinct groups. In one group, speech appears to reside in the left hemisphere, as it does in right-handers. The other two groups have anomalous speech representations, either in the right hemisphere or in both hemispheres. The reasons for these organizational differences remain unknown.

## 15-6 Intelligence

Intelligence is easy to spot but difficult to define. Obvious differences exist across as well as within species, and we find varied forms of intelligence among humans within our own culture and in other cultures. Intelligence is unrelated to differences in brain size within a species or to any obvious gross structural differences among members of the species. Intelligence may be related to synaptic organization and processing efficiency. A review by Jung and Haier concluded that differences in intelligence are linked to structural and functional variations in certain cortical brain regions; they proposed the parieto-frontal integration theory of intelligence (P-FIT) based on their model. The parallel network neuroscience theory (NNT) proposes different networks for crystalized and fluid intelligence.

## 15-7 Consciousness

Consciousness, the mind's level of responsiveness to impressions made by the senses, emerges from the complexity of the nervous system. We discussed three theories, that seek to explain how consciousness emerged and its neural basis. *Evolutionary theory* suggests consciousness arose as a product of increased complexity requiring more complex nervous systems, which eventually led to systems that could mediate a sense of self. *Global neuronal workspace theory* proposes that consciousness emerges from information integrated in the frontal–parietal networks and distributed across the brain. *Information integration theory* suggests consciousness emerges from our ability to integrate information generated by the posterior cortex. Ongoing parallel experiments in six independent laboratories are using noninvasive imaging techniques to better understanding the neural correlates of consciousness.

# Key Terms

anomalous speech representation, p. 557

association cortex, p. 531

attention, p. 535

binding problem, p. 533

brain connectome, p. 540

cell assembly, p. 529

cognition, p. 527

cognitive neuroscience, p. 539

consciousness, p. 562

contralateral neglect, p. 536

convergent thinking, p. 559

dichotic listening, p. 548

divergent thinking, p. 560

executive function, p. 537

extinction, p. 536

hyperconnectivity, p. 542

intelligence A, p. 560

intelligence B, p. 560

mirror neuron, p. 538

neuroeconomics, p. 545

perseveration, p. 538

psychological construct, p. 526

social neuroscience, p. 543

synesthesia, p. 558

syntax, p. 527

theory of mind (ToM), p. 543

---

# Selected Resources from

**Neuroscience in Action:** Thinking about Thinking: Cognition, Attention, and Planning

**Videos**

Attention

Why is Attention Important?

Cognitive Development

Split Brain Functioning

The Split Brain: Lessons on Language,

Vision, and Free Will

Understanding Intelligence

How Intelligent are Animals?

Hallucinations: Causes and Experiences

**LearningCurve**

**Practice Quiz**

William Taufic/Getty Images

# What Happens When the Brain Misbehaves?

# 16

## RESEARCH FOCUS 16-1

### Posttraumatic Stress Disorder

Life is filled with stress. Indeed, we routinely cope with a myriad of stressors. But some events are so physically threatening and emotionally shattering that they have long-term consequences. For about 10% of people, flashbacks, disturbing dreams, and persistent thoughts can interfere with their daily activities long after the physical danger from such an event has passed. These symptoms can lead to emotional numbness and a diagnosis of **posttraumatic stress disorder (PTSD)** (Dyer & Corrigan, 2021).

Traumatic events that may result in PTSD include violent assault, natural or human-caused disaster, accident, and war, as well as the stresses of certain types of work. For example, as many as 30% of veterans of the wars in Iraq (2003–2011) and Afghanistan (2001–2021) — many not directly exposed to combat — developed symptoms of PTSD, including intrusive, unwanted thoughts related to stressful events, negative mood, and altered arousal and reactivity responses. These same effects can occur in other people who encounter trauma, such as firefighters, police officers, and medical workers.

Therapy for PTSD includes cognitive-behavioral therapy, which is effective in about half of all cases; lifetime stress assessment therapies; and pharmacological treatments. One approach is **virtual reality (VR) exposure therapy**, a controlled virtual immersion environment combining realistic street scenes, sounds, and odors that allows people to relive traumatic events, develop coping strategies for them, and extinguish their emotional response to the trauma. The Virtual Iraq and Afghanistan Simulation is customized for war veterans: it starts with benign events — such as children playing — and gradually adds increasingly stressful components, culminating in such traumatic events as a roadside bomb exploding in the virtual space around an armored personnel carrier,

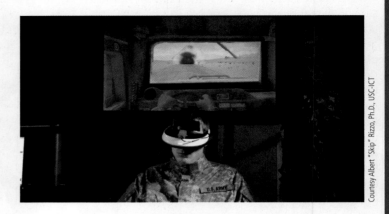

Courtesy Albert "Skip" Rizzo, Ph.D., USC-ICT

illustrated here. VR exposure therapy is also used *prior* to stress exposure for soldiers, police officers, firefighters, and other first responders as a means of preventing PTSD. At the present time, VR treatment — like many other treatment approaches to PTSD — remains difficult to assess experimentally using a double-blind protocol (Meyerbröker & Morina, 2021).

There is also interest in why many people do *not* develop PTSD following extremely stressful events, as well as in the extent to which PTSD is associated with other health events, including previous stressors, diabetes, and head trauma. That said, assessment and treatment options for many of those individuals who endure PTSD are poor; many people drop out of treatment programs, and many others receive no assessment or treatment at all. In addition, many treatment approaches and studies fail to address issues of inclusion related to sex and ethnography.

---

**posttraumatic stress disorder (PTSD)** Syndrome characterized by physiological arousal brought on by recurring memories and dreams related to a traumatic event for months or years after the event.

**virtual reality (VR) exposure therapy** Controlled virtual immersion environment that, by allowing individuals to relive traumatic events, gradually desensitizes them to stress.

**phenylketonuria (PKU)** Behavioral disorder caused by elevated levels of the amino acid phenylalanine in the blood and resulting from a defect in the gene for the enzyme phenylalanine hydroxylase; the major symptom is severe developmental disability.

Understanding of PTSD, detailed in Research Focus 16-1, Posttraumatic Stress Disorder, illustrates how thinking on the brain's role in health is still evolving. Largely as a result of symptoms displayed by returning Vietnam War veterans, in 1980 the *Diagnostic and Statistical Manual of Mental Disorders, Third Edition* (DSM-III) introduced PTSD as a mental disorder. Other investigators then pointed out similarities in symptoms among war veterans, rape victims, people subjected to accidents and natural disasters, and people who encountered trauma as a result of their occupations.

The many discussions of behavioral disorders and diseases presented throughout this book serve to describe how knowledge about brain function contributes to our understanding and treatment of brain disorder and disease. Our focus in this chapter is the central role of the brain in diagnosis and treatment.

### 16-1

# Multidisciplinary Contributions to Brain and Behavior

Neuroscientists now recognize that the brain is influential in many disease conditions. Brain health is influenced by life experiences, genetics, and epigenetic effects transmitted across generations.

Consider the condition **phenylketonuria (PKU)**, in which apparently healthy newborn babies begin to develop an array of puzzling symptoms that lead to severe physical and cognitive disability. They develop a musty odor in the breath, skin, or urine, and

**Learning Objectives**
- Define the field of clinical neuroscience.
- Contrast the DSM and RDoC classification systems.
- Summarize the general causes of disordered behavior.
- Describe some of the methods used to treat disorder.

they begin to have skin rashes and seizures. With time, their development is delayed, they become hyperactive, and they develop emotional, social, and intellectual problems and psychiatric disorders.

As complex as the condition may appear, a single brain abnormality can cause PKU. An autosomal recessive disorder affecting more than 10,000 newborns each year globally, PKU is the most common inherited metabolic disease. It results from a defect in the gene for phenylalanine hydroxylase (PAH), an enzyme that breaks down the amino acid phenylalanine; thus, this defect causes excess amounts of phenylalanine to build up in the brain. Phenylalanine is a precursor molecule for a number of other neurotransmitters, including norepinephrine and dopamine. An abnormality in PAH can be caused by more than 1000 different naturally occurring mutations in the PAH gene. To inherit PKU, both parents must carry a defective version of this gene. The recessive condition can, in some circumstances, confer resistance to certain fungal toxins.

PKU can be treated by diet—that is, by restricting dietary intake of phenylalanine. Foods high in protein, including beef, fish, cheese, and soy, contain large amounts of this amino acid. Following a strict diet in infancy prevents brain damage, and maintaining a controlled diet throughout life ensures protection. Expectant mothers who have had PKU might provide an in utero environment with high phenylalanine levels, and this, too, can be controlled if the mother restricts her dietary intake of phenylalanine. Nevertheless, a full understanding of PKU treatment requires a greater understanding of cultural, sex, and ethnographic differences in diet and protein metabolism.

As the examples of PTSD and PKU illustrate, behavioral studies, by their very nature, investigate the whole organism through methodological approaches that include genetics, genetic engineering, and epigenetic mechanisms. But an understanding of the whole organism requires an understanding that there are vast individual differences between people based on sex differences, differences in ethnography, cultural practices, and family history, among other factors. Similarly, an understanding of the brain's structure and function leads to the understanding that individual brains differ in their responses to stimuli and experiences. Where one person may develop PTSD, for example, another person exposed to similar circumstances may not; and while one person may benefit from one kind of treatment, another person with the same condition may benefit from a different kind of treatment.

Section 3-3 reviews genetics, genetic engineering, and epigenetic mechanisms; Section 7-5 explores techniques for measuring genetic and epigenetic influences.

## Clinical Neuroscience

Before we delve into the discussion of brain disorders, let's first review the professional landscape of those who study and treat them. A wide variety of professionals are involved in diagnosing and providing therapy for behavioral disorders. Psychologists deal with problems at the level of behavior, psychiatrists deal with problems related to brain dysfunction, and neurologists deal with problems related to nervous system damage. Psychologists likely have PhDs, and psychiatrists and neurologists have degrees in medicine; all have special training in some aspect of treatment, belong to professional societies, and are licensed to provide their services. The professional character of health care is reflected in the years of education required to become a health-care worker, the complexity of services that health-care providers perform, and the licensing required for health-care workers to receive financial compensation from health-care insurance companies or government agencies. Many readers of this book may decide to pursue a health-care profession.

Behavioral disorders—which are traditionally classified as social, psychological, psychiatric, or neurological—reflect the assessment and treatment roles different professional groups play. As our understanding of brain function increases, the lines between behavioral disorders are blurring. Increasingly, practitioners are synthesizing their insights into a unified understanding of behavior and brain, a **clinical neuroscience** that views the brain as the ultimate source of behavior and analyzes the diseases and disorders that affect it.

Professional health-care workers should be considered the last line of defense for brain health, however. The World Health Organization, founded in 1948, provides a definition of health that includes emotional, environmental, financial, intellectual, occupational,

**clinical neuroscience** Specialty in the field of neuroscience that focuses on the diagnosis and treatment of diseases and disorders affecting the brain and central nervous system.

physical, social, and spiritual health. This description gives rise to multifaced missions that vary from development of vaccinations for disease and parasites to efforts to improve social and economic welfare. In recognition of this multidimensional understanding of health and well-being, many companies and organizations feature wellness programs for their employees with missions that include enabling members to pursue a well-balanced lifestyles within a supportive and equitable work environment. Another outcome of this wide view of well-being is the understanding that the actual frontline workers for an individual's health are their family, friends, and community. Indeed, family members are often the primary caregivers for people with diseases or disorders and are among the most affected by it; as such, they join practitioners as participants in treatment.

With this understanding of the multidisciplinary nature of brain and behavior in mind, we will now survey behavioral, psychiatric, and neurological disorders in the following sections. In each section, we examine how disorders are classified, treated, and distributed in the population and review established and emerging treatments.

# Behavioral Disorders

The brain is complex. We do not yet understand all its parts and their functions, nor do we know precisely how the brain produces consciousness, a sense of well-being, and a sense of self. Still, significant advances have led to the realization that, while under some circumstances the brain copes competently with life's challenges, under other circumstances it is not up to the task.

We now recognize that the brain is composed of hundreds of interacting structures. We also know that the functions of these brain parts depend upon ongoing expression of genes, interactions of myriad chemicals, and functioning and connections of glia and neurons. Finally, we understand that behavioral disorders can be caused by genetic abnormalities, abnormalities in nervous system development over the life span, and environmental and epigenetic effects that modulate genetic and developmental expression. Nevertheless, as abundantly illustrated in earlier chapters, many processes underlying our functions are unconscious: they operate outside our awareness.

## Diagnosing Behavioral Disorders

The National Institute of Mental Health (NIMH) estimates that, in a given year, about one in four people in the United States has a diagnosable behavioral disorder, and nearly half of the population has such a disorder over their lifetime. Only a minority receive treatment of any kind, and even fewer receive treatment from a mental health specialist. Large-scale surveys of neurological disorders show a similar pattern of prevalence. Together, behavioral, psychiatric, and neurological disorders are the leading cause of disability after age 15.

The contrast between PTSD and PKU described at the beginning of this section illustrates the difficulties in understanding behavioral disorders. Both conditions present with an array of symptoms that seem equally complex. For PTSD, the complexity remains; by comparison, for PKU, the explanation is simpler because its cause is known and there is an effective treatment.

Knowledge about behavioral disorders is hampered by the subjective nature of behavior. Most diagnostic information gathered about a patient's behavior comes from both the patient and the caregivers and family members who know the patient and are often better diagnosticians than the professionals who have limited interactions with the patient (Sacrey et al., 2015). Nevertheless, people are often not objective observers of their own behaviors or those of a loved one. They tend to be selective in noticing and reporting symptoms. If you believe that someone has a memory problem, for example, you are more likely to notice memory lapses that you would ordinarily ignore.

Nor are people often specific in identifying symptoms. Simply identifying a memory problem is not sufficient. Treatment requires knowing exactly what type of memory deficit underlies a problem. Loss of memory for words, for places, or for habits—each has a different underlying pathology and involves a different brain system.

Just as patients and their loved ones make diagnosis difficult, so too do diagnosticians. Behavioral information about patients may be interpreted differently by general

Sections 14-2 and 14-3 explain a range of memory deficits.

physicians, psychiatrists, neurologists, psychologists, social workers, and others. Evaluators with different conceptual biases shape and filter the questions they ask and the information they gather.

## Classifying Behavioral Disorders

Classification systems have a long history in science, where they are applied to gain insights into biological processes and to generate theories to explain those processes. Many classification systems have been developed to explain psychological, psychiatric, and neurological disorders; indeed, each of the professional groups focused on these areas has its own classification system, which is frequently revised in light of new knowledge. In addition, the World Health Organization has developed an extensive classification of diseases, *The International Classification of Diseases*, which is used by many countries to compile statistical data related to health. Although it provides an extensive overview of disease, this classification is not primarily directed toward disease diagnosis and treatment.

The first set of criteria for diagnoses in behavior was developed in 1972. Since that time, two parallel sets of criteria have gained prominence. The best-known, most widely used classification is the American Psychiatric Association's ***Diagnostic and Statistical Manual of Mental Disorders*** **(DSM)**, now in its revised fifth edition, DSM-5-TR. The intent of this system is to aid diagnosis and treatment. **Table 16-1** outlines the classification scheme for behavioral disorders in the DSM-5-TR.

The other classification system, launched by NIMH, is the *Research Domain Criteria* (RDoC; pronounced "R doc"). With this classification system, NIMH is not trying to provide a diagnostic guide or replace current diagnostic systems. Instead, the goal of the RDoC is to understand the nature of mental health and illness in terms of varying degrees of dysfunction in general psychological/biological systems. Thus, whereas the DSM begins from the premise that labeling a condition will lead to understanding of the condition and ways of treating it, the RDoC assumes that understanding of basic biological function will lead to understanding of malfunction and treatment.

**Table 16-2** lists some of what we know about PKU using RDoC units of analysis: genes, molecules, cells, circuits, and so on. Note that the underlying problem becomes less apparent with the procession of entries in the table. In fact, it is not possible to predict the specific biochemical abnormality from information at the neurological, behavioral, or social level—exactly where the most accessible information resides.

Classification systems, such as *taxonomy* (the branch of biology that groups organisms according to their common characteristics and relationships), have advanced our knowledge of brain structure and function. Likewise, classifications of behavioral disorders produced by the behavioral sciences have advanced our understanding of the role of the brain in behavioral disorders. Yet all classification systems have limitations. The DSM-5-TR is arbitrary and unavoidably dependent on prevailing cultural views. Naming disorders or systems is problematic as well. The term *idiot* once designated a person with a low IQ score. When the term became pejorative, it was replaced with the term *retarded*. That term is now considered pejorative as well, and the DSM-5-TR uses the term *intellectually disabled* instead.

Another criticism is epitomized by the statement "just because you name a disorder does not mean it exists." In a sense, Emily Dickinson expresses this idea in the opening line of her poem "Much Madness": "Much Madness is divinest Sense—To a discerning Eye."

For example, if all behavioral disorders could be analyzed as readily as PKU, neuroscience research could quickly yield cures for each of them. For PKU, the distinctive smell detected by one mother in her baby's urine was the first link in a chain of discoveries that led to the identification of elevated phenylalanine. Many disorders do not result from a

**TABLE 16-1** Summary of DSM-5-TR Diagnostic Classification of Disorders

| Diagnostic category |
| --- |
| Neurodevelopmental disorders |
| Schizophrenia spectrum and other psychiatric disorders |
| Bipolar and related disorders |
| Depressive disorders |
| Unspecified mood disorder |
| Anxiety disorders |
| Obsessive-compulsive and related disorders |
| Trauma- and stressor-related disorders |
| Dissociative disorders |
| Somatic symptom disorder and related disorders |
| Feeding and eating disorders |
| Elimination disorders |
| Sleep–wake disorders |
| Sexual dysfunctions |
| Gender dysphoria |
| Disruptive, impulse-control, and conduct disorders |
| Substance-related and addictive disorders |
| Neurocognitive disorders |
| Personality disorders |

*Source:* Information from American Psychiatric Association (2022).

***Diagnostic and Statistical Manual of Mental Disorders*** **(DSM)** The American Psychiatric Association's classification system for psychiatric disorders.

The Basics in Section 1-3 provides an overview of taxonomy.

**TABLE 16-2** PKU: RDoC Pathogenesis of a Behavioral Disorder

| Level of analysis | Known information |
| --- | --- |
| Genes | Inborn metabolism error; recessive defective gene (autosomal) with about 1000 variants |
| Molecules | Conversion of phenylalanine to tyrosine impaired, elevating levels of phenylalanine and its metabolites in the blood, which occurs before and after birth |
| Cells | Decrease in neuron size and dendritic length; lowered spine density; reduced glutamine activity |
| Circuits | Decreased or damaged myelin and decreased cortical pattern organization |
| Physiological behavior | Reduced enzyme activity; intellectual impairment with an onset that varies with the gene abnormality; slow growth; seizure; abnormal EEG |
| Self-report | IQ score below 50 (in 95% of participants); significant loss of meaningful life and productivity if untreated |
| Treatment | Dietary intake of phenylalanine restricted; enzyme substitution |

single genetic abnormality, however, and the causes of most disorders remain conjectural. The major problem remains: diagnosis of a disability is based mainly on behavioral symptoms, and behavioral symptoms give few clues to specific neurochemical or neurostructural causes.

## Causes of Disordered Behavior

Section 3-3 discusses the genetic bases of several disorders, as well as epigenetic mechanisms and the innovative field of genetic engineering.

Neuroscientists presume that abnormal brain functioning results in disordered behavior. In a general sense, there are at least six general causes of abnormal brain function:

1. *Genetic errors* that affect a chromosome (Down syndrome), a constellation of genes (as with schizophrenia), a single gene (as in Huntington disease), or a single nucleotide polymorphism (as in *BDNF* [brain-derived neurotrophic factor] alterations).

2. *Epigenetic mechanisms* at work prenatally, later in life, and even in succeeding generations. Most of our genes are continually active, and our behavior and our environment can modify their activity.

Clinical Focus 3-3 describes the genetic basis of Huntington disease; Clinical Focus 5-2, neural degeneration in Parkinson disease; Clinical Focus 2-3, symptoms and after-effects of stroke; and Clinical Focus 4-3, myelin breakdown in multiple sclerosis.

3. *Progressive cell death* resulting from neurodegenerative causes (as in Parkinson or Alzheimer disease). In some cases, a single abnormal protein can initiate a cascade of events that results in progressive cell death.

4. *Rapid cell death* (as in stroke or traumatic brain injury), in which the circulatory system is interrupted or the brain is concussed or penetrated.

5. *Loss of neural function and connections,* like that seen in disorders such as multiple sclerosis and myasthenia gravis, in which an individual's own immune system attacks neural elements.

6. *Life stress,* including inadequate developmental opportunities, poor nutrition, and PTSD.

At the microscopic level are genetic errors, such as those responsible for Tay-Sachs disease and Huntington disease. Intermediate categories include one-time events, such as infections, injuries, and toxins. At the macro level, nutrition, stress, and negative experiences are prominent actors. Of course, many of these factors interact. Genetic vulnerability to stress, infection, or pollution may be the immediate cause of some disorders. In other cases, no direct genetic predisposition is needed: disordered behavior arises strictly from epigenetic factors, such as stress and negative experiences, which influence gene expression and function.

The Index of Disorders on the inside cover lists all the behavioral disorders discussed in this book, but they constitute a mere fraction of the total number of known disorders.

**Table 16-3** lists some likely causal categories underlying behavioral disorders.

## Treating Behavioral Disorders

Treatments for behavioral disorders need not be direct biological or medical interventions. Just as the brain can alter behavior, so behavior can alter the brain. Behavioral treatments focus on key personal and environmental factors that influence how a person acts. As behavior changes in response to treatment, the brain is affected as well.

Take, for example, the treatment for *generalized anxiety disorders* attributed to chronic stress. People who endure a persistently high anxiety level often engage in maladaptive behaviors in an effort to reduce their distress. While they require immediate treatment with antianxiety medication, long-term treatment entails changing their behavior. Generalized anxiety disorder is not simply a problem of abnormal brain activity, but also the product of personal and social factors that fundamentally alter the person's perception of the world.

Perhaps you are thinking that behavioral treatments may help somewhat in treating brain dysfunction, but the real solution must lie in altering brain activity. Since every aspect of behavior is the product of brain activity, behavioral treatments *do* act by changing brain function. If a child has a problem in school—say, in reading or math—extra instruction is an accessible solution. If people can change how they think and feel about themselves or some aspect of their lives (such as their competence at math), this change has taken place because talking about their problems or resolving a problem alters how their brain functions. In a sense, then, a behavioral treatment is

**TABLE 16-3** Some Causes of Selected Behavioral Disorders

| Cause | Disorder |
|---|---|
| Genetic error | Tay-Sachs disease |
| Hormonal | Androgenital syndrome |
| Developmental | Autism |
| Infection | Encephalitis |
| Injury | Traumatic brain injury |
| Toxins | MPTP poisoning |
| Poor nutrition | Korsakoff syndrome |
| Stress | Anxiety disorders, PTSD |
| Negative experience | Developmental delays |

a biological intervention. Behavioral treatments may be helped along by drug treatments that make the brain more receptive to change through behavioral therapy. In this way, drug treatments and behavioral treatments can have synergistic effects, with each helping the other to be more effective. We discuss pharmacological treatments to many disorders in the sections that follow.

Your behavior is a product of all your learning and social experiences. An obvious approach to developing a treatment is to recreate a learning environment that replaces a maladaptive behavior with an adaptive behavior. Thus, the various approaches to behavioral treatment use principles derived from experiment-based learning theory. A few of these approaches are discussed next.

**Behavior Modification** **Behavioral modification** applies well-established learning principles to eliminate unwanted behaviors. Therapists apply principles developed in studies of learning by reinforcement conducted in laboratory settings, including operant and classical conditioning. For example, if a person is debilitated by a fear of insects, rather than looking for inner causes, the behavioral therapist tries to replace the maladaptive behaviors with more constructive ways of behaving. These might include training the individual to relax during systematic exposure to unthreatening insects (butterflies), followed by gradual exposure to more threatening insects (bees). This form of habituation (adaption to a repeatedly presented stimulus) is called *systematic desensitization*.

**Cognitive Therapy** **Cognitive therapy** operates from the perspective that thoughts intervene between events and emotions. Consider the possible responses to losing a job. One reaction could be "I'm a loser; life is hopeless," but an alternative thought is "The job was a dead end. The boss did me a favor. I can do better." And another is "I was thinking of moving on from this job and improving my education." The first reaction might lead to depression, whereas the others would not. Cognitive therapies challenge a person's self-defeating attitudes. This type of therapy is important for people with brain injuries as well, because it is easy for people to think they are crazy or stupid after suffering a brain injury. Cognitive-behavioral therapy is discussed further in Section 16-2.

**Neuropsychological Therapy** If a relative or friend had a stroke and became aphasic (unable to speak), you would expect that person to attend speech therapy—a behavioral treatment for an injured brain. The logic in speech therapy is that by practicing (relearning) the basic components of speech and language, the individual should be able to regain at least some lost function. The same logic can apply to other types of behavioral disorders, whether motor or cognitive.

Therapies for cognitive disorders resulting from brain trauma or dysfunction aim to retrain people in the fundamental cognitive processes they have lost and to exploit those that remain. Although cognitive therapy seems as logical as speech therapy after a stroke, it assumes that behavior can be changed without deference to the brain. Neuropsychologists operate on the idea that understanding the brain can lead to neurocognitive programs that can improve functional outcomes within the limitations of a brain injury. For example, understanding that a person will always be limited in a specific ability after a brain injury allows the therapist to concentrate on improving compensatory behavior. For example, if use of a hand or a leg is compromised after stroke, learning to use a prosthetic assistant may be more useful than physiotherapy alone.

**Emotional Therapy** In the 1920s, Sigmund Freud developed the idea that talking about emotional problems enables people to gain insight into the causes of those problems and can serve as treatment. Talk cures and other forms of psychological intervention may be broadly categorized as psychotherapies.

Since Freud's time, many ideas have been put forth about the best type of therapy for emotional disorders. A key realization here is that for many disorders, whether neurological or psychiatric, medical treatments are not effective unless patients also receive **psychotherapy**. Indeed, the only effective treatment in many cases lies in addressing the unwanted behaviors directly—in acquiring the skill rather than taking the pill.

**behavioral modification** Treatment that applies learning principles, such as conditioning, to eliminate unwanted behaviors.

**cognitive therapy** Therapy based on the perspective that thoughts intervene between events and emotions, so the treatment of emotional disorders requires changing maladaptive patterns of thinking.

**psychotherapy** Talk therapy derived from Freudian psychoanalysis and other psychological interventions.

Consider a 25-year-old woman pursuing a promising career as a musician who suffered a traumatic brain injury in an automobile accident. After the accident, she found that she was unable to read music. She soon became depressed. Part of her therapy required her to confront her disabling cognitive loss by talking about it rather than simply stewing over it. Only when she pursued psychotherapy did she begin to recover from her intense depression.

For many people with emotional impairments resulting from brain disease or trauma, the most effective treatment for depression or anxiety is to help them adjust by encouraging them to talk about their difficulties. Group therapy provides such encouragement and is standard treatment in brain injury rehabilitation units.

**Physical Activity and Music as Therapy**  Exercise and music have positive effects on peoples' attitudes, emotional well-being, and brain function. They are important in maintaining health and are useful as therapy once health is compromised. Physical exercise demands visual control of movement. Music affects arousal and activates the motor cortex and the premotor cortex. Listening to music can improve gait in persons with Parkinson disease and stroke, and can reduce pain after surgery. Likewise, learning to play a musical instrument is beneficial therapy. Singing, a useful adjunct to rehabilitative speech therapy, enhances the ability to enunciate. Physical activity, including dancing and playing sports, combined with computer-based physical therapies, improves well-being and counteracts the effects of depression.

Section 10-4 observes that practitioners have only just begun to tap the power of music as a therapeutic tool.

Exercise boosts your mood because it boosts your dopamine levels.

**Real-Time fMRI**  Using **real-time fMRI (rt-fMRI)**, individuals learn to change their behavior by controlling their own brain activation patterns. rt-fMRI is a behavior-modification technique that uses biofeedback and was first used to treat intractable pain, which produces a characteristic brain activity pattern. For example, if individuals can see their brain activity via functional magnetic resonance imaging (fMRI) in real time as they feel pain, they can be trained to reduce the neural activity and thus lessen their pain. rt-fMRI uses a form of operant conditioning in which the gradual modification of a person's behavior increases the probability of reward. Think of rt-fMRI as a form of neural plasticity in which the individual learns new strategies, guided by brain activation information. When individuals decrease brain activation in regions associated with pain, for example, they report decreased pain perception.

One potential treatment application of rt-fMRI is in monitoring brain activation in the context of behavioral therapy. Patients need not be consciously aware of the therapy's objectives: induced brain changes or other biomeasures, whether conscious or unconscious, can prove beneficial.

Because fMRI is expensive, applications of rt-fMRI have not been widely assessed, but similar real-time techniques based on electroencephalography (EEG) activity or other physiological measures can be beneficial and economical. Furthermore, innovations in wearable devices are making biofeedback methods accessible for a wide range of treatment and monitoring applications in the home (Bowman et al., 2021).

**Virtual Reality Therapy**  The principle behind virtual reality (VR) therapy is that participants enter or interact with a virtual world displayed on a computer screen or through goggles. One example is the Virtual Iraq and Afghanistan Simulation described in Research Focus 16-1. The participant can experience sights, sounds, and even smells that mimic situations related to acquiring the behavioral disorder—in this case, PTSD. In modified VR therapy, the participant interacts as a character in a computer game. Winning the game necessitates making adaptive choices; maladaptive choices result in losing the game. Video-game technology applied to VR therapy had been reported to be useful for treating a wide range of disorders, from phobias to impaired limb use after stroke (Vieira et al., 2021).

**real-time fMRI (rt-fMRI)**  Behavior-modification technique in which individuals learn to change their behavior by controlling their own patterns of brain activation.

## 16-1 Review

Before you continue, check your understanding. Answers to Self-Test appear at the back of the book.

1. The most widely used classification of disorders, intended as an aid in diagnosis and treatment, is the _____.

2. Causes of disordered behavior include _____, _____, _____, _____, and _____.

3. For most psychiatric disorders, the causes are unknown, but _____ is an exception.

4. How does the approach to classification taken by the RDoC contrast with the approach taken by the DSM?

## 16-2

# Psychiatric Disorders

*Psychiatric disorders*, which are assumed to be due to brain malfunction, include a wide range of disorders summarized by the DSM-5-TR. We focus here on the three general behavioral categories—psychoses, mood disorders, and anxiety disorders—that are the most studied and best understood. **Figure 16-1** summarizes their prevalence. Schizophrenia, bipolar disorder, and major depression affect a small number of people, but their costs—in loss of social relationships, productivity, and medical care—are disproportionately large.

**Learning Objectives**
- Describe the symptoms and causes associated with schizophrenia.
- Describe the major mood disorders, and summarize the relationships between stress and mood.

## Schizophrenia Spectrum and Other Psychotic Disorders

*Psychoses* are disorders in which a person loses contact with reality and is subject to irrational ideas and distorted perceptions. Among the varieties of psychosis, schizophrenia is the most common and best understood. Nevertheless, schizophrenia takes many forms, and whether it is a single disorder or several disorders that share some symptoms is uncertain. The complexity of behavioral and neurobiological factors that characterize schizophrenia makes it especially difficult to diagnose and classify. Understanding schizophrenia is an evolving process and far from complete.

### Diagnosing Schizophrenia

The DSM-5-TR lists six diagnostic symptoms of schizophrenia:

1. Delusions—beliefs that distort reality

2. Hallucinations—distorted perceptions, such as hearing voices

3. Disorganized speech, such as incoherent statements or senselessly rhyming talk

4. Disorganized behavior or excessive agitation

5. Catatonic behavior—extreme inactivity, the opposite extreme of agitation

6. Negative symptoms, such as blunted emotions or loss of interest and drive, all characterized by the absence of some healthy response

Schizophrenia may produce a wide range of symptoms, and individual differences in behavioral effects exist as well. Voluminous research related to the origins and causes of schizophrenia has emerged, but the three lines of research summarized in this section have transformed ideas about its genetics, its development, and its associated brain correlates.

**Genetics** It is recognized that genetics contributes to schizophrenia, as does environment. The more closely related an individual is to someone diagnosed with schizophrenia, the more likely that person is to develop the condition. The concordance of schizophrenia

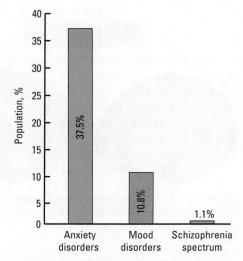

**FIGURE 16-1 Prevalence of Some Psychiatric Illnesses** Data from National Institute of Mental Health, http://www.nimh.nih.gov/health/statistics/index.shtml.

in identical twins is high: 80% is the most recent estimate. That the concordance for schizophrenia is not 100% means that environmental factors must also play a role.

Genome studies involving many thousands of people have identified about 300 different mutations on 10 different genes that predispose an individual to schizophrenia. At least two factors complicate the interpretation of genetic studies, however. First, genetic disorders in one ethnographic population may not be found in another population. Second, the candidate genetic abnormalities for schizophrenia are also found in many other conditions, including major depression, bipolar disorder, anxiety disorders, and autism. The commonality among these genes may be that they all contribute to brain development and, therefore, mutations in these genes may contribute to a variety of abnormalities in brain development that subsequently produce behavioral symptoms (Priol et al., 2021).

**Development** Schizophrenia is usually diagnosed in young adulthood, but a body of evidence suggests that it originates much earlier, even prenatally. Its expression in adulthood must therefore await the conclusion of a host of developmental processes that ultimately shape the adult human brain. That schizophrenia has developmental origins has many implications.

First, environmental factors acting through epigenetic mechanisms are likely to influence brain development such that only a subset of at-risk individuals develop adult schizophrenia. Second, identifying developmental factors that contribute to schizophrenia provides the best opportunity for intervention to reduce the risks of developing it. Any potential cure for schizophrenia will depend on early detection and remediation through epigenetic mechanisms (Richetto et al., 2021).

**Brain Correlates** The world-wide Enhancing NeuroImaging Genetics through Meta-Analysis (ENIGMA) project is directed toward describing brain changes associated with schizophrenia and its genetic variants (Thompson et al., 2021). Before describing some of the general changes uncovered through these efforts, we point out that many different brain changes occur in people diagnosed with schizophrenia. Magnetic resonance imaging (MRI) analysis of the brain and its metabolic activity can be undertaken to answer questions related to the specific changes associated with any individual case.

Brain features generally associated with schizophrenia include enlarged ventricles and a thinner cortex, especially in the medial temporal regions and frontal cortex, suggesting cell loss occurs in these areas. The positron emission tomography (PET) images in **Figure 16-2** illustrate metabolic changes in adult-onset schizophrenia. The scan on the left reveals an obvious abnormality in prefrontal cortex activity compared with the scan on the right, from an adult who does not have schizophrenia.

Imaging technology suggests that there are similarities in the brain changes associated with schizophrenia across a wide range of ages. Some aspects of neuronal and fiber composition of the temporal lobes and the frontal lobes change over the course of development, as indicated by variations in their density, which can be seen with MRI. The cortical maps constructed by Judith Rapoport and coworkers (2012) reveal that the children in their study who developed schizophrenia showed a remarkable loss of gray matter in the cerebral cortex between the ages of 13 and 18 (**Figure 16-3**). Imaging of individuals with childhood-onset schizophrenia suggests that the condition begins in utero and is characterized by excessive pruning of short-distance cortical connections (Rao et al., 2015). Research by Watsky and colleagues (2018) has also found many similarities in brain changes in childhood-onset schizophrenia and adult-onset schizophrenia, which shows that there is continuity between the conditions.

Additional brain changes associated with schizophrenia include alterations in neuronal structure resulting in abnormal dendritic fields in cells in the dorsal prefrontal

HANK MORGAN/Science Source

**FIGURE 16-2  Adult-Onset Schizophrenia**
Note the abnormally low blood flow in the prefrontal cortex at the top of the PET scan in the brain of an adult with schizophrenia (*left*) compared with that of an adult who does not have schizophrenia (*right*).

Average annual loss (%)

0   −1   −2   −3   −4   −5

Typical adolescents          Participants with schizophrenia

**FIGURE 16-3  Childhood-Onset Schizophrenia**
Three-dimensional maps derived from MRI scans reveal that, compared with healthy teenagers aged 13 to 18 (*left*), individuals with childhood-onset schizophrenia (*right*) have widespread loss of gray matter across the cerebral hemispheres.
Courtesy of Paul Thompson and Arthur W. Toga, Laboratory of Neuro Imaging, Keck School of Medicine of USC and Judith L. Rapoport, National Institute of Mental Health.

**(A)**

Hippocampus

Organized (healthy) pyramidal neurons

**(B)**

Disorganized (schizophrenic) pyramidal neurons

**FIGURE 16-4 Organic Dysfunction** Rather than the consistently parallel orientation of hippocampal neurons typical in healthy brains **(A)**, the orientation of hippocampal neurons in the brain of a person with schizophrenia is haphazard **(B)**. Information from Kovelman & Scheibel (1984).

**major depression** Mood disorder characterized by prolonged feelings of worthlessness and guilt, disruption of normal eating habits, sleep disturbances, a general slowing of behavior, and frequent thoughts of suicide.

**bipolar disorder** Mood disorder characterized by periods of depression alternating with normal periods and periods of intense excitation, or *mania*.

**mania** Disordered mental state of extreme excitement.

**anxiety disorder** A disorder that includes a number of conditions in which unhelpful anxiety has a negative effect on daily life.

regions (**Figure 16-4**), in the hippocampus (Cho et al., 2004), and in the entorhinal cortex (Arnold et al., 1997).

In sum, this evidence suggests that schizophrenia is associated with alterations in the temporal region and the frontal cortex. As you have learned, these areas of the brain are associated with memory, language, and decision making. The changes there result in alterations in neural networks that are engaged in functions common to everyday life (Wang et al., 2021).

## Neurochemical Correlates of Schizophrenia

Neuroscientists also consider the neurochemical correlates of brain–behavior relationships in schizophrenia. Dopamine abnormalities were the first to be linked to schizophrenia, through two lines of evidence. First, most neuroleptic drugs (i.e., drugs used to treat schizophrenia) act on the dopamine synapse. Second, drugs that enhance dopamine synaptic activity, such as amphetamine, can produce psychotic symptoms reminiscent of schizophrenia.

This dopamine theory of schizophrenia appears too simple, however, because many other neurochemical abnormalities, summarized in **Table 16-4**, are also associated with schizophrenia—in particular, abnormalities in dopamine and dopamine receptors and in gamma-aminobutyric acid (GABA) and GABA-binding sites. Evidence also suggests that changes in the *N*-methyl-D-aspartate (NMDA) glutamate receptor may be present in some people with schizophrenia, a finding that is leading to the development of new classes of glutamate drug therapy. Affected individuals vary widely in the extent of their abnormalities, however. How neurochemical variations might relate to the presence or absence of specific symptoms is not known. It seems unlikely, given the history of research into the relationship between biomarkers and schizophrenia, that a one-to-one relationship will be found. At this point, there remain many explanations of schizophrenia, from alternations in network structure to changes or degeneration of some features on neurons or glia (Cuttler et al., 2021).

**TABLE 16-4 Biochemical Changes Associated with Schizophrenia**

| |
|---|
| Decreased dopamine metabolites in cerebrospinal fluid |
| Increased striatal $D_2$ receptors |
| Decreased expression of $D_3$ and $D_4$ mRNA in specific cortical regions |
| Decreased cortical glutamate |
| Increased cortical glutamate receptors |
| Decreased glutamate uptake sites in cingulate cortex |
| Decreased mRNA for synthesizing GABA in prefrontal cortex |
| Increased $GABA_A$-binding sites in cingulate cortex |

*Source:* Information from Byne et al. (1999).

The dopamine hypothesis of schizophrenia is discussed in Section 6-2.

GABA is the brain's main inhibitory neurotransmitter. Section 6-2 discusses GABAergic agonists and their effects at the GABA receptor.

## Mood Disorders

Mood disorders include major depressive disorders, bipolar disorder, and anxiety disorders. The main symptoms of **major depression** are prolonged feelings of worthlessness and guilt, disruption of normal eating habits, sleep disturbances, a general slowing of behavior, and frequent thoughts of suicide. **Bipolar disorder** is a condition in which periods of mood often change, sometimes abruptly, to depression and back again to mania. **Mania**, the opposite mood extreme from depression, is characterized by excessive euphoria. The affected person often formulates grandiose plans and is uncontrollably hyperactive. **Anxiety disorders** include a number of conditions in which unhelpful anxiety has a negative effect on daily life.

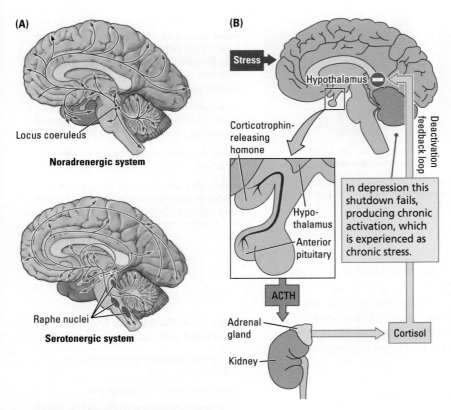

**FIGURE 16-5 Stress-Activating System**
**(A)** Medial view showing that in the brainstem, cell bodies of noradrenergic (norepinephrine) neurons emanate from the locus coeruleus (*top*), and cell bodies of the serotonergic activating system emanate from the raphe nuclei (*bottom*). **(B)** When activated, the HPA axis affects mood, thinking, and, indirectly, cortisol secretion by the adrenal glands. HPA deactivation begins when cortisol binds to hypothalamic receptors.

The relationship between the stress response and plasticity is discussed in Section 14-4.

This research confirms studies on the effects of stress on hippocampal function reported in Sections 7-5 and 8-4.

**HPA axis** Hypothalamic–pituitary–adrenal circuit that controls the production and release of hormones related to stress.

# Major Depression

Both brain and environment contribute to major depression. Predisposing factors related to brain anatomy and chemistry may contribute more to mood changes in some people, whereas life experiences contribute mainly to mood changes in other people.

Life experiences can act as stressors on the brain, which require a mobilization of antistress responses to protect the brain. The depression that any individual might feel when frustrated by life experiences may be part of an antistress response. If stress persists and the antistress response is not quickly effective, brain inflammation with continuing depression may follow. Although the stress response, including neuroinflammation, can contribute to many brain diseases, including Alzheimer and Parkinson disease, we will limit our discussion here to its association with depression.

**Reactivity to Stress** A significant psychological factor in understanding depression is reactivity to stress. A bewildering number of life, health, and brain factors—including economic or social failure, disruption of the circadian rhythm, deficiencies of vitamin D and other nutrients, pregnancy, brain injury, diabetes, cardiovascular events, childhood abuse, and metabolic disorders including being overweight, among many others—are stress events.

One explanation of the effects of stress posits that neural function is first mobilized but can become overwhelmed. For example, monoamines (the noradrenergic and serotoninergic activating systems diagrammed in **Figure 16-5**A) modulate hormone secretion by the hypothalamic–pituitary–adrenal system (called the **HPA axis** for short and illustrated in Figure 16-5B). When we are stressed, the HPA axis is stimulated to secrete corticotropin-releasing hormone, which stimulates the pituitary to produce adrenocorticotropic hormone (ACTH). ACTH circulates through the blood and stimulates the adrenal medulla to produce cortisol. Normally, cortisol helps us deal with stress. If we cannot cope, or if stress is intense, the excessive cortisol can wield a negative influence on the brain by inducing effects such as neuroinflammation, thereby damaging the feedback loops the brain uses to turn off the stress response.

**Neuroinflammation** Inflammation is one result of the body's complex response to injury. You undoubtedly recognize the signs of peripheral inflammation—redness and heat due to increased blood flow to a site of injury, swelling caused by the accumulation of fluid, pain due to the release of chemicals that activate pain receptors, and reduced function due to these influences. Acute inflammation is usually associated with the protection and repair of tissue but if the repair process is not successful, chronic inflammation can result. Many different disease conditions can be traced back to chronic inflammation, including asthma, arthritis, and potentially depression.

Stress and a wide range of brain injuries and infections can result in the combination of brain injury and either acute or chronic neuroinflammation. Microglia are active participants in the brain's inflammatory response to injury; they secrete a range of chemicals called cytokines that play active roles in the subsequent repair processes. If the repair is successful, other microglia participate in ending the inflammatory response. If it is not successful, chronic inflammation can result. Chronic inflammation can lead to reduced neuronal function, including decreases in the activity of the noradrenergic and serotoninergic neural systems responsible for modulating mood. The consequence is the symptom of enduring depression.

**Treatment** Conventional antidepressant drugs such as the selective serotonin reuptake inhibitors (SSRIs) are directed toward increasing levels of serotonergic and other transmitters that are proposed to be related to depression. Antidepressants effectively increase transmitter function and stimulate brain repair. For example, fluoxetine (Prozac) stimulates both BDNF production and neurogenesis in the hippocampus, resulting in a net increase in granule cells, described in Research Focus 16-2: Antidepressant Action and Brain Repair.

Because neuroinflammation is proposed to be implicated in depression, anti-inflammatory drugs have also been suggested as potential treatments for depression (Roohi et al., 2021). In addition, reports suggest that ketamine, a glutamate antagonist and so-called club drug, can rapidly and temporarily reverse symptoms of depression. This finding suggests that the neuroinflammatory processes associated with depression may influence many neurotransmitter functions, including those of glutamate.

Although we have emphasized biological correlates of depression, the best treatment need not be a direct biological intervention. **Cognitive-behavioral therapy (CBT)** is an excellent—and perhaps the best—therapy for depression (Huibers et al., 2021). It focuses on challenging the person's beliefs and perceptions. The objective is to identify dysfunctional thoughts and beliefs that accompany negative emotions and to replace them with more realistic ones.

Simply pointing out that a person's beliefs are faulty is not likely to be effective, however, because it probably took months or years to develop those beliefs. The neural circuits underlying faulty beliefs must change, just as the strategies for developing new ones must change. In a real sense, then, CBT is effective if it induces neural plasticity and changes brain activity, and if it is helped along by other treatments.

**cognitive-behavioral therapy (CBT)** Problem-focused, action-oriented, structured treatment for eliminating dysfunctional thoughts and maladaptive behaviors.

For further discussion of medications to treat depression, see Section 6-2. Clinical Focus 6-4 explains the threat of suicide attendant to untreated major depression.

**Principle 10:** Neuroplasticity is the hallmark of nervous system functioning.

## Anxiety Disorders

Anxiety often accompanies depression, but anxiety disorders can also occur as a separate condition. Anxiety disorders include phobias, panic disorders, agoraphobia, obsessive-compulsive disorder, PTSD, and generalized anxiety disorder.

### RESEARCH FOCUS 16-2

## Antidepressant Action and Brain Repair

Continuous stress and poor coping skills contribute to excessive cortisol levels in the brain and to depression and anxiety. Granule cells in the hippocampus, which are especially sensitive to cortisol, can die when cortisol levels are either reduced, as shown in the figure, or increased excessively.

These hippocampal cells may themselves play a role in regulating cortisol levels: they may be the switch that turns off the brain's stress response. Their absence leaves the HPA axis unchecked. Subsequently, the increased cortisol levels contribute to more neuron death and to depression and anxiety. It's a vicious circle.

That antidepressants take some weeks to produce their positive effects on behavior and that new neurons take some weeks to migrate to and become incorporated in the hippocampus suggest that the antidepressants' mechanism of action is to enhance hippocampal function—in essence, to replace the neural switch that turns off the stress response.

A remarkable finding emerged from studies of how selective serotonin reuptake inhibitors (SSRIs) affect the hippocampus. The SSRIs increased neurogenesis in the subgranular zone, cell migration into the dentate gyrus, and the number of functioning cells there (Yohn et al., 2020).

The literature on hippocampal neurogenesis is the most prolific in neuroscience, encompassing more than 9000 papers, and scientists continue to debate whether hippocampal neurogenesis takes place in humans. Nevertheless, neurogenesis research indicates that phenomena we perceive as bad (such as deprivation in infancy, conflict, stress, poor diet, and most drugs) depress neurogenesis, and phenomena we perceive as good (such as exercise, enriched environment, sufficient sleep, and a healthy diet) enhance neurogenesis. Finding the signaling pathways that enhance neurogenesis may reveal the relationships among altered cognition, memory, depression, and the effects of antidepressant drugs (Kornhuber & Gulbins, 2021).

Hippocampus

**Healthy rat hippocampus** **Neuronal degeneration**

Courtesy of Dr. Simon Spanswick, Dept. of Psychology, University of Calgary.

We are all subject to anxiety, usually acutely in response to stress, but less commonly as chronic reactivity (an increased anxiety response) even to seemingly minor stressors. Anxiety reactions certainly are not pathological; they are an evolutionary adaptation for coping with adverse conditions. But anxiety can become pathological and make life miserable. Anxiety disorders are the most common psychiatric conditions. The DSM-5-TR lists 10 classes of anxiety disorders that together affect 15% to 35% of the population at some point in their lives (see Figure 16-1).

Why some people show pathological anxiety to stimuli to which others have a milder response is a central question. One hypothesis, covered in the earlier section on depression, is that stressful experiences early in life increase susceptibility to a variety of behavioral disorders, especially anxiety disorders.

The mechanism by which GABAergic agonists reduce anxiety is described in Section 6-2.

**Treatment** Although anxiety disorders were once treated primarily with GABA-enhancing benzodiazepines, such as Valium, today they can also be treated with SSRIs, such as Prozac, Paxil, Celexa, and Zoloft, that act on noradrenaline and serotonin. Antidepressant drugs do not act immediately—a fact that suggests the treatments must stimulate some gradual change in brain structure, much as these drugs work in treating depression.

One more time: a pill is not a skill.

Cognitive-behavioral therapy, which we described in the discussion of depression, is effective in treating anxiety. The most effective behavioral therapies expose and reexpose people to their fears in an effort to extinguish emotional responses to otherwise benign events. For example, treating a phobic fear of germs requires exposing the person repeatedly to potentially germy environments, such as public washrooms, until the discomfort abates.

## 16-2 Review

Before you continue, check your understanding. Answers to Self-Test appear at the back of the book.

1. Schizophrenia is a complex disorder associated with neurochemical abnormalities in _____, _____, and _____ receptors.

2. Schizophrenia is associated with pronounced anatomical changes in the _____ and _____ cortices.

3. The monoamine-activating systems that have been the focus of the most investigation related to understanding depression are _____ and _____.

4. The most effective treatment for depression and anxiety disorders is _____.

5. Describe the relationship between neuroinflammation and major depression.

6. Describe the main difficulty in linking genes to schizophrenia.

### Learning Objectives

- Describe the symptoms and outcomes associated with TBI.
- Define the different types of stroke and the effects and treatments associated with each.
- Define the types of epileptic seizure.
- Describe the common feature of myelin disorders, and summarize the symptoms of MS.
- Define neurocognitive disorders, and describe the brain changes and symptoms associated with Alzheimer and Parkinson diseases.
- Summarize the prion theory of progressive neurocognitive disorders.

## 16-3

# Neurological Disorders

Neurological disorders are disorders in which the brain is clearly damaged. They include traumatic brain injury, stroke, epilepsy, multiple sclerosis, and neurocognitive disorders.

## Traumatic Brain Injury

*Traumatic brain injury* (*TBI*) is a wound to the brain that usually results from a blow to the head, also called a *concussion*. It is the most common form of brain damage in people younger than age 40. TBI commonly results from the head making impact with other objects—as can occur in automobile and industrial accidents and in sports injuries. TBI can also follow blows to the chest that result in a rapid increase in blood pressure, which can damage the brain indirectly.

Children and elderly people are more likely to injure their head in a fall than are others; likewise, males between 15 and 30 often incur brain injuries, especially in

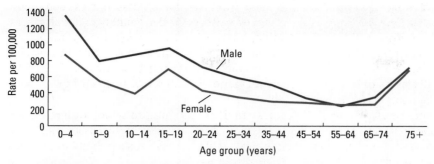

**FIGURE 16-6 Incidence Rates of Head Trauma** Based on combined reports of emergency room visits, hospitalizations, and deaths, this chart graphs the estimated frequency of TBI in males and females across the life span. Data from Centers for Disease Control and Prevention (2010).

automobile and motorcycle accidents (**Figure 16-6**). Children's chance of having a significant TBI before they are old enough to drive is 1 in 30, and at all ages males are more likely to suffer TBI than females.

TBI is a concern for both professional and amateur athletes—especially those who play football, ice hockey, lacrosse, and soccer, and who ride horses—as well as for individuals on active military duty. Sports incidents account for about 20% of TBIs, and the U.S. Army Institute of Surgical Research reports that TBI affects more than one in five U.S. soldiers wounded in war. Some of the symptoms of concussion are listed in **Table 16-5**.

Concussions, especially repeated concussion, can initiate a sequence of brain changes that result in altered behavior and dementia long after the initial event. A large-scale longitudinal study of this phenomenon is now under way involving football and ice hockey players who have a history of concussion and who have agreed to donate their brains for postmortem analysis (Silverberg et al., 2021). Examination of the brains of deceased professional football players who had a history of concussion and severe postconcussion symptoms (described in Clinical Focus 16-3: Concussion) has revealed extensive, diffuse loss of cerebral tissue.

## Symptoms and Outcomes of Brain Trauma

TBI can cause direct damage to the brain. Trauma can disrupt the brain's blood supply, induce bleeding and cause swelling (leading to increased intracranial pressure), expose the brain to infection, and scar brain tissue (with the scar being a focus for later epileptic seizures). The disruption in blood supply tends to be brief, but a parallel disruption of energy production by neuronal mitochondria, which can persist for weeks, is related to many postconcussion behavioral symptoms.

TBI is commonly accompanied by a loss of consciousness that may be brief (minutes) or prolonged (coma). The duration of unconsciousness can serve as a measure of the severity of damage because it correlates directly with mortality, intellectual impairment, and deficits in social skills. The longer a coma lasts, the greater the possibility of serious impairment or death becomes.

Two kinds of behavioral effects result from TBI: (1) impairment of specific functions mediated by the cortex at the coup (the site of impact) or contrecoup (opposite side) lesion, as illustrated in **Figure 16-7**, and (2) more generalized impairments from widespread trauma throughout the brain. Discrete impairment is most commonly associated with damage to the frontal and temporal lobes, the brain areas most susceptible to TBI. (See the images of the tissue samples in Clinical Focus 16-3.)

**TABLE 16-5 Signs and Symptoms of Concussion**

| |
|---|
| Headache or a feeling of pressure in the head |
| Temporary loss of consciousness |
| Confusion or feeling as if in a fog |
| Amnesia surrounding the traumatic event |
| Dizziness or "seeing stars" |
| Ringing in the ears |
| Nausea |
| Vomiting |
| Slurred speech |
| Delayed response to questions |
| Appearing dazed |
| Fatigue |

Clinical Focus 1-1 recounts one psychologist's experience of living with TBI. Section 14-5 details a dancer's recovery from TBI.

In longitudinal research, over time investigators repeatedly observe or examine subjects with respect to the study's variable(s).

**FIGURE 16-7 Mechanics of TBI** Pink and blue shading mark the brain regions most frequently damaged in closed-head injury. A blow can produce a contusion both at the site of impact and on the opposite side of the brain, due to rebound compression.

A variety of mechanical forces cause traumatic brain injuries as a result of a blow to the head.

Damage at the site of impact is called a coup (shown in pink).

← Direction of blow          Direction of blow →

Pressure resulting from a coup produces a contrecoup on the opposite end or side of the brain (shown in blue).

Movement of the brain may shear nerve fibers, causing microscopic lesions, especially in the frontal and temporal lobes. Blood trapped in the skull (hematoma) and swelling (edema) cause pressure on the brain.

## ◎ CLINICAL FOCUS 16-3

# Concussion

Early in 2011, 50-year-old former Chicago Bears defensive back Dave Duerson shot himself in the chest and died. He left a note asking that his brain be studied. Duerson had played 11 years in the National Football League, won two Super Bowls, and received numerous awards.

As a pro player, Duerson endured at least 10 concussions, but none seemed serious enough to cause him to leave a game. After retiring from football, he went to Harvard and obtained a business degree. He pursued a successful business career until he began to have trouble making decisions and controlling his temper.

Eventually, Duerson's business and marriage failed. After his suicide, the Center for the Study of Traumatic Encephalopathy in Boston did study his brain. The center is conducting postmortem anatomical analyses of the brains of other former athletes as part of a long-term longitudinal study.

**Dave Duerson's Brain** Staining for tau protein highlights degenerating brain tissue (dark brown areas) in the frontal cortex and medial temporal lobe of these coronal sections through Duerson's anterior right hemisphere. Damage to the subcortical basal ganglia in the sections' central portions (yellowish areas) is sparse by comparison.

Duerson's diagnosis, **chronic traumatic encephalopathy (CTE)**, is a progressive degenerative disease found in individuals with a history of multiple concussions and other closed-head injuries. (A variant long associated with boxing is *dementia pugilistica [DP]*.)

The effects of concussion often go unrecognized. For those people who are injured, little apparent pathology appears after relatively short periods of rest, the usual treatment. Nevertheless, the relationship is well established between concussion and a range of degenerative diseases that occur later in life — neurocognitive disorders, including Alzheimer disease, as well as Parkinson disease, motor neuron disease, and CTE.

The relationship between concussion in early life and later degenerative brain disease suggests that concussion can initiate a cascade of pathological events that, over the course of the years, develop into CTE. CTE is characterized by neurofibrillary tangles, plaques, and neuronal death. Cerebral atrophy and expanded ventricles due to cell loss are typical in advanced cases. As shown in the accompanying images, researchers test for cell death by staining for accumulation of the tau protein, which is associated with neuronal death and so is a sensitive marker for brain trauma.

Many unknowns about CTE persist. Can just one concussion initiate a cascade that results in brain degeneration, or are many concussions required? Are some individuals especially susceptible to CTE? Should blows to the head that result in no pronounced symptoms be distinguished from blows that result in loss of consciousness?

That many well-known athletes have developed CTE has generated public awareness of the consequences of concussion. This understanding has caused some people to evaluate their participation in some sports and is leading to changes in contact sports to make them safer for the brain (Van Pelt et al., 2021). Rule changes, protective behavior, protective gear, and wearable devices that can gauge concussion are becoming more widely used in sports given the now-recognized risks of concussion and CTE.

---

**chronic traumatic encephalopathy (CTE)**
Progressive degenerative disease caused by multiple concussions and other closed-head injuries, characterized by neurofibrillary tangles, plaques, cerebral atrophy, and expanded ventricles due to cell loss.

More generalized impairment results from minute lesions and lacerations scattered throughout the brain. Movement of the hemispheres in relationship to one another causes connecting fibers to tear, especially those of the corpus callosum. This results in a decrease in complex cognitive functions, including mental speed, concentration, and overall cognitive efficiency.

Individuals with TBI complain of poor concentration or lack of ability, and their personality and social behavior may be affected. Many fail to do things as well as they could before the injury. Few people with TBI who have sustained severe head injuries are able to resume their studies or return to gainful employment. If they do reenter the workforce, they do so at a lower level than before their accident. One frustrating problem with TBI is misdiagnosis: the chronic effects of the injury are often invisible, as they are not accompanied by any obvious neurological signs or abnormalities.

## Recovery from Traumatic Brain Injury

Recovery from head trauma is difficult to gauge due to the absence of systematic studies and any agreed-upon classification for TBI (Tenovuo et al., 2021). That said, the recovery process may continue for 2 to 3 years following the initial event, though most cognitive recovery occurs in the first 6 to 9 months after the injury. Recovery of memory functions appears to occur more slowly than recovery of general intelligence, and recovery of memory is poorer than for other cognitive functions.

Although the prognosis for significant recovery of cognitive functions is good, optimism about the recovery of social skills or personality traits, areas that often show significant changes with TBI, is less rosy. Numerous studies support the conclusions that quality of life—assessed in terms of social interactions, perceived stress levels, and enjoyment of leisure—is reduced after TBI and that this reduction is chronic.

**ischemic stroke** A stroke resulting from a blocked blood vessel.

**hemorrhagic stroke** A stroke resulting from bleeding from a blood vessel.

# Stroke

Stroke is an interruption of blood flow due to either blockage or bleeding of a vessel. **Ischemic stroke** is a result of blockage to a vessel; **hemorrhagic stroke** is a result of bleeding from a vessel. Bleeding could result from a cerebral aneurysm, a bulge with resulting weakening of a blood vessel (see Clinical Focus 16-4: Cerebral Aneurysms).

A stroke sets off a sequence of damage that progresses, even if the blood flow is restored, as might occur after ischemic stroke. Changes at the cellular level can seriously compromise not only the injured part of the brain but other brain regions as well.

## Effects of Stroke

Consider what happens after a stroke interrupts the blood supply to a portion of the brain. In the first seconds to minutes, as illustrated in **Figure 16-8**, changes begin in the affected regions' ionic balance, including changes in pH and in the properties of the cell membrane. These ionic changes result in several pathological events:

1. Release of massive amounts of glutamate results in prolonged opening of calcium channels in cell membranes.

2. Open calcium channels, in turn, allow toxic levels of calcium to enter the cell, not only producing direct toxic effects but also instigating various cellular changes that may potentially prove toxic to the cells.

3. Brain tissues become inflamed and swollen, threatening the integrity of cells that may be far removed from the stroke site. As in TBI, an energy crisis ensues as

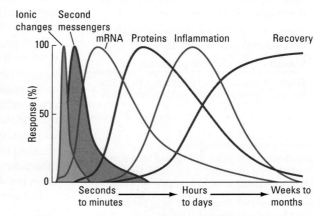

**FIGURE 16-8 Results of Ischemic Stroke** A cascade of events takes place after blood flow is blocked as a result of stroke. Within seconds, ionic changes at the cellular level spur changes in second-messenger molecules and RNA production. Changes in protein production and inflammation follow and resolve slowly, in hours to days. Recovery begins within hours to days and continues for weeks to months or years.

---

◉ **CLINICAL FOCUS 16-4**

## Cerebral Aneurysms

C. N. was a 35-year-old nurse described by Isabelle Peretz and her colleagues (1994). In December 1986, C. N. suddenly developed severe neck pain and a headache. A neurological examination revealed an aneurysm in the middle cerebral artery on the right side of her brain.

An *aneurysm* is a bulge in a blood vessel wall caused by weakening of the tissue, much like the bulge that appears in a bicycle tire at a weakened spot (see the figure). Aneurysms in a cerebral artery are dangerous: if they burst, severe bleeding and consequent brain damage result.

In February 1987, C. N.'s aneurysm was surgically repaired, and she appeared to have few adverse effects. Postoperative brain imaging revealed, however, that a new aneurysm had formed in the same location but in the middle cerebral artery on the opposite side of the brain. This second aneurysm was repaired 2 weeks later.

After her surgery, C. N. had temporary difficulty finding the right words when she spoke, but more importantly, her perception of music was changed. She could no longer sing, nor could she recognize familiar tunes. In fact, singers sounded to her as if they were talking instead of singing. But C. N. could still dance to music.

Aneurysm in middle cerebral artery

Bulge in bicycle tire

Figure 5-4 shows how calcium affects neurotransmitter release; Figure 5-16 illustrates how metabotropic receptors can activate second messengers.

Clinical Focus 2-3 describes the symptoms and aftereffects of stroke.

| Use the F.A.S.T. Test to Spot Stroke |
|---|
| **Face**    Ask for a smile to check both understanding and muscle control. |
| **Arms**    Check if one arm is weak by asking the person to raise both arms. |
| **Speech**    Listen for slurred speech. |
| **Time**    If you see any symptom, call 911 or the local emergency services number right away. |

**diaschisis** Neural shock that follows brain damage in which areas connected to the site of damage show a temporary arrest of function.

**neuroprotectant** Drug used to try to block the cascade of poststroke neural events.

Experiment 11-3 describes research with monkeys that contributed to the development of constraint-induced therapy for people.

**FIGURE 16-9 Constraint-Induced Therapy** A person who has experienced stroke that leads to impaired mobility of the right hand has the use of the unimpaired hand constrained by a cloth covering, forcing the person to use the impaired limb.

mitochondria reduce their production of adenosine triphosphate (ATP), resulting in less cerebral energy.

4. A form of neural shock occurs. During this **diaschisis**, areas distant from the damage are functionally depressed.

5. Stroke may also be followed by changes in the injured hemisphere's metabolism, its glucose utilization, or both. These changes may persist for days. For example, after a cortical stroke, metabolic rate has been shown to decrease about 25% throughout the hemisphere.

## Treatments for Stroke

The ideal treatment for ischemic stroke is to restore blood flow before the cascade of pathological events begins. Tissue plasminogen activator (t-PA) is a clot-busting drug, but must be administered within 3 to 5 hours to be effective. Currently, only a small percentage of people who experience stroke arrive at the hospital soon enough to receive t-PA therapy—in large part because stroke is not quickly identified, transportation is slow, or the stroke is not considered an emergency. (The table to the right offers some suggestions for identifying a potential stroke event.)

The effectiveness of treatment with t-PA is further complicated by the fact that it is often difficult to determine the type of stroke—that is, ischemic or hemorrhagic—upon initial examination. For example, if stroke is accompanied by a fall, it may be unclear whether the person's symptoms are due to a stroke that caused the fall, or a fall that resulted in TBI. In the former case, t-PA would be an appropriate treatment to remove a blood clot from ischemic stroke; in the latter case, t-PA might exacerbate bleeding in the brain indicative of hemorrhagic stroke, resulting in more catastrophic damage.

Other drugs, called **neuroprotectants**, can be used to try to block the cascade of postinjury events, but to date there are no truly effective drugs. Clinical trials based on animal studies are currently searching for effective neuroprotectant drugs.

When the course of a stroke leads to dead brain tissue, the only treatments that can be beneficial are those that facilitate plastic changes in the remaining living brain tissue, with associated compensatory behavior. Examples include speech therapy and physical therapy, virtual reality, computer games, and robotic machines.

Some simple behavioral treatments are surprisingly effective. One is *constraint-induced therapy,* pioneered by Edward Taub in the 1990s (Uswatte et al., 2018). Its logic confronts a problem in poststroke recovery related to *learned nonuse*. Individuals with stroke who have motor deficits in a limb often compensate by overusing the intact limb, leading to an accompanying decrease in the use of the impaired limb such that the function of that impaired limb actually regresses.

In constraint-induced therapy, the intact limb is held in a sling for several hours per day, forcing the person to use the impaired limb (see **Figure 16-9**). Any treatment that forces individuals to practice behaviors extensively is successful. An important component of these treatments, however, is a posttreatment contract in which people continue to practice after the formal therapy is over. If they fail to do so, the chances for learned nonuse and a return of symptoms are high (Hayward et al., 2021).

Another common effect of stroke is loss of speech. Specific speech therapy programs can aid in the recovery of speech. Music and singing, both of which are mediated in part by the right hemisphere, can augment speech therapy after left hemisphere stroke.

Many attempts have been made to use either direct cortical stimulation or transcranial magnetic stimulation (TMS) in combination with behavioral therapy as a stroke treatment. The idea is to induce plasticity in regions adjacent to the dead tissue, with the goal of enhancing the efficiency of the residual parts of the neuronal networks. These treatments have proved beneficial in individuals with good residual motor control, but again those with larger injuries show much less benefit, presumably because the residual neuronal network is insufficient to support recovery (Breining & Sebastian, 2020).

# Epilepsy

Epilepsy is characterized by recurrent self-generated seizures, which register on EEG as highly synchronized neuronal firing indicated by a variety of abnormal waves. About 1 person in 20 has at least one seizure in their lifetime, usually associated with an infection, fever, and hyperventilation during childhood (6 months to 5 years of age). Most children who experience a seizure do not develop epilepsy, a disease that affects between 0.2% and 4.1% of the population.

**FIGURE 16-10  MRI Showing Angioma**
Structural or metabolic epilepsy may result from brain malformations such as angioma, or AV malformation, shown on this dorsal view MRI. Abnormal cerebral blood vessels (in white) form a convoluted pattern, including a balloon-like structure (blue area at lower right) that caused the death of brain tissue around it in the right occipital cortex.

SPL/Science Source

## Classifying Seizures

Causes of epileptic seizures are categorized as genetic, structural/metabolic, or unknown. *Genetic epilepsy* results directly from a known genetic defect. Causes of *structural/metabolic epilepsy* include brain malformations and tumors (see **Figure 16-10** for one example), acquired disorders such as stroke and trauma, and infections. The *unknown* category encompasses causes yet to be identified.

**Table 16-6** summarizes the great variety of circumstances that appear to precipitate seizures. The range of circumstances is striking, but seizures do have a consistent feature: they are most likely to occur when a person is sleeping.

The International League Against Epilepsy (ILAE) has developed a classification system of epilepsy based on where seizures begin in the brain, the level of awareness during a seizure, and other associated seizure factors. **Focal seizures** arise from a synchronous, hyperactive local brain region. Thus, focal seizures may have motor, sensory, autonomic, and/or psychogenic features, depending on where they are located. If focal seizures involve memory regions of the brain, for example, memory and awareness can be altered (impaired awareness seizure). **Generalized seizures** start at a focal location and then spread rapidly and bilaterally to distributed networks in both hemispheres. In *primary generalized epilepsy*, seizures begin in more widespread neural networks. Seizure diagnosis is improved by the use of a wearable EEG recording device that records their time, duration, and location (Bruno et al., 2021).

People having a generalized seizure may cycle through the four stages charted in **Figure 16-11**: (1) normal EEG record before onset; (2) onset and tonic phase, in which the body stiffens; (3) clonic phase, in which the person makes rhythmic movements in time with the large, highly synchronized discharges; and (4) a period of depressed EEG activity after the seizure ends.

**TABLE 16-6** Factors That May Precipitate Seizures in Susceptible Persons

| Emotional stress |
| --- |
| Sleep deprivation |
| Tiredness |
| Alcohol |
| Fever |
| Flickering lights |
| Noncompliance |
| Menstruation |
| Physical exercise |
| Health |

*Source:* Information from Ferlisi & Shorvon (2014).

Clinical Focus 4-1 describes a diagnosis of epilepsy and shows an EEG being recorded.

**focal seizure**  Seizure that arises at a synchronous, hyperactive, localized brain region (at a focus).

**generalized seizure**  Seizure that starts at a focal location, and then spreads rapidly and bilaterally to distributed networks in both hemispheres.

**FIGURE 16-11  Generalized Seizure Patterns**  Examples of EEG patterns recorded during a generalized seizure. Dots on the hemispheres below indicate the approximate recording sites. Column numbers mark the seizure's stages: (1) normal record before the attack; (2) onset of seizure and tonic phase; (3) clonic phase; and (4) a period of depressed EEG activity after the seizure ends. *Abbreviations:* LT and RT, left temporal and right temporal; LF and RF, left frontal and right frontal; LO and RO, left occipital and right occipital.

Left                    Right

## Treating Epilepsy

Most seizures self-terminate. In the condition termed *status epilepticus*, the seizure's driving force does not abate, often due to a brain insult or to drug withdrawal. Status epilepticus can be life-threatening, and drug intervention with a fast-acting GABA agonist or glutamate antagonist is required to end the seizure. The recommended time limit before intervention is 5 minutes. Longer-lasting seizures are unlikely to self-terminate.

The first-line treatment for epilepsy is drugs to inhibit seizure development and propagation. Among the diverse range of mechanisms that drugs employ to raise seizure thresholds are enhancing the action of the inhibitory neurotransmitter GABA and stabilizing the inactive state of sodium channels. Most people with epilepsy work with their physician to find a drug and dosage that cause the fewest side effects. In 30% to 40% of people with epilepsy, however, antiseizure drugs fail to completely control the condition; this is known as *intractable epilepsy*. The most common treatment for intractable epilepsy in adults is surgical resection of epileptogenic tissue, which has a success rate of about 70%. Deep brain stimulation (DBS) may also prove useful for intractable epilepsy: bilateral stimulation of the anterior thalamus has been successful in reducing seizure frequency. While DBS shows promise, however, more research is needed (Foutz & Wong, 2021).

## Disorders of Myelin

Myelin is the glial coverings made by the oligodendroglia in the peripheral nervous system (PNS) and the Schwann cells in the central nervous system (CNS). A large number of acquired and inherited disorders are associated with myelin, ranging from the most common disorder, *multiple sclerosis* (MS), to several rare genetic disorders. Disorders of myelin can be local. *Optic neuritis*, for example, may affect only one eye, and *transverse myelitis* may affect only one spinal cord segment. Other myelin disorders are more general; for example, MS can affect myelin in almost any part of the nervous system. Because of its frequency, we will focus our discussion of myelin disorders on MS.

Myelin and other types of glial cells and neurons are described in detail in Section 3-1.

### Multiple Sclerosis

MS is characterized by myelin loss in both motor and sensory tracts and nerves. Brain imaging with MRI, as shown in **Figure 16-12**, identifies areas of sclerosis in the brain as well as in the spinal cord. Worldwide, about 2 million people have MS; in this population, women outnumber men about 2 to 1. MS is most prevalent in northern Europe and northern North America, and it is rare in Japan and in more equatorial countries. Depending on the region, the incidence of MS ranges from 2 to 150 per 100,000 people, making it one of the most common structural nervous system diseases.

Remission followed by relapse is a striking feature of MS: in many cases, early symptoms initially are followed by improvement. The course varies, running from a few years to as long as 50 years. A person with MS may eventually be affected by paraplegia and confined to a wheelchair or to bed.

Proposed causes of MS include bacterial infection, virus, environmental factors including pesticides, an immune response of the CNS, misfolded proteins, and lack of vitamin D. Often, multiple cases occur in a single family. Many genes have been

**FIGURE 16-12 Diagnosing MS** Imaged by MRI, discrete MS lesions appear as dark patches all around the lateral ventricles and in the brain's white matter.

associated with MS, but no clear evidence indicates as yet that MS is inherited or transmitted from one person to another.

Research has focused on the relationship between MS and the immune system, and findings suggest that MS is an **autoimmune disease**. The ability to discriminate between a foreign pathogen in the body and the body itself is central to immune system functioning. If this discrimination fails, the immune system makes antibodies to the person's own body; in the case of MS, the immune system makes antibodies to myelin.

As various organisms' genomes have been sequenced, it has become apparent that all have many genes in common. Thus, the proteins found in different organisms are surprisingly similar. And here is the problem for the human immune system: a foreign microbe may contain a protein that is nearly identical to the body's own protein. If microbe and human share a common gene sequence, the immune system, in attacking that microbe, can end up attacking itself. This process is known as *horror autotoxicus* (Latin for "horrible self-toxicity"). The idea is that some microbial protein sequences are homologous with structures found in myelin, which leads to an attack against the microbe and a person's own myelin, as illustrated in **Figure 16-13**. Thus, immune responses to a variety of disease conditions, including COVID-19, the cause of the 2020–2022 pandemic, have been reported to incidentally cause neuroinflammation and potentially demyelination (Sriwastava et al., 2021).

The fact that MS is more common in extreme northern and southern latitudes has raised the possibility that inadequate direct sunlight, which is necessary for the body to synthesize vitamin D, factors into precipitating the condition. The question remains whether an acute or a longstanding vitamin D deficiency is relevant to this relationship. Perhaps a vitamin D deficiency interacts with other factors to increase susceptibility to MS. For example, a number of genes are involved in the transport and absorption of vitamin D, and variants of these genes are related to low levels of vitamin D, even in individuals who consume diets containing adequate amounts of vitamin D and/or are exposed to adequate amounts of sunlight (Boltjes et al., 2021).

Section 4-3 discusses the function of the myelin sheath, and Clinical Focus 4-3 elaborates on multiple sclerosis as an autoimmune disease.

**FIGURE 16-13 Damage to the Myelin Sheath Caused by MS** *Sclerosis* comes from the Greek word for "hardness."

**autoimmune disease** Illness resulting from the loss of the immune system's ability to discriminate between foreign pathogens in the body and the body itself.

**neurocognitive disorder** Acquired and persistent syndrome of intellectual impairment characterized by memory and other cognitive deficits and impairment in social and occupational functioning.

# Neurocognitive Disorders

**Neurocognitive disorders** are those in which there is a decrease in the level of overall function due primarily to a decrease in cognitive function. These disorders are classified as either major or mild, depending on the extent to which they allow a person to live independently. The percentage of older people in the general population has increased steadily over the past several decades. Neurocognitive disorders affect 1% to 6% of the population older than age 65 and 10% to 20% of those older than age 80, so the incidence of neurocognitive disorders has also increased with the aging of the overall population.

Neurocognitive disorders involve an acquired and persistent syndrome of intellectual impairment. Their two common, essential features are (1) loss of memory and other cognitive deficits and (2) impairment in social and occupational functioning. Causes can be divided into two broad categories: degenerative and nondegenerative (**Table 16-7**). In the following sections, we will limit our discussion to Alzheimer and Parkinson disease, two degenerative neurocognitive disorders with very different trajectories.

## Alzheimer Disease

Alzheimer disease, a major neurocognitive disorder and one of the most common causes of degenerative neurocognitive disorder, is known to reduce life span. Three predisposing factors have been identified for Alzheimer disease: age, sex, and genetics. Alzheimer disease most often begins in people older than the age of 65. Women are more likely both to develop Alzheimer disease and to have more severe symptoms, suggesting a hormonal influence.

**TABLE 16-7 Degenerative and Nondegenerative Neurocognitive Disorders**

| Degenerative | Nondegenerative |
|---|---|
| Alzheimer disease | Vascular dementias (e.g., multi-infarct dementia) |
| Extrapyramidal syndromes (e.g., progressive supranuclear palsy) | Infectious dementia (e.g., acquired immunodeficiency syndrome [AIDS] dementia) |
| Wilson disease | |
| Huntington disease | Neurosyphilis |
| Parkinson disease | Posttraumatic dementia |
| Frontal temporal dementia | Demyelinating dementia (e.g., multiple sclerosis) |
| Corticobasal degeneration | |
| Leukodystrophies (e.g., adrenoleukodystrophy) | Toxic or metabolic disorders (e.g., vitamin $B_{12}$ and niacin deficiencies) |
| Prion-related dementias (e.g., Creutzfeldt-Jakob disease) | Chronic alcohol or drug abuse (e.g., Korsakoff syndrome) |
| Chronic traumatic encephalopathy (CTE) | |

*Source:* Information from Charney et al. (2017).

**(A) Healthy brain**

**(B) Brain with Alzheimer disease**

**(C)**

Posterior parietal cortex

Inferior temporal cortex

**(D)**

Limbic cortex

Entorhinal cortex

**FIGURE 16-14 Cortical Degeneration in Alzheimer Disease** Contrast between **(A)** the brain of a healthy elderly adult and **(B)** the brain of an elderly adult that shows shriveling due to cell shrinkage characteristic of Alzheimer disease. Distribution and severity of degeneration on **(C)** lateral and **(D)** medial aspects of the brain in an average Alzheimer case. The darker the area, the more pronounced the degeneration is. White areas are spared, with only basic changes being discernible in them. (A and B: Laura Hemmy/Nun Study, University of Minnesota.)

Clinical Focus 14-3, on Alzheimer etiology, includes a micrograph of an amyloid plaque.

Neurofilaments are a type of *tubule* that reinforces cell structure, aids its movement, and transports proteins.

Figure 14-17 shows how glutamate can affect NMDA and AMPA receptors to promote learning by association.

| Normal adult pattern | Early Alzheimer disease | Advanced Alzheimer disease | Terminal Alzheimer disease |

**FIGURE 16-15 Stripped Branches** The dendritic trees of individuals with Alzheimer disease degenerate and their neurons atrophy, worsening their symptoms, including memory loss and personality changes.

Incidence of Alzheimer disease is high in some families, suggesting that genetic causes may be a factor in 40% to 70% of cases. Nevertheless, many other factors influence susceptibility to Alzheimer disease, including personal lifestyle, environmental toxins, high levels of trace elements such as aluminum in the blood, an autoimmune response, a slow-acting virus, and reduced blood flow to the cerebral hemispheres.

Until recently, the only way to identify and study Alzheimer disease was via postmortem pathology examination, and this method is still the only way to provide a definitive diagnosis. Early diagnosis in the course of the disease—or even before disease onset—is an obvious goal that aids in treatment and prevention. As the disease progresses, widespread changes occur in cortical structures and in many neurotransmitter systems. Neuropsychological testing and brain imaging are used in diagnosis, but early diagnosis occurs in only about 25% of cases, with a lower rate in marginalized populations (White et al., 2021).

The principal neuroanatomical change in Alzheimer disease is the emergence of amyloid plaques (clumps of abnormal protein), chiefly in cortical areas. Increased plaque concentration in the cortex has been correlated with the magnitude of cognitive deterioration. Plaques are generally considered nonspecific phenomena because they can be found in people without Alzheimer disease and in those with neurocognitive disorders caused by other known events.

Another anatomical correlate of Alzheimer disease is neurofibrillary tangles (accumulations of microtubules from dead cells) found in both neocortex and allocortex. Neurofibrillary tangles have been described mainly in human tissue and have also been observed in people with Down syndrome and Parkinson disease.

Finally, the neocortical changes correlated with Alzheimer disease are not uniform. As **Figure 16-14** shows, the cortex atrophies and can lose as much as one-third of its volume as the disease progresses. But cellular analyses at the microscopic level reveal that some areas, including the primary sensory and motor cortices (especially the visual and sensorimotor cortices), are relatively spared. The frontal lobes are less affected than is the posterior cortex. The more widespread cause of cortical atrophy appears to be a loss of dendritic arborization (**Figure 16-15**).

In addition to cell loss and shrinkage, changes take place in the remaining cells' neurotransmitters. In the 1970s, researchers believed that a neurotransmitter replacement could be a treatment option. The prime candidate neurotransmitter was, and still is, acetylcholine (ACh), and one treatment developed for Alzheimer disease is medication that increases acetylcholine levels in the forebrain. Cholinergic agonists given orally or as a skin patch can be helpful early in the disease. Unfortunately, Alzheimer disease has proved far more complex, as widespread cell damage occurs and transmitters other than ACh clearly are changed as well. Noradrenaline, dopamine, and serotonin are reduced, as are the NMDA and AMPA receptors for glutamate. Clinical trials of treatments for Alzheimer disease number in the hundreds but show limited success in producing a cure or treatment.

## Parkinson Disease

Parkinson disease is a condition in which movement is slowed, though it is also associated with many other alterations in movement, emotion, and cognition. Parkinson disease is estimated to afflict as much as 1% of the population, with the incidence rising sharply in old age. This disease is primarily related to degeneration of the substantia nigra and attendant loss of the neurotransmitter dopamine released in the striatum. Thus, it offers insights into the roles played by the substantia nigra and dopamine in movement control.

That Parkinson symptoms vary enormously illustrates the complexity inherent in understanding a neurological disorder. The degeneration of a well-defined set of cells is central to the disease, but many other brain areas are also affected, so the symptoms are not the same in every person.

Symptoms begin insidiously, often with a tremor in one hand and slight stiffness in distal parts of the limbs. Movements may become slower, with the face becoming masklike, eventually with loss of eye blinking and facial emotional expression. Thereafter, the body may stoop and the gait may become a shuffle, with arms hanging motionless at the sides. Speech may slow and become monotonous, and difficulty swallowing may cause drooling. At the onset of symptoms, a person may display symptoms of neglect—they may not be aware of the changes.

Although the disease is progressive, the rate at which symptoms worsen varies; only rarely is progression so rapid that a person becomes disabled within 5 years. Usually 10 to 20 years elapse before symptoms cause incapacity.

Momentary partial remission may also occur in response to interesting or stimulating situations. Neurologist Oliver Sacks (1998) recounted an incident in which a stationary patient with Parkinson disease leaped from his wheelchair at the seaside and rushed into the breakers to save a drowning man, only to fall back into his chair immediately afterward and become inactive again. Remission of some symptoms in activating situations is common but usually not as dramatic as in this case. Simply listening to familiar music can help an otherwise inactive individual get up and dance, for example. Or a person who has difficulty walking may ride a bicycle or skate, seemingly effortlessly. A person who seems immobilized can quickly catch a ball that is thrown. The ability of a person to respond to these activating stimuli is useful in physical therapy, and physical therapy is important because it may slow disease progression.

Because some symptoms of Parkinson disease entail the appearance of abnormal behaviors (positive symptoms) and others the loss of normal behaviors (negative symptoms), we consider both major categories.

**Positive Symptoms**  Positive symptoms manifest in movements thought to be inhibited (i.e., held in check) in unaffected people but released from inhibition in the process of the disease. Positive symptoms include:

1. *Tremor at rest.* These tremors manifest as alternating movements of the limbs and hand tremors, with a pill-rolling quality, as if a pill were being rolled between the thumb and forefinger.

2. *Muscular rigidity.* Increased muscle tone simultaneously in both extensor and flexor muscles is particularly evident when the limbs are moved passively at a joint. In *cogwheel rigidity*, movement is resisted, but with sufficient force, the muscles yield for a short distance and then resist movement again.

3. *Involuntary movements.* Small movements or changes in posture, sometimes referred to as **akathisia**, or *cruel restlessness*, may accompany general inactivity, but these movements often occur for no apparent reason.

**Negative Symptoms**  Negative symptoms include movements that can no longer be produced, including:

1. *Disorders of posture.* An inability or difficulty to maintain a part of the body in its normal position in relationship to other parts, such as a drooping head, poor posture, or the inability to maintain one's balance when sitting or standing.

2. *Disorders of righting.* A person in a supine position has difficulty standing or rolling over.

3. *Disorders of locomotion.* A person has difficulty initiating stepping, shuffles with short footsteps when walking, and displays **festination**, faster and faster steps leading to running.

4. *Hypokinesia.* This condition is characterized by slow movement, a blankness of facial expression, a lack of blinking or of swinging the arms when walking, and a lack of spontaneous speech.

Section 5-2 discusses neurotransmitters associated with dopamine. Clinical Focus 5-2 discusses the discoveries that led researchers to understand the connection between Parkinson disease and dopamine and recounts the story of Joy Milne, a health-care worker whose unique ability to smell Parkinson disease led to a change in how the disorder is diagnosed.

Clinical Focus 5-4 describes Sacks's case history of administering L-dopa to patients with Parkinson disease. Sacks, whose writings enriched the neurological literature, died in 2015.

*Positive symptoms* are behaviors not typically seen in people. *Negative symptoms* are the absence of typical behaviors or inability to engage in an activity.

**akathisia**  Small, involuntary movements or changes in posture; motor restlessness.

**festination**  Tendency to engage in a behavior, such as walking, faster and faster.

**Cognitive Symptoms** Although Parkinson disease is usually viewed as a motor disorder, changes in cognition occur. Psychological symptoms in individuals with Parkinson disease are as variable as the motor symptoms. Nonetheless, a significant percentage of them show cognitive symptoms in emotion, memory, and thought processes. People may sit for hours, apparently lacking the will to begin or continue any activity. Parkinson disease is often considered to be a neurocognitive disorder because individuals with this disease do not appear to be processing the content of conversations. In fact, they may simply be processing it very slowly. Cognitive slowing in persons with Parkinson disease has some parallels to Alzheimer disease.

Clinical Focus 5-5 describes the case of a person who experienced Parkinson-like symptoms after using synthetic heroin that contained MPTP.

**Causes Of Parkinsonism** The ultimate cause of Parkinson disease—loss of cells in the substantia nigra—may result from disease (such as encephalitis or syphilis), from drugs (such as MPTP [1-methyl-4-phenylpyridinium], a contaminant that has been found in synthetic heroin and damages dopamine cells), or from unknown causes. *Idiopathic* causes—those related to the individual—may include environmental pollutants, insecticides and herbicides, concussion, or genetic factors. Demographic studies of people who contract the disease at a relatively young age have prompted the suggestion that water and air might contain environmental toxins that work in a fashion similar to MPTP.

Joanne Rathe/Boston Globe/Getty Images

Rhythmic movement helps people with Parkinson disease restore the balance between positive and negative symptoms. Those who participate in specially designed Dance for Parkinson groups led by the Mark Morris Dance Center, like the one pictured here, report that moving to music helps them regain muscle control. Exercise, including tai chi and boxing, also reinforces treatments directed toward replacing depleted dopamine.

**Treating Parkinson Disease** The cure for Parkinson disease is either to stop degeneration of cells in the substantia nigra or to replace them. Neither goal is achievable at present. Thus, current treatment is pharmacological and behavioral, directed toward support and comfort.

Physical therapy consists of simple measures, such as heat and massage, to alleviate painful muscle cramps, as well as training and exercise to cope with debilitating movement changes. Used therapeutically, music and exercise can improve other aspects of behavior, including balance and walking, and may actually slow the course of the disease.

The objective of pharmacological treatment is increasing the activity in whatever dopamine synapses remain. L-Dopa, a precursor of dopamine, is converted into dopamine in the brain and enhances effective dopamine transmission, thereby lessening the disease's symptoms. Drugs such as amantadine, amphetamine, monoamine oxidase inhibitors, and tricyclic antidepressants can stimulate the remaining dopamine neurons, so they may also lessen symptoms. Anticholinergic drugs, such as atropine, scopolamine, benztropine (Cogentin), and trihexyphenidyl (Artane), block the brain cholinergic systems that seem to show heightened activity in the absence of adequate dopamine activity.

As the disease progresses, however, drug therapies become less effective because there are fewer dopamine neurons to stimulate. One effect of the decrease in available dopamine is that the number of dopamine receptors increases. Consequently, the action of the remaining dopamine on the increased number of receptors begins to produce side effects that include abnormal movements. Once the side effects become severe, treatments that stimulate dopamine release are no longer useful. Some drug treatments that directly stimulate dopamine receptors have been reported to result in increased sexuality and an increased incidence of compulsive gambling.

Section 7-1 describes the use of lesions and DBS in treating Parkinson disease. Figure 11-13 charts how the globus pallidus internal, a structure in the basal ganglia, regulates movement force.

Two surgical treatments described later in this section are based on the idea that increased activity of globus pallidus (GPi) neurons inhibits motor function. A lesion of the internal part of the GPi can reduce rigidity and tremor. Hyperactivity of GPi neurons can also be reduced neurosurgically by electrically stimulating the neurons via DBS (see Figure 16-19 later in this section). A stimulating electrode is permanently implanted in the GPi or an adjacent area, the subthalamic nucleus. Persons who undergo this therapy carry a small electric stimulator that they can turn on to induce DBS and so reduce rigidity and tremor. These two treatments may be used sequentially: when DBS becomes less effective as the disease progresses, a GPi lesion may be induced.

A still-experimental Parkinson treatment involves increasing the population of dopamine-producing cells. One way is to transplant embryonic dopamine cells into the basal ganglia. In the 1980s and 1990s, this treatment was reported to have varying degrees of success; the results were muddied, however, by many poorly conducted studies with inadequate preassessment and postassessment procedures. Newer treatments are directed toward improving the integration of grafts with the brain and stimulating stem cells to replace lost neurons (Silva et al., 2022).

# The Prion Theory of Progressive Neurocognitive Disorder

Alzheimer and Parkinson disease have some similarities. The best-studied similarity between the two diseases is the **Lewy body** (**Figure 16-16**), a fibrous ring that forms within neuronal cytoplasm and is thought to correspond to abnormal neurofilament metabolism. Until recently, the Lewy body was most often found in the region of the midbrain substantia nigra and believed to be a hallmark of Parkinson disease, as amyloid plaques were viewed as a marker of Alzheimer disease. In fact, Lewy bodies appear in several neurocognitive disorders, including Alzheimer disease. There are even reports of people with Alzheimer-like neurocognitive disorders, such as Lewy body dementia, who have no plaques and tangles but who do have extensive Lewy bodies in the cortex. Symptoms of these diseases may be similar because they have similar origins.

Indeed, the idea that several diseases marked by brain degeneration may have a similar origin is central to prion theory (the term *prion* is short for "proteinaceous infectious particle"), advanced in 1982 by Stanley B. Prusiner, who received the 1997 Nobel Prize for his work. A **prion** is an abnormally folded protein that causes other similar proteins to adopt the abnormal fold (**Figure 16-17**). The abnormal fold renders the protein less functional.

Prions tend to clump together, forming protein aggregates that contribute to cell death. Prions can also infect neighboring brain and body cells, resulting in general brain degeneration and muscle wasting. As this gradual infection proceeds, it causes progressive neurodegeneration. A prion can have a genetic origin, have a spontaneous origin, result from trauma and other causes, or be acquired by ingesting food that contains a prion.

Prions were identified during investigation of various degenerative brain diseases in humans and other animals. Creutzfeldt-Jakob disease, a rare human degenerative disease that progresses rapidly, gained public prominence in the 1990s, when some people contracted a similar condition after eating beef from cattle that had displayed symptoms of *bovine spongiform encephalopathy* (*BSE*). BSE is a degenerative brain condition accompanied by muscle wasting. BSE, in turn, is similar to a condition in sheep called *scrapie* (so named because the animals scrape or scratch themselves) that also features wasting of brain and body. *Chronic wasting disease* is a similar condition found in deer and elk.

The infectious nature of one such infection was observed in the Fore tribe of Papua New Guinea in the 1950s. A large number of Fore were dying of a muscle-wasting condition called *kuru* (meaning "to shake" in Fore). It turned out that the Fore were contracting kuru by practicing ritual cannibalism: they ate the brains of dead relatives (some of whom had died of kuru), which the Fore believed would preserve their spirits. In an experiment to investigate the condition, body parts from people who had kuru were fed to a chimp that then contracted the disease. The infectious agent in this condition is a prion.

In Parkinson disease, the misfolded protein is proposed to be *alpha-synuclein*. It accumulates, largely in substantia nigra cells, to form a Lewy body. In Alzheimer disease, the misfolded proteins are *amyloid beta* (Aß) and *tau protein*, which form amyloid plaques and mainly affect cortical cells. According to one explanation, prion proteins may be produced by gut bacteria (Brás & Outeiro, 2020). Once formed, the prions migrate via the vagus nerve to the brain (**Figure 16-18**). These prions may arrive in the brain many years before symptoms of disease begin.

The prion theory opens new avenues for investigating degenerative disease treatments, including drugs that remove prions, block prion formation, or alter proteins that are prone to misfolding (Brás & Outeiro, 2020). In addition, the many lifestyle

**FIGURE 16-16  Midbrain Lewy Body** Lewy bodies (arrow) characteristic of Parkinson disease are found in the brains of people with other disorders as well.

The *infection* as referred to in the definition of prion is not one caused by casual contact.

**FIGURE 16-17   Disease Process** *Left:* Prion proteins typically fold into helices and pleated sheets. *Right:* In misfolding, part of the normal protein changes into a beta helix. The result is an infectious disease-causing prion.

**Lewy body** Circular fibrous structure found in several neurocognitive disorders; forms within the cytoplasm of neurons and is thought to result from abnormal neurofilament metabolism.

**prion** From *proteinaceous* and *infectious*; an abnormally folded protein that causes progressive degenerative neurocognitive disorders.

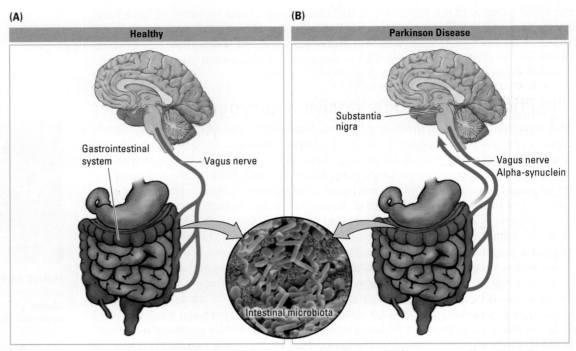

**FIGURE 16-18 Gut Prion Sources (A)** Normal relationship between the vagus nerve and gut containing beneficial bacteria in which the nerve regulates gut activity. **(B)** Harmful gut bacteria produce a prion, which migrates to the brain via the vagus nerve.

attributes—including healthy diet, exercise, and education—that seem to confer some resistance to degenerative diseases may be effective because they help the body resist the formation and effects of prions. Selective cattle breeding for protein alleles that do not produce misfolding prevents BSE. Inserting a misfolding-resistant human protein allele into mice renders them resistant to prion disease. Any treatment developed for humans could potentially treat BSE in cattle, scrapie in sheep, and wasting disease in deer and elk, and any treatment for these animals could help humans.

## Age-Related Cognitive Loss

Most people who grow old do not develop a neurocognitive disorder, but virtually everyone experiences some level of age-related cognitive loss, even while living an active, healthy, productive life. Aging is associated with declines in perceptual functions (especially vision, hearing, and olfaction) and declining motor, cognitive, and executive (planning) functions as well. Older people tend to learn at a slower pace and typically do not attain the same mastery of new skills as do younger adults.

Noninvasive imaging studies reveal that aging is correlated with decreased white-matter volume, probably related to myelin loss. This condition is reparable. There is little evidence of neuronal loss in typical aging, although a reduction in neurogenesis in the hippocampus does occur. Compared with younger people, older people tend to activate larger regions of their attentional and executive networks (parietal and prefrontal cortices) when they perform complex cognitive and executive tasks. This increased activation correlates with reduced performance on tests of working memory, as well as on attentional and executive tasks.

Two lines of evidence suggest that age-related declines in function can be slowed. The first focuses on aerobic exercise to enhance general health and improve the brain's plasticity via increased neurogenesis, gliogenesis, and trophic factor support. The second involves brain exercise employing training strategies that enhance neural plasticity and reverse learned nonuse.

Most of us know the frustration of losing a skill—whether it's trigonometry or tennis—after getting out of practice. Skill loss does not reflect neurocognitive disorder,

**Brain Workout** Engaging in cognitively stimulating activities can prevent neural networks and general cognitive function from declining with age.

but simply a use-it-or-lose-it effect. Training programs designed to stimulate plasticity in the appropriate cerebral circuitry include motor, auditory, or visual system–based cognitive and/or attentional training. Brain training is designed to stimulate plasticity rather than to rehabilitate specific losses.

Brain-aging changes take place in the context of the entire body's aging. For example, a neurocognitive disorder may reflect the effects of a chronic cerebrovascular disorder, marginal high blood pressure. Marginal elevations in blood pressure can lead to cerebral microbleeds, especially in white matter. The cumulative effect of years or even decades of tiny bleeds may lead eventually to increasingly disturbed cognition. This condition may first appear as a *mild cognitive impairment* (*MCI*) that slowly progresses, with cumulative microbleeds, toward a neurocognitive disorder. For this reason, a healthy lifestyle that preserves the healthy function of the body also contributes to an enduring healthy brain.

View the progression of these microbleeds, or silent strokes, at https://www.youtube.com/watch?v=J3fb0CaDpEk.

# Treatments for Neurocognitive Disorders

The ultimate goal for behavioral neuroscience is to apply knowledge to generate treatments that can restore a disordered brain to a range of healthy functioning. This goal is daunting because the first task—learning what causes a particular behavioral disturbance—is so difficult. Few behavioral disorders have a cause as simple as PKU does. Most, like schizophrenia, are complex. A more achievable goal is to make small advances by improving current treatments, developing new treatments, and analyzing the causes of disease. Available treatments, while extensive, fall into four general categories:

1. *Neurosurgical.* The skull is opened, and some intervention is performed on the brain.

2. *Electrophysiological.* Brain function is modified by stimulation through the skull.

3. *Pharmacological.* A chemical that affects the brain is either ingested or injected.

4. *Behavioral.* Treatment manipulates the body or the experience, which in turn influences the brain.

## Neurosurgical Treatments

Neurosurgical manipulation of the nervous system is largely reparative, as when tumors are removed or arteriovenous (AV) malformations corrected. Typically, such neurosurgical interventions are successful. Advances include improved imaging of a target for surgery—as the surgery takes place—and methods that allow diseased tissue to be destroyed without opening the skull. For example, *radiosurgery* uses energy, such as X-rays directed from different sources, to converge on a target and destroy abnormal cells. Individual X-rays lack the energy to damage healthy cells through which they pass: tissue is destroyed only where multiple beams converge.

Treatment for Parkinson disease entails inactivating brain regions that produce tremors and regions participating in the production of muscular rigidity that impairs movement. An electrode is placed in the motor thalamus, and an electric current is used to damage neurons responsible for producing the unwanted effects. Alternatively, in **deep brain stimulation (DBS)**, an electrode fixed in place in the globus pallidus or subthalamic nucleus is connected to an external electrical stimulator that the person can activate (**Figure 16-19**). The stimulation can inactivate cells responsible for unwanted effects, thereby restoring more normal movement (Knight et al., 2015).

DBS is also used experimentally to treat TBI and behavioral dysfunctions such as obsessive-compulsive disorder and major depression (De Jesus et al., 2021). Electrodes implanted in the brain are well tolerated and remain effective for several years. Electrical stimulation can have an activating effect, relieving depression or compulsive behaviors. Stimulation may also make brain tissue more plastic and receptive to other treatments. During stimulation, individuals can learn more effective thought and behavioral patterns. For many conditions, DBS remains an experimental option of last resort. It is not a permanent cure: when the stimulation stops, beneficial effects are reduced—hence the importance of coupling DBS with cognitive-behavioral therapy.

Brain tumors are the topic of Clinical Focus 3-2. AV malformation, or angioma, is imaged in Figure 16-10.

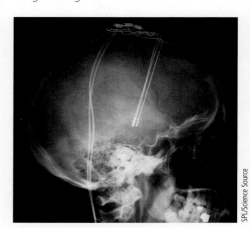

SPL/Science Source

**FIGURE 16-19 Deep Brain Stimulation** X-ray of a human brain showing electrodes implanted in the thalamus for DBS.

**deep brain stimulation (DBS)** Neurosurgery in which electrodes permanently implanted in the brain stimulate a targeted area with a low-voltage electrical current to facilitate behavior.

Another highly experimental neurosurgical strategy draws on the fixed sequence of prenatal brain development from cell division and cell differentiation to cell migration and synaptogenesis. If a brain region is functioning abnormally or if it is diseased or dead, as occurs in TBI or after a stroke, it should be possible to return this region to the embryonic state and regrow a healthy region. The use of *induced neurogenesis* has a science fiction ring but may someday be feasible. In laboratory rats, for example, stem cells can be induced by *neurotrophic factors* to generate new cells that can migrate to the site of an injury.

Figure 14-26 shows neurogenesis induced in a rat brain to repair a cortical stroke.

In the 1980s, neurosurgeons experimented with implanting fetal stem cells in adult brains. The success achieved with this approach was limited due to difficulties in cell placement, connections, and rejection by the transplant recipient's immune system. Another restorative idea comes from the discovery that multipotent stem cells in other body regions, such as bone marrow and skin, appear capable of manufacturing neural stem cells. Indeed, using appropriate manipulations, any cell can potentially be returned to a stem cell state. The advantage is that the person's own cells are not rejected by the immune system.

Figure 8-8 diagrams the origins of specialized brain cells from multipotent neural stem cells.

If people's own multipotent stem cells prove able to generate neural stem cells, it should be possible to extract stem cells, place them in a special culture medium to generate thousands or millions of cells, and then insert these stem cells into the damaged brain. The cells would be instructed to differentiate appropriately and develop the correct connections. Stem cell transplantation is taken seriously today as a potential treatment for many neurological conditions, including Parkinson disease, TBI, and stroke, but it remains largely at an investigative stage (Zhao et al., 2021).

## Electrophysiological Treatments

Treating the mind by treating the body is an ancient notion. In the 1930s, researchers used insulin to lower blood sugar and produce seizures as a treatment for depression. By the 1950s, insulin therapy had been replaced by electroconvulsive therapy (ECT), the first electrical brain stimulation treatment.

ECT was developed as a treatment for otherwise untreatable depression, and although its mode of action was not understood, it did prove useful. Less frequently used today, ECT sometimes remains the only treatment for people with severe depression. One reason may be that it stimulates the production of a variety of neurotrophic factors, especially BDNF, which in turn restores inactive cells to a more active mode.

Neurotrophic factors are nourishing chemical compounds that support neuronal growth, development, and viability.

Problems with ECT include the massive convulsions that electrical stimulation causes. Large doses of medication are required to prevent them. ECT also leads to memory loss, a symptom that can be troublesome with repeated treatments. A noninvasive technique called transcranial magnetic stimulation (TMS) uses magnetic rather than electrical stimulation. Magnetic stimulation can be applied to a localized brain region; anesthesia is not necessary. To date, TMS has been approved by the U.S. Food and Drug Administration as a treatment for depression. Clinical applications, reviewed in Research Focus 16-5: Treating Behavioral Disorders with Transcranial Magnetic Stimulation, are growing.

Clinical Focus 6-4 describes a case in which ECT was used to treat major depression. Figure 7-8 diagrams how TMS works.

## Pharmacological Treatments

Several accidental discoveries, beginning in the 1950s, led to a pharmacological revolution in the treatment of behavioral disorders. Here are some key examples:

1. The development of phenothiazines (neuroleptics) to treat schizophrenia stemmed from a drug used to premedicate surgical patients. In the decades that followed, new neuroleptic drugs became increasingly more selective, and they remain effective today.

2. A new class of antianxiety drugs was invented: the anxiolytics. Medications such as Valium quickly became—and remain—the most widely prescribed drugs in the United States.

3. L-Dopa provided the first drug treatment for serious motor dysfunction in Parkinson disease. Once taken, L-dopa is converted into and replaces dopamine lost due to Parkinson disease.

Clinical Focus 5-4 describes case studies in the use of L-dopa to treat Parkinson disease.

## ⊚ RESEARCH FOCUS 16-5

# Treating Behavioral Disorders with Transcranial Magnetic Stimulation

In transcranial magnetic stimulation (TMS), a magnetic coil placed over the scalp induces an electrical current in the underlying brain regions. TMS can be applied to localized brain regions (focal areas)

In clinical therapy for depression, TMS influences neural activity in a localized brain area.

Marcello Massimini/University of Milan

thought to be implicated in specific disorders. Manipulation of the magnetic field can stimulate an area of cortex as small as a quarter, the cortical surface only, or deeper layers of brain tissue.

The primary clinical use of TMS, which the U.S. Food and Drug Administration formally approved in 2008, is for depression. Numerous studies report positive effects using TMS, but the required duration of treatment and the duration of beneficial effects remain under investigation.

The effects of brief pulses of TMS do not outlive the stimulation. *Repetitive TMS* (rTMS), which involves continuous stimulation for up to several minutes, produces longer-lasting effects than TMS. Small but promising studies have also extended the possible benefits of TMS to schizophrenic auditory hallucinations, anxiety disorders, neurocognitive disorders, hemiparesis, and pain syndrome.

Among the problems in all studies of TMS are questions related to the duration and intensity of stimulation, as well as to the area stimulated. Each person's brain is slightly different, and to ensure that appropriate structures are stimulated, an MRI must be performed on each subject.

Does TMS stimulation make the brain more plastic? If so, can learning be enhanced? The key idea is that when TMS is delivered, it produces a change in cortical excitability. This change then facilitates learning. Indeed, the therapeutic effects of motor or cognitive training can be improved when combined with TMS (Bhattacharya et al., 2021).

---

The power of such drugs to change disordered behavior revolutionized the pharmaceutical industry.

The central goal is to develop drugs that can act as "magic bullets" to correct the chemical imbalances found in various disorders and that have fewer side effects than the drugs currently available. Both goals have proved difficult to achieve.

Pharmacological treatments have significant downsides. Acute and chronic side effects top the list, and long-term use may cause new problems. Consider a person who takes an antidepressant medication. The drug may ease the depression, but it may also cause decreased sexual desire, fatigue, sleep disturbance, and reduced cognitive functioning. Thus, although a medication may be useful for getting a person out of a depressed state, it may produce other symptoms that are themselves disturbing. Furthermore, in depression related to a person's life events, a drug does not provide the behavioral tools needed to cope with an adverse situation. One final time, "A pill is not a skill."

Negative side effects of drug treatments are evident in many people whose schizophrenia is being treated with neuroleptics. Antipsychotic drugs act on the mesolimbic dopamine system, which affects motivation, among other functions. The side effects emerge because these drugs also act on the nigrostriatal dopaminergic system, which controls movement. Individuals who take neuroleptics eventually develop motor disturbances. For example, **tardive dyskinesia**, an inability to stop the tongue, hands, or other body parts from moving, is a motor symptom of neuroleptic administration. Side effects of movement disorders can persist after treatment with the psychoactive medication has stopped. Taking drugs for behavioral disorders, then, does carry risk. Rather than being magic bullets, these medications often act like shotgun shells, whose pellets scatter wider than the intended target.

Despite their drawbacks, drugs do prove beneficial for many people. Improved drug chemistry promises to reduce side effects, as do improved delivery modes that bring a drug to a target system with minimal effects on other systems. One improved delivery system, illustrated in **Figure 16-20**, uses nanoparticles called *liposomes*, which are

Section 6-2 classifies psychoactive drugs and their therapeutic effects.

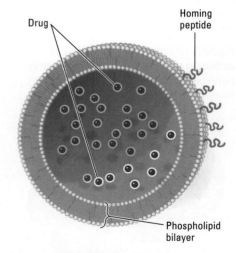

**FIGURE 16-20 Liposome for Drug Delivery** Biosynthetic vesicles can deliver microscopic drugs or DNA to the body's cells. Synthetic biology is discussed in Section 7-1.

---

**tardive dyskinesia** Inability to stop the tongue or other body parts from moving; motor side effect of neuroleptic drugs.

biosynthetic molecules 1 to 100 nm (nanometers, or billionths of a meter) in size. One natural biological nanoparticle, with a radius of about 40 nm, is the synaptic vesicle that houses a neurotransmitter for delivery into the cell's extracellular space. Liposomes consisting of a synthetic vesicle with a homing peptide on the surface can, in principle, be constructed to carry a drug across the blood–brain barrier and deliver it to specified types of neuron or glial cells within the nervous system.

## 16-3 Review

Before you continue, check your understanding. Answers to Self-Test appear at the back of the book.

1. _____, a wound to the brain resulting from a blow to the head, is the most common form of brain damage for people younger than age 40.

2. Interruption of blood to the brain is called _____, and if prolonged, it can result in _____.

3. The most common form of myelin disorder is _____.

4. Although superficially appearing to be very different diseases, Parkinson and Alzheimer disease are proposed to be caused by _____, which suggests that they may be part of a common disease spectrum.

5. Name two strategies that can reduce or reverse neurological and cognitive decline with aging.

## 16-4

# Research Challenges

Even if the problems of diagnosis were solved, major obstacles to investigating behavioral disorders would still exist, as is recognized by the National Institute of Health's BRAIN Initiative. This initiative provides funding for research that targets the following problems.

## Organizational Complexity

The nervous system far outstrips other body systems in terms of complexity. The brain contains a wider variety of cell types than does any other body organ, and nervous system cells and their connections are plastic: they change with experience. These features present a complex challenge to understanding healthy and disordered functioning.

## Systemic Complexity

As our understanding of brain and behavior has progressed, it has become apparent that multiple receptor systems serve widely varied functions. For example, the brain's major activating systems—those that employ acetylcholine, dopamine, norepinephrine, serotonin, and GABA—are diffuse, with little specificity between biochemistry and behavior. The neurotransmitter GABA affects some 30% of the brain's synapses. When people ingest a GABA agonist (such as a benzodiazepine) to treat anxiety, multiple effects on behavior become apparent. So it is with most drug treatments.

## Neuronal Plasticity

The nervous system can adapt to extreme stress or injury. Even the nigrostriatal dopaminergic system's close relationship to Parkinson disease is enigmatic (**Figure 16-21** illustrates the extent of this system). It is impossible to tie dopamine depletion to a consistent behavioral syndrome. Two people with Parkinson disease can exhibit vastly different symptoms, even though the common basis of the disease is a loss of neurons from the substantia nigra. Furthermore, only when the loss of dopamine neurons exceeds about 60% to 80% do investigators see clinical signs of Parkinson disease. Are all those dopamine cells not needed? That is unlikely, but this finding highlights the

### Learning Objectives

- Summarize some of the challenges facing research into neurological disorders.

Figure 5-19 summarizes major neural activating systems; Figure 6-8 shows how psychoactive drugs affect the GABA$_A$ receptor.

**FIGURE 16-21 Nigrostriatal Dopamine Pathways** Axons of neurons in the midbrain substantia nigra project to the basal ganglia, supplying dopamine to maintain healthy motor behavior. Dopamine loss contributes to muscle rigidity and dyskinesia in Parkinson disease.

brain's considerable compensatory plasticity. When a disease progresses slowly, the brain has a remarkable capacity for adapting.

## Compensatory Plasticity

Even the best technology produces uncertain relationships. MRI may show that a person with MS has many nervous system lesions, yet behaviorally that person may display few outward symptoms. Just as brain lesions do not always produce behavioral symptoms, behavioral symptoms are not always linked to obvious neuropathology. Clearly, people display compensatory plasticity: they can change their behavior to adapt to neural change, just as they can display disordered behavior without obvious brain pathology.

## Technological Resolution

Some people have notable behavioral problems after a brain trauma, yet no obvious signs of brain damage appear on their MRIs. An infant's brain may initially seem healthy, only to display severe cerebral palsy later. The resolution of an imaging technology may lack sufficient power to detect subtle neuronal changes, such as a drop in dendritic spine density or injury so diffuse that it is hard to identify. Given the current diagnostic methods for both behavioral disorders and neuropathology, identifying disorders and their causes is seldom easy.

Chapter 7 summarizes the benefits and deficiencies of a number of imaging technologies.

## Modeling Simplicity

A major avenue for investigating the causes of disorders is to develop and study animal models. Monkeys, rats, and mice with specific lesions of the nigrostriatal dopamine system are used to model Parkinson disease. Animal models can lead to significant advances in understanding neural conditions and their treatment, but the insights they provide into the neurobiology behind behavioral disorders can be oversimplified.

Section 7-8 reviews the benefits of creating animal models of disorders.

The fact that a drug reduces symptoms does not necessarily mean that it is acting on a key biochemical aspect of the pathology. Aspirin can get rid of a headache, but that does not mean the headache is caused by the receptors on which aspirin acts. Similarly, antipsychotic drugs block dopamine $D_2$ receptors, but that does not mean schizophrenia is caused by abnormal $D_2$ receptors. Schizophrenia quite possibly results from a disturbance in glutamatergic systems, and for some reason dopamine antagonists can either rectify the abnormality or, alternatively, produce effects on behavior that counteract the behavioral effects of schizophrenia.

## Modeling Limitations

Modeling human disorders is complex, and critical thinking is imperative when you encounter media reports about studies that describe possible cures for human behavioral diseases. Caution is especially in order when it comes to psychiatric disorders whose causes remain unknown. Furthermore, many symptoms of disorders such as schizophrenia and anxiety are largely cognitive. Objectively identifying any cognitive processes mimicked by a laboratory model is a difficult task.

## 16-5

# Posttraumatic Growth and Apathy

We began this book with the case of Fred Linge, who described his nontraditional therapy of faith, hope, and love to aid in his recovery from TBI. People have remarkable abilities to change their goals and an equally remarkable ability to compensate in response to disease and brain injury. This ability to learn to cope is referred to as **posttraumatic growth**. Factors that promote posttraumatic growth include social support, high levels of activity, a high number of life events, the availability of paid work, stable relationships after injury, and the presence of religious faith and/or a high

**Learning Objectives**
- Describe some of the factors that facilitate recovery or compensation following brain injury.

**posttraumatic growth** The ability to cope with and compensate for deficits resulting from brain injury and disease.

Tommy McHugh with one of his sandstone sculptures. To learn more and view McHugh's art, go to http://www.tommymchugh.co.uk.

**posttraumatic apathy** Condition characterized by diminished motivation and purposeful behavior following brain injury or disease.

level of purpose (Grace et al., 2015; Powell et al., 2012). In short, posttraumatic growth involves much of the nontraditional therapy described by Fred Linge.

Posttraumatic growth can also lead to expression of behaviors and skills that might otherwise not have been exploited. Consider this movie plot: a person sustains a blow to the head and then becomes a better person. Do pathological changes in brain and behavior sometimes lead to behavioral improvement in real life? A report by Jim Giles (2004) on Tommy McHugh's case is thought provoking.

McHugh (1949–2012), a heroin addict, committed multiple serious crimes and spent a great deal of time in jail. Later, he suffered a cerebral hemorrhage (bleeding into the brain) from an aneurysm. The bleeding was repaired surgically with a metal clip on the leaking artery. After he recovered from the injury, McHugh's personality changed. He took up painting, which he had never done before, and became a successful artist.

The phenomenon in which an individual acquires a new skill after an injury is called *acquired savant* syndrome, and it reflects the extent to which posttraumatic growth can progress. Many other reports describe people who have developed new musical or artistic talents after their injuries; a registry has been created to document such cases (Treffert & Treffert, 2021).

Just as coping with brain injury can be aided by posttraumatic growth, it may be hampered by **posttraumatic apathy** (Green et al., 2021). Apathy is a condition characterized by diminished motivation and purposeful behavior. The involvement of growth and apathy as behaviors mediated by the brain must be recognized as consequences of brain injury.

Formal therapy and drug treatment of brain disease is clearly helpful, as we have documented. Nevertheless, posttraumatic growth can also be enhanced with old-fashioned but readily available methods, social support, employment, and a sense of purpose. The enhancement of posttraumatic growth can also serve as a countermeasure to posttraumatic apathy.

# Summary

## 16-1 Multidisciplinary Contributions to Brain and Behavior

Contemporary understanding of brain and behavior provides new insights, explanations, and treatments for brain disorders. Health professionals who treat behavioral disorders are forging a unified understanding of mind and brain. Clinical neuroscience is a specialty that focuses on the diagnosis and treatment of diseases and disorders affecting the brain and central nervous system.

Disorders can be classified according to their presumed etiology (cause), symptomatology, or pathology. The classification systems developed by psychologists, psychiatrists, and neurologists overlap, and each is revised from time to time. Clearly, better comprehension of the causes of disorders will lead to better classification systems. Advances in genetics and brain imaging will aid this effort. The table summarizes the range of available treatments, from highly invasive neurosurgery to noninvasive electrophysiology, and from moderately invasive pharmacology to behavioral treatments.

## General Treatment Categories

| Neurosurgical | Behavioral |
|---|---|
| *Direct intervention* | *Manipulation of experience* |
| DBS | Behavior modification |
| Stem cell transplantation | Cognitive, cognitive-behavioral therapy |
| Tissue removal or repair | Neuropsychological |
| **Electrophysiological** | Emotional therapy, psychotherapy |
| *Noninvasive manipulation* | |
| ECT | Physical activity, music |
| TMS, rTMS | rt-fMRI |
| Pharmacological | VR exposure and other computer-based simulations |
| *Chemical administration* | |
| Antibiotics or antivirals | |
| Psychoactive drugs | |
| Neurotrophic factors | |
| Nutrition | |

## 16-2 Psychiatric Disorders

Psychiatric disorders, including psychoses, mood disorders (such as major depression), and anxiety disorders, are assumed to be caused by brain malfunction. Psychoses, of which schizophrenia is the most common and best understood, are characterized by loss of contact with reality. Schizophrenia can produce a wide range of symptoms, influenced by individual differences, and its causes have genetic, developmental, anatomical, and neurochemical correlates. Mood disorders include major depression and anxiety disorders. Psychological factors in understanding depression relate to the brain's reactivity to stress. Anxiety disorders often accompany depression, but can also occur separately.

### 16-3 Neurological Disorders

Neurological disorders are the result of damage to the brain. Traumatic brain injury (TBI) is a wound to the brain as a result of a blow to the head or body. Mild TBI, which includes concussion, is currently the subject of a large-scale longitudinal study. Stroke is an interruption of blood flow due to blockage (ischemic) or bleeding (hemorrhagic) of a vessel, which can cause a cascade of pathological events. Epilepsy is characterized by recurrent seizures, which can be recorded on an EEG. Seizures can be focal or generalized, and treatment can be pharmacological or, in cases of intractable epilepsy, surgical. Multiple sclerosis is an autoimmune disorder that results in damage to the myelin sheaths that encase the axons, and eventually leads to paraplegia.

Neurocognitive disorders involve progressive loss of function in neurons, or the loss of neurons themselves. Memory loss and an acquired and persistent syndrome of intellectual impairment characterize many neurocognitive disorders, including Alzheimer and Parkinson diseases. The prion theory of progressive neurocognitive disorders suggests that these disorders may be caused by abnormally folded proteins. Treatments for neurocognitive disorders include neurosurgical, electrophysiological, and pharmacological therapies.

### 16-4 Research Challenges

Most behavioral disorders have multiple causes, including genetic, epigenetic, biochemical, anatomical, and social–environmental variables—all of them interacting. Although innovations in research methods, imaging technology, and genetic and epigenetic discoveries have vastly improved our capacity to diagnose and treat disorders, researchers are confronted with several major obstacles when investigating behavior, including organizational complexity, systemic complexity, neuronal plasticity, compensatory plasticity, technological resolution, modeling simplicity, and modeling limitations.

### 16-5 Posttraumatic Growth and Apathy

People with a behavioral disorder can achieve remarkable recovery while still dealing with their disabilities, a capacity called posttraumatic growth. They can also show posttraumatic apathy, a condition characterized by little interest in recovery. Factors that promote posttraumatic growth include social support, high-activity levels, a high number of life events, having paid work, new stable relationships after injury, milder disability, and having religious faith and/or having a high level of purpose.

## Key Terms

akathisia, p. 589

anxiety disorder, p. 577

autoimmune disease, p. 587

behavioral modification, p. 573

bipolar disorder, p. 577

chronic traumatic encephalopathy (CTE), p. 582

clinical neuroscience, p. 569

cognitive therapy, p. 573

cognitive-behavioral therapy (CBT), p. 579

deep brain stimulation (DBS), p. 593

*Diagnostic and Statistical Manual of Mental Disorders* (DSM), p. 571

diaschisis, p. 584

festination, p. 589

focal seizure, p. 585

generalized seizure, p. 585

hemorrhagic stroke, p. 583

HPA axis, p. 578

ischemic stroke, p. 583

Lewy body, p. 591

major depression, p. 577

mania, p. 577

neurocognitive disorder, p. 587

neuroprotectant, p. 584

phenylketonuria (PKU), p. 568

posttraumatic apathy, p. 598

posttraumatic growth, p. 597

posttraumatic stress disorder (PTSD), p. 568

prion, p. 591

psychotherapy, p. 573

real-time fMRI (rt-fMRI), p. 574

tardive dyskinesia, p. 595

virtual reality (VR) exposure therapy, p. 568

## Selected Resources from  Achieve

**Neuroscience in Action:** TBI and Stroke: Assessment and Outcomes of Brain Damage

**Videos**

Wendy Suzuki: The Brain-Changing Benefits of Exercise

Cognitive Therapies

Therapeutic Effectiveness: The Placebo Effect

Chronic Traumatic Encephalophathy (CTE): A Growing Problem

The Science of CTE

Anxiety Disorders

Child Anxiety Disorder: Clinical Features and Treatment

Depression

Why Do Depression and Anxiety Go Together?

Schizophrenia

Schizophrenia: New Definitions, New Therapies

Alzheimer's and the Brain

Alzheimer's Research Within Families

**LearningCurve**

**Practice Quiz**

ANSWERS TO SECTION REVIEW SELF-TESTS

## CHAPTER 1

### REVIEW 1-1
1. Traumatic brain injury (TBI)
2. central nervous system (CNS); peripheral nervous system (PNS)
3. forebrain; cerebellum
4. inherited; learning *or* experience
5. Research on embodied behavior proposes that we understand each other not only by listening to words, but also by observing gestures and other body language. In addition, it proposes that we think not only with silent language, but also with overt gestures and body language.
6. Your answer should explore the idea that our behavior consists of many unconscious functions that are robotlike as well as learning-dependent conscious functions that are AI-like.

### REVIEW 1-2
1. mentalism; dualism; materialism
2. natural selection
3. minimally conscious state *or* MCS
4. *in any order:* Mendelian genetics; epigenetics
5. Descartes theorized that demonstrations of language and memory were central to the presence of a mind, a concept carried forward in Turing's imitation game, which was devised to test consciousness. The ability of nonhuman animals to use language and retain the relationship between words and concepts is the focus of a number of experimental communication studies.
6. In formulating the theory of natural selection, Darwin relied on observation to conclude that living organisms are related and pass traits from parents to offspring. Mendel used experimentation to show that heritable factors underlie phenotypic variation among species.

### REVIEW 1-3
1. muscles
2. nerve net; brain
3. cladogram
4. Brain size is related to new forms of locomotion and movement, such that increases in the size of brain structures accommodate more complex movement.
5. Human beings belong to the animal kingdom, and an understanding of our common ancestry with and relationship to other animals can give us insights into the development of human brains and behavior.

### REVIEW 1-4
1. common ancestor; chimpanzee
2. multiple hominin species
3. packing density
4. energy
5. A neuron's energy cost is relatively constant across species, so any adaptation to support this energy cost is beneficial. The ability to prepare food through hot and cold cooking allows humans to maximize the energy obtained from food, which supports activities other than those directed at food foraging and fosters genetic mutations that trade movement strength for movement skill.
6. Brain cell count, neuron size, and packing density in specific brain regions can all be used to describe brain complexity and behavioral capacity, and these measures can be used to draw comparisons and contrasts across species. For example, similarities in the number of neurons in the cortex of apes and elephants suggest that they should have equivalent cognitive abilities, which they do.

### REVIEW 1-5
1. species-typical behavior
2. *g*
3. Flynn effect
4. multiple intelligences
5. memes
6. In comparing different species, a larger brain correlates with more complex behavior. In comparing individuals within a species, brain size and intelligence are only remotely related. Instead, the complexity of different brain regions is related to behavioral abilities. Humans, for example, vary widely in body size and in brain size, as well as in having different kinds of intelligence. All these factors make any simple comparison of individuals' brain sizes and intelligence impossible.
7. Researchers have proposed that humans have a number of intelligences. Like other traits, genetic and phenotypic variation in intelligence has adaptive value, both in making the group resistant to environmental change and disease and in fostering innovation.

## CHAPTER 2

### REVIEW 2-1
1. behavior; brain
2. *in any order:* frontal; temporal; parietal; occipital

3. neuroplasticity (*or* plasticity)
4. white matter; gray matter
5. tracts; nerves
6. Compare your diagram or description with Figure 2-2B.

### REVIEW 2-2
1. *in any order:* forebrain; midbrain; hindbrain
2. These studies indicate there are multiple evolutionary paths to intelligence.
3. The forebrain has expanded dramatically over the course of vertebrate evolution. However, archaic brain forms have not been discarded or replaced as more complex nervous systems have emerged. Thus, the forebrain's expansion is an elaboration of functions already present in the other brain regions and leads to its functioning on multiple levels.

### REVIEW 2-3
1. spinal cord
2. hindbrain; midbrain; diencephalon
3. cerebellum
4. allocortex; neocortex; *in any order:* sensory; motor; integrative (*or* cognitive)
5. **F**unction, **A**natomy, **C**onnections, and **T**opography
6. Unlike other parts of the brain, which tend to connect to only certain other parts of the brain, the neocortex connects to almost all other parts of the brain, so it is involved in a vast range of functions.

### REVIEW 2-4
1. *in any order:* cranial nerves; spinal (peripheral) nerves
2. left
3. *in any order:* head; internal organs and glands
4. The law of Bell and Magendie states that sensory (afferent) spinal nerve fibers are dorsal (in humans, posterior) and that motor (efferent) spinal fibers are ventral (in humans, anterior). This law allows neurologists to predict the location of spinal cord damage accurately, based on changes in sensation or movement.

### REVIEW 2-5
1. ganglia
2. sympathetic; parasympathetic
3. The ANS operates largely outside our conscious awareness, whether we are awake or asleep, to regulate the vegetative functions essential to life.

4. The ENS contains a wide range of neuron types, chemical transmitters, glial cells, and complex neural circuits, similar to the brain.

5. Psychobiotics are live organisms that, when ingested in adequate amounts, can benefit people who have a behavioral disorder.

**REVIEW 2-6**

1. Neuronal circuits are series of synaptically interconnected neurons. They can be considered functional units because the nervous system requires circuits to sense the world and control movements.

2. *in any order:* olfactory system; somatic nervous system; ANS; ENS

3. *in either order:* excitation; inhibition

4. Any individual's perceived reality is only an approximation of what is actually present. An animal's representation of the world depends on the nature of the sensed information and the circuitry and networks in the animal's brain.

## CHAPTER 3

**REVIEW 3-1**

1. *in either order:* neurons; glial cells

2. *in either order:* exciting; inhibiting

3. *in any order:* sensory neurons; motor neurons; three types of interneurons: stellate cells, pyramidal cells, and Purkinje cells

4. *in any order:* ependymal cells; astrocytes; microglia; oligodendroglia; Schwann cells

5. astrocytes

6. Robots are capable of producing goal-oriented actions, as well as sensing the world around them and coordinating actions in response, much as animals do. Researchers can thus construct robotic models to confirm hypotheses about human nervous system function, such as the excitation and inhibition of neurons. Information derived from this work can also be used to further refine robot models to more closely function like an animal's nervous system.

7. Researchers working in neuromorphic computing and other approaches to AI look to understand the structure and function of the brain so they can build more powerful computers that will respond and adapt to uncertainty and ambiguity in the natural world—a process called machine learning.

**REVIEW 3-2**

1. *in any order:* cell membrane; nucleus; endoplasmic reticulum (*or* ER); Golgi bodies; microtubules (*or* tubules); vesicles

2. *in any order:* channels; gates; pumps

3. DNA; RNA; protein

4. endoplasmic reticulum (*or* ER); Golgi bodies; microtubules; exocytosis

5. By using most of the proteins that it makes, a cell enables itself to interact with other cells and to modify their behavior. The collective action of cells mediates behavior.

6. A protein's shape and its ability to change shape are central to its function. Though proteins can vary somewhat in structure and remain functional, misfolded proteins (called prions) can wreak havoc in more than 100 nervous system diseases by causing other proteins to misfold.

**REVIEW 3-3**

1. 23; protein

2. alleles

3. mutation

4. Down syndrome; trisomy

5. recessive; dominant

6. CRISPR (*or* clustered regularly interspaced short palindromic repeat) *or* CRISPR/Cas9; spacer; RNA (*or* gRNA, guide RNA)

7. Gene methylation *or* DNA methylation

8. Mendelian genetics concentrates on inheritance patterns—that is, which genes parents pass to their offspring, and those offspring pass to succeeding generations. Epigenetics is the study of how the environment and experience can affect the inherited genome.

9. Genes expressed in a cell are influenced by factors within the cell and in the cell's environment. Epigenetic mechanisms, such as histone modification, gene methylation, and mRNA modification, can influence gene function by blocking a gene to prevent transcription or by unlocking a gene so that it can be transcribed. Environmental and experiential factors, including stress or reductions in stress, can induce changes in our brain that make us unique individuals.

## CHAPTER 4

**REVIEW 4-1**

1. electricity

2. stimulation; recording

3. *in either order:* concentration gradient (from an area of relatively high concentration to an area of lower concentration); voltage gradient (from an area of relatively high electric potential to an area of lower electric potential)

4. We discovered how to record from the giant axons of the North Atlantic squid; how to use an oscilloscope to measure small changes in voltage; and how to craft microelectrodes small enough to place on or in an axon.

5. Ion channels in cell membranes may open to facilitate ion movement, close to impede ion movement, or pump ions across the membrane.

**REVIEW 4-2**

1. resting potential; ions

2. semipermeable; negative

3. hyperpolarization; depolarization

4. excitatory postsynaptic potentials (EPSPs); inhibitory postsynaptic potentials (IPSPs)

5. When multiple EPSPs or multiple IPSPs occur in rapid succession, they will combine to depolarize or hyperpolarize the membrane—this is temporal summation. Similarly, multiple EPSPs or multiple IPSPSs occurring close together on the membrane will combine to depolarize or hyperpolarize the membrane—this is spatial summation.

**REVIEW 4-3**

1. cell body; initial segment; axon

2. action potential; nerve impulse

3. absolutely refractory; relatively refractory

4. Nerve impulses travel more rapidly on myelinated axons because of saltatory conduction: action potentials leap between the nodes separating the glial cells that form the axon's myelin sheath.

5. Some neurons have voltage-activated channels on their dendrites that allow the reverse movement of an action potential into the neurons' dendritic fields.

**REVIEW 4-4**

1. ion channel

2. sensory receptor cell; voltage-activated

3. motor; muscles

4. autoimmune; acetylcholine

5. Each different type of membrane channel performs a different function, including generating the transmembrane charge, mediating graded potentials, and triggering the action potential. The varieties of channels evolved as new species of animals and new behaviors evolved.

## CHAPTER 5

**REVIEW 5-1**

1. chemical synapses; gap junction (*or* electrical synapse)

2. experience; learning

3. axodendritic; axosomatic; axomuscular; axoaxonic; axosynaptic; axoextracellular; axosecretory; dendrodendritic

4. dendrite; cell body *or* soma

5. (1) A chemical transmitter is synthesized inside the neuron and then (2) packaged and stored in the axon terminal. Next, when an action potential reaches an axon terminal, it is (3) transported to the presynaptic membrane and released into the synaptic cleft. The transmitter (4) binds to and activates receptors on the postsynaptic membrane. The transmitter is (5) degraded or removed.

### REVIEW 5-2

1. *in any order:* synthesis; release; receptor action; inactivation

2. *in any order:* small-molecule transmitters; peptide transmitters; gaseous transmitters; lipid transmitters; ion transmitter

3. *in either order:* acetate, choline; acetylcholinesterase *or* AChE

4. lipid; postsynaptic

5. An ionotropic receptor's pore or channel can be opened or closed to regulate the flow of ions through it, directly effecting rapid and usually excitatory voltage changes on the cell membrane. Metabotropic receptors, which are generally inhibitory and slow acting, activate second messengers to indirectly produce changes in cell function and structure.

### REVIEW 5-3

1. acetylcholine *or* ACh; cholinergic; cholinergic; noradrenergic

2. *in either order:* serotonin *or* 5-HT; dopamine *or* DA

3. *in any order:* cholinergic; dopaminergic; noradrenergic; serotonergic

4. This idea has been attractive for a long time because a clear relationship exists between DA loss in the substantia nigra and Parkinson disease, and because acetylcholine and norepinephrine are clearly related to somatic and autonomic behaviors. But for other neurotransmitter systems in the brain, establishing clear one-to-one relationships has proved difficult.

### REVIEW 5-4

1. neurohormones; pituitary gland; releasing hormones; brain

2. *in any order:* peptides; amino acids; lipids; steroids

3. homeostatic; gonadal; glucocorticoids

4. anabolic (*or* anabolic–androgenic) steroids; muscle mass; masculinizing

5. epinephrine; cortisol

6. The hippocampus is important in ending the stress response by regulating cortisol levels. If the cortisol level remains elevated owing to prolonged stress, eventually it will damage the hippocampus.

7. Neurotransmitters are released by presynaptic neurons and influence adjacent postsynaptic neurons. Neuromodulators diffuse from a neuron to produce effects on receptors in an entire brain region. Hormones are released by neurons or other tissue and are distributed throughout the body and brain via the circulatory system. All three can be chemically identical, but are distinguished by the distance they travel from their release point.

## CHAPTER 6

### REVIEW 6-1

1. Psychoactive drugs; psychopharmacology

2. blood–brain barrier; brain

3. synapses; agonists; antagonists

4. tolerance; sensitization

5. *in any order:* feces; urine; sweat; breath; breast milk

6. (a) Drug use at home is unlikely to condition drug-taking behavior to familiar home cues, so tolerance is likely to occur.

    (b) Novel cues in a work setting may enhance conditioning and so sensitize the person who uses drugs only occasionally.

### REVIEW 6-2

1. Caffeine; adenosine

2. GABA$_A$; Cl$^-$ *or* chloride ion

3. serotonin

4. endorphins

5. release; reuptake; D$_2$

6. Psychotropic drugs act on many neurotransmitter systems, including acetylcholine, anandamide, dopamine, epinephrine, glutamate, norepinephrine, and serotonin.

### REVIEW 6-3

1. Behavioral myopia

2. Substance use disorder (*or* SUD); addiction

3. psychomotor activation; mesolimbic dopamine system

4. women; men

5. Behavioral myopia theory suggests that intoxicated individuals are unusually responsive to local and immediate cues, so the environment excessively influences their behavior, while consequences go ignored.

### REVIEW 6-4

1. liking (pleasure); tolerance; wanting (craving); sensitization

2. frontal cortex; brainstem; mesolimbic dopamine system (pathways); basal ganglia

3. epigenetics

4. drugs; other life experiences

5. A reasonable approach to treatment views substance use disorder in the same way as chronic behavioral addictions and medical problems are viewed: as a lifelong challenge for most people.

## CHAPTER 7

### REVIEW 7-1

1. *in either order:* brain function, behavior; neuropsychology

2. sectioning; staining; multiphoton imaging

3. touchscreen platforms

4. G protein–coupled receptors (*or* GPCR)

5. Brain-stimulation methods include using electrical pulses, as in DBS; magnetic fields, as in TMS; ultrasonic beams, as in HIFU; chemicals, by administering drugs; or the transgenic techniques of optogenetics (which employs light), chemogenetics (which employs synthetic drugs to interact exclusively with designer receptors), or genetic engineering, in the case of CRISPR-Cas9 techniques. GRAB technology uses fluorescent proteins at the receptor to allow researchers to visualize neurotransmitter–receptor interactions.

### REVIEW 7-2

1. *in any order:* single-cell recording; EEG; ERP; MEG

2. action

3. graded

4. magnetic; cell (*or* neuron) groups

5. EEG is much less expensive than MEG.

### REVIEW 7-3

1. *in either order:* computed tomography (*or* CT) scan; magnetic resonance imaging (*or* MRI)

2. neural connections (*or* fiber pathways); brain metabolites

3. brain injury *or* brain damage

4. CT produces X-ray images of one object from many angles and then uses scanning software to combine them into a three-dimensional image of the brain.

### REVIEW 7-4

1. *in any order:* functional magnetic resonance imaging (*or* fMRI); optical tomography (*or* fNIRS); functional positron emission tomography (*or* PET)

2. radioactively labeled molecules; neurochemical

3. cerebral blood flow

4. Resting-state images in PET and rs-fMRI can identify abnormalities in brain

function. rs-fMRI can also identify functional connections in the resting brain.

### REVIEW 7-5

1. biochemical; *in either order:* microdialysis; voltammetry

2. concordance rates

3. DNA; gene expression

4. Epigenetic studies show that life experiences can alter gene expression and that these changes are associated with changes in neuronal structure and connectivity. Altered neuronal organization, in turn, is associated with changes in behavior.

### REVIEW 7-6

1. *in any order:* temporal resolution; spatial resolution; invasiveness

2. *any one or more:* EEG, ERP, *and/or* fNIRS

3. Answers will vary but should touch on one or more of the methods described in Table 7-2. For example, cerebral voltammetry can be used to measure the change in dopamine concentration in the nucleus accumbens following the introduction of corticosterone, as was done by Wheeler and his colleagues.

### REVIEW 7-7

1. *in either order:* natural; artificial

2. biologically; *in any order:* development, structure, physiology, cognitive abilities

3. Your answer should draw on the potential for advances across any number of fields, including medicine, law, commerce, and education, to name just a few. But your answer should also consider dangers in our ability to control AI and predict its use.

### REVIEW 7-8

1. neuroethics

2. behavioral

3. Animal Welfare Act

4. Animal experimentation can help researchers better understand the functions of the human and nonhuman body, brain, and behavior, as well as develop medicines and treatments for humans and other animals.

5. The field of neuroethics is interested in the ethical implications of our use of the tools of science—what are the potential risks to individuals and to society of certain applications and of the information that may be gained from them, and what parameters should be considered to avoid these risks.

### CHAPTER 8

### REVIEW 8-1

1. behavior

2. neural circuits

3. *any three in any order:* hormones; sensory experience; injuries; genes; factors associated with SES

4. Behaviors cannot emerge until the requisite neural structures are sufficiently mature.

### REVIEW 8-2

1. neural tube

2. neurogenesis; gliogenesis

3. *in either order:* cell adhesion molecules (*or* CAMs); tropic factors

4. hippocampus

5. Dynamic changes in frontal lobe structure (morphology) are related to the development of intelligence.

### REVIEW 8-3

1. independent finger movements *or* the pincer grasp

2. vocabulary; sound processing

3. growth spurts

4. temporal lobe; basal ganglia

5. Correlation does not prove causation: changes in either behavior or the brain are likely to interact such that neither directly causes the other.

### REVIEW 8-4

1. chemoaffinity hypothesis

2. accelerate; shorten

3. testosterone; estrogens

4. critical periods *or* sensitive periods

5. Adolescence is a time of rapid brain change related to pubertal hormones and psychosocial stressors, both of which heighten the brain's vulnerability to disorders.

### REVIEW 8-5

1. critical

2. SIDS *or* sudden infant death syndrome

3. visual *or* sensory

4. The brain retains its plasticity, or capacity to change, adapt, and learn, throughout our lifetimes.

5. Egg cells are formed early in female development and are not easily changed by experience. Because sperm is constantly being renewed, gene expression in males is more likely to be altered by experience and passed on through the germline.

### CHAPTER 9

### REVIEW 9-1

1. Sensory receptors

2. Receptive; density

3. *in either order:* thalamus; cortex

4. subjective

5. Each modality has many receptors and sends information to the cortex to form topographic maps.

### REVIEW 9-2

1. retinal ganglion cells *or* RGCs

2. P *or* Parvocellular; M *or* magnocellular

3. *in either order:* geniculostriate; tectopulvinar

4. facial agnosia *or* prosopagnosia

5. The dorsal stream to the parietal lobe processes the visual guidance of movements (the *how*). The ventral stream to the temporal lobe processes the visual perception of objects (the *what*). Information related to *where* is conveyed through both the *how* and *what* pathways.

### REVIEW 9-3

1. receptive fields

2. photoreceptors; retinal ganglion; lateral geniculate nucleus

3. topographic map

4. corpus callosum

5. The fovea is represented by a larger area in the cortex than the visual field's periphery. Thus, more processing of foveal information occurs in region V1 compared to processing of peripheral information.

### REVIEW 9-4

1. bars of light

2. temporal

3. trichromatic theory

4. opponent

5. RGCs are excited by one wavelength of light and inhibited by another, producing two pairs of what seem to be color opposites—red versus green and blue versus yellow.

6. Our unconscious assumptions are a necessary component of our visual system's color constancy. Respondents to "The Dress" assumed a light source (either sunlight or incandescent light), and that assumption then influenced their perception of the dress color.

### REVIEW 9-5

1. hemianopia

2. scotomas

3. monocular blindness

4. optic ataxia

5. Damage to the dorsal stream produces deficits in visually guided movements. Damage to the ventral stream produces deficits in object recognition.

### REVIEW 9-6

1. amblyopia

2. temporal

3. echolocation; auditory

4. Our visual system, like our other sensory systems, is continually being altered by experience. Individuals who have

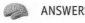

incurred some injury to a structure in the visual pathway can show significant recovery as their brains adapt and change to accommodate the injury, through rewiring of the pathway.

## CHAPTER 10

### REVIEW 10-1

1. air pressure waves *or* compression waves *or* sound waves
2. *in either order:* frequency, amplitude; complexity
3. *in any order:* loudness; pitch; prosody; quality *or* timbre
4. temporal
5. Delivery speed, or the number of sound segments that can be analyzed per second, distinguishes speech and musical sounds from other auditory inputs. Nonlanguage sounds that are about 5 segments per second are heard as a buzz, yet we are capable of understanding speech delivered at nearly 30 segments per second. Random or aperiodic sounds are perceived as noise.

### REVIEW 10-2

1. ossicles *or, in any order,* hammer, anvil, and stirrup
2. inner hair cells; cochlea *or* organ of Corti
3. *in either order:* basilar; tectorial
4. auditory *or* cochlear; auditory vestibular *or* eighth
5. inferior colliculus; medial geniculate nucleus
6. The planum temporale is larger in the left hemisphere, and Heschl's gyrus is larger in the right hemisphere. In most people, this anatomical asymmetry correlates to a functional asymmetry: the left temporal cortex analyzes language-related sounds, whereas the right temporal cortex analyzes music-related ones.

### REVIEW 10-3

1. tonotopic
2. cochlea
3. *in either order:* superior olive; trapezoid body
4. audition for action
5. The brain detects a sound's location via two mechanisms. Neurons in the brainstem (hindbrain) compute the ITD, the time difference in a sound wave's arrival at each ear. Other neurons in the brainstem compute IID, the difference in sound amplitude (loudness) in each ear.
6. Because the implantation process requires destruction of the organ of Corti and the basilar membrane, external sounds can no longer be perceived except those from the cranial nerve

stimulator. The cochlear implant, however, detects sound via a microphone processor, and translates the amplitudes and frequencies of incoming sound waves into electrical stimulation that is passed directly to the appropriate locations on the cochlear nerve.

### REVIEW 10-4

1. language; music
2. *in any order:* Broca's area; supplementary speech area; face area of motor cortex
3. Wernicke's
4. Broca's
5. perfect (*or* absolute) pitch; amusia *or* tone deafness
6. Three lines of evidence support the idea that language is innate: the universality of language, the natural acquisition of language by children, and the presence of syntax in all languages.

### REVIEW 10-5

1. epigenetic
2. left
3. spectrogram
4. Birdsong dialects demonstrate that the songs young birds hear influence how they sing.
5. As noted at the beginning of the chapter, the ability to produce and perceive music likely preceded language in the hominin evolutionary history, as did the neural mechanisms allowing for the processing and production of music. That other animal species demonstrate an enjoyment of musical sounds beyond their social or biological function indicates that the appreciation of music that compelled our hominin ancestors to spend valuable time crafting and using instruments extends to other animals as well, suggesting even deeper roots in our genetic lineage.

## CHAPTER 11

### REVIEW 11-1

1. *in either order:* hierarchical; parallel
2. (*in any order*) prefrontal; premotor; motor (*or* M1)
3. brainstem
4. spinal cord
5. Quadriplegia is cessation of sensation and movement in the arms and legs that results from complete severing of the spinal cord at the C1–C2 level. Paraplegia results from a cut below the cervical nerves and involves paralysis and loss of sensation only in the legs and lower body.
6. The forebrain—particularly the frontal lobe—is involved in planning,

selecting, and coordinating our skilled movements. The brainstem produces adaptive species-typical movement and coordinates complex actions such as standing and walking. Nerves running through the spinal cord execute movement. In addition to relaying information from the brain to the body, the spinal cord contains some complex motor programs, though the brain is needed to guide these movements.

### REVIEW 11-2

1. *in either order:* body, action
2. Position-point
3. lateral corticospinal; anterior corticospinal
4. trunk; *in either order:* limb (*or* arm), finger (*or* digit)
5. muscles; *in either order:* flexes, extends
6. Body maps, which are found across the primary motor cortex, correspond to different parts of the body (with body parts sized relative to the brain areas associated with them). Action maps represent actions organized into functional movement categories.
7. Researchers theorize that motor neurons in the spinal cord have an action map similar to those in the motor cortex. Thus, despite their isolation from the brain following injury, movement might still be organized by spinal interneurons and motor neurons following electrical stimulation.

### REVIEW 11-3

1. basal ganglia; force
2. hyperkinetic; hypokinetic
3. errors
4. Both diseases are associated with damage to the basal ganglia, a structure that likely plays a role in regulating movement force. In hyperkinetic disorders, such as Huntington disease, damage leads to too much force and excessive movement. In hypokinetic disorders, such as Parkinson disease, too little force is applied, leading to insufficient movement.
5. Both the cerebellum and the cerebrum are involved in related sensory, motor, and cognitive functions. They have increased in tandem over the development of the human species as the capacity for more complex behavior has increased.

### REVIEW 11-4

1. hapsis; proprioception; nociception
2. posterior; anterior
3. pain gate
4. periaqueductal gray matter *or* PAG
5. vestibular; balance

6. Phantom limb pain is a form of central pain, which is the experience of pain in the absence of an ongoing ailment. It may be related to abnormalities in the reorganization of cortical maps following amputation of a limb, or it may be related to persistent activity in the cortical map related to the amputated limb.

7. Without proprioception, sensory information about body location and movement is lost and can be regained only by using vision.

### REVIEW 11-5

1. body
2. action
3. apraxia
4. dorsal visual; ventral visual
5. Studies have demonstrated that unpredictability plays a role in the tickle perception. Because we can predict when we are about to tickle ourselves, we do not perceive the tickle sensation in these cases.
6. Answers to this question should address the communal nature of tickling (i.e., we cannot tickle ourselves), which suggests that it is a form of communication between two individuals. Additionally, the laughter from tickling is distinct from other forms of laughter, and can help to strengthen bonds between individuals, as can other forms of play.

### CHAPTER 12

### REVIEW 12-1

1. rewarding
2. stimulation
3. androgen
4. innate releasing mechanisms *or* IRMs
5. In general, behavior is controlled by neural circuits that are modulated by a wide range of factors.

### REVIEW 12-2

1. regulatory; nonregulatory
2. hypothalamus
3. pituitary gland
4. The behavioral column is composed of brainstem regions devoted to social behaviors, ingesting, and exploration and foraging behaviors. These functions are modulated by the cerebral hemispheres. The hypothalamus acts to organize these cerebral inputs and produce feedback loops that regulate cerebral information to orchestrate homeostasis and motivate behaviors.

### REVIEW 12-3

1. olfactory epithelium
2. orbitofrontal cortex *or* orbital frontal cortex *or* OFC

3. allele of the taste receptor gene *TAS2R38*; taste buds
4. (*in any order*) Parkinson disease, dementia, COVID-19
5. According to Rozin and others, our neural system for controlling our behaviors via input from our chemical senses became harnessed to a cognitive evaluation system that was then able to respond to more abstract things, such as people, groups, and actions. This evaluation system was later extended to include moral offenses, such as violations of fairness and of taboos.
6. There is a vital link between human olfaction and social behavior. A growing body of evidence indicates that humans can identify their own odor, the odor of kin versus non-kin, and the odor of friends versus strangers, and that these different odors activate different regions of the brain.

### REVIEW 12-4

1. *in any order:* lateral hypothalamus; ventromedial hypothalamus; paraventricular nucleus
2. enteric
3. Osmotic; hypovolemic
4. Cognitive factors that control eating include thinking about food and the association between environmental cues and the act of eating. The constant pairing of environmental cues with eating can result in the cues alone motivating eating behavior. Some eating disorders have a cognitive component.

### REVIEW 12-5

1. *in either order:* hypothalamus; amygdala
2. *in either order:* organizing effects; activating effects
3. medial preoptic area; the amygdala
4. default (*or* default mode)
5. Variations in epigenetics effects could lead to different architecture and function of the hypothalamus among heterosexual, homosexual, and transgender individuals.

### REVIEW 12-6

1. *in any order:* constructivist; appraisal; neuropsychological
2. *in any order:* hypothalamus; amygdala; prefrontal cortex
3. Emotions are associated with a wide range of human behaviors and physiological responses; they encompass thoughts and plans related to past experience and future activity, suggesting the influence of different neural systems. The experience of emotions is subjective, making their components difficult to localize in the brain. The language used to describe

emotion varies from culture to culture, such that emotion words that may translate from one language to another do not necessarily describe the same brain activity and do not necessarily capture the context in which emotions occur. Lastly, fMRI, the tool typically used to measure brain activity, does not provide a natural context for having an emotional experience.

4. (1) Tameness and loss of fear; (2) indiscriminate dietary behavior (eating many types of formerly rejected foods); (3) greatly increased autoerotic, homosexual, and heterosexual activity with inappropriate object choice (e.g., the sexual mounting of chairs); (4) tendency to attend and react to every visual stimulus; (5) tendency to examine all objects by mouth; and (6) visual agnosia, an inability to recognize objects or drawings of objects.

### REVIEW 12-7

1. rewarding
2. (*in either order*) wanting; liking
3. dopamine; *in either order:* opioid, endocannabinoid
4. Intracranial self-stimulation is a phenomenon in which animals learn to turn on a stimulating electric current to their brain, presumably because it activates the neural system that underlies reward.

### CHAPTER 13

### REVIEW 13-1

1. circadian; circannual
2. free-running
3. Zeitgeber
4. the sun
5. Light is the most effective input in entraining an animal's circadian rhythms, and sunrise is the most effective light Zeitgeber. In fact, when animals live in latitudes where constant light and constant dark are experienced over months, their biological clocks turn off.

### REVIEW 13-2

1. superchiasmatic nucleus *or* SCN
2. retinohypothalamic
3. intrinsically photosensitive retinal ganglion cells (*or* ipRGCs)
4. slave
5. Experimental evidence suggests that the circadian rhythm can put a time stamp on a behavioral event, rendering it easier to recall at the same time in the circadian cycle in which it occurred previously.
6. Sunrise is the most effective Zeitgeber for entraining our circadian rhythms. Furthermore, melatonin, which

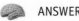

activates the parasympathetic rest-and-digest system and suppresses other physiological events in the body, promotes sleep during the dark portion of the circadian cycle, making it difficult to sleep during the day. Sleeping late in the morning disrupts these physiological processes that are mediated by our circadian cycle.

## REVIEW 13-3

1. polysomnography (or PSG)
2. in either order: N-sleep (or NREM sleep); R-sleep (or REM sleep)
3. in any order: brain activity; muscle tone; eye movement
4. five; longer
5. Interpreting dreams is difficult because it is possible that the interpreter will impose their own explanation, or spin, on the dreams.
6. Wearable devices are an affordable alternative to laboratory methods and can capture many of the same metrics as PSG, providing individuals with a good snapshot of their sleep patterns. However, the measurements derived from wearables are much less sensitive than those obtained with PSG technology, which remains the gold standard for the analysis of sleep.

## REVIEW 13-4

1. in any order: adaptation; restoration; support for memory
2. the synaptic homeostasis memory theory of sleep
3. place; NREM (or N-)
4. microsleep
5. hippocampal ripples (or ripples)
6. This theory suggests that different types of memories are stored during different sleep states: explicit memory is stored during N-sleep and implicit motor memory is stored during R-sleep.
7. Gardner broke the record for consecutive hours staying awake. In doing so, he demonstrated that the negative effects of sleep deprivation (e.g., hallucinations, cognitive and memory lapses), though serious, were temporary and did not lead to lasting impairment. Further research has concluded that limited periods of sleep deprivation do not produce prolonged physiological alterations.

## REVIEW 13-5

1. reticular activating system or RAS
2. arousal; awareness
3. peribrachial area
4. We have separate neural systems for keeping us awake while we are still (cholinergic) and when we move

(serotonergic). Sensory events activate our cholinergic neurons, making us attentive, and movement activates our serotonergic neurons, maintaining arousal levels.

5. The RAS in the brainstem is associated with sleep–wake behaviors and behavioral arousal. Projections from the RAS extend along the dorsal and ventral pathways to numerous cortical areas that are implicated in N-sleep and R-sleep behaviors. Stimulation or injury to any of these areas will have an effect on specific sleep–wake behaviors, but no single structure is responsible for sleep.

## REVIEW 13-6

1. insomnia; hypersomnia
2. drug-dependent insomnia
3. in either order: R-sleep; N-sleep
4. REM sleep behavioral disorder or REM (R-sleep) without atonia; subcoerulear
5. Orexin is a peptide neurotransmitter that helps to maintain wakefulness, and orexin cells connect to many brain regions to activate related systems. Orexin is probably one of many factors related to waking behavior, as animals with narcolepsy and reduced orexin can be awake but then collapse into sleep.
6. Various symptoms of sleep disorders are often symptoms of other disorders, and often coincide, such that it is difficult to diagnose certain specific disorders. Furthermore, individuals are often unaware of the sleep disturbances or disorders, or may be inclined to dismiss any sleep disruptions that they experience rather than seeking medical or clinical help.

## CHAPTER 14

## REVIEW 14-1

1. Pavlovian or classical
2. operant or instrumental
3. implicit; explicit
4. Episodic
5. Memory is not localized to any particular brain circuit or region. Rather, multiple memory circuits vary with the requirements of the memory task.

## REVIEW 14-2

1. in either order: hippocampus; amygdala
2. basal ganglia
3. Lashley searched for explicit memory in the perceptual and motor systems of his animal subjects using invasive tests designed mostly for implicit memory. Milner studied a patient who underwent bilateral removal of the medial temporal lobe and used behavioral tests of both explicit and implicit memory.

## REVIEW 14-3

1. in either order: hippocampus; neocortex or cortex
2. implicit
3. amygdala
4. consolidation
5. Emotional experiences stimulate hormonal and neurochemical activating systems that stimulate the amygdala. The amygdala, in turn, modulates the laying down of memory circuits in the rest of the brain.
6. Murray, Wise, and Graham's evolution accretion model includes the proposal that every cortical area participates in memory via specialized neural circuits, a concept that includes more regions of the brain than most other models. More significantly, these authors propose a true explicit memory system unique to humans that arose as a result of expansion of the human brain, and which allows us to "observe" events in time (including those that we recall) from the perspective of a participant—to essentially construct narratives around our experience.

## REVIEW 14-4

1. in either order: habituation; sensitization
2. long-term potentiation or LTP; long-term depression or LTD
3. GABAergic or inhibitory
4. in either order: synapse number; neuron number
5. hippocampus
6. behavioral sensitization
7. Plastic changes in neural networks can interfere with behavior essentially by learning behaviors that interfere with healthy function. Examples are addiction and PTSD.

## REVIEW 14-5

1. in any order: learning new ways to solve problems; reorganizing the brain to do more with less; replacing the lost neurons
2. in either order: direct cortical stimulation; deep brain stimulation or DBS
3. neurotrophic
4. Functional improvement after brain injury reflects compensation rather than recovery.

## CHAPTER 15

## REVIEW 15-1

1. in order: attending to; identifying; making meaningful responses to
2. language; flexibility
3. neuron
4. Much of human thought is verbal. Language allows us to categorize

information and provides a way to organize our behavior around time.

**REVIEW 15-2**

1. association; cognition
2. temporal; parietal
3. plan; organize
4. Mirror
5. The multimodal cortex allows the brain to combine characteristics of stimuli across different sensory modalities, whether we encounter the different stimuli together or separately.
6. Neurons in the mirror neuron system (MNS) respond to one's own actions and those of others. The MNS is widely distributed throughout the brain and has been shown to play a role in the brain's understanding and performance of actions. Therapies based on the concept of the MNS, such as action observation treatment, in which patients watch videos and attempt to imitate the action they see, can aid in recovery of motor ability following damage or disease, and can help in the development of precision skills in neurologically normal participants.

**REVIEW 15-3**

1. cognitive neuroscience
2. brain connectome
3. cerebellum
4. social interactions
5. theory of mind (*or* ToM)
6. decision making
7. *in any order:* Understanding others; understanding oneself; self-regulation; social living

**REVIEW 15-4**

1. *in either order:* spatial behavior; music
2. *in either order:* controlling voluntary movement sequences; language
3. corpus callosum
4. Because the hemispheres process information differently, they think differently. The existence of language in the left hemisphere allows it to label computations and thus make inferences

that the right hemisphere cannot. Our understanding of this asymmetry has implications for our study of certain behaviors and disorders.

**REVIEW 15-5**

1. *in either order:* sex; handedness
2. neural circuits
3. synesthesia
4. Gonadal hormones influence brain development and shape neural circuits in adulthood.

**REVIEW 15-6**

1. *g* factor *or* general intelligence; convergent; divergent; intelligence A; intelligence B; parieto-frontal integration; network
2. structural; functional
3. epigenetic
4. Neuroimaging studies show that efficiency of prefrontal–parietal circuits is related to standard intelligence measures and that executive function is related to gray-matter volume in the frontal lobe. The parieto-frontal integration theory proposes that specific cortical regions connected by white matter underlie intelligence and that individual differences in intelligence are related to structural and functional differences in these regions. Network neuroscience theory, in contrast, proposes that there are different brain networks for crystallized and fluid intelligence—these two networks are considered segregated subsystems.

**REVIEW 15-7**

1. Consciousness
2. ventral visual (*or* ventral); dorsal visual (*or* dorsal)
3. *Evolutionary theory* suggests that as organisms became more complex, more complex nervous systems were needed to coordinate activity, which led to the development of incentives and rewards, and thus to emotions, and eventually to a sense of self, or consciousness. *Global neuronal workspace theory* proposes that consciousness emerges from information integrated in the

frontal–parietal networks and distributed across the brain. *Information integration theory* suggests consciousness emerges from our ability to integrate information generated by the posterior cortex.

**CHAPTER 16**

**REVIEW 16-1**

1. *Diagnostic and Statistical Manual of Mental Disorders or* DSM-5
2. *in any order:* genetic errors; epigenetic mechanisms; progressive cell death; rapid cell death; loss of neural connections
3. PKU *or* phenylketonuria
4. The RDoC seeks to understand biological functions as a way to understand disorders and their treatment. The DSM begins by identifying a condition and then seeks to understand and treat that condition.

**REVIEW 16-2**

1. *in any order:* dopamine; glutamate; GABA
2. *in either order:* temporal; frontal
3. *in either order:* noradrenergic (*or* norepinephrine); serotonin
4. cognitive-behavioral therapy *or* CBT
5. Inflammation is one of the body's responses to injury, but in cases where the repair process is not successful, chronic inflammation can result. Chronic inflammation-like effects in the brain can lead to decreased activity of the noradrenergic and serotoninergic systems that modulate mood, leading to depression.
6. Many genetic and epigenetic influences contribute to every behavior, including schizophrenia.

**REVIEW 16-3**

1. Traumatic brain injury *or* TBI
2. ischemia; stroke
3. multiple sclerosis *or* MS
4. loss of cells from the substantia nigra
5. Aerobic exercise and brain training are strategies for enhancing or stimulating neuroplasticity as we age.

## A

**absolutely refractory** The state of an axon in the repolarizing period, during which a new action potential cannot be elicited (with some exceptions) because gate 2 of sodium channels, which are not voltage activated, is closed.

**acetylcholine (ACh)** First neurotransmitter discovered in the peripheral nervous system and central nervous system; activates skeletal muscles in the somatic nervous system; either excites or inhibits internal organs in the autonomic nervous system.

**action map** Representation of the body performing actions in the sensory or motor cortex; also, any topographical representation of the body in action by a neural area.

**action potential** Large, brief reversal in the polarity of an axon membrane.

**activating effects** Hormonal actions that influence activities in the adult brain.

**activating system** Neural pathways that coordinate brain activity through a single neurotransmitter; its cell bodies lie in a brainstem nucleus; axons are distributed through a wide central nervous system region.

**addiction** A complex brain disorder characterized by escalation, compulsive drug taking, and relapse.

**afferent** Conducting toward a central nervous system structure.

**agonist** Substance that enhances neurotransmitter function.

**akathesia** Small, involuntary movements or changes in posture; motor restlessness.

**allele** Alternative form of a gene; a gene pair contains two alleles.

**allocortex** Part of the cerebral cortex ("outer bark"), composed of three or four layers; plays a role in controlling motivational and emotional states as well as in certain forms of memory.

**alpha rhythm** Regular brain wave pattern in an electroencephalogram with a frequency ranging from 7 to 11 Hz; found in most people when they are relaxed with eyes closed.

**Alzheimer disease** Degenerative brain disorder related to aging; first appears as progressive memory loss and later develops into generalized dementia.

**amblyopia** Condition in which vision in one eye is reduced as a result of disuse; usually caused by a failure of the two eyes to look in the same direction.

**amino acid hormone** Chemical messenger derived from amino acid, most commonly tyrosine.

**amnesia** Partial or total loss of memory.

**amphetamine** Synthetic compound that increases the neurotransmitter dopamine in the synaptic cleft by reversing the dopamine transporter.

**amplitude** Stimulus intensity; in audition, roughly equivalent to loudness; graphed by the increasing height of a sound wave.

**amusia** Tone deafness; inability to distinguish between musical notes.

**amygdala** The part of the brain that participates in species-typical behaviors, emotion, and emotional memory; from the Greek word for "almond," reflecting the general shape in the medial temporal lobe.

**anabolic steroid** Class of synthetic hormones related to testosterone, which have both muscle-building (anabolic) and masculinizing (androgenic) effects; also called *anabolic–androgenic steroid*.

**androgen** Class of hormones that stimulate or control masculine characteristics, and that play a role in levels of sexual interest in humans.

**anencephaly** Failure of the forebrain to develop.

**anomalous speech representation** Condition in which a person's speech zones are located in the right hemisphere or in both hemispheres.

**anorexia nervosa** An eating disorder characterized by exaggerated concern with being overweight that leads to inadequate food intake and often excessive exercising; can lead to severe weight loss and even starvation.

**antagonist** Substance that blocks neurotransmitter function.

**anterior spinothalamic tract** Pathway from the spinal cord to the thalamus that carries information about pain and temperature toward the brain.

**anterograde amnesia** Inability to remember events subsequent to a disturbance of the brain such as head trauma, electroconvulsive shock, or neurodegenerative disease.

**anterograde synaptic transmission** Process that occurs when a neurotransmitter is released from a presynaptic neuron and binds to a receptor on the postsynaptic neuron.

**anxiety disorder** Any of a number of conditions in which unhelpful anxiety has negative effects on daily life.

**aphagia** Failure to eat; may be due to an unwillingness to eat or to motor difficulties, especially with swallowing.

**aphasia** Inability to speak or comprehend language despite the presence of normal comprehension and intact vocal mechanisms. *Broca's aphasia* is the inability to speak fluently despite the presence of normal comprehension and intact vocal mechanisms. *Wernicke's aphasia* is the inability to understand or to produce meaningful language even though word production remains intact.

**apoptosis** Genetically programmed cell death.

**apraxia** Inability to make voluntary movements in the absence of paralysis or other motor or sensory impairment, especially an inability to make proper use of an object.

**association cortex** Neocortex outside the primary sensory and motor cortices; functions to produce cognition.

**associative learning** Linkage of two or more unrelated stimuli to elicit a behavioral response.

**astrocyte** Star-shaped glial cell that provides structural support to central nervous system neurons and transports substances between neurons and blood vessels.

**atonia** Reduced muscle tone; a condition of maximally low muscle inactivity produced by motor neuron inhibition.

**attention** Narrowing or focusing awareness to a part of the sensory environment or to a class of stimuli.

**attention-deficit/hyperactivity disorder (ADHD)** Developmental disorder characterized by core behavioral symptoms including impulsivity, hyperactivity, and/or inattention.

**autism spectrum disorder (ASD)** The range of cognitive symptoms, from mild to severe, that characterize autism; severe symptoms include greatly impaired social interaction, a bizarre and narrow range of interests, marked abnormalities in language and communication, and fixed, repetitive movements.

**autoimmune disease** Illness resulting from the loss of the immune system's ability to discriminate between foreign pathogens in the body and the body itself (i.e., an abnormal immune response by the body against substances and tissues normally present in the body).

**autonomic nervous system (ANS)** Part of the peripheral nervous system that regulates the functioning of internal organs and glands.

**autoreceptor** Self-receptor in a neuronal membrane, which responds to the same transmitter released by the neuron; part of a negative feedback loop allowing the neuron to adjust its output.

**axon** Root, or single fiber, of a neuron that carries messages to other neurons.

**axon collateral** Branch of an axon.

**axon hillock** Juncture of the soma and an axon.

## B

**back propagation** Reverse movement of an action potential into the soma and dendritic field of a neuron; postulated to play a role in the plastic changes that underlie learning.

**basal ganglia** Subcortical forebrain nuclei that coordinate voluntary movements of the limbs and body; connected to the thalamus and to the midbrain.

**basic rest–activity cycle (BRAC)** Recurring cycle of temporal packets (about 90-minute periods in humans), during which an animal's level of arousal waxes and wanes.

**basilar membrane** Receptor surface in the cochlea that transduces sound waves into neural activity.

**behavior** A collection of coordinated movements that are internally generated, often in response to external stimuli.

**behavioral modification** Treatment that applies learning principles, such as conditioning, to eliminate unwanted behaviors.

**behavioral myopia** "Nearsighted" behavior displayed under the influence of alcohol, wherein local and immediate cues become prominent; remote cues and consequences are ignored.

**behavioral neuroscience** Study of the biological bases of behavior in animals, including humans.

**behavioral sensitization** Escalating behavioral response to the repeated administration of a psychomotor stimulant such as amphetamine, cocaine, or nicotine; also called *drug-induced behavioral sensitization* and sometimes simply *sensitization*.

**beta rhythm** Fast brain-wave activity pattern associated with a waking electroencephalogram.

**bilateral symmetry** Body plan in which those organs or parts present on both sides of the body are mirror images in appearance. For example, the hands are bilaterally symmetrical, whereas the heart is not.

**binding problem** Philosophical question focused on how the brain ties single and varied sensory and motor events together into a unified perception or behavior.

**biological clock** Neural system that times behavior by producing biorhythms.

**biorhythm** A natural rhythm in a behavior or bodily process.

**bipolar disorder** Mood disorder characterized by periods of depression alternating with normal periods and periods of intense excitation, or *mania*.

**bipolar neuron** Sensory neuron with one axon and one dendrite.

**blind spot** Retinal region where axons forming the optic nerve leave the eye and where blood vessels enter and leave; has no photoreceptors and is thus said to be blind.

**blob** Region in area V1 that contains color-sensitive neurons, as revealed by staining for cytochrome oxidase.

**blood–brain barrier** Protective partition between the blood and the brain formed by tight junctions between the cells that compose blood vessels in the brain; prohibits entry of an array of substances, including toxins, into the brain.

**body map** Representation of the human body in the sensory or motor cortex; also, any topographical representation of the body by a neural area.

**brain connectome** Map of the complete structural and functional fiber pathways of the human brain in vivo.

**brainstem** Central structure of the brain (including the hindbrain, midbrain, thalamus, and hypothalamus) that is responsible for most life-sustaining, unconscious behavior.

**Broca's area** Speech area that functions with the motor cortex to produce the movements needed for speaking.

## C

**carbon monoxide (CO)** Gaseous neurotransmitter; activates cellular metabolism.

**cataplexy** State of atonia, as in R-sleep, occurring while a person is awake and active; linked to strong emotional stimulation.

**cell adhesion molecule (CAM)** Chemical molecule to which specific cells can adhere, thereby aiding in migration.

**cell assembly** Hypothetical group of neurons that become functionally connected via common sensory inputs; proposed by Hebb as the basis of perception, memory, and thought.

**cell body (soma)** Core region of the cell containing the nucleus and other organelles for making proteins.

**central nervous system (CNS)** The brain and spinal cord, which together mediate behavior.

**cerebellum** Major brainstem structure specialized for learning and coordinating movements; assists the cerebrum in generating many behaviors.

**cerebral cortex** Heavily folded and layered tissue that forms the outer structure of the forebrain; composed of the neocortex and allocortex.

**cerebral palsy (CP)** Group of disorders that result from brain damage acquired perinatally (at or near birth).

**cerebral voltammetry** Technique used to identify the concentrations of specific chemicals in brains.

**cerebrospinal fluid (CSF)** Clear solution of sodium, chloride, and other ions that is produced in the ventricles inside the brain and circulates around the brain and spinal cord until it is absorbed beneath the arachnoid layer in the subarachnoid space.

**cerebrum (forebrain)** Major structure of the forebrain, which consists of two mirror-image hemispheres (left and right) and is responsible for most conscious behavior.

**channel** Opening in a protein embedded in the cell membrane that allows the passage of ions.

**chemical synapse** Junction at which messenger molecules are released when stimulated by an action potential.

**chemoaffinity hypothesis** Proposal that neurons or their axons and dendrites are drawn toward a signaling chemical that indicates the correct pathway.

**chemogenetics** Transgenic technique that combines genetics and synthetic drugs to activate targeted cells in living tissue.

**cholinergic neuron** Neuron that uses acetylcholine (ACh) as its main neurotransmitter; *cholinergic* applies to any neuron that uses ACh as its main transmitter.

**chordate** Animal that has both a brain and a spinal cord.

**chronic traumatic encephalopathy (CTE)** Progressive degenerative disease caused by multiple concussions and other closed-head injuries, characterized by neurofibrillary tangles, plaques, cerebral atrophy, and expanded ventricles due to cell loss.

**chronotype** Time type; individual variations in circadian activity.

**circadian rhythm** Day–night rhythm.

**cladogram** Diagram representing the relationship between organisms with branch points signifying possible common ancestors.

**clinical neuroscience** Specialty in the field of neuroscience that focuses on the diagnosis and treatment of diseases and disorders affecting the brain and central nervous system.

**clinical trial** Consensual experiment directed toward developing a treatment.

**cochlea** Inner ear structure containing the auditory receptor cells.

**cochlear implant** Electronic device with wires that is implanted surgically into the inner ear; the wires carry transduced sound waves that directly excite the cranial nerve, allowing a deaf person to hear.

**cognition** Act or process of knowing or coming to know; in psychology, refers to thought processes; in behavioral neuroscience, refers to identification and planned response to stimuli.

**cognitive-behavioral therapy (CBT)** Problem-focused, action-oriented, structured treatment for eliminating dysfunctional thoughts and maladaptive thought and reasoning processes.

**cognitive neuroscience** Study of the neural bases of cognition.

**cognitive therapy** Therapy based on the perspective that thoughts intervene between events and emotions, so the treatment of emotional disorders requires changing maladaptive patterns of thinking.

**color constancy** Phenomenon whereby an object's perceived color tends to remain constant relative to other colors, regardless of changes in illumination.

**coma** Prolonged state of deep unconsciousness resembling sleep.

**common ancestor** Forebear of two or more lineages or family groups; ancestral to both groups.

**compensation** Following brain damage, the neuroplastic ability to modify behavior from that demonstrated prior to the damage.

**competitive inhibitor** A drug that competes with another drug for a receptor site; an

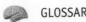

example is naloxone, which acts quickly to block opioid action by competing with the opioid for binding sites.

**computational neuroscience** Quantitative approach using biologically plausible mathematical models to mimic the development, structure, physiology, and cognitive abilities of the nervous system in an effort to better understand them; also called *mathematical neuroscience*.

**computed tomography (CT)** X-ray technique that produces a static three-dimensional image (called a CT scan) of the brain in cross section.

**concentration gradient** Difference in the relative abundance of a substance among regions of a container; allows the substance to diffuse from an area of higher concentration to an area of lower concentration.

**concussion** Alteration in brain function that results from sudden shaking or blows to the head and can lead to severe brain damage, especially after repeated injury; symptoms may be temporary and affect memory, consciousness, vision, coordination, and mood, among other effects.

**conditioned response (CR)** In Pavlovian conditioning, the learned response to a formerly neutral conditioned stimulus (CS).

**conditioned stimulus (CS)** In Pavlovian conditioning, an originally neutral stimulus that, after association with an unconditioned stimulus (UCS), triggers a conditioned response (CR).

**cone** Photoreceptor specialized for color and high visual acuity.

**connectome** All the pathways connecting regions of the central nervous system.

**consciousness** The mind's level of responsiveness to impressions made by the senses.

**consolidation** Process of stabilizing a memory trace after learning.

**constraint-induced therapy** Procedure in which restraint of a healthy limb forces a person to use an impaired limb to enhance recovery of function.

**contralateral neglect** Ignoring a part of the body or world on the side opposite (contralateral to) that of a brain injury.

**convergent thinking** Form of thinking that searches for a single answer to a question (such as 2 + 2 = ?); contrasts with *divergent thinking*.

**corpus callosum** Band of white matter containing approximately 200 million nerve fibers, which connects the two cerebral hemispheres to provide a route for direct communication between them.

**cortical column** Anatomic organization that represents a functional unit six cortical layers deep and approximately 0.5 mm across, perpendicular to the cortical surface.

**corticobulbar tract** Bundle of nerve fibers that directly connects the cerebral cortex to the brainstem nuclei that control facial muscles.

**corticospinal tract** Bundle of nerve fibers that directly connects the cerebral cortex to the spinal cord; it branches at the brainstem into an opposite-side lateral tract, which informs movement of limbs and digits, and a same-side anterior tract, which informs movement of the trunk; also called *pyramidal tract*.

**cranial nerves** The 12 nerve pairs that control sensory and motor functions of the head, neck, and internal organs.

**critical period** Developmental window during which some event has a long-lasting influence on the brain; also called *sensitive period*.

**culture** Learned behaviors that are passed on from one generation to the next through teaching and imitation.

**cytoarchitectonic map** Map of the neocortex based on the organization, structure, and distribution of the cells.

## D

**deafferentation** Loss of incoming sensory input, usually due to damage to sensory fibers; also, loss of any afferent input to a structure.

**decibel (dB)** Measure of the relative physical intensity of sounds.

**declarative memory** Ability to recount what one knows, by detailing the time, place, and circumstances of events; often lost in amnesia.

**deep brain stimulation (DBS)** Neurosurgical technique in which electrodes implanted in the brain stimulate a targeted area with a low-voltage electrical current to produce or facilitate behavior or give relief from psychiatric conditions.

**default network** Brain network of interacting regions of the frontal and parietal lobes that have highly correlated activity when a person is not engaged in some targeted activity.

**delta rhythm** Brain-wave activity pattern with a frequency of 1–3 Hz.

**dendrite** Branching extension of a neuron's cell membrane; greatly increases the cell's surface area; collects information from other cells.

**dendritic spine** Protrusion that greatly increases the dendrite's surface area; typical point of dendritic contact with the axons of other cells.

**depolarization** Decrease in electrical charge across a membrane, usually due to the inward flow of sodium ions.

**dermatome** Body segment corresponding to a segment of the spinal cord.

***Diagnostic and Statistical Manual of Mental Disorders* (DSM)** The American Psychiatric Association's classification system for psychiatric disorders.

**diaschisis** Neural shock that follows brain damage in which areas connected to the site of damage show a temporary arrest of function.

**dichotic listening** Experimental procedure for simultaneously presenting a different auditory input to each ear through stereophonic earphones.

**diencephalon** The "between brain," which integrates sensory and motor information on its way to the cerebral cortex.

**diffusion** Movement of ions from an area of higher concentration to an area of lower concentration through random motion.

**diffusion tensor imaging (DTI)** Magnetic resonance imaging method that can image fiber pathways in the brain by detecting the directional movements of water molecules.

**dimer** Two proteins combined into one.

**disinhibition theory** Explanation holding that alcohol has a selective depressant effect on the brain's frontal cortex, which controls judgment, while sparing subcortical structures responsible for more innate behaviors, such as desire.

**diurnal animal** Organism that is active chiefly during daylight.

**divergent thinking** Form of thinking that searches for multiple solutions to a problem (how many ways can a pen be used?); contrasts with *convergent thinking*.

**dopamine (DA)** Amine neurotransmitter involved in coordinating movement, attention, learning, and reinforcing behaviors.

**dopamine hypothesis of schizophrenia** Idea that excess dopamine activity causes symptoms of schizophrenia.

**dorsal stream** Visual processing pathway from region V1 to the parietal lobe; guides actions relative to objects.

**dorsolateral prefrontal cortex (dlPFC)** Brodmann areas 9 and 46; makes reciprocal connections with the posterior parietal cortex and superior temporal sulcus; responsible for selecting behavior and movement with respect to temporal memory.

**Down syndrome** Chromosomal abnormality resulting in intellectual impairment and other abnormalities, usually caused by an extra chromosome 21.

**dualism** Philosophical position that both a nonmaterial mind and a material body contribute to behavior.

**dyslexia** Impairment in learning to read and write; probably the most common learning disability.

**dystonia** Disorder in which muscles contract involuntarily, causing repetitive or twisting movements.

## E

**echolocation** The ability to use sound to locate objects in space.

**efferent** Conducting away from a central nervous system structure.

**electrical stimulation** Passage of an electrical current from the uninsulated tip of an electrode through tissue, resulting in changes in the electrical activity of the tissue.

**electrocorticography (ECoG)** Graded potentials recorded with electrodes placed directly on the surface of the brain.

**electroencephalogram (EEG)** Graph of electrical activity from the brain, which is mainly composed of graded potentials from many neurons.

**electrographic seizures** Abnormal rhythmic neuronal discharges; may be recorded by an electroencephalogram.

**embodied behavior** Theory that the movements we make and the movements we perceive in others are central to communication.

**emotion** Cognitive interpretation of subjective experiences that can influence thought and behavior.

**emotional memory** Memory for the affective properties of stimuli or events.

**encephalization quotient (EQ)** Jerison's quantitative measure of brain size obtained from the ratio of actual brain size to expected brain size, according to the principle of proper mass, for an animal of a particular body size.

**end plate** On a muscle, the receptor–ion complex that is activated by the release of the neurotransmitter acetylcholine from the terminal of a motor neuron.

**endocannabinoid** Molecules made by the body that have a similar structure to cannabinoids.

**enteric nervous system (ENS)** Mesh of neurons embedded in the lining of the gut, running from the esophagus through the colon; controls the gut.

**entorhinal cortex** Cortex located on the medial temporal lobe surface; provides a major route for neocortical input to the hippocampal formation; often degenerates in Alzheimer disease.

**entrain** To determine or modify the period of a biorhythm.

**ependymal cell** Glial cell that makes and secretes cerebrospinal fluid; found on the walls of the brain's ventricles.

**epidermal growth factor (EGF)** Neurotrophic factor; stimulates the subventricular zone to generate cells that migrate into the striatum and eventually differentiate into neurons and glia.

**epigenetics** Differences in gene expression related to environment and experience.

**epinephrine (EP)** Chemical messenger that acts as a neurotransmitter and as a hormone to mobilize the body for fight or flight during times of stress; also known as *adrenaline*.

**episodic memory** Autobiographical memory for events pegged to specific place and time contexts.

**equilibrium (reversal potential)** The membrane potential of an individual ion, at which there is no net (overall) flow of that particular ion from one side of the membrane to the other.

**estrogen** Variety of sex hormones responsible for the distinguishing female characteristics.

**event-related potential (ERP)** Complex electroencephalographic waveform related in time to a specific sensory event.

**evolutionary psychology** Discipline that seeks to apply principles of evolution to understand the causes of human behavior.

**excitation** Increase in the activity of a neuron or brain area.

**excitatory postsynaptic potential (EPSP)** Brief depolarization of a neuron membrane in response to stimulation, making the neuron more likely to produce an action potential.

**executive function** Cognitive processes associated primarily with the frontal lobe that plans behavior and makes decisions.

**exocytosis** An active process by which chemical substances are carried in vesicles to the outer cell membrane, fuse with it, and release their contents.

**explicit memory** Conscious memory: subjects can retrieve an item and indicate that they know the retrieved item is the correct one.

**extinction** In neurology, neglect of information on one side of the body when it is presented simultaneously with similar information on the other side of the body.

**extrastriate (secondary visual) cortex (V2–V5)** Visual cortical areas in the occipital lobe outside the striate cortex.

**eyeblink conditioning** Experimental technique in which subjects learn to pair a formerly neutral stimulus with a defensive blinking response.

**F**

**facial agnosia** Face blindness; the inability to recognize faces; also called *prosopagnosia*.

**fear conditioning** Conditioned emotional response between a neutral stimulus and an unpleasant event, such as a shock, that results in a learned association.

**festination** Tendency for a behavior to speed up, such as walking, faster and faster.

**fetal alcohol spectrum disorder (FASD)** Range of physical and intellectual impairments observed in some children following significant alcohol exposure during gestation.

**filopod (pl. filopodia)** Process at the end of a developing axon that reaches out to search for a potential target or to sample the intercellular environment.

**focal seizure** Seizure that arises at a synchronous, hyperactive, localized brain region (at a focus).

**forebrain** Evolutionarily the most recent addition to the brain; coordinates advanced cognitive functions such as thinking, planning, and language; contains the allocortex, neocortex, and basal ganglia.

**fovea** Central region of the retina specialized for high visual acuity; its receptive fields are at the center of the eye's visual field.

**free-running rhythm** Rhythm of the body's own devising in the absence of all external cues.

**frequency** Number of cycles a wave completes in a given time.

**frontal lobe** Lobe of the neocortex that lies anterior to the central sulcus and beneath the frontal bone of the skull.

**functional magnetic resonance imaging (fMRI)** Magnetic resonance imaging technique that measures brain activity indirectly by detecting changes associated with the ratio of oxygenated and deoxygenated blood; often used to measure cerebral blood flow during cognitive testing or resting.

**functional near-infrared spectroscopy (fNIRS)** Noninvasive technique that gathers light transmitted through cortical tissue to image oxygen consumption; a form of optical tomography.

**G**

**G protein** Guanyl nucleotide–binding protein coupled to a metabotropic receptor; when activated, binds to other proteins.

**gamma-aminobutyric acid (GABA)** Amino acid neurotransmitter; typically opens $Cl^-$ channels and therefore inhibits neurons.

**ganglia** Collection of nerve cells that functions somewhat like a brain.

**gap junction** Area of contact between adjacent cells in which connexin proteins in each cell form connecting hemichannels; when open, the hemichannels allow ions to pass between the two cells; also called an *electrical synapse*.

**gate** Protein embedded in a cell membrane that allows substances to pass through the membrane on some occasions but not on others.

**gender identity** An individual's concept of self as male, female, neither, or both.

**gene** DNA segment that encodes the synthesis of a particular protein.

**gene (DNA) methylation** Epigenetic process in which a methyl group attaches to the DNA sequence, suppressing or enabling gene expression.

**generalized seizure** Electrographic seizure that starts at a focal location, and then spreads rapidly and bilaterally to distributed networks in both hemispheres.

**geniculostriate system** Projections from the retina to the lateral geniculate nucleus to the visual cortex.

**genotype** Particular genetic makeup of an individual.

**glabrous skin** Skin that does not have hair follicles but contains larger numbers of sensory receptors than do hairy skin areas.

**glial cell** Nervous system cell that supports the function of neurons; provides insulation, nutrients, and support, and aids in repairing neurons and eliminating waste products.

**glioblast** Product of a progenitor cell that gives rise to different types of glial cells.

**glucocorticoid** One of a group of steroid hormones, such as cortisol, secreted in times of stress; important in protein and carbohydrate metabolism.

**glutamate (Glu)** Amino acid neurotransmitter; typically opens the Na$^+$ and Ca$^{2+}$ channels and therefore excites neurons.

**gonadal (sex) hormone** One of a group of hormones, such as testosterone, that control reproductive functions and strongly influence sexual appearance as male or female.

**graded potential** A small voltage fluctuation across the cell membrane.

**gray matter** Areas of the nervous system composed predominantly of neuronal cell bodies and capillary blood vessels.

**growth cone** Growing tip of an axon.

**growth spurt** Sporadic period of sudden growth that lasts for a finite time.

**gyri (sing. gyrus)** Small protrusions or bumps formed by the folding of the cerebral cortex.

## H

**habituation** Learned behavior in which the response to a stimulus weakens with repeated presentations.

**hair cell** Specialized neurons in the cochlea tipped by cilia; when stimulated by waves in the cochlear fluid, the cilia bend and generate graded potentials in inner hair cells, the auditory receptor cells.

**hapsis** Perceptual ability to discriminate objects on the basis of touch.

**hemisphere** Literally, half a sphere, referring to one side of the cerebrum.

**hemorrhagic stroke** A stroke resulting from bleeding from a blood vessel.

**hertz (Hz)** Measure of sound wave frequency (repetition rate); 1 hertz equals 1 cycle per second.

**heterozygous** Having two different alleles for the same trait.

**hindbrain** Evolutionarily the oldest part of the brain; contains the pons, medulla, reticular formation, and cerebellum, the structures that coordinate movements.

**hippocampus** From the Greek word for "seahorse"; distinctive allocortical structure lying in the medial temporal lobe; participates in memory and spatial navigation and is vulnerable to the effects of stress.

**histamine (H)** Neurotransmitter that controls arousal and waking; important in immune response, but can cause the constriction of smooth muscles; when activated in allergic reactions, constricts the airway and contributes to asthma.

**homeostatic hormone** One of a group of hormones that maintain the internal metabolic balance and regulate the physiological systems in an organism.

**homeostatic mechanism** Process that maintains critical body functions within a narrow, fixed range.

**hominin** Term referring to all forms of humans, living and extinct.

**homonymous hemianopia** Blindness of the entire left or right visual field.

**homozygous** Having two identical alleles for a trait.

**HPA axis** Hypothalamic–pituitary–adrenal circuit that controls the production and release of hormones related to stress.

**Huntington disease** Hereditary disease characterized by chorea (ceaseless involuntary jerky movements) and progressive dementia, ending in death.

**hydrocephalus** Buildup of fluid pressure in the brain and, in infants, swelling of the head, if the flow of cerebrospinal fluid is blocked; can result in intellectual impairment and death.

**hydrogen sulfide (H$_2$S)** Gaseous neurotransmitter; slows cellular metabolism.

**hyperconnectivity** Increased local connections between two related brain regions.

**hyperkinetic symptom** Excessive involuntary movement, as seen in Tourette syndrome.

**hyperphagia** Compulsive overeating that leads to significant weight gain.

**hyperpolarization** Increase in electrical charge across a membrane, usually due to the inward flow of chloride ions or the outward flow of potassium ions.

**hypersomnia** Disorder of falling asleep at inappropriate times, or a difficulty staying awake.

**hypokinetic symptom** Paucity of movement, as seen in Parkinson disease.

**hypothalamus** Diencephalon structure that contains many nuclei mediating regulatory functions such as hunger and thirst.

**hypovolemic thirst** Thirst produced by a loss of overall fluid volume from the body.

## I

**implicit memory** Unconscious memory: includes skills, conditioned responses, or recall of events, upon prompting that is not intentional.

**imprinting** Formation of an attachment by an animal to one or more objects or animals at a critical period in development.

**induced pluripotent stem cells (iPSCs)** Cells created from the body's tissues that can differentiate into nearly all cell types found in the body.

**inhibition** Activity that decreases the action of a neuron or brain area.

**inhibitory postsynaptic potential (IPSP)** Brief hyperpolarization of a neuron membrane in response to stimulation, making the neuron less likely to produce an action potential.

**initial segment** Area near where the axon meets the cell body, which is rich in voltage-gated channels that generate the action potential.

**innate releasing mechanism (IRM)** Hypothetical mechanism that detects specific sensory stimuli and directs an organism to take a particular action.

**insomnia** Symptom of a number of disorders characterized by an inability to fall asleep, stay asleep, or experience satisfactory sleep.

**insula** Multifunctional cortical tissue located within the lateral fissure; contains language- and taste perception–related regions and neural structures underlying social cognition.

**intelligence A** Hebb's term for innate intellectual potential, which is highly heritable and cannot be measured directly.

**intelligence B** Hebb's term for observed intelligence, which is influenced by experience and other factors in the course of development; measured by intelligence tests.

**interneuron** Association cell interposed between a sensory neuron and a motor neuron; in mammals, interneurons constitute most of the brain's neurons.

**ionotropic receptor** Embedded membrane protein that acts as (1) a binding site for a neurotransmitter and (2) a pore that regulates ion flow to directly and rapidly change membrane voltage.

**ischemic stroke** A stroke resulting from a blocked blood vessel.

## J

**jet lag** Fatigue and disorientation resulting from rapid travel through time zones and exposure to a changed light–dark cycle.

## K

**Klüver–Bucy syndrome** Behavioral syndrome, characterized by compulsive investigation and hypersexuality resulting from bilateral injury to the temporal lobe.

**Korsakoff syndrome** Permanent loss of the ability to learn new information (anterograde amnesia) and to retrieve old information (retrograde amnesia) caused by diencephalic damage resulting from chronic alcohol use disorder or malnutrition that produces a vitamin B$_1$ deficiency.

## L

**lateralization** Localization of function primarily on one side of the brain.

**law of Bell and Magendie** Sensory fibers are dorsal/posterior and motor fibers are ventral/anterior, with an exception.

**learned taste aversion** Acquired association between a specific taste or odor and illness; leads to an aversion to foods that have the taste or odor.

**learning** Relatively permanent change in an organism's behavior as a result or experience.

**learning set** Rules of the game; implicit understanding of how a problem can be solved with a rule that can be applied in many different situations.

**Lewy body** Circular fibrous structure found in several neurocognitive disorders; forms within the cytoplasm of neurons and is thought to result from abnormal neurofilament metabolism.

**light pollution** Artificial light that can change activity patterns and so disrupts circadian rhythms.

**limbic system** A conceptual system controlling affective and motivated behaviors and certain forms of memory, whose key anatomy lies between the neocortex and brainstem; includes the cingulate cortex, amygdala, and hippocampus, among other structures.

**lipid hormone** Chemical messenger derived from lipids such as arachidonic acid, which acts on membrane receptors; also known as *eicosanoid.*

**locked-in syndrome** Condition in which an individual is aware and awake but cannot move or communicate verbally because of complete paralysis of all voluntary muscles except the eyes.

**long-term depression (LTD)** Long-lasting decrease in synaptic effectiveness after low-frequency electrical stimulation.

**long-term potentiation (LTP)** Long-lasting increase in synaptic effectiveness after high-frequency stimulation.

**luminance contrast** Amount of light an object reflects relative to its surroundings.

**M**

**magnetic resonance imaging (MRI)** Technique that produces a static three-dimensional brain image by passing a strong magnetic field through the brain, followed by a radio wave, then measuring a radiofrequency signal emitted from hydrogen atoms.

**magnetic resonance spectroscopy (MRS)** Magnetic resonance imaging method that uses the hydrogen proton signal to determine the concentration of brain metabolites.

**magnetoencephalogram (MEG)** Magnetic potentials recorded from detectors placed outside the skull.

**magnocellular (M) cell** Large visual system neurons in the lateral geniculate nucleus that are sensitive to light, and that mediate light and dark perception and movement.

**major depression** Mood disorder characterized by prolonged feelings of worthlessness and guilt, disruption of normal eating habits, sleep disturbance (e.g., insomnia), a general slowing of behavior, and frequent thoughts of suicide.

**mania** Disordered mental state of extreme excitement.

**masculinization** Process by which exposure to androgens (male sex hormones) alters the brain and stimulates an individual to develop mal reproductive organs and secondary sexual characteristics (e.g., facial hair and deepening of the voice).

**materialism** Philosophical theory that behavior can be explained as a function of the nervous system without recourse to the mind.

**medial forebrain bundle (MFB)** Tract that connects the brainstem structures with various parts of the limbic system; includes fibers for activating projections of dopamine, norepinephrine, and acetylcholine.

**medial geniculate nucleus** Major thalamic region concerned with audition.

**medial pontine reticular formation (MPRF)** Nucleus in the pons that participates in R-sleep.

**melatonin** Hormone secreted by the pineal gland during the dark phase of the day–night cycle; influences daily and seasonal biorhythms.

**meme** An idea, a behavior, or a style that spreads from person to person within a culture.

**memory** Ability to recall or recognize previous experience.

**Mendelian genetics** Principles of inheritance demonstrated in experiments by Gregor Mendel, based on the observation that heritable factors (genes) pass from parent to offspring.

**Ménière disease** Disorder of the middle ear resulting in vertigo and loss of balance.

**meninges** Three layers of protective tissue—dura mater, arachnoid, and pia mater—that encase the brain and spinal cord.

**mentalism** Explanation of behavior as a function of the nonmaterial mind.

**metabolic syndrome** Combinations of medical disorders, including obesity and insulin abnormalities, that collectively increase the risk of developing cardiovascular disease and diabetes.

**metabotropic receptor** Embedded membrane protein with a binding site for a neurotransmitter linked to a G protein; can affect other receptors or act with second messengers to affect other cellular processes, including opening a pore.

**metaplasticity** Interaction among different plastic changes in the brain.

**microdialysis** Technique used to determine the chemical constituents of extracellular fluid in freely moving animals.

**microelectrode** A microscopic insulated wire or a saltwater-filled glass tube whose uninsulated tip is used to stimulate or record from neurons.

**microglia** Glial cells that originate in the blood, aid in cell repair, and scavenge debris in the nervous system.

**microsleep** Brief sleep period lasting a second or so.

**midbrain** Central part of the brain; contains neural circuits for hearing and seeing as well as for orienting movements.

**mind–body problem** Difficulty of explaining how a nonmaterial mind and a material body interact.

**minimally conscious state (MCS)** Condition in which a person can display some rudimentary behaviors, such as smiling or uttering a few words, but is otherwise not conscious.

**mirror neuron** Cell in the primate premotor and parietal cortex that fires when an individual observes an action taken by another individual.

**monoamine oxidase (MAO) inhibitor** Drug that blocks the enzyme monoamine oxidase

from degrading such neurotransmitters as serotonin, norepinephrine, and dopamine.

**monosynaptic reflex** Reflex requiring one synapse between sensory input and movement.

**motivation** Internal state of an organism that acts to initiate or energize behavior; from the Latin *motivus,* meaning "a moving cause."

**motor neuron** Cell that carries efferent information from the brain and spinal cord to make muscles contract.

**motor sequence** Movement modules preprogrammed by the brain and produced as a unit.

**multiple sclerosis (MS)** Nervous system disorder resulting from the loss of the myelin sheath around axons in the central nervous system.

**mutation** Any alteration of a gene that yields a different version of its protein.

**myelin** Glial coating that surrounds axons in the central and peripheral nervous systems; prevents adjacent neurons from short-circuiting.

**N**

**natural selection** Darwin's theory explaining how new species evolve and how existing species change over time; individuals with different characteristics (phenotypes) have differential reproductive success leading populations of living organisms to adapt and change.

**neocortex (cortex)** Outermost layer ("outer bark") of the forebrain that is visibly folded in humans and other large-brained animals; composed of about six layers of cells.

**neoteny** Process in which juvenile stages of predecessors become adult features of descendants; idea derived from the observation that more recently evolved species resemble the young of their common ancestors.

**Nernst equation** Calculates the equilibrium potential (also referred to as the *Nernst potential*) for an ion based on its charge (i.e., its valence) and its concentration gradient across the membrane.

**nerve** Large collection of axons coursing together *outside* the central nervous system.

**nerve growth factor (NGF)** Neurotrophic factor that stimulates neurons to grow dendrites and synapses and in some cases promotes the survival of neurons.

**nerve impulse** Propagation of an action potential on the membrane of an axon.

**nerve net** Simple nervous system that has no center, but rather consists of neurons that receive sensory information and connect directly to other neurons that move muscles.

**netrin** Chemoattractive tropic molecule that guides axon growth.

**neural Darwinism** Hypothesis that competition among neurons for connections and metabolic resources is like natural selection in organisms.

**neural network** Functional group of neurons that connects wide areas of the brain and spinal cord.

**neural plate** Primitive neural tissue that gives rise to the neural tube.

**neural stem cell** Self-renewing multipotential cell that gives rise to any of the different types of neurons and glia in the nervous system.

**neural tube** Structure in the early stage of brain development from which the brain and spinal cord develop.

**neuritic plaque** Area of incomplete necrosis (dead tissue) consisting of a central protein core (amyloid) surrounded by degenerative cellular fragments; often seen in the cortex of people with neurocognitive disorders such as Alzheimer disease.

**neuroblast** Product of a progenitor cell that gives rise to any of the different types of neurons.

**neurocognitive disorder** Acquired and persistent syndrome of intellectual impairment characterized by memory and other cognitive deficits and impairments in social and occupational functioning.

**neuroeconomics** Interdisciplinary field that seeks to understand how the brain makes decisions.

**neuroethics** Discipline concerned with the ethics of medical and biological research, which also incorporates the meaning of being human from the perspective of philosophy of mind, psychology, theology, and law.

**neuromodulators** Neurotransmitters that alter the firing and synaptic characteristics of other neurons, typically over an extended period.

**neuron** Specialized nervous system cell engaged in information processing.

**neuronal circuit** A series of neurons interconnected by synapses that subserve a function when activated.

**neuropeptide** Short, multifunctional amino acid chain (fewer than 100 amino acids); acts as a neurotransmitter and can act as a hormone.

**neuroplasticity** The nervous system's potential to modify itself physically or chemically in response to environmental change and to compensate for age-related changes and injury.

**neuroprosthetics** Field that develops computer-assisted devices to replace lost biological function.

**neuroprotectant** Drug administered to block the cascade of post-trauma neural events.

**neuropsychology** Study of the relationships between brain function and behavior in humans.

**neurotransmitter** Chemical with an excitatory or inhibitory effect when released by a neuron onto a target.

**neurotrophic factor** Chemical compound that supports growth and differentiation in developing neurons and may act to keep certain neurons alive in adulthood.

**nitric oxide (NO)** Gaseous neurotransmitter; acts, for example, to dilate blood vessels, aid digestion, and activate cellular metabolism.

**nociception** Perception of pain, temperature, and itch.

**node of Ranvier** The part of an axon that is not covered by myelin.

**nonregulatory behavior** Behavior unnecessary to an animal's basic survival needs.

**non-REM sleep (N-sleep)** Slow-wave sleep; associated with rhythms having slower waves with larger amplitude.

**noradrenergic neuron** From *adrenaline*, Latin for "epinephrine"; a neuron containing norepinephrine.

**norepinephrine (NE)** Neurotransmitter that accelerates heart rate in mammals; found in the brain and in the sympathetic division of the autonomic nervous system; also known as *noradrenaline*.

**nuclei (sing. nucleus)** A group of neurons forming a cluster that can be identified using special stains.

## O

**obesity** Excessive accumulation of body fat.

**obsessive-compulsive disorder (OCD)** Behavior characterized by uncontrollable repetitive thoughts (obsessions) and compulsively repeated acts (such as hand washing).

**occipital lobe** Lobe of the cerebral cortex that lies beneath the occipital bone.

**ocular dominance column** Functional column in the visual cortex that is maximally responsive to information coming from one eye.

**oligodendroglia** Glial cells in the central nervous system that myelinate axons.

**operant conditioning** Learning procedure in which the consequence (such as obtaining a reward) of a particular behavior (such as pressing a bar) increases or decreases the probability of the behavior occurring again; also called *instrumental conditioning*.

**opponent process** Explanation of color vision that emphasizes the importance of the apparently opposing color pairs: red versus green and blue versus yellow.

**optic ataxia** Deficit in the visual control of reaching and other movements.

**optic chiasm** Junction of the optic nerves, one from each eye, at which the axons from the nasal halves of the retinas cross to the brain's opposite side.

**optogenetics** Transgenic technique that combines genetics and light to excite or inhibit targeted cells in living tissue.

**orbitofrontal cortex (OFC)** Prefrontal cortex behind the eye sockets (the *orbits*); receives projections from the dorsomedial nucleus of the thalamus; central to a variety of emotional and social behaviors, including eating; also called *orbital frontal cortex*.

**organizing effects** Hormonal actions that influence the organizational development of the fetal brain.

**organoid** Artificially grown, simplified, three-dimensional, miniature versions of organ parts, including brain tissue.

**orienting movement** Movement directed to sensory input, such as turning the head to see the source of a sound.

**oscilloscope** Device that uses an electron beam to serves as a sensitive voltmeter, registering changes in voltage over time.

**osmotic thirst** Thirst that results from a high concentration of dissolved chemicals, or *solutes*, in body fluids.

**ossicle** Bone of the middle ear; either the hammer, anvil, and stirrup.

**otoacoustic emissions** Spontaneous or evoked sound waves produced within the ear by the cochlea that escape from the ear.

## P

**pain gate** Hypothetical neural circuit in which activity in fine-touch and pressure pathways diminishes the activity in pain and temperature pathways.

**parahippocampal cortex** Cortex that surrounds the hippocampus; located in the medial temporal lobe.

**paralysis** Loss of sensation and movement due to nervous system injury.

**paraplegia** Paralysis of the legs due to spinal cord injury.

**parasomnia** Unusual or unwanted behavior that disrupts sleep.

**parasympathetic division** Part of the autonomic nervous system that acts in opposition to the sympathetic division—for example, preparing the body to rest and digest by reversing the alarm response or stimulating digestion.

**parietal lobe** Lobe of the neocortex that lies beneath the parietal bone of the skull.

**Parkinson disease** Motor system disorder correlated with dopamine loss in the substantia nigra; characterized by tremors, muscular rigidity, and reduction in voluntary movement.

**parvocellular (P) cell** Small visual system neuron in the lateral geniculate body that is sensitive to color.

**Pavlovian conditioning** Learning achieved when a neutral stimulus (such as a tone) comes to elicit a response after its repeated pairing with some event (such as delivery of food); also called *classical conditioning* or *respondent conditioning*.

**peptide hormone** Chemical messenger translated from cellular RNA; a short string of amino acids.

**perception** Subjective interpretation of sensations.

**periaqueductal gray matter (PAG)** Nuclei in the midbrain that surround the cerebral aqueduct joining the third and fourth ventricles; PAG neurons contain circuits for species-typical behaviors (e.g., female sexual behavior) and play an important role in the modulation of pain.

**peribrachial area** Cholinergic nucleus in the dorsal brainstem having a role in R-sleep behaviors; part of the reticular activating system, which projects to the medial pontine reticular formation.

**period** Time required to complete an activity cycle.

**peripheral nervous system (PNS)** All the neurons in the body outside the brain and spinal cord.

**perirhinal cortex** Cortex lying next to the rhinal fissure on the ventral surface of the brain.

**perseveration** Tendency to emit repeatedly the same verbal or motor response to varied stimuli.

**persistent vegetative state (PVS)** Condition in which a person is alive but unaware, unable to communicate or to function independently at even the most basic level.

**personalized medicine** A medical model whereby treatment is tailored to the individual.

**phenotype** Set of individual characteristics (physical or behavioral traits) that can be seen or measured.

**phenotypic plasticity** An individual's capacity to develop into a range of phenotypes.

**phenylketonuria (PKU)** Behavioral disorder caused by elevated levels of the amino acid phenylalanine in the blood and resulting from a defect in the gene for the enzyme phenylalanine hydroxylase; the major symptom is severe developmental disability.

**pheromone** Odorant biochemical released by one animal that acts as a chemosignal and can affect the physiology or behavior of another animal.

**photoreceptor** Specialized retinal neuron that transduces light into neural activity.

**pituitary gland** Endocrine gland attached to the bottom of the hypothalamus; its secretions control the activities of many other glands of the body.

**place cells** Hippocampal neurons maximally responsive to a specific location in an animal's environment.

**plasticity** Body's potential for physical or chemical change; enhances its adaptability to environmental change and its ability to compensate for injury. (In the brain and nervous system, this potential is called *neuroplasticity*.)

**polysomnography (PSG)** Sleep measurement method that combines measures of multiple sleep events, including brain activity, muscle activity, and ocular activity, to give a representation of an individual's sleep patterns.

**position-point theory** Idea that the motor cortex functions to move a body part to a point in space.

**positron emission tomography (PET)** Imaging technique that detects changes in blood flow by measuring changes in the uptake of compounds such as oxygen or glucose; used to analyze the metabolic activity of neurons.

**posterior spinothalamic tract** Pathway in the posterior segment of the spinal cord that contains fine-touch and pressure sensory fibers.

**postsynaptic membrane** Membrane on the transmitter, or input, side of a synapse.

**posttraumatic apathy** Condition characterized by diminished motivation and purposeful behavior following brain injury or disease.

**posttraumatic growth** The ability to cope with and compensate for deficits resulting from brain injury and disease.

**posttraumatic stress disorder (PTSD)** Syndrome characterized by physiological arousal brought on by recurring memories and dreams related to a traumatic event for months or years after the event.

**preparedness** Predisposition by an animal to emit behavior to certain sensory stimuli.

**presynaptic membrane** Axon terminal membrane on the transmitter, or output, side of a synapse.

**primary auditory cortex (area A1)** Asymmetrical structures within Heschl's gyrus in the temporal lobes; receives auditory input from the ventral region of the medial geniculate nucleus.

**primary visual cortex (V1)** Cortex in the occipital lobe that receives visual input from the lateral geniculate nucleus; also called *striate cortex*.

**priming** Using a stimulus to sensitize the nervous system to a later presentation of the same or a similar stimulus.

**prion** Derived from the terms *protein* and *infection*, *proteinaceous* and *infectious*; an abnormally folded protein involved in progressive neurocognitive disorders.

**procedural memory** Ability to recall a movement sequence or how to perform some act or behavior.

**progenitor cell (precursor cell)** Cell derived from a stem cell that migrates and produces a neuron or a glial cell.

**proprioception** Perception of the position and movement of the body, limbs, and head.

**prosody** Melodic tone of the speaking voice.

**protein** Folded-up polypeptide chain that serves a particular function in the body.

**psyche** Synonym for *mind*; a nonmaterial entity once proposed to be the source of human behavior (specifically, consciousness, imagination, opinion, desire, pleasure, pain, memory, and reason).

**psychoactive drug** Substance that acts to alter mood, thought, or behavior; used to manage neuropsychological illness, but also may be taken recreationally.

**psychobiotics** Treatment that uses live bacteria (probiotics) or compounds to enhance the growth of gut bacteria (prebiotics).

**psychological construct** Idea or set of impressions that some mental ability exists as an entity; examples include memory, language, and emotion.

**psychomotor activation** Increased behavioral and cognitive activity so that at certain levels of consumption, the person using a drug feels energetic and in control.

**psychopharmacology** Study of how drugs affect the nervous system and behavior.

**psychosurgery** Any neurosurgical technique that damages the brain but is intended to improve behavior.

**psychotherapy** Talk therapy derived from Freudian psychoanalysis and other psychological interventions.

**pump** Protein in the cell membrane that actively transports a substance across the membrane.

**Purkinje cell** Distinctively shaped interneuron found in the cerebellum.

**pyramidal cell** Distinctively shaped interneuron found in the cerebral cortex.

**Q**

**quadrantanopia** Blindness of one quadrant of the visual field.

**quadriplegia** Paralysis of the legs and arms due to spinal cord injury; also referred to as *tetraplegia*.

**quantum (pl. quanta)** The number of neurotransmitter molecules, equivalent to the content of a single synaptic vesicle, that produces a just-observable change in the depolarizations of the postsynaptic terminal.

**R**

**radial glial cell** Path-making cell that a migrating neuron follows to its appropriate destination.

**rapidly adapting receptor** Body sensory receptor that responds briefly to the onset of a stimulus on the body.

**rate-limiting factor** Any chemical in limited supply that restricts the pace at which another chemical can be synthesized.

**real-time fMRI (rt-fMRI)** Behavior-modification technique in which individuals learn to change their behavior by controlling their own patterns of brain activation.

**receptive field** Region of sensory space (e.g., skin surface) in which a stimulus modifies a receptor's activity.

**reconsolidation** Process of restabilizing a memory trace after the memory is revisited.

**referred pain** Pain that arises in one of the internal organs but is felt on the surface of the body.

**regulatory behavior** Behavior motivated to meet an animal's survival needs.

**reinforcer** In operant conditioning, any event that strengthens the behavior it follows.

**relatively refractory** The state of an axon in the later phase of an action potential, during which higher-intensity electrical current is required to produce another action potential; a phase during which potassium channels are still open.

**releasing hormone** Peptide released by the hypothalamus that increases or decreases hormone release from the anterior pituitary.

**REM sleep (R-sleep)** Rapid eye movement sleep; REMs are associated with waking-like brain-wave pattern displayed by the neocortical electroencephalographic record.

**resting potential** Electrical charge across the insulating cell membrane in the absence of stimulation; a store of potential energy produced by a greater negative charge on the intracellular side relative to the extracellular side.

**resting-state fMRI (rs-fMRI)** Magnetic resonance imaging method that measures changes in oxygenation levels when the individual is resting (not engaged in a specific task).

**reticular activating system (RAS)** Large reticulum (mixture of cell nuclei and nerve fibers) that runs through the core of the brainstem; associated with sleep–wake behavior and behavioral arousal; also called the *reticular formation*.

**reticular formation** Brainstem area in which nuclei and fiber pathways are mixed, producing a netlike appearance; associated with sleep–wake behavior and behavioral arousal.

**retina** Light-sensitive surface at the back of the eye consisting of neurons and photoreceptor cells.

**retinal ganglion cell (RGC)** One of a group of retinal neurons with axons that give rise to the optic nerve.

**retinohypothalamic tract** Neural route formed by axons of photosensitive retinal ganglion cells (pRGCs) from the retina to the suprachiasmatic nucleus (SCN); allows light to entrain the SCN's rhythmic activity.

**retrograde amnesia** Inability to remember events that took place before the onset of amnesia.

**reuptake** Inactivation of a neurotransmitter when membrane transporter proteins bring the transmitter back into the presynaptic axon terminal for reuse.

**rod** Photoreceptor specialized for functioning at low light levels.

## S

**saltatory conduction** Fast propagation of an action potential at successive nodes of Ranvier; *saltatory* means "leaping."

**schizophrenia** Behavioral disorder characterized by delusions, hallucinations, disorganized speech, blunted emotion, agitation or immobility, and a host of associated symptoms.

**Schwann cell** Glial cell in the peripheral nervous system that myelinates sensory and motor axons.

**scotoma** Small blind spot in the visual field caused by migraine or by a small lesion of the visual cortex.

**scratch reflex** Automatic response in which an animal's hind limb reaches to remove a stimulus from the surface of its body.

**second messenger** Chemical that initiates a biochemical process when activated by a neurotransmitter (the first messenger).

**segmentation** Division into a number of parts that are similar; refers to the idea that many animals, including vertebrates, are composed of similarly organized body segments.

**selective serotonin reuptake inhibitor (SSRI)** Drug that blocks 5-hydroxytryptamine (5-HT) reuptake into the presynaptic terminal; most commonly used to treat depression.

**semaphorins** Class of chemorepulsive molecules that deflect axons from inappropriate regions.

**sensation** Registration by the sensory organs of physical stimuli from the environment.

**sensitization** Learned behavior in which repeated administration of a stimulus results in the progressive amplification of a response.

**sensory neuron** Cell that detects or carries sensory information into the spinal cord and brain.

**serotonin (5-HT)** Amine neurotransmitter; helps to regulate mood and aggression, appetite and arousal, perception of pain, and respiration.

**sexual dimorphism** Differential development of brain areas in the two sexes.

**sexual orientation** A person's pattern of sexual attraction—to the opposite sex, to the same sex, or to both sexes.

**sleep apnea** Inability to breathe during sleep, causing a sleeper to wake up to breathe.

**sleep paralysis** Inability to move that occurs briefly when a person is awake, usually just falling asleep or waking up.

**sleeping beauty syndrome** A rare condition in which the affected individual has recurring bouts of excessive sleeping.

**sleepwalking** N-parasomnia in which the sleeping person may sit up, walk around, and, in some extreme cases, perform complex activities, such as cooking or driving; also called *somnambulism*.

**slowly adapting receptor** Body sensory receptor that responds as long as a sensory stimulus is on the body.

**small-molecule transmitter** Quick-acting neurotransmitter synthesized in the axon terminal from products derived from the diet.

**social neuroscience** Interdisciplinary field that seeks to understand how the brain mediates social interactions.

**somatic nervous system (SNS)** Part of the peripheral nervous system that includes the cranial and spinal nerves to and from the muscles, joints, and skin, which produce movement, transmit incoming sensory input, and inform the central nervous system about the position and movement of body parts.

**somatosensory neuron** Brain cell that brings sensory information from the body into the spinal cord.

**sound wave** Mechanical displacement of molecules caused by changing pressure that possesses the physical properties of frequency and amplitude, and their complex interaction; also referred to as *compression wave*.

**spatial summation** Addition of one graded potential to another, when the potentials occur close in space.

**species** Group of organisms that can interbreed.

**species-typical behavior** Behavior that is characteristic of all members of a species, such as the songs or dances of birds or the eating behavior of animals.

**stereotaxic apparatus** Surgical instrument that holds the head to permit a researcher or neurosurgeon to target a specific part of the brain.

**steroid hormone** Fat-soluble chemical messenger synthesized from cholesterol.

**storage granule** Membranous compartment that holds several vesicles containing a neurotransmitter.

**stretch-activated channel** Ion channel on a tactile sensory neuron that becomes activated in response to stretching of the membrane, initiating a nerve impulse.

**striate (striped) cortex** Primary visual cortex (V1) in the occipital lobe; shows stripes (striations) on staining.

**striatum** Caudate nucleus and putamen of the basal ganglia.

**stroke** Sudden appearance of neurological symptoms as a result of severely reduced blood flow.

**substance use disorder (SUD)** A diagnostic term for a pattern of drug use in which people rely on a drug chronically and excessively, allowing it to occupy a central place in their life.

**subunit** Protein molecule that assembles with other protein molecules.

**subventricular zone** Lining of neural stem cells surrounding the ventricles in adults.

**sudden infant death syndrome (SIDS)** Unexplained death while asleep of a seemingly healthy infant younger than age 1 year.

**sulci (sing. sulcus)** Grooves in brain matter, as are found in the neocortex or cerebellum.

**supplementary speech area** Speech production region on the left frontal lobe dorsal surface.

**sympathetic division** Part of the autonomic nervous system that arouses the body for action, such as mediating the involuntary fight-or-flight response to alarm by increasing heart rate and blood pressure.

**synapse** Spatial junction between one neuron and another; forms the information transfer site between neurons.

**synaptic cleft** Gap separating the neuronal presynaptic membrane from the postsynaptic membrane.

**synaptic vesicle** Membranous compartment that encloses a fixed number (*quantum*) of neurotransmitter molecules.

**synesthesia** Ability to perceive a stimulus of one sense as the sensation of a different sense, as when sound produces a sensation of color; literally, "feeling together."

**syntax** Set of rules for putting together words; proposed to be unique to human language.

**synthetic biology** Design and construction of biological devices, systems, and machines not found in nature.

**T**

**tardive dyskinesia** Inability to stop the tongue or other body parts from moving; motor side effect of neuroleptic drugs.

**Tay-Sachs disease** Inherited birth defect caused by the loss of genes that encode the enzyme necessary for breaking down certain fatty substances; appears 4 to 6 months after birth and results in intellectual disability, physical changes, and death by about age 5.

**tectopulvinar system** Visual projections from the retina to the superior colliculus to the pulvinar (thalamus) to the parietal and temporal visual areas.

**tectum** Roof (area above the ventricle) of the midbrain; its functions are sensory processing, particularly visual and auditory, and the production of orienting movements.

**tegmentum** Floor (area below the ventricle) of the midbrain; a collection of nuclei with movement-related, species-specific, and pain perception functions.

**temporal lobe** Lobe of the neocortex that lies beneath the temporal bone of the skull.

**temporal summation** Addition of graded potentials to each other, when the potentials occur close in time.

**terminal button (end foot)** Knob at the tip of an axon that conveys information to other neurons.

**testosterone** Sex hormone secreted by the testes and responsible for the emergence of typically masculine characteristics.

**thalamus** Diencephalon structure through which information from all sensory systems is organized, integrated, and projected into the appropriate region of the neocortex.

**theory of mind (ToM)** Ability to attribute mental states to others.

**theta wave** Brain waves with a frequency ranging from 4 to 11 Hz.

**threshold potential** Voltage on a neural membrane at which an action potential is triggered by the opening of sodium and potassium voltage-activated channels; about −50 mV relative to the extracellular surroundings; also called *threshold limit*.

**tolerance** Decrease in response to a drug with the passage of time.

**tonotopic representation** In audition, structural organization for processing of sound waves from lower to higher frequencies.

**topographic** Representing function in different areas of the central nervous system.

**topographic map** Spatially organized neural representation of the external world.

**topographic organization** Neural spatial representation of the body or areas of the sensory world perceived by a sensory organ.

**Tourette syndrome** Disorder of the motor system characterized by involuntary vocalizations (sometimes including curse words and grunting sounds) and odd, involuntary movements of the body, especially of the face and head.

**tract** Large collection of axons coursing together *inside* the central nervous system.

**transcranial magnetic stimulation (TMS)** Procedure in which a magnetic coil is placed over the skull to stimulate the underlying brain; used either to induce behavior or to disrupt ongoing behavior.

**transgender** Possessing personal characteristics that transcend traditional gender boundaries and corresponding sexual norms; identification with a gender different from that expected based on the sex assigned at birth.

**transgenic animal** Product of technology in which one or more genes from one species is introduced into the genome of another species to be passed along and expressed in subsequent generations.

**transmitter-activated channel** Receptor complex that has both a receptor site for a chemical and a pore through which ions can flow.

**transmitter-activated receptor** Protein that has a binding site for a specific neurotransmitter and is embedded in the membrane of a cell.

**transporter** Protein molecule that pumps substances across a membrane.

**traumatic brain injury (TBI)** Wound to the brain that results from a blow to the head.

**trichromatic theory** Explanation of color vision based on the coding of three primary colors: red, green, and blue.

**tricyclic** Drug, characterized by its three-ring chemical structure, that blocks 5-hydroxy-tryptamine (5-HT) reuptake transporter proteins.

**tripartite synapse** Synapse between a presynaptic neuron, a postsynaptic neuron, and an astrocyte.

**tropic molecule** Signaling molecule that attracts or repels growth cones.

**tumor** Mass of new tissue that grows in an uncontrolled manner and is independent of surrounding structures.

**U**

**unconditioned response (UCR)** Unlearned, naturally occurring response to an unconditioned stimulus (UCS), such as salivation when food is in the mouth.

**unconditioned stimulus (UCS)** Stimulus that naturally and automatically (unconditionally) triggers an unconditioned response (UCR).

**V**

**ventral stream** Visual processing pathway from region V1 to the temporal lobe that mediates perception, as opposed to action mediated by the dorsal stream.

**ventricles** Cavities in the brain that make and contain cerebrospinal fluid.

**ventrolateral thalamus** Part of the thalamus that carries information about body senses to the somatosensory cortex.

**vertebrae (sing. vertebra)** The bones that form the spinal column.

**vestibular system** Somatosensory system comprising a set of receptors in each inner ear that respond to body position and to movement of the head.

**virtual reality (VR) exposure therapy** Controlled virtual immersion environment that, by allowing individuals to relive traumatic events, gradually desensitizes them to stress.

**visual field** Region of the visual world seen by the eyes.

**visual-form agnosia** Inability to recognize objects or drawings of objects.

**visuospatial memory** Use of visual information to recall an object's location in space.

**voltage-activated channel** Gated protein channel that opens or closes only at specific membrane voltages.

**voltage gradient** Difference in electric potential between two regions that allows a flow of current if the two regions are connected.

**voltmeter** Device that measures the strength of electrical voltage by recording the difference in electrical potential between two points.

**vomeronasal organ (VNO)** Collection of neurons that detect pheromones; it plays a role in reproduction and social behavior in many mammals, though its specific function in humans is disputed.

**W**

**wanting-and-liking theory** Explanation holding that both wanting and liking mediated by separate neural systems underlie addiction; also called *incentive sensitization theory*.

**Wernicke's area** Secondary auditory cortex (planum temporale) lying behind Heschl's gyrus at the rear of the left temporal lobe; regulates language comprehension; also known as the *posterior speech zone*.

**white matter** Areas of the nervous system composed mainly of myelin-sheathed axons.

**wild type** Typical allele (most common in a population).

**withdrawal symptom** Any of the physical and psychological behaviors displayed when drug use ends.

**Z**

**Zeitgeber** Environmental event that entrains biological rhythms; German for "time giver."

**zinc** An ion transmitter that is packaged and stored in vesicles and when released, interacts with several receptors.

**zoopharmacognosy** Behavior in which nonhuman animals self-medicate.

## CHAPTER 1

Berwick, R., & Chomsky, N. (2016). *Why only us: Language and evolution.* MIT Press.

Blum, M., & Blum, L. (2021). A theoretical computer science perspective on consciousness. *Journal of Artificial Intelligence and Consciousness, 8*(1), 1–42.

Challa, H. J., Bandlamudi, M., & Uppaluri, K. R. (2021, August). Paleolithic diet. *StatPearls.* https://www.statpearls.com/nursepractitioner/ce/activity/37317

Challenger, M. (2021). *How to be an animal: A new history of what it means to be human.* Penguin.

Changeux, J. P., Goulas, A., & Hilgetag, C. C. (2021). A connectomic hypothesis for the hominization of the brain. *Cerebral Cortex, 31,* 2425–2449.

Churchland, P. (1986). *Neurophilosophy: Toward a Unified Science of the Mind-Brain.* MIT Press.

Conca, F., Borsa, V. M., Cappa, S. F., & Catricalà, E. (2021). The multidimensionality of abstract concepts: A systematic review. *Neuroscience and Biobehavioural Reviews, 127,* 474–491.

Conroy, G. C., Lamont, R. W., Bridges, L., Stephens, D., Wardell-Johnson, A., & Ogbourne, S. M. (2021). Conservation concerns associated with low genetic diversity for K'gari-Fraser Island dingoes. *Scientific Reports, 11,* 9503.

Darwin, C. (1871). *The descent of man, and selection in relation to sex.* J. Murray.

Darwin, C. (1963). *On the origin of species by means of natural selection, or the preservation of favored races in the struggle for life.* New American Library. (Original work published 1859.)

Darwin, C. (1965). *The expression of the emotions in man and animals.* University of Chicago Press. (Original work published 1872.)

Deary, I. J. (2000). *Looking down on human intelligence: From psychometrics to the brain.* Oxford Psychology Series, No. 34. Oxford University Press.

Derex, M., & Mesoudi, A. (2020). Cumulative cultural evolution within evolving population structures. *Trends in Cognitive Science, 24*(8), 654–667.

Descartes, R. (1972). *Treatise on man* (T. S. Hall, Trans.). Harvard University Press. (Original work published 1664.)

Dunbar, R. (1998). *Grooming, gossip, and the evolution of language.* Harvard University Press.

Edlow, B. L., Claassen, J., Schiff, N. D., & Greer, D. M. (2021). Recovery from disorders of consciousness: Mechanisms, prognosis and emerging therapies. *Nature Reviews Neurology. 17*(3), 135–156.

Eibl-Eibesfeldt, I. (1970). *Ethology: The biology of behavior.* Holt, Rinehart and Winston.

Flynn, J. R. (2012). *Are we getting smarter? Rising IQ in the twenty-first century.* Cambridge University Press.

Fonseca-Azevedo, K., & Herculano-Houzel, S. (2012). Metabolic constraint imposes tradeoff between body size and number of brain neurons in human evolution. *Proceedings of the National Academy of Sciences of the United States of America, 109*(45), 18571–18576.

Gardner, H. (2006). *Multiple intelligences: New horizons.* Basic Books.

Gardner, R. A., & Gardner, B. T. (1969). Teaching sign language to a chimpanzee. *Science, 165*(3894), 664–672.

GBD 2016 Neurology Collaborators. (2019, May). Global, regional, and national burden of neurological disorders, 1990–2016: A systematic analysis for the Global Burden of Disease Study 2016. *Lancet Neurology, 18*(5), 459–480.

Gordon, A. D., Nevell, L., & Wood, B. (2008). The *Homo floresiensis* cranium (LB1): Size, scaling, and early *Homo* affinities. *Proceedings of the National Academy of Sciences of the United States of America, 105*(12), 4650–4655.

Gould, S. J. (1981). *The mismeasure of man.* Norton.

Gross, C. G. (1995). Aristotle on the brain. *The Neuroscientist, 1*(4), 245–250.

Gunz, P., Neubauer, S., Falk, D., Tafforeau, P., Le Cabec, A., Smith, T. M., Kimbel, W. H., Spoor, F., & Alemseged, Z. (2020). *Australopithecus afarensis* endocasts suggest ape-like brain organization and prolonged brain growth. *Science Advances, 6*(14), eaaz4729.

Hebb, D. O. (1949). *The organization of behavior: A neuropsychological theory.* Wiley.

Herculano-Houzel, S. (2018, April 1). The evolution of human capabilities and abilities. *Cerebrum,* cer-05-18.

Herculano-Houzel, S. (2019). Life history changes accompany increased numbers of cortical neurons: A new framework for understanding human brain evolution. *Progress in Brain Research, 26*(250), 179–216.

Herculano-Houzel, S., Avelino-de-Souza, K., Neves, K., Porfirio, J., Messeder, D., Mattos Feijó, L., Maldonado, J., & Manger, P. R. (2014). The elephant brain in numbers. *Frontiers in Neuroanatomy, 8,* 46.

Heron, W. (1957). The pathology of boredom. *Scientific American, 196*(1), 52–56.

Herringa, R. J., Birn, R. M., Ruttle, P. L., Burghy, C. A., Stodola, D. E., Davidson, R. J., & Essex, M. J. (2013). Childhood maltreatment is associated with altered fear circuitry and increased internalizing symptoms by late adolescence. *Proceedings of the National Academy of Sciences of the United States of America, 110*(47), 19119–19124.

Jacobson, E. (1932). Electrophysiology of mental activities. *American Journal of Psychology, 44*(4), 677–694.

Jerison, H. J. (1973). *The evolution of the brain and intelligence.* Academic Press.

Johanson, D., & Edey, M. (1981). *Lucy: The beginnings of humankind.* Warner Books.

Jones-London, M. (2020). NINDS strategies for enhancing the diversity of neuroscience researchers. *Neuron, 107*(2), 212–214.

Kunz, A. R., & Iliadis, C. (2007). Hominid evolution of the arteriovenous system through the cranial base and its relevance for craniosynostosis. *Child's Nervous System, 23,* 1367–1377.

Li, M. L., Tang, H., Shao, Y., Wang, M. S., Xu, H. B., Wang, S., Irwin. D. M., Adeola, A. C., Zeng, T., Chen, L., Li, Y., & Wu, D. D. (2020). Evolution and transition of expression trajectory during human brain development. *BMC Evolutionary Biology 20,* 72.

Linge, F. R. (1990). Faith, hope, and love: Nontraditional therapy in recovery from serious head injury, a personal account. *Canadian Journal of Psychology, 44*(2), 116–129.

Marcé-Nogué, J., Püschel, T. A., Daasch, A., & Kaiser, T. M. (2020). Broad-scale morphofunctional traits of the mandible suggest no hard food adaptation in the hominin lineage. *Scientific Reports, 10,* 6793.

Milton, K. (2003). The critical role played by animal source foods in human (*Homo*) evolution. *Journal of Nutrition, 133*(Suppl. 2), 3886S–3892S.

Natale, S. (2021). *Deceitful media: Artificial intelligence and life after the Turing test.* Oxford University Press.

Roberts, S. G. B., & Roberts, A. I. (2020). Social and ecological complexity is associated with gestural repertoire size of wild chimpanzees. *Integrative Zoology, 15*(4), 276–292.

Savage-Rumbaugh, S. (1999). Ape communication: Between a rock and a hard place in origins of language—What non-human primates can tell us. In B. J. King (Ed.), *Origins of language: What non-human primates can tell us* (pp. 115–188). School of American Research Press.

Schultz, A. K., Wu, J. N., Ha, S. Y. S., Kim, G., Slade, S. B., Rivera, S., Reidenberg, J. S., & Hu, D. L. (2021). Suction feeding by elephants. *Journal of the Royal Society Interface, 18*(179), 20210215.

Scolding, N., Owen, A. M., & Keown, J. (2021). Prolonged disorders of consciousness: A critical evaluation of the new UK guidelines. *Brain, 144*(6), awab063.

Shearer, C. B. (2020). A resting state functional connectivity analysis of human intelligence: Broad theoretical and practical implications for multiple intelligences theory. *Psychology & Neuroscience, 13*(2), 127–148.

Terkel, J. (1995). Cultural transmission in the black rat: Pinecone feeding. *Advances in the Study of Behavior, 24,* 119–154.

Tononi, G. (2012). *PHI: A voyage from the brain to the soul.* Pantheon Books.

Tooley, U. A., Bassett, D. S., & Mackey, A. P. (2021). Environmental influences on the pace of brain development. *Nature Review Neuroscience, 22,* 372–384. https://doi.org/10.1038/s41583-021-00457-5.

Villmoare, B., Kimbel, W. H., Seyoum, C., Campisano, C. J., DiMaggio, E. J., Rowan, J., Braun, D. R., Arrowsmith, J. R., & Reed, K. E. (2015). Early *Homo* at 2.8 Ma from Ledi-Geraru, Afar, Ethiopia. *Science, 347*(6228), 1352–1355.

Watson, S. K., Townsend, S. W., Schel, A. M., Wilke, C., Wallace, E. K., Cheng, L., West, V., & Slocombe, K. E., (2015). Vocal learning in the functionally referential food grunts of chimpanzees. *Current Biology, 25*(4), 495–499.

Weiner, J. (1995). *The beak of the finch.* Vintage.

Wilson, M. L. (2021). Insights into human evolution from 60 years of research on chimpanzees at Gombe. *Evolution and Human Science, 3,* e8.

Zeberg, H., & Pääbo, S. (2020). The major genetic risk factor for severe COVID-19 is inherited from Neanderthals. *Nature, 587,* 610–612.

Zwir, I., Del-Val, C., Hintsanen, M., Cloninger, K. M., Romero-Zaliz, R., Mesa, A., Arnedo, J., Salas, R., Poblete, G. F., Raitoharju, E., Raitakari, O., Keltikangas-Järvinen, L., de Erausquin, G. A., Tattersall, I., Lehtimäki, T., & Cloninger, C. R. (2021, April 21). Evolution of genetic networks for human creativity. *Molecular Psychiatry*. Epub ahead of print. https://doi .org/10.1038/s41380-021-01097-y

## CHAPTER 2

Avetisyan, M., Schill, E. M., & Heuchkeroth, R. O. (2015). Building a second brain in the bowel. *Journal of Clinical Investigation, 125*(3), 899–907.

Barton, R. A. (2012). Embodied cognitive evolution and the cerebellum. *Philosophical Transactions of the Royal Society B, 367*(1599), 2097–2107.

Baumann, O., Borra, R. J., Bower, J. M., Cullen, K. E., Habas, C., Ivry, R. B., et al. (2015). Consensus paper: The role of the cerebellum in perceptual processes. *Cerebellum, 14*, 197–220.

Brodmann, K. (1909). *Vergleichende Lokalisationlehr der Grosshirnrinde in ihren Prinzipien dargestellt auf Grund des Zellenbaues.* J. A. Barth.

Fiorito, G., & Scotto, P. (1992). Observational learning in *Octopus vulgaris. Science, 256*(5056), 545–547.

Gilbert, S. F., & Epel, D. (2009). *Ecological developmental biology: Integrating epigenetics, medicine, and evolution.* Sinauer.

Glasser, M. F., Coalson, T. S., Robinson, E. C., Hacker, C. D., Harwell, J., Yacoub, E., Ugurbil, K., Andersson, J., Beckmann, C. F., Jenkinson, M., Smith, S. M., & van Essen, D. C. (2016). A multi-modal parcellation of human cerebral cortex. *Nature, 536*(7615), 171–178.

Goyal, M., Demchuk, A. M., Menon, B. K., Eesa, M., Rempel, J. L., Thornton, J., Roy, D., Jovin, T. G., Willinsky, R. A., Sapkota, B. L., Dowlatshahi, D., Frei, D. F., Kamal, N. R., Montanera, W. J., Poppe, A. Y., Ryckborst, K. J., Silver, F. L., Shuaib, A., Tampieri, D., Williams, D., ... ESCAPE Trial Investigators. (2015). Randomized assessment of rapid endovascular treatment of ischemic stroke. *New England Journal of Medicine, 372*(11), 1019–1030.

Hatcher, M. A., & Starr, J. A. (2011). Role of tissue plasminogen activator in ischemic stroke. *Annals of Pharmacotherapy, 45*(3), 364–371.

Keyhanian, K., Umeton, R. P., Mohit, B., Davoudi, V., Hajighasemi, F., & Ghasemi, M. (2020). SARS-CoV-2 and nervous system: From pathogenesis to clinical manifestation. *Journal of Neuroimmunology, 350*, 577436.

Sender, R., Fuchs, S., & Milo, R. (2016). Are we really vastly outnumbered? Revisiting the ratio of bacterial to host cells in humans. *Cell, 164*(3), 337–340.

Sharma, N., Chakrabarti, S., & Grover, S. (2016). Gender differences in caregiving among family-caregivers of people with mental illness. *World Journal of Psychiatry, 6*(1), 7–17.

Sokolov, A. A., Miall, R. C., & Ivry, R. B. (2017). The cerebellum: Adaptive prediction for movement and cognition. *Trends in Cognitive Sciences, 21*(5), 313–332.

van Essen, D. C., & Glasser, M. F. (2018). Parcellating cerebral cortex: How invasive animal studies inform noninvasive mapmaking in humans. *Neurons, 99*(4), 640–663. https://doi .org/10.1016/j.neuron.2018.07.002

Zeiler, S. R. (2019). Should we care about early post-stroke rehabilitation? Not yet, but soon. *Current Neurology and Neuroscience Report, 19*(3), 13. https://doi.org/10.1007/ s11910-019-0927-x.

## CHAPTER 3

Anirudh, K. V. S., Jasti, T., & Kandra, P. (2021, May 25). CRISPR/Cas9 in cancer: An attempt to the present trends and future prospects. *Biotechnology and Applied Biochemistry*. https://doi .org/10.1002/bab.2200.

Bainbridge, M. N., Wiszniewski, W., Murdock, D. R., Friedman, J., Gonzaga-Jauregui, C., Newsham, I., Reid, J. G., Fink, J. K., Morgan, M. B., Gingras, M. C., Muzny, D. M., Hoang, L. D., Yousaf, S., Lupski, J. R., & Gibbs, R. A. (2011). Whole-genome sequencing for optimized patient management. *Science and Translational Medicine, 3*(87), 87re3.

Bonnerjee, D., & Bagh, S. (2021). Application of CRISPR-Cas systems in neuroscience. *Progress in Molecular Biological Translation Science, 178*, 231–264.

Brooks, J. (2016, May 5). How many pages does it take to print out someone's genetic code? *KQED Science.*

Carulli, D., & Verhaagen, J. (2021). An extracellular perspective on CNS maturation: Perineuronal nets and the control of plasticity. *International Journal of Molecular Science, 22*(5), 2434.

Check, E. (2007, June 1). James Watson's genome sequenced. *Nature News.* https://doi .org/10.1038/news070528-10.

Frolows, N., & Ashe, A. (2021, June 7). Small RNAs and chromatin in the multigenerational epigenetic landscape of *Caenorhabditis elegans. Philosophical Transaction of the Royal Society of London B: Biological Science, 376*(1826), 20200112.

Herculano-Houzel, S., Manger, P. R., & Kaas, J. H. (2014). Brain scaling in mammalian evolution as a consequence of concerted and mosaic changes in numbers of neurons and average neuronal cell size. *Frontiers in Neuroanatomy, 8*, 77.

Hernaiz-Llorens, M., Martínez-Mármol, R., Roselló-Busquets, C., & Soriano, E. (2021). One raft to guide them all, and in axon regeneration inhibit them. *International Journal of Molecular Science, 22*, 5009.

Jardim-Messeder, D., Lambert, K., Noctor, S., Pestana, F. M., de Castro Leal, M. E., Bertelsen, M. F., Alagaili, A. N., Mohammad, O. B., Manger, P. R., & Herculano-Houzel, S. (2017). Dogs have the most neurons, though not the largest brain: Trade-off between body mass and number of neurons in the cerebral cortex of large carnivoran species. *Frontiers in Neuroanatomy, 11*, 118.

Kaati, G., Bygren, L. O., Pembrey, M., & Sjöström, M. (2007). Transgenerational response to nutrition, early life circumstances and longevity. *European Journal of Human Genetics, 15*(7), 784–790.

Kenny, A., Plank, M. J., & David, T. (2018). The role of astrocytic calcium and TRPV4 channels in neurovascular coupling. *Journal of Computer Neuroscience, 44*, 97–114.

Meng, H.-R., Suenaga, T., Edamura, M., Fukuda, A., Ishida, Y., Nakahara, D., & Murakami, G. (2021). Functional MHCI deficiency induces ADHD-like symptoms with increased dopamine D1 receptor expression. *Brain Behavior and Immunity, S0889-1591*(21), 00196-3.

Miller, M. B., Reed, H. C., & Walsh, C. A. (2021). Brain somatic mutation in aging and Alzheimer's disease. *Annual Review of Genomics and Human Genetics, 22*, 239–256.

Ostrom, Q. T., Patil, N., Cioffi, G., Waite, K., Kruchko, C., & Barnholtz-Sloan, J. S. (2020). CBTRUS statistical report: Primary brain and other central nervous system tumors diagnosed in the United States in 2013–2017. *Neuro-Oncology, 22*(12 Suppl 2), iv1–iv96.

Pérez-Rodríguez, D. R., Blanco-Luquin, I., & Mendioroz, M. (2021). The participation of microglia in neurogenesis: A review. *Brain Sciences, 11*(5), 658.

Ramón y Cajal, S. (1909–1911). *Histologie du systeme nerveux de l'homme et des vertebres.* Paris: Maloine.

Rynes, M. L., Surinach, D. A., Linn, S., Laroque, M., Rajendran, V., Dominguez, J., Hadjistamoulou, O., Navabi, Z. S., Ghanbari, L., Johnson, G. W., Nazari, M., Mohajerani, M. H., & Kodandaramaiah, S. B. (2021). Miniaturized head-mounted microscope for whole-cortex mesoscale imaging in freely behaving mice. *Nature Methods, 18*(4), 417–425.

Salzberg, S. L. (2018). Open questions: How many genes do we have? *BMC Biology, 16*, 94.

Sisodiya, S. M. (2021). Precision medicine and therapies of the future. *Epilepsia. 62*(Suppl. 2), S90–S105.

Stricker-Shaver, J., Novati, A., Yu-Taeger, L., & Nguyen, H. P. (2018). Genetic rodent model of Huntington disease. *Advances in Experimental Medicine and Biology, 1049*, 29–57.

Takano, T., & Soderling, S. H. (2021). Tripartite synaptomics: Cell-surface proximity labeling in vivo. *Neuroscience Research, S0168-0102*(21), 00099-7.

Urnov, F. D. (2021). The Cas9 hammer and sickle: A challenge for genome editors. *CRISPR Journal, 4*(1), 6–13.

Waddington, C. H. (1956). Genetic assimilation of the bithorax phenotype. *Evolution, 10*(1), 1–13.

Wang, J., Zhuge, X., & Zhuge, F. (2021). Hybrid oxide brain-inspired neuromorphic devices for hardware implementation of artificial intelligence. *Science and Technology of Advanced Materials, 22*(1), 326–344.

Webb, B. (2020). Robots with insect brains. *Science, 368*(6488), 244–245.

Yang, S., & Ye, K. (2021). Recent advances in understanding the adaptive evolution of metabolic genes and traits. *Current Opinion in Clinical Nutrition and Metabolic Care, 24*(4), 308–314.

## CHAPTER 4

Bartholow, R. (1874). Experimental investigation into the functions of the human brain. *British Medical Journal, 1*(700), 727.

Beghi, E. (2020). The epidemiology of epilepsy. *Neuroepidemiology, 54*(2), 185–191.

Bender, K. J., & Trussell, L. O. (2012). The physiology of the axon initial segment. *Annual Review of Neuroscience, 35*, 249–265.

Cendes, F., Theodore, W. H., Brinkmann, B. H., Sulc, V., & Cascino, G. D. (2016). Neuroimaging of epilepsy. *Handbook of Clinical Neurology, 136*, 985–1014.

C. O., Personal correspondence with author, July 14, 2021.

Crotty, P., Sangrey, T., & Levy, W. B. (2006). Metabolic energy cost of action potential velocity. *Journal of Neurophysiology, 96*(3), 1237–1246.

Descartes, R. (1972). *Treatise on man* (T. S. Hall, Trans.). Harvard University Press. (Original work published 1664.)

Eccles, J. (1965). The synapse. *Scientific American, 21*(1), 56–66.

Hodgkin, A. L., & Huxley, A. F. (1939). Action potentials recorded from inside nerve fiber. *Nature, 144,* 710–711.

Höfflin, F., Jack, A., Riedel, C., Mack-Bucher, J., Roos, J., Corcelli, C., Shultz, C., Wahle, P., & Engelhardt, M. (2017). Heterogeneity of the axon initial segment in interneurons and pyramidal cells of rodent visual cortex. *Front Cell Neuroscience, 11,* 332.

Khalilov, I., Minlebaev, M., Mukhtarov, M., & Khazipov, R. (2015). Dynamic changes from depolarizing to hyperpolarizing GABAergic actions during giant depolarizing potentials in the neonatal rat hippocampus. *Journal of Neuroscience, 35*(37), 12635–12642.

Pan, Z.-H., Lu, Q., Bi, A., Dizhoor, A. M., & Abrams, G. W. (2015). Optogenetic approaches to restoring vision. *Annual Reviews of Vision Science, 1,* 185–210.

Patra, D. P., Hess, R. A., Abi-Aad, K. R., Muzyka, I. M., & Bendok, B. R. (2019). Roberts Bartholow: The progenitor of human cortical stimulation and his contentious experiment. *Neurosurgery Focus, 47*(3), E6.

Reich, D. S., Lucchinetti, C. F., & Calabresi, P. A. (2018). Multiple sclerosis. *The New England Journal of Medicine, 378*(2), 169–180.

Rezania, K., Soliven, B., Baron, J., Lin, H., Penumalli, V., & van Besien, K. (2012). Myasthenia gravis, an autoimmune manifestation of lymphoma and lymphoproliferative disorders: Case reports and review of literature. *Leukemia & Lymphoma, 53*(3), 371–380.

Rho, J., Sankar, R., & Stafstrom, C. E. (Eds.). (2010). *Epilepsy: Mechanisms, models, and translational perspectives.* CRC.

Schiess, M., Urbanczik, R., & Senn, W. (2016). Somato-dendritic synaptic plasticity and error-backpropagation in active dendrites. *PLOS Computational Biology, 12*(2), e1004638.

Sterley, T.-L., Baimoukhametova, D., Füzesi, T., Zurek, A. A., Daviu, N., Rasiah, N. P., Rosenegger, D., & Bains, J. S. (2018). Social transmission and buffering of synaptic changes after stress. *Nature Neuroscience, 21*(3), 393–403.

Stys, P. K. (2013). Pathoetiology of multiple sclerosis: Are we barking up the wrong tree? *F1000Prime Reports, 5,* 20.

**CHAPTER 5**

Anand, A., Patience, A. A., Sharma, N., & Khurana, N. (2017). The present and future of pharmacotherapy of Alzheimer's disease: A comprehensive review. *European Journal of Pharmacology, 815,* 364–375.

Ballard, A., Tetrud, J. W., & Langston, J. W. (1985). Permanent human parkinsonism due to 1-methyl-4-phenyl-1, 2, 3, 6-tetrahydropyridine (MPTP). *Neurology, 35*(7), 949–956.

Barbeau, A., Murphy, G. F., & Sourkes, T. L. (1961). Excretion of dopamine in diseases of basal ganglia. *Science, 133*(3465), 1706–1707.

Barth, C., Villringer, A., & Sacher, J. (2015). Sex hormones affect neurotransmitters and shape the adult female brain during hormonal transition periods. *Frontiers in Neuroscience, 20,* 9–37.

Birkmayer, W., & Hornykiewicz, O. (1961). Der L-3, 4-Dioxyphenylalanin (L-DOPA) Effekt bei der Parkinson A Kinase. *Wiener Klinische, 73,* 787–789.

Bourgin, J., Cachia, A., Boumezbeur, F., Djemaï, B., Bottlaender, M., Duchesnay, E., Mériaux, S., & Jay, T. M. (2015). Hyper-responsivity to stress in rats is associated with a large increase in amygdala volume: A 7T MRI study. *European Journal of Neuropsychopharmacology, 25*(6), 828–835.

Chidambaram, S. B., Rathipriya, A. G., Bolla, S. R., Bhat, A., Ray, B., Mahalakshmi, A. M., Manivasagam, T., Thenmozhi, A. J., Essa, M. M., Guillemin, G. J., Chandra, R., & Sakharkar, M. K. (2019). Dendritic spines: Revisiting the physiological role. *Progress in Neuropsychopharmacology & Biological Psychiatry, 92,* 161–193. https://doi.org/10.1016/j.pnpbp.2019.01.005.

Clauss, J. A., Avery, S. N., & Blackford, J. U. (2015). The nature of individual differences in inhibited temperament and risk for psychiatric disease: A review and meta-analysis. *Progress in Neurobiology, 127–128,* 23–45.

Dere, E., & Zlomuzica, A. (2012). The role of gap junctions in the brain in health and disease. *Neuroscience & Biobehavioral Reviews, 36*(1), 206–217.

Ehringer, H., & Hornykiewicz, O. (1960/1974). Distribution of noradrenaline and dopamine (3-hydroxytyramine) in the human brain and their behavior in the presence of disease affecting the extrapyramidal system. In J. Marks (Ed.), *The treatment of Parkinsonism with L-dopa* (pp. 45–56). MTP Medical and Technical Publishing.

Hamilton, T. J., Wheatley, B. M., Sinclair, D. B., Bachmann, M., Larkum, M. E., & Colmers, W. F. (2010). Dopamine modulates synaptic plasticity in dendrites of rat and human dentate granule cells. *Proceedings of the National Academy of Sciences of the United States of America, 107*(42), 18185–18190.

Harris, J. P., Burrell, J. C., Struzyna, L. A., Chen, H. I., Serruya, M. D., Wolf, J. A., Duda, J. E., & Cullen, D. K. (2020). Emerging regenerative medicine and tissue engineering strategies for Parkinson's disease. *NPJ Parkinson's Disease, 8*(6), 4.

Kellar, D., & Craft, S. (2020). Brain insulin resistance in Alzheimer's disease and related disorders: mechanisms and therapeutic approaches. *The Lancet: Neurology, 19*(9), 758–766. https://doi.org/10.1016/S1474-4422(20)30231-3.

Lajud, N., & Torner, L. (2015). Early life stress and hippocampal neurogenesis in the neonate: Sexual dimorphism, long-term consequences and possible mediators. *Frontiers in Molecular Neuroscience, 8,* 3.

Landré, L., Destrieux, C., Baudry, M., Barantin, L., Cottier, J. P., Martineau, J., Hommet, C., Isingrini, M., Belzung, C., Gaillard, P., Camus, V., & El Hage, W. (2010). Preserved subcortical volumes and cortical thickness in women with sexual abuse-related PTSD. *Psychiatry Research, 183*(3), 181–186.

Langston, W. J., & Palfreman, J. (2014). *The case of the frozen addicts.* Pantheon.

Magee, J. C., & Cook, E. P. (2000). Somatic EPSP amplitude is independent of synapse location in hippocampal pyramidal neurons. *Nature Neuroscience, 3*(9), 895–903.

McAllister, B. B., & Dyck, R. H. (2017). Zinc transporter 3 (ZnT3) and vesicular zinc in central nervous system function. *Neurosciences & Biobehavioral Reviews, 80,* 329–350.

McEwen, B. S. (2019). Hormones and behavior and the integration of brain-body science. *Hormones and Behavior, 119,* 104619. https://doi.org/10.1016/j.yhbeh.2019.104619

McGowan, P. O., Sasaki, A., D'Alessio, A. C., Dymov, S., Labonté, B., Szyf, M., Turecki, G., & Meaney, M. J. (2009). Epigenetic regulation of the glucocorticoid receptor in human brain associates with childhood abuse. *Nature Neurosciences, 12*(3), 342–348.

Mechoulam, R., & Gaoni, Y. (1967). The absolute configuration of delta-1-tetrahydrocannabinol, the major active constituent of hashish. *Tetrahedron Letters, 12,* 1109–1111.

Mechoulam, R., Hanus, L. O., Pertwee, R., & Howlett, A. C. (2014). Early phytocannabinoid chemistry to endocannabinoids and beyond. *Nature Neuroscience Reviews, 15*(11), 757–764.

Moore, T. J., Glenmullen, J., & Mattison, D. R. (2014). Reports of pathological gambling, hypersexuality and compulsive shopping associated with dopamine receptor agonist drugs. *JAMA Internal Medicine, 174*(12), 1930–1933.

Morgan, J. (2016). Joy of super smeller: Sebum clues for PD diagnostics. *The Lancet: Neurology, 15*(2), 138–139. https://doi.org/10.1016/S1474-4422(15)00396-8

Nagy, J. I., Pereda, A. E., & Rash, J. E. (2017). On the occurrence and enigmatic functions of mixed (chemical plus electrical) synapses in the mammalian CNS. *Neuroscience Letters, S0304-3940*(17), 30755-3.

Palfreman, J. (2015). *Brain storms: The race to unlock the mystery of Parkinson's disease.* Scientific American/Farrar, Straus and Giroux.

Parkinson, J. (1989). An essay on the shaking palsy. In A. D. Morris & F. C. Rose (Eds.), *James Parkinson: His life and times* (pp. 151–175). Birkhauser. (Original work published 1817.)

Sacks, O. (1976). *Awakenings.* Doubleday.

Sapolsky, R. M. (2004). *Why zebras don't get ulcers* (3rd ed.). Henry Holt.

Sapolsky, R. M. (2005). The influence of social hierarchy on primate health. *Science, 308*(5722), 648–652.

Scudellari, M. (2017). Your body is teeming with weed receptors. *The Scientist.* https://www.the-scientist.com/?articles.view/articleNo/49810/title/Your-Body-Is-Teeming-with-Weed-Receptors/

Totland, M. Z., Rasmussen, N. L., Knudsen, L. M., & Leithe, E. (2019). Regulation of gap junction intercellular communication by connexin ubiquitination: Physiological and pathophysiological implications. *Cell and Molecular Life Sciences, 77*(4), 573–591. https://doi.org/10.1007/s00018-019-03285-0

Tréatikoff, C. (1974). Thesis for doctorate in medicine. In J. Marks (Ed.), *The treatment of Parkinsonism with L-dopa* (pp. 29–38). MTP Medical and Technical Publishing. (Original work published 1919.)

Trivedi, D. K., Sinclair, E., Xu, Y., Sarkar, D., Walton-Doyle, C., Liscio, C., Banks, P., Milne, J., Silverdale, M., Kunath, T., Goodacre, R., & Barran, P. (2019). Discovery of volatile biomarkers of Parkinson's disease from sebum. *ACS Central Science, 5*(4), 599–606. https://doi.org/10.1021/acscentsci.8b00879

Ungerstedt, U. (1971). Adipsia and aphagia after 6-hydroxydopamine induced degeneration of the nigrostriatal dopamine system in the rat brain. *Acta Physiologica (Scandinavia), 82*(Suppl. 367), 95–122.

Upmanyu, N., Jin, J., Ganzella, M., Bösche, L., Malviya, V. N., Zhuleku, E., Politi, A., Ninov, M., Silbern, I., Urlaub, H., Riedel, D., Preobraschenski, J., Milosevic, I., Jahn, R., &

Sambandan, S. (2021). Co-localization of different neurotransmitter transporters on the same synaptic vesicle is bona-fide yet sparse. *bioRxiv*. Epub ahead of print. https://doi.org/10.1101/2021.06.30.449903

Weilinger, N. L., Lohman, A. W., Rakai, B. D., Ma, E. M., Bialecki, J., Maslieieva, V., Rilea, T., Bandet, M. V., Ikuta, N. T., Scott, L., Colicos, M. A., Teskey, G. C., Winship, I. R., & Thompson, R. J. (2016). Metabotropic NMDA receptor signaling couples Src family kinases to pannexin-1 during excitotoxicity. *Nature Neuroscience, 19*, 432–442.

Widner, H., Tetrud, J., Rehngrona, S., Snow, B., Brundin, P., Gustavii, B., Björklund, A., Lindvall, O., & Langston, J. W. (1992). Bilateral fetal mesencephalic grafting in two patients with Parkinsonism induced by 1-methyl-4-phenyl-1, 2, 3, 6-tetrahydropyridine (MPTP). *New England Journal of Medicine, 327*, 1556–1563.

## CHAPTER 6

Asarnow, J. R., Porta, G., Spirito, A., Emslie, G., Clarke, G., Wagner, K. D., Vitiello, B., Keller, M., Birmaher, B., McCracken, J., Mayes, T., Berk, M., & Brent, D. A. (2011). Suicide attempts and nonsuicidal self-injury in the treatment of resistant depression in adolescents: Findings from the TORDIA study. *Journal of the American Academy of Child and Adolescent Psychiatry, 50*(8), 772–781.

Ayano, G., Tesfaw, G., & Shumet, S. (2019). The prevalence of schizophrenia and other psychotic disorders among homeless people: A systematic review and meta-analysis. *BMC Psychiatry, 19*(1), 370.

Becker, J. B., & Chartoff, E. (2019). Sex differences in neural mechanisms mediating reward and addiction. *Neuropsychopharmacology, 44*(1), 166–183.

Berridge, K. C. (2018). Evolving concepts of emotion and motivation. *Frontiers in Psychology, 9*, 1647.

Birks, J. S., Chong, L. Y., & Grimley Evans, J. (2015). Rivastigmine for Alzheimer's disease. *The Cochrane Database of Systematic Reviews, 10*(4), CD001191.

Bjørklund, G., Mutter, J., & Aaseth, J. (2017). Metal chelators and neurotoxicity: Lead, mercury, and arsenic. *Archives of Toxicology, 91*(21), 3787–3797.

Bradley, C. (1937). The behavior of children receiving benzedrine. *American Journal of Psychiatry, 94*(3), 577–581.

Brown, A. R., Owen, S. F., Peters, J., Zhang, Y., Soffker, M., Paull, G. C., Hosken, D. J., Wahab, M. A., & Tyler, C. R. (2015). Climate change and pollution speed declines in zebrafish populations. *Proceedings of the National Academy of Science of the United States of America, 112*(11), 1237–1246.

Campbell, N. A. (1996). An interview with Eloy Rodriguez. In *Biology* (4th ed., p. 23). Benjamin Cummings.

Charlson, F. J., Ferrari, A. J., Santomauro, D. F., Diminic, S., Stockings, E., Scott, J. G., McGrath, J. J., & Whiteford, H. A. (2018). Global epidemiology and burden of schizophrenia: Findings from the Global Burden of Disease Study 2016. *Schizophrenia Bulletin, 44*(6), 1195–1203.

Cherian, S. V., Kumar, A., & Estrada-Y-Martin, R. M. (2020). E-cigarette or vaping product–associated lung injury: A review. *American Journal of Medicine, 133*(6), 657–663.

Cho, J., Spence, M. M., Niu, F., Hui, R. L., Gray, P., & Steinberg, S. (2020). Risk of overdose with exposure to prescription opioids, benzodiazepines, and non-benzodiazepine sedative-hypnotics in adults: A retrospective cohort study. *Journal of General Internal Medicine, 35*(3), 696–703.

Comer, R. J., & Comer, J. S. (2021). *Fundamentals of abnormal psychology* (9th ed.). Worth.

Cortese, S. (2019). Debate: Are stimulant medications for attention-deficit/hyperactivity disorder effective in the long term? *Journal of the American Academy of Child and Adolescent Psychiatry, 58*(10), 936.

Cowan, R. L., Roberts, D. M., & Joers, J. M. (2008). Neuroimaging in human MDMA (Ecstasy) users. *Annals of the New York Academy of Sciences, 1139*(1), 291–298.

Cristino, L., Bisogno, T., & Di Marzo, V. (2020). Cannabinoids and the expanded endocannabinoid system in neurological disorders. *Nature Reviews in Neurology, 16*(1), 9–29.

Day, J., Savani, S., Krempley, B. D., Nguyen, M., & Kitlinska, J. B. (2016). Influence of paternal preconception exposures on their offspring: through epigenetics to phenotype. *American Journal of Stem Cells, 5*(1), 11–18.

Dube, S. R., Felitti, V. J., Dong, M., Chapman, D. P., Giles, W. H., & Anda, R. F. (2003). Childhood abuse, neglect, and household dysfunction and the risk of illicit drug use: The adverse childhood experiences study. *Pediatrics, 111*(3), 564–572.

Durell, T. M., Kroutil, L. A., Crits-Christoph, P., Barchha, N., & Van Brunt, D. E. (2008). Prevalence of nonmedical methamphetamine use in the United States. *Substance Abuse Treatment, Prevention, and Policy, 3*, 19.

Everitt, B. J. (2014). Neural and psychological mechanisms underlying compulsive drug seeking habits and drug memories: Indications for novel treatments of addiction. *European Journal of Neuroscience, 40*(1), 2163–2182.

Fraioli, S., Crombag, H. S., Badiani, A., & Robinson, T. E. (1999). Susceptibility to amphetamine-induced locomotor sensitization is modulated by environmental stimuli. *Neuropsychopharmacology, 20*, 533–541.

Freud, S. (1974). *Cocaine papers* (R. Byck, Ed.). Penguin. (Original work published 1884.)

Griffin, J. A., Umstattd, M. R., & Usdan, S. L. (2010). Alcohol use and high-risk sexual behavior among collegiate women: A review of research on alcohol myopia theory. *Journal of American College Health, 58*, 523–532.

Han, B., Compton, W. M., Mojtabai, R., Colpe, L., & Hughes, A. (2016). Trends in receipt of mental health treatments among adults in the United States, 2008–2013. *Journal of Clinical Psychiatry, 77*(10), 1365–1371.

Hardee, J. E., Weiland, B. J., Nichols, T. E., Welsh, R. C., Soules, M. E., Steinberg, D. B., Zubieta, J.-K., Zucker, R. A., & Heitzeg, M. M. (2014). Development of impulse control circuitry in children of alcoholics. *Biological Psychiatry, 76*(9), 708–716.

Herd, C. P., Tomlinson, C. L., Rick, C., Scotton, W. J., Edwards, J., Ives, N., Clarke, C. E., & Sinclair, A. (2018). Botulinum toxins for the prevention of migraine in adults. *Cochrane Database of Systematic Reviews, 6*(6), CD011616.

Hillemacher, T., Weinland, C., Lenz, B., Kraus, T., Heberlein, A., Glahn, A., et al. (2015). DNA methylation of the LEP gene is associated with craving during alcohol withdrawal. *Psychoneuroendocrinology, 51*, 371–377.

Hodebourg, R., Murray, J. E., Fouyssac, M., Puaud, M., Everitt, B. J., & Belin, D. (2019). Heroin seeking becomes dependent on dorsal striatal dopaminergic mechanisms and can be decreased by N-acetylcysteine. *European Journal of Neuroscience, 50*(3), 2036–2044.

Isacsson, G., & Rich, C. L. (2014). Antidepressant drugs and the risk of suicide in children and adolescents. *Paediatric Drugs, 16*, 115–122.

Isbell, H., Fraser, H. F., Wikler, R. E., Belleville, R. E., & Eisenman, A. J. (1955). An experimental study of the etiology of "rum fits" and delirium tremens. *Quarterly Journal of Studies on Alcohol, 16*(1), 1–35.

Kapadia, M., Zhao, H., Ma, D., Hatkar, R., Marchese, M., & Sakic, B. (2014). Zoopharmacognosy in diseased laboratory mice: Conflicting evidence. *PLOS ONE, 9*(6), e100684.

Kenny, P. J. (2007). Brain reward systems and compulsive drug use. *Trends in Pharmacological Sciences, 28*(3), 135–141.

Koob, G. F., Buck, C. L., Cohen, A., Edwards, S., Park, P. E., Schlosburg, J. E., Schmeichel, B., Vendruscolo, L. F., Wade, C. L., Whitfield, T. W., Jr., & George, O. (2014). Addiction as a stress surfeit disorder. *Neuropharmacology, 76*(Part B), 370–382.

Krasnova, I. N., & Cadet, J. L. (2009). Methamphetamine toxicity and messengers of death. *Brain Research Reviews, 60*(2), 379–407.

Lecendreux, M., Konofal, E., Cortese, S., & Faraone, S. V. (2015). A 4-year follow-up of attention-deficit/hyperactivity disorder in a population sample. *Journal of Clinical Psychiatry, 76*, 712–719.

Lee, B. Y., Park, S. Y., Ryu, H. M., Shin, C. Y., Ko, K. N., Han, J. Y., Koren, G., & Cho, Y. H. (2015). Changes in the methylation status of DAT, SERT, and MeCP2 gene promoters in the blood cell in families exposed to alcohol during the periconceptional period. *Alcohol: Clinical and Experimental Research, 39*(2), 239–250.

Lent, J. K., Arredondo, A., Pugh, M. A., & Austin, P. N. (2019). Ketamine and treatment-resistant depression. *American Association of Nurse Anesthesiology Journal, 87*(5), 411–419.

MacAndrew, C., & Edgerton, R. B. (1969). *Drunken comportment: A social explanation*. Aldine.

McGreal, C. (2018). *American overdose: The opioid tragedy in three acts*. Public Affairs.

Mead, E. A., & Sarkar, D. K. (2014). Fetal alcohol spectrum disorders and their transmission through genetic and epigenetic mechanisms. *Frontiers in Genetics, 5*, 154.

Meyer, M. F., Powers, S. M., & Hampton, S. E. (2019). An evidence synthesis of pharmaceuticals and personal care products (PPCPs) in the environment: Imbalances among compounds, sewage treatment techniques, and ecosystem types. *Environmental Science and Technology, 53*(22), 12961–12973.

Mohammad, S., Page, S. J., Wang, L., Ishii, S., Li, P., Sasaki, T., Basha, A., Salzberg, A., Quezado, Z., Imamura, F., Nishi, H., Isaka, K., Corbin, J. G., Liu, J. S., Kawasawa, Y. I., Torii, M., & Hashimoto-Torii, K. (2020). Kcnn2 blockade reverses learning deficits in a mouse model of fetal alcohol spectrum disorders. *Nature Neuroscience, 23*(4), 533–543.

National Institute on Drug Abuse, National Institutes of Health. (2016). *2015–2016 National Survey of Drug Use and Health*. https://www.drugabuse.gov/national-survey-drug-use-health.

Nehlig, A. (2010). Is caffeine a cognitive enhancer? *Journal of Alzheimer's Disease, 20*(Suppl. 1), S85–S94.

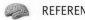
Nguyen, B. M., Kim, D., Bricker, S., Bongard, F., Neville, A., Putnam, B., Smith, J., & Plurad, D. (2014). Effect of marijuana use on outcomes in traumatic brain injury. *American Surgery, 80*(10), 979–983.

Nicol, J. J., Yarema, M. C., Jones, G. R., Martz, W., Purssell, R. A., MacDonald, J. C., Wishart, I., Durigon, M., Tzemis, D., & Buxton, J. A. (2015). Deaths from exposure to paramethoxymethamphetamine in Alberta and British Columbia, Canada: A case series. *CMAJ Open, 3*(1), E83–E90.

Nutt, D. (2019). Psychedelic drugs—a new era in psychiatry? *Dialogues in Clinical Neuroscience, 21*(2), 139–147.

Nutt, D., Erritzoe, D., & Carhart-Harris, R. (2020). Psychedelic psychiatry's brave new world. *Cell, 181*(1), 24–28.

O'Donnell, J. K., Halpin, J., Mattson, C. L., Goldberger, B. A., & Gladden, R. M. (2017). Deaths involving fentanyl, fentanyl analogs, and U-47700—10 states, July–December 2016. *CDC: Morbidity and Mortality Weekly Report (MMWR) Weekly, 66*(43), 1197–1202.

Oleson, E. B., & Roberts, D. C. (2009). Parsing the addiction phenomenon: Self-administration procedures modeling enhanced motivation for drug and escalation of drug intake. *Drug Discovery Today: Disease Models, 5*(4), 217–226.

Parrott, A. C. (2013). Human psychobiology of MDMA or "Ecstasy": An overview of 25 years of empirical research. *Human Psychopharmacology, 28*(4), 289–307.

Popova, S., Lange, S., Bekmuradov, D., Mihic, A., & Rehm, J. (2011). Fetal alcohol spectrum disorder prevalence estimates in correctional systems: A systematic literature review. *Canadian Journal of Public Health, 102*, 336–340.

Preller, K. H., Burt, J. B., Ji, J. L., Schleifer, C. H., Adkinson, B. D., Stämpfli, P., Seifritz, E., Repovs, G., Krystal, J. H., Murray, J. D., Vollenweider, F. X., & Anticevic, A. (2018). Changes in global and thalamic brain connectivity in LSD-induced altered states of consciousness are attributable to the 5-HT2A receptor. *eLife, 7*, e35082.

Raman, S. R., Man, K. K. C., Bahmanyar, S., Berard, A., Bilder, S., Boukhris, T., Bushnell, G., Crystal, S., Furu, K., KaoYang, Y.-H., Karlstad, Ø., Kieler, H., Kubota, K., Lai, E. C.-C., Martikainen, J. E., Maura, G., Moore, N., Montero, D., Nakamura, H., … Wong, I. C. K. (2018). Trends in attention-deficit hyperactivity disorder medication use: A retrospective observational study using population-based databases. *The Lancet: Psychiatry, 5*(10), 824–835.

Reese, E. D., Yi, J. Y., McKay, K. G., Stein, E. A., Ross, T. J., & Daughters, S. B. (2019). Resting state connectivity predicts distress tolerance and is associated with cocaine use. *Journal of Clinical Medicine, 8*(12), E2135.

Reinstatler, L., & Youssef, N. A. (2015). Ketamine as a potential treatment for suicidal ideation: A systematic review of the literature. *Drugs, 15*(1), 37–43.

Roberts, N. P., Roberts, P. A., Jones, N., & Bisson, J. I. (2015). Psychological interventions for post-traumatic stress disorder and comorbid substance use disorder: A systematic review and meta-analysis. *Clinical Psychological Reviews, 38*, 25–38.

Robinson, T. E., & Becker, J. B. (1986). Enduring changes in brain and behavior produced by chronic amphetamine administration: A review and evaluation of animal models

of amphetamine psychosis. *Brain Research Reviews, 396*(2), 157–198.

Robinson, T. E., & Berridge, K. C. (2008). The incentive sensitization theory of addiction: Some current issues. *Philosophical Transactions of the Royal Society of London, 363*(1507), 3137–3146.

Robinson, T. E., & Kolb, B. (1997). Persistent structural adaptations in nucleus accumbens and prefrontal cortex neurons produced by prior experience with amphetamine. *Journal of Neuroscience, 17*(21), 8491–8498.

Robson, P. J. (2014). Therapeutic potential of cannabinoid medicines. *Drug Testing and Analysis, 6*(1–2), 24–30.

Roitman, P., Mechoulam, R., Cooper-Kazaz, R., & Shalev, A. (2014). Preliminary, open-label, pilot study of add-on oral Δ9-tetrahydrocannabinol in chronic post-traumatic stress disorder. *Clinical Drug Investigations, 34*(8), 587–591.

Sacks, J. J., Gonzales, K. R., Bouchery, E. E., Tomedi, L. E., & Brewer, R. D. (2015). 2010 national and state costs of excessive alcohol consumption. *American Journal of Preventive Medicine, 49*(5), e73–e79.

Sevincer, A. T., & Oettingen, G. (2014). Alcohol myopia and goal commitment. *Frontiers in Psychology, 4*, 169–175.

Sousa, A., & Dinis-Oliveira, R. J. (2020). Pharmacokinetic and pharmacodynamic of the cognitive enhancer modafinil: Relevant clinical and forensic aspects. *Substance Abuse, 41*(2), 155–173.

Stroud, C. B., Davila, J., Hammen, C., & Vrshek-Schallhorn, S. (2011). Severe and non-severe events in first onsets versus recurrences of depression: Evidence for stress sensitization. *Journal of Abnormal Psychology, 120*(1), 142–154.

Substance Abuse and Mental Health Services Administration (SAMHSA). (2015). National Survey on Drug Use and Health (NSDUH). Table 5.6B—Substance use disorder in past year among persons aged 18 or older, by demographic characteristics: Percentages, 2014 and 2015.

Teixeira-Gomes, A., Costa, V. M., Feio-Azevedo, R., Bastos, M. L., Carvalho, F., & Capela, J. P. (2015). The neurotoxicity of amphetamines during the adolescent period. *International Journal of Developmental Neuroscience, 41*, 44–62.

United Nations. (2021). *World Drug Report 2021.* United Nations Office on Drugs and Crime.

Urban, N. B., Girgis, R. R., Talbot, P. S., Kegeles, L. S., Xu, X., Frankle, W. G., Hart, C. L., Slifstein, M., Abi-Dargham, A., & Laruelle, M. (2012). Sustained recreational use of ecstasy is associated with altered pre and postsynaptic markers of serotonin transmission in neocortical areas: A PET study with [11C]DASB and [11C]MDL 100907. *Neuropsychopharmacology, 37*(6), 1465–1473.

Wadgave, U., & Nagesh, L. (2016). Nicotine replacement therapy: An overview. *International Journal of Health Sciences, 10*(3), 425–435.

Wenger, J. R., Tiffany, T. M., Bombardier, C., Nicholls, K., & Woods, S. C. (1981). Ethanol tolerance in the rat is learned. *Science, 213*(4507), 575–577.

Wright, G. A., Baker, D. D., Palmer, M. J., Stabler, D., Mustard, J. A., Power, E. F., Borland, A. M., & Stevenson, P. C. (2013). Caffeine in floral nectar enhances a pollinator's memory of reward. *Science, 339*(6124), 1202–1204.

Yager, L. M., Pitchers, K. K., Flagel, S. B., & Robinson, T. E. (2015). Individual variation in the motivational and neurobiological effects of an opioid cue. *Neuropsychopharmacology, 40*(5), 1269–1277.

Yamada, J., Sato, C., Konno, K., Watanabe, M., & Jinno, S. (2020). PSA-NCAM colocalized with cholecystokinin-expressing cells in the hippocampus is involved in mediating antidepressant efficacy. *Journal of Neuroscience, 40*(4), 825–842.

## CHAPTER 7

Agboola, O. S., Hu, X., Shan, Z., Wu, Y., & Lei, L. (2021). Brain organoid: A 3D technology for investigating cellular composition and interactions in human neurological development and disease models in vitro. *Stem Cell Research & Therapy, 12*(1), 430–446.

Brown, A. R., Antle, M. C., Hu, B., & Teskey, G. C. (2011). High frequency stimulation of the subthalamic nucleus acutely rescues neocortical movement representations and motor deficits following 6-hydroxydopamine administration in rats. *Experimental Neurology, 231*(1), 82–90.

Bueller, J. A., Aftab, M., Sen, S., Gomez-Hassan, D., Burmeister, M., & Zubieta, J.-K. (2006). BDNF Val66Met allele is associated with reduced hippocampal volume in healthy subjects. *Biological Psychiatry, 59*(9), 812–815.

Cacucci, F., Yi, M., Wills, T. J., Chapmans, P., & O'Keefe, J. (2008). Place cell firing correlates with memory deficits and amyloid plaque burden in Tg2576 Alzheimer mouse model. *Proceedings of the National Academy of Sciences of the United States of America, 105*(22), 7863–7868.

Damasio, H., & Damasio, A. R. (1989). *Lesion analysis in neuropsychology.* Oxford University Press.

Dong, A., He, K., Dudok, B., Farrell, J. S., Guan, W., Liput, D. J., Puhl, H. L., Cai, R., Duan, J., Albarran, E., Ding, J., Lovinger, D. M., Li, B., Soltesz, I., & Li, Y. (2020). A fluorescent sensor for spatiotemporally resolved endocannabinoid dynamics in vitro and in vivo. bioRxiv. Cold Spring Harbor Laboratory. https://doi.org/10.1101/2020.10.08.329169

Farrell, J. S., Colangeli, R., Dong, A., George, A. G., Addo-Osafo, K., Kingsley, P. J., Morena, M., Wolff, M. D., Dudok, B., He, K., Patrick, T. A., Sharkey, K. A., Patel, S., Marnett, L. J., Hill, M. N., Li, Y., Teskey, G. C., & Soltesz, I. (2021). In vivo endocannabinoid dynamics at the timescale of physiological and pathological neural activity. *Neuron, 109*(15), 2398–2403.e4. https://doi.org/10.1016/j.neuron.2021.05.026

Farrell, J. S., Gaxiola-Valdez, I., Wolff, M. D., David, L. S., Dika, H. I., Geeraert, B. L., Wang, X. R., Singh, S., Spanswick, S. C., Dunn, J. F., Antle, M. C., Federico, P., & Teskey, G. C. (2016). Postictal behavioural impairments are due to a severe prolonged hypoperfusion/hypoxia event that is COX-2 dependent. *eLife, 5*, e19352.

Forlim, C. G., Klock, L., Bächle, J., Stoll, L., Giemsa, P., Fuchs, M., Schoofs, N., Montag, C., Gallinat, J., & Kühn, S. (2020). Reduced resting-state connectivity in the precuneus is correlated with apathy in patients with schizophrenia. *Scientific Reports, 10*(1), 2616.

Fox, P. T., & Raichle, M. E. (1986). Focal physiological uncoupling of cerebral blood flow and oxidative metabolism during somatosensory stimulation in human subjects. *Proceedings of* the National Academy of Sciences of the United States of America, 83(4), 1140–1144.

Fraga, M. F., Ballestar, E., Paz, M. F., Ropero, S., Setien, F., Ballestar, M. L., Heine-Suñer, D., Cigudosa, J. C., Urioste, M., Benitez, J., Manuel, B.-C., Sanchez-Aguilera, A., Ling, C., Carlsson, E., Poulsen, P., Vaag, A., Stephan, Z., Spector, T. D., Wu, Y.-Z., Plass, C., & Esteller, M. (2005). Epigenetic differences arise during the lifetime of monozygotic twins. Proceedings of the National Academy of Sciences of the United States of America, 102(30), 10604–10609.

Ghosh, K. K., Burns, L. D., Cocker, E. D., Nimmerjahn, A., Ziv, Y., Gamal, A. E., & Schnitzer, M. J. (2011). Miniaturized integration of a fluorescence microscope. Nature Methods, 8(10), 871–878.

Gonzalez, C. L. R., Gharbawie, O. A., & Kolb, B. (2006). Chronic low-dose administration of nicotine facilitates recovery and synaptic change after focal ischemia in rats. Neuropharmacology, 50(7), 777–787.

Haubensak, W., Kunwar, P. S., Cai, H., Ciocchi, S., Wall, N. R., Ponnusamy, R., Biag, J., Dong, H.-W., Deisseroth, K., Callaway, E. M., Fanselow, M. S., Lüthi, A., & Anderson, D. J. (2010). Genetic dissection of an amygdala microcircuit that gates conditioned fear. Nature, 468(7321), 270–276.

Iglesias, A. H. (2020). Transcranial magnetic stimulation as treatment in multiple neurologic conditions. Current Neurology and Neuroscience Reports, 20(1), 1. https://doi.org/10.1007/s11910-020-1021-0

Kolb, B., & Walkey, J. (1987). Behavioural and anatomical studies of the posterior parietal cortex of the rat. Behavioural Brain Research, 23(2), 127–145.

Lee, D. J., Lozano, C. S., Dallapiazza, R. F., & Lozano, A. M. (2019). Current and future directions of deep brain stimulation for neurological and psychiatric disorders. Journal of Neurosurgery, 131(2), 333–342.

Little, S., & Brown, P. (2020). Debugging adaptive deep brain stimulation for Parkinson's disease. Movement Disorders, 35(4), 555–561.

Livet, J., Weissman, T. A., Kang, H., Draft, R. W., Lu, J., Bennis, R. A., Sanes, J. R., & Lichtman, J. W. (2007). Transgenic strategies for combinatorial expression of fluorescent proteins in the nervous system. Nature, 450(7166), 56–62.

Lomber, S. G., & Payne, B. R. (1996). Removal of two halves restores the whole: Reversal of visual hemineglect during bilateral cortical or collicular inactivation in the cat. Visual Neuroscience, 13(6), 1143–1156.

Mayor, A. (2018). Gods and robots: Myths, machines, and ancient dreams of technology. Princeton University Press.

McGowan, P. O., Sasaki, A., D'Alessio, A. C., Dymov, S., Labonté, B., Szyf, M., Turecki, G., & Meaney, M. J. (2009). Epigenetic regulation of the glucocorticoid receptor in human brain associates with childhood abuse. Nature Neuroscience, 12(3), 342–348.

Miller, C. T., Hale, M. E., Okano, H., Okabe, S., & Mitra, P. (2019). Comparative principles for next-generation neuroscience. Frontiers in Behavioral Neuroscience, 13, 12. https://doi.org/10.3389/fnbeh.2019.00012

Morris, R. G. M. (1981). Spatial localization does not require the presence of local cues. Learning and Motivation, 12(2), 239–260.

Mychasiuk, R., Schmold, N., Ilnytskyy, S., Kovalchuk, O., Kolb, B., & Gibb, R. (2011). Prenatal bystander stress alters brain, behavior, and the epigenome of developing rat offspring. Developmental Neuroscience, 33(2), 159–169.

National Research Council of the National Academies. (2011). Guide for the care and use of laboratory animals (8th ed.). The National Academies Press.

O'Keefe, J., & Dostrovsky, J. (1971). The hippocampus as a spatial map. Brain Research, 34(1), 171–175.

Ogawa, S., Lee, T. M., Kay, A. R., & Tank, D. W. (1990). Brain magnetic resonance imaging with contrast dependent on blood oxygenation. Proceedings of the National Academy of Sciences of the United States of America, 87, 9868–9872.

Oomen, C. A., Hvoslef-Eidem, M., Heath, C. J., Mar, A. C., Horner, A. E., Bussey, T. J., & Saksida, L. M. (2013). The touchscreen operant platform for testing working memory and pattern separation in rats and mice. Nature Protocols, 8(10), 2006–2021.

Parra-Damas, A., & Saura, C. A. (2020). Tissue clearing and expansion methods for imaging brain pathology in neurodegeneration: From circuits to synapses and beyond. Frontiers in Neuroscience, 14, 914.

Penfield, W., & Jasper, H. H. (1954). Epilepsy and the functional anatomy of the human brain. Little, Brown.

Phillips, B. U., Lopez-Cruz, L., Hailwood, J., Heath, C. J., Saksida, L. M., & Bussey, T. J. (2018). Translational approaches to evaluating motivation in laboratory rodents: Conventional and touchscreen-based procedures. Current Opinion in Behavioral Sciences, 22, 21–27.

Pinti, P., Tachtsidis, I., Hamilton, A., Hirsch, J., Aichelburg, C., Gilbert, S., & Burgess, P. W. (2020). The present and future use of functional near-infrared spectroscopy (fNIRS) for cognitive neuroscience. Annals of the New York Academy of Sciences, 1464(1), 5–29.

Posner, M. I., & Raichle, M. E. (1997). Images of mind. W. H. Freeman.

Quadri, S. A., Waqas, M., Khan, I., Khan, M. A., Suriya, S. S., Farooqui, M., & Fiani, B. (2018). High-intensity focused ultrasound: Past, present, and future in neurosurgery. Neurosurgery Focus, 44(2), E16.

Ramírez, N. F., Lytle, S. R., & Kuhl, P. K. (2020). Parent coaching increases conversational turns and advances infant language development. Proceedings of the National Academy of Sciences of the United States of America, 117(7), 3484–3491.

Rojczyk-Gołębiewska, E., Pałasz, A., Worthington, J. J., Markowski, G., & Wiaderkiewicz, R. (2015). Neurolight: Astonishing advances in brain imaging. International Journal of Neuroscience, 125(2), 91–99.

Scoville, W. B., & Milner, B. (1957). Loss of recent memory after bilateral hippocampal lesions. Journal of Neurology, Neurosurgery, and Psychiatry, 20, 11–21.

Sejnowski, T. J. (2018). The deep learning revolution. MIT Press.

Spanswick, S., Lehmann, H., & Sutherland, R. J. (2011). A novel animal model of hippocampal cognitive deficits, slow neurodegeneration, and neuroregeneration. Journal of Biomedicine and Biotechnology, 527201. https://doi.org/10.1155/2011/527201

Spanswick, S., & Sutherland, R. J. (2010). Object/context-specific memory deficits associated with loss of hippocampal granule cells after adrenalectomy in rats. Learning and Memory, 17(5), 241–245.

Spinney, L. (2005). Optical topography and the color of blood. The Scientist, 19, 25–27.

Szyf, M., McGowan, P., & Meaney, M. J. (2008). The social environment and the epigenome. Environmental Molecular Mutagenetics, 49(1), 46–60.

Tisdall, M. M., & Smith, M. (2006). Cerebral microdialysis: Research technique or clinical tool. British Journal of Anaesthesia, 97(1), 18–25.

Wess, J., Nakajima, K., & Jain, S. (2013). Novel designer receptors to probe GPCR signaling and physiology. Trends in Pharmacological Sciences, 34(7), 385–392.

Wheeler, D. S., Ebben, A. L., Kurtoglu, B., Lovell, M. E., Bohn, A. T., Jasek, I. A., Baker, D. A., Mantsch, J. R., Gasser, P. J., Wheeler, R. A. (2017). Corticosterone regulates both naturally occurring and cocaine-induced dopamine signaling by selectively decreasing dopamine update. European Journal of Neuroscience, 46(10), 2638–2646.

Whishaw, I. Q. (1989). Dissociating performance and learning deficits in spatial navigation tasks in rats subjected to cholinergic muscarinic blockade. Brain Research Bulletin, 23(4–5), 347–358.

Whishaw, I. Q., & Kolb, B. (2005). The behavior of the laboratory rat. Oxford University Press.

## CHAPTER 8

Ames, E. W. (1997). The development of Romanian orphanage children adopted to Canada. Final report to Human Resources Development, Canada.

Anda, R. F., Felitti, V. J., Bremner, J. D., Walker, J. D., Whitfield, C., Perry, B. D., Dube, S. R., & Giles, W. H. (2006). The enduring effects of abuse and related adverse experiences in childhood: A convergence of evidence from neurobiology and epidemiology. European Archives of Psychiatry and Clinical Neuroscience, 256(3), 174–186.

Andrews, D. S., Lee, J. K., Harvey, D. J., Rogers, S. J., Nordahl, C. W., & Amaral, D. G. (2021). A longitudinal study of white matter development in relation to changes in autism severity across early childhood. Biological Psychiatry, 89(5), 424–432.

Arai, K., & Lo, E. H. (2017). Gliogenesis. In L. R. Caplan, J. Biller, M. C. Leary, E. H. Lo, A. Thomas, M. Yenari, & J. H. Zhang (Eds.), Primer on cerebrovascular diseases (2nd ed., pp. 91–95). Elsevier.

Bastiaanssen, T. F. S., & Cryan, J. F. (2021). The microbiota-gut-brain axis in mental health and medication response: Parsing directionality and causality. International Journal of Neuropsychopharmacology, 24(3), 216–220.

Berens, A. E., & Nelson, C. A. (2015). The science of early adversity: Is there a role for large institutions in the care of vulnerable children? Lancet, 386(9991), 388–398.

Blakemore, S. (2018). Inventing ourselves: The secret life of the teenage brain. Public Affairs Books.

Blum, D. (2002). Love at Goon Park. Perseus Books.

Bock, J., Rether, K., Grogerr, N., Xie, L., & Braun, K. (2014). Perinatal programming of emotional brain circuits: An integrative view from systems to molecules. Frontiers in Neuroscience, 8(8), 11.

Bond, A. M., Ming, G.-L., & Song, H. (2015). Adult mammalian neural stem cells and neurogenesis: Five decades later. Cell Stem Cell, 17(4), 385–395.

Bourgeois, J.-P. (2001). Synaptogenesis in the neocortex of the newborn: The ultimate frontier for individuation? In C. A. Nelson & M. Luciana (Eds.), *Handbook of developmental cognitive neuroscience* (pp. 23–34). MIT Press.

Casey, B. J., Galvan, A., & Somerville, L. H. (2015). Beyond simple models of adolescence to an integrated circuit-based account: A commentary. *Developmental Cognitive Neuroscience, 17,* 128–130.

Changeux, J.-P., & Danchin, A. (1976). Selective stabilization of developing synapses as a mechanism for the specification of neuronal networks. *Nature, 264,* 705–712.

Clarke, R. S., Heron, W., Fetherstonhaugh, M. L., Forgays, D. G., & Hebb, D. O. (1951). Individual differences in dogs: Preliminary report on the effects of early experience. *Canadian Journal of Psychology, 5*(4), 150–156.

Cowan, C. S. M., Callaghan, B. L., & Richardson, R. (2016). The effects of probiotic formulation (*Lactobacillus rhamnosus* and *L. helveticus*) on developmental trajectories of emotional learning in stressed infant rats. *Translational Psychiatry, 6*(5), e823.

Cowan, W. M. (1979). The development of the brain. *Scientific American, 241*(3), 116.

Cussotto, S., Clarke, G., Dinan, T. G., & Cryan, J. F. (2019). Psychotropics and the microbiome: A chamber of secrets… *Psychopharmacology, 236*(5), 1411–1432.

Dean, D. C., Planalp, E. M., Wooten, W., Schmidt, C. K., Kecskemeti, S. R., Frye, C., Schmidt, N. L., Goldsmith, H. H., Alexander, A. L., & Davidson, R. J. (2018). Investigation of brain structure in the 1-month infant. *Brain Structure and Function, 223*(4), 1953–1970.

Dettmer, A. M., & Suomi, S. J. (2014). Nonhuman primate models of neuropsychiatric disorders: Influences of early rearing, genetics, and epigenetics. *ILAR Journal, 55*(2), 361–370.

Dias, B. G., & Ressler, K. J. (2014). Parental olfactory experience influences behavior and neural structure in subsequent generations. *Nature Neuroscience, 17*(1), 89–96.

Dietsche, B., Kircher, T., & Falkenberg, I. (2017). Structural brain changes in schizophrenia at different stages of illness: A selective review of longitudinal magnetic resonance imaging studies. *Australia and New Zealand Journal of Psychiatry, 51*(5), 500–508.

Epstein, H. T. (1979). Correlated brain and intelligence development in humans. In M. E. Hahn, C. Jensen, & B. C. Dudek (Eds.), *Development and evolution of brain size: Behavioral implications* (pp. 111–131). Academic Press.

Eriksson, P. S., Perfilieva, E., Björk-Eriksson, T., Alborn, A. M., Nordborg, C., Peterson, D. A., & Gage, F. H. (1998). Neurogenesis in the adult human hippocampus. *Nature Medicine, 4*(11), 1313–1317.

Faiz, M., & Morshead, C. M. (2018). Stem cells to function. In R. Gibb & B. Kolb (Eds.), *The neurobiology of brain and behavioral development* (pp. 99–132). Elsevier.

Franke, K., & Gaser, C. (2019). Ten years of *BrainAGE* as a neuroimaging biomarker of brain aging: What insights have we gained? *Frontiers in Neurology, 10,* 789. https://doi.org/10.3380/fneur2019.00789.

Franke, K., Ristow, M., & Gaser, C. (2014). Gender-specific impact of personal health parameters on individual brain aging in cognitively unimpaired elderly subjects. *Frontiers in Aging Neuroscience, 6,* 94.

Fuhrmann, D., Knoll, L. J., & Blakemore, S.-J. (2015). Adolescence as a sensitive period of brain development. *Trends in Cognitive Sciences, 19*(10), 558–566.

Geng, F., Botdorf, M., & Riggins, T. (2021). How behavior shapes the brain and the brain shapes behavior: Insights from memory development. *Journal of Neuroscience, 41*(5), 981–990.

Gershon, E. S., & Rieder, R. O. (1992). Major disorders of mind and brain. *Scientific American, 267*(3), 126–133.

Geschwind, D. H., & Rakic, P. (2013). Cortical evolution: Judge the brain by its cover. *Neuron, 80*(3), 633–647.

Gibb, R., Gonzalez, C., & Kolb, B. (2014). Prenatal enrichment and recovery from perinatal cortical damage: Effects of maternal complex housing. *Frontiers in Behavioral Neuroscience, 8,* 223.

Goldstein, J. M., Seidman, L. J., Horton, N. J., Makris, N., Kennedy, D. N., Caviness, V. S., Jr., Faraone, S. V., & Tsuang, M. T. (2001). Normal sexual dimorphism of the adult human brain assessed by in vivo magnetic resonance imaging. *Cerebral Cortex, 11*(6), 490–497.

Gonzalez-Santana, A., & Diaz-Heijtz, R. (2020). Bacterial peptidoglycans from microbiota in neurodevelopment and behavior. *Trends in Molecular Medicine, 26*(8), 729–743.

Guerrini, R., Dobyns, W. B., & Barkovich, A. J. (2007). Abnormal development of the human cerebral cortex: Genetics, functional consequences and treatment options. *Trends in Neurosciences, 31*(3), 154–162.

Harker, A., Raza, S., Williamson, K., Kolb, B., & Gibb, R. (2015). Preconception paternal stress in rats alters dendritic morphology and connectivity in the brain of developing male and female offspring. *Neuroscience, 303,* 200–210.

Harlow, H. F. (1971). *Learning to love.* Albion.

Hebb, D. O. (1947). The effects of early experience on problem solving at maturity. *American Psychologist, 2,* 737–745.

Hedderich, D. M., Menegaux, A., Schmitz-Koep, B., Nuttall, R. Zimmerman, J., Schneider, S. C., Bäuml, J. G., Daamen, M., Boecker, H., Wilke, M., Zimmer, C., Wolke, D., Bartmann, P., Sorg, C., & Gaser, C. (2021). Increased brain age gap estimate (*BrainAGE*) in young adults after premature birth. *Frontiers in Aging Neuroscience, 13,* 158. https://doi.org/10.339/fnagi.2021.653365.

Hensch, T. K. (2018). Critical periods in cortical development. In R. Gibb & B. Kolb (Eds.), *The neurobiology of brain and behavioral development* (pp. 133–152). Academic Press.

Herholz, S. C., & Zatorre, R. J. (2012). Musical training as a framework for brain plasticity: Behavior, function, and structure. *Neuron, 76*(3), 486–502.

Hessl, D., Libero, L., Schneider, A., Kerns, C., Winder-Patel, B., Heath, B., Lee, J., Coleman, C., Sharma, N., Solomon, M., Nordahl, C. W., & Amaral, D. G. (2021). Fear potentiated startle in children with autism spectral disorder: Association with anxiety symptoms and amygdala volume. *Autism Research, 14*(3), 450–463.

Ho, T. C., Colich, N. L., Sisk, L. M., Oskirdo, K., Jo, B., & Gotlib, I. H. (2020). Sex differences in the effects of gonadal hormones on white matter microstructure development in adolescence. *Developmental Cognitive Neuroscience, 42,* 100773.

Hodel, A. S., Hunt, R. H., Cowell, R. A., van den Heuvel, S. E., Gunnar, M. R., & Thomas, K. M. (2015). Duration of early adversity and structural brain development in post-institutionalized adolescents. *Neuroimage, 105,* 112–119.

Horn, G., Bradley, P., & McCabe, B. J. (1985). Changes in the structure of synapses associated with learning. *Journal of Neuroscience, 5*(12), 3161–3168.

Huttenlocher, P. R. (1994). Synaptogenesis in human cerebral cortex. In G. Dawson & K. W. Fischer (Eds.), *Human behavior and the developing brain* (pp. 137–152). Guilford Press.

Jenkins, S., Harker, A., & Gibb, R. (2018). Maternal preconception stress alters prefrontal cortex development in Long-Evans rat pups without changing maternal care. *Neuroscience, 394,* 98–108.

Jurkowski, M. P., Bettio, L., Woo, E. K., Patten, A., Yau, S.-Y., & Gil-Mohapel, J. (2020). Beyond the hippocampus and the SVZ: Adult neurogenesis throughout the brain. *Frontiers in Cellular Neuroscience, 29,* 293. https://doi.org/10.3389/fncel.2020.576444.

Kelly, J. R., Minuto, C., Cryan, J. F., Clarke, G., & Dinan, T. G. (2017). Cross talk: The microbiota and neurodevelopmental disorders. *Frontiers in Neuroscience, 11,* 490.

Kinney, H. C. (2009). Brainstem mechanisms underlying the sudden infant death syndrome: Evidence from human pathologic studies. *Developmental Psychobiology, 51*(3), 223–233.

Kolb, B. (2021) Sensitive periods for recovery from early brain injury. In S. Andersen (Ed.), *Current topics in behavioral neuroscience: Sensitive periods of brain development.* Springer.

Kolb, B., & Gibb, R. (1993). Possible anatomical basis of recovery of function after neonatal frontal lesions in rats. *Behavioral Neuroscience, 107*(5), 799–811.

Kolb, B., Gibb, R., & Gorny, G. (2003). Experience-dependent changes in dendritic arbor and spine density in neocortex vary with age and sex. *Neurobiology of Learning and Memory, 79*(1), 1–10.

Kolb, B., Mychasiuk, R., Muhammad, A., Li, Y., Frost, D. O., & Gibb, R. (2012). Experience and the developing prefrontal cortex. *Proceedings of the National Academy of Sciences of the United States of America, 109*(Suppl. 2), 17186–17193.

Kovelman, J. A., & Scheibel, A. B. (1984). A neurohistologic correlate of schizophrenia. *Biological Psychiatry, 19*(12), 1601–1621.

Kuhl, P. K. (2011). Early language learning and literacy: Neuroscience implications for education. *Mind, Brain, and Education, 5*(3), 128–142.

Lee, J. K., Andrews, D. S., Ozonoff, S., Solomon, M., Rogers, S., Amaral, D. G., & Nordahl, C. W. (2020). Longitudinal evaluation of cerebral growth across childhood in boys and girls with autism spectrum disorder. *Biological Psychiatry, 90*(5), 286–294.

Lenneberg, E. H. (1967). *Biological foundations of language.* Wiley.

Lenroot, R. K., Gogtay, N., Greenstein, D. K., Wells, E. M., Wallace, G. L., Clasen, L. S., Blumenthal, J. D., Lerch, J., Zijdenbos, A. P., Evans, A. C., Thompson, P. M., & Giedd, J. N. (2007). Sexual dimorphism of brain development trajectories during childhood and adolescence. *NeuroImage, 36*(4), 1065–1073.

Lorenz, K. (1970). *Studies on animal and human behavior* (Vols. 1 and 2). Harvard University Press.

Lu, L. H., Leonard, C. M., Thompson, P. M., Kan, E., Jolley, J., Welcome, S. E., Toga, A. W., & Sowell, E. R. (2007). Normal developmental changes in inferior frontal gray matter are associated with improvement in phonological processing: A longitudinal MRI analysis. *Cerebral Cortex, 17*(5), 1092–1099.

Marin-Padilla, M. (1993). Pathogenesis of late-acquired leptomeningeal heterotopias and secondary cortical alterations: A Golgi study. In A. M. Galaburda (Ed.), *Dyslexia and development: Neurobiological aspects of extraordinary brains* (pp. 64–88). Harvard University Press.

Moore, K. L. (1988). *The developing human: Clinically oriented embryology* (4th ed.). Saunders.

Moreno-Jimenez, E. P., Terreros-Roncal, J., For-Garcia, M., Rabano, A., & Llorens-Martin, M. (2021). Evidences for adult hippocampal neurogenesis in humans. *Journal of Neuroscience, 41*(12), 2541–2553.

Mychasiuk, R., Gibb, R., & Kolb, B. (2011). Prenatal stress produces sexually dimorphic and regionally specific changes in gene expression in hippocampus and frontal cortex of developing rat offspring. *Developmental Neuroscience, 33*(6), 531–538.

Myers, D. G. (2015). *Psychology* (11th ed.). Worth Publishers.

Nelson, C. A., Zeanah C. H., & Fox, N. A. (2019). How early experience shapes human development: The case of social psychosocial deprivation. *Neural Plasticity, 2019*, 1676285.

Nelson, C. A., Zeanah, C. H., Fox, N. A., Marshall, P. J., Smyke, A. T., & Guthrie, D. (2007). Cognitive recovery in socially deprived young children: The Bucharest Early Intervention Project. *Science, 318*(5858), 1937–1940.

Noble, K. G., & Giebler, M. A. (2020). The neuroscience of socioeconomic inequality. *Current Opinion in Behavioral Sciences, 36*, 23–28.

Noble, K. G., Houston, S. M., Brito, N. H., Bartsch, H., Kan, E., Kuperman, J. M., Akshoomoff, N., Amaral, D. G., Bloss, C. S., Libiger, O., Schork, N. J., Murray, S. S., Casey, B. J., Chang, L., Ernst, T. M., Frazier, J. A., Gruen, J. R., Kennedy, D. N., Van Zijl, P., … Sowell, E. R. (2015). Family income, parental education and brain structure in children and adolescents. *Nature Neuroscience, 18*(5), 773–778.

O'Hare, E. D., & Sowell, E. R. (2008). Imaging developmental changes in gray and white matter in the human brain. In C. A. Nelson & M. Luciana (Eds.), *Handbook of developmental cognitive neuroscience* (pp. 23–38). MIT Press.

Overman, W., Bachevalier, J., Turner, M., & Peuster, A. (1992). Object recognition versus object discrimination: Comparison between human infants and infant monkeys. *Behavioral Neuroscience, 106*(1), 15–29.

Paterson, D. S., Trachtenberg, F. L., Thompson, E. G., Belliveau, R. A., Beggs, A. H., Darnall, R., Chadwick, A. E., Krous, H. F., & Kinney, H. C. (2006). Multiple serotonergic brainstem abnormalities in sudden infant death syndrome. *Journal of the American Medical Association, 296*(17), 2124–2132.

Payne, B. R., & Lomber, S. G. (2001). Reconstructing functional systems after lesions of cerebral cortex. *Nature Reviews Neuroscience, 2*, 911–919.

Petanjek, Z., Judaš, M., Šimić, G., Rašin, M. R., Uylings, H. B. M., Rakic, P., & Kostović, I. (2011). Extraordinary neoteny of synaptic spines in the human prefrontal cortex. *Proceedings of the National Academy of Sciences of the United States of America, 108*(32), 13281–13286.

Piaget, J. (1952). *The origins of intelligence in children*. Norton.

Piccolo, L. R., Merz, E. C., He, X., Sowell, E. R., & Noble, K. G. (2016). Age-related differences in cortical thickness vary by socioeconomic status. *PLOS ONE, 11*(9), e0162511.

Purpura, D. P. (1974). Dendritic spine "dysgenesis" and mental retardation. *Science, 186*(4169), 1126–1127.

Rakic, P. (1974). Neurons in rhesus monkey cerebral cortex: Systematic relation between time of origin and eventual disposition. *Science, 183*(4123), 425.

Rapoport, J. L., Giedd, J. N., & Gogtay, N. (2012). Neurodevelopmental model of schizophrenia: Update 2012. *Molecular Psychiatry, 17*(12), 1228–1238.

Riesen, A. H. (1982). Effects of environments on development in sensory systems. In W. D. Neff (Ed.), *Contributions to sensory physiology* (Vol. 6, pp. 45–77). Academic Press.

Rogenmoser, L., Kernbach, J., Schlaug, G., & Gaser, C. (2018). Keeping brains young with making music. *Brain Structure and Function, 223*(1), 297–305.

Romeo, R. R., Leonard, J. A., Robinson, S. T., West, M. R., Mackey, A. P., Rowe, M. L., & Gabrieli, J. D. E. (2018a). Beyond the 30-million-word gap: Children's conversational exposure is associated with language-related brain function. *Psychological Science, 29*(5), 700–710.

Romeo, R. R., Segaran, J., Leonard, J. A., Robinson, S. T., West, M. R., Mackey, A. P., Yendiki, A., Rowe, M. L., & Gabrieli, J. D. E. (2018b). Language exposure relates to structural neural connectivity in childhood. *Journal of Neuroscience, 38*(36), 7870–7877.

Rutter, M. (1998). Developmental catch-up, and deficit, following adoption after severe global early privation. *Journal of Child Psychology and Psychiatry, 39*(4), 465–476.

Schnack, H. G., van Haren, N. E., Brouwer, R. M., Evans, A., Durston, S., Boomsma, D. I., Kahn, R. S., & Hulshoff Pol, H. E. (2014). Changes in thickness and surface area of the human cortex and their relationship with intelligence. *Cerebral Cortex, 25*(6), 1608–1617.

Seki, T. (2020). Understanding the real state of human adult hippocampal neurogenesis from studies of rodents and non-human primates. *Frontiers in Neuroscience, 14*, 839. https://doi.org/10.3389/fnins.2020.00839.

Sherman, L. E., Rudie, J. D., Pfeifer, J. H., Masten, C. L., McNealy, K., & Dapretto, M. (2014). Development of the default mode and central executive networks across early adolescence: A longitudinal study. *Developmental Cognitive Neuroscience, 10*, 148–159.

Sherwin, E., Bordenstein, S. R., Quinn, J. L., Dinan, T. G., & Cryan, J. F. (2019). Microbiota and the social brain. *Science, 366*(6465), eaar2016.

Snyder, J. S. (2019). Recalibrating the relevance of adult neurogenesis. *Trends in Neurosciences, 42*(3), 164–178.

Sorrells, S. F., Paredes, M. F., Zhang, Z., Kang, G., Pastor-Alonso, O., Biagiotti, S., Page, C. E., Sandoval, K., Knox, A., Connolly, A., Huang, E. J., Garcia-Verdugo, J. M., Oldham, M. C., Yang, Z., & Alvarez-Buylla, A. (2021). Positive controls in adults and children support that very few, if any, new neurons are born in the adult human hippocampus. *Journal of Neuroscience, 41*(12), 2554–2565.

Sowell, E. R., Thompson, P. M., Leonard, C. M., Welcome, S. E., Kan, E., & Toga, A. W. (2004). Longitudinal mapping of cortical thickness and brain growth in normal children. *Journal of Neuroscience, 24*(38), 8223–8231.

Sowell, E. R., Thompson, P. M., & Toga, A. W. (2004). Mapping changes in the human cortex throughout the span of life. *The Neuroscientist, 10*(4), 372–392.

Sperry, R. W. (1963). Chemoaffinity in the orderly growth of nerve fiber patterns and connections. *Proceedings of the National Academy of Sciences of the United States of America, 50*(4), 703–710.

Tooley, U. A., Bassett, D. S., & Mackey, A. P. (2021). Environmental influences on the pace of brain development. *Nature Reviews Neuroscience, 22*, 372–384. https://doi.org/10.1038/s41583-021-00457-5.

Tottenham, N. (2014). The importance of early experiences for neuro-affective development. *Current Topics in Behavioral Neuroscience, 16*, 109–129.

Tottenham, N., & Galvan, A. (2016). Stress and the adolescent brain: Amygdala-prefrontal cortex circuitry and ventral striatum as developmental targets. *Neuroscience and Biobehavioral Reviews, 70*, 217–227.

Twitchell, T. E. (1965). The automatic grasping response of infants. *Neuropsychologia, 3*(3), 247–259.

VanTieghem, M., Korom, M., Flannery, J., Choy, T., Caldera, C., Humphreys, K. L., Gabard-Durnam, L., Goff, B., Gee, D. G., Telzer, E. H., Shapiro, M., Louie, J. Y., Fareri, D. S., Bolger, N., & Tottenham, N. (2021). Longitudinal changes in amygdala, hippocampus and cortisol development following early caregiving adversity. *Developmental Cognitive Neuroscience, 48*, 100916.

Wallace, P. S., & Whishaw, I. Q. (2003). Independent digit movements and precision grip patterns in 1–5-month-old human infants: Hand-babbling, including vacuous then self-directed hand and digit movements, precedes targeted reaching. *Neuropsychologia, 41*(124), 1912–1918.

Weiss, S., Reynolds, B. A., Vescovi, A. L., Morshead, C., Craig, C. G., & van der Kooy, D. (1996). Is there a neural stem cell in the mammalian forebrain? *Trends in Neurosciences, 19*(9), 387–393.

Werker, J. F., & Tees, R. C. (1992). The organization and reorganization of human speech perception. *Annual Review of Neuroscience, 15*, 377–402.

Yakovlev, P. E., & Lecours, A.-R. (1967). The myelogenetic cycles of regional maturation of the brain. In A. Minkowski (Ed.), *Regional development of the brain in early life* (pp. 3–70). Blackwell.

Zuccolo, L., DeRoo, L. A., Wills, A., Smith, G. D., Suren, P., Roth, C., Stoltenberg, C., & Magnus, P. (2016). Pre-conception and prenatal alcohol exposure from mothers and fathers drinking and head circumference: Results from the Norwegian Mother–Child Study (MoBa). *Scientific Reports, 6*, 39535.

Zuchero, J. B., & Barres, B. A. (2015). Glia in mammalian development and disease. *Development, 142*(22), 3805–3809.

## CHAPTER 9

Bálint, R. (1909). Seelenlähmung des "Schauens," optische Ataxie, räumliche Störung der Aufmerksamkeit. *Monatschrift für Psychiatrie und Neurologie, 25*, 51–81.

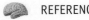

de Gelder, B., Tamietto, M., van Boxtel, G., Goebel, R., Sahraie, A., van den Stock, J., Stienen, B. M. C., Weiskrantz, L., & Pegna, A. (2008). Intact navigation skills after bilateral loss of striate cortex. *Current Biology, 18*(24), R1128–R1129.

Farah, M. J. (1990). *Visual agnosia.* MIT Press.

Freud, E., Culham, J. C., Plaut, D. C., & Behrmann, M. (2017). The large-scale organization of shape processing in the ventral and dorsal pathways. *eLife, 6,* e27576.

Garcea, F. E., Chen, Q., Vargas, R., Narayan, D. A., & Mahon, B. Z. (2018). Task- and domain-specific modulation of functional connectivity in the ventral and dorsal object-processing pathways. *Brain Structure and Function, 223*(6), 2589–2607.

Goodale, M. A., Milner, D. A., Jakobson, L. S., & Carey, J. D. P. (1991). A kinematic analysis of reaching and grasping movements in a patient recovering from optic ataxia. *Neuropsychologia, 29*(8), 803–809.

Haak, K. V., & Beckmann, C. F. (2018). Objective analysis of the topological organization of the human cortical visual connectome suggests three visual pathways. *Cortex, 98,* 73–83.

Hasson, U., Nir, Y., Levy, I., Fuhrmann, G., & Malach, R. (2004). Intersubject synchronization of cortical activity during natural vision. *Science, 303*(5664), 1634–1640.

Held, R. (1968). Dissociation of visual function by deprivation and rearrangement. *Psychologische Forschung, 31,* 338–348.

Jerison, H. J. (1973). *The evolution of the brain and intelligence.* Academic Press.

Kline, D. W. (1994). Optimizing the visibility of displays for older observers. *Experimental Aging Research, 20*(1), 11–23.

Kuffler, S. W. (1952). Neurons in the retina: Organization, inhibition and excitatory problems. *Cold Spring Harbor Symposia on Quantitative Biology, 17,* 281–292.

Laha, B., Stafford, B. K., & Huberman, A. D. (2017). Regenerating optic pathways from the eye to the brain. *Science, 356*(6342), 1031–1034.

Lehky, S. R., & Tanaka, K. (2016). Neural representation for object recognition in inferotemporal cortex. *Current Opinion in Neurobiology, 37,* 23–35.

Lim, J.-H. A., Stafford, B. K., Nguyen, P. L., Lien, B. V., Wang, C., Zukor, K., He, Z., & Huberman, A. D. (2016). Neural activity promotes long distance, target-specific regeneration of adult retinal axons. *Nature Neuroscience, 19,* 1073–1084.

Milner, A. D., & Goodale, M. A. (2006). *The visual brain in action* (2nd ed.). Oxford University Press.

Mundinano, I.-C., Chen, J., de Souza, M., Sarossy, M. G., Joanisse, M. F., Goodale, M. A., & Bourne, J. A. (2019). More than blindsight: Case report of a child with extraordinary visual capacity following perinatal bilateral occipital lobe injury. *Neuropsychologia, 128,* 178–186.

Norman, L. J., & Thaler, L. (2019). Retinotopic-like maps of spatial sound in primary "visual" cortex of blind human echolocators. *Proceedings of the Royal Society: Biological Sciences, 286*(1912), 1–9.

Oswald, J., Kegeles, E., Minelli, T., Volchkov, P., & Baranov, P. (2021). Transplantation of miPSC/mESC-derived retinal ganglion cells into healthy and glaucomatous retinas. *Molecular Therapy Methods in Clinical Development, 21,* 180–198. https://doi.org/10.1016/j.omtm.2021.03.004

Patel, G. H., Sestieri, C., & Corbetta, M. (2019). The evolution of the temporoparietal junction and

posterior superior temporal sulcus. *Cortex, 118,* 38–50.

Purves, D., Augustine, G. J., Fitzpatrick, D., Katz, L. C., LaMantia, A.-S., & McNamara, J. O. (Eds.). (1997). *Neuroscience.* Sinauer.

Quinn, J., Musa, A., Kantor, A., McClements, M. E., Cehajic-Kapetanovic, J., MacLaren, R. E., & Xue, K. (2021). Genome-editing strategies for treating human retinal degenerations. *Human Gene Therapy, 32*(5–6), 247–259. https://doi.org/10.1089/hum.2020.231

Sacks, O., & Wasserman, R. (1987, November 19). The case of the colorblind painter. *The New York Review of Books, 34,* 25–33.

Shibuki, K., Wakui, I., Fujimura, T., Tomikawa, M., & Hasegawa, S. (2020). Rapid recovery from cortical blindness caused by an old cerebral infarction. *Frontiers in Neurology, 11,* 69. https://doi.org/10.3389/fneur2020.00069

Szentagothai, J. (1975). The "module-concept" in cerebral cortex architecture. *Brain Research, 95*(2–3), 475–496.

Tanaka, K. (1993). Neuronal mechanisms of object recognition. *Science, 262*(5134), 685–688.

Tanaka, S., Miyashita, M., Wakabayashi, N., O'Hashi, K., Tani, T., & Ribot, J. (2020). Development and reorganization of orientation representation in the cat visual cortex: Experience-dependent synaptic rewiring in early life. *Frontiers in Neuroinformatics, 14,* 41. https://doi.org/01.3389/fninf.2020.00041

Wallisch, P. (2017). Illumination assumptions account for individual differences in the perceptual interpretation of a profoundly ambiguous stimulus in the color domain: "The dress." *Journal of Vision, 17*(4), 5.

Weizkrantz, L. (1986). *Blindsight: A case study and implications.* Oxford University Press.

Wiesel, T. N., & Hubel, D. H. (1965). Comparison of the effects of unilateral and bilateral eye closure on cortical unit responses in kittens. *Journal of Neurophysiology, 28*(6), 1029–1040.

Wong-Riley, M. T. T., Hevner, R. F., Cutlan, R., Earnest, M., Egan, R., Frost, J., & Nguyen, T. (1993). Cytochrome oxidase in the human visual cortex: Distribution in the developing and the adult brain. *Visual Neuroscience, 10*(1), 41–58.

Yuan, F., Wang, M., Jin, K., & Xiang, M. (2021). Advances in regeneration of retinal ganglion cells and optic nerves. *International Journal of Molecular Science, 22*(9), 4616. https://doi.org/3390/ijms22094616

Zihl, J., von Cramon, D., & Mai, N. (1983). Selective disturbance of movement vision after bilateral brain damage. *Brain, 106*(2), 313–340.

## CHAPTER 10

Bermudez, P., Lerch, J. P., Evans, A. C., & Zatorre, R. J. (2009). Neuroanatomical correlates of musicianship as revealed by cortical thickness and voxel-based morphometry. *Cerebral Cortex, 19*(7), 1583–1596.

Bertram, R., Hyson, R. L., Brunick, A. J., Flores, D., & Johnson, F. (2020). Network dynamics underlie learning and performance of birdsong. *Current Opinion in Neurobiology, 64,* 119–126.

Bregman, A. S. (2005). Auditory scene analysis and the role of phenomenology in experimental psychology. *Canadian Psychology, 46*(1), 32–40.

Chomsky, N. (1965). *Aspects of the theory of syntax.* MIT Press.

Clark, G. M. (2015). The multi-channel cochlear implant: Multi-disciplinary development of electrical stimulation of the cochlea and the

resulting clinical benefit. *Hearing Research, 322,* 4–13.

Daniel, E. (2007). Noise and hearing loss: A review. *The Journal of School Health, 77*(5), 225–231.

Drake-Lee, A. B. (1992). Beyond music: Auditory temporary threshold shift in rock musicians after a heavy metal concert. *Journal of the Royal Society of Medicine, 85*(10), 617–619.

Geissmann, T. (2001). Gibbon songs and human music from an evolutionary perspective. In N. L. Wallin, B. Merker, & S. Brown (Eds.), *The origins of music* (pp. 103–124). MIT Press.

Hyde, K. L., Lerch, J. P., Zatorre, R. J., Griffiths, T. D., Evans, A. C., & Peretz, I. (2007). Cortical thickness in congenital amusia: When less is better than more. *Journal of Neuroscience, 27*(47), 13028–13032.

Kenna, M. A. (2015). Acquired hearing loss in children. *Otolaryngologic Clinics of North America, 48*(6), 933–953.

Kim, K. H. S., Relkin, N. R., Young-Min Lee, K., & Hirsch, J. (1997). Distinct cortical areas associated with native and second languages. *Nature, 388*(6638), 171–174.

Knudsen, E. I. (1981). The hearing of the barn owl. *Scientific American, 245*(6), 113–125.

Marler, P. (1991). The instinct to learn. In S. Carey and R. German (Eds.), *The epigenesis of mind: Essays on biology and cognition* (p. 39). Erlbaum.

Naples, J. G., & Ruckenstein, M. J. (2020). Cochlear implant. *Otolaryngologic Clinics of North America, 53*(1), 87–102.

Norman, L. J., Dodsworth, C., Foresteire, D., & Thaler, L. (2021). Human click-based echolocation: Effects of blindness and age, and real-life implications in a 10-week training program. *PLOS ONE, 16*(6), e0252330.

Nottebohm, F., & Arnold, A. P. (1976). Sexual dimorphism in vocal control areas of the songbird brain. *Science, 194*(4261), 211–213.

Pereira, A. P. S., Marinho, V., Gupta, D., Magalhães, F., Ayres, C., & Teixeira, S. (2019). Music therapy and dance as gait rehabilitation in patients with Parkinson disease: A review of evidence. *Journal of Geriatric Psychiatry and Neurology, 32*(1), 49–56.

Pinker, S. (1997). *How the mind works.* Norton.

Purves, D. (2017). *Music as biology: The tones we like and why.* Harvard University Press.

Rauschecker, J. P. (2012). Ventral and dorsal streams in the evolution of speech and language. *Frontiers in Evolutionary Neuroscience, 4,* 7.

Romanski, L. M., Tian, B., Fritz, J., Mishkin, M., Goldman-Rakic, P. S., & Rauschecker, J. P. (1999). Dual streams of auditory afferents target multiple domains in the primate prefrontal cortex. *Nature Neuroscience, 2*(12), 1131–1136.

Sunitha Suresh, B. S., De Oliveira, G. S., Jr., & Suresh, S. (2015). The effect of audio therapy to treat postoperative pain in children undergoing major surgery: A randomized controlled trial. *Pediatric Surgical International, 31*(2), 197–201.

Teie, P. U. (1998). Noise-induced hearing loss and symphony orchestra musicians: Risk factors, effects, and management. *Maryland Medical Journal, 47*(1), 13–18.

Teng, S., & Whitney, D. (2011). The acuity of echolocation: Spatial resolution in the sighted compared to expert performance. *Journal of Visual Impairment & Blindness, 105*(1), 20–32.

Thaler, L., Arnott, S. R., & Goodale, M. A. (2011). Neural correlates of natural human echolocation in early and late blind echolocation experts. *PLOS ONE, 6*(5), e20162.

Thaler, L., De Vos, R., Kish, D., Antoniou, M., Baker, C., & Hornikx, M. (2018). Human echolocators adjust loudness and number of clicks for detection of reflectors at various azimuth angles. *Proceedings of the Royal Society B: Biological Sciences, 285*(1873), 20172735.

Thompson, C. K., Meitzen, J., Replogle, K., Drnevich, J., Lent, K. L., Wissman, A. M., Farin, F. M., Bammler, T. K., Beyer, R. P., Clayton, D. F., Perkel, D. J., & Brenowitz, E. A. (2012). Seasonal changes in patterns of gene expression in avian song control brain regions. *PLOS ONE, 7*(4), e35119.

Trehub, S. E., Schellenberg, E. G., & Kamenetsky, G. B. (1999). Infants' and adults' perception of scale structures. *Journal of Experimental Psychology: Human Perception and Performance, 25*(4), 965–975.

Zatorre, R. J., Evans, A. C., & Meyer, E. (1994). Neural mechanisms underlying melodic perception and memory for pitch. *Journal of Neuroscience, 14*(4), 1908–1919.

Zatorre, R. J., Evans, A. C., Meyer, E., & Gjedde, A. (1992). Lateralization of phonetic and pitch discrimination in speech processing. *Science, 25*(5058), 846–849.

### CHAPTER 11

Aflalo, T. N., & Graziano, M. S. (2007). Relationship between unconstrained arm movements and single-neuron firing in the macaque motor cortex. *Journal of Neuroscience, 27*(11), 2760–2780.

Alexander, R. E., & Crutcher, M. D. (1990). Functional architecture of basal ganglia circuits: Neural substrates of parallel processing. *Trends in Neuroscience, 13*(7), 266–271.

Asanuma, H. (1989). *The motor cortex*. Raven Press.

Bao, B., Duan, L., Wei, H., Luo, P., Zhu, H., Gao, T., Wei, X., Li, J., Li, Y., Chai, Y., Zhang, C., & Zheng, X. (2021). Changes in temporal and spatial patterns of intrinsic brain activity and functional connectivity in upper-limb amputees: An fMRI study. *Neural Plasticity, 223*, 8831379. https://doi.org/10.1155/2021/8831379

Black, K. J., Kim, S., Yang, N. Y., & Greene, D. J. (2021). Course of tic disorders over the lifespan. *Current Development Disorders Reports, 8*(2), 121–132.

Blakemore, S. J., Wolpert, D. M., & Frith, C. D. (1998). Central cancellation of self-produced tickle sensation. *Nature Neuroscience, 1*(7), 635–640.

BRAIN Initiative Cell Census Network (BICCN). (2021). A multimodal cell census and atlas of the mammalian primary motor cortex. *Nature, 598*, 86–102.

Brinkman, C. (1984). Supplementary motor area of the monkey's cerebral cortex: Short- and long-term deficits after unilateral ablation and the effects of subsequent callosal section. *Journal of Neuroscience, 4*(4), 918–992.

Bukhari, Q., Ruf, S. F., Guell, X., Whitfield-Gabrieli, S., & Anteraper, S. (2021). Interaction between cerebellum and cerebral cortex, evidence from dynamic causal modeling. *Cerebellum*. ePub ahead of print. https://doi.org/10.1007/s12311-021-1284-1.

Cole, J. (1995). *Pride and a daily marathon*. MIT Press.

Corkin, S., Milner, B., & Rasmussen, T. (1970). Somatosensory thresholds: Contrasting effects of postcentral-gyrus and posterior parietal-lobe excisions. *Archives of Neurology, 23*(1), 41–58.

Critchley, M. (1953). *The parietal lobes*. Arnold.

Evarts, E. V. (1968). Relation of pyramidal tract activity to force exerted during voluntary movement. *Journal of Neurophysiology, 31*(1), 14–27.

Fleury, L., Panico, F., Foncelle, A., Revol, P., Delporte, L., Jacquin-Courtois, S., Collet, C., & Rossetti, Y. (2021). Non-invasive brain stimulation shows possible cerebellar contribution in transfer of prism adaptation after-effects from pointing to throwing movements. *Brain and Cognition, 151*, 105735.

Foster, E., Wildner, H., Tudeau, L., Haueter, S., Ralvenius, W. T., Jegen, M., Johannssen, H., Hösli, L., Haenraets, K., Ghanem, A., Conzelmann, K.-K., Bösl, M., & Zeilhofer, H. U. (2015). Targeted ablation, silencing, and activation establish glycinergic dorsal horn neurons as key components of a spinal gate for pain and itch. *Neuron, 85*(6), 1289–1304.

Granata, G., Valle, G., Di Iorio, R., Iodice, F., Petrini, F. M., Strauss, I., D'anna, E., Iberite, F., Lauretti, L., Fernandez, E., Romanello, R., Stieglitz, T., Raspopovic, S., Calabresi, P., Micera, S., & Rossini, P. M. (2020). Cortical plasticity after hand prostheses use: Is the hypothesis of deafferented cortex "invasion" always true? *Clinical Neurophysiology, 131*(10), 2341–2348.

Graziano, M. S. A. (2009). *The intelligent movement machine: An ethological perspective on the primate motor system*. Oxford University Press.

Hess, W. R. (1957). *The functional organization of the diencephalon*. Grune & Stratton.

Huber, L., Finn, E. S., Handwerker, D. A., Bönstrup, M., Glen, D. R., Kashyap, S., Ivanov, D., Petridou, N., Marrett, S., Goense, J., Poser, B. A., & Bandettini, P. A. (2020). Sub-millimeter fMRI reveals multiple topographical digit representations that form action maps in human motor cortex. *Neuroimage, 208*, 116463.

Inanici, F., Brighton, L. N., Samejima, S., Hofstetter, C. P., & Moritz C. T. (2021). Transcutaneous spinal cord stimulation restores hand and arm function after spinal cord injury. *IEEE Transactions on Neural Systems and Rehabilitation Engineering, 29*, 310–319.

Kaas, J. H. (1987). The organization and evolution of neocortex. In S. P. Wise (Ed.), *Higher brain functions* (pp. 237–298). Wiley.

Kalueff, A. V., Stewart, A. M., Song, C., Berridge, K. C., Graybiel, A. M., & Fentress, J. C. (2016). Neurobiology of rodent self-grooming and its value for translational neuroscience. *Nature Reviews Neuroscience, 17*(1), 45–59.

Karl, J. M., Kuntz, J. R., Lenhart, L. A., & Whishaw, I. Q. (2018). Frame-by-frame video analysis of idiosyncratic reach-to-grasp movements in humans. *Journal of Visualized Experiments, 2018*(131), 56733. https://doi.org/10.3791/56733

Kawala-Sterniuk, A., Browarska, N., Al-Bakri, A., Pelc, M., Zygarlicki, J., Sidikova, M., Martinek, R., & Gorzelanczyk, E. J. (2021). Summary of over fifty years with brain–computer interfaces: A review. *Brain Sciences, 11*(1), 43.

LaFollette, M. R., O'Haire, M. E., Cloutier, S., Blankenberger, W. B., & Gaskill, B. N. (2017). Rat tickling: A systematic review of applications, outcomes, and moderators. *PLOS ONE, 12*(4), e0175320.

Lashley, K. S. (1951). The problem of serial order in behavior. In L. A. Jeffress (Ed.), *Cerebral mechanisms and behavior* (pp. 112–136). Wiley.

Liu, Y., Vannuscorps, G., Caramazza, A., & Striem-Amit, E. (2020). Evidence for an effector-independent action system from people born without hands. *Proceedings of the National Academy of Sciences U.S.A. 117*, 28433–28441.

McHugh, C., Taylor, C., Mockler, D., & Fleming, N. (2021, May 6). Epidural spinal cord stimulation for motor recovery in spinal cord injury: A systematic review. *NeuroRehabilitation, 49*(1), 1–22.

Melzack, R. (1973). *The puzzle of pain*. Basic Books.

Melzack, R., & Wall, P. D. (1965). Pain mechanisms: A new theory. *Science, 150*(3699), 971–979.

Morelli, N., & Hoch, M. A. (2020). A proposed postural control theory synthesizing optimal feedback control theory, postural motor learning, and cerebellar supervision learning. *Perceptual and Motor Skills, 127*(6), 1118–1133.

Mountcastle, V. B. (1978). An organizing principle for cerebral function: The unit module and the distributed system. In G. M. Edelman & V. B. Mountcastle (Eds.), *The mindful brain* (pp. 7–50). MIT Press.

Mylopoulos, M. (2021). Oops! I did it again: The psychology of everyday action slips. *Topics in Cognitive Science*, ePub ahead of print.

National Spinal Cord Injury Statistics Center. (2020). *Facts and figures at a glance*. University of Alabama at Birmingham. https://www.nscisc.uab.edu/Public/Facts%20and%-20Figures%202020.pdf

Nudo, R. J., Wise, B. M., SiFuentes, F., & Milliken, G. W. (1996). Neural substrates for the effects of rehabilitative training on motor recovery after ischemic infarct. *Science, 272*(5269), 1791–1794.

Park, J., Coddington, L. T., & Dudman, J. T. (2020). Basal ganglia circuits for action specification. *Annual Review of Neuroscience, 43*, 485–507.

Penfield, W., & Boldrey, E. (1937). Somatic motor and sensory representation in the cerebral cortex as studied by electrical stimulation. *Brain, 60*, 389–443.

Pons, T. P., Garraghty, P. E., Ommaya, A. K., Kaas, J. H., Taum, E., & Mishkin, M. (1991). Massive cortical reorganization after sensory deafferentation in adult macaques. *Science, 252*(5014), 1857–1860.

Quadrelli, E., Bartoli, B., Bolognini, N., Cavanna, A. E., Zibordi, F., Nardocci, N., Turati, C., & Termine, C. (2021). Automatic imitation in youngsters with Gilles de la Tourette syndrome: A behavioral study. *Child Neuropsychology, 27*(6), 782–798.

Ramachandran, V. S., & Rogers-Ramachandran, D. (1996). Synaesthesia in phantom limbs induced with mirrors. *Proceedings of the Royal Society: Biological Science, 263*(1369), 377–386.

Rocha, L. S. O., Gama, G. C. B., Rocha, R. S. B., Rocha, L. B., Dias, C. P., Santos, L. L. S., Santos, M. C. S., Montebelo, M. I. L., & Teodori, R. M. (2021). Constraint induced movement therapy increases functionality and quality of life after stroke. *Journal of Stroke and Cerebrovascular Disease, 30*(6), 105774.

Roland, P. E. (1993). *Brain activation*. Wiley-Liss.

Rothwell, J. C., Taube, M. M., Day, B. L., Obeso, J. A., Thomas, P. K., & Marsden, C. D. (1982). Manual motor performance in a deafferented man. *Brain, 105*(3), 515–542.

Sacks, O. W. (1998). *The man who mistook his wife for a hat: And other clinical tales*. Touchstone Books.

Schieber, M. H. (2011). Dissociating motor cortex from the motor. *Journal of Physiology, 589*(Pt 23), 5613–5624.

Sereno, M. I., Diedrichsen, J., Tachrount, M., Testa-Silva, G., d'Arceuil, H., & De Zeeuw, C. (2021). The human cerebellum has almost 80% of the surface area of the neocortex.

*Proceedings of the National Academy of Sciences of the United States of America, 117*(32), 19538–19543.

Shahsavani, N., Kataria, H., & Karimi-Abdolrezaee, S. (2021). Mechanisms and repair strategies for white matter degeneration in CNS injury and diseases. *BBA Molecular Basis of Disease, 1867*(6), 166117.

Stankevicius, A., Wallwork, S. B., Summers, S. J., Hordacre, B., & Stanton, T. R. (2021). Prevalence and incidence of phantom limb pain, phantom limb sensations and telescoping in amputees: A systematic rapid review. *European Journal of Pain, 25*(1), 23–38.

Stewart, K., Lewis, J., Wallen, M., Bear, N., & Harvey, A. (2021). The Dyskinetic Cerebral Palsy Functional Impact Scale: development and validation of a new tool. *Developmental Medicine and Child Neurology, 1867*(6), 166117.

Thach, W. T. (2007). On the mechanism of cerebellar contributions to cognition. *Cerebellum, 6*(3), 163–167.

Thach, W. T., Goodkin, H. P., & Keating, J. G. (1992). The cerebellum and the adaptive coordination of movement. *Annual Review of Neuroscience, 15,* 403–442.

Therrien, A. S., Howard, C., & Buxbaum, L. J. (2021). Aberrant activity in an intact residual muscle is associated with phantom limb pain in above-knee amputees. *Journal of Neurophysiology, 125*(6), 2135–2143.

van Nispen, K., Mieke, W. M. E., van de Sandt-Koenderman, E., & Krahmer, E. (2018). The comprehensibility of pantomimes produced by people with aphasia. *International Journal of Language and Communication Disorders, 53*(1), 85–100.

von Holst, E. (1973). *The collected papers of Erich von Holst* (R. Martin, Trans.). University of Miami Press.

Windt, J. M., Harkness, D. L., & Lenggenhager, B. (2015). Tickle me, I think I might be dreaming! Sensory attenuation, self–other distinction, and predictive processing in lucid dreams. *Frontiers in Human Neuroscience, 8,* 717.

Winkler, S. M., & Bryant, G. M. (2021). Play vocalizations and human laughter: A comparative review. *Bioacoustics, 30*(5), 499–526.

Xie, W., Shu, T., Liu, J., Peng, H., Karpeta, N., Marques, P., Liu, Y., & Duan, M. (2021). The relationship between clinical characteristics and magnetic resonance imaging results of Ménière disease: A prospective study. *Scientific Reports, 11*(1), 7212.

### CHAPTER 12

Ackerly, S. S. (1964). A case of paranatal bilateral frontal lobe defect observed for thirty years. In J. M. Warren & K. Akert (Eds.), *The frontal granular cortex and behavior* (pp. 192–218). McGraw-Hill.

Adams, D. R., Kern, D. W., Wroblewski, K. E., McClintock, M. K., Dale, W., & Pinto, J. M. (2018). Olfactory dysfunction predicts subsequent dementia in older U.S. adults. *Journal of the American Geriatric Society, 66*(1), 140–144.

Anderson, D. J., & Adolphs, R. (2014). A framework for studying emotions across species. *Cell, 157*(1), 187–200.

Arnold, A. P., Reue, K., Eghbali, M., Vilain, E., Chen, X., Ghahramani, N., Itoh, Y., Li, J., Link, J. C., Ngun, T., & Williams-Burris, S. M. (2016). The importance of having two X chromosomes. *Philosophical Transactions of the*

*Royal Society of London B: Biological Sciences, 371*(1688), 20150113.

Bao, A.-M., & Swaab, D. F. (2011). Sexual differentiation of the human brain: Relation to gender identity, sexual orientation and neuropsychiatric disorders. *Frontiers in Neuroendocrinology, 32*(2), 214–226.

Barrett, L. F., Adolphs, R., Marsella, S., Martinez, A. M., & Pollak, S. D. (2019). Emotional expressions reconsidered: Challenges to inferring emotion from human facial movements. *Psychological Science, 20*(1), 1–68.

Bartoshuk, L. M. (2000). Comparing sensory experiences across individuals: Recent psychophysical advances illuminate genetic variation in taste perception. *Chemical Senses, 25*(4), 447–460.

Bechara, A. (2017). Revisiting Phineas Gage: Lessons we learned from damaged brains. In B. Kolb & I. Q. Whishaw (Eds.), *Brain & behaviour: Revisiting the classic studies* (pp. 113–129). Sage.

Berridge, K. C. (1996). Food reward: Brain substrates of wanting and liking. *Neuroscience and Biobehavioral Reviews, 20*(1), 1–25.

Berridge, K. C., & Kringelbach, M. L. (2015). Pleasure systems in the brain. *Neuron, 86*(3), 646–664.

Berridge, K. C., & Robinson, T. E. (1998). What is the role of dopamine in reward: Hedonic impact, reward learning, or incentive salience? *Brain Research Reviews, 28*(3), 309–369.

Berridge, K. C., & Robinson, T. E. (2003). Parsing reward. *Trends in Neuroscience, 26*(9), 507–513.

Berridge, K. C., & Robinson, T. E. (2016). Liking, wanting and the incentive-sensitization theory of addiction. *American Psychologist, 71*(8), 670–679.

Brunetti, M., Babiloni, C., Ferretti, A., Del Gratta, C., Merla, A., Olivetti Belardinelli, M., & Romani, G. L. (2008). Hypothalamus, sexual arousal and psychosexual identity in human males: A functional magnetic resonance imaging study. *European Journal of Neuroscience, 27*(11), 2922–2927.

Buss, D. (2014). *Evolutionary psychology: The new science of the mind* (5th ed.). Taylor & Francis.

Butler, R. A., & Harlow, H. F. (1954). Persistence of visual exploration in monkeys. *Journal of Comparative and Physiological Psychology, 47,* 257–263.

Buzaki, G. (2011). *Rhythms of the brain*. Oxford University Press.

Carus-Cadavieco, M., Gorbati, M., Ye, L., Bender, F., van der Veldt, S., Kosse, C., Börgers, C., Lee, S. Y., Ramakrishnan, C., Hu, Y., Denisova, N., Ramm, F., Volitaki, E., Burdakov, D., Deisseroth, K., Ponomarenko, A., & Korotkova, T. (2017). Gamma oscillations organize top-down signaling to hypothalamus and enable food seeking. *Nature, 542*(7640), 232–236.

Cohen-Kettenis, P. T., & Pfafflin, F. (2010). The DSM diagnostic criteria for gender identity disorder in adolescents and adults. *Archives of Sexual Behavior, 39*(2), 499–513.

Collins, B. E., Greer, C. B., Coleman, B. C., & Sweatt, J. D. (2019). Histone H3 lysine K4 methylation and its role in learning and memory. *Epigenetics & Chromatin, 12,* 7. https://doi.org/10.1186/s13072-018-0251-8

Curtis, V., & de Barra, M. (2018). The structure and function of pathogen disgust. *Philosophical Transactions of the Royal Society B, 373*(1751), 20170208. https://doi.org/10.1098/rstb.2017.0208.

Daly, M., & Wilson, M. (1988). *Homicide*. Aldine.

De Wall, C. N., MacDonald, G., Webster, G. D., Masten, C. L., Baumeister, R. F., Powell, C., Combs, D., Schurtz, D. R., Stillman, T. F., Tice, D. M., & Eisenberger, N. I. (2010). Acetaminophen reduces social pain: Behavioral and neural evidence. *Psychological Science, 21*(7), 931–937.

Dubois, J., Oya, H., Tyszka, J. M., Howard, M., Eberhardt, F., & Adolphs, R. (2017). Causal mapping of emotion networks in the human brain: Framework and initial findings. *Neuropsychologia, 145,* 106571. https://doi.org/10.1016/j.neuropsychologia.2017.11.015

Dunsmoor, J. E., Kubota, J. T., Li, J., Coelho, C. A. O., & Phelps, E. A. (2016). Racial stereotypes impair flexibility of emotional learning. *Social Cognitive and Affective Neuroscience, 11*(9), 1363–1373.

Eisenberger, N. I. (2012). The neural basis of social pain: Evidence for shared representations with physical pain. *Psychosomatic Medicine, 74*(2), 126–135.

Eisenberger, N. I., & Moieni, M. (2020). Inflammation affects social experience: Implications for mental health. *World Psychiatry, 19*(1), 109–110. https://doi.org/10.1002/wps.20724.

Eliyan, Y., Wroblewski, K. E., McClintock, M. K., & Pinto, J. M. (2021). Olfactory dysfunction predicts the development of depression in older U.S. adults. *Chemical Senses, 46,* bjaa075.

Everitt, B. J. (1990). Sexual motivation: A neural and behavioral analysis of the mechanisms underlying appetitive and copulatory responses of male rats. *Neuroscience and Biobehavioral Reviews, 14*(2), 217–232.

Field, T. M., Woodson, R., Greenberg, R., & Cohen, D. (1982). Discrimination and imitation of facial expression by neonates. *Science, 218*(4568), 179–181.

Friedman, J., Barrett, L. F., Wormwood, J. B., & Quigley, K. S. (2019). Applying the theory of constructed emotion to police decision making. *Frontiers in Psychology, 10,* 1946.

Garcia, J., & Koelling, R. A. (1966). Relation of cue to consequences in avoidance learning. *Psychonomic Science, 4,* 123–124.

Gerkin, R. C., & Castro, J. B. (2015). The number of olfactory stimuli that humans can discriminate is still unknown. *eLife, 4,* e08127.

Glickman, S. E., & Schiff, B. B. (1967). A biological theory of reinforcement. *Psychological Review, 74*(2), 81–109.

Gorski, R. A. (1984). Critical role for the medial preoptic area in the sexual differentiation of the brain. *Progress in Brain Research, 61,* 129–146.

Harvard Medical School. (2020). *The diet review: Special health report*. Harvard Health Publishing.

Hummer, T. A., Phan, K. L., Kern, D. W., & McClintock, M. K. (2017). A human chemosignal modulates frontolimbic activity and connectivity in response to social stimuli. *Psychoneuroendocrinology, 75,* 15–25.

Insel, T. R., & Fernald, R. D. (2004). How the brain processes social information: Searching for the social brain. *Annual Review of Neuroscience, 27,* 697–722.

Jacobsen, C. F. (1936). Studies of cerebral function in primates. *Comparative Psychology Monographs, 13*(3), 1–68.

Kagan, J. (2018). Brain and emotion. *Emotion Review, 10*(1), 79–86.

Khorashad, B. S., Manzouri, A., Feusner, J. D., & Savic, I. (2021). Cross-sex hormone treatment and own-body perception: Behavioral and brain connectivity profiles. *Scientific Reports, 11*(1), 2799.

Klüver, H., & Bucy, P. C. (1939). Preliminary analysis of the temporal lobes in monkeys. *Archives of Neurology and Psychiatry, 42,* 979–1000.

Kolb, B., & Nonneman, A. J. (1975). The development of social responsiveness in kittens. *Animal Behavior, 23*(2), 368–374.

Kolb, B., & Whishaw, I. Q. (2021). *Fundamentals of human neuropsychology* (8th ed.). Macmillan Learning.

Kosse, C., & Burdakov, D. (2018). Fast and slow oscillations recruit molecularly distinct subnetworks of lateral hypothalamic neurons *in situ*. *eNeuro, 5*(1), 0012–0018.

Kragel, P. A., Kano, M., van Oudenhove, L., Ly, H. G., Dupont, P., Rubio, A., Delon-Martin, C., Bonaz, B. L., Manuck, S. B., Gianaros, P. J., Ceko, M., Reynolds Losin, E. A., Woo, C.-W., Nichols, T. E., & Wager, T. D. (2018). Generalizable representations of pain, cognitive control, and negative emotion in medial frontal cortex. *Nature Neuroscience, 21*(2), 283–289.

Kringelbach, M. L., & Berridge, K. C. (2017). The affective core of emotion: Linking pleasure, subjective well-being, and optimal metastability in the brain. *Emotion Review, 9*(3), 191–199.

Kringelbach, M. L., & Phillips, H. (2014). *Emotion: Pleasure and pain in the brain*. Oxford University Press.

Kross, E., Berman, M. G., Mischel, W., Smith, E. E., & Water, T. D. (2011). Social rejection shares somatosensory representations with physical pain. *Proceedings of the National Academy of Sciences of the United States of America, 108*(15), 6270–6275.

Kung, K. T. F., Brown, W. V., Constantinescu, M., Noorderhaven, R. M., & Hines, M. (2016). Early postnatal testosterone predicts sex-related differences in early expressive vocabulary. *Psychoneuroendocrinology, 68,* 111–116.

Levenson, R. W., Lwi, S. J., Brown, C. L., Ford, B. Q., Otero, M. C., & Vertaen, A. (2017). Emotion. In J. T. Cacioppo, L. G. Tassinary, & G. G. Berntson (Eds.), *Handbook of psychophysiology* (4th ed., pp. 444–464). Cambridge University Press.

Little, A. C., Jones, B. C., & DeBruine, L. M. (2011). Facial attractiveness: Evolutionary based research. *Philosophical Transactions of the Royal Society B: Biological Sciences, 366*(1571), 1638–1659.

Lundstrom, J. N., Boyle, J. A., Zatorre, R. J., & Jones-Gotman, M. (2008). Functional neuronal processing of body odors differs from that of similar common odors. *Cerebral Cortex, 18*(6), 1466–1474.

Luo, Z., Hou, C., Wang, L., & Hu, D. (2019). Gender identification of human cortical 3-D morphology using hierarchical sparsity. *Frontiers in Human Neuroscience, 13,* 29.

MacLean, P. D. (1949). Psychosomatic disease and the "visceral brain": Recent developments bearing on the Papez theory of emotion. *Psychosomatic Medicine, 11*(6), 338–353.

Manzouri, A., & Savic, I. (2018). Cerebral sex dimorphism and sexual orientation. *Human Brain Mapping, 39*(3), 1175–1186.

Manzouri, A., & Savic, I. (2019). Possible neurobiological underpinnings of homosexuality and gender dysphoria, *Cerebral Cortex, 29*(5), 2084–2101.

McCarthy, M. M., Auger, A. P., Bale, T. L., De Vries, G. J., Dunn, G. A., Forger, N. G., Murray, E. K., Nugent, B. M., Schwarz, J. M., & Wilson, M. E. (2009). The epigenetics of sex differences in the brain. *Journal of Neuroscience, 29*(41), 12815–12823.

McCarthy, M., de Vries, G. J., & Forger, N. G. (2017). Sexual differentiation of the brain: A fresh look at mode, mechanisms, and meaning. In D. W. Pfaff & M. Joels (Eds.), *Hormones, brain, and behavior* (3rd ed., pp. 3–32). Academic Press.

Melis, M., Haehner, A., Mastinu, M., Hummel, T., & Barbarossa, I. T. (2021). Molecular and genetic factors involved in olfactory and gustatory deficits and associations with microbiota in Parkinson's disease. *International Journal of Molecular Science, 22*(8), 4286.

Meunier, N., Briand, L., Jacquin-Piques, A., Brondel, L., & Penicaud, L. (2021). COVID 19-induced smell and taste impairments: Putative impact on physiology. *Frontiers in Physiology, 11,* 1882.

Meyer, M. L., Williams, K. D., & Eisenberger, N. I. (2015). Why social pain can live on: Different neural mechanisms are associated with reliving social and physical pain. *PLoS One, 10*(6), e0128294.

Money, J., & Ehrhardt, A. A. (1972). *Man and woman, boy and girl*. Johns Hopkins University Press.

Mwilambwe-Tshilobo, L., & Spreng, R. N. (2021). Social exclusion reliably engages the default network: A meta-analysis of Cyberball. *NeuroImage, 227,* 117666.

Narayanan, N. S., & DiLeone, R. J. (2017). Lip sync: Gamma rhythms orchestrate top-down control of feeding circuits. *Cell Metabolism, 25*(3), 497–498.

Olds, J., & Milner, P. (1954). Positive reinforcement produced by electrical stimulation of septal area and other regions of rat brain. *Journal of Comparative and Physiological Psychology, 47*(6), 419–427.

Olsson, S. B., Barnard, J., & Turri, L. (2006). Olfaction and identification of unrelated individuals: Examination of the mysteries of human odor recognition. *Journal of Chemical Ecology, 32*(8), 1635–1645.

Phoenix, C. H., Goy, R. W., Gerall, A. A., & Young, W. C. (1959). Organizing action of prenatally administered testosterone propionate on the tissues mediating mating behavior in the female guinea pig. *Endocrinology, 65*(3), 365–382.

Ritchie, S. J., Cox, S. R., Shen, X., Lombardo, M. V., Reus, L. M., Alloza, C., Harris, M. A., Alderson, H. L., Hunter, S., Neilson, E., Liewald, D. C. M., Auyeung, B., Whalley, H. C., Lawrie, S. M., Gale, C. R., Bastin, M. E., McIntosh, A. M., & Deary, I. J. (2018). Sex differences in the adult human brain: Evidence from 5216 UK biobank participants. *Cerebral Cortex, 28*(8), 2959–2975.

Rouadi, R. W., Idriss, S. A., & Bousquet, J. (2021). Olfactory and taste dysfunctions in COVID-19. *Current Opinion in Allergy and Clinical Immunology, 21*(3), 229–244.

Rozin, P., Haidt, J., & Fincher, K. (2009). From oral to moral. *Science, 323*(5918), 1179–1180.

San-Cristobal, R., Navas-Carretero, S., Martinez-Gonzalez, A., Ordovas, J., & Martinez, J. A. (2020). Contribution of macronutrients to obesity: Implications for precision nutrition. *Nature Reviews: Endocrinology, 16*(5), 305–320.

Scherer, K. R., & Moors, A. (2019). The emotion process: Event appraisal and component differentiation. *Annual Review of Psychology, 70,* 719–745.

Seeley, R. J., & Woods, S. C. (2003). Monitoring of stored and available fuel by the CNS: Implications for obesity. *Nature Reviews Neuroscience, 4*(11), 885–909.

Siegel, J. K., Kung, S. Y., Wroblewski, K. E., Kern, D. W., McClintock, M. K., & Pinto, J. M. (2021). Olfaction is associated with sexual motivation and satisfaction in older men and women. *Journal of Sex Medicine, 18*(2), 295–302.

Skinner, B. F. (1938). *The behavior of organisms*. Appleton-Century-Crofts.

Smith, D. V., & Shepherd, G. M. (2003). Chemical senses: Taste and olfaction. In L. R. Squire, F. E. Bloom, S. K. McConnell, J. L. Roberts, N. C. Spitzer, & M. J. Zigmond (Eds.), *Fundamental neuroscience* (2nd ed., pp. 631–667). Academic Press.

Swanson, L. W. (2000). Cerebral hemisphere regulation of motivated behavior. *Brain Research Reviews, 886*(1–2), 113–164.

Weis, S., Patil, K. R., Hoffstaedter, F., Nostro, A., Yeo, B. T. T., & Eickhoff, S. B. (2020). Sex classification by resting state brain connectivity. *Cerebral Cortex, 30*(2), 824–835.

Williams, J. A., Bartoshuk, L. M., Fillingim, R. B., & Dotson, C. D. (2016). Exploring ethnic differences in taste perception. *Chemical Senses, 41*(5), 449–456.

Wise, R. A. (1980). The dopamine synapse and the notion of "pleasure centers" in the brain. *Trends in Neurosciences, 3*(4), 91–95.

Woolford, S. J., Sidell, M., Li, X., Else, V., Young, D. R., Resnicow, K., & Koebnick, C. (2021). Changes in body mass index among children and adolescents during the COVID-19 pandemic. *JAMA, 326*(14): 1434–1436. doi:10.1001/jama.2021.15036.

Woolley, C. S., Gould, E., Frankfurt, M., & McEwen, B. S. (1990). Naturally occurring fluctuation in dendritic spine density on adult hippocampal pyramidal neurons. *Journal of Neuroscience, 10*(12), 4035–4039.

World Health Organization. (2021). *Fact sheets: Obesity and overweight*. http://www.who.int/news-room/fact-sheets/detail/obesity-and-overweight.

Zhang, Y., Luo, Q., Huang, C.-C., Lo, C.-Y. Z., Langley, C., Desrivières, S., Quinlan, E. B., Banaschewski, T., Millenet, S., Bokde, A. L. W., Flor, H., Garavan, H., Gowland, P., Heinz, A., Ittermann, B., Martinot, J.-L., Artiges, E., Paillère-Martinot, M.-L., Nees, F., … & IMA-GEN consortium. (2021). The human brain is best described as being on a female/male continuum: evidence from a neuroimaging connectivity study. *Cerebral Cortex, 31*(6), 3021–3033.

## CHAPTER 13

Agorastos, A., Nicolaides, N. C., Bozikas, V. P., Chrousos, G. P., & Pervanidou, P. (2020). Multilevel interactions of stress and circadian system: Implications for traumatic stress. *Frontiers in Psychiatry, 10,* 1003.

Allen, S. F., Gardani, M., Akram, A., Irvine K. R., & Akram, U. (2021). Examining the factor structure, reliability, and validity of the Disturbing Dreams and Nightmare Severity Index (DDNSI) consequences sub-component. *Behavioral Sleep Medicine, 19*(6), 783–794.

Alzate-Correa, D., Aten, S., Campbell, M. J., Hoyt, K. R., & Obrietan, K. (2021). Light-induced changes in the suprachiasmatic nucleus transcriptome regulated by the ERK/MAPK pathway. *PLoS One, 16*(6), e0249430.

An, Z., Merrill, N. J., Lee, K., Robin, R., Hayat, A., Zapfe, O., & Piccoli, B. (2021). A two-step model of human entrainment: A quantitative study of circadian period and phase of entrainment. *Bulletin of Math and Biology, 83*(2), 12–24.

Aschoff, J. (1978). Circadian rhythms within and outside their ranges of entrainment. In I. Assenmacher & D. S. Farner (Eds.), *Environmental endocrinology* (pp. 171–181). Springer.

Azeez, I. A., Igado, O. O., & Olopade, J. O. (2021). An overview of the orexinergic system in different animal species. *Metabolism and Brain Disease, 36*(7), 1419–1444.

Bais, B., Hoogendijk, W. J. G., & Lambregtse-van den Berg, M. P. (2021). Light therapy for mood disorders. *Handbook of Clinical Neurology, 182,* 49–61.

Binkley, S. (1990). *The clockwork sparrow.* Prentice Hall.

Blumberg, M. S. (2015). Developing sensorimotor systems in our sleep. *Current Directions in Psychological Science, 24*(1), 32–37.

Bolsius, Y. G., Zurbriggen, M. D., Kim, J. K., Kas, M. J., Meerlo, P., Aton, S. J., & Havekes, R. (2021). The role of clock genes in sleep, stress, and memory. *Biochemical Pharmacology, 191,* 114493.

Buijs, R. M., Soto Tinoco, E. C., Hurtado Alvarado, G., & Escobar, C. (2021). The circadian system: From clocks to physiology. *Handbook of Clinical Neurology, 179,* 233–247.

Cain, S. W., Verwey, M., Szybowska, M., Ralph, M. R., & Yeomans, J. S. (2007). Carbachol injections into the intergeniculate leaflet induce nonphotic phase shifts. *Brain Research, 1177,* 59–65.

Carter, K. A., Hathaway, N. E., & Lettieri, C. F. (2014). Common sleep disorders in children. *American Family Physician, 89*(5), 368–377.

Charest, J., Samuels, C. H., Bastien, C. H., Lawson, D., & Grandner, M. A. (2021, June 21). Impacts of travel distance and travel direction on back-to-back games in the National Basketball Association. *Journal of Clinical Sleep Medicine.*

Chen, C.-Y., Logan, R. W., Ma, T., Lewis, D. A., Tseng, G. C., Sibille, E., & McClung, C. A. (2016). Effects of aging on circadian patterns of gene expression in the human prefrontal cortex. *Proceedings of the National Academy of Sciences of the United States of America, 113*(1), 206–211.

Cheung, B. Y., Takemura, K., Ou, C., Gale, A., & Heine, S. J. (2021). Considering cross-cultural differences in sleep duration between Japanese and Canadian university students. *PLoS One, 16*(4), e0250671.

Cordi, M. J., & Rasch, B. (2021). How robust are sleep-mediated memory benefits? *Current Opinion in Neurobiology, 67,* 1–7.

Corrêa C. C., Blasca, W. Q., & Berretin-Felix, G. (2015). Health promotion in obstructive sleep apnea syndrome. *International Archives of Otorhinolaryngology, 19*(2), 166–170.

de Lecea L. (2021). Twenty-three years of hypocretins: The "Rosetta stone" of sleep/arousal circuits. *Frontiers in Neurology and Neuroscience, 45,* 1–10.

Dement, W. C. (1972). *Some must watch while some must sleep.* Stanford Alumni Association.

Dopheide, J. A. (2020). Insomnia overview: epidemiology, pathophysiology, diagnosis and monitoring, and nonpharmacologic therapy. *American Journal of Management Care, 26*(4 Suppl), S76–S84.

Edelman, G. M. (1989). *The remembered present: A biological theory of consciousness.* Basic Books.

Farhadian, N., Khazaie, H., Nami, M., & Khazaie, S. (2021). The role of daytime napping in declarative memory performance: A systematic review. *Sleep Medicine, 84,* 134–141.

Fatemeh, G., Sajjad, M., Niloufar, R., Neda, S., Leila, S., & Khadijeh, M. (2021, January 8). Effect of melatonin supplementation on sleep quality: A systematic review and meta-analysis of randomized controlled trials. *Journal of Neurology.*

Fischer, D. B., Boes, A. D., Demertzi, A., Evrard, H. C., Laureys, S., Edlow, B. L., Liu, H., Saper, C. B., Pascual-Leone, A., Fox, M. D., & Geerling, J. C. (2016). A human brain network derived from coma-causing brainstem lesions. *Neurology, 87*(23), 2427–2434.

Freud, S. (1900). *The interpretation of dreams.* Franz Deuticke.

Gale, C., & Martyn, C. (1998). Larks and owls and health, wealth, and wisdom. *BMJ, 317*(7174), 1675–1677.

Gandhi, M. H., & Emmady, P. D. (2021). Physiology, K complex. *StatPearls.* https://www.statpearls .com/articlelibrary/viewarticle/31499/

Gerrard, J. L., Burke, S. N., McNaughton, B. L., & Barnes, C. A. (2008). Sequence reactivation in the hippocampus is impaired in aged rats. *Journal of Neuroscience, 28*(31), 7883–7890.

Hall, C. S., Domhoff, G. W., Blick, K. A., & Weesner, K. E. (1982). The dreams of college men and women in 1950 and 1980: A comparison of dream contents and sex differences. *Sleep, 5*(2), 188–194.

Hanson, J. A., & Huecker, M. R. (2021). Sleep deprivation. *StatPearls.* https://www.ncbi.nlm .nih.gov/books/NBK547676/

Helfrich-Förster, C., Monecke, S., Spiousas, I., Hovestadt, T., Mitesser, O., & Wehr, T. A. (2021). Women temporarily synchronize their menstrual cycles with the luminance and gravimetric cycles of the Moon. *Scientific Advances, 7*(5), eabe1358.

Hobson, J. A. (1989). *Sleep.* Scientific American Library.

Hobson, J. A. (2002). Sleep and dream suppression following a lateral medullary infarct: A first-person account. *Consciousness and Cognition, 11*(3), 377–390.

Hobson, J. A. (2004). *13 dreams Freud never had: A new mind science.* Pi Press.

Hulsegge, G., Proper, K. I., Loef, B., Paagman, H., Anema, J. R., & van Mechelen, W. (2021). The mediating role of lifestyle in the relationship between shift work, obesity and diabetes. *International Archives of Occupational and Environmental Health, 94*(6), 1287–1295.

Jones, B. E. (1993). The organization of central cholinergic systems and their functional importance in sleep–waking states. *Progress in Brain Research, 98,* 61–71.

Jouvet, M. (1972). The role of monoamines and acetylcholine-containing neurons in the regulation of the sleep–waking cycle. *Ergebnisse der Physiologie, 64,* 166–307.

Kay, D. B., & Buysse, D. J. (2017). Hyperarousal and beyond: New insights to the pathophysiology of insomnia disorder through functional neuroimaging studies. *Brain Sciences, 7*(23), 1–19.

Kelley, D. D. (1991). Sleep and dreaming. In E. R. Kandel, J. H. Schwartz, & T. M. Jessell (Eds.), *Principles of neuroscience* (pp. 741–777). Elsevier.

Khodasevich, D., Tsui, S., Keung, D., Skene, D. J., Revell, V., & Martinez, M. E. (2021). Characterizing the modern light environment and its

influence on circadian rhythms. *Proceedings of Biological Sciences, 288*(1955), 20210721.

Kinney, H. C., Korein, J., Panigrahy, A., Dikkes, P., & Goode, R. (1994). Neuropathological findings in the brain of Karen Ann Quinlan. The role of the thalamus in the persistent vegetative state. *New England Journal of Medicine, 330*(21), 1469–1475.

Klinger, E. (1990). *Daydreaming.* Tarcher (Putnam).

Lamberg, L. (2003). Scientists never dreamed finding would shape half-century of sleep research. *Journal of the American Medical Association, 290*(20), 2652–2654.

Lucas, S. J., Michel, C. B., Marra, V., Smalley, J. L., Hennig, M. H., Graham, B. P., & Forsythe, I. D. (2018). Glucose and lactate as metabolic constraints on pre-synaptic transmission at an excitatory synapse. *The Journal of Physiology, 596*(9), 1699–1721.

Malcolm-Smith, S., Koopowitz, S., Pantelis, E., & Solms, M. (2012). Approach/avoidance in dreams. *Consciousness and Cognition, 21*(1), 408–412.

Maquet, P., Laureys, S., Peigneux, P., Fuchs, S., Petiau, C., Phillips, C., Aerts, J., Del Fiore, G., Degueldre, C., Meulemans, T., Luxen, A., Franck, G., Van Der Linden, M., Smith, C., & Cleeremans, A. (2000). Experience-dependent changes in cerebral activation during human REM sleep. *Nature Neuroscience, 3*(8), 831–836.

Matar, E., McCarter, S. J., St Louis, E. K., & Lewis, S. J. G. (2021). Current concepts and controversies in the management of REM sleep behavior disorder. *Neurotherapeutics, 18*(1), 107–123.

McCommis, K. S., & Butler, A. A. (2021). The importance of keeping time in the liver. *Endocrinology, 162*(2), bqaa230.

Monecke, S., Brewer, J. M., Krug, S., & Bittman, E. L. (2011). Duper: A mutation that shortens hamster circadian period. *Biological Rhythms, 26*(4), 283–292.

Moruzzi, G., & Magoun, H. W. (1949). Brain stem reticular formation and activation of the EEG. *Electroencephalography and Clinical Neurophysiology, 1*(4), 455–473.

Nesan, D., Feighan, K. M., Antle, M. C., & Kurrasch, D. M. (2021). Gestational low-dose BPA exposure impacts suprachiasmatic nucleus neurogenesis and circadian activity with transgenerational effects. *Scientific Advances, 7*(22), eabd1159.

Pacheco, A. T., Bottorff, J., Gao, Y., & Turrigiano, G. G. (2021). Sleep promotes downward firing rate homeostasis. *Neuron, 109*(3), 530–544.e6.

Phillips, A. J., Czeisler, C. A., & Klerman, E. B. (2011). Revisiting spontaneous internal desynchrony using a quantitative model of sleep physiology. *Journal of Biological Rhythms, 26*(5), 441–453.

Pothukuchi, K. (2021). City light or star bright: A review of urban light pollution, impacts, and planning implications. *Journal of Planning Literature, 36*(2), 155–169.

Putilov, A. A., Dorokhov, V. B., & Poluektov, M. G. (2017). How have our clocks evolved? Adaptive and demographic history of the out-of-African dispersal told by polymorphic loci in circadian genes. *Chronobiology International, 35*(4), 511–532.

Quinlan, J., & Quinlan, J. (1977). *Karen Ann: The Quinlans tell their story.* Doubleday.

Ralph, M. R., & Lehman, M. N. (1991). Transplantation: A new tool in the analysis of the mammalian hypothalamic circadian pacemaker. *Trends in Neurosciences, 14*(8), 363–366.

Raven, P. H., Evert, R. F., & Eichorn, S. E. (1992). *Biology of plants*. Worth Publishers.

Reiter, R. J. (1980). The pineal and its hormones in the control of reproduction in mammals. *Endocrinology Review, 1*(2), 120.

Richter, C. P. (1965). *Biological clocks in medicine and psychiatry*. Charles C. Thomas.

Roffward, H. P., Muzio, J., & Dement, W. C. (1966). Ontogenetic development of the human sleep–dream cycle. *Science, 152*(3722), 604–619.

Rosenberg, R., Citrome, L., & Drake, C. L. (2021). Advances in the treatment of chronic insomnia: A narrative review of new nonpharmacologic and pharmacologic therapies. *Neuropsychiatric Disease and Treatment, 17*, 2549–2566.

Sateia, M. J. (2014). International Classification of Sleep Disorders, Third Edition. *Chest Journal, 146*(5), 1387–1394.

Scarpelli, S., Gorgoni, M., Alfonsi, V., Annarumma, L., Di Natale, V., Pezza, E., & De Gennaro, L. (2021). The impact of the end of COVID confinement on pandemic dreams, as assessed by a weekly sleep diary: A longitudinal investigation in Italy. *Journal of Sleep Research, 20*, e13429.

Schenck, C. H., Bundlie, S. R., Ettinger, M. G., & Mahowald, M. W. (1986). Chronic behavioral disorders of human REM sleep: A new category of parasomnia. *Sleep, 25*(2), 293–308.

Schmidt, C., Peigneux, P., Cajochen, C., & Collette, F. (2012). Adapting test timing to the sleep–wake schedule: Effects on diurnal neurobehavioral performance changes in young evening and older morning chronotypes. *Chronobiology International, 29*(4), 482–490.

Schreiner, T., Petzka, M., Staudigl, T., & Staresina, B. P. (2021). Endogenous memory reactivation during sleep in humans is clocked by slow oscillation-spindle complexes. *Nature Communications, 12*(1), 3112.

Scott, H., Lack, L., & Lovato, N. (2020). A systematic review of the accuracy of sleep wearable devices for estimating sleep onset. *Sleep Medicine Reviews, 49*, 101227.

Shankar, A., & Williams, C. T. (2021). The darkness and the light: Diurnal rodent models for seasonal affective disorder. *Disease Model Mechanisms, 14*(1), dmm047217.

Siegel, J. (2004). Brain mechanisms that control sleep and waking. *Naturwissenschaften, 91*(8), 355–365.

Silber, M. H., Buchfuhrer, M. J., Earley, C. J., Koo, B. B., Manconi, M., & Winkelman, J. W. (2021). The management of restless legs syndrome: An updated algorithm. *Mayo Clinic Proceedings, 96*(7), 1921–1937.

Sivertsen, B., Friborg, O., Pallesen, S., Vedaa, Ø., & Hopstock, L. A. (2021). Sleep in the land of the midnight sun and polar night: The Tromsø study. *Chronobiology International, 38*(3), 334–342.

Spiesshoefer, J., Linz, D., Skobel, E., Arzt, M., Stadler, S., Schoebel, C., Fietze, I., Penzel, T., Sinha, A.-M., Fox, H., Oldenburg, O., & on Behalf of The German Cardiac Society Working Group on Sleep Disordered Breathing Ag-Deutsche Gesellschaft Für Kardiologie Herz Und Kreislaufforschung E V O. (2019). Sleep—The yet underappreciated player in cardiovascular diseases: A clinical review from the German Cardiac Society Working Group on Sleep Disordered Breathing. *European Journal of Preventative Cardiology, 28*(2), 189–200.

Tisdale, R. K., Yamanaka, A., & Kilduff, T. S. (2021). Animal models of narcolepsy and the hypocretin/orexin system: Past, present, and future. *Sleep, 44*(6), zsaa278.

Tononi, G., & Cirelli, C. (2016). Sleep and synaptic down-selection. In G. Buzsáki & Y. Christen (Eds.), *Micro-, meso-, and macro-dynamics of the brain* (pp. 99–106). Springer.

Uchida, S., Soya, S., Saito, Y. C., Hirano, A., Koga, K., Tsuda, M., Abe, M., Sakimura, K., & Sakurai, T. (2021). A discrete glycinergic neuronal population in the ventromedial medulla that induces muscle atonia during REM sleep and cataplexy in mice. *Journal of Neuroscience, 41*(7), 1582–1596.

Valli, K., & Revonsuo, A. (2009). The threat simulation theory in light of recent empirical evidence: A review. *American Journal of Psychology, 122*(1), 17–38.

Vanderwolf, C. H. (2002). *An odyssey through the brain, behavior and the mind*. Kluwer Academic.

Wilson, M. A., & McNaughton, B. L. (1994). Reactivation of hippocampal ensemble memories during sleep. *Science, 265*(5172), 676–679.

Yamazaki, E. M., Antler, C. A., Lasek, C. R., & Goel, N. (2021). Residual, differential neurobehavioral deficits linger after multiple recovery nights following chronic sleep restriction or acute total sleep deprivation. *Sleep, 44*(4), zsaa224.

Zada, D., Sela, Y., Matosevich, N., Monsonego, A., Lerer-Goldshtein, T., Nir, Y., & Appelbaum, L. (2021). Parp1 promotes sleep, which enhances DNA repair in neurons. *Molecular Cell, 81*(24), 4979–4993.

Zaidi, F. H., Hull, J. T., Peirson, S. N., Wulff, K., Aeschbach, D., Gooley, J. J., Brainard, G. C., Gregory-Evans, K., Rizzo, J. F. III, Czeisler, C. A., Foster, R. G., Moseley, M. J., & Lockley, S. W. (2007). Short-wavelength light sensitivity of circadian, pupillary, and visual awareness in humans lacking an outer retina. *Current Biology, 17*(24), 2122–2128.

Zhang, H., Khan, A., Chen, Q., Larsson, H., & Rzhetsky, A. (2021). Do psychiatric diseases follow annual cyclic seasonality? *PLoS Biology, 19*(7), e3001347.

## CHAPTER 14

Aoued, H. S., Sannigrahi, S., Doshi, N., Morrison, F. G., Linsenbaum, H., Hunter, S. C., Walum H., Baman, J., Yao, B., Jin, P., Ressler, K. J., & Dias, B. G. (2019). Reversing behavioral, neuroanatomical, and germline influences of intergenerational stress. *Biological Psychiatry, 85*(3), 248–256.

Arvanitakis, Z., Capuano, A. W., Lamar, M., Shah, R. C., Barnes, L. L., Bennett, D. A., & Schneider, J. A. (2018). Late-life blood pressure association with cerebrovascular and Alzheimer disease pathology. *Neurology, 91*(6), e517–e525.

Avila, J., & Perry, G. (2021). A multilevel view of the development of Alzheimer's disease. *Neuroscience, 457*, 283–293.

Bailey, C. H., Kandel, E. R., & Harris, K. M. (2015). Structural components of synaptic plasticity and memory consolidation. *Cold Spring Harbor Perspectives in Biology, 7*(7), a021758.

Binder, J. R., Desai, R. H., Graves, W. W., & Conant, L. L. (2009). Where is the semantic system? A critical review and meta-analysis of 120 functional neuroimaging systems. *Cerebral Cortex, 19*(12), 2767–2796.

Bliss, T. V., & Lømø, T. (1973). Long-lasting potentiation of synaptic transmission in the dentate are of the anaesthetized rabbit following stimulation of the perforant path. *Journal of Physiology, 232*(2), 331–356.

Bonnici, H. M., Chadwick, M. J., Lutti, A., Hassabis, D., Weiskopf, N., & Maguire, E. A. (2012). Detecting representations of recent and remote autobiographical memories in vmPFC and hippocampus. *Journal of Neuroscience, 32*(47), 16982–16991.

Bonnici, H. M., & Maguire, E. A. (2018). Two years later—Revisiting autobiographical memory representations in vmPFC and hippocampus. *Neuropsychologia, 110*, 159–169.

Cahill, L., Babinsky, R., Markowitsch, H. J., & McGaugh, J. L. (1995). The amygdala and emotional memory. *Nature, 377*, 295–296.

Candia, V., Wienbruch, C., Elbert, T., Rockstroh, B., & Ray, W. (2003). Effective behavioral treatment of focal hand dystonia in musicians alters somatosensory cortical organization. *Proceedings of the National Academy of Sciences of the United States of America, 100*(13), 7942–7946.

Chang, F.-L. F., & Greenough, W. T. (1982). Lateralized effects of monocular training on dendritic branching in adult split-brain rats. *Brain Research, 232*(2), 283–292.

Corkin, S. (2002). What's new with the amnesic patient H.M.? *Nature Reviews Neuroscience, 3*, 153–160.

Corkin, S., Amaral, D. G., Gonzalez, R. G., Johnson, K. A., & Hyman, B. T. (1997). H.M.'s medial temporal lobe lesion: Findings from magnetic resonance imaging. *Journal of Neuroscience, 17*(10), 3964–3979.

Damasio, A. R., Tranel, D., & Damasio, H. (1989). Amnesia caused by herpes simplex encephalitis, infarctions in basal forebrain, Alzheimer's disease and anoxia/ischemia. In F. Boller & J. Grafman (Eds.), *Handbook of neuropsychology* (Vol. 3, pp. 149–166). Elsevier.

Davis, M. (1992). The role of the amygdala in fear and anxiety. *Annual Review of Neuroscience, 15*, 353–375.

Day, J. J., Kennedy, A. J., & Sweatt, J. D. (2015). DNA methylation and its implications and accessibility for neuropsychiatric therapeutics. *Annual Review of Pharmacology and Toxicology, 55*, 591–611.

Dias, B. G., Maddox, S., Klengel, T., & Kessler, K. J. (2015). Epigenetic mechanisms underlying learning and the inheritance of learned behaviors. *Trends in Neuroscience, 38*(2), 96–107.

Dittrich, L. (2016). *Patient H.M.: A story of memory, madness, and family secrets*. Random House.

Dobrovolsky, A., Bogin, V., & Meloni, E. G. (2019). Combining xenon inhalation with trauma memory reactivation to reduce symptoms of posttraumatic stress disorder: Case report, justification of approach, and review of the literature. *The Primary Care Companion for CNS Disorders, 21*(5), 18nr02395.

Eriksson, P. S., Perfilieva, E., Björk-Eriksson, T., Alborn, A.-M., Nordborg, C., Peterson, D. A., & Gage, F. H. (1998). Neurogenesis in the adult human hippocampus. *Nature Medicine, 4*(11), 1313–1317.

Fuster, J. M. (1995). *Memory in the cerebral cortex*. MIT Press.

Fuster, J. M., Bodner, M., & Kroger, J. K. (2000). Cross-modal and cross-temporal association in neurons of frontal cortex. *Nature, 405*, 347–351.

Galaburda, A. M., Sherman, G. F., Rosen, G. D., Aboitiz, F., & Geschwind, N. (1985). Developmental dyslexia: Four consecutive patients with cortical anomalies. *Annals of Neurology, 18*(2), 222–233.

Gapp, K., Jawaid, A., Sarkies, P., Bohacek, J., Pelczar, P., Prados, J., Farinelli, L., Miska, E., & Mansuy, I. M. (2014). Implication of sperm RNAs in transgenerational inheritance of the effects of early trauma in mice. *Nature Neuroscience, 17*(5), 667–669.

Gazzaniga, M. S. (Ed.). (2000). *The new cognitive neurosciences.* MIT Press.

Gould, E., Tanapat, P., Hastings, N. B., & Shors, T. J. (1999). Neurogenesis in adulthood: A possible role in learning. *Trends in Cognitive Sciences, 3*(5), 186–191.

Gould, E., Tanapat, P., McEwen, B. S., Flugge, G., & Fuchs, E. (1998). Proliferation of granule cell precursors in the dentate gyrus of adult monkeys is diminished by stress. *Proceedings of the National Academy of Sciences of the United States of America, 95,* 3168–3171.

Hebb, D. O. (1947). The effects of early experience on problem solving at maturity. *American Psychologist, 2,* 737–745.

Hebb, D. O. (1949). *The organization of behavior: A neuropsychological theory.* Wiley.

Hornickel, J., Zecker, S. G., Bradlow, A. R., & Kraus, N. (2012). Assistive listening devices drive neuroplasticity in children with dyslexia. *Proceedings of the National Academy of Sciences of the United States of America, 109*(41), 16731–16736.

Ivanco, T., Racine, R. J., & Kolb, B. (2000). The morphology of layer III pyramidal neurons is altered following induction of LTP in somatomotor cortex of the freely moving rat. *Synapse, 37*(1), 16–22.

Jacobs, B., Schall, M., & Scheibel, A. B. (1993). A quantitative dendritic analysis of Wernicke's area in humans: II. Gender, hemispheric, and environmental factors. *Journal of Comparative Neurology, 327*(1), 97–111.

Jacobs, B., & Scheibel, A. B. (1993). A quantitative dendritic analysis of Wernicke's area in humans: I. Lifespan changes. *Journal of Comparative Neurology, 327*(1), 83–96.

Josselyn, S. A., Kohler, S., & Frankland, P. W. (2017). Heroes of the engram. *Journal of Neuroscience, 37*(18), 4647–4657.

Kaas, J. (2000). The reorganization of sensory and motor maps after injury in adult mammals. In M. S. Gazzaniga (Ed.), *The cognitive neurosciences* (pp. 223–236). MIT Press.

Kempermann, G. (2019). Environmental enrichment, new neurons and the neurobiology of individuality. *Nature Reviews Neuroscience, 20*(4), 235–245.

Kempermann, G., Kuhn, H. G., & Gage, F. H. (1998). Experience-induced neurogenesis in the senescent dentate gyrus. *Journal of Neuroscience, 18*(9), 3206–3212.

Kolb, B., Cioe, J., & Comeau, W. (2008). Contrasting effects of motor and visual learning tasks on dendritic arborization and spine density in rats. *Neurobiology of Learning and Memory, 90*(2), 295–300.

Kolb, B., Cote, S., Ribeiro-da-Silva, A., & Cuello, A. C. (1997). Nerve growth factor treatment prevents dendritic atrophy and promotes recovery of function after cortical injury. *Neuroscience, 76*(4), 1139–1151.

Kolb, B., & Gibb, R. (2014). Searching for the principles of brain plasticity and behavior. *Cortex, 58,* 251–260.

Kolb, B., Gibb, R., & Gorny, G. (2003). Experience-dependent changes in dendritic arbor and spine density in neocortex vary with age and sex. *Neurobiology of Learning and Memory, 79*(1), 1–10.

Kolb, B., Li, Y. Robinson, T. E., & Parker, L. A. (2018). THC alters morphology of neurons in medial prefrontal cortex, orbital prefrontal cortex, and nucleus accumbens and alters the ability of later experience to promote structural plasticity. *Synapse, 72*(3).

Kolb, B., Morshead, C., Gonzalez, C., Kim, N., Shingo, T., & Weiss, S. (2007). Growth factor–stimulated generation of new cortical tissue and functional recovery after stroke damage to the motor cortex of rats. *Journal of Cerebral Blood Flow and Metabolism, 27*(5), 983–397.

Kronbichler, L., & Kronbichler, M. (2018). The importance of the left occipitotemporal cortex in developmental dyslexia. *Current Developmental Disorders Reports, 5*(1), 1–8.

Lashley, K. S. (1960). In search of the engram. Symposium No. 4 of the Society of Experimental Biology. In F. A. Beach, D. O. Hebb, C. T. Morgan, & H. T. Nissen (Eds.), *The neuropsychology of Lashley* (pp. 478–505). McGraw-Hill. (Reprinted from R. Sutton (Ed.), 1951, *Physiological mechanisms of animal behavior* pp. 454–482. Cambridge University Press.)

Le, J., Thomas, N., & Gurvich, C. (2020). Cognition, the menstrual cycle, and premenstrual disorders: A review. *Brain Science, 10*(4), 198.

LePort, A. K. R., Mattfeld, A. T., Dickinson-Anson, H., Falon, J. H., Stark, C. E. L., Kruggel, F., Cahill, L., & McGaugh, J. L. (2012). Behavioral and neuroanatomical investigation of highly superior autobiographical memory (HSAM). *Neurobiology of Learning and Memory, 98*(1), 78–92.

LePort, A. K. R., Stark, S. M., McGaugh, J. L., & Stark, C. E. L. (2017). A cognitive assessment of highly superior autobiographical memory. *Memory, 25*(2), 276–288.

Liu, Z., & Cheung, H.-H. (2020). Stem cell-based therapies for Parkinson disease. *International Journal of Molecular Science, 21*(21), 8060.

Loftus, E. F. (1997). Creating false memories. *Scientific American, 277*(3), 70–75.

MacDougall, M., & Fine, A. (2014). The expression of long-term potentiation: Reconciling the priests and the positivists. *Philosophic Transactions of the Royal Society B: Biological Science, 369*(1633), 20130135.

Maguire, E. A., Gadian, D. G., Johnsrude, I. S., Good, C. D., Ashburner, J., Frackowiak, R. S., & Frith, C. D. (2000). Navigation-related structural change in the hippocampi of taxi drivers. *Proceedings of the National Academy of Sciences of the United States of America, 97*(8), 4398–4403.

Mahncke, H. W., Bronstone, A., & Merzenich, M. M. (2006). Brain plasticity and functional losses in the aged: Scientific bases for a novel intervention. *Progress in Brain Research, 157,* 81–109.

Martin, A., Kronbichler, M., & Richlan, F. (2016). Dyslexic brain activation abnormalities in deep and shallow orthographies: A meta-analysis of 28 functional neuroimaging studies. *Human Brain Mapping, 37*(7), 2676–2699.

McCormick, C., Barry, D. N., Jafarian, A., Barnes, G. R., & Maguire, E. A. (2020). vmPFC drives hippocampal processing during autobiographical memory recall regardless of remoteness. *Cerebral Cortex, 30*(11), 5972–5987.

McCormick, C., Moscovitch, M., Valiante, T. A., Cohn, M., & McAndrews, M. P. (2018). Different neural routes to autobiographical memory recall in healthy people and individuals with left medical temporal lobe epilepsy. *Neuropsychologia, 110,* 26–36.

McGaugh, J. (2004). The amygdala modulates the consolidation of memories of emotionally arousing experiences. *Annual Review of Neuroscience, 27,* 1–28.

Meloni, E. G., Gillis, T. E., Manoukian, J., & Kaufman, M. J. (2014). Xenon impairs reconsolidation of fear memories in a rat model of post-traumatic stress disorder (PTSD). *PLOS ONE, 9*(8), e106189.

Miller, C. A., Gavin, C. F., White, J. A., Parrish, R. R., Honasoge, A., Yancey, C. R., Rivera, I. M., Rubio, M. D., Rumbaugh, G., & Sweatt, J. D. (2010). Cortical DNA methylation maintains remote memory. *Nature Neuroscience, 13*(6), 664–666.

Milner, B., Corkin, S., & Teuber, H. (1968). Further analysis of the hippocampal amnesic syndrome: 14-year follow-up study of H.M. *Neuropsychologia, 6*(3), 215–234.

Mishkin, M. (1982). A memory system in the brain. *Philosophical Transactions of the Royal Society of London: Biological Sciences, 298,* 83–95.

Mishkin, M., Suzuki, W. A., Gadian, D. G., & Vargha-Khadem, F. (1997). Hierarchical organization of cognitive memory. *Philosophical Transactions of the Royal Society of London: Biological Sciences, 352*(1360), 1461–1467.

Murray, E. (2000). Memory for objects in nonhuman primates. In M. S. Gazzaniga (Ed.), *The new cognitive neurosciences* (pp. 753–763). MIT Press.

Murray, E. A., Wise, S. P., & Graham, K. S. (2017). *The evolution of memory systems.* Oxford University Press.

Mychasiuk, R., Muhammad, A., Ilnystskyy, S., & Kolb, B. (2013). Persistent gene expression changes in NAc, mPFC, and OFC associated with previous nicotine or amphetamine exposure. *Behavioural Brain Research, 256,* 655–661.

Mychasiuk, R., Muhammad, A., Ilnystskyy, S., Kovalchuk, O., & Kolb, B. (2016). Chronic stress induces persistent changes in global DNA methylation and gene expression in the medial prefrontal cortex, orbitofrontal cortex, and hippocampus. *Neuroscience, 322,* 489–499.

Nudo, R. J., Plautz, E. J., & Milliken, G. W. (1997). Adaptive plasticity in primate motor cortex as a consequence of behavioral experience and neuronal injury. *Seminars in Neuroscience, 9*(1–2), 13–23.

O'Keefe, J. (2006). Hippocampal neurophysiology in the behaving animal. In P. Andersen, R. Morris, D. Amaral, T. Bliss, & J. O'Keefe (Eds.), *The hippocampus book* (pp. 475–548). Oxford University Press.

O'Keefe, J., & Nadel, L. (1978). *The hippocampus as a spatial map.* Oxford University Press.

Parmar, M., Grealish, S., & Henchcliffe, C. (2020). The future of stem cell therapies for Parkinson disease. *Nature Reviews Neuroscience, 21*(2), 103–115.

Patihis, L., Frenda, S. J., LePort, A. K. R., Petersen, N., Nichols, R. M., Stark, C. E. L., McGaugh, J. L., & Loftus, E. F. (2013). False memories in highly superior autobiographical memory individuals. *Proceedings of the National Academy of Sciences of the United States of America, 110*(52), 20947–20952.

Ragert, P., Schmidt, A., Altenmuller, E., & Dinse, H. R. (2003). Superior tactile performance and learning in professional pianists: Evidence for meta-plasticity in musicians. *European Journal of Neuroscience, 19*(2), 473–478.

Ramachandran, V. S. (1993). Behavioral and magnetoencephalographic correlates of plasticity in the adult human brain. *Proceedings of the*

*National Academy of Sciences of the United States of America, 90*(22), 10413–10420.

Ramón y Cajal, S. (1928). *Degeneration and regeneration of the nervous system.* Oxford University Press.

Reynolds, B., & Weiss, S. (1992). Generation of neurons and astrocytes from isolated cells of the adult mammalian central nervous system. *Science, 255*(5052), 1707–1710.

Richlan, F. (2020). The functional neuroanatomy of developmental dyslexia across languages and writing systems. *Frontiers in Psychology, 11,* 155.

Robinson, T. E., & Kolb, B. (1997). Persistent structural adaptations in nucleus accumbens and prefrontal cortex neurons produced by prior experience with amphetamine. *Journal of Neuroscience, 17*(21), 8491–8497.

Robinson, T. E., & Kolb, B. (2004). Structural plasticity associated with drugs of abuse. *Neuropharmacology, 47*(Suppl. 1), 33–46.

Sainsbury, R. S., & Coristine, M. (1986). Affective discrimination in moderately to severely demented patients. *Canadian Journal on Aging, 5,* 99–104.

Sapolsky, R. M. (1992). *Stress, the aging brain, and the mechanisms of neuron death.* MIT Press.

Schacter, D. L. (1983). Amnesia observed: Remembering and forgetting in a natural environment. *Journal of Abnormal Psychology, 92*(2), 236–242.

Sekeres, M. J., Winocur, G., Moscovitch, M., Anderson, J. A. E., Pishdadian, S., Martin Wojtowicz, J., St-Laurent, M., McAndrews, M. P., & Grady, C. L. (2018). Changes in patterns of neural activity underlie a time-dependent transformation of memory in rats and humans. *Hippocampus, 28*(10), 745–764.

Sherry, D. F., Jacobs, L. F., & Gaulin, S. J. C. (1992). Spatial memory and adaptive specialization of the hippocampus. *Trends in Neuroscience, 15*(8), 298–303.

Sirevaag, A. M., & Greenough, W. T. (1987). Differential rearing effects on rat visual cortex synapses: III. Neuronal and glial nuclei, boutons, dendrites, and capillaries. *Brain Research, 424*(2), 320–332.

Sirevaag, A. M., & Greenough, W. T. (1988). A multivariate statistical summary of synaptic plasticity measures in rats exposed to complex, social and individual environments. *Brain Research, 441*(1–2), 386–392.

Skinner, B. F. (1938). *The behavior of organisms.* Appleton-Century-Crofts.

Sonntag, K.-C., Song, B., Lee, N., Jung, J. H., Cha, Y., Leblanc, P., Neff, C., Kong, S. W., Carter, B. S., Schweitzer, J., & Kim, K.-S. (2018). Pluripotent stem cell-based therapy for Parkinson's disease: Current status and future prospects. *Progress in Neurobiology, 168,* 1–20.

Squire, L. R., Genzel, L., Wixted, J. T., & Morris, R. G. (2015). Memory consolidation. *Cold Spring Harbor Perspectives in Biology, 7*(8), a021766.

Stewart, J., & Kolb, B. (1994). Dendritic branching in cortical pyramidal cells in response to ovariectomy in adult female rats: Suppression by neonatal exposure to testosterone. *Brain Research, 654*(1), 149–154.

Sugar, J., & Moser, M. B. (2019). Episodic memory: Neuronal codes for what, where, and when. *Hippocampus, 29*(12), 1190–1205.

Sutherland, R. J., Sparks, F. T., & Lehmann, H. (2010). Hippocampus and retrograde amnesia in the rat model: A modest proposal for the situation of systems consolidation. *Neuropsychologia, 48*(8), 2357–2369.

Tallal, P. (2012). Improving neural response to sound improves reading. *Proceedings of the National Academy of Sciences of the United States of America, 109*(41), 16404–16407.

Therrien, A. S., Howard, C., & Buxbaum, L. J. (2021). Aberrant activity in an intact residual muscle is associated with phantom limb pain in above-knee amputees. *Journal of Neurophysiology, 125*(6), 2135–2143.

Thorndike, E. L. (1898). Animal intelligence: An experimental study of the associative processes in animals. *Psychological Review Monograph Supplements, 2,* 1–109.

Tsechentscher, N., Ruisinger, A., Blank, H., Diaz, B., & von Kriegstein, K. (2019). Reduced structural connectivity between left auditory thalamus and the motion-sensitive planum temporale in developmental dyslexia. *Journal of Neuroscience, 39*(9), 1720–1732.

Tulving, E. (2002). Episodic memory: From mind to brain. *Annual Review of Psychology, 53,* 1–25.

Turner, A., & Greenough, W. T. (1985). Differential rearing effects on rat visual cortex synapses: I. Synaptic and neuronal density and synapses per neuron. *Brain Research, 329*(2), 195–203.

Woollett, K., & Maguire, E. A. (2011). Acquiring "the knowledge" of London's layout drives structural brain changes. *Current Biology, 21*(24), 2109–2114.

Woolley, C. S., Gould, E., Frankfurt, M., & McEwen, B. S. (1990). Naturally occurring fluctuation in dendritic spine density on adult hippocampal pyramidal neurons. *Journal of Neuroscience, 10*(12), 4035–4039.

## CHAPTER 15

Adamaszek, M., D'Agata, F., Ferrucci, R., Habas, C., Keulen, S., Kirkby, K. C., Leggio, M., Mariën, P., Molinari, M., Moulton, E., Orsi, L., Van Overwalle, F., Papadelis, C., Priori, A., Sacchetti, B., Schutter, D. J., Styliadis, C., & Verhoeven, J. (2017). Consensus paper: Cerebellum and emotion. *Cerebellum, 16*(2), 552–576.

Adolphs, R., Gosselin, F., Buchanan, T. W., Tranel, D., Schyns, P., & Damasio, A. R. (2005). A mechanism for impaired fear recognition after amygdala damage. *Nature, 433,* 68–72.

Barbey, A. K. (2018). Network neuroscience theory of human intelligence. *Trends in Cognitive Sciences, 22*(1), 9–20.

Basten, U., Hilger, K., & Fiebach, C. J. (2015). Where smart brains are different: A quantitative meta-analysis of functional and structural brain imaging studies on intelligence. *Intelligence, 51,* 10–27.

Bilder, R. M., & Reise, S. P. (2019). Neuropsychological tests of the future: How do we get there? *Clinical Neuropsychology, 33*(2), 222–245.

Boly, M., Massimini, M., Tsuchiya, N., Postle, B. R., Koch, C., & Tonini, G. (2017). Are the correlates of consciousness in the front or back of the cerebral cortex? *Journal of Neuroscience, 37*(40), 9603–9613.

Braga, R. M., Van Dijk, R. A., Polimeni, J. R., Eldaief, M. C., & Buckner, R. L. (2019). Parallel distributed networks resolved at high resolution reveal close juxtaposition of distinct regions. *Journal of Neurophysiology, 121*(4), 1513–1534.

Bugnar, T., Reber, S. A., & Buckner, C. (2016). Ravens attribute visual access to unseen competitors. *Nature Communications, 7,* 10506. https://doi.org/10.1038/ncomms10506

Calvin, W. H. (1996). *How brains think.* Basic Books.

Castiello, U., Paulignan, Y., & Jeannerod, M. (1991). Temporal dissociation of motor responses and subjective awareness. *Brain, 114*(6), 2639–2655.

Cattaneo, L., & Rizzolatti, G. (2009). The mirror neuron system. *Archives of Neurology, 66*(5), 557–560.

Chomsky, N. (2010). Some simple evo-devo theses: How true might they be for language. In Larson, R., Deprez, V., & Yamakido, H. (Eds.). *The evolution of human language* (pp. 54–62). Cambridge University Press.

Crick, F., & Koch, C. (1998). Consciousness and neuroscience. *Cerebral Cortex, 8*(2), 97–107.

Damasio, A. (2012). *Self comes to mind: Constructing the conscious brain.* Vintage.

Dediu, D., & Levinson, S. C. (2013). On the antiquity of language: The reinterpretation of Neandertal linguistic capacities and its consequences. *Frontiers in Psychology, 4,* 397. https://doi.org/10.3389/fpsyg.2013.00397

Diamond, M. C., Scheibel, A. B., Murphy, G. M., Jr., & Harvey, T. (1985). On the brain of a scientist: Albert Einstein. *Experimental Neurology, 88*(1), 198–204.

Dolins, F. L., Klimowicz, C., Kelley, J., & Menzel, C. R. (2014). Using virtual reality to investigate comparative spatial cognitive abilities in chimpanzees and humans. *American Journal of Primatology, 76*(5), 496–513.

Duncan, J., Seitz, R. J., Kolodny, J., Bor, D., Herzog, H., Ahmed, A., Newell, F. N., & Emslie, H. (2000). A neural basis for general intelligence. *Science, 289*(5478), 457–459.

Elam, J. S., Glasser, M. F., Harms, M. P., Sotiropoulos, S. N., Andersson, J. L. R., Burgess, G. C., Curtiss, S. W., Oostenveld, R., Larson-Prior, L. J., Schoffelen, J.-M., Hodge, M. R., Cler, E. A., Marcus, D. M., Barch, D. M., Yacoub, E., Smith, S. M., Ugurbil, K., & Van Essen, D. C. (2021). The human connectome project: A retrospective. *NeuroImage, 244,* 118543.

Feinstein, J. S., Adolphs, R. M., & Tranel, D. (2016). A tale of survival from the world of patient S. M. In D. G. Amaral & R. Adolphs (Eds.), *Living without an amygdala* (pp. 1–38). Guilford.

Frith, C., Perry, R., & Lumer, E. (1999). The neural correlations of conscious experience. *Trends in Cognitive Sciences, 3*(3), 105–114.

Gatti, D., Rinaldi, L., Cristea, I., & Vecchi, T. (2021) Probing cerebellar involvement in cognition through a meta-analysis of TMS evidence. *Scientific Reports, 11,* 14777. https://doi.org/10.1038/s41598-021-94051-5

Gaulin, S. J. (1992). Evolution of sex differences in spatial ability. *Yearbook of Physical Anthropology, 35*(S15), 125–131.

Gazzaniga, M. S. (1970). *The bisected brain.* Appleton-Century-Crofts.

Gazzaniga, M. S. (1992). *Nature's mind.* Basic Books.

Gazzaniga, M. S., Ivry, R. B., & Mangun, G. R. (1999). *Cognitive science: The biology of the mind.* Norton.

Genç, E., Fraenz, C., Schlüter, C., Friedrich, P., Hossiep, R., Voelke, M. C., Ling, J. M., Güntürkün, O., & Jung, R. E. (2018). Diffusion markers of dendritic density and arborization in gray matter predict differences in intelligence. *Nature Communications, 9*(1), 1905.

Ghanzanfar, A. A., & Schroeder, C. E. (2006). Is neocortex essentially multisensory? *Trends in Cognitive Science, 10*(6), 278–285.

Glasser, M. F., Coalson, T. S., Robinson, E. C., Hacker, C. D., Harwell, J., Yacoub, E., Ugurbil, K., Andersson, J., Beckmann, C. F., Jenkinson, M., Smith, S. M., & Van Essen, D. C. (2016). A multi-modal parcellation of human cerebral cortex. *Nature, 536*(7615), 171–178.

Goldstein, J. M., Seidman, J. L., Horton, N. J., Makris, S., Kennedy, D. N., Caviness, Jr., V. S., Faraone, S. V., & Tsuang, M. T. (2001). Normal sexual dimorphism of the adult human brain assessed by in vivo magnetic resonance imaging. *Cerebral Cortex, 11*(6), 490–497.

Gray, J. R., & Thompson, P. M. (2004). Neurobiology of intelligence: Science and ethics. *Nature Reviews Neuroscience, 5,* 471–482.

Guell, X., Gabrieli, J. D. E., & Schmahmann, J. D. (2018). Triple representation of language, working memory, social and emotion processing in the cerebellum: Convergent evidence from task and seed-based resting-state fMRI analyses in a single large cohort. *Neuroimage, 172,* 437–449.

Guilford, J. P. (1967). *The nature of human intelligence.* McGraw-Hill.

Haier, R. J. (2017). *The neuroscience of intelligence.* Cambridge University Press.

Hebb, D. O. (1949). *The organization of behavior.* McGraw-Hill.

Hebb, D. O. (1980). *Essay on mind.* Lawrence Erlbaum.

Heyes, C. (2015). Animal mindreading: What's the problem? *Psychonomic Bulletin and Review, 22*(2), 313–327.

Hickok, G. (2014). *The myth of motor neurons.* Norton.

Hubbard, E. W. (2007). Neurophysiology of synesthesia. *Current Psychiatry Reports, 9,* 193–199.

Ingalhalikar, M., Smith, A., Parker, D., Satterthwaite, T. D., Elliott, M. A., Ruparel, K., Hakonarson, H., Gur, R. E., Gur, R. C., & Verma, R. (2014). Sex differences in the structural connectome of the human brain. *Proceedings of the National Academy of Sciences of the United States of America, 111*(2), 823–828.

Ionta, S., Costantini, M., Ferretti, A., Galati, G., Romani, G. L., & Aglioti, S. M. (2020). Visual similarity and psychological closeness are neurally dissociable in the brain response to vicarious pain. *Cortex, 133,* 295–308.

Jung, R. E., & Haier, R. J. (2007). The parieto-frontal integration theory (P-FIT) of intelligence: Converging neuroimaging evidence. *The Behavioral and Brain Sciences, 30*(2), 135–154.

Kemmerer, D. (2021). What modulates the mirror neuron system during action observation? Multiple factors involving the action, the actor, the observer, the relationship between the actor and observer, and the context. *Progress in Neurobiology, 205,* 102128. https://doi .org/10.1016/j.pneurobio.2021.102128.

Kennedy, D. P., & Adolphs, R. (2012). The social brain in psychiatric and neurological disorders. *Trends in Cognitive Sciences, 16*(11), 559–572.

Kimura, D. (1967). Functional asymmetry of the brain in dichotic listening. *Cortex, 3*(2), 163–178.

Kimura, D. (1973). The asymmetry of the human brain. *Scientific American, 228*(3), 70–78.

Kimura, D. (1999). *Sex and cognition.* MIT Press.

Kolb, B., & Stewart, J. (1991). Sex-related differences in dendritic branching of cells in the prefrontal cortex of rats. *Journal of Neuroendocrinology, 3*(1), 95–99.

Kolb, B., & Whishaw, I. Q. (2021). *Fundamentals of human neuropsychology* (8th ed.). Macmillan Learning.

Lee, S., Parthasarathi, T., & Kable, J. W. (2021). The ventral and dorsal default mode networks are dissociably modulated by the vividness and valence of imagined events. *Journal of Neuroscience, 41*(24), 5243–5250.

Lieberman, M. D. (2007). Social cognitive neuroscience: A review of core processes. *Annual Review of Psychology, 58,* 259–289.

Lieberman, M. D., & Eisenberger, N. I. (2015). The dorsal anterior cingulate cortex is selective for pain: Results from large-scale reverse inference. *Proceedings of the National Academy of Sciences of the United States of America, 112*(49), 15250–15255.

Loui, P., Li, H. C., Hohmann, A., & Schlaug, G. (2011). Enhanced cortical connectivity in absolute pitch musicians: A model for local hyper-connectivity. *Journal of Cognitive Neuroscience, 23*(4), 1015–1026.

Luders, E., Cherbuin, N., Thompson, P. M., Gutman, B., Anstey, K. J., Sachdev, P., & Toga, A. W. (2010). When more is less: Association between corpus callosum size and handedness lateralization. *NeuroImage, 52*(1), 43–49.

Luria, A. R. (1972). *The man with a shattered world.* Basic Books.

Maginnity, M. E., & Grace, R. C. (2014). Visual perspective taking by dogs (*Canis familiaris*) in a Guesser–Knower task: Evidence for a canine theory of mind? *Animal Cognition, 17,* 1375–1392.

Mancuso, M., Di Tondo, S., Costantini, E., Damora, A., Sale, P., & Abbruzzese, L. (2021). Action Observation Therapy for upper limb recovery in patients with stroke: A randomized controlled pilot study. *Brain Science, 11*(3), 290. https://10.3390/brainsci11030290

Mashour, G. A., Roelfsema, P., Changeux, J.-P., & Dehaene, S. (2020). Conscious processing and the global neuronal workspace hypothesis. *Neuron, 105*(5), 776–798.

Melloni, L., Mudrik, L., Pitts, M., & Koch, C. (2021). Making the hard problem of consciousness easier. *Science, 372*(6545), 911–912.

Meyer, M. L., Davachi, L., Ochsner, K. N., & Lieberman, M. D. (2019). Evidence that default network connectivity during rest consolidates social information. *Cerebral Cortex, 29*(5), 1910–1920.

Mlodinow, L. (2009). *The drunkard's walk: How randomness rules our lives.* Vintage Books.

Moran, J., & Desimone, R. (1985). Selective attention gates visual processing in the extrastriate cortex. *Science, 229*(4715), 782–784.

Mukerjee, M. (1996). Interview with a parrot [field note]. *Scientific American, 274*(4), 24.

Newsome, W. T., Shadlen, M. N., Zohary, E., Britten, K. H., & Movshon, J. A. (1995). Visual motion: Linking neuronal activity to psychophysical performance. In M. Gazzaniga (Ed.), *The cognitive neurosciences* (pp. 401–414). MIT Press.

Olkowicz, S., Kocourek, M., Lucan, R. K., Portes, M., Fitch, W. T., & Herculano-Houzel, S. (2016). Birds have primate-like numbers of neurons in the forebrain. *Proceedings of the National Academy of Sciences, 113*(26), 7255–7260.

Olulade, O. A., Seydell-Greenwald, A., Chambers, C. E., Turkeltaub, P. E., Dromerick, A. W., Berl, M. M., Gaillard, W. D., & Newport, E. L. (2020). The neural basis of language development: Changes in lateralization over age. *Proceedings of the National Academy of Sciences (USA), 117*(38), 23477–23483.

Pailian, H., Carey, S. E., Halberda, J., & Pepperberg, I. M. (2020). Age and species comparisons of visual mental manipulation ability as evidence for its development and evolution.

*Scientific Reports, 10*(1), 7689. https://doi .org/10.1038/s41598-020-64666-1

Pepperberg, I. M. (1990). Some cognitive capacities of an African grey parrot (*Psittacus erithacus*). In P. J. B. Slater, J. S. Rosenblatt, & C. Beer (Eds.), *Advances in the study of behavior* (Vol. 19, pp. 357–409). Academic Press.

Pepperberg, I. M. (1999). *The Alex studies.* Harvard University Press.

Pepperberg, I. M. (2006). Ordinality and inferential ability of a grey parrot (*Psittacus erithacus*). *Journal of Comparative Psychology, 120*(3), 205–216.

Podgórski, P., Waliszewska-Prosół, Zimny, A., Sasiadek, M., & Bladowska, J. (2021). Resting-state functional connectivity of the ageing female brain—differences between young and elderly female adults on multislice short TR rs-fMRI. *Frontiers in Neurology, 12,* 1015. https://doi.org/10.3389/fneur.2021.645974.

Poldrack, R. A., Baker, C. I., Durnez, J., Gorgolewski, K. J., Matthews, P. M., Munafò, M. R., Nichols, T. E., Poline, J.-B., Vul, E., & Yarkoni, T. (2017). Scanning the horizon towards transparent and reproducible neuroimaging research. *Nature Reviews Neuroscience, 18*(2), 115–126.

Proulx, M. J., Todorov, O. S., Aiken, A. T. M., & deSousa, A. A. (2016). Where am I? Who am I? The relation between spatial cognition, social cognition, and individual differences in the built environment. *Frontiers of Psychology, 7,* 64.

Rasmussen, T., & Milner, B. (1977). The role of early left brain injury in determining lateralization of cerebral speech functions. *Annals of the New York Academy of Sciences, 299,* 355–369.

Ritchie, S. J., Cox, S. R., Shen, X., Lombardo, M. V., Reus, L. M., Alloza, C., Harris, M. A., Alderson, H. L., Hunter, S., Neilson, E., Liewald, D. C. M., Auyeung, B., Whalley, H. C., Lawrie, S. M., Gale, C. R., Bastin, M. E., McIntosh, A. M., & Deary, I. J. (2018). Sex differences in the adult human brain: Evidence from 5216 UK biobank participants. *Cerebral Cortex, 28*(8), 2959–2975.

Rizzolatti, G., & Sinigaglia, C. (2016). The mirror mechanism: A basic principle of brain function. *Nature Reviews Neuroscience, 17,* 757–765.

Rizzolatti, G., Fabbri-Destro, F., Nuara, A., Gatti, R., & Avanzini, P. (2021). The role of mirror mechanism in the recovery, maintenance, and acquisition of motor abilities. *Neuroscience and Biobehavioral Reviews, 127,* 404–423.

Sachs, M. E., Ellis, R. J., Schlaug, G., & Loui, P. (2016). Brain connectivity reflects human aesthetic responses to music. *Social Cognitive and Affective Neuroscience, 11*(6), 884–891.

Sala-Llonch, R., Bartres-Faz, D., & Junque, C. (2015). Reorganization of brain networks in aging: A review of functional connectivity studies. *Frontiers in Psychology, 6,* 553.

Sawamoto, N., Honda, M., Okada, T., Hanakawa, T., Kanda, M., Fukuyama, H., Konishi, J., & Shibasaki, H. (2000). Expectation of pain enhances responses to nonpainful somatosensory stimulation in the anterior cingulate cortex and parietal operculum/posterior insula: An event-related functional magnetic resonance imaging study. *Journal of Neuroscience, 20*(19), 7438–7445.

Seydell-Greenwald, A., Ferrara, K., Chambers, C. E., Newport, E. L., & Landau, B. (2017). Bilateral parietal activations for complex visual-spatial functions: Evidence from a visual-spatial construction task. *Neuropsychologia, 106,* 194–206.

Sperry, R. (1968). Mental unity following surgical disconnection of the cerebral hemispheres. *The Harvey Lectures, Series 62*, (pp. 293–323). Academic Press.

Stein, B. E., & Rowland, B. A. (2011). Organization and plasticity in multisensory integration: Early and late experience affects its governing principles. *Progress in Brain Research, 191*, 145–163.

Stein, B. E., Stanford, T. R., & Rowland, B. A. (2020). Multisensory integration and the Society for Neuroscience: Then and now. *Journal of Neuroscience, 40*(1), 3–11.

Sternin, A., Burns, A., & Owen, A. M. (2019). Thirty-five years of computerized cognitive assessment of aging—Where are we now? *Diagnostics, 9*(3), 114. https://doi.org/10.3390/diagnostics9030114

Stewart, J., & Kolb, B. (1994). Dendritic branching in cortical pyramidal cells in response to ovariectomy in adult female rats: Suppression by neonatal exposure to testosterone. *Brain Research, 654*(1), 149–154.

Tholen, M. G., Trautwein, F.-M., Böckler, A., Singer, T., & Kanske, P. (2020). Functional magnetic resonance imaging (fMRI) item analysis of empathy and theory of mind. *Human Brain Mapping, 41*(10), 2611–2628. https://doi.org/10.1002/hbm.24966

Tonini, G. (2012). *Phi: A voyage from the brain to the soul*. Pantheon Books.

Umiltà, M. A., Kohler, E., Gallese, V., Fogassi, L., Fadiga, L., Keysers, C., & Rizzolatti, G. (2001). I know what you are doing: A neurophysiological study. *Neuron, 31*(1), 155–165.

Van Overwalle, F., Manto, M., Cattaneo, Z., Clausi, S., Ferrari, C., Gabrieli, J. D. E., Guell, X., Heleven, E., Lupo, M., Ma, Q., Michelutti, M., Olivito, G., Pu, M., Rice, L. C., Schmahmann, J. D., Siciliano, L., Sokolov, A. A., Stoodley, C. J., van Dun, K., … Leggio, M. (2020). Consensus paper: Cerebellum and social cognition. *Cerebellum, 19*(6), 833–868.

Wada, J., & Rasmussen, T. (1960). Intracarotid injection of sodium amytal for the lateralization of cerebral speech dominance: Experimental and clinical observations. *Journal of Neurosurgery, 17*(6), 266–282.

Waller, D., & Nadel, L. (Eds.). (2013). *Handbook of spatial cognition*. American Psychological Association.

Wang, R., Liu, M., Cheng, X., Wu, Y., Hildebrandt, A., & Zhou, C. (2021). Segregation, integration, and balance of large-scale resting brain networks configure different cognitive abilities. *Proceedings of the National Academy of Sciences (USA), 118*(23), e2022288118.

Witelson, S. F., & Goldsmith, C. H. (1991). The relationship of hand preference to anatomy of the corpus callosum in men. *Brain Research, 545*(1–2), 175–182.

Witelson, S. F., Kigar, D. L., & Harvey, T. (1999). The exceptional brain of Albert Einstein. *Lancet, 353*(9170), 2149–2153.

Woollett, K., Spiers, H. J., & Maguire, E. A. (2009). Talent in the taxi: A model system for exploring expertise. *Philosophical Transactions of the Royal Society B, 364*(1522), 1407–1416.

Yeo, B. T. T., Fienen, F. M., Sepulcre, J., Sabuncu, M. R., Lashkari, D., Hollinshead, M., Roffman, J. L., Smoller, J. W., Zöllei, L., Polimeni, J. R., Fischl, B., Liu, H., & Buckner, R. L. (2011). The organization of the human cerebral cortex estimated by intrinsic functional connectivity. *Journal of Neurophysiology, 106*(3), 1125–1165.

Yong, Z., Hsieh, P. J., & Milea, D. (2017). Seeing the sound after visual loss: Functional MRI in acquired auditory–visual synesthesia. *Experimental Brain Research, 235*(2), 415–420.

## CHAPTER 16

American Psychiatric Association. (2022). *Diagnostic and statistical manual of mental disorders* (5th ed., Text Revision). American Psychiatric Association.

Arnold, S. E., Rushinsky, D. D., & Han, L. Y. (1997). Further evidence of abnormal cytoarchitecture in the entorhinal cortex in schizophrenia using spatial point analyses. *Biological Psychiatry, 142*(8), 639–647.

Bhattacharya, A., Mrudula, K., Sreepada. S. S., Sathyaprabha, T. N., Pal, P. K., Chen, R., & Udupa, K. (2021, July 9). An overview of non-invasive brain stimulation: Basic principles and clinical applications. *Canadian Journal of Neurological Science/Journal Canadien Des Sciences Neurologiques*, 1–39.

Boltjes, R., Knippenberg, S., Gerlach, O., Hupperts, R., & Damoiseaux, J. (2021). Vitamin D supplementation in multiple sclerosis: An expert opinion based on the review of current evidence. *Expert Reviews in Neurotherapy, 21*(6), 715–725.

Bowman, T., Gervasoni, E., Arienti, C., Lazzarini, S. G., Negrini, S., Crea, S., Cattaneo, D., & Carrozza, M. C. (2021). Wearable devices for biofeedback rehabilitation: A systematic review and meta-analysis to design application rules and estimate the effectiveness on balance and gait outcomes in neurological diseases. *Sensors (Basel), 21*(10), 3444.

Brás, I. C., & Outeiro, T. F. (2020). Alpha-synuclein: Mechanisms of release and pathology progression in synucleinopathies. *Cells, 10*(2), 375.

Breining, B. L., & Sebastian, R. (2020). Neuromodulation in post-stroke aphasia treatment. *Current Physical and Medical Rehabilitation Reports, 8*(2), 44–56.

Bruno, E., Böttcher, S., Viana, P. F., Amengual-Gual, M., Joseph, B., Epitashvili, N., Dümpelmann, M., Glasstetter, M., Biondi, A., Van Laerhoven, K., Loddenkemper, T., Richardson, M. P., Schulze-Bonhage, A., & Brinkmann, B. H. (2021). Wearable devices for seizure detection: Practical experiences and recommendations from the Wearables for Epilepsy And Research (WEAR) International Study Group. *Epilepsia, 62*(10), 2307–2321.

Byne, W., Kemegther, E., Jones, L., Harouthunian, V., & Davis, K. L. (1999). The neurochemistry of schizophrenia. In D. S. Charney, E. J. Nesthler, & B. S. Bunney (Eds.), *The neurobiology of mental illness* (p. 242). Oxford University Press.

Centers for Disease Control and Prevention. (2010). Traumatic brain injury in the United States: Emergency departments visits, hospitalizations, and deaths, 2002–2006. Centers for Disease Control and Prevention, U.S. Department of Health and Human Services.

Charney, D. S., Nestler, E. J., Sklar, P., & Buxbaum, D. (Eds.). (2017). *The neurobiology of mental illness*. Oxford University Press.

Cho, R. Y., Gilbert, H., & Lewis, D. A. (2004). The neurobiology of schizophrenia. In D. S. Charney & F. J. Nestler (Eds.), *The Neurobiology of Mental Illness* (2nd ed., pp. 299–310). Oxford University Press.

Cuttler, K., Hassan, M., Carr, J., Cloete, R., & Bardien, S. (2021). Emerging evidence implicating a role for neurexins in neurodegenerative and neuropsychiatric disorders. *Open Biology, 11*(10), 210091.

De Jesus, O., Fogwe, D. T., Mesfin, F. B., & Das, J. (2021, September 3). Neuromodulation surgery for psychiatric disorders. In *StatPearls* [Internet]. StatPearls Publishing.

Dyer, K. F. W., & Corrigan, J. P. (2021). Psychological treatments for complex PTSD: A commentary on the clinical and empirical impasse dividing unimodal and phase-oriented therapy positions. *Psychological Trauma, 13*(8), 869–876. https://doi.org/10.1037/tra0001080.

Ferlisi, M., & Shorvon, S. (2014). Seizure precipitants (triggering factors) in patients with epilepsy. *Epilepsy & Behavior, 33*, 101–105.

Foutz, T., & Wong, M. (2021, September 2). Brain stimulation treatments in epilepsy: Basic mechanisms and clinical advances. *Biomedical Journal*, S2319-4170(21)00110-4.

Giles J. (2004). Neuroscience: Change of mind. *Nature, 430*(6995), 14.

Grace, J. J., Kinsella, E. L., Muldoon, O. T., & Fortune, D. G. (2015, August 14). Post-traumatic growth following acquired brain injury: A systematic review and meta-analysis. *Frontiers in Psychology, 6*, 1162.

Green, S. L., Gignac, G. E., Watson, P. A., Brosnan, N., Becerra, R., Pestell, C., & Weinborn, M. (2021, April 26). Correction to: Apathy and depression as predictors of activities of daily living following stroke and traumatic brain injuries in adults: A meta-analysis. *Neuropsychological Review*, Epub ahead of print. https://doi.org/10.1007/s11065-021-09509-0

Hayward, K. S., Kramer, S. F., Dalton, E. J., Hughes, G. R., Brodtmann, A., Churilov, L., Cloud, G., Corbett, D., Jolliffe, L., Kaffenberger, T., Rethnam, V., Thijs, V., Ward, N., Lannin, N., & Bernhardt, J. (2021). Timing and dose of upper limb motor intervention after stroke: A systematic review. *Stroke, 52*(11), 3706–3717.

Huibers, M. J. H., Lorenzo-Luaces, L., Cuijpers, P., & Kazantzis, N. (2021). On the road to personalized psychotherapy: A research agenda based on cognitive behavior therapy for depression. *Frontiers in Psychiatry, 11*, 1551.

Knight, E. J., Testini, P., Min, H.-K., Gibson, W. S., Gorny, K. R., Favazza, C. P., Felmlee, J. P., Kim, I., Welker, K. M., Clayton, D. A., Klassen, B. T., Chang S.-Y., & Lee, K. H. (2015). Motor and nonmotor circuitry activation induced by subthalamic nucleus deep brain stimulation in patients with Parkinson disease: Intraoperative functional magnetic resonance imaging for deep brain stimulation. *Mayo Clinic Proceedings, 90*(6), 773–785.

Kornhuber, J., & Gulbins, E. (2021). New molecular targets for antidepressant drugs. *Pharmaceuticals (Basel), 14*(9), 894.

Kovelman, J. A., & Scheibel, A. B. (1984). A neurohistologic correlate of schizophrenia. *Biological Psychiatry, 19*(12), 1601–1621.

Meyerbröker, K., & Morina, N. (2021). The use of virtual reality in assessment and treatment of anxiety and related disorders. *Clinical Psychology and Psychotherapy, 28*(3), 466–476.

Peretz, I., Kolinsky, R., Tramo, M., Labrecque, R., Hublet, C., Demeurisse, G., & Belleville, S. (1994). Functional dissociations following bilateral lesions of auditory cortex. *Brain, 117*(Pt 6), 1283–1301. https://doi.org/10.1093/brain/117.6.1283

Powell, T., Gilson, R., & Collin, C. (2012). TBI 13 years on: Factors associated with post-traumatic growth. *Disability Rehabilitation, 34*(17), 1461–1467.

Priol, A.-C., Denis, L., Boulanger, G., Thépaut, M., Geoffray, M.-M., & Tordjman, S. (2021). Detection of morphological abnormalities in schizophrenia: An important step to identify associated genetic disorders or etiologic subtypes. *International Journal of Molecular Science, 22*(17), 9464.

Rao, J., Chiappelli, J., Kochunov, P., Regenold, W. T., Rapoport, S. I., & Hong, L. E. (2015). Is schizophrenia a neurodegenerative disease? Evidence from age-related decline of brain-derived neurotrophic factor in the brains of schizophrenia patients and matched nonpsychiatric controls. *Neurodegenerative Diseases, 15*(1), 38–44.

Rapoport, J. L., Giedd, J. N., & Gogtay, N. (2012). Neurodevelopmental model of schizophrenia: Update 2012. *Molecular Psychiatry, 17*(12), 1228–1238.

Richetto, J., & Meyer, U. (2021). Epigenetic modifications in schizophrenia and related disorders: Molecular scars of environmental exposures and source of phenotypic variability. *Biological Psychiatry, 89*(3), 215–226.

Roohi, E., Jaafari, N., & Hashemian, F. (2021). On inflammatory hypothesis of depression: What is the role of IL-6 in the middle of the chaos? *Journal of Neuroinflammation, 18*, 45.

Sacks, O. W. (1998). *The man who mistook his wife for a hat: And other clinical tales.* Touchstone Books.

Sacrey, L.-A., Zwaigenbaum, L., Bryson, S., Brian, J., Smith, I. M., Roberts, W., Szatmari, P., Roncadin, C., Garon, N., Novak, C., Vaillancourt, T., McCormick, T., MacKinnon, B., Jilderda, S., & Armstrong, V. (2015). Can parents' concerns predict autism spectrum disorder? A prospective study of high-risk siblings from 6 to 36 months of age. *Journal of the American Academy of Child and Adolescent Psychiatry, 54*(6), 470–478.

Silva, R. C., Domingues, H. S., Salgado, A. J., & Teixeira, F. G. (2022). From regenerative strategies to pharmacological approaches: Can we fine-tune treatment for Parkinson's disease? *Neural Regeneration Research, 17*(5), 933–936.

Silverberg, N. D., Iverson, G. L., ACRM Mild TBI Definition Expert Consensus Group, and the ACRM Brain Injury Special Interest Group Mild TBI Task Force. (2021). Expert panel survey to update the American Congress of Rehabilitation Medicine definition of mild traumatic brain injury. *Archives in Physical Medical Rehabilitation, 102*(1), 76–86.

Sriwastava, S., Tandon, M., Podury, S., Prasad, A., Wen, S., Guthrie, G., Kakara, M., Jaiswal, S., Subedi, R., Elkhooly, M., & Lisak, R. P. (2021). COVID-19 and neuroinflammation: A literature review of relevant neuroimaging and CSF markers in central nervous system inflammatory disorders from SARS-CoV2. *Journal of Neurology, 268*(12), 1–31.

Tenovuo, O., Diaz-Arrastia, R., Goldstein, L. E., Sharp, D. J., van der Naalt, J., & Zasler, N. D. (2021). Assessing the severity of traumatic brain injury: Time for a change? *Journal of Clinical Medicine, 10*(1), 148.

Thompson, P. M., Jahanshad, N., Schmaal, L., Turner, J. A., Winkler, A. M., Thomopoulos, S. I., Egan, G. F., & Kochunov, P. (2021, October). The Enhancing NeuroImaging Genetics through Meta-Analysis Consortium: 10 years of global collaborations in human brain mapping. *Human Brain Mapping.* https://doi.org/10.1002/hbm.25672.

Treffert, D. A., & Treffert, D. A. (2021). The sudden savant: A new form of extraordinary abilities. *Wisconsin Medical Journal, 120*(1), 69–73.

Uswatte, G., Taub, E., Bowman, M. H., Delgado, A., Bryson, C., Morris, D. M., Mckay, S., Barman, J., & Mark, V. M. (2018). Rehabilitation of stroke patients with plegic hands: Randomized controlled trial of expanded constraint-induced movement therapy. *Restorative Neurology and Neuroscience, 36*(2), 225–244.

Van Pelt, K. L., Puetz, T., Swallow, J., Lapointe, A. P., & Broglio, S.P. (2021). Data-driven risk classification of concussion rates: A systematic review and meta-analysis. *Sports Medicine, 51*(6), 1227–1244.

Vieira, C., Ferreira da Silva Pais-Vieira, C., Novais, J., & Perrotta, A. (2021). Serious game design and clinical improvement in physical rehabilitation: Systematic review. *JMIR Serious Games, 9*(3), e20066.

Wang, X., Cheng, B., Roberts, N., Wang, S., Luo, Y., Tian, F., & Yue, S. (2021). Shared and distinct brain fMRI response during performance of working memory tasks in adult patients with schizophrenia and major depressive disorder. *Human Brain Mapping, 42*(16), 5458–5476.

Watsky, R. E., Gotts, S. J., Berman, R. A., McAdams, H. M., Zhou, X., Greenstein, D., Lalonde, F. M., Gochman, P., Clasen, L. S., Shora, L., Ordóñez, A. E., Gogtay, N., Martin, A., Barch, D. M., Rapoport, J. L., & Liu, S. (2018). Attenuated resting-state functional connectivity in patients with childhood- and adult-onset schizophrenia. *Schizophrenia Research, 197*, 219–225.

White, L., Ingraham, B., Larson, E., Fishman, P., Park, S., & Coe, N. B. (2021, October 13). Observational study of patient characteristics associated with a timely diagnosis of dementia and mild cognitive impairment without dementia. *Journal of General Internal Medicine.* https://doi.org/10.1007/s11606-021-07169-7.

Yohn, C. N., Shifman, S., Garino, A., Diethorn, E., Bokka, L., Ashamalla, S. A., & Samuels, B. A. (2020). Fluoxetine effects on behavior and adult hippocampal neurogenesis in female C57BL/6J mice across the estrous cycle. *Psychopharmacology (Berl), 237*(5), 1281–1290.

Zhao, L., Liu, J.-W., Shi, H.-Y., & Ma, Y.-M. (2021). Neural stem cell therapy for brain disease. *World Journal of Stem Cells, 13*(9), 1278–1292.

Note: Page numbers followed by f indicate figures; those followed by t indicate tables.